INSIDE AFRICA

BOOKS BY JOHN GUNTHER

INSIDE AFRICA

INSIDE U.S.A.

INSIDE LATIN AMERICA

INSIDE ASIA

INSIDE EUROPE

THE RIDDLE OF MACARTHUR

EISENHOWER

ROOSEVELT IN RETROSPECT

BEHIND THE CURTAIN

DEATH BE NOT PROUD

D DAY

THE TROUBLED MIDNIGHT

INSIDE

AFRICA

by

JOHN GUNTHER

Author of INSIDE EUROPE, INSIDE ASIA
INSIDE LATIN AMERICA and INSIDE U.S.A.

HARPER & BROTHERS
New York

INSIDE AFRICA

Copyright 1953, 1954, 1955, by John Gunther
Printed in the United States of America

All rights in this book are reserved. No part of the book may be used or reproduced in any manner whatsoever without written permission except in the case of brief quotations embodied in critical articles and reviews. For information address Harper & Brothers, 49 East 33rd Street, New York 16, N. Y.

Library of Congress catalog card number: 55-8022

To JANE

The "I" in this book is mostly "we."

CONTENTS

A Note by Way of Preface   xxi

PART ONE: The North and the East

1. Dark Continent Becoming Light   3
2. The Sultan of Morocco   20
3. Moroccan Backdrop   38
4. Arab World in North Africa   56
5. The French, the Nationalists, the Americans   72
6. Lord of the Atlas   93
7. Tangier and Tetuan   107
8. Brief Word about Algeria   120
9. Inside Nowhere—the Sahara   130
10. The Tunisian Complex   146
11. Libya, or a Child Learning to Walk   163
12. Crisis and Development in Egypt   183
13. Nasser to Naguib to Nasser   201
14. The Nile and the Sudan   223
15. Haile Selassie, Emperor of Ethiopia   247
16. More about Ethiopia, Eritrea, and the Somalis   274
17. Foreword to Bantu Africa   285
18. Kenya: The Land and People   310
19. Kenya: British Rule in Africa   334
20. Kenya: The Mau Maus   358
21. East Africa: Animals   379
22. The Wonderful World of Tanganyika   396
23. Hope and Crisis in Uganda   421

PART TWO: The South and the West

24. The Union of South Africa: Successors to Malan   449
25. The Union: Country, Towns, and Issues   484

26.	The Union: The Blacks and the Browns	516
27.	The Union: Gold, Diamonds, and South West Africa	545
28.	Medicine Murder in Basutoland	568
29.	Portuguese Africa	585
30.	The Rhodesias and Central African Federation	602
31.	More About Rhodesia and Nyasaland	620
32.	Congo I: Belgian Policy in Africa	646
33.	Congo II: Uranium, Giants, Pygmies	669
34.	French Rule in Black Africa	691
35.	A Visit to Dr. Albert Schweitzer	712
36.	Introduction to British West Africa	735
37.	Complexities and Achievements in Nigeria	746
38.	Nigeria—Its Inflammatory Politics	765
39.	The Nigerian North	776
40.	Prime Minister Nkrumah of the Gold Coast	790
41.	House of Commons in Black Miniature	807
42.	The Gold Coast and the Golden Stool	819
43.	Mr. Tubman of Liberia	843
44.	Monrovian Doctrine	859
45.	Dakar and French West Africa	871
46.	. . . And to Conclude	884
	Acknowledgments, Bibliography, and Sources	893
	Index	925

Chart, showing characteristics of each country, pages xii-xix

MAPS

Africa, showing author's trips, page 10

Area maps, each covering several countries, will be found on pages 23, 165, 249, 313, 451, 693, 737.

The darkest thing about Africa has always been our ignorance of it.
—GEORGE H. T. KIMBLE

Oh, Africa, mysterious land!
Surrounded by a lot of sand
And full of grass and trees,
And elephants and Africanders
And politics and salamanders
And native rum in little kegs
And savages called Tuaregs . . .
And tons of diamonds, and lots
Of nasty, dirty Hottentots
And coolies coming from the East
And serpents, seven yards long at least
And lions, that retain
Their vigor, appetites, and rage
Intact to an extreme old age,
And never lose their mane . . .
Vast continent! Whose cumbrous shape
Runs from Bizerta to the Cape.
—THE MODERN TRAVELLER

Always something new out of Africa.
—PLINY THE ELDER

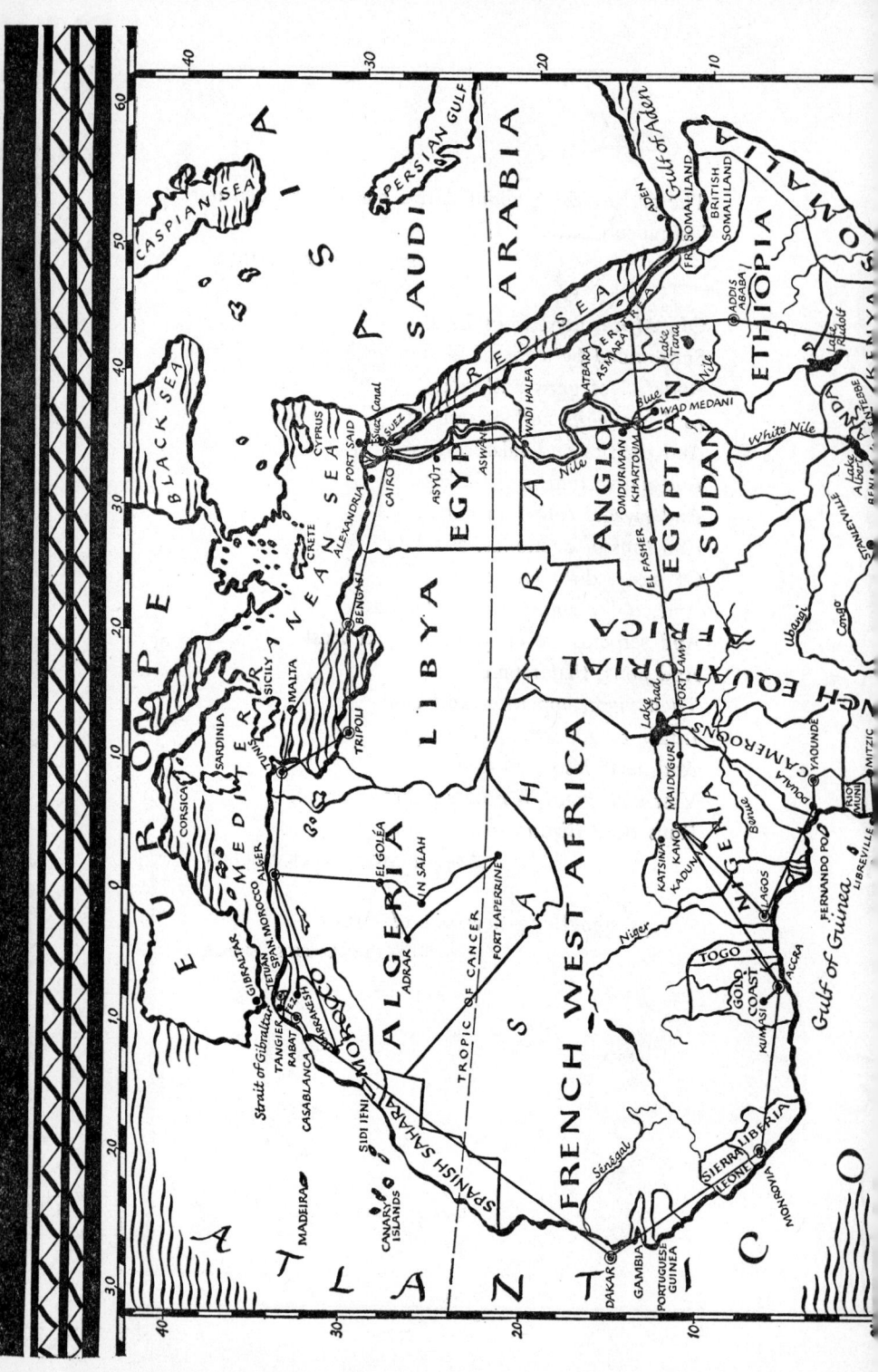

COUNTRY	AREA (square miles)	CAPITAL	POLITICAL STATUS	DESCRIPTION	POPULATION (approximate)
ALGERIA	847,500	Algiers	Part of France	Sahara is its magnificent backyard. Home of Foreign Legion and Garden of Allah. Nationalist insurrection in 1954	8,764,000
ANGOLA	481,351	Nova Lisboa	Portuguese overseas province	Mostly wilderness, little known and largely undeveloped. But Africa's only transcontinental R. R. starts here. No nationalism yet. Has forced labor	4,111,796
BASUTOLAND	11,716	Maseru	British "High Commission Territory"	Embedded in Union of S.A.; lonely mountains; medicine murder; men in blankets	561,289
BECHUANALAND	275,000	Mafeking	British "High Commission Territory"	Mostly desert; lively tribal spirit. Much discontent following Tschekedi-Seretse crisis	296,754
CAMEROONS (British)	34,000	Buea	UN Trust Territory (British)	Administered from Nigeria; now split into two halves	1,051,000
CAMEROONS (French)	166,800	Yaoundé	UN Trust Territory (French)	Jungle Africa growing up quickly; strong incipient nationalism but loyal to France	3,065,000
CONGO	904,974	Léopoldville	Belgian Colony	Limitless reservoir of richness only partly developed. Firm Belgian rule; economic progress but no civil liberties. Not even Belgians vote. Abounding in color, picturesqueness. Perhaps the most exciting country in Africa except politically. Rain forest; pygmies; black magic	12,000,000
EGYPT	386,000	Cairo	Independent	Bridge between three continents; intellectual headquarters of Arab world. Strong influence over rest of Africa, takes a cautious neutralist position. Home of oldest civilization known to mankind; after centuries of foreign rule now vigorously on its own. Powerful, prolific, expansionist	Between 21,000,000 and 22,000,000
ERITREA	47,875	Asmara	Federated with Ethiopia	Once an Italian Colony. Desert-*cum*-mountain shelf on Red Sea. See text	1,103,000
ETHIOPIA	409,266	Addis Ababa	Independent	Magnificent high plateau; history goes back 3,000 years; Christian; vivid recent progress; dominated by Emperor	12,000,000 (?)
FERNANDO PO	800	Santa Isabel	Spanish colony	Island off unhealthiest part of Africa; slavery and forced labor here in old days	33,980

RACIAL COMPOSITION	A FEW PRINCIPAL TRIBES	RELIGION	CHIEF PROBLEMS	PRINCIPAL PRODUCTS	POLITICAL PARTIES	LEADERS (colonial governors not included)
About one million French; otherwise mostly Arab	Arab; Kabyles	Moslem; Christian	Assimilation of Arabs into French system; education; economic development; birthrate	Wine Figs Iron ore Phosphates	UDMA (Democratic Union of Algerian Manifesto) MTLD (Movement for Triumph of Democratic Liberties) Ulema	Ferhat Abbas (UDMA) Messali Hadj (exiled) (MTLD)
Overwhelmingly black African	Few important	Pagan; strong Catholic influence	Illiteracy 97%; economic backwardness	Coffee Maize Sugar Palm oil	None	
Only 1,689 Europeans	Basuto	Pagan but strongly Christianized	Export of manpower to Union	Wool Mohair	Basutoland National Congress	Paramount Chieftainess 'Mantsebo
Only 2,379 Europeans	Bamangwato	Mostly Pagan	Relations with Union; economic development; expulsion of Seretse	Pastoral products Hides, cattle, Butter Gold & silver		Tschekedi Khama; Seretse Khama
Handful of Europeans	Fulani; Fang; Bakoko	Pagan; some Christians	Political development associated with Nigeria	Cocoa Palm kernels Bananas Rubber	Linked to Nigerian Parties	Dr. E. M. L. Endeley
About 13,000 Europeans	Dozens widely differentiated	Pagan; some Christians and Moslems	"Assimilation"	Cacao Bananas Coffee Palm kernels Oil	UPC (Union des Populations des Camerouns); Kamerun National Congress	Um Noyobe Ruben (UPC) "Prince" Mango Bell
Overwhelmingly African; only about 60,000 Europeans	Too many to mention; see text	Mostly Pagan, but with strong Catholic influence	Communication; education; how to let Africans advance further economically without building up political pressure	Palm oil Cotton Coffee Coal Copper Diamonds Gold Uranium	None permitted	
Alien population about 1.2% of total	Largely detribalized; some Nubians and Bedouin	Moslem	Diseases like bilharzia; fact that 96.5% of land is uninhabitable desert; birthrate; political consolidation under Nasser	Cotton Onions Rice	Liberation Rally (old parties suppressed)	Colonel Gamal Abdul Nasser (Prime Minister)
About 17,000 Italians	Some Sudanese, some Arabs	50-50 Coptic Christian and Moslem	Growing pains under new Ethiopian parenthood	Coffee Barley Tobacco Sesame	Unionist Party	Ado Tedla Bairn (Chief Executive)
A few European and American officials, etc.	Amhara; Galla; Danakil	Coptic Christian but many Pagans and Moslems	National integration; communications; education. See Text.	Cattle Hides & Skins Coffee Wax, Wheat	None	Emperor Haile Selassie
Solidly black	Bubis	Pagan; some Catholics	Mainland labor in cocoa fields	Cocoa Coffee		

COUNTRY	AREA (square miles)	CAPITAL	POLITICAL STATUS	DESCRIPTION	POPULATION (approximate)
FRENCH EQUATORIAL AFRICA	969,111	Brazzaville	French "overseas territory"; member of French Union	Home of Dr. Schweitzer. FEA stretches all the way from Congo to Libya; has four great territories, e.g., Chad. 3,000,000 cattle; 320 miles of RR; 46 secondary schools	4,436,500
FRENCH WEST AFRICA	1,815,768	Dakar	French "overseas territory"; member of French Union	Six times bigger than Texas; comprises eight highly varied territories, like Senegal, Ivory Coast, Mauretania, Niger, Dahomey, etc.; fast-growing political consciousness; 360,000 camels; 54 movies	17,000,000
GAMBIA	3,974	Bathurst	British Colony & Protectorate	A small British enclave on West Coast surrounded by French territory	275,000
GOLD COAST	79,000	Accra	British Colony & Protectorate	On the Guinea Coast. Has African Prime Minister Nkrumah and is on brink of self-government; probably will be the first black dominion. Scene of Volta project, and lives on cocoa. Politically one of most effervescent countries on continent. Very rich	4,500,000
KENYA	224,960	Nairobi	British Colony & Protectorate	Sublime highland scenery; white settlers; Mau Maus. A tourist & safari paradise; lions four miles from center of Nairobi. See text for politics	5,700,000
LIBERIA	43,000	Monrovia	Independent	An American stepchild, fantastically backward. Only Negro republic in world except Haiti. Much corruption. Considerable economic progress lately	1,500,000 (?)
LIBYA	679,343	Tripoli (also Benghazi and Sébha)	Independent	A "box of sand." Once an Italian colony; strong American, British, and Egyptian influence; newest country in the world except Central African Federation	1,174,000
MADAGASCAR	229,438	Tananarive	French "overseas territory", member of French union	Enormous offshore island, not really part of Africa	4,350,700
MOROCCO (French)	153,870	Rabat	French Protectorate (part of Sherifian Empire)	One of the most challenging, colorful, and important countries in the world. Sultan expelled because of fierce pressure of Nationalist movement. Some danger of Communist penetration. Important U. S. military air bases are located here	8,617,387
MOROCCO (International Zone)	225	Tangier	Part of Sherifian Empire under International Administration	"Most successfully administered international city in world," resembles old treaty ports in China. See text	170,000

RACIAL COMPOSITION	A FEW PRINCIPAL TRIBES	RELIGION	CHIEF PROBLEMS	PRINCIPAL PRODUCTS	POLITICAL PARTIES	LEADERS (colonial governors not included)
Only about 24,000 Europeans	Everything from bush people to desert nomads	Pagan; Moslem	Assimilation of native communities into French system; lack of communications; backwardness	Cotton Timber Coffee Diamonds Gold Cocoa Palm kernels		
63,000 French *colons* & other Europeans	Hundreds; see text	Pagan; Moslem	Political development; strong growth of nationalism; many French *colons* moving into Dakar	Peanuts Palm kernels Coffee Groundnut oil Cocoa	RDA (Rassemblement Democratique Africain); parties emerging and important in each territory	Leopold Sedar Senghor Felix Houphonet-Boijny (RDA)
Overwhelmingly black; only 222 Europeans	Mandingo	94% Moslem	Economic troubles	Peanuts	Gambia Moslem Congress; Gambia Democratic Party	Wallace Johnson
99.8% African; only about 6,770 Europeans	Ashanti; Fanti; Akan	Pagan, Christian, Moslem	Political integration; advance toward full political freedom from British	Cocoa Gold	Convention People's Party	Kwame Nkrumah (Prime Minister)
42,000 Europeans, 158,000 Asians, 5½ million Africans	Kikuyu; Masai; Kamba; Nandi; Swahili; Turkana	Pagan and Christian	Stamping out Mau Mau terrorism; building up of new multiracial government; reduction of color bar and racial tension	Sisal Coffee Farm products	United Country Party (moderate white settlers) Kenya Africa Union	Michael Blundell E. W. Mathu Jomo Kenyatta (in jail)
All black except a few foreign advisors, missionaries, etc.	Mandingo; Kru; Grebo; Vai	Christian; Pagan; a few Moslems	Communications; public health; poverty and lack of education	Rubber Iron ore	True Whig	William Vacanarat Shadrach Tubman (President)
Some Italians still	Senussi	Moslem	Disunity	Olive oil Dates Esparto grass		King Idris I
Mostly Malagasys	Hova	Moslem; Pagan; Christian	Political assimilation; building up of better economy	Coffee Cloves Vanilla Graphite Cassava	National Council of Madagascar	
300,000-350,000 French *colons*; 50,000 other Europeans	Arabs Berbers	Moslem (except for Europeans)	Nationalism; economic development	Fish Wine Wool Phosphates	Istiqlal (suppressed)	Sidi Mohammed Ben Moulay Arafa el Alaoui (Sultan) (Mohammed VI) Sidi Mohammed Ben Youssef (Sultan deposed) (Mohammed V) Allal el Fassi (exiled) Hadj Ahmed Belafrej (exiled) Hadj Thami Glaoui el Mezouari (Pasha of Marrakesh)
Perhaps 60,000 French, Spanish, etc.	Arabs	Moslem (except for Europeans)	Mostly commercial		No parties	Mendoub of Tangier

COUNTRY	AREA (square miles)	CAPITAL	POLITICAL STATUS	DESCRIPTION	POPULATION (approximate)
MOROCCO (Spanish)	18,009	Tetuan	Spanish Protectorate (part of Sherifian Empire)	Smaller, poorer than French Zone. Staging ground for Spanish army	1,082,000
MOZAMBIQUE	297,731	Lourenço Marques	Portuguese overseas province	Here Portuguese try to keep nationalism down by the Assimilado System. Strong South African influence	5,732,767
NIGERIA	372,674	Lagos	British Colony and Protectorate	Divided into three great regions; 250 tribes; several hundred languages. One of the most inflammatory countries in world, coming into embrace of modern times overnight. Ancestors of most American Negro slaves came from here or nearby. Very powerful and progressive nationalist movement; country may soon reach self-government	31,500,000
NORTHERN RHODESIA	284,745	Lusaka	Part of Central African Federation (British)	Cities look like American frontier towns in Wild West days. Economy built on copper	1,866,000
NYASALAND	37,374	Zomba	Part of Central African Federation (British)	Dr. Livingstone's favorite country. A beautiful country, dominated by its lake. Has few white settlers as such, but they control economy. Africans highly developed	2,352,500
PORTUGUESE GUINEA	13,948	Bissau	Portuguese overseas province	A tropical backwater, largely unknown	517,249
RIO MUNI (Spanish Guinea)	10,039	Bata (chief town)	Spanish colony	Forlorn and derelict enclave, administered from Fernando Po	134,000
RUANDA-URUNDI	20,120	Usumbura	UN Trust Territory (Belgian)	Administration almost indistinguishable from that of Congo. Most dramatic scenery in Africa. Home of pygmies and giants both	3,904,799
SIERRA LEONE	27,925	Freetown	British Colony and Protectorate	One of oldest, stablest British territories	1,767,213
SOMALIA	198,000	Mogadiscio	UN Trust Territory (Italian)	On "Horn of Africa." Scheduled to be independent in 1960	1,000,000
SOMALILAND (British)	67,936	Hargeisa	British Protectorate	People largely nomads, but townsmen show strong political advance	640,000
SOMALILAND (French)	8,376	Djibouti	French "overseas territory"; member of French Union	A decrepit little territory	55,000
SOUTHERN RHODESIA	150,327	Salisbury	Part of Central African Federation (British)	A white settlement state par excellence, but still has wonderfully varied tribal life. Federated with N. Rhodesia and Nyasaland as an effort to keep "Gold Coast from moving east and Union from moving north." Idea is to create multi-racial state but under white control	2,095,000

RACIAL COMPOSITION	A FEW PRINCIPAL TRIBES	RELIGION	CHIEF PROBLEMS	PRINCIPAL PRODUCTS	POLITICAL PARTIES	LEADERS (colonial governors not included)
Large Spanish colony	Arabs; Riffi	Moslem (except for Europeans)	Spaniards give more leeway to nationalists than do French in their zone	Minerals Wool	Islah (Reform Party)	Abdel Kholek Torres
Overwhelmingly black African	Various	Pagan; some Christians; many Moslems	Economic backwardness; illiteracy	Sugar Maize Cotton Copra		
Overwhelmingly African; only 11,700 Europeans	Ibo; Yoruba; Hausa	Pagan; Moslem; Christian	Unity of three chief regions; nationalist pressure for freedom from Britain by 1956	Peanuts Coal Tin and other minerals	NCNC (National Council of Nigeria & the Cameroons) Action Group Northern People's Congress	Dr. Nnamdi Azikiwe (NCNC) Obafemi Awalowo (Action Group) Ahmadu, the Sardauna of Sokoto (NPC)
About 97.5% African; only 45,000 Europeans	Angoni; Barotse; Wemba; Batoka	Pagan; some Christians	Industrial color bar; race relations	Copper Tobacco	Federal Party Northern Rhodesian African Congress	Sir Roy Welensky Harry Nkumbula
4,703 Europeans	Yaos; Angoni; Nyanja	Pagan but strongly Christianized	African participation in new federation (against will of most)	Tobacco Tea Tung	Nyasaland National Congress	J. S. Sangala
Almost solidly black	Various	Pagan; a few Christians	Backwardness	Rice Palm oil		
Solidly black except for few white officials		Pagan; a few Christians	Practically nothing is known about this region	Cocoa Coffee		
Handful (3,733) of Europeans	Watutsi	Pagan; strong Catholic influence	Overpopulation; education; economic development	Tin Coffee Gold Cotton Hides		Mwami of Ruanda
Only 598 Europeans	Mende; Temne	Pagan; Christian	Strong nationalist stirrings; race relations	Iron ore Palm kernels Diamonds Kola nuts	National Council for the Colony of Sierra Leone; Sierra Leone Peoples Party	M. A. S. Margai (chief minister)
Overwhelmingly African	Somali	Mostly Moslem	Growth of nationalism	Bananas Cotton	Somali Youth League	Abdullahi Issa
Overwhelmingly African	Somali; Afar	Moslem	Growth of nationalism	Spices Hides Skins	Somali Youth League	
Overwhelmingly African	Somali	Moslem and Pagan	Largely commercial	Hides Salt		
About 92.5% African; 160,000 Europeans	Mashona; Matabele	Pagan; many Christians	Political development; color bar; race relations	Tobacco Chrome	Federal Party	Sir Godfrey Huggins

COUNTRY	AREA (square miles)	CAPITAL	POLITICAL STATUS	DESCRIPTION	POPULATION (approximate)
SUDAN	967,500	Khartoum	Anglo-Egyptian Condominium	A magnificent country, mostly desert but watered in part by the Nile. Profound political vitality and effervescence. Scheduled to become fully independent by 1956, if it does not join Egypt	8,309,663
SPANISH SAHARA	105,409	Villa Cisneros	Spanish Colony	A desert wasteland, little known. Run from Tetuan	40,000
SWAZILAND	6,704	Mbabane	British "High Commission Territory"	Enclave between Union and Portuguese territory. Remarkable tribal life	185,215
TANGANYIKA	342,706	Dar es Salaam	UN Trust Territory (British)	Mt. Kilimanjaro, Serengeti game country, Williamson's diamond mine, and many other picturesquenesses. Political development beginning. Good administration; not much color bar	7,800,000
TOGOLAND (British)	13,041	Ho	UN Trust Territory (British)	Once German; now split into British and French fragments	382,717
TOGOLAND (French)	21,235	Lomé	UN Trust Territory (French)	Closely resembles other Guinea Coast countries	970,983
TUNISIA	48,195	Tunis	French Protectorate	Much more educated and responsible nationalist movement than in Morocco; severe disorders recently; French colonialism on the way out	3,416,000
UGANDA	93,981	Entebbe (also Kampala)	British Protectorate	A "model" colony in the heart of Africa, luxuriant, under a modern planned economy regime. Strong political fermentations. Native life unrivaled for color	4,962,749
UNION OF SOUTH AFRICA	472,494 (790,219 including South-West Africa)	Pretoria (also Cape Town)	Independent (but member of British Commonwealth)	Home of inheritors of Dr. Malan and theory of Apartheid (complete racial segregation). Complex and perhaps insoluble three-way crisis in race relations. Economy based on the mines, owned by whites and worked by black labor. Politics painful, but country has great vigor and beauty, packed with tradition	12,646,375 (13,076,729 including South-West Africa)
ZANZIBAR	1,020	Zanzibar	Sultanate under British protection	Island off East Coast near Equator; an Indian Ocean Shangri-La	265,000

SOURCES: Statesmen's Year Book; World Geo-Graphic Atlas; various almanacs and government reports.

RACIAL COMPOSITION	A FEW PRINCIPAL TRIBES	RELIGION	CHIEF PROBLEMS	PRINCIPAL PRODUCTS	POLITICAL PARTIES	LEADERS (colonial governors not included)
Overwhelmingly Arab and Black African	Shilluk; Dinka; Nuer; Zande; Beja	Moslem and Pagan	Political rivalries and development	Cotton Gum arabic	UMMA Party (Independence) National Unity Party	El Sayed Sir Abdel Rahman el Mahdi Pasha ("Sar")(UMMA) El Sayed Sir Ali Mirghani Pasha ("Sam") Sayed Ismail Ahmed El Azhari (Prime Minister)- (National Unity Party)
Practically all African	Mostly Arabs and Berbers	Moslem	Poverty; lack of communications	Ambergris in coastal towns		
Only 3204 Europeans	Swazi	Pagan	Relations with Union; economic development	Cattle Asbestos		Sobhuza II.
7,700,000 Africans; 71,000 Asians; 16,000 Europeans	Masai; Chagga; Sukumo; Swahili	Mostly Pagan but plenty of Moslems and some Christians	Economic development; conquest of tsetse fly; political integration	Sisal Coffee Cotton Diamonds Beeswax	TANU (Tanganyika African National Union)	Mangi Mkuu Tom Marealle Julius K. Nyerere
51 Europeans	Ewe	Pagan mostly	Whether to join Gold Coast or not	Cocoa	C.P.P. (Gold Coast) Togoland Congress	S. G. Antor
Only 841 Europeans	Ewe	Pagan mostly	Political assimilation	Cacao Coffee Palm kernels Copra Cotton	Comité de l'Unité Togolaise	Sylvanus Olympio
280,000 French and other Europeans	Largely detribalized; some Bedouin	Moslem	Nationalism; also the birthrate — pop. goes up by 80,000 per year	Olive oil Wine Cork Phosphates Iron ore	Neo-Destour	Sidi Mohammed Lamine Pasha (Bey of Tunis) Habib Bourguiba (Exiled)
99.2% African (50,300 Indians and 7,600 Europeans as against 5¼ million Africans)	Baganda; Toro; Ankole; Hima	Pagan with marked Christian admixture	Kabaka crisis; political development	Cotton Coffee	Uganda African Congress	Edward William Frederick David Walugembe Mutebi Luwangula Mutesa (The Kabaka) Mutesa II (Deposed)
8,500,000 Africans 2,600,000 Europeans 1,000,000 Colored and mixed 360,000 Indians	Zulu; Xhosa; Herero; Bushmen; Ovambo	Dutch Reformed Church (Europeans); Pagan and miscellaneous Christian (Africans)	Racial tension and disharmony	Corn Grapes Wool Iron ore Diamonds Gold Uranium	Nationalist Party United Party Liberal Party African National Congress South African Indian Congress	Johannes Gerhard Strijdom (Prime Minister)
200,000 Africans 45,000 Arabs 16,000 Indians 306 Europeans	Arabs	Moslem	Disease known as "Sudden Death" afflicting clove trees	Cloves		Sultan Khalifa II

A Note by Way of Preface

THIS, the fifth Inside book, is an attempt to describe all of Africa in so far as it is possible to do so in a single volume. It is an obvious companion, a fellow, to *Inside Europe* (which was published as long ago as 1936), *Inside Asia*, *Inside Latin America*, and *Inside U.S.A.* The scope of this book, whatever its shortcomings and malproportions may be, is continental; I have tried, whether successfully or not, to cover the entire immense and explosive continent. Many admirable books on various parts of Africa exist, but very few attempt to deal with it as a whole. Even Lord Hailey's classic *African Survey* is limited to Africa below the Sahara, and it does not by any means cover all of that.

I began to collect material on Africa a good many years ago—in 1931 or even before—and have been assembling it systematically ever since. I did not, of course, know at that time what use I would make of this, much less that I would ever write a book called *Inside Africa*. In 1926, 1929, 1936, and 1943 I visited parts of Africa, and flew across it twice. Then in 1952–53 my wife and I traveled in Africa for long steady months, and saw it from stem to stern, from top to bottom. This was the most difficult, crowded, and exhausting as well as stimulating trip I have ever taken. There are forty-four countries or political subdivisions in Africa today, and of these we saw most, including all those important. We visited 105 different towns, and took fifty-four different trips by air. During one period of twenty-five days we slept in sixteen different places, and in one stretch of five weeks we had (breakfast excluded) exactly one meal alone. Altogether we traveled more than 40,000 miles, which is sixteen times the air distance across the United States, and much longer than the circumference of the earth at its stout waistline, the Equator.

Not many people realize that Africa is almost four times bigger than the United States. You could drop the continental United States into Africa four times and the edges would scarcely touch. And of course it is infinitely more complex than the United States, less homogeneous, spectacularly more varied within itself, newer, and more volatile. Morocco differs from Swaziland more than Iceland differs from Peru. Almost the whole continent is in an uproar.

A NOTE BY WAY OF PREFACE

Africa is not an easy continent to travel in. In general, either to save time or because no other means of transportation were available, we flew from capital to capital; then, almost without exception, we managed to make at least one trip by automobile into the surrounding bush or hinterland. Even airplane travel is difficult; Africa is the place where airplanes run on Tuesdays—maybe.

A great deal of Africa is not at all what the visitor may expect. Most is not sultry and forbidding jungle, but eroded desert, savanna, and hard, high, spiny plateau country, with a minimum of vegetation. Time and time again I thought that I was in Wyoming or Montana. Even the cities have the dusty, fabricated look of early American frontier towns. If you want to see a naked savage, you have to go out and look for him, and this process may be laborious. Much of Africa—of course I am generalizing broadly—is not even particularly hot. I never found a place, except possibly Khartoum, as hot as Houston in a heat wave, or as uncomfortable as Washington. Nor is much of it necessarily unhealthy to visitors who take reasonable precautions. At any rate neither my wife nor I ever had a degree of fever or a stomach ache from an African complaint.

During the course of our trip I worked hard with my ears and took notes on conversations with 1,503 people. I was not looking for adventure. I was looking for facts. And in Africa, more than in most continents, facts are not always easy to come by. African statistics are fantastically unreliable for the most part. Several African countries—let alone cities—have never had a census. Three reference books on my desk, all unimpeachably standard, give three different figures even for such an item as the total area of Africa. At least this makes research into Africa a challenge. Its mysteries consist of more than just the contours of the Mountains of the Moon.

But as to the people we met—

All I can do is thank them all. My real bibliography is people. We talked to pygmies, giants, kings, and slaves. We talked to white settlers, black insurrectionaries, prime ministers, nationalists, and witch doctors. We met such picturesque leaders in picturesque domains as the Sultan of Zanzibar, the Asantehene of Ashanti, the Mwami of Ruanda, the Mahdi of Khartoum, the Kabaka of Buganda, the Wali of Tripolitania, the Pasha of Marrakesh, the Emir of Kano, and many others. Also we met peasants in these realms who are lucky if they have a grass roof over their heads, or earn fifty dollars a year.

In general, but not always in detail, the structure of this book follows the chronology of our trip. I have not used the conventional pattern of dividing Africa into two separate entities, north and south of the Sahara, but instead

A NOTE BY WAY OF PREFACE

have broken the work into two large groupings: (1) North and East; (2) South and West. Because Africa is so little and so inaccurately known I have included more history—also more direct personal observation—than in the other Inside books. But the root design, the basic manner of approach, is the same. I have tried to give a conspectus of the whole gigantic continent with at least passing reference to every major problem—human, social, religious, racial, economic, political. All that the ordinary reader needs to know about Africa will, I hope, be found in this book. That is one reason why it is so long. I had no idea when I began it that it would turn out to be almost as long as *Inside U.S.A.*

We begin Part I with an introductory survey, and then make progressive contact with issues all the way from North Africa to the Mau Maus in Kenya. Our first stop is Morocco, where our trip began. We look at French administration in Algeria and Tunisia; dip briefly into the splendid, lustrous world of the Sahara; proceed then to the wastes of Libya, the youngest country in the world; inspect revolutionary Egypt and its enormous stepchild the Anglo-Egyptian Sudan; penetrate into Ethiopia and graze on the edges of Red Sea Africa; descend then into Black Africa proper and sketch the outlines of British policy and rule in East Africa; and survey the fascinatingly varied worlds of Kenya, Tanganyika, and Uganda. Then, skipping to the south, we open Part II with the Union of South Africa, with its racial tensions and stupendously difficult and perhaps insoluble problems; visit the three "High Commission" territories; glance at Portuguese Africa briefly; progress northward to the new Central African Federation embracing the Rhodesias and Nyasaland; survey the magnificent world of the Congo and see what the Belgians have done there; look at French Africa again; and emerge finally into the promise and sunshine of the West Coast, where experiments of great germinating force are taking place particularly in the Gold Coast and Nigeria. The arc of Part II stretches from the successors of Malan to Nkrumah. It is a very wide and challenging arc indeed.

J. G.

PART ONE

The North and the East

I speak of Africa and golden joys.
—HENRY IV, Act V, Scene 3

For better or for worse the old Africa is gone and the white races must face the new situation which they have themselves created.
—JAN CHRISTIAAN SMUTS

CHAPTER 1

Dark Continent Becoming Light

In Africa think big. —CECIL RHODES

AFRICA is not in some respects a Dark Continent at all; it is flashing with vivid light. Much of it is luminous—in fact incandescent. This is because, among other reasons, it presents the spectacle of millions upon millions of people being transformed almost overnight from a primitive, tribal way of life to aggressive membership in modern society. Africa is like an exploding mass of yeast. Its fermentations are not merely political and economic, but social, cultural, religious. It is springing in a step from black magic to white civilization, although there are plenty of Africans who still believe in black magic. The grandchildren of Dr. Livingstone's porters go to Oxford. Today's Africa may not know exactly where it is going, but it is on the march, and marching fast—toward western standards.

This is the first great point to make about contemporary Africa—its emergence with exaggerated speed into the embrace of modern times. The problems arising inevitably from this evolution are so difficult, so abrasive and perplexing, that they cannot be described in an inch; much of this book will be taken up with them. The second great point is a contrary point. While partaking with confused zeal of much that the western world has to offer many parts of Africa are at the same time attempting to throw off the political shackles of the West. Africans want our education and techniques, our mode of life and standard of living, but not our domination or exploitation. Of course there are millions of Africans still too ignorant, too backward, childlike, and uneducated to know what nationalism means, or to care two strings of beads whether they are politically free or not. Nevertheless the nationalist note is being sounded almost everywhere; there are scarcely any educated Africans who are not nationalist to some degree or other, for good or ill. Africa, like practically every other undeveloped place in the world, seeks to be free of old-style colonialism with its deprivations, abuses, and anachronisms.

This fabulous and challenging continent is vital to the western world not merely because it is important strategically and is packed with vital raw materials, but because it is our Last Frontier. Much of Asia has been lost; Africa remains. But Africa lies open like a vacuum, and is almost perfectly defenseless—the richest prize on earth. What is more it is defenseless in a period of Cold War. Besides it pants for development. If we do not help it to develop, somebody else will. But it is a black continent, not white, and so problems of agonizing complexity arise in such fields as race relations and the creation of "plural" societies. Another reason why Africa is so exhilarating—and important—is that it contains peoples in every known stage of political development, from the most blatantly primitive to the most sophisticated. There are independent states, self-governing dominions, quasi-dominions, protectorates, colonies, trusteeships, territories the status of which is ambiguous or contested, and large areas which, no matter how they are governed, are still purely tribal or feudal. Africa is a kind of living laboratory, a paradise for the political scientist as well as anthropologist—which means that it is still rich with opportunities if we are wise enough to seize them.

Is the white man finished in Africa?

Are Africans capable of self-government?

If imperialism is dead, what is going to take its place?

Could Communism capture Africa, as it has captured much of Asia?

Can the colonial powers save their position by reform?

These are among the questions to which we must address ourselves, but the answers are not easy.

AFRICA: SOME ITEMS IN PHYSIOGNOMY

The historically decisive characteristic of the African continent is its inaccessibility.

—W. M. MACMILLAN

Africa covers not less than 11,262,000 square miles, and is as big as the United States, western Europe, India, and China put together; its area is one-fifth that of the entire land surface of the globe. It rises out of the Atlantic, the Mediterranean, the Red Sea, the Indian Ocean, and the Antarctic, a continental mass shaped like some monstrous liver or kidney. The coastline has few indentations. Africa is the most impregnable of continents, and hence the least developed. Not only is its periphery difficult to penetrate; so is the interior plateau. It is the most tropical of continents, and the one most afflicted by diseases that have profound economic as well as human consequences. For instance, two-thirds of all Tanganyika (which is half again as big as Texas) is uncultivable on account of the tsetse fly, an insect which exists nowhere else in the world except Africa. Much of Africa is desert, brittle grassland, and heavy rain forest; less than 10 per cent of the total land is arable.

Africa is an important depository of raw materials, and the surface has scarcely been thumbed as yet. It produces something like 98 per cent of the diamonds of the world, 55 per cent of its gold, and 22 per cent of its copper, as well as large quantities of various strategic minerals, like manganese, chromium, and uranium. Africa produces about two-thirds of the world's cocoa and three-fifths of its palm oil, and has immense reserves of water power. It could grow every crop on earth. But if Africa is rich, it is also poor. This is one of the overriding paradoxes. It exports only about 3 per cent of the total world export of raw materials, and does not even produce enough food to feed itself. Erosion is remorselessly eating the land away. Thus arises a double point: Africa is not only vital for what it already has, but is incomparably the greatest potential source of wealth awaiting development in the world. No continent has ever beckoned with more fruitful opportunities.

On Africa's 11,262,000 square miles live 198,000,000 people, divided into a fantastic number of different tribes. These are astoundingly variegated. This will be demonstrated time and time again in these pages. Most ethnologists say—the subject has thorns—that there are three main racial groups: Hamites, Negroes, and "Bantus." Another group is that of the Bushmen, but these exist only in isolated parts of southern Africa, and are extinct as a force. Hamites are technically speaking white. "Bantu" is properly not a racial but a linguistic term; it is commonly used, however, as a convenient blanket word for most African peoples, dark-skinned but not always as dark as pure Negroes, who cover most of Africa below the bulge. As to "Negro" that too is an extremely imprecise and unsatisfactory term. There are hundreds of different types of Negro, Negroid, and Negrillo peoples. Speaking roughly the Negroes are those who occupy parts of Central Africa and most of the West Coast. A further complication is that profuse admixtures of peoples have occurred, and are still occurring; Hamitic Ethiopians have crossed with Semitic Arabs; Hamitic Berbers have crossed with Negroes from the French Sudan; Negroes and Bantus are inextricably commingled in the Congo, Nigeria and elsewhere.

The 198,000,000 people of Africa speak something like *seven hundred* main different languages. There are generally conceded to be 10 principal Semitic languages, 47 Hamitic, 182 Bantu, and no fewer than 264 Sudanese. These latter and their offshoots are the main "Negro" languages. Between 200 and 300 of these languages have in recent years been given written form; complete Bibles exist in 33, and the New Testament in 70. Parts of the Bible are in at least 200 others. Only 3 languages, aside from Arabic, ever achieved their own written script before the white man came—Amharic, the language of Ethiopia; a variety of Berber known as Tamachek; and a Liberian language called Vai. All others today use our ordinary English lettering, when they are written down at all.

The main religious groups among Africans are Moslem, pagan or animist, and Christian. Reliable statistics are impossible to get but probably there are about 60,000,000 Moslem Africans, mostly concentrated on the northern shelf and along the East Coast, 112,000,000 pagans, and 21,000,000 Christians. Mohammedanism, as we shall see presently, is a powerfully expanding and pervasive force.[1]

Now we must have one more figure and then we are done with statistics for a time. It is a very significant figure indeed. It is moreover an almost unbelievable figure, and it is the heart of the African problem. *The total white European population of Africa is probably only five million.* Everybody else on the continent—with the exception of some 600,000 Indians and minor colonies of Lebanese, Syrians, and the like—is of *African* stock. Africa is a continent containing 193,000,000 Africans, mostly black or brown, and not more than 5,000,000 European whites. Yet the white man rules. Moreover of this total number of 5,000,000 Europeans two and a half million are concentrated in South Africa and 1,600,000 in French North Africa; in other words there are only about a million white Europeans in all the rest of Africa, immeasurably vast and with a heavily proliferating black population. The white man is overwhelmingly outnumbered.

Let us make these figures even more striking by breaking them down. In Nyasaland, for instance, there are 2,400,000 black Africans as against 4,073 white Europeans; in French Togoland, 970,983 as against 841; in Sierra Leone 1,766,615 as against exactly 598. Nigeria, the largest African country in population, has more than thirty *million* people, of whom only 11,750 are white Europeans. The white man in Nigeria is consequently outnumbered by more than 2,500 to one. In the "white settler" countries the percentage of Europeans is larger, but still small; Kenya, for instance, has 5,500,000 black Africans, but not more than 42,000 whites.

Such statistics tell us—with as much obviousness as an elephant in a

[1] There are also large Moslem communities in West Africa.

drawing room—why nationalism has such force. Only too patently 11,750 white men cannot keep 30,000,000 black men from becoming free once the 30,000,000 black men decide that they *want* to become free. No European country has the power to keep such a majority permanently down, if it does not want to be kept down and has enough education to be able to assert itself.

THERE ARE TWO AFRICAS

The northern coast of Africa, that is to say the southern coast of the Mediterranean, is to a certain extent not Africa at all except in the geographical sense. In Roman times it was much more part of "Europe" than Scandinavia or even Britain. Today Morocco, Algeria, Tunisia, and particularly Egypt are not as different as one might think from southern Spain, Greece, or Turkey. Their civilization derives from Europe and the Middle East; they are Mediterranean countries, much closer to Europe than to Black Africa.

The Sahara is often called a sea of sand, and it really is a sea—a sea, moreover, that separates Europe from Africa more than the Mediterranean does. The French in particular always recognize that Africa is divided into two separate entities by the Sahara; they almost never use the blanket term "Africa" but differentiate instead between "North" Africa and *Afrique noire*. Above the Sahara, Africa is Europe; below, Africa is Africa. The Sahara itself, both a barrier and a bridge, is a kind of no man's land—or rather all man's land—in between.

This is not to say that there are no unifying factors in Africa. We shall encounter several as this book proceeds, though not many. One is Islam. Another, in a totally different category, is bilharzia, a waterborne disease that made—and makes—disastrous inroads in Egypt and has now climbed up the Nile and is spreading insidiously in the lakes and rivers of Central Africa and the Rhodesias.

I should put in a word here about African communications. They are frightful. Difficulties in air travel are as nothing compared to travel on the ground. The British have been in Kenya, a show-piece colony, for fifty years, but the roads there would make a Tibetan blush; some are worse than western American roads before the advent of the automobile. But at least Kenya *has* roads; there are immense tracts of Africa with none at all. To get from Khartoum, say, to Asmara in Eritrea, a distance of four hundred miles, will take about six weeks overland—if the weather is good. Even to send a telegram between these two points entails an element of delicious risk. If you want to telephone from Johannesburg to Lagos, two major capitals, the call must be routed through London. On a pan-Africa basis there are practically no communications. No transcontinental highway exists from east to west, and the north-south roads, from Algiers or Cairo to the Cape, are still paths for adventurers. The Algiers route traverses the Sahara, and that from Cairo has an unpaved gap more than a thousand miles long. The railroads, with some exceptions, are almost as feeble as cable cars. Nothing like a rail network on an all-African level is even dreamed of, and the continent has only 5.6 per cent of the world's total railway mileage.

Another point in this general realm is that political frontiers have little natural reality. For the most part they mark off where the rule of one white man stops and another starts, but not much else. They were made in the old days mostly by latitude and longitude—"written in the heavens"— by Europeans because the interior was almost totally unexplored.[2] Even today nobody can tell from the terrain where, for instance, the southern Sudan ends and northern Uganda begins. A tribe like the Masai lives on both sides of the Kenya-Tanganyika border, and pays little attention to what "country" it is in.

SOME MORE PRELIMINARY POINTS

What does Africa . . . stand for?
—H. D. THOREAU

1. The poverty of most Africans out in the bush, or even in the cities, is something almost beyond the power of the western imagination to grasp. Geographers have today what they call "caloric" maps, showing the intake of food of peoples in various parts of the world. Bantu Africa has the lowest rate on the globe. The average wage of an unskilled worker in East Africa is $3.00 to $4.00 per month; the per capita income ranges between $14.00 and $28.00 *per year*.[3]

2. Similarly the backwardness of Africa has to be seen to be believed. The illiteracy rate for the continent as a whole is probably 90 per cent. But in such realms as "backwardness" one must be careful to think of Africa in proper perspective. People who talk indiscriminately about Africans being "primitive" are being primitive themselves. What is backwardness, anyway? It is perfectly true that millions of Africans have never

---

[2] Harry R. Rudin, "Africa in Perspective," *Journal of International Affairs*, Vol. VII, No. 2, 1953, a brilliantly comprehensive brief article.

[3] *Africa: New Crises in the Making*, by Harold L. Isaacs and Emory Ross, Foreign Policy Association.

been to a movie and believe in spells cast by their witch doctors; but it is also true that in Nigerian tribal wars fighting stopped for the day after the first man was killed. Africans have not had—as is only too obvious—our advantages. It is interesting to recall in this connection such facts as that there were 41,633 homes in Kentucky with no toilet or privy as of recent date, that in Puerto Rico there are only 497 physicians for a population of 2,210,703, that no fewer than 1,500,000 American boys were rejected by the draft in World War II because they could not read and write, that in the United States today an automobile is stolen every 2.3 minutes, and that 34,763 American citizens were killed in automobile accidents in 1954.

3. Africans have astoundingly different levels of political development even within the same area. I talked to a British governor who said that "his" people were at least thirty-five years behind those of Nigeria. He added quickly, "But this does not mean that we have thirty-five years!" The pace of events everywhere in Africa is very fast. Reform, education, training for administration, must come at once, or it will be too late—that is, the Africans will refuse to accept further tutelage under European rule.

4. It should be carefully noted, however, that a great many Africans have no sense of affiliation beyond their families, clans, or tribes.

5. Politics quite aside, much of the continent is erupting. Something like 40,000,000 natives have left their tribes, have taken up residence in the towns and villages, and are seeking a new way of life. The social mixups and problems caused by this mass uprooting are formidable indeed. So long as Africans remain tribal, as in parts of the Congo and Portuguese Africa, they are not a problem except in the field of local administration. It is when the tribal life breaks down and they attempt to enter white urban society that their status and future becomes such a complex and agonizing issue. But the process cannot be stopped. Once the white man invaded the black man's Africa; now it is the black man who invades the white man's Africa. Hence there are two possibilities for the future, a head-on collision between black and white, with disastrous consequences for both, or the gradual, eventual emergence of plural societies, that is, coexistence.[4]

6. I should interpolate here a line about use of the word "native," as in the paragraph above. Africans do not like to be called "natives" nor do they care much for "black" or even "Negro." They like to be called "Africans." When occasionally I use "blacks" or "natives" for "Africans" I do not mean this as an affront.

7. I like Africans but they are not always easy to know or get along with. The friendlier a European (or American) is, the more suspicious the

[4] "Plural society" is defined in Chapter 19 below.

African may be. It is often a risk for an African to be friendly. Some have a strong note of childishness. They are sometimes truculent, schizophrenic, and full of inferiority and insecurity which they may express by exaggerated superiority. An African Negro, to be able to enter the western world at all, has had to bridge an inordinately wide, difficult, and painful gap in his own community; moreover he will have had to face, like as not, intense bigotry and intolerance from colonial Europeans. Schizophrenia? It is never easy to be a man of two worlds. It is hard enough to be a man of one.

8. Most Europeans in Africa have extremely little knowledge of any Africans except servants or subordinate employees. Many have never met a sophisticated, westernized, well-educated African. They think instinctively that *all* Africans are inferior, and cannot take them seriously as human beings.

9. Many Europeans think that Africans, if they become free, will make a botch of freedom. But this remains to be seen. They also say that African exploitation of Africans could be worse than European, and that the "new" Africa will not be "democratic." One reason behind this latter hypothesis, which the experience of the Gold Coast incidentally disproves so far, is the supposition that Africans, who have lived mostly in tribal societies, do not have much tradition of the freedom of the individual. Another is that the electorate is immature, and there are few trained leaders. It has been hard enough to make democracy work in Burma or Indonesia. (Or for that matter in Germany, Nicaragua, or New Jersey.) It will be harder still in Tunisia and the Sudan. Yet it would be silly to insist that the task is hopeless or impossible.

AFRICAN HISTORY: A FIVE-MINUTE GLIMPSE

Nobody knows what filled the vast cornucopia of Africa with its first inhabitants, nor does anybody know with much certainty who these were. The origin of the Negro is as obscure as that of the Chinese. Some historians think that Africa, rather than Central Asia, is the birthplace of the human race. After all this is the continent of the great anthropoids. One thing that we do know, coming to comparatively recent times, is that Egypt has had an uninterrupted civilization for more than 6,000 years; the story of Carthage is well known, and so is that of the Arab conquests of North Africa. In the Middle Ages various Negro or semi-Negro kingdoms, like the Mandingo, flourished briefly in the Sahara and then collapsed. The Berbers took Timbuktu in 1433. But most of Africa, particularly below the Equator, is still untouched by the prongs of our knowledge; its history is almost totally opaque. Rock paintings in South Africa give us tantalizing glimpses of life among the early Bushmen many thousands of years ago—they show a strong resemblance to paleolithic rock painting in Spain. Centuries later a civilization capable of producing works of art existed in Nigeria, as the Benin bronzes show. But in the main Africa south of the Sahara has little history until the white man came. Ruins out of which secrets might be wrested are few, and written records do not exist.

The first exploration of the African coastline, which is 16,100 miles long, was Phoenician; the Carthaginian explorer Hanno got as far as Sierra Leone in 520 BC. Bold Greek voyagers sailed around the edges of Africa, but could no more penetrate it than a water bug can penetrate a stone. The modern period of exploration begins with the Portuguese, who made voyages of the most extraordinary scope and enterprise in the time of Prince Henry, justly called the Navigator (1394-1460). Bartholomeu Diaz rounded the Cape of Good Hope in 1488, and Vasco da Gama touched on the Kenya coast on his way to India ten years later. Almost everywhere around Africa we shall find niches made by the early Portuguese. Then came Dutch, Danish, Spanish, French, and British voyagers and traders.

Slavery was the ugly dominant note in African history for at least 250 years, roughly from 1562 to the early 1800's. It is impossible to underestimate the importance of this today in psychological and other realms. Africans, having been slaves, do not want to be slaves again. Of course Africans themselves played a large role in the enslavement of other Africans. One should also mention the fact that the United States of America is 10 per cent a black nation today, because of slaves from Africa; one out of every ten living American citizens has an African ancestor. Central and South America—particularly that splendidly civilized country Brazil—have African strains too obvious to mention.

Slavery in Africa, which was an extremely lucrative business, occurred simultaneously on both sides of the continent; Europeans marauded for slaves or bought them on the West Coast; Arabs did the same thing in the north and east. The European slavers sold their produce to the West Indies and the United States, until the traffic was abolished; the Arabs sold to the Arabian peninsula, Turkey, and the Middle East. The slave trade, though presumably outlawed, continued to be practiced in some parts of Africa until comparatively recent times; when Dr. Albert Schweitzer arrived in French Equatorial Africa in 1913 remnants of the traffic still existed. Liberia was defaced by a vicious scandal over slavery, in which members of the government were involved, as recently as 1930.[5] But the slave traffic

---

[5] Charges appeared in the Manchester *Guardian* on October 15, 1953, that Saudi Arabians still bought slaves, procuring them from the Somalis and Ethiopia.

no longer exists anywhere in Africa on an organized basis, on a wholesale scale, or with the connivance of legitimate authorities.

Africa below the Equator did not begin to be opened up till the nineteenth century.[6] Until then, in the words of Miss Margery Perham, one of the most renowned of contemporary authorities on Africa, "it was a coast, not a continent." In 1800, as may be readily proved by maps of the day, 90 per cent of Black Africa was still unknown. Then French and British explorers penetrated the Niger area, and two Portuguese (strikingly enough they were half-castes) crossed the continent from ocean to ocean for the first time; the journey took them nine *years*, from 1802 to 1811. Later came spectacular bursts of exploratory activity, which have entered the world's folklore. Livingstone began his epochal discoveries in 1849, Speke solved the "riddle of the Nile" in 1862, and Stanley in 1875-76 explored the Congo. A wide furrow was cut by Christian missionaries, the importance of whose work, particularly in education, has been incalculable. In another dimension, the Suez Canal was opened in 1869. This, however, came about not so much because of interest in Africa *per se*, but to shorten the route to India. The fact that Africa has been developed so recently is a gravid factor in today's affairs; whole countries have been created in the lifetime of people who are not only still alive, but who are not particularly old. Kenya did not exist as such till the early 1900's; Nigeria is younger than Anthony Eden. Africa, the oldest continent, is also new.

The imperialist race for Africa began seriously in the 1870's, and was mostly completed by 1898. (British penetration of the West Coast began long before this, but it was predominantly commercial rather than political.) Roughly thirty years sufficed for carving up the continent. In 1875 there were (the Boer republics in South Africa excepted) four independent "countries" in Africa—Morocco, Liberia, Ethiopia, and Zanzibar. European invaders distinguished themselves by "avarice, treachery, hypocrisy, and brutality."[7] They swindled large tracts of land out of native kings by giving them worthless loops of beads; they made "treaties" by planting a flag. Major actors were King Leopold II of Belgium, who created and personally owned the Congo "Free" State, and—indirectly—Prince Bismarck. There came any number of episodes which need not concern us, some cynical, some romantic—the race between the British and the French for the Sudan, the race between Britain and Germany for the Cameroons, and a remarkable

---

[6] Except South Africa. The history of the Union has altogether different roots and takes a different course. Another country (above the Equator) with its own special self-contained history is Ethiopia.

[7] Evelyn Waugh, *Waugh in Abyssinia*, p. 5.

DARK CONTINENT BECOMING LIGHT

swap involving Zanzibar and, of all places, Helgoland in the North Sea. All that need be said at this juncture is that by the turn of the century, or shortly thereafter, the continent was largely in the hands of Great Britain, France, Belgium, Italy, Portugal, Spain, and Germany. Africa was a melon, and it was duly portioned out.

COLONIALISM: ITS DAYS ARE NUMBERED

About colonialism in Africa two main things should be said, without reference to various immoralities and injustices in the system. (1) It did a great deal of good. (2) It is dying.

The benefits the colonial system brought to Africa, even if it brought abuses too, are incontestable. Perhaps much of what the white man did was selfish, since it was for the benefit of the white communities themselves; nevertheless the record stands for itself. The Europeans may have ravaged a continent, but also they opened it up to civilization. Colonialism made today's nationalism possible, and opened the way to democracy. The Europeans abolished slavery, and ended tribal warfare. They created communications, improved the standard of living, developed natural resources, introduced scientific agriculture, fought to control malaria and other diseases, established public health controls, gave natives only an inch away from barbarism stable administration and a regime based in theory at least on justice and law. (The white man's law, of course.) Most important, they brought Christianity and western education. Not much education, but some. And there had been practically none before.

Why, if the white man has done so much good, is he on the way out in large parts of Africa? Why is old-style colonialism, the rule of the white powers, dying if not dead? There are all manner of reasons. Ethics —the pervasive feeling that it is morally wrong for one nation to rule another. After all Africa is the African's own continent. Diminishing returns—the fact that the expense of continued repressive (or even unrepressive) rule outbalances the return. Force costs money. Christianity—the missionaries taught that all men are equal under God. Woodrow Wilson— who preached the self-determination of small nations. Two calamitous world wars—which destroyed the European imperial system, and gave Africans good opportunity to learn about the frailties of their white masters. Two hundred thousand Africans fought (as colonial troops or otherwise) in World War I; five hundred thousand fought in World War II.[8] The Atlantic Charter and the United Nations Charter—both of which furnished

---

[8] See the Foreign Policy Association pamphlet cited above.

hope to colonial peoples everywhere. The example of India and the Middle East—where non-white governments have established successful rule. Above all, the population ratio and the growing force of African nationalism itself. Five million whites cannot permanently rule 193,000,000 Africans.

A great deal of Africa—most—is of course still under colonial rule, and in the Congo, several French territories, and Portuguese Africa this is not likely to be upset for many years to come. But patterns are changing. Outright repression is no longer in vogue, except in the Union of South Africa, the sorest spot on the continent. Not only is the white man defensive; he is frightened (even in the Union). Hence the major trend in much of white Africa today is a peculiar combination of stubborn defiance of the growing power of natives, together with attempts to save the situation and prolong colonial rule by a steady—if slow—process of amelioration and concession. Sensible Europeans know that the price of peaceable European survival on the continent is reform.

But what will take the place of European regimes, if they go? Are Africans capable of self-government? Of course not in many areas. But the question no longer has much relevance, strange as this may seem. I met many Africans, particularly on the East Coast, who conceded frankly that they were not remotely ready for full self-government as yet. The question is nevertheless irrelevant because, whether they are fit or not, nationalist Africans feel that they must start somewhere, sometime, and learn government by practicing it. They would much prefer to have bad government of their own than good government by a white outsider. The only way to learn how to walk is—to crawl.

COLOR BAR

Next to nationalism this is the most important and harassing issue in Africa, at least below the Sahara. The two subjects are inextricably interrelated, because it is color bar more than anything else that makes Africans turn nationalist. Color bar means what Americans call segregation, or Jim Crow—it is a blanket term for all the discriminations and injustices practiced against blacks and semi-blacks by their white rulers or by the white community. One must not think of an African in the Congo bush as being on the same level as a Negro in Harlem. He is nowhere nearly as advanced as that. But he can resent wanton maltreatment just as keenly, and want to improve his status. Moreover he belongs not to a minority, as in the United States, but to an overwhelmingly preponderant majority. Some problems in race relations appear to be insoluble, particularly in the

Union. They must be faced nevertheless. It is color bar, above everything, that makes Africa boil with discontent. It is the root cause of African inferiority, which in turn leads to resentment and revolt; it warps the minds of white man and black man both. Self-government will, of course, presumably mean the end of color bar, since a free African country will not be likely to discriminate against its own people, at least on the grounds of race.

Other principal African grievances against colonial rule have to do with (a) education; (b) economic exploitation. The European masters have by and large starved education in most of Africa. As a single case in point we might mention that in Kenya there are exactly 35 secondary schools for 5,500,000 Africans; the total enrollment is 3,555 boys and 451 girls. In regard to exploitation consider that Europeans in South Africa extract from the African earth gold worth several hundred million dollars a year, but that the mine owners pay their African labor a wage ranging from 33 to 42 cents per day. A salient fact about Africa as a whole is that the European position rests almost exclusively on the use—and often exploitation—of cheap black labor.

THE PATTERN OF TODAY'S AFRICA

The colonial problem cannot be solved without equitable distribution of wealth everywhere.
—WENDELL WILLKIE

There are four independent countries in Africa today, run by Africans —Liberia, Libya, Ethiopia, and Egypt.[9] A fifth, the Union of South Africa, is also independent (although a member of the British Commonwealth) but it is certainly not run by Africans.

The Anglo-Egyptian Sudan (which covers 967,500 square miles, an area one-third the size of the entire United States) will, as a result of the 1953 treaty between Britain and Egypt, become fully independent probably in 1956, or join Egypt. It is to all practical purposes independent now. The Gold Coast, on the underside of the western lobe of the continent, one of the richest colonies in the world, has an African prime minister and cabinet and a largely African legislature, and is scheduled to become a fully self-governing dominion, within the British Commonwealth, by 1956 or perhaps sooner. It will probably be the first "Black Dominion." Nigeria (which has more than twice as many people as the Union of South Africa)

---

[9] A critic might well say that Libya hardly stands on its own feet as yet, but for the purposes of this quick survey it must be included among the independent states.

has also been promised independence, with certain qualifications, by 1956.

Somalia, on the horn of Africa, which like Libya was once an Italian colony, is now being administered by the United Nations, and by an agreement already reached is to become independent in 1960.

Southern Rhodesia has for years had a special position as an almost fully self-governing colony, and has recently been joined with Northern Rhodesia and Nyasaland to compose the new Central African Federation. It is generally assumed that this entity will in time reach dominion status.

One should also mention what might be called "United Nations" Africa. No fewer than six African countries as well as Somalia are, technically at least, "trust" territories of the United Nations. They were former German colonies. Each is administered by a European power—Tanganyika by the British, Togoland and the Cameroons by both British and French, and Ruanda-Urundi by the Belgians—but the fact that they are trusteeships makes the European rulers, who have to report to the UN several times a year, particularly sensitive to their responsibilities. Time and time again the UN has been extraordinarily useful to African nationalists of several other countries as well, because it provides an international forum at which they can present grievances. Moreover it does a great deal of useful welfare work not only in the trust territories but everywhere in undeveloped Africa. Also it is worth noting that Article 73 of the UN Charter states that the member powers, in every colonial area, recognize that the interests of the native inhabitants are *"paramount."*

Omit from this brief summary the Union, the Central African Federation, and the UN trust territories. Even so the African states already self-governing or near to becoming so comprise 87,052,000 out of Africa's 198,000,000 people, on 3,458,471 square miles out of 11,262,000. From the point of view of people, 44 per cent of African Africa is free or almost free; from the point of view of area, 31 per cent.

*

Five European powers rule the rest.[10]

French Africa. Area, 4,022,150 square miles; population, 44,152,600. From the standpoint of territory France is by far the largest African power. French policy is based on the concept of assimilation, i.e., to make Africans in the long run Frenchmen. The French do not train natives for eventual self-government, which is the gist of the British system, but try instead to channel off nationalist discontent by (in theory) opening up the doors of

---

[10] This brief section is designed to be no more than a quick *hors d'oeuvres* to much more substantial treatment of the subject later.

French culture, French civilization, to the Africans in their charge. But their techniques differ sharply north and south of the Sahara. We shall inspect Morocco, Tunisia, and Algeria in the chapters immediately following. In the south—*Afrique noire*—French rule has a much more moderate basis than on the Mediterranean bench. Every African in all the vastness of French West Africa, French Equatorial Africa, Madagascar, and so on is a citizen of *France*, with privileges and duties more or less equal —again in theory—to those of a French citizen in Rouen or Bordeaux. This means among other things that, except socially, there is comparatively little color bar. Moreover electors in these areas send their own representatives to Paris. No fewer than 52 out of the total of 626 members of the National Assembly are African, and there are 38 African senators out of 320.

British Africa. The British rule or administer 62,433,645 people, living on 2,025,719 square miles. Of the total population perhaps 280,000— no more—are white.[11] British methods, like French, differ radically from country to country. For instance, color bar is marked on the East Coast, and in particular in the Rhodesias, but hardly exists in the West. White settlement is forbidden in Nigeria, but Kenya is the stronghold of a European settler minority that will fight to the last bitter inch to maintain white supremacy. It is also the home of the dangerous and expensive Mau Mau revolt. But certain broad principles underlie British policy everywhere, no matter what local divergencies there may be. One is Indirect Rule, which means administration through the mechanism of native chiefs. Great Britain is the only colonial power that maintains an avowed official policy, the ultimate objective of which is to train Africans for complete self-government, within the Commonwealth. This does not mean that the British intend to get out of Africa next week, or that they will not ruthlessly deal with people who displease them. It does mean that, little by little, in slow stages, they are giving Africans serious political responsibilities. Perhaps the pace is not fast enough. Plenty of criticisms can be leveled against Britain all the way from the Gambia to Basutoland, but every British colony of consequence has by this time *some* kind of arrangement, no matter how vestigial, by which Africans are taking part in their own government.

There are several reasons for this policy. Once I heard the late Ernest Bevin define it in three words: "Give — and keep." He meant, of course, that by voluntary withdrawal at a propitious time, the British will retain

[11] And of these 240,000 no fewer than 160,000 are concentrated in Southern Rhodesia. I have not included the Union of South Africa in these figures. It is "British" in name only.

the good will of the Africans in the area concerned, strengthen the Commonwealth rather than risk weakening it by continued rule against the will of the inhabitants, and emerge ethically generous and at the same time possessed of full political and economic advantages. Britons believe in right, they believe in justice, they believe in the ineluctable processes of history, and they believe in keeping their bread buttered right side up. They know full well that a handful of Europeans cannot possibly keep the entire continent of Africa in permanent subjugation, except by methods that cost too much. Then vivid moral and idealistic factors come into play, as we shall see often before this book is done. I met a young District Officer in the Mau Mau country who told us, "When the British Commonwealth has to rule by force alone, it is finished."

Belgian Africa. This means the Congo, which covers 924,300 square miles and has twelve million people, of whom roughly 60,000 are Europeans. The essence of the Belgian system is to buy off discontent by giving economic opportunity. Nobody in the Congo can vote (not even Belgians), and the Congolese have few, if any, civil rights or liberties; but they have good wages, good social services, and freedom from most of the worse irritants of color bar. The system is working well. Little evidence exists of active (as apart from passive) nationalism or political unrest.

Portuguese Africa. This consists mostly of two enormous colonies, Angola and Mozambique, which between them have a population of around 9,500,000 on 778,000 square miles. Legally they are overseas provinces of Portugal itself. The natives have had little access to the fermentations of the world outside, and are years behind those in most of the rest of Africa. One interesting Portuguese innovation is the *assimilado* system, as we shall see below. Also Portuguese Africa still has forced labor.

Spanish Africa. Population, 1,495,000; area, 134,700 square miles. This too we shall deal with in due course later.

IS THE WHITE MAN FINISHED IN AFRICA?

Of course not. He will probably not be finished for a long, long time—if he behaves himself. It would be a grave pity if he were finished, because he still has tremendous contributions to make. Africa needs development, it needs tutelage. Who does not? But development and tutelage cannot take place in an atmosphere poisoned by political repression and racial tension. Let us repeat: the price of peaceable European survival on the African continent is reform; moreover reform expressed in concrete political terms, and with a timetable.

DARK CONTINENT BECOMING LIGHT 19

The Governor General of the Belgian Congo, who cannot be accused of any partiality for nationalism, told us, "It is dangerous to educate Africans. It will be more dangerous not to educate them." Once an African is educated, he can at least be reached.

Finally a word on Communism.[12] Most African nationalists I met pretended, at least, to abhor the Communists and all their works; but this attitude may not last forever. There are certainly some African leaders today who hate the British, the French, the Belgians enough to be willing to take aid from the Communists, when they need it and if they can get it. They have nowhere else to turn. If we, of the western world, do not help Africans to fulfill their legitimate aspirations, some will turn to Communism in our place. It will be a bad joke for them, but a worse joke on us. Already there are areas where the Communists are almost in a position to take over the nationalist movement. This, if it should happen, would be a tragedy not merely for the Africans involved, but for the whole democratic world. If Communism is ever let loose on the great mass of black illiterates, among the intolerably poor and crushed in the submerged regions of the continent, a development might arise like that in China. And we will have lost Africa, as China has been lost.

*

Enough by way of introduction. Let us explore now, country by country, Africa with all its mixedupness, magnificence, color, squalor, and vibrating challenge for the future.

[12] This subject too we shall explore in detail in many passages below, particularly in Chapter 46.

CHAPTER 2

The Sultan of Morocco

Deposing me will not solve the Moroccan problem.
  —THE FORMER SULTAN OF MOROCCO
Free as an Arab. —RALPH WALDO EMERSON

So WITH the Sultan of Morocco we begin this long journey around the least known and most copious of continents. There are, of course, two sultans. The pallid and inept old gentleman who acceded to the Moroccan throne on August 21, 1953, and who has had a distressingly uncomfortable reign so far, only reached his exalted position because the French deposed and exiled his predecessor. Many people think that the exiled Sultan, even if he is completely out of action at present, is the rightful ruler of his country. We will deal with these two rococo personages in turn. The gist of the situation in Morocco is a tense, ugly struggle for power between rival forces which they personify. The old Sultan represents the nationalists, the new Sultan the French.

The reigning Sultan, he who is on the spot in Morocco today—"on the spot" in the colloquial as well as literal sense of the phrase—is named Sidi Mohammed Ben Moulay Arafa el Alaoui. He is at once a pope, a king, a puppet, and a prisoner.

The Sultan—any sultan—is a pope, because he is the supreme religious head of his community. Before he can reign he must be anointed with power by the Ulema of Fez, a congregation of Moslem holy men corresponding roughly to the College of Cardinals in Rome. The Sultan is a king, an authentic monarch in his own right, because Morocco is—in theory at least—an independent state which the French "protect." Morocco has been ruled by a succession of native dynasties since the ninth century AD, and its official name—even under the French protectorate—is still the Sherifian Empire. The Sultan is a puppet, since he has to do what the

THE SULTAN OF MOROCCO

French tell him to do, or lose his job. France established its protectorate over Morocco in 1912, and has been the effective authority in the country ever since. Finally, any sultan is a prisoner because of the paradoxical point that the French, even if their authority is supreme, cannot rule without him. They have to have a sultan on the throne, in order to maintain the pretense that Morocco is an "independent" country, which pretense suits their convenience. The present Sultan is a figurehead, an obedient prisoner (whereas his predecessor was disobedient) but to a certain extent the French are his prisoners too.

PAUSE FOR STATION IDENTIFICATION

Everybody knows that Texas is a large exuberant state full of oil and millionaires. Nobody, writing a book about Asia, would have to pause to explain that Japan is an island, heavily populated by imitative, industrious people with black hair and yellow skin. The word "Japan" instantly brings forth familiar images. One of the difficulties in writing about Africa is that, time and time again, we shall have to break narrative pace and pause for the most rudimentary exposition. Most Americans—Europeans too—have only faint knowledge of the significance of names that we shall be using constantly, even those as familiar as "Berber." I do not think that the average reader of this book will know automatically where Marrakesh is, or what is the difference in status between Tangier and Tetuan. Morocco is, it happens, more familiar than much of the rest of Africa; it does, after all, convey *some*thing—even if no more than a brand of leather—just as Egypt connotes the Pyramids, sand, and the Nile. I will not have to define the Nile. But I am not sure that I can mention the Atlas, which is almost as important to Morocco as the Nile is to Egypt, without having to take time out to explain what the Atlas is. We will constantly be impaled on a vexing dilemma—whether to take practically nothing for granted and risk being otiose by describing what the reader already knows, or to irritate and puzzle him by using words like "Sherifian" without explanation, and driving him to an encyclopaedia.

Furthermore, even if we know a good deal about Morocco already, we may know it wrong. For instance, the word "Moor" gives most people an instinctive association with "dark" or "black." Everybody knows the term "blackamoor." No doubt *Othello* and *The Merchant of Venice* are partly responsible for this. In actual fact Moors are not a Negro people at all, though many have interbred with Negroes. Ethnically they belong to the caucasian race, and some Moors are paler than Senator McCarthy or Rita Hayworth.

HIS MAJESTY THE SULTAN

Sidi Mohammed Ben Moulay Arafa el Alaoui, Commander of the Faithful, was born in Fez in 1889, and is a wealthy landowner.[1] He is an uncle of the former Sultan, and a cousin of several other recent sovereigns. He is a member of the Alaouite family and is a Sherifian, or lineal descendant of the Prophet Mohammed, one of whose titles was Sherif of Mecca. All Moroccan sultans in the modern age have been Sherifians. But as a matter of blunt fact nobody, at this date, can know with reasonable accuracy whether a man is a true Sherifian or not. Genealogy is far from being an exact science in Moslem lands, and, even if it were, few people would be able to trace their ancestry back for more than thirteen hundred years. Mohammed died in AD 632, and left no sons. But we shall run into so-called Sherifians everywhere in Moslem Africa. They resemble American descendants of folk who crossed the Atlantic on the *Mayflower*. There must be hundreds in Fez alone, perhaps thousands. Your chauffeur or bootblack may well be a Sherifian.

The Alaouite house, which has been the reigning dynasty since 1668, is supposed to derive from the Caliph Ali, the son-in-law of the Prophet, through his daughter Fatima. Its members held large amounts of land in the Tafilalet oasis, below the Atlas mountains. They were Arab, not Berber. Now it is important to understand that the royal succession in Morocco is not necessarily hereditary in our western sense. All over Africa we will find succession to be an extraordinarily intricate and varying phenomenon. The Moroccan sultanate does not automatically pass from father to eldest son, or to any son, though a son is preferred. The successor must be a relative, a Sherifian, but that is all. Similarly England has been ruled by several different royal houses, but all claim descent from the Plantagenets. A new sultan is, in theory, supposed to be the best or strongest male relative available. He is chosen (again in theory) by the Ulema of the Kairouyine mosque in Fez,[2] one of the holiest institutions in Islam. In actual fact the French Resident General in Morocco suggests a candidate to the Ulema, and this candidate is then "elected" to the sultanate.

---

[1] "Sidi" may be variously translated as "Prince," "Lord," "Chief," or even "Monseigneur." "Ben" means "son of."
[2] Kairouyine may be spelled in several different ways, for instance Kairoween and Qarawiyin. The French version is Karouiine. In general in these chapters I will conform to English rather than French usage. Most African names are difficult enough in any case, and Fez for example is easier on Anglo-Saxon eyes than Fès.

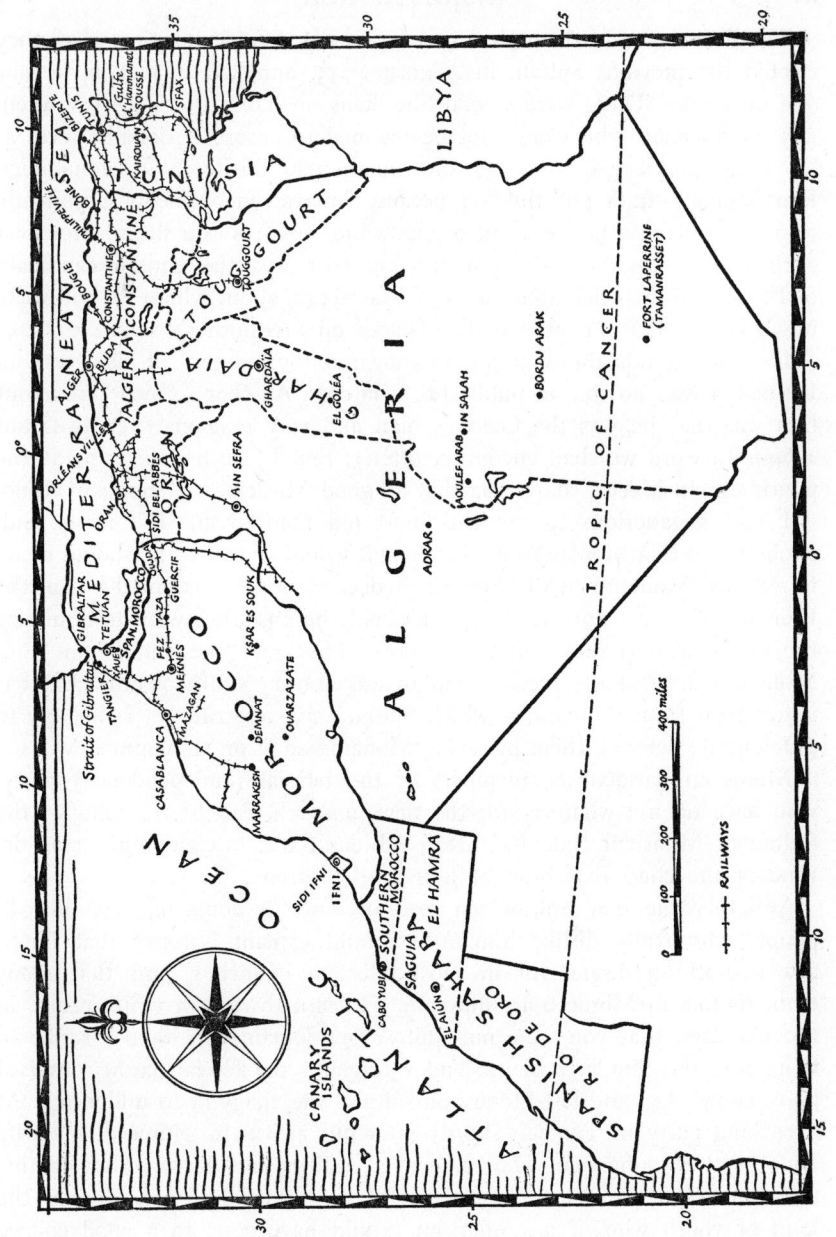

The French found themselves in a somewhat difficult position when they ejected the previous Sultan, in August, 1953, and had to pick up a new one overnight. There were several Sherifians on hand, but France wanted, (1) an *old* man who would not be inclined to absorb nationalist ideas as his reign progressed, and (2) one completely docile. Sidi Mohammed Ben Moulay Arafa got the job because he was inconspicuous, perfectly respectable from a family point of view, and colorless as a sheep. Moreover —the most important thing about him—he was the chosen candidate of El Glaoui, the celebrated Pasha of Marrakesh, about whom we will write much below. He is related to the Glaoui on his mother's side.

Even so, he was almost totally unknown at the moment of his accession. He had played no role in public life whatever. All that seemed sure about him was that he was the Glaoui's man and very religious. Yet he is not a *harji* (a word we shall encounter often); that is, he has never made the pilgrimage to Mecca, something that all good Moslems are supposed to do.

I find it laborious to call this inert old man by his full name, Sidi Mohammed Ben Moulay Arafa. Properly it would seem that he should be referred to as Mohammed VI, since his predecessor was Mohammed V. But the French seldom use numerical titles, probably because they want to minimize the historical importance of the dynasty. They say "the Sultan" or "Sidi Mohammed." But the previous Sultan was also a "Sidi Mohammed." If it is not clear from the context which Sultan I am referring to, I shall try to differentiate between them by saying Mohammed V or Mohammed VI.

Moroccan nationalists, members of the Istiqlal (Independence) party, who have no use whatever for the new monarch, call him scoffingly "the Sultan of Monsieur Bidault," because Bidault was foreign minister at the time of the coup that brought him to the throne.

Whether the new Sultan can read or write is doubtful, according to people who really dislike him. We should explain at once that illiteracy is nothing disgraceful in most Moslem countries, and that many eminent folk in Morocco are illiterate. To learn to read or write meant, in the old days, that you were not quite a gentleman; you hired a scribe to write for you. Similarly in pre-Tudor England the feudal barons despised book knowledge, and left literary pursuits to the clergy or to underlings. At a cocktail party in Tangier, shortly after our arrival in Morocco, my wife and I met a young man who came of a wealthy and distinguished family, and who was a painter about to have his first show in Paris. He was the kind of youth who, if an American, would have gone to a good college without question. But this young man had never been to school at all. He was totally illiterate. What is more this did not worry him—or his friends— in the least.

THE SULTAN OF MOROCCO

When Mohammed VI moved into the imperial palace at Rabat, he insisted for the first few days on cooking his own meals, according to a widely accepted story. He thought that somebody loyal to the previous regime might try to poison him.

The Sultan of Morocco—any sultan—is necessarily one of the richest men in the world, not only from the point of view of money but by reason of the services he can command. Not even the British monarch lives on such a scale. There are about sixty royal palaces in Morocco, and the imperial staff probably numbers ten thousand. This is still the feudal world in full, blazing opulence. The Sultan gets three hundred million francs a year, or around $850,000, for the upkeep of himself and family. I asked General Augustin Guillaume, who was Resident General when we visited Morocco, where all the money came from. "From the people." "And where do they get it?" "From the soil." Guillaume paused a moment and added, "At least they get it from the soil if it rains. If it doesn't rain enough, there isn't any money."

Parenthetically we should add that the present Sultan—in marked contrast to Mohammed V—is a frugal man, rich in his own right, and not greedy. One reason why a sultan is paid such a large salary is that, as a rule, he must maintain a personal establishment of enormous dimensions. By Islamic tradition, he cannot turn any claimants away from his board, and in time is bound to accumulate hundreds or even thousands of retainers. Instances of this occur all over Moslem Africa. At every Moslem court we visited we met dozens of hangers-on. Another reason why sultans are paid so well is to keep them tractable.

Mohammed VI's family life—in this too he differs sharply from the previous Sultan—is respectable. His wife is a lady named Lalla Henia, who is a granddaughter of a former monarch named Moulay Hassan. They have five children, and have always lived in secluded privacy. Mohammedans are, as everybody knows, allowed to have four wives—or rather I should say four wives *at a time*—but few men ever take their full complement. Also they may have as many concubines as their purse or vitality can afford. But the new Sultan has, so far as is known, no consort except Lalla Henia. Incidentally she is not a "queen," since the institution of queenship is unknown in Morocco. The reason for this is probably the traditionally inferior position of women in Moslem society, a subject we shall pursue further in a later chapter. A woman in Morocco, even if she is born of a Sherifian family, does not pass the rank on to her children. Titles are hereditary only in the male line.

The chief hold of the Sultan on his people is religious. Morocco is by and large an extraordinarily orthodox and devout country by Islamic standards. But also the Sultan has, or had, substantial temporal powers. To explain this we must interpolate a word about the peculiar structure of Moroccan government, which till 1953 was an absolute—not a constitutional—monarchy, one of the last left in the world. The French want, at all costs, to maintain the pretense that they are merely "advisers" who rule in the Sultan's name. Hence a kind of parallel structure has always existed, with the French administration on one side, and what is known as the *Makhzen,* or Sultan's personal government, on the other.

Now under this double system of government the Sultan could, if he wanted to, assert himself in several ways, even if the real power always remained French. For instance, executive and judicial functions are not separated in Morocco. The Sultan is the supreme judicial authority—even in criminal cases—in any legal matter concerning Moroccans. Also Morocco has no legislature, and the Sultan himself had sole legislative power to the extent that he could issue decrees that had the force of law if the French approved of them. Moreover the French could not enact a law themselves without the Sultan's counter-signature. The previous Sultan infuriated the Residency by repeatedly going "on strike," so to speak, withholding his signature to various *dahirs* (laws) and thus creating an administrative deadlock. This was a chief reason for his dismissal. The new Sultan will, of course, be easier to handle. But the French are taking no chances. Various reforms went into effect recently clipping his wings and in fact stripping him of almost all secular authority. The *Makhzen* is now the shadow of a shadow, devoted largely to supervision of religious institutions and foundations.

On the other hand the French, in order to strengthen their own position, have to do what they can to build up the new Sultan's prestige and popularity. Their major task in Morocco at the moment is to rally the people around their new man. They even call him a "nationalist" (of the moderate wing) as a sop to nationalist sentiment. Nobody has any future anywhere in Africa these days unless he is *some* sort of nationalist, even the Sultan of Morocco.

SULTAN IN EXILE

The deposed Sultan, Sidi Mohammed Ben Youssef, is a character much more complex, colorful, and ornate. He reached the throne in 1927, when he was a boy of seventeen, and was the eighteenth member of his dynasty to become monarch. He was the third son of the preceding Sultan; the French, in choosing him, passed over his two elder brothers. At that time they wanted a young man, not old, whom they thought would be malleable, who knew French, and who seemed intelligent and promising. He turned out to be a scorpion in their bed.

French hatred of Mohammed V became boundless. For one thing they complained about his avariciousness and extravagance. He collected automobiles the way an ordinary man might collect neckties. His salary, the French say, was only a minor part of his gross income. When he ascended the throne he was penniless; when he left he was worth between four and five billion francs.[3] How much of this capital he was able to take with him to exile is unknown, nor is it certain that it would be of much use to him in Madagascar, even if he has it. Mostly his fortune was built up (again according to the French) by loot collected from the caids and pashas, or by other gifts.

Again we pause to explain. A pasha is a provincial governor or head of a municipal administration; a caid is, more or less, a rural magistrate or leader of a tribe.[4] All pashas and caids in Morocco are, in theory, appointed by the Sultan (of course with French concurrence), and men wanting these lucrative posts have to pay for them. This was—and perhaps still is—part of the accepted process of government. It is nothing new to history. In Roman times provinces were farmed out to governors who paid for their jobs and then recompensed themselves by looting at will. In New York City (let us say) the cop on the beat may extract tribute from the citizenry, part of which he passes on to those higher up. But in Morocco things were done with a more exuberant flourish. Not only did the pasha pay handsomely for his appointment, but every year, on the occasion of three Moslem holidays, he was obliged to bestow on the Sultan other gifts, known as *heydias*.[5]

Mohammed V, he who is now cooling—or warming—his heels in the waters of the Indian Ocean, was a youngish man of lusty spirit. He liked to have women around. He had two wives, and forty or fifty—perhaps more—concubines. It would have been unthinkable for him to have passed any day without at least a brief moment in the engaging company of one of these ladies. Moors are, as is notorious, strongly sexed. The ex-Sultan's first wife, a woman of about forty-five, was known officially as "the Mother of

[3] Calculating the franc at 350 to the dollar this would make between $11,140,000 and $14,250,000.
[4] Correctly caid should be spelled Qā'id. Many Arabic words contain macrons and apostrophes to indicate sounds that cannot be accurately rendered in English. There are even two types of apostrophe, the *hamza* (') and the *ain* (').
[5] See *World Today*, October, 1953, a publication of the Royal Institute of International Affairs, London. Another source of a sultan's income was his position as head of the judiciary. People paid for "justice" in cases involving contracts, property, and the like.

the Sultan's Children"; the younger wife, about twenty-five, was called "the Favorite." Both women are Berbers, not Arabs; the younger is paler. The elder was a woman of the upper classes, the younger a servant girl. She was a gift to the Sultan from the Glaoui of Marrakesh, in the days before the two men quarreled. The girl was a firebrand, people told us, who fascinated the old Glaoui because she was impossible to tame; he sent her up to Rabat, the capital, as a curiosity, and she showed such strength of character, as well as delectable appeal, that the Sultan eventually married her.

Neither wife seemed to have had much jealousy of the other, though of course nobody knows what went on inside the harem. They were sometimes seen together. For instance, they called twice a year together on the wife of the French Resident, and behaved with correct dignity. General Guillaume himself never met them, because it would have been unthinkable for them to be seen by any man, let alone a foreigner. When they visited the Residency half the premises were shut off, doors locked, and male servants rigidly excluded, so there could be no possibility of any accidental encounter. On any expedition the two wives were of course heavily veiled—muffled in white from top to toe.

Among the ex-Sultan's concubines several were French, according to rumors of the time, several were Negro, and one was supposed to have been English or American. The Sultan, on being deposed, wanted to take no fewer than twenty-eight of these ladies with him into exile; eight did actually accompany him, and it was officially announced by Paris that thirteen others would be allowed to join him later. Departure of the harem from Rabat was picturesque. The women accompanying His Majesty, whether wives, daughters, concubines, or servants, were all dressed identically, in white robes completely concealing their persons. They resembled helmeted firefighters in asbestos suits or female knights, if there are any such, in the hoods of the Ku-Klux Klan.

Mohammed V was, despite his extravagances, a remarkably democratic character in some respects. Of all his automobiles, the one he preferred to drive himself was a pint-sized Renault. He liked to build things with his own hands, and even to run a bulldozer. He played good tennis—almost of tournament quality—and one of his favorite partners was a cook from the royal kitchens. He was pudgy, but athletic, and he liked to ride, to shoot, and to hunt wild boar.

He seldom received outsiders, and almost always used an interpreter. One official attached to the court told me that his advisers always knew that he was in a good mood if he wore white robes and had shaved. If not, a stormy session was ahead. This touch is archtypically Arab; it could be out of *The Arabian Nights.*

The French would never have deposed Mohammed V for bad manners, or for being fond of money and pretty women, or even for being a despot. About his personal life they cared little. What they did dislike was his association with nationalism, and this is what cost him his throne.

His masters were, moreover, uneasy about the way he was bringing up his children, of whom he has had five by his first wife. These range from Prince Moulay Hassan, the oldest boy who is in his late twenties, to a daughter aged ten. The Sultan gave remarkable freedom to the two elder daughters, Lalla Aisha and Lalla Malikn, who are around twenty-two and twenty respectively. They were allowed to go shopping unescorted on the streets of Rabat, wore western dress without veils, and behaved, in general, almost as young ladies might in Jersey City—even to the extent of hanging around milk bars and listening to jitterbug music. They had their photographs taken and put on display, and, something totally unprecedented, made talks on the radio.

No one, when we were in Rabat, could explain exactly why the Sultan gave his daughters—in contradistinction to his wives and concubines—such unconventional leeway. But the French apparently thought that it represented a nationalist "plot." It proved, they said, that the Sultan must be strongly under the influence of the Istiqlal, which, as a modern nationalist party, believes (more or less) in the emancipation of women.[6]

A more serious issue concerned His Imperial Highness Prince Moulay Hassan. This boy, after education in France, became a spirited nationalist, and was a marked influence on his father. But also the Sultan, on his side, sought to soften the views of his impetuous, free-willed son. Prince Moulay Hassan's indiscretions were, according to the French, insufferable. For instance, on one occasion he gave his father a handsome motorcar, and announced publicly that it was the gift of the "Crown Prince." Now, as we have already pointed out, the Sherifian throne is not necessarily hereditary, and the young man had no right to assume—or announce—that he was heir apparent. The French were aghast that Moulay Hassan could be actively harboring the idea of being Mohammed V's successor. They would never have let him reach the throne.

The United States has, as is well known, several immense military air bases in Morocco, and keeps a substantial garrison in the country. The Residency sought from the beginning to sterilize His Majesty from all contact, official or unofficial, with the American installations. He was Sultan

[6] See below, in Chapters 4 and 5, for the position of women in Morocco.

of Morocco but he was not even told about negotiations for the bases when these began. Nor was his consent asked or gained. The French bypassed him completely. They had a right to do so, since by terms of the protectorate treaty they are exclusively charged with the conduct of Morocco's exterior relations; the Resident General is by law the Sultan's foreign minister as well as minister of war. Then one day Prince Moulay Hassan, acting on his own initiative, hopped in a car, went out to the base near Rabat, and called openly on the officers in charge. This may sound like a small business, but it had a considerable symbolic significance. Plenty of Moroccans, even if pro-American, feel a natural concern about the fact that their country, without its consent ever being asked, is now a part of the American defense system. If the United States bombs Moscow from Rabat, then it is conceivable that Rabat could be bombed by Moscow. Willy-nilly Morocco will be party to the next world war. It was this situation that the youthful Moulay Hassan sought to dramatize. The French were furious.

One must be careful to point out that Mohammed V was not by any means a particularly aggressive or inflamed nationalist. He was not. He was a sultan. He was not within a million miles of being as nationalist as Nasser in Egypt or Nkrumah in the Gold Coast. He did not want to make a revolution against France. He wanted partnership with France. He stood for Moroccan independence in time, on decent terms, and he would have liked the French to name a date for the eventual termination of the protectorate, but he was not a positive insurrectionary. He came to be identified with the Istiqlal movement and what it stood for, but he was not its leader. Most nationalist intellectuals recognized his symbolic value, but had small use for him as a human being. They hate feudalism and the paraphernalia of an Oriental past almost as much as they hate French rule.

STORY OF THE COUP

It would take a sizable book to tell this in full detail. For a good many years the ex-Sultan, though he talked back to his overlords on occasion, behaved with correct acquiescence. He was a self-indulgent satrap, little more. What, finally, made him turn against the French? I asked General Guillaume this question, and got a surprising answer: "President Roosevelt."

Guillaume did not say this altogether seriously. There were, of course, other provoking factors, such as World War II itself, the German conquest of France, and in particular the American landings on French territory

THE SULTAN OF MOROCCO

in North Africa.[7] It stunned the Moors to discover that France was not a strong power, but weak and divided. President Roosevelt came to the Casablanca Conference early in 1943, and during its course invited the Sultan to dine with him. Apparently this meeting was a momentous landmark in His Majesty's intellectual development. Also, incredible as the fact may be, it marked the first time since 1912 that any sultan had *ever* been permitted to see a foreign dignitary alone, without French advisers standing by. Mr. Roosevelt, who was notable for his dislike of old-style colonial methods, told the Sultan frankly that he thought Morocco should be independent in time. This, at least, is what the French *say* Mr. Roosevelt said. Then, from Hyde Park, the President wrote him a letter, to which he is supposed to have added a longhand postscript, advising him to try to keep Morocco's mineral resources intact—safe from further foreign exploitation.

From this time on, according to the French, the ex-Sultan "went sour." Hitherto they had seldom bothered to think of him at all except derisively as a figurehead, but now they had to acknowledge that he was a potential rival force. The Sultan spoke in Tangier (1947) declaring that Morocco would insist on its full rights as a protectorate. He visited Paris (1950) and asked for a new treaty with France, on better terms. He emphasized Moroccan kinship with the rest of the Arab world, demanded various reforms, and looked for succor to the UN. Tension climbed within Morocco. General (now Marshal) Alphonse-Pierre Juin was Resident General during most of this period.[8] He was a tough and zealous guardian of French interests. Meantime the Istiqlal (which had been founded in 1943) became more powerful and insurgent day by day and was, the French say, heavily infiltrated by Communists. The Residency—which is responsible to the Quai D'Orsay in Paris—felt that it was facing not merely a nationalist revolt but a Communist conspiracy. How much truth there was to this, as of that date, is uncertain. Istiqlal people are stout in their denials of Communist association.

Now a powerful actor began to exert decisive influence—El Glaoui, the Berber leader and Pasha of Marrakesh, who has always been on the French side. This formidable chieftain was, in theory, subordinate to the

---

[7] The French charge that the Sultan was a collaborationist with the Nazis during the Vichy period. So were many French.
[8] Juin was, it happens, born in Bone, Algeria, and laughingly calls himself an "African." He was dismissed from his post as vice-chairman of the French Supreme War Council early in 1954. This had nothing to do with Morocco. Juin was trying to make his own policy against French adherence to the European Defense Community.

Sultan, and owed him fealty; in fact he was practically an independent potentate, and thumbed his nose at Rabat whenever he felt like it. Late in 1950 he called angrily on the Sultan, and accused him of being responsible for nationalist unrest in several of his Berber villages. The Glaoui protested that he, the Sultan, a descendant of the Prophet Mohammed, ought to be ashamed of himself for dealing with revolutionaries and Communists. Furious, the Sultan showed the Glaoui the door. "Go, dog," are the words he is supposed to have used. The Glaoui went. Reaching his own quarters, he muttered dryly that the monarch's behavior had saved him seven million francs, which was the sum he had brought with him as "tribute" to His Majesty. As a result relations between the Sultan and Glaoui ceased. This was a situation that played perfectly into the French hand.

In February, 1951, came the celebrated "Juin incident." Marshal Juin demanded of the Sultan, among other things, that he sign a statement denouncing the Istiqlal, and threatened to depose him if he did not do so. This crisis was resolved by a compromise.

Meantime the Glaoui's Berber horsemen left their hill stations, descended into the plains, and assembled in martial display outside Fez, Rabat, and other towns, as a threat to His Majesty. In their heavy burnouses (cloaks) and carrying aged flintlock muskets, they made a spectacular, if tattered, show of force. They did not care much about politics. They wanted loot. They did not get it. The Glaoui was forced to disband them, and they returned to their homes crestfallen and hungry, because at the last moment Paris refused to go along with Juin's plans to use the Glaoui's demonstration as a pretext for getting rid of the Sultan then and there. One personage who took an important role in this decision to save the monarch at that time was Vincent Auriol, the President of France; another was the American Ambassador, David K. E. Bruce.

There followed strikes, riots, and disturbances, spread over a year. Juin finished his tour of duty, and was succeeded by Guillaume. The Arab states persisted in efforts to get the Moroccan question aired before the UN, which the French resisted. The Sultan went so far as to issue unilateral communiques, something he had never done before. Then in November, 1952, came his annual Speech from the Throne. The French originally instituted this ceremony to build up the sultanic prestige, and by tradition it is the one pronouncement the monarch can make every year which is composed entirely within the palace, and which the Residency does not see before it is delivered. The Sultan took a moderate line. He thanked the French for all they had done for Morocco, but said that the time would come when the country must get rid of its "baby clothes."

THE SULTAN OF MOROCCO

Then on December 7 severe rioting broke out in Casablanca. We shall allude to this in more detail later. The French at once outlawed the Istiqlal, smashed its entire organization, and threw a thousand or more nationalists into jail. This was the beginning of the end for the Sultan. He had committed himself so deeply to the Istiqlal by this time that he had no other important following. Once the Istiqlal was broken, he was broken too.

*

It was the Glaoui who administered the *coup de grâce,* which came nine months later. Guillaume was absent in France on a brief holiday; apparently he had no premonition of serious trouble. One story is that the permanent French officials in Rabat, who were relentless in their hatred of the Sultan, moved behind Guillaume's back. Anyway he was doomed. In particular the French *colons* (settlers) were now determined to get rid of him, no matter how. Moreover most of the conservative pashas and caids had irrevocably turned against him, because of his association with the nationalists, the *Lumpen-proletariat* of the towns. The feudal pashas hated the "riffraff" of urban agitators, who, if they ever came to power, would certainly take away their own feudal privileges. The caids do not like the big cities. It was a revolt of country bishops against the pope. There are twenty-three pashas and 323 caids in Morocco, and the Glaoui had already (as early as May) got 270 of these to sign a petition to the French government demanding that the Sultan be dismissed.

Climax came in August, 1953. Again the Glaoui's gaunt, cloaked horsemen rode toward Fez and Rabat, ready for the kill. Guillaume flew back to Morocco posthaste. He surrounded the palace with French troops, so that the Sultan would be "protected," but then took advantage of the situation to present him with a new series of demands. The Sultan's own requests for reforms were dismissed. Helpless, the monarch agreed to Guillaume's stipulations. On August 12 the Glaoui summoned his chief supporters, two thousand in all, to Marrakesh and forced the French hand by declaring the Sultan to be deposed. The French did not know quite what to do. The Glaoui was their man, and the Sultan was broiling in the skillet; but they were still reluctant to take such a supreme and irrevocable step as dismissal of the sovereign.

Guillaume asked for delay, but the Glaoui was not to be deterred. On the fifteenth his conclave deprived the Sultan of all his spiritual powers. Nationalist riots occurred in Oujda, Casablanca, and elsewhere, by way of protest. The situation was further complicated by the fact that these were the days of an important Moslem religious festival—it was as if the fate of the United States were being determined on July 4. Guillaume told Paris how things stood, and the French government, which was fiercely divided, finally gave him permission to oust the Sultan. Promptly he surrounded the palace with armed forces again, and informed Mohammed V that he had to go. The formal deposition occurred on August 20.

The new Sultan was promptly confirmed in office by the *Makhzen,* and enthroned in Rabat. Thousands of fundamentalist Moslems—countrymen and Berbers—lined the route he took from Marrakesh. But in Rabat itself hardly an Arab was to be seen. Tanks and armored cars patrolled the dead, stricken streets. It was a sallow enthronement. Also the French took the precaution of arresting all known nationalists of any prominence who had survived the clean sweep after the Casablanca riots.

Mohammed V was hustled out of the country by air to Corsica. He had never flown before, and at the airport tried desperately to stave off the flight. He said that he had "claustrophobia" and asked to see a doctor on the ground that his heart was weak. His own doctor could not be found, and a French physician hurriedly summoned gave him a cursory examination, saying, "Your Majesty, you have the heart of a young girl!" Off he flew. Few Moroccans of the court were there to see him go. But one important member of the **entourage,** whom most people had suspected of being a French spy, confounded them by showing such emotion at the departure of His Majesty that he fainted on the spot.

ITEMS IN AFTERMATH

As soon as he arrived in Corsica, Mohammed V began to issue protests and complaints. He said that somebody had rifled his baggage (which went on a different plane) and the French authorities conceded that this was correct and that "certain articles" had been removed including a revolver and some razors.[9] He demanded financial compensation to the extent of ten billion francs, and presented to President Vincent Auriol an itemized list of property losses that included single goats and olive trees.

Abruptly on January 25, 1954, he was hoisted out of Corsica, and sent to Madagascar. He was accompanied by his youngest wife (who was six months with child), a fistful of concubines, and his two sons. The French thought that Corsica was too close to Morocco, and wanted to get him further away. In Corsica he might possibly attempt to escape, or be rescued by Arab or Spanish plotters. General Franco had withheld recognition from the new

[9] New York *Times,* August 27, 1953.

Sultan, and Moorish leaders in the Spanish Zone of Morocco refused to accept him as the legal ruler. This was an unpleasant blow to the French, and relations with Spain became strained almost to a breaking point.

It had been planned at first to send Mohammed V all the way to Tahiti. He was allowed to remain in Madagascar after pledging himself solemnly (April, 1954) to abstain from all political activity.

*

Immediately after the Sultan was deposed the United States informed the French government of its "strong displeasure" at this action, which it viewed with "deep concern."[10] On the other hand the State Department, with the future of the American air bases in Morocco at stake, had no desire to make unnecessary trouble for France. The United States took the Sultan's side in a remote academic way, and the French side practically. America and Britain both moved to head off protests made by the Arab bloc at the UN. But at least fifteen nations went on record to some degree or other in protesting at the French action.[11] That there should be such widespread pro-Moroccan sentiment has little except theoretical interest at the moment, but it was a severe annoyance to the French. They boycotted various UN sessions. General Guillaume went so far as to charge (February, 1954) that a world-wide plot was being hatched against France everywhere in Africa. In particular the French resent inflammatory broadcasts by the Cairo radio, which are widely heard throughout Morocco.

NEW REIGN AND REFORM

Immediately Mohammed VI took the throne the French began to institute some long overdue reforms. Partly this was in order to conciliate liberal opinion in Paris. These reforms, for the most part, exist so far merely on paper, and it is difficult to define precisely the status of each. (1) Morocco is no longer to be considered an absolute monarchy. The government is

---

[10] Homer Bigart in the New York *Herald Tribune*, August 23, 1953.

[11] Egypt, Iraq, Iran, Syria, Lebanon, Saudi Arabia, Yemen, Afghanistan, Burma, India, Indonesia, Pakistan, Liberia, the Philippines, and Thailand. This makes about as solid an Afro-Asian bloc as can be imagined. It is striking that Liberia and the Philippines, which usually follow American policy closely, did not do so. Subsequently a formal Arab-Asian proposal for full sovereignty for Morocco within five years was only defeated by a vote of twenty-eight to twenty-two. In December, 1954, Pakistan infuriated the French by suggesting blandly at the UN that the International Bank for Reconstruction and Development (World Bank) "take over" France's "enormous financial interest" in Morocco. *New York Times*, December 12, 1954.

being overhauled "with a view to making Morocco a modern country." (2) French and Moroccan administration is to be enmeshed, and the foundation laid for some parliamentary or semi-parliamentary system in the future, with elected municipal councils. (3) The judicial system is to be thoroughly revamped, so that the pashas and caids will no longer have judicial as well as executive powers. A pasha will not be both policeman and judge, as has been the case heretofore. (4) A new labor charter will be written. (5) New legislation is promised in the field of civil liberties. Morocco, one should remember, has been under martial law uninterruptedly since 1914.

Meantime, as noted above, the French drastically cut down on the powers and privileges of the Sultan himself. Legislation will, in the future, go into effect in certain circumstances whether the monarch signs decrees or not, and he can no longer automatically hold up *dahirs* by withholding his consent. The Day of the Throne ceremony has been abolished; this is to keep any future sultan from making pronouncements on his own. Above all, it is henceforth forbidden for the pashas and caids to give him gifts—i.e., bribes or "refreshers"—on the Moslem holidays when such gifts were formerly *de rigueur*.

Simplicity was the keynote of the new reign, in so far as it was possible for the new Sultan to give any keynote at all. He asked people not to call him "Majesty," since this was a title deserved only by God, and even went so far as to encourage young women to drop their veils. He urged his people to spend more time at prayer, and dismantled the private menagerie of Mohammed V, ordering twenty-two lions to be sold to a circus. No longer do courtiers have to be barefoot in his presence, and prostration and genuflection have been abolished.

Nationalist agitation, even though most nationalist leaders were in jail or in concentration camps out in the Sahara, has occurred without respite since the beginning of the new reign. There was almost as much political violence as in Tunisia, which is saying a lot. Bombings took place intermittently, and in six months 101 people were killed and 230 wounded. Twice the Sultan himself survived attempts at assassination. In September, shortly after his accession, he went to a ceremony in Rabat on horseback, and an Arab carpenter tried to run him down in a car—a novel method of projected murder. The Sultan was knocked off his horse, but escaped serious injury. In March, 1954, terrorists in Marrakesh exploded two grenades in a mosque where Mohammed VI was praying in company with the Glaoui. The formidable old Glaoui pulled a pistol out of his pocket and shot the assailant himself. A news photographer caught the Sultan an instant after the grenade exploded; the picture is one of the most mournfully dramatic I have ever seen. Looking like a whipped child, the monarch wipes blood from his forehead with the edge of his cloak, which is smeared and spattered with blood. A servant or courtier in the picture has been so shocked that his features break out into a kind of stunned, crazy smile. The Sultan was only slightly hurt. His features betray astonishment, pain, a numb humiliation, and above all sorrow. An inch behind him a guard's rifle sticks out, like a mockery.

*

The French were forced after this to double all their security measures, and it was announced that anybody disloyal to the new Sultan would be expelled from the Moslem community, i.e., excommunicated. The Arab reply to this was something borrowed from India—a weapon the French fear more than terrorism—threat of a passive resistance campaign and civil disobedience.

THE GRAND VIZIER

One remarkable personage in Morocco is the venerable Prime Minister or Grand Vizier, Hadj Mohammed El Mokri. He is, as of the moment of writing, not less than 103 years old! None the less he is still spry and in fair command of his faculties; he took his usual holiday in France last year, exactly as if he were a youth of seventy, still smokes cigars, and still runs the Sultan's personal government. This old and durable gentleman—the facts are incredible—was born in 1851, when Millard Fillmore was President of the United States and Louis Napoleon was Emperor of France. He represented Morocco at the Algeciras Conference in 1906, and was considered at that time to be one of the country's mature statesmen. He has been Grand Vizier without interruption since 1920—in five different sultanates; sultans come and go, but the ancient and indestructible Grand Vizier remains. Few politicians in history can rival the record of thirty-four solid years in office. He was supposed to be loyal to Mohammed V; yet he carried on under Mohammed VI without the flicker of an aged eyelash. He has always been staunchly pro-French. Naturally the old man's personal as well as political influence is profound, if only through the labyrinthian web of his family relationships. One of his daughters married El Glaoui, the Pasha of Marrakesh; another married a former sultan, Moulay Hafid; one of his sons is Pasha of Casablanca. The Grand Vizier has a marked sense of humor, and is apt to be coquettish about his age. He asked a visitor recently, "How old do you think I am?" The visitor replied that he did not look a day over eighty, and the Grand Vizier was vastly pleased. A French official said of him once, "In this man death has died."

CHAPTER 3

Moroccan Backdrop

> How the European has established colonies is explained by his nature, which resembles that of a beast of prey.
> —FRIEDRICH NIETZSCHE
>
> French rule is bliss.   —MARSHAL LYAUTEY

FRENCH NORTH AFRICA consists of three countries, Morocco, Algeria, and Tunisia, which have marked individual characteristics; one old saying is that Morocco is a lion, Algeria a man, and Tunisia a pretty woman. (Tunisian nationalists, who are among the most virile and explosive in Africa, will not thank me for saying this.) Morocco and Tunisia are the only two Moslem countries left in the world—Algeria is a special case—that have not yet achieved national independence.[1]

The French have been in Algeria since 1830, Tunisia since 1881, and Morocco since 1912; the qualities of their rule differ in each. Morocco and Tunisia are protectorates, but not protectorates of exactly the same kind; Algeria is considered to be part of France itself, as French as Oregon—or the Panama Canal Zone—is American. But not all of Algeria is equally French, as we shall see, from the point of view of political rights. Neither Morocco nor Tunisia belongs to that recently invented catchall, the French Union, and they have no parliamentary representation in Paris. On the nationalist side there are differences too. Morocco is the most backward of the three countries, Algeria the most quiescent (though a fierce small revolt occurred in Algeria in 1954), and Tunisia the most advanced. Tunisian nationalism is much more educated and mature than Moroccan nationalism.

All three countries are part of what we generally call the Arab world—that is their predominant native population is Semite or Hamite by race,

[1] Except the Anglo-Egyptian Sudan which is scheduled to become fully independent in 1956.

Arabic by language, and Moslem by religion.[2] The population of all three is about 20,000,000, of whom 1,600,000 are French. Most French are concentrated in Algeria. All three countries are poor by western standards, so poor that they cannot feed themselves, but an effervescent economic development is under way, particularly in mining and hydroelectric projects. Even so, economy is still largely pastoral. There are many more camels in North Africa than automobiles, more date palms than tractors.

Who and what run French North Africa? (1) The French government. (2) Islam. (3) A Moslem feudal class that lives off the land. (4) French *colons* (settlers).

Morocco, together with Algeria and Tunisia, is called by the Arabs the Djezira-el-Maghreb, or Island of the West. Morocco itself is Maghreb-el-Aksa—Farthest West. In early times there was no particular distinction between the three countries, and the frontiers are almost totally artificial, like most African frontiers. The Romans called the area Mauretania (whence our word Moor) but the Mauretania on the maps today is something different, a territory in French West Africa. In modern times Europeans came to think of North Africa as "Barbary," and its littoral as the Barbary Coast. Technically, in the pirate days, this stretched from Salé, next to Rabat, all the way around the elbow of the Atlantic and Mediterranean, along the whole of the shores of Algeria and Tunisia, into what is now Libya. This was the fierce arc the Barbary pirates sailed.[3]

The original inhabitants of the Maghreb were Berbers. Then followed successive waves of conquest by Phoenicians (who founded Carthage in Tunisia), Greeks, Romans, Vandals, Franks, Byzantines, Arabs (twice), Turks (who did not reach Morocco), and, in modern times, the Portuguese, Spanish, and French. This confused heritage has made North Africa very much of an ethnological mixed bag. It is risky to try to simplify this, but in the main there are, it would seem, four main divisions of peoples today. First, the Berbers, who are Hamites. Second, the Semites, and this category includes both Arabs and Jews. Third, Negroes. They come into the picture because both Arabs and Berbers raided south for slaves. Fourth, the Europeans. I am not referring merely to contemporary settlers. The Moors raided on the seas as well as the sands. Their national industry was piracy. They lived on loot, human and otherwise, and brought forcibly into the Maghreb great numbers of captured European (Christian) slaves.

Finally, by way of introduction, we should reiterate the point that North Africa—at least its coast—is not merely Africa, but Europe. Most French

[2] I know full well that the Berbers are not Arabs, but we will discuss the Berbers later.

[3] Another old European name for the Maghreb was "Africa Minor."

people think of Morocco, Algeria, and Tunisia as prolongations of France itself, politically, economically, emotionally, strategically. Morocco in particular is considered to be "occidental"; General Guillaume has described it as "an unattached fragment of the European continent." Morocco commands Gibraltar, and its history is inextricably intertwined with Spain. The basin of the Mediterranean is indivisible; this great sea separates two worlds, but also joins them.

Superfinally, North Africa is part of Asia too. Profound Asiatic influences —one need only mention Islam—have penetrated it. So, at outset, we should keep in mind that we are dealing with an area that is European, African, and Asian all at once.

WHAT IS A MOOR?

What, then, is a Moor? This may seem to be a simple question, but it is not altogether easy to answer. In our first evening in Tangier I asked it of a mixed group of learned folk, and the resulting discussion lasted several hours and almost produced mild fisticuffs.

The simplest definition is geographical. A Moor is any African living in Morocco, no matter of what race or religion. Folk in Algeria and Tunisia are not Moors, properly speaking, though they may have Moorish background and characteristics.

Any other definition leads us into prickly difficulties. A Moor cannot be defined simply as a *Moslem* inhabitant of Morocco, since there are Christian and Jewish Moors. But most Moors (Arabs and Berbers) *are* Moslem.

"Moslem," "Arab," and "Moor" are sometimes used synonymously, but this usage is not correct. "Moslem" is basically a religious term, and "Arab" is ethnic or linguistic. A Pakistani is a Moslem, but he is not an Arab. And there are millions of Moslems in the world who are not remotely Moors— for instance in Russian Turkestan, China, Afghanistan, Indonesia, and the Philippines. It is interesting, however, that Moslems in the Philippines are called Moros, a name that obviously derives from Moor. A final odd point is that Moors themselves do not use the word "Moor," at least in Morocco. It is a strictly European term.[4]

MOROCCO: DIVISIONS AND DISTINCTIONS

Morocco, a complex entity, is itself divided into three parts—the French Zone, the Spanish Zone, and the International Zone which consists mostly

---

[4] See "Nationalism in Morocco," by Nevill Barbour, *Middle Eastern Affairs*, November, 1953.

MOROCCAN BACKDROP

of the city of Tangier. The three together form the Sherifian Empire, though Spain, as noted in the chapter preceding, does not at the moment recognize the suzerainty of the new Sultan. In theory, the Sultan rules all three Moroccos. I remember my astonishment, entering Tangier for the first time, upon seeing "Sherifian Empire" on police forms and other official papers; I had always thought of Tangier as completely extraterritorial and international. If we must be statistical occasionally in the course of this book, let us at least gulp the statistics down quickly. French Morocco covers 153,870 square miles, and is about the size of California; the precise population is unknown, but is between eight and nine million. Of these perhaps 350,000 are French; there are also about 50,000 other non-Africans, mostly Spaniards. The area of the Spanish Zone is 18,009 square miles, and the population 1,082,000. Tangier is a small ganglion of territory (225 square miles) completely encased in the Spanish area, and has roughly 170,000 people.

Morocco—taking it as a whole—has at least four concrete distinctions. (1) It faces west as well as north, and is thus an Atlantic as well as a Mediterranean community. It is the extreme western projection of the Moslem world.

(2) Unlike Algeria and Tunisia, it was never conquered by Turkey. The Turks in their earth-shaking movements captured the Balkans, Egypt, Arabia, and most of the Middle East and the southern Mediterranean coast, but they never penetrated to Morocco.

(3) Partly for this reason, Morocco is the most undefiled, the least contaminated, of all Islamic states, except possibly Saudi Arabia itself. It is a country secretive and resistant to hurry or change. I have visited every Islamic country in the world except two, but I never felt such a dense, closed-in atmosphere as in Morocco. Here one breathes deep of the most formidable and ancient essences.

Of course European—and American—influence has come to towns like Tangier and Casablanca. The old impregnability will, in time, be broken down. Nothing could be more remarkable than the contrast between, say, the neon-lit avenues of Casablanca and a feudal *kasbah* (castle) in the Atlas. All over Africa, time and time again, we shall see the old and the new pressing against each other side by side. The fact remains that Morocco is still forty years or more behind such a country as, say, the Lebanon. In some respects it is as hidden, as opaque, as fundamentalist, as Tibet or Afghanistan.

(4) Morocco is much more closely associated with Spain than Algeria or Tunisia, quite aside from the fact that part of it is a Spanish protectorate. After all, Moors and Arabs occupied Spain for more than seven hundred years, and when they were finally forced out—in the same year that Colum-

bus discovered America—they brought much that was Spanish back with them to Africa, and this influence has persisted strongly to this day. Conversely, just as Spain still marks Morocco deeply, Morocco still marks Spain. What is a Spaniard, in fact, if not a Catholic Moor?

Years ago when I lived in Vienna people liked to say that the Balkans began on the other side of Landstrasse Hauptstrasse. Similarly it is often said, and truly, that Africa begins at the Pyrenees.

A COLD COUNTRY WITH A HOT SUN

One misconception about Morocco is that it is always hot. The country can, of course, be hot, just as Saskatchewan can be hot, and in summer below Mogador you can fry an egg by putting it out in the sand. But, hot as it may be at times, it is never tropical in the sense that Black Africa is tropical. Ask any GI who landed at Casablanca in 1942 and slogged through the frozen mud en route to Tunisia if North Africa is always dry and hot. In 1954 snow cut off whole regions of the Atlas for weeks at a time, and supplies had to be dropped to villages by parachute. Morocco can be whipped by Atlantic gales almost like Newfoundland or Cape Hatteras.

Marshal Lyautey, the formidable and fancy colonial administrator who created modern Morocco, once said, "Morocco is a cold country with a hot sun." I heard this sapient remark quoted at least fifty times.

*

There are three different Atlas ranges—the High, the Middle, and the Anti-Atlas—and their lustrous corrugated peaks rise to more than 12,000 feet. They cut Morocco off from the rest of Africa, and have greatly contributed to its isolation, its impregnability. Behind Marrakesh they are snow-clad for much of the year, and provide a dazzling white Alpine backdrop to the endless smooth rose and amber of the desert. The contrast is so piercing that the spectacle seems to be a mirage. It is as if enormous mounds of ice cream should rise incongruously out of an ocean of consomme.

Marshal Lyautey in his blunt way divided Morocco into two parts—"*Maroc utile*" and the rest of the country. A more scientific division is between the *bled-el-makhzen*, the solidly pro-French districts adjacent to the towns, which are (or were) loyal to constituted authority, and the *bled-es-siba*, or unruly countryside. Sometimes, however, the word "bled" is used to refer collectively to the whole of the feudal south; the French usually call this the "Shluh" or "Chleuh" country. It is striking that, until the reign of the deposed Sultan, no Moroccan sovereign had ever exercised complete authority over more than a quarter of his domain. It was France which knit the country together, purified it, and gave it substance. Many Moroccans still think of themselves as residents of Fez, or Oujda, or Agadir, rather than as "Moroccans." A Tunisian is a Tunisian, but a Moroccan can be a lot of things.

A WORD ABOUT MOROCCAN HISTORY, BUT JUST A WORD

In the eighth century AD bits and pieces of the Arab world, which stretched from Baghdad to Cordoba, began to break off. This was the origin of Morocco. A rebellious local governor shook off the caliphate yoke, set up his own rule, and founded the Moroccan Empire in AD 788. It has lasted ever since—almost 1,200 years. This sultan was poisoned a few years after his accession by a fluid, disguised as perfume, sent to him by Harun el Rashid, whose name is known to all readers of *The Arabian Nights*. The first capital was the old Roman town of Volubilis, near Meknes; Fez became the capital in 808. The centuries that followed are packed with conspiracy and violence, overshot with an opaque, silklike Oriental haze.

Moorish nationalists, sentimental about their past, like to talk about the "civilization" their forebears produced, and even compare this to that of the Great Moguls in India. And, it is true, Fez retained its identity as a center of learning for century after century, and some notable architecture was produced and still survives. But Morocco has nothing to compare with the Alhambra in Granada or the Taj Mahal. The Moors liked to build, but also they liked to destroy. Rather than keep a mosque or other building in proper repair they preferred to tear it down. In general, a period of anarchy followed every reign. The new Sultan, holding power precariously until, like as not, he was poisoned or otherwise removed by a rival, spent most of his energies collecting loot.

One extraordinary and fiendish character was the Sultan Moulay Ismail who ruled for fifty-five years between 1672 and 1727. He was thus a contemporary of Louis XIV, one of whose daughters he wanted to marry. This Moulay Ismail was a criminal monster of extreme picturesqueness. He set out to build at Meknes, near Fez, a capital that would outdo Versailles. The royal stables alone were three miles long, and contained 12,000 horses; slaves who worked on these and other grandiose structures were, if they did not give satisfaction, cemented alive into the walls. Moulay Ismail aroused a considerable amount of interest (perhaps envious) abroad. Louis XIV sent an ambassador to his court, to ascertain if reports commonly heard could possibly be true. The ambassador sent word back in confirmation that, in one period of six weeks, thirty-one children were born to the Sultan, and that on one occasion he received him (the ambassador) with hands and arms bloody to the elbow, because he had just lopped off the heads of several slaves. Moulay is supposed to have had 549 wives, as well as concubines by the thousand, since he seldom used a woman twice. Of his children 867 survived him. Hundreds of his daughters were strangled at birth. He imported vast numbers of Saharan Negroes to Meknes, systematically mated them to Moorish women, and set about to establish by this means a kind of Praetorian Guard of specially bred half-castes. The Guard still exists, but is recruited by different methods. He had several hundred thousand slaves, of whom 25,000 were captured Christians. He is supposed to have killed 36,000 people with his own hand. Some he tied between planks, and then sawed them in half. His favorite amusement, which shows a certain amount of athletic skill, was to cut off a slave's head with one sweep of his scimitar, while mounting a horse. Courtiers attending him had to catch his saliva before it reached the ground whenever he spat, and his excrement was carefully preserved and given as tokens of esteem to ladies in the harem. Any time Moulay wore anything colored yellow, it meant that he was going to kill everybody in sight.[5] But also this noxious old man was an able soldier and administrator, who united most of Morocco and made it tranquil and prosperous; he was an extremely devout and accomplished theologian and once sought to convert King James II of England to Islam.

Morocco deliquesced after Moulay Ismail, although several sovereigns did what they could to establish effective rule. In the 1870's the reigning monarch went so far as to ask the United States to establish a protectorate over the country; he knew that it could not survive without help, but did not want it to become the victim of any European power.

Morocco fell prey to the imperialist grab and scramble early this century. It had no cohesion or will to survive. By 1902 the French were established as the paramount power; then came an Anglo-French agreement by which France got a free hand in Morocco in exchange for a British free hand in Egypt. Spain also played a role in this arbitrary and cynical maneuvering. Another major actor was Germany in the person of Kaiser Wilhelm, who demanded a share of the Moroccan spoils. France, with British support, bought him off by giving him a large slice of French Equatorial Africa adjacent to the Cameroons. Then, taking advantage of anarchical quarrels within Morocco itself, the French in 1912 marched on Fez, and duly estab-

---

[5] Several of these incredible details come from the *Guide Michelin*, which never makes a mistake. Also I have drawn on Galbraith Welch, *North African Prelude* and Edith Wharton's *In Morocco*.

lished their protectorate. Had it not been for *German* pressure—a striking point—this event, the root of all Moroccan history ever since, might not have happened. By bribing Germany in Africa below the Sahara, France got what it wanted in the north. Morocco was a pawn, a bobbin, in *European* politics —an item in Franco-German rivalry across the Rhine.

The protectorate was, however, established with the Sultan's invitation and consent, and French policy ever since has always been "in the name of and for the benefit of the Sultan." Why should France, even today, bother to contend that Morocco is still a "sovereign" state? Mostly this is because at the beginning the French could not annex Morocco openly without provoking international condemnation. Then as time went on it became a political convenience to keep Morocco a protectorate. France held the substance of power, but could always palm off part of the responsibility. Colonialism went out of fashion and it gave Paris satisfaction to be able to say that Morocco was not a colony but a protected "independent" power. But why, today, does France not permit Morocco to take its place along with other French territories as a member of the French Union? If Madagascar is fit to belong, why not Morocco? The French assert that, in fact, they did offer membership in the Union to the last Sultan, but that the offer was rejected. It has not been made again. France does not want to give Morocco a new and improved status out of fear that this will inflame Moroccan nationalism further. The pretext is that the country is not "ready." The French are, it would seem, making the same fatal blunder that they made in Indochina—withholding concessions altogether or giving them too little and too late.

After 1912 came the rule of the illustrious soldier and colonial administrator General (later Marshal) Louis Hubert Gonzalve Lyautey. He was Resident General till 1925, and during all those years ran Morocco singlehanded. Lyautey had an extraordinarily ripe imagination and was packed with character. He was one of the authentic creators of modern Africa. He was indisputably a great man. Also he was a prima donna and a fuss-pot. He loved negotiation, to which he addressed himself with supple finesse, and hated battle. Sensibly, he thought that it was much better policy to win over a tribe than slaughter it. I have even heard French officers of high rank say that he was a "terrible" soldier. During the pacification campaigns his lieutenants even did their best to keep him from visiting the front. One saying about him was that as a soldier he was a good academician, and as an academician a good soldier. But Lyautey had enormous strength in other directions. He liked to govern and to build. Casablanca is his creation. He loved—adored—the Moors, and got along with them splendidly. He invented the policy of "co-sovereignty"—governing in the Sultan's name—and of trying to rule within the framework of existing Islamic institutions. He was a proconsul of the old school, who really knew and understood native peoples, like Lord Cromer in Egypt or, to make a more contemporary analogy, Douglas MacArthur. In the end Lyautey lost his job, as MacArthur did, because he persisted in making his own policy in defiance of the home government.

When Lyautey took command in 1912, Morocco did not have a single bridge or inch of railway. It was a "feudal slum," nothing more or less. Roads, hospitals, schools, were miserable beyond description, if they existed at all. It had no printing press, no maps, and little public order. The Sultan's sway did not extend for more than a few miles outside Meknes and Fez, and it was as much as one's life was worth to travel deep into the countryside. There can be no doubt whatever that Lyautey's accomplishment was immensely beneficial and creative in the physical sphere. We do not need to list in this space the French achievements in forty-three years, achievements particularly outstanding in the realms of public health, public works, road building, development of national resources, scientific agriculture, and so on.

But even if French administration was beneficial plenty of Moroccans fought against it for years. Much of this resistance was Berber, not Arab. The towns were pacified quickly but out in the hills and particularly below the Atlas stubborn tribesmen had to be cleaned out inch by inch. Military operations on a substantial scale actually had to go on until 1934—for more than twenty years—and the country was not officially "pacified" until that year.[6]

If you glance at a Michelin map today you will see that Moroccan roads are of three categories, those open without restriction at any time, those open only by day, and those which may not be traversed at all without military authorization. Even Fez and Marrakesh are in restricted areas where travel is technically forbidden without a permit. More than half the country outside the coastal area is still officially classified as a *zone d'insecurité*.

SOME MOROCCAN CITIES

The capital of French Morocco, RABAT (population 161,416) has one chief business—government. It is the seat of the Résidence Générale and the Imperial Palace, and has wide pleasant streets, handsome villas behind

---

[6] General Guillaume has been quoted as saying, "Not one of the native tribes came over to us. Not one submitted without a fight. Not one of them accepted us without having been conquered by arms." From an Istiqlal pamphlet, *Morocco under the Protectorate*, published in New York.

brightly flowering shrubbery, and the general atmosphere of a "made" capital, like Canberra or Washington, D.C. It has little of the antique charm of Fez, but is full of piquant contrasts. American GI's from the nearby bases saunter down streets traversed by Moslem women so heavily veiled that they look like tall white thumbs. In a leading hotel gentlemen may choose between plumbing in the Turkish manner, that is, a hole in the floor between pedals, or a western water closet.

Correctly the city is named Rabat el Fatif, which means Camp of Victory. The ruins of an old Arab settlement date back to the twelfth century; the French town was built from scratch forty years ago. When Marshal Lyautey entered it on horseback in 1912, to look over the site, he saw French workmen putting up new buildings in the *medina* (Arab quarter). "Tear those down at once," commanded Lyautey. He set the policy then and there that the new French cities in Morocco should never encroach on the old Arab towns, but should be parallel communities close by. Lyautey is, of course, buried in Rabat. He died in France (in 1934) but left instructions that his body should be transposed to Morocco. He wanted to lie in the Shella, an ancient castle that contains tombs of several Moorish potentates. He ordered some cedars to be planted there, while he was still Resident General, to flank what he hoped would be his final resting place. Somebody protested, "But it will take a hundred years for the cedars to grow!" Lyautey responded, "All the more reason to plant them now."[7]

But in actual fact he does not repose in the Shella, because Islamic custom forbade his being buried in a Moslem holy place. His tomb is a *marabout* (shrine) not far away; he himself wrote the inscription it bears:

HERE LIES
LOUIS HUBERT GONZALVE LYAUTEY
WHO WAS THE FIRST RESIDENT-GENERAL OF FRANCE IN MOROCCO
1912-1925
HE DIED IN THE CATHOLIC RELIGION
WHOSE LAST SACRAMENTS HE RECEIVED
WITH FAITH.
PROFOUNDLY RESPECTFUL OF THE ANCIENT TRADITIONS
AND OF THE MOSLEM RELIGION
PRESERVED AND PRACTICED BY THE PEOPLE OF THE MAGHREB
AMONGST WHOM HE HAS DESIRED TO REST IN THIS LAND
WHICH HE HAS LOVED SO WELL
MAY GOD KEEP HIS SOUL IN ETERNAL PEACE.

[7] Several of these details are from an admirable small guide to Morocco published in Casablanca, *The True Morocco*, by F. H. Mellor.

Politically Rabat has a somewhat strained—even painful—atmosphere these days. Arabs are forbidden to assemble in the streets, even in groups of two or three, and the police watch everybody. American visitors may have their papers rifled, and the European community is on edge. I never succeeded in seeing a single conspicuous nationalist in Rabat; all were in jail. In essence Rabat gave the feeling I have had in, say, places like Warsaw under Pilsudski or even Rome in the early days of Mussolini; there was no outright sense of terror (such as existed in Berlin under the Nazis) but plenty of intimidation, tension, and bad nerves.

The Pasha of Rabat belongs to the Tazi family; that is to say he is the equivalent of a Roosevelt or Astor. He is a very pale Moor, whom the Europeans call (when he is not present) "Pinky."

The sultan's palace is, like most of the royal residences in Morocco, shabby and unsubstantial in external appearance. Few people know what florid and arcane wonders may lie within. Its most conspicuous feature (and this too is typical) is the enormous open court—seemingly as big as the Place de la Concorde—which it faces. Such courts, known as *mechouars*, are used as parade grounds where, in normal times, the monarch receives homage from massive congregations of his people.

A sister city to Rabat, across the miserable small river Bou Regreg, is Salé. This is purely a Moorish community, and, like Tetuan, is a headquarters for modern-minded Moslem intellectuals. Salé was an old pirate town, and Cervantes was imprisoned here. The saying is that Rabat and Salé will never be friends "until the sands become raisins and the river milk."

North of Rabat is PORT LYAUTEY, where the United States maintains an important naval base. Its significance is that, if we ever need to invade North Africa again, a functioning naval installation is ready on the spot. The Pasha of Port Lyautey, by name Moulay Hassan Ben Ali Quazzani, was removed from his office by the French in December, 1952, because he was a strong nationalist, and was accused of dealings with the Istiqlal; he was one of the few pashas loyal to the deposed Sultan. He is also one of few contemporary Moroccans of rank to have made a mixed marriage. His wife is an American.

*

If Rabat is Morocco's Washington, the great city of CASABLANCA (population around 600,000) is its New York. This fast-growing and vivid metropolis, built on the Atlantic below Rabat, is the commercial, financial, and industrial heart of the country. About one-third of the population is French. By European standards a city of six hundred thousand does not seem very big, but it is big for Africa; in fact Casablanca is the fourth or fifth largest city on the continent.[8]

Forty years ago Casablanca was a collection of fisherman's huts; today it resembles nothing so much as Rio de Janeiro, or even Miami, with a façade of white buildings, most of them bright with glass and hung with balconies in the modern manner, on a smoothly foaming ocean. It is the fourth largest "French" port and last year handled more tonnage than Marseilles. Casablanca has metropolitan hotels, big *brasseries* with interior balconies like those in Brussels, and restaurants affiliated with parent houses in Paris. Also in the outskirts it has a *bidonville* (shantytown) where wretched Arabs live in buildings, if they can be called buildings, made out of five-gallon gasoline cans hammered flat. The slums of Africa are not an ennobling sight. Casablanca does not remotely resemble a celebrated movie named for it, nor was this movie ever allowed to be shown here. Its atmosphere is almost totally commercial. One point of striking interest is the Bousbir, which is supposed to be the largest and most spectacular brothel area in the world. It is a distinct city within a city, and contains something like 11,000 registered prostitutes. These are mostly Moorish, but practically every nationality—as well as age—is represented. A girl costs anything from 15 cents up. Most young girls enter the Bousbir on a six-month contract; then, having accumulated a dowry, they return to their native hills, marry, and presumably live happily ever after.

Morocco is the only country in the world where the United States still retains and exercises extraterritorial rights; these derive from a treaty made by Andrew Jackson in 1836, and provide, in the general manner of extraterritorial (or "capitulatory") treaties, that American citizens resident in Morocco are exempt from certain local laws, and can be tried for most offenses only by an American consular court. The United States is the only power still to have extraterritorial privileges in Morocco; the British and Spaniards gave up theirs long ago. Probably the State Department would be glad to relinquish exercise of an authority that almost everybody concedes to be an outworn imperialist anachronism, but at the moment extraterritoriality serves a useful purpose, because of the American air bases in Morocco. Also Casablanca has a small but aggressive American business community, consisting mostly of GI's who stayed on after the war. They got into a ferocious fight with the French recently because they claimed that extraterritoriality exempted them from regulations about import li-

---

[8] I say "fourth or fifth" because African statistics are so unreliable. For instance, nobody knows the exact population of Ibadan, Nigeria, which may be bigger than Casablanca.

censes and the like, and the consequent legal tangle went all the way to the International Court of Justice at The Hague. During the trial attorneys representing the French Republic charged that the United States was seeking to "impose its own quasi-protectorate on Morocco."[9] The verdict was a compromise.

In December, 1952, occurred the Casablanca riots. French and Moorish accounts of this tragedy differ sharply. The spark setting off the explosion was the assassination of Farhat Hached, the Tunisian trade union executive and nationalist leader. This occurred near Tunis, a long way from Casablanca, on December 5, but the repercussion in Morocco was almost instantaneous. In protest, Moroccan trade unionists declared a day of mourning and a general strike. Shops were closed, and crowds gathered in the streets. The outbreak would never have taken place if the authorities had not attempted to break the strike. On December 7 police penetrated into the Arab quarter to arrest nationalist leaders, and severe fighting broke out, which continued into the next day. Tear-gas bombs were dropped from airplanes, and French troops used machine-gun fire against mobs of demonstrators. These had few firearms but used weapons like knives and sharpened shoehorns. The mobs might well have been subdued by no more serious weapons than firehoses. Seven Europeans were killed by the infuriated Arabs, and their bodies horribly mutilated.[10] No one knows how many natives died, because Arabs never leave their dead where they fall, but try to haul them off for secret burial. The nationalists say that 1,208 Arabs were killed; the French say thirty-three.

This wretched affair caused profound shock in Paris and elsewhere. There were protests from both left and right at what was called wanton and needless bloodshed. One group of French Catholics, led by the Nobel prize winner François Mauriac, publicly compared the killings to the Guernica atrocity in Spain and the Italian bombings in Ethiopia. The local French citizenry was held largely responsible.

*

If you like your romance dark FEZ is probably the most romantic city on earth. It might have been dreamed up by Edgar Allan Poe—almost sinister in its secretiveness, a twisted city, warped and closed. Fez has 202,000 people, lies inland in a secluded valley, and is the intellectual,

---

[9] *New York Times*, August 30, 1952. Moroccans, even nationalists, on the whole like extraterritoriality, since it implies that Morocco *is* a sovereign state.

[10] If an Arab kills somebody in anger he is likely to cut off the victim's penis and stuff it in the corpse's mouth.

spiritual, and artistic capital of Morocco. It is as different from Casablanca as, say, Baghdad is from Liverpool. Walls cut it off somberly. Most streets are too narrow for any automobile or even bicycle traffic; they are corridors or stairways made of dirt, mud, or cobbles. The *souk* (market or bazaar) is the most labyrinthine I ever saw. What is a *souk*? A department store which manufactures some of its goods on the spot. Here, in an enclosed limited space, a city submerged within a city, the purchaser may buy anything from live goats to *majoun* (candied hashish), from DDT to attar of roses. The great virtue of any Oriental bazaar is that it concentrates all possible shopping needs in a single restricted area. But the *souk* of Fez is a far cry from Woolworth's. There are no fixed prices, and it positively stinks both of richness and of rot.

Fez, the native city, has in abundance almost everything that we think of as "Moslem"—wet alleys choked with donkeys, fountains playing in hidden courtyards, the plangent call of the muzzein from spidery minarets, gardens bound in glossy tile, mosques that have never been entered by a westerner, and everywhere the Moorish arch with its acorn top. Also Fez has something unusual among Arab cities—copious water. One of its sights is a spiked gate, on which the decapitated heads of criminals used to be impaled; another is a sanctuary where even the sultan could not pursue his enemies; still another is the Kairouyine mosque, to which is attached one of the best known universities in the Islamic world. Here students huddle in cold cells, get bread once a day, learn by listening in loose groups to ancient sages, and are not yet taught that the world is round. Four out of its two thousand students are women.

In medieval times some eight thousand Spanish families fled from the Cordoba caliphate, and settled in Fez; their descendants are still here, and give the city a strong Andalusian underlay. Jewish influence, which likewise came from Spain, is similarly marked, and a great number of prosperous Fezis have Jewish blood. The people are the palest I saw in Morocco, even paler than most Berber hillmen. Fez is, par excellence, the city of the upper Arab bourgeoisie, and it is a rich community. It is an extremely sophisticated city. Meknes is oafish by comparison. Fezis look down on the Berbers to the south as illiterate ruffians. The legend is that, in older days, your host at dinner would offer you your choice among his concubines. Fez is also a poor city. At the railway station, waiting for a train after midnight, I saw what seemed to be a disorderly heap of mail sacks piled on each other. They were Arabs sleeping in their burnouses.

There is no United States Consulate in Fez, and the American flag flies on only one building. This is a *fondouk,* or inn, founded by an American lady from Boston, which is at present run by a Frenchman, Guy Delom, who embraced Mohammedanism some years ago. Most fondouks lie at the outskirts of Moorish towns, where the caravans come to rest; camels and other animals sleep in the courtyard, and human beings in stalls facing a balcony above. This fondouk is peculiar in that it serves sick and injured animals, not men; wayfarers bring in ailing camels, donkeys, goats, and other beasts to what is probably the most unusual veterinary establishment in the world. Nobody could possibly overstate the wanton, childish cruelty with which domestic animals are treated in most of Africa.

The most eminent living Fezi today is the Sherif Adbelhai el Kittani, chief of the Moslem Confraternities of Morocco, an excessively reactionary organization. He is strongly pro-French, and played a prominent role in the intrigues that dehorsed the last Sultan. Nevertheless Fez is a major stronghold of nationalist sentiment; it is politically radical although orthodox religiously. The bazaars had to be closed after fierce rioting in August, 1954, caused by nationalist resentment against French repressive measures. Twenty-five hundred troops of the Foreign Legion occupied the whole *medina*. A French officer told me, "Here it is not like Marrakesh. Here they hate us even with their eyes."

*

Fez is Europe, but closed; Marrakesh is Africa, but open. Fez is black, white, and gray; Marrakesh is red. The name "Morocco" derives from this ancient Berber capital, and the rouged sands of the Sahara wash it. This is the great market town for the northwestern desert tribes. But Marrakesh itself, under the cream-white canopy of the Atlas, is a proliferating mass of blossom. Here are orange trees and cypresses slim as pencils, bougainvillaea and hibiscus, gardens boiling with roses, date palms etched like saws against the sky, and jacaranda the color of candied violets.

MARRAKESH (population 238,237) is the biggest city in Morocco after Casablanca, and dates from 1062. Parts of it were torn down when Sultan Moulay Ismail needed building material for Meknes, and have never been rebuilt. It is a sister town to Seville, and the same architect helped design both cities. It has a celebrated red tower, the Koutoubia, which resembles closely the Giralda in Seville; one of the most romantic and satisfying hotels in the world, the Mamounia; and the rambling ocher palace of El Glaoui, its gaunt and Damascene-like pasha. But the first thing that Marrakesh reminded me of was—oddly enough—Russia. We lunched at a villa where Berber workmen, using tools that have not changed form in a thousand years, were repairing a flower-hung garden wall. As they patted the clay they chanted a song peculiar to their trade, the Song of the Builders of the Walls of Marrakesh, as Russian boatmen once sang the Volga Boat Song. The next thing I thought of was Japan, because Arab (or Berber) houses, which are practically devoid of furniture, give the same quality of utter repose and removed and private elegance that houses in Kyoto do. Also Arab meals—I shall describe one presently—have a ceremonial quality and ritualistic pattern much like those in Japan.

Nevertheless Marrakesh as a whole gives a totally African impression. The pulse is that of Saharan Africa at its most intense beat. The streets are much less gnarled, less cramped, than in Fez. Even in the market one gets an occasional glimpse of sky, through splintered roofs, as if it were seen through a pierced tent. Never, not even in prewar Istanbul, have I seen people so drenched with primitive, vivacious color. Here are sienna-colored Tuareg in indigo veils, and Senegalese black as blindness. Skins are mahogany, bronze, chocolate, beige, russet, tar-paper. Tribesmen bring in wool and goats, and go out with sugar, spices, and brilliantly dyed cloth. We saw a prancing white stallion up for display, gruesome heaps of camel meat, and leather *baboushes* (slippers) in gold and blue. In the dye market are lambent pools of ultramarine and scarlet. We visited the camel market, to see the lively trade in these obdurate beasts, watched how bearded merchants guide their donkeys with a wand like a chopstick, avoided beggars of the most adhesive and avaricious persistence, looked at children with their faces half eaten off by sores, sniffed at spices, and listened to the bells of the water carriers, who transport their precious cargo in goatskins strapped to their backs, and are hung with brass pots, pans, and dippers.

This kaleidoscopic, spectrum-colored market reaches climax, comes to a boil so to speak, and spews out and over, in an open space, the size of half a dozen American city blocks, called the Djemma el Fna, or Place of Death. This is one of the supreme sights of Africa or anywhere else. It is not a place of death at all, but life. It is a combination of *souk* (being jammed with portable stalls), a parade ground like the Rambla in Barcelona, and a place of public entertainment—Coney Island. One curious point is that, even in the heat of the day, countrymen who have come to stare unbelievingly and with wonder at what the Djemma el Fna has to show, are huddled in the heaviest clothes. This is because they cannot afford a *fondouk*, and have no place to leave extra garments; they wear everything they own, and bring their animals along. *Mauretania* by Sacheverell Sitwell has a description of this fabulous, orgiastic public square that is unrivaled. The best time to visit it is at dusk. Small flares light up each vibrating oval of entertainers—the snake charmers, the fire eaters, the scribes taking down letters, the storytellers enthralling a rapt audience, the magicians with their live doves. One sight not easily forgotten is the chain of blind beggars that cuts its way through the throbbing crowds, holding itself together by clasped hands.

Marrakesh has such inexpressible poetic aroma that one is apt to forget prosaic details like the typhus epidemic of 1937, when 25,000 people died. And now (the two subjects are not related) it has a casino, with entertainment fresh from Paris, where one may lose money effluently at roulette or *chemin-de-fer*, pretend that one is in a civilized place like Biarritz or Cannes, and not be bothered by sword swallowers.

ECONOMICS, A DREARY SUBJECT

How can Morocco support a town like Casablanca, with its 600,000 people and mushroom velocity of growth? What are the bases of Moroccan economy? How does the country live?

Part of the answer is minerals. Near OUJDA, the sixth biggest Moroccan town, is an impressive mining development, in which American interests are heavily involved, based on zinc and lead. The chief mines are at Zellidja. As to other minerals, manganese is important (with production up from 80,000 tons in 1938 to 426,000 in 1952), as are strategic materials like cobalt and antimony. Also Morocco is the second biggest producer of phosphates in the world; the phosphate enterprises, which employ 10,000 workers, are the property of the state, and are administered by the Office Cherifien des Phosphates.

Morocco has a "Plan," which operates in four-year periods; this is one concept that the Russians have contributed to the Dark Continent; almost all African countries have their Four-, Five-, or Ten-Year Plans. The Moroccan balance of trade is heavily adverse, with France by far the best customer, but trade with the United States is becoming more important year by year. American aid to Morocco amounted to $76 million in the last year of the Marshall Plan; total American contributions to French Africa as a whole probably reach $250,000,000.

One item heavy with potentiality for the future is hydroelectric development. Great dams are being built. Morocco is short on coal and thirsty for power; its consumption of electricity has quintupled since 1938, and is now up to 700,000,000 kilowatt hours per year, with the demand still enormously exceeding the supply. There is sharp competition for water in Morocco, almost as in Colorado. Whom will the new water, created or put to work by projects now under way, belong to? The industrial class wants it for power in the towns; equally the farmers want it for irrigation. If the towns take too much for electricity, agriculture will correspondingly suffer. And agriculture—despite the rising importance of minerals—is still by far Morocco's biggest source of wealth.[11]

Other pressing problems are the birth rate, and how, in future, to feed a phenomenally expanding population. Morocco had 3.4 million people in 1921, and has more than eight million today; the population goes up at the terrific rate of 100,000 per year, and is expected to double by 1980. Morocco itself may not be fertile, but its people are.

[11] Fisheries are important too. Safi is the largest sardine port in the world.

CHAPTER 4

Arab World in North Africa

> *The contact of Islam elevates and spiritualizes these [African] peoples.*
> —ANDRÉ GIDE
>
> *Islam lacks spiritual originality and is not a religion with profound thoughts on God and the world. . . . It has preserved all the instincts of the primitive religious mind and is thus able to offer itself to the uncivilized and half-civilized peoples of Asia and Africa as the form of monotheism most easily accessible to them. . . . Islam can be called a world religion only in virtue of its wide extension.*
> —ALBERT SCHWEITZER

ONE-THIRD of all Arabs in the world live in North Africa, and in French North Africa alone there are 247 different Arab tribes; to generalize about them is not easy. But let us go into some aspects of Arab character and attributes. GI's who served in North Africa during the war will perhaps remember the pocket guides distributed by the army, describing native customs and giving hints on how to get along with Arabs. They were a miniature cross between Baedeker and *Vogue's Book of Etiquette*. (They were also full of mistakes, Arab friends tell me.) But they gave generally a good simplified picture. Arabs operate on a lunar or intercalary calendar and their Sunday is Friday. Arab boys do not like to fight with their hands, and urinate sitting down. One should never shake hands with Arabs vigorously; they have delicate fingers, and hate a hearty handshake. Arabs are apt to become hysterical at the sight of blood, never wash in still water, take their shoes off entering a mosque, and do not eat pork. GI's were admonished not to loiter near mosques, and not to bring dogs to a picnic (to the Arab the dog is religiously unclean). Do not—the booklet proceeds—make passes at Arab women or try to yank their veils off, never perform a private function in public near Arabs, do not cut native bread with a knife but tear it apart with the fingers, do not offer Arabs a drink, do not undress near Arabs, do not use the word *indigène* (native), and remember that "a man may wear skirts and still be a man."

Arabs smoke, but if they are good Moslems they do not drink alcohol. This rule is, however, often violated. By and large in primitive areas the taboo on alcohol is still strict; in cosmopolitan towns like Tunis it is breaking down. Further afield, in Egypt for instance or the Lebanon, I have seen Moslems drink like fish or Irishmen. In Morocco I never saw an Arab take a drink. Occasionally a venturesome youth will sip a glass of wine; if so he is apt to feel sickened later, ashamed of himself, and unclean. The fact that, in the ordinary course of events, Arabs do not drink has greatly assisted the sale in North Africa of American soft drinks, like Coca-Cola. Of course one also finds Coca-Cola in countries where people do drink alcohol; in fact one finds it almost everywhere. Africa is being inundated by this beverage consisting of sugar, bubbles, and a syrup with an arcane formula and mysterious appeal.

The two worst Arab traits are probably (a) cruelty, and (b) homosexuality. Traditionally Arabs are—or can be—as cruel as the Chinese, or even more so. In Fez I heard of a servant, traveling with a caravan, who told his master that his slippers hurt. The master had him shod in molten metal, so that what remained of his feet were incased in iron for the rest of his life. If a great many youthful Arabs are homosexual, there is a good reason for it. There are not enough women to go around. First, the fact that Moslems may have four wives naturally decreases the number of women available to those not rich enough to be polygamous. Second, an Arab youth has, by and large, practically no social contacts with young girls of his own milieu; such western phenomena as courtship, petting, and the like are—or have been until recently—utterly unknown. To sleep with a girl before marriage is (among people of the upper class) virtually impossible. Hence the Arab youth finds his sexual outlet either with prostitutes or among members of his own sex. Prostitution, on its side, leads to promiscuity and disease, and probably 65 per cent of all people in Morocco have venereal disease.

Arabs have an interest in the erotic both delicate and profuse, as any reader of their literature well knows. Even the French, of all people, are shocked at times by Arab salacity and lasciviousness. Recently authorities in Fez confiscated, on grounds of sheer indecency, some "art" calendars printed with Arabic mottos. But these were taken from Arab classic verse! Even the simplest Arab proverb is apt to have a sexual connotation, for instance, "Silk was invented so that a woman could go naked in clothes."

Sexual symbolism is particularly marked in Moslem architecture. The Moorish arch, which may be seen in thousands of buildings from Seville to Isfahan, and which is basic to the design of a whole civilization, is in the shape of a hollow phallus.

We do not need to describe Arab costume except to mention in passing that it can be extraordinarily attractive and practicable. The basic garment —for men—is the *djellaba,* a kind of gown with a hood, which is cool (allegedly) when the weather is warm, and warm when the weather is cool; it keeps out dust and sand, and is at once coat, hat, robe, overcoat, blanket, and pajamas. Sometimes a burnouse (a larger hooded cloak) is also worn. If an Arab sleeps outdoors, he turns his burnouse upside down and puts his feet in the hood. Turbans are a whole long story by themselves. By a man's turban may you know him—his status in society, his tribe, his occupation. Many Arabs of the upper class carry poniards; originally to bear a poniard meant that a man was not a slave. A poniard has its inside edge sharpest. As to women, their inner garments are covered usually by a white wrapper, or drape, that clothes most of the body impenetrably. In cities like Tangier or Algiers odd combinations may occur. Underneath the lady's exterior sheath (if she is rich) may be a suit or dress by Christian Dior; sometimes, beneath the hem of the white cloak which makes most of her look like a walking sheet, glittering western shoes with high heels are seen, tripping along the pavement almost like small birds.

Moors make faithful servants in European households, but they are hard to train if they are fresh from the hills. They find it difficult to move a chair through a door, or put a bottle on a shelf. This, I heard it explained, is because they have been brought up in tents, where the walls are elastic, and bulge easily under pressure; they do not understand instinctively the dimensions of a fixed, solid universe. About Arab capacities in handicrafts there are two theories. One is that nobody in the world can rival an Arab for delicate and fastidious work done by a chisel held—between his toes. The other is that the Arab will do anything to a building rather than repair it. He will patch—but not repair. Another remark is a parody of a famous phrase by Winston Churchill: "Give us the job, and we will finish the tools."[1]

Most Arabs are profoundly democratic in their personal instincts, and have fanatic loyalty to their friends and their own kind. A slave can be your brother. They are rigid fatalists, and a phrase heard without end is *Inshallah,* "If God wills it" or "With the will of God."

[1] "An Arab is a man who will pull down a whole temple to have a stone to sit on," says one proverb.

Old-style Moors in towns like Fez or Salé are fond of mysticism, but have little interest in science or formalized thought. They will go to a lecture—maybe—on St. Theresa of Ávila, but not one on Voltaire or Racine. They have small curiosity about external literature; Shakespeare is hardly known. Yet in their own fields they have exquisitely sensitive minds. A French barrister told us that Paris could become dull, but Fez never, because people in Fez were so exceptionally varied in their interests, so responsive and "refined." The rich, of course, do no work; they live on the land, like the rich in Spain, and exist mostly for the satisfaction of their sensual desires. Naturally they tend to resist anything that disrupts their mature complaisance, their life in a beautiful house bound by latticed courtyards, where secluded fountains play. Another characteristic in the realm of the mind is that—my friends say—Arabs are the most fluent and treacherous liars on earth.

A French official told us that it was impossible to make a Moor a good lawyer or engineer. Of course this is nonsense. It may have been true thirty years ago but it is not true today. Morocco has, to be sure, very few native lawyers or professional men, but this is because education has been brutally starved by the French administration. Other Arab countries are swamped with a rising intelligentsia, and Morocco will follow suit in time. Everywhere in the Arab world a major characteristic, a dominating phenomenon, is thirst, thirst, thirst, for education.

Arabic is a Semitic language, and like Hebrew is written from right to left. One reason why it is so difficult to learn is that it is compact, almost like a form of shorthand. Also, as we know, several of its sounds have no precise equivalent in English or French, and the fact that it is short on vowels makes transliteration doubly irksome. The word for mountain is spelled *jbl* in Arabic; it appears in various European translations as *djebel, jebel, jabal, dzhabel, giabel,* and *giebel*. The English sentence "This is the man I spoke of" would, in Arabic, appear as *"Tas mn I spk f."* The root KTB means "to have to do with writing," and may be modified into an almost preposterously difficult number of forms, as to wit:

maktub	something written
kitab	book
kutab	books
katib	writer
kattab	prolific writer
maktabet	library
kutubi	bookseller
kitabat	writing
kaatib	scribe

kaataba	to write
kitab	a writ
uktub	write!
yektubaani	two are writing
seyektub	will write soon
yektub	will write later

And so on ad infinitum.[2]

Educated Arabs who know classic Arabic can, of course, read a book or newspaper whether it is published in Rabat, Baghdad, or Peshawar, but it by no means follows that they will easily understand one another's speech. Arabic is, in fact, a whole lot of languages—like English. Recently an American language officer, with a perfect knowledge of literary Arabic, was transferred from Damascus to Algiers. He could scarcely make himself understood. He was like somebody from Mobile, Alabama, moved to the Orkneys. But within the limited orbit of North Africa most Arab-speaking peoples can understand one another, although differences and difficulties increase as a person moves eastward. The Arabic spoken in Morocco is much less pure than elsewhere along the coast, partly on account of Berber admixtures. A citizen of Casablanca will get on well enough in Algiers, but in Libya he may have trouble, and in Egypt more trouble still.

THE ISLAMIC CREED

Islam alone of the missionary faiths has not withered in the land of its birth and once the religion of the Prophet has entirely conquered a country it has never yet been ejected therefrom.
—ALAN H. BRODRICK

Now we must try to explore what Arabs believe in. Literally Islam means "submission" or "resignation" to the will of God; figuratively it means the world and creed of all Moslems in the world.

Mohammedans, if they make any pretense to orthodoxy at all, subscribe to five practices: (i) They recite *There is no God but Allah, and Mohammed is the Prophet* (literally, messenger or "sent-one") *of Allah*. (ii) Pray five times a day, with face toward Mecca. The prayers, which may be performed in any place—even out in the street or in a bazaar—take the form of a mild gymnastic exercise. (iii) Give alms to the poor up to 10 per cent of their income. This practice, let us interpolate at once, is by no means universally observed. (iv) Keep the holy month of Ramadan, during which no food, water, or sexual intercourse may be had between dawn and sunset.

---

[2] From a useful small pamphlet published in Tripoli, Libya, by the United States Information Service, *Tripolitania, The Country and Its People*, by Mohammed Murabet.

Anyone who has ever visited a Moslem country during Ramadan knows what a fierce strain it imposes on all who celebrate it, particularly servants. By dusk, especially if the season is hot, people are in a frenzy; then they stay up half the night feasting and carousing. (v) At least once in a lifetime make the pilgrimage to Mecca. A Moslem who has done this adds the title *hadj* to his name, and wears a distinctive turban. There are tens of thousands of *hadjs* in North Africa. In addition, a good Moslem is supposed to answer the call of the caliph for a jehad, holy war. But Islam as a whole has no caliph these days, and the call has not sounded for a brace of centuries.

Mohammedanism has, in theory, no hierarchal structure or priests, although every mosque has certain officials, and North Africa is sprinkled with holy men called *marabouts*.[3] Many Mohammedans—perhaps the majority—believe not only in Islam, but in assorted spooks, spirits, and superstitions, depending on their background and locality. We have all heard about djinns. Most Moslems (like most Italians and Spaniards) believe in, hate, and avoid the Evil Eye. We in western worlds should feel no superior complacency about such symbols. Plenty of Americans hate to have a black cat cross their path. Another manifestation of Moslem belief is the phenomenon known as *baraka*. This means the quality of blessing, or benediction, that a good or wise man may bestow on others, by the mere fact of association or simple contact. General Naguib of Egypt is a conspicuous example of a man possessed with *baraka* to a signal degree. The concept of *baraka* is somewhat difficult to understand. It has little to do with a man's secular greatness or authority. Gandhi had immense *baraka*; Nehru has almost none. Lord Halifax has *baraka*, but not Winston Churchill. Among eminent Moslems with little if any *baraka* are—to choose at random—the former Grand Mufti of Jerusalem and the Aga Khan.

The gospel of the Moslems is, of course, the Koran (correctly, *Qur'ān*, which means "recitation") which Mohammed took down from heaven as the words reached his earthly ear. The creed of Islam, as he invented and developed it, borrowed a good deal from both Judaism and Christianity, and had astonishing vigor, freshness, and emotional appeal. Mohammed (AD 570-632) is not considered by his followers to be God himself, but merely the greatest prophet of God.[4] He was an extraordinarily complex visionary

---

[3] This word can also mean a shrine or tomb.
[4] Once more we must mention the difficulty of transliterating Arabic into English. There are at least a dozen ways to spell Mohammed. Most correct is Muḥammad, and do not forget the dot under the "h." I am conforming to simplified American usage in saying Mohammed. Similarly I propose to stick to "Moslem" instead of the British "Muslim." In France Mohammedans are commonly called "Musulmans," as they are in India, but the French do not capitalize the "m."

and man of genius. He was both a zealot and very practical. He forbad alcoholic liquor because he thought Arabs drank too much. He devised a calisthenic system of prayer so that the sedentary would get exercise. He outlawed pork partly for sanitary reasons. He married eleven times, and invented the attractive principle that paradise, filled with beautiful virgins, belongs only to his believers. He was unique among the founders of great religions in that he sought to establish temporal as well as spiritual power, and he set in motion one of the greatest surges of military conquest ever known.

One main characteristic of Islam is its clean directness, its clarity and simplicity. The believer has a pure, uplifting contact with a monotheistic god, and can pray anywhere—even out in the fields. Most Moslems, if only because their religion is so easy to comprehend and practice, and promises such picturesque and succulent rewards, consider themselves to be distinctly superior to members of other creeds. This superiority, this consciousness of membership in an elite class, is a powerful cement binding Islamic communities together. Many Mohammedans look down on Christians with supercilious contempt. A minor example of this is that Moors use the term "European gold" for counterfeit money, and call the dipper-like gadget that makes a toilet work "a Christian cap."

For several generations after Mohammed the outstanding fact about Islam was its inflammatory militancy. The Koran (xlvii, 15) says: "And when ye meet those who mis-believe—then strike off their heads until ye have massacred them." Over and over again, it was emphasized that he who died in battle would go straight to paradise, all sins forgiven. If a man had wounds, they would be "as resplendent as vermilion and odoriferous as musk." Mohammed's formidable successors the Caliphs Abu Bakr (his father-in-law), Omar (brother-in-law), Othman, and Ali (cousin, son-in-law, and adopted son) and their highly competent generals made such conquests as mankind had not seen since Alexander, and which have never been surpassed except perhaps by Napoleon. In the space of little more than a hundred years the terrific impact of Islam was felt from China to the gates of Paris.

By no means were these invading conquerors under the green crescent flag mere destroyers. They brought a tremendous culture in their wake—architecture, work in tile and fabrics, poetry, algebra. To the Arabs we owe our system of numerical notation, the use of paper, much stimulus to exploration, the survival of Greek classics which first reached the West in Arabic translation, and much early knowledge in such fields as optics, horticulture, and medicine. But the Moslems had, by and large, comparatively little political sense. They had small interest in stable administration or the evolution of sound governmental procedures. Politically the Arab world split up at the time of Ali, the fourth caliph, and has never been united since. From 1517, when the Turks conquered Egypt, until the aftermath of the Great War in 1918—for four hundred years—there was no independent Arab (as distinct from Moslem) state, except Morocco in a manner of speaking. Arab nationalism, if there ever was such a thing, had perished.

The story of its revival is far too long and abstruse to go into here. As everybody knows, the Arab "awakening" between World Wars I and II produced a fascinating variety of struggling but independent nationalisms— in Syria, Iraq, Saudi Arabia, and so on. This movement has now spread to Africa. The Arab or Arab-speaking countries that are members of the United Nations today have a steadily maturing and articulate world influence.

ISLAM: ITS PENETRATIVE FORCE

If you should wish to be converted to Islam this can be done in five minutes.[5] The ceremony takes only a minimum of preparation and is almost instantaneous. You must make a statement of faith, and repeat the phrase that there is no God but Allah, and that Mohammed is his sent-one, adding that you fully understand this, believe in it with the heart, will recite it correctly and without hesitation, and profess it until death. Aside from this, no indoctrination or apprenticeship is necessary. A simple business!

This is one reason why Mohammedanism has made such immense inroads in contemporary Africa. Moslems comprise almost one-third of the total population of the continent today—60,359,000[6] out of 198,000,000—and they are expanding further all the time. Outright Moslem areas, aside from these that we are dealing with at present in French North Africa, are Libya, Egypt, the Sudan, the Somalis, part of Ethiopia, Zanzibar, much of the so-called Swahili Coast, a good deal of French West Africa and French Equatorial Africa, and much of Nigeria and the Gold Coast. There are probably ten million Moslems in Nigeria alone. Islam has leaped straight across the Sahara, saturated much of the land beneath it, and penetrated the Bantu regions to the south.

[5] Ibrahim Dagher in a special North African issue of *Current History*, April, 1954.
[6] Of these 37,585,000 are Arabic-speaking. About ten per cent of this total can read and write.

Islam has no racial bias; hence there is no bar to the conversion of Bantus or Negroes. It has spread so pervasively among pagans and animists because, among other things, its procedures are so simple and its appeal so concrete. All that a man has to do—in order to be assured of life hereafter in a paradise filled with pretty girls—is to pray five times a day and so on. He does not even have to go to church. Moreover Islam permits him four legal wives on earth, which Christianity has not yet got around to doing. It confronts him with no abstruse theological problems; he does not have to occupy himself with conundrums about the Holy Ghost. Finally, in the words of one authority, "it permits him to retain most of his basic superstitions and belief in the omnipotence of spirits." Also Islam gains strongly by reason of the rivalry between various Christian sects; pagans see the spectacle of protestant and Catholic missionaries competing in the same area, and do not understand how this harmonizes with the principle of a universal Christian God.

Another point is that, as Alan H. Brodrick[7] puts it: "Islam is a social system as well as a religion . . . and a social system that gives to the believer a conviction of equality with all other believers." Often Islam has been called the most democratic of the great religions of the world.

Europeans in Africa—or elsewhere—are on the contrary very seldom converted to Islam, unless they happen to be isolated specialists in Arab culture. These are often homosexual. Nor do Moslems easily become Christian. (In the Levant, particularly Beirut, there are a great many Christian Arabs, but these derive for the most part from families that were Christian *before* the Arab advent.) For a long time it was practically axiomatic among Christian missionaries that Mohammedans were impossible to convert. But Roman Catholics, particularly in the United States, have not given up hope of making mass inroads in the Moslem world. Consider the following from the *African Angelus*, a missionary publication:

WILL MARY CONQUER 200,000,000 MOHAMMEDANS?

> Bishop Fulton J. Sheen has more than once called attention to the fact that Our Lady of Fatima has a Mohammedan name . . . The Moslems have a devotion to Mary as the Mother of Christ, and it could be that their eventual conversion to Catholicity will come through her . . . As for the Koran's devotion to Mary, it was a strange mixture, but it has left the Moslems with a Marian tradition. Mary may be the key to the conquest of Moslemism by Christ. Only a flood of grace will accomplish the feat. History shows that such floods of grace have sometimes been released . . .

[7] In his valuable brochure *North Africa*, p. 18.

MOHAMMEDANISM AND NATIONALISM

In a sense Islam (like Roman Catholicism) has no frontiers within itself; this is why most Moslem states—despite struggles for intellectual leadership like the one going on presently between Egypt and Pakistan—form such a cohesive bloc.[8] The unifying factor in Arab nationalism is religion. The French in North Africa, for this reason, have to proceed cautiously in religious matters. They try not to interfere with Moslem institutions as such, which might give the nationalists opportunity to make political protest on religious grounds; on the other hand they do their best to keep the church in close rein. Even sweepers in mosques are "civil servants" getting salaries from the French administration.[9] Many Frenchmen think that Marshal Lyautey's basic policy of governing as far as possible within the Moslem framework has been a disastrous impediment to progress. "If we could only abolish Islam, our task would be infinitely easier," I heard one official say. "The only solution for Morocco is to laicize it, as Kemal Ataturk laicized Turkey."

The nationalists, on their side, have a double point of view. First, Islam is an extremely conservative force by and large, and this obstructs progress. For instance, if women had the vote, took part in education, and were unveiled, they could be of paramount value to the nationalist movement. But, second, the great mass of nationalists *are* necessarily Mohammedans, many of them orthodox and devout, and the nationalist movement would collapse if it affronted their basic religious principles. The nationalists want, in a word, two things at once—to modify the arbitrary feudal power of the church, and at the same time take advantage of its unifying force.

Can a Moslem be a Communist? Certainly. Similarly many Roman Catholics in Italy and Poland are Communists, although in theory this would seem to be impossible. Communist infiltration into the Moslem world is an increasingly dangerous problem. But Islam on the whole is certainly a strong anti-Communist entity and comparatively few Moslems are outspoken Communists so far.

WORD ABOUT THE BERBERS

In the house of a Moor do not speak Arabic. —THOMAS FULLER

We face now the Berbers, who were the original inhabitants of North Africa. Arab civilization is, in several aspects, no more than a thin, brittle

---

[8] "Modern Nations and Islam," by Robert Montagne, *Foreign Affairs*, July, 1952.
[9] "North African Dilemma," by Philip Deane, London *Observer*, November 8, 1953.

veneer on a hard Berber underlay. Probably 45 per cent of the people of Morocco, 30 per cent of those of Algeria, are still Berber, but in Tunisia most Berbers have disappeared.

Over centuries there have been profound interminglings between Arab and Berber, and many people are a mixture of both stocks. Folk known as "Arabized Berbers" and "Berberized Arabs" exist, but only an anthropological hairsplitter can tell the difference between them.

Morocco has upwards of three million pure Berbers, divided into 375 different tribes or sub-tribal groups. By and large Berbers are fairer than Arabs; some have blue eyes. Berbers, like Arabs, are Mohammedans, but are less orthodox; for instance, some eat pork. An old apothegm is that "a Berber is not a true Moslem, but only thinks he is." A good many Berbers were converted to Christianity before the Arabs came and engulfed them; St. Augustine was a Berber. Berbers have their own language, which is totally unlike Arabic (of course many Berbers know Arabic too) and which does not exist in written form, except in the case of one Saharan offshoot. Berbers have no written records, and there is no Berber literature. A French orientalist once tried to transliterate spoken Berber into the Roman alphabet but the result was not successful. French officers who have to learn both languages told us that whichever is learned first makes it almost impossibly difficult to learn the other.

Generally speaking Arabs are town dwellers (at least in the north) or rural nomads; Berbers are "settled mountain agriculturalists."[10] As a rule Arabs are better educated than Berbers, more modern-minded, and much more nationalist. The Istiqlal has made some headway among Berbers in southern Morocco, but not much. Arabs and Berbers dislike one another by and large. Berbers are seldom homosexual, and despise Arabs for being so widely addicted to this vice. Arabs despise Berbers because they marauded into the Sahara and Senegal, brought back Negro women, and married them. Some Berbers are, as a result, black as asphalt—they appear to be pure Negro—and yet are technically considered to be white. Today most Berbers are monogamous. Berbers are much more warlike than Arabs (Arabs of the present day, at least) and for centuries they resented rule, if rule it could be called, by the Sherifian (i.e., Arab) Sultanate in Fez. The intervention of France in 1912 came partly because of Berber risings. The French infinitely prefer Berbers to Arabs by and large. They regard them much as the British in prewar India regarded the tall Moslem warriors of the North-West Frontier, who were considered to be overwhelmingly superior to the Hindus of the plains. "Berbers are *men!*" the French like to say. At least 80 per cent

[10] Brodrick, *op. cit.*, p. 20.

of Moroccan troops in the French army today are Berber. Basic French policy in Morocco has, for years, been an effort to play off Arab against Berber, Berber against Arab—a classic implementation of the axiom "Divide and Rule."

Historically Berber origins are an impenetrable mystery. One theory is that they were a Celtic-Iberian mixture, who came across the Straits of Gibraltar from Spain many thousands of years ago; another is that they were originally Phoenician, deriving from the Levant. There may have been several different Berber strippings or layers. The name comes from a Greek root meaning "foreign" and is the origin of words like "barbarian" and "Barbary." The Berbers themselves do not use this term, but call themselves *Jmazighen*, which means "free men."

THE JEWISH COMMUNITY IN MOROCCO

This is important and substantial. There are probably half a million or more Jews in North Africa, most of them in Morocco; this is one place in the world where Jews and Arabs have, until recently, managed to get on together tolerably well. Jews occupy several strata in society. In Tangier, for instance, the Sephardic Jews who came from Spain in the fifteenth century are a privileged and wealthy class, more Spanish than the Spanish; there are exclusive clubs in Tangier with an 80 per cent Jewish membership. At the other extreme are Jews in villages behind the Atlas, who are segregated into ghettos and live in circumstances of the utmost degradation, misery and squalor. The Jewish quarter of any Moorish city is known as the *mellah*, which derives from the word "salt." The Jews were those who pickled in salt the heads of the Sultan's enemies, so that these would not deteriorate when put out on public display, like taffy-apples.

The Jews are the bankers and money-changers throughout North Africa—so much so that many Arab markets close on Saturday, the Jewish day of rest. Arabs cannot, of course, become bankers themselves (at least in theory) because they are forbidden by the Koran to charge interest. As to politics most Moroccan Jews—those of the upper class anyway—are on the whole a pro-French and conservative element. They have not forgotten, however, that they were harshly treated by Vichy (which extended the Nuremberg laws to North Africa), and they want more security. Moroccan Jewry has been called a "kind of protectorate within the protectorate." On the other hand the Jews have no definite citizenship status in Morocco. They are excluded by and large from the civil service, and are subject (except in Tangier) to Moslem religious law, "which does not even recognize the oath of a Jew to be valid."[11] Many Moroccan Jews view with apprehension the rise of Arab nationalism, and a substantial exodus to Israel has begun.

A MOORISH WEDDING

Near Tetuan, the capital of Spanish Morocco, is a mountain village called Xauen (pronounced Shau-un), softly brilliant in its coloring, fragrant with flowers, and inexpressibly remote. It had never been visited by a Christian until the Spanish army opened it up in the Rif war in the 1920's. We clambered through the pale rocky alleys of this town, luminous with sunlight on chalk, looked at its pretty little mosques in pastel colors, and suddenly walked into a Moorish wedding.

First came musicians playing shrill pipes and beating rude drums shaped like tambourines; they wound down a crooked narrow hill into a brightly colored square, where old men sat cross-legged on the ground, silent and serene in their white-hooded capes. Then arrived bearded elders of the bride's family, some of them limping on sticks, and a woman in a red and white striped cloth bearing aloft large green and yellow candles. Next came more musicians, blowing echoes against the rocks, and then a group of eight panting young men carrying a paper box on long poles. This box was not very big and was shaped like a hat, or narrow tent, square at the bottom and pointed at the top. It was heavy and the boys bent under it, crying out and singing as other musicians and candle bearers followed, including a cordon of wildly playing flutists. But our eyes were fixed on the opaque box, which was disappearing out of sight now, in a torrent of colored silk streamers. Concealed in this box was the bride.

This was all we saw of the ceremony. Nobody sees much more. The bride was being carried to the home of her fiancé, where the nuptials would take place. Bride and groom have, of course, never met—never laid eyes on one another. When she arrives at his house, nobody is there except a female Negro servant. The groom himself is out celebrating with his bachelor friends. The bride is lifted out of the box—her feet must not touch the ground—and she waits until he arrives. She may have to wait a long time. It is he who controls every aspect of the ceremony. He comes in, and presently they dine together, while members of the family wait outside, shrieking and pounding out music. No doubt the man and woman survey each other with considerable curiosity. The bride is usually thirteen or fourteen; the groom may be of any age. When the marriage is consummated the Negro

---

[11] Late in 1954 a Commission of American Jews visited Morocco and made a public appeal for "the end of discrimination against the 340,000 Jews in Tunisia and Morocco." *New York Times*, November 10, 1954.

servant tosses a bloodstained handkerchief out of the window to the crowd below, as proof of the bride's virginity. Legend is that she usually has a live chicken handy, whose throat may be slit if necessary.

The nuptial feast may be the last meal the bride ever takes with her husband in the whole course of her life, because by rigid Moslem convention men almost invariably eat alone; women of the household dine later on what scraps remain. For the rest of her days the young woman is, in effect, her husband's slave. She almost never leaves his house; literally, she may not be permitted to go outside more than once or twice in her entire lifetime; if she does emerge she must of course be heavily veiled. She lives entirely with the women of her husband's household, or alone. She seldom even sees members of her own family, even if they are resident in the same town. Once a year—perhaps—her mother may call on her. Once a year—perhaps—she may be permitted to visit a sister or female cousin. Arabs are very jealous sexually. No other male except the husband, in orthodox families, is *ever* permitted to see the wife's exposed face.

But what about courtship before the marriage? This does not in the normal course of events exist. All arrangements are made, long in advance, by close-knuckled negotiation between the two families. It is usually the father of the groom who initiates a "romance"; he scouts about to see what young ladies are available, and then approaches the prospective bride's father. Sometimes the mother of the groom-to-be calls on the girl's mother. Thereafter the details are largely financial. The groom's family pays the bride's family whatever sum is decided on; the bride is purchased like a bicycle or a sack of millet. Of course in a small town news of what is happening gets around. Probably the fiancé hears tidbits of gossip about his bride-to-be from friends. He may even "peek"—discreetly—when she takes a walk (of course she will be veiled) to get some knowledge of her contours and appearance. He will like it best if she seems to have a very small nose and mouth and eyes as big as possible.

The "engagement" may last for months, and during this period the young lady is deliberately fattened up. She lives on olive oil and sweets, because to be plump is fashionable. During the ceremonies immediately preceding the wedding, she is not permitted to smile. If she shows any sign of animation or pleasure, this is supposed to indicate that she has had a loose past. Before the wedding she is bathed and anointed; her hands and feet are painted with henna, and all hair is removed from her body. The groom shaves his skull.

If the groom does not like the bride on the wedding night, he may "repudiate" her at once, that is, refuse to live with her. In this case his father gets most—but not all—of the purchase price back. Once married, the husband may divorce the wife at will; divorce on his part is automatic on any pretext. All that is necessary is to go to the local pasha's court, make a declaration, and pay 700 francs ($2.00). But a man cannot divorce and remarry the same girl more than *three times*. This regulation became necessary because many young husbands divorced their wives in hot-tempered haste after a lovers' quarrel, and then repented and remarried them.

The husband may at any time marry other wives, or take concubines, although the wife (except in some exceptional circumstances) cannot divorce the husband. A man's world! As to children there is no distinction in Koranic law between those legitimate or illegitimate.[12] Sons are welcomed, daughters lamented. If a daughter is born to a man his friends commiserate with him on such bad luck. A woman is nothing.[13]

A word on polygamy. For several reasons it is going out of fashion in North Africa. First, wives cost money. Two, three, or four wives cost a great deal of money, and only the substantially rich can afford to be polygamous these days. Second, the love factor. Moslems are, after all, human beings. A man may actually fall in love with his wife, even if he has never once laid eyes on her till he sees her on the nuptial couch, and consequently may have no desire to marry again. Third, a Moslem married to more than one woman must, by Islamic custom, give exactly the same treatment—financial, social, personal—to *each* wife. Despite this injunction, there are bound to be jealousies and quarrels in multi-wife households, and many Arabs nowadays stick to just one wife if only to avoid such friction.

We met one Arab in an Algerian oasis who was the object of considerable local interest. He was a male nurse in the local hospital, and he got a large salary for that area—about $160 per month. He had a full complement of four wives, and was the envy of the entire community, because he was rich enough to maintain four separate dwellings, with a wife in each. And we heard about one Tunisian lady, about forty, who had had a serious quarrel with her husband because he did *not* take another wife. Wife No. 1 wanted him to marry a strong young girl to do the housework.

*

Despite all this the concept of romantic love is gaining ground in North Africa, and impulses for the emancipation of women are being felt. It will be a long time before twenty-year-old Ahmed can take eighteen-year-old Miss

---

[12] "Moroccans believe that the child sleeps indefinitely and comes into this world only when he awakens." *Moroccan Horizons,* by Catherine Tolliver.

[13] An additional point is that a Moslem may marry anybody he likes—Jewish or Christian—but a Moorish woman cannot marry anybody not a Moslem. Children must follow the *father's* religion.

Fatima, who lives in the next block, to have a cup of coffee in the nearby hotel, write her a love letter, or suggest an automobile ride in the moonlight. Nevertheless the tyranny of the veil has begun to lift, and there are some indications of progress and reform; for instance, some mothers in wealthy families are insisting on marriage contracts for their daughters, to protect their interests. One reason is education. More and more Moslem girls are going to school. Once a girl gets even a rudimentary education, she is less apt to be a willing slave. (But in most Arab countries, the ratio of boys going to school as compared to girls is still roughly 500 to one.) Another is the movies—Hollywood is teaching Moslem women how American women live. On the other hand, it is difficult for many Moslem wives to attend movies. For instance in Tangier it is, believe it or not, legally forbidden for a Moslem woman to go to the movies at all; in Spanish Morocco attendance is segregated, and women go by themselves in the afternoon.

A French doctor in El Golea, an oasis deep in the Sahara, told us that he had attended twenty-seven Moslem women in childbirth last year. For a male doctor, let alone a European, even to have been permitted to *see* a Moslem woman would have been unthinkable some years ago. Children were always delivered by midwives, or, in poor circles, by the mothers alone. In Tunisia, we met a youthful artist with six girl cousins. Their mother has insisted that all six go to France to learn vocations. And in Casablanca unveiled ladies, who are called *évoluées*, have organized something unprecedented—an American-style woman's club, devoted to feminist activity.

Young women who do, despite every obstacle, manage to become *évoluées* are likely to have a rough time in some respects—the price of emancipation can be high. Few Moslem youths dare to associate with them, and they are mercilessly snubbed by the French. Also a girl who has "evolved" may absorb western influence too quickly and without much discrimination—she may think that to become westernized means nothing but to chew gum and wear dungarees. American girls resident in Casablanca say that they lack "drive."

CHAPTER 5

The French, the Nationalists, the Americans

The French will stay in North Africa as long as France exists. But does France exist?

—ABDEL KRIM

IN MAY, 1954, General Guillaume was replaced as Resident General of Morocco by a civilian diplomat, Francis Lacoste. This was a sensational event. It came immediately after the fall of Dienbienphu in Indochina, and was probably precipitated to an extent by that disaster. There was no personal reflection on Guillaume. But his policy had become unworkable. From the day Mohammed V was deposed, Morocco became steadily more turbulent; instead of settling down tranquilly; nationalist activity did not diminish, but increased. French repressive measures only made matters worse, and Morocco, like Tunisia, almost seemed to be heading toward civil war. And France, facing a desperate end to the situation in Indochina, simply could not afford to have more trouble elsewhere.

Guillaume was, and is, the most attractive French officer of high rank I ever met. He has tenacity and a peasant-like earthiness. A solidly intelligent man, he is a scholar as well as a soldier, a famous linguist (he speaks eight languages), and the author of books on such subjects as the Berber language and the pacification of the Atlas tribes. He served a great many years in Morocco as a youthful officer, and knows it better than France, down to every gulch and almond tree. A nice thing about him was that he was made a colonel by Pétain, a brigadier general by Giraud, a major general by De Gaulle, and a full general by Vincent Auriol. To anybody who knows French politics—or human character—this means a lot.[1]

---

[1] For a time, under De Gaulle, he served as French military attaché to Moscow. He knows Russian, and wrote a standard work on the Red army. De Gaulle insisted that his military attaché in Russia fulfill three conditions—know Russian, have the rank of general, and be a veteran of both world wars. Guillaume was the only man in the whole French army who satisfied all three stipulations.

Guillaume is a practical man, who like all French bourgeois respects the intellect, but he is impatient of abstractions. He sees things in black or white. He detests the Moroccan nationalists, and thought that anybody who had any dealings with them at all was an enemy of France. "You have to be for us or against us," he kept saying. "There can be no middle ground." And this, of course, is why he lost his job since, whether the French like it or not, nationalism *has* to be dealt with as a legitimate force, and some distinction made between moderates and terrorists.

American policy perplexed Guillaume mightily. He told me that he thought that it was little short of demented of us to spend half a billion dollars on our Moroccan bases on the one hand, and with the other give asylum in New York to nationalist "insurrectionaries." Sometimes French governments perplexed him too. I asked him what gave him most trouble— Cairo, Washington, the UN, Moscow, or Morocco itself. He laughed: "Paris."

Francis Lacoste, Guillaume's successor, is a professional diplomat of long experience. He has served in Peking, Belgrade, and Washington, and has been French delegate to both the Atomic Energy Commission of the UN and the Security Council. He was the son of a well-known artist, Charles Lacoste, and has a literary heritage. He is in his late forties, and is cultivated, responsible, and adroit. He knows Morocco well, because he served three years there as representative of the Quai d'Orsay to General Juin, and as such was Juin's chief advisor. He was much too open-minded for Juin. Nor did the *colons* like him. This is not to say that Lacoste is any flaming liberal who is going to give Morocco away. Terrorism must, of course, be stamped out, but he knows that the imposition of force alone will not solve the Moroccan problem.

Mr. Lacoste is the tenth Resident General since Lyautey. That this post, the highest that France can bestow in overseas administration, should go to a career diplomat is rare; usually it is a plum gnawed by soldiers or politicians. One odd point is that no French foreign minister since the war has ever visited Morocco, although it lies in the jurisdiction of the Quai d'Orsay. Mr. Schuman, Mr. Bidault, and so on have been too busy elsewhere. This is one reason why the permanent staff of the Residency has always tended to make its own policy.

*

That notable patriot and courageous and sensible human being Pierre Mendès-France became prime minister in May, 1954, and at once turned his attention to Morocco (and Tunisia). He set up a new cabinet department to deal with Moroccan and Tunisian affairs, and did his best not merely to clear up the existing mess in both countries, but to chart out a workable future. The Mendès-France approach was fresh-minded, brisk, and realistic. Perhaps he did not go far enough. But he made a lively new beginning. For Morocco he promised a wide political reform, based on the concept of eventual home rule. He refused, on the other hand, to restore the old Sultan, and made it clear that French privileges would be safeguarded. Even so right-wingers in Paris fought his North African proposals with bitter venom, and so—playing their own wily game—did the Communists. Mendès-France won two votes of confidence (August 27 and December 11) but on the latter date his margin was much decreased. In February, 1955, he faced once more an unholy coalition of extreme right and extreme left, and was beaten by 319 votes to 273. Men who did not want to modify even by an inch the terms of the French tenure in North Africa turned out of office the best prime minister France has had since the war. It is important to remember for the future that it was an *African* issue that helped cause the fall of this Paris government.

THE FRENCH CASE

La seule excuse pour la colonisation, c'est le médecin.
—MARSHAL LYAUTEY

This lies in at least two dimensions—moral intellectual and that of physical accomplishment. The French, the most civilized people on earth, are so proud of their *mission civilisatrice* that they sometimes assume that this alone justifies their presence in Morocco. Moreover they are by no means willing to agree that nationalism is, of itself, a cure-all; they do not accept "the dogma that the only way to make a country evolve is to grant it sovereignty." And what would independence, if gained, produce? It is not at all certain, as General Guillaume himself once pointed out, "that national freedom for a country necessarily makes for *liberty*."[2] What price the nationalist movement, say the French, if it serves merely to turn Morocco back to feudal chaos, or exploitation by carnivorous Moors, or the Communists?

Self-determination for small peoples may be worthy in theory, the French say, but first one must define "people." Are the Moroccans a "people"? It is either "a bad joke or a scandal," Guillaume thinks, that a handful of conspirators in Cairo should dare to speak for "human rights" in, of all places, Morocco. But we are entitled to ask what the aim of French policy is, since

---

[2] "The French in North Africa," by General Augustin Guillaume, *Atlantic Monthly*, July, 1953.

the present system is working so badly, and may lead to chaos. Again let me quote Guillaume, who told us, "What we should strive for is the creation of a Franco-Moroccan *community*, with both sides as partners." But on what terms? No one knows. What rights will the junior partner have?

The *Economist* of London printed in 1951 an article called "Little Change Since Lyautey," which contained the following description of French colonial policy in contrast to British:

> France, if it has distantly admired the British Empire, has never appreciated the medley of mercantilism, missionaries, medicos, and public schoolboys which, with a seasoning of high aristocrats, has won the British such success among native peoples. The French conception of administration, at home as well as abroad, is essentially Napoleonic and Roman. It is something which is rigidly superimposed upon a supposedly chaotic society: it is the will of the central government overriding the local clashes of opinions and interests. Above all, the administration is a thing which, while it may well be torpedoed by the free play of opinion and parliamentary democracy, has absolutely nothing to gain from them. It is this profound distrust of politicians and the disunity that they naturally bring which has made it so hard instinctively for the French abroad to countenance even the most gentle movements of indigenous populations towards political expression . . . The emergence of native assemblies is the proconsul's ultimate nightmare. Thus the concepts of a Lyautey: *la force; la grandeur; le désintéressement; la simplicité* . . . There is always a gulf between the vague progressive liberalism of English colonial thought since 1918 and the precise (if only fragmentarily realised) French aim of assimilation.

French opinion specifically about Moroccan nationalism includes several points:

1. Morocco was not a true country until the French came, and it was they, the French, who made Moroccan statehood possible, by rescuing Morocco from barbarism, pacifying it, and giving it stable rule. Moroccan "nationalism," if it exists at all, never existed until the war, and is a French invention.

2. If it was not a French invention, it was "created" by the Germans and Spaniards during the war, in order to embarrass France, and is encouraged now by anti-French elements in the United States and the UN. Nationalism is really nothing but a nasty new kind of internationalism.

3. The average Moor has no interest in national freedom. He is almost totally inert politically. If he does want to be free this derives not from idealism but out of a desire to retaliate against his enemies. Moroccan nationalism means little except vengeance.

4. Even granting that the nationalist concept may have validity, it has been grossly abused by charlatans—a noisy minority of demagogues (mostly educated in Paris, alas) who have no real roots in the population, who are universally corrupt, and who would exploit the masses much more flagrantly than the French. Think of what Egyptians have done to Egypt!

5. Anyway, Morocco is nowhere near being capable of self-government, because among other things it has no trained leaders or educated electorate. Moreover there are practically no natives with technical education—agricultural engineers, veterinaries, railway experts, architects, and the like. To make the country capable of self-government, capable of direct management of its own affairs, will take a generation at least.

When one turns to physical accomplishment the French record is, of course, considerable. France has been in Morocco only since 1912, which is not more than a few seconds away historically speaking. As I have already mentioned, Morocco at that time had no roads, no harbors, no mines, no public health. In 1912 there was exactly one hospital, a mental institution where all the patients were chained together by an iron collar. French enterprise has built in forty-three years 28,000 miles of road, 1,100 miles of railroad, eight modern ports, and ninety-four airfields and landing strips. The standard of living of the country has advanced enormously, and industrialization is proceeding fast. "More than 200,000 Moroccans work in modern factories which provide a million people with a livelihood," General Guillaume wrote recently.[3] Day by day work goes on in agricultural development, irrigation, housing schemes, health control, increase in the production and use of electric power, and education, though this latter is the weakest spot in the French case. The record in public health is particularly impressive. Old epidemic scourges, like smallpox, plague, and typhus, have been wiped out, and admirable work has been done against malaria. In 1952 Moroccan hospitals, 481 in all, gave fifteen million free consultations, almost all to Moroccans. The budget—again to quote Guillaume—gives more money to schooling than "most of the independent countries of the Near East." Finally to mention a variety of items, Morocco had in 1912 roughly a million acres planted to wheat; today's figure is ten million. There are 24,500,000 citrus trees as against a handful. In 1931 there were 2,649 radios in the country; today, 170,000, of which 80,000 belong to Moroccans. In 1947, there were eighty-two cinemas; today, 130. Some 13,000 Moroccans own motorcars, and the

[3] *Atlantic Monthly*, cited above. Also see an eloquent article by Guillaume, "The French Accomplishment in Morocco," *Foreign Affairs*, July, 1952.

country has one telephone for every 180 inhabitants, a record as good as that of Norway or Australia.

Also one should remember that this accomplishment came during a period when France had to fight two world wars, in one of which she suffered a severe defeat, and when it was having perpetual financial difficulties. Moreover warfare went on in Morocco itself for more than twenty years.

Morocco costs the home country a good deal, so much so that in 1952 France—the French taxpayer—contributed half the Moroccan budget, $51,000,000 out of $105,000,000. But the French get much out of Morocco in exchange. For one thing the country is of immense importance both strategically and in the realm of prestige; for another it is an essential bridge to French possessions south of the Sahara; for another it produces handsome revenues for French mining and other commercial interests; for another it is a vital source of military man power. During the fighting in Indochina troops from Morocco and elsewhere in French Africa made up most of the French army, because *French* conscripts do not serve overseas unless they volunteer to do so. Finally, and most important, Morocco provides a living for some 300,000 Frenchmen—the *colons* who have established residence there.

If Morocco is so manifestly valuable, why have not the French adopted a more rational, more farseeing political policy, the better to hold it peaceably? Did they learn nothing from the loss of Syria and the Lebanon, or from the bloody, humiliating defeat in Vietnam?

Half a dozen factors, they say, tend to make Morocco "safe." One is that it is so far west, isolated from the rest of the revolutionary Arab world by the Sahara and Algeria. Another is that Moroccans are by and large so "incompetent." Another is that, even if incompetent, the substantial majority is still loyal. Still another is that as French administration proceeds with its good works, knitting the country together with new roads, opening it up and modernizing it, the chances are that nationalist sentiment will be easier to control. Finally, the French can, they think, always count on the support of the Berbers, who are much better fighters than the Arabs in the towns.

THE COLONS—FRENCH "WHITE SETTLERS"

There are 300,000 French citizens in Morocco—some estimates say 350,000—and these constitute a profoundly exacerbating factor in local politics.

The "white settler" problem is not peculiar to Morocco; it is a dominant and vexing issue in much of Africa. It has become almost axiomatic that political tensions will be most acute where white settlers are most conspicuous, as in Kenya. Countries in which the European authorities themselves strictly limit—or forbid—white settlement by fellow Europeans are on the whole those most tranquil and progressive, like the Congo, Tanganyika, and the Gold Coast.

Usually white settlement produces trouble for the simple reason that African natives by and large hate to have their land taken away, even as would Swiss or Welshmen. The white settler may stimulate the standard of living and bring in public improvements, but he is nevertheless resented as an interloper. Land is something almost sacred to the average African, no matter how poor it may be. In Morocco five thousand *colons* own about one-tenth of all cultivable land.[4] Tens of thousands more own other land. But hundreds of thousands of Moroccans have no land at all, must work on the white farms, and are miserably underpaid. So long as white *colons* and Moorish peasants rub shoulders, smoke will come if not flame. Contact plus exploitation almost inevitably makes for conflict.

French craftsmen and professional men serve their own colony in Morocco, and practically every engineer, manufacturer, lawyer, doctor, manicurist, hotel proprietor, barman, or salesgirl in a good shop, comes from France. Likewise the civil service is French, down to the lowliest station. One issue is voting rights for all these. The French want to give their residents of Morocco, who are of course not Moroccan citizens, the suffrage when a constitutional reform is worked out; this the Moroccan nationalists fiercely resist, because it would greatly lessen their own future voting power. The French on their side say, "We live here. We work here. We make the country what it is. Why *shouldn't* we vote?"

The *colons* have a powerful lobby in Paris, both in the Senate and Assembly, and for years they have virtually "run" the Residency, through their local interests and political pressure on the Quai d'Orsay. Oddly enough a Frenchman is apt to lose some of his best quality when he leaves Marseilles. Once across the Mediterranean, he seems to acquire totally new and different characteristics, probably because his latent provincialism becomes intensified. One Moroccan told us, "The French are so nice in Paris, and so awful here."

The more intransigent *colons* talk on occasion about making a revolt against Paris, and founding their own republic in Morocco. They despise men like Mendès-France, say that French policy is far too conciliatory

---

[4] "Morocco: The Struggle Neither Side Can Win," by Claire Sterling, *Reporter*, April 13, 1954, a brilliantly informative article.

THE FRENCH, THE NATIONALISTS, THE AMERICANS

rather than the reverse, and want Moroccan nationalism wiped out forcibly once for all. Similarly we will find white settlers in Kenya who talk wildly about secession from the British Commonwealth. Of course "secession" would be impossible in Morocco if only because of considerations of security. One *colon* told us, "If our troops ever leave Morocco, every French family here will be murdered the next day."

COLOR BAR IN FRENCH MOROCCO

For the first time in relation to a particular country we mention color bar. (It will not be the last.) Officially color bar does not exist at all in French North Africa, for two good reasons (a) Arabs and Berbers are "white"; (b) the basic tenet of French policy is assimilation. Hence, formal segregation is ruled out. On the other hand all manner of severe discriminations are practiced against Moors, particularly in economic fields and education. In the social sphere the French say that their behavior is based on a "culture bar," not color bar; exactly the same thing may be heard in Kenya and the Rhodesias. Few Frenchmen would refuse an invitation to dinner with the Pasha of Marrakesh, or hesitate to ask a prominent caid to a reception; if a Moor is rich enough, prominent enough, and culturally acceptable, he may be admitted to the periphery of French society.[5]

If an educated Moor manages to get to Paris and take part in cultural life there, the French attitude becomes altogether different, because in Paris social mixing between Frenchman and *indigène* is encouraged. In fact it might almost be said that a Moorish student in Paris is considered dangerous if he *does* consort with his own kind. Once a Moor is far enough along financially, socially, and intellectually to be getting an education *in France*, the French want him to mingle with themselves rather than his own people, at least to an extent. Their hope is to make *Frenchmen* out of educated Moors, who will thus be deflected out of the nationalist movement and become dutiful clerks in a law office, undertakers or surrealist poets, loyal to *la belle France*.

In Morocco almost all French people, talking to a Moor to his face, use the familiar second person, not out of intimacy but as if they were talking to a child. To say "vous" gives the *indigène* too much dignity, the *colons* think. Behind their backs, Frenchmen almost universally refer to Moors as

[5] "Segregation is much worse in the American south than in Morocco"—so we heard one French lady angrily exclaim. "We do not have Jim Crow buses here!" I repeated this to a Moorish friend, who laughed. "I wish we did have segregated buses. We outnumber the French so greatly that it is *they* who would be segregated—two or three seats to a bus!"

members of the *salerace* (pronounced as if it were one word, and meaning "dirty people"), or *salesarabs*, also run together as one word.[6]

"LO! THE POOR INDIAN!"

Half a dozen times in Morocco people reproached us severely not merely for the way Americans treat Negroes, but for our behavior to the Indians. In fact red Indians pursued us all through Africa. There were days in the Rhodesias (as an example) much later in our trip when, it seemed, nobody talked about anything else. "Think what you did to your Indians! You exterminated *your* natives! Nothing that we have done here is anything like so despicable as your treatment of your hopeless redskins. Americans ought to be ashamed of themselves. We try to educate our blacks, and yet you dare to criticize us, you who *murdered* your whole aboriginal population!" The argument has point. Yet there are all manner of answers to it. Today, at least, non-reservation Indians in the United States have full citizenship, intermarry with other Americans if they feel like it, serve in the army, can get any kind of job, and may rise to almost any position in society. We have come a long way toward tolerance since outrages perpetrated against the Five Civilized Tribes and the Nez Percé, even though reservation Indians may be wretchedly treated still. Anyway the fact that Americans have behaved abominably toward Indians does not excuse Europeans of the present day for doing the same thing. Another point is, of course, that the original Indian population of the United States had nothing like the development that most North Africans have today, and were relatively much less numerous.

*

Indians in India likewise come in for frequent mention in Morocco, and two points are usually made. One is that the British were crazy—stark, raving mad—ever to have given up India. The other is that they lost India out of weakness, a "mistake" that the French do not intend to repeat. The fact that India, Ceylon, Pakistan, Burma and so on have become free serves, on the whole, to make France doubly tenacious about holding what parts of Africa it has.

[6] This has one paradoxical effect in the realm of Moorish costume. Most young Moors, especially if they are pale, no longer wear the tarboosh or fez, which instantly identifies them as being Moslem. "I don't wear a fez any more," one nationalist told me, "because I am sick and tired of hearing a dirty Frenchman call me a dirty Arab." So, in order to preserve nationalist consciousness, Moors give up one of its chief badges.

THE ISTIQLAL AND NATIONALISM

The chief Moroccan grievances against France are the following, aside from the basic feeling that it is morally wrong for one nation to rule another.

1. Morocco has never been allowed to have a national election, and there are practically no democratic procedures, much less an elected assembly or parliament. What the political scientists call "responsible" government does not exist, that is, government by a cabinet and legislature responsible in some measure to the people. Every British colony or protectorate in Africa has, by this time, at least the beginnings of responsible government, under which Africans are being systematically trained to take over their own affairs.[7] Nothing remotely like this goes on in Morocco, nor do any Moroccans sit in Paris as members of the French Senate or National Assembly. Africans from all other French overseas areas (except Tunisia) do sit in Paris as regularly elected legislators, with definite responsibilities not only to their own people but to the French Union as a whole, but there are none from Morocco. The country is, in short, nothing more or less than a French-run subject state.

A subsidiary irritant is that the protectorate has no time limit. Never have the French given any promise of future independence, or even a time table; nobody ever talks in terms of dates, as do the British in Nigeria and the Gold Coast, and as the United States did in the Philippines. Some Moroccans are convinced that the French have no intention of ever giving up Morocco, and plan to maintain the protectorate in perpetuity, with the eventual aim of making Morocco, like Algeria, frankly a part of France.

Moreover Moroccans are permitted practically no share in administration, even on the lower levels. "Of the forty-five thousand people on the Residency's payroll, only sixty are Moors, most of them doormen or menial clerks. Only one Paris graduate holds a position of any responsibility at all."[8] Thus, as the nationalists see it, the French are able to assert that Morocco is incapable of self-government because no native administrators are available, while at the same time they make it impossible for such administrators to be trained—a neatly vicious and impenetrably closed circle.

2. Civil liberties do not exist. There is no freedom of the press, or of speech, or of assembly. The country has been in a state of siege—the equiv-

[7] Except British Somaliland.
[8] From the Claire Sterling article cited above. Recently a school for Moroccan administrators was at last opened in Rabat, but very few Moors attend.

alent of martial law—for more than forty years. There is no penal code or code of civil law. Freedom of movement is severely restricted; nobody can move around the country without permission. Even the Moroccan Boy Scout organization has been disbanded. Political expression and organization are forbidden; anybody can be arrested for almost anything at any time. The number of Moroccan nationalists in concentration camps is unknown, but probably runs into the thousands. While we were in Marrakesh a schoolteacher asked members of her class what they would like for Christmas. One little girl piped up, "A machine gun!" Probably she meant this as a joke, but her father was arrested the next day.

3. *Education.* A member of a great Moroccan family, who is not anti-French, told me, "Two things you may be sure of. There is no justice in this country, and no education." It is a principal nationalist complaint not merely that the French starve education, but that they do so deliberately, because of course education will in time inevitably tend to strengthen the nationalist movement. Once a child learns how to read and write, he is halfway to freedom. By keeping people illiterate the French keep them submerged. Moreover they operate their educational institutions with glaring bias. Ninety-four per cent of French children of school age in Morocco go to school; something less than 10 per cent of Moroccan children of school age go to school. The French say that this means that 174,860 Moroccan children now attend primary schools, as against 11,000 in 1911. True. But it also means that roughly 1,800,000 Moroccan children do *not* attend primary schools. As to higher education the figures are even more striking. Only about 15,000 Moorish boys are in high schools, and 350 in universities. For a Moroccan child to get a decent education is almost hopelessly impossible.

Everywhere in Africa we shall find education to be a pivotal preoccupation, the root problem of problems. Why do native Africans yearn for education with such passionate avidity? Because, among other reasons, they know that it is education that gives the white man his superiority. Why do various colonial administrations—not just the French—refuse to give it to them? Because the European powers do not want to spend the money, because they fear the creation of an African educated class, and because it was the conventional view for many years that African youngsters were scarcely to be distinguished from stray dogs on the street.

4. *Military Service.* The French deny hotly that any Moroccans are forcibly impounded into the French army and it is quite true that many young Moors volunteer freely for service. The nationalists assert, however, that even if the law forbids impressment an occasional Arab or Berber

THE FRENCH, THE NATIONALISTS, THE AMERICANS 83

boy may wake up to find himself in a French uniform in West Germany or elsewhere without being absolutely sure how he got there. Perhaps the local caid was trying to curry favor with the Residency by raising "volunteers." Another point of resentment in the military sphere is the size of the *French* garrison that Morocco is obliged to support—around 50,000 officers and men.

5. Public Health. Most nationalists concede that the French have done an admirable job in this field, but say that they would have had to do it anyway, to safeguard the interests of the local European population.

6. Economic Matters. The French system is, the nationalists say, to feed the sparrow by feeding the horse; France is, needless to say, the horse, and Morocco the sparrow. A hugely disproportionate slice of the budget goes to the salaries of French functionaries. The French do not pay anything like a fair share of the tax burden, but get most of the benefits. More has been spent on housing projects for 350,000 Europeans than for the entire Moroccan population. Most of the riches of the country lie in French hands, and in every field Moroccans are wantonly exploited.

7. Trade Unions. Dispute has gone on about this issue for years, and it was a chief source of friction between the Residency and Istiqlal before the deposition of the Sultan. The French want at all costs to prevent the unionization of Moroccan labor on an over-all basis, because this would obviously give Moors a stunningly convenient mechanism for political as well as economic action. Moroccans, as of the moment, are not allowed to have unions of their own, but they may join *European* unions. This has produced a peculiar situation, inasmuch as the principal French unions in Morocco are affiliated to the Confédération Général de Travail, which is Communist-dominated from Paris. So the French, by refusing to let Moorish workmen form their own unions, turned them over in effect to the Communists—not the result intended! On the other hand this paradox has in a curious way benefited the French to a degree, because they now have an excuse for hanging the "Communist" tag on Istiqlal members who belong to the CGT. It is better, some French think, to draw off Moorish workmen into a Communist organization where they will be subject to all manner of controls that have nothing to do with Morocco, rather than let them belong to purely Moroccan and fully autonomous local unions which would inevitably become mainsprings of the nationalist movement.[9] Meantime the Istiqlal denies stoutly that its union membership (about

---

[9] This paradox has been explained by Sal Tas, "After Egypt, Morocco," *New Leader*, December 17, 1951. Also see Alexander Werth, "Report on Morocco," *New Statesman*, June 13, 1953.

70,000) is Communist to any appreciable extent. The nationalists have taken over the Communists in the CGT rather than vice versa.

*

A word on the Istiqlal (pronounced "*Ist*-ikk-lal") itself. Its history closely resembles that of other African nationalist groups we shall encounter. It was founded in 1943, out of a merger of various smaller parties; youthful Moroccan intellectuals had set up patriotic societies early in the war, and even before this a Moroccan "Committee of Action" existed in Paris, supported by the French Popular Front of those days. Then for a brief period the Istiqlal led a fairly respectable existence, notably during the liberal administration of Eirik Labonne, who was Resident General in 1946–47. It was never formally recognized as a "party," but was permitted to exist. Eleven Istiqlal "deputies" even sat in what was called the Moroccan College of the Council of Government; but they quit this group—or were expelled from it—after conflict with Marshal Juin.

Today, of course, the Istiqlal has no legal existence of any kind, and since the Casablanca riots of 1952 has been driven completely underground although some of its members may be met in Tangier. It has two principal leaders, and its "capitals," Tangier aside, are New York and Cairo. In New York, associated with the Moroccan Office of Information and Documentation, is Hadj Ahmed Belafrej, one of the original founders of the party, who was expelled from French Morocco in 1937. I have had several talks with him and his associates. He is a small, precise, levelheaded man in his early forties, well educated and a moderate. In Cairo is Allal el Fassi, whom the French consider to be much more dangerous and inflammatory. He was a teacher by profession, and before the war spent a long period of forced exile in French Equatorial Africa, having been charged with revolutionary activity. He is violently anti-Communist. When he was fifteen (a nationalist already) he wrote a poem "My People Will Know Me," the opening lines of which are:

> How is it that after fifteen years I am still
> a child and playing,
> While my people, with their hands bound,
> cannot find the way to their desire.[10]

Both these gentlemen exasperate the Residency extremely, but el Fassi more than Mr. Belafrej. Why, the French ask, *why*, should respectable people in New York and Cairo pay attention to a pair of nationalist fanatics utterly unknown (so they allege) in their own country? Not one Arab in a thousand and not one Berber in ten thousand, the French insist,

---

[10] From the Nevill Barbour article cited above.

THE FRENCH, THE NATIONALISTS, THE AMERICANS

have ever even heard of either. The thought that they could ever run a government is preposterous—insane. They simply *cannot* be taken seriously, the French say. I labor this point because the same thing is heard all over Africa about rising nationalists, not only in French territories. The old colonials resolutely refuse even to consider the possibility that Africans can be growing up.

One nationalist I met in Tangier talked more or less as follows: "We don't dislike France. We are not against the French, but only against exploitation and their colonial methods." (Indeed I have never met a nationalist in any French area who did not love Paris.) "Of course we are not ready for self-government yet, but we are on the way. There may be a handful of old Moorish functionaries against us, but they are of no consequence—worn-out quislings. How can we win without the application of force? Only an occidental would ask that question. Of course we do not have the physical force necessary to throw the French out now. What counts is our *esprit*, our moral principles, our *will*. When eight million Moroccans are solidly united by the desire to become free, nothing can keep them from eventually becoming free. The more the French clamp down on us, the more they help our cause. But we do not believe in extremism. We do not want to have to become extremists. The chief danger in Morocco and elsewhere in North Africa is that the people, under continued stress and provocation, will get out of hand, eventually dismiss *us*, and then take on more extreme leaders, like the Communists. What is our greatest asset? Youth. Anybody with youth and hope is bound to be on our side."

Half a dozen times—perhaps oftener—we heard statements remarkably like this in other parts of Africa. Nationalist leaders in distant countries, who could have had no contact whatever with this man in Tangier, said the same thing almost word for word.

Some observers I met thought that Morocco would be free in five years, some not for twenty years, some not for a generation or longer. My own feeling is that independence cannot come soon except possibly as a by-product of some much larger event like a general war. It was World War II that freed Syria and the Lebanon, and the French are not likely to be dislodged from Morocco except by some similar convulsion. But nationalism gains a stronger grip on people day by day. Even Marshal Juin said once, "Of course *every* Moroccan is a nationalist."

NATIONALISTS AND THE POSITION OF WOMEN

It was interesting to talk to nationalists about the position of women. One would assume that they would automatically welcome the emancipation of women, since it is the woman who trains the child, and an educated woman is much more likely to train a child to modern directions than one still buried in a harem. Segregation of women is a principal force holding back progress on every level. This cannot be disputed. Yet the nationalists have to steer a wary course. (A.) They must deal with the masses, and cannot afford to alienate devout Moslems; they cannot risk a quarrel with the Islamic church, because the unifying force of Islam is their best weapon against France. (B.) Many women do not want to be emancipated, even if this should be to their benefit. The Istiqlal does not want to affront this large segment of the population, to say nothing of their husbands. (C.) Most important, if women become unveiled it will be easier for the *French* to assimilate them, which the nationalists want to avoid at all costs.

The French, on their side, try to maintain intact much of the old feudal structure, including the status of women, in order to keep the country better under control; it suits their political purpose to have women veiled. Their excuse is that it is their duty to preserve ancient Moslem "culture."

THE COMMUNIST PROBLEM IN MOROCCO

The Communist party is, of course, legal in France; it has been illegal in Morocco since the Casablanca outbreak in 1952. The French insist that it continues to have great power underground, and that the Istiqlal is thoroughly infiltrated with Communism, which the Istiqlal says it is not. As already mentioned, the chief breeding ground for Communists is the labor movement, which is largely under the control of the Communist-run CGT. Communism was not a big preoccupation in Morocco until comparatively recently, if only because the country still had a basically feudal structure. Now with industrialization proceeding briskly the situation is quite different. Also the French have been quick, in the last year or two, to take advantage of American fear and hatred of Communism and to bid for American sympathy by stressing to the utmost the alleged Communist elements in the Istiqlal. In all fairness, one should mention again that the Istiqlal denies vehemently that it has any Communist affiliations at all. Basically it is the party of the upper bourgeoisie. Its leaders say that if the French are seriously perturbed about Communism in Morocco, they should begin by dealing with it at home. After all ninety-two Communists sit in the National Assembly in Paris, and it is not the Istiqlal's business if a *French* trade union happens to be dominated by Communists.

Soviet policy is, in the abstract, to foment trouble in all the Arab nations, attack colonialism, discredit the West, and filter into local nationalist

THE FRENCH, THE NATIONALISTS, THE AMERICANS 87

parties if possible. Africa is, however, not particularly high in Soviet priorities at the moment. It may become high later. Africa may well be tomorrow's Asia.[11] One incidental point, not often appreciated, is that both Soviet Russia and Communist China are very substantial Moslem powers. The Soviet Union, because of its large Moslem populations in Turkestan, Mongolia, and Central Asia, probably in fact has more Moslem inhabitants than any country in the world except Pakistan and possibly Indonesia. Recently at the UN Sir Gladwyn Jebb, the British Ambassador, pointedly asked Arab delegates who were attacking the French administration in Morocco why they did not similarly demand a debate on Russian treatment of Moslems in the Soviet Union. The Russian delegate replied that it was a "crude slander" to assume that the Moslem peoples in Soviet territory were anything but "happy."[12]

The best answer to Communist penetration or agitation in colonial Africa is, of necessity, reform. The Russian cause feeds best on nationalist grievances, particularly if these are authentic. The easiest way to throw a country into the arms of Moscow is to mistreat the people. But the West (speaking of the Communist menace in Africa as a whole) faces a seemingly unpleasant dilemma in this regard. We will come across this repeatedly in these pages. If Country X, let us say, gives a colonial people no reform at all and continues to rule purely by repression, this will probably in the end produce disorders out of which Communism will gain. On the other hand, if Country X gives large political concessions and educates its people to the point where they are capable of governing themselves the risk must be faced that the Communists may take over the newly formed independent government. This has not, however, happened as yet anywhere in Africa, and there is little imminent danger of its happening. Educated nationalists are, by and large, fiercely anti-Communist, if only because they have long been subject to colonial rule. They have no relish to get rid of one imperialism in order to pass to the dominance of another much more predatory and sinister.

As to Morocco and North Africa the chief points of danger are (a) ignorance and (b) despair. The average unschooled Berber or Arab has no conception at all of what Communism is, and does not understand its menace. To those more sophisticated, the chief thing that Communism offers is hope of change. Obviously the nationalists have little chance of making a successful revolution by themselves, and they certainly are not going to get help from Great Britain or the United States. Russia is the

[11] See Chapter 46 below.
[12] Thomas J. Hamilton in the *New York Times*, October 9, 1953.

only country to which they can turn. Moreover Russia, despite its own imperialism, is the professed enemy of colonialism and the western colonial powers. The price of continued arbitrary suppression of the nationalist movement will be to throw it eventually into the hands of Communism. Hence, as moderates see it, the best solution lies in education and steady reform. But not everybody believes that moderation will be possible. One friend in Rabat told us, "In a decade Morocco will be a Russian colony —or American."

THE AMERICAN AIR BASES IN MOROCCO

Technically these bases are not American at all, but French, although they were built by the United States, serve a particular American purpose, and are manned by American troops—in fact they are as American as Omaha, Nebraska. Yet from a juridical point of view they belong to France, and the French flag flies over them; they are under French (not Moroccan) sovereignty, the French own the land, and if we ever leave Morocco they will revert to France, although the installations we have built are American property, and we could take our gas tanks and hangars back home if we so desire.

These were the conditions Paris insisted upon when negotiations for the bases began in 1950. The Moroccans were not consulted or informed in any way about these negotiations. The Cold War was getting hot at that time, Americans were fighting in Korea, and fear of a general war between the United States and Russia gripped the Pentagon. It was considered imperative that we should at once, with little regard for cost, plunge into the adventure of creating five giant Air Force bases in Morocco. We were willing to give the French practically anything they asked for. Speed was of the essence. Why was Morocco chosen instead of Tunisia or Libya, which are a thousand miles or more nearer to Moscow? For one thing Morocco has an Atlantic frontage, whereas the Mediterranean is a bottleneck. For another Morocco is less vulnerable to counterattack. And as a matter of fact the new bases are not, by contemporary standards, far from Russian targets. From Casablanca to Moscow is only 2,400 miles, an easy four hours by jet.

Earth began to move in April, 1951, and in an incredibly short time two of the five installations were operational. The job was the biggest ever undertaken by the United States army engineers, and the largest American military project abroad since the war. Civilian contractors helped. The work was done in such a hurry that it was botched in some respects, much repair work has been necessary on the runways, and Congress has at one time or another investigated charges of waste, graft, and inefficiency. As of the moment of writing three of the five projected bases are in use. The five (not counting headquarters of the Fifth Air Division at Rabat) are Sidi Slimane, Nouasseur, Ben Guerir, Boulhaut, and El Djema Sahim. If war comes, it is from these—among others elsewhere—that our atomic bombers will take off.

Nouasseur, which we visited en route from Casablanca to Marrakesh, is the chief supply and repair depot. I never realized before what a lot of things the American taxpayer's money goes for. Nouasseur is not merely an airfield, one of the largest in the world; it is a city, rough at the edges it is true, but a veritable city just the same. About six thousand Moroccan families had to be displaced to make room for it. The construction work alone at Nouasseur cost $115,000,000, and its equipment about the same. There are 600,000 square feet of building space just for machine shops and the like. We looked at the pits where gasoline is housed. There are twenty-three of these, each capable of pumping fuel into an aircraft at the rate of 600 gallons per minute. But what impressed me most was the warehouses. Here practically everything that an army, or a city, may conceivably need in a long war is stocked in quantity, from canned meat to nuts and bolts. I don't suppose it can be possible, but I think I saw ten thousand brooms.

Then we proceeded to Ben Guerir, which at that time was not as close to completion as Nouasseur. But the runway (14,000 feet, one of the two or three longest in the world) could be used; it is built of two layers of macadam on solid rock, and looks like a gray moon flattened out. It is longer than Central Park.[13]

The total American forces in Morocco number 7,500. The Air Force wanted 32,000 as a minimum, so that among other things anti-aircraft defenses would always be copiously manned, but the French refused to allow us any such number of men. Other complications came up on such matters as wage scales—for instance, a Moroccan truck driver gets about half what a French truck driver gets, who in turn gets half what an American gets—but on the whole relations between French, Americans, and Moors have been remarkably harmonious. American influence has been pronounced in developing skills in Moroccan labor. The Americans broadcast a daily program on Radio-Maroc, which is designed for the GI's, but thousands of Moors listen in, and for the first time in their lives hear American music,

---

[13] There are problems in running bases like these that have nothing to do with air power. For instance GI's will not eat French bread, though this is generally considered by connoisseurs to be the best in the world. But our troops do not like it, and so bakeries had to be built for making typically American bread composed largely of thin air.

talks, and entertainment. In the long run this may have a certain political as well as cultural effect. Most Americans, we should add parenthetically, have a naturally friendly feeling for the Moors. This phenomenon can be irritating to the French. They do not like to see American girls—stenographers, civilian employees, and the like—go out with Moorish boys. One American on the staff of Radio-Maroc was visited by the police recently, who gave him a list of certain Moroccans with whom he *must* not be seen publicly. "If you have to meet these people," he was told, "meet them in their houses, but not in the bars or cafés. It is bad for our morale."[14]

The French may not like to admit it, but the Americans in Morocco greatly strengthen their position. The bases give the United States a vital interest in preserving the status quo in Morocco, which in turn serves French interest. We cannot afford to let Morocco blow up, in view of our huge military investment there. France is holding the Moroccan tiger by the tail, and we have to hold on too. On the other hand I have heard Frenchmen deplore our Moroccan commitments, saying that the fresh air we have let into North Africa will be bound to assist the nationalists in the long run, whether we want this result or not. One told me, "The Moroccan bases will unavoidably produce strain between the United States and France some day. But relations between our two countries must remain good at all costs, for the sake of world peace. So please build your bases somewhere else. Go to Spain!"

As a matter of fact this is exactly what the United States has done, but not for this reason. Late in 1953, after negotiations extremely stiff and difficult, Generalissimo Franco granted to the United States the right to build air bases in Spain. These, being newer and nearer Europe, may in time reduce the importance of the Moroccan bases, or even render them supererogatory. The Pentagon went into Spain mainly because it wanted installations close to the Pyrenees to provide fighter cover in Europe if disaster should come to France in World War III, but also because of the unstable political situation in Morocco. It is an old military axiom that no base is worth much if it is situated in potentially hostile territory.

The nationalist point of view varies between two extremes. One is that the United States is now a direct participant in the French "rape" of Morocco, and, without its consent, has automatically made Morocco a party to the next world war. The other is that it is a good thing to have the

---

[14] Since the August, 1954, nationalist riots American military personnel have been under orders not to wear civilian clothes while off duty, for fear that they may be mistaken for Frenchmen and shot by terrorists. New York *Herald Tribune*, November 26, 1954.

Americans around, because they will influence the French to be more temperate.

AMERICAN POLICY IN FRENCH NORTH AFRICA

It has always been a basic tenet of American foreign policy "to support the orderly development of dependent areas toward self-government . . . in conformity with the principles of the United Nations charter."[15] Speaking to the nation during the Indochina crisis on May 7, 1954, Secretary of State Dulles said, "The United States, as the first colony in modern history to win independence for itself, instinctively shares the aspirations for liberty of all dependent and colonial peoples. We want to help and not hinder the spread of liberty. We do not seek to perpetuate Western colonialism."

If this be true, why does not the United States express more concretely its sympathy with nationalist groups in Morocco and elsewhere in Africa? Why, if we have such a deep "instinctive" feeling for nationalism, do we almost invariably support the French against the nationalists? There are at least three answers. (1) In the present historical phase, Paris is worth more to us than Fez. We want French military help in Europe, and so we must logically ride along with France. Moreover North Africa is the tail of the French kite; step on the tail, and the kite won't fly. If war comes, a strong and friendly France will be essential to the American national interest. Above all, France must be kept above water. (2) Morocco is not by any stretch of the imagination fit for self-government as yet. (3) We have our own Moroccan bases to protect.

It would probably be correct to say that United States policy exists on two planes, immediate and long-range. For the next few years we can afford to take no chances. We must work with the French because we cannot afford to work without them. Perhaps then in the future, at some date now remote, we can support the growth of nationalist sentiment and the satisfaction of legitimate nationalist aspirations. This view reflects a prevailing mood in Washington today not merely in regard to Morocco but toward most of colonial Africa. We shall encounter it again before this book is done. The United States sympathizes with nationalist aspirations, yes, but we do not want to upset the European boat. But this policy of ambiguity and delay has grave dangers. It may lose us Africa, the greatest of all prizes in a period of cold war. Paris may be more important to us than Fez *today*, but this may not be true ten or even five years from now. Western Europe has to be on our side in any case; but parts of

[15] From a State Department release after the deposition of Mohammed V.

Africa may be in a position to make their own policy in the future, and they may not choose us. They may take a neutralist position, like India, or even go Communist. The easiest way to *make* them go Communist is to deny them opportunity for development and freedom. For the United States to associate itself exclusively with the colonial powers and ignore or snub nationalist African sentiment is shortsighted in the extreme.

Not long ago overzealous American officials in North Africa, anxious not to affront French susceptibilities, went to the crazy length of cutting out references to "independence" from a speech by the President of the United States on the Fourth of July! Even the French laugh at us and despise us for being so craven.

Meantime, on the Washington level, the United States hopes piously that the French, out of their own self-interest, will come to behave more reasonably, more liberally, in Morocco. Nobody can suppress a nationalist movement forever by chucking people into jail, if only because nationalism thrives on suppression. What the United States wants is a stable, peaceable Morocco, which means that sooner or later major concessions will have to be made to Moroccan nationalism.

CHAPTER 6

Lord of the Atlas

> *Morocco is saved. Now I can die happy.*
> —THE PASHA OF MARRAKESH, after dismissal of the last Sultan.

WE HAVE mentioned El Glaoui, the Pasha of Marrakesh, several times in these chapters, and now we must treat of him in more detail. This picturesque old chieftain is one of the most remarkable characters we met in all Africa. He is a kind of Oriental Charles the Bold, who fought 121 pitched battles in his youth, has been wounded thirty-two times, and is proud of the number of men he has killed with his own hand. Also he has a dark, almost feline quality of grace. He has been called the Metternich of Morocco, and has the sophistication of a really first-rate cardinal. The key to his policy is that, like good cardinals, he has always been consistent.

The Glaoui is called other things too—"Lord of the Atlas," the "Black Sultan," and "the Gazelle of the Sus," the Sus being the rich, fertile valley below Marrakesh, between the Atlas ranges, which he holds in fief. His full name is correctly Hadj Thami Glaoui el Mezouari; "Thami" is his given name, and "Glaoui" that of his tribe. "Pasha of Marrakesh" is his principal title. His domains cover several thousand square miles, in which live at least a million Berbers, perhaps more; his private "army" of Berber warriors, who owe him unequivocal fealty, numbers about 300,000. Probably the Glaoui is the last feudal lord on earth with so many armed men at his disposal. (They are not, however, armed in the modern fashion, but carry romantically old muskets.) Then too as Pasha of Marrakesh he is chief administrator—for the French—of much of southern Morocco. It is as if, in the United States, a subpresident with his own militia had virtually autonomous authority over Texas, Arizona, and New Mexico.

The Pasha's political strength lies mostly in the fact that he has always played the French side. But he would resent hotly being called a puppet, and indeed he is not a puppet as the new Sultan is, but is rather a French associate, a valued ally. He likes the French, and they like him. He is proud of his position. I will not forget his expression when a tactless French lady told him patronizingly in a mixed group that France could always count on him because he knew on which side his bread was buttered. He was not only angry, but deeply hurt.

The Glaoui was, as we know, the preponderant force in the intrigue that got rid of the former Sultan. He hated Mohammed V with fixed passion, and it was seemingly a signal victory to get him ousted. But it may not turn out that way—not quite—because with the old Sultan gone the Glaoui has lost some of his bargaining power. The French no longer need him so much. On the other hand the new Sultan is a Glaoua, and was the Glaoui's man.

The Pasha is tall, very dark, gaunt, and with a handsome face that carries an engaging note of rascality. His antique hands are wrinkled like walnuts, and he has a winning smile. He is over eighty now, but still fit physically. Eighty is no age at all for a Moor. He has an elder brother, Sidi Hassi, who is ninety-six, and who is still an active administrative officer—his title is "Pasha of the Kasbah."

The Glaoui is a devout Moslem, and has made the pilgrimage to Mecca no fewer than five times. He has never touched alcohol in his life, but he has no objection to serving it profusely to European guests. He plays good golf, and his private course near Marrakesh is supposedly the best in North Africa. He is renowned for his physical prowess as well as courage and gift for direct action; once he broke up a riot in the *medina* by laying about him with a whip. He likes to stay in luxurious hotels in London and Paris, and takes the cure once a year at Vichy or some similar spa. He knows French, but speaks it haltingly; as a rule he talks in Arabic (or Berber) through an interpreter. His efficient secretary, Albert E. Berdugo, comes from Tangier, and is of an old Jewish family; that the Pasha of Marrakesh should have a Jewish aide surprises people who do not know how well the Moorish and Jewish communities generally get along in Morocco.

One of the Pasha's great enthusiasms is Winston Churchill, who has several times visited him in Marrakesh, and partaken of his sumptuous hospitality. He admires in particular how much Sir Winston can eat and drink. The Pasha is a very rich man indeed, but once, before World War II, he was temporarily hard up and the French had to lend him money. One of his palaces, which he uses as a guest house for European visitors, is unexampledly ornate, furnished in what Oriental taste considers to be the correct manner. One of the bathrooms has two huge tubs. The Pasha's idea was that a husband and wife visiting him might enjoy the experience of bathing together in the same room. The source of his wealth is, of course, the people. His official biographers say that he maintains substantial agricultural properties in southern Morocco, and the legend is that every shopkeeper in Marrakesh works for him one day a week; he owns manganese, cobalt, asbestos, lead, uranium, and gold mines. An unfriendly critic, the well-known French writer Claude Bourdet, says that the Glaoui grinds down his serfs like an old-time robber baron, and is a merciless exploiter through the mechanism of his own police and tax collectors. The peasants have to give him what is called "spice"—gifts whenever he sets out on a trip, or on the occasion of holidays and feasts—as well as free labor when he demands it. He has a complete personal monopoly of the local output of saffron, almonds, and olives, and pays for these articles only 50 per cent of the normal market price. Mint may not be sold by others until he has disposed of his own mint crop.[1]

El Glaoui rose out of the Imézouaren family, and his forebears have been powerful locally for more than two hundred years. At the turn of this century three different feudal families fought to control the Atlas passes. The young Glaoui was a stalwart fighter. Once his raiders reached the outskirts of Oujda. An elder brother, Si Madani, was head of the family at this time and Lord of the Sus. This gentleman took a leading role in ousting the late Sultan Abdel Aziz, who was deposed in 1907, just as the Glaoui himself took an important part in deposing Mohammed V forty-six years later. In 1908 the Glaoui became Pasha of Marrakesh, and except for one short interval he has held this position ever since. He was Pasha when the French came in 1912, and made the great decision of his life when, under his brother's leadership, he decided to welcome rather than resist them. As a matter of fact he and his brother fought *with* France to oust a usurper in Marrakesh. The Glaoui and Marshal Lyautey became close friends. When World War I broke out Lyautey summoned him to say that he might have to send the French garrison in Morocco back to Europe to fight against the Germans, and asked him what would happen in Marrakesh if the French withdrew. The Pasha replied in effect, "Leave it to me." Lyautey did so, and the whole of the Sus stayed quiet, although French pacification of the Berber tribes had only just begun. Oddly enough the garrison of Marrakesh itself consisted in 1914 mostly of *Germans* in the French Foreign Legion!

Later the Glaoui became a principal instrument of the French "pacification" of Morocco. He fought and subjugated his own countrymen on behalf of France. In World War II he worked hard and cleverly for the Allied cause. He refused to have anything to do with the German Armistice Commission during the Vichy period, kept his tribesmen back in the hills

[1] *Temps Moderne*, Paris, July, 1953.

with their arms secure, and staunchly welcomed the American landings at Casablanca in 1942 and the reassertion of legitimate French authority.

Naturally the Glaoui's family connections ramify through the whole of Moroccan official society. His elder brother El Madani was once Grand Vizier, and he is a son-in-law of the present Grand Vizier, El Mokri.

The Glaoui himself has at present, it is believed, four wives and four principal concubines. Probably he has had twenty or thirty children, but nobody would be likely to know for sure.[2] Of these six sons and two daughters are well known, though the daughters are, of course, never seen by outsiders. I heard them described as "wilted flowers"; they sit indoors most of the time, and are seldom even permitted into the palace courtyards, lest they be tainted by the glimpse of some unauthorized male. When they take an automobile ride not only are they heavily veiled, but the windows of the car are screened.

The Glaoui's household, as we observed it, seemed harmonious, pleasantly civilized, and much more relaxed than most in this milieu. The father dotes on his sons, while ruling them with a fibrous hand. Sometimes visitors see a homely scene—one of the boys sitting casually on the balcony outside his office, waiting for him to appear, and then greeting him with devoted respect and affection. The wives are not veiled within the palace, and mix freely with the children, whether they are *their* children or not. The Pasha seldom has a meal with them—or even with his grown sons—but he is never far away, and knows all that goes on. The boys went to good French schools, and were made to learn French from infancy. In fact, to improve their French, they were even forbidden to speak Arabic to each other at home. Similarly in India in the old days potentates insisted that their children speak only English. The sons are not allowed to smoke—at least in El Glaoui's presence. Sometimes he slyly tries to tempt them with forbidden cigarettes, to see if they will have will power enough to resist. He is ambitious for all the boys, and makes them work hard; it is his dearest wish that one will some day become Grand Vizier. All have dignity, grace, and charm.

The eldest son, whose mother was a Circassian, is Si Brahim, the Caid of Telouet.[3] He is in his early thirties, and is a complex youngster, who seems to be as strong and delicately turned as a spring; he is pale, good-looking, and reserved to an almost sinister-seeming degree. Telouet is the

---

[2] Ibn Saud, the late King of Arabia, who had multitudinous sons, liked to say, "In my youth I created my country. Now in my old age I populate it." The Glaoui might almost make the same remark.

[3] "Si" means "Mister," more or less.

ancestral fortress of the Glaoui tribe, and Brahim, as its caid, has considerable local power. Probably he will be his father's successor as Pasha, but nobody can be sure.

Si Sadek, another son, is a judge in the Pasha's court at Marrakesh—an attractive young man with a highly refined, acute, and serene intelligence. He wanted to go to Harvard Law School, but his father kept him so busy that he could not get away. (To become a judge under Koranic law takes eleven years of study.) Recently the Pasha asked Sadek what he would like most for a birthday present; he expected some such answer as a Cadillac, but Sadek's reply was, "A pilgrimage to Mecca with my mother." Si Hassan, another son, is a painter of distinction, who recently had a successful one-man show at the Wildenstein gallery in New York, after several exhibitions in Paris. He and Sadek have the same mother. Hassan, like Sadek, is exceptionally cultivated and attractive, and his paintings have gaiety, sweep, and color. Still other sons are Si Mohammed, Caid of Ait Ourir, Si Abdullah, Caid of Fetouaka, and Si Ahmed, one of his father's lieutenants in Marrakesh. Another boy, who was also brilliant and promising and who would almost certainly have been his father's successor if he had lived, was Si Mehdi. He was educated at St. Cyr, became an officer in the French army, and after a gallant career was killed in Italy in World War II.

*

Visiting the Pasha is, naturally, an experience of the most piquant quality. We were summoned to the Marrakesh palace. Outside the walls were rough-looking guards, dressed in the ragamuffin way of most Moors, without arms or uniforms. They reminded me of retainers outside palaces in Mexico, who are similarly nondescript and look like the most menacing of loafers. Penetrating one gate, we walked through three successive courtyards, each paved only with dirt (to make easier footing for the horses) and of a strange irregular shape. The impression is of a kind of slipshod crazy quilt—a miniature Hampton Court cut out of angular mud. On the porch of the Pasha's own residence squatted an enormously fat unveiled Negro woman, chatting casually with a high official. The appointments inside are astonishing. I felt as if I were in the Alhambra redecorated by a dealer in Victorian antiques. Rooms are tiled in yellow, pale blue, and an insidiously brilliant green, with tall wooden ceilings painted in gilt and other colors. Sèvres porcelain, Imari chinaware, Turkish clocks, are part of the décor. There are narrow benches set against the walls, and practically no other furniture.

The Glaoui received us for our first visit in his business quarters, and these are modest. Against one wall I saw a painting of Marrakesh by Mr. Churchill, placed atop a very large iron safe. The safe had a nice cozy look. Then the Pasha showed us a set of leather-bound autographed books, kept on a special shelf, that the British prime minister had sent him, together with—of all odd things—a portrait of Churchill and Stalin, autographed by the former but not the latter.[4] The Pasha looked ageless. He looked like a black tulip made of steel. He wore a striped brown-and-white *djellaba* over an inexpensive American-style soft shirt and foulard tie. With one eye half closed, the Pasha addressed us soberly. He has strong opinions. The main thing he said was that, if the French ever leave Morocco, the result will be anarchy and bedlam. He is for France because he thinks French rule is the best. He gave me the impression of a man individualistic and completely fearless, a cross between Robin Hood and Rupert of Hentzau, who did not comprehend, spry as his intellect is, anything at all of the pressures of the modern world. But we did not talk long. Our host just wanted to look us over. Then we were asked to dinner.

A DINNER WITH THE PASHA

Nothing in gastronomy is more exotically enticing than an Arab *diffa* or banquet. We went to several. First Hassan and Sadek gave us a "simple" lunch as a kind of dress rehearsal, so that we could learn in privacy what to expect and how to comport ourselves. Then General Guillaume drove us one day to a town called Demnat, where he was bestowing a decoration on a venerable caid. This was a full-dress feast. At the gates of the city armed horsemen on white chargers fired their muskets in salute, and pranced in fierce display. We were given ceremonial offerings of dates and milk, and heard for the first time the most extraordinary sound that North Africa provides—the high sibilant whistle, which is almost a whinny, a neigh, made by the long files of women from the town, who line the castle walls, and, as they begin to oscillate in a slow rhythmic dance, let loose this penetrating horselike chant.

Guests at a Moorish meal sit on cushions or low divans, with a large white napkin laid over their knees. You may use this, but not too conspicuously, to clean the lips, but not the fingers.[5] You may hold bread in your left hand—bread is in large soft chunks—but otherwise the left hand

---

[4] This was one of the few times I ever saw any books in an Arab or Moorish household. Arabs do not go in much for libraries.

[5] Even in the best houses napkins are apt to be old and full of rough darns; cloth is precious in North Africa. Sometimes they do not match. Africa is the continent where nothing matches.

is not supposed to touch food, because of a Moslem custom having to do with bodily cleanliness. Except in special cases there are no knives, forks, spoons, plates, or other implements. The tablecloth is put on the floor, to catch crumbs. You eat with your right hand, taking everything from a common dish, and if you are a purist you use only the thumb and first two fingers. The fingers are not supposed to touch the mouth. To lick the fingers, no matter how greasy they may become, is bad form; but I have seen it done. These procedures are simple enough with some types of food, but not all. *Couscous* is difficult. Or try picking up a blazingly hot fried egg with three fingers and get it into your mouth without touching the lips or spilling. Unskilled people use wads of bread as a cleanser. Bones and similar debris are tossed on the floor or table.

First—at a typical feast—a servant arrives with a copper kettle, or pitcher with a thin spout, and pours water into a bowl over the hands of each guest. (At the conclusion of the meal, this ceremony takes place again, and soap is provided.) Next comes mint tea, thick and sticky. Then *plat* after *plat* arrives; each makes a separate course. Food is brought in on very large trays or in casseroles, and is kept warm by being covered with tall canopies made of straw, like fancifully shaped hats. Then, as in a Chinese meal properly served, you reach over to the common dish, which all share, and choose a morsel to your taste. Women of the household are never present at a *diffa*. Each dish, if anything is left, is passed on down to the women who are waiting in a different part of the castle or dwelling. When the wives and concubines have finished, it goes on in turn to male servants, then to female servants, and finally to retainers, hangers-on, or slaves.

It was interesting to watch French people of the most impeccable refinement, who might have been characters out of Marcel Proust, eat Moorish meals. They ate with their fingers with the most obvious gusto and relish; in fact they seemed to be possessed by a mad glee while tearing a hot slippery chicken apart with their bare hands. I offered the remark at one dinner that eating without implements was a simple enough indication of a suppressed tendency to revert to childhood, and a lady replied that, indeed, in the Faubourg St. Germain where she was brought up she had been strictly forbidden ever to touch food with her hands, had always yearned to do so, and now took a special perverse joy in doing it.[6]

But let me proceed to our dinner *chez* the Pasha. Twenty bearded

---

[6] One lady I know cannot always quite manage to swallow some of the odd delicacies that may be provided at a *diffa*, like certain internal organs. Such items she surreptitiously sticks away into her slab of bread, hoping that this evasion will not be seen.

retainers, looking like a line of owls, saluted our arrival at the palace. We entered a small room with maroon-striped settees, green curtains, and a flaming yellow carpet—Moslems love clashing colors—and with arched windows and a vaulted ceiling. One guest this evening was a celebrated French official, the Préfet of Casablanca; another was a barefooted, white-robed Arab octogenarian, the Caid of Mogador. A cold wind whipped through the doors and windows, which are usually kept open at ceremonies of this kind, no matter how chilly it may be outside. (At a luncheon birds may fly in and out.) The Glaoui, who had been sitting alone on a hassock, rose to greet us. He wore Arab dress (and carried a poniard) except for Argyll socks and a bright red necktie. At once we moved across a courtyard filled with orange trees to another division of the palace, where an American-style bar was functioning. Of course the Glaoui and the Caid did not drink the cocktails that were offered, which were a brilliant pink in color. The bar amuses the Pasha, as it might amuse any sophisticated host. Dinner was announced by a major-domo who entered abruptly and twitched the Glaoui's elbow, in the peculiar informal manner of Moorish servants. We went outdoors again, crossed another courtyard, and emerged finally into a room big enough to seat two hundred. The chief colors here were pink, lettuce-green, white, and purple. The Pasha, with a chortle of satisfaction, slid out of his slippers unobtrusively, climbed gaily over a hassock, sat down on a divan, and invited us to sit around him. This is what we ate:

First, a pale green soup composed of almonds, peas, and bits of white fish. (This was a concession to the uncouth West. We were even allowed plates and spoons. Moors know full well that existence is impossible to a Frenchman unless dinner begins with soup.)

Second, a whole roast lamb, served naked and intact. This, the staple course at an elaborate Moorish meal, is known as a *mechoui*. With infinite dexterity the Glaoui broke into the hot crackling skin, and seized from underneath specially tender morsels, which he passed on with his fingers to my wife. Often a lively competition occurs among guests to get the meat deepest down, from the ribs, where it is particularly fat and tender. This procedure may sound gross, but is not. Nobody tears off big chunks of flesh. People eat slivers and delicate strips. Sometimes at a big *diffa* the course following this is *another* whole roasted lamb, prepared with some sort of sauce to differentiate it from the first.

Third, a *pastilla*. This *plat*, which takes a full forty-eight hours to prepare, is the pride of a good Moorish cook. It is a pie, almost three feet in diameter, the crust of which is an inordinately fine, flaky *mille-feuilles*, on which a design is made with powdered sugar. Underneath, as a bold guest dents the crust, and usually burns his finger doing so, will be found a miscellany of shrimp, tripe, sweetbreads, olives, liver, *cervelles*, mussels, and fried eggs. It is a veritable treasure nest, and delicious beyond speech.

After this we had four more main courses in sober succession—squabs with a sauce like none other I have ever tasted before or since, a kind of hot, liquid and milky hollandaise; a covey of whole roast chickens, stuffed with olives and swimming in a lemon dressing; a ragout of lamb, onions, eggplant, and hard-boiled eggs; and a second, different ragout—slices of lamb laid tenderly atop a bed of peas and almonds. Then came a dish of strangely shaped pretzels seasoned with molasses, the equivalent of the sherbet still served occasionally at formal dinners in the West; it is sweet, and a refresher before what is to come.

Couscous was next. This, the basic food of Morocco for rich and poor alike, is made of semolina. The mound of grain may contain anything else from cool-skinned grapes to chunks of mutton; that of the Pasha came with turnips, carrots, and hazelnuts. *Couscous*, like rice in Japan, is always served toward the end of the meal so that you can fill up if you are still hungry, and it is bad manners to take too much. It is hard to manage with the fingers, since it is almost as dry as sand. The Glaoui is one of the world's foremost manipulators of *couscous* balls. We watched him fascinated. He picks up a handful of the hot grain, tosses this in his palm without touching it with the fingers, and gently bounces it in the hollow of his hand until by some miracle it forms a cohesive ball; this he then pops into his mouth, catching it on the fly. It was like watching a man, with one hand, make and eat golf balls.

At last came a cake made of frozen figs and tangerines. The Pasha picked up his napkin, and with a flourish dropped it on the tablecloth; this is the conventional gesture to indicate that the meal, any meal, is over. During all this we of the West drank champagne. The old Caid, who never said a word during dinner, sipped lemonade steadily with a peculiar hissing gurgle. Finally—the end is the beginning—we had mint tea again, the universal drink of North Africa, which is supposed to be an aphrodisiac.

*

After dinner ladies of the harem danced for us, first five Berber girls, then five Arabs. That we should be allowed to see them (and they to see us) was an exceptional experience. The Berber girls were somewhat stout, and danced what is known as an *Aouache*. One had golden castanets, which made a bell-like sound. In the background, a male musician played something that seemed to be a musical saw set athwart a long mandolin; the sound was like no other I have ever heard. The dancers had their shoulders and arms covered, but with sleeves slit so that the skin was visible; legs and ankles were completely concealed, and this gave a curious provocative quality to the rhythm of the dance. The movement, as the girls made a vibrating circle, was mostly with the hips and feet.

Then came the Arabs, who were slimmer, prettier, and more sophisticated. The musician was a violinist and the performance more deliberately erotic. The girls wore turbans, draped so that the hair could be seen (or it was caught up with bright ribbons), blouses with the arms bare, and clanking golden chains and bracelets. They carried small drums, called *gambri*, the beating of which accentuated the flexing of their bodies. Their movements spread from the belly both up and down; even the head oscillated in a sexual motion, and the dance came to a climax when each girl, bending forward and back sharply, while still rotating her torso, plucked at her sash.

This was the first native dancing we saw in Africa. No dancers that we encountered later—and we looked for dancing in every country—were more enthralling.

INTO THE KASBAH COUNTRY

This book, I repeat, is not a record of travel or personal experience; it is a book of politics and information. But it is impossible to give a fair picture of some African countries without brief description of some trips we took. After Marrakesh we crossed the High Atlas by car and descended into the wild stubborn terrain beyond. For the first time I began to get a direct intimate view of primitive Morocco. Before this we had talked and listened. Now we saw.

Marrakesh was misty when we left it early on a December morning. A light beige dust danced against the palms, which looked like big frayed daisies. Up the road we climbed and circled, through steep craggy passes. Then we saw snow, speckled with rock, the color of Roquefort cheese. Around a sharp bend sat a row of crouching Arabs, and I reflected for the fortieth time that these can be the most fixed and immobile people on earth. They might have been white rocks, stone markers to keep us from going off the cliff. Then I saw that they were not Arabs at all; they *were* white rocks.

Lunch at the Kasbah of Telouet. Caid Brahim had sent word ahead, and here in his ancestral castle we had a monumental *diffa*. A *kasbah* is by conventional definition a fort or castle, and Telouet is one of the most historic and romantic in Morocco.[7] It seems to be part of the hill it sits

---

[7] Also the word *kasbah* can mean the old part of an Arab city, as in Algiers.

on, and its squat crenelated towers command peremptorily the plain below. The walls, made of baked mud, have literally been carved out of the surrounding earth. Somberly, Telouet gives forth an almost forbidding sense of power, darkness, and mystery. Richard Coeur de Lion would have liked it, and so would Metro-Goldwyn-Mayer. Even today, it is supposed to have fastnesses and dungeons out of which men, once incarcerated, have never emerged. Some *kasbahs* date from the Arab conquest of Morocco, and have changed little since. Most have no plumbing or electric light. They look like what Europeans think of as "crusaders'" castles, except that the towers are square, not round.

After lunch, by instructions of the Caid, dances were put on for us, in the open air of a blazing white, irregularly paved courtyard. The audience consisted of three—my wife, myself, and our chauffeur. The performers numbered hundreds. The entire village was turned out. About twenty male musicians squatted in an irregular pool in the center of the court, caressing their drums. Around them then assembled an oval loop of dancers, ranging from children to old women who might have been seventy. They took their positions, it seemed, more or less by age, and wore every combination and variety of color; they had green turbans, and pointed purple slippers, and gold coins jangling from necklaces around their brown throats, and skirts the color of a fire engine. The dance began with a kind of shuffle, as the loop of women moved solidly first in one direction, then the other, with an insistent rhythmic clapping of the hands. The effect as a whole was of a slow shimmy performed by a centipede. Then in the space between the pool of musicians and the circle of seesawing women solo dancers moved like peacocks, with their proud heads erect. The beat of the drums became heavier, more resonant. This went on for an hour or longer. A black triangle of shade cut deeper into the court, as it does late in the afternoon at a bullfight. Suddenly the dancers were dismissed. They darted across the yard and toward the harem like pretty scampering hens. It was time for them to eat. I hope they got the remnants of the Lucullan feast we had.

That night we reached Ouarzazate and here we saw the same kind of dance, but in circumstances even more beautifully exceptional—by firelight. Our host was the Khalifa Hadj Ahmed Ou Tzoujjouart, and the ceremony took place in his *kasbah* in the town, by name Taourirt.[8] This is one of the loveliest of Moroccan *kasbahs*. Flaky red walls and square flat towers are pierced not merely by loopholes which have been there for two

---

[8] If I have these names wrong it is because even the local French authorities were not certain how to spell them.

hundred years, but by modern windows with broad white frames—a typical Moroccan incongruity. Again we saw the inner pool of squatting musicians and the loop of women around them, making two concentric ovals. The circle of women, depending on the rhythm of the dance, contracted and expanded as if a white noose had been laid on the earth and was being manipulated like a lariat. It was bitterly cold. You made your choice of being singed by the enormous crackling fire, which was burning at the side of the musicians, or freezing. Sparks from the tamarisk boughs swept and sprinkled over the dancers. Flames jutted out, spread their orange plumage across the court, and flapped back and forth like banners incandescent in the wind. The reds, the purples, the salmon-pinks, the clashing greens, were given a phosphorescent glow, as if by fireflies, and the whole scene melted gradually into chiaroscuro—gray, white, and black.

This is not primitive Africa. It is feudal Africa. There is a big difference. I do not think that anywhere else in the world could a feudal baron, living in a castle that might have come out of a Moorish Grimm, summon by a flick of his finger two hundred women who are not only members of the harem, but principals in a *corps de ballet*. One chieftain in the neighborhood is still so aloof, so impregnably independent, that he recognizes the suzerainty of neither the Sultan nor the Glaoui, but only of the French. Until France came most of the noblemen in this vicinity were incessantly at war with one another. Family fought against family, tribe fought tribe, as in Europe in the twelfth century. Meantime the peasants—serfs—built the *kasbahs*, with their warped geometrical designs, piece by piece. As reward, they were housed and fed. Today little has changed except that fighting has stopped. The serfs are not, technically speaking, slaves any longer, since they are free to go; but where would they go? Formerly they got no wages—what would they need money for—but this is changing now. People do want money. They want to buy Coca-Cola and chewing gum and take trips into the towns. They want radios, better food, and education for their children. Life still has a wonderful quality of dignity and repose in these brittle old *kasbahs*, but there is a perceptible air of uneasiness, a groping movement toward fulfillment and change. I left the *kasbahs* of Taourirt and Tifoultout, which is outside Ouarzazate, with two contrary impressions: (a) these are the Middle Ages; (b) they are over.

Ouarzazate is also, of course, a modern town, an important French military outpost controlling the roads down into the Sahara. The local French commandant, an officer of the Service d'Affairs Indigène, told us about his work. The last resistance was not stamped out in the nearby mountain range known as the Black Djebel, or Sarro, until 1933. In other words warfare was still going on with these intractable Berbers when Hitler seized power in Germany, and when Mr. Roosevelt was first elected President. The French administrative officers are devoted, disciplined, and experienced, and have much more amicable relations with the natives than their colleagues in the large towns. They are like the District Commissioners whom we will meet later in British Africa, experts in everything from anthropology to irrigation. They are at once policemen, magistrates, and governors. A boy of thirty, with an European staff of not more than three or four, may be in charge of a territory as big as Oklahoma.[9]

Ouarzazate has one main street, about fifty yards long, and two thousand people, of whom two hundred are French. The temperature can reach 110 degrees Fahrenheit in the summer. The sight I enjoyed most, next to the *kasbahs*, was the general store, run by a Greek. It resembles closely the general store in Twin Corners, Montana, or Greensboro, Vermont. The frigidaire has cold beer, ham is sliced by a machine made in Toledo, and you can buy anything from a can of sardines to a monkey wrench.

From Ouarzazate two roads stretch out which are among the most interesting in all Africa, one going southeast to Zagora, along the celebrated Valley of the Dra, the other projecting eastward through an equally celebrated valley, that of the Dades, which is solid with crumbling *kasbahs*. We chose the latter. Five minutes after we were on the road, it became clear to us—if we needed to know it—that indeed Africa is a continent of contrasts. We passed first a long line of camions carrying manganese, and then a stately camel caravan.

En route to Tinerhir the earth becomes positively crimson, and the mountains hold a savage yellow light. Villages rise out of rock like sculptures by Gutzon Borglum. The *kasbahs*, as squat and rectilinear as baby skyscrapers cut off at the middle, are sometimes only a quarter of a mile apart; some seem deserted, but each houses a family group, say a hundred people. Tinerhir is not much of a town, but it has a comfortable *gîte d'étape*, or resthouse. Here buildings are decorated with fancy mud prickles, which the French call dog ears; these are a characteristic of Saharan Africa. At Tinerhir we began to pass out of the Glaoui's territory. The people have a different look. We saw tall women in blue veils, smeared with indigo. Children wear topknots like the Chinese—to have this pigtail makes it easier for Mohammed to reach out and carry them aloft to heaven. In the Tinerhir area are 30,000 natives and thirty French. The local commandant has no troops,

---

[9] One small point of interest is that the French, who are a sublime people but who have little gift for friendship, do not have much camaraderie amongst themselves. One officer took us to the home of another. They had been stationed in the same village for years, but they still called each other's wives "Madame" with the utmost stiffness, and the junior of the two did not know where the bathroom was in the senior's house. Possibly he had never been in it before.

not even a company of *Goumiers*. He rules by prestige alone. Of course he can summon force at any time. Tinerhir, like most Saharan towns, has an immense walled open enclosure in its center, bigger than Trafalgar Square; this was originally a parade ground. At one side I saw a shiny new Texaco station, and on the other a Mobiloil gas pump. Even in Saharan Africa, Americans compete. We visited the market. The big thing on sale was a consignment of fresh donkey dung, used for fuel. I began to understand, after some of the dreariness of Tinerhir, why Moroccans like to go to Marrakesh. It is for the same reason that people in upper New York State make a pilgrimage to Radio City, even if Radio City has no snake charmers.

The next day we turned north, after a stop at Ksar-es-Souk, which is the capital of a desert area as big as Belgium. Its walls are red, and it commands the Tafilalet oasis. A peculiar coat of dust formed on the top of our car; I looked again, and saw that it was frost. Then at a village called Midelt we became handsomely snowbound—on New Year's Eve. The *chasseneiges*, snow plows, had broken down. We had to make a ten-hour detour over brittle *pistes* (dirt roads) in the back country, to avoid the blocked passes, and finally reached the enveloping majesty of Fez. So we had had a glimpse, all too brief, of the old Morocco. Our chauffeur said as we bade him good-by, "Do not forget that this is a hard country, *monsieur*. With Negroes in the Sahara there can be understanding. With these Moors, No." A sick dog moaned in the courtyard. We went into the Palais Jamai, one of the most enchanting of hotels, and there a Parisian waiter was making crepes suzette with as exquisitely fixed attention as if he were feeding a hummingbird with an eye dropper.

FRENCH MOROCCO—TO SUM UP

First. Two civilizations that have points of harmony as well as conflict are being fused together.

Second. The French still make use of feudal institutions, both in the structure of government and otherwise, to further their own interests.

Third. Obviously Morocco has a long way to go before being ready for self-government. Nevertheless, the nationalist movement cannot be dismissed, and is growing stronger all the time.

Fourth. The French have done a great deal for Morocco, but not nearly enough.

Fifth. Morocco is not only part of Europe, but part of the United States, since it lies within NATO frontiers.

CHAPTER 7

Tangier and Tetuan

> *Tangier the White . . . posted like a sentinel on the most northern part of Africa.*
> —PIERRE LOTI

TANGIER is an oddity. It reminded me of treaty ports in China in the old days. Once after visiting the Far East I wrote that Shanghai was a complex political ulcer on the face of China, and almost the same thing might be said about TANGIER in relation to North Africa, although it is much smaller. Like the lustrous Chinese cities of the past, it is full of rich tax dodgers, and has an atmosphere of fastidious duplicity. It deals heavily in gold, as Shanghai dealt in silver. It is famous for spies, smugglers, and pirates; trials for piracy still take place occasionally before the consular courts. It is a major haven for expatriated homosexuals and other outcasts in their wanderings around the world, as was Peiping. Many of its most refined citizens take dope, though this is in the form of a derivative of hashish, not opium. But the chief parallel with the China of the old international settlements is that, although it is part of the Sherifian Empire, Tangier is governed by an international regime and its citizens have international protection. It has been called "the only successfully governed international city in the world."[1]

Also Tangier is unique in that its European residents live virtually tax-free and are unencumbered by the various regulations that are standard everywhere else in the world. There is no income tax, no sales tax, no gift tax, no inheritance tax. Rich Britons, whose estates would be wiped out by death duties at home, can leave substantial fortunes if they establish residence in Tangier. The banking laws are so lax that practically anybody can

---

[1] There are three different postal administrations; most citizens trust the British above the others. You can mail a letter from the British post office in Tangier with British stamps exactly as if you were in Stratford-on-Avon or Llanerchymedd. The British also maintain their own post office in Tetuan, the capital of Spanish Morocco.

open or run a bank, whether or not he has any authentic capital, and banks do not have to publish balance sheets or other statistics. There are money changers on every street corner. Similarly anybody can form a corporation and be almost totally exempt from the usual technical controls; no inspection of financial institutions is required. There are no currency or exchange restrictions whatever, and anybody can trade in any kind of money. Most important of all, any person can become a legal resident of Tangier by moving there, if he has a valid passport. Nor are visas required for citizens of countries belonging to the international administration. For anybody inclined to be a crook, Tangier thus offers a setting almost too perfect to be believed, although four different codes of law are in force.

The population is supposed to be 170,000, but statistics of this sort are unreliable as they are everywhere in Africa. Of the total perhaps 110,000 are Moors. The Spanish is the largest of the European communities, and Tangier has 20,000 Jews, who have their own representation in the legislature and their own rabbinical courts. There are three types of Jew—the old stock almost indistinguishable from Moors, those that came from Spain in medieval times, and contemporary refugees from Central Europe. When I asked "Who runs Tangier?" one answer was "the Jews." (Others were the real estate operators, the Mendoub or representative of the Sultan, France, the Spanish police, the financial community, and Mr. Archer, the international administrator.)

What does Tangier live on, if there are no direct taxes? A large percentage of the budget comes from a flat 12½ per cent duty charged on all imports, except some luxuries which pay only 7½ per cent. Tangier is thus not quite a free port, but almost. What in effect happens is that the Arab population, which is of course the poorest as well as the most numerous, pays for the European rich. This is because the Arabs have to buy tea, sugar, textiles, and other imported staples, and bear the brunt of the customs duty charged on these. It is the *indigènes*, crushed by insufferable poverty as they may be, who support the international community.

For the prosperous, Tangier is a kind of mattress—an old sock—stuffed with gold. Anybody can buy, sell, or store gold in any quantity or form; especially cast pocket-sized ingots are a favorite item. Gold comes to Tangier for a variety of reasons—mostly these days from frightened men of property in western Europe. Suppose, let us say, a Frenchman sells his family estates; he may prefer to have his proceeds in Tangier in gold rather than in paper francs at home. Many transactions occur through Switzerland. Tangier is so attractive a haven for fugitive gold not only because of the free exchange market but because it is under both British and American protection. It is accessible—at the mouth of the Mediterranean—and its older banking houses have a nice reputation for discretion. But the Tangier gold holdings, though picturesque, are not big. This African metropolis is not Fort Knox. Probably its total gold holdings do not amount to more than $50,000,000. Recently an American wanted on the spur of the moment to buy $30,000 worth; he had to go to half a dozen banks before he got it all.

One curiosity about contemporary Tangier is its "radio power." It is one of the great wireless crossroads of the world, partly because of peculiar meteorological characteristics; there is little interference from such celestial phenomena as the aurora borealis, and transmission is generally possible twenty-four hours a day twelve months a year. With Tangier as a relay point, practically any target in Europe can be reached with the accuracy of a pair of calipers. RCA has an important installation in Tangier, so has Mackay, and so has the Voice of America.

Fez is archtypically a Moslem city, and Casablanca a European city; Tangier is a mixture of both, and full of stimulating contrasts. As so often happens in a Mediterranean town, the brothel area lies immediately behind the cathedral. Expatriated millionaires live in dilapidated Arab palaces, the patios of which contain aggressively ancient fig trees surrounded by shiny aluminum modern furniture. From one house which is as contemporary as next week's *New Yorker* one can see, a stone's throw away, both the prison platform where people were bastinadoed not long ago and the windowless insane asylum still in use. One point of colorful interest is the American Legation. This, originally the home of a Moorish prince, lies on the edge of the *medina*, and is the oldest American diplomatic station in the world. It has housed representatives of the United States uninterruptedly since 1791. Moroccans are fond of pointing out that theirs was the first country in the world to recognize the independence of the United States, and that George Washington is the author of a celebrated letter written to a Sherifian majesty in 1789. They do not always add that the chief reason for our interest in Morocco in those days was the depredations of the Barbary pirates.[2]

As always in a Moslem city, women add a sharp colorless note of color. Most that you see in Tangier are so heavily muffled in white veils that they look like wads of Kleenex. Should you by chance see an unveiled woman, she is probably a peasant from the mountainous Rif. Purdah is extremely strict for townspeople. A woman walking alone with a man on the street is actually subject to arrest, and I have already mentioned that Tangerine women are forbidden to go to movies.

[2] Incidentally the lighthouses of Trafalgar and Tarifa, from which our word "tariff" comes, are both visible from the residence of the American minister.

TANGIER: ADMINISTRATION AND POLITICS

But first a word on Tangier's history, which is pungent.[3] In modern times it was occupied first by the remarkable Portuguese, who left notches almost everywhere on the African coasts. Apparently the first suggestion that Britain take it over came from General Monk, later the Duke of Albemarle. He wrote a dispatch in 1657 as follows: "There is a castle in the Streight's mouth which the Portugals have called Tangar, on Barbary Side, and which, if they part with it withal, it would be very useful to us, and they make very little use of it, unless it be for the purpose of getting Blackamoors . . . An hundred men will keep the castle and half a dozen Frigates there would stop the whole trade in the Streights to such as shall be enemies of us."[4]

Monk's suggestion was not taken up at once, but in 1662 Portugal did give Tangier—and also Bombay!—to Britain as part of the dowry of Princess Catherine of Braganza on her marriage to Charles II. There can scarcely be an example in history of a lady contributing so much geography to her spouse. But in 1684 the British abandoned Tangier (not Bombay) because it had become "a nest of papacy where Irish troops and Romish bastards could disport themselves unchecked." One illustrious British regiment, first raised in 1661 to hold Tangier castle, continued to be called the "Tangier Regiment" until modern times.

The British never gave up strategic interest in Tangier, for the overriding reason that, with Gibraltar, it corks the Mediterranean. Lord Nelson once said, "Tangier must always remain in the hands of a neutral power like Morocco, or England must own it." This is the root reason why Tangier is internationalized today. The British were able to keep France, Spain, and Germany from seizing it by the device of setting it up as an international community. Mother and father to contemporary Tangier is the Algeciras Conference of 1906. Then in 1923 Britain, France, and Spain signed an instrument known as the Tangier Statute, which set up the International Zone and is still the basis of its organic law. In 1945 when World War II was drawing to a close a treaty dealing with Tangier was negotiated in Paris by Britain, France, the United States, and the Soviet Union. The Americans and Russians did not play a strong role in this, because of lack of direct interest in the area. The conference confirmed the organization and powers of

[3] It is uncertain incidentally whether Tangier was named for the fruit, or vice versa. Actually tangerines are called mandarins in Tangier.
[4] "A Note on Morocco," *Bulletin of International News*, April 3, 1943.

the multi-nation Committee of Control that runs Tangier today, and gives it one of the most novel forms of government in the world.[5]

By reason of its participation in the 1945 conference Russia could become a party to the Tangier government at any time, but it has never exercised this privilege. This is a striking fact, and why the Russians have never chosen to assert themselves in the International Zone is a matter of unceasing local speculation. They do not even maintain a consulate in Tangier. At first the Russians refused to share in the city's administration because they would not sit down at the same table with representatives of Franco Spain. Three seats on the legislature are, in theory, still held open for Soviet membership. No doubt there would be vigorous protests if Russian representatives ever did actually appear. Meantime the local citizenry has no doubt that, even if they are not officially represented in the region, the Soviets know everything worth knowing about what goes on.

*

Eight nations sit on the Committee of Control which administers Tangier —the United States, Great Britain, France, Spain, Italy, Belgium, Portugal, and the Netherlands, all of which were signatories to the original Algeciras Conference. They are in the normal course of events represented on the Control Committee by their regular diplomatic or consular representative resident in Tangier. The Committee also appoints an executive officer known as the Administrator who by tradition must always represent one of the smaller powers. The present administrator, an adroit and engaging Portuguese, is José Archer.[6]

Also there is a Legislative Assembly, appointed in part by the Committee of Control, i.e., by the representatives of the eight powers. Tangier must be the only "country" in the world with a "legislature" partly named, so to speak, by London, Washington, Rome, Madrid, and so on. Three Americans are members of this Assembly, who are, so far as I know, the only citizens of the United States alive who sit in a foreign "parliament." There are also three British in the Assembly, four French, four Spaniards, three Italians (by reason of a new arrangement), and one Belgian, one Portuguese, and one

---

[5] Parenthetically, one should mention that the Spaniards moved in on the International Zone in 1941, and occupied it till 1945. They thought in 1941 that France was beaten, that England would never again play a decisive role in the Mediterranean, and that they could simply march in and take over the area with impunity. The pretext was that Tangier should be "neutral," but it is a matter of historical fact that Spain at that time was an Axis ally, and planned to enter the war soon on the Axis side.

[6] Mr. Archer was succeeded by a Belgian diplomat recently.

Netherlander. Three others represent the local Jewish community, and six are Moors. These are appointed by the Mendoub (delegate of the Sultan), who is closely bound to the French. He controls the Jewish as well as his own Moorish votes and always votes with France, so that as a general rule the French are invincible. Yet all this happens on territory which is part of the Sherifian Empire, and where Moroccan "sovereignty" is supposed to be a trust of all the powers!

Mr. Archer had a job that called for all his manifest competence. The administrator—any administrator—has eight different bosses to please, of eight different nationalities, as well as the Mendoub. Moreover most of the Europeans are not much interested in Tangier per se or the fate of Tangerines; they are career diplomats interested in advancing themselves by pleasing their own governments. Officials under the administrator are of various nationalities. The regular police force is run by a Belgian, and in addition there is a special police detachment under the Spaniards. Finance is British, justice Italian, customs French, public welfare Spanish, and so on. But what about the Moorish inhabitants of Tangier, who number 64 per cent of the population? The plain fact is that they are out of luck. It is almost impossible for an Arab to get a good job in the administration. There are all manner of other discriminations. The Committee of Control and the Administrator have, in theory, no authority whatever over the *native* population; their responsibility applies solely to the international community. So there are in reality two parallel governments in Tangier. The Arabs are left to the refined mercies of the Mendoub.

There has never been an election in Tangier, and there are no political parties or independent press. The Control Committee can veto any measure passed by the legislature. Public opinion has no way to express itself, except by word of mouth; sometimes scribes read out manifestos (the "spoken press") in the mosques or bazaars. Nevertheless Tangier is an important headquarters for Moroccan nationalism, and the city is full of Istiqlal sympathizers and refugees, who do their best to keep out of the sight of French agents planted everywhere. The reason why nationalism flourishes—even if half underground—lies obviously in the fact that the area is both international *and* part of Morocco. The chief weapon of the authorities against nationalist expression is Article Ten of the 1923 statute, which forbids agitation and propaganda, and provides that anybody offending against peace and order may be expelled. On the whole it has been applied leniently; nationalists are not apt to get into trouble unless they become obstreperous. The administration, as I heard it put on high authority, "shuts its eyes to nationalism, so long as nationalism keeps reasonably quiet." There are several curiosities in regard to Article Ten. One is that any member of the Committee of Control, for instance the American minister or British consul general, can order to be expelled from Tangier any national of his own country. Nowhere else in the world has any American official such summary power.

The French authorities do their best to keep out of their zone anybody whom they think may be inflammatory, and use Tangier as a watchtower to this end. Recently five Egyptian newspaper representatives, who had had no trouble getting visas for French Morocco in Egypt, paused briefly in Tangier on their way to Rabat. They were stopped flat in their tracks by the French in Tangier, who refused them permission to proceed. This produced a lively scandal because the Spaniards in Morocco then leaped in and, with a full fanfare of hospitality, invited the Egyptians to visit *their* zone, and see how well things were going on there in contrast to French Morocco. The Spaniards like to irritate and frustrate the French on occasion.

MENDOUB OF TANGIER

This bleached-out old gentleman, by name Si Ahmed Tazi, is the personal representative of the Sultan in the International Zone, a sub-lieutenant of God, and a dutiful French puppet. His palace is charming if somewhat moldy; he is worthy enough, but not particularly stimulating intellectually. Entering his palace we passed through a long ragged line of retainers, typically Moorish in their subtle combination of shabbiness and splendor. They seemed to have a peculiar status in the household, and were all at once humble, watchful, and proprietary. If you moved, they moved, but silently. I said to our escort, "They look like slaves," and our escort replied dryly, "That's what they are."

SPANISH ZONE IN MOROCCO

Spain envisages tomorrow a free and great Moroccan people....
—GARCIA FIGUERAS

Spanish Morocco, across the Mediterranean from Gibraltar, lies in two layers. Narrow coastal strips containing the cities of Ceuta and Melilla are technically considered to be part of Spain itself, and are under the direct rule of Madrid, exactly as if they were in Europe. The rest—the Spanish Zone proper—is a division of the Sherifian Empire, like French Morocco. It covers about a tenth of the whole of Morocco, and is much poorer than the French Zone.[7] The Spaniards hold it as subtenants, so to speak. They

---
[7] But it has a Five-year Plan.

do not, like the French, have a direct treaty with Morocco; their rights derive from arrangements with France (dating from 1912), not with the Sultan.[8]

But, strange as it may seem, the Spaniards get along with the Moroccans better on the whole than the French do. They take their Moroccan commitments with great seriousness. The native ruler is known as the Khalifa (literally, lieutenant or viceroy), and is named Sidi Moulay Hassan Ben el Mahedi. He is a member of the Sherifian dynasty, and is in theory appointed to his exalted position by the Sultan, whom he represents. Actually Madrid decides who the Khalifa shall be, and he is no more than a ceremonial mouthpiece of the Spanish government. The Spanish High Commissioner, corresponding to the Resident General in French Morocco, is Lieutenant General Rafael Garcia Valiño. Such is the prestige given to his post that he is generally regarded as the second most important man in Spain after Generalissimo Franco himself.

TETUAN, the capital, with some 90,000 people, has character. Tangier is froth and tinsel; Tetuan is rooted into the earth. Tangier has a brilliant European glitter, and eats and drinks money; Tetuan is a sober city, dignified and clean; it does not wear its heart on its sleeve, and conveys a note of secrecy and command. In my first hour there I did not see a single person on the streets in European dress, not even a policeman; yet it is as Spanish as the Escorial. Its *souk*, or market, is sublime. It is colorful to an extreme, but fixed and orderly. Chains of blind lead the blind, as in Marrakesh, but they seem to know where they are going. The people are poorer, but there are not so many beggars. We saw hashish sold openly on the streets (if you could call them streets) and sipped mint tea so strong that it burned the tongue. And here women wear shrouds that seem darker than those in French Morocco, so that they resemble toadstools.

Behind Tetuan rise the hills of the Rif, which is still almost an impenetrable area. Here the great Moorish chieftain Abdel Krim rose in the early 1920's and fought both Spanish and French to a standstill until he surrendered to overpowering force in 1926. If he had had only Spaniards to fight, he might well have pushed them into the sea. But the French could not afford to have Spanish Morocco beaten, and hence intervened. It took the elite of their army to crush Abdel Krim. This was not a border insurrection; it was a full-dress war. The French have been sensitive to what goes on in Spanish Morocco ever since. They do not want any more Abdel Krims. Today the Rif is totally quiet, but there is scarcely a village or

---

[8] A curious point is that the United States does not recognize Spanish Morocco as a legal entity. C. L. Sulzberger in the New York *Times*, February 5, 1952.

mountaintop without a Spanish garrison. Abdel Krim himself, after his capitulation, was exiled to the French island of Réunion in the Indian Ocean. After some years Paris decided to move him to metropolitan France, but by means of a neatly executed plot he managed to escape while his ship was passing through the Suez Canal, and is now living in Cairo. The Egyptian government will not turn him over to French (or Spanish) hands. In Cairo we had a long talk with Abdel Krim; he is physically frail these days, but alert, and has a luminous humor, subtlety and intelligence. Like many orientals, he likes to give point to his conversation by gestures with his delicate, fastidious hands. We asked him what he thought of Mohammed V, and nothing could have been more pictorially emphatic than his gesture of thumbs down. He said that the Sultan was a patriot "only for himself." We asked him about the Glaoui. With swift, gay, naughty fingers he slipped his hand in and out of a pocket, as if to indicate that the Glaoui's political views were largely based on considerations of finance.[9]

France and Spain had a stiff, unpleasant, and still unresolved quarrel in 1953-54 following the deposition of Mohammed V. The Spaniards have so far refused to recognize the legality of this, which is acutely embarrassing to France. The French are having troubles enough in their own zone. If the Spanish Zone, which has a million people, should actually break away from the Sherifian Empire, the results for Paris could be catastrophic. France even sent warships into Spanish Moroccan waters (January 20, 1954), ostensibly for "long-range target" practice, in protest at the Spanish attitude. Then in Tetuan 30,000 people applauded wildly when 430 caids presented a petition to General Garcia Valiño, repudiating the new Sultan "since he was imposed arbitrarily by France in contempt of the wishes of the Moroccan people," and refusing to accept him as ruler. What did Generalissimo Franco do? He did something unprecedented. He expressed his "utmost satisfaction" at this anti-French demonstration! There followed

[9] Vincent Sheean saw Abdel Krim in Cairo not long ago and paraphrased as follows his views on American foreign policy: "At the end of the war there was a superb opportunity for the United States, basing itself upon the ... Atlantic Charter, to rally all the colonial and oppressed peoples to a new organization of human society. This opportunity was missed and the American power chose instead to support colonial empires everywhere, no matter how shaky they might be, in southeast Asia, Africa, and the East. The colonial and oppressed peoples now find that the only power which professes belief in their ability to rise is Soviet Russia. This was a gross general error in American policy, . . . and will cost us all dear. . . . France cannot be restored and the North African peoples will find their opportunity to revolt. The partition of Palestine, coming on top of a series of such errors in judgement, threw the Arab world against the Americans in whom they had believed, and introduced Russia to the Mediterranean. A period of grave and unnecessary struggle, with unpredictable results, is now inevitable." *Virginia Quarterly Review*, Winter, 1951.

prolonged and exacerbated discussions between Paris and Madrid, with a stalemate as the upshot.

One result of this impasse has been a singular paradox. Many Moroccan nationalists and even Communists, who have always thought of Franco as Mephistopheles or worse, now praise him warmly, and even talk of him as the "defender" of the Arab world, which is, indeed, one of the things he would like to be.

Spanish tactics in Morocco are, of course, part of a larger general picture. As France and Great Britain seemingly grow weaker, Spain is the more tempted to speak in a louder, brassier voice. The Spaniards are pushing hard to get Gibraltar, and would like extremely to reacquire Tangier. Anything that diminishes French or British prestige plays to their hand.

ASPECTS OF SPANISH POLICY

The rulers of Moslem Spain never subjugated Morocco. It was the Moors who conquered Moslem Spain.
—ALAN H. BRODRICK

Spanish policy in Morocco differs from French in several ways:

First, the Spanish Zone is highly militarized, which tends to keep it quiet. The chief value of Spanish Morocco to Spain is its usefulness as a staging and training ground for the army. Much more than the French, the Spanish administration is run by the military, and there are probably as many as 100,000 troops in the Spanish Zone.

Second, Spaniards have as we know a strong Moorish underlay and resemble Moors closely in all manner of respects. Most Spaniards like the Moors, understand them, and know how to get along with them. There is no attempt to impose a policy of assimilation. Moors are pretty well let alone. One young Moor told me, "The French despise us—the Spaniards treat us with respect."

Third, The Spanish Zone has not been seriously exploited by white *colons*, and there are few, if any, discriminations in the realm of color bar. In the leading hotel in Tetuan we saw a Moorish chieftain having lunch. Maybe this is a small point, but we never saw the same thing in Rabat or Casablanca.

Fourth, Franco himself has a close personal association with the Moors. He served in Morocco for many years, and without Moorish troops he could not have won his civil war. His Elite Guard in Madrid is composed of Moors.

Fifth, The Generalissimo wants to cultivate as good and close relations as possible with all the Arab states, particularly those in the Mediterranean basin. To this end conciliation of his own Arabs is a necessity. Recently the Secretary General of the Arab League in Cairo paid a state visit to Madrid, and publicly expressed his approval of Spanish policy.

Sixth, Franco apparently fears that French Morocco faces a long period of instability, and he wants to keep his own zone sterilized away from this. Hence, it is sensible to be moderate.

This is not to say that Spanish Morocco, in contrast to French, is any paradise for the Moroccan. It is not, even though Spain has promised its Moors eventual self-rule. The Spanish Zone in all manner of respects is not only a feudal backwater, but the walled-off preserve of a grossly totalitarian dictatorship. The secret police are everywhere. Nevertheless some astonishing ameliorations may be cited. Recently Garcia Valiño proclaimed ostentatiously a widespread amnesty for political prisoners; hundreds were released from jail. The Istiqlal is perfectly legal in the Spanish Zone (which doubly infuriates the French) and so is its offshoot the Islah, or Reform Party. A nationalist newspaper is permitted to exist (of course it is carefully controlled), and when we were in Tetuan it was announced that free primary education would soon be guaranteed for the entire Moorish population. Advanced students are encouraged to go to Egypt. Several Moors have risen to high rank in the Spanish army—there is even a Moorish general, Mohammed ben Meziàm, who recently became Captain General of Galicia on the mainland. To sum up, Spanish policy, in contradistinction to French, seeks to make use of local nationalism, even if this means encouraging it to a degree, rather than antagonizing it. The strings of control by Madrid are never loosened, but they are wrapped up in the silk of "co-operation." One Spanish official told us, "We know perfectly well that we cannot last forever here, but we intend to last as long as possible."

Of course any nationalist foolish enough to engage in overt revolutionary activity would get the shortest of short shrifts. No colonial rulers are tougher than Spaniards. The chief ameliorative factor probably lies in the realm of race relations and color bar. A Moor, if he is treated badly, at least has the satisfaction of being treated badly by somebody almost of his own kind, not by a race-conscious super-white superior.

Leader of the Islah is Abdel Khalek Torres, whom we met in Tangier. He is outspoken enough, but basically moderate; he is well educated, and above all wants education for his people. He said that he did not like to make trouble for the Spanish. "Our nationalism is not xenophobic. We do not want to be a great nation, but we could fulfill a useful role by being a link between Europe and Africa. All we want is to be free."

Moroccan nationalists on the pan-Morocco level do not, at the moment, pay much attention to the Spanish Zone. Spanish Morocco is a sideshow compared to French Morocco if only because the Spanish Zone will inevitably follow the French. Casablanca is the key to Morocco's future, not Tetuan.

Finally, a word on the Khalifa. Nobody seems to be sure what attitude this portly middle-aged gentleman takes on politics. The Spaniards seal him off even more hermetically than the French seal off the Sultan. The Khalifa may have acute awareness of his viceregal prerogatives, but seldom gets a chance to exercise them. He came into the news in 1949 by marrying a young lady named Princess Lalla, in circumstances of the most florescent pomp. His bride was the daughter of a former sultan, Abdel Aziz, who died in exile in Tangier, and a British mother. She is a modern young woman, and goes about unveiled. The wedding ceremonies lasted three weeks, and cost $600,000; Franco's gift to the bride was $50,000. The average wage of a Spanish Moroccan worker is 25 cents a day.

MORE ABOUT SPANISH NORTH AFRICA

Other Spanish colonies in North Africa (not counting the Canary Islands) are a derelict void. One is Ifni, a minuscule enclave in French Morocco on the Atlantic. It produces ambergris. Nearby are two adjoining regions, the Southern Protectorate of Morocco, which is part of the Sherifian Empire, and Spanish Sahara, a separate entity. This latter is divided into two zones, Rio de Oro and Sekia el Hamra. All these are run by the High Commissioner in Tetuan, and very little indeed is known about them. There are unkempt settlements and a few miserable coastal towns, but the hinterland is raw emptiness. Rio de Oro covers 73,762 square miles, and probably does not contain more than 23,000 people. The capital of Sekia el Hamra, by name Smara, is harder to reach than Lhasa in Tibet, and is quite probably the loneliest town in the world. No one would talk in these backward, degraded regions of Spanish "conciliation" or "cooperation."

NATURE NOTE IN XAUEN

I have already mentioned Xauen. It is where we saw the wedding. Here the street cleaners, women who pick up dung with their bare hands, wear a costume that consists of a big straw hat tied on with a pink-and-white-striped shawl, a yellow jacket from which green sleeves project, skirts sharply striped in red, white, and black, and blue shoes.

Near a mosque that looked like a pink porcelain toy we went into a café with a dirt floor and a few wooden tables; in a dark corner some Arab boys were doing something. We heard broken moans, and then a peculiar whimpering, as if bubbles of pain were breaking through clenched teeth. But it was the sound of an animal, not a human being. The boys had caught a hedgehog, and were skinning it alive. We asked them why. "To hear it cry."

CHAPTER 8

Brief Word about Algeria

Algerians became French before they became Algerian.
—GENERAL AUGUSTIN GUILLAUME

ALGERIA is an integral part of France, although separated from it geographically, and this makes it a special entity. Its African inhabitants are in the technical sense of the word full French citizens (although few Moslem women vote) and its three northern departments, Algiers, Constantine, and Oran, have the same status as departments inside metropolitan France itself, like Seine-et-Oise or Alpes-Maritimes. There are no legal restrictions of any kind against natives in these departments, and moreover they retain their rights of personal status—in regard to marriage, property, and the like—under Koranic law, thus having the best of both worlds. From this point of view it would seem that Algeria represents the French policy of colonial assimilation at its best and most fruitful. Algeria is far ahead of Morocco constitutionally, and much more advanced than any territory in Black Africa. But has all this solved the Algerian "problem," and is Algeria *really* a part of France? No.

People often say that the capital, ALGIERS (population 315,210) is indistinguishable from a seaport on the French mainland, Toulon or even Marseilles. Indeed it has plenty of French characteristics—kiosks, boulevard cafés, mansard roofs, and neatly combed gardens behind black iron pikes. It does not remotely resemble Marrakesh or even Tangier. It is bourgeois and respectable. It has good bookshops and good restaurants. The French always believe in feeding the mind and body both. The fact remains that Algiers, beneath its sound French awning, is still an Arab city. Comparatively few Arabs in Arab dress are to be seen on the streets except in the celebrated Kasbah, but—deep down—they are still there, silent, wary, and inescapable. They are the permanent substratum, the flesh beneath the skin.

Algeria covers 847,500 square miles, and is thus roughly four times the size of France; its population is around nine million, of whom perhaps a million are European. Of the eight million *indigènes* about two million are Kabyles, who are a Berber offshoot; they are mountain people, shepherds and olive growers, more pro-French than the lowland Arabs, and partly Christianized. Another important community is that of the M'zabites, a people so peculiar that they have been called both the "Jews" and "Quakers" of the Moslem world. Their capital is the desert city Ghardaïa; they are intensely puritanical and fiercely acute men of business.[1] Many retail shops in Algiers are M'zabite. When a M'zabite dies, he is supposed to be buried at his birthplace, and the bodies are sometimes shipped down to Ghardaïa by taxicab.

Not all the million Europeans in Algeria are French by any means; there are a good many Spaniards and some Italians. The Jewish community, which has had full French citizenship since 1870, numbers 130,000. Some French, particularly among the wealthier *colons*, represent families that have lived in Algeria for four generations or even longer. They have a long history of despising the Arabs (nowhere does one hear the phrase *"salesarab"* more than in Algiers) but they have inevitably acquired some Arab characteristics. Having lived off this land, they take indelible color from it. The French in Algeria might almost be said to represent a new kind of separate "Mediterranean" nationality.

Now another point. The three northern departments, with their Cezanne-colored vineyards and sharply terraced hills so much like those on the Riviera, comprise less than one-tenth of the area of the whole country. Below the coastal fringe are the Southern Territories, mostly desert. The illimitable Sahara is Algeria's backyard. These enormous territories (the total population of which is only 816,992) are *not*, like the coastal departments, part of France on the governmental level. They are part of *Algeria*. They are administered not from Paris but from Algiers. Maybe this sounds like hairsplitting, but the details are important. The Southern Territories do not send their own deputies to Paris and are, in substance, colonies *of* Algeria. What really runs them is the French army. This situation has produced heated political pressures lately, because of the discovery of oil in the desert regions. If oil becomes immensely lucrative, like that in Saudi Arabia, to whom will its revenues go? If Algeria should be the sole beneficiary, it might well become richer than France itself. Paris would like whatever income oil may produce in time to be diffused through the whole French budget; Algiers, on its side, wants the major share. One recent proposal in Paris was that the Southern Territories should be detached altogether from Algeria and transformed into a separate autonomous unit,

---

[1] Ghardaïa is also well known for its dancers, chiefly the Ouled Naïls.

with Algiers bypassed and the region put under the direct authority of France. Algerians, particularly the *colons*, resisted this plan with passion.

Not much oil has been found so far, though something like $150,000,000 has been spent looking for it in Algeria and Tunisia. A French company, half owned by the government, is producing about 100,000 tons a year from one field near Algiers. Hopes are hot and high for future strikes. Both Shell and Caltex have initial prospecting rights, and are negotiating for more. American companies operating in Algeria must be one-third owned by a French subsidiary. All over the northern Sahara we saw teams of geologists and geophysicists, prodding into the desert sand, building camps, and waiting for oil to flow.

ALGERIA AND MOROCCO: HOW THEY DIFFER
There is no elite in Algeria
—PHILIP DEANE

Taking it as a whole Algeria differs profoundly from Morocco. It is bigger, richer, and more Europeanized. Also—

1. Algeria was never a real country, a national entity, like Morocco. The Turks took it early in the sixteenth century; then local soldiers of fortune established their own quasi-government in 1710, under a dignitary known as the Dey. Algeria became the pirate state par excellence. The Dey's buccaneers discovered that they could profitably sell white slaves to blacks as well as vice versa, and preyed all over the Mediterranean, capturing European ships.

2. The French have deeper roots here than in Morocco. They took Algeria in 1830: the pretext was that a French consul calling on the Dey had been insulted by being slapped on the face. What a far cry it is from this to Dienbienphu! France has thus had 125 years to extend its regime in Algeria, as against seventy-four for Tunisia and only forty-three for Morocco. The country was "absorbed" into metropolitan France in 1848, and the process of Europeanization has gone on ever since. Arab culture was plowed under.

3. Algeria is not a theocratic state like Morocco—it has no Islamic monarch.

4. The social structure is curiously mixed up. Not all the European settlers are rich *colons*, nor are all the Arab beggars. Algeria is one country in Africa where European immigrants can be the proletariat, and prosperous Arabs the bourgeoisie.[2]

[2] See "Cross-Tides of North African Revolt," by Herbert Luethy, *Commentary*, November, 1952.

5. Many Algerians emigrate to France; they cannot be kept out any more than Puerto Ricans can be kept out of the United States, since they are French citizens. There are perhaps 300,000 Algerians on the mainland today, mostly unskilled labor, and they present grave problems in housing and employment.

6. The Communists cannot be outlawed or the Communist party suppressed, as in Morocco, since Algeria is part of France and the Communist party is legal in France. You can buy Communist newspapers on any kiosk in Algiers.

Perhaps we should add a word about the position of women in Algeria. A French journalist I know has Arab friends whom he has met every day for twenty years; yet he has *never* seen one of their wives. Most Arab women, here as in Morocco, live totally useless lives except to bear children; they cannot sew a button or cook an egg. But emancipation is coming to Algerian women faster than to those Moroccan. Many young girls—particularly students—go around unveiled, and some even sit in the cafés; some get jobs as salesgirls in the shops, or work as servants in European homes. Women of fashion, who are in strict purdah at home, wear European dress if they take a trip to Paris, leaving their veils behind.

Algeria has Biskra, the original "Garden of Allah," which is a somewhat shabby oasis these days. It is the birthplace of the novelist Albert Camus. It has the old capital city of Tlemçen, which looks like a Moorish town, and heroic Roman ruins at Timgad and Tebessa. Timgad was built by the Emperor Trajan (a Spaniard) in AD 100. Algeria is as crowded with Roman ruins as a churchyard with skulls. Algeria has Colomb-Béchar, where coal and iron are now being mined in moderate quantities; this marks, the French say, "the debut of industrialization of the Sahara." Colomb-Béchar is also the center of French army work with guided missiles. Finally Algeria has Sidi bel Abbes, the headquarters of the most famous military body in the world—the French Foreign Legion. Half of its 30,000 troops, if the truth must be told, are German.[3]

POLITICS AND NATIONALISM IN ALGERIA

Early in May, 1945, savage riots broke out in the neighborhood of Constantine. This was the first important uprising to take place anywhere in North Africa in the modern period.[4] It was the kick-off of contemporary

---

[3] The mayor of Sidi bel Abbes is (or was) a Communist, the only Communist sitting in the Algerian Assembly.
[4] The Rif War excepted.

Arab nationalism, but other than purely nationalist factors were involved. Drought had destroyed the crops, and produced an unexampled famine. The trouble started when police tried to interfere with a demonstration celebrating V-E Day. Some 50,000 Arabs fought. The French concede that roughly 1,500 of these (and 102 Europeans) were killed; the Arabs say that their total casualties were between twenty and thirty *thousand*. These figures, given out by the Arab League in Cairo, must almost certainly be exaggerated.[5]

The French at once took stock after this unpleasant episode and set about making a new policy for Algeria. The *Statut de l'Algérie* was passed in 1947, after violent debate. Today, as a result, Algerian participation in government is on two levels.

First, in Paris. Algeria elects thirty deputies to the National Assembly, exactly as if it were situated in metropolitan France, fourteen to the Council of the Republic (Senate), and eighteen to the Assembly of the French Union at Versailles. Fifteen of the thirty deputies, seven senators, and nine Union councilors are Moslem, i.e., Algerian natives. Any time they vote together they can be the balance of power in *French* politics. They could, in theory, decide whether or not France would join the United States in a war against Russia. But as a matter of fact they are split along the lines of political parties in France itself, and never vote as a bloc. Moreover most are completely subservient to big French interests. The total membership of the French Assembly (the old Chambre des Députés) is 626. If Algeria had representation strictly according to population, it would have 125 deputies in this body, not merely thirty. But this would produce a complete *reductio ad absurdum*—"France would be in danger of being assimilated by her own empire," instead of vice versa. We shall find these themes repeated when, a great many pages from now, we reach French West Africa.

Second, in Algeria. An Assemblée Algérienne exists, which sits in two separate colleges or houses, one exclusively Arab, one partly so. The president is alternately a Frenchman and a Moslem. This body, which handles the local budget and other home-rule matters, has considerable authority. It was created not merely as a sop to Algerian nationalists, but to the French *colons* on the spot, who did not want Paris to have exclusive control of their finances. Elections to the Assembly are in theory by direct, secret, and universal suffrage, exactly as in France. Actually the French administration pulls the strings, and episodes have occurred almost comically corrupt. For instance, more people may "vote" in a constituency than are on the

[5] *World Today*, February, 1948.

electoral rolls, as in Kansas City. In the final analysis, no matter how the total membership divides, the French Governor General has decisive authority. Most deputies are puppets, and the French derisively call them "Beni-Oui-Ouis," yes-men.

European *colons* own two-thirds of the arable land in Algeria, and control the entire wine production, which is the basis of the country's economy; Algeria produces something like 1,300,000 tons of wine per year, most of which goes to France. Seventy large landowners own no less than 500,000 acres.[6] French interests control the banks, shipping, the mines, local traction, utilities, and most cereal production. That the *colons*, a minority of one in nine, should have such predominant economic power is, of course, a fundamental nationalist grievance, especially since the Arabs themselves are so wretchedly poor. Sixty per cent of the indigenous rural population is officially classed as "destitute."

The *colons* know their own strength full well, and have given Paris almost as many headaches as the nationalists. Several times their extremist leaders have threatened to secede from France, and form their own independent republic to be part of a "Union of North Africa." But this threat can hardly be more serious than the similar threat in Morocco, since Algeria could not exist economically without France.

Algeria has no fuel to speak of and consequently little industry; so it costs the home country a lot of money. Of a recent budget of seventy-two billion francs, twenty-eight billion came from the French federal budget, i.e., from Paris. Algeria is a luxury. Marxist writers comment without end on the "exploitation" of colonial peoples by imperialist powers, but colonies often cost more than they earn. On the other hand France and Algeria complement each other nicely in several spheres, and the partnership is commercially valuable to both. Algeria is a splendid market for French-manufactured goods, and so on. France needs Algerian wheat and wine. But why, if the country is so expensive to the French taxpayer, does France insist on holding on to it at all costs? The answers, as in the case of Morocco, lie mostly in the realm of sentiment and strategy. Would the United States willingly give up Alaska or Hawaii? France, without North Africa, would be like Denmark. And let us revert to the *colons* once again —Algeria gives living space and earning space to a million Frenchmen.

There is no official color bar in Algeria; nor is there much contact between Frenchman and Arab. At an official reception, a few Arabs may be present as "demonstration" pieces. If an Arab reaches such a minor post as head of a section in a ministry, this is considered to be a sensational

[6] Philip Deane in *The Observer*, November 8, 1953.

"advance." Of course most Arabs, if from the countryside, are too illiterate
—as yet—for social or official intercourse. Probably not more than 2 per cent
of the native population in the big towns can read or write; in the rural
areas, not more than half of one per cent. An Arab boy, if he gets far
enough along to go to college, will try to Europeanize himself as soon as
possible, because only by being proficient in French can he possibly advance.
At the University of Algiers the Arabic classes are almost empty. One night
a week is, however, "Arab night" at the Algiers Opera. Here modern
Arab plays, mostly from Egypt, are presented; contemporary Arab drama
is in a lively state of development. The audience consists mostly of westernized and sophisticated members of the Arab community, who go to
see plays in their own tongue almost as if they were going slumming. The
legend is that the French secret police have every person who attends
regularly identified.[7]

To conclude: Algerians are French citizens, yes, but the "equality" is
on paper only. It is not what is written in the law that counts, but attitude
of mind. What the *colons* want is cheap, unskilled, uneducated labor, not
Arabs in their drawing rooms. There will never be equality, even among
citizens, until the Arabs have equal access to education. And this is, of
course, the chief native grievance, next to economic discrimination. The
French have been in Algeria for 125 years, but not till 1952 did the Paris
government ever give the country one penny for Arab education. At present
only about one-sixth of Arab children of school age go to school, which
means that well over a million are totally excluded from education—a disgraceful situation. On the other hand schools are not segregated, but mixed.
If an Arab child does manage to get to school, he sits side by side with
French children.

*

Before World War II various Algerian leaders formed nationalist parties
which merged, split confusingly, disappeared, and appeared again, sometimes with Communist support, sometimes not. The Atlantic Charter, among
other things, stimulated desire for freedom. At present there are four
different Algerian nationalist groups:

1. The UDMA, or Democratic Union of the Algerian Manifesto, led
by Ferhat Abbas, which is conservative and moderate. It wants independence
in theory, in the form of a republic federated to France, and it rejects the
French policy of assimilation, which Mr. Abbas calls an "inaccessible

[7] One movie house shows Egyptian films in Arabic. Arab subtitles are never inserted
in French films, on the theory that uneducated natives are only interested in
"action."

chimera," on the other hand it is willing to accept "guidance" by France in defense and foreign policy. Abbas has a French wife, enlisted in the French army during the war, and lives and dresses in the western manner. He was imprisoned briefly after the outbreak in May, 1945. Though an Arab party, the UDMA does its business in French, not Arabic.

2. A much more volatile and radical group, the MTLD (Movement for Triumph of Democratic Liberties), whose leader is a vivid personality named Messali Hadj. He is a former Communist, and the *colons* charge him with instigating the 1945 "insurrection." He has twice been exiled to French Equatorial Africa for extended periods, and is now interned in France at a town named Les Sables–d'Olonne. His followers want full independence at once, and are usually known as "Messalis." There are no MTLD deputies in Paris or Algiers, and the French would take practically any steps to keep any from being elected.

3. A religious group that takes its name from the word *ulema*. Mostly its members are Moslem "Protestants," who want to reform archaic elements in the Islamic church. Its leader is Sheikh Bachir Brahimi, who is well known all over the Arab-speaking world. His special interest is education. He was founder and first president of an organization trying to co-ordinate Moroccan, Tunisian, and Algerian nationalist groups.

4. The Communists. These cannot, as mentioned above, be legally suppressed, and their influence is strong. The three other nationalist parties are now bound with them in a newly constituted "Algerian Front"; the moderates say that they will be able to throw the Communists out "later." Recently the Communist party polled more than a hundred thousand votes in a municipal election.[8] One source of its strength is the Confédération Général de Travail, which, as in Morocco, is the leading trade union. The Communist newspaper, the *Alger Republicain*, is the only one in Algeria that encourages Arabs to join its staff, and it makes a special point of trying to get circulation from educated Arabs. Also, an odd incidental point, it is probably read more by non-Communists than any Communist paper in the world, because the other Algiers newspapers, owned by *colons*, are so imperviously reactionary. There is no liberal press. Communist Arabs (who by and large take their orders from the French Communist party in Paris) stand for reform within Islam as well as out. They want not merely freedom from the French, but from the religious hierarchy. Does a Moslem, if a Communist, allow his wife to go about unveiled? I found it difficult to get an accurate answer to this question.

Russia maintained a consulate in Algiers for some years, and then

---

[8] "Algeria—France's Next Indo-China?" by Claire Sterling, *Reporter*, May 25, 1954.

abruptly closed it down in October, 1951, without explanation. Not until Egypt will we reach an African country that has any Soviet embassy, legation, consulate, or other official installation. There is no Soviet representative at all in French Africa.

The chief thing working against the French in Algeria is, in long perspective, the Arab birthrate; the population increases by 250,000 a year. Algeria had 1,500,000 people in 1900, has 9,000,000 today, and will probably have 18,000,000 in thirty years. One reason for a growth so extreme is, of course, the admirable measures taken by the French in sanitation and public health. They may suffer political calamity—in the end—as a paradoxical result of their own good works. But if the French will never be able to absorb the rapidly multiplying Arabs, neither will the Arabs ever be able to absorb the French.

ALGERIAN REVOLT IN 1954

In November, 1954, a small but serious armed rebellion broke out against French authority in eastern Algeria, much to the chagrin of Paris. Morocco and Tunisia were being troublesome enough; to have militant nationalism spread to Algeria, conventionally thought of as perfectly secure and tranquil, was a humiliating shock. The official French view is that nationalism cannot be legally "countenanced" in Algerian territory since this is an integral part of France itself; the various nationalist groups described above were tolerated as "escape valves." Even so the French have in recent days not been so sure of Algeria as they pretended to be. One index of this is that only about 3 per cent of Algerian Moslems eligible for service in the French army were actually called up; the others—97 per cent!—are not considered reliable enough.

The November insurrection caught the French almost completely by surprise, if only because, at the moment, Prime Minister Mendès-France was doing his utmost to establish conciliation with Morocco and Tunisia. Gangs of nationalist terrorists, who were well organized and apparently operated under a careful plan, broke loose. Eight Frenchmen were murdered in localities stretching over a wide area; garrisons were cut off and outposts attacked in places as remote as Biskra. The rebels even had hopes, it seemed, of establishing a permanent focus of resistance in the Aurès Mountains. The French, who have about 10,000 troops in Algeria, flew in paratroopers and other reinforcements in considerable number, and after a week the rebels were put down and order restored. Ringleaders were, the French say, *fellaghas* (terrorists) from Tunisia across the border. What disconcerted

BRIEF WORD ABOUT ALGERIA 129

France most was that these were able to penetrate into Algeria for more than a hundred miles almost overnight, and found ready sympathy among Algerians. The French also blame the Cairo radio for the stimulus it gave the insurrectionaries. But there was also a possibility that the uprising might have been organized in part from the French mainland, particularly in mining towns like Lille where there are large colonies of Algerian workers. Police combed through the Algerian population all over France, and in Algeria itself the MTLD was outlawed and suppressed.

In January, 1955, just before his dismissal, Mendès-France sought to repair Algerian bridges by sending to Algiers a new Governor General in the person of Jacques Soustelle, an accomplished publicist and intellectual, who for years along with André Malraux has been closely associated with General Charles De Gaulle.

CHAPTER 9

Inside Nowhere—the Sahara

I DON'T need to be measured for a space jacket, and I am never going to stand in line waiting for the first tickets to the moon. I have already seen the moon. That is I have seen Tamanrasset in the Sahara, the chief town of the Hoggar and home of the blue-veiled Tuareg. The Tamanrasset region is positively lunar in its bleak grandeur, its quality of moon-dipped, freezing loneliness.

Even the etiolated trees look lunar, the few that exist. They are a species of willow, greenish white, almost like bushes washed with silver paint—spiky, gnarled, and both brilliant and forbidding. As for the mountains, they are lunar to a conspicuous degree. A million or so years ago (geologists will forgive my imprecision) the fires under the Sahara vomited up a few hundred million tons of earth, and so made the macabre formation known as the Hoggar.

The lava spurted up, and then, so to speak, froze. Hence, today, separate peaks rise like scattered puffballs, solitary and individual; they do not form part of a range. They look like the mushroom clouds that shoot out of the atomic bomb. And, indeed, something like the atomic bomb—a volcanic explosion of immense magnitude—produced them when the earth of the Sahara split. But these puffballs are not clouds. They are savagely solid formations of cold red rock.

I can list several words that suggest the shape of mountains; in tamer countries they look like sugar loaves, or tents, or caterpillars. But the mountains of the Hoggar near Tamanrasset take abnormal forms. They resemble frightful miscarriages of nature, like a monkey with three heads; they look like thumbs sticking out of a cracked glove, or a woman's breast with the nipple torn out, or a collapsed snake.

During the day, the Cyclopean sun eats up all the color, but at dawn and sunset, the mountains are radiantly painted with gamboge, slate-blue, purple, coral, and above all crimson-rose. And there is no life in them whatever. At night arrive the stars. Everybody knows what desert stars are like, but not everybody knows the Hoggar stars, which hang down, just overhead, like enormous silver cherries. The Tuareg have a story about the planet Venus, saying that she was a naughty goddess who sold her father into slavery to gain beauty, and was punished by being fixed in cold space forever. We watched her blink.

One day we drove a few miles out into the desert, beyond the place where the *piste* (unimproved road) stops.

My wife said, "Look—a lake!"

The silver shimmering water lay on the horizon like a shallow flat disk of mercury. It was our first mirage.

Within a week, we had seen so many mirages—sometimes they lay glistening on three sides of the horizon at once—that we did not even pause to look at them.

I had always been told that the Sahara was notable for being flat, hot, and full of sand. Around Tamanrasset it is about as flat as Switzerland and, in winter, cold as a cadaver. As for sand, it was several days before we found any, but when we did there was plenty.

The Sahara is, of course, an area so vast and so diversified that it is impossible to generalize about it. There are oases in the Sahara with a million palms, moist as wet blotters; there are also areas so blindingly hot and arid that they have never yet been traversed. In Arabic, the word "Sahara" means "emptiness," or "nothing."

FLIGHT TO TAMANRASSET

Practically all communication in the Sahara is by way of the oases; one travels like a golf ball, hopping from green to green. Our route was Algiers-El Goléa-Adrar-Aoulef-Tamanrasset. The plane goes once a week, and is an old DC-3 operated by Air France; we are a long, long way now from the kind of commercial air service familiar in the United States or western Europe. Half the space is for cargo, strapped by thongs to the naked sides of the fuselage and carpetless metal floor. The roof is painted white, partly to deflect the sun's heat, partly because white is the easiest color to see in the desert, and sometimes even the best-run planes have forced landings. Bus and automobile tops are similarly white on vehicles devoted to Saharan travel.

This Air France route is the life line of the western Sahara. It sucks life into the desert from the north like a hose. We left Algiers at 4:45 on a winter morning bristling with wind and rain. At El Goléa, two hours away, the sun was burning a big yellow hole on the horizon but it was so cold that my hands were numb. The Saharan airports have no runways in our sense; they are nothing but primitively marked strips pared off the desert. At each the haphazard routine was the same. We would discharge cargo—a bundle of newspapers, a crate of tomatoes, a cask of butter—into waiting arms. The weekly arrival from the Mediterranean is a big event. French soldiers always stood about, to gossip with our crew. Some were Zouaves. The non-coms wore blue kepis, baggy black pantaloons, and native sandals of any color—scarlet, gold, magenta, pale blue—with their toes sticking out. Arabs always lay about in their burnouses, as inert as logs.

We arrived in Tamanrasset—almost halfway across the Sahara—late that afternoon, and felt instantly swallowed up by the Saharan void. I have never known any place so startlingly silent. If a leaf falls, it sounds like a firecracker. The remoteness is immeasurable. It was a crazy touch to learn that radio reception here is best from, of all places, Monte Carlo. Our guest house was an ocher-red building made of baked mud, like an adobe structure in New Mexico, but with the color more intense. Most buildings in Tamanrasset are designed to withstand summer heat, with thick walls and small windows; they do not even have fireplaces, and in winter are ice cold. They carry latticed designs on their exterior walls, made of mud and shaped like paper patterns cut out by a child. The surfaces are faintly corrugated by long shallow scoops, made by the fingers of those who built them. Later I looked at the mountains, which have the same kind of hollow furrows, clawed out by the wind. Hand of God, hand of man, leave the same marks in Tamanrasset.

The mud houses are apt to melt down if it rains, and vicious storms can come in the autumn, but once it did not rain in Tamanrasset for seven solid years. The altitude is 4,822 feet, and in August the shade temperature can reach 126 degrees. But while we were there it was only moderately hot by day, if freezingly cold at night. Life goes by zigzags. The thermometer can drop sixty degrees—literally—between noon and night. We wore light tweeds by day, and slept shivering in sweaters and an overcoat.

This is still part of the Southern Territories of Algeria—though the frontier of French Equatorial Africa is only 250 miles away—and TAMANRASSET is capital of an administrative area called the *Annexe* of the Hoggar; this covers 375,000 square kilometers and is thus three-quarters the size of France. The town has about 2,000 people, of whom 135 are French. It has no bank, no newspaper, no plumbing, no telephones, and the electricity works for only three hours a day, from 6 to 9 P.M. I have never seen before shops so rawly primitive as the few that line Tamanrasset's single street, dark as caves, windowless, and selling padlocks, combs, and odd bits of cloth.

Tamanrasset compares to Ouarzazate as Ouarzazate compares to Fez or Fez to London. Existence here has certain primitive complexities. If you have a cat you must be careful not to let it out by night. The local Negroes love to eat cats, because catmeat makes them strong (so they say) and their women fertile.

Our host was a young French military officer, Captain Lecointre, the chief administrator of the Hoggar region, and a former *Méhariste*, or member of the Camel Corps. His military duties are few, since the area has been pacified since 1916. He needs practically no troops, except Camel Corps men out on patrol. But, like the administrators in the Atlas region, he keeps quite busy—as governor, judge, and superintendent of such realms as sanitation, agriculture, engineering, maintenance of the *pistes*, the economy of the area, and public health. "Life can be very hard here," he told us. "I like it." We sat before his small, smoky fire—wood is more precious than platinum—and I stared suddenly at the ceiling. It was made of rough boughs of *ételle*, a kind of tamarisk, still clothed in bark, and set under a straw matting, the kind of matting normally used for covering a floor. It was the first time in my life I ever saw a floor used as a ceiling.

One thing that Captain Lecointre does not have to worry about is nationalism, which is utterly unknown in these regions. The population is altogether docile and friendly, and almost everybody we passed on the silent, buff-colored streets muttered a gentle *"Bon jour."* Tamanrasset is the principal Tuareg center, but few Tuareg are to be seen, since these nomads live in tents or mobile encampments in the surrounding desert; they have no villages or towns. The local traders are mostly M'zabites, and there is a small Arab community composed of ex-soldiers. One day a beggar stopped us; he was a Sherifian, a lineal descendant of Mohammed. He said he had had nothing to eat for four days. He was not telling the truth. The bulk of the population is Negro. This was the first predominantly Negro town, if it can be called a town, that we saw in Africa. The poorest Negroes live in their own quarter, a clayey shantyville on the outskirts; similarly do poor Negroes live in hovels where American cities fray at the edges. These Negroes were, until comparatively recent times, slaves of the Tuareg nobles, and some would like to be slaves again, because it was easier to work as a servant for nothing than break rock on the roads for wages. In fact, when the French administration freed the slaves, many refused to leave their masters. Today, the Negroes have little push or sense of responsibility. Their heritage is to understand nothing but command. Being slaves, they had no reason to learn anything. The Arabs get along with them quite well, but despise them. I sent an Arab boy on an errand, and offered him a small tip. He refused it proudly with the words, "Do you think I am a Negro?"

There are no date palms in Tamanrasset, which makes it unique among Saharan oases. Once palms were abundant, owned by the Tuareg nobles. The Tuareg shared grain with their slaves, but not dates, even though the Negroes tended the trees. In resentment the Negroes began to neglect them, and in time they died. Now, to obtain dates, the Tuareg have to travel to some neighboring oasis. Trade is largely a matter of barter; for dates, they give sheep or grain. One afternoon outside the local inn—vividly French, boiling with a robust bonhomie, and packed with bearded non-coms in billowing pantaloons—we saw Tuareg swords for sale, but we never found any shields, which are becoming very scarce; they are made of antelope skin and are taut as parchment. A few yards away is the *fondouk*, the native hostel for men and animals; here tall men in blue gowns slept beside their camels. One rose as we approached, and with calisthenic genuflexions prayed to Mecca.

There are some remarkable sights in and near Tamanrasset, deriving from local history and folklore. One is Mount Laperrine, which commands the oasis like a savage fingerless red hand. It is not particularly high, about 11,000 feet, but few people have ever climbed it except professional Alpinists; lumps of lava break off, and make any ascent treacherous. It was named for a French general who crashed in an airplane not far away, and died of thirst before he could be rescued.[1] Then we saw the *bordj* (shelter) where the celebrated Père de Foucauld lived, and where he was killed in 1916 by Senussi Arabs. About Charles de Foucauld one could write much. He is one of the substantial heroes of French Africa. He was a dissolute, worldly youth, an army officer of great promise, who retired melodramatically into the desert, embraced religion, devoted himself to mysticism, aroused much enmity as well as adulation, and founded an order based on the most extreme asceticism, called the Petits Frères du Sacré Coeur. Its membership is not large today, but it still exists. Also near Tamanrasset is Abalessa, where an ancient Tuareg queen held court, the heroine of Pierre Benoit's novel *L'Atlantide*. Below—far below—are almost mythical Saharan cities like Gao on the Niger, Agadès, and Zinder, the goal of camel caravans. Tamanrasset is the hub of a spider web of *pistes* faintly scratched on the desert that reach all the way to Kano (in Nigeria), Lake Chad, and Fort Lamy, 2,680 kilometers away.

But Tamanrasset itself provides enough romantic color for anybody not a glutton, if only because of the Tuareg in their shrouds of indigo.

[1] Tamanrasset was originally named Fort Laperrine, and still appears as this on some maps.

THE BLUE-VEILED MEN

One reason why Tuareg[2] are so striking is that it is the men, not the women, who wear veils. These are of a magnificent deep blue, dyed by indigo. The dye is, however, not very fast, and is apt to smudge, like carbon paper, so that the very skins of the Tuareg nobles seem blue. Moreover, they use blue eye paint, ringing the lids, and the women are tattooed. The men muffle their faces even while eating and drinking, passing up food from underneath the veils. I never saw a male Tuareg face. These nobles are tall men, with a splendid bearing, and the combination of white hood and blue veil makes them resemble armored, helmeted creatures out of science fiction. They look like blue bullets with a blunt white tip.

How did the practice arise for men, not women, to be veiled? One explanation is that the Tuareg wanted to differentiate themselves from the Arabs. Ask a Targui about this and the usual answer is that it is a matter of such ancient custom that nobody knows. Probably the old Tuareg simply sought to protect their faces from the merciless sun. Also, a proud people, they wanted to hide any wounds they might receive in battle, so as not to be humiliated before their women. Now the veil is a convenient device, if only because it makes the men virtually anonymous. Talk with a Tuareg noble is an interesting experience, in that it is impossible to read his face.

Use of the color blue is easier to explain. Tuareg *like* blue, just as American women like pink or red for fingernails. Also, blue is a good color for cutting off rays of the sun.

No one knows much about the origin of the Tuareg. They are a Hamitic people, probably descendants of the Berbers, and were headstrong warriors, camel raiders, and slave traders till the French came to the Sahara. Unlike other Berbers, they have a written language. The characters are fascinatingly rectilinear, and vowels do not exist. This is more or less the way my name looks in Tamachek, which is what the Tuareg language is called:

```
    ⵅⵉ           ⵅⵉ+:
    J N         G N T R
```

The Tuareg are a matriarchy. A man named Akhamouk, known as the Aménocal, is king, but rank is passed on by the women, not the men. If an Aménocal should marry a lady not of the royal line, his children

[2] Correctly—but I don't want to be pedantic—"Tuareg" is the plural form of the word. The singular is Targui.

could not succeed. We shall find this matriarchal system of inheritance almost universal when we reach Black Africa.

There are two distinct classes among Tuareg—nobles and vassals. The chief distinguishing mark of the noble is that he does no work. Work is solely the province of vassals, and no vassal may ever rise to become a noble. He is fixed in this status for life. But if a male vassal marries a female noble (such marriages are rare) the children are noble. Contrariwise, children of a male noble and a female vassal are not noble, strange as this may seem. There are three noble tribes, the Kel-Rela, Taïtok, and Tedjehe-Mellet.

The Tuareg marry late as a rule, and, unlike almost all other Moslems, are monogamous. Tuareg girls—nobles and vassals alike—are among the few women in the Islamic world who ever have a chance to flirt, since they do not wear veils. If a girl is a vassal, she may be deflowered before marriage with impunity; if a noble, she may not.

The Tuareg are poor, frugal, and clean. The venereal rate among Arabs in the neighborhood is 90 per cent; among Tuareg, nil. They are law-abiding, and crime is virtually unknown. They are almost never homosexual, as Arabs often are. They live on their herds of sheep, traveling by camel from pasture to pasture. (There is a fair amount of pasture in this part of the Sahara, where the mountain slopes collect rain.) When they need money, they go into the nearest town and sell a camel to the butcher. The basis of their diet is camel's milk and farina; meat is far too dear. They eat with spoons, not with their fingers as Moors do.

*

The schoolmaster in Tamanrasset is Claude Blanquernon, as solid and splendid a person as any I ever met, and one of the world's foremost authorities on the Tuareg. It was he who invented "nomad schools" in the Sahara. He wanted to get education out into the tribes. He could only do so by camel. So he traveled with a Tuareg tribe for the whole length of the school year, as it moved grazing its herds from camp to camp—a one-man school on camel-back for seven months, teaching as he went along. Now, three young Frenchmen have similar jobs in the Hoggar area, and this system of instruction, greeted with incredulity at first, is firmly entrenched. Blanquernon is a real pioneer.

This striking character (he and his wife are Normans) took us out to see some Tuareg. It happened, by luck, that a detachment of nobles had camped nearby; otherwise, since they are perpetually on the move, it might have been laborious to find any. (Only two Tuareg have, incidentally, *ever*

INSIDE NOWHERE—THE SAHARA 137

left their desert homeland. One was taken to Paris as a curiosity by Père de Foucauld some forty years ago; one was flown to Constantine, Algeria, in 1951, by our friend M. Blanquernon, in order—of all things—to vote. The French wanted to have at least one Targui at the Algerian election then taking place. Blanquernon showed him a steamship in the harbor and explained what made it go. "Ah, just like a teapot!" he replied.)

We set out in an open truck. With us were two Tuareg nobles who had come into town, and who volunteered to show us the way. They sent their camels back to the camp, led by a vassal, but carefully kept their saddles with them, in our truck; these are objects of considerable beauty, with the front shaped like the hilt of a giant sword. We were the first Americans these Tuareg had ever seen. They had heard about New York, though. It was a large city like Adrar or El Goléa, but without camels and beyond the sea.

We drove over a hard, rattling crust of gravel toward the Tuareg camp. Excited children clung to the truck like flies, and had to be brushed off, until we passed out of the town. But we could not brush off small birds that followed us; these are called *boula-boula*, and the Tuareg say that they can talk to them. We left the *piste* and bumped over red granite rocks and clumps of talha, a variety of thorny mimosa. We knew we were getting somewhere when we saw a few goats; then a breath-taking line of white camels stood profiled against a rim of ruddy hill.

The ceremonial tent, where we were greeted, was made of copper-colored leather, stretched flat between poles; a red rug projected out on the ground. A fire was laboriously made, out of scraps and twigs, and we sat down, cross-legged, until water for the tea was boiling. "They ruin themselves to get tea," M. Blanquernon explained. We had brought a small gift of sugar.

In the tent were the brother-in-law of the Aménocal, by name Mustapha; his wife, the sister of the Aménocal; another lady who was the widow of the previous Aménocal; and one of the Aménocal's nephews—a regal company indeed. I happened to be wearing an old leather waistcoat, soft with use; this and its zipper were objects of amazed curiosity. One by one each nobleman made the zipper work, and kept patting the leather, as if no leather so pliable had ever been seen before.

The ladies, unveiled, in blue robes, shy, like frightened birds, sat back timidly in the tent. But soon, unable to resist their curiosity, they came forward and began to finger softly my wife's jewelry, especially a small St. Christopher's medal. M. Blanquernon explained what this was. One of the nobles at once grinned, and pointed to some good luck charms—made of leather, like tobacco pouches—that *he* wore to ward off evil. The world is, after all, one.

First we had camel's milk, which is creamy and delicious, served to all from a common bowl, to which each person puts his lips. Then came the tea, poured in a thick stream from a tiny pot held high above the glasses. It was strong and sweet, and took a long time to prepare, because the fire was so puny. Ceremoniously, we each had to drink three cups.

What did the Tuareg talk about, as M. Blanquernon interpreted? Mostly about what a farmer in Montana might talk about, or a herdsman in Northumberland—crops, prices, the weather, local gossip. A few weeks before, Blanquernon had gone out into the desert to take a tape recording of the Aménocal's voice. The Aménocal, curious about the machine, asked how much it cost, and had been horrified to learn that it was worth four camels. This anecdote was repeated with great relish. Then one of our hosts told our fortune by swiftly drawing quick, delicate designs with his finger in the sand. We offered everybody cigarettes. These the men put aside carefully because they do not smoke, eat, or take money in front of women.

When we left, we gave one of the ladies a lift to the vassals' camp a few miles away. It was the first time in her life she had ever been in an automobile.

EN ROUTE NORTH

An expedition by car across the Sahara is an interesting business. There are elaborate regulations to fulfill and precautions to be taken, even on such an easy route as the one we took.[3] Anybody crossing the desert in his own conveyance must notify the authorities of the exact route contemplated, and post a sizable bond as a deposit toward the expenses of a rescue car that will be sent out if, after twenty-four hours, the destination is not reached. You must carry shovels, wire netting, pails, and rope, as well as food and water. People have died of thirst on the brink of a well, because they could not get their pails down deep enough. Nowadays few Europeans ever get lost in this part of the desert, because of the severe precautions imposed by the Service Saharienne. Still, an Englishman died on the road from Tamanrasset to Zinder last winter. Natives die more frequently, largely because they have become somewhat careless. They think that, with the increase in travel, a car will be bound to come along sooner or later, if they

---

[3] The Sahara was never crossed by automobile until the 1920's.

INSIDE NOWHERE—THE SAHARA

are lost or waterless. Sometimes rescuers do happen to come along. And sometimes not.

The French say that in summer, without water, a man lost in this region cannot expect to live more than twelve or fourteen hours. A full day in full sun between dawn and sunset will kill him.

American Air Force authorities, who have made exhaustive surveys of desert conditions for the benefit of crashed fliers, are more optimistic. This table from an official pamphlet called *Survival*[4] shows approximately how many days you can survive and how far you can travel depending on your water supply:

MAXIMUM DAYTIME TEMPERATURES IN SHADE	ENTIRE WATER SUPPLY PER MAN	APPROXIMATE SURVIVAL DAYS RESTING IN SHADE AT ALL TIMES	APPROXIMATE SURVIVAL DAYS —WHEN TRAVELING ONLY AT NIGHT AND RESTING IN SHADE BY DAY. ALSO DISTANCE YOU CAN TRAVEL	
VERY HOT 100 F. & above	No water	2 −5	1 −3 days	20 miles
	1 quart	2 −5½	2 −3½ days	20 miles
	2 quarts	2 −6	2 −3½ days	25 miles
	4 quarts	2½−7	2½−4 days	30 miles
MODERATELY HOT 80–100 F.	No water	5 −9	3 −7 days	20–40 miles
	1 quart	5½−10	3½−7½ days	20–45 miles
	2 quarts	6 −11	3½−8 days	25–50 miles
	4 quarts	7 −13	4 −9 days	30–60 miles

But the word "shade" is the catch. We saw stretches of the Sahara a hundred miles long without a single speck of shade.

It may be useful to keep the following symptoms in mind, if your truck breaks down. If you become dehydrated to the extent of 1 to 5 per cent of your body weight, there will be thirst, anorexia, flushed skin, impatience, sleepiness, increased temperature, and nausea. For a loss of 6 to 10 per cent, dizziness, headache, dyspnea, decreased blood volume, cyanosis, indistinct speech, and inability to walk. For 11 to 20 per cent, delirium, spasticity, swollen tongue, inability to swallow, deafness, shriveled skin, and anuria.[5] I met a Belgian diplomat who almost died in the Nubian desert. What he remembers most is that his tongue became so swollen that he could not speak, his lips split, and for weeks after his rescue he was thirsty

---

[4] AAF Manual 64-0-1, published by Headquarters, Army Air Force, June, 1945.
[5] From *Afoot in the Desert, A Contribution to Basic Survival*, published by the Air University, Maxwell Air Force Base, Alabama, which in turn uses a chart from *Physiology of Man in the Desert*, by E. F. Adolph and Associates, New York.

all the time. If you die your body will remain in good condition for some months or even longer, because of its desiccation.

French officers talk about the heat as if it were something living. One told us that, from May 15 to October 15, the average temperature inside his house at Adrar, day and night, was 95 degrees Fahrenheit. In the shade outside, it could reach 122 degrees; in the sun, 140 degrees. "It is hot," he said gravely, "but supportable." Once he ordered fifty kilograms of potatoes from Ghardaïa, a few hundred miles up the road; when they arrived, they weighed forty kilograms, and were inedible. The heat had sucked ten kilograms of water out of them in fourteen hours. While he told us this story, we were shivering with cold.

Our own trip overland from Tamanrasset had every element of picturesqueness, but no danger; this was winter, and we were lucky. We rode with two French non-coms in a type of military vehicle called a *savanne*—a tough, squat, high-bodied car that can go anywhere over sand or rocks, like a rabbit. The *pistes* were not too bad; I have known worse roads in Scotland and Vermont, but not over such extended distances. It took us a long, hard day to reach Arak (395 kilometers), another to get to In Salah (275 kilometers), and a third to reach that wonderful oasis, El Goléa (420 kilometers) where seventeen hidden springs pump water at the rate of 22,000 cubic meters per minute. Yet El Goléa sits on a thin belt of rock directly between the two most feared areas in the whole Sahara, the Great Western Emptiness (*Grand Erg Occidental*) and the Great Eastern Emptiness (*Grand Erg Oriental*).

First day, Tamanrasset to Arak. We drove eleven hours, and never saw another vehicle except one. This was a SATT bus (of the Société Africaine des Transports Tropicaux), en route to Algiers all the way from Fort Lamy, which was twelve *days* late. It had repeatedly broken down, and we rescued and took with us one of its passengers. Nearby was a cluster of blanched camel skeletons. The *piste* is a wide track, a stony belt almost indistinguishable from the desert it cuts across. We saw only one sign of habitation during the entire day, a cluster of Arab huts, and not a single gas pump in 395 kilometers. One *carrefour* pointed the way to Gao, 1,200 kilometers away; not one town exists in all this distance. There were occasional signs to indicate wells—*eau sanitaire*—and at one point we crossed the Tropic of Cancer, neatly marked.

The mountains looked like elephants, like swollen gourds, like crushed duffel bags. If this road had signs saying "Falling Rocks" like those in New York State, there would have been a dozen in a hundred miles. Our car crawled and slid among rocks like a lizard. Our chauffeur every few minutes stopped abruptly, lifted up his carbine, and shot out of the window at gazelles. Half a dozen times we left the *piste* to chase gazelles through the dense forest of rocks, without descending from the car. We never got one. The chauffeur kept grunting, "I think I *touched* that one!" or "A near miss!"

Arak is a *bordj* deep in a crater; it is here only because the regulations provide that there must be a shelter every 250 miles. Nothing exists at Arak except this shelter, nothing else whatever. We had an extraordinarily good dinner (the two main courses were potatoes) and the host, who may see a European once every two weeks or so, told us about the rock paintings characteristic of this part of the Sahara. The trip we made this day would have taken between two and three weeks to do by camel. Until twenty-odd years ago, there was no other way to do it.

Second day, Arak to In Salah. All signs of vegetation ceased. Before this there had been isolated patches of desert scrub, enough for goats to feed on. But now we passed through a barren wilderness of nothing but stones. In the distance, slopes of white sand lay against the red mountains, and looked like flanks of snow. At noon we spread blankets out on rough black gravel and had a picnic. To my amazement a living thing appeared—a fly. Then obvious signs of civilization began to appear. The kilometer posts were neater, and were spaced five kilometers apart instead of ten. The *piste* became more controlled, and did not meander so much; we no longer had the sense of driving in an interminable dry rocky river bed. But we passed no single car all day, nor did we see a single human being, until we hit a camp of oil prospectors near the outskirts of In Salah.

In Salah has forty-three French, 5,000 *indigènes* (mostly Negro) and 80,000 palms. Mud prickles adorn the orange-colored buildings, and clay gates and walls carry the familiar cutout frieze. This oasis is much less picturesque than Tamanrasset, but nearer Europe; there is electric light till 10 P.M. The *souk* was the emptiest and most forlorn I have ever visited. Flies clung to children like lumps of licorice.

What makes an oasis, God or man? In general one will be formed wherever date palms can reach subterranean moisture; oases are usually at low points, where water creeps invisibly down through the sand and rocks. Then elaborate engineering work is necessary to make irrigation channels, tap springs, and improve their flow. There are, so to speak, three different layers or levels of vegetation in a well-tended oasis—the dates above, citrus and other fruit trees in their shade below, and vegetables and flowers on the ground. The water pumped in these groves is, only too manifestly, the lifeblood of the Sahara; each oasis is a heart. For years it has been a grandiose dream to "irrigate" parts of the Sahara, particularly in the area of the *chotts* (dried-up lakes), and scientific research to this end goes on constantly. Only about one-sixth of the Sahara as a whole is sand. When President Roosevelt visited North Africa he talked about a Saharan TVA. If you can get water to gravel, crops will grow, and the desert could burst into bloom. But the difficulties are almost insurmountable, partly because communications are so scant. For instance, in the entire vastness of the French Sahara, which is wider than the United States, there are only two north-south roads. One of these is the one we were on.

Third day, In Salah to El Goléa. For two hours we saw nothing, not even a scrap of bush. The desert here is black, not yellow; the very rocks are sunburned black. We reached the great Tademait Plateau, and climbed it almost as one would climb a flight of stairs. We saw a long camel caravan at the top, marching slowly against the sky; it looked so much like caravans in movies that it was hard to believe that it was real. We had lunch at an oil camp in Fort Miribel, and saw a signpost almost outrageously romantic—Bidon Cinq, 1,379 kilometers; Tombouctou 2,293; Fort Lamy 3,907. Here at Fort Miribel a Dutch prospecting team is working for Shell of Algiers. There have been no actual oil discoveries in this area as yet. Many who love the Sahara do not like these developments. One French officer told us, "For twenty years we have been trying to teach the natives to grow crops, to develop a satisfactory agriculture, to learn about irrigation, to live decently on the land. Now come the oil invaders, and everybody rushes off to work in their camps. Oil may enrich the Sahara. Also, it may ruin it."[6]

Then we passed onto the brittle rocky channel between the great emptinesses, the solid sandy ergs, and our car had a minor breakdown. Sand in the carburetor. There were mirages on three sides, glittering, shimmering, brighter than silver. I walked over the earth, which had the consistency of foam crushed solid, and said to my wife, "Look at the frost." Actually there had been a drop of cold rain, but my joke was poor. What we were walking on was salt.

El Goléa is one of the great, smiling, voluptuous oases. We stayed in the comfortable SATT hotel; rough palm fronds made a fire at night, and in bed we had metal bottles filled with boiling water, much more efficacious than a rubber hot-water bag. By day we waded in the dunes, which slide

---

[6] In 1952 a company called BEIN (Bureau for African Industrialization) was set up with a $30,000,000 annual subsidy from the French government to make an economic survey of the Sahara and investigate such possible innovations as "solar batteries" to provide power. (*New Statesman*, August 7, 1954.) Meantime a British company, headed by the well-known forestry expert Richard St. Barbe Baker, has been formed to investigate ways to "arrest the progress" of the Sahara by an afforestation program. The Sahara at present spreads "thirty miles a year."

massively in on the oasis from each side and take on every color—puce, amber, fawn, white—as the vibrating sunlight changes; the sand is soft and fine, and you can sink in it to your knees. When the winds blow along the ridges of these formidable smooth dunes, the natives say that the sand is "smoking."

When the French came to El Goléa there were 6,000 date palms in the oasis; today, 127,000. Water spurts out of the ground all year, with no seasonal fluctuation, from a stable water table—good water, fit to drink. A good many French people buy a stand of palms in El Goléa, as an investment, the way Americans buy real estate in Florida. Few, however, come to El Goléa to live, beautiful as it is in the spring and fall. In summer it is so hot that even airplane traffic has to stop, and provisioning is done by truck and camel. The total French population is only 150, and of these 110 are oil men newly arrived; the natives number about 10,000, mostly Arabs and a variety of Berber known as Zenetes. When the slaves were freed, the French had to give them part of the oasis, where they still maintain their own community; otherwise they would have starved. One old Negro lady remembers with pride that she was bought, because of her beauty, for a record price—50 kilograms of salt.[7] Nowadays it takes about sixty trees to support a family.

The great sight of El Goléa is the slate-colored Vieux Ksar, or fort, dominating a bleak hill nearby. It has been there for nine hundred years. A Swiss engineer was asked recently if any modern architect could build such a structure, out of mud, without steel, without nails, without cement, and hope to have it last that long. Answer: "No." Here until recent times a Zenete queen held fashionable and pompous court. The highest reward one of her warriors could get, for valor on the field of battle, was a night in her company; in exceptional cases, two nights or even three. The Arabs at the end captured this Ksar through treachery, and slaughtered every man, woman, and child it contained. It became French in 1891. One oil man working in El Goléa today is the son of a French officer who died taking it, and who is buried at its summit. (Père de Foucauld is also buried in El Goléa; his remains were moved here from Tamanrasset in 1929.)

We spent one afternoon with the White Fathers in El Goléa, and saw the school run by their associates, the Soeurs Blanches. Their building looks like nothing I ever saw in the realm of architecture; the roof is covered solidly by smooth white cupolas, like beehives, to break the rays of the sun. The order of White Fathers was founded by Cardinal Charles Lavigerie in 1874, with the design of Christianizing Moslems in Africa, and is justly

[7] Of course this happened before the French abolished slavery.

celebrated. Its members wear immaculate white robes, and are always bearded; many are men of the most exquisite cultivation, who have done much good work for education all over Africa. In the Sahara there are practically no attempts at proselytism by the Pères Blancs any longer, because it is almost impossible—in this region—to convert a Mohammedan. Father Lusson in El Goléa told us, "The Moslems here do not *bend* either to the forces of reason or of history." This was the first time that we saw the work of the White Fathers. Later, particularly in Ruanda-Urundi and the Congo, we met them several times again.

At the El Goléa hospital the resident doctor told us that, in ten years, he has never had a case of appendicitis in a native, or seen a cancer. Elsewhere in Africa we subsequently found doctors who reported this same extraordinary thing. Tuberculosis? "None as yet in the Sahara. We may bring it in."

CAMELS

These are odd beasts—so measured, slow, and supercilious to their menial tasks. A good riding camel costs thirty to thirty-five thousand francs ($85-$100), a baggage camel around twenty thousand ($57). But most people do not buy camels; they grow them. The favored color for a smart riding camel is called *azrem*—a pale pinkish eggshell. There is little affinity between the camel and his master; few camels are named, as a dog or a horse is named, and I never came across anybody who said that a camel recognized him, even after months of being ridden by the same person. A camel is adult at seven years, and has a working life up to about the age of fifteen.

Normally, a camel can do fifteen miles a day; twenty-five is exceptional even in cool weather. In winter, a camel can go literally for months without water, *if* he has access to good pasture, and is not working; if working, he can live without water for ten or twelve days in good pasture, and five or six days in bad. In summer, no matter what the pasture is, he must have water every other day.

The *Méharistes*, officers and men of the Camel Corps, go out in a platoon of fifty or sixty men, and are in motion almost the whole year; they inspect tribes, watch the pasturage, administer justice, look at wells, and punish thieves. They carry medicine and a radio. Each officer has four camels, two of which march while the other two wait in pasture; each noncom has two. The French like camels trained by a variety of Arab nomads known as the Chaamba. Female camels are never used, and the males are castrated. In a forced march, a platoon may lose 25 per cent of its animals. The world's record for camel travel was made many years ago by a French officer who did almost five hundred miles in eleven days, without losing a single beast.

The basis of caravan traffic is, of course, trade. A caravan can consist of anything from six to two hundred camels; forty to fifty is the average. If you see a cluster of two or three camels, it is a family on the move. Arabs leading caravans find their way by an almost superhuman instinct for terrain. They will remember a basic dune pattern even if half of it has blown away.

Camels always travel by soft ground, if possible, never on the *pistes*, because hard ground splits their hoofs. But their worst enemy is mud. They are less fatiguing to ride than horses, provided they do not gallop. They are fragile beasts, and have one disconcerting characteristic; if tired or sick, they never appear to be in trouble, but die at once without warning. Generally, you can tell the state of health of a camel by the hardness of his hump. If a camel is overworked or underfed (they eat a lot) the hump diminishes; when it is put to good pasture the hump will grow again, if the beast is not too old. For every day that a camel is "forced," it needs a full week's rest.

I asked if camels would ever be replaced by the marvelous, omnipresent jeep. No. There are at least three reasons. First, gasoline costs money. Second, even a jeep cannot traverse the great ergs. Third, you cannot eat a jeep if it dies.

CHAPTER 10

The Tunisian Complex

Rain is the best governor. —Tunisian proverb

TUNISIA, which is probably the most inflamed country in all Africa at the moment (except Kenya), dominates the neck of the central Mediterranean. Bizerte, its great naval base, is only about a hundred miles from Sicily. Nobody thinks of it nowadays, but Tunisia was a serious matter of contention, like Corsica and Nice, between France and Italy in the heyday of that unfortunate gorilla, Benito Mussolini. Italy wanted to take the rich Tunisian littoral from France. Today the struggle for power is altogether different, and involves the United States, the United Nations, the Arab world of the Middle East, and much else. It is a straight-out, implacable fight between France and Tunisian nationalists.

Tunisia differs in marked degree from Morocco and Algeria, with which it is commonly associated:

Item. It is considerably smaller, more compact, and better developed.

Item. Like Morocco, it is a French protectorate and is theoretically an "independent" sovereign state. In actuality, of course, it is ruled from Paris, but it is not part of France, like Algeria, nor is it a member of the French Union. The French occupation dates from 1881. The nominal ruler is called the Bey.

Item. It is substantially richer than Morocco in agriculture, but not so rich in minerals. The economy is based on grain, wine, phosphates, cork, and olives. The old story has it that when a Tunisian peasant picks up an olive, he says, "This is my gold." Minor curiosities in production are henna, pistachios, and shaddocks. There are not so many *colons* in proportion to total population as in Algeria.

Item. Basically the people are Arab, and few Berber traces remain. Many Arabs are of a variety we have not encountered before—nomads in black tents, desert Bedouin. The townsmen do not think of themselves as "Arabs," but as Tunisians. The country has a strong urban bourgeoisie, a *native* middle class.

Item. Tunisia is much more westernized than Morocco, closer to Europe, and more advanced. The Islamic structure is not so impenetrable. Mosques in Tunisia are open to Europeans, and many more women are *évoluées* than in Morocco. In the big towns women are beginning to drop the veil.

Item. Tunisia, unlike Morocco, had no strongly entrenched feudal lords, and the tribal structure is not so fixed. There was no need for a prolonged military "pacification."

Item. Partly as a result of all this, Tunisian nationalism is more educated and articulate than that of Morocco or Algeria; Tunisia has an intellectual elite that knows exactly what it wants and where it is going.[1] The French cannot easily dismiss Tunisian nationalism as anything fabricated, weak, or spurious; it is an undeniably serious force, with deep indigenous roots. After a few days in Tunis I asked if there was *any* Tunisian not a nationalist. The reply was a bitter joke: "Only the prime minister." The prime minister of that day was, though a patriot, trying to work with the French. And *that* prime minister is no longer in power.

We have in Tunisia three main factors to survey—the beylical circle, the French, and the nationalists. The nationalist party, corresponding to the Istiqlal but stronger, is called the Néo-Destour (New Constitution), and became legal in 1954 after a long period of suppression. We can omit or gloss over many details because, *mutatis mutandis*, we have already seen a parallel development in Morocco, but Tunisia is much more turbulent, with political expression better organized.

But first let us glance briefly at the physical backdrop of the country.

LOOKING AT TUNIS AND ITS ENVIRONS

Tunisia is roughly the size of Tennessee (48,195 square miles), and has 3,600,000 people, of whom 240,000 are Europeans. There are large Italian and Jewish colonies—80,000 each.[2] Half the country is desert. TUNIS (population 364,00) is a capital without much character. It reminded me of a city in the Levant, like Beirut, or even a miniature Cairo, plus a dash

---

[1] Tunisians are volatile and garrulous. Abdel Krim, the old Rif leader, told us when we met him in Cairo—perhaps not altogether seriously—that the Tunisians would never make a successful revolution because "they talk too much."

[2] The Jewish community has full Tunisian nationality and equality under the law. It is better treated than that in Morocco, but this is not to say that it is treated well. More and more Tunisian Jews are emigrating to Israel.

of France; the people are a heterogeneous medley, and the Arab lacquer is slippery. This produces an odd effect; Tunis is Europeanized and yet not European, and this makes it seem more conventionally "Oriental," more Turkish, than purer Moslem cities. This is a bastard town, a far cry from Marrakesh or Fez.

In the courtyard of a modern office building I saw a sign, "Religious and Political Discussion Forbidden in this Area." Waiting in a minister's anteroom I suddenly heard a man screaming. It was a purely animal scream—hysterical, persistent, and uncontrolled. It came from the minister himself, who was rebuking a subordinate.

This is all Hannibal country. The ruins of Carthage, which are not much to see, are only a few miles away. Nearby is one of the most charming suburbs in the world, Sidi Bou Said, where buildings are predominantly white and blue; against the brilliantly whitewashed plaster the powder-blue décor looks like cornflowers. History has left some odd footprints in this area. King Louis IX of France, Saint Louis, took Carthage in 1270, died there, and is regarded by the local Arabs as a *marabout*. The Leaning Tower of Pisa is supposed to have been built out of stones from Carthage. The White Fathers have an important headquarters here; it is called their "brain trust." And, of all things, the song "Home, Sweet Home" was written here; its author, John Howard Payne, was American consul in Tunis in the 1840's.

From Tunis we drove inland to Kairouan,[3] founded in 673 AD. and one of the holiest cities of the Islamic world; three pilgrimages to Kairouan are the equivalent of one to Mecca. Its celebrated mosque, built rather on the lines of Cordoba, is a mad extravaganza; there are hundreds of columns, and most have capitals of different styles; nothing matches. In another mosque, known as the Mosquée du Barbier, three hairs from the beard of the Prophet Mohammed are carefully preserved. The mosques are open to infidels here, because, the Tunisians say, the French "desecrated" them by forcing their way into them during the military conquest of Tunisia, and they have been open ever since. There was no Lyautey in Tunisia.

The *souk* in Kairouan is not so picturesque or enclosed as those in Morocco, and perhaps cleaner; grain, vegetables and so on do not lie directly on the ground, but on straw mats or in baskets. While we were visiting it a bomb exploded near the city gates. A French policeman shrugged with mild bad temper, "Another outrage by the Anglo-Americans!" Apparently he

---

[3] This has any number of other spellings like Qairwan and Al-Qayrawan. It has no present connection with the mosque and university in Fez of similar name, but they are linked historically.

THE TUNISIAN COMPLEX

thought that the United States and Great Britain subsidize the Tunisian nationalists.

We passed the hill where Aeneas and Dido are supposed to have made love, and then a village with the nice name Aphrodisium, where the King of the Vandals had his summer palace. We passed Roman monuments, of a minor sort, without number; anybody digging a well in this area, or even planting crops, will almost certainly unearth bits of Roman marble. You can fill your pockets with loot—genuine antiquities—in an afternoon.

Nearby is the town Enfidaville, where the youthful André Gide had a remarkable initiation into amatory experience, and came to Hammamet on the sea, which the Romans called Putput. Here is a modern house often called by connoisseurs the most beautiful in the world. Hammamet, like Taormina, is a minor capital for sophisticated expatriots. Everything about this part of Tunisia is quintessentially Mediterranean. We passed on to Sousse, where many Maltese live today, and which was the Roman Hadrumetum; Caesar landed here in 46 BC. Further south is the singular island of Djerba, where a community of Jews has lived uninterruptedly for 1,900 years. This is supposed to have been Circe's island. Still further south is Sfax, which the British novelist Ronald Firbank thought was the most beautiful city in the world.[4]

*

When people say that "North Africa" was once the granary of Rome they mean Tunisia. As a matter of fact the old Roman name for Tunisia was *Afrikiya*, and today Tunisian nationalists call it by an Arab version of this, "Ifriqiyah." If, people sometimes ask, Tunisia and its periphery were fertile enough to have fed Rome, why cannot these regions be made more productive now? Why cannot the desert be reclaimed? If the Romans were capable of irrigating the Sahara, why cannot we do likewise? There are several reasons. For one thing the Romans had unlimited slave labor; for another the population Rome had to support in Europe was not very big. Actually Tunisia grows twenty times more grain nowadays than it did in Roman times, but all of this—and more—has to be used at home. The Romans did some wonderful things in Tunisia. Maps are still in use that follow line by line Roman maps, charting out the best areas for irrigation channels and olive culture.

In pre-Roman times a forest belt must have covered much of northern Tunisia, and perhaps stretched all the way to the Atlantic. Ritchie Calder, in a provocative article in the *New Statesman* called "Hannibal and His

[4] Sitwell, *Mauretania*, p. 224.

Elephants,"[5] points out that there are two kinds of desert, "climatic" and "man-made." A climatic desert is one where, even if underground water courses exist, the rainfall is not enough to sustain vegetation; a man-made desert is one "where life, in the form of vegetation and hence of animals and humans, has existed, but where man's intervention has destroyed it." There must have been genuine forests near Carthage centuries ago, because otherwise Hannibal could not have had elephants. (Indeed even in southern Algeria my wife and I saw rock paintings many thousands of years old that depicted elephants and other jungle beasts.) But a variety of forces combined to obliterate these ancient forests, and turn the terrain into desert. For one thing Vandals and Arabs destroyed the Roman aqueducts which fed the land with water. Even today, "the ravaging of trees and shrubs is a fetish with the desert nomads," because they crave wood for fuel. What the nomads do not destroy the goats eat up. Nevertheless, Mr. Calder and other experts have high hopes that the Tunisian and other man-made deserts can be made productive again. Afforestation is not an impossibility, even in the deep Sahara.

*

Tunisian history has notable color, but we already know the general pattern. There were confused centuries of Turkish rule, and then violently corrupt periods under various autonomous beys and devs. The French took Tunis partly by reason of a deal with the British; Lord Salisbury "gave" Tunisia to France in exchange for a free hand in Cyprus.[6] This occurred mostly because the British feared Germany; Bismarck, strange as it may seem, made Tunisia French, as he helped to make Morocco French. As in many parts of Africa, we have the spectacle of native lands, native peoples, traded and booted about as if they were lumps of putty. The good old imperialist partitioners cut up Africa like an ox. But it is still alive.

BEY OF TUNIS

Few people of consequence in the contemporary world can have more medieval characteristics than the Bey of Tunis. He positively reeks of the Dark Ages—and not merely those of Europe, but of Asia. It happens that he is of amiable disposition; otherwise he might be a Turkish despot of the murderous thirteenth century. This elderly gentleman (he was born

[5] May 6, 1954.
[6] Lord Salisbury told France that some of the desert territory it was getting had only "very light soil." A. J. Toynbee in the London *News Chronicle*, August 24, 1935.

in 1881) must be the last monarch left in the world to maintain a private troupe of dwarfs. One of his passions is alchemy; he likes to mix secret brews and potions in his laboratory. He is also fascinated by astrology, and is an enthusiastic astronomer. His knowledge of science cannot, however, be highly advanced, since he knows no western language, and even his Arabic is primitive.[7]

I asked a French official if the Bey, like the Sultan of Morocco, made a Speech from the Throne every year; the answer was, "Ridiculous!—How could he?—He cannot read or write." He is supposed to sign his name with a rubber stamp. One rumor is that the Bey began life as an artisan, and he still likes to do things with his hands; his palaces contain thousands of clocks, with which he tinkers constantly. He looks like an Oriental version of the late Kaiser Wilhelm, with a soaring but stiff mustache. I asked if he dined in the western or eastern fashion, and received the answer, "No one would know." President Eisenhower's salary would be roughly $12,000,000 per year if he, Eisenhower, were paid the same percentage of the national budget that goes to the Bey. But oddly enough the beylical group does not exhibit marked signs of extravagance; the French say that its members are too stupid and unimaginative even to know how to spend money. What I liked most when we visited the Throne Room in the Dar El Bey (palace) in Tunis—a monstrously Victorian structure—was a small projecting alcove with low windows. Directly underneath this lies a route into the bazaar, and here the Bey, unobserved, can watch the passers-by, like a child playing at being a spy.

The Bey is properly called Sidi Mohammed Lamine Pasha; he is a "sovereign" but not a king, and is addressed as His Highness, not His Majesty. Officially, by French style, he is *Possesseur du Royaume de Tunis, Souverain actuel*, and the throne is described as his *dépositoire*. He has ruled since 1943, when his predecessor, a personage named Mohammed El Moncef Bey, was rudely kicked out of office and exiled to Pau.[8] The Bey comes of a Greek or Cretan family that has been in power in Tunis uninterruptedly since 1705; it replaced a truly fabulous cutthroat dynasty founded by a renegade Corsican named Murad. The Bey's father was also a Bey, but there were two others in between.

Here we reach something inordinately strange. The beys do not inherit by primogeniture, nor are they chosen by a *ulema*, as in Morocco. The

---

[7] See "The Bey of Tunis," by George W. Herald, *United Nations World*, December, 1952. Sitwell also mentions the dwarfs.

[8] Marshal Juin, a great kicker-out of potentates, played a role in this. Moncef was accused of being a collaborationist. See "Crisis and Reform in French North Africa," by Charles-André Julien, *Foreign Affairs*, April, 1951.

succession goes to the *oldest*—not the youngest—properly accredited member of the beylical family. This anomaly derives from Turkish days, when a child or youth, if heir apparent, was almost certain to be assassinated. A brochure available in Tunis names eighty-three royal personages with the rank of *prince du sang de la famille beylicale actuelle,* listed by date of birth; the oldest was born in 1862, and the youngest in 1941. The present Bey was number four on this list when he reached the throne. In addition to the eighty-three princes there are about 160 other beylical individuals. Mostly these make a slatternly if gilded crew. Because of their prestige and position they are forbidden to work, and must be supported by the public payroll. The Bey's eldest son is Sidi Chedley Ben Mohammed Lamine Bey; he was born in 1910 and is number twenty-eight on the inheritance list. It is extremely unlikely that he will ever accede to the throne, if only because he is an ardent nationalist and the French hate him. The heir presumptive at present is a dignitary known as the "Bey du Camp." This title was bestowed traditionally on the most prominent person likely to succeed the Bey; then he was given a military command and packed off into the hinterland to keep him from making trouble at home. The present Bey du Camp is named Azzedine Bey, and was born in 1882. He is supposed to be insane. The new monarch, if it turns out to be Azzedine, will be almost as old as the present one. Following Azzedine on the list are three other princes now in their sixties. The ruler of Tunis is almost always an *old* man before he can reach the throne. Sons have no chance.[9]

The present Bey has, so far as is known, only one wife, who is never seen; she is a Negress, and is called the "Beza." Commonly she is said to descend from stock not distinguished; in fact she is supposed to have come out of a *gourbi,* or mud hut. The Bey and his consort have nine daughters and three sons. One daughter, Princess Zakia, is the wife of Dr. Ben Salem, a former Minister of Health and an outspoken nationalist; he was arrested and interned by the French in 1952. The Princess herself has been accused of being a member of a ring of conspirators providing weapons for terrorists.[10] Modern times have, it seems, even reached the family of the sovereign. Most emancipated Tunisian nationalists do not like the royal circle, on the ground that most of its members are worthless parasites; they concede, however, that it has a certain value as an instrument to reach the masses.

---

[9] Azzedine Bey was assassinated by a nationalist terrorist after these lines were written. So was Colonel René de Benoit de Lapaillonne, a French officer who for some years headed the Bey's private guard.
[10] New York *Times,* April 30, 1952.

THE TUNISIAN COMPLEX

The Bey of Tunis differs from the Sultan of Morocco in several important respects. (a) He is not a Sherifian, not a descendant of the Prophet. (b) Politically, he is much more inert. (c) He has no religious authority over the community, since Tunisia is not a theocratic state.

The French do not have much regard for the Bey, but, since they want to preserve the fiction that Tunisia is a "sovereign" state, they cannot do without him. This has not prevented them from surrounding his palace with troops and threatening the use of force when, on occasion, he has refused to sign decrees. But they are loath to use too much force because this would throw him further into the nationalist camp, nor can they possibly afford to eject him from office at the moment and replace him with somebody else, so soon after the deposition of the Sultan of Morocco. The Bey is, on the other side of the fence, under considerable steady pressure from intellectuals in Cairo—also Pakistan—to take the nationalist side more firmly. He becomes more nationalist all the time, if covertly. To sum up, both the French and nationalists find this anachronistic old gentleman useful, but they both know well that the whole beylical hierarchy is an outrageous excrescence and bar to Tunisian progress.

THE FRENCH IN TUNISIA

These exist in three main groups, the civil service, garrison, and *colons*. The first numbers 9,800, which the Tunisians think is a figure grossly large; even postmen in the *medina* are French. The garrison, which has repeatedly had to be reinforced, has something between 25,000 and 40,000 men. Of *colons* there are about 160,000. Many French in Tunisia are not truly French at all; thousands are naturalized Italians, and thousands more are Algerian. Also many Corsicans live in Tunisia, on whom the metropolitan French look down almost as Americans look down on Puerto Ricans. Some *colons* are poorer than all but the poorest *indigènes,* and are thought of not merely as second-class citizens but as definite menaces to government. As I heard it put, "They are not numerous enough to stay and become a stable element in society, but they are too numerous to push out." One Residency official told us frankly, "The *colons* very much impede our task." I asked him what his task was and he replied with an engaging gesture that the French (of the governing class) had two ambitions which were of necessity conflicting: first, to remain; second, to assist the Tunisians gradually—*very* gradually—to self-government.

The French are proud of their achievements in Tunisia since the Treaty of Bardo in 1881 and the Agreement of La Marsa in 1883, by which their occupation was legalized. There has been very little "hit and run" exploitation; few, if any, Frenchmen have made vast fortunes out of Tunisia. They think of it as part of France, and hence do not play tricks with it, any more than they play tricks with France itself. Tunisia had in 1881 practically no roads and 117 miles of railroad; today it has 8,990 miles of road, 1,350 of railroad. There are four modern ports, handling more than four million tons of shipping per year, two large dams with more projected, 45,000 acres of land under irrigation, and an annual production of electric power amounting to 180 million kilowatts, with more to come. The population has doubled in twenty years, thanks largely to admirable French work in public health. In 1881 there were 1,136,000 acres planted to grain; today, 3,300,000 acres (of which 617,000 are owned by Europeans). There are 24,000,000 olive trees, 50,000 industrial workers, 40,000 people self-sustaining through handicrafts (as in Morocco handicrafts play an extremely important role in the economy), and seventy-six agricultural co-operatives. Fifty-eight per cent of the total budget is contributed by France, and 14.1 per cent of this goes to education. There are 190,000 Tunisian boys in the public schools, and, a noteworthy fact, 34,300 girls. A French official statement says, "On the basis of prevailing demographic conditions, the Department of Education plans to attain universal education by 1969."

Nevertheless by midsummer of 1954 Tunisia had come perilously close to civil war. Why? France has done a lot, but the Tunisian nationalists, like those in Morocco, do not consider "a lot" to be enough. The biggest abrasive factor is probably psychological. The French simply do not *like* Tunisians, and cannot resist treating them with indifference or contempt. Another obstacle to reform has been lack of money. But in fields that do not necessarily cost much money there is much that France could do for Tunisia, if it genuinely wants to improve relations. Let the Tunisian flag be flown more often, and the French flag less. Allow more participation by the UN in welfare work in Tunisia. Permit the American Consulate to be raised to the rank of Legation, which would stimulate Tunisian pride. Give the Tunisian press access to news sources other than French; at present the press agencies in Paris have a monopoly on all news disseminated. Let Tunisians, even if they are not yet fully qualified, assist in work on irrigation, seed improvement, well-digging, erosion control, and so forth, so that they do not have the feeling that the French think of them only as manual laborers. Emphasize vocational education. Relax the visa restrictions that make it impossible for most citizens of other Moslem countries, like Egypt, to visit Tunisia. Teach Arabic in the public schools as well as French. Give more non-political jobs to Tunisians. (For instance, the Director of

Antiquities must, by law, be a Frenchman "in perpetuity.") Get more Tunisians into government, give them substantial-sounding titles, and let them cut their teeth on administrative problems. Permit Tunisia to have all-Tunisian units in the French army. Try to emphasize the Tunisian as well as French contribution to the national welfare, and make it clear that rule by force alone is a concept that the French themselves know to be out of date.

Most French officials realize well enough that they must reform; the question is whether or not reform will come soon enough. Foreign Minister Schuman announced late in 1951 that full "internal" autonomy for Tunisia was the eventual aim of French policy, but he did not set a date, or even mark out a timetable, and he did not use the word "independence." Even so, the Schuman statement was an important forward step. No such announcement has, for instance, ever been made about Morocco. The French concede that, in time, Tunisia must be free to an extent; otherwise it could too easily go the way of Indochina. The United States makes pressure on Paris to liberalize; so does the Middle East. And there are plenty of French themselves who deplore repression. "The severest critics of French policy in Tunisia are to be found in France itself," one recent commentator says. Many citizens detest old-style colonialism, if only because it almost always defeats its own purpose in the end. Even among *colons* in Tunisia there are strong liberal elements. During the summer crisis in 1954 forty French civic leaders in Tunisia appealed to the Mendès-France government to lighten, not increase, oppressive measures on the spot.

Nevertheless, it may be taken as axiomatic that the French will never give up two things, unless they are forced out by war. First, control of Tunisian foreign policy. Second, the massive naval installations at Bizerte. I asked a *colon* why. "Because Tunis is the key to our European house."

*

Almost at once, on assuming office in 1954, Mendès-France addressed himself to the Tunisian problem. In August he flew dramatically to Tunis on a brief, pregnant visit, and promised Tunisia immediate home rule. As a result an all-Tunisian government was formed; a moderate nationalist, Tahar Ben Amer, took office as prime minister, and three members of the Néo-Destour, the chief and most inflammatory nationalist party, became ministers in a cabinet of ten. This was a very large concession indeed on the part of the French. At once political tension became less, and for the moment at least terrorism diminished. A definite agreement on home rule was reached—after stiff negotiations—in April, 1955.

THE NÉO-DESTOUR AND NATIONALISM

The Tunisian nationalist movement goes back many years. As long ago as 1857 reform groups were active in Tunisia, and before World War II two patriotic organizations came into being called the "Young Tunisians" and "Old Turbans." One reason for their disaffection was a French proposal to open up part of the *habous* land (property in the custody of religious foundations) to white colonization; as always, white settlement makes for trouble. After World War I Tunisian nationalists went to the Paris Peace Conference to plead their case before President Wilson, and the first genuine nationalist party, called the Destour, was formed. An insurgent wing broke off to found the Néo-Destour in the early 1930's; the French outlawed this, together with other nationalist groups, in 1938, and the Néo-Destour had no legal existence from that date until 1954, when Mendès-France restored it to legality.[11]

Most Tunisian nationalists are Paris-educated, and even if they propagandize in Arabic they speak French among themselves. They have close intellectual ties to Egypt, and dismiss such a country as Libya as a "savage" state; they think of fellow nationalists in Morocco or Algeria as hopelessly "feudal" or "bourgeois," and indeed they are substantially more mature than Moroccans. Another point is their addiction to monologue, exhortation, and theoretical dialectics. Until recently they have not seemed (to the French, at least) to be very practical people, even if educated. I asked His Excellency Salah Eddine Ben Mohammed Bacchouche, who was prime minister when we visited Tunisia, what the nationalists "wanted." He pointed to his behind. "The seat—the *fauteuil*—power! But they have no idea what to do with it." (Nationalists would, of course, deny this allegation strongly.)[12]

To list the chief grievances of Tunisian nationalists is hardly necessary; by implication at least we know most of them already. The *colons* own

---

[11] However, it was "recognized" on occasion, even if illegal, and several Néo-Destourians were members of Tunisian governments before 1954. Valuable historical background on Tunisian nationalism may be found in "The Tunisian Nationalist Movement, Four Decades of Evolution," by Benjamin Rivlin, *Middle East Journal*, Spring, 1952.

[12] What Mr. Bacchouche's office reminded me of most, even though it is situated in the Dar El Bey, was the City Hall in Chicago or Boston. It crawled with retainers seeking jobs, clamoring for interviews, and wheedling favors. People in Boston do not, however, wear tarbooshs or frayed Arab robes.

a disproportionate share of land, and the tax structure is wickedly discriminatory. There should be more money for public health, for social welfare, and for education. The Tunisians feel a basic lack of trust in the validity of French promises. Also France deliberately makes it impossible for Tunisia to build up a cadre of administrators and technicians, which is the one thing it needs most, because then the pat argument that Tunisia is incapable of manning a government would no longer hold good. Above all, Tunisians resent being a subject people.

There has never been a general election in Tunisia, although the French have been here for seventy-four years, and civil liberties are unknown. Martial law has been in force since World War II. There is no elected legislature. There is no freedom of the press, or of speech, or assembly. Everybody assumes as a matter of course that his mail is opened. There are about 6,000 political prisoners in Saharan concentration camps, sent there without any process of law whatever. I talked to one youthful lawyer who had recently been released from the camp at Foum Tatahouime. There was no explanation when he was sent there, and none when he was released. ("A sword of Damocles, *monsieur!*") The French do not call these internees political "prisoners," but say that they are merely *éloignés*, "those taken away."

The two chief distinctions of the Tunisian nationalist movement are (1) it is strongly allied to what is probably the best run and most powerful trade union organization anywhere in Africa above the Rhodesian Copper Belt. (2) It has a real leader, even though he is in exile at the moment, Habib Bourguiba. For the first time in this book we come across an African nationalist of genuine stature, a man who might fairly be compared to leaders like Ho Chi Minh—though he is not a Communist—or even Jawaharlal Nehru.

Bourguiba is about fifty, a lawyer, educated in France and with a French wife; in appearance and quality he is almost indistinguishable from a cultivated Parisian. He was the founder of the Néo-Destour and then its president. His career has alternated between exile and nationalist action. In September, 1934, he was packed off to the Sahara and released in 1936 when the Popular Front came to power in Paris; then in 1938 he was arrested when the Néo-Destour was dissolved. Came the war. The Germans (who were in occupation of Tunisia from November, 1942, to May, 1943) let Bourguiba out of jail, but although he spoke for Tunisian freedom on the Bari (Italy) radio and elsewhere, he was never an outright Axis collaborationist.[13] Even the French most hostile to him concede that Bourguiba

[13] Rivlin, *op. cit.*

was always "honest." He was arrested again when the French resumed their administration of Tunisia, escaped, and made his way to Cairo. In 1946 he visited the United States. Early in 1952, after returning to Tunisia, he was arrested once more, following an "insurrectionary" speech. Also he had been putting pressure on the Bey to appeal to the United Nations for intervention in Tunisia, and the French, who resent deeply any nationalist intrigues within the palace, had to take fancy steps to keep the Bey quiet. Bourguiba was exiled to an island called La Galite, forty miles north of Bizerte, uninhabited except by a few lobster fishermen. But after a time this seemed to the French to be uncomfortably near Tunis and early in 1954 he was shipped to an island off the coast of Brittany, Groix, where he was interned until the Mendès-France government let him move to Chantilly, near Paris. He has not yet (at the moment of writing) been permitted to return to Tunis.

Bourguiba's qualities are in the main what they might be expected to be. He is an intellectual, and at the same time an effective and in fact inflammatory mass orator. He is vigorously anti-Communist, and would like to be a friend of the West. He has little personal rancor against the French, and his Seven Point program, the basis of the Néo-Destour program, represents the responsible rather than the extreme nationalist point of view, although it goes very far. Most Tunisians think that he will "inevitably" be free Tunisia's first prime minister.

When Bourguiba was interned in 1952 the leadership passed to the labor executive Farhat Hached, who was quite well known in the United States. In 1951 he spoke before the convention of the American Federation of Labor at San Francisco, and was the first African trade union leader to establish close relations with men like William Green of the AF of L and James B. Carey of the CIO. Farhat Hached was murdered near Tunis on December 5, 1952. This murder, as we know, set off the Casablanca riots in Morocco; its repercussions are not stilled yet, either in Morocco or Tunisia. Hached's car was ambushed in broad daylight and he was machine-gunned to death. His murderers, who have never been caught, were members of a secret vigilante organization set up by *colons* and known as the Red Hand, according to Tunisian nationalists. Also the French police may have been involved, and another theory is that the Communists, who hated Hached, might have been responsible. But most evidence points to the Red Hand.

Hached's murder was an unmitigated tragedy not only for Tunisia but for France. He was composed and competent, an organizer rather than an agitator. He believed above all in the unity of Tunisia. Even more than

Bourguiba, he would have made an excellent prime minister. The old Destour, the Néo-Destour, the beylical circle, the Jews, all felt close to him, and responded to his practical, enlightened leadership.

The Red Hand never concealed its intention to assassinate Farhat Hached, if possible. This organization is fanatically right-wing and inflamed, and thinks of the *nationalists* as "enslavers" of the country. Also it hates Americans. The United States, even more than the Soviet Union, is considered to be the villain, and Hached was often attacked for his associations with the American labor movement. Besides he had won his way into the Bey's confidence, which doubly infuriated French extremists. Here is part of a Red Hand manifesto issued shortly before the Hached murder:

> *Against the Enslavement of Tunisia*
>
> by the imperialist American grocers,
> the exterminators of the Red [Indian] race,
> the assassins of the Porto-Ricans,
> the maintainers of black slavery,
> the hangmen of the Philippines
>   Rally to the RED HAND
> Against Farhat Hached the American.
>   Rally to the RED HAND
> Against the rottenness of the accomplice
>   Beylical court.
>   Rally to the RED HAND
> Which will make of this country a French
>   land of liberty in the old tri-colored tradition of 1789.
>
> *Liberté-Egalité-Fraternité*
>
> Free men, Tunisian brothers,
>   Moslems, Christians, Jews
> For our threatened independence,
> To safeguard our ancient Mediterranean
>   civilization,
> Arab and Latin
>   RALLY TO THE RED HAND[14]

Trade unions are so important in Tunisia and elsewhere in Africa because in several countries they provide the *only* mechanism available to nationalists for organization, if political parties are forbidden. All other vehicles of expression are cut off. But unionization almost invariably leads to bitter conflict with the governing authorities. First, the *sine qua non* of economy everywhere in French North Africa is cheap native labor. If labor is well

---

[14] From *Farhat Hached*, a pamphlet published in New York (July, 1954) by the Tunisian Office for National Liberation, by Bahi Ladgham.

paid, profits will not be so high; hence employers fight the advance of unionism relentlessly. Second, trade union activity inevitably takes on a nationalist character. Struggle in the economic sphere becomes political, and the unions find themselves fighting not merely the *colons* but the government.

The labor situation in Tunisia is roughly the following. The dominant union, of which Hached was undisputed boss, is the UGTT (Union Générale des Travailleurs Tunisiens). It has between 80,000 and 100,000 members, and is affiliated with the ICFTU, or International Confederation of Free Trade Unions, which is the anti-Communist world trade union body. Tunisians, unlike Moroccans, have won the right to belong to a strong *native* union organized on a national basis and not subservient to Paris; moreover, they have a link to free labor movements elsewhere in the world. It was Farhat Hached who organized the UGTT in 1944. To do so he had to break away from the Communist-dominated CGT in which he had also been a leading force. He drew most of the CGT membership into his own new union, even though this was profoundly anti-Communist.

A Communist union does, however, still exist in Tunisia, the USTT or Union Syndicale des Travailleurs de Tunisie, which *is* affiliated to the CGT and the Communist-run World Federation of Trade Unions. But it is not nearly as strong as the UGTT.

Curiously enough the Communist party is still legal in Tunisia. Its numerical strength is small. Probably the French permit it to exist in the hope that it will compete with the Néo-Destour and thus divide the nationalist movement. But if the Communists *should* ever filter into the Néo-Destour in such strength as to take it over, this would be a catastrophe for France as well as Tunisia. Bourguiba himself has said that if the nationalist movement is totally suppressed, the Tunisian people will turn to Communism in sheer despair.

It is, as always, exceptionally difficult to talk about the menace of Communism in any French territory without consideration of what may occur some day in Paris. Obviously, if *France* should ever go Communist, there is no limit to what might happen.

Finally, we should make the point that, even if Tunisia is aflame with terrorism, a substantially good possibility of solution still exists. The main reason for this is that Tunisians have such a marked French veneer; assimilation has been going on for more than seventy years. Few nationalists envisage any denouement without *some* French participation, if only because they know perfectly well that they have not enough men as yet to run a government alone. They know, too, that it is to their own interest to have

French protection in the Mediterranean. What Tunisia wants is political education, social advance, self-respect, domestic autonomy, friendship with France, and a close community with the Moslem states to the east. Its ideal would be Dominion Status on the British model. The French can still save Tunisia, if they will put into effect their promise of autonomy.

COURSE OF RECENT EVENTS

Tunisia, unlike Morocco and Algeria, has a cabinet form of government, though without any elected legislature. Actually there are two cabinets. The ministers are all Tunisian, but each ministry has a French "director" of equal authority. In March, 1952, the prime minister, Mohammed Chenek, and his entire cabinet were arrested and tossed into the Sahara, an event unparalleled even in French colonial history. No government in Tunisia has been really stable from this date until the present. The French allowed elections to be held in April, 1953, for *caïdat* (rural) and municipal councils, and in the rural districts 60 per cent of the registered voters went to the polls. This was an important step, and the French called the results a "triumph." But in the chief towns nationalists boycotted the proceedings, which made them useless.

Later in 1953 a new Resident General, Pierre Voizard, was appointed. This was timed to coincide with the meeting of the UN General Assembly, so that the French could say that a new Tunisian regime was just getting under way, and should not be judged until it had its feet on the ground. Voizard did not have an easy time. On one occasion he was angrily mobbed not by nationalists but by outraged French *colons*. Then Mendès-France replaced Voizard by General Boyer de Latour du Moulin, who had been French Commander in Chief in the country. On the one hand Mendès-France sensibly promised reform; with the other he sought to protect legitimate French interests.

What made most trouble during much of this period were the *fellagha*, nationalist terrorists who marauded through the countryside and kept it in an uproar. Many *fellagha*, the French say, were nothing more or less than simple bandits operating under the cloak of the nationalist cause, but this did not make them easier to deal with. Until the Mendès-France regime legalized the Néo-Destour and pledged autonomy for the country, political assassinations went on at the unbelievable rate of one per day. Tunisians killed; then Frenchmen killed in revenge; then Tunisians killed again.

In both 1952 and 1953 the Tunisian "case" made big news at the United Nations in New York. The United States slipped and slithered on this. First the American delegation took the Tunisian side, and then abruptly reversed itself. Events in general followed more or less those involving Morocco, but the Tunisian petitions were submitted with more force. Eleven Asian-Arab countries asked support for a resolution demanding that Tunisia should be granted independence "within three years." This was sidetracked, and a compromise adopted. In 1954 the story was much the same. Meantime in Cairo the rector of Al Azhar University, one of the supreme institutions of learning in the Moslem world, issued a statement in association with other religious leaders condemning the French in North Africa in language seldom heard before, and appealing to Moslems everywhere to boycott France "commercially, industrially, politically, and culturally."[15] Moslems the world over were asked to cease buying French goods, and to raise funds for the aid of their oppressed brethren in North Africa.

*

So now we conclude with French North Africa, and turn to Libya and Egypt, the first independent countries we meet in the course of this long journey.

[15] Albion Ross in the New York *Times*, December 17, 1953.

CHAPTER 11

Libya, or a Child Learning to Walk

From the halls of Montezuma to the shores of Tripoli...
—HYMN OF THE UNITED STATES MARINES

... That triumph of Imagination, the Libyan Association.
—THE MODERN TRAVELLER

LIBYA, the youngest country in the world, is packed with bizarre curiosities. Few Americans—even granting that they know where it is—appreciate its vastness. It is bigger than all western Europe, and one-fifth the size of the United States. If you superimpose Libya on a map of the United States and put Tripoli at Chicago, it will stretch from Des Moines to the tip of Florida. Most of this considerable area is worthless desert. (But Saudi Arabia was once "worthless" desert—and look at it now.) Libya fronts on the Mediterranean, but it projects deep into the Sahara, and is riverless. It can rain cats and dogs along the coast—as I will freely attest—but it has practically no fresh water except well water at widely scattered oases. As a result it is probably the poorest country in the world as well as the newest; only 2 per cent of the land is productive, and the average income probably does not exceed $35 per person a year.

In all the Libyan immensity there are only about 1,150,000 people, mostly Bedouin nomads. Libya has no bank of its own, no native doctor of medicine, not more than 225 miles of railway, and an army that numbered, when I was there, fifty-eight men. People drink a dessert made of mint tea and hazelnuts. It has a wind, the notorious *ghibli*, which sprays brown sand from the Sahara over the coastal towns, brings the heat on occasion to 120 degrees, and is locally regarded as the most unpleasant wind in the world.[1] It contains

---

[1] The hottest shade temperature ever known, 136.4 degrees, was recorded in the Libyan desert only a few miles south of Tripoli. Libya also has the lowest place on the African continent, 436 feet below sea level.

the city of Tobruk, which anybody interested in the African campaigns of the last war will remember, and the splendid ruins of Cyrene, from which came the most ravishingly lovely statue of Venus ever known.

Libya, this child learning to walk, was formerly an Italian colony. In its contemporary phase it has three foster parents—Great Britain, the United States and the United Nations—and a solicitous big brother, Egypt. It has a king, by name Idris, the newest king in the world. Libya is the eighth member of the Arab League, and one of the eleven or twelve independent Moslem countries in the world. It has a strategic importance beyond what one would assume from its desiccated remoteness. For instance, the United States maintains an important air base near Tripoli, called Wheelus Field. Libya is the first nation ever put on its feet, such as they are, by the UN. Whether or not it survives will have vivid repercussions in much of Africa and elsewhere. It is a test case (unfortunately on ground arid in the extreme) of how well a new nationalism can work.

Is Libya viable? Let us explore.

The most striking thing about the United Kingdom of Libya, as it is called officially, is that it is not merely one country, but three. Its major problem is national integration—how to make its separate parts cohere. The three areas are:

1. *Tripolitania.* Capital, Tripoli; population about 800,000. The stock is basically Berber. This is the western section of the country, more Europeanized than the rest, and more advanced. There are still about 45,000 Italians in and around Tripoli—mostly merchants and farmers—and Italian investments are still considerable. This is in sharp contrast to Cyrenaica, the eastern section, where the Italians are much more fiercely hated, and where very few remain—only 118 to be exact out of a former 47,000. Tripolitania and Cyrenaica differ sharply, they do not like each other, and communications between them are difficult and scant. Recently the United States Information Service showed a movie depicting Cyrenaica to an audience in Tripoli. People exclaimed in surprise, "Why, those people in Cyrenaica are just like us, after all!" American influence is strong in the Tripoli region partly on account of the proximity of Wheelus Field; it would be wrong, however, to say (as is sometimes said) that the United States "dominates" Tripolitania. If anybody dominates it the British do.

2. *Cyrenaica.* Capital, Benghazi; population, roughly 300,000. (Benghazi and Tripoli have equal rank as "co-capitals" of Libya as a whole.) Cyrenaica is the home of a celebrated Arab people known as the Senussi—who hardly exist in Tripolitania—and adjoins Egypt. It looks back to a Greek past, in contrast to Tripolitania where the heritage is largely Roman and Carthaginian.

The Italians had to wage two long, difficult, and expensive wars with the Senussi before Cyrenaica was conquered; resistance did not end till 1932. In World War II, Cyrenaica saw much more fighting than Tripolitania; Benghazi suffered no fewer than 1,080 air raids, and changed hands five times, as the British Eighth Army and Marshal Rommel's Afrika Korps pursued each other across the desert. Today British influence is still marked.

3. *The Fezzan.* Capital, Sébha; population, about 50,000. This is largely terra incognita—the desert region south of Tripoli that flanks Tunisia, the southern territories of Algeria, and both French West and French Equatorial Africa. When I was in Libya it was impossible to fly from Tripoli to Sébha except via Tunis, whence a French plane penetrated into the Fezzan once a fortnight. The Fezzan was liberated by the Free French forces of General Leclerc, and a detachment of the French Foreign Legion is still stationed there. The frontiers are not yet finally delimited. No one seemed to know, when I asked, if a border town called Gadamès, an almost mythical city on the ancient caravan route to the south, was technically in French territory or in Libya, although there is no doubt in the mind of the Libyan government that it is Libyan. Gadamès exists in two layers; part of the city lies underground. In Sébha, I was told, only fourteen people are literate enough to be able to use a library. The French are not particularly popular in Libya; people say that whereas something new and vital is being built—created—in Tripolitania and Cyrenaica, the French try to keep the Fezzan strictly under old-style thumbs. Nor do the French, on their side, look to the Libyan experiment with much favor. Naturally, if Libya proves in time that it is capable of self-government, the argument will be redoubled that Morocco and Tunisia, which are infinitely more advanced, are equally competent to run their own affairs.[2]

Some remarkable peoples, aside from the Senussi and Tuareg in the southern desert, inhabit Libya. One should at least mention in passing the Troglodytes, authentic cave dwellers who live for the most part underground, and the Khologhli, descendants of Libyan women who interbred with a special brand of Turk, the Janissaries.

LOOKING BACKWARD

Libya, this "box of sand," is the youngest country in the world, having been born on December 24, 1951; it is also one of the oldest. "Libya" was originally an Egyptian word, and in both Greek and Roman times was the

[2] Agreement for the withdrawal of French troops from the Fezzan was reached in January, 1955.

general name for all Africa west of Egypt.³ One can peel off Libyan history layer by layer. Few countries have known dominion by such a variety of masters. (a) First came the Phoenicians, who pushed the aboriginal Berbers back and founded colonies on the coast well before the settlement of Carthage, perhaps as early as 1000 BC (b) After Carthage was destroyed by Rome in 146 BC a Numidian (=nomad) kingdom held power briefly. (c) Julius Caesar "liberated" Libya, and several centuries of Roman rule duly followed. The Romans built—on a Carthaginian foundation—cities like Sabratha and Leptis Magna which are the sites today of incomparably noble ruins, among the most beautiful in the world.⁴ (d) Cyrenaica during these centuries had a different development, and was dominated by Greece for roughly 1,200 years, from 600 BC to AD 600. (e) The Vandals, after reaching Spain, crossed the Mediterranean and pushed the Romans out of Libya. (f) In the time of Justinian occurred a short revival of Roman power focussed from Byzantium. Then (g) the Arabs came in 643 AD and swept everything else away.

But we are just beginning. The Berbers (h) hit back at the Arabs and managed to reconquer part of the country from them. (i) In the eleventh century Egypt sent two Arab tribes, the Beni Hillal and the Beni Suleim, who had settled in the upper Nile valley, into Libya. These are the foundation of the Arab stock in the country today. (j) A brief period of Norman rule followed, directed from Sicily. (k) Spain took over part of the coast in 1510; the Spaniards wanted to make their southeastern flank safe, and wipe out the Barbary pirates who were using Tripoli as a base. (l) Spain handed Libya over to the Knights of Malta in 1530. (m) Turkey began to be active in the Mediterranean, and in 1551 sent out two conquering expeditions; one took Cyprus, the other Libya. (n) A remarkable Turkish official on the spot, Ahmed Caramanli, made a revolution in 1711 and seized power in Libya. Under the Caramanli dynasty Libya had an independent status, which the Turkish government recognized, until 1835. (o) Turkey then reassumed power and Libya became a province of the Sublime Porte until the Turks were ousted by the Italians in 1911–12. (p) Italian rule lasted till World War II, with Tripolitania and Cyrenaica united into a single colony. Before this the two provinces had *always* had separate identities. Even under Rome Libya was divided. (q) During World War II the Germans and British alternated in possession. (r) A British caretaker government main-

---

³ The correct name of the country today is Al Mamlaka Al Libiyya Al Muttahida.
⁴ Sacheverell Sitwell's *Mauretania* has a fascinating account of these. Leptis was built by the Roman Emperor Septimius Severus, who had African Negro blood and who died (AD 211) in, of all places, York, England.

tained administration from 1945 to 1950. (s) Libya, with the British still remaining a dominant force, passed to United Nations jurisdiction, and finally became an independent state.

*

French, British, Portuguese, Belgian, and Spanish colonial policies in Africa are part of the substance of this book, and to make the record complete we should perhaps interpolate a brief line here about Italian policy, though the Italian colonial empire has disappeared. (Somalia on the Horn of Africa is, however, being administered by Italy under a ten-year United Nations trusteeship.) Libya was by far Italy's most important colony until the conquest of Ethiopia in 1935–6. Italy came late to the African grab. There was not much left to take. The Italian war against Turkey (1911–12) was completely cold-blooded and ruthless, made with the calculated intention of seizing African territory from the decaying Sultan; Mussolini himself—a youthful socialist in those days—violently opposed this imperialist adventure. Twenty years later the same Mussolini postured in Libya as a conquerer, and then set in motion the aggressions that led to World War II by invading Ethiopia.

Libya—particularly Cyrenaica—cost Italy a fantastic amount of trouble. The Cyrenaicans simply refused to be subject peoples. They even fought (during World War I) with the Turks *against* the Italians. Two prolonged, full-dress Italo-Senussi wars occurred in 1911–17 and 1923–32. One heroic Senussi leader, Omar Al Mukhtar, a very considerable personage indeed, held out to the last in the Kufra oasis. When the Italians finally got him they hanged him publicly—although he was gravely wounded—before an audience of 20,000 tribesmen forced to attend the ceremony. It is an index of the toughness—and patriotism—of the Cyrenaicans that they lost *one-third* of their total adult male population before they were so decimated and exhausted that they had to surrender.[5]

The story is often told, but resolutely denied by the Italians, that during these campaigns the late Marshal Graziani invented a novel method of intimidation and punishment, that of grabbing a local sheikh, taking him up in an airplane, identifying him with a placard tied around his neck, and pitching him overboard—alive—on whatever village happened to be in need of "pacification."

Italian policy in Africa was based on the principle of "demographic colonization." The African areas were to serve the explicit purpose of drawing off surplus Italian population at home, like leeches applied to a swollen body.

[5] An admirable account of all this is in *The Sanussi of Cyrenaica*, by E. E. Evans-Pritchard. Also see "The Nationalist Movement in Libya," *World Today*, July, 1946.

LIBYA, OR A CHILD LEARNING TO WALK 169

This policy was encouraged by every possible means, but only about 92,000 Italians ever settled in Libya, about half of whom went there before Mussolini. The Italian system did not give much to the African. In Tunisia, French *colons* were the masters, but they did at least hire African labor; Italian landowners, on the other hand, sought to import Italian labor. They built good roads, but did practically nothing for native education or public health. There was little training for self-government, as under the British, or encouragement to become assimilated, as under the French. Nationalist expression (in the pre-Fascist era) was of course forbidden, and civil rights unknown. Overt nationalists were simply jailed or shot. Then Mussolini, who had good sense in some matters, sharply modified this policy. He wanted to re-create a Roman Africa. To this end he had to try to win Arab good will. He built up "Arab-Fascist" formations, and boasted that he would be a "father" to Islam. Also the Italians (like the Belgians) did their best to produce a good economy, out of which the Africans might gain material benefits. The standard of living in prewar Tripoli was much higher than it is today. (Nationalism costs money.) Finally, in all fairness, it should be pointed out that Italian techniques in colonization were established before the present era, when old-fashioned colonial policies were still considered to be respectable, and when nobody dreamed that an educated African could be anything but a marionette or tool. Today, if Italy had an outright colony, there is no reason to think that its administration would not be enlightened.

Libya jumped from one regime to another overnight. In Tripoli I met an outstanding political figure, and I asked him—innocently enough—if he had a long nationalist background. He looked embarrassed, and then told me that he had been a major in the Italian army.

The mechanisms whereby Libya did finally achieve independence were curious. "Freedom was not so much gained as foisted on the country," a British observer says. The great powers could not agree on what to do with it, and Libya became free in the end mostly for want of any other solution. For years disposal of the former Italian colonies, Libya in particular, was a knotty problem. The Council of Foreign Ministers wrestled with it first, and then the UN Assembly. The British, who were paying the bills, wanted to divide the country, that is, make Tripolitania and Cyrenaica separate entities. They wanted to be able to protect British strategic interests in Cyrenaica at least, even if Libya proved to be incapable of survival as a whole. And Mr. Eden had announced in 1942 that Cyrenaica, where the Senussi had fought so staunchly, would never be permitted to return to Italian rule. The British have a lively interest in Cyrenaica because it gives them an admirable frontage on the Mediterranean, close to Egypt; it makes a convenient staging ground for British troops, and helps to compensate for the imminent loss of Suez.

As to American policy it favored a "collective trusteeship" for Libya under the UN, to run for ten years, after which the problem could be dealt with anew. This would probably have been the most sensible solution. For various reasons it fell through. Italy and the Arab bloc (the so-called Rome-Mecca axis) opposed it, and so did the Soviet Union. Then the Russians asked for a trusteeship of their own over Tripolitania; this proposal alarmed everybody. In 1949 the Bevin-Sforza scheme—named for the British and Italian foreign ministers of the period—proposed a three-way partition of Libya, with the French getting a trusteeship over the Fezzan, the British over Cyrenaica, and the Italians over Tripolitania. People shrieked. It seemed fantastic that the UN should want to give part of Libya back to the *Italians*, the beaten enemy. But the Bevin-Sforza plan was defeated by only one vote. Negotiations had to begin all over again, and, in the end, as people became bored with the topic, Libya's future was settled with almost indecent haste. It was decided late in 1950 that the country should become independent before December 31, 1951, which meant that the whole machinery of government had to be set up in a little more than a year.[6]

HIS MAJESTY KING IDRIS I

The name of the King of Libya is officially al-Sayyid Mohammed Idris al-Mahdi es Senussi. "Idris" means "Enoch." The monarch is in his middle sixties now, and is a thoughtful, somewhat frail old gentleman. His dominating characteristics are erudition, piety, and suspiciousness. Nothing has ever mattered much to him except freedom, if not for all of Libya, at least for Cyrenaica. He has considerable elevation of character and a subtle intelligence. He knows no western language, but is an Arabic scholar of advanced attainments, and is probably the most sophisticated as well as learned head of state in the Moslem world. His chief defect is lack of force.

We saw him not in Tripoli or Benghazi but in Cairo, where he was recuperating from a recent illness. That he had been away in Cairo for an extended period—"an absentee monarch"—caused much criticism in Libya. He makes plans with a good deal of secrecy, and moves by sudden whim; nobody in Libya knew (at that time) when he would return. King Idris

---

[6] During the final negotiations one UN delegate is supposed to have said to a colleague, "At three o'clock this afternoon we free Libya." His colleague replied, "Impossible. We freed Libya yesterday." From "The Newest State and Monarch," by Judd L. Teller, *The Reporter*, March 4, 1952.

LIBYA, OR A CHILD LEARNING TO WALK

and his suite lived in Cairo at the Mena House, a celebrated hotel near the Pyramids. He had elaborate quarters there—most of one floor. Outside his rooms sat a delegation of magnificent white-robed tribal sheikhs, slim, cloudily silent, and immobile; they looked like white fingers, with nails for faces. They had been waiting to see him (he had been too ill to receive anybody) for three solid weeks. A page summoned us and I thought that we were being led to some anteroom where a chamberlain would prepare us for the audience with His Majesty. But we were ushered, without intermediation, directly into the royal presence. Of course an interpreter was present. Idris has a bushy mustache and gold-rimmed glasses; he wore a blue cloak and short tarboosh. He sat in the middle of a sofa, and we faced him in chairs a few feet away. My first impression was that this was an extremely gentle man. I have always, for some reason, had difficulty talking to Arab potentates; they do not give out readily, and Idris has the reputation of being even more reticent than most. So it was a welcome surprise to find that he talked readily—and with charm and humor. A chuckle runs in his voice. Idris may be frail, but his wits are still sharp. Talking about Morocco he said that French policy was bound to produce—unfortunately—exactly that which it wanted to prevent, namely, a permanent state of disorder which the Communists would exploit. Talking about the United States, he asked us—with a bright gleam—why we worked so hard to liberate countries behind the Iron Curtain, which would probably turn out to be enemies no matter what, while we neglected countries that would always be our friends, like Tunisia and Morocco.

King Idris fills a double role—he is both the secular monarch and religious head of his people. In the familiar Moslem pattern, as old as Islam itself, he was a religious figure first, and then turned to politics. Idris is the grandson of the founder of the Senussi order, and hereditary leader of the Senussis. We must have a word about these peculiar people. They are dervishes, with a tradition both fiery and devout. Like the Wahabis in Saudi Arabia, they are extremely strict Moslems, reformists who want to return to the original hard-and-fast purity of Islam. The movement was founded by "the Grand Senussi" (grandfather of Idris) who was born near Tlemçen, in Algeria, in 1787; it spread out into the desert among the Bedouin so strongly that, by the end of the nineteenth century, the Senussis had established what has been called "a theocratic empire," spilling over political frontiers. This was then broken up by the British, French, and Italians. But the Senussis continued to maintain their cohesion and identity, partly by reason of a remarkable institution known as the *zawia*. The *zawias* are a combination of town hall and seminary, where the teachings of the fraternity are kept alive; almost every village and oasis has one, though the Italians destroyed a great number of them in the Senussi wars.

King Idris was born in 1889 in the Jaghbub oasis in Cyrenaica, and has been head of the Senussi order since 1917. In time he became the Emir of Cyrenaica, and was recognized as such by the Italians for a brief period. In 1923 Italian policy stiffened, and Idris retreated to exile in Egypt. During World War II he assisted the British greatly in their desert campaigns, and, after the Axis forces were chased out of Libya in 1943, he returned to his country after twenty-one uninterrupted years of exile. In 1949 the British made him Emir of Cyrenaica again, while waiting for a final UN decision on Libya as a whole. A national constituent assembly proclaimed him King of Libya in 1950, although the country did not yet formally exist.

Naturally Idris is better known and liked in Cyrenaica than in Tripolitania. Some Tripolitanians scoff at him as a "shepherd chieftain," and say that he was "put over" on the country. There was an attempt to assassinate him in Tripoli when he was still Emir of Cyrenaica, and he has tended to avoid visiting Tripoli ever since.

Idris has a strong family sense, and is heavily superstitious. In 1952 he decided to rebury his father (who had died in a remote oasis) in Benghazi. While the body was enroute by truck the worst *ghibli* in twenty years singed the country with hot flying sand. Idris decided that this was a bad omen, stopped the truck, and sent his father's remains back to their original resting place.

King Idris has no male heir, which is a tragedy for the country. He was married first in 1897, when he was only eight years old; this was a purely ceremonial wedding, made for family reasons. He has never had more than one wife at a time. Two subsequent marriages ended in divorce, when they produced no living issue. Then in 1932 Idris married again; his wife was a cousin (born in 1911), named Al Sayyida Fatima Al Shifa bint al-Sayyid Ahmad al-Sharif. She has had no fewer than fourteen miscarriages. During her last pregnancy, in 1952, three American doctors from Wheelus Field attended her steadily. She bore a son early in 1953, but the infant lived for only a few hours. As a result of all this Idris has designated his brother, by name Rida, as crown prince and heir to the throne, with the succession going then to Rida's eldest son. Rida, who is known as Deputy King and who lives in Tripoli, is a jovial, socially minded man, quite different from the retiring Idris. The royal family, which has thirty-eight male members—all of whom have to be supported by the state—is fiercely split. Some thirty-two of the thirty-eight princes, who belong to a different branch of the Senussi family, have strongly opposed Idris on occasion.[7]

Idris and Queen Fatima (who of course is never seen) live most of the time at Leyte, a few miles from Benghazi. Here an underground stream flows, which was the original River of Forgetfulness of the ancient Greeks, and which contributed the word "lethal" to the English language. The royal palace was formerly an Italian casino. Also the King has a summer capital at El Baida, in the hilly region called Jebel el Akhdar, 140 miles east of Benghazi. The whole diplomatic corps has to establish temporary residence in this vicinity each summer, although its living facilities are meager and communications practically non-existent. When Idris visits Tripoli he uses the palace once occupied by Marshal Balbo. All this means that Libya, a country with fewer people than Arkansas, has in effect four capitals, if you include El Baida and Sébha in the Fezzan. Moreover Idris has lately been spending most of his time in Tobruk, near the Egyptian border—presumably to make it easier to get away if he should have to leave the country quickly.

Recently Libya got its own national currency for the first time, but the issue had to be withdrawn and another substituted, because Idris objected to the use of his effigy on the banknotes; strict Moslems do not like to have their faces portrayed. The King's Speech from the Throne last year showed, more than ever before, the strong influence of Egypt on his domain. An Egyptian delegation is drawing up a new legal code for the country, and 120 Libyan students have gone to Egypt on scholarships. Idris did not get on well with Farouk (who was pro-Italian and thought that Idris was too pro-British) but he has a close relation with the Nasser regime. Early in 1954 Idris visited Spain (as did President Tubman of Liberia—Spain has a marked interest in the independent African states). Recently Libya scored its first "triumph" in foreign policy by being accepted as a member of the Arab League. But a Russian veto kept it out of the UN, even though it is a United Nations child.

In October, 1954, Ibrahim Ahmed Al Shalhi, the Minister of Palace Affairs, and by all odds the man closest to the King, was murdered. He was *nazir* of the Royal Household, and had almost unlimited power; his origins were obscure, and one story is that he was a slave brought up by members of the Senussi family and trained to be Idris' bodyguard; he was barely literate, but even so became the undisputed *éminence grise* of the regime. Al Shalhi was assassinated by a young man named Sherif Mohieddin Al Senussi, a nephew of both Idris and Queen Fatima. A similar sensation would occur if, let us say, the prime minister of Japan should be murdered by one of the

[7] "Dangers of Tribal Unrest in Libya," London *Times*, October 21, 1954.

Emperor's cousins. Al Shalhi was bitterly hated by most members of the royal circle, but his death was a catastrophe for Idris.

Some episodes extraordinary even for an Oriental monarchy took place after Al Shalhi's death. Idris purged several members of the government. Then the *entire royal family* (except the Queen and the Crown Prince) were deprived of their titles and privileges, and nine conspicuous princes including the son of the Crown Prince were packed off to exile in a forlorn oasis 150 miles south of Benghazi. The nineteen-year-old prince who murdered Shalhi was, despite his youth and royal blood, executed in February, 1955.

To sum up: In the present phase Idris is the only person capable of holding Libya together, but he himself hardly seems capable of doing so. At least he steadily favors his native Cyrenaica over Tripolitania, and as a result resentment by the richer and more advanced Tripolitanians has become the chief political issue of the country. Earnest Libyan patriots who want above all to make the federal system work are caught in a cruel dilemma, because if they attack the King they defeat their own best interests by making the country weaker.

THE TOWN OF TRIPOLI AND ITS POLITICS

Libya itself is wretchedly poor, but TRIPOLI (population around 130,000) is one of the best built, cleanest, and generally most attractive cities in North Africa. The Italians know how to build cities, and they spent billions of lire on Tripoli. The name means "Three Cities"; in Roman times Tripoli made a trinity with Sabratha and Leptis Magna. The most imposing edifice today is the Castello, or fort, which once housed the Caramanli family. Tripolitanian architecture is madly mixed up—masts of old ships jut out of Arab courtyards, and Roman columns are morticed into Turkish walls. British influence vies with Italian; it would be hard to decide which is the best modern building, Barclay's Bank or the Banca di Roma. People light cigarettes with Italian *fiammiferi* and drink a hideous local fluid known as Kitty Kola. Many street names, like the Via Ariosto, are still Italian, and the leading hotel has a vigorous Italian-style night club and casino. Slogans like *Viva il Ré* are chalked on walls—also I saw a few hammers and sickles. A substantial Jewish community still exists, although thousands of Jews fled to Israel after an ugly pogrom in 1945. Arab women wear a costume known as the barracan; this is a cloak worn like a blanket, which covers the whole body and head but leaves one eye exposed, and is thus the equivalent of a veil as well.

Libya is in the sterling area, and it was fascinating to learn that the whole country contained, when we were there, only *one* American businessman, the representative of an oil company. I should imagine that this is the only nation in the world (Communist areas excluded) where the entire American business community consists of one person.

But the most interesting sight in Tripoli has to do with the United States —the old Protestant cemetery, where five American sailors lie buried. They were members of the crew of the USS *Intrepid*, which was blown up in Tripoli harbor during the Barbary wars. An American force landed near Tripoli and planted the Stars and Stripes there on April 27, 1804. The United States did not invade Africa again until 1942.

*

When the UN began to lay the framework for a Libyan government it was discovered that there were only seventeen native university graduates in the entire country.[8] To set up an administration was like trying to build a house without wood or nails. The amazing thing is that, after so brief a period, the experiment should be working as well as it does. A government *is* functioning after a fashion. It even has a Five-Year Plan. The King appoints a cabinet, which performs its duties conscientiously, and elections have taken place (February, 1952) in which a remarkable percentage of people voted.

Many British advisors have been kept on, survivors of the postwar administration; these do not represent the British government, but are strictly Libyan officials. When we visited the *Wali* (governor) of Tripoli we found British assistants in practically every office. But slowly these Britons, especially on the lower levels, are being weeded out, as enough Libyans become trained to take their places. Syrians and Palestinians have come in too.[9] We found some outspoken anti-British sentiment in Libya, but the country could not survive without British help, and all sensible Libyans know it. The budget deficit since independence has been about $4,000,000 out of $12,000,000, and London makes this up. In July, 1953, after long negotiation, a formal treaty of alliance was signed between the United Kingdom and Libya. It assured further British financial aid for twenty years (at the rate of $10,500,000 per year for the first five years) and gives the British permission to maintain "certain armed forces" in the country. I asked two Britons why they had such interest in Libya as a whole, as apart from Cyrenaica. First

---

[8] Not a big figure, but probably bigger than the number in Liberia, Ethiopia, or Eritrea at the same time. Some people I met doubted the number seventeen. "Just try to find 'em!" they said.

[9] Arab Palestinians, not Israeli Jews.

answer: "These chaps did a lot for us in the war, and we can't let them down." Second answer: "We do not want a vacuum here."

Libya is, meantime, proceeding with plans for the development of its own "army," which will be British-trained. Why on earth should the country want an army? (A) All national states have armies, and so Libya must have one. To have a national force bearing arms gives the Libyans self-respect. (B) The cabinet includes a minister of defense, and this dignitary can hardly be taken seriously if he has no military apparatus under him. (C) An army gives politicians something to play with, a phenomenon that has been known in countries more advanced than Libya.

One interesting Libyan, Mahmoud Bey Muntasir, was prime minister from the inception of government till February, 1954, when he resigned partly on account of ill-health, but also because of a serious political difference with the King. He is an able man, Italian-educated. Later he became ambassador to London. Muntasir hated Al Shalhi. The point at issue was whether Libya should be ruled like an old-style theocratic state, with the prime minister nothing but a Grand Vizier under the King's (and Al Shalhi's) orders, or whether it should adapt itself to modern times, with the King governing within the terms of the Federal Constitution. Incidentally one of the justices of the Libyan Supreme Court is an American. Muntasir was succeeded as prime minister, after an interval, by an energetic official named Mustafa ben Halim. He is an engineer, who had lived most of his life in Egypt, and was almost unknown in Libya at the time of his appointment. He visited the United States in the summer of 1954, after a trip to Turkey. Both Turkey and the Arab League have strong diplomatic designs on Libya. Turkey would like to see Libya part of the "team" it is setting up with Iraq and Pakistan; the Arab League wants to keep it close to Cairo.

An opposition leader of consequence, now exiled to Saudi Arabia, is Beshir Bey Sadawi. He was markedly anti-West, and led a party with Communist indoctrination.

The person whom I liked best in Libya, a wise and salty old personage, is the Sheikh Mohammed Abu Al-Asad Al-Alem, the Grand Mufti of the country. He is half blind and over seventy; last year he married a third wife, a girl in her teens. This does not mean that he is not a very holy personage. In fact he is such a devout Moslem that *my* wife was not allowed to accompany me when I saw him; the Mufti never receives foreign women, even if they are veiled. Nowhere else in Africa, even in remote parts of Nigeria and in the Sudan, did we find any Moslem dignitary so strict.

The Mufti, who is strongly pro-British and pro-American, had some shrewd observations to make about the Libyan scene. What Libyans need, he said, is what all people need—money and skills. "Get some food into our bellies, get some knowledge into our heads."

POINT FOUR AND WHEELUS FIELD

British influence is, then, decisive in Libya if only because the United Kingdom finances the government. But the impact of the United Nations and the United States is also strongly felt. Libya is the scene of the fourth largest Point Four program in the world, administered by the Foreign Operations Administration. Only Indonesia, Pakistan, and India have bigger Point Four establishments and these countries are of course much bigger than Libya. The United States spent in Libya $2,270,000 in 1951–53, and the American staff numbers about sixty.

One might almost say that Libya is a veritable school; its whole population, directly or indirectly, is being instructed by American and UN advisors. Altogether men representing twenty-six different nationalities are on the scene, and their work is of the most challenging importance. More than anywhere else in Africa, except possibly Liberia, technicians representing the UN and the United States are trying to educate an entire country, put it on its feet, and make it work. No doubt there has been extravagance and ineptitude in the administration of the Mutual Security Program here and elsewhere. But in Libya at least it is rendering service far beyond its cost. Instead of cutting Point Four appropriations the American government should amplify them many times. Money could not be better spent. The best of all ways to keep Africa on our side is to give it generous, constructive financial aid.

Point Four and the UN operate (in Tripolitania) in four major fields—public health, natural resources, agriculture, and education. A variety of tutors are at work—accountants, tax experts, statisticians, agronomists, authorities on hides and skins, range management specialists, foresters, and specialists in date palms, textbooks, child psychology, and manual training.

In public health the major problem is trachoma, the incidence of which is enormous beyond belief; about 90 per cent of all Libyan children have or have had trachoma. Patiently, demonstration teams are teaching the population the use of DDT to keep down flies, which spread the disease. If trachoma is caught in time, blindness will not result. But it takes months to treat a child—or adult—successfully, and most Libyans do not understand the necessity for regular stringent treatment; they have to be *taught* from the bottom up. Venereal disease is another vexing problem. Somebody told an eminent Libyan recently that 90 per cent of the prostitutes in Benghazi have gonorrhea. "How lucky it is that men don't catch it!" was his innocent reply.

As to natural resources and agriculture, the main effort is to increase food crops. In the Fezzan people get only eight hundred calories a day on the average, which means virtual starvation. But it is extremely difficult to make the Fezzan folk repair their wells, learn new agricultural methods, and so on, which might give them more food. American experts are surveying the desert, mapping underground water resources, and trying to improve crop quality. Efforts are being made to step up production of one of Libya's few distinctive products, esparto grass, which is used for making fine paper. Farmers are being taught to grade their wool more accurately, and separate out the "dung tags" that kept it from a high-priced market; the value of Libyan wool has substantially increased as a result. Also three forest nurseries have been established, and 160,000 seedlings planted. This is a part of something fancily known as the "sand dune stabilization project." Finally in this realm, the United States sent an important shipment of wheat to Libya in December, 1953, when drought produced something close to a famine.[10]

Education is a whole long story in itself. Here we strike a note that will be many times repeated in this book. Libya, like practically every other place in Africa, is education-mad. "The thirst for education is like that of a man trying to suck water out of sand," one UN specialist told me. Compulsory primary education is now in prospect, and Point Four and the UN are working hard to establish the necessary public-school system. The American emphasis is largely on teacher training and a technical school for skilled trades, like carpentry and plumbing. Out in the oases schools operate in three shifts. Communities volunteer to create their own embryo schools. Of course the obstacles are innumerable. A blackboard—even a pencil—is a rare and expensive object. Here too we run against the chief of all embarrassments to progress in a Moslem land—the position of women. Arabs do not want their daughters to go to school, and the ratio of boy students to girls is about a hundred to one.

Libya has no university, and would like Point Four to build one. But no university can have much utility until there are enough high-school graduates

---

[10] Report to Congress on the Mutual Security Program, Washington, 1953. One troublesome obstacle to economic reform is the donkey, a notably inefficient animal. But the Libyans will not give up their donkeys, because donkey dung gives them fuel and donkeys turn their water wheels. Point Four is not so crazy as to want to abolish donkeys, but it would like to see them used more economically. The American advisors are pro-camel as well as anti-donkey. A donkey provides nothing but dung and draft power; a camel gives milk, fiber, meat, leather, and long-range transportation as well.

LIBYA, OR A CHILD LEARNING TO WALK 179

to fill it. A good many Libyan boys are, however, now studying at universities abroad. They will become before long leaders of the nation. An incidental point—in connection with adult education—is that four of seven directors of government bureaus in Tripolitania have recently completed special training courses under Point Four supervision. One should also mention the admirable work of the United States Information Service and its libraries. Films (mostly on American subjects) have to be shown in shifts, so numerous and avid is the audience. The library has six hundred books in Arabic; people who can read at all want to read *any* book, altogether without reference to title, author, or subject; it is impossible to keep any book in Arabic on the shelves for more than a few minutes. Finally, the American authorities have distributed 150 radios throughout the country; these go for the most part to clubs, seminaries, and other organizations, where they serve a wide collective audience.

*

Wheelus Field, seven miles from Tripoli, is the big American military installation here. Technically speaking it is not an Air Force "base," but merely a "field." There is no infringement of Libyan sovereignty, and the land utilized has been leased from 1,400 different individual owners of property. The Americans have, however, had a long wrangle with the Libyan government over terms and contracts.[11] Wheelus, which is maintained and run by extraordinarily expert young American officers, has a variety of purposes. For one thing it is an essential stop on the global routes of the United States Military Air Transport Service. Again, it has plenty of space and ideal flying weather most of the time, and American planes stationed in Germany and elsewhere come down here for gunnery practice. It is not primarily designed for retaliation against Russia in the event of war, like the American bases in Morocco. Wheelus is the oldest United States Air Force installation in Africa. More than six hundred American children attend

[11] "The Air Force was in the position of a man who builds a mansion on a lot without buying the lot first." American investment in Wheelus Field is between $50,000,000 and $100,000,000, and the Libyans wanted the United States to pay a great deal more rent than it was paying. (Robert C. Doty in the New York *Times*, February 13, 1954.) Agreement over the base came in September, 1954, after protracted negotiations. The American government agreed to pay Libya $45,000,000 over a period of twenty years, and to give other economic assistance to the country. The United States thus joined Great Britain as a chief element in keeping Libya alive financially. The country is living, as it has been nicely said, "on its geography." The American agreement was bitterly opposed by some Libyan nationalists. They did not want to commit themselves to being part of the American defense system. King Idris had to remove from office at least one important official in order to achieve ratification of the agreement in the Libyan parliament.

its school, and these make a rare sight for Africa. On the property when we visited it—and not far from the 11,000-foot runway—was a most exceptional and curious object, the stadium Mussolini built for the Tripoli automobile race track. This, made of solid concrete, was the largest cantilever structure in the world, and it took a long time before American engineers were able to pull it down.

BENGHAZI AND CYRENAICA

Communication by commerical air routes is not very good in North Africa, to put it mildly. Services across Libya (or even between Tunis and Tripoli) are scant. Maybe there will be a plane once a week—or maybe not.[12] Through the courtesy of Henry S. Villard, American minister to Libya, we got a lift on a United States Air Force plane from Tripoli to Benghazi. It was amazing to see from the air the brief, sharp limits of the Tripoli oasis. It looks like a green eye in an enormous face of sand. The sand creeps right up to the edges of the eye. The oasis—to change the metaphor—might have been made by a cooky cutter. We reached Benghazi at dusk, and circled the field for an interminable time, because Libyan boys had to put out flares to mark the landing strip. These were kerosene torches which they lit by hand. A far cry from Idlewild!

BENGHAZI is a miserable city, I think the most miserable we saw in all Africa except Monrovia in Liberia. It was half destroyed by bombing during the war, and even today gangs of workmen are shoveling up debris fifty yards from Graziani's old palace. Disposal of scrap has been a big and profitable business. People live on their own city—literally. Benghazi seems to be a million miles from Tripoli, although the flight only takes three hours; here we are in Africa, not Europe, and a slatternly Africa at that. Bedouins and their camels pitch camp just off the main streets. The population is about 60,000, of whom perhaps 20,000 are literate; the circulation of the local daily is 3,000, which is quite good for Libya. The name Benghazi derives from an old Egyptian legend, and means Bernice. This lady was the daughter of a Ptolemy who was murdered by her own son. Before this, when her husband was absent at the wars, she promised to give a lock of hair to Aphrodite if he returned safely; he did, and a cluster of stars near the constellation Leo is still called Bernice's Hair.

---

[12] A British company, Silver City Airways, recently procured a concession to operate internal airways in Libya. "Although the service is intended primarily to carry general cargo, special rates will be quoted for camels, goats, horses, sheep, and cattle." London *Times*, December 22, 1953.

LIBYA, OR A CHILD LEARNING TO WALK

There are a good many contemporary points of interest. The Cyrenaica Defense Force, a British detachment composed of Arabs, makes an odd impression because its men wear kilts and play bagpipes, in imitation of a Scots regiment. The local cathedral, built by the Italians, has twin bulbous domes, and is known irreverently as Mae West. A number of German technicians have been hired by the local British garrison—veterans of Rommel's Afrika Korps who were prisoners of war. The shortage of trained Libyans is so desperate that several educated men, who had made successful careers abroad, were literally *forced* to return and take up government service, under threat of reprisals on their families. They were, in effect, kidnaped by their own new nation.

The Arabs here are much stricter than those in Tripoli. They do not drink alcohol at social gatherings (whereas in Tripoli we encountered plenty of mixed drinking) and are more inclined to wear native dress. Of course they never, under any circumstances, bring their wives to a public (or private) function. If you want to make a sensation at a dinner party in Benghazi, ask any Arab guest if he thinks that women should be unveiled. But the winds of the modern world blow even in Cyrenaica. No fewer than *seventeen* young Arab women now attend public schools. I do not mean this is a joke. It is a significant development. So is the fact that a well-born Moslem girl, only sixteen, announced to her family recently that she was leaving home to become a teacher, because it humiliated her that almost all Cyrenaican schoolteachers had to be men imported from Syria or Egypt. No Arab country—let us repeat—will ever achieve true civilization until the women are emancipated.

The best people we met seemed to be of the royal house or close to it. Americans who still have an atavistic suspicion of monarchical institutions may be disconcerted by this phenomenon. And there are plenty of princelings and the like—all over Africa and the Middle East—who are spoiled, feudal, and corrupt. Nevertheless they represent a class that, by and large, has had two priceless advantages, wealth and consequent opportunity for education. So they stand out.

The United States has a substantial Point Four program in Cyrenaica, which like that in Tripoli does valuable work. As in Tripoli, the American Library is thronged, and the demand for literature in both Arabic and English far outruns the supply. This institution should have thousands of books, not a few hundred; if Washington would spend even a little more money, it could make a world of difference. Women readers (a few women *can* read) have to be segregated, and use a special closed-off room. Bitterness over Israel presents another problem. About two hundred Jews still live in

Cyrenaica; these are permitted to use the library only on Saturday afternoons. One day an attendant discovered that the flag of Israel had been crudely scissored out of the dictionary, no doubt by some outraged Arab. The Jews were quick to retaliate. Next week, flags of all the Moslem states were gone!

Below Benghazi is the Sand Sea of Calanscio, which is probably the most impenetrable desert on earth. Below this is Kufra, famous as the "lost oasis"; it was not seen by a white man till a German explorer got there in 1881, and has not been seen often since. You can reach Kufra from Benghazi in ten days by jeep, or forty by camel, but you will not find much there. In 20,000 square miles there are 432 people. The two loneliest men in the world are supposed to have been two officers, one British, one French, who spent most of World War II in Kufra with the assignment of keeping watch on each other.

*

To conclude—is Libya viable? Of course not, unless it manages to stay united and continues to receive foreign aid. Its future, like that of any child, depends on how well it is brought up. Give it games, give it food, give it schooling, and it can develop. This, the newest member of the family of nations, has a useful role to fulfill, and there is no inherent reason why it cannot do so. If it is frail, give it a brace. As a matter of fact it is walking quite briskly already. Libya does not cost very much, and North Africa needs a free country here. The cost of preserving Libya will be less than surrendering it to chaos or to Communism.

CHAPTER 12

Crisis and Development in Egypt

> *Every one of us is able in his own way to perform a miracle.*
> —COLONEL GAMAL ABDUL NASSER
>
> *Certain areas of Egypt are cultivated by irritation.*
> —SCHOOLBOY BONER

THE most important event in the history of modern Egypt occurred on July 23, 1952, when a handful of youthful military zealots seized power. Ever since, events have flowed with precipitous velocity. The long and short of the present situation is that the army junta still rules the country and rules it well, but faces difficulties in putting its ambitious and far-reaching reforms into positive, beneficent effect.

For thirty years or more the struggle for power in Egypt was triple— between the British, the palace, and the Wafd (nationalist party). The 1952 *coup d'état* cut across all three of these traditional pivots of force, and as a result Egypt has had to adjust itself to an altogether different equilibrium. The army struck, in a sense, against the British, the palace, *and* the Wafd. Egypt was laid open like a rotting melon. On this, the junta sought to build.

Nasser-Naguib ousted the fat King, abolished the titles of "Pasha" and "Bey,"[1] proclaimed a republic, suspended the constitution, dissolved the old political parties, built up the Liberation Rally as a new supra-party machine, struck against feudalism, staked out a land reform, and sought to punish those guilty of corruption—in a word, they turned a brisk, stimulating new page in Egyptian history. But whether their *coup d'état* will turn out to be a genuine, permanent *revolution* remains to be seen.

---

[1] "Pasha" and "Bey" are somewhat loose terms in Egypt; roughly they correspond to "Lord" and "Sir." Several times, soon after these titles were forbidden, we met people in Cairo who gave us their cards, and scratched out the word "Bey" after their names; they had not had time to have new cards made. Generally in these chapters I use "Pasha" to indicate members of the old ruling landlord class, but plenty of flaming nationalists were pashas.

Hopes are high and rule is firm, even though the junta has had to fight on two fronts—against the feudal landlords and old aristocracy on the one side, and the politico-religious fanatics of the Moslem Brotherhood (now suppressed) on the other. It faces fierce enmity from both right and left, although this is to oversimplify a situation of inordinate fluidity. What holds it up mainly is the army and the "street"—that is, the people at large, the masses, the mob. But the street is fickle. Moreover it is hungry. Nasser has to keep feeding it. Communists filter into the "street," and so do other troublemakers. Communists even penetrated into the Moslem Brotherhood.

Another point is that the junta itself has undergone severe internal crises, despite the dedicated idealism of its leaders. The original coup was fertilized and executed by one of the most remarkable of contemporary revolutionaries, Gamal Abdul Nasser. He rules Egypt, although he is only a thirty-seven-year-old lieutenant colonel. His "front man" during the early period of the revolutionary struggle was General Mohammed Naguib,[2] but Naguib has disappeared as a factor and is now, at the moment of writing, under house arrest. Revolutions have a habit of eating their own creators as well as children. But the first accomplishments of the regime were in the main performed while Naguib was still in titular command, and plenty that happened—as I know from having watched him on the spot—was his work as well as Nasser's. Up to a point it is impossible to differentiate between the contribution of the two men, once devoted friends and allies, now separated by a grievous chasm. So from time to time I will use the locution "Nasser-Naguib" to describe the bold unit they once made.

The new government becomes more stable month by month, but Nasser himself might conceivably be forced out of office or assassinated before these lines reach print. On the other hand, a man of force, acumen, and deep moral and intellectual conviction, he may well evolve into a kind of Egyptian Ataturk, and remain in power for years to come. His chief source of power is that he really stands for something, the liberation and advancement of the masses. He gives people what they have seldom had before, *hope*. No wonder Egyptians call his movement the "blessed" revolution.

For a long time the British ruled Egypt outright, or at least tried to do so. Then came a period when it served their purpose to have Egyptian governments as soft and pliable as possible, so that they could be easily manipulated. Any quarrel between Egyptians always played into the British hand. All this is ended. The chief claim to fame of Nasser-Naguib so far is, in fact, that Britain is no longer a *direct* power in Egypt at all. Two events of surpassing international importance have taken place since the military clique

[2] Pronounced "Na-geeb."

took office—the agreement of February 12, 1953, providing for self-government in the Sudan (largely negotiated by Naguib) and the subsequent agreement of October 19, 1954 (largely negotiated by Nasser), whereby the British promise to evacuate Suez.

Egypt is on its own—at last.

EGYPT: THE PHYSICAL PICTURE

> Who shall doubt "the secret hid
> Under Cheops' pyramid"
> Was that the contractor did
>   Cheops out of several millions:
> Or that Joseph's sudden rise
> To Comptroller of Supplies
> Was a fraud of monstous size
>   On King Pharaoh's swart Civilians?[3]
>   —RUDYARD KIPLING

Egypt is so well known that we can skip much. We do not need to mention such renowned characters in Egyptian history as Rameses II and Alexander the Great, Cleopatra and Napoleon. The Egyptians derive from the oldest civilization known to mankind, and have the longest history.[4] Their written records go back six thousand years or more. But for century after century they have for the most part been subject to the dominion of outside conquerors. Ethiopians, Persians, Greeks, Romans, Arabs, Turks, Mamelukes, left their heelprints on the sandy body of Egypt. The country was ruled uninterruptedly by foreigners from 525 BC, the date of the Persian invasion, until 1936 when the British gave it independence. Even the "Egyptian" ruling class in the last 150 years has been largely alien.

"People who live in deltas are apt to be soft." I do not know whether this generalization holds good everywhere, but I heard it made of Egyptians several times. They are complacent folk by and large—or at least they have been complacent till modern nationalism woke them up. "These are the easiest people in the world to govern, if somebody *will* govern," a British official told me. One eminent Arab scholar put it this way: "We are like the Nile. We are not a violent people, but very steady. Occasionally there come eruptions, and afterward we revert back to normal. Our life comes from the Nile. We have the consciousness of being part of a steady, powerful, continuous stream—the Nile flows through us, and gives us power and

---

[3] From "A General Summary" from *Departmental Ditties and Ballads and Barrack Room Ballads*, by Rudyard Kipling, reprinted by permission of Mrs. George Bambridge, Doubleday and Company, Inc., and the Macmillan Company of Canada.

[4] With the possible exception of Mesopotamians.

patience. If an Egyptian politician struts too much, we *laugh* him out of office. Make some jokes at his expense, and soon he finds himself completely isolated. The only way to reach an Egyptian is through his heart."

Egyptians have, it would seem, changed little throughout the centuries. You can see almost everywhere (particularly in the south) people today who are living images of Rameses or Nefertiti. On the other hand—a curious point—Egyptians do not have much consciousness of their superb Pharaonic heritage. One theory to account for this is that the Arabs, when they took Egypt, did their best to wipe out traces of what had existed before. Nowadays Egyptian education makes a strong point of the country's ancient history, and strives to make people proud of it. Another point is that, although it has seen so many conquerors, Egypt remains remarkably homogeneous. The country replenished its blood from Nubia, from the desert Bedouin, and from Greece, Turkey, and the Levant, not from peoples far away.

Egyptians are likely to have a marked sensitiveness and inferiority about their background; if a man rises to be something out of the ordinary, it is assumed as a matter of course that he must be foreign. I even heard the remark, "That chap Nasser is so able—he must have a drop of Turkish blood somewhere." As a matter of fact Nasser is a pure Egyptian of Arab stock.

Egyptians speak Arabic, and Egypt is the "capital" of the Arab world, but Egyptians are not Arabs. They have strong Arab characteristics, and Cairo is the most fecund center of Arab culture in the world, but they are a people quite unique and apart. Most cultivated Egyptians have much closer ties to Europe than to Asia or the rest of Africa, and dislike being thought of as "African." Some Egyptians are almost as dark-skinned as Negroes, but their orientation is to the Mediterranean, not to Black Africa. I attempted to explain patiently to a Cairene official what my trip was about. "Ah," he said finally, "you are going to write a book about Africa *and* Egypt!"

Egypt is predominantly Moslem, of course, but one interesting Christian community exists—that of the Copts. These are members of one of the oldest Christian churches in the world. The Copts are an extremely conservative group, active in trade and the bureaucracy; their main focus is the town of Asyut on the Upper Nile; probably there are 1,100,000 Copts in Egypt altogether. They are often called the "oldest" Egyptians, since they descend from those who refused to intermix with the Arabs at the time of the Islamic conquest of Egypt in AD 640. (One of Mohammed's wives was, however, a Copt.) Nowadays though Coptic females may occasionally marry Moslem males, marriages between male Copts and Moslem females are

CRISIS AND DEVELOPMENT IN EGYPT

extremely rare. When one of ex-King Farouk's sisters, Fathia, married a Copt, pressure from the Moslem community forced him to disown and disinherit her. General Naguib during his tenure of office took what were considered to be extraordinary steps to maintain a solid, good relationship with the Coptic community; for instance, he was the first prime minister in Egyptian history ever to send official greetings to the Copts on their Christmas Day, January 7.

Also some 65,000 Jews live in Egypt, who form an aggressive and powerful community concentrated mostly in Cairo and Alexandria. With these too Naguib, a firm believer in religious tolerance, sought amicable relations. Although he was—and is—a profoundly devout Moslem and was a conspicuous army commander in the Egyptian war against Israel (1948-49), he worked hard for religious amity between Arabs and Jews within Egypt itself.[5] He often visited the principal synagogue in Cario, and had cordial relations with its rabbi. His Christmas card in 1952 was a picture of a mosque, a synagogue, and a Coptic church together, under the inscription, "Religion is for God; the country is for all."

Finally we should have a word about the Nubians. These are black people from the Upper Nile, with tribal scars carved in their cheeks; they have a complex history going back to the remotest antiquity, and are largely employed these days as house servants in Cairo and the cities. The Nubian desert flanking their riverain villages is so desolate that it practically makes the rest of the Sahara look like a garden. Also Egypt has some 50,000 Bedouin nomads in this area, desert dwellers who live in portable black tents. The Nubian (sometimes called Berberine) homes and villages are curious. Almost every wall has a plate, cup or saucer set into the exterior plaster; these are trophies from the hotels or houses where the Nubians work as cooks and the like, and are proudly displayed as a kind of badge of metropolitan experience.

*

We have come a long way now from the Africa of feudal Morocco, the Saharan wastes, and Libya. Egypt as a whole compares to the Fezzan as, let us say, New York City compares to a village in Tehuantepec. Egypt—the Arabic name for the country is Misr—not only has a past; it has a present. This is a vital, brilliant, and exciting country, bursting with contemporary reality. It has a modern railway system, good roads (at least in the Nile Delta) and a flourishing virile commerce. Its national income, almost three

[5] Incidentally Egypt and Israel are *still* at war technically speaking. A truce stopped the actual fighting, but no peace treaty has ever been signed.

billion dollars a year, is very high for Africa, and it has a markedly articulate press and radio. Take merely the matter of people in the educated class—politicians, jurists, scientists, men of affairs. When I began this chapter I planned to include a brief Egyptian "Who's Who"; I had to drop the idea for lack of space, since to give even the lightest sampling of Egypt's intellectual wealth I would have had to include at least a hundred names. Still: it is ludicrous to attempt even the briefest, barest sketch of Egypt without mentioning at least—to pick at random—men of such challenging distinction as Abdul Rahman Azzam, the former secretary general of the Arab League, or Dr. Mahmoud Fawzy, the subtle-minded and delicately voiced foreign minister.

One remarkable personality is a woman, Madame Doria Shafik. She is a poetess of distinction, a journalist and publisher, the leader of the Egyptian feminist movement, a signal political force, and, together with all this, one of the most exotically beautiful women in the Middle East. Madame Shafik is the founder and leader of the Bent el-Nil (Daughters of the Nile). Egypt has had a lively feminist movement for at least thirty years, which stands for the emancipation of women, full equality in suffrage, and the like; it fought polygamy and the veil.[6] Madame Shafik—her story is far too long to tell in this space—is the contemporary leader of Egyptian feminists. She is thirty-seven, a Ph.D. from the Sorbonne, and the mother of two children; one of her magazines has a position comparable to that of the *Ladies' Home Journal* in the United States. Early in 1951 she led a corps of militant suffragettes into the Cairo parliament; in 1954 she went on an eight-day hunger strike, in an effort to force Nasser-Naguib to give full voting rights to women.[7]

CAIRO (in Arabic El Kahira) is by far the biggest city in Africa and is probably the richest and most sophisticated. Its population has risen from somewhere around a million twenty years ago to more than two and a half million today, and it is the largest city in the Moslem world. It covers an area twice that of Paris. There are only two cities in all Africa with a population of more than a million, and both are Egyptian: Cairo and ALEXANDRIA, which Alexander the Great founded in 331 BC and built in the shape of a

---

[6] Only about 4 per cent of Egyptian males are polygamous these days, and most women wear western dress, at least in the upper classes. A great many men still walk the streets of Cairo in costumes that look like white nightgowns, but comparatively few women are veiled.

[7] Naguib did not want to go so far as this, but in other respects the Egyptian government seeks zealously to protect women and their interests. A decree of December 10, 1953, provides that any man caught "flirting" with a woman on the streets shall be subject to seven days in jail. New York *Herald Tribune*, December 11, 1953.

Macedonian cloak. Cairo has the Pyramids and that nice old noseless lady the Sphinx; it has buses made in England run by chauffeurs made in the Sudan; its aristocracy has weekend lodges on the edge of the desert called "tents," and houseboats on the Nile extraordinarily luxurious and effete. Cairo has a grasping mercantile class and slums packed with blind beggars; it has the greatest Islamic institution of learning in the world, Al Azhar University, and a splendid modern secular university as well,[8] with 27,000 students between them; it has streets that look as if they might be in Chicago, and others where the palms rise like slim vases for a hundred feet, and then burst into an umbrella of green bloom. Part of the glamour of Cairo went forever when Shepheard's Hotel, with its celebrated terrace, was burned down in the riots of January, 1952. The most breath-taking objects of art I have ever seen are the golden ornaments and utensils taken from the tomb of King Tutankhamen, now on permanent display at the National Museum. The telephone girls in the Cairo hotels have to be quinquelingual, and sometimes they know a sixth language—Turkish—in addition to the Arabic, French, English, Greek, and Italian that are obligatory. In Cairo you can eat a dessert made of olives soaked in honey. Out by Mena House one of the camels is named Miss Telephone, and another Baby New York City.

Cairo has changed beyond belief since I first saw it a score of years ago. The difference is not merely in such realms as neon lighting, air conditioning (so rare in most of Africa), and the cliffs of modern apartment buildings along the river. In the 1930's and during the war fashionable Cairo had practically the texture of a British town. There were all manner of Oriental trimmings, to be sure, and East met West in a maelstrom of conglomerate internationalism, but the basic overlay was British. Nowadays Britons are not much in evidence. The garrison has long since been evacuated, and not since 1936 has any British High Commissioner driven regally through the streets in an armored cavalcade. The cafés and bars are packed with Egyptians, not Englishmen. (Many Egyptians, even if they are good Moslems, drink.)

Just one word on the Pyramids. A pyramid is a tomb, no more and no less. The Egyptian pharaohs built their tombs so big for the same reason that a monarch in Europe liked to leave behind him a big palace, and also to make their remains totally secure. A pyramid is the most indestructible of architectural shapes. A tower may fall; a wall may crumble. But nothing is ever apt to disturb the masonry in a structure like the Great Pyramid of Cheops, which contains 2½ million blocks of stone and weighs 4,883,000 tons. How was it possible for the ancient Egyptians to erect such enormous monuments?

[8] Once called Fuad University and now known as the University of Cairo.

(1) Slave labor. (2) The Nile. The stone blocks were floated on barges to the foot of the desert, when the Nile reached the proper level, and then hauled up ramps by the muscle power of thousands of slaves. No people have ever believed in a future life more unquestioningly than the old Egyptians; hence, their tombs were provisioned with every necessity, from food to vehicles, from weapons to cosmetics. Grains of wheat found in Luxor have in recent years been planted in France; after five thousand years, they produced a crop. The pharaohs took every conceivable precaution to render their tombs permanently inviolate; yet they were ravaged and looted by marauders almost from the beginning. A great deal of nonsense has been written about mummification. Actually the process, though it still has aspects not completely cleared up, presents no big technical problems; the secret is not so secret as the composition of the embalming fluid the Russians used for Lenin, or what goes into some American soft drinks. First the internal organs of the dead Pharaoh were withdrawn from the body through the nearest orifice; for instance, the brain was siphoned out through the nostrils.[9] The body was then pickled in a kind of brine for an indeterminate period. It was then dried out, rubbed with resin, and wrapped very tight in rags dipped in resin. When a mummy is uncovered today, the flesh is death-colored, a dull ivory; on exposure to the air it instantly turns black.

Most Egyptologists think that the chances of finding another tomb as fabulously rich and grandiose as that of King Tutankhamen are remote. Few royal tombs remain nowadays that are not accounted for. Yet scarcely a month passes without some new discovery—major or minor—in the Egyptian sand. In 1954 no less a trophy than the Cheops funeral ship was discovered in a sealed corridor near the Great Pyramid. To find this here was like walking into a bank every inch of which is familiar and coming across an unknown and unsuspected vault with a million dollars in it.

What Cairo—and Egypt—live on mostly is cotton; without cotton (and the Nile) the country would die. Egypt produces the finest long-staple cotton in the world, and from cotton it gets not less than *four-fifths* of its foreign exchange, i.e., its imports; few countries have an economy more vulnerable. The cotton yield per acre is 438 pounds as against 339 in the United States. Cotton was introduced into Egypt by Mohammed Ali in the 1820's, and, strangely enough, the American Civil War forty years later made it the basis of Egyptian wealth; when Lancashire could not buy cotton from the American south, the British textile industry had to turn to Egypt instead.[10] For years the British played politics with Egyptian cotton; they were by far

---

[9] C. W. Ceram, *Gods, Graves, and Scholars*, p. 169.
[10] See Emil Ludwig, *The Nile*, p. 545.

the best customer and—until recently—could always keep the country in line by limiting their cotton purchases. The Nasser regime wants, if possible, to broaden the basis of Egyptian economy, and make it less critically dependent on one export crop. For instance, a big petroleum hunt is going on, with several American companies participating. To have permitted this marks a substantial reversal in Cairo policy. For a long time the Egyptians, being on the point of getting rid of the hated British at last, would not tolerate even the faintest idea of letting other "imperialist" interests enter the country. But Nasser wants above all to bridge the yawning, desolate gap in Egypt between rich and poor. And, as Dorothy Thompson pointed out in a recent brief article, the Nasser government cannot begin to share wealth on any extensive scale until new wealth is created.

Nasser's plans are so ambitiously wide in this direction as to be almost grandiose. Political consolidation must come first, but Nasser and his men never cease to think in terms of future long-range economic development, so that the standard of living of the masses as a whole may be raised. General Naguib, when he was still prime minister, told me pithily that "no exploitation can be worse than overexploitation." He added, *"Egyptians* have been exploited, but not Egypt. Let us try to make the great wealth of Egypt available to the *people*." I asked four different Egyptians of the most varied background what the country needed most. All answered with a single identical word, "Production." One huge project, which will cost more than $500,-000,000 and take ten years to build, is a new dam, the Saad el Ali (High Dam) scheme. This will be in the form of a "pyramidal granite rock field half a kilometer thick," to be situated near Aswan; if all goes well, it will increase the total arable land in the country from 6,000,000 to 8,000,000 acres, and increase national production by $450,000,000 per year.[11] At least three other auxiliary projects, one to be partially financed by Point Four aid from the United States, are designed to make more land cultivable, stimulate rice production, convert 700,000 acres of one-crop land in Upper Egypt to perennial irrigation, and increase the agricultural yield per acre.[12] A large fertilizer plant, to cost $72,000,000 and capable of producing 375,000 tons of nitrates annually, is to be built and worked by electricity from Aswan Dam. There are all manner of other projected industrial developments. A German company, Demag of Duisburg, is building a $45,000,000 iron and steel plant at

---

[11] These and details below are from an article by Nasser, "The Egyptian Revolution," in *Foreign Affairs*, January, 1955. See also Dana Adams Schmidt in the New York *Times*, October 22, 1954. One projected scheme is to reclaim "50,000 acres ... by piping water under the Suez Canal to the Sinai desert, for use in resettling Arab refugees from Palestine."

[12] More on the problem of the land below.

Helwan, to make use of iron ore reserves near Aswan. It will be owned 51 per cent by the Egyptian government. Factories for paper, jute, beet sugar, automobile tires, and so on, are in the planning stage. A minimum wage law was passed, and about $200,000,000 has been budgeted for immediate social services.

*

One curse of Egypt is illiteracy; another is disease. Probably three-quarters of the population cannot read or write. But this is a misleading figure, because it includes women, who until comparatively recent years had no access to schooling at all; the illiteracy figure for males alone is around 50 per cent. Even so, it is only too obvious that it is going to be difficult in the extreme to make representative government work well in Egypt—or work at all—until these figures are modified. Education (as in all African countries) is the most imperative and pressing problem that the government faces. In 1920, under the British, the budget for education was roughly £1,000,000; today, it is more than £20,000,000. In 1922, there were exactly three public secondary schools in the whole of Egypt; today, 765. I have even heard Egyptians—progressive Egyptians—say, "We are going too fast. The university is too big. There are too many students. There will be no jobs for them, and, just as in the Balkans in the old days, they will become postal clerks and then revolutionaries. Moreover our standards of education are not good enough. We must at all costs avoid the peril of creating a *half*-educated class."

Many Oriental countries go through a period, long or short, when they probably *need* dictatorship. Nasser's chief justification for arbitrary rule is that he acts solely as an agent or deputy of the people, until they are educated enough to handle the responsibilities of full self-government themselves. Of course other dictators have said this before. One trouble with dictators is that, as a rule, they are tempted to keep on dictating after the need for them has passed. "Dictatorship is like a giant beech tree—very fine, but nothing grows underneath it," Stanley Baldwin once said. Nasser, however, is a man of such strong basic good will and intelligence as well as patriotism that he is not likely to fall into the mistakes dictators so often make.

In Egypt and elsewhere in Africa the "quick-death" diseases—pneumonic plague, smallpox, typhus—have by and large been beaten; the debilitating or disabling maladies remain. Almost all Egyptians have amoebic dysentery at one time or other, and 64 per cent are believed to suffer from intestinal worms. There is no place in the world, I imagine, where the visitor sees so much blindness, particularly among children, as in Egypt. Trachoma, ocular gonorrhea, and other eye diseases, carried mostly by flies, are appallingly prevalent. Egypt has, in fact, 150,000 totally blind persons and probably 3,570,000 victims of trachoma—figures proportionately higher than anywhere else in the world.[13] The disease that causes most trouble is, however, something else—an extraordinary ailment known as bilharzia, a form of schistosomiasis sometimes called the "snail disease." The case may very well be made that the most important issue in Egypt is not the price of cotton or the future intentions of Colonel Nasser, but this miserable complaint bilharzia. Almost 50 per cent of all Egyptians have it. Only rarely is it immediately fatal, but it causes profound weakness and debilitation over years, through irritation of the liver, bladder, and other organs. Bilharzia is a disease of water, and anybody can catch it—not only in Egypt but in many other parts of Africa—by simple contact with infected water. You can get it by swimming, fishing, paddling, or even boating in water where the snail happens to exist. All over Africa the traveler will be well advised to remember the maxim, "Never wash in *still* water," because agitated or running water is less apt to be infected. The disease is a particularly serious problem in Egypt because the fertile parts of the country are irrigated by the Nile, and peasants at work in the fields—especially rice fields—are unavoidably in contact with water most of the time. Bilharzia is caused by a tiny parasite, so sharp and agile that it can enter the skin even if there is no fissure, which passes part of its life cycle in the body of a variety of snail, which in turn lives in Nile or other water.

EGYPT: THE PERMANENT REALITIES

> The higher Nilus swells,
> The more it promises: as it ebbs, the seedsman
> Upon the slime and ooze scatters his grain,
> And shortly comes to harvest.
> —ANTONY AND CLEOPATRA, ACT II, SCENE 5

First, the land. Egypt covers 386,198 square miles (about twice the size of California) but of this *not less than 96.5 per cent* is uninhabitable desert. The tiny inhabitable area consists of the Nile valley, its Delta, and a few scattered oases. Only about six million acres in the whole of Egypt are under cultivation. Cultivation is made possible by irrigation from the basic fact of the country's existence, the River Nile.

[13] Kennett Love, New York *Times*, November 26, 1953. The Rockefeller Foundation and other American (and United Nations) institutions have a long record of useful service in matters of Egyptian public health, particularly in regard to eye complaints.

Second, population pressure. Egypt had by the 1947 census—none has been taken since—a population of 19,087,304. Today the figure is probably between twenty-one and twenty-two million. Practically all of these millions are squeezed into the green fertile thread of the Nile valley, with the result that the density of population here is the highest in the world, about 1,600 per square mile.[14] Moreover the population has for years grown at an astonishing pace, and will presumably continue to do so. It has increased by 100 per cent in forty years, and soars nowadays at the unbelievable rate of 350,000 per year. "The only thing that grows in Egypt and stays in the country," said my friend the university professor, "is the population. We are a nation smothered by ourselves." He paused with an ironic chuckle. "One fault is that most of our four thousand villages do not have electric light. There is nothing for the people to do after sundown except have sexual intercourse."

Make more land. Make fewer people. Either of these solutions would alleviate the problem, but neither is easy. The desert is difficult to irrigate, and the rank and file of Egyptians are not educated enough to understand the necessity for birth control.[15] A possible future remedy may be industrialization, as indicated above, and Nasser has marked ambitions in this direction. The lesson of history is that as industrialization increases and the standard of living goes up, the birthrate tends to diminish. As things stand today the only check on the irresistible advance of population is infant mortality. This reaches in Egypt the staggering figure of 129 per 1,000 (as against 29.2 per 1,000 in the United States). The average life expectancy of an Egyptian at birth is only about thirty-seven years.

Not only are millions of Egyptians jammed together in the narrowest of spaces; inequalities in the ownership of land are extreme. There are about 2,700,000 landowners in all; of these more than two million own less than an acre each. Eighty-five per cent of the total population of Egypt is altogether landless. But 2,000 rich pashas own no fewer than 1,200,000 acres; *36 per cent of all cultivable land in the country is in the hands of one-half of one per cent of the population.*

The Egyptian pashas were—until recently—not only probably the richest class of their kind in the world, in comparison to the rest of the people,

---

[14] The density of population per square mile of cultivated land in the United States is 210.

[15] Strikingly enough the Rector of Alexandria University recently made a public pronouncement to the effect that nothing in Moslem theology forbids birth control. But it will be a long time before birth control percolates down to the masses. Many patriotic young Egyptians—instead of marrying several wives before they are twenty—now defer marriage until they are in their mid-thirties and then remain monogamous. They do not want to add the burden of surplus children to the nation.

but the most corrupt. During the war when I visited Egypt the saying was that forty new millionaires were created every month, largely through graft. Ex-King Farouk was the country's largest single landowner. He derived from a tradition opulent and extravagant beyond belief; his grandfather the Khedive Ismail owned one-fifth of *all* cultivable property in the entire country, and nevertheless borrowed from Europe the neat sum of $495,000,000 in a reign lasting sixteen years. In recent times it has been calculated that a full 50 per cent of the Egyptian national income went to 1.5 per cent of the population.[16] Another exacerbating factor was that the landowning aristocracy had, by and large, practically no interest in the country (except to draw money out of it); it sprang from the Turks and did not even consider itself to be Egyptian.

In contrast the lot of the submerged millions of fellahin on the soil (*fellah*=plowman) was miserable beyond description. It still is. The fellah lives with his water buffalo in mud, slime, and penury. A recent survey by Rockefeller Foundation scientists found that living standards in Egyptian villages were lower than anywhere in the civilized world, and that the *average* income in Egypt is only about $87 per year.

Nasser-Naguib on reaching power set out at once to make a land reform. It is too early to estimate the results. In principle the big estates are to be broken up, and all individual land holdings limited to two hundred acres. What the lush aristocracy thought of this can easily be imagined. Screams of bloody murder reverberated up and down the Nile. Some people were even stupid enough to whisper balefully the word "Communism!" Of course nothing could possibly be a more fruitful hotbed for Communist agitation than Egyptian society unreformed, with the fellah permanently glued to his mire. Reforms like those that Colonel Nasser seeks to put into effect are, it is only too manifest to people of good will, the best possible defense *against* future Communist advance.

A HANDFUL OF DATES

And they spoiled the Egyptians.
—EXODUS 12:36

1805–1849. Modern Egyptian history begins with the remarkable military adventurer and despot Mohammed Ali, founder of the dynasty which lasted till Nasser-Naguib ousted the contemptible Farouk. Mohammed Ali was born in Macedonia of Albanian descent and did not have a drop of Egyptian

[16] *The Emergence of Modern Egypt*, published by the Foreign Policy Association, p. 35.

blood. He commanded a detachment of Albanian mercenaries in the service of the Turks, who sent him to Egypt to fight Napoleon. He stayed there after the French withdrew, and created his own rule. Technically Egypt remained part of the Ottoman Empire but in actuality it was ruled for the next century by Mohammed Ali and his successors, who were known (till 1922) as Khedives. Mohammed Ali was a savage in some respects—a famous episode is his treacherous murder of the Mamelukes—but a man of commanding grasp and stature. He died in 1849.

In 1953 the Egyptian government passed a law confiscating the property of all of Mohammed Ali's descendants, i.e., the royal family. About 350 Egyptians and sixty Turkish citizens resident in Egypt were affected, and the total sum involved was put at $558,000,000.

1882. The British occupation of Egypt began, and lasted for fifty-four years. The provoking factor leading to British intervention was the rise to power of the first fellah ever to play an important role in Egyptian history, a peasant leader named Ahmed Arabi. Arabi was the founder of modern Egyptian nationalism.[17] The British were watching affairs in Egypt with possessive care, because the Suez Canal had been opened in 1869 and Egypt, even more obviously than before, was an irreplaceably vital pivot in communications to India and beyond. Moreover the reign of the Khedive Ismail had exploded in a phantasmagoric carnival of corruption and extravagance. Both the British and French felt that Arabi's rise, no matter how amply it was justified by the Khedivial tyranny, menaced their interests. The British bombarded Alexandria to destroy Arabi's military power and occupied Cairo. Arabi was sent off to exile in Ceylon. Nominally Egypt still remained a Turkish dominion under its own autonomous Khedive, but the British became rulers in fact, and Sir Evelyn Baring (later Lord Cromer) ran Egypt practically singlehanded for more than twenty years.

For the first time in this book we assess British colonial intentions. The British did not culpably grab off Egypt as a matter of explicit imperial policy. The evolution was much more subtle and complex than that. Mr. Gladstone was a convinced, if spasmodic, anti-imperialist. One biographer of Lord Cromer puts it this way: "It may indeed be said without hesitation that . . . Mr. Gladstone's governments were looking in any direction except that in which they were moving. They were caught up in the tide and swept along in the direction of a military occupation, but they went protesting, and when they found themselves in possession of the country, they did so to their own dismayed astonishment and utterly against their will."[18] Conquest

---

[17] In 1954 the Nasser government made a grant of £20,000 to his descendants, in recognition of his role in Egyptian history.
[18] Ludwig, *op. cit.*, p. 559, quotes this from Lord Zetland.

CRISIS AND DEVELOPMENT IN EGYPT 197

it was; but conquest despite itself—in the name of God, trade, and the Pax Britannica.

In 1883, immediately after the occupation, Lord Granville announced that Great Britain intended to withdraw her forces from Egypt "as soon as the state of the country ... will admit of it." But in 1955 British forces had not yet left Suez.

Policy in London was one thing; policy as advocated by empire builders out in the field was something else again. The following passage is from Richard Burton, the celebrated explorer and Orientalist, and is a summary of his recommendations in regard to Egypt in 1888. It gives a rare, pungent whiff of what imperialism was like in the good old days:

> First and far away, annex Egypt and all its territory entirely; but if the Government does not decide on this bold stroke, at least have no half-measures ...
> Oblige the Sudanese to give up their arms, and abolish the useless expense of the Egyptian Army and Navy.
> Garrison with English troops Alexandria, Cairo, Suez, Ismailíyyeh, Port Said, Suákin, Masáwwah, one fortress at Perim, one at Rossier (the point between Suez and Akabah), and one fortress on the Akabah side.
> Station one Man-of-War at each of the following posts:—Alexandria, Port Said, Suez, Suákin, Masáwwah; a gunboat at Perim, Rossier, Ismailíyyeh, and one close to Akabah; say two gunboats in the Suez Canal, and two in the Red Sea to look after the Slave-trade.
> Banish Ismail's sons for ten years ...
> Forbid Slave-trade, and hang at the next tree or nearest yard-arm all Slave-dealers caught red-handed after date of proclamation.[19]

But also Burton recommended exemption of the peasantry from taxes for five years, full religious liberty, building of railways and irrigation projects, education, freedom of foreign trade, and industrialization. "Help the Egyptians to improve themselves." Also: "After seven years, give them a free press; they are not fit to have any press just now."

Colonel Nasser wrote in *Foreign Affairs* (January, 1955): "From the outset the British sapped the strength and moral energies of Egypt. Foreign business, which under the system of privileges known as the Capitulations operated free from all taxation, easily dominated the emerging Egyptian commercial class."

Nasser proceeds to plead his case:

> They [the British] always said they were on the point of leaving, and always found an excuse to stay. At first they claimed they were in Egypt to protect the foreigners against the Egyptians, although the

---

[19] *Life of Sir Richard Burton*, by Isabel Burton, Vol. II, pp. 295-6.

foreigners never asked for their protection; then they claimed they had to stay to protect the Christian and Jewish minorities against the Moslems, overlooking the fact that the Christians and the Jews had joined the Moslems in demanding the withdrawal of the British forces from Egypt. The defense of the Suez Canal and the maintenance of their lines of communication with India and their Far Eastern Empire were further pretexts. When World War II came they said they could not go because the Suez Canal was an important base, and after World War II they explained that they had to stay to safeguard the interests of the free world.

I asked a senior British diplomat in Cairo to summarize the pros and cons of British rule since 1882. "There is no doubt that we were very, *very*, VERY naughty. On the other hand we did a great deal for Egypt. We built the Aswan Dam."

This quotation is a nice example of typical upper-class self-criticism and understatement. The British did much more for Egypt than build the Aswan Dam. Two points at least should be made on the British side: first, their techniques in the early days did no more than reflect the temper of the times; perhaps they are immoral by today's standards, but they were not immoral in the light of international conventions then; second, British policy in Egypt served not only imperial but democratic world interests. It would not have been pleasant to have had Germans in charge of Suez in either World War I or II. Also: Egypt would not be as well equipped for independence as it is today had not it been for British tutelage. Still again: British rule may have been "manipulative," but it was never tyrannical. London might have made Egypt an outright colony at any time, but never did so.

1914. On the outbreak of World War I Great Britain did, however, make Egypt a "protectorate," thus finally severing the tie with Turkey.

1918. The first of the great nationalist parties of modern Africa, the Wafd (the name means "delegation" in Arabic) came into being under the patient, implacable leadership of Zaghlul Pasha. He had a command of the Egyptian masses almost like that of Gandhi in India. I met Zaghlul in Cairo many years ago. He had a face like a parchment mask and a mind like a vise. He was subtle as a snake charmer, tenacious, and tough as gristle. In 1919 came a serious insurrection against the British, led by Zaghlul. In 1921 came a passive resistance campaign, patterned by Zaghlul on the civil disobedience movement in India.

From Zaghlul's day to this, practically all Egyptian politicians except outright tools have been anti-British. Parties formed and re-formed, and the Wafd had many sinuous ups and downs, but basic nationalist policy always remained the same—freedom from British rule.

1922. The British were forced to bestow on Egypt an agreement giving the country limited independence; the protectorate was terminated, and Fuad (father of Farouk) assumed the title of King. But the British reserved to themselves liberty of action in four supremely important spheres: protection of foreign interests, security of imperial communications, defense, and the Sudan. Even so Egypt had come a long way forward. A constitution was written, the Wafd won a terrific electoral victory; in 1924 Zaghlul (after several periods of exile) became prime minister.

1924. Sir Lee Stack, the British *sirdar* (commander-in-chief) of the Egyptian army and Governor General of the Sudan, was assassinated by a nationalist fanatic. Great Britain took sharp reprisals, particularly in regard to the Sudan.

1927. Zaghlul died, and was succeeded as leader of the Wafd by Nahas Pasha, the son of a fellah.

1936. Signature of a new Anglo-Egyptian treaty ended a period of prolonged strain, intrigue, and inflammatory discontent. Egypt gained virtually complete independence. The British High Commissioner became an ambassador, and British troops left Cairo. Egypt was admitted to the League of Nations as a sovereign state in 1937. There were two reasons for British willingness to give Egypt independence at last. One was basic. The pattern is familiar, and will be more familiar before this book is done. It is that the British had the shrewdness and good sense to realize that they were hurting their own best interests by seeking to remain in Egypt against the will of the overwhelming bulk of the population. To remain was too expensive. Their position could not be maintained without endless and monstrous cost. They would gain rather than lose by getting out. A second, subsidiary reason was the Italian invasion of Ethiopia, which alarmed British and Egyptians both.

1942. Egypt stayed technically neutral during World War II until 1944 although the British—and Americans—used Cairo as an essential base for operations everywhere in the Middle East. It served the allied purpose to have Egypt remain what was euphemistically called "a non-fighting ally." In blunt fact, plenty of leading Egyptians—and several officers then youthful and unknown who are conspicuous in the Nasser circle today—wanted the Axis to win the war, not the British. They were delighted when Marshal Rommel and his Afrika Korps pounded close to the gates of Cairo. Then on February 4, 1942, came a fantastic imbroglio. Farouk (who had succeeded his father and who was strongly under Italian influence) had a pro-Axis prime minister named Aly Maher, an able citizen who is still a considerable force in Cairene affairs. The British demanded that Farouk throw him out in favor of somebody more complaisant to the Allies. Farouk refused. Thereupon the

British surrounded Abdin palace in Cairo, the royal residence, with tanks and by a *coup de main* forced Farouk to accept their candidate.

This was, incredibly enough, none other than Nahas Pasha, leader of the nationalist Wafd. The British were in a peculiar position. They wanted a strong man with the widest possible popular support, and Nahas was the only such personage available. The Wafd, on its side, though dedicated from its foundation to expelling the British from Egypt, had by this time become much less anti-British than before. To rule at all, the Wafd had to play the British game to an extent, if only to be stronger vis-à-vis the pro-Axis palace. It is true that the wily Nahas had been making fiery anti-British speeches almost up to the moment of his appointment. Doubtless one reason why the British chose him was to shut him up. Anyway he was forced on Farouk as prime minister.

1951. King Farouk denounced the 1936 treaty and assumed the title King of the Sudan as well as King of Egypt. At this period Egyptian politics were dominated by the "Unity of the Nile Valley" concept. The British protested that abrogation of the treaty was illegal, but there was little they could do about it.

1952 (January 26). Cairo was sacked and in part burned by a mob. Nobody to this day knows for certain who organized this holocaust of pillage and arson. One persistent story is that Communists in the Polish legation in Cairo were the instigators. In the mob itself were dissidents from almost every camp, including the Moslem Brotherhood, anti-British folk at large, and thousands of young men and women who, like a lynch mob in the old American South, joined the demonstration for the fun of it, to let off steam, or because they had nothing else to do.

1952 (July 23). The Nasser-Naguib coup.

CHAPTER 13

Nasser to Naguib to Nasser

> It [the Arab world] has known what it wanted to do away with, but it has not known what it wanted to build . . . The problem was to restore human dignity to Egypt.
> —GAMAL ABDUL NASSER

> Convicted Pashas shiver as they flounder
>   in the river,
> And Nile-green Incorruptibles emerge . . .
>
>   The need for a detergent
>   Admittedly was urgent,
> But what can wash the waters of the Nile?
> —SAGITTARIUS

LIEUTENANT COLONEL Gamal Abdul Nasser (correctly Gamel Abd Al Nasir) was born on January 5, 1918, and is of modest bourgeois background. His father was a post-office clerk in Alexandria; his mother was the daughter of a businessman. From the age of seventeen Nasser had strong revolutionary tendencies. He was several times arrested for participation in student riots. He went to the Renaissance Secondary School in Cairo, studied law for a time, and then decided to devote himself to the army. He was commissioned in 1938, served for a time in the Sudan, and fought against the Jews in Israel. But even while campaigning in Palestine he records that he was fully aware that the "real" battleground would be Egypt itself. One turning point of his life came in February, 1942, when, as mentioned above, the British unleashed tanks and machine guns against Farouk's palace. Nasser had no particular use for Farouk, even in those days, but he was the King, and that he should be humiliated and browbeaten so flagrantly seemed to Nasser an intolerable affront to Egyptian dignity. What an irony it is that it should have been the same Nasser who, ten years later, destooled the profligate King and hurled him out of the country!

Nasser is a tall, large, gracefully built man with remarkable eyes and a big rudder of a nose. His personal habits are exemplary. He lives with complete lack of ostentation in a modest Cairo villa, and his personal life has been happy. He has five youthful children. He is a devout Moslem, and does not touch alcohol. He has acute interest in politics all over the world, and is one of the few African—or European—statesmen who subscribe to such periodicals as *Foreign Affairs* not by ordinary post but by airmail. The dominating aspect of his character is disinterestedness plus force. He cares nothing for himself; all that interests him is the life of Egypt. He is much more reserved and less turbulent than most Egyptians, and his businesslike clarity of manner shows little of the inferiority-superiority sensitiveness and lack of poise that distinguish many of his compatriots.

This is not to say that he has ever lacked emotion. I heard him described as a man of ice—and fire. He took part during the war in an attempt to force the release of the deposed prime minister, Aly Maher, from detention; he looked for guidance for a time to such notorious extremists as Hadj Amin El Husseini, the exiled Grand Mufti of Jerusalem; he was an early member of the Moslem Brotherhood, and on one occasion even flirted with the idea of assassinating the King.

What is more, Nasser took active part in another murder plot which, however, miscarried. He has described this himself, in a series of three articles for the Egyptian magazine *Akher Saa*, entitled "The Philosophy of the Egyptian Revolution," which he wrote in 1953.[1] Few documents of our time are more revealing. It is a rare thing, to put it mildly, for a man who is running a country to confess that only a few years before he had been leader of a murder squad. He does not reveal the name of the intended victim, but describes in considerable detail his own emotions. At this time he and his fellows were convinced that nothing but "positive action," that is political assassination, could save Egypt. His prose is somewhat flowery:

> I remember one night which marked the turning point of my ideas and dreams on this score. We had prepared a group for action and selected a person who we decided must cease to exist. We observed his habits and laid down a detailed plan. We were going to shoot him down as he returned to his home in the night.
> We set up an attack group to do the shooting, a covering force to protect the attack group, and a third group to organize the getaway. The appointed night came, and I went out with the attack group. Everything went according to plan . . .
> The squads concealed themselves in their chosen positions; and when the marked man came by, bullets were sent in his direction.

[1] I have had access to a privately circulated translation of these. They were printed in part in the London *Observer*, October 10, 17, and 24, 1954.

The execution squad withdrew while the covering force protected its retreat, and the getaway to safety began. I started the motor of my car, and drove away from the theater of the positive action we had organized.

But suddenly there resounded in my ear the sounds of screaming and lamentation and the wailing of a woman, the crying of a baby, and then a continuous agitated call for help . . .

I arrived at my house and threw myself on my bed, my mind in a furor and unceasing turmoil in my heart and conscience. The sounds of screaming and lamentation, wailing, and the calls for help continued to ring in my ears.

I didn't sleep all night . . .

Was I right? I answered myself with conviction: I acted for the sake of my country.

Were these the only possible means? I replied, in some doubt: What else could we do?

Is it really possible to change the future of our country by eliminating this or that person, or is the problem deeper than this? . . .

We dream of the glory of the nation. But which is more important, to eliminate those who ought to be eliminated or to bring forward those who should be brought forward?

Then Nasser describes his violent emotion of relief the next morning when he learned that the shots had gone wild, and the victim had escaped without serious injury!

Nasser's articles are of absorbing interest, showing as they do the convulsion of agony that gripped his mind, and also how half-baked some of his thinking was. Ceaselessly he reflected on the weakness of his country, its degradation and shame. Egypt had to be redeemed; it had to be saved not merely from the British[2] but from itself; it had to be made strong, united, free, with a new cleanliness of spirit, with corruption and selfishness abolished. But how?

Nasser took the lead at last in organizing the Free Officers Committee, composed of some four hundred youthful men, most of them under the rank of major. In effect, it is still this body that rules Egypt today. At the top were nine or ten of his closest comrades, who came to be called the *Binbashi* ("major" in Turkish). But even while he was creating this hard corps of revolutionary organization, he continued to be harassed by torturing self-doubt. In his articles he stresses the point over and over again that his role—and the army's—was dictated by fate, by circumstance. What was going on in Egypt was like the Pirandello play, *Six Characters in Search of an Author*. Events were looking for a man, not vice versa. "It was not the army that defined its role in the events that took place; the opposite is closer

---

[2] Nasser uses the locution "the Imperialism" as a synonym for "British."

to the truth. The events and their ramifications defined the role of the army in the great struggle to free the nation." Yet he asks himself—was it *necessary* for the army to do what it did?

Conscientiously he seeks to explore the philosophical background to his action, as well as his own motives. He asks himself, "When did I discover the seeds of revolution within myself?" He thinks that they must have been planted in his subconscious in early childhood, put there "by the generation before us." He records that even as a child he burst into a rebellious shout every time he saw an airplane in the sky:

> Ya 'Azeez, Ya 'Azeez
> Dihiya takhud al-Ingleez!
>
> Oh Almighty, Oh Almighty,
> Disaster take the English!

*

Between the Cairo riots (January 26, 1952), and Nasser's coup (July 23, 1952), the Farouk regime crumbled fast. The desperate King tried one futile prime minister after another. The Wafd had become a feeble, sordid simulacrum of what it had been in the days of old Zaghlul. Corruption was positively orchidaceous. One item making for bitterness was a scandal—shocking even for Egypt—over munitions. Profiteers in Cairo had deliberately supplied the army at the front in the Palestinian War with defective or worthless arms and ammunition, and had made huge profits by this evil enterprise. Senior officers showed their displeasure by electing as chairman of the Officers Club a general almost unknown to the country at large, but one who had made a reputation for decency and courage in the fighting in Israel—Mohammed Naguib—against the King's candidate. Nasser says in his articles that these events were subsidiary—that the coup was inevitable, and was bound to have come in any case—but they played nicely into his hand. Once the King lost the loyalty of the army, he was doomed.

Nine officers composed Nasser's original Revolutionary Council, which grew out of the original Free Officers Committee. Naguib was not among them, but was brought into it because the clique needed an older man, a soldier with authority and prestige, to give it respectability. Nasser plotted the coup, and then sold it to Naguib. The junta, under Nasser's guidance, moved in the early hours of July 23 with force and precision. Tanks commanded strategic points in Cairo, and radio broadcasts announced to the nation that the army had moved "to purify itself." There was no bloodshed or disorder. There were no demonstrations against foreigners—if only because Nasser did not want to give the British any pretext for stepping in.

An incidental point is that the plotters maintained close contact with the American embassy as soon as the coup got underway, and got strong sympathy from Americans in Cairo.

Farouk was forced to abdicate on July 26, and left the country. For a time a regency ruled and then, on June 18, 1953, the monarchy was abolished. The junta set up Aly Maher as its first prime minister, but he did not last long; Naguib replaced him as prime minister and then became president as well.

What ailed Farouk? First, greed; second, lasciviousness. Cairo gossip has it that, following an injury in an automobile accident some years ago, his whole character suddenly changed. From being a slim, handsome young man he became very fat; from being a personage reasonably serious—if spoiled— he turned into a self-indulgent playboy. I met him in Cairo several times during the war. He showed a good deal of dash and spirit—also vanity and capriciousness. Like most kings, he lived in a peculiar private world of his own. Some of his mannerisms were, even then, excessive. Leaving a night club one evening he reached in his pocket for a handful of coins and slithered them over the dance floor with the gesture of a child skipping stones across water; no doubt this was his manner of tipping the waiters. The thing he talked to me about most, politics aside, was whether or not he would be a success in Hollywood and how, above everything else in life, he wanted to meet Miss Ginger Rogers. His income was around £2,000,000 per year, and he had four palaces, two yachts, a squadron of "personal aviation," and carloads of erotica. One thing may be said about Farouk with the utmost assurance; not a soul in Egypt regretted his departure outside of his own small loop of henchmen, and probably not a soul survives who wants him back.

*

In the articles cited above Colonel Nasser strikes an important fundamental note in this passage:

> Our real crisis in my view is that we are going through two revolutions, not merely one. Every people on earth goes through two revolutions, a political revolution by which it wrests the right to govern itself from the hand of tyranny or from the army stationed upon its soil against its will; and a social revolution involving the conflict of the classes and which settles down when justice is secured to the inhabitants of the united nation.
>
> Peoples preceding us on the path of human progress have passed through two revolutions, but they have not had to face both at once . . . But as for us, the terrible experience through which our people is going is that we are having both revolutions at once.
>
> The political revolution, to be successful, must attain the objective

of uniting all the elements of the nation, binding them together solidly, and instilling the ideal of self-abnegation for the sake of the country as a whole. But the social revolution, from the moment of its first appearance, shakes values and loosens principles, and sets the citizenry as individuals and as classes to fighting each other. It gives free rein to corruption, doubt, hatred . . . and egotism.

We are caught between the millstones of the two revolutions we are fated now to be going through. One revolution makes it obligatory for us to unite and love one another and fight side by side to the death; the other forces dissention upon us in spite of our desires, we are blackened by hatreds, and each of us thinks only of himself.

In spite of these reflections Nasser apparently hoped that, once he threw out the King and set up a new government, the people would automatically rally to him and stay rallied, in pursuit of the shining ideals of the revolutionary movement. Indeed mass demonstrations of unprecedented size and enthusiasm—demonstrations such as Egypt had never seen before, with hundreds of thousands of people massed in the streets—did take place. This was when Naguib was titular leader of the junta. But to have a lot of people out in the streets is not the same thing as successful government. To re-create a country overnight is not easy, or, as Nasser puts it, "to develop the mature political consciousness that is an indispensable preliminary for a sound democracy." There had to be the sternest kind of activity on at least three fronts—first to get the mechanics of government into smooth operation, second to clean out and punish personages guilty of corruption and other crimes in the previous regime, and third to make the new government secure against the danger of a counter coup.

The Council of Revolutionary Command—executive body of the junta—was increased in membership from nine to fourteen, and then pared down to eleven. Its motto was Unity, Order, Work. But even here at the very top, trouble came. Two at least of the original group have been ousted and either exiled or imprisoned. One of these was a Communist. The Council contains several red-hot socialists today, but no Communists. The word in Cairo at the beginning—among bitter enemies of Nasser-Naguib—was that the junta was "90 per cent Fascist, 10 per cent Communist." This was a gross exaggeration, if only because the inner struggle for power was based on personalities, not ideology. If the government took measures that savored strongly of state capitalism, it was because private capitalism had ceased to function fruitfully. Things were astoundingly mixed up.

Nasser-Naguib borrowed ideas from Fascism, but they were much less totalitarian and extremist than those who opposed them. Their methods may have been totalitarian, but not the basic aim. Membership in the new

Liberation Rally was voluntary, not obligatory. There was no accent on force for force's sake. Almost at once every effort was made to work out a system of constitutional reform, and pave the way for free elections and the resumption of democratic government. The army was the protector of the people, and the revolution was in the people's name.

One early watchword was "Clean up!" The junta set out to rub some of the slime off Egypt's oily surface. A three-man revolutionary tribunal was set up, more or less on the model of the French Revolution, under the chairmanship of a youthful air officer, Abdel Latif Boghdady, who was minister of war.[3] The sentences it meted out were mild on the whole—except in a few instances of outright treason. The purge affected almost every sphere of Egyptian society, and a weird collection of characters met judgment. All political leaders of the Wafd, Liberal Constitutional, and Saadist parties who had held ministerial office between 1942 and 1952 were deprived of all political rights until 1964. This made a clean sweep of the old politicians. Dozens of army officers, career diplomats, and university professors were purged. Nahas Pasha—now known simply as Mustafa el Nahas—was jailed, and his wife, Zeinab el Wakil, who had been one of the real rulers of Egypt in the last days of the monarchy, was found guilty of fraud and corruption and had some $3,000,000 worth of property confiscated. Two of the leading journalists in the country, the brothers Mahmoud Abul Fath and Hussein Abul Fath, got suspended sentences of ten and fifteen years respectively, on charges of corruption. A former prime minister, Ibrahim Abdel Hadi, who had been involved in scandals during the Palestine war, was actually sentenced to death for "high treason and conspiracy with a foreign power." This sentence was, however, later commuted. Several personages in Farouk's entourage got long sentences, as did one member of the short-lived regency council and at least two Wafdist ministers. The notorious Fuad Serag el-Din, who had been secretary general of the Wafd party and a cabinet minister of commanding power, got fifteen years. But Egyptians are an unrevengeful people. Soon almost all these sentences were suspended.

One persistent, almost ineradicable source of dissidence and turmoil was the Moslem Brotherhood. This, a body which combined extreme nationalist aims with a kind of fundamentalist religious fanaticism, was not so much a party as a movement. It grew up after World War II, and had several million members at the height of its power. It wanted freedom from Britain above all, believed in political terrorism, and assassinated two Egyptian prime ministers and other folk. At one time Nasser, as I have

[3] Later this zealous officer became minister of municipal and rural affairs; seldom in Egypt has anybody made things hum more.

already mentioned, belonged to this organization, and so probably did several other members of the cabinet and the Council of Revolutionary Command. Also it was penetrated strongly by Communists. Nasser-Naguib tried to co-operate with the Brotherhood at first. A certain identity of purpose linked them, particularly in religious matters. But they were bound to come into conflict, if only because there was not room in Egypt for two revolutionary mass movements. The Brotherhood began to make agitation against the government, and in January, 1954, it was suppressed; 450 of its leaders were arrested, two thousand local headquarters were shut down, and $8,500,000 of its funds were confiscated. But it refused to stay suppressed. Its supreme "guide," Hassan El Hodeiby, was released from jail after a time and trouble began anew. In October came an attempt by members of the Brotherhood to assassinate Nasser; eight shots were fired against him, but he escaped untouched. This time the government moved against the Brotherhood in real earnest, and it was crushed and broken up to such an extent that it is doubtful if it can ever rise again. Six members implicated in the murder plot against Nasser were hanged, and so was its secretary general, Abdel Kader Auda. El Hodeiby, an old friend of Nasser's, was "sent in irons to Toura prison to break stones for the rest of his life."[4]

The October episode also served to end General Naguib as a political force. He was removed from office (November, 1954) and placed under arrest. Probably he had nothing to do with the plot against Nasser, but Brotherhood terrorists said that they planned to make a new revolutionary government under his (Naguib's) leadership. Whether or not the General was aware of this conspiracy to make use of him is unknown.

*

The breakup of the Nasser-Naguib relationship is one of the saddest of contemporary political episodes. Naguib had great quality and brought much to the revolution. The two men complemented each other nicely. Nasser was the brain, the theoretician, the organizer; Naguib was the doughty and incorruptible man of action, wildly popular with the masses. For a time there was a profound fondness between the two partners as well as close political affiliation. What, in the end, caused the split? First, pressures within the army. Second, Naguib wanted a quick return to a normal parliamentary regime, but Nasser thought that the people were not yet ready. Naguib is much more moderate than Nasser, much less inclined to push through a truly revolutionary program on a long-range basis. Third, temperamental differences growing into acute bitterness and jealousy.

[4] *World Today*, February, 1955.

NASSER TO NAGUIB TO NASSER

Nasser for a long time stoutly denied reports that he intended to get rid of Naguib and take over his functions. He said, "I am too young. Besides, I am too fond of him."

As of the time I visited Egypt in preparation for this book, Nasser had no public post at all; Naguib had everything. He was prime minister, commander-in-chief of the Armed Forces, minister of defense, head of the Army Revolution, leader of the National Liberation Rally, and chairman of the Council of Revolutionary Command. Later he became president of the Republic as well.

Nasser first emerged into public view when he became deputy prime minister and minister of the interior on July 18, 1953. Before that, very few people indeed outside the inner circle even knew his name. Seldom has any country experienced a more sinuous merry-go-round than what followed. We must foreshorten the story drastically. Conflict between the two men became open, Nasser was the stronger, and on February 25, 1954, Naguib was forced to resign from all his major posts. Nasser became prime minister and chairman of the Council of Revolutionary Command. But the announcement of this changeabout produced such a fierce storm in Cairo that it had to be revoked; also intense pressure from the Sudan, where Naguib was universally regarded as a savior and a hero, forced Nasser to reconsider. Nasser, having got rid of the front man, found that he was so popular that he had to be taken back. So after three days of commotion Naguib reassumed the presidency, but not the premiership. But almost immediately —on March 8—came another development, caused by a crisis over votes within the junta itself. A compromise was worked out whereby Naguib lost control of the Council of Revolutionary Command, but became prime minister again. On March 27–29 a further complex evolution came, with such attendant tension that a state of emergency had to be declared in Cairo. Naguib remained nominally president and premier, but his power disappeared. Then on April 17, for the second time within two months, Nasser (who had become deputy prime minister) replaced him as prime minister. Finally came the November explosion over the Moslem Brotherhood, and Naguib passed entirely from the scene. Nasser took over the chairmanship of the Council of Revolutionary Command and the duties of head of state, though the actual office of president was left vacant.

A BRIEF GLIMPSE OF NAGUIB

We should have one more word about Naguib the man. He deserves further mention if only because of his remarkable distinction of character. When I talked with him I thought that he was one of the two or three most attractive men I had ever met in public life anywhere. He has certainly not got Nasser's intellectual qualities, but his human qualities are marked. He has a fine natural modesty. He is humane, selfless, sensible, and with a lively sense of humor, something unusual among makers of national revolutions.

The General was gregarious, and liked to get around. At a crowded reception in Cairo when he was at the height of his power, he noticed a man standing alone. He asked his hostess to identify him, and got the reply, "Oh, that's Mr. X., the dullest man in Cairo." Naguib promptly went up to Mr. X., took him into a corner, and talked to him earnestly for ten minutes. Later the hostess asked, "Why *did* you waste your precious time on *that* man?" Naguib replied, "He looked lonely, and I felt sorry for him." At about this same time I asked somebody who did not like Naguib what it was that he disliked about him: "Oh, he's always kissing babies."

When my wife and I met him the first thing I noticed in his office was a large scroll on the wall saying simply "God" in Arabic, and then a cluster of eight telephones on his desk. One of these rang as we started to talk. Naguib picked up the phone himself, listened a moment, and then discovered that the connection had failed. "Broken," he muttered cheerfully, and handed the instrument to an aide who was standing by. So as not to waste time, he continued his conversation with us, while the aide waited, with the receiver at his ear, for the phone to work again—a curious little scene.

Naguib's force and courage were incontestable; he was wounded three times in the Palestine war. I asked him about hardships in his youth. He said nothing, but with a peculiar smile unrolled the sleeve of his left arm, where an ugly scar was visible. He explained that when he was a boy of eight, already pledged to nationalism for Egypt and the Sudan, he had put a spike in a fire and driven it into the flesh of the arm, to prove his determination and manhood before his elders.

Naguib was born in the Sudan fifty-five years ago. His father, an Egyptian, came of an army family; his mother was half Sudanese. That he should have risen out of the Sudan, and is partly Sudanese himself, is striking. He has the implacable, bracing patriotism of the frontiersman, the semi-exile. It is, of course, a familiar phenomenon that dictators should be born just outside the countries they come to rule. Hitler was an Austrian, and Stalin a Georgian; Pilsudski was born in Lithuania, and Kemal Ataturk in Greece. Kemal was one of Naguib's most cherished early heroes.

Our talk took place the day before the Anglo-Egyptian accord on the Sudan was reached, and Naguib was about as busy as a man could be. But when we offered to leave, he would not let us go. Nor did he know, at that moment, whether he and the British would actually achieve a Sudanese settlement or not. Yet, once we started to talk, he spoke with the utmost calmness, simplicity, and detachment, as if the Sudan did not even exist. His speech (in English) is slow; he grasps for the correct word, while puffing at a pipe which he filled by breaking off bits of a cigar. He mentioned subjects as varied as books he read as a child, the future of Suez, how he got degrees in both commerce and law (at night school—while he was a junior officer), the Egyptian birthrate, his childhood ambition to be a doctor, and his profound belief in God.

His attitude to the British is peculiar. At great, almost monotonous length he described his distrust and hatred of British policy; yet his attitude toward individual Englishmen seemed to be almost affectionate. We shall come across this paradox again in connection with nationalists in British Africa. Actually Naguib would never have had any career at all had it not been for the education British rule made it possible for him to get. He grew up in Wad Medani in the Sudan, where his father was a district commissioner under the British. He went to Gordon College in Khartoum. And personal intercession by British officers got him into the Egyptian army and assisted his steady rise.

Over and over again, talking of Egypt, Naguib mentioned the necessity for self-denial, for sacrifice and renunciation. "What Egypt needs is discipline, unselfishness." He cared nothing for pomp or money and has always been as honest and generous as sunshine. As prime minister, he got a salary of $6,864 per year; as a major general in the army (he refused to accept promotion to a full generalship), he got $3,456. He lived on this latter sum, and never moved from the unpretentious house where he lived for seventeen years. His wife is never seen. Good Moslems do not show their wives.

I asked him how he took the load off, how he relaxed. He just laughed, telling us that, earlier in the week, he had got up at six one morning, and worked till 6 P.M. He went home for a bite of dinner, returned to his office, and then worked through the night till 8 A.M. He went home again, got three and a half hours' sleep, and then stayed at his desk till midnight. Incidentally while rising in the army rank by rank he managed to learn Hebrew, French, German, and Italian as well as English.

No government can ask prolonged self-denial of people unless it gives them hope, and this was what Naguib symbolized in the early days of the coup. Another source of power was his accessibility. He made himself intimately, physically close to great masses of the people; he was a dictator out in the market place. Finally, Naguib had—and has—*baraka*, the quality of being able to bestow blessing or benediction, so that he becomes a kind of link between man and the Almighty.

NASSER: A LINE IN ESTIMATE

To return to Nasser. What he needs most, as is only too obvious, are time and political tranquillity. He cannot get the former without the latter. To rule successfully he must hold the good will of the people at large, and not let his government degenerate into a purely military junta, exercising authority capriciously. But to rule at all he has to hold the reins firm, and this he cannot do—for the time being at least—without maintaining arbitrary rule.

One thing can be said without question—already he has done more for Egypt in a couple of years than the royal family did in a hundred and fifty. He is absolutely honest and has never asked anything for himself. The very fact that he is both dedicated and honest is a phenomenon so puzzling to old-style Egyptians that they cannot "understand" him. I heard him described as a "simple man with a complex mind." But, after all, that is better than being a complex man with a simple mind.

What Nasser and his men lack most is concrete managerial experience. No doubt they have made mistakes, but it would be a tragic day for Egypt and the world if they should be overturned and the country should succumb to forces more revolutionary or, worse, be sucked back into the sloth, greed, and infamy of the old regime.

EGYPT: INTERNATIONAL

What makes Egypt one of the most important countries in the world, let alone Africa, is of course its geographical position as a bridge between continents. Colonel Nasser, in the articles cited above, even goes so far as to say that Egypt, both European and African, is also part of southwestern Asia. Indeed nothing separates it from what we normally think of as "Asia" except the Red Sea and Sinai Peninsula. Egypt commands the eastern Mediterranean and controls the short sea route from Europe to the Indies and China. Moreover it is vital to the defense of all the Middle East. No wonder the free world wants Egypt, this pivot and prize, to be on its side.

Egyptian foreign policy has several aspects, aside from the overriding double problem of getting the British out of the Sudan and Suez. This, it is assumed, will be finally achieved by 1956.

Arab League. This body is not an agency of the Egyptian government, but Egypt is by far its most important member. Its headquarters are in Cairo, and an Egyptian, Abdel Khalek Massouna, is its secretary general, in succession to the legendary Abdul Rahman Azzam, who was purged by Naguib. The Arab League is not supra-national, but its members are bound by a mutual defense pact. It is a kind of bloc, focusing pan-Arab policy, encouraging a common point of view, and stimulating Arab nationalism. Egypt wants as close a cohesion as possible between the Arab states of the Near and Middle East. The trouble is that the Arab countries do not easily cohere. Personal, religious, and political difficulties make effective unity difficult.

Egypt exerts, however, a considerable influence at the United Nations and elsewhere as sponsor-at-large of the Arab cause, no matter how disunited the Arab world may be locally. The Egyptians have steadily supported nationalist aspirations in Morocco and Tunisia, as we know, and this has produced intermittent serious tension between Egypt and France.

In the summer of 1954 Egypt and Saudi Arabia agreed to "pool their resources in war industries, armaments, defense, and military training."[5] Farouk and Ibn Saud were bitter enemies; Nasser and Ibn Saud's heir are close friends. Saudi Arabia has, on account of petroleum, riches almost unparalleled in the world; if Arabian wealth should become available to Egypt as a result of the new defense arrangements, Egypt could become a powerful military state. In August, 1954, Colonel Nasser made the pilgrimage to Mecca. He announced that Moslems all over the world should turn the ceremony of the pilgrimage into a concrete weapon for political unity; such a statement is unprecedented in Islamic history. At about the same time Major Salah Salem, Egyptian minister of National Guidance and for Sudanese Affairs, a picturesque and able character who is generally regarded as Nasser's closest friend and right-hand man, flew to the Lebanon and Syria to strengthen Egyptian bonds in the Levant.

Israel. Scarcely a day passes without some painful incident on the Israel-Egyptian border, or in consequence of the Egyptian blockade of Israeli shipping. In January, 1955, two young Israelis were hanged in Egypt after being convicted of "espionage and sabotage." One was a French citizen and doctor of medicine. He was alleged to be leader of a "Zionist spy ring" that, among other things, had attempted to burn down the United States information Service libraries in Cairo and Alexandria.

No relations of any kind exist as yet between Egypt and Israel. Jews from Israel are not allowed into the country, and it will be a long time before the present truce is followed by a real peace. A great many Egyptians still

[5] Kennett Love in the New York *Times*, June 12, 1954.

have active military fear of Israel; they say that they would not hate Israel so fiercely if it were not so "warlike"; some even go to the hysterical length of fearing that, when the British go, the Israelis will seize the Suez Canal. I also heard an Egyptian remark, "The real reason why we dislike Jews is that we are so much like them."

Nasser himself is not inflammatory or extravagantly anti-Semitic, any more than was Naguib. In fact he has recorded the deep admiration he felt for Jewish strength and tenacity in winning freedom from the British, and how he sought to learn from the Palestinian example. He did his duty as a soldier against Israel, but he has little animus against individual Jews.

Neutralism, the United States, and Middle East Defense. The easiest way to summarize a situation agonizingly fluid and complex is to say that Egypt is on the fence, but with leanings toward the West. Late in 1951 the United States and the western powers proposed the creation of a Middle East Defense Organization to be called MEDO, which would be a supplement to NATO in western Europe. Egypt refused to have anything to do with this, and the project had to be dropped. Without Egyptian adherence it was useless. When I asked Naguib if he would ever permit establishment of an American military base in Egypt, his reply was a cheerful—but indignant—snort. The last thing any Egyptian government could tolerate is the establishment of any new western military installation on its territory, no matter how worthy its aim might be.

Nasser once put the matter more temperately, saying that "mutual defense pacts between the Arab world and the western powers would have to wait until the Arabs had overcome their residual suspicion of western imperialist intentions."

An eminent professor at the University of Cairo said to us, "Why cannot you Americans understand realities? We know that, in the present juncture of international affairs, you think that you must play with the British. But we cannot trust the British—yet. Therefore we cannot trust you. Meantime you are making the same mistake elsewhere that you made in Morocco. You are temporizing between platonic statements of support for the aspirations of Moslem nationalism and direct military support of the oppressors of Moslem nationalism. You should realize that it will serve your own best practical purpose to have us free, because we will be a stronger and better ally free. What good is Morocco to you now? Not much. But if you had negotiated with the Sultan instead of the French, Morocco would be your grateful and faithful friend."

The situation in Egypt was further complicated by the fact that, while the negotiations over Suez were proceeding, the British did not want

American arms to flow into Egypt. People in Cairo say moreover that American economic aid was deliberately withheld from Egypt, in order to force the Egyptians into agreeing to accept the MEDO proposals. Another irritating crisis came when Nasser tried to buy $3,500,000 worth of arms from Spain. British pressure on Madrid stopped this, but later London withdrew its own embargo on the shipment of arms to Egypt, which had been in force since 1951. (Originally this embargo was promoted by the United Nations in an effort to localize the Egyptian war with Israel.)

Meantime the United States, having snubbed Egypt (or having been snubbed by it), turned north and east instead. The American government made arms available to Pakistan, and Pakistan concluded (February, 1954) an important pact with Turkey. Egypt has always been somewhat jealous of Pakistan, and now it woke up to see a projected chain of free world defense arrangements and installations staked out across the whole Mediterranean and the Middle East, into the heart of Asia, with itself conspicuously excluded. Then (early in 1955) came the announcement shocking in the extreme to Cairo that Iraq intended to sign a defense agreement with Turkey, which would mean pulling Iraq out of the Egyptian orbit and the virtual breakup of the neutralist Arab League. The Egyptian government did everything in its power to frustrate this maneuver, but without success.

Meantime, however, the historic Anglo-Egyptian settlement over Suez had been reached. As a result Cairo began to show more cordiality to the West. In November, 1954, the United States agreed to make available to Egypt $40,000,000 for economic development. Cairo had hoped for $100,000,000. Later Nasser stated that Egypt could not enter a formal defense pact, but would stand on the side of the West in the event of any Soviet aggression in the Middle East, in particular against the Turks, and would accept military aid if it were "unconditional."

Various organs of the United Nations are active and fruitful in Egypt, like the Children's Emergency Fund and UNRWA, which deals with the tragic plight of Arab refugees from Israel. The United States maintains a Point Four organization in Egypt, which has done fine work in several fields, from the planting of edible desert grasses to the building of 60,000 latrines in villages. "In-service training of Egyptian public health nurses has begun. To improve the egg and meat yield of poultry, 100,000 baby chicks are being brought in. Two American experts developed a new water-repellent, sun-dried brick type of dwelling, cheap to build, and twenty demonstration houses are being erected. In addition, 200 Egyptian technicians are being trained in the United States. Other programs are being planned."[6]

[6] *Middle Eastern Affairs*, February 1953.

Point Four appropriations are, however, not very large and there is a little joke in Cairo to the effect that the program "should be called Point One-and-a-Half." The total American expenditure in Egypt was only $3,425,000 for 1951-53. As well dust the Pyramid of Cheops with a whiskbroom as try to make really significant contributions to a country like Egypt with so paltry a sum.

Soviet Union and Communism. Relations between Cairo and Moscow are, as the diplomats say, "correct." Recently Major Salah Salem announced on behalf of the Egyptian government that "Egypt would cooperate with all states on either side of the Iron Curtain which supported her aims, but . . . with none which withheld freedom and dignity from Egypt."[7] One eminent Cairene told us with engaging candor, "The Cold War puts us in a truly devilish position. It is very difficult indeed to choose between the United States and the Soviet Union. We fear you both." Early in 1954 the Egyptian and Soviet governments raised the legations in their respective countries to the status of embassies. Al Azhar University has students from Soviet Moslem areas. More important, the Egyptians have made aggressive efforts to improve trade with Moscow and its satellites. A commercial treaty with the Soviet Union was signed in March, 1954, and imports from Russia to Egypt increased 35 per cent in a recent nine-month period (from £6,500,-000 to £10,000,000); exports from Egypt to Russia increased by nearly 2,000 per cent, from £581,000 to £10,000,000.[8] Concurrently, Egyptian trade with Britain fell. Also Cairo is buying heavily from East Germany, and has signed a trade agreement with Rumania; Egyptian missions have visited Poland, Czechoslovakia, and Hungary, and the country would like extremely to sell cotton to Red China.

But on the domestic side of the fence Egypt is rigidly, resolutely anti-Communist. The Communist party has of course been suppressed, and the authorities vigilantly seek to stamp out subterranean Communist activity.

Early in 1955 Colonel Nasser reiterated a familiar note in the *Foreign Affairs* article already cited:

> There would not be any Communist infiltration in any part of the Middle East and Africa if the United States could develop a courageous policy—and the only morally correct one—of supporting those who are anxious to get rid of foreign domination and exploitation. Real independence would be the greatest defense against Communist—or any other type—of infiltration or aggression. Free men are the most fanatical defenders of their liberty, nor do they lightly forget those who have championed their struggle for independence.

[7] London *Times*, February 11, 1954.
[8] *Time*, January 14, 1953.

Germany. For the first time in this book we encounter the strong impact and influence of West Germany on an African country. Bonn is acutely interested in Cairo—and vice versa. About six hundred German technicians are employed by the Egyptian government, working on several levels—military, engineering, railroads, and the like. "Nasser could never have made his coup without his German advisers," I heard it said. Probably this is an overstatement, but German technical skill has been helpful to the junta in several conspicuous areas. A German tank officer is supposed to be in charge of the mechanization of the Egyptian armed forces, and a German naval specialist is at work on marine matters. A chief advisor to the Central Planning Board is a well-known German, Dr. Wilhelm Voss. Cairo has a German-language newspaper and a German chamber of commerce. Three hundred German firms held a trade fair in the city recently; German missions repeatedly visit the country, and one recent arrival was no less a personage than Dr. Hjalmar Horace Greeley Schacht. Egypt wants hard-money credit from Germany, and offers cotton in exchange; German exports to Egypt are rising at a fantastic rate. An American official told me, "Nasser will blow up in time, there will be a war some day, and then the Germans will fulfill their dream of the *Drang Nach Osten*—they will inherit all this part of the world."

(Germany has lively incipient interests almost everywhere in Africa, not merely in Egypt. The Germans are particularly active in the Gold Coast, Nigeria, the Portuguese territories, and to an extent in the Union—wherever, in a word, there is a vacuum to fill in trade or otherwise. Also Bonn is encouraging African students to come to Germany for university training, and an elaborate "Africa House" is being built at Stuttgart.)

Egyptian Attitude to Black Africa. This has two aspects. First, Egypt is a powerful force behind the spread of Islam in the world; naturally, it hopes to see as much of Black Africa as possible go Moslem. "It is not true," the representative of a great foreign power told us in Cairo, "that the Dark Continent is getting lighter. It is getting darker. What will be the effect of the immense reserves of black African manpower as they spread irresistibly out into the world? Africa is like a bottle with the cork being pulled out. One temperate, civilizing force is Islam. Therefore the more Africans who are converted to Mohammedanism the better."

Second, Egypt regards itself as a kind of mother and father to African nationalist movements everywhere, and the case might be made that it has its own subconscious "imperialist" designs on the continent. Colonel Nasser's hatred of colonialism is of course genuine, but Egyptian policy is not always altogether altruistic. The Cairo radio broadcasts to the African East Coast in

Swahili—and does so with such anti-British venom that London has lodged official protests. An organization known as the League for Colored Peoples has its headquarters in Cairo, and, under Indian leadership, meetings in Cairo are projected of an All-African Congress. Colonel Nasser wrote in his "Philosophy of the Revolution": "We cannot under any circumstances remain aloof from the terrible and sanguinary [sic] struggle going on in Africa today between five million whites and 200,000,000 Africans . . . The peoples of Africa will continue to look at us, who guard the northern gate and who constitute their link with all the outside world. We will never . . . be able to vacate our responsibility to support with all our ability the spread of enlightenment and civilization to the remotest depths of the jungle . . . The Dark Continent is now the scene of a strange and excited turbulence . . . We shall not, in any circumstances, be able to stand idly by in the face of what is going on in Africa in the belief that it will not affect or concern us . . . I will continue to dream of the day when I will find in Cairo a great African Institute dedicated . . . to an enlightened African consciousness, and to sharing with others from all over the world in the work of advancing the peoples of the continent."

One of Nasser's chief associates, who yields to no one in his hatred of colonialism, gave us a slightly different picture. He said that the two things that counted most in Black Africa were "the germ" and "happiness." First, there must be effort to conquer disease; second, to fill out people's *time*, by giving them opportunities for self-development. "An African in the bush works no more than two and a half months a year. What shall we do with his surplus time? People must be allowed to develop according to the tempo and rhythm to which they are accustomed. Do not go too fast. Even Egypt is not yet ready for the New York subway."

A FEW PARAGRAPHS ABOUT SUEZ

The Suez Canal, which has been aptly called "the richest ditch on earth," connects the Mediterranean and the Red Sea. It links Europe with Asia through a slice of Africa 103 miles long. It is one of the few great canals of the world without locks. More than ten thousand ships go through the Suez Canal every year, a traffic two and a half times greater than that of Panama; sometimes they are stacked dozens deep awaiting transit. One reason for a large increase in business lately is the movement of American tankers carrying oil from Saudi Arabia.

The Canal was, as everybody knows, built largely through the vision of the French diplomat and man of affairs Ferdinand de Lesseps. After ten years of arduous work it was officially inaugurated on November 17, 1869. The Emperor Franz Joseph of Austro-Hungary and the Empress Eugénie, wife of Louis Napoleon, were guests at the inaugural, and Verdi wrote *Aïda* to celebrate the event.[9] The British for a dozen years did everything possible to block building of the canal, fearing that it would make India too accessible to rival powers. Then in 1875 Prime Minister Benjamin Disraeli, without consulting parliament, bought £4,000,000 worth of shares in the canal from the Khedive Ismail; Disraeli borrowed the money from the Rothschilds. Ever since, the British government has owned roughly 43 per cent of the company's valuable stock, and it has been a lucrative investment.

Majority control of the company (*Société Universelle du Canal Maritime de Suez*) still, however, rests with private French owners. Its headquarters are in Paris. Lately the Egyptian government has exerted steady and successful pressure to share more fully in operating the canal and get a larger proportion of its revenues. Ninety-five per cent of the labor force working on it must be Egyptian, according to a recent law. The original concession ran for ninety-nine years, and expires in 1968. By terms of another recent agreement the whole canal property will revert to the Egyptian government on that date. For imperialism both public and private, time is running out.

*

So much for the canal proper. The British base in the Canal Zone is something else again. This was built up over a course of forty years during the British occupation of Egypt. Obviously Suez was crucial to imperial communications—a veritable nexus of empire—and needed protection. The base has nothing to do with the administration of the canal. It merely happens to be adjacent. The base is totally a British military enterprise. In 1954 (when the Anglo-Egyptian agreement for its evacuation was negotiated and signed) it was still by all odds the biggest overseas military installation in the world, and probably the most powerful. It stretched along the canal for two-thirds of its length, and covered no fewer than 9,714 square miles. It had a total personnel of 83,000 British troops, 50,000 tons of ammunition, 300,000 tons of ordnance equipment, ten airfields, and the usual paraphernalia of a base of such magnitude—dock yards, warehouses, cantonments, and the like. To build it cost 1.4 billion dollars, and it contained $700,000,000 worth of supplies; its annual expense to the British

---

[9] The Metropolitan Opera in New York gave a special performance of *Aïda* on November 30, 1954, to commemorate the one hundredth anniversary of the signature of the first agreement between de Lesseps and the Egyptian authorities.

taxpayer has been calculated at $140,000,000. These figures, consequential as they are, do not reflect the full importance of Suez. What made it count in the British imagination above all was its symbolic power. It was like Singapore in the old days, an iron stake driven impregnably, immovably, into one of the supreme crossroads of the world, on which flew with stiff pride the Union Jack.

But times, as they say, change.

That the British held on in Suez after evacuating Cairo in 1936 became an increasingly intolerable affront to Egyptian sovereignty. Moreover by terms of the 1936 Anglo-Egyptian agreement London had promised to restrict its Suez garrison to 10,000 men. But somehow—partly on account of World War II—this grew to 83,000. The Egyptians felt as New Yorkers might feel if Long Island were cut off and garrisoned in force by a hated alien power. An area containing a million people and three chief cities—Port Said, Ismailia, and Suez—were under illegal foreign occupation. The British did their best to be inconspicuous, and leaned over backward to avoid incidents. But it is difficult to keep 83,000 men permanently inconspicuous. The Egyptians used the fact that the British were there at all as a pretext for incessant anti-British agitation on a wide political scale. Egyptian terrorists and "commando squads" raided into the Zone and made havoc. The Moslem Brotherhood preached a "holy war" to liberate the canal from the foreign interloper. By 1951 a nasty little guerrilla war was raging. No British life was safe. The British, exasperated beyond measure, took severe reprisals and forty-six Egyptians were killed in a battle near Ismailia. This was one reason for the burning of Cairo on "Black Saturday," January 26, 1952. Infuriated Egyptian mobs retaliated by putting to the flames anything they could reach—like Shepheard's Hotel—that savored of alien power, even though the British had left Cairo sixteen years before.

Meantime, on its side, London had a number of good reasons in several sharply different fields for thinking that it might be a good idea to relinquish the Suez base. (1) What good is a base if it lies in irreversibly hostile territory? Fifty thousand troops of the Suez garrison had to be there merely to protect the 33,000 who actually ran the base. (2) A base like Suez is an anachronism these days, Egyptian hostility quite aside. It is too concentratedly vulnerable to hostile air attack, particularly by such a weapon as the H-bomb or even the A-bomb. (3) Suez kept 83,000 British troops bottled up who might be more usefully trained elsewhere, and cost a prodigious amount of money to maintain. It was a good staging ground, but Cyrenaica or Cyprus might be better. (4) Suez had a double function—it not only served to defend the canal and imperial communications, but was a wonderfully convenient mechanism for exerting pressure *on* Egypt. But the era when Great Britain could attempt to dominate Egypt by the threat of military force was gone forever. Hence, the base lost much of its *raison d'être*. (5) Britain wants a stable, tranquil and friendly Middle East, something almost impossible to achieve in the face of overt Egyptian enmity. Nobody could get anywhere in building a new defense system in the area until the British evacuated the canal.

There was some talk that the United Nations might be called in as mediator. But the United States could not accept this, since it might have created a precedent for some future intervention by the United Nations in regard to the *Panama* Canal.

One difficulty was that the British did not object so much to getting out, but were worried greatly about who might replace them, in case the Egyptians should prove incapable of defending themselves against aggression. Another was British sensitiveness over a recent series of diplomatic defeats—for instance in Iran—which made it difficult to recede further under pressure without grave loss of prestige. On the other hand the breakdown over Persian oil taught the British that there was such a thing as being too stubborn for too long.

Once the Sudan problem was amicably settled and out of the way, the road to agreement on Suez became easier. The Suez accord followed inevitably from the Sudan accord.[10] This is not to say that negotiations were easy. On the contrary they were delicate, prolonged, and abstruse. The chief Egyptian negotiator was Nasser; the chief British negotiator, until illness forced his temporary absence, was Sir Ralph Stevenson, the brilliantly accomplished and realistic British ambassador to Egypt. The agreement, as finally reached in 1954, calls for withdrawal of British military forces from Suez within twenty months, that is by June 18, 1956. But for seven years four thousand British *civilian* technicians, under Egyptian administrative control, are to remain in order to supervise maintenance of the installations. Also the British have the right to return in force if the Soviet Union attacks any Arab League country—or Turkey—within the next seven years.

Extremists on both sides did what they could to fight ratification of the accord, but failed. Forty conservative backbenchers in London, who held that withdrawal was a shameful "scuttle," were finally voted down. The Churchill government would have fallen on this issue if the Labor party

---

[10] One should mention, however, that as far back as 1946 the late Ernest Bevin and the Egyptian prime minister Sidky Pasha successfully negotiated a Suez agreement. But it failed of ratification in the Egyptian parliament, largely over the status of the Sudan.

had not abstained from voting. I would incidentally give a good deal to know what Sir Winston, who is not one to surrender any imperial position lightly, thought privately of the agreement. But no matter what he thought, he had to accept it. In Egypt the Moslem Brotherhood bitterly opposed Nasser to the last moment and beyond. Its members wanted to get the British out of the Zone bag and baggage and at once, without qualification or delay. One reason why the Brotherhood (what is left of it) hates the agreement so fanatically is the curious one that Britain is empowered to re-enter Suez if Turkey, a *lay* Islamic state, is attacked. The Brotherhooders call the Turks infidels, and do not want to compromise Egypt by assisting them in any way.

Among moderates in Egypt—and the Sudan—the effect of the Suez agreement was like that of lancing a boil. For the first time since 1882, Egypt will have (by 1956) no British garrison on her soil; for the first time in almost 2,500 years, she will have complete national sovereignty.

*

So now except for a few words to come about the Nile we conclude with the northern tier of Africa, the Africa of the Mediterranean littoral and the upper Sahara, the Africa close to Europe. Let us turn south to the Sudan and then to the great world of Black Africa below.

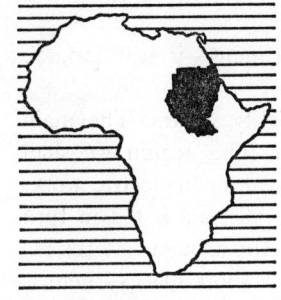

CHAPTER 14

The Nile and the Sudan

> *Aut Nilus, Aut Nihil.* —LATIN PROVERB
>
> *The Nile may be the father of civilization and the wisdom of the Egyptians may have spread north, east, and west, but till less than a century ago the source of the great river was a mystery and the peoples beyond to the south remained sunk in darkness.*
>
> —W. M. MACMILLAN

NASSERS and Naguibs may come and go; the Nile remains. This stupendous river, at once fixed and elastic, with its swampy roots and flowering Delta, has often been compared to a palm tree, but it more closely resembles the shaft of an esophagus, or alimentary canal, through which the stuff of Egypt's life passes. The thick, fruitful silt of the Delta was once topsoil in faraway Uganda and Ethiopia. Nothing can be more striking than to stand on the Kasr el Nil embankment in Cairo, during the crest of the Nile flood, and reflect that this hot muddy torrent consisted originally of Congo snow. Originally? Before that the Nile was rain in the Indian Ocean and South Atlantic.

The Nile (nobody knows the origin of the name) is the most gravid river in the world. It is not the most beautiful or most spectacular. But it is the only river about which it may be said that, without it, an entire country would die. It is also the longest river in the world, measuring 4,160 miles as against 3,988 for the Mississippi-Missouri and 3,900 for the Amazon, and for most of its course is the straightest. Its basin covers 1,100,000 square miles, or roughly one-tenth of the whole of Africa. It loses between a quarter and a half of its total flow before it reaches the Mediterranean, oozing endlessly away into papyrus swamps or burned up by the fierce desert sun, but when it finally does empty itself into the sea its rate of discharge—after a journey longer than the width of the American continent—is still 420,000 cubic feet a second.[1]

There are several Niles, all part of the same mighty stream. The main branch has its source in Lake Victoria in Uganda. This region we shall inspect in due course later, with mention of the great hydroelectric works now in construction at Owen Falls.[2] Of course Lake Victoria is fed in turn by mountain rivers originating in Tanganyika and the Congo. At its beginning the river is known as the Victoria Nile for a short space—there is also an Albert Nile—and then becomes the *White Nile*. This loops upward into the Sudan and is almost lost for a time in the Sudd swamps, the largest and most impenetrable swamp area in the world. The White Nile then straightens itself out, gains confidence and pluck, and flows like a giant pipe through the whole of the Sudan.

The *Blue Nile* rises at Lake Tana in Ethiopia. The two branches meet at Khartoum, the capital of the Sudan, to become the main Nile and push northward into Egypt. The White Nile is more sluggish than its sister, and much steadier. Eighty-four per cent of the total flow of the main Nile comes from the turbulent and dashing Blue Nile, which carries down to the desert its wild highland heritage. In spate the Blue Nile holds no less than "300 to 400 times more water than at low point." The slope of the *main Nile* is gentle, and is interrupted by a series of celebrated cataracts. One extraordinary and unique thing about the Nile is that, almost alone among the master rivers, it gets little sustenance from tributaries. About two hundred miles north of Khartoum it meets the Atbara, but this is dry for more than half the year. Then for 1,700 river miles—all the way to the Delta—it receives no other stream at all. This is the loneliest, the most self-sufficient, and the most powerful river in the world.

Egypt is made fertile, phenomenally fertile where it is touched by the magic finger of the river, by the process known as flooding. Once a year the Nile swells up like a cobra, rises over its banks, and spills its vast burden of surplus water out into the burning desert. When it recedes the land is impregnated with moisture, i.e., life. The "miracle" of the Nile flood has been known, watched, and measured since the days of the Pharaohs— probably before. The river rises about twenty-six feet at Aswan, twenty-three at Cairo. It takes three weeks for the flood to travel downstream and reach Aswan and then Cairo; the peak point comes between August and mid-September.

---

[1] The Nile has never been described better than by Winston Churchill in *The River War*. Sir Winston first visited Egypt and the Sudan more than half a century ago, but what he wrote still holds good today.

[2] See Chapter 23 below.

THE NILE AND THE SUDAN

Flood (= surplus) water is called "untimely" water; there is so much of it in the flood season that it cannot be used; it charges down to the Mediterranean unharnessed, carrying with it millions upon millions of tons of real estate. But except during the flood Egypt does not get *enough* water for its purposes, which is the heart of the problem. Of the total Nile flow, about one-fifth is "timely" (at once usable), one-fifth untimely and not storable, three-fifths untimely but storable.[3]

Two types of irrigation exist in Egypt, "basin" and "perennial." Under "basin" (natural) irrigation the river does freely what it wants. South of Luxor, for instance, the Nile is allowed simply to burst over its banks and saturate the desert where it wills, exactly as it did ten thousand years ago. Thousands of square miles of land become lakes. But the soil is made moist and pregnable only for a brief period; the Nile does not provide anything like enough water for irrigation the year around. "Perennial" (manmade) irrigation is effected by canals and other devices whereby water may be stored, channeled, and made available and useful when the Nile is low, and is thus an essential supplement to basin irrigation.

To master and harness the Nile further is one of the greatest of all African —or world—problems, and obviously involves not only Egypt and the Sudan but Uganda, Ethiopia, and other countries. What the Nile needs is a permanent, superscale, international TVA. The difficulties are almost insuperable. Take merely the matter of inaccessibility and primitiveness of communications. The fact may not be believed, but in the whole of the Sudan the Nile is spanned by only four bridges in a total of 2,144 river miles, and all these are clustered in one small area near Khartoum. *There is no bridge at all* over the Nile between a point north of Owen Falls (in Uganda) and Kosti, 198 miles south of Khartoum—a distance of almost three thousand miles.

Egypt has the Aswan Dam and half a dozen barrages, including the Delta Barrage north of Cairo. Colonel Nasser, as I have already mentioned, hopes to erect a giant new dam near Aswan, which will be capable of holding and "storing the whole of the Nile flood." There are two important dams in the Sudan, the Jebel Auliya on the White Nile below Khartoum and the Sennar on the Blue, which fertilizes the Gezira area. Another is to be built soon. One project which could be of inestimable value is a scheme to drain the Sudd swamps, by garrotting the Nile into a 186-mile-long canal near Jonglei, in the southern Sudan. This, by saving huge amounts of Nile water that seep out into the marshland wilderness and are totally lost, could transform the productivity of both Egypt and the

[3] *Sudan Almanac*, 1953, p. 39.

Sudan. Ways must also be worked out to store more water on a modest scale, and feed it to the fields as needed, month by month. Engineers talk of a "century of storage"; that is, the safe accumulation of enough water to make planning possible, not merely on the basis of months or years, but decades.[4] Few problems in the world offer greater challenge to the creative intelligence and good will of mankind.

Egypt has virtually no water except that which the Nile provides, because rainfall is scant or non-existent. But parts of the Sudan have rain (Khartoum gets fifteen inches in a good year) and the country is not quite so unequivocally dependent on the Nile. Since the river flows through the Sudan before it reaches Egypt, Egypt is not only dependent on the Nile but on the Sudan as well for all its water supply. Practically every aspect of Egyptian policy toward the Sudan is based on the absolutely vital necessity of safeguarding its source of water *in* the Sudan.

Egypt and the Sudan divide water on the basis of ratios established by the Nile Waters Agreement of 1929, with Egypt receiving all but about 8 per cent. The Sudanese would like to get a much higher proportion. As things stand at present Sudanese irrigation projects rest on how much water has to be reserved for Egypt. If a government hostile to Egypt should ever take power in the Sudan, could the Sudanese cut off Egypt's water, and make the country die of thirst? This is a moot point. Some engineers say yes. Of course the Nile could not be entirely cut off, but if the Sudanese dams were *opened* at certain junctures (not closed), the whole of the Nile overburden would crash into Egypt and would be too much for the Egyptians to control, with the result that they would probably lose 20 to 25 per cent of their water available for irrigation. But the Sudanese would lose irrigation water too.

GREAT WORLD OF THE SUDAN

We reach now the Sudan itself, one of the most fabulous countries of the world. Its status is unique, and since 1899 it has been a condominium, ruled in theory jointly by Britain and Egypt. The only other condominiums I can think of in the world are Canton and Enderbury islands in the Pacific and the New Hebrides. On February 12, 1953, as we noted in a preceding chapter, came the epochal pact between the British and Egyptians over the Sudan. This, in effect, gave notice of termination of the condominium, and since January 1, 1954, the Sudan has been almost completely on its own—a newly arrived state in the family of nations. But ties with Egypt

[4] Cf. *Time*, March 7, 1949.

remain extremely close. The Sudan is bound to Egypt by more than just the Nile. In fact the chief stipulation of the 1953 accord is that the Sudan shall have the right within three years to choose its own future—whether to maintain itself on an independent basis or join Egypt. Meantime British control, which was dominant for half a century, has been virtually extinguished, although British influence in some directions may remain.

The Sudan—even if it links itself to Egypt by 1956—is a totally different entity from Egypt. Let us proceed.

Politically the Sudan is, I think, the most exciting country we saw in all Africa with the possible exception of Nigeria. This is not a nation half dead at birth, like Libya. It has the intense virility of something newly born and its vibrant will to live derives from sound old roots. The Sudan sounds a note unlike any we have met in Africa so far—of animation, confidence, and spontaneity. It is crowded with zest to get ahead; it boils and sparkles with euphoria. I even heard a youthful Sudanese say, "Our country is going to be like the United States; we will try to combine here the best of both Africa *and* Europe." On a different level he went on enthusiastically, "We want more than just good roads, good schools, good hospitals. We want good *movies* too!"

Geographically the Anglo-Egyptian Sudan (which is still its official name) is a kind of viaduct between Mediterranean and African Africa. The name means "Land of Blacks." But plenty of Sudanese are not very black. The country is not to be confused with the French Sudan (part of French West Africa), which is two thousand miles away. One thing to emphasize is its vastness, its almost illimitable immensity. It covers 967,500 square miles, and so is almost four times the size of Texas—if anything can be four times the size of Texas.

There are about 9,000,000 Sudanese, and although the country's nationalism is fervently articulate it is not altogether easy to define exactly what "a" Sudanese is. Putting it as briefly as possible, most (but not all) Sudanese are of mixed Arab and Negro blood superimposed on an older Hamitic stock. The distinction is marked between the urban population (about a million) and the tribes out in the desert and equatorial jungle. The bureaucrats in the towns, with their brittle veneer of western education, despise the nomads and tribesmen, and call them savages. As a matter of fact, man for man, many of these "savages" are far superior to the *Lumpen-proletariat* in the towns. They can be magnificent specimens physically and have their own highly developed standards of conduct and honor. Moreover, despite their primitive uncouthness, they have by and large a happy way of life. Most of course are still illiterate. Some of the most famous tribes in

Africa are Sudanese, like the Bejas or Fuzzy-Wuzzys who spring from the Red Sea area.[5] Among the Nilotic peoples are the Nuers, the Shilluks, and the Dinkas, about which there could be pages of abstruse—and fascinating—anthropological description. There are about 820,000 Dinkas and 350,000 Nuers. Most southern Sudanese are elaborately cicatrized with beads of scar tissue adorning their bodies; in some tribes adolescent boys have their incisor teeth gouged out by spears. They are a wonderful people with cattle. They have little political consciousness (so far) but an immense sense of superiority and racial pride; they are inclined to patronize British officials for "the unfortunate whiteness of their skins." Male Dinkas may occasionally be seen near Khartoum, although their natural habitat is far away to the southwest. They are tall men who customarily, even today, go around stark-naked and stand on one foot like storks, supported by long staves.

During the war I stopped briefly at El Fasher, capital of Darfur Province. The surrounding desert looks like a "petrified ocean." This was for a long time regarded as the most remote place in Africa, the furthest spot from any coast. Darfur covers 138,540 square miles—an area almost as big as Japan—and until 1916 had its own identity as a quasi-independent kingdom. Below is Wau, the capital of the Dinka country. Here we encounter—for the first time in this book—big game typically African, like elephant and hippopotamus. Another remote and exotic Sudanese town is Malakal (population 13,000), capital of the Upper Nile Province; here the Shilluks still have their own "king." One chieftain—of the Moru—has the nice name Jumbo.

The Sudan has a favorable balance of trade, and has not had a budget deficit since 1912. There is no income tax. The chief export crops are cotton (by a long way) and gum arabic. "Seven eighths of the world's supply of gum arabic is shipped from Port Sudan."[6] The staple food of the people is *dura*, a kind of millet.

Two other preliminary points might be mentioned. One is that the Sudan (in its desert regions at least) is one of the hottest places on the world's surface. Once—in April, 1903—a temperature of 126.5 degrees was recorded at Wadi Halfa. Khartoum is the only city I have ever been in—and we visited it in winter—where I could feel heat from the street burn through the soles of my shoes. Egypt and Libya have some unpleasant winds, but nothing to match the *haboob* of the Sudan, which in June blows desert dust as black as smoke from an oil fire over the parched, quivering towns.

[5] Traditionally so-called by the British because of their mops of unruly long hair.
[6] *1001 Facts about the Sudan*, a pamphlet published by the Sudanese government.

Another is the propulsive force of the Sudanese group of languages. These, 264 in number, have crossed Africa all the way to the West Coast; Yoruba in Nigeria and Ewe and Twi under the west African bulge are Sudanic languages. Similarly the Nilotic peoples have spread their virile blood far afield, as witness the Masai in Kenya and the giant Watutsi in Ruanda-Urundi, who are cousins to the Hamitic Sudanese.

NORTH AND SOUTH IN THE SUDAN

The chief line of demarcation in the country is between north and south. The northerners, who number around 6,500,000, are mostly Arabic-speaking, Moslem by religion, and strongly under Egyptian influence. They belong—to speak roughly—to the world of Europe and the Levant. The 2,500,000 southern Sudanese are totally different—pagan, primitive, darker-skinned, and with their own native languages. A good many southern tribesmen have, however, in the past half century become Christianized. Antipathy between north and south goes far back. General Gordon wrote about Equatoria, the southernmost Sudan province, "When you have got the ink that has soaked into blotting paper out of it, then slavery will cease in these lands."[7] This was written in the 1880's, and Gordon was quite wrong. It did not take many years to abolish slavery in the Sudan. Feudal lords—as in several Moslem countries—may still have family retainers whose status is virtually that of slaves, but organized slavery and the slave traffic have long ceased to exist. The fact remains that in the old days the northern Arabs raided perennially into the black south and carried off hundreds of thousands of slaves. The southern Sudan was a kind of pool, a reservoir, of black manpower mercilessly drained. To this day old-style northern Sudanese think of the southerners as "slaves," and the south still holds to a sharp atavistic fear of marauders from the north.

Nationalist Sudanese say today that the fissure between north and south is artificial, and was built up and made use of by the British to serve their own ends—*divide et impera*. In reality (say the nationalists) their country *is* an authentic homogeneous unit, politically, economically, and geographically. The southern languages are different, true, but almost everybody knows pidgin Arabic or English. Everything in the southern Sudan flows inevitably downriver (up on the map) to the north. Certainly it is true that the British have not in recent history assisted north-south intercourse very much. In particular they tried to block conversion of the pagan southerners to Islam, because they wanted to keep the southern Sudan as a kind of

[7] Quoted by Lytton Strachey in *Eminent Victorians*, p. 229.

counterbalance to the influence of Moslem Egypt in the north. Northern traders were not allowed into the south without special license, nor could southerners come north. It was easier for a Sudanese in Malakal to get to Uganda than to Khartoum. The whole southern area was closed off, like a secret enclave, under its own administration. But quite possibly these "machinations" by the British were an effort to protect the southern Sudanese, not vice versa.

The future of the south was the chief impediment in negotiations for the 1953 accord. The British hesitated to turn over peoples so primitive to exclusive Sudanese—or Egyptian—dominion. They did not want to see the south a prey to exploitation, political or otherwise. They thought that the south should be given time to decide its future for itself. In reply the Sudanese (and Egyptians) accused the British of trying to set up a kind of Pakistan in the Sudan, which would eventually be made to join Kenya and Uganda. Actually there was nothing that Britain wanted less than to be saddled with the southern Sudan. But it did hope for a fair deal for its pagan and Christian peoples, helpless against political onslaught from the north.

Not only was the southern Sudan a closed area under British rule; so in a manner of speaking was the whole country. Visitation was not encouraged. Even today there are only four towns—in a territory as big as all western Europe—with hotels where Europeans can stay with any comfort—Khartoum, Wadi Halfa, Port Sudan, and Juba, the capital of Equatoria. Incredibly enough the United States was not permitted to have any diplomatic representation in the Sudan until 1951. Khartoum, one of the key cities of the world, had no American ambassador, minister, or consul.[8]

FROM CAIRO TO KHARTOUM

This trip, unless you travel by air, takes three stages. The celebrated "white train" (really a dirty cream color) with its European *wagon-lits* scuffles out of Cairo in the evening and reaches LUXOR early the next day. Here you may visit some of the most majestic and melancholy ruins ever made by man, and watch snake charmers seduce cobras out of hidden niches in the rocks. You proceed by train to a town called Shallal near the Aswan Dam, and board a blunt-nosed scow, which is really three marine vehicles strapped together. First-class passengers travel in the middle structure. One of our British friends sighed, "Everything is run by the Wogs now. I can remember when people on these boats *dressed for dinner!*"

[8] One is reminded of India in the old days. Not till the eve of World War II did the British permit foreign diplomatic representation at New Delhi; the United States was represented in India only by consular officials in Calcutta and Bombay.

Below Aswan the Nile broadens out to become a pellucid sheet of lake. Along the shallow, sandy banks the palms are submerged so that only the tufts show—an unnatural spectacle—and the Nubian villages look like a fringe of lace. Shops along the shore are mobile—feluccas with curved sails carrying provisions from dock to dock. At night not a light is visible on the whole river. The heat would satisfy Cerberus.

Abu Simbel, where Rameses II still guards the Nile from his vantage point in what is surely the most isolated, time-worn and immovably serene of all temples, is a sublime sight. It was a shock to learn that it will disappear forever—so will the whole town of Wadi Halfa and its environs—if Colonel Nasser's mammoth dam is built. All this area will be permanently flooded to make the new Nile reservoir.

At WADI HALFA, having entered the Sudan, you board a train again. This is regarded by most British who have lived long and proudly in the Sudan as the best train in the world, and indeed it is extraordinarily good. You learn now (if you have not already learned it) that this is hot country. The train is fawn-colored, with roomy compartments like those on Indian trains; there are only seven windows to a car, and these are glassed in blue and shuttered heavily. In the dining car a Sudanese major-domo in a magnificent uniform serves seven-course meals with the suave aplomb of Mr. Henri Soulé at Le Pavillon; the napery sparkles and the silver shines. For breakfast you get authentic Oxford-vintage marmalade. But this train, for all its smart evocation of the *ancien régime*, is part of a railway system owned by the Sudanese state, and is manned by members of one of the most powerful —and radical—labor unions in all Africa.

The run from Wadi Halfa to Khartoum takes twenty-seven hours. The train cuts straight across the desert first, and then winds its way along the Nile. The desert stations do not have names but only numbers, and stand fifty miles apart. The stationmasters are Greek; no other people could stand the loneliness. The most famous stop is No. 6, because this has water. At all the others, water for the trains has to be brought by train. Each station has a cluster of conical brick huts, where the local personnel live; these are pure white (to reflect the sun) with dead black caps. At once, descending at these stations and watching people, you feel an acute sense of the profound difference between the Sudan and Egypt. A certain atmosphere of rapacity is gone. Children are cleanly dressed, and have fewer sores; veiled women wear pure white flowing robes, and do not beg. On the public buildings the British and Egyptian flags fly side by side, as is obligatory under the condominium. A young Sudanese passenger told us with emotion, "We have no flag as yet. But within a year *those* flags will be down."

HISTORY, KHARTOUM, AND THE GEZIRA

No country has been more a prisoner of external forces than the Sudan. It is busy trying to make its own history now. In 1819 Mohammed Ali sent his armies into the Sudan and conquered it; thereafter Egyptian rule, which was unimaginably cruel, slothful, and corrupt, lasted till the 1880's. About 1881 rose the corrosive prophet and warrior who became famous the world over as the Mahdi (= messiah); his real name was Mohammed Ahmed. He built up an army of dervishes, and in the name of God fought a fierce rebellion against British and Egyptians both. He was what nowadays we would call a fanatic nationalist with overpowering religious overtones. The Mahdi was a very considerable personage indeed. He claimed to be a descendant of the Prophet Mohammed. He died young—at thirty-seven —but before his death he freed most of the Sudan from Egyptian tyranny.

Forced to their knees by this inflammatory patriot, the Egyptians turned to London for help. What followed is a romantic tragedy known to everybody. After prolonged vacillation the British government sent General Charles George ("Chinese") Gordon to safeguard British interests and superintend the Egyptian withdrawal, which had finally been decided on. Gordon was not (as is often thought) dispatched to Khartoum to conquer the Sudan, but to help evacuate it. But he was a cranky absolutist character and he made his own policy. The Mahdi's forces advanced on Khartoum and after a long siege took it in 1885. Gordon was killed by dervish spears on the steps of the palace that is now the seat of the Governor General, three days before a relief expedition arrived to save him. Thirteen years later the British took their revenge. In 1898 General Sir Horatio Kitchener (later Lord Kitchener of Khartoum—the Egyptians called him "Kitchener Rex") wiped out the dervishes once and for all at Omdurman. This was a battle in the grandest old style. The Anglo-Egyptians lost forty-eight killed; the dervishes lost 9,700. One of Kitchener's officers was none other than the youthful Winston Churchill. It is somehow startling to recall that Sir Winston had his baptism of fire leading a cavalry charge on the banks of the Nile fifty-seven years ago. His own description of this contains some truly purple prose.[9]

The Mahdi had died (a natural death) in 1885, shortly after Gordon was killed. Kitchener had his tomb opened and sacked and his remains thrown into the river. The Mahdi's successor was another notable Sudanese religious fanatic and nationalist, by name Abdullahi and known usually as the Khalifa

[9] *A Roving Commission*, p. 182 et seq.

(lieutenant). He was pursued after the slaughter at Omdurman and caught and killed in Kordofan in 1899.[10]

In 1899 joint Anglo-Egyptian rule was set up over the Sudan—the condominium. But although Egypt had theoretically equal status as a codominus, the British ran the country. Kitchener was commander-in-chief and Governor General for ten long years (1889-99) and Sir Reginald Wingate for seventeen more, until 1916. Proconsuls had capacious terms in those days. The Egyptians tried to hold on to their juridical rights, but they had little to say.[11]

After the murder of Sir Lee Stack in 1924 the British administration became even more exclusive. But Egypt was capable of making mischief diplomatically, and, as Egyptian nationalism grew more powerful, so did Egyptian resentment at being ignominiously squeezed out of the Sudan. In 1951 a Wafdist government unilaterally abrogated the condominium and proclaimed Farouk "King of the Sudan." The British refused to accept this. Meantime *Sudanese* nationalism was also growing steadily in pitch and volume.

The Sudan, because of its condominium status, was never and is not now a member of the British Commonwealth. The Foreign Office, not the Colonial Office or the Commonwealth Relations Office, handled Sudanese affairs. An organism called the Sudan Agency maintained offices in London, but this was not part of the *British* government. In fact the local administration in Khartoum had extraordinary—almost autonomous—powers. It was run by Englishmen of course, but these constituted a Sudanese government. Until recent years the most important man in the Sudan by far, its real boss, was not the Governor General appointed from London but the Civil Secretary rising out of the *local* civil service.[12] Khartoum always had a kind of veto power over London.

*

[10] Another event immediately after Omdurman was the celebrated "Fashoda" crisis. This almost caused a war between Britain and France. A French column under Colonel Marchand—the French had designs on the Sudan too—planted the tricolor at Fashoda on the Nile near Khartoum. Political pressure imposed by London on a timid Paris forced him out.
[11] The condominium agreement states that the Governor General shall always be appointed by the *Egyptian* government with the concurrence of the British government, but this formula was nothing but a fiction. The Governor General was always British.
[12] Several confusions attend these matters. In theory the chief representative of *Egypt* in the Sudan is still the *British* governor, since Britain and Egypt are co-domini. When a British official in Khartoum uses the word "we" he can mean the British, the Egyptians, or the Sudanese. Of course after 1956 there will be no British governor or civil secretary.

All this background comes to vivid life on even the briefest visit to KHARTOUM. This city, pivotal to the future of Africa, is actually three cities—Khartoum itself (population 79,000) largely governmental; Khartoum North (41,000) an industrial suburb; and Omdurman (128,000) across the river, which is the Arab town. The name means "Elephant's Trunk." Khartoum was founded by the Egyptians in 1823, destroyed by the Mahdi's dervishes, and rebuilt by Kitchener in 1899. He laid it out—with what magisterial self-righteousness and confidence!—in the shape of a Union Jack.

This served a good tactical purpose—machine guns could easily command the long slanting streets with their numerous intersections—but it makes for a traffic problem now. Street signs are scarlet, and some are in three languages—English (on top), Arabic, and Greek. Kitchener Avenue along the Blue Nile is one well-known thoroughfare. I asked a British friend how long it would be before this was renamed Nasser Boulevard. He replied grimly, "At any rate I will wager that it will never be named for a Sudanese." Events may well prove him wrong.

The British have been in Khartoum for more than fifty years, but it has no sewage system; "night soil" is still collected by camel-drawn carts. Even in important British houses there are no flush toilets. British standards—as always—follow a complex insular pattern. Night soil is all right. Morals are something else again. A few Balkanesque night clubs exist drearily in Khartoum, with girls of assorted nationalities. One troupe when we were there had a Viennese, a Greek, an Italian, a Finn, a Frenchwoman, two Hungarians, and a Portuguese. But *English* women are not allowed to be night-club entertainers or prostitutes in the Sudan.

Khartoum was an important stop in the aerial route across Africa used during World War II by American and Allied transport planes. Few GI's will remember it with relish.

Khartoum's chief distinction is, of course, that it lies at the confluence of the Blue and White Niles. Winston Churchill described the city as a "spout." I was much impressed by the lights over the big bridge—some white, some blue—but this has no deliberate symbolic significance. The White Nile is whitish—if not actually white—at Khartoum, whereas the Blue is a dirty brownish color. The two rivers maintain their separate identities for miles after they leave Khartoum, even though they have become parts of the same thick stream. Swimming is possible in the river near Khartoum (if one has no fear of bilharzia) because heavy steamboat traffic has frightened away the crocodiles.

Another important distinction is that Khartoum is the seat of University College. This is an amalgamation of the Kitchener School of Medicine and one of the most renowned of all institutions of learning in Africa, Gordon Memorial College, which gives degrees honored by the University of London, and is the only school of such standing in the whole of eastern British Africa except Makerere in Uganda. The United Kingdom gave its endowment fund a free gift of £1,000,000 recently in recognition of the Sudanese contribution to World War II. There are about five hundred students taking degrees in law, medicine, public administration, engineering, and agriculture. The college has no official connection with the Sudanese government, but no government at all would be possible without it, because it trains the governing class. Here, under British tutelage, Sudanese youth has for half a century received higher education. The irony is of course striking that practically all students turned out by Gordon College become vigorous nationalists. By fostering an institution of this kind, the British, a phenomenally puzzling people, deliberately plant the seeds of their own doom. But they go ahead and do it anyway.

Omdurman across the Nile, on the western bank, was built by the Khalifa, as a modern and "model" African city, to replace Khartoum when the latter was burned down. It is still almost purely African. Its principal sights today are the Khalifa's mosque, a hideous silver structure, and the Mahdi's tomb, which has been rebuilt (by the British). The most remarkable mass demonstration I saw in Africa, and one of the most remarkable I have ever seen anywhere, occurred in Omdurman on February 20, 1953. More than one hundred thousand people gathered in the blazing open square near the mosque, to celebrate the signature the previous week of the Anglo-Egyptian accord promising independence to the Sudan. It was the largest crowd in the country's history. Leaders of rival parties spoke, and old enemies embraced. Flags flew everywhere—the black flag of the Prophet Mohammed, the black-yellow-green flag of the Mahdi, and the red-white-black flag of the Egyptian Liberation Rally; thousands of these were made overnight, stitched together out of any kind of cloth, and with the stripes going any which way. But we saw no Union Jacks. On a rude podium (bricks kept tumbling off it) a spout of gas flame made a hissing illumination. Music from European violins got mixed up with music from native drums. Almost everybody wore white gowns, and looked like ghosts come to vivid life. The crowd cheered, shrieked, and chanted, as if crazed by joy. But the chief note of interest was something else. The Sudanese authorities had little experience of handling such a mass of people, and few police were available. Boys with staves led visitors to their places. But the proceedings were swift and to the point, and there was no disorder or confusion of any kind.

*

From Khartoum we drove down to visit Gezira and have a glimpse of Wad Medani (population 57,000), capital of the Blue Nile Province. The Gezira is a narrow triangle between the White and Blue Niles, and resembles the "Fertile Crescent" of Mesopotamia in miniature. It covers one million acres, has 26,000 tenant farmers, and is the best run and most productive project of its kind in Africa. It dates from the opening of the Sennar Dam in 1925; the original capital came from the United Kingdom. The scheme is "a joint enterprise between the [Sudanese] government on behalf of the people, the tenant farmers and the management."[13] Forty per cent of the profits go to the Sudanese government (and this constitutes a substantial share of the country's public revenue), forty per cent to the tenant farmers, and the rest to the Gezira Board, a public agency which runs the enterprise. "The tenant enjoys a higher standard of living and greater land security than any other small holder in the Middle East."

The Gezira project is—to define it in a word or two—a scheme to grow long-staple cotton and other crops by means of irrigation. Holdings are restricted to forty acres, and the tenant plants—in strict rotation—ten of these to cotton, five to grain, and two and a half to fodder. He gets free water, and the grain and fodder remain his own. Engineers say that, more than any region on the earth's surface, the Gezira provides ideal circumstances for a development of this kind. Water flows by gravity from the Blue Nile to the White, and the slope is so gentle that no erosion problem exists. The soil is impermeable clay, and loss from seepage is negligible; the canals do not have to be bound by brick or tile, and are no more than simple ditches. A million desolate acres have been made to burst with flower and seed.

Along one canal our car frightened a camel; the beast became hysterical and bolted; we followed it for miles, unable to stop it. The Jebel Auliya Dam is operated by Egyptians, not Sudanese. Our guide said, "You can tell the temper of Anglo-Egyptian-Sudanese relations by the way the Gippy guards behave. Sometimes they are polite, sometimes not." We stopped for a drink of lemonade at a supervisor's house, and carefully waited for the ladies of the household to scamper away and hide. Alien, infidel eyes do not see Moslem women in the Sudan. Along the White Nile the high land (made semi-fertile by rain) is owned by tribes; the riverain land, where it

[13] 1001 *Facts about the Sudan*, p. 12.

THE NILE AND THE SUDAN   237

has to be worked individually, is owned by individuals; people are in full transition from a nomadic (grazing) to an agricultural economy. We saw thousands of demoiselle cranes, maribou storks, and other birds. If a huntsman shoots a grouse, his Arab bearers will race pellmell to the bird to cut its throat before it is formally declared to be dead; otherwise they cannot eat it. Approaching the Gezira we became totally lost. There was no trace of any kind of track at all. Our guide said laconically, "It's hard to know where to drive when you can drive anywhere." This parched, violently dusty emptiness, obliterated by clouds of dirt, was what the whole Gezira was like before the irrigation project got under way.

The Sudan has another important reclamation and development scheme in the Zande area, nine hundred miles away near the Congo border. This too is symptomatic of the way progress is coming to much of Africa, even if it comes slowly.

IN MEMORIAM: THE SUDAN POLITICAL SERVICE

This was probably the most elite body of its kind in the world. The total personnel of the civil service in the Sudan (as of the time we were there) was about 7,000; of these about 6,000 were Sudanese, about 1,000 British. Of the 1,000 British most worked on short term contracts; only 230 were permanent career civil servants. Of these 230 only about 140 were members of the *Political* Service, which administered the country. This handful of carefully chosen, impeccably trained men, no more than 140 in all, governed 9,000,000 people in an area the size of the United States east of the Mississippi. One is reminded of the Indian Civil Service before 1939. But the Sudan Political Service was even more powerful and exclusive.

There were also 130 Sudanese in the Sudan Political Service, but their jobs were minor. All nine governors (of the nine provinces) were British when we were there; so were the deputy governors and the top-level administrators in Khartoum itself, like Sir James Robertson, the Civil Secretary. These men were the steel brace that held the Sudan together and made it function as a state.

The Sudan Political Service was probably the best paid body of its kind in the world, although salaries were not high by American standards. Members got eighty days' *annual* leave (think by comparison of Foreign or Colonial Office officials who do not get home more than once every two or three years at best) with free transportation to England and back not only for themselves but for their families; and they could retire at forty-eight. Retirement was obligatory at fifty-two. This meant as a rule that an official served in the Sudan no longer than twenty-five years, and then retired on a comfortable pension for life. Twenty-five years of work may not seem much, but the climate of the Sudan takes a great deal out of a man. Retirement was made possible at the early age of forty-eight so that it would be easier for an individual, if he wished, to find other work. For anybody looking for a job there is a considerable difference between being forty-nine and fifty-one. Significantly members of the Sudan Political Service (with a few rare exceptions) were not permitted to take up private employment *in the Sudan* after retirement. They could not become traders or settlers. Obviously this was to prevent them from utilizing their intimate knowledge of the Sudan—or exploiting their previous official position—for private gain.

Recruits for the service came mostly from the English and Scottish universities. Extraordinarily enough there was no written examination. A man would have his scholastic record looked into, but that was all. People were chosen (after being surveyed and questioned orally by a board) for their character or athletic prowess. It took a junior officer ten years to rise to the status of District Commissioner. Boys not more than a few years out of Oxford might rule a territory the size of England. Their main job was to give the Africans a sense of security and to be fair. To get a rise in pay, every officer had to pass an examination in Arabic. The most promising DC's, those with a good chance of becoming governors in time, were shifted at two-year intervals (if possible) from province to province so that their experience should be as wide as possible. Men were chosen not only for their ability to get along with Africans but with other whites, in particular if only an extremely limited number of white men lived in the neighborhood; also for their capacity to live alone. DC's in the south were nicknamed "Bog Barons." One senior official told me, "Of course we sent the *clever* lads to the northern provinces. The south is no place for a *clever* man. Anybody clever would go crazy. For the south we had to have stolid chaps, but, by Jove, what good chaps they were!"

In older days every member of the service out in the field was obliged to dress in full uniform, with boots and spurs, even if it were 100 in the shade, and ride horseback for an hour each morning—for self-discipline and to impress the Sudanese. But all "that pukka Sahib stuff"—as one governor described it to us—went out with the war. "You don't sit in a tree and shoot elephants any more. You sit in an office and add up figures."

Most British had, and have, a very high regard for the Sudanese, particularly those non-urban. "Sudanese are not like Egyptians. They don't cheat." Moreover they are *men*, like the Pathans of the North-West Frontier, the British say admiringly. "In the past few years they murdered three of our DC's. Takes a stout fellow to be able to do *that!*"

*

The chief grievance against the Political Service was that it was so expensive. The Sudanese resented the salaries and pensions the Britons got, their beautiful houses along the Nile, and also the fact that its members were part of a rigidly closed circle, all powerful and immune to criticism. Almost half the administrative budget went to salaries, the Sudanese say; moreover in half a century (they assert) the British did not spend a total of more than £17,000,000 on *Sudanese* public improvements. One politician told us, "British rule was certainly not corrupt, as Egyptian rule might have been. But it was just as certainly exploitative." I found, however, that comparatively few Sudanese had much active animus against the British; the atmosphere was nothing like so anti-British as that of Egypt. On the other hand a marked wave of xenophobia began to be felt as the Sudanese prepared to take over the government.

The British—at least most of those in the civil service—grant that the 1953 accord was unavoidable, but they think that it came too soon. Their target date for Sudanese independence was 1966. Of course events at large—not just in the Sudan—made any such remote date utterly impossible. They might as well have asked the Sudanese to wait till 2066.[14] But for reasons both selfish and unselfish many Britons felt that the Sudanese needed substantial further tutelage, that they simply were not ready for full self-government as yet. The country never even had a legislature till 1948. What is the point of attaining self-government if the self-government is too inexperienced, too undermanned and slipshod, to be able to work? To replace the 140 Britons in the Political Service 140 Sudanese had to be found—but where were they to come from? There are only about seventeen secondary schools in the country, which turn out perhaps two thousand boys a year; of the graduates of Gordon College, only about a dozen customarily go into the Political Service. The British felt, in short, that the Sudan did not have nearly enough trained man power available for the tasks of government. Also they asked whether or not a Sudanese official in the field, considering his tribal and family affiliations, could possibly be free enough of local

---

[14] One senior British official said to us, "We try to be a little *ahead* of the Sudanese moderates. We can 'give and keep' if we give *in time*." But he had gravely underestimated the velocity of Sudanese development. For the philosophy of "give and keep" see Chapter 1 above.

pressures to make a good DC, in adjudicating disputes and administering justice. Finally, they felt that there was grave danger that, as soon as they themselves were out, the Egyptians would gobble up the country.

The atmosphere in British circles in Khartoum was febrile in 1953. Stoutly, honorably, men about to give up their lifework insisted that they wished the Sudanese well. *"Hope* they can pull it off!" With a similar accent a rejected suitor might offer congratulations to his sweetheart, when she goes off to marry someone else. I have never seen more numerous (or more neatly mustached) stiff upper lips.

The Sudanese have several answers to the British. First, they make the general point that, whether or not they are completely fit for self-government, this is their right and they intend to exercise it whether for good or ill. Nationalism cannot be stopped. But, secondly, they do not concede that they cannot run the country just as well as the British did. For one thing—as to filling jobs—they say that the British gravely underestimate the number of trained Sudanese available. Moreover if no Sudanese can be found for some particular post, the new government will have no objection to keeping on a British incumbent on contract—but as a servant, not as a master. Not many Britons have, however, been willing to stay; in fact a mass exodus of British officials began in early 1955. The Sudanese say that they will bring in Germans, Swiss, and others as substitutes. Recently they turned to New Delhi and hired a group of Indian technicians—judges, surveyors, census officers, railway engineers, entomologists—although India itself is desperately short of trained personnel.

First to be "Sudanized" was the Political Service. A British Governor General still remains, but his powers have been curtailed and his post will be abolished by 1956. All nine provincial governors are now Sudanese, as well as senior civil servants in Khartoum. Then came the army. Major General R. D. Scoones, the caid or commandant of the Sudanese Defense Force, turned over his duties to his Sudanese second-in-command in August, 1954, and left the country. Since that date there have been no British military officers in the Sudan. Finally the police were Sudanized. But as a matter of fact the Sudanese had for a long time been running their own police (6,500 in number) by themselves. When the 1953 accord was signed there were only about a dozen British police officers in the entire country.

*

So the British are out now. Perhaps their regime was archaic and expensive and it was imposed on the country by force in the first instance, but what a magnificent job the British did! For fifty years their administration

THE NILE AND THE SUDAN

gave the Sudan education, justice, public order, and almost complete political tranquillity, with opportunity for development, even during periods of the most effervescent crisis. There has never been a revolt; there has never even been a sign of overt unrest. (For this one must pay tribute to the good qualities of the Sudanese as well.) Think in contrast of the French record in Morocco, a country which cannot be ruled at all except by the threat of force. Since World War II only one British battalion—say eight hundred men—has been stationed in the Sudan, and the Sudanese Defense Force never had more than thirty British officers. All this in a territory that could easily have exploded into chaos at any moment, if administration had ever been arbitrary, selfish, or unwise.

Truly the British have reason to be proud of themselves in the Sudan. And when time came for them to leave, they left like gentlemen.

THE EGYPTIAN POSITION

Practically all Egyptians take the line that, after 1956, the Sudan must inevitably become part of Egypt. The two countries (as the Egyptians see it) are brothers with the closest historical and biological association; the Sudan is the source of Egypt's lifeblood—water—and would be an ideal spill-over area for Egypt's surplus population; the Sudanese are splendid soldiers and would make Egypt a stronger military nation.

The Sudanese attitude is a good deal more complex. Sudanese and Egyptians are brothers, yes; 40 per cent of all Sudanese politicians have Egyptian blood, yes; there is no Egypto-Sudanese "problem," yes; it would be a good idea to exchange Sudanese water for Egyptian population, since the Sudan is heavily underpopulated—yes.

But the Sudanese, even if they are closely akin to the Egyptians, do not necessarily admire them. A youthful Sudanese told us, "We like Egyptians, but do not respect them; we do not like the British, but do respect them." The basic point is that after more than a century of subjugation by Egypt, Britain, and a combination of both, the Sudanese are at last on the point of being completely free. Why, having gained independence, should they surrender it to Egypt? Why, getting a chance to prove that they can run their own free country, should they throw this chance away?

To a certain extent the Sudanese are divided on this issue. Speaking roughly the urban class, which is literate and reads the inflammatory Egyptian press, is pro-Egyptian; the desert and forest dwellers on the other hand remember what their fathers told them about misrule by Cairo in the days of their grandfathers, and are suspicious of Egyptian good intentions. They see no point to jumping out of a British pan into an Egyptian fire.

Certainly, however, the Sudan would not be on the brink of full freedom had it not been for some wonderfully shrewd, effective politics by Naguib-Nasser. The Egyptian leaders knew that they could not settle their difficulties with the *British*, which was their main preoccupation, until a Sudanese settlement was reached. Naguib did something totally unexpected, which caught London by surprise. He reversed altogether the previous Egyptian policy toward the Sudan, repudiated the Farouk-Wafd "Unity of the Nile Valley" concept (at least for the time being) and suggested something outrageously practical that nobody else had ever thought of before—namely, asking the Sudanese themselves to decide their future. The British had no recourse but to agree.[15] After all Naguib was giving up *Egyptian* claims to the Sudan if it chose to remain free. Moreover his chief emissary to the Sudan, Major Salah Salem, skillfully lined up all political parties there in favor of the idea.[16] So negotiations began, and the accord of February 12, 1953, was signed.

Of course Naguib's course of action enhanced Egyptian prestige in the Sudan, and he himself, partly Sudanese anyway, became a tremendous national hero. It was pressure from the Sudan that saved him from being tried for treason after his fall-out with Nasser in 1954. Nasser wants to stay on good terms with the Sudan.

SUDANESE POLITICS AND PERSONALITIES

The Sudan is the last important Moslem country we shall encounter until this long book nears its end, although several states that we shall visit meanwhile have powerful Arab minorities, and the island of Zanzibar is Moslem. Sudanese politics have always been inextricably mixed up with religion. One aspect of the present political situation is that two religious sects are struggling for secular power.

The outstanding leaders—and bitter rivals—are known commonly by their nicknames. "Sar" and "Sam." Sar, the Mahdi, born in 1885, is none other than a posthumous son of the great Mahdi, and is considered by his

---

[15] Of course the ultimate right of the Sudanese to be free was implicit in the whole of British policy toward the Sudan, as it is in British colonial policy elsewhere. But, as explained above, the British wanted to go much more slowly. Naguib made the issue immediate, and gained great political capital by doing so.

[16] A wan British comment was, "The Egyptians had unlimited money, and play better than we do under the table."

followers to be a prophet, like his father—almost divine.[17] Orthodox Moslems, on the other hand, do not subscribe to Mahdism. Sar is correctly known as El Sayed Sir Abdel Rahman el Mahdi Pasha, KBE, CVO. The most significant thing about him is that he is spiritual leader of the UMMA (Independence) party. He does not want the Sudan to be swallowed up by Egypt; he wants it to be free. Sometimes Sar is called a British puppet—a strange thing for the son of the Mahdi to be—but this is to overstate the case. His properties have convenient access to the most valuable of all Sudanese commodities—water—and he is probably the richest man in the country.

Sam, in strict contrast to Sar, is much more fundamentalist and orthodox from a religious point of view and much more pro-Egyptian. His name is El Sayed Sir Ali Mirghani Pasha, KCMG, KCVO; he too has been knighted by the British. Of Persian origin, he leads the powerful Khatmia (anti-Mahdi) sect. He was educated in Cairo, and his main support is in the towns. If Sar is sometimes called a British puppet, Sam is sometimes called an Egyptian puppet. But Sam takes the position that he is purely a religious leader, altogether above and beyond politics. Like Sar (whom he hates) he is respectable, venerable, and rich. Though strongly pro-Egyptian now, he was once Great Britain's man. The British did their best to keep *both* Sar and Sam in camp. Long ago (when the condominium was first getting under way) London flirted with the idea of making the Sudan a kingdom with Sam as king—as a counterpoise to Mahdist strength. But Sam did not want to be king, and gradually the British transferred their support to Sar.

We did not meet Sam, but Sudanese friends took us over to Omdurman for an interview with Sar, the Mahdi. Sar has four wives, and we met two of his sons; one is about fifty and is the active head of the UMMA party; one is a youngster about seven, with an English governess. Sar does not, however, speak any English himself.[18] The wives are, of course, secluded into strict purdah; we did not even see any female retainers. Sar is tall, dark, dignified, and amiable. He wears a thick, graying beard, played with lemon-yellow beads as he talked, and (as is so often the case with potentates of this type) had on a costume that became less Oriental from north to south. His dazzling white, intricately bound turban might have come out of medieval Baghdad; his woolen socks and narrow yellowish shoes might have come from Harlem. We had tea, lemonade, and cakes with icing

[17] Once more let us mention how close people are to history in this part of the world. The Mahdi is the son—not the grandson—of the Mahdi. The present-day Governor of Kenya, Sir Evelyn Baring, is a youngish man but is nevertheless the *son* of Lord Cromer, who ruled Egypt for twenty-four years from 1883 to 1907.

[18] Nor does Sam.

colored to an almost intolerable brilliance. Present at our audience was the assistant minister of irrigation. Then entered a celebrated Sudanese personality, ninety-six years old, who has devoted most of his life to advancing the cause of education for Sudanese women, Sheikh Babikar Bedri. He was barefoot, and kissed the Mahdi's hand three times loudly. This alert, humorous old man fought at Omdurman against Kitchener fifty-seven years ago.[19]

The Mahdi asked us about the United States, and mentioned how important had been the good offices of Ambassador Caffery in Egypt in helping to achieve the Sudan accord. Then he wanted to know whether the United States really stood on the side of African nationalism—or not.

*

The first general election in Sudanese history took place in November, 1953. Seldom has any election been more picturesque. Several hundred thousand people who did not know how to read or write and who had never seen a ballot box went triumphantly to the polls; symbols were used instead of names, and voters had their fingernails etched with a kind of acid stain, which could not be washed away, to keep them from voting twice. The British accused the Egyptians of unwarrantable interference in these elections —and vice versa. But the proceeding as a whole was honest, orderly, and efficiently carried out.

The National Unity Party (pro-Egyptian) won a resounding victory. The Mahdi's party—standing for independence—made a showing much less good than anticipated. In the House of Representatives the National Unionists won 50 seats to the UMMA's 23; in the Senate 21 out of 30. Another important party is the Socialist Republican. There are about ten parties in the Sudan in all.

One should interpolate here a word about the strength, which is growing steeply, of the Sudanese labor movement. Not since Tunisia have we seen a country distinguished by trade unionism on any substantial scale, and it will be a long time before we meet another. Labor legislation is advanced in the Sudan, and there are more than eighty well-established unions. They cover everything from dock workers to medicine; there are unions for bakery assistants, schoolteachers, taxi drivers, and civil servants. Strikes are frequent.

---

[19] The Mahdi told us that he had recently received from Sir Winston Churchill an autographed copy of *The River War*, Churchill's account of the British campaign against the Khalifa. Gracefully Churchill communicated to the Mahdi (the present one) the hope that a biography would be written of his father some day from the Sudanese point of view, not from that of the British invaders. Churchill greatly admired the old Mahdi's military prowess.

THE NILE AND THE SUDAN

The labor membership is almost solidly pro-Egyptian. Considerable danger exists of Communist penetration into the unions, particularly that of the railway workers, which is the largest and most powerful in the country, with a membership near 30,000. As always the Communist party appeals to the have-nots and the newly created and inadequately educated intelligentsia. It operates from subterranean cells in Egypt. One Sudanese told me, "Most Moslems do not become Communists easily." Then he used an unexpected adjective: "We do not care for an ideology so *emaciated*."

On January 1, 1954, following the elections, the first Sudanese parliament was ceremoniously opened, and "full" self-government began, as promised by the 1953 pact. The powers of the British Governor General were curbed by the installation of a new body called the "Governor General's Commission," which can veto him in certain circumstances. This consists of five members—two Sudanese, one Briton, one Egyptian, and one Pakistani as chairman—and therefore has a four to one Moslem majority. Troubles, as was inevitable, promptly afflicted the new government as it tested its apron strings. There were severe riots in Khartoum in March, with thirty-one fatalities. In December (1954) three Khatmia ministers were expelled from the new cabinet, ostensibly because they flirted with the UMMA. Crisis followed crisis, but all were overcome.

The Prime Minister is a resonant and arresting personality, a Sam man and head of the National Unity party, by name Sayed Ismail Ahmed El Azhari. He was born in Omdurman in 1902, and is a grandson of the Grand Mufti of the Sudan; he was educated at Gordon College and then the American University at Beirut in the Lebanon. He was a teacher for many years, and president of the pro-Egyptian Ashigga party until this merged with the Unionists. He visited the United States to plead the Sudanese case before the Security Council of the UN in 1947. Twice (in 1948 and 1949) he was jailed by the British for sedition, but the terms were brief. He is a devout Moslem and fanatic nationalist. In 1954 he made a state visit to London as a guest of the United Kingdom government. He made a good impression there, and the shrewd, farseeing British saw to it that he was received not only by Sir Winston Churchill but by the Queen.

By 1956 the Sudan must choose whether it will remain independent or link up to Egypt. Cairo's position is very strong, but the Sudanese are having a brilliantly good time learning to run their own affairs. Whether the Sudan will remain the Sudan or become part of Egypt or whether a compromise will be worked out is impossible to predict at the moment. If El Azhari stays in power, a reasonable guess is that it will join Egypt and Egypt will become in consequence the second biggest country (from the standpoint of population) on the continent, and by all odds the most powerful except for the Union.

VOICE OF AMERICA IN THE SUDAN

Khartoum was the first city in Africa where we found a good many people listening closely to Voice of America programs, which are rebroadcast from a station (location top secret) in the eastern Mediterranean. One pert comment: "Your speakers know Arabic quite well, but they would be more effective if any of them had better knowledge of the countries they talk about."

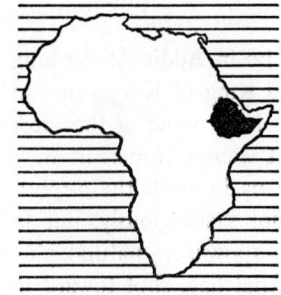

CHAPTER 15

Haile Selassie, Emperor of Ethiopia

The Aethiopians slept near a thousand years, forgetful of the world, by whom they were forgotten.
—EDWARD GIBBON

A damsel with a dulcimer
In a vision once I saw:
It was an Abyssinian maid,
And on her dulcimer she play'd. . . .
—SAMUEL TAYLOR COLERIDGE

WE REACH now a country utterly unlike any we have seen in Africa so far. Ethiopia, sometimes called Abyssinia, is a mountain fastness, a fortress, cut off to a large extent from the adjacent world by the mere fact of its altitude, an impregnable feudal kingdom lost in space. What struck us most in nonpolitical realms is that for the first time in months we saw trees—not palms, not tropical shrubbery—but stout, honest trees roughly climbing the rough slopes of mountains. The thing that struck us most politically was, of course, the person of the Emperor. Haile Selassie strides the immense wastes of the Ethiopian plateau—like a gnome.

One might almost say that the chief issue in Ethiopia is a struggle between this frail, tenacious little man *and* his country. The note he sounds is of progress, modernization, at least to the extent that difficult circumstances make this possible. Haile Selassie has committed himself to a carefully calculated effort to conquer the backwardness of his domain, and bring it into the embrace of civilization overnight. No struggle in Africa is more challenging.

A generation has grown up since the Italian conquest of Ethiopia, when Haile Selassie's proud, dainty, and adhesive figure commanded the liberal conscience of mankind. A visitor does not have to be in Addis Ababa long to find out that he is still Emperor of Ethiopia and King of Kings. In fact he runs his country, both blessed and tortured as it is by some of the most titanic forces ever let loose by nature, almost as if it were a kindergarten.

When we arrived in Addis Ababa friends drove us in from the airport. "My God, the Emperor!" exclaimed our escort—not sacrilegiously, but in the tone of a man confronted suddenly with an overpowering natural phenomenon. A big green Rolls-Royce, flying the imperial flag, shot toward us around a corner. Donkeys scattered, and, almost as if they were bending before some invisible wind, passers-by flattened themselves on the road, not merely bowing, but in full prostration. Our car—and all other cars—jerked to a stop, and our companions jumped out to the street, bowing stiffly as the imperial limousine darted past. The King of Kings, perched on cushions, bowed back politely, and then swept on. This ceremony of recognition of the Emperor is *de rigueur* in Ethiopian society.

The Emperor himself, however, takes protocol somewhat less seriously than do members of his entourage. Recently he visited Massawa, the Eritrean seaport. A group of diplomats saw him approach, and smartly jumped out of their own cars to salute him. He wagged his finger at them as if they were children behaving *too* properly.

A few days after our arrival in Addis Ababa my wife and I had the honor of being received by His Imperial Majesty (few people ever say merely "His Majesty"). I have met a good many kings, but never one like this. The extreme stiffness of the Ethiopian court dates from a tradition centuries old; even in comparatively recent times courtiers were supposed to approach the Emperor by crawling across the room. In earlier days the penalty for disrespect was cutting off the lips and tongue of the offender. When etiquette began to take on a western character, during the present Emperor's reign, the model chosen was Swedish, and Sweden has the strictest court in Europe. (Ethiopia and Sweden may seem to be odd bedfellows, but Swedish influence is profound today in several Ethiopian spheres, as we shall see below.)

I faced minor sartorial difficulties, since I had been told that I must wear a morning coat and striped trousers; I did not possess these articles, and could find nobody in Addis Ababa who had them to fit my size. Eventually I was permitted to penetrate into the imperial presence in nothing more formal than a dark suit, and nothing untoward happened. The kingdom is still standing. Carefully friends briefed us about what we had to do. On entering the Emperor's chamber three separate bows are necessary, one at the threshold, one halfway across the room, and one on being presented—

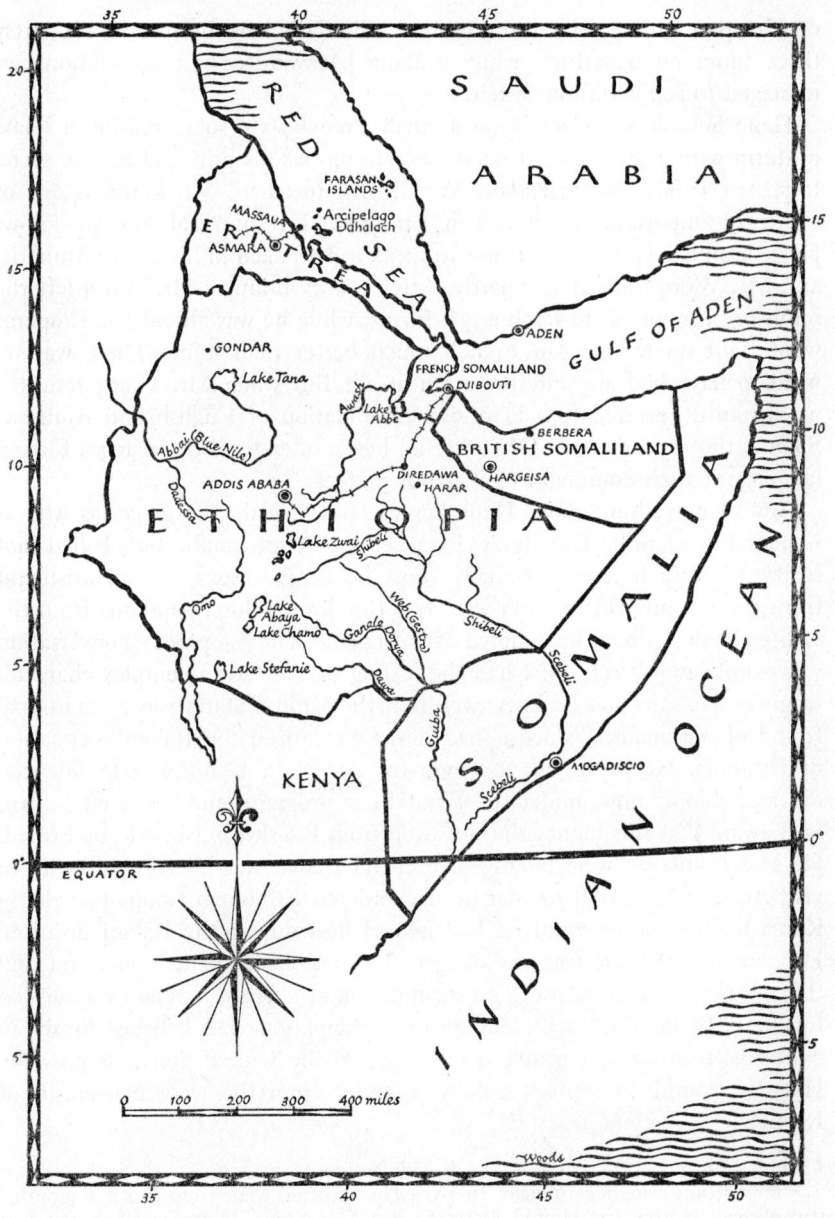

on the part of my wife three curtsies. Similarly one must bow or curtsy three times on departure, while walking backward. These stipulations we managed to fulfill without hitch.

Haile Selassie sat placidly on a small French-style sofa, wearing a khaki uniform with a placard of decorations. He rose as his principal private secretary, Ato Tafarra Worq Kidane Wold, introduced us; Mr. Worq is one of the most important dignitaries in Ethiopia.[1] His Imperial Majesty knows English quite well but prefers not to speak it; he talked in his native Amharic, and Mr. Worq translated expertly. After twenty minutes Mr. Worq left the room for a moment, to fetch a gift for us; while he was absent the Emperor went right on talking—in French much better than mine. There was no need to have had any interpretation at all! But when Mr. Worq returned we instantly reverted to a laborious combination of English and Amharic. Such is the royal custom. Of course all heads of state dislike using a foreign language if their command of it is not perfect.

Almost everything about Haile Selassie has a quality of grace, as well as impeccable dignity. Everybody has seen his photograph, but I had not realized before how exceptionally short he is. He looks like an aristocrat from the Levant. On the sofa were two tiny brown dogs, papillons from the United States, which he fondled as we talked. The Emperor's conversation was simple and direct, but I had the feeling that he was a complex character to grasp. He said that he knew well that the United States was a traditional friend of nationalism, since it had never recognized the Italian occupation of Ethiopia. He expressed gratitude for American technical and financial aid to Ethiopia now, under the Point Four program, and said that he was well aware that this money did not drop from the sky, but had to be earned. He said (while we were talking in French) that it was his *rêve* (dream) to visit America.[2] He told us that he had ordered Ethiopian troops to fight in Korea because other countries had helped *him* during the Italian invasion. He denied that there was any danger of Communism in Ethiopia and said that he would like very much to see a common defense program established for the Middle East, with American participation. He believes firmly in collective security, but wants as close ties to the United States as possible. Here we found an attitude totally different from the wary neutralism of Egypt.

[1] Once he was a translator in the British embassy.
[2] This dream was soon fulfilled. In 1954 His Imperial Majesty took a five months' trip abroad, visiting the United States for the first time. He received a resounding welcome. America fascinated him. Also he went to England (where Queen Elizabeth II conferred on him the Order of the Garter) and several countries on the continent including Yugoslavia, where he got on well with Marshal Tito.

One of His Imperial Majesty's duties this morning was inspection of the Imperial Police Staff College at Aba Dina, where a class of officers was graduating, and we were invited to attend this ceremony. The school, which is run by Swedes, proudly demonstrated its achievements. The program told us what we would see. "Brief examination in investigation of the scene of crime, with saving traces." "Demonstration of a modern equipped rushing-out-car with police and radio." Cadets did exercises in ju-jitsu, and showed us that they knew how to take fingerprints. Haile Selassie walked from exhibit to exhibit, in the piercing sunshine, amid swarms of angry and pertinacious flies. He wore a long khaki cape and a large beige-colored pith sun helmet, which made him look—I mean no disrespect—something like a mushroom.

When he entered the main room, where a throne had been set up, he rested his tiny feet on a cushion; otherwise they would not have reached the floor. He never smiled, nor looked to the right or left. Finally in the courtyard he watched the cadets get their diplomas. Each had to walk up four carpeted steps, salute in a complicated manner, and then descend backward. The Emperor shook hands with no one but a senior Swedish officer. He made a short speech, and a band played the wild, soaring notes of the Ethiopian imperial anthem. I saw a motto on the school wall: "The law whether it rewards or punishes must be applied to all without exception." Indeed one of the Emperor's most conspicuous tasks has been to make law respected. The feeble ineptness of much that we saw was heartbreaking. One boy, chosen to demonstrate his skill in mechanics, could not make the gears of a car work; another who gave a lecture on crime prevention was so dazed —numb—that he could scarcely talk. Yet it is out of beginnings like this, no matter how clumsy, that Haile Selassie's Ethiopia is being built. A loyal, honest, and efficient police is a necessity in Ethiopia—just as it should be in New York—and it cannot be created without education, education, education.

*

Now before proceeding to discuss the Emperor's character and attainments we must paint briefly a backdrop of Ethiopia itself.

WHAT MAKES ETHIOPIA UNIQUE

Four interesting phenomena are these: (1) Ethiopia is not only an independent state, but has by far the longest record of independence of any country in Africa except Egypt, and it differs strikingly from Egypt in that it has *never* been under foreign domination, except during the Italian occupation from 1936 to 1941. (2) It is Christian—indigenously Christian from the most ancient times, not Christianized by modern missionaries. (3) It is *not* a "black" or Negro nation, as most people think. Some of its people are black as Vulcan, and some have Negro blood, but Ethiopians most distinctly do not think of themselves as Negro or Negroid. (4) In Ethiopia, the equation characteristic of colonial Africa is reversed—Europeans work for Africans, not vice versa.

Let us elaborate on these four points in turn.

(1) Ethiopia remained unconquered—until Mussolini—for almost three thousand years, even during the heyday of the European scramble for Africa, for the simplest of reasons—it was too inaccessible, too mountainous and impregnable, to attack.[3] Even in Homeric times Ethiopians were known as "the farthest away of all mankind"; their country was the place where the sun was supposed to set. Ethiopia was, however, several times penetrated—but not conquered—by Europeans. The Portuguese, seeking the legendary Prester John, touched on its coasts; then in the sixteenth century came the Turks, who brought in Islam. The British sent the Napier expedition into the country in 1868, to rescue a handful of British subjects held in capitivity; the operation was a success, but cost £9,000,000. In 1895 the Italians attacked Ethiopia, but they were so badly mauled at the celebrated Battle of Adowa that they retired and left the country severely alone—as did the other great powers—till 1935.[4]

Ethiopian history goes back all the way to Solomon and the Queen of Sheba. Their son Menelik became the first ruler of the kingdom, and all Ethiopian kings—ever since—are implicitly believed to be his lineal descendants. The name "Menelik" is so revered that no monarch ever dared adopt it as his own first name, although it occurred in family names, for interminable centuries, until the great Menelik II (1889–1908) who was Haile Selassie's granduncle and the victor of Adowa. Myths that describe the origin of the dynasty are picturesque, and have been the subject of innumerable Ethiopian works of art. Sheba was Queen in the ancient Ethiopian city of Axum; she heard of Solomon's wisdom, determined to visit him, and organized a safari to Jerusalem. At a sumptuous banquet, Solomon assured her that he would not seize her virtue, since she was so highly born, if she promised in return to take nothing that belonged to him. They dined to-

---

[3] Not till 1928 was one extensive Ethiopian region, the Danakil Desert, crossed by a white man. It was the last important African area remaining unexplored. See Carlton S. Coon, *Measuring Ethiopia*, p. 80.

[4] Never before Adowa had any European invaders of Africa been beaten by a native state.

gether and he saw to it that she ate amply of foods highly spiced; then he slept in a canopied tent nearby. She woke up, thirsty, and surreptitiously took a drink of water. So Solomon said that she had broken her word, and must surrender herself to his embraces. Thus the first Menelik was conceived, and the Solomonic line brought into being. The throne is still called the Solomonic throne.[5]

Four principal provinces or "kingdoms"—Amhara, Shoa, Tigrai, and Gojjam—grew up on the isolated wilderness of the Ethiopian plateau during the Middle Ages, and fought each other perpetually. Axum was the capital from prehistoric times until 1538. The imperial crown is still kept at Axum, and this remote village was—and is—the site of some of the most stunning and mysterious objects of antiquity in the world, giant obelisks made of single blocks of granite, larger than Egyptian obelisks, the origin of which is unknown. Ethiopia needs archeologists today almost as much as it needs adding machines. Until modern times the Ethiopians were mostly a savage people. That is to say, they were probably as savage as the Visigoths, the Angles, or the Franks. They were peculiarly addicted to mutilation, and liked to cut off the hands or feet of enemies captured in battle; even today, in some remote regions, a man is not supposed to be worthy of marriage until he has killed somebody and given his fiancée the sexual organs of the victim. But let us keep in mind that as late as the reign of Queen Elizabeth I people in England were publicly hung, drawn, and quartered, a form of execution much worse than any ever devised in Africa. The African continent has no monopoly on barbarity.

In the modern period various emperors tried to knit the country together. The job was something like rolling the Rockies to the Appalachians with bare hands.

(2) The statement that Ethiopia is "Christian" needs modification, in that probably half the total population (there are no reliable statistics) is Moslem or pagan. But the government and ruling classes are almost solidly Christian (Coptic). The country might almost be called a theocracy, and Haile Selassie himself, an extremely devout Christian, more or less runs the Ethiopian national church. Remote Coptic monasteries have been functioning in Ethiopia without interruption for almost fifteen hundred years. The clergy is fantastically numerous—one authority says that one out of every five adult males is a priest—and fantastically backward; it is probably the most illiterate clergy in the world.

The Church plays such an exceptional role in Ethiopia, economically and

[5] Margery Perham's indispensable *The Government of Ethiopia*, p. 403, contains a full and flavorsome account of this old legend.

politically, that we must tell something of its origin. In about AD 340 two Phoenician boys, both Christian, were shipwrecked in the Red Sea, made their way into Ethiopia, became favorites of the King, and converted him to the Christian faith. One boy, whose name has come down to us as St. Frumentius, traveled back and forth between Ethiopia and Egypt, and in time became the Abuna (roughly, archbishop or metropolitan) of Ethiopia, under the authority of the Patriarch of Alexandria. When Frumentius died, the King asked the Patriarch to send him a new Abuna. This system—appointment of the head of the Ethiopian church by the Coptic patriarch in Egypt—went on without serious interruption from the fourth century till 1950. The head of the Ethiopian church, with vast powers, was always an *Egyptian* Copt, even though he might be a man well beyond middle age who had never been in Ethiopia before and who knew not a word of any Ethiopian language. It was as if, throughout the course of British history, the Archbishop of Canterbury always had to be a Finn or Dane. There came, inevitably, incessant struggles for power between various kings and their Abunas. To exercise influence in the secular field, the Abuna had to keep on good terms with the king. The King, on his side, had little authority if the Abuna was against him. And neither could kick the other out.

Haile Selassie set about ending this anomalous situation after his return from exile, and when the last Egyptian Abuna died he refused to accept a new one. He wanted the leadership of the church to be Ethiopian. Delicate and protracted negotiations with the Alexandrian patriarch were necessary before he had his way. He had to tread carefully because he did not want to break too sharply with tradition. In the end a new system was set up. The church became national, and the Abuna must always be Ethiopian hereafter. The Emperor nominates a man suggested by the local clergy, and this nomination is then "confirmed" by the Patriarch in Alexandria, who no longer has any role in the actual choice. Many hard-shell Copts bitterly resented the Emperor's course of action, but there was nothing they could do about it.

As to Moslems in Ethiopia they are a powerful force. Harar, the Emperor's own province, is largely Moslem; the Somali and Danakil areas are solidly Moslem, and the Callas (the great tribe south and west of Addis Ababa) are probably half Moslem; Moslem landowners make pockets over the whole country. The Emperor's attitude is to give Moslems complete religious freedom, provided that they remain loyal Ethiopians; Moslems have their own special civil rights, and are subject to their own *kadi* courts. What worries Haile Selassie most is Moslem pressure outside, rather than inside, the country. Ethiopia is, as we know, the source of the Blue Nile. Will an independent Moslem Sudan be as friendly to Ethiopia as the British were? What would be Egypt's attitude to Ethiopia if, by some conceivable chance, a Moslem Brotherhood government should take command in Cairo some fine day? Ethiopia has had its independence threatened by Moslems before, and has not forgotten.

(3) Ethiopians of the ruling class—the Amharas who live in the high central province—consider themselves to be "white" no matter what their color is, and are a terrifically proud people. The "blacks" are slaves from the Sudan or other Negroes; Europeans (including Americans) are thought of as "pink." Once the rumor spread that the United States intended to send an American Negro as ambassador to Ethiopia; this would have been a hideous *faux pas*, and luckily did not happen.

Originally Semites entered Ethiopia from across the Red Sea—thousands of years ago. They superimposed themselves on the indigenous Hamitic peoples, who were "first cousins of the early Egyptians, second cousins of the Berbers and Tuaregs, and (since the Hamite is a Caucasian) third cousins of the races of Europe."[6] Inevitably then, during the course of centuries, they fused to an extent with Nilotic peoples from the Sudan. No one would deny that plenty of racial admixture has taken place. But most members of the ruling Amhara class at least still have features markedly Caucasoid; it is only their dark skin that makes them look like Negroes. They do *not* as a rule have squat noses or bulbous lips.

Nowadays Ethiopians like to call themselves a "Sabaean" people; "Saba" means "Sheba," and the Red Sea is known locally as the "Sabaean" Sea. They look north and east rather than south or west. Even if they concede that they are "African," they belong to another world too, that of the Middle East. There is practically no contact, cultural or economic, with Black Africa. Kenya, although it borders on Ethiopia, seems further away than Saskatchewan. But the Sabaean peoples, the Greeks, the Arabs, the mixed folk of the Levant, have close bonds.

Ethiopian Jews exist; they are called Falashas, and make influential small communities in several areas, particularly near Lake Tana. They were great warriors as well as traders, and at one remote time even took over the dynasty; they think of themselves as exiles from the Promised Land, but do not know Hebrew. Certainly Haile Selassie himself must own to some faint tincture of Jewish blood, since he claims descent from Solomon.

(4) Swedes train some of the Ethiopian police, the Imperial Guard, and the military air force. The Imperial Guard is Haile Selassie's own elite

[6] Stephen H. Longrigg, A *Short History of Eritrea*, p. 10.

corps of troops—about five thousand in number—and is totally different from the Ethiopian army.[7] A considerable rivalry exists between the Guard and the army, as well as between the local Swedes and British, which the Emperor probably encourages quietly because he likes to keep people on their toes. Swedish influence in Ethiopia began with Lutheran missionaries. Just as Danes have always been interested in another remote country, Siam (Thailand), so have the Swedes always been interested in Ethiopia. The King of Sweden paid a state visit to the country when he was crown prince. After the Italian war Swedes came in to assist reconstruction. Addis Ababa has a Swedish hospital and a Swedish-Ethiopian trading company; two Swedish judges sit on the High Court, and a Swede, by name Norberg, is head of the new Telecommunications Authority set up by virtue of a loan from the World Bank in Washington.

Hiring foreigners for government jobs is, of course, necessary because so few trained Ethiopians are available or trustworthy. Also a good many foreigners have entered the country to engage in private business. Among officials the Chief Justice of the High Court is British, as is the Commissioner of Police. The French own the railroad which connects Addis Ababa with the sea at Djibouti—the only railroad in the country. It spans 486 miles, and has been called the most expensive railway in the world; it costs three times more to ship a consignment of hides from Addis Ababa to Djibouti than from Djibouti to New York. French and British are inclined to play together—in some spheres—against the Swedes and Americans. The chief trading company, A. Besse and Company, famous throughout the Red Sea world, is French, domiciled in Aden. Another important company, Mosvald, is Norwegian. An institution known as Her Majesty's Handicraft School is run by Norwegians in co-operation with Point Four; this does fruitful work against weighty obstacles; handicrafts have been virtually unknown, because well-bred Amhara women will not work with their hands. There are Canadian officials in the Ministries of Finance and Commerce, and an Israeli, born in Hungary, is advocate general and chief prosecutor. A Czech is an advisor to the Foreign Office, an Austrian is head of the Development Bank, and one important judge is a Free Pole. A Greek doctor is physician to His Imperial Majesty, and is one of the very few foreigners ever given the title "Bitwoded" (Well-Beloved). A Swiss is director of the telecommunications training

---

[7] The army is being trained by a newly arrived American military mission. Also the United States has provided Ethiopia with $5,000,000 worth of token military aid, small arms and the like, by terms of a mutual security arrangement. Previously the Ethiopian army had been trained by Japanese, Belgians, and British.

HAILE SELASSIE, EMPEROR OF ETHIOPIA

center being established by the Technical Assistance Administration of the UN. The hotel in Bishaftu, where the Swedes train the air force, is managed by another Swiss, and the road there has been variously worked on by Italians, Greeks, and Germans. A spaghetti factory is Italian. The brewmaster in the St. George Brewery is, fittingly enough, a Czech from Pilsen, and the conspicuous King George Bar on the central piazza of Addis Ababa is run by a Greek. The bandmaster of the Imperial guard band is (again fittingly) a Viennese. This plays once a week or so at the leading hotels, and may be hired out for private parties.

The German community is conspicuous; most old-time Germans call themselves Viennese, and some *are* Viennese; they came to Ethiopia as traders many years ago, and are respected. There are comparatively few Central European refugees from Hitler, because Ethiopia was under Fascist rule during the worst days of the anti-Jewish terror, and Jews gave it a wide berth. Some Germans are former Nazi storm troopers, who fled to Addis Ababa after 1945 to escape denazification trials. They cannot return to Germany, and are truly *Staatslos*. The Ras Hotel on some evenings looks and sounds almost like a restaurant in Stuttgart.

Italians still run the Ras Desta Hospital, which is curious in that Ras Desta, the great resistance chieftain for whom it was named, was murdered by Italians during the war. Most Ethiopians have a fierce, ineffaceable enmity to Italy still, but not toward individual Italians. When one of the Convairs used by Ethiopian Air Lines had a minor crash recently, sabotage "from Italy" was instantly suspected. I asked a cabinet minister if the Italians had done *anything* for the country; his face took on an expression of severe pain, and after a long pause he grudgingly replied, "Roads." Then he qualified this by adding that the roads were no good anyway, and had been built purely for strategic purposes. Practically every leading Ethiopian family lost a son, a brother, or a father, either killed in actual warfare, or shot during the Italian occupation—particularly after an attempt to murder Marshal Graziani, the Italian viceroy, who is still called the "butcher" or the "hyena." The Ethiopians are vividly proud of the fact that the Italians never caught the youthful patriot who threw the bomb at Graziani. During the last days of Italian rule, their principal officials—even the military—were practically besieged in their houses by the populace, although they had massacred most of the Ethiopian ruling class, particularly the youth, in revenge for the Graziani "incident." My wife and I met one afternoon three Ethiopian ladies of important rank; one was the wife of the minister of commerce, one the daughter of a former Ethiopian ambassador to London, and one the headmistress of a local school. Young brothers of all three had been executed, and the girls themselves spent years in a concentration camp in Italy.[8]

Among missionaries there are half a dozen main groups. (a) The Seventh-Day Adventists, who maintain a hospital. (b) The Sudan Interior Mission, one of the most celebrated institutions in Africa; its main work is in the Sudan, but it spills over elsewhere. Its personnel is largely American, British, and Canadian, and among other things it supports good bookshops. (c) The American Presbyterian Mission, which has several schools. (d) The Scandinavian Lutheran bloc—Swedes, Finns, Norwegians, Danes—which is progressive and hard-working. Instruction in the Scandinavian schools is in English. (e) The Roman Catholics, in particular Jesuit Canadians.

Haile Selassie is friendly to all the missions, because with them his limited educational and medical programs are expanded, but they are not permitted to do any proselytizing. The national church severely resents any intrusion into its religious field, and the Emperor is angry if he comes across any attempt to uncopt the Copts.

Foreign influence in Ethiopia is, then, profound. On the other hand extremely little penetration by foreign *capital* has occurred—this is one reason why the country is so poor—because the Ethiopians have a morbidly acute fear of losing any aspect of their independence, and want to keep their latent wealth all to themselves. Only two foreign concessions have been granted since 1945. One was to a Dutch company developing cane sugar, and the other to the Sinclair Petroleum Company, which has a fifty-year contract to prospect for petroleum.

THE AMERICAN ELEMENT

Finally in this realm we touch on the position of the United States, which is strong and growing stronger all the time. Including missionaries, the American colony in Addis Ababa numbers about 775 and is the largest foreign community after the Greeks. Ethiopian Air Lines, which plays an absolutely vital role in the country, is American-managed,[9] and Americans hold key posts in the three most critical ministries, foreign affairs, finance, and commerce; also Americans train the army. All Ethiopian banknotes are signed by Americans who have at one time or other served as governors of the Bank of Ethiopia. One American is director of the State Planning Board; another,

[8] On the other hand the point may be made that Italian penetration, cruel as it was, did Ethiopia some good. It gave the country a badly needed jolt. Also the Italians spent millions on public improvements which are the bedrock of the country's physical progress today.

[9] I will describe the operation of this fabulous airline in Chapter 16 below.

under UN auspices, has recently worked out a pilot project for a 50,000-acre cotton development. An American lady has for many years been supervisor to the royal household. Ethiopia has an elaborate and effective Point Four program, and the country received recently a $5,000,000 loan from the Bank for Reconstruction and Development. The Imperial Highway Authority is managed by an American, and Americans from Oklahoma A. & M. are building the Imperial Ethiopian College of Agriculture, creation of which is one of Haile Selassie's most cherished projects. Ohlin Scott, an American, is an advisor to the Ministry of Commerce, and his brother Robert K. Scott to the Finance Ministry. Two Americans are advisors at the Foreign Office, John H. Spencer (whose wife is Swedish) and Albert H. Garretson. These are all entirely "unofficial"; they do not represent the American government, but are American citizens working for Ethiopia in a private capacity. Spencer served in Ethiopia before the occupation. Both he and Garretson, a former professor at New York University and State Department official, have profound influence, not only because of their wisdom and ability but because they are very close to the Emperor. They have been called "the two most important non-Ethiopians in Ethiopia."

One reason why American prestige is high is that the United States never recognized the Italian conquest. Also since the war Haile Selassie has sought to escape from what has been described as the "all-embracing and omnipresent character of British benevolence." Britain, France, and Belgium *did* recognize the Italian occupation, and turned their embassies (or legations) into consulates. The United States, Mexico, Brazil, and the Soviet Union did not do so.

English has become the universal second language in Ethiopia. The law courts sit in both Amharic and English, and the *Official Journal* is published in both languages; instruction in the public schools is in English after the age of nine. The Emperor has a natural fondness for Amharic, but he knows perfectly well that an Ethiopian student will never be able to study, let us say, aviation techniques or atomic physics, in this language. Something western must be taught. (Similarly, years ago, German was obligatory for advanced science students in American universities, because so much technical literature was available only in German.)

RED NETWORK IN ETHIOPIA?

Rumors are sometimes heard that the Russians are a potent force in Ethiopia, and that Addis Ababa is the control point for Soviet manipulations everywhere else in Africa. This legend came originally from a British source, and gained plausibility because Ethiopia is the only country between Egypt and the Union of South Africa where Soviet Russia has any diplomatic representation at all. Russian spies sit in a large, heavily staffed embassy; the Russian hospital is a "show place"; Addis Ababa is "operational headquarters for all the Communist parties in Africa"; Russian agents continually go in and out of Ethiopia disguised as traders, and even carry arms and ammunition to the Mau Maus in Kenya—so these stories go.

The truth is different. Official Americans in Addis Ababa, who would be only too interested in all this if it were true, deny it categorically. So do the responsible British and Ethiopians.

In actual fact only three Soviet agencies exist in Addis Ababa; the legation (Russia is the only great power that has not raised its diplomatic mission to the rank of embassy), an information office patterned on the admirable libraries of the United States Information Service, and the Dejazmatch Balcha Hospital. The total Russian personnel in Ethiopia is only about fifty, and this number includes career diplomats and servants. The Soviet legation has nothing like the importance of the American or British embassies, and has no intimate contact with the Emperor; the down-at-heel information office seems to contain nothing but portraits of Stalin and books in Russian; the hospital is an old *Czarist* hospital, founded more than forty years ago. A close sentimental connection has always existed between the Russian orthodox church and the Ethiopian Coptic church; the czars sent Red Cross units to Ethiopia back in 1896.[10] Of course the Russian hospital is run by the Soviets now. Its staff is meager, and its equipment poor; it plays no role in Ethiopian life comparable to that of the Swedish or other European hospitals. Its former director, Dr. Kashmensky, was, however, popular in local society; recently (and quite possibly for this reason) he was recalled to Moscow. The Soviet minister to Ethiopia also lost his post early in 1954.

How much propaganda the Russians manage to export from Addis Ababa to the rest of Africa is unknown, but it cannot be much, if only because communications are so difficult. To get arms to the Mau Maus—even leaflets—in any quantity would be geographically and logistically impossible. Some Communist propaganda, printed in English, has been found in the local schools, and Russian agents may—as a matter of course—try to subvert Ethiopian intellectuals. In one ministry an Ethiopian-hired official (not a Russian, but a fellow traveler from Central Europe) is obstructive. But the idea that the Russians are present in Ethiopia in major force, or that

[10] Not everybody remembers that the great Russian poet Pushkin had an Ethiopian great-grandfather.

their legation could be a huge nest spawning an intercontinental network on a grand scale, is beyond the realm of belief at the moment.

STILL MORE BACKGROUND

Can the Ethiopian change his skin, or the leopard his spots?
—JEREMIAH, XIII, 23

Ethiopia is as big as France plus most of Spain; estimates of its population range from ten million to twenty—no census has ever been taken, and comparatively few people even know how old they are—with twelve million probably the most reasonable guess.[11] The name "Ethiopia" comes from the Greek, and means "burned face." Most citizens dislike the older, more conventional name for their country—Abyssinia—because this has an Arab origin and connotes "mixed." Ethiopia has 18,000,000 cattle, and exactly seven movie theaters. It is one of the most spectacularly beautiful countries in the world, and a major factor in almost everybody's life is the altitude. Among other things this helps to keep disease down, because the sunshine is so sharp. Recently an officer of the World Health Organization said of it, "A filthy country—but most sanitary!"

The word "Amhara" (mountain people) comes from Hebrew, and the language, Amharic, has its own script (as do Armenian and Georgian), and is inordinately complex; I could not find anybody who would say with certainty whether its fantastic alphabet contained 247, 256, or 259 different letters. But the Emperor has resisted attempts to Latinize it. The only place in the world, I was told, where this abstruse language is taught outside Ethiopia is the School of Oriental Studies in Paris. Few books exist in Amharic—even in Ethiopia itself—except the Bible, and it took many years before this was translated successfully.[12] Most proper names in Ethiopia have a biblical derivation. For instance, Haile Selassie means "Power of Trinity." There is no cult of Mary in the Coptic Church, but thousands of people are named Mariam; St. George is the patron saint, and Guiorguis exist beyond count.

Ethiopia has enormous reserves of subsoil wealth, but the surface has hardly been touched. Coffee is the most important crop; our word "coffee" comes, in fact, from the Ethiopian place name "Kaffa." American Point Four experts take one look at the land and can scarcely believe what they see;

---

[11] These figures do not include Eritrea, with which Ethiopia is now federated. See Chapter 16 below.
[12] The ancient Coptic language, displaced by Amharic, is Geez, which is variously spelled Ghis, Gheez, and Ge'ez. Some priests still use it on occasion, as priests in western lands may use Latin.

the plateau near Addis Ababa has a fertility probably unmatched in the world except by the American corn belt, and could become one of the greatest granaries on earth. Of course communications (except by air) are primitive in the extreme, and make progress difficult. All but one or two Ethiopian roads have approximately the status of British roads at the time of Stonehenge; in the whole country, only 2,300 miles of road exist at all. The distance from Addis Ababa to Harar, the chief town of the Emperor's home district, is 240 miles; the trip will take two full days if you have a car with four-wheel drive. Large parts of the country can only be reached by jeep, and only six cities in the entire kingdom are connected by telegraph. A scant ten others can be reached by radio—if the radio is working. Americans at work on communications pant with agony at obstacles they encounter. It may take months—literally—to get a decision on the simplest point, because of corruption, overcentralization, or rivalries between ministers.

Parts of Ethiopia are still semi-savage; it is one of the few countries in Africa where, in some areas, it is distinctly unsafe for a person to go about alone. (There are similar areas, of course, in New York City.) Some Ethopian women—until quite recently—wore their hair plaited with the bowels of oxen, and among the Gallas dead children may be hung on trees instead of being buried. Not long ago a British customs official on the Ethiopia-Kenya frontier complained to his Ethiopian colleague that his dog kept him awake, by howling all night. A few days later the dog appeared without ears. Horrified, the Briton asked what had happened. The Ethiopian officer replied, "The dog did not listen when I told it to be quiet, and so I cut its ears off."

Whether or not slavery still exists substantially is a moot point. Of course there are slaves—it is impossible to draw the line in many parts of Africa between slaves, family retainers, or servants who just don't get paid.[13] Abyssinia was for generations (along with the southern Sudan and northern Uganda) the chief source of slaves shipped to Arabia and the Yemen. When Ethiopia entered the League of Nations in 1923, Haile Selassie pledged himself to wipe out slavery, and did his best to do so. Yet the Italians say that, when they took the country, they released no fewer than 420,000 slaves. As to commercial traffic of slaves across the Red Sea, that has ceased to exist on an organized basis. Reasons are three: (1) The Emperor's own energetic anti-slavery campaign. (2) The demand from Arabia grew less, as the economic and social fabric of the Red Sea countries began to change. (3) Slave areas, particularly in the wildly remote region adjacent to the Sudan, became depopulated. Slavery diminished for the simple reason that there were no more slaves to find.

[13] Perham, *op. cit.*, has a full discussion of this.

Ethiopia had, as of the time I went there, exactly two newspapers, both of them weeklies under government control; one appeared in English and Amharic, the other in French and Amharic. A British editor[14] has described recently some of his tribulations in the wild, wonderful field of Ethiopian journalism. He wanted to change his weekly into a daily, and then found that the censor had to see everything—even topical social notes—four or five days in advance! His news stories were mercilessly cut, and political comment forbidden. Here are some stipulations laid down by the censorship:

> 1. Whenever the Emperor is mentioned his name must appear at the beginning of the article, and no other name must appear before his.
> 2. All references to the Emperor, including all pronouns, must be capitalized.
> 3. The portrait of a living person must not appear on the same page with that of a deceased person. Group photographs must not be used if any member of the group is deceased.

Ethiopians are not only extraordinarily proud but sensitive in the extreme. I heard a *Ferengi* (foreigner) who knows the country well and likes it very much say, "These are the most arrogant people in the world, and this is their most endearing quality." Social life is difficult, because officials simply forget to turn up for a dinner party, and never bother to explain. It is almost as hard to get good servants as in New York; people are too supercilious to work, unless they obtain a feudal or semi-family status. Horseback riding is Addis Ababa's chief outdoor recreation, but this entails a certain mild xenophobic risk. Playful boys are apt to hurl rocks at the wives of foreign diplomats riding out from their elegantly secluded compounds. In the schools, masters have trouble teaching the Ethiopian youth the principles of sportsmanship. If a team loses a football game, its members will be apt to ambush and waylay the victors after the match, assaulting them with sticks and stones. I heard one European teacher exclaim in despair about her class, "The poor, arrogant, helpless little *chocolates!*"

We were warned not to photograph street scenes—the only place in Africa where this happened. It is not that people fear the evil eye, which the camera represents in some African communities; the authorities do not like Ethiopian primitiveness to be exposed. Passports of all visitors are impounded for a day or two, and in Addis Ababa strict curfew closes off the streets at night. Nobody is allowed out of doors without a pass. Ethiopians do not like jokes or criticism. Recently a foreign official ordered from London a set of the works of Evelyn Waugh; he found that *Black Mischief*, Mr. Waugh's hilarious but sharp-edged parody of things Ethiopian,

---

[14] William H. Seed, "Censorship in Ethiopia," *Manchester Guardian*, October 7, 1952.

had been abstracted from the shipment. Miss Margery Perham's *Government of Ethiopia* is the best modern text on the kingdom; it is fair-minded, authoritative, and not particularly critical. But it will not be found in any bookshop in Ethiopia, and Miss Perham herself, one of the foremost living authorities on Africa, was for a long period refused a visa to the country.

Ethiopia has never had a true election, and nobody would pretend that it is a democracy. There are no political parties, no trade unions, no vehicles for the expression of opinion, and no civil liberties in our sense. A "parliament" exists, but it is altogether rudimentary; the Emperor picks the membership of the upper house himself. No political opposition is permitted. If an important official falls into disfavor, a difficult problem is created—what to do with him? In the United States a defeated senator, or a retiring member of the cabinet, can go back to his law practice or other occupation, but in Ethiopia there is no place to go, because no good jobs exist outside the government. Some fifty politicians of rank are believed, as of the moment, to be in *confino*, or forced exile, out in the desolate wastes of the plateau. They have their own servants (or slaves) and a certain liberty of action and movement; but they cannot return to Addis Ababa. In the old days the authorities waited till a prisoner was forgotten, whereupon he would be poisoned. I asked, "Can prisoners write letters?" Laughter greeted the naïveté of this remark. "Of course not. Most cannot read or write. If they dictate a letter to a scribe, the scribe will write what *he* feels like writing, and send the document to whomever *he* may gain favor from. Or he may send several contradictory letters."[15]

Corruption is widespread in Ethiopia, but by and large is on a minor scale. *Wholesale* looting, even in the provinces, has gone out of fashion, and is frowned upon; no longer will a *ras* or governor calmly expropriate *all* the tax receipts. Addis Ababa is probably less corrupt than Cairo and is certainly less corrupt than Monrovia. Nothing exists comparable to the situation in one Middle Eastern city, where even the international airport cannot be made to give proper service if the local personnel is not "subsidized" by the airlines using it.

Everything—any progress—depends ultimately on education, and the Emperor's program in this regard is the best thing in the kingdom. Nobody is "minister" of education—a vice-minister is in charge of this department—because the Emperor himself acts as minister. Approximately one third of

---

[15] Some ordinary prisoners are sent to Adola, a town in the gold fields near the Kenya border. Here they do forced labor, but are well treated. The prison population is about three thousand. A British mission visited the area lately and found conditions "good." One of the few radio circuits in Ethiopia connects the government with this prison camp.

the budget goes to education (a large percentage for Africa—and for countries not in Africa), and Haile Selassie has spent immense sums out of his personal fortune to support educational effort. About 80,000 Ethiopian children go to school. Teachers have a heartbreaking job. Children learn slowly, and overvalue what they learn; a high-school graduate will think that he is competent to be a minister. One curious point is that few children ever have toys to play with; as a result they never learn to do things with their hands as American youngsters do, and are apt to be clumsy, with no manual dexterity, in later life.

I asked a European who has worked in Addis Ababa since the war what changes he had seen. First, many fewer people are barefoot. Second, servants know how to read and write.

Finally, one should mention that the Emperor has to do practically everything himself. He is "the sole source of power and initiative" in a country which till recently had hardly "a semblance of modern administration."

NEW FLOWER

Addis Ababa—the name means "New Flower"—lies at an elevation of 7,800 feet (about the altitude of Mexico City), has perhaps 350,000 people, and looks as if it had been dropped piecemeal from an airplane carrying trash. It resembles a Tartar camp more than a modern town. Many people still live in *tukals,* round huts with clay floors and grass roofs, even on the main streets. Some neighborhoods look like suburbs in the West Indies; crude hovels lie behind stockades of tall sharpened sticks, and wildly colorful tropical vegetation bursts through rotting walls. But next door may be a modern stone building. Things are madly mixed up and scattered. Most streets are not named, and houses have no numbers. Everywhere there are eucalyptus trees, which grow so luxuriantly that they are harvested like a crop, for firewood; these were planted by Menelik, and give the town a silvery bluish tint. Addis Ababa, although wretched and tawdry beyond belief, can be beautiful at times. The surrounding hills are magnificent, with a peculiar lean, spotted look, and so is the sky. One night when we were there the full moon looked like an enormous perfect circle cut out of purple carbon paper.

Our chauffeur drove a jeep in the Korean War, and presumably thought he was still driving it. We passed a lonely row of granite pillars, with scrawny cows grazing between them. This is the Haile Selassie Imperial University. It consists—as of the moment—of nothing whatever except this unfinished façade. Work will be resumed when—the reason is interesting—there are enough *high-school* graduates to fill a university class. Of course high schools have only been operating since 1945, after the war. We passed gerries without number, gaily painted and drawn by dilapidated horses, and saw traffic signs forbidding certain lanes to mules. We looked at sites of the old gibbets, where public executions took place till recently; members of the criminal's family were obliged to attend the ceremony. We saw barefoot men outside mangy public offices, dictating to scribes, and lines of petitioners, waiting to see Official Number Three who might, in time, pass them on to Official Number Two, and finally to Number One, if enough *backsheesh* changed hands. We passed a hospital, the standard joke about which is that it has only enough barium for *half* a stomach X-ray. We saw the Opera House, which was built by the Italians, and has never housed an opera. We went to the Ras Hotel, on Churchill Road; here showcases in the lobby contained primitive medical equipment, alarm clocks, an aluminum bedpan, and tennis shoes, instead of jewels and furs. People swore to me that if we visited the State Bank we would see goats wandering about inside. Outside the office of the United States Information Service sat a really choice leper, among other beggars. Several important brothels are on a main street; others are situated on an alley called Mattress Lane where, oddly enough, there are also a few shops that sell mattresses.[16]

We happened to be in Addis Ababa during the Coptic Lent, which lasts for two months. Ethiopians may not, during this period, eat anything that comes from an animal or bird—no meat, eggs, milk, butter, cheese. They may, however, have fish, since fish are cold-blooded. One can imagine the difficulties of a European hostess entertaining official Ethiopians during this period.[17] The Ethiopian cuisine contains some famous staples, like *tej*, a mead made of fermented honey, and a fiery sauce called *wat*, so fierce with pepper that it practically makes the ears bleed. Ethiopian bread looks like an old inner tube.

*

All this, then, shows something of what Haile Selassie has to contend with. It is a lot.

[16] Up in the hilly "residential" area we noticed, night after night, a house removed from others, exquisitely lighted, and obviously patrician; this is owned by the most eminent prostitute of the town, who is supposed to accept as clients nobody under the rank of vice-minister. There were always cars and gerries parked outside, despite the curfew.
[17] Some striking oddities occur in Addis Ababa social life. Recently an American oil company, Caltex, broke the long-standing monopoly (Shell) on domestic sales of gasoline and oil, and opened a handsome filling station near the Ras Hotel. All members of the *corps diplomatique* were invited to attend the celebration of this event.

HAILE SELASSIE, EMPEROR OF ETHIOPIA

THE NEGUS: HIS LIFE AND TIMES

Haile Selassie I, Elect of God, Conquering Lion of the Tribe of Judah, King of Zion, *Negusa Nagast* (King of Kings), and Emperor of Ethiopia, was born in Harar Province in 1892. He has been the most powerful person in the country since 1917; in other words his authority has persisted undiminished for more than thirty-five years, except of course during the Italian occupation. Haile Selassie spent five years to a day, from May 5, 1936, to May 5, 1941, in exile. Mussolini cost him his throne, but he regained it in a manner of speaking because of Hitler; had not Hitler made World War II, provoking British intervention in Ethiopia, he might still be sitting in Bath, England, where he spent part of his forced sojourn abroad.

He was grandson of Menelik II, and inherits royal blood from both father and mother. The British embassy in Addis Ababa has a chart of the imperial family that covers several square yards; Ethiopian genealogy is abstruse. His father was Ras Makonnen, who was Menelik's chief diplomat and soldier. Menelik became senile in the last years, after having organized the modern kingdom. Young Haile Selassie got a western education from a French Catholic mission in Harar, and showed outstanding qualities—including ambition—very early. Menelik (before his dotage) took careful note of him, pushed him hard, and made him a *ras* when he was still a youth. *Ras*dom is not inherited; the title corresponds more to "Marshal" than to "Duke" or "Prince." Haile Selassie was called Ras Tafari at this time, and, after Menelik had tried him out in various posts, he became Vice-Governor of Harar before he was twenty-five. Menelik died, and was succeeded as Emperor by Lij Yasu (Jesus), one of his grandsons. Yasu's reign was a disaster. He offended the priestly hierarchy by embracing Islam, which is as if a King of England should suddenly become Buddhist, and committed other indiscretions. World War I was going on then, and Turkish and German influence grew steeply in Ethiopia. Came a palace revolution (1916) made mostly by the church, but in which the British and French (who wanted to frustrate Yasu) certainly played a hand. Yasu was deposed, and Haile Selassie brought forward to replace him. But he could not be made Emperor yet. The succession went to an aged and incompetent lady, the Empress Zauditu, one of Menelik's daughters, but Haile Selassie became Regent and heir to the throne. Three forces favored him: the church, his imperial lineage, and one wing of the army. Even so civil war took place until he fought and won a pitched battle with Yasu's forces. A decade of subterranean struggle followed—mostly with intractable *rases*—before he gained a firm, final grip on power. Such intrigues went on as made even Ethiopian hair stand on end.

Then (he was still known as Ras Tafari) he negotiated Ethiopia's entrance into the League of Nations, which brought him marked prestige, and wrote a new constitution giving himself wide powers. In 1928 he became King of Shoa (an important province), and in 1930, when Zauditu died, he was crowned Emperor. Old Yasu was still alive. He was not invited to the ceremony. He was, in fact, still a prisoner in chains—literally—and remained so until his death in 1935.

Haile Selassie's appearances before the League of Nations at Geneva, his defiance of Mussolini and gallant resistance to Italian conquest, are too well known to need repetition here.[18]

When further resistance against Italy was hopeless the Emperor abandoned his capital (via the French railway), although several of the tough old *rases* fought on for some months, like Ras Imru, who later became Ethiopian ambassador to Washington, and Ras Desta. A major influence in persuading him to go—after the front collapsed and further military operations were impossible—was his wife. The Emperor's justification for his departure was that nobody else could possibly represent Ethiopia in the outside world, and lead successful efforts for its resurrection. In this he was perfectly right. He spent difficult years. He went to Jerusalem first, where Abyssinian monks live in the Church of the Holy Sepulchre; the British were busy conciliating the Italians at that time, after the failure of sanctions, and did not want him in the Middle East. France, under Laval, would not have him, and he was unable—on account of Italian pressure—to establish residence in Switzerland. Finally the British took him in, and set him up in a house in Bath. Today the imperial villa in Bishaftu, near Addis Ababa, is named for this—the Villa Fairfield. After Munich the British began to see how useful Haile Selassie might, after all, turn out to be. When World War II broke out the reconquest of Ethiopia became an Allied aim, and in August, 1940, the Emperor was flown to Khartoum to further this. The Emperor "organized" the campaign—one of the most remarkable in modern military history—but British and Indian troops did most of the fighting, assisted by Ethiopian guerrillas.

*

Haile Selassie's Empress, whose name is Manan, is a most striking character. She is a very large woman, almost rhomboidal in shape; she is impassive, uncommunicative, and seldom seen. She comes from a powerful

---

[18] Today Ethiopians deny that they were "beaten" by Italy. Their way of putting it is that, after resisting much longer than anybody could have expected, they "stopped fighting."

HAILE SELASSIE, EMPEROR OF ETHIOPIA

and rich family in the Wallega country, near the Sudan; the marriage had great political significance, since it united two distant groups. Haile Selassie is her second husband. The Empress has, so far as is known, no distinct political views, except a desire to keep the monarchy intact, but in several directions she exercises a signal influence. She is extremely religious and conservative, and has a marked interest in finance.[19]

Haile Selassie and Manan have several children. Among them are:

1. Princess Tenaghne Worq, who married first Ras Desta and then Bitwoded Andargachaw Masai, at present His Imperial Majesty's viceroy in Eritrea. She is about forty.[20] She has several children, including Princess Ruth Desta, a most engaging and progressive young lady, Princess Aida, who is married to the Governor of Ombo, and Prince Samson, who went to school at Riverdale in New York City and then attended Columbia, and who has the reputation of being something of an *enfant terrible*. That is, he likes to do things like wearing colored socks with a dinner jacket.

2. The Crown Prince, by name Mardazmach Asfa Wasan, born in 1916 and educated at the University of Liverpool. He has been married twice, and recently became the father of a son, Yacob, thus establishing the royal succession into the next generation. Illness retarded him for a time. He is a serious young man, who takes after his mother in some respects; he is Governor of Dessie, which is supposed to be the second hardest administrative job in the country. (Hardest is the governorship of Gondar.)

3. Prince Masfin Makonnen, the Duke of Harar, who is in his early thirties. His wife is also of the imperial family, and they have several sons.

The imperial family is, it goes without saying, very wealthy indeed, but the Emperor himself does not have much interest in money except for worthy public purposes. The Empress, yes. (A contemporary joke is that she keeps a strongbox, stuffed with gold, under her bed.) It is, as a matter of fact, almost impossible to distinguish between the country's public finance and the private imperial funds, because the Emperor is forever financing undertakings out of his own pocket. If he visits a locality and sees that it needs a clinic or school, he will—like as not—donate the necessary funds himself.

---

[19] One might mention here a curious point, that the position of women in Ethiopia has always been exceptional. We are a long way removed now from Arab customs. Women have property rights equal to those of men, and may sue their husbands for divorce. There is no purdah. Nor are women chattel as in much of Black Africa. All this is supposed to derive from the Sheban tradition, and is exemplified by the position of the Empress.

[20] Another daughter was Princess Tsahai, born in 1920. She was the apple of her father's eye, and died in childbirth in 1942. She was trained to be a nurse at Guy's Hospital, London, and the Emperor maintains a hospital in Addis Ababa dedicated to her name.

In part the family is so rich because the Italians nationalized all public property, and this—of a value purported to be $320,000,000—fell naturally into the imperial exchequer. It provided a handsome and wonderfully convenient fund for paying off debts (if any), bestowing favors, and the like. The finest town house in Addis Ababa, resembling a French château, belongs to the Duke of Harar. Also the Emperor has income from commercial sources; for instance he owns the only modern printing press in the country, and the Empress is believed to be a heavy investor in several enterprises. By tradition, one-third of the country's gold production belongs to the Emperor; no one knows what the total amount is, but it has been estimated at a million ounces per year. Proceeds from this would, if the above figure is correct, give Haile Selassie a tidy additional income, since gold is worth $35 per ounce.

The Emperor and Empress dine out once a year at each embassy or legation in Addis Ababa; these occasions are, needless to say, marked by the most severe formality. In return the imperial family gives occasional big diplomatic receptions. Foreign guests are sometimes embarrassed because the town palace of His Imperial Majesty, even though it is an imposing structure with gates almost like those at Buckingham Palace, contains few accessible powder rooms.

Haile Selassie's chief quality is probably tenacity. What he believes in most, after Ethiopia, is himself. But he is completely dedicated and selfless in his devotion to his country, and there are few who do not respect him. He is a careful administrator, and an expert at the art of knocking heads together when he presides at cabinet meetings. He has no sports or hobbies. Nothing really interests him except the giant task of holding Ethiopia together, reforming its feudal structure, and bringing it to a self-respecting status in modern society. No man has ever had a harder job, and the contribution he has made to his country is tremendous.

Since he trusts nobody's ability fully, the Emperor has to deal with almost everything himself. He will himself scrutinize the contract for a new cook at the palace, and he annotates every important document in the diplomatic bags. One of his dominating traits is curiosity. If he sees a new type of rifle, he wants to take it apart with his own hands. At seven in the morning, say, he will announce that he intends to visit such-and-such a school; then at the school he questions the children on what they learned the day before, and what they think of their teacher. Recently one of his advisers submitted plans for a publicity brochure; the Emperor said, "No, I could build two schools for that amount of money." He loves children. One occasion at which he relaxes is a children's party he gives every year on the Ethiopian Christmas (January 7th); the son of a British diplomat tweaked his beard at one of these, saying, "Why do you wear that old beard, sir?" His courtiers were shocked, but Haile Selassie laughed.

How far does the Emperor's writ extend? For a long time the answer to this was "Not very far," because Ethiopia had virtually no communications. Today Haile Selassie wields authority over a larger area than anybody who has ever held the throne. There are still areas near the Sudan border where no real administration exists, and from the time of his accession till 1952 he avoided visiting the northern province of Tigrai, which was notorious for being restive. Nor has his power always been substantial in Gojjam, though this is not far from Addis Ababa. In a sense Haile Selassie has to run his country as pre-Tudor kings ran feudal England. If an obstreperous *ras* refuses to share tax collections with the central government and cannot be brought to heel by force or influenced by other procedures, it is just too bad.

Plots against the Emperor, mostly amateurish, are uncovered from time to time. Members of the imperial family itself are said to have been involved in an *attentat* in 1951. Normally a conspiracy does not envisage anything so nasty as killing, but merely the removal of His Majesty into a reposeful exile. Only rarely are plots uncovered by the police; usually the Emperor himself finds out about them, because as a sound working principle he has *two* men in every camp or office, who hate each other. A tells on B, B tells on A, and both tell on C if necessary.

THE EMPEROR'S CHIEF SOURCES OF POWER

We might recapitulate these as follows: (1) The fact that his line—by legend anyway—goes back to Solomon and Sheba. (2) The church. (3) Intense and ceaseless personal scrutiny of every aspect of administration. (4) His gallantry of character and other personal qualities. (5) Nobody exists who could take his place. Ethiopia is a one-man show.

The basic struggle in Ethiopia is between the feudal interests, who go back to Menelik and beyond, and those more progressive, represented by the Emperor, who is however part of the feudal interests himself.

To sum up: Haile Selassie's government is personal and its curse, like that of all palace governments, is that it is too centralized (something that cannot be helped at present) and lacks competent, trustworthy personnel. There can be no doubt that, against fantastic obstacles, the Negus has already done more for his people than any emperor in history, by bringing it from barbarism to the threshold of modern times in a generation.

MEN AROUND THE EMPEROR

The prime minister, a man of splendid dignity, good humor, and force of character, is Bitwoded Makonnen Endelkachau; he is also one of the handsomest men I ever met, a veritable Apollo carved out of ebony. His wife, a niece of the Emperor's, is Princess Yeshash Worq. Tea with them in their simply furnished modern house up in the hills is an engaging experience. They have adopted and are educating six or seven orphaned children. The prime minister served for a time as controller of the French railway, and has been close to the Emperor since the 1920's. He is not merely a politician of great sophistication, but an amateur poet, a playwright, a painter (he showed us two of his landscapes), and one of Ethiopia's few authors of radio skits. His son, who is almost as handsome as he, went to Oxford.

Another powerful member of the government is Ato Makonnen Abte Wold, who is both minister of finance (a crucial post in a country like Ethiopia) and minister of propaganda. His younger brother, a much more progressive figure, by name Ato Aklilou Abte Wold, is minister of foreign affairs, and still another brother, Ato Akaele Abte Wold, is vice-minister of education. These brothers comprise three-eighths of the total cabinet. Equally influential (perhaps more so) is the minister of the pen, whose name and title are Tsahafi Taezaz Wolde Guiorguis Wolde Yohannes, and who is also minister of justice. He has been with the Emperor since the beginning, and shared his exile in London. The minister of the pen is secretary both to the royal family and the cabinet; he issues all imperial regulations, controls the promulgation of decrees, and is, in short, the Emperor's official mouthpiece. Very little can happen in Ethiopia that Wolde Guiorguis does not know about. In general he is a balancing force between extreme conservatives (like the finance minister) and the younger element, which is represented by such men as Yilma Deressa, former minister of commerce and at present ambassador to Washington, and Menassie Lemma, the vice-minister of finance.

Officials are obliged to take care of details on a level that would be undreamed-of in a European country, because the Emperor himself sets this example. If a plane is late, the minister in charge of civil aviation may well hop down to the control tower himself.

Haile Selassie pushes the young, forward-looking men as hard and fast as he can. Only one old *ras* is a member of the cabinet at present. The recently appointed minister to India is thirty-one: the minister to Greece is twenty-nine.

ETHIOPIAN MISCELLANY

Ethiopia is the only place in the world where a goose colored blue exists, and on Lake Tana the canoes are made of papyrus. In Ethiopia extraordinary phallic monuments, made of granite and the size of bollards in the Venice lagoon, startle visitors exploring ancient meadows. Ethiopia has never to date produced a native architect, chemist, biologist, soil technician, or civil engineer. Ethiopian women of the ruling class may be so sumptuously tattooed that the markings on their throats and wrists glow like jewels. No visitor to Addis Ababa is likely to forget the institution known as the *Sbanya;* he is the night watchman outside every official's door, who deliberately wears the most ramshackle costume possible—sometimes nothing but a ragged burlap blanket with a rifle sticking out. This is in order to get tips from guests out of pity and at the same time humiliate his employers.

CHAPTER 16

More about Ethiopia, Eritrea, and the Somalis

*If it wasn't for myopia,
We could see to Ethiopia.*
—ANONYMOUS

WE TURN now to two stimulating and hopeful Ethiopian phenomena, both in the realm of aviation, which symbolize well the country's vivid interest in technical advance. I have mentioned in passing Ethiopian Air Lines. The first time I saw one of its planes—a new Convair—I blinked. Surely there has never been such a paint job on an airliner before. All EAL ships are painted a bright, orange-juice yellow, with broad, gay red and green stripes from nose to stern, and with a formidable Lion of Judah, yellow on a red plaque, emblazoned on the fuselage.

Ethiopian Air Lines is certainly one of the most remarkable airlines in the world. It began operations in 1947, starting with nothing; in 1954 it flew 2,300,000 miles with 68,000 passengers. The Ethiopian government owns it, but it is maintained and run by TWA (Trans World Airlines); most of the staff is American. What makes EAL so important is that it gives the country something it never had before, effective communications. If, ten years ago, the Emperor—or anybody—should have wished to go from Addis Ababa to the important provincial capital Gondar, only 280 miles away, the journey would have taken a full two weeks—in the dry season; during the rains, it would have been impossible. Today EAL flies to Gondar three times weekly in two hours and thirty-five minutes. Every province in Ethiopia is now served by this hop-skip-jump airline (but it hops, skips, and jumps on time) except those in the uninhabited southwestern desert. It goes into twenty-two Ethiopian towns, many more than have telegraph. More than any force except the personality of the Emperor, EAL knits the country together; if the imperial authority extends today further than it has ever extended before, this airline is largely responsible.

The manager in Ethiopia of this enterprise is one of the most exceptional Americans in Africa, Waldo G. ("Swede") Golien, who was born in North Dakota forty-five-odd years ago. Not long ago Haile Selassie wanted to visit Axum, the old capital and holy city. But, except by air, it is almost impossible to reach Axum; moreover, it is not served by Ethiopian Air Lines, and Golien had never been there. But when His Imperial Majesty gives an order, it is an order. Golien piloted a ship up to Axum himself, looked over a deserted airstrip that the Italians had built in 1935 and which had promptly, viciously, reverted to jungle, and risked a landing. He gave instructions to the local governor to clean up the runway, fill in holes, and cut down nearby trees. Two weeks later he flew into Axum again to see how this work had progressed. It was done. Then, when he was satisfied that the adventure of landing would be tolerably safe, he returned to Addis Ababa, picked up the Emperor and his party, and delivered them to Axum as if he were on a routine flight from Paris to Amsterdam.

Golien has been flying since 1927, when he was a Marine Corps pilot at Pensacola, Florida. During the war, he flew the Atlantic thirty times or more for the Air Transport Command. He went out to Ethiopia for TWA in 1947, and has been there ever since. The Emperor, who has always been fascinated by aviation, liked him, and flies with him a good deal; in fact they transact most of their business in the cockpit. Golien handles the controls, as Haile Selassie adjusts his small frame to the co-pilot's seat, perching there like some dainty little bearded bird.

"I have every confidence in Mr. Golien," he said after one flight. "Moreover, I know that God is taking care of both of us."

Golien has a fleet of eleven planes and a staff of 405, including eighteen American pilots. The minor personnel is mostly Ethiopian. There are eleven Ethiopian copilots, but none has been given command of a ship so far. This will come in time. It may take four or five years, but it will come. To get the line into smooth operation has cost headaches such as westerners can scarcely comprehend. For one thing the terrain over which EAL flies is impossibly difficult—a jagged green-brown hell. Airports are primitive and lie at terrific altitudes, and there are practically no communications on the ground. For another, even the highest Ethiopian officials had no idea of the technical complexities of major airline operation—problems in fuel supply, maintenance, accurate scheduling, and the like. Thousands of people who now ride on EAL as a matter of course, because they can do their business in no other way, never saw a timetable before, a boxed lunch, or the windsleeve on an airport.

Golien likes the Ethiopians, admires many of their traits, and appreciates warmly the co-operation he has had. Month by month, year by year, he turns more work, more responsibility, over to them. But it is hard for him to get good personnel, because the country is so desperately short of trained people, and the government takes all the educated youth it can get. One difficulty is that, even when Ethiopians are trained, they are apt to have less reasoning power than American or European boys, less sense of devotion to a job for the job's own sake.

One thing "Swede" Golien is proud of above all. His line has flown in Ethiopia for eight years now, under day-in, day-out circumstances that would make any official of the Civil Aeronautics Board faint, sob, or cut his throat, without a single fatal accident.

COUNT VON ROSEN AT BISHAFTU

Driving out from Addis Ababa to Bishaftu I felt for the first time on our trip that I was in savage Africa. We passed a band of dancers prancing in a field; they were rehearsing for some ceremonial occasion, and their costumes seemed to be an exploding mass of shields and feathers. Soon we were in Galla country. Priests on donkeys rode by, under straw umbrellas. In one village women sat placidly out in the sharp mountain sunshine having their hair done. They have fuzzy hair, which they attempt to straighten; to this end it is soaked in butter, and then woven into literally hundreds of separate tiny braids, which lie on the skull like ridges on a melon. The butter stays there till the next hair-do, and naturally becomes rancid in time.

But we saw signs of progress. Old and new kiss everywhere in Africa, even Ethiopia. Agricultural methods are improving; the earth here is jet-black fifteen feet down, and yearns for development. The tractors will be coming soon. The road is built on gumbo, solid and sticky like the gumbo in the Dakotas; it is almost impossible to keep in repair, but it is better maintained year by year. Ungainly *trenta-quatros*, trucks high-slung like Ethiopian mules, ground past us—stuffed with cereal produce and pepper for *wat*. The trucking services have grown to a point where they carry about a third as much traffic as the toylike railway, in spite of the wretched condition of the roads.

Count C. G. Von Rosen is Director of the Imperial Air Force Training Center at Bishaftu. He comes from a distinguished old Swedish family, and is an attractive figure. Once he barnstormed all over Europe as a stunt flier. He flew an ambulance plane (probably the first ambulance plane in the world) from Sweden to Ethiopia during the Italian war, and it was he who made a famous rescue of a Swedish Red Cross unit bombed by the Italians. The Emperor, admiring him greatly, asked him to come back to Ethiopia after the war and organize a military air force. This Von Rosen has done. For a time he held the world's distance record, 6,220 kilometers, for a solo pilot. Alone in a small Swedish craft, he flew from Stockholm to Addis Ababa (non-stop) in thirty-two hours. Toward the end of this flight—which was epochal no matter how lightly he talks about it—he had several uninterrupted hours in the worst sandstorm he ever saw, but he hit the Khartoum airport within three hundred yards, and then flew on without landing. He says that this was not good navigation, but pure luck. "If I had hit it within thirty miles, it would have been good navigation!"

Some three hundred Ethiopian boys go into training at Bishaftu every year; of these no more fail than would be washed out in a comparable installation in Belgium or Canada. Bishaftu was chosen as the site because it is high enough to be out of the malaria belt, but not too high for easy flying; also it is on the railroad. About a hundred Swedes—including wives and children—live here. Bishaftu is important not merely for military training per se, but as a technical school. We visited the hangars, the workshops, the dormitories. Ethiopians are, Von Rosen said, excellent pilot material. They are natural fliers, just as they are natural fighters. Ethiopian ground troops did extremely well in Korea. A certain rivalry exists between Von Rosen and Ethiopian Air Lines to get promising boys; then the government will try to grab them off—to make them clerks. Von Rosen had three Ethiopian squadrons ready for action in Korea when the war stopped there, and Bishaftu has logged about 10,000 flying hours so far, with not more than three accidents.

Von Rosen, like Golien, is close to the Emperor, and often takes him for flights over the country, sometimes with an Ethiopian pilot at the controls. The Emperor knows nearly every acre of his domain from the air. He has utterly no fear, Von Rosen says. Once he wanted to get from a remote airport to Addis Ababa in a single-motored plane. Von Rosen forbade him to make the flight. The Emperor protested with the words, "But you would take the risk yourself, wouldn't you?" "Yes," answered Von Rosen, "but I am not Emperor of Ethiopia."

THE ERITREAN SHELF

I saw parch'd Abyssinia rouse and sing.
—KEATS, *Endymion*

Eritrea, the thorny, forlorn splinter of desert-*cum*-mountain along the Red Sea north of Ethiopia proper, is now federated with Haile Selassie's kingdom. Originally (1889) it was an Italian colony; the British took it over after World War II and administered it until federation with Ethiopia in 1952.[1] The name "Eritrea" derives from Mare Erythraeum, which is what the Romans called the Red Sea; the people are largely of Hamitic origin. Eritreans are milder people than Ethiopians, less interbred with Negroes, more advanced in some respects, and not so haughty. They are small-boned, with pointed features, and do not look Negroid at all. Their chief languages, Tigrinya and Tigré, differ greatly from Amharic, and Ethiopians and Eritreans cannot understand one another as a rule. Many Eritreans fought with the Italians *against* Ethiopia in 1935-36. Today the population is more or less equally divided between Copts and Moslems, and probably totals 1,100,000. Eritrea has 190 miles of railway—for an area bigger than Pennsylvania—and sixteen cinemas. When the British came in they found, in the whole country, not a single native university graduate, and only about a dozen men with a high-school education. It was not much material out of which to try to build a government.

ASMARA, the capital, sits perched in mountains 7,765 feet above sea level, and has charm. The story is that, whereas Addis Ababa is a big village, Asmara is a small *town*. The Italians built it well, like Tripoli, with handsome wide streets, ornate public buildings, and even such refinements of civilization as a modern sewage system, something that Addis Ababa certainly hasn't got. Mussolini wanted Asmara to be a gem of the new Italian empire. It is not quite that, but it still gives the impression of being a pleasant enough small city in Calabria, or even Umbria. But the Italians starved education. They built a race track and a slaughterhouse, but no schools. The population is 85 per cent infected with venereal disease, but nobody seems to care. Piquantly celebrated bandits, known as Shiftas, exist in the immediate environs, and can make the serpentine ride down

---

[1] Temptation is always considerable to include in these pages nuggets of local history. Consider the career of Baron Münzinger. He was a Swiss who served successively as both French *and* British consul at Massawa; in 1872 he took command (together with his wife) of a freebooting *Egyptian* expedition attempting to conquer Ethiopia from Eritrean territory. This was beaten back and Egypt disappeared from the Eritrean scene, as did Baron Münzinger.

MORE ABOUT ETHIOPIA, ERITREA, AND THE SOMALIS 279

to the sea exciting and even dangerous. The local beer, by name Melotti, is excellent.

Eritrea became an autonomous—or semi-autonomous—entity attached to Ethiopia by a curious process. I have already mentioned, describing Libya in Chapter 11, how the great powers quarreled over disposition of the former Italian colonies. Nobody knew quite what to do with Eritrea, such a derelict splinter of territory. Italy wanted it back of course; also Ethiopia wanted it. The Soviet bloc and the Arab states—for totally different reasons— would have liked it to be independent. The Bevin-Sforza plan suggested partition as a compromise, with the western half of the country, 95 per cent Moslem, going to the Sudan—to which it has the closest affiliations—and the eastern highlands, which are 85 per cent Christian and which are a natural extension of the Ethiopian plateau, going to Ethiopia. This proposal had a good deal to recommend it, but the United Nations Assembly, meeting in May, 1949, turned it down by one vote. Ethiopia abstained from voting. Haile Selassie was playing a careful waiting game; he thought that, with luck, he might in the end get *all* of Eritrea, and this indeed is what happened.

So the country continued to be run (till 1952) by an efficient, progressive British "caretaker" government. But this could not go on forever. The great powers debated three alternatives. (1) Immediate independence, an impossibility because Eritrea was not capable of economic self-support. (2) Restoration to Italy, likewise an impossibility, because Italy was getting the trusteeship over Somalia, and as a former enemy could not easily be given more. (3) Federation with Ethiopia. This was tenaciously opposed by Italy and the Arab bloc—the "Rome-Mecca" Axis—but went through anyway. The Arab states wanted an independent Eritrea, which they hoped they could be able to dominate eventually. The United Nations commissioner, Eduardo Anze Mateinzo, a Bolivian, played a large role in making federation a fact, and so did Philip Jessup. The United States and several Latin American countries pushed for it strongly.[2]

Within Eritrea itself people were divided. The pro-Ethiopian Copts vigorously welcomed federation; anti-Ethiopians opposed it. They said that Eritrea was not being "federated" at all, but forcibly "annexed"—"sold down the river to Haile Selassie." Eritrea is much poorer than Ethiopia, and as soon as federation became a fact the cost of living sharply increased. Eritreans, even though they have had so little education, are more advanced

---

[2] A joke of the period said that the solution finally adopted was "a Bolivian concept of a Swiss federation adapted to an African absolute monarchy." *Time*, October 13, 1952.

politically than most Ethiopians. Under the British they had an articulate press, parties, and free elections. Hence the anti-federalists complained that they were being pulled down to a lower level of political development. They resent it that Eritrea has no channel of official communication to the outside world except through "feudal" Addis Ababa. The UN should continue to hold a watching brief, many Eritreans think. On the other hand the country is bound to derive certain concrete advantages out of federation.[3]

One reason why Haile Selassie wanted federation is that Eritrea, the "lost province," has two ports (Massawa and Assab), and gives Ethiopia access to the sea. This is important from the viewpoint of security, and for other reasons. Development of motor traffic on the Massawa-Asmara-Addis Ababa route may break the old stranglehold of the French railway. Having an ocean frontage brings Ethiopian administrators new problems. The man newly appointed to be Port Administrator at Massawa had never, until he assumed this post, seen a ship, a dock, or salt water before. The Emperor is, however, fixed in his determination to make his country a "major" Red Sea naval power.

The Eritrean constitution was drawn up by the UN. There is an assembly, split exactly 50-50 between Copts and Moslems, which elects a chief executive who serves a four-year term. At present this is an able citizen, by name Tedla Bairu, who was educated in a Swedish mission school and then in Italy. Under federation Ethiopia, not Eritrea, is responsible for foreign affairs, defense, finance, foreign and interstate commerce, customs, and communications; not much remains to Eritrea. Haile Selassie has visited Eritrea twice a year since 1952, and always receives a vivid welcome. The real ruler of the country is the Bitwoded Andargachaw Masai, his viceroy and son-in-law.

Some 17,000 Italians still live in Eritrea, who are everything from shoemakers to barmen in the hotels. Those in commerce are having a hard time now, and many have returned to Italy recently. But Italian influence is still what gives Eritrea its special color, charm and quality.

THE SECRET AMERICAN BASE IN ERITREA

Not one American in ten thousand knows it, but the United States maintains in Asmara a substantial hush-hush military base, known as Radio Marina. This is not a base in the sense that it houses aircraft, like the bases in

---

[3] Tension between federalists and anti-federalists in Eritrea produced some picturesque terrorism. One leading anti-federalist, by name Woldeab Woldemarian, must hold the world's record for having survived attempts at political assassination. He has been shot at, bombed, poisoned, and otherwise attacked seven times.

Morocco; it is highly specialized. Radio Marina has been in existence since 1942, and has some forty American officers and six hundred GI's; most are expert radio technicians. Its chief function is to be an all-weather, all-year transmission point for United States government radio communications. The weather in Eritrea favors this; so does the altitude; so does the geographical location. During the Korean War radio traffic between Washington and Korea was of course incessant, but weather conditions over the Pacific often interfered with messages. Dispatched the other way around, via Asmara, they always got through. Then, although small, Radio Marina has other uses and advantages. Broadcasts anywhere in the Middle East are easily monitored from here. To have an American communications center on the Red Sea, comfortably established, and in expert working order, might be a considerable convenience in the event of war—war in the Middle East or elsewhere. Finally, Radio Marina is a useful watchtower for American observers looking at Africa as a whole.

I was interested in all this—also in the chocolate milk shakes at the PX. Not for a long time had we tasted such indigenous American delicacies. The Emperor, visiting Radio Marina not long ago, also found these milk shakes objects of satisfaction. Radio Marina is maintained with efficiency, precision, and courteous regard for the Eritreans. Eritreans and Ethiopians are delighted to have it here, because obviously it gives the United States a stake in their country. The Chief Executive of Eritrea drops in occasionally to have a manicure, and T-bone steaks cost 55 cents. Once again, as in North Africa, I felt intense admiration for the way Americans, so far from home, manage to make the best of a difficult post, remain cheerful, do an admirable job, and never (unlike Europeans) get mixed up in local political affairs.

THE SOMALILANDS

The Somali region, known today as the Horn of Africa, was once called Regio Aromatica, because of the spices it grew, and marks the extreme eastward projection of the continent. "The Somalis," an English observer writes, "are independent people unused to any sort of central government, unaccustomed to any form of direct taxation, and intensely suspicious of the foreigner, the white man, and the Christian. The only forms of national sport are raiding one's neighbor's camels, seizing his water supplies, and emasculating his males."[4] Somalis are not considered to be Negroes, even if they are as black as coffins. Most are Moslems of ancient Hamitic stock.

[4] J. Darrell Bates, "The Somaliland Protectorate," *Corona*, May, 1953.

There are three different Somalilands containing 120 different tribes:

1. *French Somaliland.* This is the small enclave around the port of Djibouti; it ranks as an overseas territory (*Côte Française des Somalis*) of the French Union, and sends one deputy and one senator to Paris. French Somaliland has 60,000 people and 24 schools. Its budget is $4,780,000, and the French say that 17 per cent of this goes to public health. The temperature at Djibouti, an evil little city, can rise to 113 degrees when an evil hot wind called the Khamsin blows from the baked desert. French Somaliland has been called "a nest of vampires."

2. *British Somaliland.* This is much bigger and less decrepit. The British governor is the sole legislative and executive authority, and the territory is run strictly as a protectorate. The capital is Hargeisa. The 700,000 people are mostly Moslem nomads, who live by grazing. Important crops are myrrh and frankincense, and a new road has recently been built to tap the spice areas, by means of a grant from the Colonial Development and Welfare Fund. British Somaliland was the habitat for years of a slippery gentleman named Mohammed bin Abdullah, who became notorious as the "Mad Mullah." He resisted British penetration of the country for nineteen solid years (1901–1920), and kept it in exasperated turmoil during most of this period; four different military expeditions were sent against him, but he was never caught. Of course he was not "mad" at all, but a vigorous early nationalist, like Abdel Krim.

3. *Somalia,* formerly Italian Somaliland. This territory, covering almost 300,000 square miles, has a unique status. It was an Italian colony until World War II; then, after years of argument, it was restored to Italy as a trust territory under United Nations supervision, although Italy is not a member of the UN.[5] The trusteeship runs for ten years from April 1, 1950; in 1960 Somalia is to be a fully independent, sovereign state. This is the only UN trusteeship with a time limit. Also the UN has more authority in Somalia than in its other trust territories, and maintains a permanent advisory commission there. Whether the Somalis will be capable of effective self-government after only five more years of tutelage is an open question. Probably they will need a good deal of financial aid at least. Seventy per cent of the population (1,265,624) are desperately poor nomads or semi-nomads.

MOGADISCIO, the capital, is variously spelled Mukdisha, Magadisho, Mukdishu, Mogadisho, Mogadaxo, and Mogadischo. The legend is that this is the place where Mussolini sent Italians whom he *really* wanted to get rid of.

[5] Originally (1905) the Italians bought Somalia from the Sultan of Zanzibar.

MORE ABOUT ETHIOPIA, ERITREA, AND THE SOMALIS

Somalia has one of the most radical and energetic nationalist movements in all Africa, the Somali Youth League. One of its leaders, an articulate youngish man named Abdullahi Issa, has several times appeared at the UN, denouncing Italian administration. Somali nationalism goes back a long way, in spite of the primitiveness of the country; the Somalis say that they constituted a homogenous "state" until this was "Balkanized" by Britain, France, Italy, and Ethiopia in the 1880's, but it is difficult to take such a claim altogether seriously. World War II gave nationalism a strong impetus; these regions were occupied and policed by British African troops from Kenya who "brought to the Somalis a sudden realization of their own backwardness." The Somalis looked down upon them, but they "could drive and repair vehicles, operate telecommunications, and knew in their own territories a degree of economic stability."[6] So the Somali people set about trying to get ahead.

On September 22, 1950, the *New Statesman* printed a letter from E. Sylvia Pankhurst denouncing the new Italian regime as it took up the task of governing the country. Administration, she asserted, was manned by "old colonials" who had served in Ethiopia; for instance, the Secretary General of the new government was the Fascist Governor of Harar. "A very serious situation is developing ... under Italian trusteeship," Miss Pankhurst wrote. "A ruthless persecution of members of the Somali Youth League ... is under way. In the first forty-seven days after the British hand-over to the Italians more than 300 Somali Youth League members had been thrown into prison. All senior police officers ... and others employed by the British have been dismissed or imprisoned ... The trials are in secret, the courts being closed to the public."

But this was long ago. Reporting to the UN in 1953, the Italians denied charges of unrest, and adduced the progress their regime is making in education, medical services, and political reform. Actually Italy has no motive for applying repressive measures or denying the Somalia people legitimate opportunity. The Italians have no long-range interest in the country at present, and probably will be glad to get out when the trusteeship expires in 1960.

Somalia has several other political parties in addition to the Somali Youth League—for instance, the Hisbia Dighil Mirifle, organized largely on a tribal basis, and the Partito Democratico Somalo. Municipal elections in 1954 (with 38,119 voters participating) gave the Somali Youth League 141 out of 281 seats. An interesting report was issued in December 1954, by the UN mission visiting Trust Territories in East Africa. The American

[6] "The Horn of Africa," *New Statesman*, March 6, 1948.

member was Mason Sears. Mr. Sears and his colleagues treat political developments in Somalia with marked respect, and give substantial hope for the country's future. The era of resentment against Italy for resentment's sake seems to be over, and the danger of Communist penetration much reduced. (For a time the Somali Youth League in particular was supposed to be strongly infiltrated by Communists.) "All political parties," says the UN report, "seem to have accepted realistically their role in the present political set-up and are working constructively. . . ." Nationalist consciousness is strong, but it is also "responsible." All senior posts in the administration are still held by Italians.

Frontiers in this part of the world are totally artificial, and the Somalis, a volatile group of tribes, leak over the borders. A fourth Somaliland exists in the Ogaden province of Ethiopia, which, although it is part of Ethiopia, is still administered by the British.[7] Northeast Kenya is likewise largely occupied by Somalis, and there are smaller Somali enclaves along the East Coast. Somalis are not much liked by British administrators, who say that they are "deceitful" and "treacherous."

It is remarkable that the Somalis, considering their background, should have such a strong sense of political organization and effervescent nationalism, at least in the towns. The Youth League stands for unity for all the Somali regions, in a confederation to be known as "Greater Somalia." One aim is to achieve a written language, to be called Osmania.

Somali nomads in Ethiopia—not in Somalia proper—got into the news recently because they refused to allow UN and Point Four "locust control" teams into their areas. About thirty American and European technicians patrol districts in Ethiopia where huge swarms of locusts, probably coming from Saudi Arabia across the Red Sea, invade the land. Later these penetrate down to Kenya and beyond and make formidable havoc. Locusts are a pressing problem throughout much of Africa. What the control teams on the spot try to do is destroy the locusts at their source by modern insecticide techniques. But the Ethiopian Somalis would not let them enter the most heavily infected breeding areas. Airplanes were widely used for spraying locust concentrations because the Ethiopian government could not provide armed escort for the men on the ground.

[7] An Anglo-Ethiopian agreement early in 1955 provides for the return of this area to Ethiopian administration. Somalis who liked British protection in the region known as the Haud bitterly resented being turned over to Ethiopia.

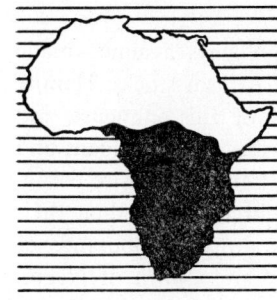

CHAPTER 17

Foreword to Bantu Africa

> *In every book I ever read*
> *Of travels on the Equator,*
> *A plague, mysterious and dread,*
> *Imperils the narrator.*
> —THE MODERN TRAVELLER

Now at last we reach Bantu Africa. This is the broad, fat pendulum of territory stretching roughly from a line a few hundred miles above the Equator all the way to the Cape—in other words all of Africa below the western bulge, an area twice as big as the United States. Of course not all Africans in this tremendous space are Bantus, but they predominate— in Kenya, Tanganyika, Uganda, the Congo, the Rhodesias, Nyasaland, the Portuguese colonies of Angola and Mozambique, parts of French Equatorial Africa, the three British "High Commission" territories in the Union (Basutoland, Bechuanaland, Swaziland), and the Union of South Africa itself.

Strictly speaking this is not "Black Africa"—what the French call *Afrique noire*. Bantus are brown, more or less, not black. Moreover, as I have mentioned in Chapter 1, "Bantu" is correctly not a racial term at all, but linguistic. Black Africa lies mostly (by conventional definition) along the West Coast above the bulge, and is the domain of pure Negroes rather than of Bantus. But of course there have been prodigious interweavings and overlappings and underlappings, and sometimes I shall use the words "Bantu," "black," and "Negro" synonymously.

Mostly in this chapter and the six that follow we deal with the huge entity known as British East Africa, which means the Colony and Protectorate of Kenya, the Protectorate of Uganda, the Territory of Tanganyika, and the remarkable non-Bantu island of Zanzibar. But also, in order to make generalizations more apposite or comprehensive, I dip at times into other Bantu or Negro areas.

286   INSIDE AFRICA

Bantus are a mixture—so at least most anthropologists assume—made thousands of years ago when pools of the two basic African stocks, Hamite and Negro, began to flow into one another. Out of this immense and turbulent process of fusion came (a) the Nilotic tribes of the Sudan, and (b) the Bantus who spread further south and west, filling the entire cornucopia of the continent. Bantus are, by and large, lighter-skinned than their parent Negroes (and lighter than some Hamites), although thousands of them may be as black as top hats. Of course they are a *form* of Negro. Most, but not all, have Negroid features—crinkly or woolly hair, squat noses, and everted lips. Most Bantus were originally forest people, who evolved into agriculturists. They were not (again speaking broadly) pastoral nomads. What distinguishes them chiefly is that they became cattle people after clearing plots in the forest; cattle are vital to their whole way of life.

Bantus rose out of the bush; many still remain in the bush, "lacustrine" or "riverain" dwellers who live deep in the rain forests and cling close to water. But large numbers of them have in recent years begun a steady, seminal march into the towns. Chauffeurs in Nairobi, mineworkers on the Rand, the industrial proletariat in Johannesburg, clerks in Entebbe, truck drivers in Salisbury, are mainly Bantu.

There are 220 different tribes in British East Africa as a whole, and about seventy in Kenya alone, most with their own languages. It is the institution of the tribe that is the principal hallmark of native Africa below the Sahara. Of course there are tribes in the north too, as we have seen, but somehow people like the Tuareg and Amharas do not seem quite as characteristic of "pure" Africa as the great Bantu and Negro tribes. One could sing a litany of tribes. In East Africa there are tribes like the Kikuyu,[1] which are veritable nations, and like the Wagogo who still "have their tails up in the trees." (One still hears exasperated and not very progressive Englishmen say in Kenya, "But the grandfathers of these wretched people were still *monkeys!*") There are tribes businesslike and sophisticated, like the Chagga who grow coffee on the slopes of Mt. Kilimanjaro, and tribes next door which have not yet reached even the dawn of social consciousness. There are tribes with men as handsome as the Nandi, tribes with men as ugly as the pygmies, tribes with a long and honorable history like the Baganda, and tribes whose members are great specialists in arrow poisons, and like to eat lion fat, which tastes catty.

There are the up-and-coming Luos (Nilotic) in Kenya, the romantically backward Toros in Uganda, the healthily progressive Wasukuma and Wanyamwezi in Tanganyika. There are the Masai (non-Bantu) who live on

[1] The Mau Mau rebellion in Kenya was made by dissident Kikuyus.

FOREWORD TO BANTU AFRICA 287

blood and milk, and the Bahayas, famous because their women are prostitutes all over East Africa. The tribes are multiform and various; each has its own unique roots, its tradition and identity. There is no end of them. They are inescapable and inexpungeable. When we go beyond East Africa into other Bantu regions the names roll out in a proliferating, interwoven stream—names that taste like pepper and can sound like thunder or a jet splitting the sky as if it were cardboard—Zulus, Bembas, Matabele, Barotse, Xhosas, Hereros, Mangbetos, Yaos, Angonis, Nyanjas, Ovambos, Kongos, Ndongas, Mbundas. These are a few names out of hundreds.[2]

Obviously it is impossible to generalize with much pith about people so widely scattered over so much of a continent. I tried in an early chapter of this book to define some Arab characteristics; it is doubly difficult to do so with Bantu or Negro characteristics. However a few tentative things may be said.

Most Bantu languages have similar qualities, and the roots of many words are the same, or approximately the same, all the way from Kenya to the Cape. The word for "man" is *umu-ntu* in Zulu, *um-tu* in Xhosa, *oman-tu* in Luganda, and *m-tu* in Swahili. The plural form, *aba-ntu* ("men") is the same in a number of languages, and from this comes the word "Bantu" itself, meaning "human beings."[3] The fact that Bantu languages are similar over such a wide area is potentially an important unifying force. Negro languages on the other flank of Africa are totally dissimilar. They differ from Bantu almost as much as English does from Japanese, and there can be a completely new language every fifty miles.

Swahili, the lingua franca of the East Coast is an "alloy" built partly out of Arab words on a Bantu grammar. It developed in the area which the Arabs penetrated, and gradually seeped inward; it was spread mostly by Europeans, because this was the first African language they were apt to learn. Swahili (properly, Kiswahili) is spoken by at least twenty million people, who live all the way from Somalia to Madagascar. Much con-

[2] There are certain stylistic difficulties which we had better face at this point. Properly the Chaggas are called the "Wachagga," the Kikuyus the "Akikuyu," and so on. This is because a prefix denotes the difference between singular and plural in most Bantu languages. Other prefixes indicate whether the people of the tribe are meant, the country, or the language. For instance, Kikamba is the language spoken by the Akamba people of the Kamba tribe. I propose to forget these distinctions so far as possible and stick to the form of the word most familiar in English, like "Basuto" or "Watutsi." Otherwise we become bogged down in such complexities as that the "Akikuyu" speak "Gegikuyu," or that people (Wahehe) of the Hehe tribe talk Kihehe in their country (Uhehe). A good guide to these matters is *East African Background*, by G. W. B. Huntingford and C. R. V. Bell. See p. 2 and 91 ff.

[3] See *A Short History of the East Coast of Africa*, by L. W. Hollingsworth, p. 5.

troversy attends the use of Swahili in British-run schools, where it is the language of instruction. Most Africans would much prefer to learn English in school, since they will have to learn it anyway if they expect to make much progress in the world. They say that it imposes too much strain on a native boy to make him learn his own language first, then Swahili as a second language, and finally English.

Swahili is fairly easy for a European to learn—much easier than Arabic, for instance—because its grammar is comparatively simple. Prefixes and suffixes are widely used, and words are built up in stepladder manner. For instance, "love" is *penda,* "to love" is *kupenda,* "I love" is *nina-penda,* "I love you" is *nina-mu-penda.*

Some African languages have tones, like Chinese, and these can be tricky in the extreme. An illuminating book, *Talking Drums of Africa,* by John F. Carrington, which traces the origins of drum language out of different tones used in speech, mentions that in the Congo language Kele, for instance, the word *ayeke* means both "let him come" and "do not let him come," depending on pronunciation. The words for "fiancée" and "rubbish pit" are written alike, but are distinguished by different tones. The sentence *alambaka boili* means both "He watched the riverbank" and "He boiled his mother-in-law."

A LINE FROM SIR PHILIP MITCHELL

The following quotation is from a report by Sir Philip Mitchell, a former governor both of Uganda and Kenya, and one of the ablest British administrators ever to serve in Africa. It has been cited by several writers to indicate the kind of job the British faced when they began the penetration of East Africa:

> They [the Africans] had no wheeled transport and . . . no animal transport either; they had no roads nor towns; no tools except small hand hoes, axes, wooden digging sticks, and the like; no manufactures, and no industrial products except the simplest domestic handiwork; no commerce as we understand it and no currency, although in some places barter of produce was facilitated by the use of small shells; they had never heard of working for wages. They went stark naked or clad in the bark of trees or the skins of animals; and they had no means of writing, even by hieroglyphics, nor of numbering except by their fingers or making notches in a stick or knots in a piece of grass or fibre; they had no weights or measures of general use. Perhaps most astonishing of all to the modern European mind they had no calendar nor notation of time . . . Before European occupation there was no way of saying "1st January 1890" or "2:30 PM." or their

equivalents in any language spoken from Abyssinia to the Transvaal, except Swahili along the coast . . . They were pagan, spirit or ancestor propitiators in the grip of magic or witchcraft, their minds cribbed and confined by superstition . . . They are a people who in 1890 were in a more primitive condition than anything of which there is any record in pre-Roman Britain.

What most impresses Europeans on the spot in East Africa today is that Africans had not invented the wheel; we heard the phrase "They didn't even know the *wheel!*" almost as often as the one about their grandfathers being up in the trees. There is no doubt that East Africa *was*, sixty years ago, almost unbelievably primitive—much more so than West Africa. No one would want to deny this. Theodore Roosevelt when he made a celebrated safari in Kenya as recently as 1910 spoke of his railway trip from the coast as a journey through "the Pleistocene."

On the other hand, even in those primitive days, Bantu tribes in East Africa had highly developed social structures. They were savages, yes, but their societies were not chaotic. They fought wars, but mostly these were no more than overgrown feuds, not mass exercises in mass slaughter like European wars. They had their own complex values and standards, which were certainly not like ours, but which they obeyed. Their rituals were complicated, but exact. They had "an elaborate social organization" and their own systems of law and justice, as well as "of council, of morals, of village and tribal organization, even in some degree of education, and very notably in mutual aid."[4] They had no pauper class, they held land by a process of communal ownership, and they were by no means ignorant of agriculture, medicine, and other sciences and crafts. And (on the West Coast at least) they produced notable works of art.

SOME OBSERVATIONS ABOUT THE BANTUS

The equator is kind only to the lazy or the very wise.
—DENIS SAURAT

Let us proceed to generalize briefly:

1. Almost all Bantu tribes (and much of what follows is true of Negro Africa also) are held together by kinship, and have a strong clannishness and cohesiveness, under a chief or chiefs. But some tribes—like the Kikuyu —did not have chiefs until the British came.[5] Normally the chief is a combination of local boss, family counselor, and tax collector. He symbolizes

---

[4] Julian Huxley, *Africa View*, p. 15.
[5] They were ruled instead by Councils of Elders.

both unity and leadership. There have been plenty of tyrant chiefs—we met some as vulgarly possessive and bad-mannered as a ward heeler in Chicago—but chiefdom is a complicated institution, and the organization of most tribes is democratic. A chief has to serve as well as lead his people, if he wants to hold his job. He cannot easily be a dictator, because the elders of the tribe (and witch doctors) will not permit it. Chiefs are appointed to their posts by a combination of circumstances; heredity usually plays a role, but not necessarily a decisive one. People whose ideas of Africa are based on childhood reading or contemporary movies are likely to think of chiefs as old-men-of-the-tribe decked out in ostrich feathers or the manes of lions, clanking with beads and holding spears aloft. Actually most chiefs nowadays wear western dress, are youthful or middle-aged rather than old, speak good English with a peculiar semi-Oxford accent, and have keen delight in such phenomena as the price of automobiles or even the novels of Joyce Cary.

Most chiefs in British territory are in effect British agents, even if they have nationalist inclinations. They have certain duties in administration and are paid salaries for their work. Some Africans even think that chiefs are a British invention! In Uganda we watched a chief hold court; in Tanganyika we listened to a chief explain ably the details of the local political situation. In some areas big chiefs are known as "paramount" chiefs. The British, by and large, interfere as little as possible with purely tribal matters. It is a very serious matter to depose a chief, and they almost never do so. District Commissioners usually have a nicely paternal attitude toward their chiefs. It is a delicious experience to hear a chief expound his plans to throw the British out of Africa, immediately after a convivial tea with him at the DC's house. The DC's usually know perfectly well what a chief is up to, and are miracles of tact. A DC will often introduce a visitor to the chief, and then quietly withdraw, saying, "My chap here will talk to you more freely if I'm not around."

2. The sheer naked primitiveness of those parts of Africa which are still primitive is perhaps best demonstrated by habits of costume and personal adornment. I shall attempt to describe some examples of native dress from time to time in the pages following. In Natal we stared almost without belief at the hairdress of young Zulu women. Girls—such pretty girls!—braid their hair, pack it with dung, and weave it with reeds to form baskets which are solid on the head, broad, and eighteen inches high. This hair-do, once arranged, is *never* taken down. The girls have to have special pillows to hold these baskets while they sleep.

3. Religion is a matter of overwhelming importance in tribal affairs, and we shall deal with some aspects of this later in this chapter. Most Africans (like most good Christians) do not think that the dead are really dead, and worship their ancestors. Often a witch doctor has more influence than the chief of a tribe, because he has access to ancestral and other spirits. A Belgian anthropologist has gone so far as to define a tribe as a "community of the living and dead" combined, in which the dead are equally powerful.[6] Moreover spirits may take earthly form as serpents, other animals, trees, and the like, and these must be "worshiped" too. Phenomena like rain, lightning, and so on are supposed to be expressions of some special power in the universe, which among other things governs the growth of crops; hence medicine men and witch doctors seek to propitiate the elements. There are few things in the arena of African life that superstition does not touch.

A dead or dying African, even if he is already a spirit or about to become one, may be treated with scant courtesy. In Kenya, near Nyeri, we saw an aged Kikuyu lying on the side of the road, left out there to die, because the Kikuyu consider a death in the home to be bad luck. Some tribes leave their dead out for the hyenas; some bury important individuals in anthills.

4. The bases of Bantu economy are, of course, the land, which is usually held in ownership by the tribe as a whole, and cattle. The Bantu has a strong feeling about the sacredness of his land, and lives and dies by the cattle on it. Most Africans in the bush live in small round floorless and windowless huts with roofs of mud or thatch. Usually there is only one circular room, which is used by human beings and animals alike; a wood fire burns perpetually, which fills it with smoke. Livingstone wrote about the Nyasas, "Fire is their only clothing at night," and in many parts of Bantu (and Negro) Africa this is still true. One does not need to elaborate on the merciless grinding poverty of most Africans. But in the villages, which are clustered along the roads, circumstances are gradually becoming better. More and more people can afford soap, kerosene, cigarettes, and even bicycles. Many of these are "Fix" bicycles, so called because they are made out of old spare parts. Thousands of bicycles move incessantly up and down the African trails and red muddy roads. There are more on the West Coast, however, than in the East.

5. Diet. Practically all black Africans are undernourished. The staple food varies from north to south—it may be manioc (cassava), bananas, or mealie meal, which is ground-up corn. Most Africans in the bush get little

[6] Hailey, *An African Survey*, p. 30.

else. Europeans often call Bantus "lazy," and indeed many of them are lazy. But sometimes, as one observer puts it, "laziness is a protection against wretchedly low wages, inconsiderate treatment, and the break-up of the home that going to work for a white master often entails." Moreover, it may be the result of faulty and inadequate diet—in particular lack of protein and fats.[7] Most Africans are crazy about meat. But they get it seldom, because game is not always available or easy to kill, and of course butcher shops are unknown except in the big towns. Most villages have no shops at all, except ramshackle stalls. Then too few Africans could afford to buy meat even if it were available. European scientists, leaders in community development, and administrators all over Africa are working on aspects of this pivotal and painful problem. In Uganda fisheries are being built up, so that Africans can get protein from fish. Why do not the Bantus kill their own cattle for meat? As well ask why a Park Avenue millionaire of social distinction does not slit his daughter's throat, and roast her for breakfast. Cattle are not (except in rare instances) meat to an African. They are draft power, milk, fuel, and, above all, wealth and the means of buying brides.

6. Cannibalism, we might add parenthetically, is now virtually extinct in Bantu Africa. But I met a British judge who had sentenced a man in Uganda to death as recently as 1937 for boiling and eating a baby. Sometimes on long safaris Europeans change their porters every fifty miles or so, so that these can return to their homes without danger of ambush in hostile territory. There were several reasons for cannibalism anthropologically speaking—for instance the widespread belief that if you killed an enemy and ate his heart or other organs, his spirit entered into your body and gave you added strength and courage. Another was certainly craving for meat. A youthful human thigh was more tender, and probably tasted better, than a muscular haunch of antelope. Human beings are, by and large, easier to kill than game, and besides there are many types of game which, on account of various taboos, some tribes refuse to eat.

First in the Kenya hinterland and then in Uganda and particularly the Congo, we began to see Africans with filed teeth. The teeth are not sharpened with an actual file as a rule, but are chipped down with a chisel. Cannibalism is supposed by some authorities to have been the genesis of this custom, which is now persisted in as a matter of decoration. Sharp teeth presumably gave a better bite, for human as well as animal meat. Another point— perhaps not strictly relevant—is that the tenderizing agents now coming into common use everywhere in the United States derive from an African

---

[7] "To compel the African to be 'less lazy' on his present diet is like trying to make steel with one candle." *Tomorrow's Continent*, by Peter Penn and Lucie Street.

plant, a kind of papaya. Africans in some areas have used it to soften up animal tissue for generations.

7. A white man, if he behaves himself, is not likely to be molested by natives anywhere in Africa south of the Sahara—excepting in such areas as the Johannesburg slums or the Kenya Highlands where, obviously, the Mau Mau insurrection makes a special case. There is no danger whatever in African travel, except from wingèd things like insects or airplanes. The deepest thickets in the bush are safer, by and large, for a law-abiding traveler than Central Park at night. Africans have their own strict codes of behavior. Almost all early explorers, like Livingstone, pay tribute to the peaceableness of Africans, their decorousness and humility, although of course there have been dramatic exceptions to this rule. Today even savages in isolated territory usually welcome the sight of a white man, because the chances are that he may shoot some game and share it. Natives are strictly forbidden in most of Bantu Africa to possess or use firearms, just as they are forbidden (in theory) to drink hard liquor.

8. Pigmentation. I should have known better but I was astonished, in a Congo hospital, to see that a newly born African baby was pink, not black at all. The darkening of the skin comes later. A good many different hypotheses have been advanced to account for this; one is that it is a defense given by nature against tropical sun. As a matter of fact a really jet-black African is comparatively rare, except in Senegal and the Sudan. Africans may be of any color from pale yellowish brown to beige, chocolate, bronze, soot, or asphalt. Many Africans have a peculiar bodily odor (to the European sense of smell) which some authorities think may be related to their pigmentation.[8] In French Africa this odor is often referred to irreverently as *fleur d'Afrique*. Finally the frizzy hair of Africans is not a hallmark of primitiveness or backwardness, as many ignorant people believe. The *Encyclopaedia Britannica* says: "In respect to . . . hair, the white man stands in closer relation to the higher apes than does the Negro."[9]

9. Among experts on Africa arguments may be pursued without end in regard to the basic intelligence and educatability of Negroes. Much scientific work has been done on skull measurements and the like. It is extraordinarily difficult to generalize about African mental patterns. Most Bantus have excellent memories—if they are interested in a subject—and a good mimetic quality; most lack a sense of time. They are a mystery only to white people who make no effort to understand them. How often did we hear comments like, "They are hysterical somewhere in the *back*

---

[8] Conversely, Europeans have a bodily odor peculiar to the African.
[9] From the article on Negroes.

of their heads," or "You can never tell what they're *really* thinking," or even "If we only had a way to *reach* them!"

Take such a matter as their philosophical attitude to, let us say, punishment. Prisons were unknown in Africa before the white man came. It seemed extraordinarily silly to primitive Africans that offenders against society should be cooped up and fed at the public expense. They had other methods of punishment, like fines or flogging.

Africans perhaps seem to be backward (and enormous numbers of them *are* backward undeniably) partly because of the fast tempo of recent developments. Family; clan; tribe—these constituted till yesterday their total orbit. Now they face overnight concepts as difficult as "nation" and "world."

There are certainly millions of stupid Africans, just as there are millions of stupid Russians, Americans or what you will; this does not mean that there are not other millions who, given tutelage, opportunity, and confidence, will not turn out to be just as intelligent as white men. The brain has no color. Everyone knows that some Chinese and Indian brains are as good, or better, than European brains. No anthropological justification exists for assuming that any people are inferior purely on grounds of color.

Let us say once more that almost all Africans, no matter where they live or what kind of skins they have, crave education. They do not get anything like the facilities for education they deserve, which is obviously one reason why they may seem childish or confused or ridiculously pretentious even after they have had some education, because to learn only a little increases their tendency to inferiority. In Kenya only about 8 per cent of Africans of school age go to school. The British had Zanzibar for twenty-six years before opening any school at all.

It is frequently said that what Black Africa needs most is *vocational* education—the training that will make men bricklayers, pipe fitters, undertakers, soil engineers, pharmacists, aircraft mechanics, rather than lawyers or clerks. True. But only too obviously grounding in the three R's must come first. *Can* illiteracy be wiped out? Of course. Look at the example of the Philippines. Look at what is happening in India.

V. K. Krishna Menon, the Indian representative at recent meetings of the Trusteeship Council of the UN, made a prescient remark when, discussing African advance to independence; he said, "Now that we have given these people the vote, let us sit down to educate our masters."

10. Black Africans give on the whole a sense of being a sunny people, overcheerful perhaps, melodious, inquisitive, and, in spite of everything, happy. They are much warmer, gentler, more relaxed, than Arabs or the scornful, arrogant Ethiopians. An allied point is their volatility, their

physical effervescence (no matter how lazy they may be) and gregariousness and delight in music, art, and spectacle. Anybody who has traveled in backwoods Africa will know what I mean by this. You may drive for hours along a forest road in Uganda and not see a soul between villages. Have a flat tire, and instantly, in a matter of seconds, there will be a dozen Africans appearing miraculously out of the bush from nowhere, thronging the road, watching, chortling. And it is the easiest thing in the world to pick up an outrider, without having the faintest idea where he came from. Stop for a moment—particularly at night—and presto! a grinning African has perched on the seat next to your chauffeur. It is very strange.

FEMALES OF THE SPECIES

Africans like to carry things on their heads, and do so with an exquisite sense of balance. Everybody knows this. The old story is that if you give an African a wheelbarrow, he will carry even this on his head. I have seen on the heads of walking Africans—particularly women—everything from bottles standing upright to a mattress. Small children are usually slung over the back and tied on, so that the woman (who may be carrying another baby in her belly) has her hands free for other duties, such as clubbing a donkey with a stick. Men seldom carry anything, but walk ahead, scouting out the way; this derives from older days when it was the duty of the male to watch out for wild animals or enemy raiders. As a matter of fact this division of labor does not differ very much from that in the Bronx or Wimbledon; mostly it is women who do the shopping, and transport their purchases home. I asked a District Commissioner why Africans comparatively well off, who could afford bicycles for instance, did not buy carts or other mechanical contrivances for hauling heavy material. Answer: "Women are cheaper, and do not need spare parts."

Never—not even in the Andes—have I seen women so much like beasts of burden as the Kikuyu. They do not carry their loads on their heads, but on their backs supported by a leather loop around the forehead. By the time a Kikuyu housewife has reached middle age, this belt or halter will have worn a groove—literally—across her temples. It is not unusual for a Kikuyu woman to carry two hundred pounds, particularly if she is collecting firewood from the forest groves. A donkey carries one hundred pounds; a professional porter sixty (the standard load, which must not be exceeded); a prisoner at hard labor fourteen.

Kikuyu women may be thought of as slaves; actually they have well-defined rights and privileges as well as duties, and, like most Negro women, play a substantial role in the affairs of their communities. Their circumstances differ totally from those of Moslem women in countries we have already inspected; they are not prisoners or drones; they are not languid, pudding-shaped, or veiled; they work hard, and what is more they expect reward for their labors. Among the Kikuyu—again to cite a single and perhaps special tribe—women have an unassailable right to property in their own right, which even their husbands may not infringe. Women of the Kavirondo, another Kenya tribe, may not be required to use an ax, because it is the man's duty to clear the land. Women can be fierce politicians. Many women —and even children—were conspicuous among Mau Mau terrorists. It is harder to reach them and teach them western standards than to teach men, because they have had less access to education; as a rule they know no language but their own, not even Swahili. They are not even free enough of tribal strictures to become servants in European houses, except as nursemaids in some cases; Africa, like Asia, is a continent where servants are largely male. Hence women have little opportunity to see how white people live and behave.

About marriage customs we could write unendingly. Once more, it is almost impossible to generalize. Most tribes in East Africa are polygamous, without limit to the number of wives a man may have. Reasons for polygamy are both economic and in the realm of symbolism and superstition; many Africans think that sexual prowess and in particular the ability to procreate children have an association with fertility of the soil.[10] A person's worth is not measured by the criterion of wealth in much of Black Africa, but by fecundity. But women are, on the whole, freer than in Moslem society. This does not mean that they necessarily have a good life. Fathers or husbands can be tyrants anywhere. But, generally speaking, a young Bantu girl is not packaged up and delivered to the groom sight unseen by her parents, to become an ornament in a stranger's harem; she herself can associate with young men and know the joys of courtship and even have a say in the choice of a husband; she can refuse an undesired suitor, and is seldom (at least in advanced tribes like the Chaggas) married against her will. In many tribes a bride is supposed to be a virgin, and promiscuity and infidelity are frowned upon. Husbands in some areas, if they leave home on a trip, may practice upon their wives an operation known as infibulation, that is, sewing up the vagina except for a minuscule orifice. This is carrying the antique European device of a chastity belt far indeed, and is a cruel and painful process. All over Black Africa—for instance, among the Kipsigis—

[10] Hailey, *op. cit.*, p. 30.

a wife is forbidden by custom to conceive a child while suckling one. Children are not weaned until they are two years old or older as a rule, and most births are thus spaced out at salutary intervals.[11] One theory to account for this is that conception "poisons" the mother's milk, because semen has got into it. Sexual intercourse itself is not forbidden, and rude forms of birth control are practiced.[12]

There are, of course, an infinite number of special arrangements and taboos. Kikuyus (like Japanese) do not kiss on the lips. Incest is the worst of crimes, and homosexuality is uncommon—in fact in some tribes (like the Kikuyu again) unknown. In several tribes a powerful taboo forbids any contact between a man and his mother-in-law, even socially. Widows in most tribes are apt to have a miserable time; in some a widow is inherited by the deceased man's next oldest brother, who is obliged to marry her. A woman is supposed never to be left unprotected, and the tribe wants to safeguard her land, if any. There are even places where, if no male relative is available, the widow "marries" another woman in order to help take care of her stock. A woman can, in theory, become the "stepfather" of another woman's children.

Two other phenomena in this field are significant, bride-price and female circumcision. "Bride-price" means what it says; it is the sum paid by a man for his wife to the bride's family—a practice universal throughout East, Central and South Africa. A marriage cannot possibly take place without it, except occasionally among detribalized Africans in the towns. The bride-price is, nine times out of ten, paid in cattle. When cattle are not available cash, merchandise, services, or a combination of all these may be used; the prospective groom may hire himself out to the bride's father for work in the fields, and so on. In Kenya a bride costs from three heifers up or its equivalent. Bride-price is, it should be pointed out, more than a merely commercial phenomenon. A father's children are, together with his cattle, the "capital" of the family, on which it is only fair that he should have some return; if he loses a daughter, he should get an animal or two in exchange. The ability to pay bride-price demonstrates that the groom is serious in his intentions, and has reached a certain status in society. It assures good will on the part of the tribe, and is a kind of contractual augury and insurance for a happy marriage.

Circumcision is not universal among Black Africans by any means. In some

[11] *Mau Mau and the Kikuyu*, by L. S. B. Leakey, p. 19.
[12] Edwin W. Smith, *Knowing the African*, and Leakey, have much piquant detail on these matters. Also see Jomo Kenyatta, *Facing Mount Kenya*, pp. 156, 162, 173.

tribes—for instance, the Angoni, Luo, Chewa, and Bemba—males are not circumcised, and the Masai are *half* circumcised, so that a flap of foreskin hangs down like a rudder. In tribes that do circumcise males, the operation as a rule takes place when the boy reaches puberty, not in infancy, and is performed on the basis of what are known as "age groups." It is done en masse—the ceremony has an extremely important symbolic significance—and boys are stratified for life into classes depending on their age at the time. Analogously graduates of an American university are grouped by class. Each age group is named for some special person or event, and these names can be highly picturesque; one in Tanganyika was recently called "Syphilis," because of a local outbreak of this disease at the time of circumcision. Others have been *Namunyu* (hyena), *Lumiri* (for a small bird that ate the crops), *il-Kupai* (white swords), *il-Kishumu* (the raiders), and Airplane.[13]

Female circumcision is an ugly and complex story. That such an operation is possible at all, to say nothing of the fact that it is widely practiced, is a shock to many westerners. Kikuyus without exception practice female circumcision; so do Merus, Kambas, some Nandis, Hehes, Dorobos, and others. Some tribes do not, like the Zulus in South Africa. There are two types of female circumcision. In the form least revolting and least damaging it consists of removal of the clitoris; in some tribes the *labia majora* and *minora* are also amputated. The operation usually takes place when a girl is anywhere from ten to fourteen, and is part of a group ceremony. No matter how skillfully or aseptically it is performed it may, of course, have the most disastrous consequences. I have never heard a satisfactory explanation for this odious, degrading practice. Africans deny that it is designed to render a woman incapable of sexual pleasure, so that she may be more docile; clitoridectomy does *not*, they say, necessarily destroy sexual enjoyment. Jomo Kenyatta, the Kikuyu leader now in prison for alleged complicity in the Mau Mau rebellion, has written at length about female circumcision in *Facing Mount Kenya*, and he not only defends but extols it in the most lyrical terms; his description of a public circumcision ceremony makes it sound like a picnic at Vassar. Female circumcision, particularly among the Kikuyu, has been an important political problem in Kenya. Christian missionaries attacked the practice and sought to stamp it out; Kikuyu nationalists (even if they were privately ashamed of it) resented outside pressure to make them change their ways. In consequence female circumcision not only became an issue binding Kikuyus together, but a factor stimulating their hatred of all phases of white colonial control.

[13] These names, as well as details about the position of women, are from Huntingford, *op. cit.*

Finally we should mention the important fact that, almost everywhere in Black Africa, inheritance of rule is matrilineal. The old-woman-of-the-tribe is often more important than the old man. The succession passes to some male born of a *female* member of the dynastic line, and therefore a brother or nephew succeeds rather than a son.

WITCHCRAFT AND BLACK MAGIC

The fundamental conception of magic is identical with that of modern science; underlying the whole system is faith, implicit but real and firm, in the order and uniformity of nature.
—SIR JAMES FRAZER

Mumbo-jumbo will hoodoo you.
—VACHEL LINDSAY

Belief in magic is almost universal throughout Black Africa, and so is fear of witchcraft. Magic and witchcraft are quite different. In the Congo for instance there are two kinds of witch doctors. One is the *nkanga* or simple magician or medicine man, who brews herbs, prescribes potions, and often has remarkable success in curing illness. He *is* a kind of doctor. But his healing power comes not only from his potions, but because he is supposed to have intimate contact with the tribal spirits. The other is the *boloki*, the devil of the community and a nasty customer. He is a sorcerer who casts spells, and is hired to do injury to others. If mere incantations fail, he may resort to poison. There are, it might be noted in passing, about 570 different African plants known to western science that are poisonous to some degree or other. No doubt the *bolokis* know many more. A favorite place to carry poison, after it has been purchased from the witch doctor, is under the little fingernail. You dip your finger unostentatiously in the drink of the victim, and he is done for.

The origin of witchcraft, most anthropologists think nowadays, is that it gives the primitive African a sense of power against the elemental forces of nature. Man alone is not strong enough to cope with nature, which may express itself with unexampled capriciousness and brutality, and so he is driven to rely on the supernatural for assistance. In a way witchcraft is the African's substitute for our conception of the Almighty. In western religions, the concept of God is the link between the human being and the mysterious forces of the universe; similarly Africans believe in spirits. Moreover they maintain close alliance with their ancestors, as we have already pointed out, and the witch doctor is a convenient mechanism (like a Shinto priest) to this end. Another point is that few really primitive Africans believe that anybody ever dies a "natural" death. A spell must have been put on the dead man, or he would not have died. If a man is sick, it merely means that he is bewitched. Hence, Africans hire witch doctors to put spells on their enemies, or to avert spells put on themselves by others.

A university-educated African in Durban said to a European friend, "Yes, I know that a European doctor may be able to cure us better than a native medicine man, but he would not be able to tell us *who gave us the disease.*"

We in the United States or Great Britain should think twice before we dismiss the primitive beliefs of Africans as balderdash, or laugh at their occult customs. I saw a dead parrot on sale as a fetish (it was wrapped in cornhusks) in one African bazaar; disgusting, of course. But we use fetishes like foxtails on automobiles. Do you, in Brooklyn or Bognor Regis, like to walk under ladders, sit down thirteen at dinner, or light three cigarettes from the same match? Do you ever knock on wood?

Some African superstitions may seem gruesome, but they usually have a certain basis in logic. In a Congo town we ran into a pretty girl carrying twins; she wore smears of pale yellowish paint on her forehead and both cheeks, and the babies had circles of the same color—it seemed almost phosphorescent—on their temples. The purpose of this paint was to exorcise evil spirits, since twins have a curse on them. Many African tribes believe that a double birth is unnatural; it can only mean that one of the twins has been sired by a spirit, not the husband. In fact till recently in some parts of Africa, twins were killed as soon as they were born; it was the mother's job to do this, and the conventional method of execution was to stuff the nostrils full of dust.

Witchcraft is probably increasing, not decreasing, among bush people at the moment because Africans tend to cling to their old superstitions and religious forms more strongly, in the face of the western impact that is breaking up the tribes and destroying many of their other customs. They have a redoubled need for personal security as the security provided in older days by the tribe begins to disappear. They prefer to belong to spirits rather than to nothing. As a result one may see striking juxtapositions. Africa, as we know, is a continent very mixed up. In Natal we visited the shop of a briskly enterprising *inyanga* (witch doctor) and saw on exhibition and for sale the customary assortment of fetishes like the bladders of fowl and blown-up sheep's intestines. But on the wall was a sign in neatly printed English: IF YOU HAVE NOTHING TO DO, DO NOT DO IT HERE.

Witch doctors wear peculiar costumes as a rule. We saw several fully decked out. Usually one adorns himself with trophies collected from animals, like baboon tails; he is often masked, and his chief weapons are his bones, which are the vertebra of some animal killed in a ritualistic manner. To find

FOREWORD TO BANTU AFRICA

out what he needs to know, or to cast a spell, he tosses these bones down, as we play dice, and watches the design they form. Such ceremonies are, of course, secret, in communities where black magic is against European law. The witch doctor would no more be seen in public in full regalia than would the Dowager Countess of Whatnot walk down Piccadilly naked. In Swaziland—as an example—the full regalia, worn in private, is frightening to an extreme; the witch doctor wears python skins which flow out of his headdress for a distance of eighteen feet or more, carries a whip made of the tails of wildebeest, and is hideously masked. But people who know about these things can identify him even when he is in normal dress, because he wears in his long hair, as a sign of his profession, a tiny chain of blue and white beads, so fine as to be almost imperceptible. Other secret signs exist. It is the essence of witch-doctoring that few people in a community know who the witch doctor really is.

How does a man become a witch doctor? In Portuguese East Africa the aspirant goes out into the woods alone, and lives on berries and roots, as a first step in mortification and the learning of his craft. A period of meditation follows, and then instruction from senior witch doctors. Often a son follows his father into the business. He may not be considered fully eligible to practice until he has survived the ordeal by python. This means that he must retire into the jungle until he finds a certain river, encounter a python (which are numerous in that particular river) near the bank, and kill it underwater, armed with only a knife. The python's skin then becomes the most precious part of his regalia.

Not only does witchcraft have a firm grip on most Africans, but it sometimes produces effects bewildering to Europeans. Some years ago, in a backward area in Mashonaland (Southern Rhodesia), there lived a young girl called Nechiskwa. Her tribe was the Wataware, and she had been dedicated from birth to be a rain goddess. Life depends, of course, on the coming of the rain. This rain goddess, Nechiskwa, lived alone with her mother on a remote mountain. No one ever saw her, except a witch doctor named Chigango. For some reason, the rains did not come to the land that year. The tribesmen, stimulated by Chigango, decided that somebody must have interfered with the arcane powers of the rain goddess; they seized on a young man named Manduza, accused him of defiling her by having had intercourse with her, and burned him to death. Instantly, the rains began. Rain poured unendingly, and the crops were saved.

The British authorities, who may have to tolerate witchcraft but who do not like murder, arrested Chigango and three other men, and sentenced them to terms in jail. Promptly the rains stopped. Chigango was eventually let out of jail, and at once the rains began again. How are phenomena like these to be explained? Purely by coincidence? Perhaps.

In Barotseland, a year or two ago, a young girl died after a sudden illness. The villagers called in the local witch doctor, hoping that he would be able to tell them who had bewitched her, and thus caused her death. He tied her corpse to a rope, and swung it out from the limb of a tree, while the villagers stood close by, watching. Whoever was first touched by the swinging body was the murderer, the witch doctor said. After a few circles it touched the head of the sister of the *imduna*, or village headman, and the witch doctor thereupon pronounced her to be the guilty person. She would have been killed, but, managing to escape, she fled to the nearest District Commissioner, who promptly advanced on the village, arrested the witch doctor, and sentenced him to a year in jail. The next day, the woman who told the DC her story was eaten by a lion. Coincidence? Perhaps.

In Livingstone, Northern Rhodesia, a British medical officer told me the story of Mubwa, the half-man, and the maiden who lost her sight. The Mubwa lived at Mongu, in the Zambesi region. He never walked normally, but hopped on one leg, which was why he was called the half-man. This horrible creature had a limitless appetite for young girls, whom he would lure out into the bush. Sometimes they would return after a month or two; sometimes they did not. One girl in the village, having noted the fate of her playmates, refused to go when the half-man said she must be his next consort. The villagers, indignant at the half-man's methods, sided with the young girl, and concealed her in a hut for protection. They burned herbs all night in the hut, and the Mubwa, defeated by these herbs (which were provided by an anti-Mubwa witch doctor), withdrew.

But he had his revenge. The young girl, emerging from the hut the next morning, had become stone blind.

My doctor friend was called to investigate this episode. He was convinced at first that it must be a case of hysterical blindness. But he examined the girl, and found that the optic nerve had been destroyed. Yet she herself, and everybody in the village, swore that her eyesight had been entirely normal a few days before.

There is no drug, or illness, known to western science that can produce this type of destruction of the optic nerve overnight. What happened? No one knows. But the half-man is in jail, and so is the witch doctor who brewed the herbs.

At Mwalule, in the Chinzali district of Northern Rhodesia, the natives think that a certain burial place is holy. Here their chiefs have been interred for generations. They dislike extremely to have any outsiders visit this cemetery, and say that if any white man penetrates it, evil will certainly befall him. A European new to the area went into the sacred spot by mistake. Returning to the nearby headquarters of the DC, he was killed by an extraordinary accident. A flagpole cracked suddenly, falling on his head. The next day the DC went out to the burial ground himself to investigate. Driving back, his truck got out of control, and crashed down a hillside into a shallow river. He was pinned under the wreck and drowned in eighteen inches of water.

Coincidence?

Perhaps.

ON SCARIFICATION

Many Sudanese have slashed cheeks; tattooing is common among the Saharan tribes, in Ethiopia, and elsewhere; but in Black Africa we encounter a much more elaborate phenomenon in this field, that of cicatrization. I saw in the Congo and later on the West Coast men and women who do not merely wear tribal identifications on their cheeks, but whose skin is carved over a sizable surface into the most intricate and stylized designs, so that parts of their bodies look like textiles. The skin is a kind of canvas on which flamboyant patterns are permanently drawn. "Drawn" is too mild a word. They are etched. Not only is the skin punctured and slashed, but the wounds are deliberately irritated so that keloids, or lumps of heavy scar tissue, will be formed. The scars and lumps have a deep ritualistic significance, and among much else they are supposed to augment sexual appetite.

Professor Melville J. Herskovits, of Northwestern University, one of the most renowned of contemporary anthropologists, has written a full and extraordinarily revealing account of cicatrization as it is practiced in Dahomey.[14] A young girl receives twelve sets of cuts in all; the first six are usually administered immediately after her first menstruation; then comes a pause for a year. Some girls—they are greatly admired—are Spartan enough to be able to go through the whole process at one sitting. The ceremony is public, and is a festival-like event. Men, however, are not permitted to watch the infliction of one particular set of cuts on the girl's thighs.

Professor Herskovits, who lived with this Dahomy tribe for an extended period, classifies the twelve series of cuts as follows. 1. A straight zigzag across the bridge of the nose, called "there-one-sees-place." 2. Another zigzag near

[14] *Dahomey, an Ancient West African Kingdom.* Dahomey is a region in French West Africa, beyond the province of this chapter, but I include this passage here for convenience.

the hair, for identification. 3. Fine parallel lines near the temples, a sign of beauty. When a woman is in love, these cuts are supposed to become livid, and pulsate "like the heart." 4. The "kiss-me" cut, a circle on the left cheek. 5. A series of fifteen to twenty-four separate incisions on the back, near the third vertebra, called "man-go-turn-look." If a husband goes on a trip, his wife's back is the last thing he sees as she turns to go into their dwelling when he says farewell. 6. Three horizontal cuts on the side of the neck, the "good-to-touch" lumps which a man caresses in sexual play. 7. Designs on the base of the spine, made to the girl's individual order. They are called *gblimé* or "pass-over" cuts. In embraces "a man passes his hands over them." 8. A total of eighty-one different cuts made on each inner thigh, called *zido*, or "push me" cuts. 9. Six cuts making an hourglass design on the back of the hand. 10. A cut under the navel, often in the form of a lizard. 11. Three parallel rows of cuts over the shoulders. 12. Links between the breasts.

A WORD ABOUT MISSIONARIES

Before we Christianize Africans, should we not Christianize ourselves?
—DENIS SAURAT

The first missionaries in East Africa were German, affiliated however to British missionary societies. They were, of necessity, not only missionaries but explorers. Ludwig Krapf was the first white man ever to see Mount Kenya (1849), and another German, by name Rebmann, discovered Mount Kilimanjaro in 1848.[15] The most celebrated of all missionaries, who was also one of the greatest explorers who ever lived, was of course a Scot, David Livingstone. He was an astonishingly persistent and durable personality. Nobody could have been a more stoutly devout Christian, but contrary to the legend which usually portrays him with a Bible in one hand, a musket in the other, he was not primarily interested in militant evangelism. What absorbed him was not merely saving souls but mapping Africa and abolishing the slave trade. All over eastern, central, and southern Africa we shall encounter his beneficent tread. Anybody interested in Livingstone—or Africa—should read *Livingstone's Last Journey*, by Professor Reginald Coupland, an admirable biographical study. From first to last Livingstone was an explorer—and against what obstacles! He

---

[15] It is indeed extraordinary that heroic mountains higher than the Matterhorn and only a few hundred miles from the sea should never have been even seen by a white man till a little more than a century ago. We need no better tribute to the historical inaccessibility of Africa, its hidden and impenetrable darkness. Cf. *Kilimanjaro and Its People*, by Charles Dundas.

left a mark that will never be erased, by setting the pattern for Christian penetration of Africa that continues fruitfully to this day.

There are about 4,500 American Protestant missionaries alone in Africa below the Sahara today; the three denominations most active are the Methodists, the northern Presbyterians, and the Seventh-Day Adventists.[16] Probably American Protestants all told spend $10,000,000 a year on missionary work in Africa; this is a considerable sum, more than the United States government spends on all its Point Four projects on the entire continent, and almost as much as the combined education budgets of Kenya, Uganda, and Tanganyika in 1952.

Roman Catholics are also active, particularly in Ruanda-Urundi and the Congo. Of the total Christian population of Africa, around 21,000,000, some 7½ million are Catholic. One reason why Roman Catholicism appeals to primitive Africans is, of course, its devotion to miracles, its respect for mystery. Also its stronghold, where most of its adherents are concentrated, is the Belgian Congo, where it has official state support; Catholics have a virtual monopoly on education in the Congo. The Catholic missions apply much attention to the training of *African* priests; one eminent white Jesuit told me, "Our aim is to put ourselves out of business," on the theory that, to be fully effective in the long-range future, the Roman Catholic church in Africa must be a *native* church. Catholics are very proud—justly so—of the fact that more than 9,700 of their priests and seminarians in Africa are African already; of their total of three thousand sisters 71 per cent are African. Catholics have, in general, a progressive attitude on such items as color bar, and the imperative need for social and economic advance by Africans.[17]

Many Africans are perplexed and confused by the rivalry between Christian denominations. In Uganda not too long ago—in the late 1880's—this caused an actual war, which was bloody and unpleasant, and probably the only war since the Middle Ages fought purely for religious reasons. Catholic and Protestant Africans, inflamed by doctrinal zeal, tore at each other's throats, until the British stepped in and restored order.

Missionaries are on occasion criticized on all manner of grounds, and not merely because they put beautiful naked girls in Mother Hubbards, or teach that bigamy is wrong. (Almost everywhere in bush Africa one hears the story of the well-meaning missionary who persuades a chief to give up his surplus wives, and is subsequently dumfounded with remorse when he finds

---

[16] *Time*, May 25, 1953.
[17] In Uganda people told us that Catholic boys were better servants than Protestant, because their education made them more amenable to discipline.

that the chief, taking his teaching to heart, has fed these ladies to the leopards.) The principal grievance, which may not be the fault of the local missionary at all, is that Christianity is too complex a doctrine for Africans to absorb easily, and that conversion "unsettles" them, taking them away from their tribal beliefs without giving them a substitute they fully comprehend. The Christian gospel can be a markedly disruptive force in an animist society, because it teaches something that primitive peoples have little knowledge of—the importance of the individual.

We met some remarkable missionaries (both British and American, both Catholic and Protestant). Most these days are not predominantly evangelical. They want to convert and save souls, yes, but the major effort is in more secular domains—getting ophthalmological treatment to a village, or improving its water supply, or teaching a boy how to build a roof or change a tire. The work missionaries have done for education is immeasurable all over the continent below the Sahara. Without them, there would have been no education at all until very recent years.

One of the worst sights I saw in Africa was, however, an American mission run by backward folk from Tennessee, practically without funds and hopelessly handicapped by various factors. A dysentery epidemic had swept the school. Children slept in cages curtained with chicken wire—orange crates or similar boxes piled up on top of one another against a wall, like a sectional bookcase. In these tiers, babies whimpered, groaned, and cried, in pools of their own making.

DISEASES AND THE TSETSE FLY

On a Nile steamer we met a killer, a hunter, of peculiar type—he was an American, a doctor of medicine, a research scientist representing one of the great New York foundations, and a specialist in trypanosomiasis, sleeping sickness. He was going down to the southern Sudan to direct the systematic, organized slaughter of several hundred thousand wild animals, beasts in the bush. Clearing out game—exterminating it utterly over broad areas—is one method of attempting to block the ravages of the tsetse (pronounced *tetzee*) fly, which carries sleeping sickness to men and animals. A good deal of controversy attends this method. To destroy game in such quantities is obnoxious, and may upset the balance of nature in a region. But it has been used with some success in Zululand, the Rhodesias, and elsewhere. Another method, much more humane, is the clearing out of belts of bush in a given territory, so that the fly has no vegetation in which to live and breed. But such wholesale eradication of trees and bush is an expensive process. Recently it has been tried with considerable success in Uganda. After six years of work eradicating bush and breaking the association of the fly with animals, particularly buffalo, almost 3,500,000 acres of land have been reclaimed, and made fit for economic use.

The tsetse fly is one of the most fascinating of pernicious insects. It exists in twenty-one different species of the genus *Glossina*, and the disease it transmits occurs in several forms. The fly is medium-sized, and lives on only one commodity—blood. It breeds by preference in shady thickets, and has a comparatively short range of flight, but is swift. It looks very much like the kind of fly one sees in temperate climates around barns, but it can easily be distinguished from ordinary flies by the fact that its wings do not project sideways, but overlap crosswise on the back. Its bite is sharp and painful—a deep, blood-sucking stab. But the tsetse fly, even though it is one of the most damaging creatures in the world, is not the real villain. It does not cause trypanosomiasis, but merely carries it. The real villain is a trypanosome, or parasite, which lives in the bloodstreams of various beasts—lions, zebras, buffaloes, antelopes, even frogs and crocodiles. These animals are hosts to the trypanosome, but are immune to it. When the fly bites an infected beast, it may spread the disease if it subsequently bites another beast not immune. Domestic cattle are not immune and therefore cannot exist healthily in fly-infested territory. One principal trypanosome attacks only cattle, but two other varieties at least—*T. gambiense* and *T. rhodesiense*—attack human beings as well. Much scientific work is going forward on elucidation of these mysteries. A new antitoxin, antricyde, has been valuable to an extent in checking the disease in cattle.

More than four *million* square miles of Africa are "under the fly," an area much bigger than the whole United States; the tsetse belt stretches all the way across Africa from the Sudan to the Union, brushing both coasts. This does not mean that every nook and cranny of this Brobdingnag block of territory is contaminated; if that were so, life would all but cease on the African continent. But very large areas *are* contaminated, at least to the extent that cattle cannot be freely grazed. If African areas now under the fly could be cleared of it, the productivity of the continent would be increased almost beyond measure, to say nothing of the fact that a tremendous amount of human suffering would be eliminated.

Sleeping sickness in human beings is not a particularly serious disease if it is caught in time. Europeans almost never die from it these days, although they may have long bouts of debilitating illness. But Africans—with little access to prompt diagnosis and treatment—do often die. If treatment does not begin within a month after infection, the malady is fatal in the long run to Europeans and Africans alike. The trypanosome lodges in the salivary glands, and then spreads to the brain and spinal cord.

*

Africa has malaria, tuberculosis, leprosy, syphilis, elephantiasis, yaws. Cancer is, however, almost unknown among Africans, and diseases of filth, like cholera and plague, are uncommon. Africa is, by and large, a cleaner continent than Asia. Some diseases that afflict Africans—bilharzia, guinea worm, onchocerciasis ("river blindness," caused by a parasite that invades the eye), blackwater fever, tropical or phagedenic ulcer, various types of filariasis —have menacing names and sound peculiarly horrible, but the worst African disease is something more prosaic that we have already mentioned— malnutrition. One might add that probably 90 per cent of all black Africans have intestinal worms of one sort or other. Some illnesses well known in Europe, but not much of a problem medically, are shockingly prevalent in Africa, for instance hernia. Doctors at mission stations perform an incredible number of hernia operations, more than for any other serious complaint. There are three main reasons for this: (1) Rude surgery during childbirth, which leaves an infant with a defective, swollen navel. (2) Faulty diet, which causes the stomach to swell out. (3) The physical strain of bending, lifting, and carrying heavy bundles on the head.

AFRICANS AS ARTISTS

African music, African art scarcely lie within the province of this book, which is long enough already. Everybody knows that in recent years primitive African art has strongly, pungently marked contemporary western painting and sculpture. Wooden figures, bronzes, gold ornaments, fetishes, and extraordinary ceremonial masks have won an important place in museums and the houses of private collectors everywhere. Bold and violent distortion of limbs and features is characteristic of African sculpture, but there are also a calculated balance of forms and intricacy of carving. One must not underestimate the subtlety and sophistication of these works of art. The motivation of African art is largely religious, like European art before and during the Renaissance. But African art is difficult to measure in European aesthetic terms. It cannot be separated from the atavistic life of Africans, and its symbolic association with superstition. Masks are often terrifying because they are created to ward off evil spirits. Figures express ancestor worship, fertility, and so on. Many spectacular and beautiful objects were made originally to be used in tribal dancing, and they give pictorial expression to what the dance was supposed to call forth.

Nobody can travel much in Africa without running into manifestations of the deep, innate aesthetic sensibility of Negroes. We visited the market at Moshi, Tanganyika, and saw fruit and vegetables on trays—every pepper, every bit of chile, so arranged as to make a harmonious pattern for the whole. I have seen the same thing in village markets in Mexico. Even individual peas are set in designs—triangles, circles, pentagons—so that they resemble games that children play with marbles. On a road in Ruanda-Urundi we passed a gang of workmen, breaking rock with picks. They hammered in unison, *keeping time* as they worked.

African music is based largely on the drum. In the field of popular music there have been few American or European songs in the contemporary period that have not felt the impact of this African instrument and its fierce beat. Most African music is characterized by continual repetition of a short rhythmic pattern. Again, the music is inextricably bound up with religious ceremony. Music is composed as a prayer for rain, for success in hunting, or for longevity. Drums are a long story. They may be made exclusively of wood—logs hollowed out with a slit—or of wood and hide; elephant ears are a favorite hide for this purpose. Some anthropologists think that the drum first came into use as a mechanism for driving away the spirits of the dead. African drums in the forest can be heard over a considerable distance, probably up to seven or eight miles, and relays of drummers can transmit "spoken" messages with astonishing speed and accuracy—a point more than a hundred miles away may be reached in two hours. Drums never cease beating in some parts of tropical Africa. Sometimes they drive lonely DC's mildly crazy.

CHAPTER 18

Kenya: The Land and People

> What is to be their [the Africans'] part in shaping the future of their country? It is, after all, their Africa.
> —WINSTON CHURCHILL IN 1908

I SUPPOSE I liked Kenya better than any country we saw in Africa—politics aside. This jewel in the imperial crown may be somewhat tarnished, but it is a jewel nevertheless, crackling with iridescence. I will not mention except in passing things so well known as Kenya's magical combination of tropical climate and a piercing altitude, its exuberant frontier spirit, its extraordinarily dramatic beauty of landscape—above all the brilliantly blue, high, pellucid sky, with clouds pinned on it like lumps of chrysanthemum. Kenya has always been a taut, unruly, slightly crazy country—the old saying is that it was "a place in the sun for shady people." When we were there it was as tightly strung as piano wire, which it still is, in consequence of the Mau Mau rebellion which has completely dislocated the normal life of the colony. Mau Mau means murder among other things, and I have never met people so trigger-happy as in Kenya. At our first dinner party in Nairobi (later the experience became banal) I discovered that ladies of gentle breeding, in diaphanous evening dress, carried revolvers in their gold mesh bags, which clanked ominously when they were dropped casually on coffee tables. A youth who looked as if he had just come off a cricket field said with cold, sinister pride that he had shot and killed five Africans so far, and hoped that there would be more to come.

The struggle for power in Kenya is triple. Here we face a trilemma, if such a word exists, not merely a dilemma. The participants are British, Africans, and, a factor we have not encountered before, Indians. If Kenya is a triangle, its hypotenuse is color bar. Moreover the British themselves are divided into two camps. The main cleavage for a long time was between

Government House, that is the Colonial Office, that is London, on the one side, and emigrant white settlers on the Kenya land on the other. Nowadays the lines of division are more complex. On one side is a coalition between government and the moderate white settlers, which stands for an easing of racial tension and the eventual working out of a plural society in Kenya; on the other are white die-hards who stand for unmitigated, unending white supremacy, no matter what the cost.

Kenya is at war, and the Mau Mau uprising naturally dwarfs everything else in the country, but there are points of interest that go far beyond this tragic and exasperatingly nasty guerrilla conflict. Nor can Mau Mau be understood without some comprehension of the background.

KENYA: LAND AND POPULATION

No African people wants to stay the way it is.
— W. M. MACMILLAN

Kenya is slightly larger than France, or Arizona and Colorado combined. In all this territory, there is only one navigable river, the Tana, and this is not navigable for all its length. There are two rainy seasons, but almost three-quarters of the land is useless for agriculture, because of lack of water. Kenya is equatorial, but it is not (except in the steaming lowlands on the coast) what we customarily think of as "tropical." The earth does not ooze between the toes when you walk barefoot—if you are foolish enough to do so—as it does in some other parts of Africa. It is hard, abrasive, brittle, resistant. Most of Kenya is high, open scrubland or savanna, and much is outright desert. When Hollywood discovered Africa a few years ago and movie teams took their first pictures near Nairobi and sent the rushes home, executives in California yelled and screamed that this country could not possibly be "Africa." They wanted moist, torrid jungle in the Tarzan tradition, and so the camera squads had to penetrate further inland, to Uganda, Ruanda-Urundi, and the Congo.

Not only is Kenya (for the most part) arid; it is poor. It has no mineral wealth to speak of, no petroleum, no waterpower. The country lives by agriculture—mixed farming—and the chief exports are tea, coffee, pyrethrum (an insecticide), and other vegetable and animal products. Kenya has what is politely known as a "deficit economy"; that is, it is always broke. The trade balance is massively adverse, and the colony—especially since the Mau Mau outbreak—has to be bailed out by London regularly.

There are three main geographical divisions: (1) The steamy coastal strip, with its port Mombasa, which still belongs in theory to the Sultan of Zanzibar. The British pay this venerable potentate, whom we shall meet later, £16,000 a year rent for this vital area. (2) The Northern Frontier Province, which comprises more than half the whole country, and is mostly a desert wasteland. This is still a restricted area, in which travel is not permitted without special authority. The authority is, however, easy enough to procure. But patriotic Kenyans are sensitive about the fact that such a large percentage of their territory is still walled off from contact, as well as being economically useless. (3) The central plateau, with altitudes ranging from 3,000 to 10,000 feet. Here are the rich, fertile White Highlands, which cover 16,000 square miles and are the citadel of white settlement.

Kenya was named for Mount Kenya, a formidable icy 17,040-foot peak rising almost directly on the Equator, higher than Mont Blanc or any peak in the continental United States. It was first climbed by Sir Halford Mackinder in 1899. The word "Kenya" comes from a Bantu word meaning ostrich, which symbolized to Africans the alternation of black rock and white glacier on the mountain's ugly, fierce-looking summit. Another mountain of consequence is Elgon (14,140 feet) on the Uganda border. One should also mention the range of the Aberdares, on the northern fringe of the White Highlands; like Mount Kenya they are important to our story since they lie in the heart of the Kikuyu country and their shaggy wooded slopes and bamboo forest make perfect cover for Mau Mau terrorists.

One thing that particularly distinguishes East and Central Africa from the rest of the continent is its radiant chain of Great Lakes. Kenya lacks rain and river water, but it has Victoria Nyanza, one of the most impressive lakes in the world.[1] Aside from Victoria, which is shared by Kenya, Tanganyika, and Uganda, there are also Lake Rudolf, which lies in northern Kenya and touches Ethiopia; Lake Tanganyika, which separates Tanganyika from Ruanda-Urundi; the constellation Lake Albert-Lake Edward-Lake Kivu between Uganda and the Congo; and Lake Nyasa, which forms most of the frontier between Tanganyika and Nyasaland. These lakes are of surpassing beauty and interest, and they play a lively role in the geography, communications, and economy of the whole region—giant pores through which hundreds of thousands of square miles breathe.

Associated with the Great Lakes is the extraordinary geological phenomenon known as the Rift Valley. It is as painfully absurd to give this one paragraph in a book about Africa as it would be to give one paragraph to the Mississippi in a book about the United States. The Rift Valley is a stupendous, monumental fracture in the earth's surface, that stretches for almost four thousand miles from the Jordan Valley in Israel across the

[1] More on Lake Victoria in Chapter 23 below.

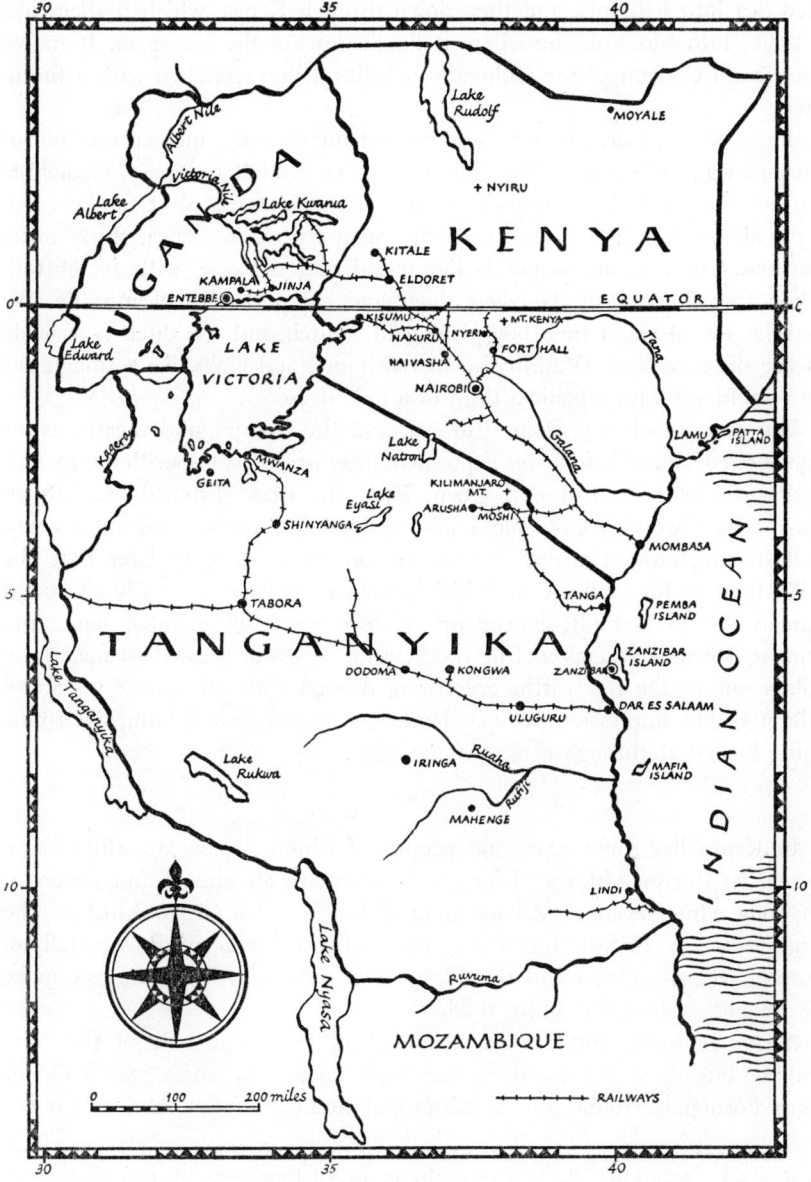

Red Sea into Ethiopia, and then down through Kenya, which it slices like a knife, into Mozambique where it finally reaches the sea again. It makes the Grand Canyon of the Colorado look like a line scratched with a toothpick.

There are, in fact, two Rift Valleys, not merely one, since an offshoot of the main gigantic crack follows the lakes from Rudolf to Nyasa. Geologists are not one in their attempts to explain how this great split in the earth came about. The best place to see the main Rift is in Kenya, thirty miles northwest of Nairobi, where it lies naked and exposed, with its bottom 1,500 feet down, and its edges sheer and sharp. In it volcanos lie like marbles tossed about by a boy playing in a ditch, but the ditch is as wide as the distance from Washington to Baltimore, and looks like a trough cut by a bulldozer with a blade a third of a mile deep.

We flew into Kenya from Ethiopia, and the country underneath, as we approached Nairobi, took on a peculiar intensity of color, with sharp reds and spikes of savagely bright green. Even the trees glistened like bits of glass. There were green-tufted knobs and knolls, narrow twisting ravines, and steeply terraced farms. It was not surprising to learn later that the Kikuyu word for "village" is "ridge," because every community of round *bandas* (huts) is built sharply on its own prong of elevated land, and separated from its neighbors by rocky walls. The sun seemed to magnetize colors out of the raw earth; everything danced with an almost unnatural vibrancy. The impression was of a landscape in exaggerated form, like something looked at through a magnifying glass.

*

In Kenya live some 5,700,000 people, of whom 42,000 are white Europeans. In British Africa a "European" means, to all intents and purposes, anybody white; even an American in Kenya is a European. Most of the Europeans are British, but there are sizable colonies of Poles, Italians, Scandinavians, and particularly Boers—South Africans—who in fact make up 22 per cent of the white total.[2]

Asians in Kenya number an estimated 158,000. The bulk of these are Indian, but there are about 24,000 Arabs along the coast, 7,000 Goans from Portuguese India, and a substantial number of Pakistanis. Also the

---

[2] There are terminological tricks to this use of the word "European." For instance, in Kenya Egyptians and Palestinian Arabs are called Europeans, though Arabs from Arabia are Asian; people from the Seychelles in the Indian Ocean are European or Asian "according to the degree of pigment in their skin." (Hugh Latimer in the *Observer*, June 27, 1954.) But by and large in every British colony the "European" community means the British.

KENYA: THE LAND AND PEOPLE

Somalis, who live mainly in the Frontier Province, are officially classified as Asian, presumably because they are not Negroes.

Everybody else in Kenya, roughly 5,500,000 out of 5,700,000 people, is an African. A fact never to be forgotten, even if Kenya seemed for many years to be an ideal haven for secure white settlement, is that this is overwhelmingly, overridingly, an *African* country. Kenya is 97 per cent African; blacks outnumber whites by 132 to 1.

A WORD ABOUT KENYA HISTORY

> Nor could his eye not ken . . .
> Mombasa and Quiloa and Melind,
> And Sofala, through Ophir, to the realm
> Of Congo and Angola further south.
> —PARADISE LOST

Kenya, the *enfant terrible* of colonies, a fool's paradise as it has often been called, a haunt of muscular ne'er-do-wells, is only about half a century old. But, as the quotation above from Milton indicates, several of its coastal cities have been known to mankind for hundreds of years. Kenya lies on the Indian Ocean, and this has been a pool for seafaring traders since time immemorial; Arab settlements on the Kenya coast probably date back three thousand years. Trade came to these ports from as far away as China. The first modern explorers were the venturesome Portuguese; Vasco da Gama stopped at Malindi in 1498, and Mombasa has Fort Jesus, now used as a prison, which was built in 1593. But the Portuguese never penetrated far inland. The back country was totally unknown, except to Arab traders and slave raiders, until the mid-nineteenth century when the modern era began of exploration, invasion by Christian missionaries, and political expropriation by the contemporary European powers.

The British acquired Kenya, which was known originally as British East Africa or the East African Protectorate, by a process embodying several motives. They had established themselves on Zanzibar, and naturally looked inland. One reason for penetration was undoubtedly humanitarian—to abolish the Arab slave trade. Zanzibar was the chief entrepôt for this evil traffic, and it turned even the coldest British stomach sick. Whole provinces of Africa were decimated to provide eunuchs for Turkish harems, or levies for Moslem armies all the way from Baghdad to Bengal. "Think what we have saved today's Africans *from!*" exclaimed Michael Blundell, Leader of the Europeans in the Kenya legislature and now minister without portfolio, when he talked to us about the background of Kenya history.

Second, the British had a motive more utilitarian—they wanted to open up East Africa to trade. The Imperial British East Africa Company was organized in 1888; it had close links to the government, but its aims were predominantly commercial.[3] Presently it became clear, however, that no private or chartered company had the resources or power to develop by itself such a huge and conglomerate territory as East Africa. Its acquisitions could not be held without political and military help. So, in 1895, the Foreign Office took over Kenya from the company, and it became formally part of the British Empire. These events were not part of a carefully laid Machiavellian plot. As has been the case almost everywhere in British Africa, commercial exploitation *preceded* political aquisition. It may be argued that penetration by private business interests made subsequent political appropriation inevitable. There was a close identity of interest. But as a matter of fact powerful forces in London in those days steadily opposed any territorial expansion by the British. Plenty of British liberals, like Mr. Gladstone, did *not* want the burden of new African commitments. The Empire grew partly by a miraculous series of accidents. One decisive factor was the ambitious German interest in Africa at that time. The British took Kenya and Uganda to keep Germany from getting them, and appeased Germany in other spheres.

It may be asked why European contact with the East Coast of Africa came so late in contrast to the West Coast. The British have been active in one way or other in Nigeria, for instance, for more than three hundred years, whereas penetration of the Kenya upcountry did not begin seriously till the 1890's. After all the East Coast was (and is) healthier than the West, just as capable of development, and had in those days greater strategic interest, on account of the Indian Ocean. Probably the answer lies in the fact that the Suez Canal was not opened till 1869. The African East Coast was too hard to reach.

The two chief operating forces in the history of Kenya have been first, the railroad; second, white settlement. Kenya is a child of its railroad, but originally this was built to tap and exploit Uganda, not Kenya; Kenya was a kind of by-product, arising almost by accident on the railroad's iron path. No more romantic story than that of the Uganda Railroad can possibly be imagined. The British government, with considerable reluctance, decided in 1895 to initiate the project. The difficulties seemed almost insurmountable. The line had to climb from Mombasa on the coast through desert, bush, and forest completely unexplored, to a plateau 7,000 feet high; it then had to dip down 1,500 feet through the Rift Valley, up again to the

---

[3] It was also committed by its charter to assist in the abolition of the slave trade. Idealistic, commercial, and political aims were inextricably interwoven.

KENYA: THE LAND AND PEOPLE

Kikuyu Escarpment at 8,500 feet, and descend again to Lake Victoria.[4] African labor was not skilled enough to be of much use, and 32,000 Indians were brought in; these are the main origin of the present Indian communities in East Africa.

On one section of track, before the iron beams could be thrust through the wilderness, three thousand out of four thousand Busoga porters died of disease.[5] Work at another point was stopped for weeks by the celebrated man-eating lions of Tsavo. After two years of effort the line had penetrated inland no further than 181 miles. The initial funds, £3,000,000, were exhausted, and critics in London called the venture the "Lunatic Line." In 1899 the track finally reached the site of what is now Nairobi, 330 miles from Mombasa, and victory was in sight. But the last stretch—to Kampala in Uganda, 879 miles from the sea—was not completed till 1926. In the early days distinguished passengers, like Theodore Roosevelt, rode on an open bench astride the cowcatcher as the train pushed through the most marvelous game country in the world. It still is. In 1953 animal fatalities on the line, which is now operated by a state administration called East African Railways and Harbors, amounted to 113, including twenty-one giraffe and one elephant. By tradition, if the train is full, the railway is obliged to put on an extra carriage if a passenger will otherwise miss his steamship connection at Mombasa. The most lucrative freight comes nowadays from Uganda, but the railway remains Kenya's life line in more ways than one.

White settlement in Kenya began with Lord Delamere, who dominated the colony singlehanded for almost thirty years. Hugh Cholmondeley, third Baron Delamere, was born in Cheshire, had unquenchable enterprise and energy, and loved sport. He made several hunting expeditions in Somaliland, and was one of the first white men to penetrate Kenya from the north (1898). He fell in love with the country, and determined to settle in its cool, rich highlands. Delamere's story, a frontier epic, is too well known to pursue here; it may be studied in full detail in Elspeth Huxley's fascinating *White Man's Country*. There came to Delamere various setbacks and indecisions, but in 1903 the government gave him a grant of 100,000 acres at Njoro, and here he built Equator Ranch. The authorities were at this time eager to open the highlands to productive settlement, if only to bring revenue to the railway. Delamere tried sheep, cattle, and wheat in turn, and built up another huge property in the Rift Valley. Several times the forces of nature, in the form of diseases like rinderpest and East Coast fever,

---
[4] *Introducing East Africa* p. 29.
[5] *Africa Emergent*, by W. M. Macmillan, p. 33.

which afflict livestock, almost broke him. He always came back. At one time he had 40,000 sheep at Soysambu, and got twenty bushels of wheat per acre on other properties. He went into creameries, flour mills, and the meat and wool business. He was father to the other settlers. He "advised, helped, threatened, and cajoled various governors and secretaries of state," always with the single ambition of making Kenya a white settlers' paradise, until his death in 1931.

One odd, little-known historical fact is that, in 1903, the British government of the day offered the Kenya Highlands to the Jews as a National Home for the Jewish people. This was, of course, before colonization of Kenya by white British settlers got fully under way. The Zionist leaders in London debated acceptance of the offer, and finally rejected it in 1905. The imagination is stimulated by the thought of various changes that might have been wrought in the contemporary world if Dr. Weizmann and his associates had accepted this remarkable proposal. The White Highlands would be today's Israel.

Kenya and Uganda were going to be joint countries with a single capital at first, but in 1904 they were separated and frontiers drawn. Kenya was transferred from the Foreign Office to the Colonial Office in 1905, and became a protectorate. It was not officially named "Kenya" until it reached presumptive adulthood and was promoted to be a crown colony in 1920. One must never forget how astonishingly new most of Africa is.

KENYA'S BASIC PROBLEM: THE LAND

Poor soil makes poor people, and poor people make poor soil worse.
—PROFESSOR R. L. ROBB

To return to white settlement. The curse of Kenya ever since Delamere's first acquisitions has been the problem of the land. It is the one dominant factor that has persisted through every shift and turn of politics to this day, and it has of course become inextricably part and parcel of the racial issue because the land occupied by the settlers was—and is—*African*. The land problem is an extremely abstruse and controversial subject. It is not true, as some Africans like to assert today, that Africans were forcibly dispossessed from the Highlands in any great number. In fact much of the area was empty or only sparsely or irregularly occupied; the Masai came in every few years to graze their stocks, and then left. Nevertheless it is incontestable that, as white settlement spread, more and more Africans became displaced. One source of acute misunderstanding was that Africans thought that they were merely renting their land; the Europeans assumed that they were buying it. The Kikuyus claim in particular that they were swindled out of substantial areas, and the British broke one supposedly sacrosanct treaty with the Masai, in order to augment European holdings. The whites always contrived in one way or other to get the *best* land, and this the Africans naturally resented. In sixteen months (1903-4) 220,000 Highland acres were transferred to 342 individual Europeans, and moreover huge tracts—blocks of 300,000 acres or more—went to European syndicates.[6] In 1901 there were exactly 13 European settlers in the whole of Kenya; in 1911, 3,000; in 1921, 9,000. A law was enacted, the celebrated Crown Lands Ordinance, which gave the Governor the right (with certain restrictions) "to grant, lease, or otherwise alienate in His Majesty's behalf any Crown lands for any purpose and on any terms and conditions as he may think fit."[7] Another ordinance defined the borders of the White Highlands (16,000 square miles) and forbade *any* ownership in this whole area by anybody not a white European.[8] "A European farmer is even prohibited from employing a non-European as manager." The net result of all this was to make Kenya—in sharp contrast to Uganda, Tanganyika, and the British colonies on the West Coast—a white settlement state par excellence. Again, the best way to present the picture is by way of a few blunt figures. The total white population of Kenya is 42,000 but only about 4,000 whites are active settlers on the land, and only about 7,000 in all are engaged in agriculture. Roughly Kenya has 68,700 square miles of arable land. A minute handful of Europeans has 16,000 square miles or 24 per cent of this; five and a half *million* Africans have to get along as best they can on the rest.

The White Highlands are so fertile that two harvests are possible every year. The rainfall is not much more than in Great Britain, malaria and sleeping sickness are unknown; the altitude is bracing, and the climate brilliant. An important point, which we shall deal with in more detail below, is that *Africans* also live in the White Highlands; these are mostly Kikuyus, of whom about a million (in normal times) are squeezed into 2,000 square miles. Compare this to 16,000 square miles for three to four thousand Europeans! Africans outside the Highlands have their own land too, but this is much less desirable. Scrutiny of a large-scale map of Kenya, on which the tsetse fly areas are marked, is interesting. Hardly an inch of the territory reserved for European settlement is "under the fly." But

---

[6] According to *Land Hunger in Kenya*, by Mbiyu Koinange and Achieng Oneko, a pamphlet published in London by the Union of Democratic Control.

[7] The government was eager to make land productive, and hence gave it away, in order to stimulate traffic on the railroad. The same thing occurred in the United States.

[8] But some of the 16,000 square miles is parkland.

African areas all over Kenya, the habitat of tribes like the Meru and Embu, are thickly fly-infested.

When Winston Churchill visited East Africa in 1907 the prospect that the Highlands might become a white community enthralled him; he even dared to predict that some day there might be as many as 30,000 Britons living there! But Mr. Churchill, a prudent as well as farseeing observer, added a note of extraordinarily prescient warning, that it was "scarcely worth while even to imagine the Highlands of East Africa denuded of their native inhabitants and occupied solely by Europeans . . . It is a grave defect for a community to found itself on the manual labor of an inferior race, and many are the complications and perils that spring therefrom."[9] Mr. Churchill could not have been more right. From that day to this, appalling complications have arisen from the juxtaposition of white and black on the same Kenya land.

The chief tribes—Masai, Kikuyu, Kamba, and so on—have their own "reserves." These are not compounds or areas to which people are forcibly confined, nor do they resemble Indian reservations in the United States. Mainly they are districts where native rights are protected and where whites may not own land.[10] Altogether the reserves in Kenya cover 52,000 square miles, but not all of this is fit for agriculture.

Conscience plays a large and honorable role in British statecraft; gradually through the years it became obvious to men of good will in Whitehall that it simply was not right that Africans should be done out of their land indiscriminately, even if white settlement obviously made it more productive and benefited the colony as a whole. The alienation process, as Lord Hailey puts it, "got out of hand." So a Native Lands Trust Board was set up, certain native areas were declared untouchable, and the process of white colonization was stopped in these. On the other hand British policy was indecisive and ambiguous. The British knew that they had to march with the times and deal fairly with Africans, but they also had to protect the interests of loyal, sound Britons already resident in Kenya. African expression of grievances steadily became more concrete and vociferous, but any time that the Colonial Office did anything for the Africans, the white settlers on the spot rose in wrath.

Two highly inconvenient and incandescent factors made matters worse. (1) The three reserves set up for the Kikuyu tribe—Kiambu, Nyeri, and Fort Hall—cover about two thousand square miles, and are known together with other areas as the Kikuyu Land Unit. But unfortunately these

[9] *My African Journey*, published in 1908.
[10] "British East Africa," *Atlantic Monthly*, January, 1954.

KENYA: THE LAND AND PEOPLE

were not—and could not be—a true unit. Instead they were for the most part composed of tiny fragments of territory meshed into and around the White Highlands like patches in a quilt.[11] Hence, it has been impossible to draw any clean frontiers between white and non-white areas in the Kikuyu region. Everywhere there are enclaves of Kikuyu territory in or near white territory, and vice versa. (2) The Kikuyus are the biggest, most advanced, and most important tribe in Kenya, and number about 1,200,000. They have *doubled* in population in twenty-five years (so has the rest of the African population of Kenya) and inevitably their reserves became overcrowded to suffocation. The density of population reached in some areas four hundred to the square mile, and it became impossible for them to support life on the amount of land they had. Moreover erosion and poor agricultural methods wore the land out. As a result many Kikuyus left the reserves and either went to work in Nairobi, or moved into the white settler areas, where they became known as *squatters*. This is, however, an unfortunate and misleading word, since it connotes the occupation of a plot of land without permission. But the Kikuyu squatters, far from being intruders, were welcomed into white territory because without them it could not have been farmed or worked. A kind of plantation system developed. The Kikuyus were hired as farm labor by the European settlers, and given wages and a place to live—perhaps a two-acre plot or *shamba*—in return. They were not miscreants or interlopers, but a perfectly stable, respectable, and hard-working tenant farmer class.

When we were in Kenya there were about 750,000 Kikuyus in the reserves, 250-300,000 squatters, and perhaps 75,000 in Nairobi. The squatter system worked for a time fairly well, despite injustices. But as a result of the Mau Mau crisis it blew up. A series of outrages occurred, particularly in the Thompson's Falls area, and the British, in an attempt to break up the terrorist gangs, forcibly moved some Kikuyu squatters from their farms in the Highlands back to the reserve. This frightened other squatters and they too began to trek back into the reserves which were already crowded to the last inch. Altogether something like 60,000 squatters have left the white farms voluntarily, and 20,000 by compulsion. The result has been double: (a) the white farms are starved for labor; (b) the reserves were smothered by this enormous influx of farmers for whom there was no food, no land.

An extremely difficult situation also arose in Nairobi, even before the Mau Mau outbreak. The thousands of Kikuyus there led a kind of double

---

[11] "Kenya, The Land, and The Mau Mau," by Derwent Whittlesey, *Foreign Affairs*, October, 1953.

life—which was also a half life—with their roots still on the land but their jobs in the town. Because of lack of housing and intolerable social conditions in Nairobi most left their wives and children back on their farms, and so became a kind of floating semi-urbanized black proletariat in a white city. This has not only produced profound social instability, but what has been called a "spiritual convulsion" in the sensitive Kikuyu people. Thousands upon thousands of families were broken up.

SWEET WATER NOT SO SWEET

Nairobi is the capital of Kenya by accident. A better location for the capital, and the one first planned, was Limuru, twenty-eight miles further up country, and at a higher elevation. But men pushing ahead with the railway found the site of Nairobi pleasant, and they stopped there with the result that a camp grew up which became a headquarters, and in turn the capital. It is an exciting drive today from Nairobi up to Limuru with rugged pockets of the Kikuyu reserve interlaced between shiny European farms. Nairobi means "Sweet Water" (for cattle) in the Masai language. It lies just over a mile high, at 5,453 feet, and is an important station on the Great North Road that (in theory) runs uninterruptedly through the whole length of what used to be British Africa from the Mediterranean to the Antarctic. When Mr. Churchill visited it in 1907 its European population was 380. Today it has roughly 169,000 inhabitants, and is by far the largest city in East Africa—with 16,000 white Europeans, 44,000 brown Indians, and 109,000 black Africans, of whom 75,000 are Kikuyus.

Nairobi is a chic little city, and thoroughly cosmopolitan. Your doctor is a Pole, your manicurist an Italian, your tailor a Hungarian. It has a national theater, smart office buildings, night clubs of European genre, day clubs rigidly British and colonial, and almost any comfort civilized man desires. This is not Benghazi or Addis Ababa by a million miles. Nevertheless Nairobi, for all its sophistication and somewhat synthetic elegance, is not Paris or London either—it is still a frontier town, raw at the edges, and provincial. One thing that gives it special quality is, of course, the stinging exhilaration of its weather. It is not particularly hot, but the altitude makes you feel that the sun is only ten feet away. Another distinction is the great game park on the edges of the city, one of the superb sights of Africa, which I shall describe in a later chapter. Nairobi is the safari capital of the world.

Nairobi was, and is, the focus of an international smart set, mostly British but with other nationalities represented, that live on froth and cream, lead playful lives in surpassingly beautiful surroundings, avoid taxation at home, and have fun shooting lions and sleeping with one another's wives. More than any city in Africa (except possibly Tangier) it attracted the corrupt rich, as well as adventurers looking for quick fortunes. This lacquered group was, by and large, utterly oblivious to the caldron it was sitting on. It had no conception whatever of the seething forces that were transforming Kenya minute by minute from an enchanted playground to an arena choked with blood and hate. Yet Nairobi is only six miles away from the nearest Kikuyu reserve. More than once I heard sober British officials say about the fashionable sybarites, *"They had it coming to them!"*

Nairobi is, of course, basically as British as beef or rugger, but with a special coloration. A cocktail party is a "sundowner," and a "safari" can be a walk around the corner. One Nairobi club is so exclusively the citadel of the white settler community that, for a long time, government officials of the highest rank found it difficult to become members. While we were in Nairobi the town was rocking because the Governor, no less, had brought in a Jew to lunch, who was supposed to be the first Jew ever to have crossed its threshold. The dining room is built in two wings, purportedly so that people recently divorced did not have to risk the embarrassment of running into their former wives or husbands. Nairobi is a piquant mixture of the conventional and unconventional. Only people utterly sure of themselves can dare to be quite so unconventional as the British often are. I called on a member of the government late one afternoon and, in shirt sleeves, he drove me back to my hotel in an open truck.

The stranger to British Africa will find in Nairobi all manner of curiosities that, after a few days, he comes to take for granted. Perhaps it is not worth mentioning that everybody has a box in the post office; letters are seldom addressed to a street or number, because (as in most of British Africa) mail delivery is unknown. I was also impressed by a peculiar phenomenon that I encountered several times at formal dinner parties; gentlemen do not go to a toilet after separating from the ladies, but walk out on the lawn, and in the equatorial darkness stand in a row facing a hedge or garden wall, and there relieve themselves while murmuring a low toast, "To Africa."[12]

Nobody wears sun helmets any more. This is a striking development and pages might be written about its implications. Topees or sun helmets

---

[12] Incidentally Nairobi veterans like to think of their city as cosmopolitan, not tropical, and they frown on the use in the evening, no matter how hot it is, of white dinner jackets. "If you *must* wear white," an old settler recently counseled his son, "at least wear a red tie with it, so people will think that you are joking or are an American."

are still worn in the Congo and French Africa, but in most of British Africa, even if it is a hundred in the shade the year round, they have become as obsolete as a peruque. But *Africans* often wear them! I met British officials born in Kenya who said that, when they were children, it was an absolutely accepted article of faith that, if a white man ventured out of doors without a helmet, the sun would instantly kill him on the spot. One thing that ended helmets (and the heavy spinal pads that were often worn with them) was the example of American GI's during the war. These (and British soldiers too) wore forage caps or went bareheaded in places even more sunshiny than Kenya, for year after year, and nobody dropped dead at all. Anyway the sun helmet is no longer with us.[13]

We happened to be in Nairobi during the blistering height of the Mau Mau crisis, and the city was unendurably tense. Almost everybody carried arms. Revolvers were hard to buy—the only ones left in the shops were, oddly enough, either Czech or Italian—and it became a criminal offense for a European to lose a weapon; a Scandinavian youth was actually sentenced to two months in jail and fined £100 when he was *robbed* of three automatic pistols. The authorities were, then as now, exerting every effort to keep firearms from getting into the hands of the terrorists. We in our hotel felt the strain and pressure keenly, because Kikuyu suspects were screened daily in a transit camp across the street. We watched raids—boys being picked up and carried off in trucks caged with wire netting. But the "emergency," as the crisis was called, did not affect much the ordinary lives of humble European citizens of Nairobi, except that business was hurt because tourists stayed away. I went to a chiropodist one day, who muttered in disgruntlement that *he* had never seen a Mau Mau and that the crisis was nothing but "a lot of talk." That very night, three loyal Kikuyus were cut to pieces at a police post not six miles away.

The oddest, sharpest side light on the emergency I encountered in polite fields came at a luncheon at Government House. Lady Mary Baring, the wife of the Governor, politely steered the conversation into French whenever it became politically interesting because servants who knew English might understand what was being said, and this was thought to be inadvisable. The staff had just been screened—at Government House!—and some Mau Mau suspects had been found.

THE INDIAN COMMUNITY

Nairobi is also an Indian town, so much so that it looks like a suburb of Bombay. On one typical street the shops follow one another like this:

---

[13] But see Chapter 35 below.

KENYA: THE LAND AND PEOPLE

Dharamshi Lakhamshi & Co.
Dhirajlal & Co.
Khimji Bhimji & Bros.
Walli Jiwa & Co.
Arjan Singh & Co.
Haria Cash Stores.
Bahadur Singh & Bros.
Kurji Karsanji.
Karmali Suleman & Sons. Ltd.

Not only do Indians virtually control retail trade in the Kenya cities—Mombasa is even more Indian than Nairobi—but they dominate the countryside. Hardly a town in Kenya is without a lively, colorful line of Indian shops. The chief Indian quality is an adhesive industriousness. The Indians did not (like the British) stop work for tea or waste time playing games; they did not close up shop for the weekend; they worked like smiling beavers; above all they did not discriminate against *African* trade, as Britons did. Indeed, they welcomed with sinewy arms anybody who had money to spend, without the slightest regard to race.

The British could not operate their colonies without Indians, because they are not only traders but make up a large element in the professional class and skilled trades as well. They are lawyers, contractors, garage owners, dentists, post-office clerks, linotypers, railway officials, bookkeepers; above all they fill the middle sections of the civil service and bureaucracy.

Indian association with East Africa goes back much further than the railroad in the 1890's.[14] Indeed it goes back probably for several thousand years. Greek travelers in the first century AD mention traffic in the Indian Ocean between Asia and Africa, and so, a long time later, does Marco Polo. It was an Indian pilot who guided Vasco da Gama across the Indian Ocean in 1498. Not only did Indian traders come to East Africa; Africans—slaves—were shipped back to India. The Nyzam of Hyderabad had an African guard in the Middle Ages, the great Emperor Urengzeb maintained a Negro admiral in Bombay, and several Bengal princes had Negro blood. An incidental point is that the Indian rupee, not sterling, was the East African currency until the end of World War I.

The Indian community today contains both Hindus and Moslems, as well as a few Sikhs and Parsees. The Khoja Moslems, known as Ismailis, belong to that fabulous old gentleman the Aga Khan, and number about 40,000 in Kenya alone. Some years ago the Aga Khan made an important declaration of policy, to the effect that his adherents, no matter how proud

---

[14] The Indians say, incidentally, but without much expression of resentment or malice these days, that their forebears who entered Kenya as railway labor were disgracefully hoodwinked and swindled. They were promised land or their passage back to India, and in most cases got neither.

they might be of their Indian origin, should consider themselves to be African, not Asian—they should not, in other words, behave as transients on African soil any longer, but act like permanent citizens in a new home. "You belong to East Africa now," he announced in effect. This statement had far-reaching social and political results.

Two leading Indians in Kenya, A.B. Patel (Hindu) and Ibrahim E. Nathoo (Moslem), the local representative of the Aga Khan, are cabinet ministers today. We were fortunate enough to pass a good deal of time in Mr. Nathoo's company, and a more discerning, amiable, and civilized host cannot be imagined. The president of the Kenya Indian Congress is N.S. Mangat, a Queen's Counsel. In his presidential address in 1954 he attacked race prejudice in the European community, and took a nationalist line so vigorous that many Britons were affronted.

The Indians are caught in the middle of Kenya—on top of the Africans, but below the British. Numerically, racially, economically, they hold the middle position. As a result many feel slighted and insecure. Two factors have been their sheet anchor on the whole—first the feeling that British government on the top level will be just and impartial and will protect their interests, no matter how silly the local colonials may be about color bar; second, the growing importance of India itself as an international force in the contemporary world.

Logically, if only because they are in the middle, the Indians should be a bridge between the other two communities, but it has not worked out this way. The British fear the increasingly closer association of Indians with Africans, because this will presumably serve in time to give uneducated Africans an educated Indian leadership—while at the same time they refuse to admit any but a handful of Indians to their own circles. Even Mr. Nathoo would have trouble getting into a British-run hotel.

Many Britons despise Indians racially and hate them as economic competitors; they even like the Africans better, because Africans have traditionally "known their place" and are less foreign. This British attitude is based in large part on complete lack of understanding. To the average colonial Briton the Indian is not only obnoxious but an impenetrable psychological puzzle, and he simply closes the walls of his community to him, not merely out of snobbery but in self-defense.[15]

There are political apprehensions too. One allegation is that Mr. Nehru has territorial designs on Kenya and intends to take it over some fine day and use it as a reservoir for his surplus population. Then too the British

---

[15] I heard one British official complain, "All Indians say 'Yes, *but*—' to everything and they are litigious even before breakfast."

fear Nehru's impact on Africa because he is not merely a leading Indian statesman eager to defend the rights of Indians in Africa, but the principal champion of anti-colonialism in the world. His words carry profound weight. Another apprehension has to do with Mau Mau. As the Mau Mau crisis worsened it was almost impossible for the British to conceive that Africans, by themselves, had the capacity to organize such an intricate and prolonged conspiracy; hence they said that "the Indians" must be behind it. Also the British disliked and feared the influence of Shri Apa B. Pant, who was Indian High Commissioner to East Africa until 1954. The British deny that they asked for his recall. Mr. Pant made a great name for himself in Kenya. He was (and is) handsome, an ardent believer in the rights of Africans, and brilliantly intelligent. He had close personal relations with African nationalists, and the charge was heard that he "meddled in politics" and deliberately influenced Africans to be even more anti-British than they were.

Pant knew a lot of Africans. (Of course it was his legitimate business to know them.) These Africans *perhaps* had, in turn, secret contact with Mau Mau leaders. So ran the line of argument trying to link India to the Mau Maus.

Other British grievances are that African students are being given scholarships in India, and that the Delhi radio has started broadcasting in Swahili. Anything that links India and nationalist Africa perturbs the British.

Of course educated Africans, looking for intellectual and social companionship in Kenya, had absolutely nowhere else to turn except to Indians, because the British refused to have any contact with them whatever. British attitudes in the stupid realm of color bar served to throw Africans into Indian arms.

But some African leaders dislike and fear Indian influence because the Indians monopolize skilled jobs to such an extent and control the middle bureaucracy. Africans, as more become educated, will not be able to find decent jobs, because the Indians have them all. The Indian answer to this is that if racial barriers are broken down and economic development for all peoples assured, there will be enough jobs for everybody.

Finally, the British fear above everything else the possible future application of the Indian concept of passive resistance, civil disobedience, to affairs in Kenya.[16] Mr. Gandhi, one of the supreme political geniuses of all time, invented this concept and made it work. It is one of the most powerful political engines (if used against a civilized people like the British) ever known, because it is the only means yet devised whereby a colonial people, *without arms,* can win a revolutionary struggle. Suppose five and a half

[16] This happened in Egypt as we know, and is happening to an extent in Morocco.

million Africans in Kenya should some day be able to discipline themselves to the rigors of a civil disobedience campaign, and move against constituted authority by this method. After all, a fact never to be forgotten, the total number of Europeans in Kenya is only 42,000. Civil disobedience could wreck the country.

The Indians, however, have utterly no interest in disrupting Kenya. Not only have they behaved with complete loyalty and co-operation during the Mau Mau crisis, which hurt them severely, but they went through it without becoming frightened, angry, or hysterical.

COLOR BAR IN NAIROBI

Here in Kenya we encounter color bar as a really paramount issue for the first time in this book. The main reason for the tension that has always afflicted Nairobi is that its society has three-way segregation. The visitor, arriving at the Nairobi airport, is given dramatic indication of this at once; there are toilets for "European Gentlemen" and "Asian Gentlemen"—none for Africans at all! Europeans employ Africans as chauffeurs, gardeners, houseboys, and so on, and patronize Indian shops because they could not function as a society without the services these provide, but beyond this, except in official circles, contact scarcely exists. Europeans live in one world; Indians in another; Africans in a third. Kenya is a three-layer cake, and the Africans, although an enormous numerical majority, have to be content with the lowest layer. That this makes for a thoroughly stifling and poisonous situation is too obvious to need elaboration, as sensible Europeans know full well. The Rt. Rev. Leonard J. Beecher, the Anglican Bishop of Mombasa and one of the principal ecclesiastical authorities in the country, said in a courageous speech in April, 1954, that Kenya had to work out a plural society or "would perish within five years."

The most serious discriminations against Africans in Kenya are, of course, economic and political. The white man's entire position in Kenya, as elsewhere in Africa, rests on black labor, and he not only denies the black man decent wages but does not allow him to vote. In a subsequent chapter I shall mention basic African grievances in some detail. As to Indians, one thing that rankles is segregation in the hotels. An Indian may be a millionaire, or the descendant of a family incomparably more illustrious than that of a Lancashire salesman in Nairobi on a business trip, or a scholar of exquisite distinction with a sheaf of university degrees, but he will not be permitted to cross the threshold of most white homes, clubs, or hotels. Africans do not feel so keenly about hotels, because few can afford them.

KENYA: THE LAND AND PEOPLE

The British are more rigid about Africans than Indians. The idea that a *black* man might gain entrance to a good hotel or restaurant is almost as unthinkable to the white community as it would have been twenty years ago—let us not forget American provincialisms in this field—in Natchez, Mississippi. But little by little the old taboos and barriers are breaking down. My wife and I did something utterly unprecedented in Nairobi. Twice we had African guests to cocktails in our hotel cottage. Don't ask me how we did it. But the walls of the hotel are still standing.

Sir Philip Mitchell set up the United Kenya Club with a mixed white, black, and brown membership, in an effort to broaden the social arena. This was an encouraging experiment, but it did not work out too well. African members were enthusiastic at first, and then bitterly disillusioned because, as I heard it put, white members who greeted them politely in the club "did not recognize them out in the street."

Most hatred of blacks by whites in Kenya and other white settler countries has (as in the United States) a sexual origin, and is based on fear. One settler exploded to us, "The difference between the United States and Kenya is that in America people who 'pass' pass white. But here they will pass black." But as a matter of fact very few Africans indeed have much interest in marrying the white man's daughter. White men are much more apt to have liaisons with black women than vice versa. The average Kenya African is a long way removed from any thought of miscegenation; the subject is totally unreal. What he wants is not mulatto children, but education for his own kind, economic opportunity, political rights, and a sense that he has some share in the development of what is, after all, his own country. Above all Africans want to *belong*.

White die-hards defend their prejudice on the ground of "culture," not "color," as they do in parts of French North Africa. This is an encouraging sign, in that it shows that people have become ashamed to base discrimination solely on considerations of race; they refuse to mingle with Africans—so they say—not because of their color but "their lack of cultural development." I even heard one titled lady say passionately that the real point at issue was not color bar or even culture bar but "water closet bar." Indians, she screamed, stand on the seat, and Africans use the floor.

THE WHITE SETTLERS

Any African country with a substantial white settler population faces trouble these days for reasons too obvious to mention. The system is not only iniquitous but unworkable, if large areas of black land are expropriated without proper compensation. The countries getting along best in Africa today do not permit large-scale white settlement at all, even if they are run by whites. But it would be naïve in the extreme to think of the whole white settler class in Kenya, for instance, as a gang of robber barons, despoiling black Africans at will. It is true that they underpay black labor and that their political views are largely conservative, but they are not strictly speaking a *feudal* community at all. Some still have sizable estates, but the present trend is all toward the breakup of the really big holdings, and the average farm today covers only about a thousand acres. Most white settlers are not baronial at all; they are yeomen farmers. They are frontiersmen, and resemble closely American homesteaders in the days when the West was being opened up. They carved out their own holdings, slaved to improve them, and do not want to lose what they have gained. Most are neither effete nor rich.[17]

Farming in Kenya is by no means a matter of sunshine and roses; recurrent economic crises have wiped settlers out wholesale. A newcomer today, by terms of official government advice, must have a capital of at least £12,000 "and borrowing facilities" if he expects to make a success of a Kenya farm.[18]

Even though they constitute a small group the settlers are vigorously articulate and have marked character. Many, in Kenya, strove to re-create a form of society they had lost at home. They wanted to get way from the red tape and petty restrictions of life in England, with its humdrum patterns, and live in a free, spacious country where, by God, every man saluted the Union Jack at sundown, and where an African was just a damned nigger and an Indian a wog. They were not so much interested in farming itself; they wanted "Africa"—its open spaces, the challenge of a new frontier, its isolation and remoteness. They were looking not merely for profits, but for Shangri La as well.

The early settlers—again like American homesteaders—were a hard-boiled, free-willed lot. In 1923 the Colonial Office, marching with the times, felt obliged to widen the basis of the Kenya administration, and five Indians and one Arab were given seats in the legislative body. That was thirty years ago—no one dreamed then of giving *Africans* seats! To give representation to Indians was bad enough. The settlers rose in fury. They had imagination,

---

[17] Technically speaking most Kenya farmers do not "own" their land. Distribution by the government of freehold land stopped thirty or more years ago, and nowadays the Crown holds title to it all. Leases formerly ran to ninety-nine years, but this did not give assurance that a family would be sure of its property for more than two or three generations, and now the usual lease is for 999 years. To have land on such terms is, of course, tantamount to outright ownership.

[18] *Kenya: Your Queries Answered*, p. 56.

KENYA: THE LAND AND PEOPLE 331

they believed in direct action, and they were contemptuous of law. They even went so far as to hatch a plot for kidnapping the Governor of the time, and setting up their own regime. The conspiracy was exposed in time.

Even today, partly as a result of the Mau Mau uprising, die-hards talk on occasion of "secession" from the Commonwealth. They will make a Boston Tea Party, throw off the "yoke" of London, and fight a white settlers' revolt as George Washington did. Then will come the establishment of a straight-out white supremacy state, with no nonsense about it, like that in the Union of South Africa. About a fifth of Kenya white settlers were pro-Malan while Dr. Malan was in power. But threats of secession cannot be taken seriously, if only because Kenya is utterly dependent on the British Treasury.

Most white settlers dislike the Colonial Office and want to run their own affairs—not merely the lunatic extremists. They say that they are *Kenyans*, not British, and that although they are loyal to the Crown they must have more decisive power in their own government. The leading Kenya politicians have lived in Kenya, not London, most of their adult lives, and they want administration that springs out of their own local roots. They dislike intensely the system whereby they are ruled, in effect, by a governor who has no fixed residence in the country—he may have been in Trinidad before and be off to Hong Kong on his next post—and by a parliament in Westminister that has no real stake in Kenya itself. Colonial affairs are not debated more than two or three times a year in the House of Commons, and the Colonial Secretary has much on his mind aside from Kenya. Above all, Kenya may become a plaything of British domestic politics. A vote crucial to the development of the colony may be decided not on Kenyan terms at all, but in line with local British tensions between the Conservative and Labor parties. In a word the white settlers want exactly what the Africans want, strange as this may seem—more self-government.

*

We drove out to spend a weekend with Michael Blundell at his farm near Nakuru.[19] At that time Mr. Blundell was Leader of the European Elected Members on the Kenya Legislative Council, and an important figure; today he is much more important, not only as chief of the new United Country Party but as a member of the cabinet—the first actual cabinet Kenya has ever had—which was set up early in 1954. He is minister without portfolio—that is, trouble shooter at large—and an extraordinarily engaging character.

---

[19] The road to Nakuru is, by common consent, the only good road in Kenya; it was built by Italian prisoners of war. Most Kenya roads turn to red gumbo when it rains, but this one has a surface.

Michael Blundell is a Yorkshireman, about forty-eight, who came to Kenya when he was eighteen, to carve out his future and a living. He worked at all manner of jobs, and for a time managed a coffee estate. He saved enough money to buy some land, and built the farm we saw. Blundell is towheaded, direct, evocative, and vigorous. I do not know how much formal education he has had; seldom have I met anybody with a more acute intelligence or a livelier, pithier sense of phrase. Like most good Yorkshiremen, he has humor, and this alone is enough to make him a refreshing phenomenon in tortured Kenya. But the chief thing to say about Mr. Blundell, of the earth earthy, is that he is a born leader, packed with magnetism, bounce, and defiance. Also he has plenty of ambition. He will almost certainly be Kenya's first prime minister—I am as sure about this as about any prophecy I have ever made in my life—when the colony arrives at independent government.

The Blundell property covers about 1,200 acres, and lies at 7,500 feet. All this area was virgin wilderness forty years ago. Mainly Blundell grows vegetables for canning—beets, peas, beans, and particularly asparagus; he is going to be the asparagus king of East Africa some day. For fun he has a garden. Flowers are not my province; all I can say is that I have never seen such flowers—spring, summer, and autumn flowers bloom all at once, from June through December. In normal times, Blundell has 150 African farmers (squatters); they get a two-and-a-half-acre plot, their food and supplies, and 25 shillings a month cash. Women—of whom he employs thirty or forty—are paid sixpence a day. This whole region was wire-taut when we were there. Blundell had lost about forty of his workers; either they had been taken by the police as Mau Mau suspects, or had drifted back to the reserves. Even those Kikuyu who remained refused to work, because they were awaiting the verdict in the trial of Jomo Kenyatta, their leader, which was then going on; they had put down their tools in a kind of strike, until they knew Kenyatta's fate. We looked at the forest slopes where terrorists are being "winkled" out, and almost had the feeling that we were being besieged. On a hillside we saw the name BLUNDELL spelled out in big white stones; several settlers in the neighborhood do this so that aircraft patrols can locate themselves.

It was here, in a garden glowing with scarlet cannas and golden Peruvian lilies, that we first became intimately—if incongruously—conscious of the way the "emergency" deformed the life of Kenya. Blundell's life has been threatened several times, and he was armed, of course; so were we. Friends lent my wife a pistol that looked to me as big and unwieldy as a cannon. Blundell has a bodyguard, who—literally—never for a moment left his side. Two African policemen steadily made their rounds of the sturdily

KENYA: THE LAND AND PEOPLE

built house but, we were told cheerfully, nobody knew whether they were to be seriously trusted or not. At dusk, every window was locked shut, and shades drawn; the assembled company pulled out their revolvers, and propped them next to their cups of tea. The guns, cocked, were actually laid out on the table. Nor did anybody sit with his back to a window or door. This sounds like nonsense. It was not nonsense. Very few Europeans (as we shall see) have been killed by the Mau Mau; but many of those who did meet death were murdered by their own servants, or by Africans in whom they had complete trust, who took them by surprise, knifing them while they were in a bath, or while eating dinner. It was no use having your gun in a coat pocket across the room. One refinement at Blundell's was that, after using our bathroom, we were instructed to lock the door from the *outside*, so that if an intruder should climb through the bathroom window he could not get further into the house. Going from room to room, people locked each door. After dinner a puppy nibbled at a lady's handbag, and she shrieked; the loaded gun inside might go off.

Somehow, life goes on. It even goes on with humor. The Blundells have a six-year-old daughter, Susan. The village police were much astonished when a Kikuyu was caught outdoors after curfew; proudly he showed them a chit of paper Susan had given him, "Pass this man. He is one of our farmers and a good chap. Signed. Susan Blundell."

Blundell talked vividly about Kenya problems. He likes to characterize himself as "an extremist of the center." He is not by any stretch of the imagination what a silly or stupid American southerner would call a "nigger-lover"; but he stands for a fair deal for the African, and wants to see color bar eliminated. He does not hate the Mau Maus because they are black, but because they are terrorists. "Thinking about everything in terms of race is the curse of this country," he said succinctly. He has vast pride in his farm, and he thinks a great deal of young Susan's future; he does not want white privileges done away with, and he does not think that it will ever be possible for Kenya to have an exclusively African government. But he is sensible enough to know that Kenya, let alone young Susan, has no future at all unless some kind of racial harmony is built up. No government, he insists, can function if it is based on suppression by Europeans of the legitimate advance of the African people. "I believe that to be impossible, and, above all, I believe it to be morally wrong." So what Blundell and his friends are trying to work out is an effective compromise, the creation of a state in which whites, blacks, and browns will all have opportunity as well as some degree of political representation.

More about Mr. Blundell later. Let us proceed.

CHAPTER 19

Kenya: British Rule in Africa

You can do wonders with an Englishman if you make him feel ashamed of himself.
—NEGLEY FARSON

LONG ago in Chapter 1 we mentioned briefly some of the characteristics of British rule in Africa. The main thing to repeat is that the British, for good or ill, and for a variety of motives both practical and idealistic, pursue a broad general policy of training their Africans for eventual self-government, within the Commonwealth. This is an altogether different policy from that of any other colonial power. The British, on the assumption that if they give freedom they will keep good will, are committed to the principle of an eventual *African* Africa, even if this should entail their own withdrawal in the long future. The risk must be taken, since a contrary policy involves risks greater.

In 1923 the Duke of Devonshire, than whom no one could have been more Tory, and who was Colonial Secretary at the time, made an astonishing statement about Kenya in particular:

> Primarily Kenya is an African territory, and His Majesty's Government think it necessary definitely to record their considered opinion that the interests of the African natives must be *paramount* [italics mine], and that if and when those interests and the interests of the immigrant races [i.e., the British and Indian] should conflict, the former [i.e., the African] should prevail . . . In the administration of Kenya His Majesty's Government regard themselves as exercising a trust on behalf of the African population . . . the object of which may be defined as the protection and advancement of the Native races.

In 1930 Lord Passfield, better known as Sidney Webb, was Colonial Secretary in a Labor government, and reiterated the principles of the

Devonshire White Paper. The ultimate objective for Kenya, Passfield said, was Dominion Status—that is to say, full self-government within the Commonwealth, with the right to secede—but he added the important disclaimer that self-government would not be possible until the native community was more advanced.

So the British, not only in Kenya but elsewhere in Africa, are committed to Dominion Status—but not too fast. This ambiguous position has produced difficulties without end. How can "paramount" interests be defined to the satisfaction of British and Africans both? What if the African child, resisting tutelage, wants to get rid of his British parent before he is fully grown up? Healthy evolution demands partnership—but on what terms? How can a people be trained for self-government, if they are not given enough education to be able to practice it? And so on. The heart of the dilemma is *pace*, which in turn depends on trust.[1] What point has self-government if this comes too soon and leads to feudalism, Communism, dictatorship, or chaos? On the other hand the pressure of events has produced a situation whereby the British can no longer rule by force alone, even if they should want to, and cannot continue long to govern at all—in some colonies—without full consent of the governed. The chief reason for this is that they are so overwhelmingly outnumbered. It costs too much to stay.

The British want to hold on as long as they can, for selfish as well as unselfish reasons, but people who call them "insincere" on the basic principle—that of preparing colonial peoples for eventual self-government—should reflect a little about recent Commonwealth history. India is free, and so are Pakistan, Ceylon, and Burma. The British freed Iraq and Jordan after a period of tutelage, withdrew from Libya, and gave up Israel. In South Africa they helped the Union to develop into a free, self-governing Commonwealth, and have made tremendous concessions in Egypt and the Sudan. Of course their hand was forced. No one would deny that. But they did not fight to hold on stubbornly after the fight was lost, with consequent civil war and the growth of Communism, as the French did in Indochina and may be doing in Morocco. The British retired with dignity, superiority, and grace—almost in the manner of a schoolmaster dismissing a graduating class. "It is interesting," one colonial administrator mentioned to me, "that there has been no serious threat of Communism in any territory the British have ever evacuated."

Africa is still by far the largest colonial domain remaining to Great

---

[1] See Negley Farson, *Last Chance in Africa*, p. 52, and a remarkable article by J. H. Huizinga, "White Witchcraft in Kenya," *Kenya Weekly News*, March 27, 1953. I have drawn on this for several phrases below.

Britain. About four-fifths of all British colonial subjects (not including citizens of the Dominions) are African. But British power, British prestige and influence, have been steadily, remorselessly whittled down. Every schoolboy knows the old maps, showing British areas in a nice rich pink all the way from Egypt to the Cape. But Egypt has been gone since 1936, and the Suez and the Sudan are going. South Africa is still a member of the Commonwealth, but has become increasingly anti-British, and it may very well secede some day and set itself up as a non-British independent state. Moreover the Union may at almost any time swallow up the three British protectorates embedded in its territory, Basutoland, Swaziland, and Bechuanaland. In the west of Africa, the Gold Coast is coming close to Dominion Status, and Nigeria is not far behind.

British rule is exceptionally elastic, and its methods differ widely from colony to colony; the emphasis is all on variety, not the opposite. And, for all their blunders and vagaries, the British have consistently sought to be progressive, liberalizing, and humane. They give justice. Their legislative assemblies, even if embryonic, give opportunity for protest. There is no British colony even remotely in the position of, say, the Spanish Sahara. But the British, even if benevolent, have been afflicted by all manner of troubles in Africa lately. One of the things that annoys them most is that, in these days, benevolence does not necessarily pay off. Uganda, the "model" state, is sullen and strained after the forced deposition of the Kabaka; many Africans in Nyasaland resisted to the uttermost incorporation into the new Central African Federation; and in Kenya the Mau Mau rebellion has wrought appalling havoc.

A final preliminary point—London is still the "capital" of Africa. The Empire is no more than a shadow of its former self, but London remains unalterably imperial. British rule gave leadership to the whole continent, not merely to British areas; men like Livingstone set an example from coast to coast. Africa is deep in the British bone. London set the mode and pulled the strings. Even today, British financial interests dominate the economy of the Union, and are heavy investors in Portuguese and Belgian enterprises. London is not merely the political capital of British colonies, but an international capital as well in all manner of respects—for instance, it is the headquarters of the International Locust Control Organization and other humanitarian and scientific enterprises almost without number. One important body is the Commission for Technical Co-operation in Africa South of the Sahara (CGTA) to which representatives of six nations are attached, and another is the Scientific Council for Africa South of the

KENYA: BRITISH RULE IN AFRICA

Sahara, which, under the direction of Dr. E. B. Worthington, has done fruitful work.

Most curiously, London is also the capital of *African* Africa, so to speak. It has any number of organizations, white, black, and mixed, devoted not to imperialist but to *anti*-imperialist causes. Here are the headquarters of the Africa Bureau, the Anti-Slavery Society, the Fabian Colonial Bureau, the Congress of Peoples Against Imperialism,[2] the West African Students Union, the League of Colored People, and many other groups, to say nothing of institutions in an altogether different category, like the Royal African Society. In London, the most imperial of cities, one may find Englishmen of fascinating variety and consequence—men like the Rev. Michael Scott—devoting their lives to the cause of *African* liberation. Moreover London is the best center for informed journalism about Africa. One might almost say that the "capital" of Africa is the office of the London *Observer*, if it is not Nuffield College at Oxford.

SOME DEFINITIONS

> For two or three generations we can show the Negro what we are: then we shall be asked to go away. Then we shall leave the land to those it belongs to, with the feeling that they have better business friends in us than in other white men.
> —LORD LUGARD

Indirect Rule. This is the basic British system throughout Africa, and means that government is carried out as far as possible by the Africans themselves, through the mechanism of their own chiefs. Up to a certain level Africans run their own administration, under British supervision. Lord Lugard, one of the most remarkable of all British empire builders, who created both Uganda and Nigeria in a manner of speaking, invented this clever and useful device. The British hold the reins; the Africans do the work. The Africans have the responsibility for such unpleasant details as tax collection; then the British spend the money.[3] But at the same time Indirect Rule gave thousands upon thousands of Africans concrete training in the arduous and complex business of governmental administration. It transformed them from savages to civil servants. It also helped to preserve African institutions; it has always been a fundamental British premise never to interfere, if humanly possible, with African tribal customs. The British almost never replace; they adapt. But Indirect Rule could only function well where tribes had a strong tradition of chiefdom, and where

---

[2] Almost all African nationalist parties are affiliated to this organization.
[3] In Africa, of course, to support the local administration.

the tribal organization remained more or less intact; it cannot apply to the hundreds of thousands of contemporary Africans who have become detribalized, and have entered into the towns.[4] Probably the days of Indirect Rule are numbered, but it was a wonderful idea while it lasted. By being "indirect," it made direct rule possible.

Dual Mandate. This means what it says—that the British in Africa commit themselves deliberately to a double responsibility. Lugard's own words defining Dual Mandate were: "On the one hand, the abounding wealth of the tropical regions of the earth must be developed and used for the benefit of mankind; on the other hand, an obligation rests on the controlling Power not only to safeguard the material rights of the natives, but to promote their moral and educational progress."

Plural Society. The standard definition of this is "a society comprising two or more elements or social orders which live side by side, yet without mingling, in one political unit."[5] Sometimes the adjective "multiracial" is used instead of "plural" if different races are involved. India, Malaya, French Canada, and the United States are examples of plural societies—where "various communities, differing from one another in culture, religion, race, or language," live within "a single political framework." The basis is equality of rights and partnership. A plural society does *not* mean one in which mixed marriages have led to racial fusion, as in Brazil. Such a society is not known technically as plural, but as "mixed." Of course a plural society may in time evolve into one mixed. This is what opponents of the plural society concept fear.

The opposite concept, based on rigid suppression and segregation of blacks and browns, is that of permanent and exclusive white supremacy, as in South Africa.

In parts of British Africa the problem of a future plural or multiracial society does not arise, because colonies like the Gold Coast and Nigeria are something else again—they are *black* societies, and will remain so.

The real trouble spots are—let us repeat—countries with substantial white populations, like Kenya, where extremist whites have sought to maintain undiluted white supremacy in the face of an overwhelmingly predominant black population, and have vigorously resisted any impulse toward racial partnership. (It is an interesting point that, conversely, blacks in a black country like Uganda also furiously oppose the idea of a plural society, because this will mean that more *white* influence will come in.) The present

---

[4] *Attitude to Africa,* a Penguin Special, p. 20.
[5] *Ibid.,* p. 45, quoting J. S. Furnivall, *Netherlands India.* Apparently the term was invented by Mr. Furnivall.

official trend in British territories with sizable white populations (Kenya and the Rhodesias) is toward the creation by slow stages of plural, multi-racial systems. The ideal is of friendly communities living in the same country side by side, with racial tension lessened or if possible eliminated, but without actual racial fusion.

Colony and Protectorate. These are confusing terms, which overlap. For instance, Kenya—the British, as always, are supple rulers—is *both* a colony and a protectorate. The coastal strip which is theoretically the property of the Sultan of Zanzibar is the protectorate; the rest is the colony. In practice the distinction means little, but to be punctilious we should mention some legal respects in which colonies and protectorates do differ. In general, a protectorate is (or was) supposed to be a more backward area, which needed "protection"; a colony has a higher status, and is more on its own. Also a colony is British territory "under the Crown," whereas in a protectorate the Crown exercises authority but the territory is not formally "annexed." A resident of a colony today, no matter of what color, is a British national; the resident of a protectorate is merely "a British protected person." But hold on! There are infinite subtleties to be dealt with in this field. For instance, Michael Blundell, though born in Britain, is a Kenyan and carries a Kenya passport. But he is a British subject, and a citizen of the United Kingdom and Colonies.

INSTITUTION OF THE GOVERNOR

At the top of the structure in every British colony or protectorate is the Governor. He is appointed by the Colonial Office in London, is the representative of the Crown, and is a combination of head of state and prime minister. Or, to put it in slightly different terms, he symbolizes the Queen, while performing executive duties roughly like those of a President of the United States. A governor almost always has a knighthood, and is called "His Excellency" or referred to informally as "H.E." Sometimes military men or political personages become governors, but most come out of the ranks of the colonial service; they start their careers at the lowest rung, as District Officers, and rise step by step. We met seven or eight governors, and stayed with several; to a certain extent they all conform to a type, and represent the basic Colonial Office policy of "Wait, Look, and Listen," but they differ vastly in personality. Twining in Tanganyika is as different from Cohen in Uganda as, let us say, the late Ernest Bevin was from Stafford Cripps.

A man usually becomes governor in his late forties or early fifties, and this is the climax of his career. As a rule he serves three or four years, but in emergencies or special circumstances this may be stretched to six years or longer. Sir Philip Mitchell was Governor of Kenya from 1944 to 1952. A governor, if successful, may have a second bout of being governor in another territory. But usually, after reaching one of the major African posts, he retires from the colonial service, to make room for younger men still on the ladder. Most governors, who are generally extremely distinguished men and still in the prime of life at retirement, serve the British nation further by taking on all sorts of jobs, public or private, after they leave Africa. There are about forty-five governors in all, scattered all over the world from Fiji to the Caribbean. In Africa the most important governorship is usually considered to be Nigeria, with Kenya a close second.

Governors in every British colony or protectorate live in what is known as Government House; this is a combination of palace, home, office, and hotel. Government Houses are usually spacious, have expertly trained servants, and are full of guests. In your room will be a schedule of mealtimes, laundry lists, and so forth, exactly as in a hotel—a really *good* hotel. The Governor is, one must always remember, the embodiment of the monarch at home, and, no matter how personally informal he himself may be, the atmosphere of his House is apt to be rigorous. Guests are expected to be punctual for an appointment. There is a distinct difference in any Government House between 11:30 A.M. and 11:31. If you are asked to dinner, the invitation may read "8:25 for 8:30," meaning that you are to be present at 8:25 P.M. without fail, because the Governor himself will enter the room at 8:30—on the dot. To be late would be a worse solecism than sliding to first base, or wearing a hat in church. Some governors are sticklers, some are not; some eat lunch in shorts. Whether a governor is a snob or not, the institution of Government House has, inevitably, become overlaid with the most elaborate and intricate snobberies; there are Europeans in most African capitals who would—almost—kill themselves to be invited to a small Government House lunch or dinner. I have in Kenya met Britons of the utmost charm, professional accomplishment, and good breeding; but the kind of job they hold is not quite "right" and never, no matter whether they stay in Nairobi for twenty years, will they ever see the inside of Government House, any more than, let us say, the manager of a steel works in the Midlands would ever be invited to Buckingham Palace.

Every governor has an aide-de-camp (ADC), who assists him with his official and social duties. These young men—sometimes army officers, sometimes relatives from London, sometimes old friends—are a combination of hall porter, house manager, bridge partner, accountant, chaperon, mail clerk, boating companion, and chef du protocol. Cohen in Uganda has a *female* ADC, and a highly competent young lady she is. Times do change.

*

The Governor of Kenya who succeeded Mitchell, Sir Evelyn Baring, had the ill luck to take his post at the very moment that the Mau Mau troubles seriously began. His term of office has consequently been painful. Sir Evelyn Baring has a fine heritage. He is the son of Lord Cromer, and has had a vivid and varied career. He was High Commissioner in South Africa at the time of the crisis over Seretse Khama, and was severely criticized for the line he took on this; as a result, a cautious man anyway, he sought in Kenya to be doubly cautious, so much so that he was sometimes called "weak." Baring is a tall handsome man, with a deep booming laugh and a profile strikingly like that of John Barrymore; he is sensitive, high-minded, and just. He should have been a perfect "white settler's governor," but he was too liberal, too temperate, to go all the way on their side; hence some extreme die-hards practically thought of him as a traitor to his class. But he was unpopular with the Africans too, much as he had their legitimate interests at heart; any governor was bound to be unpopular during the Mau Mau crisis, because he had to take measures against almost the whole of the African community. Sir Evelyn Baring is one of the most aristocratic aristocrats I have ever met, and the atmosphere of Government House in Nairobi is almost that of eighteenth-century England, caking a little at the edges. Lady Mary Baring is the daughter of an earl, the principal private secretary is a Howard, and one of the ADC's is a Ridley. People emerged down corridors as if they had just stepped out of antique frames. They were fastidious, generous, with beautiful manners and refinement—healthy people too—but they made Government House in Kenya resemble a stately island lost in time, drowned in forces nobody could comprehend.

One day tension was so acute (just before the Kenyatta verdict) that the front doors were bolted, in case an African mob should try to make a demonstration. Business, however, had to go on. So a small notice was hung on the outer doors to the effect that visitors should apply for entrance to the ADC's door around the corner. The notice was written in longhand on blue Government House note paper. Such imperturbability! It was as if a general about to defend a fortress should tell his besiegers not to tread on the lawn.

THE "ATTACK" ON GOVERNMENT HOUSE

In blunt fact any frontal assault by Africans on Government House would have been impossible. But white settlers—not Africans—*did* make a kind of attack on it a few months before. This episode, almost unprecedented in British colonial history, occurred on January 26, 1953, and was like an attempt to sack the White House with Eisenhower in it by a mob of outraged *Republicans*, not Democrats. The story of this demonstration was discreetly hushed up in the British press, and so far as I know nothing has ever been printed about it in America at all.

What happened was this:

Some days previously a white settler named Ruk, his wife (who had done much humanitarian work among the Kikuyus), and their only son had been cut to pieces by Mau Mau terrorists. The Mau Maus seldom kill Europeans; in fact, as of that date, only *nine* Britons had been killed in the whole course of the outbreak, but the Ruk murders were peculiarly atrocious, and the white citizenry, feeling that Baring's government was not dealing with the crisis firmly enough, became almost insanely aroused. A group of settlers determined to demonstrate at Government House. The organization was mostly spontaneous, but word of what was planned got around. Late at night on the 25th, Colonel Howard, the Governor's secretary, telephoned Michael Blundell, as leader of the Europeans in the legislature, to ask his advice about what to do if the demonstration materialized. Blundell sagely counseled him to remove all *African* police from the Government House environs. (The Kenya police force is largely African, under British officers.) Blundell knew that the sight of black Africans, acting as *police*, would infuriate the crowd. But his advice was not taken.

Next day, on the 26th, Europeans began to assemble. Nobody knows who gave them orders. People stopped other people, especially those driving in from the country, and said, "Go to Government House—the Governor wants to see you." By noon about 1,500 people, including many women, had gathered; most were armed. Black police barred their way, and, as Blundell had predicted, they became enraged. They shouted for the Governor to appear, but he did not appear. The crowd howled in derision, and someone yelled, "He'd have to telegraph Whitehall for permission!"

The demonstrators did not mind showing their disrespect for the Colonial Office, but, in a nice British way, they wanted to prove their loyalty to the Crown. A man called out, "There seems to be some doubt about our intentions, so I suggest that we give three cheers for Her Majesty the Queen." This was promptly done.

KENYA: BRITISH RULE IN AFRICA 343

The Sultana of Zanzibar was a guest at Government House that day, and she peeked out of an upper window, along with Lady Mary Baring, to see what all the commotion was about—1,500 armed men and women yelling their heads off on Government House lawn. Somebody saw the pale brown features of the Sultana through the window, and a cry went up, "They even have niggers in the house!" (Of course this distinguished lady is not Negro at all, but an Arab.)

Two white politicians appeared, to announce that Sir Evelyn Baring would not receive members of the crowd, and would not come out to talk to them, because this would create an unfortunate precedent if, on some future day, black or brown crowds should ever choose to demonstrate before the house of the Queen, trying to force the hand of the Crown.

At this the demonstrators became doubly enraged, and marched forward. The African police tried to push them off the terrace back to the grass. The crowd agreed to move back peaceably if the police moved back too. The scramble that followed was not dignified. The crowd moved back; the police did not move back; the crowd thought it had been double-crossed, and surged forward again. Women jabbed cigarette ends into the bare arms and legs of black policemen. Their cordon broke. Half a dozen European police made a human barrier to keep the mob from smashing its way through the buckling doors. Then came relief—in the form of Mr. Michael Blundell.

Forty years of evolution in Kenya could have been destroyed that day, if the African police had been obliged to fire on a white mob, or if the white mob had fired on their own kind and marched into the house. Blundell singlehanded kept this from happening.

He had for several hours been in conference with the Governor, pleading for a more resolute policy toward the emergency in general. A governor is held in great awe in colonial circles; Blundell had even interrupted Baring's *breakfast*, a horrifying thing to do. Now Blundell heard the crowd hammering at the doors, and, racing down the corridor, he saw *African* servants, trying to protect the Governor, straining to hold the doors shut. Blundell got out by another exit, sailed into the crowd, and began to talk. He could not be heard. He beckoned desperately toward the house and somebody within tossed a blue brocaded chair out of a window. Blundell climbed up on this. He tried to assuage the crowd and expostulate with it. He managed to get the black police to withdraw. Then, to persuade the white demonstrators to disperse, he went out on a long limb and promised them three things—appointment of an over-all military commander, mobilization of civilian man power, and the setting up of an emergency council.

Blundell himself, on behalf of the Europeans, had for several weeks been urging adoption of these three measures. The government had resisted them, apparently on the assumption that such drastic steps, which would virtually acknowledge that a state of civil war existed, were not necessary.

The crowd broke up, satisfied with Blundell's pledge. Blundell, exhausted, went into Baring's office. The Governor, with perfect composure and detachment, and having apparently expressed no pronounced curiosity as to what had been going on, was reading a book quietly. Blundell said, not knowing what the response would be, that he had *committed* him to the three controversial measures. Baring thanked him, and gave him a stiff Scotch and soda, which Blundell was glad to have.

THE PATTERN OF BRITISH RULE

What we are trying to create here is something between the Gold Coast and the Union.

—E. A. VASEY

Several observations may be made about the development of democratic procedures in British colonies.

1. Above the Governor, in ascending order, are the Colonial Office, the Secretary of State for the Colonies (who must of course be a member of the British parliament), the Cabinet, the House of Commons, and the Crown—in other words, Her Majesty's Government in London. The Governor is responsible to all of these, but he is not responsible to a *local* electorate.

2. No colonial constituencies are represented in the House of Commons. In France numerous deputies from Africa sit in both the National Assembly and the Senate; the British system does not permit this, although in theory an African-born person resident in England could stand for the House of Commons. There are several Canadian-born MP's representing British constituencies.

3. Most British colonies and protectorates in Africa have an Executive Council, commonly called the EXCO. This is appointed by the Governor, and is equivalent to a cabinet, in that each member has limited administrative authority over a certain field—native affairs, finance, education, public health, and so on. But it is not a true cabinet in the British sense because the members are not chosen out of a parliament.[6] An EXCO corresponds more closely to the American cabinet, in which members are responsible to the President only.

[6] Except in the Gold Coast. West Africa is much more advanced politically than East.

KENYA: BRITISH RULE IN AFRICA

4. Underneath the EXCO is the LEGCO or Legislative Council. This passes the local budget and most local laws. The degree of its power depends on the general state of advance of the colony. In most LEGCO's there are several categories of members, and this is a matter, no matter how dull or complex it may seem, that we must go into briefly. First—in Kenya, for instance—are the *official* members. These are senior British civil servants who run the various government departments, and hold their seats ex-officio. Then come *unofficial* members, who are appointed by the Governor out of the community at large. Finally some members are *elected*. The basic political situation in every British colony depends on the ratio between official, unofficial (appointed), and elected members. So long as officials and unofficials outnumber the elected members, the executive branch of government fully controls the legislature.

Moreover, the LEGCO cannot dismiss a government, even it it outvotes it on some bill. The EXCO is not compelled to resign, as a British cabinet must resign if it is beaten on an important issue in the House of Commons. This, more than any other factor, has produced parliamentary frustration among the whites in Kenya. They can divide against the government, but cannot unseat it. They can register their disapproval of a government, but cannot throw it out.

5. London reserves to itself other safeguards. For instance, a governor in most colonies has what are known as "reserved powers"; these are, however, almost never used. The Colonial Office can, in certain exceptional cases, invalidate legislation passed by a colony. Above all, in cases of extreme emergency (as happened in British Guiana recently) the Queen-in-Council, which means in effect the United Kingdom Government, can suspend the constitution of a colony and establish rule by decree.

6. There has never been a general election in Kenya. "You cannot put your whole destiny in the hands of black illiterates," one estimable member of EXCO put it to me. The white settlers, as things stand today, will never tolerate a free African electorate, since Africans outnumber them by 132 to 1. The elections that do take place in Kenya (every four years) are based on the "communal" system of prewar India; the Europeans and Indians vote separately, each for members of their own community, and Africans until recently did not vote at all. But—very important—a beginning has been made to give Africans some voting power. In 1952, for the first time, an embryonic electoral college was set up for Africans, who were then allowed to vote for picked African candidates but on the basis of a poll extremely small.

This division of privilege cannot last forever, for the simple reason—let us say it again—that in the long run Europeans can only remain peaceably in Kenya with the consent of the African population at large. There can be no stable government on the basis of a purely European vote. What the British fear most is that the pressure of today's events will not give them the *time* necessary for educating a big African electorate. Because equally there can be no stable government if Africans are not equipped to govern, or if the Africans do not develop leaders whom the British can respect. One should also mention that within a generation *educated* Africans and Indians together will outnumber the European community. This makes all the more imperative the need to set up effective government promptly on the *sine qua non* of racial partnership.

*

When we visited Kenya the LEGCO (total membership fifty-four) had eight "official" members, all British. The two ablest were, I thought, E. A. Vasey, the member for finance and development, who has worked for a living since the age of eleven, and who came out to Kenya in 1936, and F.W. Cavendish-Bentinck, the member for agriculture and natural resources. This bloc of eight officials, together with eighteen "unofficials" appointed by the Governor, made the "government" party.[7] Fourteen *elected* Europeans (two of them women) were the white "opposition," among them Blundell and another progressive settler, W.B. Havelock. Then there were six elected Asians, one elected Arab, and several "nominated" Africans. Among these latter were Wycliffe Wyasya Work Awori, an exceptionally vivid personality; E.W. Mathu, a Kikuyu who went to Balliol; and F.W. Odede, a Luo who was arrested soon after we met him and who has been detained ever since without trial, on the charge of spreading Mau Mau among the Nyanza tribes near Lake Victoria.

Of the eight Britons on EXCO, three have lived in Kenya for twenty-five years or longer, and think of themselves as Kenyan more than as British. One told me, "I am much more an African than any damned Kikuyu."

*

Early in 1954 came what has been called the most important constitutional change in Kenya since the country's foundation. Something had to be done to make government more effective. Oliver Lyttelton, then the Colonial Secretary, "imposed" on Kenya its first multiracial government.[8] The

---

[7] Of the "unofficials" two were African and two Asian.

[8] Lyttelton, now Lord Chandos, was succeeded as Colonial Secretary by the Rt. Hon. Alan Lennox-Boyd.

EXCO was promoted to be a real cabinet, although with no prime minister. Blundell and Havelock became members of a Council of Ministers, and so did Patel, Nathoo, and one African, a non-Kikuyu named A.B. Ohanga. He is minister for local development. Several Kikuyus became undersecretaries.

The white community was split violently asunder by this development, the first "plural" government in Kenya history. There had been no political parties at all—in the true sense—until the Mau Mau crisis. The settlers were represented politically by a body known as the Kenya Elector's Union, a kind of all-inclusive lobby or pressure group. When we saw Blundell he predicted that there would be competing white political parties "within three years." They emerged more quickly than that. Blundell, Havelock, and the moderate whites organized the United Country Party to help put the Lyttelton reforms into effect. The extremist settlers refused to go along with them, and formed a white supremacy party of their own, the Federal Independence Party. Extreme vituperation has marked recent contact between the two white groups.

BRITISH: ATTITUDES AND TECHNIQUES

On the racial problem there are three schools among the Kenya whites:
1. The "knock-'em-on-the-head" school (extremist settlers).
2. The "drink-a-cup-of-tea-with-them" school, a small minority (social workers and intellectuals).
3. In between, the moderate "lead-them-by-the-hand" school—but slowly (Blundell).

Most old-timers do not hate Africans and in fact may have a considerable affection for them; they regard them as children who can be kept in line, not necessarily by being knocked on the head, but by being spanked. "Be kind to natives, and you are doomed," one haughty person informed us. It was a stunning shock to men like this, most of whom have never known Africans except as houseboys, to discover that they have, among other things, been able to achieve political organization on a substantial scale. They simply do not grasp the *tempo* of modern African development. And, like members of most privileged classes, they help to create by their own stubbornness the pressures that may in time sweep them away.

A central paradox is that the white man does not want to stay in Africa except as ruler. But he is not wanted, because he *does* rule.

We had a Kikuyu driver in Nairobi, and asked him to be on hand one evening. He replied that he could not because he was one of a group organizing a reception for Mr. D.N. Pritt, QC, the British lawyer who had flown down to defend Kenyatta. This may seem trivial. But when we mentioned it to a veteran white settler, he blew up—partly no doubt because most white settlers do not have a high opinion of Mr. Pritt. When, later, a crowd of several thousand Africans saw Pritt off at the airport, a colonial officer told us, "Now at last I am ready to concede that the Kikuyus may represent a nationalist movement."

Many Britons in Kenya, on the other hand, work for Africans with dedication and good spirit. This is a heritage from Livingstone. The great doctor said once, "The opening of the new . . . country is a matter of congratulation only in so far as it opens up a prospect for the elevation of the inhabitants."[9] Several times we met DC's who said, quite genuinely, things like "If only we can pull it off—for *them!* If only they *will* be able to make a success of it!" This is the more remarkable in that, if they do pull it off— that is, make Africans fit for self-government—they are liquidating themselves.

One youthful officer, who was in charge of more than 200,000 natives, told us, "I could run this district much better if I acted like a gauleiter, but I can't. We have an obligation to *teach* these people. It is our duty." He smiled cheerfully. "Perhaps we *consult* Africans too much, but we have to consult. We can't afford strict military rule, and anyway that is a thing of the past."

Members of UN commissions visiting Africa have been astonished on occasion by the camaraderie between Briton and African in the field, and at the way blacks feel free to talk up to their white superiors. A Belgian observer commented to his British host, "You have brought all this Mau Mau trouble on yourselves, because you are far too *nice* to the people!"

A familiar British self-castigating lament is, "Maybe we should never have come here in the first place. Maybe we have merely stirred people up, without giving them enough in return. Are they happier?" Then: "But is it *right* for us to go with the job half done? *Can* they cope with the contrapuntal mechanics of modern society? Won't they all just *return to their blackness?*"[10]

---

[9] "Elevation" may, of course, express itself in peculiarly British dimensions. One day flying into Tanganyika our companion was a provincial commissioner who, some years before, had been a junior District Officer in the area. We skimmed over a village, and this worthy, principled, donnish man almost leaned through the window of the plane in pride and excitement at something he saw. "*I* built that football field for them!"

[10] Something that has weakened the British position is, of all things, the automobile. "In the old days a DC had to walk. He really got to know the people. Now he sits at a desk drowned in paper work, and never gets out into the bush at all

*

Educated Africans are often bitter. We heard one remark, "The more backward we are, the better the settler likes it. The British *must* oppose education, because once we are educated they are on the way out. The white position rests totally on keeping us submerged." But the educated black man is also impaled, on his side, on a cruel dilemma. Not by any stretch of the imagination is Kenya ready for self-government as yet, and therefore logically the white man must remain.

*

The British, even if the full glories of Empire have faded, are still accomplished masters of the art of imperial management, and their techniques cover a wide and fascinating arc. Take even such a minor matter—perhaps not so minor—as the Honor's List. All over British Africa there are Africans, Indians, and Arabs carrying the precious initials OBE (Order of the British Empire) or something similar after their names. Such honors are keenly sought after and esteemed by almost everybody except inflamed nationalists. Some Africans even get knighthoods, though more frequently on the West Coast than the East. No neater method of rewarding achievement, assuring conformity, drawing off discontent, and bestowing high flattery has ever been invented.

Another effective device, which was used to particular advantage in India for generations and is unassailably part of the British tradition, is the use of *native* troops to keep order.[11] Until the Mau Mau crisis there were few, if any, white troops in British East Africa. They were not necessary. A celebrated military organization known as the King's African Rifles, with white officers but black troops, did the job. African boys were as eager in the old days to get into this regiment as American boys with military ambition are to get into West Point.[12]

The British even contrive, as I heard a Kikuyu put it, "to make the Africans pay for the cost of their own subjugation." Of course this is an

---

except by car." So we heard it said. Nevertheless all over East Africa (as in the Sudan) the DC still fulfills one supreme function—that of being a symbol of security.

[11] See "Black Africa Tomorrow," by W. E. B. Du Bois, *Foreign Affairs*, October, 1938.
[12] The KAR includes battalions from Kenya, Uganda, Tanganyika, and Nyasaland, together with the First Northern Rhodesian regiment. The Kenya elements are recruited mostly from the Nandi, Kamba, Meru, and Kipsigi tribes, with some Somalis.

exaggeration, but last year the poll tax on Africans contributed not less than £860,700 out of total Kenya tax collections of £5.4 million. It is a standard African grievance that part of their tax money goes, among other things, to the upkeep of *white* schools.

Without financial help from home, Kenya would collapse. The British taxpayer is, one might say, as much "exploited" for the benefit of Kenya as natives on the spot. Kenya, like the other East African colonies, has a Ten-Year Development Plan, and this is financed in part by the British government through the Colonial Development and Welfare Fund.

Important in a different category is the Colonial Development Corporation, a public company set up to promote private investment in long-range projects all over British Africa; this has resources of something like £40,000,000, with no fewer than fifty different enterprises under way, from cattle ranches to hotels and fisheries. The total British financial contribution to over-all colonial development in Africa has been $900,000,000 in the past thirty-three years.[13]

THE AMERICAN POSITION

United States interest in East Africa is not pronounced. Washington has always thought of it—indeed the whole world of the Indian Ocean—as predominantly a British sphere. Americans are not particularly admired or well liked in Kenya; I heard remarks like "You lost our empire for us, because of your dollar pressure!" The Foreign Operations Administration has not paid much attention to East Africa, but this may be because the British (like the Belgians and French) determine themselves how American dollar aid, if any, shall be apportioned between the home country and the colonies. The colonies are not always favored. By and large FOA and Point Four are much less conspicuous in colonial territories than in the independent states, like Libya and Liberia. However, American technical help in such fields as hydrology, vocational training, and scientific agriculture is promised for East Africa. An American girl broadcasts regularly in Swahili on the United States Information Service radio program in Nairobi. As for private American interests, an American oil company has development licenses for a petroleum survey in northern Kenya, near the Somalia border, and an American automobile assembly plant is to be built at Mombasa. But the chief American contributions to the life of Kenya at present are in such fields as tourist traffic (the safari business has, however, been hard hit by the Mau Mau troubles) and Coca-Cola.

[13] A. Campbell in a letter to the New York *Times*, Jan. 16, 1954.

EAST AFRICA AS AN ENTITY

East Africa has, as we know, three main constituents—Kenya, Tanganyika, Uganda—and the area has as a whole a distinct cohesion and homogeneity. A good many problems are intraterritorial—locust control, lack of water, development of protein resources, rinderpest, lack of fuel. There are four and a half columns of "East Africa" entries in the Nairobi phone book, as to wit:

E.A. Airways
E.A. Blankets Syndicate
E.A. Breweries, Ltd.
E.A. Bureau of Research in Medicine and Hygiene
E.A. Conservatory of Music
E.A. Co-operative Trading Society
E.A. Income Tax Department
E.A. Industrial Equipment Co.
E.A. Posts and Telecommunications Exchange
E.A. Road Federation
E.A. Tourist Travel Association
E.A. Tsetse and Trypanosomiasis Research and Reclamation Service
E.A. Union Mission of Seventh-Day Adventists
E.A. Women's League

And so on. The currency is the same in all three territories[14] and the postage is closely similar. An over-all East Africa Command governs military affairs, and the Royal East African Navy operates in coastal waters. The railways are under a single administration, and so are telegrams, civil aviation, meteorological services, medical services, forestry, agriculture, and customs administration. The only important areas in which each territory is on its own are, in fact, local finance and education.

An East Africa High Commission, of which the Governor of Kenya is always ex-officio chairman, has existed since 1947. There is even a vestigial Central Legislative Assembly, which meets in turn in Nairobi, Kampala, and Dar es Salaam, with representatives from each of the three territories. But this body has no power of taxation, and so its authority is largely theoretical.

Why should not Kenya, Uganda, and Tanganyika be amalgamated into one federal state? The area is a nice natural unit, and incorporation of the Africans in Uganda and Tanganyika (which are almost solidly black) into a composite government would make a better balance with the Kenya whites.

[14] The shilling is divided not into pennies as in England, but into cents on the decimal system.

But, even though the idea may seem logical, there are vociferously expressed objections to federation. For one thing, the Kenya whites do not want to be further outnumbered by blacks. For another the blacks in Uganda and Tanganyika fear equally to come under the influence of white Kenya. Again, Tanganyika is a UN trust territory, and its amalgamation with Kenya and Uganda would present touchy constitutional problems. East African Federation is, in other words, not a likely prospect.[15]

We should have a word, finally, on the Capricorn Society, an organization standing for closer relations between all the East and Central African countries on a multiracial basis. Capricorn believes in federation, but not in white supremacy. Multiracial executive committees have been set up by the Capricorn people in Nairobi, Salisbury (Southern Rhodesia) and Dar es Salaam, with an ambitious program. The inventor and president of Capricorn, Colonel David Stirling, had a brilliant war record, and since 1949 has devoted himself largely to African development. Capricorn, he said recently, "rejects both white colonialism and African nationalism in favor of the development of a multiracial society in which, however, western culture and the Christian religion would be dominant."[16] The organization has an almost mystical fervor, and its membership includes Europeans, Africans and Asians.

SCENTED ISLE OF ZANZIBAR

> When the flute is played in Zanzibar, all Africa east of the Lakes must dance.
> —ARAB PROVERB

Zanzibar is the only place I have ever visited where birds nest in the chandeliers of the British Residency, and where I got sunburned in the rain. This is one of the most enticing little domains left in the world—an island some twenty miles off the East African coast near the Equator. The name comes from the Persian *zenj* (black) and means "Country of Blacks." But nowadays Zanzibar is not so much black as a mixture of various browns. It lives mostly on cloves, and the island is permeated by their aromatic scent. The streets are narrow, dark, and almost vaulted; the old houses still have massive teakwood doors, delicately carved and studded with huge brass buttons. Zanzibar is, on the surface, largely an Arab town. It gives a note of secrecy, moistness, and dilapidation. The Sultan has two auto-

---

[15] Another point is that the Tanganyika and Uganda governments are inclined to be somewhat jealous of Kenya, the big white sister; moreover they do not like it that they have to pay part of Kenya's bills.

[16] *African News*, March, 1954.

mobiles, both of which are painted scarlet,[17] and only one building in the city has an elevator. Aside from its pictorial beauty and exoticism, the chief characteristic of Zanzibar is lassitude. "After six months," an English lady told us, "everybody here feels like some awful vegetable."

Zanzibar has a unique political status, being an "independent" sultanate under the protection of Great Britain; it is part of British East Africa, but it regulates most of its own affairs and is not a member of the East Africa High Commission. The Zanzibari are proud of their semi-sovereign position, and do all they can to protect it. Zanzibar is, of course, in the last analysis run by the Colonial Office in London, and nothing is likely to happen locally that is not approved by the British Resident (he is not called a "governor"), but His Highness the Sultan does not like to admit this. British rule is as unobtrusive as possible, and the Sultan and the Resident are on placidly cordial terms.

Zanzibar and Pemba, a neighboring island under the same administration, have a population of 265,000. There are about 200,000 Africans, 45,000 Arabs, and 16,000 Indians, plus minor groups. One of these latter is an oddity among peoples—the Comorians, a Moslem community deriving from islands near Madagascar. We happened to run into a Comorian wedding, and took part in the accompanying festivities; never have I seen a more spookily gleaming spectacle. In one room were several score Moslem women —unveiled—wearing *identical* brown-and-white-flowered dresses festooned with white carnations. The bride, propped up by her groom in an inner chamber, was so paralyzed by emotion that she stood stiff and slanting like a beam of wood. Among hundreds of celebrants, my wife and I were the only westerners, and I was the only man in the whole gathering except musicians and the groom.

The Africans on Zanzibar are divided into two elements—the indigenous "Shirazi" who date from the most ancient times, and who were first conquered by Persians from Shiraz in the eighth century AD, and the "immigrants"—that is, Africans descended from slaves imported by Arabs into Zanzibar from Tanganyika, Nyasaland, and elsewhere in comparatively recent years. The Indians are likewise split up into several communities. The richest and most influential belongs to the Aga Khan.

Africans and Arabs have interbred widely over the course of centuries, and there are probably few Africans today (except recent arrivals) without some touch of Arab blood—and vice versa. The Indians, however, have never mixed at all with either the African or Arab population. Arabs are the aristocracy, the Indians control retail trade, and the Africans work on the

[17] One is an Armstrong-Siddeley, one a Humber.

land. Almost all the clove estates are owned by Arabs or Swahilis. No white settlement is allowed, and there are no European-owned clove properties; the industry is, however, managed by a British-run Clove Growers Association. The infinitesimal European community—306 people in all—consists largely of officials.

Zanzibar has an extraordinarily intricate history. Arabs from Arabia, the Persian Gulf, and elsewhere in the Middle East occupied it and in time spread over to the mainland and founded the Zenj Empire which covered a long coastal strip all the way from Somalia to Mozambique. Arab domination was broken by the Portuguese after 1498. Two centuries later the Arabs ousted the Portuguese and Zanzibar became the biggest—and most hideous—slave entrepôt in the world. Here a literally black market flourished. A man cost less than a goat. The early British explorers called Zanzibar "Stinkibar." In 1832 the Sultan of Muscat, in Oman on the Persian Gulf, moved his capital to Zanzibar, the better to supervise and cash in on the Midas-like profits of the slave trade. Zanzibar had hitherto been a colony in his dominions. This was as if, in a manner of speaking, the United States should have shifted its capital from Washington to Havana in order to keep in closer touch with affairs in Cuba. The ruling house of Zanzibar has been Muscatine ever since.

British missionaries, explorers, and traders appeared on the scene soon after. Zanzibar became their base for penetration into East Africa in the name of the Pax Britannica; Burton, Speke, Livingstone, Kirk, and others used it as a perch. But strangely enough the United States, not Great Britain, was the first western power to establish an actual consulate in Zanzibar (1836).[18] The British did their best to abolish the slave trade, and at the same time maintain amicable relations with successive sultans. Gradually slavery disappeared, but there are old people still alive today who were slaves in their youth—just as men born slaves could be found in the United States until very recently. Eventually Zanzibar became British as a result of an extraordinary deal between Bismarck and Lord Salisbury. The Zenj holdings on the mainland were breaking up, and Germany sought to grab them off. The British gave the Germans Helgoland in the North Sea (1890) in return for a pledge to restrict their East African activities to what is now Tanganyika, and to leave Zanzibar alone. One island was, in effect, swapped for the other.[19] London then consolidated its position in Zanzibar and it became

[18] *Introducing East Africa*, p. 24. A corollary point is that Muscat was the first country with which the United States ever negotiated a foreign treaty. It was designed to protect American sailors on Indian Ocean coasts.

[19] At the same time, to conciliate the French, the British gave up claims to Madagascar.

a British protectorate, although the British had repeatedly promised various sultans to respect its independence.

The present Sultan, by name Seyyid Sir Khalifa Bin Harub, GCMG, GBE, Khalifa II, has been on the throne for forty-four years, and has thus reigned longer than any monarch in the world. Three times he has attended coronations of British monarchs. He was born not in Zanzibar but in Muscat, the source of the family fortunes, in 1879; his dynasty has held rule uninterruptedly for eleven generations. He was a brother-in-law of the preceding Sultan. The British liked and trusted him, and in offering him the throne they chose well. He has always been a pliable—if stately—potentate.

One morning we had a pleasant meeting with the Sultan, who is dignified and intelligent. In general he gave the same impression as other Moslems of similar rank we had met, like King Idris of Libya and the Mahdi of Khartoum. He looks younger than his years, and is a tall man with a heavy short brown-black-white beard; he wore a white robe with red edging and a white and gold embroidered turban. He likes to drive around his island in one of his fire-engine red cars, with only the minimum of escort; he stops here and there, and chats amiably with his subjects. He is neither rich nor greedy, and the British say that the key to his character is kindliness. He bantered with us gently about what words we knew in Swahili (I could only muster two or three, like *simba* for "lion," *bwana* for "master," and *pole-pole* for "slow") and sought to impress upon us the fact that Zanzibar was not merely the most beautiful island in the world, with its glowing beaches, but the most peaceful.

Not only did we meet the Sultan; we met his queen, the youthful and pretty Sultana. Arab potentates, no matter how elderly, always seem to get on well with young wives. This was the first—and only—time we met female royalty in an Arab country. The Sultana wore a western dress, and asked us shyly about things in America and Paris and mentioned how pretty Rita Hayworth was but said that she had seemed "tired" in Zanzibar, which she visited when she was still the daughter-in-law of the Aga Khan. The Sultana only came out of purdah a year or two ago, and, when we saw her, had never been outside Zanzibar except for brief visits to Mombasa and Nairobi. Until she went to Kenya she had never in her life walked down a street or been in a shop.

Zanzibar not only has an authentic monarch; it has an authentic royal pretender, by name Seyyid Soud bin Ali. He is a son of the present Sultan's predecessor, and feels that he was unjustly passed over for the throne. But he makes no trouble, and the British pay him a modest subsidy—reputedly £65 per month—to keep him quiet. His sons are on the official payroll too.

Next to the configuration of the town itself, the most romantic thing about Zanzibar is the long line of dhows in the harbor. These ships, some of which displace four hundred tons or more, are propelled entirely by sail. The dhow traffic depends, of course, on the monsoons, which are as regular as metronomes. From December to February the monsoon blowing from north-north east blows the dhows in from India and the Persian Gulf; then from April to September the wind exactly reverses itself and blows them neatly back. Between monsoons, the Arab crews have a good time in Zanzibar. The straight run from the northern tip of Pemba to Cutch, in India, under the full monsoon, takes two weeks, which is not bad time at all. The westbound dhows bring dates, camels, rugs, and a thatching material called *makuti*; they go back with mangrove poles (for building purposes), shark fins, and perhaps smuggled ivory and rhino horns. Sometimes as many as three hundred dhows are parked in Zanzibar between monsoons.

Zanzibar and Pemba produce 80 per cent of the cloves of the world, and the islands live largely on this fragrant commodity. There are about three million clove trees on Pemba, about a million on Zanzibar itself. The crop is worth from three to four million pounds sterling a year, and the biggest market is Indonesia, where cloves are shredded and mixed with tobacco to make scented cigarettes. India is also an important market. Cloves are the buds of a tree resembling the myrtle. Oil from the stems makes vanillin, a substitute for pure vanilla, and is exported in considerable quantity to the United States. The clove trees were introduced to Zanzibar by an early sultan, who imported them from Mauritius, where they had arrived originally from the Moluccas. The clove industry in Zanzibar today faces grave peril, because the trees have been attacked by a mysterious disease known as Sudden Death. Actually this colorful name is a misnomer, since the malady seems to be associated with senility in the tree, and the trees die gradually, not at once. Another disease called "dieback" is a problem, and so is a coconut pest called *Theraptus*. Nobody knows whether Sudden Death is caused by a virus, a fungus, or by some other instrument of fatality, nor has anybody been able so far to work out a preventive or cure. Sudden Death could kill Zanzibar. The only remedy is to plant new trees, which is expensive.

Zanzibar, even if it may seem to be a cloistered Indian Ocean paradise, does not escape modern political pressures. In June, 1954, the Arab newspaper *Al Falaq* was suppressed and its editor given a choice of a steep fine or a jail sentence, for publishing pro-Communist propaganda and attacking British policy. *Al Falaq* was the organ of the local Arab Association, an important body.

KENYA: BRITISH RULE IN AFRICA

The Zanzibari have several grievances. One is that the Sultan is completely under the thumb of the British Resident and a British private secretary "imposed" on him. Another is that the British altogether dominate the local LEGCO, which has a majority of official members all of whom are appointed by the Resident, and stress unduly the fragmentation of the island between Africans, Indians, and Arabs.[20] Modern-minded Zanzibari want to encourage the growth of a single political organization uniting all the racial groups. Finally, they are strongly irredentist. They look hungrily on the Kenya coastal strip which is technically their territory still, but which the British hold under lease from the Sultan. The mainland Zanzibari are, they say, ruled by Nairobi, whereas they should be under Zanzibar itself.

[20] There are three Arab, two African, one European, and two Indian unofficial members. By tradition the European is always the British manager of the local branch of the National Bank of India.

CHAPTER 20

Kenya: The Mau Maus

When two elephants fight it is the grass that suffers.
—KIKUYU PROVERB

MAU MAU (pronounced like "cow-cow") is the name of an African terrorist society in Kenya, organized mostly in the Kikuyu tribe. The movement is based on secrecy, and its adherents are bound together by a malign oath. "Mau Mau" may mean the organization itself, or any individual member. Its origin is obscure, and it has a complex mystical base; it arose not merely out of Kikuyu grievances against the British, but because of a profound social and psychological upheaval in the Kikuyu people. Its immediate aim is to cause trouble; the eventual aim is probably nothing less than to drive the white man out of Africa. Basically it is a reaction against white society.

The Mau Mau outbreak began in the autumn of 1952 and continues to this day. It has gravely disrupted the normal life of Kenya, and produced a situation close to civil war. Its cost to the British has been £26,500,000 so far, and is almost immeasurable in other than financial fields.

Mau Mau is beyond doubt an anti-white, anti-European movement, but one striking thing about it is, as I have already mentioned, that the terrorists have killed extremely few white men—only fifty-three in more than two years; of these only twenty-five were civilians. Twenty-one Asians have been killed and several thousand loyal Africans. How can the deaths, tragic as they were, of only a handful of Europeans and Asians paralyze an entire community? The best answers to this are that Mau Mau may be a premonition of the future as well as a manifestation of the present, that it has created a semi-revolutionary situation even if the European casualties have been so light, that there would have been many more deaths if precautions were not so strict, and that the murderers are hard to catch. It does not take many murders to create an amosphere of fear and hysteria. Nobody knows who is going to be killed next. Why have not the Mau Mau gangsters attacked more European officials? I never heard a really satisfactory answer to this question. Probably the chief reason is that Europeans are so well protected.

By far the greatest number of those butchered by the Mau Mau are, then, Africans. Why were these slain? Mostly because they were Kikuyus who remained loyal and accordingly refused to take the Mau Mau oath, in spite of formidable pressures to make them do so, or because they became informers. The Mau Mau wanted above all (like gangsters in Chicago) to enforce conformity.

The Mau Maus, on their side, have lost at least eight thousand men killed. The British, with the life of the colony at stake, have acted against terrorists (when they could lay their hands on them) with merciless severity. No fewer than 505 Kikuyus have been executed so far. Even more notable is the fact that only 223 of these 505 were hanged for actual murder. One hundred and seventy-two were hanged for unlawful possession of firearms, 88 for "consorting" with terrorists, 14 for administering unlawful oaths, 6 for "acting with intent to further terrorism," and 2 for procuring supplies for terrorists.[1] All these offenses are capital crimes in Kenya under the emergency. Liberal opinion in London has been much aroused by the infliction of punishment so Draconian for crimes other than outright murder. Moreover these figures refer only to legal executions. Hundreds of other Kikuyus, terrorists or merely people suspected of being terrorists, have been shot out of hand. Any white man had the right to challenge any African in the danger areas while we were in Kenya, and shoot to kill if he did not respond.

"I saw a Kuke jump off the train as it was pulling into the station this morning," a white hunter told us blandly. "I pulled out my gun and called 'Halt!' and, damn it all, the fellow halted. I could have bagged him easily."

OUT IN THE MAU MAU COUNTRY

There are other British types. We drove out to Fort Hall, which was officially known as "a maximum danger area," and District Officer J. H. Candler, a cheerful, blond, vigorous young man, met us. He was thirty-two. We squeezed into his Land Rover, and took off. He carried a revolver and a Bren gun, and in the front of the car were stacked three shotguns. An *askari* (native policeman) sat on the rear seat, his rifle cocked.

Candler's boyishness, his robust zest and idealism, impressed me. He spoke out: "I love Africa. I love these people—even the Kukes. I hate to leave my work here, even to go home on leave. Reckon I'm a bit of a savage myself.

[1] *East Africa and Rhodesia*, July 22, 1954.

This crisis has set us back thirty years. What we have to do is restore confidence—confidence and trust in *us*. This bloody wretched terror must be stamped out, but only the Kikuyus themselves can solve the Kikuyu problem. We can help, we *must* help, but this is Africa, and the Africans have to learn how to manage this country by themselves. If they don't want us any more, why, we'll have to pack up and go. We can't run the Empire by force any longer."

Candler slammed on the brakes, as a Kikuyu suddenly stepped out of the bush onto the bright red sticky road. He exclaimed "Ah!" cheerfully and handed him one of the shotguns, with six cartridges. This Kikuyu was an informer—a native working with the British against the Mau Maus. He had been attacked twice, but miraculously got away with his life. I cannot describe adequately how the Kikuyu's teeth glistened, how his eyes rolled with relief, as he fondled the precious shotgun proudly. It had been promised to him for a long time. Now he was armed, and he could defend himself and repel attack. "Good show!" cried Candler, as we set off again. "Can't afford to lose that chap."

The road wound through rough ravines, green as rust on copper, and over steep country where the soil has been almost eroded to death. We saw a dead dog, and Candler slammed on the brakes again. He wanted to see if it had died a natural death, or had been strangled by the Mau Mau. To frighten other Africans, and to show the power of their secret omnipresence, the terrorists often kill or mutilate animals—sometimes they crucify them—and expose their carcasses in some conspicuous spot.

This dog had died naturally, and we went on.

I asked Candler what the chances of ambush were on this particular section of lonely road closed in by thick, dark vegetation that looked like green smoke.

"About one in thirty. Two ambushes here last week."

The British troops and police have several aims, Candler told us calmly. First to catch terrorists, of course. Second—more important basically—to prove to the people at large that they, the British, are stronger, more powerful, than the Mau Maus. One weapon to this end is collective punishment. "It's cruel, but it works." If a murder is committed, all people in the immediate area are subject to fines. The punishment the Kikuyus hate and fear most is confiscation of their livestock. They would rather lose their women than their cattle. "But we hate to have to punish innocent people. We want to *bring them around!*"

Most murders are committed by outside gangs who descend on the *shambas* at night. Hence, the British have stopped all bus traffic, and a

KENYA: THE MAU MAUS

strict curfew is in force. As a result the entire economic life of the region has broken down. Women cannot get their produce to market, and thousands of squatters who moved into the reserve from the adjacent Highlands are near starvation.

Mau Mau methods of murder are, as everybody knows, peculiarly atrocious. Aside from stolen firearms, the terrorists have three chief weapons: the *panga*, a long, heavy knife like a machete; the *simi*, a double-edged sword shaped like a scythe; and the *rumgu*, a nail-studded wooden club. When the Mau Maus kill with *pangas*, the victim may be literally sliced to pieces or chopped to bits. One reason for this is that every member of the attacking gang must join in the kill by actual participation with a weapon, so that all are equally guilty and nobody can inform on anybody else. Often the eyeballs of the victim are removed, so that he cannot "see" after death who his killers were. The Kikuyus are profoundly superstitious people.

Of all things connected with Mau Mau, the most exceptional—as well as horrible—is the oath. When a Kikuyu enters into the organization, or is forcibly inducted into it, he takes an oath, which is one reason why the movement has such a compulsive hold on people. If a member attempts to give up his allegiance, thus breaking his oath, other Mau Maus will do their best to track him down and murder him. Oath taking has always been part of the tradition of the Kikuyu tribe, and oaths per se do not have any sinister connotation. Methods of administering the hideous Mau Mau oath vary in different districts, but the general procedure is something like this, Candler told us. The candidate for admittance is brought at night to a lonely forest hut, and crawls through an arch of banana leaves, muttering an incantation seven times. The number seven is important, and refers to the seven orifices of the human body. Then the eyes are gouged out of a sheep, and placed over the candidate's eyes, temporarily blinding him, while he licks a mixture of blood, excrement, and juices from the sheep's eye. He repeats the oath, which is administered by a witch doctor or elder of the tribe, phrase by phrase; this commits him among other things to murder anybody who may be assigned to him as a victim, even if it is a close relative or his best friend. Other ceremonies take place too obscene for mention. An incidental point is that there is a sizable initiation fee, ranging up to 62.50 shillings ($8.75), the equivalent of a month's wages or more. This makes the oath doubly serious, and collection of these fees gives considerable economic power to the Mau Mau organization.

We drove from Kangema to a village called Kanyenyena, through the heart of the Kikuyu country. We sat in on a *barazza* (conference, literally "veranda") between Candler and his men in the neighborhood. Not far away is the sacred acacia tree which marks the spot where the tribe sprung into existence six or seven hundred years ago. Presently we reached a bare, shallow hillside, and here came the climax to our journey. Mr. Candler was superintending a purification or "de-oathing" ceremony this day, and we were privileged to watch it. Very few people indeed, except officials, have ever seen one of these ceremonies; my wife was the first white woman ever to have been present at one. In some ways it was the most remarkable single experience we had in Africa.

The idea of employing witchcraft, which the British have been trying to stamp out for a generation, as a weapon for combating other witchcraft was repugnant to many Britons, and it was adopted only with deep reluctance. In brief, the aim of the authorities is to break the formidable grip of Mau Mau on the Kikuyus by giving them a different, alternative, more powerful oath, administered by one of their own witch doctors loyal to the British cause. The new oath is supposed to do away with the necessity of obeying the Mau Mau oath, and clear people of the taint of having taken it. But the text of the counteroath is framed so that nobody has to admit that he *has* ever actually taken the Mau Mau oath, even if he has.

"The last time we had an oath ceremony, two Kikuyus fainted dead away," Mr. Candler told us. "They were terrified of what the Mau Maus might do to them later. Stout fellows, to dare to take our oath."

Hills surrounded a bowl of grass, and here three groups of Africans were waiting out in the sparkling sun. The largest, numbering about three hundred, sat clustered in a loose circle, almost as if in an amphitheater, solemn, silent, with their black close-cropped heads glistening in the strong light. These were villagers who, whether they had ever been Mau Maus or not, were prepared to risk their lives by taking the cleansing oath, renouncing Mau Mau, and swearing fealty to Queen Elizabeth. They had come quite voluntarily. They wanted to prove their loyalty.

The second group was smaller—about thirty men—made up of Kikuyus arrested for alleged complicity in Mau Mau, or who had been convicted of minor violations of law. They sat on a different hill, and were guarded by a handful of *askaris*. They were brought here by the authorities to learn a lesson from the ceremony. If they renounced terrorism and took the oath, their sentences might be remitted. They looked sullen.

Members of the third group stood isolated across the orange-red road, armed with spears. They were members of the local Home Guard, recruited from loyal Kikuyus who were willing to fight Mau Mau to the death and risk their lives doing so. Contemptuously, they refused to mix with the other groups. They were haughty and defiant. Candler introduced us to their chief. His house had been burned down twice by terrorists, and his wife murdered. His costume was a short brown burlap sack over one shoulder, and he wore a brown fedora hat with a feather. His ears were pierced, with the loop hooked up over the top of the ear.

The fresh sunshine seemed to be blown toward us by the sharp wind. Impatiently we waited for the native witch doctor, who, under Candler's supervision, would administer the cleansing oath. Black faces, with rolling white eyes, watched us, as a portable desk was set up at the bottom of the hollow. Candler made a speech in Swahili, which was then interpreted into Kikuyu by one of his native assistants. In each language, we could catch untranslatable English words like "home guard."

Illustrated propaganda leaflets were passed around, and, still squatting on the ground like school children, the Kikuyu read these intently. They chattered and nudged one another. Candler then announced that thirty men would be chosen out of the three hundred, admitted to the Home Guard, and given spears. The group crackled with excitement.

At last a truck drove up, and the witch doctor arrived. He was a tall, elderly African whose father and grandfather before him had been witch doctors. He wore a hat of black feathers with a white plume, gold bracelets, a long robe, and a red scarf around his neck fastened by a large safety pin. An assistant witch doctor, in staid European dress, accompanied him carrying a small cardboard suitcase. He walked with neat little steps lugging the incongruous-looking suitcase. In this was the Githathi, or sacred stone.

This stone, holy to the Kikuyus, is a lump of gray-red rock, pierced by seven holes that symbolize the seven openings of the human body. Carefully it was taken out of the suitcase and propped on a tri-forked stick, in front of Mr. Candler and the venerable witch doctor. People shuddered. One Kikuyu opened his mouth, and his teeth, like the ends of piano keys, chattered. The magic represented by the holy stone is very strong magic indeed.

One by one, men sitting on the lip of hill advanced to where the witch doctor sat. They walked with a nervous falter and then bent forward, rigid and slanting, almost as if in a trance. The witch doctor gave each in turn a sheaf of sharp, stiff bamboo twigs. With sober intensity they plunged these one at a time into the seven orifices of the sacred stone, jabbing them back and forth with a quick, heavy rhythm, while muttering the oath—all of this in the name of Queen Elizabeth!

The oath, translated into English, goes as follows:

> If I have never taken the Mau Mau oath, I will never take it voluntarily. If I do, let this oath slay me.

If I am forced to take the Mau Mau oath, I will report and confess. If I fail to do this, let this oath slay me.

I will do everything I can to help the government suppress Mau Mau. If I do not, let this oath slay me.

If I am made to vomit [repudiate] this oath, let this Githathi slay me.

If in future I do not supply to the government any information, already known to me or which I will know in the future, let this oath slay me.

I swear that I am and always will be a loyal subject of Her Majesty's Government and Queen Elizabeth.

Cheerfully, buoyantly, Mr. Candler superintended the proceedings. He might have been refereeing a football game. "I don't think there are more than thirty or forty outright malefactors, thugs, in this whole area with 100,000 people. I could handle this whole business myself, if I could catch those thirty or forty." Decency and optimism radiated out of this young man.

Next week six of the Home Guard men who stood silently with their spears across the road while we watched the ceremony were murdered. A few months later Candler himself was killed. He was ambushed and shot down by the Mau Maus on the same road we had taken that sunny morning. I hope his murderers have been caught and given the punishment they deserve.

KENYA, THE KIKUYU, AND KENYATTA

> *Mau Mau is only the first of these compulsive African protests. The fact that its obscenities have so far been met only by brutal and completely uncomprehending repression has intensified the racial hatred which is tearing Kenya apart. In South Africa the White Herrenvolk is big enough to hold its own in a race war for many years. In Kenya, and indeed in all East Africa, it can only save itself from extinction by abdicating its privileges while there is still time. But that means giving up the dream of White ascendancy; and, though there are stirrings of conscience in Nairobi, I met no one who seriously contemplated doing that.*
> —R. H. S. CROSSMAN

I have already written a good deal about the Kikuyu (pronounced "Kick-oo-you"), but much still remains to be said. The Kikuyus are the largest and most powerful tribe in Kenya and one of the most outstanding in all Africa. We have come a long way now from primitive peoples like the Fuzzy-Wuzzys or the Danakils. In most of this book hereafter, we shall be dealing with African tribes much more advanced.

But the first time I saw a Kikuyu elder, up in the highlands near Nyeri,

I thought from a distance that he had the most extraordinary earrings I had ever seen—great loops stretching down almost to the shoulder, and hung with bells. Then, coming closer, it became apparent that these were not only earrings, but *ears*. Kikuyus often pierce the lobes of their ears and hang weights on them, so that the lobes become hollow nooses, or loops, on which ornaments—even padlocks—may be suspended. The more ornaments a man carries in his ears, the more respected is he in the community. If by ill luck one of the lobes breaks, he gravely loses face.

The Kikuyus are polygamous, and have strong religious instincts; they have always been used to elaborate rituals. They live in a highland area and have a balanced diet; so they are a healthy people by and large. They were forest dwellers originally, who became expert agriculturalists; few people in Africa—or elsewhere—are better farmers. When they began to erupt out of their reserves, on account of population pressure and for other reasons, and spread and seep into the towns, they became Europeanized (at least on the surface) with marked speed and ease; they learned skilled trades quickly, and became good chauffeurs, carpenters, and so on. Eighty per cent of workers on the railway are—or were—Kikuyu. They are lively, enterprising, and ambitious.

One thing remarkable about their tribal organization is that, like the Ibos in Nigeria—whom they resemble in other respects—they had no chiefs. The British, trying to make Indirect Rule work, improvised chiefs and sought to impose them on the Kikuyus, but the effort was a failure. The Kikuyus were too democratic, too individualistic, too suspicious of western influence, and too deeply devoted to their anciently entrenched institutions. Their organization is not based on direct authority or a chain of command, but on a honeycomb system, built on age groups. This decentralized, cellular organization made the Kikuyus particularly vulnerable to Mau Mau penetration, and at the same time added greatly to the difficulties of the British. The Mau Maus were "hydra-headed." Lop off one polyp, and another grew. The Kikuyus would also, by reason of their organization, provide a perfect field for large-scale Communist infiltration into Kenya, if that should ever come. The cell structure is already there.[2]

Multitudes of Kikuyus, who are industrious as well as clever, went to mission schools, and became Christian. But in many cases the crust of Christianity was thin. The tribesmen deserted their own gods, but did not absorb the new God fully; this has contributed substantially to their instability. Moreover some Kikuyus, having become genuinely Christian, dis-

[2] See the London *Times*, "Nationalism in Kenya," November 13, 1952, and "Background to Mau Mau," March 1, 1954.

covered that many European Christians were not truly Christian at all, and did not practice what they preached; this caused sharp disillusion and resentment. Their own *separatist* Christian churches arose and flourished, and various pseudo-Christian sects came into being, which helped lead the way to Mau Mau. These were, taking into consideration the differences in background, something like the crackpot revivalist groups that have been pestiferous in California and the American south. They were led by black fundamentalists, who in time came to revolt against all authority.[3]

Also, a remarkable point, the Kikuyus had gumption and resource enough to organize their own school system, something almost unprecedented for Africa. It was badly needed. The Kenya government provided practically no schools for Africans until the 1930's, and the Kikuyus boycotted the Christian mission schools, because of their resentment at missionary attacks on female circumcision.[4] So the Kikuyus, to take care of their own youth, created the Kikuyu Independent Schools Association. To make this work they had to have teachers as well, and a man of great vision, Peter Koinange, founded the Kenya Teachers College at Githunguri. Later Jomo Kenyatta became the principal and leading influence of this. Inevitably these schools became hotbeds of Kikuyu nationalism. They were suppressed by the British authorities after the outbreak in 1952.

Long before the Mau Mau crisis the Kikuyus had their own political organizations. As far back as 1922 the Kikuyu Central Association was formed by Harry Thuku; its objective was to regain the "lost lands" in the White Highlands. Jomo Kenyatta was Secretary General of this body, and it steadily became more overtly anti-white and nationalist. It was dissolved and outlawed by the government during World War II. Then it rose again in the form of the Kenya African Union, commonly known as "KAU," in 1944. This was not exclusively a Kikuyu organization, but sought to draw membership from other tribes. It was well organized, with Jomo Kenyatta as president, and soon had almost a hundred thousand members. The British, probably with a good deal of reason, thought that it was nothing but the old insurrectionary KCA on a broader base and under a new name, and they watched its activities with care. But almost all African politicians of consequence became members of the KAU, including those most respectable, and it was difficult for the authorities to move against it. KAU leaders deny hotly that their organization ever had anything to do with the Mau Mau outbreak. The fact that a man may be anti-British does not, they say reasonably enough, necessarily mean that he believes in violence and murder.

[3] Negley Farson (*Last Chance in Africa*) describes these sects fully. Also see Leakey, *Mau Mau and the Kikuyu*, pp. 91-92.
[4] See Chapter 17 above.

The British, on the contrary, believe now that the KAU was the secret fountainhead of Mau Mau, and it was suppressed and outlawed in June, 1953. But its leading members (except Kenyatta and F. W. Odede) were not arrested or interned, and several KAU men, even though the organization itself does not legally exist, still hold their posts in LEGCO or on other organs of the government, like Eliud Mathu and W.W.W. Awori.

We happened to be in Nairobi when Odede, the vice-president of KAU and a member of LEGCO, was picked up by the police at 4 A.M., held without trial, and spirited away to a place of internment near Mombasa. He has not yet been tried. The authorities do not want to risk another trial like that of Kenyatta. What interested me most about Odede's arrest was the attitude of several of his closest African associates. The British claimed not only that they had evidence that Odede was a member of Mau Mau, but that he had been spreading subversive doctrine in tribes other than Kikuyu. His African friends in Nairobi could not believe that Odede, their colleague whom they saw every day, could possibly be a secret member of the Mau Mau conspiracy and a terrorist.

Finally, the Kikuyus not only had their own churches, schools, and political organization; they had a real leader, Jomo Kenyatta. He was—and is —an extraordinarily interesting man. Kenyatta was educated in a Scottish mission school near Nairobi, and is about sixty. He was an orphan, and the missionaries named him "Johnstone"; he did not know his own name. He worked as a kitchen boy, a carpenter, and an inspector for the Nairobi waterworks. Kenyatta could not be kept down. He had brains, push, and magnetism. He joined the KCA when it was formed in 1922, and within a few years became its leader. By 1928 he was publisher of a Kikuyu-language newspaper in Nairobi. Then in 1929 he went to Europe, and lived outside Africa for the next seventeen years.

Mostly he lived in London. He married an English girl, and had a child by her. He studied at the London School of Economics, became a protégé of Professor Malinowski, the well-known anthropologist, and wrote a book almost blatant in its pride of Kikuyu national customs, *Facing Mount Kenya*. It was during the London years that he adopted the name Kenyatta, with its obvious symbolic connection with his country, Kenya.[5] For the most part he lived as African students in those days usually lived in England; he was poor; he experienced plenty of discrimination and humiliation; yet he found friends and intellectual companionship. Never for a second did he lose his burning, defiant interest in his homeland. With Kwame Nkrumah (now prime minister of the Gold Coast) he helped organize a left wing pan-Africa congress that met in Manchester in 1945. Also Kenyatta visited

[5] London *Observer*, November 2, 1952.

Russia several times, something that Nkrumah never did, and studied anthropology at the University of Moscow. He was well received—the Russians made a practice then as now of trying to capture bright African students—and he would hardly even have gone there if he had not been a strong Communist sympathizer, but so far as is known he was never an outright member of the party.

Kenyatta returned to Kenya in 1946. At once he became the dominating factor in the Independent Schools Association and the KAU. His main focus of influence was the Teachers College. He stood far above other Kikuyu leaders, if only because of the force and sting of his personality. He was (and is) a heavy-set man, uncouth, powerful looking, with flamboyant habits in dress and dramatic mannerisms—vain, hypnotic, and capricious. Over the Kikuyus, he began to have an influence almost magical; in particular his appeal was overwhelming to Kikuyu women.

Kenyatta is an archetypical example of the westernized, educated Kikuyu —so one might assume. But read the dedication with which he begins his book:

> To . . . all the dispossessed youth of Africa; for perpetuation of communion with ancestral spirits through the fight for African Freedom, and in the firm faith that the dead, the living, and the unborn will unite to rebuild the destroyed shrines.

Then he mentions proudly that his grandfather was a seer and a magician, and that he has witnessed the performance of magic rites many times "in my own house and elsewhere."

When the Mau Mau movement began to appear aboveground, the British asked Kenyatta to help put it down. He agreed to try. They were astounded at the crowds that came to hear him. Any time that he was scheduled to speak, audiences unprecedented in Kenya arrived, numbering 25,000 people or more. The British say that in these speeches Kenyatta double-crossed them; that while telling his followers to give up Mau Mau because terrorism was evil and the KAU a law-abiding organization, he gave secret signs indicating that his real views were the opposite. He could have stopped the movement, the British insist, if he had really wanted to, because his word was law. He told the Kikuyus to stop drinking British beer, and they stopped drinking British beer. He told them to stop wearing British hats, and they stopped wearing British hats. But he did *not* tell them with full sincerity to give up Mau Mau, and the movement spread like wildfire, instead of diminishing. Even after his arrest—in fact even during the trial—we heard time and time again, "The only man in the world who can stop this outbreak is Jomo Kenyatta, and he could stop it in ten minutes."

He did not do so, and once he was taken into custody it was impossible to ask him to do so, because this would have given him too much prestige.

Jomo Kenyatta was arrested on October 21, 1952, on the charge of being "manager" of Mau Mau, and went on trial in November. The trial lasted for more than five months, and was one of the most spectacular ever held in a British colony. It had aspects that, in the views of many, did not add luster to British traditions of justice and fair play. The court did not sit in Nairobi, but in a remote inaccessible village called Kapenguria in the Northern Frontier district, where a schoolhouse was requisitioned for the purpose. Kenyatta and his five codefendants were represented by Mr. Pritt, QC, and a group of Negro and Indian lawyers from outside Kenya, and the magistrate conducted the hearings with technical correctness, but the inconveniences to a full and calm bestowal of justice were considerable. Kapenguria is in the midst of the wilderness; people had to sleep in a town, Kitale, thirty miles away; visitors could not enter the heavily guarded area without special passes; even drinking water had to be brought from Kitale. Mr. Pritt complained on one occasion that he did not even *get* a drink of water during the first four weeks at Kapenguria. He also complained that his mail was opened and his telephone tapped. This the British authorities denied indignantly. There was an acute shortage of trained secretarial help, and some testimony had to be taken down in longhand. There was no law library, and sometimes when people wanted documents they could only be had in Nairobi three hundred miles away. The atmosphere was one of turbulence and intimidation. People said of the magistrate who was called out of retirement to hear the case, "If he finds Kenyatta guilty the Mau Maus will murder him; if he doesn't, the white settlers will."

Kenyatta was found guilty on April 8, 1953, and sentenced to seven years in jail. The most extraordinary precautions were taken throughout Kenya, especially in Nairobi, as the day of judgment approached. Some Africans I knew went to Uganda, because they feared a general massacre of blacks by whites if he was acquitted. Following the verdict came complicated legal events. Kenyatta's appeal went all the way to the Privy Council, but was dismissed in July, 1954. Later his property (31.24 acres) in Kaimbu was confiscated, and it was announced that, after his seven years were up, he would be further "subject to restriction orders," that is, he would be obliged to remain in forced exile indefinitely in the Northern Province.

*

No matter what African tribe had happened to live in or near the White Highlands, trouble would have come in time. But that this tribe should have happened to be the volatile, strongly self-conscious Kikuyu, with its combination of violent tribal tradition and brittle veneer of European education, exacerbated the friction that was bound to develop anyway.

Most Britons in Kenya despise Kikuyus; I heard one settler say with perfect seriousness, "There are no Kikuyus on the Nairobi football team. Something must be wrong with a man who doesn't go in for football." Another said, "We have educated the Kukes much too fast. They should have had two hundred years, not forty, to jump from barbarism to the present. They are no more fit for government than to be pilots of jet aircraft. They read *Shakespeare* in the most *filthy* huts!"

Revealingly enough, the British do not recruit Kikuyus into the King's African Rifles, just as they did not allow Bengalis to enter Indian regiments in the old days in India. The Kikuyus, like the Bengalis, were considered to be too intellectualized and unreliable. (The British do not recruit the warlike Masai into the KAR either, but for a totally different reason; the Masai are too martial to be amenable to discipline.)

Coupled with all this was another factor—British ignorance of the Kikuyus. They were a traditional "enigma." Settlers and Kikuyus had lived side by side for fifty years, but very few Englishmen ever bothered to learn their language. Swahili they would attempt to talk; Kikuyu, no. The fact is almost incredible, but of the whole white population of Kenya, around 42,000, only *two* men are believed to have a really good knowledge of the Kikuyu language. One is Professor L.S.B. Leakey, a profound authority, and the other a missionary, the Rev. William Scott Dickson. Incidentally this made it almost impossible to secure adequate interpretation at the Kenyatta trial. Kenyatta of course spoke good English, but other defendants did not. Mr. Leakey acted as an interpreter for a time, but then withdrew. The British would not risk employing a Kikuyu. Somebody suggested that the senior interpreter of the Kenya Supreme Court in Nairobi should be used, since he was presumably above reproach even if he were a Kikuyu, but the allegation was then made—later denied—that this dignitary was none other than Kenyatta's brother![6] These details are minor; what is major is that scarcely any Englishmen in Kenya could talk to the Kikuyus in their own language, and thus establish real contact with them.

One last point should be made in all fairness. I got varying estimates in Nairobi about the percentage of Kikuyus infected by Mau Mau; some people put this as high as 90 per cent, but such a figure is almost certainly an exaggeration. There are tens of thousands—perhaps even hundreds of thousands—of decent, law-abiding Kikuyus who want to end terrorism just

---

[6] London *Times*, January 8, 1953.

as much as the British do. Mr. Candler told us that, in his judgment, at least six out of every ten Kikuyus who had taken the Mau Mau oath had been forced to do so against their will.

The situation in Kenya has two parts. First, the Mau Mau terror must, of course, be stamped out. But, second, this alone will not solve the Kikuyu problem.

BRIEF WORD ON MAU MAU ITSELF

Nobody, even now, knows exactly what the term *Mau Mau* means. Its origin is obscure, although "Mau" occurs as a place name in Kenya geography—there is a Mau forest near the Delamere properties, and a declivity in the Rift Valley known as the Mau Escarpment. One theory is that Mau Mau is a distortion of *uma*, the Kikuyu word for "Quit" or "Get out!" or the Swahili for "oath" (*muma*); another is that it comes from the miaow of a cat, because the terrorists sometimes disemboweled cats in their initiation ceremonies. Still another explanation is that it means "Union of Africa Movement," with the initials reversed. One more is that it derives from an early Kikuyu princess, the daughter of a man named Muumbi who was the legendary father of the tribe.

I first heard the word in New York, before we set out for Africa and before the outbreak; Negro friends told me to watch out for an incipient terrorist movement known as Mau Mau, which was "a kind of black Ku Klux Klan." In Kenya itself, despite ample evidence, nobody paid attention to the possibility of serious trouble until the summer of 1952. For several years before that District Commissioners had been sending in intermittent warnings about organized unrest in the countryside, isolated instances of a new, queer, ominous kind of terrorism, but these were not heeded. The idea that Kenya was all peaches and cream, and that the Mau Mau insurrection was invented overnight by Joma Kenyatta, is of course ridiculous. Responsible Africans also gave warning of sinister trouble to come. Mr. Havelock, a leading white settler, told me that he and his fellows had warned the authorities time after time for more than two years that a severe crisis was impending, but that the government took no action. Sir Philip Mitchell even went so far as to say that reports that East Africa was "seething with unrest" were "inexplicable nonsense."[7] An incidental point is that Mitchell finished his term as governor in June, 1952, but Baring did not

[7] Quoted by Santha Rama Rau in "The Trial of Jomo Kenyatta," *Reporter*, March 16, 1954.

arrive to succeed him until September. For three months Kenya had no governor, and this is when the Mau Maus struck.

In 1953 outraged settlers asked for the appointment of a commission to go into the question of government laxity, negligence, and stupidity, if any, in the months preceding the outbreak. But this proposal was voted down.

As of the time we were in Kenya, many Britons had not the faintest notion of what Mau Mau really meant. It was supposed to be a movement to drive the white man out of Africa, but until Kenyatta was arrested only *one* white person had been killed. There were other factors even more mystifying. What the British hated to concede was that it could have a subtle, serious, deliberate *aim*—namely, to stir up the country to such an extent that blacks would no longer be able or willing to work for whites on the land, which, in turn, would mean in the long run that the whites could not remain profitably in Kenya. Sporadic murders, even though horrible, were one thing—a police matter. But an *organized* terrorist movement was something else again—a revolution. Moreover many Britons did not like to face the fact that *they* might have some responsibility for the outbreak. There were two schools of thought. One was that Mau Mau was not founded on legitimate grievances, but was purely and simply a return by the Kikuyus to animal savagery; the other was that colonial abuses might have had something to do with it all, and that Mau Mau was a reaction to European settlement.[8] The British government even went so far as to commission a medical officer, Dr. J.C. Carothers, to make a psychiatric study of the Kikuyu tribe, in order to throw light on these matters. His report, outlining the psychological turmoil that has afflicted the Kikuyus in recent years, makes a big point of their lack of security. The truth of the matter, of course, is that Mau Mau is a mixture of various elements. A new impulse toward nationalism and political freedom gave focus to the most ancient and primitive discontents. Spiritual unrest became discharged in racial, religious, and economic fields.

To go into more detail, fundamental reasons for Mau Mau are the following:

1. Feeling among the Kikuyus (right or wrong) that they had been defrauded of their land.

2. The squatter system, and overcrowding on the reserves. Forty per cent of agricultural Kikuyus are landless.

3. Detribalization, and the miserable uprooted lives led by the new urban proletariat in Nairobi close to the reserves.

4. Religious factors, as mentioned above.

[8] Professor Max Gluckman, an eminent social anthropologist, and Sir Philip Mitchell debated this issue with some heat in the *Manchester Guardian* recently.

KENYA: THE MAU MAUS

5. The growth of an African educated class, which gave leadership to the disgruntled masses.[9]

6. Above all, the injustices of color bar.

On a subordinate level there have been exacerbations without end. One is (the Africans say) the fact that white farmers in the most congested areas were largely South African, who dutifully mimicked Dr. Malan's implacable hatred of the Negro. Another is that, as the Commonwealth took new forms after World War II, the old true-blue variety of British civil servant tended to disappear, to be replaced (for instance, in the police) by less sympathetic folk who had never seen service in Africa before.

CHRONICLE: WHICH MAY BE SKIPPED

The actual course of events in Kenya since the crisis is beyond the province of this book. We can mention only the highest of high spots. The event bringing Mau Mau activities into the open was the murder of an aged and respected Kikuyu leader, by name Waruhiu, who was killed because he defied the Mau Maus and said that their oath was not binding if taken under duress, and in any case was contrary to Kikuyu tradition. Other outrages followed, and the British were compelled to declare a state of emergency in October, 1952.[10]

The crisis soon became far too grave for the authorities on the spot to handle alone. British troops and—much later—RAF units—arrived, and have been in action ever since. After months of muddle and delay a deputy governor was appointed to take some of the burden off Baring, and General Sir George W.E.J. Erskine assumed over-all military command.[11] The Mau Maus hid in the Aberdares and on the slopes of Mount Kenya, and were almost impossible to track down and root out. The hard core of the organization probably never exceeded seven hundred determined men, but these were enough to keep the whole land inflamed.[12]

By every means, the British sought to persuade the country folk that they had not sent in troops as oppressors or aggressors, but to protect law-

---

[9] See Oden Meeker, *Report on Africa*, p. 305.

[10] One of the first actions London took was, of all things, to send a *cruiser* to Mombasa! This was in the true imperial tradition. Fifty years before, it might even have worked. But as a threat to Mau Maus deep in the forest it had about as much effect as a toy fire engine.

[11] Erskine was succeeded by Major General G. W. Lathbury in 1955.

[12] Colin Legum in the London *Observer*, August 25, 1953. Other authorities say 2000 to 6000.

abiding Africans. About 50,000 loyal Kikuyu joined the British-led Home Guard. The Mau Mau responded to this with a hideous massacre at Lari, where several hundred perfectly innocent Africans were driven from their homes and butchered in a mass slaughter. This (March, 1953) was the worst single outrage in the whole revolt.

One singular event was the capture of the terrorist leader who called himself "General China," and an attempt, which fell through at the last moment, to use him to effect the surrender of large Mau Mau contingents. Another development—an ugly one—was a kind of head-hunting contest among Britons; prizes were given for the most Mau Maus killed in battle, and so on, until public opinion in London forced a stop to the practice. One British officer was sentenced to five years in jail for torturing suspects. It is a substantial tribute to English character that, in the midst of a crisis which tore everybody's nerves to bits, the few Britons who lost their heads and behaved badly were promptly punished—by British courts. Another development, about which pages might be written, was "Operation Anvil," one of the most spectacular man hunts in all history. Some fifty *thousand* Kikuyu in Nairobi were arrested and screened in an attempt to break up the connection between Kikuyu leadership in the city and the terrorists out in the countryside. Those found innocent of any taint were released. But, as of the moment of writing, tens of thousands are still being held in detention camps. Nairobi has almost ceased to exist as a normally functioning city. The over-all figures are staggering. So far 165,462 Africans have been arrested in all, 136,117 screened, 68,984 tried, and 12,924 convicted.[13]

The Mau Mau movement will, in time, be crushed just as the terrorism in Malaya was finally crushed. It is almost impossible for the British to get peace by negotiation, because in that case the Africans will think that they have won. So, man by man, clump of bush by clump of bush, the whole Kikuyu area has to be painfully and laboriously combed out. One result—not unnaturally—has been the virtual cessation of emigration by whites into Kenya. Few would-be settlers want to be greeted with a *panga* in the bowels.

IS MAU MAU COMMUNIST?

No.

Allegations that the Mau Mau conspiracy is Communist-inspired, or that the terrorists are supplied with arms from Soviet Russia, or are led by

[13] *African Affairs*, July, 1954, p. 198.

KENYA: THE MAU MAUS

Russian agents, are nonsensical. No responsible British authority on the spot gives them any credence whatever.

It is true, on the other hand, that Jomo Kenyatta spent some time in Moscow, that contact has probably taken place between Mau Mau leaders and Indian intellectuals, some of whom may be Communist, and that Russian broadcasts in Swahili are heard—but to a minor extent—in East Africa. It is also true that the Russians, even if they have nothing to do with the Mau Mau uprising, will be delighted to exploit it to the uttermost.

The official Soviet line on Mau Mau is that it does not exist, but has been invented by the British imperialists to give them a pretext for maintaining colonial rule by force. The Moscow journal *Trud* wrote something characteristically idiotic early in 1954: "To justify their bloody deeds the colonizers set in motion a myth about Mau Mau, a secret terrorist organization operating allegedly in Kenya ... In reality, no such organization has ever existed."[14]

Official relations between the Kenya government and the Soviet Union are quite normal. Recently Kenya began to export beef to Russia for the first time.

MAU MAU: WILL IT SPREAD?

This is a worrying possibility particularly if Mau Mau should seep into those tribes from which native police and the King's African Rifles are mainly recruited. Luckily—for the British—most other tribes in Kenya, like the Masai and the Kamba, dislike Kikuyus, and are reluctant to join any movement which they dominate. There is very little intertribal sense in Kenya. But one of the defendants in the Kenyatta trial was a Luo, and in June, 1954, about 170 Wakamba were arrested for complicity in Mau Mau. About 3,000 Wakamba are believed to have taken the Mau Mau oath so far, and this is a serious matter. The Wakamba number 600,000, and occupy the strategic center of the country.

Boundaries between colonies mean nothing to most Africans, and they have always been permitted free movement between Kenya, Tanganyika, and Uganda. But Uganda and Tanganyika do not want any Mau Mau troubles, and so strict frontier controls have been established. Kikuyus already in Tanganyika (also some Masai) have made trouble,[15] and Uganda is stopping any suspicious Kikuyus from entering the country. Every effort is, in short, being made to confine Mau Mau strictly to the Kikuyus and keep it inside Kenya.

[14] Quoted by *East Africa and Rhodesia*, April 8, 1954.
[15] See Chapter 22 below.

SOME AFRICAN GRIEVANCES AND ATTITUDES

When we were in Nairobi Africans could not:
1. Buy a drink of hard liquor[16]
2. Go out at night without a pass
3. Carry arms
4. Assemble publicly or privately, even in groups of three or four, or listen to their leaders
5. Buy land in the White Highlands
6. Grow coffee or sisal, except under certain restrictions (The Africans say that the British imposed this ban to keep coffee and sisal prices up.)
7. Go to "white" restaurants, night clubs, movies, and the like, or use a European public toilet
8. Put on their own dances or *ngomas*, or give playlets traditional to tribal life
9. Vote (except in the most vestigial way)

*

Grievances over education, low wages and intolerably bad housing conditions existed of course long before the Mau Mau emergency, but have become intensified. One sore point has been that Africans in the civil service get only three-fifths of the pay of whites (the famous "three-fifths rule") for the same work. This injustice is so manifest that, at long last, steps are being taken to rectify it. Until the 1954 reforms not a single African had ever reached a major post in the Kenya civil service.[17] Perhaps they did not have sufficient education. But also they had been deliberately kept from education and thus denied any possibility of advance.

Before the crisis, there were at least twenty Kikuyu newspapers, which were read avidly by a substantial audience. Today there are none; all have been suppressed. An official known as the Registrar of Printing Presses can, in effect, shut down any publication. As a result Africans have no

---

[16] Alcohol, except beer, has been forbidden to natives in most of East, Central, and South Africa ever since the Congo treaties partitioning the continent, which were reaffirmed in 1919 by the Treaty of St. Germain en Laye. The ban on spirits was not designed as a repressive measure, but on the contrary was put into effect to protect Africans from the evils of the liquor traffic. Of course, the fact that they could not drink legally made them easier to control. Similarly reservation Indians in the United States were forbidden alcohol. The prohibition is fiercely resented nowadays. It makes Africans feel not only that they are inferior citizens, but children, and a huge traffic exists in illegal alcohol.

[17] *Attitude to Africa*, a Penguin Special, p. 49.

contact with themselves except by word of mouth. Moreover, as mentioned above, the Independent Schools and the Teachers College have been closed.

Education is the most painful of all topics in Kenya. I have already mentioned that there are only thirty-five high schools in the entire country for 5½ million Africans!—and only a small percentage of African children of primary school age actually go to school. "As soon as we educate them," I heard a white man say, "they kick us in the teeth." And I heard a black man say, "They do educate a few of us and some of us even get to Oxford; then they kick *us* in the teeth."[18]

But the grievance that outrides all other grievances is the thwarted feeling of most Africans, Mau Mau crisis or no Mau Mau crisis, that they are outcasts in their own country, inferiors who do not belong fully to society. But Africans—some of them—can still laugh, even if the laughter is sardonic. For instance, it pleases them vastly that the two British colonies that are insolvent, Kenya and Southern Rhodesia, are those with the largest proportion of white settlers.

I asked two African members of LEGCO if they thought that Kenya was fit for self-government as yet. They both answered at once, "Of course not." But they want a declaration of intention from the British government and, if possible, a timetable.

KENYA: TO SUM UP

One. Bullets alone cannot solve the Mau Mau problem. No less a person than General Sir George Erskine, who was British commander-in-chief, said, "There is no military answer to Mau Mau; it is purely a political problem of how Europeans, Africans, and Asians can live in harmony."[19]

Two. Mau Mau is, in essence, a war between black and white, and every educated African on the continent is watching it. It is not too much to say that the future of the white man in Africa depends on the outcome. I do not mean that, if the Mau Mau movement spreads, the Africans can push the Europeans into the sea. But they can make it appallingly difficult and expensive for them to stay.

Three. No solution is possible for Kenya's troubles without African participation. The dream, held by some Britons, of making it a white supremacy state in perpetuity, is gone forever.

---

[18] It should also be pointed out that there are plenty of Africans who *oppose* education for their children. They think that they learn "wrong things" and that the process is too expensive. Many parents depend for part of their living on the labor of their children. Negley Farson discusses this in *Last Chance in Africa,* pp. 122 and following.

[19] Quoted in an article by Colin Legum in *London Calling,* May 6, 1954.

Four. The beginnings of multiracial government have come, but this cannot possibly work successfully unless Africans get a higher standard of living (and "standard of living" means more than just pounds and shillings) and until color bar is broken down. Also there must be (a) land reform; (b) more education; (c) an attempt to build up villages and a middle class.

Five. Kenya needs development cryingly, but, as is only too obvious, white capital will not come into the country unless it is peaceable. Kenya has, in a word, no economic future at all unless it solves its racial problem.

Six. Kenya is nowhere near being ready for self-government as yet, and still needs a prolonged period of tutelage, but tutelage cannot proceed in an atmosphere poisoned by disharmony. The British want to make out of it something like the Central African Federation in Rhodesia and stay indefinitely, but this will be impossible in the long run if they do not face squarely the fact that Kenya is an African country.

CHAPTER 21

East Africa: Animals

> The lion will never attack a White, if he can get a Black.
> —THE MODERN TRAVELLER
>
> Th' unwieldy elephant,
> To make them mirth, us'd all his might, and wreath'd
> His lithe proboscis.
> —PARADISE LOST

LIONS can travel at a speed of about thirty-five miles an hour, if they are charging you or in a hurry to get away, and they are fantastically strong; a large lion can drag away a whole zebra—something that it would take ten men to lift. The lion is the king of beasts, but a pair of wild dogs can drive him off a hill. Invariably, however, he retires with dignity. The full moon strongly affects lions. The lion's honeymoon lasts about three weeks, and during this period neither partner likes to be disturbed. (We came across a pair of honeymooning lions near Nairobi; they rolled around in the tall grass frolicking and nudging one another robustly with the utmost good spirits; the male tired of this pastime after a while, and, crossing the road, wandered past our station wagon, scraping its fender.) The male stays near his mate during her pregnancy, 108 days, and often continues to be a family man till the cubs are grown, say at eighteen months. The female is in heat once every three years; this is a device on the part of nature to give her ample time to protect her young until the new litter comes along. Sometimes the male becomes bored with his family, and wanders off; sometimes he returns and, if in a bad temper and the lioness is not watching carefully, will eat a cub or two. It is the female, not the male, who as a rule kills game for the family. In the old days, if a man was badly mauled by a lion, chances of recovery were apt to be slim, because filth in the lion's mouth almost always caused serious infection; nowadays if medical help is nearby and penicillin is available, superficial wounds are seldom fatal. But five hundred Africans were killed by man-eaters near Ubena, Tanganyika, in 1946–47. Eating the body of another animal, the lion begins at the tail, and then works forward.[1] The largest number of lions ever seen in a single pride by Colonel Mervyn H. Cowie, director of the Royal National Parks of Kenya, was thirty-three. A pride of nine killed three wildebeests sixty yards from the main runway of East African Airlines, at Nairobi West Airport, while we were in Kenya in 1953. There are lions all over Africa from the Niger to the Zambesi and below, except in the central Congo. The bush there is too heavy for their comfort. Lions are inclined to be lazy, and are tolerant if not attacked. Their roar can be audible at a distance of six or seven miles. A good lion weighs 450 pounds.

The rhinoceros is a beast both stupid and unpleasant; he may weigh as much as a ton and a half, and can charge at twenty miles per hour. He has bad eyesight and a bad temper, and is one of the few African animals which, unprovoked, will attack a jeep or car. In half a dozen houses in Nairobi we saw snapshots proudly displayed of rhinos charging vehicles. Rhinos look both armorplated and antediluvian. They cover their own dung, rooting it up and over with their horns; these are not, as is commonly supposed, made of ivory, but consist of closely packed hair, which can be loose at the tip. Nevertheless the horns are hard as iron. The largest ever taken in Kenya measured 56½ inches. They have the reputation, when powdered and eaten, of being a powerful aphrodisiac, and a big market for them is India. People tell all sorts of tall stories about rhinos. One is of the man who burned out the clutch of his car traveling near Nairobi; he calmly shot the nearest rhino, repaired the clutch with rhino hide, and proceeded on his way unperturbed. Trapping a rhinoceros is a somewhat formidable undertaking. The beast is caught by a noose, and then tired out by being chained to a log attached to a truck.

By and large the hippopotamus is a harmless beast, unless you scratch his submerged back with a canoe. He is sometimes useful, because he clears waterways choked with papyrus and other vegetable matter; also his manure helps to make plankton grow, on which fish feed; on the other hand he does much damage to native crops. Hippos can weigh up to three tons, reach a length of fourteen feet, and have reddish sweat. They can stay under water for about four minutes, and sometimes for brief intervals they walk on river bottoms completely submerged. Natives like hippo fat, which is used as a substitute for tallow, grease, and butter.

Nobody ever gets tired of elephants. Lions can become boresome in time; elephants, never. Elephants differ almost as human beings do, and have

[1] According to *The Man Eaters of Tsavo*, by J. H. Patterson, pp. 23 and 87.

strikingly individual patterns of behavior. Most hunters believe that an elephant *knows* when a nearby man is armed and has hostile intentions; this is probably true of many other animals as well. An elephant will risk his life to help a wounded member of the herd to get away, or to protect his young. Elephants dig water holes for the use not merely of themselves but for other beasts. They are apt to be somewhat hysterical, particularly in old age; a senile bull elephant can be the nastiest of customers, but cows on the whole are more unpredictable. When an elephant charges he does not hold his trunk out and aloft, but carefully curls it up and tucks it against his chest; the trunk is delicate, and too valuable to risk in combat. The trunk alone of a big elephant can weigh several hundred pounds. Some connoisseurs think that the trunk is good to eat, although rich; you cut off a slice near the forehead, and then boil and roast it. Elephants destroy a great many trees, but also plant them, by carrying seeds in their droppings. Near Mount Kenya it takes about a square mile of forest to support a single elephant. Elephants like to make love in the water, and take about half an hour for the process, which is noisy. This is the only animal in which the male has a heat period, and one of the few whose udders are between the front limbs, not in back. Elephants kiss with their trunks.

Half the fun of a visit to East Africa is hearing about elephant hunters. Specialists—and amateurs as well—talk of the technique of difficult "brain spots" as *aficionados* discuss a bullfight, or ballet lovers praise an *entrechat six*. The whole business is wrapped up in a technical, almost ritualistic mythology. Elephants are fun to watch, too, but your white hunter will not let you get as near to them as to lions, even if you are in a car. It is a bad sign if the elephant stamps his rear feet. Few people who, as the local phrase is, have been "beaten up" by an elephant live to talk about it; you can be beaten up by rhinos, buffaloes, and so on, and still have a good chance to get away more or less intact; with elephants, no. But I met two men who had survived encounters with elephants; one was a professional hunter, and one an amateur. Each carries lasting marks—the professional is deaf in one ear, having been swatted on the side of the head by the beast's trunk; the amateur has a crippled arm and shoulder, where the elephant grazed him in passing. To skin an elephant is a massive job. It can take five or six skinners three days. As a rule it is one day's work merely to get the tusks out; these are embedded in the skull for approximately one-third of their total length, and the task needs skill, or valuable ivory will be chipped. The best method is to let the head rot for six or seven days, until the surrounding tissue has become soft. Some hunters in a hurry build a fire on the elephant's head. People talk blithely about tusks weighing one hundred pounds or more, but these are rare; a good weight is eighty. Ivory poaching and smuggling is still a fairly big business in some parts of East Africa; ivory is worth between 15 and 17 shillings a pound, and the best market is India. It is smuggled out on Arab dhows, the tusks often being concealed in huge pots of ghee.

African elephants cannot be domesticated or tamed, although on a limited scale work in this direction has been done in the Congo. No one has ever seen an African elephant in a circus. This is the great difference between African and Indian elephants, which are much easier to handle. Indians like to say, not altogether seriously, that their elephants are less savage because India has had a longer civilization than Africa.

Buffaloes are much less interesting and intelligent than elephants, but are equally dangerous. You can have a long argument by asking any group of safari experts which is the most dangerous animal in Africa—lion, leopard, rhino, elephant or buffalo. Various schools have rival favorites, but almost everybody agrees that a *wounded* buffalo is the most vindictive and menacing phenomenon that the average hunter will ever have to face. A buffalo, even if not wounded, is capable of stalking and even ambushing a man.[2] Buffaloes charge with head up and eyes wide open, and at an imposing speed. A big one stands close to five feet high at the shoulder, and its horns can be almost five feet long.

Crocodiles are ugly beasts, they can be twenty feet long, and often devour their own young. If a crocodile seizes a man, he will drown him and then keep him underwater for some hours, to soften him up before eating him. The most difficult animal to photograph successfully is probably the leopard. Carl Akeley, one of the most renowned of modern naturalists, once strangled a leopard with his bare hands. A leopard (according to Akeley) kills by springing at the throat, and at the same time tearing out the stomach of his victim with his hind paws. The rarest animal in East Africa is generally thought to be a kind of antelope called the bongo, which lives secluded in bamboo forests; I know one hunter who has worked in Africa for thirty years and has never seen a bongo alive; I know another who was once charged by one. The animal most perishable in captivity is probably the Colobus monkey. The fastest is the cheetah. An animal good to eat, if properly roasted, is the cane rat (*Thryonomys swinderianus*). Recently scientists have been assigned by the United States navy to make a study of the circulatory system of the giraffe, in an effort to determine how the blood rises in its long tube of neck; this may have application to medical problems in high-altitude aviation. Giraffes intertwine their necks when making love.

[2] Buffaloes sick with rinderpest or other ailments are particularly savage.

Any venomous snake can be dangerous; probably the worst is the black mamba. It has "hypodermic" fangs, and has even been known (like cobras) to chew when it bites. A mamba will attack a man without provocation, and death can supervene in three minutes if the bite is "full" and strikes the head, neck, or a blood vessel. Pages might be written about snake lore. We saw only one dangerous snake in Africa—a cobra which rose in the road and spat against the side of our car in Uganda. Nobody need die of snake bites, even from mambas, if anti-snake-bite serum is available; mamba victims can be saved if large amounts of serum are given fast enough.[3] The trouble is that people in the bush are apt to be far away from quick, adequate means of treatment. Snake poison kills (in some varieties) by paralyzing the nerves that control respiration; death comes from suffocation. In Tanganyika we had the great good fortune of several hours of talk with C.J.P. Ionides, one of the world's foremost authorities on reptiles. Mr. Ionides, who is British in spite of his Greek name, and who works as a ranger deep in the Tanganyika forest, is a hunter and collector of almost mythical renown. He should be prevailed upon to write a book about himself some day. He threw his watch away in 1927, and has never carried one since; the birds tell him the time. He looks like a faun. He lives in a place eighty-three miles from the nearest white man. He has had some fancy narrow escapes. Whenever the Coryndon Museum in Kenya needs a really rare specimen, it sends Mr. Ionides out to get it. He has shot gorilla for this museum, bongo (the expedition took three months), the yellow-backed duiker (a species of small antelope which took him seven weeks of hard work to find), and addax in the Sahara. But his chief interest is snakes. He has a passion for snakes. The London Zoo and Natural History Museum are full of his specimens. He has discovered six new varieties of African reptile, four of which are named for him, and he can talk about snakes—their charm, their perversities, their distinctions—for hour after magic hour.

The relation of animals to each other is a fascinating subject, which has not been sufficiently explored by zoologists. Elephants, lions, and buffaloes pretty much leave one another alone, but a lion will on occasion attack a small elephant if he finds him alone, and habitually preys on buffaloes in some areas. Lions are sometimes treed by elephants. Occasionally when elephants cross a stream hippopotamuses try to bite off their tails. Elephants and rhinos dislike each other, and often squabble, but buffalo and elephant calves have been known to play together. Between the rhino and buffalo there is usually armed neutrality. Baboons get along well with bushbuck

---

[3] Victims of bites from the gaboon and rhinoceros vipers can, however, only be saved by a special serum.

and other antelope, hopping along near them and sometimes (so it has been sworn to me) taking rides piggyback. All small animals fear the leopard, and practically all hate hyenas. Recently in Uganda a field officer of the Tsetse Control Department found the carcasses of a leopard and hartebeest close together. They had killed each other in a fight.

THE KENYA NATIONAL PARKS

Nature teaches beasts to know their friends.
—CORIOLANUS, II, i, 6

Animals are, of course, one reason why Africa is unique among continents. Nowhere else in the world is game to be found in such variety and profusion, and nowhere can it be seen in a wild state with so little effort, particularly in East Africa where high, open plains make for good visibility. Moreover there is no continent where animals are so important in the pattern of normal daily life; Africans live in close proximity to savage animals, fear them, eat them, and worship them. Animals play a dominant role in almost all African mythology and fetishism, and are the basis of much hearty folklore. But a white man in the normal course of events could travel the length and breadth of Africa and never see a wild animal at all if it were not for the great national parks and game reserves.

These are phenomenally interesting. I do not mean merely that they give you a chance to see a lion close up, or tickle an elephant with a walking stick. They preserve game. They keep Africa Africa. They give living space to some of the noblest beasts ever to walk the earth, and make it possible for the continent to remain for some years anyway the most abundant and enthralling repository of wildlife known to man.

The parks are zoos in reverse. It is man who is caged, not the animal. So long as the man stays in his cage, which is his automobile, he is as safe as in the subway. Animals (except rhinos) practically never attack a car or other vehicle. But they are—make no mistake about it—*wild* animals. One theory to account for the fact that a man is almost perfectly safe is that the animal does not normally associate human beings with automobiles. Perhaps the smell of metal and gasoline conceals the scent of man. Just as we are not afraid of even the most ferocious beasts when they are caged, so animals are not fearful of us while we wear rubber tires for shoes. Or perhaps—so I have heard it seriously attested—the animal simply thinks that the automobile is another kind of big beast with round feet.

There are two simple, basic rules in the great parks. First, never get out of your car. Second, use of firearms is completely forbidden. Since the animals are never shot at, and in most cases have never even heard the sound of a gun, they feel secure although most will scamper or slink away if a car comes too close. But we happened once on a cheetah which had just killed a Thomson's gazelle, and watched him for half an hour from a distance of about thirty feet. And once—in Uganda—we were chased by a buffalo.

On the other hand animals in the parks are not accustomed to man on foot. You stay in your automobile not only to protect yourself, but to protect the animals. The parks are not fenced (for the most part) and if lions, let us say, became used to the sight of men on foot who did them no harm they would be tempted sooner or later to wander into the towns, where they might attack people and get shot.

Experts like Mervyn Cowie, who was born in Kenya, told us that large game fifty years ago was at least twenty times more plentiful than today. Several things killed animals off—the advance of the towns, the growth of native settlement, cattle farming, and traffic on the roads which upset animals so that they do not breed. Hence the parks have become transcendently important as a means of giving sanctuary to what game remains. In the literal sense of the word, their role is vital. Most wild animals are, strange to say, somewhat frail. Another factor causing game to diminish was (and still is) native poaching. But the main point is that no room remains nowadays for the really enormous herds, except that which the parks provide. White tourists on safari do not, it might be added, cause serious damage to the game population; they do not kill enough to matter and in fact they probably help in the long run to conserve game, since they frighten away poachers.[4]

British, Belgians, Rhodesians, South Africans, Portuguese, have all created national parks and game reserves. The word "park" is a misnomer, because the terrain is usually unimproved and wild. These reserves and parks are, I think, the finest things we saw in Africa. Among the most spectacular are the real giants, like the Kruger National Park in South Africa and the Albert National Park in the Congo, which covers a million acres. One pioneer suggesting the creation of these great game sanctuaries in Africa was the American Carl Akeley. Particularly was I impressed by the quality of the men who run these parks nowadays. The wardens and

---

[4] White poachers sometimes become game wardens, if they reform; some eminently reputable characters have been poachers on occasion, particularly for ivory in the old days in the Congo. Some professional white hunters likewise go into the National Park Service, or become wardens, when they give up hunting.

rangers have discipline, devotion, love for animal life, and respect for the forces of nature; they are not merely accomplished naturalists, but superb sportsmen and human beings.

The national parks and reserves in Kenya cover more than 24,000 square miles, proportionately the biggest area given to such purposes by any country in the world. There are six national parks and six reserves. The largest is the Tsavo (eight thousand square miles) famous for its elephants.[5] The difference between a park and a reserve is that the former is a permanent sanctuary, devoted exclusively to game, whereas native farmers or nomads are permitted to live on the reserves. In northern Tanganyika are the Serengeti Plains, between Mount Kilimanjaro and a celebrated extinct volcano, Ngorongoro; here roam the most spectacular assemblages of animals still left in the world. With reasonable luck, the visitor may see ten thousand head of game in an afternoon.

*

The park we saw first, and the one I liked best in some respects, is only four miles outside Nairobi. Its virtue is its accessibility. Others are much bigger, with a wider variety of animals, but they are not always easy to reach. To visit the Kruger, probably the most famous of them all, entails a long and somewhat tedious journey from Johannesburg. But the Nairobi park lies immediately adjacent to the city itself, between the Ngong River and the Masai reserve. You can go there by taxi from any point in Nairobi for a few shillings, and the ride should not take more than a quarter of an hour.

One evening after dusk in the Nairobi park, while we were hoping to see lions, we passed a car and the occupants hailed us desperately. It is quite easy to get lost here; few of the roads are marked, and traffic is light; there are no petrol pumps or refreshment stands. The car had had a breakdown and we gave its passengers a lift back into town. If we had not happened to come along two extremely frightened English ladies might have had to spend the night in their vehicle, since to get out and walk would have been dangerous (as well as forbidden). Automobiles are not checked

---

[5] A recent Tsavo report reads, "The inaccessibility of the eastern section makes prevention of the subtle and disastrous murder of the beasts [by poachers] a most difficult problem. On one occasion five rangers . . . arrested a Wakamba. One ranger was left to guard the prisoner while the others carried on down the Tiva. The ranger was attacked by other Wakamba using poisoned arrows, and he was forced to flee for his life." Poachers often kill elephant cows, and leave the calves to die of starvation. The poison used, which is deadly, comes from the Mrishu tree, and is called *Acokanthera friesiorum.*

going in or out of the park, and if you run out of fuel or get lost, you wait till morning unless a ranger finds you. I mention this minor episode merely to indicate that a "park" in Africa is not Hampstead Heath or the Bois de Boulogne.

The Nairobi park covers forty square miles, and has between ten and fourteen thousand wild animals of about forty different species. Not only are some of the kings here, but a spectacular variety of smaller beasts— the clawless otter, which lives on fish but has to be taught to swim; the zorilla, a kind of vampire skunk; the bat-eared fox, a pretty little creature sometimes eaten by birds of prey; and small carnivores like the civet, the genet, and the caracal. And here, twenty minutes from the biggest city in East Africa, I began to get some conception of what the African earth was like, with its yellow-barked, flat-topped acacias biting their way through the crust of brittle soil, acacias of half a dozen different kinds but almost always leveled off at the top as if pressed down to make a mattress, a thorny mattress it would be. But not all the land is baked or bearded with suntanned bush. The profusion of bird life is bewildering. You can see everything from ostrich to migratory wagtails on their way to Europe, from secretary birds, the most picturesque animal I have ever seen with feathers, to larks small enough to put in a pie. There are even some human beings in the park—old Somali warriors whom the authorities have never dispossessed from their slippery-looking huts. And over everything is the high bright Kenya sky, foaming with enormous pink, cream-colored, and slate-blue clouds, so incandescent that they look as if they have fires inside.

FAREWELL TO TREETOPS

Treetops was burned by the Mau Maus in May, 1954; we were lucky enough to have seen it before it was too late. Treetops was unique, and the fact that a bit of touristy hocus-pocus was attached did not spoil it at all. It became famous all over the world in 1952 because a young lady named Elizabeth climbed its ladder a princess, and came down a queen. While she was spending the night at Treetops word came from London that her father, King George VI, was dead.

Treetops was a nest in a large, multiple-limbed fig tree in the Aberdere forest near Mt. Kenya. It was an adjunct to the Outspan Hotel in Nyeri. Platforms were built into the upper branches of the tree, which was heavily populated by baboons, and from a ledge thirty feet above the ground visitors (who slept in the tree and were made soundly comfortable) could look down on a pool of mud, spicy with salt, where animals came each night to bathe, play, and feed. Probably it was the only place in the world where the innocent onlooker, without risk and indeed while having an excellent dinner, could watch large wild animals who were absolutely oblivious of the fact that human beings were observing them. It was a kind of periscope out in the forest, a peephole thirty feet up in the leaves. It even had an artificial "moon"—a soft spotlight which copied the moon's glow, so that even on the dimmest night the animals could be seen.

The ceremony on arrival, after a walk through the forest (rude stepladders are built on the trees at intervals of twenty yards, so that you can climb up if an elephant or rhino charges you), is neatly colorful. Bags and equipment are hoisted up by rope, the visitors ascend by a long ladder, and then the ladder is pulled up into the tree. There is no way to get down except to jump. I felt that to jump might be worthwhile, when I stumbled into a very large and ill-tempered baboon in the men's room on the lower platform. We were cautioned to talk as little as possible, and to tread softly, because although the animals could not see us or catch our scent, the least sound would frighten them away. So there we were hung up in space, held back by wire netting and holding on to the twisted boughs of the tree which projects through the sleeping quarters and platforms at improbable angles. A rifle shot cracked out; this is a forest reserve, with no shooting of animals permitted, and so (our host observed blandly) it must have come from somebody nearby firing at a Mau Mau. I asked him if he trusted his servants and he laughed, "Of course not." Then, in the drowsy gloom, animals began to move out of the forest and creep slowly, warily, with infinite caution, to the foot of our tree. First came some rhinos. They looked phosphorescent. A bushbuck peeked out of the woods, and shyly advanced; it took him half an hour to cross fifty yards. Then came the red forest duiker, waterbuck, a giant forest hog, several varieties of monkey, and, at the end, seventy-five buffalo. But elephants—the prize show at Treetops—did not favor us that night. The salt lick was too dry.

AMATEURS ON SAFARI

Later we took a short safari to the Amboseli country,[6] a reserve in the plains below Mount Kilimanjaro, near the Tanganyika border. The Great North Road, which has the surface of a moderately rough laundry board,

---

[6] This was arranged through the courtesy of Michael Dunford, manager of the East Africa Tourist Travel Association, and Safariland, Ltd. Our white hunter was Mark Howard-Williams.

took us out of Nairobi. We heard about the hyena that ate not merely the garbage, but the garbage can, at the local hotel, and about the rhinoceros which met a bulldozer. Result: a draw. The *bandas* here have steeply pitched roofs, to throw the rain off, and are made of a kind of reed that swells when wet and is supposedly waterproof. We passed one Masai village which, when we saw the site again the next day, had disappeared; the Masai had burned it and moved somewhere else. The acacias are mustard-colored. We saw ostrich scooting through the dust, elands, fastidious giraffes, impala leaping gracefully, little dik-diks, and herds of zebras with their steatopygous behinds. Elephants had knocked down trees everywhere, so that the boughs made a wild tangle of dead wood, white like bones. Elephant droppings look like big square balls of closely woven brown twine.

Nearing Ol Tukai, where we spent the night, we saw two animals moderately rare—the long-necked giraffe-like antelope called a gerenuk, and the oryx with its tall straight horns. And then a leopard streaked off the flat limb of an acacia. This made our white hunter very happy. You can spend weeks here without seeing a leopard so close. We crossed the dry lake itself, which looks like an immense flat reddish brown layer of tortoise shell, grooved with hundreds of long parallel corrugations. These are tracks made by the game. We swerved suddenly, near the camp, and our safari wagon dove and bucked into thick bush. I did not know for a moment what we had come across. Elephants. There were three, under a clump of dry yellow trees, not more than sixty yards away, flanked by a silent group of Thomson's gazelle. The elephants watched us, and then crossed over the bush slowly, stately and enormous; the trunk looks like a fifth leg.

Within a hundred yards of the warden's camp were smashed trees that had been knocked down by elephants. I asked why they did not similarly knock down the flimsy cabins we slept in. "The elephant is a wise old gentleman, and does not want to get into trouble."

We climbed a broad, steep hill at dusk, and our luck became spectacular. Within an arc of a hundred degrees, we saw rhinoceros, buffalo, and elephants again. Our luck became more spectacular. Miles away a light blinked. Somebody was signaling us. We drove across rock and up and around tough gnarled little hills and then down through packed bush to a patch of barren field, where we found friends who wanted to share with us their own good luck. In a copse were fourteen lions; five or six were cubs, but fourteen lions is a lot to see at once. One lioness yawned, stretched, glared at us, and then strode off. A male, nicely maned, lay by himself in tattered open grass. We got as close to him as the base line to the net on a tennis court. He lifted his head, inspected us with deliberation, sniffed, cleared his throat, weighed for a moment the problem we presented —and then turned over on his back, grunted, and went to sleep. This was the first, and only, time in my life I have ever been snubbed by a lion.

Returning to camp we stopped suddenly near a hyena eating something. We were very quiet. My wife whispered, "Wouldn't it be wonderful if the hyena laughed?"

The hyena laughed.

*

Never having had a gun in my hand in my life, except in a shooting gallery, where I never even hit a stationary duck, I should not write much about safari matters. The reader is firmly advised to turn to Mr. Hemingway.

White hunters in East Africa are organized into a kind of trade union, the Professional Hunters Association, which maintains the most admirably strict standards. There is also a trappers' association. The hunters have about twenty full members, mostly British, and about a dozen associates. New members go through a year's probationary period. Entrance is by secret ballot, and perhaps it would be more correct to call the organization a club rather than a union. Some hunters, perfectly reputable and of the highest professional accomplishment, prefer to stay outside the association, and are lone wolves. The essence of the safari business is the narrow escape. Animals are fun, so is camping out, so are trophies, but what really tickles the imagination on a safari, what people really like to talk about, is how that lion almost, but not quite, got them. As a matter of fact only one European client has ever been killed by an animal in East Africa while in the company of a recognized white hunter; several hunters have, however, been killed, and many have been badly mauled. Two were killed in Tanganyika in 1952, one by a wounded buffalo, one by an elephant.

The two big firms in Nairobi are Safariland and Ker and Downey. Either will give you a sublimely good time under the most impeccably expert and stalwart guidance. There are two basic rules. No animal may be shot from a car or from any point within two hundred yards of a car; you have to walk that far anyway. A wounded animal that gets away counts on your license as one killed, and such a contretemps must be reported in writing to the nearest warden. The character of safaris has changed a good deal in recent years. Before the war, comparatively few clients were Americans; now they make up 90 per cent of the trade. Before the war, about 80 per cent of people came for shooting, about 20 per cent for photography;

now these percentages are reversed. And even people who shoot may spend almost as much time with their cameras as with their guns. Camera work can be, up to a point, almost as dangerous as shooting, because ordinarily the photographer has to work at closer ranges; on the other hand photographs may be taken without getting out of your automobile, and the problem of how to deal with a beast enraged by being wounded does not arise. White hunters do not particularly like to take out people who cannot shoot at all, but it has been done. Safaris even exist nowadays for people who neither shoot nor photograph, but go just to look; short "game-viewing" safaris are widely popular.

The standard rate at present for a regular safari for two people with one white hunter for thirty days is £890. This averages out to about $80 a day, and is amply worth it. The safari people provide a hunting car and three-ton truck, tentage, food, medicine, porters, and of course the hunter; the client pays for his own licenses, ammunition and film, alcohol and tobacco. Guns may be rented if you do not possess them.[7] Weather can be tricky in Africa, but the best months for a safari are from July to October and December to early March, to avoid both the long and short rains. The amount of logistical work that goes into a proper safari is often underestimated. A minimum of thirteen Africans will be aboard—cook, cook's boy, hunter's boy, personal boy for each client, skinner, sweeper, messboy, gunner's boys, and three porters. In camp, at least half a dozen separate tents or dwellings are necessary. You can have a hot bath almost any time, drink wine off ice, and wear a dinner jacket if you want to. The standard of cuisine will be as good as in any tolerable African hotel, and better than in most. In Kenya an over-all "major license" for game costs £50, and is valid for a year. This will give the visitor one lion (but not in the Masai district, which costs extra), one cheetah, one hippopotamus (but only on Lake Victoria or within five miles thereof), three buffalo, four zebra, one eland (males only), one bongo (if you can find him) and plenty of antelope, gazelle, and smaller beasts. A special license is necessary for elephant, costing £75 for the first (the tusks must exceed thirty pounds each) and £100 for the second. Two elephants are the limit. Rhinoceros (two only) cost £15 each beyond the regular license, giraffe (two males only) £15, leopard (one only) £10, ostrich (two only) £2, and the Colobus monkey 10 shillings each up to a total of two.

What professional hunters hate most is a greedy client, one who has no love for animals or feeling about game, and who shoots out his whole

---

[7] Ladies innocent of hunting should be told not to wear bright colors.

license. Few do. If your white hunter pleases you, the way to show your appreciation is to give him an elephant license, worth £75. Then he can go out and kill and sell some ivory.

QUEEN ELIZABETH PARK IN UGANDA

Death is an elephant.
—VACHEL LINDSAY

Here the director and chief warden, K. de P. Beaton, who has written several books of animal lore, took us on a brief expedition. This is the newest of the great game sanctuaries in East Africa; it was opened in June, 1952, and covers some 1,500 square miles, not all of which have been surveyed. The animal population includes, 3,000 elephants, 3,000 hippopotamuses, and between eight and nine thousand buffaloes; some of these are migratory to the Congo and back. The land was mostly uncultivable and uninhabited, because of the tsetse fly; at the time of our visit it was still in process of being "degazetted" as a sleeping sickness area. Years ago sleeping sickness caused a grievous epidemic here, and thousands of Africans died; it was only checked by moving all the inhabitants out of the contaminated area. The fly remains, but, since it seldom has a chance to feed on infected human beings, it is not dangerous. If a fly should bite a man who *has* sleeping sickness, and then bite other men, the disease might recrudesce again, as it might in many other parts of Africa. So the whole region is kept under careful scrutiny and medical control.

The Queen Elizabeth Park has unparalleled interest and unspoiled richness of animal life, especially among ungentle beasts. Much of it is still virgin bush. It compares to the park in Nairobi more or less as the wildest stretches of the Canadian Rockies compare to Boston Common. At some seasons here one may see the stupendous bush fires that are characteristic of much of Africa; the rank surface grass is set on fire, so that sweet grass for the game will come up. The smoke from these fires can sometimes be seen for a hundred miles.[8] We entered the Queen Elizabeth Park from Kishwamba, and from the terrace of the lodge we could see, down on the baked plains, large herds of buffaloes and elephants. We crossed the river channel that connects Lake George and Lake Edward, by a creaking pontoon ferry, and in Mr. Beaton's jeep drove bouncing over rough shaggy country, where craters of extinct volcanos lie one after another raw and exposed like huge inverted anthills. The game here is not accustomed to man yet, or even to automobiles, and is wary. But we got close enough to

---

[8] In the Congo incidentally the Belgians do not burn grass (except by accident) on the theory that such fires do not occur in the pure nature cycle.

one elephant to count the white birds sitting on its back, and close enough to a buffalo to smell it, when it made it clear that our attention was unwelcome. The hippos are too big to be afraid, and too unintelligent to be cautious. We got out of the jeep and stood on a slushy river bank within a few yards of hundreds of these gross, slimy monsters. They make a formidable racket, their cry being a curious cross between a roar, a croak, and a bleat.

On one island here are three marooned elephants. They swam there, but will not swim back, and nobody has been able to contrive a way to rescue them.

One warden told us, "Our days are numbered here—all over East Africa. These blasted countries will be free in twenty years. What will be done about poaching or hunting after that? The Africans will kill every animal they can find—for meat. They are absolutely famished for meat. The park will be cleaned out in no time. Maybe we can put the reserves under the UN and save all these beautiful beasts from going into the pot."

SOME ANIMAL TIDBITS

Government game reports show, no matter how official and prosaic their phraseology may be, that drama and danger from animals are still part of the day-to-day life of Africans. The following passages are from the annual document (1951) put out by the Game and Fisheries Department of Uganda:

> In April . . . an old African lady was charged by a hippopotamus which had wandered five miles from the nearest water. The lady is reported to have climbed a tree and then been bitten on the buttocks by the hippo. She was saved by villagers who speared and killed the animal.

> The Game Ranger stationed in the Northern Province was given an amusing account by a Madi as to how elephants raided his cultivation. The Madi who told the story was mystified as to how the elephants got into his shamba as the ground around the shamba was very hard and the spoor frequently could not be found. He said that he believed that the only way that the elephant could come in was by air. Their method was to wait until they got to within a short distance of the shamba when they collected a lot of grass and leaves which they made into a bung; this they inserted in the anal orifice. They then waited patiently for their stomachs to become so distended that they became airborne. As soon as they were in the air they propelled themselves forward by flapping their ears. When they reached the shamba they pulled out the bung allowing the air to escape and so came quietly

down to earth. When they had finished their depredations they did the same thing again and so flew back to the Game Reserve!

The best lion story of the year comes from an African who sent his motor bicycle into a well-known garage in Kampala for repairs. After detailing the list of repairs required the letter continued, "Personally, I am very ill on account of a collision with a lion (on the Masaka-Mubende road at Mile 110) whereby the motorcycle fell on me and it sustained severe injuries, and one of my legs got broken. On account of the shock, the lion did not harm me."

A most unusual casualty occurred not long ago. A Madi speared a buffalo which went off into a muddy swamp. The hunter went after it and came on the buffalo which charged him; neither was able to move very fast on account of the mud which was up to the hunter's knees and the buffalo's belly. While retreating before the buffalo the African fell on his back and the brute reached out and bit the man in the abdomen removing his genitalia. The unfortunate Madi later died in hospital. This is a curious reversal of the common practice amongst certain tribes of devouring the testes of buffaloes in order to increase their virility.

A report was received from Lango in October of the tragic death of a 13-year-old African boy who is alleged to have been swallowed alive by a python. The boy is stated to have been returning from church with two friends when he was seized by the great snake. The terrified screams of the two other children eventually brought other people on the scene but by then the snake had nearly swallowed the boy. Beating with sticks caused the reptile to disgorge the boy, but by then he was dead.

In February a license holder in North Acholi shot a bull [elephant] in a herd. The animal collapsed with its front legs half crossed and a young elephant, a few months old, was trapped between them. It set up a tremendous outcry, but the combined efforts of several men managed to move one of the dead animal's legs slightly and the youngster pulled itself free. After surveying the hunters with a look of aggressive and righteous indignation it shambled off after the herd.

An interesting report was received from the Uganda Fish Marketing Corporation's Station at Kasenyi in Toro. Lions were heard round the station during one night and also considerable other noise; the following morning a hippopotamus was found in a moribund condition within forty yards of the houses. A lion had been attacking it for the greater part of the night and while it had not been able to kill it, it had actually eaten part of the back leg. The unfortunate hippopotamus was immediately destroyed by an Honorary Game Ranger.

IOLA

One animal we heard a good deal about was Iola. She was a lioness, brought up from infancy by Chief Warden W.H.M. Taberer, who was stationed at that time at the Tsavo National Park. One of his rangers one day frightened a pride of lions, which made off, leaving a cub behind; it had been born a few hours before, and weighed one and three-quarters pounds. The cub was named Iola, and became before long the most famous lion in Africa, as well as a devoted member of the Taberer family. It was she who was the lioness in the movie *Where No Vultures Fly* (called in the United States *Ivory Hunter*), a picture telling with fine gusto and distinction the story of the Kenya animal reserves.

Iola was a born actress, and so gentle that it was hard to make her fierce enough to suit the purposes of her passage in the scenario. The Taberers' five-year-old daughter took rides on her golden back. Iola was good looking, vain, generous, and unpredictable. She was tame enough to wrestle with people (occasionally she would lick off patches of their skin), but not as a circus lion may be tame; she was a *wild* animal. She was astonishingly intelligent, and would obey simple commands like a good dog. Sometimes at Amboseli, when the Taberers moved there, she would get tired of sleeping in a tree and leap calmly into bed with some member of the family, or even a visitor to the camp; she scared people half to death, but never harmed anybody. Once she "adopted" a cub, who fed by sipping warm milk which the Taberers poured over her belly. Iola ate a hundred pounds of meat a week, plus two goats. Daintily when she was given meat out of the refrigerator she would slosh it around in her drinking water, to warm it up. She was unbelievably strong. When she was a year old she took a side of eland that weighed 150 pounds and *jumped* with it into a tree.

When Iola was almost two and weighed 297 pounds, the Taberers decided reluctantly that they could keep her no longer. She was getting to be too big. She had never attacked anybody, but lions are temperamental, and she did not know her own strength; she liked to play, and she might have pawed a child in fun, with disastrous consequences. Arrangements were made to send her to the zoo in Dublin, where lions are well cared for, and she was shipped up to Nairobi by truck, in a wooden crate. She had never been caged before. In Nairobi she was to have been put into a stronger metal cage, and flown to Ireland. But the night she arrived she broke out of the crate at the Nairobi airport, escaped, and prowled toward the town. She saw a bull terrier in a garden, and advanced to play with it. She had always got on splendidly with domestic animals. A farmer in a nearby house saw, to his astonishment, a blond lioness grasp at the dog, and shot her.

CHAPTER 22

The Wonderful World of Tanganyika

On the day a man is born his life is measured.
——CHAGGA PROVERB

WE ENTERED Tanganyika from Kenya by way of Mount Kilimanjaro, driving across the Athi Plains. This great mountain (the name means "Shining Mountain" in Swahili) has some remarkable distinctions. For one thing it is the highest mountain in Africa; it is more than three and a half miles high, higher by a mile than any peak in the continental United States. It is 3,784 feet higher than Mont Blanc, 5,920 feet higher than the Jungfrau. For another it rises only three degrees from the Equator, but wears a cap of snow the year around. That a mountain can be imperturbably, permanently ice-covered in this steamingly hot part of the world makes it doubly challenging. For another it is not cramped or crowded by other mountains; it is not part of a range but lifts itself out of the earth isolated and alone. No foothills clutter its smoothly corrugated flanks.[1]

Kilimanjaro is actually two mountains, not just one. Its highest summit, Kibo (19,340 feet) is not a peak but a shallow dome, connected by a long saddle to another summit, Mawenzi (16,897 feet)—a rough sharp peak speckled with black rock, and only covered with snow intermittently. Kibo is the elevation usually seen in photographs, and is always snow-clad. Here, encircled by a crust of ice and volcanic ash, is Kilimanjaro's crater, 6,000 feet across. The base of the mountain as a whole covers an area fifty-five

---

[1] True, a mountain named Meru is only twenty-five miles away to the west, and reaches the respectable height of 14,970 feet; but Kilimanjaro is so stupendous and otherwise gives such an impression of unassailable might and grandeur that Meru looks insignificant, if you look at it at all.

miles by thirty-five—an indication of its immensity. It looks like the round back of a prehistoric monster climbing out of mist.

People who live in its charmed area—both Europeans and Africans—have a strong, almost mystical feeling about it, calling it "the mountain" as if there could be no other mountain. I heard phrases like "Good chap, that ranger—soundest man with elephants on the mountain," or "Ghastly bore of a fellow—can't understand what *he's* doing on the mountain." Also Kilimanjaro has produced some splendid native folklore. One story resembles closely the Greek myth about Atalanta of Calydon. Parts of the mountain are supposed to have arisen because a boy, fleeing from an evil spirit, dropped lumps of earth behind him as he ran.

Kilimanjaro was discovered by a German missionary, Johannes Rebmann, in 1848. People did not believe him at first when he reported the existence of a huge ice-capped peak almost on the Equator. Then other missionaries, government agents, and explorers confirmed Rebmann's story, and in 1884 the mountain and its hinterland became British territory. Later—the imperialist scramble for Africa was beginning—it went to Germany. One legend is that Queen Victoria gave it to Kaiser Wilhelm as a birthday present. The Kaiser had complained that she had two African mountains with snow on top (the other being Mount Kenya) whereas he had none. Whether this story is true or not the transfer of territory was duly made. Today the frontier between Kenya and Tanganyika follows two perfectly straight lines, except for a kind of whorl, or ring, encircling Kilimanjaro so that the mountain is on the Tanganyika side, which was German until World War I.

Kilimanjaro was not climbed till 1889, when a German scientist, Dr. Hans Meyer, made the first ascent of Kibo. The topmost protuberance is still called Kaiser Wilhelm Point, the name given it by Meyer. For many years nobody knew exactly how high the mountain was, because scientific observation is difficult in this area, and the crater was not fully explored until 1930. Nowadays Kibo (not Mawenzi) is comparatively easy to climb. It presents no technically difficult or dangerous mountaineering problems. Expeditions, in fact, go up regularly; the trip takes three days up, two down, and costs $38.50. One unusual character, Dr. R. R. Reusch, a local American missionary of Russian origin, who has a passionate interest in the mountain, has climbed it no fewer than sixty-five times.

Kilimanjaro gives life. It plucks purple clouds out of the monsoon from the Indian Ocean, makes rain, and carries forests on its back. Rivers flow down its slopes, create turbulent gardens, and become lakes. It is one of the most useful mountains in the world, as well as most romantic. The leopard made renowned by Ernest Hemingway in "The Snows of Kilimanjaro" still lies frozen near the summit. In days of travel we could not get away from Kilimanjaro. We saw it from the most unexpected angles; it followed us like some colossal polar bear breathing out a pallid, cold, formidable smoke through tropical foliage. Sometimes clouds would separate just before sundown to expose its beveled dome—pink, mauve, ivory, and sable. Thin shafts of white cloud usually pierce the top, and—if I may change the metaphor drastically—resemble the paper frills on lamb chops.

Many Africans, even those Europeanized, still think of Kilimanjaro as God's throne. They pray to it, and one superstition strongly held is that a woman must not walk between a man and the mountain, because this will make him sterile. All fertility in the region comes from Kibo, and when a man dies, he is buried facing it. Few Africans in the region (except some emancipated guides and porters) would dream of ascending it, for fear of offending the spirits it contains.

Chief Tom Marealle, our host in Moshi, took a moderate, rational view, saying, "We feel about the mountain the way the British feel about the Thames—it is part of our inheritance, our tradition." A subordinate chief leaned across the table and challenged Tom. "But even you pray to it, don't you, Chief?" Mr. Marealle paused a moment and then replied, "Yes—for rain." Another chief then volunteered ingenuously, "I pray to it too, but secretly." Later from another African I heard a more positive affirmation, "God came from this mountain, and *is* the mountain."

ARUSHA, MOSHI, AND THE KILIMANJARO "CORRIDOR"

This area, though it is part of Tanganyika, differs altogether from anything else in Tanganyika. It is an enclave with special characteristics of its own, and has close affiliations with Kenya across the border.

ARUSHA lies on the slopes of Mount Meru, and commands a sublime view of Kilimanjaro across Lake Duluti; it has 4,600 people, and, oddly enough, sits at an altitude of 4,600 feet. On its main street a sign notifies you that Arusha is not only situated in the exact middle of British East Africa, but is exactly halfway between Cairo and the Cape. Times of sunrise and sunset do not vary by more than half an hour during the year. Arusha is a polyglot, westernized little town; it has a Greek community, several Germans predating World War I, and some German Jewish refugees postdating World War II. Nearby is the biggest depot in the world for selling trapped animals to zoos, and the Arusha gardens, under the icy forehead of the great mountain, are of surpassing luxuriance and beauty. Here are poinsettias colored salmon pink, croton bushes with flaming orange leaves, and Sodom apples—a tiny yellow fruit which the Mau Mau stick in the eye-sockets of animal (and human) victims, after the eyes are torn out.

In normal times about 16,000 Kikuyus live in Tanganyika, and some joined Mau Mau. A state of emergency had to be declared in the Kilimanjaro district in 1953. One reason for this (the British say) was that a loyal tribe, the Waarusha, threatened to take violent countermeasures against the Kikuyus themselves, if the British did not. The authorities arrested the leading Mau Mau conspirators, screened thousands more, and deported other thousands back to Kenya.

This is mostly white settler country, though not on the scale of the White Highlands in Kenya. White settlement is not anything like the problem in Tanganyika that it is in Kenya, but several thousand square miles in the Kilimanjaro sector are held by white farmers. "I wish we could cede the whole lot over to Kenya," one high British official told me, "Arusha really ought to be in Kenya." Some settlers are South Africans who have been in the area many years; several are recent South African refugees *from* Malan. Many are poor. But their hardness of life does not match that of the natives—many of them landless—who live in the shadow of the white farms. The poorest and most primitive community I saw in all Africa was near Arusha. Corn is stored up in the trees, which consequently seem to be hung with strange-looking nests or baskets, to keep it out of the reach of giant rats who infest the huts on the ground.

Animals are a lively and colorful problem throughout all the Kilimanjaro region. Locusts can destroy a farm overnight, and so can a variety of finch known as the dioch. One enterprising citizen of the neighborhood invented a novel method of dealing with finches lately—he trapped them by dousing his fields with quantities of molasses, on which they stuck. At a sugar plantation on the Pangani River (where the molasses came from), crocodiles are a nuisance. Our host showed us proudly a suitcase made out of the hide of one monster, shot soon after he had devoured a Negro worker. "Part of that poor boy must be right here in the skin," he averred. Nearby is a farm where an eleven-year-old girl gained local celebrity by calling to her mother in a matter-of-fact voice, "Please tell father that that elephant is in the rose garden again." On one farm we were the guests of Mr. G.R.A.M. Johnston, who was a famous Royal Air Force pilot during the war, and is now a Tanganyika settler. He showed us a most unusual and curious contrivance—two 44-gallon oil drums sealed together, with a door at one end and a peep-hole at the other. In this, lying flat on the ground, Mr. Johnston had lain all the night before waiting for a lion that had been eating his stock. Bait was strapped to a tree nearby. The lion came; Mr. Johnston shot; the lion—minus one ear—got away.

MOSHI (population 7,475, altitude 2,900 feet) is the kind of town Somerset Maugham, if he ever wrote about Africa, might have invented. Moshi means "smoke"—spume from the mountain. Gardens, like those in Arusha, are one thing; wet tropical *vegetation,* such as one finds in Moshi, is something else again. Moshi is a railway town and contains various other appurtenances of civilization, but, under Kilimanjaro's frigid cone, it is also a kind of hothouse growing bananas. The banana is, of course, the staple food of all this part of Africa; people stew, bake, steam, boil, fry, and roast bananas. Bananas make soup; they make porridge; they even make alcohol. In fact this is one of the comparatively few places in the world where the banana is a drink. Then too this versatile fruit is used as a fiber, and a process is being worked out to dry bananas and sell them like figs, and also to manufacture banana powder.

Another important crop, pyrethrum, looks like a small chrysanthemum. It is mildly poisonous, with a soporific effect, and a favorite story is of the rhinoceros who wandered by mistake into a patch of pyrethrum, ate some, and at once—all two tons of him—keeled over and went quietly to sleep.

But the basis of Moshi's life and in fact the economic base of the whole Kilimanjaro region is something more prosaic—coffee. Some 32,000 African coffee planters are banded together here in what is probably the most successful co-operative undertaking in East Africa, the Kilimanjaro Native Co-operative Union, Ltd. This is managed by the African growers themselves, with a European secretary, A.L.G. Bennett, and is a notably successful undertaking. Old-fashioned people who do not think that Africans are capable of handling their own affairs should visit the smart, efficiently run headquarters of this co-operative in Moshi. It has shops, a printing press, laboratories, a recreation center, and better hotel rooms than the Graham Greenish hotel for Europeans in the town. This organization has given vigor and freshness to the whole community, and opens the way toward what Africa needs above all—the creation of a prosperous middle class.

THE MASAI AND THE CHAGGA

By many the Masai are thought to be the most "romantic" tribe in Africa. We encountered our first *moran*—Masai warrior—on an upcountry road near Moshi; he carried a tuft on his spear to indicate that he walked on an errand of peace, and had his face daubed with red ocher paint. Almost all Masai are tall, splendidly built, and handsome; they are not quite so handsome when they smile, because they have two of their front teeth—the lower incisors—knocked out; one theory to account for this custom is that it enabled a man to eat and drink if he had lockjaw, which in older days was a frequent affliction. Up to a certain age, Masai boys and girls sleep together indiscriminately, and practically all have syphilis. It does not seem to hurt their looks. Their social organization is complex, based on age groups. They carry ornaments in their pierced ears (like the Kikuyu), and sometimes these are metal rings a foot in diameter. Some wear a solid disk-shaped bib of beads below the throat, and bind their arms and legs with concentric loops of copper wire; this may come from the nearest telephone pole, if any. Often a Masai may be wearing twenty-five or thirty pounds of metal. Masai women always have their hair cropped; men wear it plaited into a queue until marriage. Sometimes youthful Masai wander into a European beauty shop in Arusha or Tanga, and stare with envious wonder at the even more complicated ways in which white women do their hair.

The Masai are Nilo-Hamitic in origin, and have a Caucasoid cast of feature, like Ethiopians. One German authority (not a Nazi) offered the theory some years ago that they are the original forefathers of the Jews. They have their own highly distinctive non-Bantu language, and are contemptuous of education; their children do not as a rule go to school. For a tribe so celebrated, the Masai are comparatively few in number; there are probably only about 45,000 in Tanganyika, and 60,000 more in Kenya across the border. "To get vital statistics of the Masai is the hardest job in East Africa," we heard. In Tanganyika they roam over 24,000 square miles, and have 600,000 head of cattle and another 600,000 sheep and goats. They live by grazing stock, and almost never do any other kind of work. "Best cattle people in the world."

What impresses most visitors to the Masai is their diet; they live almost exclusively on milk and blood from their cattle. The blood—drawn from the neck of the living cow through a reed—and milk are imbibed directly as fluids, or reduced to a kind of mash. The blood drawing is done secretly at stated ceremonious intervals. A British official who lived among the Masai for five years told us that he had never once seen the ceremony performed. And a European doctor informed us, "The secret of Masai vitality is their diet. I could withdraw protein from the Masai, feed them nothing but carbohydrates, and turn them into Kikuyu in no time. Similarly I could make Masai out of Kikuyu if I had enough blood and milk." Masai do not even eat chickens, and seldom kill game for food. As a result creatures like zebras are astonishingly tame in the Masai country. They do, however, famously kill lions for fun, and to gain manes for their headdresses—kill them with spears.

The Masai are a fierce, proud, and lonely people, great warriors in the old days, but tranquil now except for their addiction to cattle-rustling. They look down superciliously on the neighboring tribes, and seldom become servants in the towns. But, largely because of inherited venereal disease, their population remains static, and this worries elders of the tribe. Masai have been encouraged lately to marry Kikuyu and Chagga women. But the Chagga are wary of them, and the best they can get is usually somebody more primitive, like the Waarusha.

The Masai have no nationalism in the modern sense; all they want is to be let alone. Yet even these splendidly barbaric herdsmen are beginning to feel the touch of modern times. Because of their wealth in cattle, they have for a long time paid the highest poll tax of any tribe in Tanganyika, 30 shillings per year. The government approached them recently with a development plan—largely to improve their water supply and fight sleeping sickness—and they agreed at once to accept this, although it meant that their taxes would be doubled. It will not be many years before the Masai drive Chevrolets, and get their milk and blood from a refrigerator.

*

The Chagga (properly, "Wachagga"), who also live in the Kilimanjaro district, are so different from the Masai that it is hard to believe that two such dissimilar people can belong to the same continent, let alone the same small area. "What *is* an African?" one is tempted to ask. There are about 300,000 Chagga, on the eastern, southern, and western slopes of the mountain; they are an advanced tribe, westernized and sophisticated to an extent; they are businessmen, merchants, schoolteachers, and above all coffee growers; they own 12,000,000 coffee trees. Their paramount chief, Thomas Marealle, known usually as Chief Tom, resembles a Masai warrior about as much as the president of Harvard resembles Tarzan of the Apes.

The Chagga have their own flag, national anthem, and federated organization, and are about 70 per cent Christian. They have no vernacular press as yet (as the Kikuyu had before the emergency) but this is coming. Their tribal council is an important body, and they have their own schools, hospitals, and judicial system. The British are responsible for law and order since, after all, Chaggaland is part of Tanganyika, but the Chagga are proud of the fact that the local DC's come to their council meetings as "invited" guests. The Chagga collect their own taxes—their finance is based partly on a poll and property tax, partly by a cess on coffee—and like to say that their budget, £110,000 per year, is exactly what the budget was in Britain when William the Conqueror came in 1066.

I was much impressed by Chief Tom. This is an able and progressive citizen. He speaks perfect English, wears western dress, and appears to be in his late thirties. He is known as the Mangi Mkuu (Big Chief); members of his family have been chiefs uninterruptedly for thirteen generations. His salary, paid by the Chagga themselves, is £1800 per year, and he holds office for life, but the appointment is not hereditary. Chief Tom was elected to the paramountcy in 1951, after a lively political fight; the British opposed him at first, not on personal grounds but because they thought that the institution of paramountcy was undemocratic. The Chagga had never had a "paramount" chief before.

Chief Tom is not at all anti-British, but he has reasoned and precise views on what is going on in the colonial world. We met him in the offices of the KNCU, the coffee co-operative. He talked about the land, and how the worst thing about white settlement was not merely that it takes land away from the native, but forces him into the position of being part of a submerged black working class on white estates, thus increasing the possibility of racial conflict. He thinks that the British, for all their good intentions, still govern by a "divide and rule" policy—they try to keep the tribes apart. He talked a good deal about the position of women and how vital it was to encourage them to get jobs. Women with jobs are very rare in primitive Africa. He talked too about political opportunities in a multi-racial society, and the necessity for development. "Yes. But development *for whom?*"

*

The British have "pet" tribes. They certainly respect Tom Marealle, but they do not really *like* the Chagga people, any more than they like the Kikuyu. The favorite British tribe by all odds is the Masai, even if its members are still semi-savages. Or perhaps the British are so fond of the Masai *because* they are still savages. There is always a tendency among old colonials to distrust and dislike educated tribes. The more civilized and emancipated a tribe becomes, the more trouble it is likely to make, because education almost inevitably produces discontent. Similarly in Morocco the colonial French prefer the homespun Berbers to the glib, educated Arabs in the towns.

The biggest tribe in Tanganyika, numbering about a million and a quarter, is the Sukuma. Like the Chagga, the Sukuma people have recently formed a federation out of separate chiefdoms—fifty-one in all. Their principal leader is the youthful Chief Kidaha Makwaia, who went to Oxford and was the only African member of the Royal Commission set up in 1952 to study the land problem in East Africa. Sukumuland is the seat of one of the largest and potentially most fruitful development projects in Africa.[2]

One should also mention a small tribe, the Wameru, which lives in the Kilimanjaro area. Some Wameru were forcibly evicted from their land in consequence of a resettlement scheme in their region, and angrily brought the case all the way to the UN in New York.

TANGANYIKA: THE BASIC STRUCTURE

Paternal rule and the cult of good government sometimes stand in the way of . . . self-government.
—V. K. KRISHNA MENON

Tanganyika, a trust territory of the UN administered by the British, is an enormous entity. The Kilimanjaro area is only a minute fraction of the whole. The country has roughly as many thousand square miles as there are days in the year, covering slightly less than 365,000 square miles, and is the second largest British territory in Africa; among colonial areas in the whole Commonwealth only Nigeria is bigger. Whereas the Moshi-Arusha enclave is moist and juicy, most of the rest of Tanganyika is arid—so much so in fact that only about 34 per cent of the land has any use at all. Water, if you could find it, might make the whole territory blossom; geologists, I heard it said, should go in for deep drilling of water exactly as they do for oil. Another factor making Tanganyika largely a waste land is that two-thirds of the total area is, as has been mentioned before, infected by the tsetse fly. The spine of the country is the railroad (built by the Germans for strategic purposes) that cuts westward from Dar es Salaam to Kigoma. The road system is for the most part abominable. No all-weather road exists connecting Lake Tanganyika (as big as Maryland) with the coast. To drive from Moshi to Dar es Salaam will, with luck, take three hard days, although the distance is only 240 miles; there is not a single garage on the route, and no water; there are two petrol pumps, and one hotel. Incidentally Tanganyika has some of the most striking prehistoric rock paintings in Africa, and is believed to be the original home of the dinosaur.

On Tanganyika's vastness live approximately 7,800,000 people, of whom the overwhelming majority—99.1 per cent—is African. Substantial Indian and Arab (Swahili) communities have deep roots in the country, and so do some Somalis. The white European population numbers less than

---

[2] In May, 1954, Kidaha resigned his chiefdom—an unusual thing to do—in order to go into the government civil service.

20,000. Once more we have the spectacle of a minuscule thimbleful of Europeans sprinkled like salt over an immense, impermeable black African mass.[3]

Tanganyika gives a note of tolerance, compromise, and relaxation—particularly in racial matters—in marked contrast to Kenya. There are several reasons for this:

1. The European population is mixed up and cosmopolitan. One flourishing community is that of the Greeks, who are far too sensible as businessmen and otherwise to worry much about color bar. Originally the Greeks came into Tanganyika, like the Indians in Kenya, to build the railroad. They outnumber the British, and contribute substantially to the country's worth.[4]

2. White settlers are, as we have noted, conspicuous in the Kilimanjaro "corridor" and there are large sisal plantations owned by Europeans along the coast, but only 1.3 per cent of the total land of Tanganyika is white-owned, and only about a thousand Europeans in all are engaged in agriculture. Most Britons in Tanganyika are transients, working as officials or in commerce, who do not intend to stay in the country permanently. The rights of the Africans to their land are carefully safeguarded; any transaction involving more than five thousand acres has to go all the way to the Colonial Secretary in London for approval. Tanganyika is, in a word, anxious to avoid the mistakes attending white settlement that have brought tragedy to Kenya; on the other hand it wants and welcomes *some* European farmers, because these set a good example for the African in agricultural methods and other respects. There are about 180,000 landless Africans in the country. Land hunger and low wages are troublesome problems. One index of the appalling poverty of the country is that only 450,000 Africans are "gainfully employed."

3. Tanganyika is a "geographical expression" rather than a nation, with 120 different tribes. Most of these are self-contained, isolated from their neighbors by language and other barriers, and primitive; hence, little field exists so far for the growth of a genuinely nationalist movement. Also the fact that Tanganyika is flanked on two sides by Belgian and Portuguese territory serves to keep inflammatory ideas out. Moreover most Tanganyikans (except Kikuyus in the corridor) are peaceful. During the worst of

---

[3] Tanganyika would be a much more populous country—in fact it would be almost as big as the Union of South Africa—if the westward provinces of Ruanda and Urundi had not been separated from it and given to Belgium (under League of Nations mandate) after World War I. The population of Ruanda-Urundi, a UN trust territory under Belgium, is close to 4,000,000.

[4] Of the 405 farmers in the Kilimanjaro area employing ten or more workers, 134 are Greek, 80 British, 69 South African, 12 Indian, and 6 African. The others are of twelve nationalities including Americans, Swiss, Italians, Danes, and Dutch.

the Mau Mau crisis in Kenya the number of white troops in Tanganyika was about—thirty!

4. The personality of the Governor, Sir Edward Twining, has played a substantial role in promoting a healthy political and racial atmosphere. Twining is a bluff, hearty man of boundless vision and energy, as British as mutton, who can wear his white plumes with effortless regality; but he is close to the earth, he likes and understands Africans, and he believes in progress and reform. Like Arden-Clarke on the Gold Coast, he began his career as a humble District Officer. He has rubbed shoulders with the African out in the bush for thirty years, but when it is proper to put on pomp, he does this with such a buoyant flourish that the Africans love it.[5] Above all they trust him. Twining's hobby is the history of European crown jewels. His wife is a doctor of medicine. Few governors have ever rendered greater service to a community than Twining, and he is universally respected and admired.[6] He took us for a brief excursion outside Dar es Salaam—without an ADC—and plodded through villages on foot, giving counsel to individual Africans, patting their children on the head, and in general giving forth a spirit of confidence, fair play, and bonhomie.

5. Tanganyika is a UN trust territory, which gives its educated Africans an added feeling of security. But Chief Tom Marreale told us, "The UN is our sheet anchor only because the British co-operate with it loyally. The UN would be worthless if some other kind of government ever came into power."

Finally, a word on color bar. The contrast to Kenya is acute, because color bar in Tanganyika is not an agonizing day-in-day-out preoccupation. The trend is all toward harmony and amelioration. The atmosphere in racial relations is based on status, not segregation; we even met Africans in the homes of DC's. Minor social discriminations still exist in clubs and the like, but few people in government count noses on a racial basis. There are no native reserves as such, and—most important—no pass laws; by and large any African can go anywhere he likes at any time. Twining told us, "We are trying to build up a community where merit is the criterion, not color." He told us too that the creation of a genuine multiracial structure in which the races co-operate cordially without miscegenation was something that no country has ever achieved in history before.

[5] After all a governor's plumes and an African chief's headdress represent the same thing—authority.

[6] Vernon Bartlett writes the following in *Struggle for Africa* (page 208): "I once saw the governor, at a Government House garden party, looking on with calm and confidence while an Indian school girl, with a bow and arrow and unbelievable skill, shot apples off Lady Twining's head for the benefit of Red Cross funds."

The capital of Tanganyika, DAR ES SALAAM (population 75,000), is a hot, sticky town on the Indian Ocean, well built because it was built by the Germans, with an atmosphere largely Arab-*cum*-Indian. The name means "Port of Peace." Its mayor is an Indian, the Hon. Abdulkarim Karimjee, who derives from a Yemenite family that came to the Africa mainland from Zanzibar four generations ago. Imagine Nairobi with an Indian mayor! The municipal council is divided 7-7-6-1 among Europeans, Africans, Asians, and an Arab. Dar es Salaam has a welfare center donated to the town by a wealthy Greek, and the price of a wife for your cook has gone up from 50 to 600 shillings in ten years. In November, 1953, several hippopotamuses entered Dar es Salaam from a creek near the airport, and terrorized the African quarter of the town. Dar es Salaam, like Zanzibar, is an important center for followers of the Aga Khan, and it was here that this ornate and distinguished potentate was weighed in diamonds on August 10, 1946. At the time he weighed 239 pounds, and the diamonds, mostly industrial stones of inferior quality, were borrowed from South Africa and insured for £30,000.

Dar es Salaam has an enterprising small radio station, which began operations not long ago with little more equipment than a microphone and a blanket hung over a wall; now its programs—in English and Swahili—are heard as far away as Norway. The entire technical staff is African. Sir Edward Twining was the father of this development. Radio has, as is only too obvious, a future of illimitable proportions all over Africa. And when TV comes, what fun Africans will have! They possess a marked gift for self-expression, are born dancers and actors, appreciate entertainment avidly, and have few inhibitions. "We have taken all the joy out of their lives," one high British official told us. "We ignore their tribal dances, and try to give them—cricket. It's awful. We teach them to read, and give them no reading matter that amuses them. The unforgivable sin of British imperialism is not exploitation but that it has made life dull."

TANGA, some miles up the coast from Dar, is an interesting town. The name means "sail," and the population is about 24,000. This is the center of the sisal industry, and its leading citizen is Eldred F. Hitchcock, the "King of Sisal." Mr. Hitchcock, a peppery small bearded Englishman, is the largest employer of African labor in East Africa, and is a model employer too. He believes in profits, and also in good racial relations; one cannot come without the other.[7] Sisal makes rope, and about 80,000 tons of it go to the United States each year; it is by far Tanganyika's

---

[7] Some of his workers are Mwians from Portuguese Angola. Their women wear plates in their lips.

biggest export. "The sisal plant," Mr. Hitchcock told us, "is a daffodil weighing three hundred pounds." It came to Africa from Florida, through the mechanism of a remarkable German botanist, by name Hindorf. If it had not been for the fact that sisal is a difficult crop, there might not have been a Munich in 1939. Neville Chamberlain started out life as a sisal planter in the Bahamas, and only returned to Britain and entered politics when he found that this obdurate vegetable was too hard to grow.

What distinguishes the Tanganyika coastal cities like Dar and Tanga from the hinterland is that the coast has a past. Persians, Arabs, Indians, Portuguese, have traded on this shore for centuries, and Tanga in particular, again like Zanzibar, is the seat of an ancient Arab culture. The Arabs play a skillful political game these days between Indians and the African community; they are mostly a strong conservative force. They are not like Arabs in Egypt and the Sudan, and they do not care much for western institutions; unlike up-and-coming tribes in the back country, they have little interest in nationalism. Mr. Hitchcock[8] told us that there were probably not three people in Tanga—all agitators from outside—who wanted to throw the white man out. In a dozen ways, the texture of native life here is altogether different from that anywhere else in East Africa except Zanzibar. We were startled to see little public cafés along the streets, a sight unimaginable in Arusha.

Tanganyika was the scene of the worst fiasco in recent British colonial history, the groundnuts (peanuts) scheme. An investment of £36,500,000 had to be written off by the British government as a dead loss. The project was a child of the Labor government and for a time was in the hands of a subsidiary of the United Africa Company, which in turn is part of the Unilever interests; the design was to raise enormous quantities of peanuts (on a tract first set at more than three million acres) to provide margarine, oil, and fats for Britain during the days of strict rationing after the war. The scheme fell through in 1950, and has been abandoned now except for experimental activity. Almost everything went wrong. For one thing the site was short of water (which should have been known beforehand), and when the rains did come they turned the bricklike soil to mud. For another, mechanical equipment did not work.

Some lively new economic developments are under way today, with good hope of success. A deep water port is being built at Mtwara, and the Shell interests are looking for oil in profitable quantities on Mafia Island, off the coast below Dar. Most attention is being focused on communications and water. More than £16 million have been allotted to road building in the

---

[8] He was knighted in 1955, and is now Sir Eldred Hitchcock.

next few years. Gogoland, the desert of Tanganyika, has more rainfall per annum than Kent, the garden of England, but all of it falls in a limited period; the problem is to harness and conserve water. The motto for work in this area is naturally "Gogo Forward." The Sukumuland reclamation project will, if it works, raise the living standards of a million people largely by eradication of the tsetse fly and water control through a system of dams and reservoirs. Tanganyika has some odd distinctions in the realm of economics; for instance it is the first producer of beeswax in the world.

STANLEY-LIVINGSTONE

Ujiji, on the eastern shore of Lake Tanganyika, near Kigoma, is where Henry M. Stanley found Livingstone in 1871. "Found" is not quite the correct word. It was fairly well established and known to many that this was where Livingstone must be; the problem was how to get there. Stanley, as the world knows, did it. Livingstone did not particularly need to be "rescued"; he was in poor health, but otherwise not in danger. But he was more than glad to see Stanley, and to spend the next few months with him. He had not seen a white man for more than six years.

Stanley's own account of the meeting and the famous phrase it evoked, one of the most celebrated ever uttered by mortal man, goes like this:

> Selim said to me, "I see the Doctor, sir. Oh, what an old man! He has got a white beard." And I—what would I not have given for a bit of friendly wilderness, where, unseen, I might vent my joy in some mad freak, such as idiotically biting my hand, turning a somersault, or slashing at trees, in order to allay those exciting feelings that were well-nigh uncontrollable. My heart beats fast, but I must not let my face betray my emotions, lest it shall detract from the dignity of a white man appearing under such extraordinary circumstances.
>
> So I did that which I thought was most dignified. I pushed back the crowds, and, passing from the rear, walked down a living avenue of people, until I came in front of the semicircle of Arabs, in the front of which stood the white man with the grey beard. As I advanced slowly towards him I noticed he was pale, looked wearied, had a grey beard, wore a bluish cap with a faded gold band round it, had on a red-sleeved waistcoat, and a pair of grey tweed trousers. I would have run to him, only I was a coward in the presence of such a mob—would have embraced him, only, he being an Englishman, I did not know how he would receive me. So I did what cowardice and false pride suggested was the best thing—walked deliberately to him, took off my hat, and said: "Dr. Livingstone, I presume?"
>
> "Yes," said he, with a kind smile, lifting his cap slightly.

I replace my hat on my head, and he puts on his cap, and we both grasp hands, and I then say aloud:

"I thank God, Doctor, I have been permitted to see you."

He answered, "I feel thankful that I am here to welcome you."[9]

Ujiji has not changed much in eighty years, except that it is bigger. It is, in fact, with 11,000 inhabitants, the biggest village—as apart from town—in East Africa. No white men live in it except missionaries.

TANGANYIKA: A WORD ON HISTORY AND POLITICS

Tanganyika is, as we know, the former German East Africa; it was German (along with what is now Ruanda-Urundi) from the 1880's to World War I. German penetration began with a striking character, Dr. Karl Peters, who within four months of his arrival on the coast in 1884 acquired a territory as big as Bavaria, mostly by buying it for a trifle from the local chiefs. Peters was a private citizen. He planned to sell his tracts to German colonists. He was laughed at in Germany as a visionary. Then quickly the implications of his work became clear to the Wilhelmstrasse, and he was given an Imperial Charter of Protection. The Sultan of Zanzibar, who held theoretical sovereignty over all this territory, was bought off outright with a grant of £200,000, and the German East Africa Protectorate came into being.[10]

The Germans then spread inland, but they did not completely pacify the huge area they occupied until 1910. One native chief, Quawa, could not be subdued, and shot himself (1898) to avoid surrender. The Germans took his skull to Berlin as a trophy, and were obliged to return it to Tanganyika by a clause in the Treaty of Versailles. In 1903-5 occurred a remarkable and tragic event, the Maji-Maji rebellion made chiefly by the Angoni tribe in southern Tanganyika. The Angoni, an offshoot of the Zulus, are a bold, warlike people. They did not like the Germans and rose fiercely against them. Their movement was in some respects extraordinarily like today's Mau Mau uprising—a desperate struggle against white encroachment on black land, in which political grievances were inextricably merged with pagan mysticism. The Germans put down Maji-Maji with unexampled thoroughness, efficiency, and ferocity. Instead of shooting individual ter-

---

[9] From *African Discovery*, an anthology by Margery Perham and Jack Simmons, pp. 209-10.

[10] Ironically enough the British still profit by this old German arrangement with the Sultan. They pay today's Sultan an annual £16,000 fee for their lease of the Zanzibar domains on the Kenya coast, but none for Tanganyika, on the ground that the Germans "bought" the territory. See *A History of German East Africa*, by the Hon. C.C.F. Dundas, Government Printer, Dar es Salaam, 1923.

THE WONDERFUL WORLD OF TANGANYIKA 411

rorists, they burned crops, starved villages, and razed the entire countryside. More than 120,000 Africans died. Even today the Southern Province of Tanganyika, the "Cinderella Province," has not fully recovered from the German terror half a century ago. The economy of the region has never been successfully rebuilt.

German East Africa was conquered by the British (assisted cardinally by South Africans and Indians) in 1914-18. German exploits during this period, under their formidable commander General von Lettow, are dealt with later in this chapter.

Few German traces remain in Tanganyika today, except in architecture. Almost everywhere, the *bomas* (government headquarters—literally, fences or enclosures) built solidly and soundly by the Germans in most towns of consequence are still in use. Rule by Berlin was not totally a matter of suppression and bloodshed by any means. The Germans (like the Belgians) taught Africans skilled trades, and turned them into good carpenters and blacksmiths; administration of civil law was stern, but just; and they gave the country what is still the matrix of its communications system. Many Tanganyikans of the older generation remember Germans with respect, and even affection. Several times I heard British officials say ruefully, "The Africans liked Germans better than they like us, because we are too soft."[11]

Between the wars, the British pretty well ran Tanganyika on a care and maintenance basis for the old League of Nations, and paid comparatively little attention to it. In 1938, to buy off Hitler, London seriously entertained the idea of giving the territory back to Germany, but Hitler would not have it. In 1939, after the outbreak of World War II, plans were made to use Tanganyika (and British Guiana) as havens for refugee Jews from Germany, but the project did not materialize.

*

British policy today is double—to help Tanganyika develop toward self-government, but not too fast for its own good. Tanganyika is manifestly unfit for anything like complete self-government as yet if only because (a) it is still largely a collection of tribes, (b) the great bulk of the population is illiterate. Meantime, its chief distinguishing mark is—let us repeat—a much healthier racial atmosphere than in any other country in East or Central Africa.

One British remark I heard was, "We're more than eager to let the people here have responsible government—if only to show them how difficult it is to make it work."

---

[11] One odd point is that many Africans today are supposed to dislike the British system of trial by jury. If a juryman finds a prisoner guilty, he may have a curse put on him by the condemned man, and be visited balefully by a witch doctor.

Be this as it may be there is no suffrage as yet in Tanganyika—there has never been a general election—and all members of LEGCO are appointed by the Governor; there are no elected members. Moreover the "official" (government) members have a majority (of one) over those "unofficial," who represent the various communities. But in 1954 came an interesting reform. Europeans, Africans, and Asians now have parity—nine members each—on the unofficial side of the legislature. This may seem a small business, but it took years of work to put it through, because it was vociferously opposed by whites who felt that it gave blacks and browns too much power. The previous ratio was seven Europeans, four Africans, and three Asians. Of course the 9-9-9 system (which is soon to become 10-10-10) does *not* give proportionate representation to the three racial groups, since nine European members represent fewer than 20,000 people whereas the nine Africans represent more than 7,000,000.[12] Moreover the Asian delegation representing some 75,000 people is split three ways—Arabs 2, Moslems 4, Hindus 3—which gives it a Moslem majority, and the Moslems usually take a straight-out British line.

Tanganyika Africans have no nationalist organization comparable to the Kenya Africa Union or the Uganda National Congress, but it is only a question of time before one emerges. More and more people are coming to think of themselves as "African" (other than members of separate tribes) and even as "Tanganyikan." One Provincial Commissioner told us that, twenty years ago, he would have predicted flatly that any growth of pan-Tanganyika sentiment was an impossibility, no matter over how long a span of time. "Now I know that I was wrong."

The chief African grievances are the ban on alcohol, the tendency to alienate more land to white settlers, and, above all, lack of opportunities for education. Julius K. Nyerere, a school teacher and president of the newly organized Tanganyika African National Union (TANU), told an American reporter recently that under the present program of the government, primary education will not be available to all African children until "1986 or 1990."[13]

Every year the Tanganyika government is obliged to submit a lengthy report to the Trusteeship Council of the UN, and sometimes this gets a lively airing. In March, 1954, V.K. Krishna Menon of India had some pointedly critical remarks to make, though he went out of his way to pay tribute to the qualities of Sir Edward Twining. Here are some nuggets from his speech:

[12] Cf. Alexander Campbell, *The Heart of Africa*, p. 238.
[13] Albion Ross in the New York *Times*, June 13, 1954.

THE WONDERFUL WORLD OF TANGANYIKA   413

We are too prone to look upon these territories as areas where we are purveying civilization to backward peoples. Here is a territory which has a history going back nearly three millennia . . .

There has been little or no progress towards self-government or independence in this Territory. As regards the political aspects of the situation in Tanganyika, there is very little about which we can be happy—except, perhaps, that there has been no violent conflict. It may be that when there is no violent conflict, there is no progress . . .

In the field of education, a European child costs the Administration £223 a year, an African child costs the Administration £8-5-0 a year, and an Asian child costs £31 a year. I am sure it is not contended that the European child is so uneducable that it requires thirty times as much effort to teach him . . .

There is no way to create a multiracial society except by the introduction of a common electorate.

Later the United Nations visiting mission to Trust Territories in East Africa spent six weeks in Tanganyika, and issued early in 1955 a striking and almost unprecedented report. It noted that millions of Africans are still living on a subsistence economy, recommended important political changes (such as that the parity system in the legislature should not continue for more than five more years), and expressed flatly—and sensationally—the view that "the people of Tanganyika can achieve self-government *within the present generation* [italics mine] on the basis of a political timetable." The British colonials were profoundly shocked by this document. People in Dar es Salaam at once called it "biased"—i.e., too pro-African. The British took the unusual step of announcing immediately after its publication (and before it was debated at the UN) that its recommendations were "not acceptable to Her Majesty's Government." Talk of self-government in Tanganyika by means of an actual timetable is, the British think, almost preposterously premature.

THE LEGENDARY LETTOW

All over Tanganyika, even today, people still talk about Lettow-Vorbeck, the German general who resisted British conquest of the country in World War I. He was an enemy, one of the fiercest and most intrepid the British ever faced, but he is spoken of with admiration and something akin to awe. Lettow is still alive, aged about eighty-five, and lives in Hamburg. Few people in the United States know his name, but he was one of the most successful guerrilla fighters in military history. He never lost a battle, and although overwhelmingly superior forces squeezed him out of Tanganyika at the end, he was never beaten in the field and he only surrendered in November, 1918, because of the defeat of Germany in Europe.

Lettow was a colonel in charge of the small garrison in German East Africa in 1914. The British set out to take the country. Lettow had 218 white officers and 2,542 *askaris* (native troops). When the end came he still had 155 Europeans and more *askaris* than he started with, because natives kept on joining his forces. He fought for more than four years without pause, and covered—mostly on foot—an area larger than the eastern United States. To say that the British never caught him is to put it negatively. Von Lettow kept 300,000 British and other allied troops in the field against him, and therefore prevented them from being used on other fronts, during the whole course of the war. From first to last 130 different *generals* went into action against him, and he inflicted on the Allies about sixty *thousand* casualties, including 20,000 European and Indian dead.

Paul von Lettow-Vorbeck was born at Saarlouis, in Western Germany, in 1870, the son of a general. He became an officer, and served in the Kaiser's forces in China, South-West Africa, and elsewhere. He was a typical old-style German officer—conscientious, indefatigable, unswervingly loyal to his fatherland, and correct. But almost the first thing he did when war broke out was to kidnap the civilian German governor of the region, to keep him from surrendering.

Lettow, with his tiny force, at once surprised the British by taking the initiative; instead of retreating, he attacked. He crossed into British East Africa, and even threatened Nairobi. Then he won a brilliant night engagement at Tanga; this was one of the most stinging little defeats the British ever suffered. They had summoned reinforcements from India; Lettow lay in wait for them, and virtually annihilated them when they tried to land; the Allied casualties were two thousand, and his were fifty-four. In Tanga today the desolate little cemetery where these men lie buried is a conspicuous sight. In preparation for this battle Lettow blacked his face, and reconnoitered between the lines disguised as an African. The confusion was so extreme among the British and Indians that they said later that Lettow had "mobilized the bees" against them; it happened that swarms of bees covered the battlefield.

For several years Lettow, throwing away the rule book, feinted, attacked, and slipped away. He invented several devices—like camouflaging his men with leaves—that the Japanese used in tropical warfare a generation later. For a long time (until he captured some) he had no rifles except museum pieces made in 1871; he had no smokeless powder, no artillery except some naval guns he got off a German cruiser, no aircraft, no way to repel British aircraft, and no normal sources of supply. He had no quinine, which was vital, and so made a substitute by brewing a kind of bark; this had a frightful taste, and was nicknamed "Lettow's schnapps." He himself got malaria ten different times. Water was so short sometimes that, he records, even Europeans "drank urine." His movements were largely determined by food supply, and he collected herds of cattle, which moved with his army. When the cattle failed, his men shot hippopotamuses, and ate their fat. He manufactured boots out of buffalo hide, wove his own uniforms, and made bandages out of bark. He had no communication whatever with his own government for year after year, and there was no possible way in which he could be reinforced. An incidental point is that he was wounded in the eye, and fought the last part of the campaign half blind.

In February, 1916, the allied command put no less a personage than the South African General (later Field Marshal) Jan Christiaan Smuts in the field to beat Lettow. Even in those days Smuts was a figure of formidable renown. And with him came 43,000 fresh white South African troops. A fantastic proportion of these soon became casualties through malaria and otherwise. Lettow kept winning battle after battle.

Lettow had great admiration for his *askaris*, who were fanatically loyal to him. In order to be one with his men, he had to live the way they did. He got the best out of them by treating them with scrupulous fairness; he ate with them, slept in their huts, and shared their hardships. One luxury he permitted himself was a bicycle. He often led marches on this, and even performed his own patrols.

One thing that distinguished the East African war was chivalry. From the beginning, Lettow adopted the totally unprecedented policy of *freeing* any white European prisoners he took, even officers, if they would give their word of honor not to fight against Germany again during the course of the war. This was much more sensible than having to haul prisoners along with him, and guard and feed them. Once he ambushed a contingent, and saw to his surprise the British commander-in-chief fifteen yards away, the easiest of targets. He did not shoot, because it would not have been sporting.

Smuts repeatedly called on him to surrender; Lettow repeatedly refused. One day came a message from Smuts, a chivalrous foe, informing him that the German government had just awarded him the *Pour le mérite*—the supreme German decoration for valor, corresponding to the Victoria Cross. Von Lettow, in his dry way, wrote a nice little letter of acknowledgment to Smuts and sent it across the lines, saying that he was sure there had been some "mistake," since he did not deserve such an exalted decoration.

Slowly, by heavily increasing weight of numbers, the Allies pushed Lettow out of Tanganyika into Mozambique and then Rhodesia. They thought that the war, a gentleman's war, was consequently over. But Lettow kept right on fighting. It did not matter to him in the least what territory he was on. The end came with the armistice in Europe in 1918. Von Lettow was informed that the Kaiser had given up, and that the armistice terms included the evacuation of East Africa by Germany. Von Lettow at this moment was not being engaged by the enemy; he had good stocks of cattle and ammunition; he was in no danger of being surrounded or defeated; he could have continued the war indefinitely—probably for years. His first impulse was to fight his way from Rhodesia across the Congo and retire into Angola, where he would have been impregnable.

He considered, however, that as a German soldier faithful to the fatherland he must honor the armistice. So, undefeated, he laid down his arms. Technically speaking, he did not surrender, but merely disbanded his troops and put himself at the disposal of the British commander. Von Lettow *never* surrendered as a beaten general does.

This odd old story is not done yet—not quite.

Lettow eventually reached Germany, and retired from the army in 1920. Many years later, after the German defeat and collapse in World War II, hard times came to him. Smuts, down in Johannesburg, who had always had profound admiration and respect for him, determined to give him help. So he worked out an arrangement whereby Lettow, an *enemy* general, got a pension from the victors!

In 1953 von Lettow took a trip to Africa, thirty-five years after his gallant campaigns, and stayed some months in Irene, near Johannesburg, as the guest of "Ouma" Smuts, the elderly widow of the Field Marshal. En route back to Germany the aged von Lettow stopped off for a few days in Tanga, the scene of his first stunning victory. Word spread among Africans like a bolt of fire that the great, the indomitable, the invincible von Lettow was back on their shores again. Out of the bush came a few of his surviving old *askaris*. They saluted him, and, wet-cheeked, saw him off with cheers.

A KING OF DIAMONDS

Williamson is a lone wolf, an "off-ox" as the British say. He owns and operates the richest diamond mine in the world in the Tanganyika back country, but few people have ever seen him. He is an almost total recluse—partly on account of ill health. Blackwater fever and malaria almost killed him during the lonely, stubborn years when he was searching vainly for diamonds. He discovered his mine at last not by luck or conventional

THE WONDERFUL WORLD OF TANGANYIKA 417

prospecting, but by the strictest application of scientific principles. He worked with his head as well as hands.

Dr. John Thoburn Williamson, governor and sole director of Williamson Diamonds, Ltd., is a Canadian geologist, about forty-nine. He got his Ph.D. at McGill University in 1933, and the next year went to Rhodesia to work for a mining company. Later he set out on his own, convinced that important and valuable diamond properties could be discovered in Tanganyika. After three years of search, during which he almost starved, he marked out a small area bound by five remote, shabby villages south of Lake Victoria, where he felt that diamonds *should* logically be found, because of the configuration of the soil and special geological circumstances. And here indeed he found them.

A great deal has happened since that day fifteen years ago. The mine is located at a hamlet called Mwadui, near two fairly sizable towns, Shinyanga and Mwanza. Even so, the area is one of the least known and least visited in Africa. This is Africa stark and naked, with endless miles of parched scrub under an iron sky, the Africa of jackals and hyenas moaning under lonely stars. We could not have got there if Governor Twining had not given us a lift in his private plane.

Williamson staked out a claim, got a lease, and went to work. What was once utter wilderness is now a brisk, thriving community. There are workshops, an airstrip, streets, stores, housing for the European staff, African housing, one of the best hospitals in East Africa, and of course the installations of the mine itself. Williamson employs 2,600 African workers, 110 Europeans, and 60 Asians. His labor policy is extremely good. Williamson sold his diamonds independently on the open market, through banks in London, until 1948, when he reached an agreement with the Oppenheimer interests in Johannesburg, who were impressed by his success. In 1950 he broke off relations with Oppenheimer and stopped delivery, because he did not think he was getting a good enough price; for two years he stockpiled all his diamonds. At any time during this period he might have broken the world diamond price by suddenly dumping his accumulated production on the market. But he did not do so because, in the long run, this would have hurt his own future sales, as well as Oppenheimer sales. In May, 1952, he resumed relations with the Oppenheimers, and has a contract with them giving him the right to produce up to 10 per cent, by value, of the total world output of diamonds distributed by the Oppenheimer syndicate.

Dr. Williamson is wiry, neat, good-looking, and extremely shy and quiet. He is a bachelor as well as a strict recluse. He seldom leaves the mine, seldom uses any of his four private airplanes, and practically never receives visitors. His only hobby is books—first editions. He showed us hundreds of these, laid on tables awaiting classification. Nobody knows how rich he is, because he puts most of his money back in the business. Quite possibly he is one of the richest men in the world. He holds eighth-twelfths of the total shares of his company; there are no other stockholders except his brother, P.B. Williamson, who has three-twelfths, and his close associate the Hon. L.C. Chopra, an Indian lawyer and member of the Tanganyika legislature. Williamson gave Mr. Chopra one-twelfth of the business as a reward for help in the hard early days.

We spent a vivid, robust day sightseeing on the property, which covers five square miles in all, and is bound by a double fence of barbed wire roughly twenty miles in length. The main street of the European section is called "Downing Street." Indeed Williamson is prime minister of this closely guarded and inaccessible domain. The diamonds come from a wide, shallow open pit, where African workmen scoop out shovels of gravel into big trucks. The gravel, full of diamonds, is simply scraped or pared off. No mining operation could be easier. But the ratio of diamonds to gravel is roughly one to fifteen million; that is, fifteen million particles of gravel the size of a diamond have to be moved for each diamond found. There are several stages to the processing—washing, drying, and the like. We looked at conveyor belts and centrifuges. The last process is sorting. Two women sit in a kind of barred cage, at broad tables, and with incredible speed and dexterity pick out the diamonds from the final residue of gravel.

Williamson's mine is extraordinary—indeed unique—for several reasons. First, the diamonds are predominantly gem stones, not industrials. Second, they lie almost on the surface of the earth, ready to be scratched out like grain pecked by a chicken. Most of the great South African mines are deep underground, and are much more difficult and expensive to work. Third, the deposit is fabulously rich. In South Africa six to eight carats are customarily produced per hundred cubic yards of earth; Williamson averages 250-300. Moreover Williamson's output can be gauged with close accuracy; he knows exactly how much earth he needs to move to get a certain amount of diamonds. At present he is producing 350 carats per day. He could multiply this production many times, simply by moving more earth, but 350 carats a day is enough.

Williamson sent Queen Elizabeth, when she was still a princess, a 56-carat pink stone as a wedding present, which is valued at "more than" £100,000. He showed us a model of this formidable gem, which is almost as big as a Brazil nut. The biggest diamond Williamson ever found weighed 174 carats, but it was not of very good quality. He keeps one stone in a London bank vault that weighs 147 carats—almost three times the size of the Queen's. He does not want to sell it. Anyway there are few people in the world who could afford to buy it, even if it were for sale.

After the diamonds are separated from the last bits of gravel they go into a steel and concrete pillbox on the property, where they soak for an interval in a crock, full of acid, on the open floor.[14] The clay-colored crock looks like a cooky jar, and maybe has a hundred million dollars in it. As to the pillbox it is a veritable fort. First one of Williamson's executives took us to an adjacent building, where he ceremoniously opened a vault; in this was a safe, which he opened in turn, taking out a key. We advanced to the pillbox, and its doors swung open—but only after a complicated procedure. The combination is changed daily, and four keys—each carefully kept by a different man—have to be used before the doors will open. Williamson himself cannot get in to see his own diamonds until the four different keys are produced. Then inside the pillbox are three large iron safes, as well as the crock of diamonds on the floor. Two of the safes contain diamonds; the third has cash. Nobody except Williamson and a few intimate associates know which are which.

Diamonds are, of course, small, easy to conceal, and of a highly concentrated value; in any diamond mine theft or "seepage" is a problem. In his early years, before stringent precautions were put in force, Williamson unavoidably lost a good deal of his production—nobody knows how much. Now security measures are in the stout hands of H.E. Burgess, who spent twenty years as a chief inspector in the Criminal Investigation Department of Scotland Yard. He joined Williamson's staff three years ago, and has under him four European police officers and two hundred African police. He has at his command searchlights, dogs, and ponies who patrol the barbed wire at night. Why ponies? They are quieter than jeeps, and do not have lights.

But Williamson treats his workers with much more trust and discrimination than do mine operators elsewhere in Africa. For one thing he allows them to bring their families into the compound, which would be unheard of in South Africa. He does not X-ray his men, nor give them purges. They can quit any time they want to. They are, however, carefully searched—every bodily orifice is inspected—each time they pass through the barbed wire. One odd point is that the searcher, who is armed with a torch, is also publicly searched before the others, because if a diamond should be found on anybody, it might be charged that he had "planted" it.

Every once in a while comes the day when a batch of diamonds is removed from the pillbox, and shipped out for sale. Williamson alone takes the

[14] This is to clean them. The crock sits on the floor and not in a safe because of acid fumes.

decision on the date and amount of each shipment. He calls Mr. Burgess, and, half an hour before departure, a pilot is alerted. Nobody else is told. Burgess straps the diamonds to his person, steps into the plane, and takes off for a nearby town where the bank has a good sound vault. From here the diamonds are dispatched to London by a means incongruously prosaic—airmail.

NATURE NOTE IN SHINYANGA

From Williamson's we went to Shinyanga where we saw two boys, under the supervision of a witch doctor, put on a dance with a ten-foot python. The boys became intertwined with the snake like Laocoon, and collapsed together with it after a climax of erotic intensity, writhing on the ground with the exhausted snake lying on top of them. To the wonders of Black Africa there is no end.

CHAPTER 23

Hope and Crisis in Uganda

No land, no life. —ENOCH E. K. MULIRA

IN LONDON, en route to Africa, we met Winston Churchill at an amiable social occasion, and he said, among other things, "Don't miss Uganda!" He described with vivid gusto the source of the Nile at Ripon Falls—"flashing like a horse's tail." Later I came across an old book by Churchill, *My African Journey*, published in 1908, in which he vigorously counsels the British government of the day, "*Concentrate on Uganda.*" Mr. Churchill made some remarkable observations in this now forgotten volume, for instance, "What fun to make the immemorial Nile begin its journey by diving through a turbine!" He pointed out that "it would be perfectly possible to harness the whole river" by building a dam and hydroelectric works at its source in Uganda, and that nowhere in the world would so little masonry be needed to control such an immense amount of water. Forty-six years later, in April, 1954, Sir Winston's acute vision became a reality, when the Owen Falls Hydroelectric Scheme, one of the largest and potentially most fruitful development projects in Africa, was formally opened by Queen Elizabeth.

UGANDA: TO BEGIN WITH

The principal things to say about Uganda, aside from water power and its seething colorfulness, are these:

1. It is rich. It is the biggest producer of cotton and coffee in the British Commonwealth, and—at the moment anyway—prices of these commodities are high. The trade balance is heavily favorable—in marked contrast to Kenya or Southern Rhodesia. "If we weren't so well off, we wouldn't be so model," one official told me with a mildly ironic smile.

Before the war, Uganda exports and imports combined amounted only to seven million pounds sterling a year; today, they reach ten times this sum.[1] Of the total expenditures in 1952 (roughly £15,000,000), not less than £1,300,000 went to education. Medical services were £933,356—up from £556,000 in 1950. As much money went to veterinary services as to prisons; until recently crime was practically unknown.

Uganda has no armed forces to support, which means that income can be put to more productive use. True, a Uganda battalion is included in the King's African Rifles, but this is stationed in Kenya, not Uganda. There is not one British soldier in the country. When the Governor needed a new aide-de-camp recently, he had to send all the way to the Royal Air Force in England to get one. Nor has Uganda ever had to spend much money on police; there are only about 250 British police in the whole protectorate—population 5¼ million!

2. Almost for the first time in Africa I got the impression that this was a country where Africans were happy. To live, all they have to do is reach upward and pluck fruit from trees. But this generalization—that the people are happy—needs qualification in several vivid respects, as we shall presently see. Even if many Ugandans are carefree people individually, they do not make an altogether happy or contented community. No African country under European rule is happy, once it has reached the point of being educated enough to want freedom.

3. Uganda has a very complex geographical and political structure. Embedded in the protectorate are four ancient kingdoms, which have zealously regarded treaty relationships with Britain. The chief of these, which is also the most important province in Uganda, is Buganda.[2]

4. Not only is Uganda rich; it is advanced. The accent is on *African* development. An African Chamber of Commerce exists, and there are 11,000 African shop owners, although most retail trade is still Indian. A Credit and Savings Bank has been set up, financed in part by the government, to lend money to Africans (not whites) at moderate rates of interest. A thriving European cigarette factory in Jinja, near Owen Falls, employs African *women* workers, something almost unprecedented in this part of the world. An African Housing Estate is functioning, to assist home building, and useful work is being done by the Community Development organization, which natives translate as "Good-of-the-Country" movement. This

---

[1] I do not know why it impressed me, but among articles forbidden entrance into Uganda are condensed milk, "offensive printed matter," rat virus, birds' eggs, and toy pistols. Articles that may not be taken out are wheaten products, *beche de mer*, hippopotamus teeth, unwrought precious stones, ambergris, rice, and whisky.

[2] The others are Bunyoro, Toro, and Ankole, and each has a picturesquely titled kinglet or monarch—Bukirabasai Ja Agutamba the Umukama of Bunyoro, Rukirabasai Ja the Mukama of Toro, and Rabambasai the Omugabe of Ankole.

educates and encourages Africans in a wide variety of fields—adult education, road building, safety of water supply, preservation of game, and so forth. And Uganda has a Mobile News Service, which brings information to people out in the bush by means of trucks carrying portable radio programs.[3]

In 1908 Mr. Churchill wrote:

> In Uganda the arguments for state ownership and employment of the natural resources of the country seem to present themselves in their strongest and most formidable array . . . It would be hard to find a country where the conditions were more favorable than in Uganda to a practical experiment in State Socialism.

Here too the youthful Sir Winston proves himself a remarkably good prophet. The cotton industry has been reorganized and nationalized recently, and the coffee industry is to follow. A fund has been built up in case the price of cotton slumps; the surplus goes to development at large, and all marketing is done through an independent government agency, the Lint Marketing Board. Electricity is a state monopoly in Uganda, through the Uganda Electricity Board. So are the railways, posts and telegraphs, under joint operation with the governments of Kenya and Tanganyika. There are six hundred co-operatives of one sort or another in Uganda. Then consider the Uganda Development Corporation, Ltd., a semi-governmental agency which is broadly in charge of all economic development and planning. This operates the new and important cement industry, runs the Uganda Fish Marketing Corporation, (TUFMAC), owns the only hotel in Entebbe, and is busy on various mineral and metallurgical projects.

The prevailing tone and atmosphere in economic affairs is, in other words, reformist, humanitarian, and New Dealish, under a Ten-Year "Development Period" or plan. How socialist is Uganda? About as socialist as Britain, perhaps a shade more so.

5. *Uganda does not permit white settlement,* and officially at least there is no color bar. Again the contrast to Kenya (and the Rhodesias) is marked.

The land policy, based on the tenet that Uganda is an African country belonging to Africans, goes back to 1900 and the work of Sir Harry Johnston, one of the most prescient as well as doughty and bristly of early British administrators. The motive may have been spurious in part, since at that time it was thought that the tsetse fly made Uganda unfit for European habitation. Be this as it may be, a policy of excluding whites from ownership of land was set up, and has been maintained to this day. Except for a few

---

[3] Many Africans in Uganda are still, of course, primitive in the extreme. The government radio in July, 1954, had to drop weather forecasting from some of its programs. If the weather did not turn out to be what the forecasts said, the people protested that they were being "lied to" by the government and made a rumpus. New York *Herald Tribune,* July 16, 1954.

infinitesimal holdings, no land in Uganda is owned by Europeans, and no white man may buy land without the express permission both of the British governor and the local African administration; such permission is given only in rare cases, and after laboriously applied checks and safeguards to protect Africans from exploitation. Hence, Uganda has—so far—few of the anguishing problems that inevitably accompany white settlement.

Color bar is, as always, hard to write about, because there are so many gradations in custom and habit. Uganda has no segregation in local transportation, the railroad, or (most important) in shops or schools.[4] Africans are invited as a matter of course to Government House, if their official position warrants this; but few private mixed parties take place, and the old-style British still refuse any social contact with Negroes, except at official functions. Uganda is by no means as free of color bar as British dependencies on the West Coast like Nigeria; but it is infinitely, beyond calculation or measure, more free than Kenya, the Union, or the Rhodesias. Moreover conditions are becoming better steadily. A few years ago Dr. Ralph Bunche, one of the most useful and distinguished of living Americans, was refused admittance to a hotel in Kampala. He would be accepted without question today. Another point is that an African may drink hard liquor in Uganda—in strict contrast to most of the rest of equatorial and southern Africa—if he is respectably enough dressed to go into a bar and has the price of a gin or Scotch.

*

Uganda was then, in comparison to Kenya, a pool of good will, prosperity, and peace—until two years ago. Arriving here from Kenya, one felt an almost physical sense of a weight being lifted, of emotional as well as intellectual relief. But acute political distress and turmoil came to Uganda late in 1953, when the Kabaka (King) of Buganda, the principal African dignitary in the country, was pitched off his throne and dispatched to exile. Crisis over the Kabaka still inflames much of Uganda, and definite danger exists that the peaceful evolution of the country, its hitherto serene development toward political and economic maturity, will be gravely compromised.

UGANDA: SHAPE, SIZE, AND QUALITIES

Uganda lies close to the heart of Africa, and is shaped something like a lopsided bucket; it covers 94,000 square miles, roughly the size of West Germany, and has 5¼ million people. Fifteen per cent of its area is water.

[4] An interesting minor point is that *Europeans* are not allowed to travel third class on the railway—this is an example of color bar in reverse.

The population is overwhelmingly African; 99.2 per cent of the people are of Bantu, Nilotic, or Hamitic stock. There are 50,300 Indians, and only a handful—7,600—of white Europeans, almost all British. Of this total no fewer than 1,200 are missionaries. Uganda has been thoroughly proselytized, and of the native population 1,250,000 are Christian.

The Indians are, as in Kenya, an aggressive, industrious, and prosperous community, but they do not carry as much political or intellectual weight. The mayor of Kampala, the Hon. A. N. Maini, an enlightened personality, is however an Indian (like the mayor of Dar es Salaam in Tanganyika), and Kampala has almost as much the texture of an Indian town as Nairobi. Indians served an essential historical purpose—that of carrying trade out into the wilderness. It was the railway, of course, that brought most of them into Uganda, but a few Indian families settled here even before the British came. A good many Africans resent Indian economic power and pressure. For instance, cotton ginning (but not marketing) is virtually an Indian monopoly, and Africans want to share in this lucrative business. There are only five ginneries (co-operative) in the country run by Africans.

Before proceeding we should mention the peculiarities of Bantu nomenclature as applied to Uganda:

Uganda is the name of the country.
Buganda is the name of the ancient kingdom, now one of the four provinces of Uganda.
Luganda is the name of the language.
Kiganda is an adjective pertaining to anything that has to do with Buganda.
Muganda is the name for a native of Buganda.
Baganda is the plural of Muganda.
Ganda is an adjective relating to all, or most, of the above.

Mostly in this chapter I shall be referring to Buganda, but I shall not try to follow scrupulously the style above. It would be silly to call these distinctions ridiculous or abstruse, even if they are puzzling at first. Think what a native of Uganda has to face if, for instance, he arrives in London with no knowledge of English. He must learn *inter alia* that "Britons" of "Anglo-Saxon" origin speak "English" in an area known as "England," which is part of "Great Britain," "the United Kingdom," or "the British Isles," sing a song called "Rule Britannia," and fly a flag known as the "Union Jack." The Bantu system of prefixes is, in truth, much simpler.

The western side of Uganda is marked by the Ruwenzori Range, or "Mountains of the Moon"; that these existed has been known since Ptolemy in the second century AD, but they were not seen by a white man or explored till Stanley (1875). They are difficult mountains to climb, almost perpetually smothered by steaming cloud. To the north is the Sudan—the countries melt into each other in vast swamps, as we know—and to the south and west are the unpathed, luxuriant forests of the Congo. On the east is Victoria Nyanza, the second largest lake (after Superior) in the world; it covers an area the size of Ireland, 26,000 square miles, and lies at an elevation of 4,000 feet. Uganda is both high (though not as high as Kenya) and swelteringly hot. Here we knew that we were in the real tropics at last—and needed blankets at night.

Victoria Nyanza or Lake Victoria[5] is somewhat frustrating to those who live on its banks, because it is beautiful and inviting but impossible to swim in or even paddle in safely, because of bilharzia. And it is full of crocodiles and hippopotamuses. Hippos have been known to roam down the main streets of Jinja at dawn—and Jinja is a Europeanized town with some 7,500 people. Lake Victoria has perils above as well as below its placid surface. We flew over it three times, and I have never known pilots to be more wary in dodging innocent-looking thunderclouds. Islands in Victoria are thick with the tsetse fly, and parts of the shore are officially restricted areas, in which human beings are not allowed to dwell; this is to break contact with the islands and thus prevent the fly from getting to the mainland. Onchoceriasis has been troublesome along the Nile. This disease, which causes blindness as I have already mentioned, is carried here by a fly (*Simulium damnosum*) locally known as the "mbwa"; it breeds for the most part in *rapidly* flowing water, hunts by scent, and is apparently strongly attracted by African body odors. An enterprising medical officer, seizing on this phenomenon, gave large doses of chlorophyll to natives working at Owen Falls, with the remarkable result that they no longer attracted the "mbwa" flies. As a further happy result onchocerciasis has been largely eliminated in the area.

Uganda has two capitals, Entebbe and Kampala, which are twenty-one miles apart on one of the few good roads in this part of Africa. Until modern times the journey between them took place by rickshaw. ENTEBBE is on Lake Victoria, and is three miles north of the Equator; several times we crossed this invisible hot line separating the northern hemisphere from the southern. Entebbe is the administrative capital and chief government seat, built by the British from scratch, and containing Government House, official buildings, the residences of the British elite, and celebrated botanical

---

[5] Nyanza means "lake."

gardens. The British chose the site partly to maintain the concept that Buganda and Uganda were separate entities, partly to avoid native "squalor" in Kampala, partly because the Entebbe area was freer of the tsetse fly. Its white population today is 350. But Entebbe, such a remote and artificial-seeming town, hidden by foaming jungle, is one of the great aerial crossroads of the world. Its airport, halfway between Cairo and Johannesburg, and lying at an altitude of 3,761 feet, is one of the best in Africa, and is an indispensable stop on the transcontinental north-south routes from Europe to the Cape. By jet (until jet flight was suspended) Entebbe was only about twelve hours from London. Even without jets, you can send an airmail letter from Entebbe to London quicker than to Dar es Salaam.[6]

KAMPALA (population 38,000) is the commercial capital, and has appropriate vigor and bustle; also it is the headquarters of the Buganda government (as apart from the over-all Uganda administration headquartered at Entebbe) and is the seat of the Kabaka's palace. Like Rome and Lisbon, Kampala is built on seven hills. "How refreshing," one Briton told us, "to see a view in Africa that has an end!" The Anglican cathedral stands on one of the Kampala hills, a Roman Catholic church on another, and an Islamic mosque on a third. Religious impulses and rivalries have always played a cogent role in Uganda history.

The most valuable institution in Uganda, and one of the most valuable in all Africa, occupies still another hill—Makerere College, the only school with university rank in the whole immense distance between Khartoum and Johannesburg.[7] Makerere (its official name is the University College of East Africa and it is affiliated with the University of London) was founded in 1922, and is not purely a Ugandan institution, since it takes boys equally from Kenya and Tanganyika, as well as a few from Nyasaland, Zanzibar, and elsewhere. It gives degrees to about 250 Africans a year, and its graduates have a special status and prestige all over eastern, central, and even southern Africa. It is a great thing to have been to Makerere! Think of what special distinction an American boy would have, if he were one of a graduating class of only 250 at the *only* university in, let us say, the whole Mississippi Valley. We visited Makerere several times, and I have seldom been more impressed by an educational institution anywhere. Bernard de Bunson, the principal, is an extraordinarily wise and devoted man. Students may be

[6] To talk about the speed of modern African communications compared to those of yesterday is, of course, trite, but some items are irresistible. For instance, until the railway came, colonial officers in Uganda returning to London on leave received *three months'* extra time allowance each way, since they had to *walk* to the coast. Horses or other animal transport could not be used on account of sleeping sickness.
[7] But a university is now being built at Salisbury, Southern Rhodesia.

Roman Catholic, Protestant, or Moslem, but pagans are not admitted. The boys (and a few girls) come from about eighty different tribes, and their intellectual curiosities can be vigorous. The best students are usually Kikuyus. One recent issue of the school paper contained a lively essay on the evils of witchcraft in seventeenth-century *England*. One African grievance is that, as yet, Makerere has no school of law. Most graduates go into government service—as doctors, agricultural officers, veterinarians, and the like. The principal merit of Makerere is, obviously, that it gives African boys opportunity to contribute useful lives to their communities. Also Uganda itself is enlightened by Makerere; it gives the country dignity and substance. What would Cambridge, Massachusetts, be without Harvard? The same thing might be said—*mutatis mutandis*—about Kampala. Of course there should be dozens—scores—of other Makereres scattered throughout Black Africa. Schools like this can do more than any single thing to change the face of the continent, give it hope, give it skills, bring it to modern times. But in all British colonies put together there are only three other colleges like Makerere (Achimota in the Gold Coast, Ibadan in Nigeria, and Fourah Bay in Sierra Leone); in French Africa south of the Sahara, one; in Portuguese Africa, none. The Sudan has Gordon College, and recently the Belgians have inaugurated a small university in the Congo. And that is all.

Also near Kampala, at Budo, is a well-known preparatory school—for boys and girls both—called King's College. It was founded in 1906, and was orginially a school mainly for the sons of chiefs. Boys often go to Makerere after Budo, and become doubly elite.

UGANDA: ITS GLOW AND COLOR

African color! Here you really have it—and I do not mean color in regard to race. Again let me quote Mr. Churchill:

> I had travelled through tropical forests in Cuba and India, and had often before admired their enchanting, yet sinister, luxuriance. But the forests of Uganda, for magnificence, for variety of form and colour, for profusion of brilliant life—plant, bird, insect, reptile, beast—for the vast scale and awful fecundity of the natural processes that are beheld at work, eclipsed, and indeed effaced, all previous impressions. One becomes, not without a secret sense of aversion, the spectator of an intense convulsion of life and death. Reproduction and decay are locked struggling in infinite embraces. In this glittering Equatorial slum huge trees jostle one another for room to live; slender growths stretch upwards—as it seems in agony—towards sunlight and life.

The soil bursts with irrepressible vegetations. Every victor, trampling on the rotting mould of exterminated antagonists, soars aloft only to encounter another host of aerial rivals, to be burdened with masses of parasitic foliage, smothered in the glorious blossoms of creepers, laced and bound and interwoven with interminable tangles of vines and trailers. Birds are as bright as butterflies; butterflies are as big as birds. . . . The telegraph-wire runs northwards to Gondokoro through this vegetable labyrinth. Even its poles had broken into bud![8]

This was written almost half a century ago; for much of Uganda, particularly in the Murchison Falls area, every word of it still holds good today. But Uganda has cultivation too. We drove to Jinja, on the most beautiful forest road I have ever seen, and passed through what seemed to be an elongated breakfast; in orderly but sumptuous profusion we encountered in turn pineapple, bananas, sugar, coffee, and tea.

Bananas are the staff of life, except in the grain country to the north. Our chauffeur leaped out of the car at a village and bought a bunch, which contained maybe a hundred bananas, cost 1 shilling (14 cents), and would be his basic food for a week. Bananas are also umbrellas in Uganda. In the beating rain we several times saw women plodding along the roads, with a broad banana leaf the shape and almost the size of a canoe balanced on their heads. And as in Tanganyika, bananas are a drink—or, rather, two different drinks: *pombe,* which is banana beer, and *waragi,* a distilled spirit.

One feature of the landscape, here as elsewhere in Uganda, is the procession of giant anthills, which line the roads. They are jagged and craggy and often reach a height of twelve to fifteen feet, towering like ugly sentinels; they are bright ocher red, and resemble mountain peaks in miniature. Oddly enough the termites or ants living in these fantastic structures contribute some form of chemical change to the earth, with the result that they make good as well as readily available material for road repair—earth harder and stickier than normal.[9] At every turn, we saw vegetable curiosities. I do not think I had ever encountered a "tree tomato" before, which tastes like a gooseberry, nor have I ever seen such yellow flowering trees as the cassias in Uganda, or anything as piercingly red as the plant known as the red-hot poker. On the Ruwenzori slopes is a variety of aster that grows seven feet tall. In other fields of nature one may come across other miracles. One lake, near Katwe, is colored bright pink. The variety and luxuriance of bird life makes Uganda an ornithologist's dreamland. I never knew literally what it meant to be awakened by tropical bird songs till I stayed at Government House in Entebbe. Among animals, I should give passing mention at least

[8] *My African Journey.*
[9] Some Ugandans eat ants, and consider them a delicacy.

to the long-horned cattle in the Ankole country, which we saw driving from Entebbe to Kishwamba. They make Texas cattle look practically like mice. On this road we passed a sizable town, Mbarara, where lions still occasionally walk the streets at night, when they are sure that all two-legged animals are safely in bed. But one must never forget that Africa is, above all, a continent of the sharpest possible contrasts. For instance, in Jinja, on the other side of Uganda, the Provincial Commissioner, T.R.F. Cox, mentioned casually that he had been in Africa twenty-three years and had never once seen a lion.

What gives most color to Uganda is, however, not its vegetable or animal life but human beings. I thought in Moshi, Tanganyika, that nothing could ever equal, for almost pitiless brilliance, the costumes of women there. But the women of Uganda outdo them. They saunter along the roads, or cluster in the villages, with their marvelously unmoving heads and neatly wagging hindquarters, like figures in a ballet. They do not wear belts around their foreheads like the Kikuyu, their bodies have not shriveled, and they are smiling, serene, and beautiful. Their dresses are pulled up by a sash, with a semi-bustle in the back, and fall to the ground with a long lovely sweep. The cloth is, as a rule, not so eccentrically patterned as in Tanganyika or the Congo, but gives an impression of more solid color—rose, orange, sea-green, heliotrope, crimson. Some women in remote districts still wear bark cloth; the demerit of this, which is made by beating pulp out of fig bark, is that it may melt when it rains.

AFRICAN PATTERNS IN UGANDA

In northern Uganda years ago, naked Nilotic savages when they got money would buy three things first, in this order—a hat, an umbrella, and a bicycle. Today, all over Uganda, what people want most are sugar, cash for taxes, and cloth to make dresses for their wives. One DC told me that, no matter what happens when (or if) the British go, four heritages of their rule will remain—group photographs, the visitor's book, bicycles, and football. The Baganda in particular are crazy about family photographs.

There are upward of 250,000 bicycles in Uganda, an astonishing number; it works out roughly to one for every twenty inhabitants, man, woman, and child. The weight of this figure can be more appreciated if we keep in mind that in other parts of Africa, like Nyasaland and even the Congo which is supposed to be rich, one can travel for hundreds of miles and never see a bicycle at all. A good bicycle costs 480 shillings ($67.20) in Kampala. Even children have them; boys go to their fathers and say that they will lose face with their classmates if they have to *walk* to school. One indication of the extent of bicycle traffic is a recent crime wave—1,298 bicycles were stolen in Uganda in 1953. Bicycles can support extraordinary weights, and whole families mount them; the wife usually rides sidesaddle, with a papoose strapped to her back, while the husband works the pedals; another infant may be poised on the handlebars. In Entebbe I saw a woman riding a bicycle while carrying a large pot of banana beer balanced on her head. Bicycles can be anything from a truck to a hearse; corpses are sometimes covered with bark cloth, and carried on a bicycle to the cemetery.

The Baganda love to dance, and night clubs outside Kampala must be seen to be believed. The dance "floor" is often no more than a clay courtyard under the trees, and visitors sit on old crates and boxes. A dance is called a *ngoma*; literally this means "drama." The dancing is aggressively sexual, but not in an unpleasant sense. One evening some Indian friends took us to a ginnery, where they put on a big *ngoma*. African girls with beautiful supple bodies, a soft gleaming brown in color, climbed to a kind of dais—like a boxing ring, but without ropes—in the center of the hall; to encourage them guests tossed coins (supplied by our Indian hosts) up on the dais, and the girls, one by one, strove to outdo one another in pelvic gyrations. Later an African chief took us out to his isolated and utterly lonely cottage in the jungle, along with one favored dancer and two or three musicians with their drums, to continue these festivities. Lamps were lit; the room was so small and crowded that some of us had to sit on the floor. The chief, a burly character as black as porphyry, made the pretty girl, with her slender body and delicately pointed, pear-shaped breasts, prostrate herself before him flat on the floor. "I am chief!" he muttered in an ugly voice, and commanded her to dance. This she did with a peculiar kind of calm, calculated frenzy. Suddenly I became aware that we had an audience. It was long after midnight, but dozens of Africans had crept from nowhere out of the forest, and were gaping outside and craning their necks through the windows to see what went on—an eerie spectacle. It was on this occasion too that I saw African boys open beer bottles by snapping the metal caps off—with their teeth.

Dancing caused a nice little political crisis while we were in Uganda. The prime minister of Buganda, known as the Katikiro, outlawed "western" dancing in the bars and night clubs, because these had become haunts of vice. Husbands left their wives in favor of prostitutes who knew how to dance in the western manner, families were broken up, and poll-tax collections went down. A firebrand editor called the prime minister a "fool" for having taken such a puritanical step. He was arrested for slander, and sentenced to eighteen months' imprisonment by the Mengo (native court). A *British* judge then let him out on bail. The local parliament, or great Lukiko, endorsed the prime minister's view and the ban on western dancing was confirmed.

The student journal at Budo had this to say:

> The Baganda always boast of being the most progressive people in Uganda and East Africa as a whole, but this is a falacy [sic] of the greatest order.
> They are still under the yoke of feudal Lords, and these Lords are the people who are directing the administrative Machinery of the country. Instead of thinking of ways to develop the country, they engage themselves in political manoeuvres in order that they may be enabled to stay in office for a longer time.
> After throwing the Editor of the Uganda Post into prison on political grounds, the . . . Katikiro introduced a Bill banning all Western Ball Room dancing. The Lukiko, in a state of Frenzy coupled with the fear to oppose the Bill on the part of the Chiefs, lest they should lose their posts, passed the Bill with an overwhelming majority.
> Incidentally the Lukiko failed to say which was Western Dancing. It seems we can still carry on with the Samba, Rumba and Konga!

*

The Baganda are a proud people, much more sophisticated than their neighbors. They are not fiercely industrious like the Chagga. Even if they do no work, there will be enough to eat. They have a strong sense of justice and democracy, great regard for their own forms, and intelligence. They are good at dialectics, and make excellent debaters. Probably they are the most educable tribe (they would say "nation") in East Africa. They have few social distinctions, and the poorest peasant considers himself the equal of the prime minister. Many—even if the fruit of the trees is above them—are seriously undernourished, and suffer grievously from a shortage of fats and protein. One doctor pointed out to us how astonishingly alike boys and girls look, particularly if the girl has her hair cropped; adult males may have full breasts and scanty hair. One theory to account for this is that hormone producing elements are lacking in their food, and the masculinity of the young men declines, although one would never think this while watching them dance.[10] And near Jinja we met a chief who, incredibly enough, is one of two hundred sons of the same father.

---

[10] It is interesting in this connection that in several local languages there is no distinction between "nephew" and "niece" or even "brother" and "sister." Sometimes (particularly in the Eastern Province) men dancing at village feasts will stuff pillows under their robes, and pretend to be pregnant women.

HOPE AND CRISIS IN UGANDA

In Buganda some farmers are small landlords, some are tenants; there are no squatters as among the Kikuyu because white settlement is not permitted. An acute problem is labor shortage on the farms, because everybody wants to go into the towns. Tenants pay the landlord (African) a flat rent of 10 shillings *per year*, without regard to the size of the holding, plus a tithe of coffee, cotton, and banana beer. Taxes run between 35 and 50 shillings a year, and are collected by the local chief, who is paid a salary by the Buganda government. One chief out in the bush (his salary was 960 shillings or $126 a month, a substantial sum for this part of the world) showed us proudly his books and boxes of cash from tax receipts.[11] The average farmer only earns about 600 shillings ($84.00) a year, but there are comparatively few *landless* poor.

BACKGROUND TO UGANDA AFFAIRS

The first white man ever to set foot in Uganda was the explorer J. H. Speke in 1854, who a few years later discovered that Victoria Nyanza was the source of the Nile. Then came other explorers, like Stanley, the first to travel around the great lake and demonstrate that it was just one body of water, not five as had previously been thought. Stanley opened the way for the missionaries who followed, by striking a compact with the Buganda king of those days, a formidable personage named Mutesa I. Mutesa means "measurer."

Not only did the Baganda have a king, known then as now as the Kabaka, but a court, a system of justice, a parliament (the great Lukiko), and a code of chivalry. They had no wheeled transport or written language, but they have existed as a coherent tribe, some authorities believe, since the year AD 1000, and the royal line goes back without interruption for at least four hundred years. Particularly the Baganda were proud of the fact that they were not naked people, like many of those around them, but clothed. They could not weave, but they wore bark cloth beautifully dyed and patterned, and had a highly developed culture of a sort.

They were an impulsive people, and did not have much regard for human life in the abstract. Speke's description of his meeting with Mutesa is well known:

> The king now loaded one of the carbines I had given him with his own hands, and giving it full-cock to a page, told him to go out and shoot a man in the outer court, which was no sooner accomplished

[11] There are some wonderfully fancy names among chiefs in Uganda, particularly if they went to mission schools. One we met was William Wilberforce Kajumbala Nadiope.

than the little urchin returned to announce his success, with a look of glee. . . . The king said to him, "And did you do it well?" "Oh, yes, capitally." He spoke the truth, no doubt, for he dared not have trifled with the king; but the affair created hardly any interest. I never heard, and there appeared no curiosity to know, what individual human being the urchin had deprived of life.[12]

The missionaries began to arrive in force after 1877, first British Protestants, then French Catholics, and they proselytized with sharp vigor. But even before Speke, Arab traders had penetrated into Buganda, and left strong Moslem traces. So the struggle for religious power was not only heated, but triple. At first the Baganda had utterly no comprehension of the difference between Catholics and Protestants, but even so, many converts became fanatically devout.

Mutesa I died in 1884, and was succeeded by a vicious youthful monster named Mwanga. The first Anglican bishop assigned to Uganda, James Hannington, was murdered in 1885 on Mwanga's orders. He made the error of trying to enter the country from the north, above the lake. An oracle well known to the people stated that Uganda would be conquered if a white man ever entered the territory from this direction; Hannington, despite warnings, did this, and paid for it with his life.[13]

At about the same time occurred the tragic episode of the Uganda martyrs. A group of royal page boys became converted—some Catholic, some Protestant. In rage Mwanga (who was homosexual) ordered them to be slain. But, after they were sentenced to death, he promised to spare their lives if they would renounce Christianity. For ten days every kind of pressure was put on these brave boys; one and all, they refused to recant their new faith. The legend is that they were boiled in a pot; in actual fact, they were killed by being bound in mats and tossed into huge fires. One boy escaped, and is alive today, aged over eighty. His name is Ham Musaka, and he is one of the most respected members of contemporary Uganda society.

From Kampala we drove out to see the stone cross that marks the place where thirty-two of these boys were put to the fire. It is out in a lonely unkempt field, and looked as if nobody had visited it for years. A cruel story. But one should try to view African barbarism with per-

---

[12] From *Men in the Tropics* by Harold Evans, p. 228.

[13] Politics, too, had a role in this unhappy affair. Mwanga was strongly under Arab influence, and hated European whites. He learned that a third European power, Germany, had eyes on Uganda. So he ordered Hannington's murder as a warning; the fact that Hannington was British, not German at all, was either misunderstood by him or made no difference.

HOPE AND CRISIS IN UGANDA

spective. Europeans have been barbarous too. In the Spanish Civil War in the 1930's prisoners were bound with barbed wire, doused in gasoline, and burned alive.

In 1888-91 came the religious wars that I mentioned briefly in Chapter 17. Catholic Africans looted and burned Protestant churches; Protestant Africans looted and burned Catholic churches. The Protestants won, and Mwanga fled with the French Catholics.

Meantime Captain (later Lord) Lugard was opening the country up for the Imperial British East African Company. The Baganda are proud of the fact that they were never conquered. Penetration by the company was largely peaceable. In 1893 the British government took Buganda over, although anti-imperialist sentiment in London strongly opposed this step; in 1900 the Union Jack went up over the rest of Uganda as well, by terms of a treaty known as the Uganda Agreement, for which Queen Victoria was sponsor. Sir Harry Johnston came out as Special Commissioner and set up the administration that exists today. *Punch* celebrated the agreement with a renowned cartoon, portraying John Bull surveying with a mixture of dubiety, reluctance, and moral satisfaction a new African baby delivered into his lap.

*

Uganda is a British protectorate. It has the usual apparatus of a governor, Executive Council and Legislative Council. There are no political parties in our sense, and there has never been a national election. But steadily, if gradually, the British have extended African responsibilities and opportunities. In early 1954 the membership of LEGCO was increased from thirty-two to fifty-six, with twenty African members instead of eight. Basic British policy is what it is everywhere in Africa, that of preparing Africans by slow—sometimes very slow—stages for eventual self-government. Unfortunately in Uganda the Kabaka crisis has thrown everything askew, at least for the moment, and it is accordingly difficult in the extreme to convince nationalist Baganda of British good intentions.

What the British want to establish first is effective national unity. Obviously (they say) there cannot be self-government for every tribe, or for the four different main divisions of the country. If unity does not come first, the same danger of fragmentation that afflicts Nigeria will develop; if the British get out *too* soon, chaos will be the result, and there will be no self-government at all. Until comparatively recently the British thought that they had plenty of time in Uganda, and reforms were leisurely; now they know that time is running out faster than anybody could have dreamed possible ten years ago, and they are confronted with the familiar painful dilemma—to give concessions before Africans are equipped to take advantage of them, or to put a brake on progress which will stimulate African resentment. The same situation had to be faced in Nigeria and the Gold Coast. But there the Africans are much more highly developed, and the pace is faster.[14]

The Governor of Uganda, Sir Andrew Cohen, is a large blondish restless man. He is a professional civil servant, and has been called "the most brilliant mind in the British colonial service." Most of his work took place in London, not out in the field, before he went to Uganda, and he is one of the fathers of both the Nigeria and Gold Coast reforms, as well as Central African Federation. He has never been a DC out in the bush, and is a perfect Cambridge-Bloomsbury-Whitehall type. His pretty wife is the daughter of a don, and one of his sisters is a don. He comes of a distinguished Anglo-Jewish family, and one of his grandfathers was an MP; when he was installed as Governor, he took the oath in its Jewish form. He is an intellectual of a peculiarly fastidious and sensitive type, whose early influences were men like Keynes, Lowes Dickinson, Bertrand Russell, and, in a different field, A.E. Housman. He works fourteen hours a day, smokes cigars made by the White Fathers at Kabale, has a shy manner, likes theory, and when he talks (he talks a lot) either paces the room or likes to doodle on a blotter with a pair of scissors. Some people think that he lacks popular touch. He is forty-five.

Cohen is high-minded, an idealist, a man genuinely dedicated to the cause of African development, and a devoted believer in public service. This makes all the more tragic his conflict with the Kabaka. He wanted at all costs to avoid it.

The story is complex. One thing to keep in mind is that there are *two* governments in Uganda. The protectorate government, under Cohen, rules the country as a whole. But Buganda, the old kingdom and principal province, has its own African government as well, that of the (now deposed) Kabaka, who under normal conditions had a good deal of power. For instance, he appointed all the Baganda chiefs[15] and named part of the membership of the Parliament or Great Lukiko; out in the countryside are the Gumbolola (district) and Saza (county) administra-

[14] One complicating factor is that the aristocratic Baganda consider themselves much superior to the people in the backward provinces. Toward the savages in Karamoja they feel roughly as the master of a respectable *hôtel* in the Faubourg St. Germain might feel toward a beachcomber in Madagascar. Another is that people in Uganda are separated into mutually exclusive clans.
[15] Subject to the Governor's veto.

HOPE AND CRISIS IN UGANDA

tions, also nominally subject to the Kabaka. Moreover he had a personal cabinet of three ministers, called the Katikiro (Prime Minister), the Omulamuzi (Chief Justice), and the Omuwanika (Lord of the Treasury). One of the functions of this latter dignitary is to take care of what is known as the Royal Umbilical Cord.[16]

We had appointments with all three ministers one morning, arranged through the Resident Commissioner at Kampala; an astonishing thing happened; we arrived at the Mengo, the Palace Headquarters, at the time fixed; and not one of the three ministers showed up. That this was a deliberate affront could not be doubted, although there was nothing personal about it. No explanation or apology was forthcoming. An embarrassed secretary led us through the empty offices. This episode gave me the strong impression that, even then, months before the Kabaka's dismissal, things were not as good in Uganda as they appeared to be on the surface. Obviously the ministers refused to meet us because the arrangements had been made by the British, and probably also because we were guests at Government House, and hence (to the uninformed African mind) totally under British influence.

(I will digress for a moment to explain that the reader should not think in American or European terms when I use such a word as "offices" as in the paragraph above. I do not want to obstruct these pages with descriptive matter; yet it is vital to comprehend the *scene*. The offices of the prime minister of Buganda no more resemble those of a corporation executive in New York than a hut in Polynesia resembles the House of Commons. One must never forget the appalling, dismal decrepitude of native Africa, which is caused partly by poverty, partly by the speed and confusion of an overnight transition from medieval to modern times. Everything looks as if it were about to fall to pieces. Nothing matches. In the prime minister's room were a few pieces of ancient, blistered furniture, of the crudest sort. On blackboards were scrawled statistics of the tax collections in each *saza*, births, dates, and numbers of livestock. The figures were two years out of date.)

Associated with the figure of the Kabaka is a terrific, illustrious tradition. The present Kabaka, he whom Cohen deposed, is a great-grandson of Mutesa I and is the thirty-seventh member of his line to hold the throne. Sensibly, to give the royal blood variety and vitality, a Kabaka is always obliged to marry somebody *not* of royal blood; the Queen must, in other words, be a commoner. The Kabaka is about twenty-nine, a fastidiously

[16] Two of the three ministers must always be Anglican in religion, and the other a Roman Catholic.

—almost daintily—handsome young man, with an Ethiopian look; his name is Edward William Frederick David Walugembe Mutebi Luwangula Mutesa, His Highness Mutesa II. He went to Cambridge for several years, and almost, but not quite, won a blue in soccer. Then he served a brief term as a captain in the Grenadier Guards. He speaks English faultlessly, and his conversation is larded with such phrases as "My prime minister is a most dashing chap," or, while mingling with guests at a reception, "I say, a bit of a squash!"

A new Kabaka is, by tradition, crowned at a holy place near Budo. Approaching this, members of the royal entourage are not permitted to cross water, and the streams have to be dammed off. When a Kabaka dies, his widow or widows are obliged—in theory—to live the rest of their lives in total seclusion, in the tomb area where previous Kabakas lie buried; they are not permitted to remarry. The mother of the present Kabaka broke this rule, however, by eloping with an African schoolteacher after twelve years in the tombs. This event made such a scandal that serious political rioting followed, but the lady—her name is the Princess Irene—has been forgiven now. The present Kabaka's wife, or queen, known as the Nabagereka, is an extremely pretty girl. When we met her at a party she wore a western frock, and a courtier whispered in awe that it came all the way from Marshall and Snelgrove in London.

*

Sir Andrew Cohen invited us to attend a special meeting of the Great Lukiko, at which both he and the Kabaka spoke, and this was a vivid ceremony. In North Africa we had seen plenty of things with bite and color; but here the color flashes more intensely, with more brutal emphasis; what we saw in Kampala compared to Marrakesh as, say, Gauguin compares to Odilon Redon or even Marie Laurencin. The purpose of the Lukiko session was something quite prosaic, but important—announcement of new, democratizing reforms, whereby the people of Buganda were to be given a larger share in government.

The royal enclosure lies atop the Mengo, one of Kampala's hills, and is bound by a tall fence of elephant grass; the parliament building has a roof of tin, lined with straw. Outside, sitting under trees, were the drummers. This was the first time I heard African drums really close. The sound is that of an airplane ripping clouds apart, but thicker. Near the drummers was a congregation of women, squatting in their colored cottons so that they looked like flags draped over lumps of stone—crimson, magenta, rose.

Inside, the hall was hung with Union Jacks, and at the far end stood a dais covered with leopard and lion skins. Behind was the Buganda flag —blue, with a yellow shield on which is poised a red lion; on each side were tintype photographs of the Kabaka's ancestors. Down the aisle marched a dignitary carrying the executioner's sword, a moon-shaped blade stuck on a long wooden handle, which is also a spear. Then Sir Andrew, in a white-gold uniform and carrying his plumed hat, the emblem of his office, arrived, and so did the Kabaka, who was in native robes of black and gold, under an elaborate purple umbrella.

The legislators listened as the Kabaka's speech was translated into English, and Sir Andrew's into Luganda. When they clapped in applause, the sound was instantly taken up by the drummers outside. Sir Andrew mentioned that, in order to pay for the new reforms, taxes would have to go up. Like children, members of the congregation at once groaned deeply in protest, and this note, too, was at once picked up by the drums outside, which changed their tune to a fierce rattling grumble, which became a roar, and rolled down the hill like thunder, or a lorry full of rubber-coated stones.

After this ceremony came a reception by the Kabaka in his small palace a hundred yards away. The women, wives of the chief dignitaries of state, were now allowed to enter; happily and with poise they composed themselves, some sitting on the floor, in their costumes of bursting scarlet, chartreuse, and royal blue. Their skirts spilled on the floor like pools of dye. Some male guests wore western dress, and a few carried gray top hats. No banana wine here! Sweating waiters tore through the packed room with trays of punch. Normally servants are supposed to prostrate themselves in the presence of the Kabaka, but they did not do so this day, no doubt because it would have been difficult to serve drinks while lying flat on the floor. With the Queen was her four-year-old daughter, who, on being presented to a guest, did not curtsy but was obliged to *kneel*. The Kabaka's brother, Prince George Mawanda, is one of the largest men I have ever seen; the British have great regard for him if only because he is a redoubtable cricketer. He is older than the Kabaka, but was passed over for the succession. Also we met the Kabaka's sister, known as the Nalinya, an immensely stout woman—I would guess she weighed nearly three hundred pounds—who wore a blindingly purple dress and was splashed with even more blinding diamonds. She was a powerful influence on the Kabaka, and loved him deeply. When (some months after this) she was informed of his deposition, she dropped dead on the spot with shock.

NATIONALISM ONCE MORE

Uganda nationalists were wary of us at first; later they talked freely. We met among others Ignatius K. Musazi, a former theological student who is head of both the Federation of Uganda African Farmers and the principal nationalist political organization, the Uganda National Congress, which claims to have well over a hundred thousand members. He is an alert personality.

Uganda always had the reputation—until the Kabaka crisis—of being a kind of lotus land, a country without serious political tensions—but grave riots occurred in both 1945 and 1949, and in the former year a prime minister, Martin Luther Nsibirwa, was assassinated. But these were not, it would seem, genuinely nationalist disorders; they did not aim to overthrow the protectorate government in the cause of African freedom. The "insurrection" of 1949 was directed more against Baganda landlords and the Kabaka's feudalism than against the British.[17] The riots were manifestations of growing pains. People above the subsistence level gained access to education, did not like what they saw, and began to protest.

The Congress leaders we talked to in 1953 were more sophisticated. They were outright nationalists and they meant business. They had a definite list of grievances, and knew exactly what they wanted by way of reform. They did not take Cohen's democratization of the legislature seriously, complained that they had not been consulted about it, and said that it was nothing more than window dressing and an extension of the old sinister system of "divide and rule." The chief apprehensions of the nationalists were that more and more Europeans were coming into the country, that Uganda (which has always been free of exploitation) would eventually become an "imperialist" province if this immigration were not checked, and that new developments in mining and industry would create an industrial color bar like that in the Rhodesias. Categorically the British denied that this would ever be permitted to happen. But the nationalists remained unconvinced and restive. Uganda has always been a *black* country, not mixed, and they want it to remain so at all costs. Their fears that an amalgamated or plural society was bound to develop in Uganda could not be stilled. Positively what they hope for most is a constituent assembly for the whole country, elected by the people. The fact that the

---

[17] Also political troubles arose (as in Kenya) out of religious fermentations; people who split off from orthodox Christianity and thought that they alone bore the true faith, and had sole access to God's ear, became inflammatory.

Sudan, their close neighbor, is about to become free (or join a free Egypt) has strongly stimulated Uganda nationalism, since the proud Baganda think that they are just as advanced as the Sudanese.[18]

Until the crisis following the deposition of the Kabaka, British rule in Uganda was mild, and its pressures gentle. We talked to one engaging young man—as attractive an African as any I ever met—but naughty in British eyes, a demon, a scamp. He organized a students' strike at Makerere, and caused serious political trouble in the co-operatives and elsewhere. In French Africa he would certainly have been sent to jail; in Belgian or Portuguese Africa he might well have suffered punishment much more dire. What did the British in Uganda do? They gave this irritating and insurrectionary young man a scholarship to Cambridge! Thus they avoided making a martyr of him, and at the same time neatly got him out of the country. But there was a further motive. A British official told us, "We really *like* that young man! He will be good human material some day, useful to the country. The only way to handle him and let him grow is to give him a couple of years rubbing brains with people even brighter than he is."

THE KABAKA CRISIS

This story has sharp edges. In June, 1953, Oliver Lyttelton, then the Colonial Secretary, made a speech in London, in which he mentioned casually that East Africa might some day be federated, in other words, that Kenya, Tanganyika, and Uganda might be consolidated into a unit. This remark made little impression in London, but it was blown up out of all proportion in Nairobi, as an indication that the British government planned to create a "white dominion" in East Africa, like the new Federation in Central Africa. The repercussions in Uganda were instantaneous and severe. The Baganda in particular felt that they now had concrete, official evidence for their fears, that they were going to be forcibly attached to Kenya against their will (as the Nyasalanders had been attached to Rhodesia against their will the year before), that they would pass under the domination of white settlers, and that Uganda would in consequence cease to be a black African state, with opportunity to work out its own future. The British government sought to reassure them that

---

[18] Incidentally Uganda nationalists call the British "non-natives." Africans hate the word "native" and this is a nice little demonstration of how an insult can be twisted.

these apprehensions were groundless, and that there would be no attempt at forcible federation. But the reassurance did not assure.

First the Kabaka demanded a special independent status for Buganda so that, no matter what happened to the rest of Uganda, his own country would not be swallowed up. In other ways he refused to co-operate with Cohen. This was a very serious thing to happen in a "model" colony—conflict between the Governor and King. In September the Lukiko met, and, under the Kabaka's influence, asked that Buganda be removed from the authority of the Colonial Office and be given a timetable—fateful word!—for full independence.

Meantime the British had made elaborate proposals for constitutional reform. Cohen flew to London to consult with Lyttelton, and on his return began a series of secret conferences with the Kabaka. Cohen's predicament was difficult. He did not want to lose African good will, and spoil years of harmonious development in Uganda. But he felt that the British Government stood for the progress and modernization of Uganda much more than the Kabaka did. The Kabaka did not want the Uganda government broadened and democratized, because this would cut down his own autocratic authority, as the British saw the picture. He was an obstacle to progress.

The Kabaka on his side held that the contemplated British reforms were nothing more than a device whereby Buganda would gradually lose its identity, and that the country would be "lost" before the people even knew fully what was going on.[19] He refused to be Cohen's mouthpiece to this end. So the struggle became a contest of wills, with nothing less than the future of Uganda as a whole at stake. This being granted, Cohen had no recourse but to oust the Kabaka. The drama implicit in this conflict was of surpassing force; one need only mention the contrast in personality between the British governor and the African potentate—an incidental point being that both were Cambridge men—Cohen with his massive bulk and complete dedication to principle and intellect, the Kabaka a descendant of savages, a prisoner of ancient occult forces, brilliant and sensitive as a firefly, trying to summon all his resources to meet this alien challenge.

Cohen won, of course. The Kabaka refused to back down, and there was no alternative (the British felt) but to throw him out. On November 30, 1953, he was summoned to Government House, informed that his rule was over, and at once packed off in a plane to London. Tempers must have been very high. He was not even given the opportu-

[19] The reforms hinge to an extent on the powers and composition of the two parliaments, the Lukiko (Baganda) and Legislative Council (protectorate).

nity to inform his court or family of his dismissal, or to say good-by to them.

Various other factors entered into this unhappy tale. On a personal level the Kabaka was almost as irritated with the British as they were with him. He felt that he had been slighted at the Coronation, because he did not get a ride in a carriage like the Sultan of Zanzibar and the Queen of Tonga. Then apparently he had wanted to divorce his wife, the pretty Nabagereka, and marry her sister. He went to a very high ecclesiastical authority in England asking if it would be all right to do this, and was most firmly told that he could not.[20]

Nothing could be more quintessentially British than the fact that, when the House of Commons met early in December to hear outcries on the case, the Kabaka himself sat in the Visitors Gallery, as an honored guest, and listened to the debate. Later Mr. Musazi, the president of the Uganda National Congress, came to London to plead the cause of the Kabaka. This man would, in French or Belgian or Portuguese or Spanish territory, have been considered a dangerous revolutionary. Where did he give a press conference? In the House of Commons!

Sir Andrew Cohen was put in an almost impossible position by Lyttelton's original *faux pas*, and he acted throughout from the highest motives; but many people think that the whole affair might have been handled differently. Of course Cohen, for all his vision, never dreamed that the Kabaka would not surrender at the end. It dumfounded the British that the little Kabaka, whom they had always thought of as a playboy despot, could be so definite and dedicated. At least the government should have had some successor to the Kabaka in mind. The French did not eliminate Mohammed V in Morocco until they had Mohammed VI ready as a substitute. What the British did was to break continuity, which can be a disaster anywhere in Africa.

A profound demoralization came to Buganda as a result of this crisis, and the country has been tormented ever since. Plenty of Baganda did not like the Kabaka, but without *some* Kabaka the government could not function fully. The great drums, which in the normal course of events play out every night and can be heard for miles, are stilled; this, as an African has put it, is "as if Big Ben were no longer heard at Westminster." African congregations have deserted the European churches. The Kabaka's sister cannot be properly buried so long as he is out of the country. The outraged and humiliated Lukiko, suffering from a wound more spiritual than physi-

[20] "What Went Wrong in Uganda?" by R.H.S. Crossman, *New Statesman*, February 6, 1954.

cal, has refused to sanction the appointment of a new Kabaka, and Baganda who venerate their monarch say despairingly that the dynasty—after thirty-seven reigns—has become extinct. The Lukiko even voted to refuse to receive Queen Elizabeth II, when she visited Uganda during her royal tour in 1954.[21]

Reaction of the nationalists to all this was peculiar. The Uganda National Congress had little personal association with the Kabaka. I asked one modern-minded boy (before the crisis) what the monarch, on his side, thought of Congress; the answer was, "He couldn't care less; his only interest is to hold his job; he has a vested interest in the past." In fact—a striking paradox—the nationalists were on the same side as the *British* on most points of issue when the expulsion occurred, for instance, development of the legislature and unification of the country. But they took quick advantage of the crisis to exploit it for nationalist ends, claiming that the Kabaka represents symbolically all the deepest aspirations of the people. The situation became in a word rather like that in Morocco; men who despised the monarch as an outworn anachronism rallied to his support because they found him useful.

Cohen set up a regency, consisting of the three palace ministers, and this has worked loyally. Even so, disturbances have been steady. A boycott by Africans on retail trade, organized by the Congress, did annoying economic damage. The authorities have twice had to declare a state of emergency; important chiefs have been arrested, vernacular newspapers shut down, and politicians "rusticated," i.e., sent into exile. In an attempt to straighten out constitutional matters, a mission headed by Sir Keith Hancock, an eminent Australian authority, arrived in the country.[22] Most important, the British have attempted to remove all fears that Uganda will be sold down the river to Kenya by making a formal pledge that there will be no federation without the sanction of the Uganda people themselves, and that a self-governing state will be formed "*mainly*—[italics mine]—in the hands of Africans." If this comes about and works, the crisis will not have been in vain. But there may be difficulty later in attempts to define that little word "mainly."

[21] Ironically enough, Uganda was the only African territory on the Queen's itinerary, partly because it had the reputation of being so quiet; the visit went off without hitch, but in a strained atmosphere and to the tune of a good deal of worry about security; for instance, it was thought best that Her Majesty should not even enter Kampala.
[22] The Baganda chosen to consult with him wanted Dr. Ralph Bunche to be a member of their group, but Cohen refused to have him on the ground that the delegation should be all Bugandan.

The Kabaka himself set about enjoying himself in exile. He is being paid a stipend of £8,000 per year. His bill in a London hotel amounted for one twenty-three-day period to £1,392.

But this story is not done yet. Sensational (and to a certain extent anticlimactical) events came late in 1954. The issue simply would not stay dead. The gist of procedures complicated in the extreme is that the British backed down, and announced that the Kabaka would be permitted to return to Uganda—after an interim period—if the Baganda are willing to accept certain stipulations, chiefly that Buganda remains part of Uganda and that the Kabaka accepts a democratic, constitutional status. Several events led to this decision. One was publication of the Hancock report. One was a test case in the High Court regarding the legality of the expulsion of the Kabaka; the judgment was ambiguous. On November 16, Sir Andrew Cohen addressed a session of the Great Lukiko to announce that it would be permitted, nine months after enactment of the constitutional reforms, to decide for itself whether to choose a new Kabaka, or bring the present one back. The meeting broke up in turmoil. Cohen was never able to read more than a sentence or two of his speech, and his automobile was stoned as he left the building—an amazing thing to happen in a British colony.

Seen in the large the moral of this story is that the British had the suppleness, decency, and courage to reverse themselves on the personal issue of the Kabaka, under safeguards. But this may not be enough to save Uganda from further bitterness and struggle.*

THE OWEN FALLS HYDROELECTRIC SCHEME AND THE NILE

We end this chapter where we began. Near Jinja we looked at Ripon Falls which do indeed, as Mr. Churchill said, resemble a horse's tail. Next year, if we should happen to be in Jinja again, we would not see these white flattish falls, because they are doomed to be flooded out of existence when the Owen Falls Dam, three miles away, begins to build up its reservoir of Nile water—the "century of storage." We stood on a temporary bridge—a couple of planks—above the foaming Nile where it flows at a velocity of twenty feet per second. Here the great river is born.

Owen Falls was inaugurated by Queen Elizabeth during her visit to Uganda on April 30, 1954. For the first time in history, control of the Nile takes place at its source, and it is harnessed where its power is greatest.

* *Publisher's note.* The Colonial Secretary announced in the House of Commons on July 22, 1955, that the main deadlock over the Buganda Constitution had been resolved and that the Kabaka was to return there as soon as possible.

Mr. Churchill was right even about such technical details as the masonry. At Owen Falls, engineers are storing 15,000 times more water per unit of masonry than at Hoover (ex-Boulder) Dam in the United States. The river has the capacity to produce more power in forty-seven miles than all rivers in the whole of England, and, when completed, the turbines will have a generating capacity of 150,000 kilowatts. The total cost of the project is estimated at £22,000,000.

One major purpose of the dam is to broaden the Uganda economy, so that this will not be so vulnerable to cotton and coffee prices; presumably the dam will supply power for all manner of new ventures, from sugar to textiles. Uganda itself, however, no matter how copiously it is developed, cannot possibly consume all the power the reined Nile will produce. So plans are under way for its transmission to Kenya, the Belgian Congo, and elsewhere. Uganda, in the marrow of tropical Africa, may become one of the world's greatest exporters of—electricity.

*

So much for East Africa. We take a long jump now to encounter an entirely different type of African world, the Union of South Africa.

PART TWO

The South and the West

I hold thee fast, Africa!
—JULIUS CAESAR

There is all Africa and her prodigies in us.
—SIR THOMAS BROWNE

We [the United States] must approach Africa as Africa and not simply as a projection of Britain, France, Belgium, and Portugal . . . Africa requires a hard, fresh, and imaginative new look.
—CHESTER BOWLES

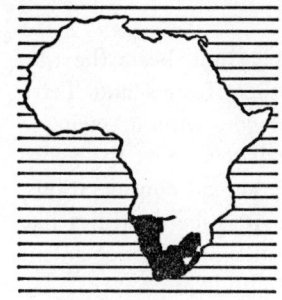

CHAPTER 24

The Union of South Africa: Successors to Malan

> So geographers, in Afric maps
> With savage pictures fill their gaps,
> And o'er unhabitable downs
> Place elephants for want of towns.
> —JONATHAN SWIFT
>
> No change, no pause, no hope.
> —H. W. NEVINSON

When, late in 1954, a relatively little-known politician named Johannes Gerhardus Strijdom succeeded Dr. Malan as prime minister of the Union of South Africa, people asked if this meant a change for the better—would not Mr. Strijdom take a more moderate line on racial policy, severance of the ties with Great Britain, and other matters? The answer is that it does not. Strijdom is even more of a fanatic than Malan, colder, bolder, younger, and more passionately inflexible. The difference between the two men is almost that between Hindenburg and Hitler.

South Africans are not Nazis, but the Strijdom government is grounded in part at least on three of the most unpleasant of human characteristics —fear, bigotry, and intolerance. It is based without qualification on the principle of unmitigated white supremacy (i.e., suppression of four-fifths of the people of the country) and it is in some respects the ugliest government I have ever encountered in the free world.

*

First, status. The Union of South Africa (in Afrikaans the name of the country is Unie van Suid-Afrika) is a fully sovereign, independent, and self-governing state, although it is a member of the British Commonwealth. The Queen is considered to be one of the three elements in the parliament (the others being the Senate and House of Assembly) and bears the title "Elizabeth II, Queen of South Africa and Her Other Realms and Territories, Head of the Commonwealth."[1] Of course—it goes without saying—the United Kingdom government has no authority whatever over the South African government, linked as they may be by some special considerations, and has no responsibility whatever for putting into practice doctrines like *apartheid*. So far as legislation is concerned the Union is as independent of London as Bulgaria or Paraguay.

Even though the tie between London and Pretoria is largely a matter of form and symbolism, fierce sentiment exists among Afrikaners to cut the relationship altogether, secede from the Commonwealth, and form a republic. This issue we will explore below. The Union has its own national anthem, *"Die Stem van Suid-Afrika,"* which is zealously promoted and revered, and its own national flag. This is a curiosity. It consists of horizontal stripes of orange, white, and blue, and in the center are placed tiny representations of the old flag of the Orange Free State, the old *Vierkleur* of the Transvaal, and the Union Jack. The Union Jack covers about one-ninetieth of the area of the flag as a whole.

The Union is the only independent country in Africa run by whites, and more than *half* of the entire white population of the continent lives here. Curiously enough, it is the only "British" country in the world in which citizens of British stock are a minority. It has two capitals, Pretoria (administrative) and Cape Town, which is the seat of the legislature. The government laboriously moves back and forth between them. The Supreme Court sits in a third city, Bloemfontein. The Strijdom cabinet wants to abolish the position of Cape Town as a capital, partly because of its British complexion, and concentrate all its workings in Pretoria.

The Union, which was constituted in 1910 following the Act of Union passed by the British parliament in 1909 (and which is still the constitution of the country) is an amalgam of four provinces. Two of these, the Cape Province and Natal, were former British colonies; the other two, the Transvaal and the Orange Free State, had formerly been independent Boer republics. Today British influence is still strong—but diminishing—in the Cape and Natal, whereas the Orange Free State and the Transvaal are still the principal strongholds of Afrikanerdom.

Second, geography. South Africa is not a big country as African countries go, and, excluding the contested area of South-West Africa, covers about 470,000 square miles. Even so, this means that it is almost the size of

---

[1] This is also the title borne by the Queen in such dominions as Pakistan and Ceylon.

France, Germany, and Italy combined. We have come a long way from equatorial Africa now. In physiognomy, the Union no more resembles Uganda than Utah resembles Venezuela. Most of it is a high, semi-arid, barren plateau (4,000-6,000 feet), and a good deal is desert. Not more than 15 per cent of the land is cultivable, and erosion is steadily, remorselessly, eating this away. The winds and waters are the cannibals of the Union. There are few important rivers, but these are energetic. The seasons are, as everybody knows, reversed, since South Africa lies in the Southern Hemisphere; January is midsummer, and winter comes in June. Everywhere lack of rain is a preoccupation. I heard one patriotic Afrikaner say, "We will, unfortunately, never be as great a country as the United States, because we lack water."

Third, population. There are in the Union a total of 12,646,375 people, of whom about 8,500,000 are Africans and about 2,600,000 are white Europeans. There are also slightly more than a million Coloreds (the name given to a special type of mulatto concentrated mostly in the Cape Province), 360,000 Indians, and 40,000 Cape Malays. In other words, the white man is outnumbered by a ratio of about four to one. In almost all African countries such ratios are much more extreme, as we know, but nowhere has the disparity between the numbers of blacks and whites produced such turmoil, anguish, and strain. This is largely because the Union excludes utterly any idea of racial partnership.

Statisticians say that the European population may be expected to double in the next thirty years, but that the African population may treble. Biology is on the dark man's side. Moreover a great many whites are poor farmers on land that is blowing away.

Another factor making for complications without end is that the European community is sharply divided within itself. There are, in round figures, about 1,500,000 Afrikaners, about 1,100,000 Britons.[2] The two groups are separated not only by their background and language, but by bitterly intense emotional, economic, and political differences. The cleavage goes far back. When Malan's Nationalists won the general election of 1948, defeating the United Party which is partly British in texture, people made the joke —not a very good joke but one quite apposite—that Malan had won the last battle of the Boer War.

No dilemma is more cruel than that faced today by the Union of South Africa. The situation is one of the most tragic, difficult, and dangerous in the world, and the problems involved appear to be insoluble. Close to ten million black and brown people are denied the most elementary rights and

[2] Of course all these are "South Africans." For terminological difficulties like this see the next section.

privileges by a divided white minority. Put in crude terms the dilemma is triangular: (A) the white minority cannot kill off the black majority, even if it should wish to do so. (B) The black majority cannot drive the white minority into the sea. (C) *Apartheid*, which is the Nationalist formula for solution, cannot be made to work except at the risk of poisoning the entire nation. Result: South Africa is not only a country gripped by crisis, but one tormented by the most paralyzing kind of fear.

Finally by way of introduction we should mention some other factors. The Union has a government which is deliberately set up on the premise of keeping a huge helot class in permanent subjugation, but this is not to say that South Africa is populated by monsters. The government may be noxious, but the people are not. There are any number of Afrikaners of the utmost political as well as personal decency. They are a hospitable people, God-fearing, industrious, and alert, with a magnificent historical tradition and frontier spirit.

The Union may face grave and perplexing crises, but it is very important to make the point that it is a strong country, not weak. This is by far the richest and most advanced nation on the continent, utterly different from any we have seen in Africa so far. It is virile, energetic, and ambitious. It has gold, diamonds, uranium, two-thirds of all the railway mileage of the continent, a thriving industrialization, and great economic power. We have come a long way now from, let us say, Tanganyika. This is Europe.

But—over everything hangs the grim pall of the racial problem. I do not think that South Africa is going to explode into civil war, and I think that the present system may last a long time, if only because of the brutal fact that the African masses are systematically denied any possibility of organization and advance. Nevertheless it is against all reason to think that a small minority of whites can keep a large majority of blacks totally submerged forever. Nobody can suppress indefinitely a whole people. Time and again I heard Afrikaners as well as British South Africans say, "Have we a future, or are we a lost people? What is going to happen to our children?" Indeed from a long-range point of view there is no "native problem" in South Africa. The problem is of white survival.

A FEW WORDS IN DEFINITION

South and southern Africa. "South Africa" means the Union; "southern" Africa means, more or less, Africa below the Zambesi, and includes not only the Union but Southern Rhodesia, Mozambique, and the three British "High Commission Territories."

European. All white people in this general area are known as "Europeans," but this term is not used officially. Citizens of the Union are "South Africans."

Afrikaner. This is a tricky word. It does not mean "African," but the opposite. An Afrikaner is, speaking loosely, any white man of non-British descent whose principal language is *Afrikaans,* the local language derived from Dutch. Most Afrikaners are of Dutch, Flemish, French Huguenot, or German stock. As to the Britons, it is not correct to call them "Britons" or "Englishmen," but I shall use these terms as a matter of convenience, since it is too laborious to say "South African citizens who speak English as a principal language and are of British descent." One small point is that the word "Afrikaner" should never be confused with "Afrikander." The latter term is an old synonym for "Afrikaner," but nowadays it means a kind of cattle. Also one might mention that the term "Dutch," although this is often used colloquially by the British community, is not a correct synonym for "Afrikaner." The Afrikaners most distinctly do not consider themselves to be Dutchmen or Netherlanders or Hollanders. There is no direct bond to the mother country at all, except in matters of religion. An Afrikaans-speaking citizen of Johannesburg is no more a "Dutchman" than a citizen of Peekskill, New York, although he may have Dutch ancestors far back.[3]

Nationalism. Through the whole course of this book so far we have become accustomed to thinking of "nationalists" as Africans who want independence from colonial rule, and of "nationalism" as a black movement. Here in the Union the equation is reversed. There are African nationalists, true, and they have an organization called the African National Congress. But it is *Afrikaner* (white) nationalism that counts in the Union, not African (black) nationalism. The party in power is the "National" party, and its members are known as "Nationalists," or "Nats" for short.

Apartheid. Another tricky word, about which we shall write much hereunder. It is pronounced "apart-ate," and means literally "separateness." There are several gradations of meaning within the word, which embodies the fundamental concept of the National party and most of the Afrikaner community, namely, racial segregation. Color bar in a restaurant or a sign on a park bench, "For Europeans Only," are examples of simple *apartheid.* There can be *apartheid* in schools, industry, recreation, and so on. The Nationalist zealots stand for complete geographical *apartheid,* which would mean splitting South Africa into two separate entities, a "Bantustan" for the

---

[3] A small actual Dutch community does, however, still exist in the Union, but this has in general closer ties to the British than to the Afrikaners.

THE UNION OF SOUTH AFRICA   455

blacks and the rest of the country for the whites. Such would be the logical culmination of the *apartheid* ideal.

Boer. This means literally "farmer." It was the old word for South Africans of predominantly Dutch extraction, who lived on the land; nowadays it is seldom used.

Native. This is the official word for "African." The government does not believe in dignifying Africans to the extent of letting them be called Africans. The term *Kaffir* is also widely used, and carries with it usually a connotation of contempt. Indians are known colloquially as "coolies."

BACKDROP TO SOUTH AFRICAN POLITICS AND NATIONALISM

South Africa has had only five prime ministers since the formation of the Union in 1910—Botha, Smuts, Hertzog, Malan, and, today, Strijdom. In few countries has power ever been concentrated in the hands of so small a number of men over a period of almost half a century. The first three were Boer generals who fought against the British in the Boer War (1899-1902), and all five were, or are, Afrikaners. But Botha and Smuts welcomed conciliation from Britain after the war, worked hard to improve relations with London, and put their faith in the development of South Africa within the imperial British framework, although they always remained tenaciously patriotic South Africans. Smuts in particular, as everybody knows, became one of the most illustrious of Commonwealth statesmen, and was often bitterly criticized in South Africa by the Nationalists for paying more attention to world affairs than to politics at home. His reputation today is considerably greater outside South Africa than in.

Was Jan Christiaan Smuts (1870-1950) a great man? I asked Alan Paton, author of *Cry, the Beloved Country*, this question when we visited Mr. Paton near Durban, and he replied, "Of course—people were willing to die for him." What is more they were willing to die for him on different sides of the fence. Smuts fought against Britain in the Boer War, and for Britain in World War I and after. He was a fascinating character. He became renowned not merely as a soldier and statesman but as a philosopher of the most lofty elevation, but his nickname in South Africa was "Slim Jannie," *slim* being an Afrikaans word meaning "crafty." His mind was coiled, thin, and tightly strung like the mainspring of a watch. Smuts had prodigious intellectual qualifications, but one of his biographers records that he never learned to read or write till the age of twelve. In his early campaigns he carried Kant, Tacitus, and a Greek New Testament in his saddlebags. He cared utterly nothing for pomp or money, and slept in a valet's room at the prime minister's house in Pretoria, his official residence for many years.[4] Also Smuts's accomplishment was massive in several fields. He worked out plans for the old League of Nations before Wilson, helped make the Treaty of Versailles, invented the term "Commonwealth" as it is used today to describe the former British Empire, and helped bring the United Nations into being at San Francisco in 1945. His first book was, of all things, an essay on Walt Whitman, and he called his philosophy "Holism." He was prime minister of the Union for an aggregate of fourteen years, and, although an Afrikaner, became undisputed leader of the United (pro-British) party. He died at eighty.

General Louis Botha (1862-1919) was, many South Africans think, a greater man than Smuts. He came of old *voortrekker* stock and had an extraordinary gentleness and sweetness of character as well as force. He was not an intellectual like Smuts. He was a man of action. But his statesmanship made possible the development of good relations between South Africa and Britain in the critical and sensitive period after the Boer War when Smuts was still hardly known except as a daring commando officer.[5] It was Botha, in a famous encounter in the Boer War, who took prisoner a youthful war correspondent named Winston Churchill. Except for several remarkably lucky accidents, each might have killed the other. Churchill's account of this pungent episode is one of the most gallant of all contemporary adventure stories.[6] Botha has, among many major claims to fame, one that is minor but engaging. When the Cullinan diamond, the greatest diamond ever known, was discovered he saw to it that it was ceremoniously presented to the British royal house. No gesture did more to heal wounds caused by the Boer War.

The founder of South African nationalism as we know it today was a personality even more remarkable, General James Barry Munnik Hertzog (1866-1942). He was a republican, although he worked well with the British on occasion. He believed in the "two streams" policy, whereby Boers and Britons might have parallel development; he did not, like Smuts, want to weld the two strains into a unity. Also Hertzog was, in a manner of speaking, the father of *apartheid*, even though this term was not invented until after his death. Smuts and Botha had comparatively little animus against Africans. Smuts was too removed intellectually to think much

---

[4] See *Botha, Smuts, and South Africa*, by A. F. Basil Williams, and "Smuts at Eighty," by Sarah Gertrude Millin, *Foreign Affairs*, October, 1950.
[5] The term "commando," widely used in World War II, is of Boer origin.
[6] "If I Had a Second Chance," by Winston Churchill, London *Observer*, November 28, 1954.

THE UNION OF SOUTH AFRICA

about color in personal terms (but he believed in segregation), and Botha died before racial relations became the harrowing, all-embracing problem that they are today. His attitude was more or less that of a benevolent plantation owner in the old American south. But Hertzog, a cranky person, believed actively in color bar. He hated Africans. He did not think that they were capable of rising in society, and did his best to keep them from having access to education, citizenship, and economic opportunity.

We cannot go into the intricate convolutions of South African party politics. The main thing to say is that, over the years, the chasm between Britons and Afrikaner nationalists steadily became deeper, wider, and more unbridgeable. Most governments were coalitions. The struggle had several aspects—between the British churches and the Dutch Reformed church, between the English language and Afrikaans, between rival concepts of Commonwealth unity and Boer republicanism. An important exacerbating factor was the intense pro-Germanism of many Afrikaners during both World War I and World War II. The Union only came into the war on Britain's side in 1914 by the narrowest of margins, and in 1939 by a majority of only thirteen in the House of Assembly. Some Boers took a line strongly resembling that of isolationists in the United States during the 1939-41 period. Some went far beyond this, and hoped ardently for a German victory. There were powerful Nazi elements in or near the Nationalist party, and several members of the present government have blatant pro-Hitler records.

In case the reader does not take at face value my description of South African politics and the emergence of nationalism as "intricate" or "convoluted," let me proceed to the extent of one brief paragraph.

Botha was the first prime minister. Party lines at this time (1910) were not fixed. Hertzog split off from Botha in 1912, and formed the Nationalist party. Smuts became prime minister for the first time in 1919, as head of what was called the South African party, and was succeeded by Hertzog, leading the nationalist opposition, in 1924. But Hertzog's own right wing made trouble. It thought that Hertzog was too conciliatory to Britain, exactly as Hertzog himself had thought that Botha had been too conciliatory to Britain. The Nationalist party always splinters off to the right, becoming more extreme each time. In 1933 Hertzog and Smuts made a coalition, and out of this the present-day United party was born. Dr. Malan then organized a group of secessionists from Hertzog, which called itself the "Purified Nationalist party," out of resentment at Hertzog's fusion with Smuts. But Smuts and Hertzog split in 1939 over entering the war (Hertzog wanted "benevolent neutrality") and Smuts became prime minister again, putting South Africa into the war on the side of the allies. Hertzog and Malan then proceeded to rejoin forces and the Purified Nationalist party became the "Reunited National party." Then Hertzog and Malan split again, and Hertzog formed the "Afrikaner" party. Dr. N. C. ("Klaasie") Havenga, who later became Malan's minister of finance, took over the Afrikaner party when Hertzog died. In 1943 the Smuts United (pro-British) party won the general election, against the combined nationalist opposition, and this held power till 1948.

Then came the big change. Malan and Havenga made a coalition, and won the 1948 election. The Nationalists have been in power ever since, and at the moment of writing it does not seem likely that they can be expelled from power for many years. The Malan group swallowed up the Havenga group, changed its name again, and became simply the "National" party. Malan himself was, people say, astonished by the extent of his victory. And it is important to note that, although Malan-Havenga got seventy-nine seats in the House of Assembly to seventy-one for the United party, they did not win a majority of the popular vote.[7] In fact they were outvoted by 140,000. But South Africa has a system of "weighted" constituencies, whereby the underpopulated rural areas or *platteland* are given augmented representation. This made Malan's majority in the legislature possible. Dr. Malan proceeded to form the first all-Afrikaner government in history. This was a logical step, but nevertheless sensational. For the first time since 1910, not a single British South African sat in the cabinet.

This 1948 election was the first ever fought in South Africa largely on the racial issue. Malan used Negroes as an issue much as Hitler used the Jews.

Came the April, 1953, general election. The country went to the polls again, and again, although the Nationalists did not win a popular majority, they captured both houses of parliament. This election has been called the most important in the nation's history. By removing the possibility of serious parliamentary opposition, it opened the way to frank totalitarianism. Again the analogy of Germany in 1932-33 is striking. Several factors helped Malan and his men to their triumph in the 1953 election. One was "weighted" representation, as in 1948. Another was the incorporation of South-West Africa, a former League of Nations mandated territory, into the Union so far as political representation was concerned; this occurred in 1950, and gave the Malanites six extra seats. Another influential factor was the Mau Mau uprising in Kenya. The nationalists told the electorate

[7] Many Afrikaners voted for the United party.

THE UNION OF SOUTH AFRICA

hysterically that Mau Mau would spread to South Africa if white supremacy was not maintained, and that only they could be trusted to maintain it.

Anyway Dr. Malan won. And the floodgates opened.

SOME AFRIKANER ATTITUDES AND CHARACTERISTICS

Before we proceed to discuss Strijdom and other members of the present cabinet, a further word of background may be useful. South Africa is one of the narrowest of countries, but it does not give up its secrets easily.

First, religion. Most Afrikaners are strict Calvinists of a peculiarly fundamentalist type, members of the Dutch Reformed church, which plays a role in the country almost comparable to that of the Roman Catholic church in medieval Spain. No doubt the upper branches of the Calvinist hierarchy contain men of the most refined and exquisite intelligence; but the rank and file are black with prejudice. "Hate is their religion," I heard it put. Moreover they believe that the power of the state is given by God; therefore, to be against the government is to be against God's will. The church is, strange as it may seem, probably the main force in the country behind *apartheid*; it teaches frankly that Negroes are an inferior race, "hewers of wood and drawers of water," who must be segregated. This, to most people, would seem to be a most unchristian doctrine, but the Boers attempt to justify it out of scripture. Natives are considered to be sons of Ham, and hence accursed.[8]

There are three different Dutch Reformed churches, the names of which are so similar that it is almost impossible to distinguish between them in English. Their differences are mainly doctrinal.

1. The *Nederduits Gereformeerde Kerk*. This is the biggest division, and the one most influential in government. It has roughly 1,100,000 members, and is the church of which Dr. Malan was a pastor. It is organized on a federal basis, but is most powerful in the Orange Free State, which it dominates. It is the most liberal of the three, but this is not saying that it is very liberal.

2. The *Gereformeerde Kerk*. This, with about 75,000 members, claims to be the original offshoot of the mother church in the Netherlands, and was founded by Van Riebeeck, the first Hollander to establish residence on the Cape.

3. The *Nederduits Hervormde Kerk*, with its chief strength in the Transvaal and a membership of about 127,000. This is the church whose members are called "Doppers," and people who do not like it make the little

---
[8] Cf. Genesis 9:18-27, and Joshua 9:21-27.

joke that it should be named the "Most Deformed" rather than the "Most Reformed" church. It is the most conservative of the three, the most obscurantist, and the most fundamentalist. Its adherents are so strict that they do not even sing hymns. Its fountainhead is the theological faculty of the University of Potchefstroom, the old capital of the Transvaal, where the Bible was translated into Afrikaans, and its rural members resemble nothing so much as backwoodsmen in the American Bible belt.

The three groups are autonomous, and have their own churches in most towns, but are linked by a consultative federal body. All three met at a congress called by the Federal Mission Council in April, 1950, and came out for complete geographical *apartheid*. This was too much even for Malan. The government knows that complete geographical division of the country is impossible. Lately have come uneasy stirrings within the churches, and there is some talk of a split on racial policy. Of course relations between the Dutch Reformed church (the generic name for the three groups taken together) and the state are entirely unofficial. The state does not "own" the church, or vice versa. But they see eye to eye on most matters, and the National party cannot possibly afford to alienate the church if only because of its influence on the smaller towns, which are the government's chief source of power. Religious instruction is compulsory in the state schools, but nonsectarian. Every member of the Strijdom cabinet is a member of the Dutch Reformed church, and so are 99 per cent of Afrikaner MP's. No Afrikaner can possibly have a successful political career if he is not an open, active member, because the church is inextricably interwoven into the fabric of daily life.

One problem worrying the church acutely is urbanization—whether it can maintain its hold on the rural youth after they go into the cities. Methodists and other denominations have made deep inroads on the Afrikaner flocks; the Methodists, to assist proselytization, now demand that all their ministers know Afrikaans. In 1953 the Anglican Bishop of Bloemfontein, the capital of the Free State, gave half his coronation sermon in English, half in Afrikaans—an unprecedented event. Another element in the struggle between the churches is race. The Dutch Reformed church is, it goes without saying, completely segregated; the Roman Catholic, Anglican, and other Christian churches are, at least in theory, open to membership by all.

Most fundamentalist Afrikaners are, it might be interpolated, violently anti-Catholic. The Piedmont hillbilly who thought that Al Smith was a secret agent of the Pope would find himself completely at home in the Transvaal. Also many Afrikaners—particularly those in government—have an ugly taint of anti-Semitism. "Anglo-Jewish imperialism" has been a traditional object of attack, exactly as in Nazi Germany, and rich Jews are pilloried in the nationalist press as "Hoggenheimers." But *official* anti-Semitism on the part of cabinet ministers is now discouraged, possibly because the Jews are an extremely powerful community—and have a lot of votes—in cities like Johannesburg. Dr. Malan even visited Israel in 1953, and apparently had a good time there.

It is the influence of the Dutch Reformed church that has, of course, helped to give the Union its fanatical puritanism. Women are not allowed in bars, and there are all manner of other "blue laws." On Sunday a visitor in a hotel must sign a book in order to get a drink. Dancing is frowned upon, but permitted. Divorce is legal, but discouraged. In some areas even fishing is prohibited on Sundays. The church has, however, never taken a prohibitionist position on alcohol, because of the importance of wine-growing to the country's economy, particularly in Cape Province. The Afrikaners are, except on matters of race, a hardheaded, canny, and realistic people.

*

Another terrific binding force is language. The Afrikaners have an almost maniacal devotion to Afrikaans, and the struggle to establish it was, they say, their major contemporary "epic." Afrikaans is spoken nowhere else in the world except South Africa, and not more than a million and a half people know it, but the Afrikaner patriots, consumed with chauvinism, like to think of it as a coming "world" language. Dr. W. W. M. Eiselen, the estimable secretary of native affairs, and before that a well-known professor at Pretoria University, said to us with genuine grief, "What a pity it is that you do not know Afrikaans!" Prime Minister Strijdom told friends not long ago how "deplorable" it was that there was no school teaching Afrikaans in Washington, DC, because this meant that children of South African officials in the United States could not be educated in their native language. Of course religion plays a cogent role in this. Afrikaners think that "mother tongue" education is a fundamental of Christianity, in that the infant Jesus "spoke the language of His mother."[9]

Afrikaans in its written form is a completely fabricated language, a political invention. It resembles Dutch, but is not Dutch. I have never heard a really satisfactory explanation why the early Dutch settlers in the Cape shook off their own language and developed a synthetic substitute. The Dutch in America did not give up Dutch except to learn English.

[9] *World Today*, April, 1947.

British, French, Spanish, and Portuguese colonists always held close to their own languages.[10] But the Afrikaners are, it is hardly necessary to repeat, a most stubborn and individualistic folk. Afrikaans gradually became the spoken language of the Boer communities. It borrowed heavily from other European languages (e.g., Flemish, French, and German) as well as Dutch, and also picked up a few words from Hottentot. Many words in Afrikaans strongly resemble parent words in Europe, and many have great charm. A "bell" is a *klokke*, "open" is *oop*, "thank you" is *dankie*, and "love" is *liefde*, *beminde*, or *stroop*. A "railroad" is a *spoorweg*, a "river" is a *rivier* or *stroum*, "pretty" is *mool*, and "Europeans only" is *Slegs vir Blankes*.

The movement to transform spoken Afrikaans into a written language began in the Cape in the 1860's. Afrikaners found it tedious to speak in one language and to write in another (Dutch or English). At first the Dutch Reformed church, which is always a firm conservative force, opposed the movement. But it grew anyway. The Act of Union (1909) provided that the country should have two official languages, Dutch and English. Then came the ferocious crusade to replace Dutch by Afrikaans, and thus put Afrikaans on a par with English, which for a decade dominated almost all "patriotic" political endeavor. The struggle was not won till 1925.

The situation today is that the Union is a bilingual state, with two official languages.[11] All government and public notices must be issued in both English and Afrikaans, and civil servants are obliged to know both. So are white school children. I heard a liberal Afrikaner say that the "wickedest" thing the nationalist government has done is separation of white children into separate language schools, because this will make it impossible for South Africa ever to become a truly united nation.[12] As to higher education, instruction at the great University at Stellenbosch in Cape Province and Pretoria University is in Afrikaans, although English is of course taught. At Witwatersrand University (in Johannesburg) and the University of Cape Town, this situation is reversed.

One Afrikaner told us that, as he grew up, he always spoke English with his mother, Afrikaans with his father. But as an adult, he says that he has found it necessary "to live" in only one language, out of fear of becoming

---

[10] One reason was of course that Dutch, Germans, and French Huguenots needed a lingua franca.

[11] The case might be made that Dutch is, technically speaking, still a third official language. Legislation and public records before 1925 were perforce in Dutch and English, not Afrikaans and English. The old statutes are now laboriously being translated into Afrikaans. Recently (for the first time in twenty-six years) a member of parliament addressed the House of Assembly in Dutch. See Leo Marquard, *The Peoples and Policies of South Africa*, p. 88, and the London *Times*, March 23, 1955.

[12] The government's position is that the child should be taught through the medium of his home language, but that he must learn the other too.

a "divided" personality. A newspaperman, who knows both languages perfectly, told me that he did 80 per cent of his work in Afrikaans, but had to write in English. He spoke English to his secretary, but dictated letters in Afrikaans. If two Afrikaners meet who speak excellent English but poor Afrikaans, they are obliged by convention to speak Afrikaans with each other. In parliament, members speak whatever language they choose; every nationalist member speaks Afrikaans (of course), and probably 90 per cent know enough English to be able to understand it. In general Afrikaners are more apt to be bilingual than British South Africans, since, to get ahead, some knowledge of English is essential. But one cabinet minister told us that the English, if they "want to remain here after we make a republic," will have to learn and do all their business in Afrikaans. In the last United party cabinet only three of the English members could speak Afrikaans; in today's all-Afrikaner cabinet, all ministers know English, although business is transacted in Afrikaans.

Has Afrikaans any literature? Even Afrikaners differ sharply in their answer to this question. Several poets, playwrights, and novelists have become conspicuous, but it is difficult to assess their talent. The vernacular press is active. Shakespeare has been translated, and has been played effectively in Afrikaans; so far as I know there have been no translations as yet of modern American classics like Hemingway or Faulkner. The demand for literature is prodigious. The first book ever to be published in Afrikaans appeared in 1861; there were only two more by 1873; 3000 in 1937; and about 10,000 today.[13] One difficulty—in preparing technical books, medical treatises, and the like—is vocabulary. Words have to be invented. The usual practice is to find out if a Dutch word exists, and then adapt it. Recently a commission visited Holland to prepare words needed in a new military manual.

A final point in this general realm: English as spoken by Afrikaners—or even by folk of British stock in the Union—has its own special quality. I do not know if philologists will agree that a special South African accent has come into being, but much of the English we heard sounded like a combination of Cockney, Australian, and even German. "Yes" is often "ya" or "yiss." "Bloody fool" is "bliddy ful."

*

Now we must mention sexual fear, biological fear, which plays a stupendous role in Afrikaner attitudes. This exists on two closely connected levels. First, fear caused merely by the fact that the whites are outnumbered by blacks and Coloreds by a ratio of four to one. If I heard the remark once,

[13] New York *Times*, July 18, 1954.

I heard it twenty times—"We don't want to be *swamped!*" Second, fear of miscegenation, fear that the white blood of the Afrikaner will sooner or later be "spotted" and "sullied" by admixtures of black and brown.

This is the root reason why Natives are, as far as possible, kept submerged politically and otherwise, the root reason for *apartheid* and its atrocious segregation patterns and outrages against humanity. The African must logically (as the Afrikaners see it) be segregated, in order to lessen as much as possible opportunities for social development and contact, so that the white stock will remain pure. Practically every argument about race relations with a rabid Afrikaner ends with some such phrase as "But you don't want a Kaffir to marry your *sister!*" The orthodox Afrikaner view is that, without *apartheid*, a mixed society is inevitable—not a plural or multiracial society, but mixed. The Union would, in other words, become Brazil.

Anybody so tactless as to mention that Brazil is an infinitely pleasant, civilized, and happy country is, of course, ruled out of bounds as a crank or "traitor." Or the remark will be made that there are not enough white genes in South Africa to make a Brazil. If fusion should ever occur, the resulting mixture will not be "coffee-colored," but something darker.

What bothers Afrikaners most about race is *color*. If the black population could overnight be given white skins, half the problem would disappear. The whites are fanatic "pigmentalists" or "pigmentocrats." In the United States, anybody with even a drop of Negro blood is a Negro. In South Africa, anybody is an African or a Colored who does not *look* sufficiently like a white. Sometimes "throwbacks" are born to Colored families—pure white children. They have so far been accepted as Europeans (when they grow up) without question. The darker a person's skin, the worse the curse. Chinese—a crazy paradox—may ride freely in the "Europeans Only" carriages on the trains. It is almost impossible for an outsider to realize the intensity with which color prejudice is held. At a recent Commonwealth Conference Dr. Malan was photographed with Mr. Nehru and the other Dominion prime ministers. When this picture was printed in the English press in Johannesburg, stout Afrikaners said that it must have been fabricated. They must have known, if they stopped to think about it, that Malan could not have avoided meeting Mr. Nehru, but even so it was literally inconceivable to them that the two men could have been photographed together.

Miscegenation is now (except in some remote *platteland* districts) extremely rare, and is strictly against the law. In the last year when mixed marriages were legally possible, there were only about seventy-five. But, as

THE UNION OF SOUTH AFRICA

is only too obvious, a good deal of miscegenation has taken place in the past, and this no doubt is what makes the Afrikaners so fantastically sensitive about color. South Africa is a country where people do not like to have their family trees too carefully scrutinized. Kingsblood Royals are not uncommon. Van Riebeeck permitted one of his men to marry a Hottentot girl, and there has been at least one other celebrated mixed marriage in the country's history. And after all the fact that almost a tenth of the total population is Colored shows that, for generations, a lively amount of holding hands must have occurred. I heard a Colored leader say (no doubt he was exaggerating), "If people with any trace at all of black blood were excluded from parliament, half the members would have to walk out." There are even Afrikaners who joke about the subject, and say to their friends lightly, "Ah, you suspect black blood in me!"

The African attitude to miscegenation is more or less that which we found in Kenya. The subject is too remote (for the vast majority) to have any relevance or interest.

I have used the word "fear" several times in this chapter but I do not want to give the impression that the Afrikaners are a craven people. They are not. They are defiant. They know that they face a problem of the most appalling difficulty and magnitude, but their attitude is far from being defensive. One editor told me proudly, "To survive, we must be supermen. This is a country fit for none but heroes." Also I should point out that a few courageous Afrikaners are, by some miracle, untainted by prejudice and take an altogether emancipated and liberal line on color. I even met one who felt, in fact, that the country had no future *without* miscegenation, since he was convinced that *apartheid* is not only evil but cannot work.

What about large-scale white immigration as a factor making for solution? This is what is being tried in the Rhodesias. One answer we heard was: "Difficult, if not impossible. We do not have enough water to support a larger population. Also this could only come from countries like Italy, and the Boers will not permit any immigration which brings in more Catholics."

*

Finally, economic and allied matters. Only about 10 per cent of the invested capital of the Union is Afrikaner. It is the British South Africans who, in the main, control industry, the mines, the banks, and so on. The British have been the merchants and traders; the Afrikaners, squeezed out of business, stayed on the land or went into the professions or government service. The fact that, speaking loosely, it is the British who are rich, the Afrikaners who are poor, has naturally tended to augment friction and bad feeling between the two communities.

This is the first country we have encountered in Africa with a large poor *white* class. I was astonished, arriving in Johannesburg, to see whites driving taxis and buses and running elevators, a sight almost unknown elsewhere on the continent. Not less than 22 per cent of the white population of the Union has been classified as "poor white," and most of this is Afrikaner. On the other hand the country is in the midst of a prodigious economic boom at the moment, a veritable industrial revolution, and the sudden wave of prosperity may change these circumstances soon.

Color is, as always, the core of almost all difficulty. I have heard it seriously argued that "Hertzog created the scum proletariat," the really *poor* poor white class. He wanted whites, not blacks, to work with their hands in the towns (whereas in most of Africa white men, as we know, never work with their hands if they can help it) in order to give the Afrikaner population greater earning power. So whites became railroad workers, road makers, transport laborers. Then, as industrialization began, they went into the factories. Hertzog was also largely responsible for the imposition of "industrial color bar" in the mines, which means that all skilled jobs go to whites. Color bar in industry costs money, but the South Africans are willing to pay the price.

Another important factor in Afrikaner character patterns is that, if crisis comes, they have no place to go. Their backs are to the wall. They are not Dutch; the idea of returning to the Netherlands is unthinkable. They cannot, either individually or en masse, return to a home country as can Britons in Africa, French, Spaniards, or Portuguese. They have made their own nation, and here they are stuck. This is another reason for Afrikaner resentment against the British. It is wounding beyond belief for an Afrikaner to hear an Englishman talk of England as "home," since he, the Afrikaner, has no European "home."[14]

Afrikaners by and large tend to remain isolated in their own communities, and seldom mix. An American official told me that he lived in Johannesburg for two years before he succeeded in getting a single Afrikaner into his home, although he had cordial social relations with scores of British.

"The Nationalists," a British editor told us, "have not tried, despite their name, to make a nation. That is their worst sin. They have had no interest at all in building up a genuine South Africa. What they want is a revival of the old Boer republics—a *Boerenasie,* farmer nation, ruled by the Afrikaner *volk* alone."

[14] Alan Paton makes a similar point in his pamphlet *South Africa Today,* p. 9.

Volkswil is a word heard almost as often as *apartheid* among Afrikaners. It means "will" or "voice" of the people, and sums up the "mystique" of Afrikanerdom. To many, *volkswil* is a concept superior to law. Nationalism is not merely a political creed, but a way of life.

*

Some Afrikaners are even more extremist than members of the present government, although it is hard to imagine how anybody could be more extreme than Swart or Verwoerd. As noted above, the tendency in Afrikaner politics is for the fanatic right wing to break off from the more moderate rightists. A former minister named Oswald Pirow, who had strong Nazi sympathies during the war, might turn up as a "man on horseback" in the event of some catastrophic emergency in the future. Early in the war an organization known as the Ossewa Brandwag (Oxwagon Fire-Guard) flourished, and was overtly Fascist; Dr. Malan refused, be it said to his credit, to have anything to do with it, and it was dissolved in 1954. A splinter group known as the Republican party arose in 1953, because it thought that the Nationalists should boycott the coronation of Queen Elizabeth. As a matter of fact the Nationalists did not, to put it mildly, celebrate this event with great vigor.

Finally, even at the risk of being obvious, let us point out that some of the best liberals in South Africa are Afrikaners. Also individual relations between many old-line Boers on the land and their Native workers are quite good. Some Afrikaner intellectuals, who entered the government out of a sense of duty, hate and fear the process of *Gleichschaltung* now going on, but have become helpless and ashamed prisoners of their position. Outside the government there are still tens of thousands of decent, honorable Afrikaners just as there were tens of thousands of decent, honorable Germans under Hitler, who look at present developments with acute dislike, dismay, and patriotic alarm. No government, no matter how infamous, can poison a whole people.

THE PERSON OF DR. DANIEL F. MALAN

Dr. Daniel François Malan (pronounced Ma-*laan*, with a slight nasal twang to the "n") is out of the picture now. He is over eighty, and lives quietly with his family in Stellenbosch. Although an elder statesman, he has little influence on the Strijdom cabinet these days. It is an open secret that he would have preferred as his successor somebody more moderate than Strijdom, like Havenga. Dr. Malan is a powerful but somewhat soggily built man with a big pale face and heavy hands; he is bald and bespectacled. He does not have a light touch, and his speeches in former days were notable for their solidity and dullness. Religion, conjoined with nationalism, has been the driving force behind his whole career. He believes literally that the Afrikaners are a "chosen" people, ordained by God to create a white Boer civilization in the African wilderness. He was a *predikant* (pastor) of the Dutch Reformed church for many years, and all his attitudes are white as crabmeat.

Dr. Malan was born in 1874 in Riebeek West, a village in Cape Province which, oddly enough, was also the birthplace of Jan Christiaan Smuts. Malan was four years younger, but the two boys had a close association during their youth; later of course they split and became bitter political opponents, but they always kept up a grudging admiration and affection for one another. Malan is partly of Huguenot descent; his father was a God-fearing and strait-laced wine farmer, whose character may be judged from the fact that the family home was named *Allesverloren*, "Everything Lost." Young Malan went to Stellenbosch University and studied philosophy and theology. He proceeded to Utrecht in the Netherlands, where he won his degree as Doctor of Divinity with a thesis on Berkeley's idealism. He did not, like his friend Smuts, fight in the Boer War. But, it seems, he had a cold, passionate hatred of the British from the earliest days. Dr. Malan served as a minister at Heidelberg in the Transvaal and elsewhere till 1915, when the secular world called him. He became editor of the newly founded nationalist newspaper, *Die Burger* of Cape Town, and was one of the leaders of the movement to make Afrikaans an official language. He entered politics in 1918, became an MP for Calvinia, rose to be leader of the Nationalist party in Cape Province, and in 1924 was appointed to be minister of education, interior, and health in the Hertzog government.

During the early days of World War II Dr. Malan made no secret of his hope that Hitler would win, and *Die Burger* was often flagrantly anti-Semitic as well as anti-British. Recently (January 28, 1953) charges were raked up that, in addition to being sympathetic to the Nazis, Malan had appealed to Hitler for aid against Britain. Malan denies this. It has also become known that, during the war, the German Foreign Office promised to "give" the Rhodesias to the Union in the event of an Axis victory.

Seen in the large, Malan's chief quality and source of power was his close personal identification with the Afrikaner *volkswil*. He has an almost miraculous capacity to know intuitively what his fellow Afrikaners are feeling, and to express their thought. Like De Valera in Eire, whom he resembles in several respects, he came to personify and crystallize the thwarted aspirations of his segment of the people. Then too, as a politician, he has always been persistent, logical, serious, and calculating. No one ever accused him of having charm; he built his policy step by step as if out of blocks of cement. He hates and fears people of black or colored skin, and has made statements about Latin American countries—also the Gold Coast—that are so naïve as to be laughable; but he has never been personally vindictive or ruthless. He would never dream of shaking hands with a Negro, but he has Colored servants, as do most of the Afrikaner ministers. If not actually "ruthless," he has certainly been harsh. One of his first acts upon becoming prime minister (1948) was to disfranchise Indians in Natal and the Transvaal. Another was to extend and make even more onerous segregation regulations in the Cape. The major acts of his government—they make a revolting display—we shall deal with later.

Perhaps, in relation to Malan and his men, we should add here a further line about religion and race. Dr. Malan, by his own lights, is not only a profoundly religious but a profoundly righteous man. What the outsider may think of as offensive or evil in the Malan philosophy is not necessarily dictated by evilness, malice, or indecency on the part of the Malanites, but by the way they interpret their own position. Their fear of being inundated by color is perfectly genuine. Of course this does not excuse the cruelties and injustices of *apartheid*. Once again the point must be made that race is at the bottom of everything. It is this obsession with color that makes the Nationalists seem so odious. Almost all their more outrageous legislation is caused by *racial* bias. If it were not for this, the Union would be thought of as a perfectly respectable member of the family of nations, intensely nationalistic and perhaps provincial, but otherwise no different from most others.

Only one so-called joke has ever been known to come from the lips of Dr. Malan. When he left Cape Town to attend the coronation of Queen Elizabeth in London, his farewell words to the deputy prime minister, Strijdom, are supposed to have been, "Brother, please don't make a republic while I'm gone."

MYSTERIOUS BROEDERBOND

One bizarre phenomenon in South African affairs is a secret society, the Broederbond (Band of Brothers). It would not be too much to say that this organization, in effect, runs the National party and hence the country. Of the ninety or more nationalist candidates who stood for parliament in 1948, about sixty were Broederbond men; ten of the present cabinet of fourteen are believed to be members.[15] Dr. Malan, people say, became a member early in the 1930's, when he made his own extreme Nationalist party in protest at the coalition between Smuts and Hertzog. The president of the Broederbond is, or was, Dr. J. C. Van Rooyen, an eminent theologian at the University of Potchefstroom. Dr. Dönges, the powerful minister of interior in the Strijdom cabinet, is supposed to have been a vice-president at one time.

The Broederbond stands for a "Christian Nationalist Calvinist Afrikaner Republic," accountable only to God. All links with Britain are to be abolished, and any Britons who choose to remain will have the status of "inferior" citizens. The Broederbond hates equally the Freemasons, the Catholics, and the Jews. Hertzog was a Freemason (so is Havenga) and quarrels over Masonry have been conspicuous in South African politics. The Broederbond, even though it fiercely opposes Masonry, has borrowed a good deal from it in several realms.

An executive council known as the *Uitvoerende*, or "Twelve Apostles," is supposed to run the Broederbond, with three "assessors" at the top. Members are knit together by their *bondsplig*, brotherly duty. There are supposed to be about 3,500 members, at least two-thirds of whom belong to the extreme fundamentalist or Dopper branch of the church.[16] Membership is, of course, secret, but on occasion Afrikaners will joke with one another, saying, "My boys in the Broederbond will get you if you don't watch out!" At the beginning only men with fathers and grandfathers born in the Union of pure Afrikaner stock were eligible to membership, but this stipulation has had to be relaxed. Candidates for membership are carefully watched—for instance to see if they commit some such dereliction as speaking English at social gatherings. Of course it is blisteringly anti-black. Once again, we encounter the nonsense of "pure" racialism in its fullest flower. Nothing like the Broederbond has ever exerted an important influence on government in any country in the world except Nazi Germany.

The organization was, it is believed, founded early in World War I by four Afrikaner zealots after a riot in which the Union Jack was pulled down and burned in a public meeting. The membership, opposing South African participation in the war on the side of the Allies, went underground. Its texture was something like that of Sinn Fein in Ireland at the same time.

---

[15] One prominent cabinet minister is supposed to have been blackballed from membership because he was not racially "pure" enough.

[16] "Apostates have revealed that of the Broederbond's 3460 members, 2039 are teachers and 356 ministers of the Dutch Reformed Church." From "Hard Choices in South Africa," by C. W. M. Gell, *Foreign Affairs*, January, 1953. See also *Time*, March 31 and May 8, 1952.

It sought friendship with the enemy of the enemy. In more recent times the Broederbond has had four main steps to its program (1) the *taalstryd,* or struggle for recognition of Afrikaans; (2) political conquest of the country through the National party; (3) improvement of the economic status of Afrikaners; (4) the eventual creation of a republic. The organization is by ten-man cells, and is complex. Every member, having proved beyond doubt the genuine quality of his *Afrikanerskap,* is supposed to have a "sphere of influence." The organization is strongest in the medical faculty at Pretoria University, the theological faculty at the University of Stellenbosch, the lower branches of the Dopper church, the old bureaucracy, and, strangely enough, the railroads.

An investigation of the Broederbond was demanded by General Smuts in 1944, out of fear that it was Fascist and had become a state within a state. The Dutch Reformed church also appointed a committee of inquiry into the organization. Public servants were subsequently forbidden by law to join the Broederbond, but there is little evidence that the society has substantially lost power.

THE GOVERNOR GENERAL

South Africa is a self-governing member of the British Commonwealth, and so has a Governor General, who represents the Crown. Constitutional practice these days favors the appointment of some local citizen to this post, not a Briton sent out from London. Governors in former days were vastly distinguished men of affairs or members of the British royal family, like Prince Arthur of Connaught and the Earl of Athlone. Those days are no more. The present Governor General, who took office in 1951, is not only an Afrikaner but—a most bizarre paradox—an avowed republican. He is Dr. Ernest George Jansen, and although he is titular head of state a visitor can journey across the length and breadth of South Africa for months at a time, and never hear his name.

Dr. Jansen is, however, a personality greatly esteemed and of elevated character. He is a Natalian, and has been a member of the Nationalist party since its foundation. He ran for parliament in 1921—after having been a member of the "Freedom Deputation" to England in 1919—and represented Vryheid in the House of Assembly for more than twenty years. He was active in the language movement. In 1924, on the formation of the Hertzog government, he became Speaker of the House, and he has held this post twice (1924-29 and 1933-43). Also he served for a time as minister for native affairs and irrigation. He is a stern personality, fair-minded, and aloof; his tenure as Governor General has been without much incident. His wife, of Huguenot descent, is a playwright in Afrikaans, and he himself is the author of several works of history.

Dr. Jansen, although a South African, symbolizes the British Crown; the representative of the United Kingdom government is, of course, somebody quite different, and is usually a senior British civil servant. The present incumbent is Sir Percivale Liesching, former permanent undersecretary in the Commonwealth Relations Office. He wears two hats, and is both High Commissioner to the Union, with ambassadorial functions, and also High Commissioner for the three British enclaves in or near the Union, Basutoland, Swaziland, and Bechuanaland.

THE PRIME MINISTER

If the European loses his color sense he cannot remain a White man.
—J. G. STRIJDOM

Johannes Gerhardus Strijdom (pronounced *Stray*-dum) is a man of medium height, lean, with dark hair and a hard square face, thin lips, and ice-cold sharp blue eyes. His features give a note of arrogance, intensity, and taut command. "Strijdom" is the old Dutch form of the name, and "Strydom" the Afrikaans form; either usage is correct, but the prime minister prefers "Strijdom."[17] He is what has been described as the most dangerous kind of fanatic—a man with a hot mind and cold heart. He is as tough as linoleum, gritty, and smiles joyfully about as often as an oyster opens its shell.

We met Mr. Strijdom and had a long talk with him, before he became prime minister, in his office in the great Union Building in Pretoria. He wore an old black suit and a black pullover. His manner was perfectly courteous and his talk quite moderate. He gestures fluently with his hands as he talks, and conveys a peculiar dark glow composed of force and confidence. He spoke English to us, Afrikaans to his secretaries who came in and out of the room. His English has a slight German-like accent, and he says "bull" for "pull" and "surwiwal" for "survival." One of the first things he said was, "Our fight here iss a fight for surwiwal."

Strijdom is of course very puritanical and religious, but he is one of the few prominent Afrikaner politicians ever to have been divorced; the fact that he has been married twice is never mentioned in the Afrikaner press. His first wife, whom he married many years ago, was an actress of distinction, who bore the stage name Marda Vanne. Her real name was Von

[17] London *Times*, December 21, 1954.

THE UNION OF SOUTH AFRICA 473

Holstein, and she was the daughter of a mayor of Johannesburg. Strijdom's second wife, whom he married in 1931, was Susanna de Klerk, the daughter of a minister of the Dutch Reformed church. They have two children. Strijdom's brother-in-law, Dr. Jan de Klerk, has been the chief organizer of the National party in the Transvaal, and is now minister of labor in the Strijdom cabinet.

Strijdom has lived most of his life in the Transvaal, but he was born (on July 14, 1893) in Cape Province, at a town called Willowmere. He studied at Stellenbosch and Pretoria, and, a vigorous athlete in his youth, was captain of the Pretoria City rugby team. He went into ostrich farming, became a civil servant, studied law, and was admitted to the bar. Then he went back to farming. He has a large Afrikander cattle farm, in partnership with his brother, near a town in the Transvaal called Nylstroom. When the early *voortrekkers* reached a small river here, they thought that it might be, of all things, the headwaters of the Nile (Nyl); hence the name. When I asked the prime minister if he still had time for farming, he answered amiably, "Only over the telephone."

Strijdom's constituency is Waterberg, which he has represented uninterruptedly since 1929. Sometimes he is called the "Lion" or the "Messiah" of Waterberg. His nickname, among people who dislike him, is "Heil Hans."

The prime minister became interested in politics in his youth, and rose rapidly in the nationalist ranks. He has always been distinguished for singleness of purpose and a completely inflexible, uncompromising point of view. (He never left South Africa and never saw Europe until a brief holiday trip in 1954, just before he became prime minister, because he did not want to be subjected to external influences.) Strijdom became in time leader of the Nationalist party in the Transvaal, and, something equally important, publisher of *Die Transvaler*, the chief Afrikaans organ in the north. This gave him a mouthpiece. In 1934 he was one of a dozen MP's who refused to join the Smuts-Hertzog coalition, and he went out into the extreme nationalist wilderness with Malan. He stayed out until 1948, when he became a member of Malan's first government. He succeeded to the prime ministership in November, 1954.

Like Senator Verwoerd and others of his fellows, he was strongly pro-Axis during the war, and has an anti-Semitic past. He talked about the "detestable" nature of "British-Jewish interests" and "the liberal democratic system" in early speeches.[18]

Today Strijdom has, as is to be expected, two main lines of thought. First, he stands not merely for *apartheid*, which is an elastic term, but in some-

[18] New York *Herald Tribune*, December 1, 1954.

thing much more fixed and final—*baasskap*, or utterly complete white domination. (Of course the concept of *apartheid* connotes white supremacy or domination, but *baasskap*—mastership—has a special additional meaning.) Strijdom believes quite frankly in a master-slave relationship. He told us, and I will not forget how he uttered the phrase, "Partnership means slow death!" Second, he wants a republic as soon as this is possible or practicable. In his very first speech as prime minister he declared that "the ultimate object of the National party was to make South Africa a republic," but he has indicated since that this is not likely for at least three years. I asked him if he could explain, in a word, why republicanism was such a compelling element in his program. He replied dryly that, no doubt, as an American, I must realize that the United States of America was happier as an independent country than it would be as a British dominion. Like all the nationalist ministers, he feels that the Commonwealth relationship imposes on South Africans "divided loyalty," which good Afrikaners cannot abide.

Until recently a kind of fissure divided the National party. On one wing was the "Keerom Street" group, composed of Cape Towners and named for the street where *Die Burger* is published and which is the nearest to a Wall Street that the Afrikaners have. The Cape Towners have always been by and large more sophisticated, more moderate, than the "Wild Boers of the Transvaal" and Orange Free State. Under Strijdom, this fissure has largely disappeared, if only because the Cape Towners, except for one or two, have been eliminated. This is a radical cabinet, a northern cabinet, and at least eleven out of its fourteen members are Strijdom men.

What are Strijdom's chief sources of power? I have mentioned his personal qualities, which are marked. More important is the fact that, like Malan, he is convinced beyond question that the God of the Dutch Reformed church has put him where he is, and he must not let God down.[19]

DR. DÖNGES AND CIVIL LIBERTIES

It is easy to get along well with Dönges. He is a civilized character, a gentleman. We saw him one afternoon when he had just returned from a little expedition outside Pretoria hunting springbok, the South African "national" antelope. We sat on thonged chairs made of stinkwood, the oddly named South African "national" wood (it has no odor) and thought

---

[19] One should, of course, remember that political figures other than Afrikaners have identified themselves with God. Think of Philip II of Spain and Mr. Gladstone.

that otherwise we might well be in Hampshire or Surrey. Dr. Dönges wears tweedy clothes, smokes a pipe, likes sport, has impeccable manners, and speaks perfect English. He gives no note of lunatic provincialism, and has a lively sense of humor.

But Dönges (pronounced Dunjus) is, next to Strijdom and Swart, probably the most powerful and menacing person in the cabinet. He has been minister of the interior since the first Malan government in 1948, and at various times has also served as minister of posts, mines, economic affairs, and finance. He was one of the editors of *Die Burger* for a time, and three times has been head of South African delegations to meetings of the United Nations. He is a devout churchman and Afrikaner, and is (or was) a leading figure in the Broederbond.

Theophilus Ebenhaezer Dönges, the youngest son of a clergyman, of old Dutch and German stock, was born at Klerksdorp, in the Transvaal, in 1895, but has been identified with the Cape most of his life. (Conversely, Strijdom was born in the Cape, but has always represented the Transvaal.) Dönges had a very good education. He went to Victoria College, Stellenbosch, the University of South Africa, and the London School of Economics. He holds the degree of LL.D. from the University of London (1925), is a barrister of the Inner Temple, and was made a king's counsel in 1939. He stood for parliament for the first time in 1941, and won a seat at Fauresmith. He has been an MP ever since, succeeded Malan as nationalist leader in the Cape Province, and has been called the "best brain" in the National party.

As Dönges sees racial matters, there are three alternatives for the white man in South Africa. (A) Permit partnership, which will inevitably lead to a mixed or coffee-colored society. (B) Quit. (C) Try to make *apartheid* work. Since the first two choices are inadmissible, the third must be taken.

Complete territorial segregation (which thorny subject we shall go into briefly in a chapter below) is not, he admits, in the realm of practical politics today. But there have to be "controls." Otherwise the Africans "would cover every inch of the country." He said frankly, "Once we give them political rights, the time will come when we will be ruled by numbers, and therefore we cannot afford to give them political rights." He does not talk about Africans with quite as much contempt as most of his cabinet colleagues, but makes remarks like "If we let 'em drink, they'd all be dead." He adopts the line that the white man should "protect" the Africans, because they are "our wards."

As minister of interior Dönges has charge of immigration, government translation (very important in a bilingual state), citizenship, the Indians (whom he would like to send bodily back to India), the Coloreds, implementation of the Group Areas Act, and much in the field of civil liberties, like censorship. In several spheres Dr. Dönges has powers above those of any court. A good many books and periodicals are forbidden entrance into the Union. Dönges told us that he had to be more "prudish" than he liked to be, because South Africa is not a "homogeneous" society, and he cannot afford to have tempers aroused that might lead to sexual crime. Anything that hints at miscegenation, or even portrays whites and blacks getting along well together, is automatically suspect. Recent publications banned make an odd assortment—Dr. Kinsey's *Sexual Behavior in the Human Male*, various works by Mickey Spillane, that beautiful novel by Stuart Cloete *Turning Wheels*, various UNESCO pamphlets about race, Richard Wright's *Native Son*, a book by Jackie Robinson, *Lady Chatterley's Lover*, comic-strip books like *Hopalong Cassidy*, and the Pittsburgh *Courier*. I asked Dr. Dönges if he thought that *Inside Africa* would be suppressed when it appeared. He laughed and said that he hoped not.

*

As of the time we were in South Africa civil liberties for the *white* population had not been much interfered with. (Abominations having to do with the blacks and browns are a different story, as we shall see soon.) White professors could say practically anything they pleased at Witwatersrand and other universities, speakers could denounce the government to *white* audiences with the utmost freedom, and the English press was unshackled. Communists or people suspected—even without evidence—of being Communists got short shrift (this question too we shall explore below), but otherwise the expression of political opinion was still free for the most part. The courts were—even if some laws were shockingly unjust —fairly administered and lenient on the whole, and few white people were jailed for political offenses. The country has a tradition of frontier spirit and outspokenness, and the fact that such strongly individualistic communities as British and Dutch lived together in a divided society promoted an atmosphere hospitable to healthy criticism.

Lately, however, developments in the field of civil liberties have taken a sharp turn for the worse. Whether Dr. Dönges himself is responsible for this is not known. Almost everything in the Union, since the advent of Strijdom, is being crudely "inspanned," yoked. The British press, although not under formal censorship, has become wary, and Johannesburg citizens are beginning to wonder if the mails are still inviolate. Well-known Union scientists have been forbidden to attend anthropological conferences abroad;

the fear is almost as great as in Soviet Russia that citizens will learn too much of what goes on in the world outside. Two bills were presented to parliament early in 1955 which cut at the very heart of civil liberties. One imposes a severe control on passports. The other—the details seem beyond belief for a civilized country—gives the police the right to attend any meeting and search any premises "without the authority of their superiors" and "without a warrant."[20] Nothing could point more ominously to the creation of a police state. And Mr. Swart has his own "Special Branch" of the police, which could easily grow into a Gestapo.

CRIME, FLOGGING, AND MR. SWART

The white man cannot survive if the black man is allowed equality of opportunity.
—C. R. SWART

Like Dönges, Swart has powers above any court. Charles Robert ("Blackie") Swart is minister of justice. He is six feet six inches tall, and for many years was the youngest and tallest man in parliament. He is still the tallest, but not the youngest. When we talked to him Mr. Swart gave forth a cheerful—even jovial—note of complacency and optimism. He was born (1894) in the Orange Free State, of old Boer farming stock. He spent most of the Boer War as a child in a British concentration camp, and has hated the British ever since. In 1914 he took part in a pro-German revolt against the Union government, when it went into the war on the side of the Allies, and was jailed briefly. Later Mr. Swart, an adventurous person, sailed for the United States, studied journalism at Columbia University, and worked in Hollywood, where he had several small parts in early movies. He returned to South Africa and entered politics in 1921, becoming a powerful figure in the Free State and secretary to General Hertzog. Later he repudiated Hertzog, and intrigued against him in circumstances unpleasant in the extreme. He was close to Malan for thirty years, and is a violent *apartheidista*, "pigmentocrat," and republican. He has been minister of justice since 1948.

The jovial, extroverted Mr. Swart has several claims to contemporary fame. One is that, as minister of justice, he has the right to "name" any person as a Communist, whether he is a Communist or not, and thus, under the terms of the Suppression of Communism Act, debar him from any public job. Also Swart can, by simple decree, forbid any man, woman, or child in the Union from living in or doing business in (or even visiting) any town or other locality in the country. Thousands of people have been effectively denied any liberty of movement.

[20] Leonard Ingalls in the New York *Times*, February 23, 1955.

It was Swart who gave sanction to a system, if he did not actually invent it, whereby ordinary prisoners may be farmed out to *private* employers if the need arises. If white farmers in an area want cheap labor, all they have to do is "hire" convicts from the government, and maintain them in their own private jails out in the *platteland*. Obviously such a system can give rise to the most noxious abuses. Finally—and most sensationally—Swart is famous for having pushed through parliament the so-called Whipping Bill, which makes flogging obligatory for certain offenses. When he introduced this bill Swart entered the Assembly carrying a cat-o'-nine-tails, and was photographed proudly handling this evil implement. Opposition deputies urged that the number of lashes authorized be reduced from fifteen to ten. (Prisoners being lashed are strapped to a board, and sometimes the beating is so severe that they are dragged off unconscious.) "What are five strokes among friends?" was Mr. Swart's reply.[21]

*

Crime is astonishingly prevalent in South Africa, and the country has more people in jail in proportion to population than any in the free world. There are at least 250,000 arrests every year, mostly of Africans picked up for infraction of the pass laws. In the Witwatersrand area alone there were 186 murders in 1945, 231 in 1948, and 472 in 1951; corresponding figures for "grievous assault" are 2,475, 3,381, and 4,776; for "serious crime" 69,036, 89,130, and—a big jump—no fewer than 158,513.[22]

Corporal punishment has been statutory for certain categories of crime for a long time in South Africa. Housebreakers are, for instance, flogged if convicted of a second offense. Lately new legislation was passed which imposes flogging, in addition to fines and imprisonment, as a possible punishment for anybody convicted of *protesting* against the segregation laws, much less breaking them. The text of this law, which was designed to crush civil disobedience, almost defies belief. Any person "who in any manner whatsoever advises, encourages, incites, commands, aids, or procures any other person . . . to commit an offense by way of protest against a law, or in support of any campaign against any law . . . shall be guilty of an offense," and may be flogged.

As of the time we visited the Union, however, no person had ever been flogged for a purely political offense. Only ordinary criminals are, in the normal course of events, likely to be subjected to this punishment. And

---

[21] London *Observer*, March 1, 1953.
[22] Gell, *op. cit.*

THE UNION OF SOUTH AFRICA 479

plenty are. Late in 1953 Mr. Swart reported to parliament that in 1952 white criminals were given a total of 760 strokes of the cat, as against 366 in 1951. Indians were given a total of 206 strokes as against 194, and Africans and Coloreds—an appalling figure—49,111 as against 27,622.

SOME OTHER MEMBERS OF THE CABINET

The Negro does not need a home. He can sleep under a tree.
—DR. DANIEL F. MALAN

The minister of external affairs and finance, Eric Hendrik Louw, is called "the pioneer of the Union's diplomatic representation abroad." He was born at Jacobsdal in 1890, and, like practically everybody else in the government, went to Stellenbosch. He first became a nationalist MP in 1924, representing Beaufort West. At various times he has been ambassador, trade commissioner, or minister to the United States (where he lived for seven years), Canada, England, France, Italy, and Portugal. His wife is a well-known violinist. Mr. Louw is suave, volatile and effervescent, but people who dislike him call him a "lightweight." He speaks with what seems to be a slight Cockney accent. He has a marked anti-Semitic past, and thinks that men like Alan Paton are "a bunch of sentimentalists." When I asked him if he was a republican, he answered, "Oh, sure." His conversation is so fluent that, at times, it explodes. He keeps in his desk a sheaf of clippings from American periodicals about outrages against Negroes in the American south, and says with a mixture of fury (at American attacks on the Union) and self-righteousness, "We have no lynching here!"

The ministry of native affairs is so powerful that it has been described as "government within a government."[23] In several fields, it rules by decree or proclamation. The minister is an outspoken extremist named Hendrik Frensch Verwoerd. He is a senator, aged about fifty-six. He studied at various German and French universities, specializing in psychology, and for some years was head of the department of sociology at Stellenbosch. Also for a time Dr. Verwoerd was editor of the *Transvaler*. One little story about him is that, when the late King George VI and Queen Elizabeth (now the Queen Mother) made their state visit to Johannesburg, he refused to allow mention of this in the *Transvaler*. The occasion was one of the biggest public festivals the city had ever seen, but Dr. Verwoerd boycotted it. Since, however, ordinary movements were bound to be disturbed on the day of the celebration, which his readers ought to be warned about for their own self-interest,

---
[23] Marquard, *op. cit.* p. 108.

he allowed to be printed a brief note to the effect that traffic congestion might occur—without explaining why!

Dr. Verwoerd did not formally enter politics until 1948, when he was elected to the Senate. He has been in charge of native affairs since that year. He is a ruthless believer in *baasskap* and *apartheid*, is supposed to have the best "academic mind" in the cabinet, is Strijdom's indispensable right hand, and is a good family man with seven children.

The mental texture of Jan de Klerk, brother-in-law to the prime minister and minister of labor, may be gauged by the following quotation from one of his recent speeches, in which he gave chromatic warning of four dangers. "The first is the 'Black danger'—the non-European in Africa is awakening and demanding a say in government. The second is the 'Red danger'—Communism. The third is the 'Yellow danger'—Africa is the springboard for India's millions. The fourth and greatest is the 'White danger'—the division among Europeans."[24] Dr. de Klerk is general secretary of the National party, but was not a member of parliament when he was appointed to the cabinet.

Barend Jacobus ("Ben") Schoeman was minister of labor for some years, and is now minister of transport. He was born in Johannesburg in 1905, left school at sixteen, and became a railway fireman, locomotive driver, and stationmaster. Later he went into dairying, entered politics in 1938, and became chairman of the Nationalist party on the Rand. He is one of the few members of the cabinet who did not rise out of the intellectual class. He was quoted recently as having said, "Negroes can do skilled work if trained for it; that is why we must not give it to them."

Another important minister and ardent nationalist (he was very close to Malan for many years) is F. C. Erasmus, who is in charge of defense. He has been called the Jim Farley of the nationalist political organization. He has set up paramilitary formations throughout the country, called *skietcommandos* (literally, shooting units), which will, if necessary, be called upon to assist national defense.

The most personable and sophisticated of the ministers, and a personality of great wit and charm, is Paul Olivier Sauer, former minister of railways and now minister of lands and irrigation. Sauer, cultivated and comparatively moderate, is the son of a famous old Cape liberal. He is full of common sense, having what the Afrikaners call "a long head," and for many years was probably the closest of all people to Malan.

The ablest person in the Malan cabinet was probably Dr. Karl Bremer,

[24] *World Today*, February, 1955.

a distinguished physician and medical authority who became minister of health and social welfare in 1951.

*

Mr. Strijdom and his men are prisoners of an ideology that must seem demented to most outsiders, and several are wildly vociferous fanatics. But it would be a grave mistake to think of this government as crazy or incompetent. It is not. It is a strong government, resolute, and able. It thinks as a team, and works like a well-co-ordinated, well-drilled team—time and again I heard ministers answer questions with phrases almost identical—and it intends to stay in power forever. Its members may be misguided, but they are logical. These men are the equal, in most personal capacities, of men in any government in the world—smart, tough, and on the ball. Much of what they do is horrifying, and in racial matters the Union today is a kind of shabby cross between Germany in 1933 and backwoods Tennessee in the 1880's, but that is no reason to minimize the force they represent.

A BOUQUET OF RECENT ACTS

> Our policy is that the Europeans must stand their ground and must remain Baas [master] in South Africa. If we reject the Herrenvolk idea and the principle that the white man cannot remain Baas, if the franchise is to be extended to the non-Europeans, and if the non-Europeans are given representation and the vote and the non-Europeans are developed on the same basis as the Europeans, how can the Europeans remain Baas . . . Our view is that in every sphere the European must retain the right to rule the country and to keep it a white man's country.
>
> —J. G. STRIJDOM

The Group Areas Act, 1950, amended in 1952. This measure, one of the most controversial ever adopted by a country, formalizes the *apartheid* concept. It has not been fully applied as yet. It provides for complete residential segregation, whereby the three main racial groups (white, Colored, and Native) will be obliged to live in different areas. The Indians are at the moment included in the Colored group. "Persons of one group will not be permitted to own or occupy property in a controlled area of another group." Even business premises may be segregated, a provision which can cause incalculable misery and hardship.

The Suppression of Communism Act, 1950. This, as we have already noted, makes the minister of justice, Mr. Swart, "sole arbiter of whether a person is a Communist or not."[25] Any person "named" as a Communist is

[25] *Economist,* February 28, 1953.

automatically forbidden to hold any position in the public service or any trade union.

The Population Registration Act, 1950, provides for the classification of the entire population into racial groups, with people ticketed, photographed, and identified according to race. The intention of the Act, which creates a kind of National Register, is partly to keep Coloreds from being able to "pass."[26]

The Immorality Amendment Act, 1950, following the *Prohibition of Mixed Marriages Act of 1949.* These two acts embody legislation unparalled in the world except by the Nuremberg laws of Nazi Germany. The Mixed Marriages Act forbade marriages between Europeans and non-Europeans, and the Immorality Act went further, making illegal any sexual relationship between Europeans and any variety of non-whites, i.e., Colored and Indian as well as Native. Previously there had been a ban on extra-marital intercourse only between whites and Africans. Nowadays it is a serious crime for a white person (even a sailor off a ship calling in Cape Town) to have intercourse with anybody non-white. Prostitution across the color line is forbidden. On the other hand Africans, Indians, and Coloreds may have mixed relations at will. The object of the law is to keep the *white* community from "contamination." One curious result of this is that an extramarital relationship between two white people, no matter how flagrant, is perfectly legal, whereas a happy marriage between a white and a non-white is a crime.

The Separate Amenities Act, 1953. This legalizes existing segregation patterns in transportation, public places, and so on, and followed the *Bantu Authorities Act, 1951,* which is concerned with Africans still on the reserves.

The Public Safety and Criminal Law Amendment Acts, 1953, together with amendments to the *Riotous Assemblies Acts.* The first empowers the government to declare a state of emergency and legislate by proclamation, if necessary; the second fixes the penalties which may be applied to persons protesting against any of the racial laws, or inciting others to do so. It is a crime in the Union "to support . . . any campaign for the repeal or modification of *any* law."[27]

The Bantu Education Act, 1953. From the long-range point of view, this is probably the most important law of all, because it gives the government complete control of African education. The mission schools will have to fall in line with government "inspanning," or close down.

The Industrial Conciliation Act, 1954. This gives the minister of labor

---

[26] Marquard, *op. cit.,* p. 152.
[27] London *Observer,* March 1, 1953.

"far-reaching powers to determine at his own discretion what occupations the members of any race may engage in."[28] In other words, industrial color bar may be made absolute.

Finally, we must mention the *Separate Registration of Voters Act, 1951,* the *High Court of Parliament Act, 1952,* and subsequent acts in the same field, which have to do with attempts by the government to set up parliament as a higher constitutional authority than the Supreme Court. These acts arose out of the fierce desire by Nationalists to remove some 48,000 Colored voters in Cape Province from the common roll, thus in effect disfranchising them. Their passage produced the most profound constitutional crisis and struggle in the history of South Africa, of which turbulent echoes are still rolling. Mr. Strijdom set out to resolve the issue once for all in 1955 by the startling—in fact stunning—device of packing *both* the Supreme Court and the Senate. The full story of his machinations to this end is one of the weirdest in contemporary history.

A hundred pages might be written about these sensational developments, which involve the "entrenched clauses" in the constitution and much else. The main reasons why the Nationalists, at all costs, wanted to destroy the voting power of the Coloreds (who have been on the common roll since the Cape achieved responsible government in 1853) are, first, racialism, and, second, the fact that the Coloreds hold the balance of power in several constituencies which the Nationalists need badly. Be it said to their honor, a striking number of honest, decent Afrikaners—even including professors at such a hotbed of Afrikanerdom as Pretoria University—rose in outrage at the indecency of the government's proposals, and did their best to thwart them.

IS SOUTH AFRICA FASCIST?

Not quite. Not yet.

---

[28] *South Africa,* by Gwendolen M. Carter, Foreign Policy Association.

CHAPTER 25

The Union: Country, Towns, and Issues

> My Motto is—Equal Rights for every civilised man south of the Zambesi. What is a civilised man? A man, whether white or black, who has sufficient education to write his name, has some property, or works. In fact, is not a loafer.
> —CECIL RHODES.
>
> Instead of rejoicing you would do better to weep: for this gold will cause our country to be soaked in blood.
> —PAUL KRUGER.

LATER in this chapter I shall deal with British affairs and attitudes, in contrast to Afrikaner, but first we must have a word about the old Dutch background, and then give a brief physical picture of today's provinces and towns. South Africa is a nation with a splendid, hard-grained history and tradition. Much of its development was like that of the American west in frontier days, and its early pioneers, creating a civilization out of barren wilderness, had a similar love of freedom, enterprise, and robustness.

History of the Union derives from a Dutch ship's surgeon named Jan van Riebeeck, who landed at Table Bay, on the Cape peninsula, on April 6, 1652, and founded there a "refreshment station" for the Dutch East India Company. British and Portuguese navigators had seen the Cape (which was originally named the Cape of Storms, not the Cape of Good Hope) long before Van Riebeeck, and Britons had in fact planted the Union Jack there in 1620, but they did not stay. The Dutch East India Company needed a station where its ships could get water, meat, and fresh provisions. It is striking that, twenty-six years before Van Riebeeck, other Dutch adventurers and businessmen founded New York City.

The Dutch community on the Cape grew slowly. It was not easy to

THE UNION: COUNTRY, TOWNS, AND ISSUES 485

penetrate into the interior, because there were few rivers. But handfuls of resolute burghers began almost at once to push out along the Mediterranean-like coastal strip and set up farms in the eastern valleys, and others became cattle ranchers in the great plateau to the north called the Karroo. Some resented rule by the Dutch East India Company; some were motivated by a spirit of adventure, money-making, and land hunger. These *trekboers* (itinerant farmers) wanted to carve out a new life and society of their own, free and isolated. They worshiped their lonely land.

In 1688 came the first Huguenots. It is impossible to overemphasize the role exerted in South Africa ever since by this vigorous community. There are thousands of Union citizens today with French names like Du Plessis and de Villiers. The Botha family derived originally from Huguenots in Lorraine, and Smuts's mother was of Huguenot descent. The Huguenots have traditionally been a leaven, a yeast, in the Netherlander dough. Also the Huguenots brought the grape into the country, and so founded one of South Africa's most lucrative and pleasant industries, viniculture.

Slavery was introduced early, in order to provide cheap labor in the farms near Cape Town. The first slaves came from West Africa—the Gulf of Guinea—which was also the chief source of slaves going to the United States. Then the Dutch began to import Malays from the East Indies, who were less expensive to acquire. The imposition of slavery had profound historical consequences. Incidentally there was a strong tendency toward *apartheid* in the Dutch even in these early times. The Company built a large hedge to keep natives out of bounds. Three hundred years later, Afrikaners are still trying to do exactly the same thing.

The local aborigines whom the Dutch encountered on their arrival and soon after were of two different types, the Hottentots and Bushmen.[1] The Hottentots were a pre-Bantu people, resident on the fringes of the Cape when the Dutch came. They were pastoralists who had come down from the north, and had little knowledge of cultivation. They were not warlike, and the Dutch overcame or absorbed them promptly. Most were wiped out in a great smallpox epidemic in the eighteenth century, and few pure Hottentots survive today. But, along with the slaves from Malaya, they are the fathers of the contemporary Cape Colored community, and also of a people of mixed blood still conspicuous in the Free State and elsewhere, the Griquas. As to the Bushmen, although sharing some characteristics with the Hottentots, they were a totally different people. Their rock paintings seem to show

---

[1] Also there were the Strandlopers or Beachrangers, a semi-Hottentot people of extreme primitiveness, who became "hangers-on of the white community." *South Africa*, by Arthur Keppel-Jones, p. 38.

Chinese influence, and their language is distinguished by peculiar sounds known as "clicks." The Dutch could not make any use of them, as they did of the Hottentots. The *trekboers* killed them off like animals, or, to put it in slightly different terms, as American pioneers of roughly the same period killed off Red Indians. But a few Bushmen still survive, and hold tenaciously to their racial, linguistic, and other characteristics. Most, like the Hottentots, have abnormally large rumps, and the legend is that they can go for days without food, living on the fat in their own buttocks. They may be found today in the Gemsbok Game Reserve, the Ermelo district of the Transvaal, in the Kalahari Desert, and on the borders of South West Africa. They are Stone Age people still.

Presently the Dutch trekkers encountered Africans much more formidable. Bantu tribes like the Xhosa, fierce and warlike, poured down from the north, and filled the same vacuum that the Boers, spreading out further along the coast, also began to penetrate. The Xhosa, like the Boers, were a cattle people. There were various conflicts and settlements. At last (in 1776) a frontier between Boer and Bantu was drawn at the line of the Great Fish River. But the Africans raided across the river to steal Boer cattle, the Boers retaliated, and what is known as the first Kaffir war (1779) took place. All this is important because it is a fixed and immovable item in the "mystique" of Afrikaners today that they, not Bantus or Negroes, were the original possessors of the country, or at least a good part of it. All over Africa the remark may be heard, with reason, that the continent is, after all, a black man's continent, which the white man took by force of arms or artifice. The South Africans deny with toilsome heat and vigor that any such argument has any validity in their own special case. They take the line (not counting Hottentots and Bushmen) that *they*, not the Bantus, possessed the country first, that it is a white man's country by priority of occupation, and that the black man, not the white, is the interloper. It is certainly true that, even in the next century, the Transvaal and Orange Free State were still empty for the most part when the Boers advanced north. So, in a manner of speaking, were the Great Plains empty when the American pioneers moved west. But there had to be six or seven serious Kaffir wars before the coastal strip and its periphery were pacified.[2]

Now entered an altogether new and potent factor. Great Britain began to play a leading role in South African events. The British seized the Cape

---

[2] A high official in Pretoria told me with a straight face, "Today, except for two small areas, all parts of South Africa that were originally occupied by the Bantus are still in the possession of the Bantus." What he meant was that the Bantu areas are native *reserves*. Whether the Bantus living there today would think of themselves as being "possessors" of these areas is, to put it mildly, open to question.

THE UNION: COUNTRY, TOWNS, AND ISSUES 487

from the Dutch in 1795, and thus began what Field Marshal Smuts named "the Century of Wrong." The British did not want the Cape, which at that time commanded the route to India and the East, to fall into the hands of Napoleon and the French. This was their principal excuse for what was, even by the standards of those days, a highhanded action. It was not (as always in that era) an *African* issue that settled the fate of Africa, but European rivalries. British possession of the Cape was confirmed by the Treaty of Paris in 1814, and settlers from Great Britain began, after the Napoleonic Wars, to stream into South Africa. Historians say that one reason for this was the economic depression that came to Britain in the 1820's. Whatever the reason the struggle for power in South Africa became from that time on triangular—between Boer, Bantu, *and* Briton. The British consolidated their position in the Cape and spread out toward Natal, and this inevitably produced a steadily increasing pressure on the Boers which pushed them away from the seacoast to the north.

In 1836 began the Great Trek. This is the greatest romantic event in Boer history. It is totally absurd to attempt to describe it in a paragraph. It conveys to the Afrikaner what Paul Revere's Ride, Custer's Last Stand, Valley Forge, and the Alamo, all convey to Americans. Several thousand Boer farmers and cattlemen with their families, traveling by ox wagon, struck inland over the *veld* (plain) and settled eventually across the Vaal River. Of course the Boers were fleeing not merely from the British, but from the forces of nature too—drought and rinderpest. After 150 years, their land had become worn out. A major historical motif everywhere in Africa has always been the struggle of man against a hard environment. It is not quite correct to use the word "fleeing" in connection with the Great Trek. The Boers did not think that they were fleeing; they were advancing. One thing prompting them to move into new lands of their own, free from British rule, was their resentment at the British abolition of slavery. The Boers did not want to be interfered with. They wanted (even as of that date) to make their own Native policy, and they resented bitterly having to give up their slaves.

Harsh battles against the Zulus, who under their bloodthirsty kings Chaka and Dingaan occupied part of Natal, distinguished the Great Trek. The Battle of Blood River (1838) crushed the Zulu power for a time. Meantime the northerly wing of *Voortrekkers* crossed the Orange River and then the Vaal, and set up their first settlements, a marvelous feat of heroism, tenacity, and endurance. Particularly did Boer women in their ox wagons demonstrate elemental fortitude. Historians who analyze the results of the Great Trek usually make two points. (1) It confirmed, if it did not actually create, the schism that exists between Boer and Briton to this day. (2) It cut the Boers off, so that they partook scarcely at all of the age of enlightenment that generally distinguished European communities everywhere in the world in the second half of the nineteenth century. If the Afrikaners are isolated today, it is the isolation that their grandfathers deliberately sought that helps make them so.

In 1852, the South African Republic (now called the Transvaal) was established by the trekkers, and in 1854 came the formation of a sister republic, the Orange Free State. For the next fifty years crisis followed crisis in the relations between the British on the Cape and in Natal (where there had been a nasty little Boer-British war in 1842) and the two Boer republics. The Boers were, beyond doubt, wickedly pushed around. The South African Republic was forcibly annexed to the British Empire in 1877 in flagrant violation of treaty arrangements, and in 1880-81 the Transvalers revolted against British rule. The situation had become intolerably complicated by two immense and seminal events, the discovery of diamonds on the Orange River (1867) and of gold on the Witwatersrand in the Transvaal in 1886. Thus both Boer republics became glittering prizes. From being stubborn little farmer "principalities," of no serious interest to the world outside, they—in particular the Transvaal—were transformed almost overnight into fabulous repositories of incalculable mineral wealth.[3]

"Oom Paul" (Uncle Paul) Kruger—pronounced Kroo-yer—became in 1883 president of the Transvaal. He is one of the indisputably great men of South African history—perhaps the greatest. He was stubborn, dour, and resolute, ruled the Transvaal virtually singlehanded for seventeen years, and is the only person I can think of offhand except one (also of Dutch extraction) who was ever elected president of a country four times. Stephanus Johannes Paulus Kruger, born in 1825, took part in the Great Trek as a boy of eleven, and fought against the Zulus. As a child he went into religious trances. He was a Dopper of Doppers. He wore as a rule a wide stovepipe hat, and had a face like a knot of solidified mucilage. A sublimely inflexible patriot, he is revered by his people with as much authentic respect and fondness as Lincoln is revered in the United States. He believed till the end of his days that the world was flat, and in his youth (the legend has it) bit off his own thumb after a hunting accident, when the wound became infected and he was far from a doctor or medical

---

[3] The British moved very quickly indeed to make the diamond fields safe British territory. Kimberley, the main site, lies in Cape Province almost directly on the Free State frontier. Griqualand West, which had been under the administration of a remarkable mulatto named Waterboer, was promptly annexed by the British government in 1868, a year after diamonds were discovered.

THE UNION: COUNTRY, TOWNS, AND ISSUES 489

supplies. Kruger married three times, and had sixteen children. He died in exile in Vevey, Switzerland, in 1904.

At about this time another fantastic and formidable character entered the South African scene—Cecil Rhodes. It would be the grossest personification of history to say that conflict between Kruger and Rhodes caused the Boer War, which broke out in 1899 and brought all these seething tendencies and forces to a tragic climax. But certainly these two ponderous and dedicated men typified Boer and British attitudes.

RHODES: COLOSSUS OF SORTS

Rhodes was one of the most brilliant and puzzling Englishmen who ever lived. He had demoniac energy and ambition, but in some respects he was a mixed-up and even unpleasant character. His imagination soared to the stars (he even had visions of annexing the planets to the British Empire) but he was capable of signing photographs which he gave to admirers with some such salutation as "Yours spitefully, Cecil Rhodes." Kruger thought that Rhodes was "unscrupulous"; Rhodes thought that Kruger was an "ox." Rhodes had what he called a "50 per cent belief" in God; calculated that his name would be remembered for four thousand years; cared nothing for money but left a fortune that has been estimated at anything between twenty-five and forty-five million pounds; added 800,000 square miles of territory to the British flag; and left no sons.[4]

Cecil John Rhodes was born at Bishop's Stortford, Hertfordshire, on July 5, 1853. His father was a vicar, and he was one of twelve children. One of his brothers died of drink. He was supposed to go into the clergy, but his health was bad; he struggled against tuberculosis and allied complaints all his life. Doctors told him to go to South Africa for his health, and he emigrated to Natal in 1870, aged seventeen. With one of his brothers he set out for Kimberley in 1872, dug for diamonds, and almost at once made a fortune. During the next few years he commuted, so to speak, between South Africa and Oxford. He attended Oxford for part of each year, and spent the long vacations in Kimberley, although the voyage back and forth took in those days an interminable time. A doctor in Oxford told him in 1873 that he had only six months to live. He became a Freemason in 1877. He was a millionaire by 1880, and founded the De Beers Mining Company, which grew into one of the greatest mining properties ever known, the De Beers Consolidated Mines, Ltd. In 1881 he entered politics, and became

---

[4] For Rhodes's adventures in the north, see Chapter 30 below; for his grave in Rhodesia, Chapter 31.

a member of the Cape Colony legislature. *Then,* aged twenty-eight, he returned to Oxford once more, took his B.A., and prepared to study for an advanced degree.

Back in South Africa, Rhodes proceeded to do for gold what he had done in diamonds, that is, make a consolidation or cartel under his control of a multiplicity of small companies. He organized the mammoth Consolidated Gold Fields in 1886, and was now the great king of gold as well as diamonds. But making money *per se* did not interest him. He wanted money for political purposes, not personal. He was not primarily concerned with business, but with power. In 1889 he set up the British South Africa Company for development of the north (Bechuanaland and what are now the Rhodesias), and in 1890 became prime minister of the Cape Colony. So at thirty-seven he was head of De Beers, head of Consolidated Gold Fields, head of the British South Africa Company, which held a charter from the British government, and prime minister.[5]

Rhodes had one dominating idea all his life. He got it early, and it never left him. It was quite simple, and Rhodes believed in it as Socrates believed in reason or Goethe in nature. His *idée fixe* was that the English-speaking peoples were the master "race" of the world, that the British Empire was the supreme achievement of history, and that all the world should, if possible, be ruled benevolently by the British crown.

All his life Rhodes kept making wills. He made wills, disposing of his gigantic properties, as a man may work out timetables for a casual summer holiday. The first of the series came when he was twenty-two; it is such an astonishing document that part of it should be quoted. He left his fortune (already considerable) in trust to the Colonial Secretary of the time and his successors for the "establishment, promotion, and development of a Secret Society," the first aim of which was to be "the extension of British rule throughout the world." The agenda included "the occupation by British settlers of the entire Continent of Africa, the Holy Land, the Valley of the Euphrates, the Islands of Cyprus and Candia, the whole of South America, the Islands of the Pacific not heretofore possessed by Great Britain, the whole of the Malay Archipelago, the seaboard of China and Japan, *the ultimate recovery of the United States of America as an integral part of the British Empire* [italics mine], the inauguration of a system of Colonial representation in the Imperial Parliament which may tend to weld together the disjointed members of the Empire, and, finally, the foundation of so great a Power as to hereafter render wars impossible and promote the best interests of humanity."

[5] *Cecil Rhodes,* by William Plomer, p. 22. Also see Cloete's *African Portraits,* from which I have drawn several of these details.

THE UNION: COUNTRY, TOWNS, AND ISSUES 491

Rhodes's grandioseness knew no bounds. He invented the dream of a "Cape to Cairo" railway (which is still not built) and offered to pay personally the cost of building a telegraph line between Salisbury, the capital of Southern Rhodesia, founded by one of his expeditions, and Uganda. Once he ordered his agents to buy for him the entire Drakenstein Valley, which he wanted for a farm, regardless of cost. This is, the necessary differences being observed, almost as if an individual Frenchmen should buy the Valley of the Rhone.

Rhodes had some marked peculiarities. So far as is known he never had anything to do with a woman in his life. Even in the rough early days in the diamond diggings he avoided women, and in later years he did not even want his associates to marry. He was a bachelor, and he liked to be surrounded by bachelors. For a long time he shared quarters with Dr. Leander Starr Jameson, his closest friend and a figure almost as controversially celebrated in South African history as Rhodes himself. Rhodes had at one period what has been described as a "romantic" friendship with a young man named Neville E. Pickering, who is variously identified by biographers as his "secretary," "friend," and "trustee." Rhodes made a will leaving his entire fortune, incredible as this fact may seem, to this young man. Later he abruptly called off the most important business deal of his life when, in Johannesburg, he got word that Pickering was ill in Kimberley. At once Rhodes ordered a coach to take him there. Pickering did not recover, and died in Rhodes's arms, saying that Rhodes had been "father, mother, brother, and sister" to him. Cancellation of the Johannesburg deal cost Rhodes £3,000,000.

He visited England in 1901, and was invited to dinner by Queen Victoria. She asked him if it were true that he was a woman-hater. He is supposed to have replied, "How can I hate a sex to which Your Majesty belongs?" She asked him, "What are you engaged on at present, Mr. Rhodes?" He replied, "I am doing my best to enlarge Your Majesty's dominions."[6]

Rhodes disliked and eschewed women, but it was a woman who made ugly some of the last passages in his life. A Polish lady, Princess Catherine Radziwill, even more emotionally extravagant than most Poles, became insanely fascinated by him, joined him on a ship from England to South Africa against his will and by a subterfuge, and turned against him when, so the story goes, he would have nothing to do with her. Apparently she misinterpreted remarks he made to her that were no more than expressions of tired or exasperated chivalry. A lawsuit followed, Rhodes had to testify

[6] *Rhodes*, by Sarah Gertrude Millin, pp. 138-39.

against her, and she went to jail; the episode (which is ignored by most Rhodes biographers) left an unpleasant sting and seems to indicate that, no matter how carefully a man may avoid women, they are apt to cause him trouble in the end.

Rhodes contributed a good deal to the history of the Cape, but his achievements there do not rival what he did in the north. Pondoland was annexed through his efforts, and the "Rhodes Fruit Farms" set the pattern for later agriculture. He donated his house near Cape Town, the Groote Schuur (Big Barn), to the nation, and Union prime ministers, when they are in residence at the Cape, use it still. He got along well with the Dutch, and had no particular animus against Africans, whom he thought of as children or "niggers."

Rhodes was a large man, and he gave an impression of solidity and heaviness. When he sat on a chair, it squeaked. He had a high falsetto voice. He was rubicund in his mature years, and some of his portraits resemble startlingly those of the late J. Pierpont Morgan. He liked to drink, and was in the early days (and even when he was prime minister) often surrounded by heavy drinkers, but he was not a drunkard, as is sometimes alleged.

What finished Rhodes in the Cape was the Jameson Raid—and "Oom Paul" Kruger. The Transvaal, as a result of the discovery of gold, was filled with *uitlanders*, immigrants. These came from various countries, including Britain, and hated the Boer government. Jameson and others concocted a crazy plot, whereby a group of raiders should enter the Transvaal from Bechuanaland, and assist an *uitlander* revolt. The confusion that followed would, they calculated, make sufficient pretext for the British (i.e., Rhodes and the Cape government) to step in, re-establish order, and take the Transvaal over. Rhodes himself was beyond doubt party to the plot, but casually. He probably did not take it very seriously. He was quite capable of being Olympian enough to think of it as a prank. Whether the British government of the day in *London* also knew about it is one of the most controversial points in imperial history. At any rate the raid (December 29, 1895) was an utter fiasco. The Kruger government held firm, the *uitlanders* never got a chance to rise, and Jameson and his men were jailed.

Rhodes was forced to resign as prime minister of the Cape four days after Jameson surrendered. His resignation as a director of the British South Africa Company followed a few months later. It was, of course, impossible for him to remain in office after the Raid, because the scandal was too flagrant. Rhodes was stunned by his dismissal, but took it well. He did not

THE UNION: COUNTRY, TOWNS, AND ISSUES 493

even rebuke Jameson. He was too fond of him. He said merely, "He has upset my apple cart." Later Rhodes told Kaiser Wilhelm that he, Rhodes, had been a "naughty boy" to have been involved in the Raid, but "never got whipped at all."[7] Rhodes's ego was such that, it seems, it never even occurred to him that the Raid *had* finished him except for a last appearance in the north. As far as the Cape itself was concerned, he went out like a light. Rhodes died at Muizenberg, near Cape Town, on March 26, 1902, aged forty-nine. The doctor who condemned the Oxford boy to death in 1873 was wrong by a quarter of a century.

*

The Rhodes scholarships have, of course, rendered a magnificent service to good will and fraternization among the English-speaking peoples of the world. One odd point is that Rhodes apparently thought at the time he set up the scholarships that the United States was still composed of only thirteen states. The scholarships have not, perhaps, had quite the effect that Rhodes anticipated. Oxford is not a university likely to teach imperialism. But they are a monument that will keep fruitful forever the memory of this extraordinary man—extraordinary, yes, but also strangely limited, predatory, and naïve.

THE FOUR PROVINCES AND THEIR CITIES

This Cape is a most stately thing and the fairest Cape we saw in the whole circumference of the Earth.

—SIR FRANCIS DRAKE

The Cape Province (area 277,113 square miles, bigger than France) is by far the largest of the four provinces of the Union of today, and has 4,417,330 people. This, as we know by now, is the most sophisticated area in South Africa, with the deepest European roots. Its flowering contours along the sea are of unsurpassed beauty, and resemble closely the French Riviera or Italy near Amalfi, but are for the most part wilder and more mountainous. In the Cape Province are Dutch villages, with their homesteads, that look as if they had been bodily transported from the Netherlands two hundred years ago, and have not changed by an iota since.[8] The Cape has succulent apple farms, beach resorts like Hermanus, the great University at Stellenbosch (named for Simon Van der Stel, one of the earliest Dutch governors), the town of Paarl which has the largest wine cellars in the

---
[7] Plomer, *op. cit.*, p. 101.
[8] One particularly lovely village is Graaff Reinet, a sheep-farming center. Here Dr. Malan served as a pastor for many years.

world, some villages that appear to be as British as villages in the Cotswolds, except that the thatch on their white-walled cottages is jet black, and, up in the northwest, the enclave surrounding Walvis Bay, where whales make love. It has valleys as abundantly fertile as the Drakenstein, and on Table Mountain alone more varieties of wild flower grow than may be found in the whole of the British Isles. Much of the Cape looks like the Engadine in spring. But also Cape Province touches on the Kalahari Desert, which is almost as empty and barren as the Sahara, and contains the vast semi-arid area known as the Karroo (=dry place) which is steadily biting its way north. Part of the low *veld* is wonderful sheep country. It is also extraordinarily empty. Flying over the Karroo, or even traversing it by train (stations are few and far between), the visitor is almost reminded of the northern Sudan. There is no resemblance at all to Equatorial Africa, with its teeming peoples packed shoulder to shoulder. Also Cape Province has KIMBERLEY, the diamond city, and the Transkei, which covers ten millon acres and is the largest Native reserve on the continent.

CAPE TOWN, capital of the province and legislative capital of the Union as a whole, is one of the most magnificently located as well as charming cities in the world. It has a golden, creamy atmosphere and a marked cosmopolitan accent, deriving from its historic role as "a tavern of the seas." Some of its public buildings have a nice old-fashioned stateliness and dignity; also it has some of the foulest slums in Africa, like Windermere. Towering behind it is Table Mountain, which really is as flat-topped as a table. Cape Town has roughly 615,000 people, of whom 260,000 are Europeans. Even here, the white population is a minority. There are 5,200 Asians, 40,000 Cape Malays, 58,900 Africans, and 238,000 Coloreds. The strictly black population is comparatively small. Residents of Cape Town are called colloquially Kapenaars or Capies, depending on whether your slang is Afrikaans or English.

Hanging down from Table Bay like an appendix, but in the shape of a crooked flint arrowhead, is the peninsula, with its tip at Cape Point. This is the most southerly point in Africa. Baboons, not too friendly, climb over your car, while you watch the brave spectacle of the waters of the South Atlantic, Indian Ocean, and Antarctic mingling. A warm current, the Agulhas, flowing from the Indian Ocean, intersects here with the icy Benguela Current sweeping up from near the South Pole. The drive to the Cape of Good Hope from Cape Town is, of course, one of the most famous in the world, but was not quite so spectacular as I had been given to expect; it resembles the Grand Corniche near Monte Carlo. Bathing can be dangerous, on account of quicksand. There are signs "American Eats" and California-like restaurants built in the shape of bulldogs. On the Indian Ocean side is the important British naval base at Simonstown.

All Africans in the western region of Cape Province (178,000) will be moved out bag and baggage "gradually," according to a government announcement early in 1955. This will be the largest experiment in geographical *apartheid* yet to take place, and will constitute one of the biggest forced movements of a population in history. Dr. Eiselen, the secretary for native affairs, did not reveal where these hapless folk will be transplanted. Excuse for the measure is that the African population of the western Cape has risen from 30,000 to 178,000 since 1921, on account of industrial development, and that the Africans are "too close" to the adjacent Colored population. The cost to human values will be immense.

Up the coast from Cape Town is PORT ELIZABETH, with roughly 70,000 whites, 30,000 Africans, 30,000 Coloreds, and a fingerful of Indians. This, except Pretoria, is the only city in the Union with a larger European than non-European population. Port Elizabeth was founded by a colony of British unemployed after the Napoleonic Wars. When Anthony Trollope visited it in 1878 there was not (he records) a single tree in the vicinity. Nowadays it is held together, kept from being blown away, by a plant known as the Port Jackson willow, which covers the dunes with a kind of scrub. Port Elizabeth has numerous monuments to the British dead in the Boer War, including one to a horse. Its economy was based for many years on ostrich feathers; when these went out of fashion it might have become derelict (as did several other smaller South African cities, like Oudtshoorn), but the growing trade in wool saved it. Nowadays it has all manner of new industry. General Motors, Ford of Canada, and British Studebaker have impressive plants here. Port Elizabeth is an "English" town, of course, and was for years a major stronghold of the United party, but in the 1953 elections the Nationalists won a seat, largely because so much Afrikaner labor has come in from the farms to the new factories. I found here a curious development in the attitude of some stout Britons, who said that, although their ties to the United Kingdom were still naturally close, they felt more kinship to New Zealand and to an extent Canada, because of the similarity in Commonwealth attitudes and problems.

Port Elizabeth has the most startling slum I saw in Africa—startling because native homes are made out of the large boxes in which imported automobiles have been crated. The companies donated the packing cases to the community. The area is called Package Town by the Europeans, and Kwa Ford by the Africans. "Kwa" means *chez*, or "at the place of." Also in Port Elizabeth is something nicknamed the "Apartheid Bridge." This is a gangway over the railway marshaling yards, which thousands of workers use. It is split down the middle by a partition, with two-thirds of the space for Europeans, the rest for Africans, although Africans using it outnumber whites by a hundred or more to one.

*

Natal is the other province still largely dominated by British South Africans; it is the least Afrikaner region in the country, and is considerably more British in mood and texture than the Cape. Also it has most of South Africa's Indians. Natal covers 35,284 square miles, about the size of Portugal, and has some 2,410,000 people. It was named for the Nativity by Vasco de Gama, when he traversed these shores (long before the Dutch came) on the way to India, as part of his spirited, stubborn quest "for Prester John and the King of Calicut." Natal, walled off from the rest of the Union by the Drakensberg Mountains, is called the Garden Province, because it has water. An important crop is sugar, and the average wage of a farm laborer is, if he is lucky, about $60 per year.[9] Natal has the Hluhluwe Game Reserve (pronounced "Slu-slu-we"), famous for white rhinoceroses, and a romantic little city, Vryheid (Freedom), which for some years maintained existence as an "independent" republic. Also Natal has Ladysmith, the site of a famous siege in the Boer War, and Zululand.

The Zulus, great warriors and cattle raiders in older days, are thoroughly tamed and docile now. We visited a Zulu *kraal* (literally, enclosure) near Durban, watched youthful pretty girls, with wonderful beadwork around their throats and bare breasts, walk down the lonely brown roads, and looked at their elders grinding mealie into meal, and brewing Kaffir beer. The name "Zulu" means "People of Heaven." Probably the Zulus are the most celebrated tribe in all Africa. About 400,000 of them still survive, and they live on a reserve covering 10,000 square miles. ESHOWE is the capital; the name comes from the sigh of wind through trees. Zulus are a Bantu people, believe devoutly in *lobola* (the local term for bride-price), and live near their cattle in round thatched huts called rondavels. They have a king, Cyprian Bhekuzulu Zulu, a boy in his middle twenties, not very well educated and completely devoid of power. He is a direct descendant of the ferocious Chaka, the greatest and most terrible of the early Zulu kings.

Zululand was grabbed off by the British and annexed to the Crown in 1887, largely to keep the Boer republics from gaining access to the sea, but also to keep the Germans out. Kaiser Wilhelm, on whose support Kruger vainly counted in the Boer War, always had a personal interest in Zululand.

[9] "African Dilemmas," by Cornelis W. de Kiewiet, *Foreign Affairs*, April, 1955.

THE UNION: COUNTRY, TOWNS, AND ISSUES 497

The Britons in Natal have a high-pitched local patriotism, and Natalians are sometimes called "hysterical" by citizens of other provinces. Natal is the only province that never had a substantial period of Dutch or Boer rule, and is the only one that can fly the Union Jack along with the South African flag as a matter of right; it insisted on this as a condition for entering the Union. There is a strong British secessionist movement in Natal, but, in the present historical phase, this can hardly be taken seriously, if only because Natal lives largely on exports to the rest of the Union. Many Natalians insist, however, that if Strijdom and his men make a republic, they will secede forthwith, create a kind of Ulster and become a separate British dominion. Whether or not this could be done legally is uncertain. A constitutional situation like that in the United States before the Civil War might develop. The grand old man of Natal is Senator Heaton Nicholls, the leader of the newly formed Union Federalist party.

Durban is the chief city of Natal, but the capital is PIETERMARITZBURG, near the beautiful section of country known as the "Valley of a Thousand Hills." It compares to Durban as, say, Springfield, Illinois, compares to Chicago. The population is about 75,000. It was named, curiously enough, not for one man but for two—Pier Retief and Gert Maritz, who were *Voortrekker* heroes in the Zulu wars. Retief was the courageous leader slain treacherously by King Dingaan of the Zulus. The Zulu name for Pietermaritzburg is something else—Umgunggundhlovu, all of which means simply "elephant." This is a pleasant, drowsy city. It is the seat of the University of Natal, the principal of which is one of the most distinguished of contemporary Afrikaners, Professor E. G. Malherbe, and has one of the best publishing houses in Africa, with the odd name Shooter and Schuter, founded by two men with names spelled differently but pronounced alike. Pietermaritzburg has lately taken on more and more of an Afrikaner complexion, because of increasing numbers of Afrikaans-speaking employees in the government services, railways, and the like. In a garden I saw flowers as spectacular as any I have ever seen anywhere, an orange-colored variety of golden-shower. But our host told us not to wander in the shrubbery too freely, because of cobras.

DURBAN looks like Brighton, with a broad façade of resort hotels facing the Indian Ocean. From all over the Union and elsewhere come tourists to bathe in its warm waters, and be hauled about in rickshas drawn by picturesquely clad Zulus, who wear horns and feathers. The rickshas are, I heard, made only in one place in the world, a town in New Jersey. Zulu beads come mostly from Venice. Beyond the hotels and metropolitan district are lines of industrial suburbs as unending as Los Angeles or *David*

Copperfield. All these were built on land that was mangrove swamp only a few years ago. Factories glaringly new rise among coconut palms, pineapples, and bananas, and the town is suffused by an odor of burning sugar cane.

Durban was named for an early British governor, Sir Benjamin d'Urban, and has about 420,000 people divided into more or less equal thirds—white, African, and Indian. Here, as in Nairobi, the racial situation is a genuine "trilemma." The city was defaced by severe race riots in January, 1949. Many British South Africans living here, although they consider themselves to be pukka sahibs and despise the Afrikaners on all manner of grounds including their racial bias, have a record of intolerance toward the Indian community that is as shameful as anything in the country. Some Britons, when they take a trip to Johannesburg, make the little joke that "they are going to the Union." The skimpiness and difficulty of communications characteristic of Africa are conspicuous here. Even today there is no railroad between Durban and Cape Town, and no direct air service between Durban and Bloemfontein. Some interesting people live near Durban. At Phoenix, in the heart of the sugar fields, is Manilal Gandhi, son of the great Mahatma. Here is where the Mahatma worked for many years, set up his first *ashram*, and preached civil disobedience. At Groutville we talked to Chief A. J. Luthuli, president of the African National Congress. At Verulam lives Jordan K. Ngubane, editor of the *Bantu Forum*, the only African-owned Negro newspaper in the country.

*

The Transvaal, like the Orange Free State, is an inland province, and has 4,800,000 people on 110,450 square miles. Roughly it has the population of Massachusetts on an area as big as Nevada. The capital is Pretoria (administrative capital of the Union as a whole as well); the chief city is of course Johannesburg. This is the richest of the four provinces, the most populous, and the most heavily industrialized. Here are the great Rand mines, and near Pretoria is Iscor, the Iron and Steel Corporation of South Africa, with its heavily expanding plant. But out in the *platteland* are some of the most miserable and desolate villages in all European Africa; each (like Quebec) is dominated by its church, although here it is a different church. The Transvaal has the high *veld*, much of which looks like Montana or Wyoming, and the bush *veld*, which is lower, moister, and more cultivable. Here are huge citrus farms. The Transvaal has Potchefstroom, the oldest city in the province and the end of the line for the *Voortrekkers* in 1838, and towns with names like Warmbaths (near Strijdom's constituency),

THE UNION: COUNTRY, TOWNS, AND ISSUES 499

Rabelais, and Pilgrim's Rest. Transvalers have been by tradition restless folk; this province has always been the heartland of the dissatisfied. The *uitlanders*, who superimposed themselves on the old Boer structure, still give it a riffraffy flavor. I have heard Nationalists say, "The decent Afrikaners come from the Orange Free State and the Cape; the Transvalers are mongrels and adventurers, *biltong* hunters."[10]

Also the eastern Transvaal has the Kruger National Park (once called the Sabi Game Reserve), which covers eight thousand square miles and is probably the most famous of all the great African sanctuaries for animal life. President Kruger himself was the father of this, and the reserve has been in existence since 1898. Some people think it has become vulgarized and "touristy." You can almost feed lions peanuts.

PRETORIA (altitude 4,593 feet) has about 150,000 whites, 120,000 blacks, and about 6,000 Indians, Malays, and other Coloreds. The Native population has been kept down by a mechanism known as "influx control," which keeps out migrant labor. The city is considerably older than Johannesburg, having been founded in 1854, two years after the Transvaal became independent. Here lived some of the greatest of the Afrikaner patriots, like Pretorius, Joubert, and Hofmeyr. Pretoria is called the "Flower of the Transvaal" and the "Jacaranda City," and the local chauvinism sometimes expresses itself even in horticultural terms; one official told me proudly, "Our jacaranda are so much handsomer than your Japanese cherry blossoms in Washington, DC." Pretoria has Church Street, which is supposed to be the longest and straightest in the Union, and the formidably massive Voortrekker Monument, which is surely as stolid and *ungemütlich* as any of its type in the world. Non-Europeans are allowed to inspect its wonders on Tuesdays between 2 and 5 P.M. Nearby is the Premier diamond mine, discovered by Sir Thomas Cullinan in 1901, and owned by the Oppenheimers. Close to the leading hotel, where a superb sausage called *boerewors* may be had for lunch, is a remarkable taxidermy shop—J. R. Ivy (Pty.) Ltd. —where you can buy eland thongs. Recently in the Pretoria zoo a litter of ligers was born, but all died. A liger is the offspring of a union between a lion and a tiger. The segregation laws are not applied to animals.

Pretoria has no newspaper published in Afrikaans, although it is the capital of Afrikaner nationalism. Of course the *Transvaler* may be had from Johannesburg, which is only thirty-six miles away. Recently the United States embassy took over a new building on Pretoria Street. A special clause

---

[10] *Biltong* is jerked meat, an esteemed national dish. The most adventurous among the *Voortrekkers* were scouts who went ahead and killed game for the rest to eat.

had to be inserted in the lease so that Africans in American employ could use the elevators.

*

Finally, the Orange Free State. So puritanical is this province that, for many years, trains were not permitted to run on Sundays. Nowadays they are allowed to pass through on Sundays, but not to originate. The Free State covers 49,647 square miles, the size of Czechoslovakia, and has 1,018,207 people. The capital is BLOEMFONTEIN, a somewhat dreary little city. This also ranks as the third "capital" of the Union as a whole, because it houses the Supreme Court or Court of Appeal. The Free State is not necessarily more fundamentalist than the Transvaal, but it has the most solidly homogenous Afrikaans-speaking population of any of the provinces, and the church consequently has crushing power. Nevertheless the Free State for many years was a moderating influence on Afrikaner sentiment and politics. It was well governed—Lord Bryce called it a "model republic" in the early days—and its people were much less unruly than the irresponsible Transvalers. One of its early presidents, Sir John Henry Brand, held office even longer than did Kruger in the Transvaal. In the modern period Hertzog, a staunch Free Stater, was a powerful conciliatory force. Today circumstances are changing largely because of industrialization, which steadily brings Afrikaner country boys of the most irrefragably backward and primitive type into the newly discovered gold fields and the towns. Never till 1953 did the National party make a clean sweep in the Free State. Previously there had always been at least one United party man.

Bloemfontein, although a principal citadel of Afrikanerdom, was founded (in 1848) by the British, not the Boers, and plenty of English-speaking families have lived here without interruption since the beginning. One of the best English-language newspapers in the Union, the *Friend*, has been published here since 1850;[11] no newspaper existed in Afrikaans until 1926. Bloemfontein has about 38,000 Europeans, with a 60-40 Afrikaner majority, 78,000 Africans, 1,500 Coloreds, and exactly *two* Indians. In the whole of the Free State, the total number of Indians is sixteen. Indians are not allowed to live in the Free State, and cannot visit it except under permit. Strikingly enough, although the Free State is the home territory of "Blackie" Swart and although Bloemfontein does not provide a very agreeable backdrop, this is usually the city chosen for the annual meetings of the African National Congress. One reason is that it is centrally located. In Bloemfontein is the "Wailing Wall" of the old Boers, which is also a

[11] One of its editors in the Boer War period was Rudyard Kipling.

THE UNION: COUNTRY, TOWNS, AND ISSUES 501

kind of Valhalla to contemporary Afrikaners—the monument erected to the 26,000 Boer women and children who died in British detention camps during the Boer War. It was charged—quite without foundation—that some of these were killed off by ground glass put in their bully beef. In the Free State British "atrocities" never ceased being a major campaign issue until Dr. Malan discovered racialism as a substitute in 1948.

A sign in the leading Bloemfontein hotel forbids entrance to the dining room of "females from the age of twelve in slacks," and "males above the age of twelve without ties or jackets."

JOHANNESBURG, CITY OF GOLD

Although it lies in the heart of the Transvaal, JOHANNESBURG (altitude 5,750 feet) is predominantly a British city, not Afrikaner. Back-country Doppers may be impressed by its wonders, but they tend to fear and despise it, first because they think of it as a wicked Babylon, second because it represents with such vitality British wealth, attainment, and prestige. They call it the *Duiwelstad*, "Devil's city." The African name is Goli, derived from "gold." Colloquially Johannesburg is often called "Joburg," but this appellation is more likely to be used by visitors than residents. Similarly citizens of Chicago seldom say "Chi," as crude outsiders do, and San Franciscans do not like the word "Frisco."

Johannesburg is the biggest city in Africa after Cairo, and by far the most important city south of the Sahara. What it reminded me of most was Houston, Texas, although Houston has no altitude and its gold is oil. In quickness of tempo, somewhat crude vitality, and brilliant aggressiveness Johannesburg is the most American of all cities in Africa. Seen from an airplane at night, it provides a spectacle almost unrivaled on the continent, with its great glowing halo of lights visible for a score of miles. It is not a very big city by European standards, but it has force. It is a real *city*. Johannesburg has, by the most recent estimates, about 950,000 people, of whom perhaps 500,000 are African. There are about 450,000 Europeans (which makes it by all odds the biggest European city in Africa) and some 20,000 Indians.

This is a rowdy city, tough, raw, confident, and energetic. In Johannesburg, as I heard it put, "the frontier has come to town." The altitude gives a sparkle to blood and mind, and it has (according to a booster pamphlet) 720 more hours of sunshine per year than Cannes or Nice. Nobody seems to be sure for whom Johannesburg was named—history moves fast. It did not exist until the discovery of gold in 1886, and thus is younger than any of its citizens under seventy. In 1890, the city did not have a single tree Today there are more than a hundred parks, and I have never seen a community with so many tennis courts. The streets do not, in several areas, carry signposts or any other means of identification that I could find, and the taxi drivers are the rudest and most ignorant I have ever encountered anywhere. The skyscrapers are of medium size, but undeniably impressive. Shops for the most part are uninviting, and their window displays suburban. Traffic is a problem, because Johannesburg has more than 100,000 automobiles, a terrific figure for Africa. Blocks are short, and the city was laid out that way because corner property was so valuable. It was instructive to watch Europeans sitting impatiently in automobiles interminably stalled by traffic, obviously getting ulcers minute by minute, while carefree Africans sailed and sauntered down the sidewalks, not worried in the least by such preoccupations as getting to the country club on time.

Johannesburg has, for a city grown up from a mining camp and now desperately eager to take on sophistication, very little night life. Why? An Italian headwaiter told me, "All the millionaires have to be at work by eight in the morning."

Literally, Johannesburg sits on gold. This is the only city I have ever been in except a much smaller one (Butte, Montana) built directly on top of the mines. There is almost as much traffic in the channels and tunnels and caverns a mile or more underneath the city streets as on them. Johannesburg squats atop a reef or ore vein that runs through the Transvaal for about a hundred miles. *Rand* means "ridge," more or less, and is short for Witwatersrand, "Ridge of White Waters." One farm sold in the 1880's for twelve oxen has produced £75,000,000 in gold so far. The total output of gold from the Rand to date has been estimated at £3,000,000,000.[12] Another item that gives Johannesburg unique distinction is above ground, not below. The surface of the city and its outskirts are covered by large flat dumps, consisting of debris hauled up from the mines and left there. They are, I was told solemnly, the biggest man-made structures on earth. The dumps keep the city from spreading out in some areas, with the consequence that land can be worth £40,000 per acre. The dumps are extraordinarily beautiful. Some look like the sand dunes on Lake Michigan, some like enormously magnified crystals. They are silver, fawn, gray, or golden. Sometimes the wind blows dust off them so that they resemble live volcanoes. The idea that they might be planted with green stuff to hold them together better has been suggested, but it is difficult to work out. One enter-

[12] From *Johannesburg, South Africa's Metropolis*, published by the South African Tourist Corporation.

THE UNION: COUNTRY, TOWNS, AND ISSUES 503

prising individual wanted to build an elaborate night club on the dump nearest to the center of town, but the project did not materialize.

When we were there the mayor of Johannesburg was Hymie Miller, who was born in Altoona, Pennsylvania. He emigrated to Cape Town, aged three, in 1910, and is a successful lawyer. Mr. Miller was a Hertzog man, and is a good Nationalist. His wife is a Johannesburg girl, and is the first mayor's wife in the history of the city ever to be born in the metropolis itself.

Johannesburg has a powerful and active Jewish community. There are 104,156 Jews in the Union (just under 5 per cent of the total European population), and of these some 50,000 live in Johannesburg. Thus the white community here is about 15 per cent Jewish. Many South Africans maintain close relations with Israel, and are ardent Zionists. Jews have risen everywhere—in business, shopkeeping, the professions, education, and even politics, and are largely responsible for the spirit of intellectual emancipation and earnest desire for cultural values that has distinguished Johannesburg in the past. Most Jewish citizens have been supporters of the United party, but not all. Some voted for Malan on the ground that "the British never did anything for us," and some even greeted the nationalist victories in 1948 and 1953 with satisfaction, because if the Nationalists had been beaten they might have held the Jews responsible. The Jews do not want to reawaken the latent anti-Semitism of the National party. Until the early 1950's Jews were not, incidentally, even allowed to be members of the National party in the Transvaal. One should also point out that there is practically no anti-Semitism in South Africa on the social level. South Africans are not inclined to be snobs, except in regard to color.

One powerful element in the economic life of the Union, focused in Johannesburg, is the Schlesinger Organization, which was founded in 1903 by I. W. Schlesinger, a New Yorker, and which is carried on by his son, John Schlesinger. It has large interests in hotels, theaters, insurance, chain stores, advertising, and travel services, and operates the largest citrus farm in the world. But above everything it dominates movies and show business not only in the Union but all over southern Africa.

I have already mentioned the shocking prevalence of crime in South Africa particularly along the Rand. There are communities here almost as much dominated by lawlessness as the gold rush camps in California, or, let us say, Chicago in the 1920's. Living in the best hotel in Johannesburg, in the center of the city, we were told that it would be unsafe to take a walk after dark—this, too, although most Africans are off the streets at night. One day we stepped into a taxi. The driver, who was surly even for Johannesburg, wrote down my name and the number of our hotel room, saying that he wanted to have these details in writing on his person, in case I should knock him on the head from behind while he was driving. This was in daylight. On another occasion I asked the hotel porter to get us a car for a trip to Sophiatown, one of the Native areas, and he replied, "You're lucky not to be going out there at night. You'd never get back alive." (Of course a similar remark might be made by a hotel porter in New York about a nocturnal trip to Harlem).

Perhaps the atmosphere of Johannesburg is hysterical, but some of the fright felt by members of the white community is justified. A British social worker, beloved by the Africans, did not want to take us to visit a "location" on a Sunday or the next day, which happened to be a holiday. The place simply was not safe on days when the residents were not at work. Women alone, even if they have their own cars, will not as a rule drive out to a dinner party in the suburbs, because the risk of assault is too great if, for instance, the automobile should have a puncture and have to stop. Johannesburg is a city where European children, even in the best areas, do not go to parks or playgrounds, and seldom roller-skate on the streets, where lovers do not dare to sit on park benches after dusk, and where nobody would dream of taking a lonely hike. Most householders sleep with a gun at the side of the bed, and many have fierce dogs—ridgebacks from Rhodesia —to guard their premises. The terror that grips Johannesburg makes for contempt of law. The American manager of a local bank told me that he "thought" that, in the dark the night before, he saw a Native intruder enter his garden. "What did you do?" "Took a pot shot at him, of course. Don't know whether I hit the beggar or not."

Youthful hoodlums are called *tsotsis*. They roam in gangs, which are picturesquely named, even as do teen-age criminals in New York. They drink a poisonous illicit booze, and smoke *dagga*, which resembles marijuana. There are white as well as Negro *tsotsis*, who have similarly been driven desperate by the grim circumstances in which they live. To a degree they resemble the savage "wolf children," *besprezornyi*, who became a serious menace to public order in Soviet Russia after the revolution.

Finally, one should mention newspapers. This is the first country which we have met in Africa (and will be the last) where a real press exists in the European or American sense.[13] The Johannesburg *Star* and *Rand Daily Mail* (also the *Cape Times* and *Cape Argus* in Cape Town) have a long record of courageous, honest journalism. About 120 newspapers are pub-

---

[13] Kenya and Southern Rhodesia have good newspapers, but they can hardly be called a "press."

lished in the Union, a number greater by far than in any other African country; most of these are not, however, dailies. The metropolitan dailies are never bilingual; the weeklies out in the *veld* usually are. The Afrikaner politicians are bitterly jealous of the power and influence of the English papers, if only because they reach a large number of Afrikaners. One reason for this (as Mr. Strijdom himself pointed out to us) is that the British dailies print more news, and even Afrikaners are interested in news. Also they are much less politically slanted, and have access to more advertising.[14] One fascinating publication, British owned but African edited and run, is the *Drum*, published in Johannesburg. It is a monthly magazine, and resembles to a degree the American *Ebony*. The *Drum* has commendable enterprise, is brilliantly edited, and has a circulation of about 70,000. This is largely concentrated in the Union, but the *Drum* is the nearest thing on the continent to a pan-African publication; for instance it sells about 12,000 copies a month as far away as the Gold Coast, and has a circulation in other countries too. The *Drum* goes in heavily for exposés, such as conditions on the convict "farms" or in the jails in Johannesburg, and these perform a substantial public service. It is a wonder that the government allows them to be printed, but in theory at least the press is still free in South Africa. One recent *Drum* article dealt with the disgraceful "tot" system in the Cape vineyards, where Native and Colored workers (even children) are paid part or most of their wages in wine, with the result that they are stupefied with alcohol most of the time, and become permanently debauched.

Also we should have at least one word about literature. Johannesburg is the scene of what might well be called a literary renascence, and a number of youthful writers have appeared of the utmost sensitiveness and promise, like Nadine Gordimer.

THE JOHANNESBURG LOCATIONS

These are as appalling as anything I have ever seen. I thought, years ago, that slums in Bombay and Shanghai were "bad," but those in this white state devoted to white supremacy are worse. A "location" is, technically speaking, a township or settlement lived in by Natives on the periphery of a city, or in a non-white area. It is not the same thing as a "compound."

---

[14] Some news stories carry not only the signature but the home address of the writer. I have never seen this oddity elsewhere, and never heard a satisfactory explanation for it. Perhaps it gives the writer an added sense of responsibility. At any rate any reader who dislikes a story knows where to find its author after office hours.

There are no women in compounds, and residence is not permanent. Compounds, as we shall see in a chapter below, are a kind of barracks housing migratory workers attached to the mines or other industries.

All Africans in Johannesburg live in locations except the mineworkers in the compounds or hostels and *single* servants in a white household. Married couples are not, by and large, employed as servants anywhere in the Union, and cannot live in the white man's home, for fear that they will produce black children and thus contaminate a white neighborhood.[15]

There are four principal locations in one area on the outskirts of Johannesburg, and we visited them all—Moroka (population 54,000), Jabavu (31,000), Orlando (97,000), and Pimville (24,000). I thought that Moroka was the worst. Orlando had a few street lights, but otherwise these suffocatingly crowded communities are totally dark at night. All except Orlando, which is the best, are fenced with wire. Moroka has no electricity except at a social service center that makes its own. Moroka and Jabavu together have *one* clinic—for 85,000 people! Orlando has one cinema, one clinic, and exactly one public telephone—for almost 100,000 people. It was this last item which interested me most, because it is an example of the deliberate, calculated effort by the authorities to make it as difficult as possible for Africans to communicate *with each other.* Any attempt at native organization will, it is hoped, be severely handicapped by difficulties in communication. Streets in the locations are not always named, and few houses (none in the district known as Kliptown) have numbers. If a person should, for some reason, want to round up half a dozen Africans in a hurry, the difficulties merely in the realm of communications would be almost insuperable.

We drove out to Orlando on the brightest, sunniest, of June mornings. If it were not for the antiseptic effect of the African sunshine, even in winter, and the naturally clean habits of most adult Africans, frightful epidemics could take place in these locations. We passed a sign, DRIVE SLOWLY—NATIVES CROSSING AHEAD, exactly like signs warning motorists in Vermont about cattle. I sat in our parked car for a moment, after we had spent an hour on the location, scribbling notes. The door was open, and the front seat empty. Our guide had left her handbag there, since she was standing only a few yards away. A tall African boy swiftly and silently came up, slipped a hand into the car, grabbed the handbag, and

---

[15] Incidentally it is a crime in the Union for an African servant to quit his job without permission, or to be "impertinent" to a master, by terms of the Masters and Servants Act. Alexander Campbell in *Time*, September 3, 1951.

started to run off. I was so surprised at robbery under such circumstances that all I could say was "Hey!" The boy called "I don't know!" dropped the bag in the dirt, and was out of sight in a flash behind a wall.

Most houses in these locations, if they can be called houses, are crumbling, crooked structures of rusty corrugated iron, bits of wood, cardboard, or even reeds, lining "streets" (there are no sidewalks) full of rocks and flowing with slime. Some houses are better built, but do not have walls solid to the roof, so that the residents have little privacy. Floors are of cement, which gives people rheumatism. Windows have to be shut at night, for fear of the *tsotsis*, and this tends to spread tuberculosis. For these "homes" Natives pay to the municipality a rent that is by no means small, considering what they earn. There are no trees—this is partly because many primitive Africans think that trees carry evil spirits. We saw a few Coca-Cola signs, and even ghastly little restaurants advertising fish and chips. But this marks a substantial advance, because until recently such amenities as Coca-Cola and restaurants were unknown, and Africans in this general area would not touch fish, which were supposed to resemble snakes and which carry a strict taboo.

There are, of course, no toilet facilities whatever in most houses, or even running water. I take the following from A *Place to Live*, a pamphlet published by the Johannesburg City Housing Committee. It carries an introduction by the Right Reverend Ambrose Reeves, the Bishop of Johannesburg, than whom no person can be more authoritative.

> The floors [of the public latrines] are of rough, badly eroded concrete skimming, with numerous depressions in which urine collects . . . ineffectively graded to insanitary and offensive sumps which have to be emptied by hand, creating a certain amount of spillage which flows down the numerous erosions into open spaces. The risers (seats) are of gumpole type, which makes usage, particularly by females, elderly persons and children, almost an impossibility, with the result that the floors are indescribably fouled.

Photographs show an open pool that catches "the overflow of urine running down from the uneven floors." Recently a child fell into one of these deep pools, and was drowned. "A population estimated at 34,000 men, women, and children share between them 561 of these foul and disgusting latrines."

The Reverend Michael Scott, the Anglican clergyman who has devoted a large share of his life to African betterment, once (before he was forbidden entrance into South Africa) took part in an interview with the minister of native affairs, Dr. Verwoerd, and other ministers, in reference to conditions in the Johannesburg locations.[16]

> We [the deputation] pointed out the seriousness of miniature townships growing up without light, water, drainage or health facilities of any kind. The Minister of Native Affairs laughed at us; we asked him if he had seen the situation for himself; he told us that he had, from a distance—he had flown over the area. He said he thought we should not worry unduly about the shantytown, that there was something rather comic [sic!] about the way these shantytowns had sprung up almost over night.

In one location, according to the document just cited, there is one doctor for 40,000 people, and 65 per cent of all children die by the age of two. Mothers, if they lack milk, give children water and mealie meal at birth, and they die like flies. Almost all children, if they survive, are likely to suffer from complaints caused by malnutrition, and more than half have intestinal worms. But thousands do survive. The locations positively pullulate with children.

South Africans of the utmost worthiness and decency, and of all ranks and creeds, do their best to ameliorate these intolerable conditions. Our guide was a representative of the African Children's Feeding Scheme, which seeks to give some modicum of proper nourishment to indigent children. Bread, specially fortified with protein, is distributed, and so is a kind of peanut butter containing a tasteless and odorless fish powder, which also provides protein. Another article is a soup powder that will produce edible soup after only thirty seconds in boiling water. Speed is an important item, because fuel is so desperately scarce.

The wage earner of a family in the locations must go into Johannesburg every day to work, and here enters another unpleasant, exasperating factor. The commuter trains are crowded beyond belief, and the workers may spend as much as *four or five hours* every day getting to their jobs and back. Sometimes it is necessary to stand in a queue for at least an hour to get a bus, and then to queue up again for a period of half an hour or longer for the train. Humane employers in Johannesburg let their help off early on payday, Friday. This is to prevent wholesale pickpocketing or assault by the *tsotsis* who mingle with the crowds at the rush hour and push their way into the teeming trains.

---

[16] *Civilization Indivisible*, by Michael Scott, a Statement for the United Nations Commission on the Racial Situation in the Union of South Africa.

THE UNION: COUNTRY, TOWNS, AND ISSUES

The miracle is that even in the locations, ghastly as they are, most Africans seem happy. They will allow nothing to deprive them of their joy of living.

REMOVAL IN THE WESTERN AREAS

On the western edge of Johannesburg is Sophiatown, a special kind of township or location. Here some 60,000 Africans lived in circumstances considerably better than in Moroka or Orlando. Part of Sophiatown was, it is true, a slum, but part was not. Here was the only place in the whole of the urban Transvaal where Natives were permitted to own their own homes.[17] Sophiatown was a decent, law-abiding little enclave. It even had a swimming pool for African children. As far back as 1944 (long before the Nationalists came to power) the idea was broached of emptying Sophiatown of its Africans, with their long-established shops, churches, and community centers, to meet the needs of the expanding white population. White suburbs had grown up nearby, and the Europeans did not want to live near Natives. After the passage of the Group Areas Act, which authorizes complete residential segregation, the Nationalist government decided to go forward with the "Western Areas Removal Scheme," and thus clear Sophiatown of its 60,000 Africans—wipe out the whole community. The City Council of Johannesburg opposed the project for humanitarian and other reasons, but was overruled. Protests came from the English-language newspapers, the United party, the Anglican church, the Jewish community, the Liberal party, and the South African Institute of Race Relations, but were not heeded. In February, 1955, the forcible eviction of Africans from Sophiatown began.

Some families that had lived here for forty years were given ten hours' notice to move. They were picked up with all their possessions by vans guarded by police, and shipped out to new homes in a development called Meadowlands, twelve miles from Johannesburg near Moroka.

Nobody was evicted from Sophiatown until new quarters were ready, and the Meadowlands housing was good, infinitely better than in the locations nearby and probably much better than in most of Sophiatown. But there were several catches. For one thing nobody in Meadowlands is allowed to buy land and own it on freehold.

The government defends the Sophiatown removals on the ground of "slum clearance." The real motives go deeper. The evictions will (when

[17] With the exception of another similar township, Alexandria.

they are fully effective) serve to make Johannesburg a whiter city, and are the first concrete steps toward converting residential *apartheid* into a reality. Moreover it uproots and in effect destroys the most prosperous, stablest, and best educated Native community in the Transvaal. If the government had genuinely wanted to do a bit of slum clearance, it might well have given its attention to the shantytowns, as a writer in the London *Times* recently pointed out. The Western Areas Removal Scheme is not only "a moral horror," but a deliberate attempt to increase African insecurity.[18]

THE BRITISH POSITION

This is to hold on at all costs. I have already mentioned that 90 per cent of the country's invested capital is in the hands of the English, who dominate commerce, big business, and the mines. When I asked a venerable Natalian of British origin whether the Afrikaners would not in time "absorb" his community, he replied with a snort, "Ever heard of a bulldog being absorbed by a damned cat?" Be this as it may be, the British South Africans are being steadily squeezed out of the upper bureaucracy, and are at a heavy political disadvantage. If any man of British stock still has, let us say, a senior job in the railways or diplomatic service, his days are numbered. I heard the most celebrated of all mine operators say ruefully, "There will never be any government here except a 'Dutch' government from now on." To an extent this is the fault of the Britons themselves. They were so busy making money that they let politics go to the Afrikaners almost by default, and are now paying the penalty.

Perhaps I gave a false impression when, in the preceding chapter, I described the glad fervor with which people of British descent talk of England as "home." They do; but this is not to say that they are not devoted to South Africa, and are not deeply patriotic South Africans. A businessman in Port Elizabeth told us, "I was born on the same day as this country, and I love it. I cannot bear to see it go down the drain." There are British families that have lived uninterruptedly in the Cape for more than four generations. In the radiant hills above Durban we met two men, both of the solidest English stock, whom I shall call Citizens A and B. There was a long political argument, and Citizen B made some rude remarks about Nationalists. When he left the room, Citizen A, who detests the Nationalists too, sighed, "That man is as old-fashioned as

[18] See the London *Times*, October 8, 1954; *Time*, February 21, 1955; and "The Grim Drama of Johannesburg," by Alan Paton, New York *Times*, February 27, 1955.

THE UNION: COUNTRY, TOWNS, AND ISSUES   511

plum pudding. He still thinks that South Africa ought to be Surrey. I do not. I am a South African!"

This is an attitude extremely important to understand, and is characteristic. British South Africans, like Australians or New Zealanders, have an authentic and vivid local identity. They may be fond of Britain, but they are certainly not British. Many, although of English origin, have never been in England.

Nobody should think that all Afrikaners are villains in regard to segregation, and all the British South Africans lily-pure. Far from it. *Apartheid* is the official Nationalist policy, but plenty of Britons believe in it too. I heard one Englishman say plaintively, when I was describing the horrors of the locations, "But you *do* believe that the Natives are all a lot of savages, don't you?" The difference between Afrikaner and Briton on racial matters is largely one of temperament and degree. The Afrikaner puts out a blunt sign, "Europeans Only!" The Briton prefers to achieve the same result more gently, perhaps by some such sign as "Natives, Please Keep Away." On the other hand it should be firmly noted that few Britons, if any, are crazily obsessed by race as a matter of public policy, as so many nationalist Afrikaners are. Britons may believe in color bar on the beaches and in the hotels (so do people in Detroit and Los Angeles), but they do not want to eliminate Natives from the economy or make them slaves. Most of the effective protest that has come against extremist measures by the government rises in British-descended circles.

South Africa is of prime importance and value to the United Kingdom on the highest levels. The Union is a very important customer indeed for all manner of British exports, and is Britain's chief source of gold. The British investment in the Union since World War II is enormous—the equivalent of almost one billion dollars. The Union has more than a million English South Africans, and is still a member of the Commonwealth. The sea route around the Cape gives South Africa considerable strategical importance, and the British naval base at Simonstown is a valuable item in what used to be called "imperial" defense. From almost every point of view —economic, political, sentimental—it serves the British interest to be on good terms with South Africa.

There are two principal obstacles to smooth relations between the United Kingdom and South Africa, aside from the British dislike of too much *apartheid* and dismay at the totalitarian course now being taken by the Union. (1) The position of the High Commission Territories, (2) republicanism.

We shall mention in a subsequent chapter some of the internal problems of the three High Commission Territories, which are British enclaves adjacent to or imbedded in the Union—Basutoland, Swaziland, Bechuanaland. Suffice it to say now that the Nationalists want all three to be incorporated into Union territory, and thus terminate British rule. The history behind this issue is extraordinarily complex. At the time of the Act of Union (1909) it was assumed as a matter of course that, sooner or later, the Union would take over the three British areas. Procedure for this was, in fact, included in the Act. But at that time, and in following years, the Union government had its plate full, and did not particularly want to embroil itself with these territories, which have their own intricate and special problems. When the Nationalists came into power in 1948, this situation soon changed. In 1953 Dr. Malan announced that he would "give" Britain five years to cede the three protectorates to the Union, and in 1954 he asked for resumption of negotiations to this end. But the Union today is not the Union of 1909-10, and the British are reluctant in the extreme to surrender the territories, and thus turn over their African wards to white supremacy fanatics. But perhaps in the long run they will find it impossible to do otherwise.

More serious and pressing is republicanism. All nationalist leaders in South Africa fervently want a republic, and to attain this is their fixed, official policy. The British would, naturally, deplore secession; they do not want the Commonwealth "club" to be broken up by withdrawal of any country, let alone by one as important as South Africa. Some chance exists that a formula will be worked out whereby the Union, like India, may become a republic but at the same time will *not* secede from the Commonwealth. Malan and Strijdom detest Mr. Nehru, but they may have to thank him for having set a precedent that might solve one aspect of the problem.

Strijdom will probably fight the 1958 general election on the republic issue. I have already noted that he has promised not to make a republic for three years. Why does he not act sooner? First, no matter how great nationalist strength is, formation of a republic (whether or not the ties with Britain were severed completely) would cause a domestic political crisis of the first magnitude. One need only keep in mind the numerical strength and monetary power of the British community. Second, severe economic losses to the country might result. Third, South Africa, so long as it retains its present status, has like Canada and Australia automatic access to "imperial" and Commonwealth secrets, particularly in the realm of strategy and defense, and these can be valuable.

Why, since South Africa is already fully self-governing and independent, should the Nationalists *want* to make a republic? What will they gain? Any Briton who asks these questions does not understand much about the Afrikaner mentality. Even if it gains them nothing, the Nationalists are absolutely determined to make South Africa a republic in time. It is an obsession with them, as the Treaty of Versailles was with Hitler. Even the most innocent symbolism exasperates them to frenzy. I heard Afrikaners say things like, "It took us a long time to get the royal family off our postage stamps, but we did it!" On a more serious level the chief justification for republicanism is, as Mr. Strijdom told us, the feeling that the country can never become truly united if its citizens have "divided" loyalty. This can only mean that he equates the word "united" with "Afrikaner," since the British community, even if it accepts loyally the status of a republic in the future, will never forget its allegiance to the Queen. Even so, Strijdom has a strong point in this argument.

Another cabinet minister put it this way. "Yes, we are free—except for *the unseen tie!* We are a conquered people. We must become a republic for the sake of our national pride." Another: "There will always be friction between Afrikaner and Englishman as long as *that girl* [sic] six thousand miles away is represented here." Another: "I am a republican because I was born one. I was born in the Transvaal when it was still an independent state. Thank God for the British! They broke our tie with Holland, and this made us self-reliant and put us on our own. Now we shall return the compliment."

OPPOSITION TO STRIJDOM

The leader of the United (*Verenigde*) party, the old Smuts party, is Jacobus Gideon Nel Strauss, nicknamed "Straussie." He is a boyish-looking man with signal charm as well as intelligence, and is a prosperous Queen's Counsel. He was born in the Cape of German stock that goes back 270 years. "South Africa is like the United States—a melting pot," he told us proudly. His home language was Afrikaans, but he speaks flawless English; his wife came of an English-speaking family. Strauss likes golf, and is a Christian Scientist. Politics got into his blood early, and he became Smuts's secretary many years ago. He has been MP for Germiston, near Johannesburg, since 1932, and was minister of agriculture in the last United party cabinet.

Mr. Strauss is attractive and able, but lacks force and popular appeal. Another important figure in the United party is the well-known Cape statesman, Sir de Villiers Graaff. The man nearest to Strauss as a technical advisor is probably Dr. F. J. Van Biljon, who ran Smuts's Social and Economic

Planning Council. The Oppenheimers are close to the United party leadership, and the party has been financed in the past partly by mining money.

Two things ail the United party, and ail it grievously. One is biology. Afrikaners outnumber Britons roughly by a ratio of three to two, and so the United party is at a permanent numerical disadvantage. Moreover the Afrikaner birthrate is higher than the British, and the Afrikaans-speaking youth is, as I heard it said, "utterly impervious to education," that is, to any possibility of change. Many thousands of Afrikaners vote, however, for the United party, not for their own Nationalists, and the Nationalists have never so far won a popular majority in the polls.

Second, the United party is almost fatally handicapped by its attitude toward *apartheid*. Mr. Strauss believes in a "step-by-step" evolution, steady "consultation" with non-Europeans, continuing economic integration, and the solution of racial problems "outside politics." But this puts him into a hopelessly ambiguous position. He seemed to be neither for *apartheid* nor against it. In the long run, to expand successfully against the Nationalists, the United party must favor a policy of "getting along" with non-Europeans, but this it cannot do without losing most of its present-day support. Still, many citizens will continue to vote for it, because it is the only effective party opposing the present government.

*

"Sailor" Malan was an opposition figure of consequence for some years, as leader of the Torch-Commandos. Adolph Gysbert Malan, a distant cousin to the former prime minister, was a celebrated RAF pilot during the war, and entered politics after his return to South Africa. The Torch-Commandos consisted largely of young men who fought valiantly for Britain against the Axis during six years of war, and then, back in the Union, were horrified to see that their own country seemed to be in danger of going Nazi. So they rose in wrath, particularly when Dr. Malan sought to disfranchise the Cape Coloreds. The Torch-Commando movement has, however, now largely diminished as a force. Its present leader is Louis Kane-Berman, of Jewish extraction, an interesting and enlightened personality.

*

In 1953 came formation of the Liberal party. Among its leaders are Senator Margaret Ballinger, who for many years has ably represented Native interests in parliament, the distinguished historian Leo Marquard (an Afrikaner), and Alan Paton. The program of the Liberal party is unprecedented in South Africa. It stands for the "creation of a common society for white and black," and welcomes African, Indian, and Colored membership. This, in the Union today, is almost tantamount to treason, and the Liberal party, still very small, has a hard row to hoe. The nationalist press sought to damn it forever by publishing with gleeful hate photographs of its first meeting, in which blacks and whites stood together on the speakers' platform. Mr. Paton told us, "There comes a time when every man has to do what he thinks is right, regardless of consequences. Perhaps our evolution will be slow. But we have to start somewhere." I met one responsible neutral journalist who said that, if a historian should write the history of South Africa in the year 2000, the outstanding event of the 1950's would not be the Malan-Strijdom advance to power but the creation of the Liberal party. For the first time since its foundation the Union has a political organization based on the ideal of racial partnership.

CHAPTER 26

The Union: The Blacks and the Browns

South Africa is a country of black men—and not white men. It has been so; it is so; and it will be so.
—ANTHONY TROLLOPE IN 1877

SEGREGATION patterns in South Africa—the patterns of social, political, economic, and emotional *apartheid*—are a kind of devil's dance. They go back to the earliest times, and have never worked, not even in the first days when Africans were scant. *How* to make segregation work is still, after three hundred years, an endless and unsolved problem. First van Riebeeck, as we have noted, built a hedge to keep Africans at a safe distance. Then came plans, never carried out, to surround the first settlements in the Cape with a moat or canal. Then, the first burghers hoped vainly, the mountains behind Cape Town would keep the Natives out. Then various small rivers became frontiers. Early in the nineteenth century people thought of setting up a "neutral belt," but this was quickly filled, because of the insatiable hunger of the trekkers for more and more land. Next came proposals for a mixed-up "checkerboard" system, with blacks restricted to certain areas. It failed. The Boer conquest of the Transvaal and Free State followed, but there were too many Africans to be killed off, and the system of reserves was constituted.[1] But now industrialization on a major scale characterizes the Union, and the reserves are, in a manner of speaking, breaking up, as more and more Africans come into the towns, seeking work.

Social patterns today resemble to an extent those of the old American south. (And how many times did I hear white Nationalists say, "What would things be like in your country if your population ratio was reversed,

---
[1] The British invented the idea of reserves, but the Boers copied it.

and you had 135,000,000 Negroes as against 15,000,000 whites!") A race-conscious white man in the Union will not shake hands with an African or Indian, or call him "Mister." In a letter, some such salutation as "Greetings!" is used to avoid saying "Mister." The parks are not segregated—but Natives cannot sit down on European benches—nor are the zoos. Interracial sport is unknown, and cemeteries and hearses are strictly segregated. In theory Africans are not allowed to drink anything but their own Kaffir beer, which is made out of Kaffir corn and has an alcoholic content of about 2 per cent, but thousands patronize illicitly the *shabeens*, speakeasies. Africans are by and large not permitted to use "fast" or passenger elevators in office buildings or elsewhere. There are very few, if any, public toilets for Africans anywhere in the white areas of the big cities. Downtown theaters and cinemas in Johannesburg are of course barred to Negroes, and so is the public library. The only non-segregated library in the entire Union is that in Johannesburg run by the United States Information Agency.

In the big hotels the concierge, doorman, headwaiters, and maids are (as a rule) all white. Waiters are Indian, and the busboys Colored. The elevator boy may be African. In sophisticated hotels, Indians and Coloreds are permitted to have dinner if they are met at the outer door by a white guest and taken to a private dining room. I never saw an African in a hotel in the Union.

Patterns in transportation are confusing. In Johannesburg there are white taxis for whites, black taxis for blacks. White buses carry whites; black buses carry blacks. Indians and Coloreds may ride on top of the white buses, or in back seats. Whites waiting for buses in residential areas have a kind of kiosk at the bus stops, where they may find shelter; blacks at the same stop stand in line out in the rain. In Cape Town segregation on the buses is not enforced, but is applied on the suburban trains. In Durban, Indians sit on the back seats of white buses. Port Elizabeth has three-way segregation in the buses. On overnight trains, Africans have their own compartments, are not allowed in the dining car, and use blankets of a special color, marked "N.E." or "Non-European." On South African Airways cushion covers and the white cloth on the top of the seats, which the head touches, have to be washed or dry-cleaned separately from those which the whites have used, if an African or Indian passenger uses them.

Shopping is not segregated in the Union (as it is in some towns in the Rhodesias); a Native can buy in any shop. Banks did not have segregated quarters until the advent of Dr. Malan. Patterns in the post offices vary. That in Cape Town is segregated, but the African division has equally good quarters and service. The Coloreds have their own post office. In Durban customers write out telegrams at the same table, but stand in different lines, and Africans usually wait longer for service. The Bloemfontein post office has separate entrances. Cape Town, all things considered, is the most relaxed city in this general field. Durban is the most explosive, although on the surface it appears to be tranquil. Tension is high in Johannesburg, but attitudes are more urbane than in, say, Bloemfontein. A white man who greets a black man publicly will be stared at and perhaps criticized, but there will not be a riot. If a white taxi driver knocks over an African on a bicycle, and a crowd assembles to watch the ensuing altercation, white onlookers will often have courage enough to take the black boy's side.

Turn to things political. The basic nationalist point of view, as I mentioned in connection with Dr. Dönges, is that Africans should have no political rights whatever. And Mr. Louw told us, "If we give them the vote, sooner or later we will have to abdicate."

No Africans in the Union have any vote at all except a handful—perhaps 4,000—in Cape Province. And these do not vote for members of parliament at large. General Hertzog took the Cape Africans off the common roll in 1936. Until then they had full voting rights if they fulfilled certain property and other qualifications. Now they vote only for *white* representatives (three in the Assembly, four in the Senate) who are charged with representing their interests. Thus 8,500,000 Africans are represented in parliament by seven members out of 209. Moreover the white MP's representing the Africans, worthy as they are, have very little power to do anything concrete for their constituents. Of course there are no African, Indian, or Colored MP's.

Economic affairs and education should also be mentioned briefly. Africans are, by terms of the so-called Color Bar Act of 1926 and other acts, excluded from practically all skilled occupations, and it is a criminal offense for a Native mineworker to quit his job, absent himself from work, or strike.[2] Africans (with a few exceptions) are not permitted to own their own homes in the cities. To allow Africans to own property would, many observers think, be the best of all possible means for averting revolutionary turmoil, because it would give them a genuine, permanent stake in the community. But this, of course, is exactly what the authorities do not want. One of the major tenets of *apartheid* is to keep Africans *from* having a secure foothold anywhere, except in the reserves. The upshot is that the great majority of urban Africans are, even if they earn good wages, excluded altogether from ever being able to buy a place to live. As to education, that is a tangled and tragic story. South Africa, we should keep in mind, has had

[2] Marquard, *op. cit.*, pp. 62 and 125.

THE UNION: THE BLACKS AND THE BROWNS

mission schools for well over a hundred years, and this is one of the few countries on the continent with second- and third-generation educated Natives. About 30 per cent of African children of school age today go to primary school, which is not a bad figure for Africa. But almost insuperable obstacles have been set up recently in the field of *higher* education. Obviously, to cut off Africans from full educational opportunity is a major weapon of *baasskap*, white supremacy. If the Africans have no elite class, they are less likely to make trouble. The Afrikaner Nationalists fear African progress much more than they fear African backwardness. Until the *apartheid* steamroller began to hit education in 1952 and 1953, there were four universities in the Union which accepted Africans, although the total number of graduates every year probably did not exceed four hundred. There were about one hundred African students at Witwatersrand, two hundred at the University of Cape Town, and a handful at the University of Natal. Classes at Natal are strictly segregated; those at Cape Town and Witwatersrand were not, but of course African students were a very small minority. Finally there was Fort Hare, an all-African college affiliated with Rhodes University at Grahamstown, partly supported by the state, and with perhaps four hundred Native and Colored students. Dr. Malan announced in December, 1953, that Cape Town and Witwatersrand would no longer accept Native students, and in May, 1955, Fort Hare was abruptly closed down—a shocking blow to African youth everywhere in the Union—on the charge that a "secret authority" existed in the student caucus. The term "secret authority" was not enlarged upon or defined. So today higher education for Africans has ceased to exist in the Union, except for a few students in Natal and the last handful still surviving at Cape Town and Witwatersrand.

Overwhelmingly, so far as the African rank and file are concerned, the things that hurt most in the whole ignominious field of segregation are (a) police brutality and (b) the pass laws. There are at least a dozen different kinds of pass—passes may be issued by any white employer or even by a child in a white household on any odd bit of paper—and most Africans in the towns are obliged to have on their persons at all times four different passes. One is a residential permit, another a lodger's permit, the third is a certificate from the employer, and the fourth may be a curfew pass. The pass laws are, moreover, inordinately complex. Professor Julius Lewin of Witwatersrand University, one of the best known and most enlightened authorities on Native law in the Union, has described how Africans, even if they *want* to obey the law scrupulously, may find it literally impossible to do so. He writes, "The legal position today of the Africans is such that the police can arrest any of them walking down the main street of Johannesburg at any time of the day or night, and any competent prosecutor will have no difficulty whatever in finding some offence with which he could be charged." In a recent year there were no fewer than 968,593 arrests for violations of the pass laws, and 861,269 convictions. The cost to the community of such an appalling crime sheet can easily be imagined. But the pass laws are a necessity to *apartheid*, because they are the chief means whereby day-to-day watch may be kept on Africans, and by which they are denied mobility without permission. No African can simply pick up and move from Johannesburg to Kimberley, or even from factory to factory or village to village, as an American Negro may move freely from Tampa, Florida, to Jacksonville and work at any kind of job. The pass laws make freedom of movement impossible. It has even been charged that they conduce to a variety of forced labor, since, if a worker cannot get a pass permitting him to move, he is obliged to find employment in the area where he happens to be located.[3]

Any Native in the Union may be arrested and confined to jail for three months without trial and without any charges being made. After three months an appeal may be lodged, but few Africans have enough knowledge of law or money to be able to do so. Another regulation is that any Native or group of Natives—even a tribe—may be moved from one area to another purely by administrative order. No authority from a court is necessary. These measures (the first has not been applied except in a few cases) do not derive from the Nationalist government, but from the Act of Union, which provides that non-European affairs are in the jurisdiction of the "Governor-General-in-Council," i.e., the government, without reference to parliament. From the very beginning, the Union set out to keep an iron hand on its Native population.

In the Transvaal, a prisoner convicted of some felony for which the sentence is six months or more is sometimes given the choice, after sentence, of serving his term in the ordinary jails and breaking rock on the roads, or going to a convict farm. In these, which I alluded to in Chapter 24 above, the farmers pay the government 9d. per day per convict used. What this amounts to is that the farmers get labor for 9d. a day, which is cheap even for Africa. The prisoners get nothing. The government keeps these farms under inspection, and supplies each farm jail with a warden. Offenders picked up in the cities for violation of the pass laws or some such minor dereliction are usually given a choice by the police, *before* going to the

---

[3] Gwendolen M. Carter, *South Africa*, a pamphlet in the Headline Series of the Foreign Policy Association, referring to a report on forced labor (1953) made by the International Labor Organization.

THE UNION: THE BLACKS AND THE BROWNS 521

magistrate, of standing trial or working on a farm for six months. The prisoner gambles. If he chooses to stand trial, he may be acquitted; on the other hand, he may get a sentence longer than six months.

To return to social patterns. The segregation restrictions apply not only to residents of South Africa, but to anyone. Late in 1953, Fransisco (Pancho) Segura, an internationally known professional tennis player, was refused a visa to the Union, presumably because he is an Ecuadorian and has Indian blood.[4] All manner of weird events may be noted in the field of sport. When the New Zealand football team visits the Union, it has to leave its Maori members at home, because they have "colored" skin. One of the best tennis players in the Union, a Colored boy named Davis Samaii, can play at Wimbledon, but not in mixed matches in Johannesburg. Recently an embarrassing crisis came in Pretoria (not in regard to sport) when a Pakistani delegation arrived to take part in a meeting of the Commonwealth Parliamentary Association. The Pakistanis had to be officially transformed into "Europeans" for the length of their stay!—in order to avoid incidents. Not everybody is so well favored. Recently the Egyptian consul general in Cape Town, a personage of the most civilized quality, was refused admittance to a local movie, because his skin looked "dark." Similarly the staff in a Johannesburg hotel not long ago refused to let the High Commissioner of the Republic of India use the elevator. American Negroes, no matter how distinguished, find it almost impossible to get visas to the Union these days. In January, 1955, the United States navy cruiser *Midway* visited Cape Town. This caused a ferocious crisis, because four hundred of its seamen were Negroes or Filipinos. At first it seemed that they would not be allowed ashore. Then, after some firm language by the American officers, the local authorities decided that the "risk" of letting the black and brown sailors land must be taken, but severe restrictions were imposed on them. The *Midway*'s officers made an interesting riposte to this. They opened the ship to all visitors on a non-segregation basis, so that Cape Towners of all varieties and colors could see for themselves what an American warship (non-segregated) was like. No fewer than 23,000 people—whites, blacks, Indians, Coloreds—accepted the invitation with alacrity, and thronged the ship for two days.

*

Union officials who defend segregation patterns and their treatment of Africans in general make half a dozen main points. (1) There is little, if

[4] *New York Times*, August 8, 1953.

any, discrimination against Africans in shops. If, in other words, a black man has money to spend, he is free to spend it. (2) Wages are, for Africa, high, and so is the standard of living. Otherwise, spokesmen for the government say, the hundreds of thousands of Natives from Mozambique, Basutoland, and Nyasaland who have emigrated to the Union would not be willing to remain. (3) The government, despite the formidable strictures of the new Bantu Education Act, does a good deal for primary education. An African child has a better chance of getting a few years of schooling at least in the Union than in most countries south of the Sahara. (4) Some semblance of a Negro press exists. (5) Negroes are recruited into the police. These are not, however, permitted to carry firearms, and they cannot arrest Europeans. (6) Conditions are "good" in the reserves. Of course it is a fundamental concept of *apartheid* that, in the strictly native areas, Africans should be tolerably well treated. Many Nationalists would like extremely to see history reverse itself, so that Africans in great number would return to their tribes. The more childlike an African is, the better the "pigmentocrats" like it. The Afrikaners cannot, however, have their cake and eat it too. They would like the Natives to stay on the reserves, a subservient and isolated "child" class, but also they want cheap black labor for industry and the mines. It was the introduction of work for wages that in the first instance broke up tribal life.

MORE ABOUT THE NATIVE COMMUNITY

> The traveller in South Africa is astonished at the strong feeling of dislike and contempt—one might almost say of hostility—which the bulk of the whites show to their black neighbors. . . . It is stronger among the Dutch than among the English, partly, perhaps, because the English wish to be unlike the Dutch in this as in many other respects. . . .
>
> The Kafirs, (sic) now divided into many tribes and speaking many languages and dialects, will lose their present tribal organization. . . . When, perhaps in the twenty-first century, the native population has reached the point of progress we have been imagining, the position may be for both races a grave or even a perilous one, if the feeling and behaviour of the whites continue to be what they are now.
>
> —LORD BRYCE IN 1899

Of the eight and a half million Africans in the Union, roughly two million live in urban areas, three million on the European farms, and three and a half million in the reserves. The principal reserves are Zululand, the Transkei, Pondoland, and Vendaland. I have just mentioned that defenders of the Union regime say that conditions on the reserves are "good." The government spends on Natives a total of about £20,000,000 per year. Nevertheless some contrary facts should be noted. The reserves constitute 9.6 per cent of the total area of the Union, but this means that eight and a half million people have less than 10 per cent of the country, whereas 2,600,000 whites have 90.4 per cent. Moreover the whites have most of the *best* land. It may be argued that, potentially, the African land was just as good as the white land, but that the black man has ruined it by overgrazing of stock and deleterious methods of agriculture.[5] There are too many cattle, which the Zulus and Xhosas and other tribes refuse to kill off, and the cattle eat up the land. The fact remains that the reserves, as at present constituted, are not adequate for the support of their population. They are agonizingly overcrowded, with about eighty people per square mile as against ten per square mile in the European rural areas; and they are capable of raising only about half the food they require. The only future for Africans in the reserves is, in the words of one writer, "slow starvation."

Conditions among the three million Africans working as laborers on the white farms are probably better, although here they may not own land, but this does not mean that they are very good. Many workers get no cash wage, but only the right to cultivate for themselves some of the master's land, in return for work part of the year.

The African community, whether living in locations and compounds in the towns or out on the land, covers a wide gamut in languages, customs, attitudes, and enlightenment. There are Africans as impeccably cultivated and intellectually distinguished as, say, Dr. Z.K. Matthews, who visited America in 1952-53 and taught at the Union Theological Seminary in New York (and as a result was treated with crude unpleasantness by South African officials when he returned home); there are also Africans who are as far removed from today as the Danakils in Ethiopia. There are Africans who write sound English prose, like Peter Abrahams, author of *Tell Freedom*, and Henry Nxumalo of the *Drum*; there are also Africans by the hundred thousand who cannot read or write at all. There are tribes (like the Zulus) sternly upright and moral for the most part, and tribes greatly addicted to homosexuality, like the Pondos. Some Africans, again like the Zulus, are pro-government on the whole; some hate the white man, and many have no political sense at all. If we went into anthropological details this chapter would have no end. In the eastern Transvaal lives a tribe, the Lovedu, which was ruled by a queen who apparently had a considerable measure of white blood; she was a rain goddess, by name Mujaji, and is supposed to have been the original of the heroine of Rider Haggard's *She*. Most black magic

[5] We shall find this same argument made in the Rhodesias.

among primitive Africans in the Union has to do with lack of water and yearning for rain.[6]

Primitiveness is, let us add, a word that needs careful definition. I have several times in the chapters above made note of this. Of course people who exorcise evil spirits by black magic and pray for rain are likely to be "backward" and "primitive." But, in their own special way, they may also be interestingly sophisticated. African medicine men use drugs unknown to (or neglected by) the European pharmacopoeia that may, like Chinese and Indian drugs, prove to have unique value. African methods of agriculture are often called "wasteful," but some agronomists think that the Native method of burning the cover of part of their crop, and then leaving it fallow for a very long period, is healthier for the soil than more aggressive western methods of crop rotation. Then too Africans by and large have a marked aesthetic sense, enjoy art, cultivate complex but satisfactory social relationships, judge character well, and believe in peace.

Africans have, of course, been much intimidated in the Union. This is the only country we visited below the Sahara where I never once saw an African stretch out his hand to be shaken.

Religious stratifications among Natives in South Africa are difficult to outline. Statistics are not reliable, but it is commonly said that one-half the Native population is Christian, one-half pagan. Just as in Kenya (and also in the Congo, as we shall see presently), a curious synthesis between witchcraft and Christian principles and practices has developed steadily. Among the Christians, the layer of Christianity is likely to be thin, if only because so many people find Christianity such a puzzling concept to understand. Some "Christian" or sub-Christian sects in the Union have the most bizarre names imaginable. The "Castor Oil Dead Church" exists, and so does the "King George VI Win The War Hallelujah Apostolic Church."

Ten years ago the gap between university-educated Africans in the towns —doctors, preachers, teachers—and tribal Africans out in the remote *veld*

---

[6] One amateur anthropologist told me that the life of the African was "circular" in these regions. He lives in a circular kraal, has circular huts, uses circular utensils, "and thinks in circles." Many Natives can draw a perfect circle freehand, but not a square. A nice witchcraft story we heard has to do with Chaka, the greatest and most cruel of Zulu kings. Chaka was having trouble with his witch doctors, who had become too powerful for his taste. One night he killed an ox secretly and smeared its blood over the kraal. Next morning he summoned his first witch doctor, and asked him who had been guilty of this offense. The witch doctor rolled his bones, and pronounced guilty someone whom he knew that Chaka disliked. Chaka said "No!" and dismissed him. Other witch doctors were summoned, with the same result. Finally came a youthful witch doctor who, in terror of his life and after much hesitation, said that Chaka himself had killed the ox. Chaka promptly made this young man his chief witch doctor, and dismissed the others from his court.

or the reserves appeared to be unbridgeable, but it is being bridged rapidly. The pace of African advance, despite all obstacles, has been astonishing. But as the chasm between different varieties of African becomes narrower, that between Africans *en masse* and Europeans has become steeper and broader, partly because the African thinks that the European has destroyed his way of life and given nothing substantial in return. Repeatedly, from Europeans who ardently wish the Africans well, we heard remarks like, "We have lost contact. We do not know what is going on in their minds." Such a phenomenon is, of course, dangerous as well as disconcerting. Africans driven underground by the hostility of the white community will take on a secret life of their own. People ask what will happen when, or if, the African loses his traditional wonderful patience and good humor. Cut off from any possibility of entering European society, the rank and file may desert their *own* educated class, and go back to their witch doctors, or even turn into Mau Maus. They are superb human material, but even the best human material can be spoiled by arrogance on the part of Europeans, deceit, or neglect, to say nothing of suppression. One wise American told me, "There are two tragedies facing South Africa. The first is that, in order to keep the black mass submerged, the white rulers must inevitably become totalitarian. The second is that the only effective African answer to this will be to turn to Communism."

Nationalism, in reference to today's Africans in the Union, is another word that should be used with some discrimination. There are no doubt hundreds of thousands of Natives educated enough to know what nationalism means, and to want it and work for it, above ground or under. But also there are hundreds of thousands who have not yet reached this state of development. They may have grudges; they may be anti-white; they may be anti-exploitation; they may be anti-today; but they are not yet politically minded Nationalists in the sense that Dr. Nkrumah's men on the Gold Coast are Nationalists. They are nowhere near being ready to control, administer, or run a modern state. Nevertheless they are not prepared to accept continuing domination by somebody else. This burdensome paradox is familiar to us from the example of Kenya. One should also emphasize again that the tempo of African development has quickened prodigiously in the past few years. This is one of the factors that has frightened the government into passing the various repressive acts mentioned in Chapter 24. Some Europeans think that feeling has already become so irreversibly bitter that conflict—even civil war—will in the long run be impossible to avoid. The white liberals who might conceivably have been in a position to influence Africans and save the situation have lost all control of the aroused African intelligentsia.

I will close this section by quoting two men, both of them reasonable and well-informed. An African doctor said with considered judgment, "The Nationalists will stay in power for a generation at least. I do not expect freedom for South Africa in my lifetime." The other was a British journalist. I said that (in contrast to the African just quoted) many people had told us that the white man would be lucky if he survived in the Union for fifty years. Reply: *"Fifty* years? Anybody who says that is a blasted optimist."

THREE AFRICAN LEADERS

We visited Dr. A.B. Xuma in his neat, pleasantly furnished small house in Sophiatown. There were bowls of fruit and flowers, a piano, and an atmosphere of modest amenity. This was before the Western Areas Removal Scheme got under way, and I do not know if Dr. Xuma has been dispossessed of his property. But his house was in the heart of the Johannesburg area that the *apartheidistas* had determined to wipe clean of Africans. Dr. Xuma is, I should say, about fifty. He is a Xhosa (pronounced Causa). He was educated at Northwestern University (Evanston, Illinois), Budapest, Edinburgh, and London. He is a doctor of medicine, and a former president of the African National Congress, the chief organization in the country representing patriotic Africans. Mrs. Xuma is a North Carolina girl, and has a nice southern voice and sense of humor. In all Africa we did not meet a more civilized, charming couple.

Dr. Xuma, who is balanced and moderate, talked first about medical affairs. There are three African doctors in Johannesburg and three more in the surrounding suburbs—a total of six for half a million people. It is almost impossible for an African to become a physician. A black medical student is not even allowed to watch an autopsy on a white man, much less to observe or assist an operation or method of treatment. It is also impossible for African doctors to serve in a white or mixed hospital, because this would mean that they might (horror of horrors!) have to give orders to a white nurse.

Apartheid, as Dr. Xuma sees it, is not only based on fear, but is a device for deliberately creating and perpetuating fear. The Nationalists have to hate, in order to maintain the *status quo,* and fear is a good mechanism for inducing hate. "If any contact between the races was to be allowed, too many white people would discover that *we* are human beings." Dr. Xuma does not have much faith in Mr. Strauss's United party and thinks that there is little difference between the parties on *apartheid,* except that the Nationalists are more aggressive. A great many Afrikaners are, he thinks, humane and honorable folk who find the present government detestable, even if it is their own. One reason (Dr. Xuma believes) for *apartheid* is the Boer War. The more inflamed Afrikaners want to put the Africans "in their place," if only because they think that the *British* pampered them. "They seek to reverse all the processes of history."

The African National Congress is not, strictly speaking, a political party, and it has no status in law. A man like Dr. Xuma describes it as "a mass liberation movement." It was founded in 1912, in the same year that Hertzog split off from Botha to form the first Nationalist party. Its chief architect, Dr. P.I. Seme, was, it happens, educated in the United States, and so was its first president, Dr. John Dube. The original membership was small; today it is 100,000 or more. Dues are 2s. 6d. per year. The government impedes the Congress at every step, makes it almost impossible for its leaders to travel or communicate freely with one another, and keeps a sharp eye on its development and affiliations, but has not suppressed it. In particular the authorities detest its former secretary general, Walter Max Sisulu. Mr. Sisulu visited Moscow once, but denies firmly that he is (or ever was) a Communist. Sisulu was arrested in 1954 and sentenced to three months in jail with compulsory labor, for alleged contravention of the Suppression of Communism Act. His "crime" was to attend a "public" meeting—at which six persons were present!

Another nationalist organization is the All-African Convention. This is a much more extreme body than the Congress. It welcomes Colored and Indian as well as African members, and is supposed to have been penetrated to some extent by the Communists. But official Communists say that it is Trotskyist.

*

Dr. James Moroka is a doughty character. He too is a doctor of medicine, and, like Xuma, is a former president of the African National Congress. Dr. Moroka got his medical education at Edinburgh and Vienna. He lives in Thabanchu, on the desolate, barren wastes of the Orange Free State plateau; this is the only locality in the Free State where Africans may own land. Dr. Moroka operates the Moroka Methodist Missionary Hospital (150 beds) at Thabanchu, the only institution in the Free State that trains African nurses. His prestige, both as a doctor and man of politics, is substantial all over the Union. It is even whispered that white patients secretly go to him for treatment, because he is such a good physician and also because they think that he may add a bit of witch-doctoring to his cures. Many white people in South Africa respect deeply Native medical lore. Dr. Moroka is more positive politically than Dr. Xuma. He is not inflammatory, but he is militant. One thing he said (when he slipped me into his dispensary for a moment between patients) was that the Afrikaner authorities get a stranglehold on Africans in the reserves by "buying the chiefs." We have seen the same sort of thing in British Africa. Dr. Moroka is a good Christian, and believes strongly in white-black co-operation. He was the founder of the All-African Convention years ago, but left it in 1947 because it harbored Communists, and went over to the Congress. He was arrested by the authorities during the civil disobedience campaign in 1952, but was soon released.

*

President of the Congress in 1952-53 was former Chief Albert J. Luthuli. He was born in Rhodesia fifty-seven years ago, of Zulu origin, and is a teacher by profession. He was educated at Adams College, near Durban, a well-known missionary institution. His father was an African Christian missionary, who went out to Rhodesia from the Union in the service of the American Congregationalist church, and he is an extremely devout Christian. He spent some years teaching at Adams—he taught music, teacher training, geography, history, and the Zulu language—and became a chief in 1935, on the invitation of his tribe (and of course with the concurrence of the government authorities). He visited India recently as representative of the South African Christian Council, and made a lecture tour, under Congregationalist auspices, in the United States.[7] One of his daughters is studying to be a doctor of medicine. We had a long talk with him at his home at Groutville, in the Umvoti Mission Reserve. Groutville was named for an American missionary who worked here in the 1830's. The circumstances of our meeting with Mr. Luthuli were dramatic. We saw him on a Sunday. The day before he had received one of Mr. Swart's noisome little communications, forbidding him to travel to any of a number of cities in the Union, restricting his movements severely otherwise, and making it an offense for him to attend any public gathering, even a church service. What did Luthuli do? He went to his village church, and preached a sermon there.

Mr. Luthuli sketched for us the history of the passive resistance ("Defiance") movement that swept South Africa in 1952, and which I shall allude to again below. As Congress president, he was intimately involved. The government authorities summoned him to Pretoria, remonstrated with him, and asked him to give up participation in the movement. They were polite,

[7] Some of these details are from an article about Mr. Luthuli in the African *Drum*, by Jordan Ngubane, February, 1953.

but he was given two weeks to decide whether to follow the government's "advice," or lose his position as chief. Luthuli, an honest and courageous man, replied that a chief, by Zulu tradition, is leader of his people first, and a government official second. The government thereupon dismissed him. This aroused so much resentment among the tribal elders that no chief has ever been appointed to replace Luthuli. But his dismissal cost him his job and livelihood.

Like Dr. Moroka, Mr. Luthuli is strongly anti-Communist. He announced recently that he would leave the Congress at once if it ever came under Communist influence. Talking to us he denied what is commonly alleged, that the Congress is dominated by Indian intellectuals. He said that it stood for close co-operation among all non-Europeans, but ran its own show.

Mr. Swart's order "localizing" Luthuli in the Groutville sugar fields had an obvious and explicit motive—to make it impossible for him to function as president of the Congress. Above everything, the president needs mobility. I had a feeling that Luthuli, a person of the utmost generousness and purity of spirit, did not realize fully how the government was closing in on him and his fellows, and was determined to exterminate them as a political force, no matter how. Luthuli showed no rancor whatever, and seemingly had little comprehension of the power and vindictiveness of his opponents. But I also got a strong sense, more than from any African in the Union, that this man, quite aside from his Christian nobility of character, was a genuine leader. He said, as we prepared to leave, "What a pity it is that the government should try to destroy for no reason the good will of our people. Why do they lie about us? We are not an enemy." But the government thinks, of course, that he *is* an enemy. His last words were, "God will see us through somehow."

COLOREDS ON THE CAPE

The Cape Coloreds (half-castes) are a fascinating community. There are more than a million of them, and they derive from the first Malays (some of them convicts) imported into South Africa by the Dutch East India Company, the Hottentots, and—the British navy! Sailors—not just British —have brought a continual infusion of fresh white blood into the Cape for more than three hundred years. In the early days the Coloreds were officially known as "Baastards." Today their name in Afrikaans is *Kaapse Kleuring*. Except for the early Hottentot strain, they have by and large practically no African blood. Their ancestors did *not* intermarry with the Bantus, any more than the Boers did. They have always been a European-minded **group,** oriented toward the white man. They have no tribal background, and even Hertzog thought of them as Europeans.[8] Many Coloreds, even today, call black Africans "Kaffirs," as the lower-class white man does. What most Coloreds want is to "pass" into the white community.

Politically there are two wings, the conservatives who hope to maintain as close ties with the Europeans as possible, and radicals who stand for a "Unity Front," which would combine Coloreds, Indians, and Africans in a common anti-European program. Comparatively little contact has taken place so far between Coloreds and Indians, and the Coloreds did not participate in the 1952 civil disobedience campaign.[9] One important Colored leader is George J. Golding, who is president of the Colored People's National Union, editor of the *Sun*, a newspaper representing Colored interests, and principal of a Colored school.

Recent legislation by the Nationalist government is designed to make "passing" by Coloreds into the white ranks difficult if not impossible. At the same time the Afrikaners do not want the Coloreds to have closer relations with Africans. They do not want to thrust more than a million people, many of them the solidest type of citizen, into the arms of the black mass, thus strengthening it and giving it leadership. Yet their psychosis about color is so inexpungeable that they would not dream of letting them filter gradually into their own white community.

In fact, even though they try to curry favor with the Coloreds—by giving them jobs in the bureaucracy and so on—the Nationalists have taken the strongest possible line against them in other fields. The Group Areas Act, if fully enforced, will cause almost as much hardship to Coloreds in Cape Town as to Natives in Johannesburg.[10] And ever since 1952 the Nationalists have convulsed the country politically with their efforts, deliberately made even at the risk of wrecking the constitution, to remove Colored voters from the common roll.

This caused passionate resentment in the Colored community. The Coloreds, a proud people anyway, have always been particularly proud of the fact that they have had full voting privileges. As these pages go to press the struggle over this issue is not finally decided, but there can be no doubt of the outcome. Mr. Strijdom has packed the Supreme Court, and, on

---

[8] Marquard, *op. cit.*, p. 147.
[9] But Indians like, if they can, to marry Colored women, if only because of the shortage of women in their own community.
[10] One Colored doctor told me that he has lived in a European quarter for seventeen years. Now, to avoid being moved out of his own house, he has to pay a kind of ransom to the authorities. What is happening is "economic strangulation of the innocent," especially if long-located *business* premises also have to be vacated.

June 16, 1955, a bill was passed in parliament increasing the membership of the Senate from forty-eight to eighty-nine, so that the government has a safe two-thirds majority. This was necessary, before the Cape voters could be disfranchised, because their right to vote is one of the "entrenched clauses" in the constitution, along with the right of English to be an official language, and these entrenched clauses cannot legally be rescinded except by a two-thirds vote of both houses of parliament sitting jointly.

If history has any logic, it seems almost certain that the Colored community, for all its pro-European instincts, will in time be forced to ally itself more closely to the Africans and Indians. The government gives it no other choice. One Colored leader told us, "The Nationalists have done more to unite non-Europeans than any government in history. Such are the ironies of white supremacy."

On the non-political level we should perhaps mention that, more than any people in South Africa, the Coloreds like to drink. Alcoholism has become a serious social problem, made more serious by the fact that wine from the nearby vineyards is cheap and readily available.

*

The Cape Malays, 40,000 in number, are classified as Coloreds, but form a separate and quite distinct community. They descend, like many Coloreds, from the early Malays brought into the Cape by the Dutch, and some are still pure Malays. They are Mohammedans, and hold strictly to themselves. They sometimes marry Moslem Indians, but not Africans, Coloreds, or Europeans as a rule. Their folksongs are remarkable, and they maintain their old crafts tenaciously, in particular the making of fine casks. They have their own quarter, which has several mosques, and their women are veiled, but lightly. They are an honest, reliable, and respectable community.

THE INDIAN COMMUNITY

There are about 360,000 Indians in the Union, of whom 300,000 are concentrated in Natal. Most are Hindus, and, as in East Africa, they are lively merchants and traders. They have not penetrated the bureaucracy and professions to anything like the extent reached in East Africa. Immigration of Indians into the Union is prohibited, and this ban goes back many years; hence, the community cannot increase in numbers by any influx from outside. Until recently Indians were permitted to return to India to marry, and bring back their wives; this is now forbidden. The Nationalists would, if possible, like to repatriate the entire Indian population, and send it back to India. By a law passed in 1927, the government offers £20 to any Indian willing to return to India, plus free transportation, but few have gone back.

Natal, people like to say, "has itself to blame for its Indians." The British brought them in in the 1860's as indentured labor to work in the sugar fields, just as they were brought into Kenya as laborers on the Uganda railroad. The Boers of the day had nothing to do with this. Indeed they promptly (1891) threw out of the Free State the few Indians who had penetrated there, and Afrikaners today bitterly blame the British for having saddled the country with its Indian "problem." Relations between South Africa and India itself are strained, to put it mildly. The more fanatic Afrikaners cannot, like extremist Britons in Kenya, charge that Mr. Nehru is plotting secretly to use Africa as a dumping ground for his surplus population, since Indian immigration into the Union is forbidden, but some do think seriously that India will some day make war on the Union, and attack it by force of arms. This is the reason for much current agitation in South Africa for building up a navy.

Discrimination in the Union against Indians follows much the same pattern as that against Africans, but in some respects is even more severe. As always in the field of segregation, macabre details may be found. An Indian traveling through the Orange Free State is not allowed to get off the train, except perhaps for a breath of air at a wayside station.[11] In Natal it is an offense for a European to give an Indian a drink even if the Indian is a guest in his house, and an Indian physician is, in theory, even forbidden to buy medicinal alcohol for sterilizing his instruments, presumably out of the fear that he may drink the stuff. Outrageous discriminations in matters of law occur frequently. One day in Johannesburg we were told over the phone that the headquarters of an Indian organization on Kork Street was being raided by the police. We took a taxi there, but the raid was already over. I heard an onlooker say to an Indian out on the street, "Did they tear the place down?" Answer: "Not yet."

If Afrikaner Nationalists hate Indians more fiercely than they hate Africans, this is largely because they fear Indian intellectual leadership and influence on the black masses. Then again Afrikaners have a more tender feeling toward Africans than Indians, if "tender" is the appropriate word, because Africans make a splendidly useful labor force, whereas Indians do not. Of course a full-fledged "pigmentocrat" must logically be anti-Indian if only because he *is* anti-Negro. If he does something for the Indians, then logically he may have to do something for the Africans in time. Similarly he must be anti-Chinese, and even anti-Japanese, although there are no Japa-

[11] Bartlett, *op. cit.*, p. 83.

THE UNION: THE BLACKS AND THE BROWNS 533

nese in the Union. If you are against any color (except white), it is necessary to be equally against all alien and suspect hues.

The principal Indian political organization is the South African Indian Congress. This was founded, back in 1898, by no less a personage than Mahatma Gandhi. It predated formation of the Union itself by twelve years, and has today about 45,000 members. It went through several phases. Roughly until 1914, when Mr. Gandhi left South Africa, it devoted itself to fighting the segregation laws. The Mahatma went to jail three times in South Africa. In the middle 1920's, when legislation against Indians became stiffened, the Congress began to take on a more overtly political complexion. In 1931 and again in 1946 there were passive resistance or civil disobedience movements, and thousands of Indians went to jail for nonviolent protest against discrimination. The emphasis today is on creation, if possible, of a United Front of all non-Europeans, with close co-operation particularly between Indians and Africans. But so far, except at the very top, contact between Indians and Africans is slight.

President of the South African Indian Congress for some years, and an outstanding personage in the Indian community, is Dr. Y.M. Dadoo. His father came to South Africa in the 1880's, and he was born in the Union. He is a doctor of medicine trained at Edinburgh. Afrikaner leaders say without pause that the Indian Congress is "completely dominated" by Communists, and cite Dr. Dadoo as a principal case in point, but whether or not he is a Communist today is uncertain. Dr. Dadoo was "immobilized" late in 1953 by a Ministry of Justice order restricting his movements. He appealed against this to the Supreme Court, and, remarkably enough, won the appeal. Another consequential Indian leader is Yosuf Cachalia, who is not a Communist. When we visited Manilal Gandhi, the Mahatma's son, near Durban, and saw the house where the Mahatma lived for many years (the original building was eaten by termites, and has now been rebuilt as a school), we asked about the Communist menace. Mr. Gandhi took a hopeful view, saying gently, "We have enough on our hands without Karl Marx." In other words responsible Indian (and African) leaders do not want Communists to enter the scene, because this will make the task of liberation more difficult. But this is not quite the whole story, as we shall see below.

"DEFIANCE" AND THE POSSIBILITY OF PROTEST

On June 26, 1952, began the "Defiance" movement led jointly by the African National Congress and the South African Indian Congress. It was a failure, but foretells much. The campaign was based on the Gandhian precept of civil disobedience, and was completely non-violent. Its object was, of course, to register on behalf of the African and Indian communities as dramatic a protest as possible against the Group Areas Act, the Bantu Authorities Act, the pass laws, and other legislation. African and Indian volunteers took a pledge of non-violence, deliberately broke some law or other—for instance by sitting in a European waiting room at a railway station, or trying to get into a public library—and thus invited arrest. The government moved with speed and vigor, and ten thousand Africans and Indians were in due course arrested. The "Defiance" movement, although it did not reach the full mass of the people, was well organized and led. That the civil resisters should behave with such discipline and fortitude startled the authorities. I have already mentioned in Chapter 18 that civil disobedience is the *one* means whereby a submerged population, without access to arms, can make a revolution. It was not lost on the government that Mr. Gandhi freed India largely by the use of this device, and moreover that it was invented, not in India at all, but in South Africa.

The "Defiance" campaign reached its peak in September, 1952, and died out by the end of the year. For the moment at least it is unlikely that a similar movement can be launched successfully, if only because so many Native leaders have been immobilized. Also, as we have already seen, the Criminal Law Amendment Act was passed in February, 1953, and was followed by ancillary legislation. Till the end of 1952 penalties were minor for civil resisters, and jail terms short. But now people breaking the public security or segregation laws are subject to much more severe action, including long prison sentences, confiscation of property, and flogging. (But, to repeat, it is only fair to add that nobody has as yet been flogged for a purely political offense.)

One striking episode in 1952 was the arrest (December 8) of Manilal Gandhi and Patrick Duncan. Mr. Duncan cannot be accused of being an African, an Indian, or a Communist. He is, in fact, the son of Sir Patrick Duncan, a former Governor General of the Union, i.e., the symbolic representation of the British (and Union) Crown.[12] Duncan, a most attractive person, is youthful and idealistic. With Mr. Gandhi, a group of Africans and Indians, and seven white men and women, he technically violated the law by entering a location at Germiston, near Johannesburg, without a permit, thus asking for arrest. The scene was colorful, because he had previously been severely injured in an automobile accident, and had to limp on crutches, to which he had tied the yellow, green, and black colors of the

---

[12] And his wife is the daughter of a director of the Bank of England. Alexander Campbell, *The Heart of Africa*, p. 129.

THE UNION: THE BLACKS AND THE BROWNS 535

"Defiance" movement. The group sang "Africa," the hymn of the African National Congress, and waited patiently to be arrested. They did not have to wait long. Mr. Gandhi was subsequently given the choice of a fine of £50 or fifty days in jail, Mr. Duncan of £100 or 100 days. Duncan got the heaviest sentence, if only because he was a white man and the son of a former Governor General. He chose to go to jail rather than pay the fine, in order to make the full sincerity of his motives manifest.

*

The only weapon left to Africans in the foreseeable future is the strike. But it is not an easy thing to make a successful strike in South Africa. There are all manner of impediments in the way of organization. Africans by and large do not have automobiles or telephones. They are isolated out in the locations or locked up in compounds. They do not have things utterly taken for granted in a western country—typewriters or electric light at night. Communications are scant, and the curfew strict. Nevertheless several strikes have taken place. There was a one-day strike of 100,000 mineworkers in 1946; now such a strike would be illegal. The most dramatic strike occurred in the Johannesburg area at about the same time, when 90,000 Africans in Alexandria *walked* ten miles to work rather than pay an increase in the bus fares. Africans in Orlando, even though they had a good rail service, walked to work in sympathy. Many were given lifts by sympathetic white motorists. The strike lasted for ten days, when the bus companies capitulated.

A successful general strike could bring Johannesburg to its knees in a week, particularly if domestic servants struck. But such a strike would be ruthlessly met by the government.

LAST WORDS ON APARTHEID

There shall be no equality between black and white either in church or state.
—FIRST CONSTITUTION OF THE TRANSVAAL

Apartheid automatically cultivates the color crisis. If somewhere in Africa tonight there is a black Hitler, dreaming of driving all white men into the sea, he must be praying for the continuation of Apartheid.
—SIR STEPHEN KING-HALL

There are men in upper Afrikaner circles as bad as Goebbels; there are also a number of perfectly genuine idealists. Strange as it may seem, the idealists think of *apartheid* as an "idealistic" concept, not the reverse, which in the long run will help the African, not harm him. The argument, which I heard several times, goes like this: "What we are trying to do is build a vertical development. This must be based on segregation—yes. But we want to give Africans every opportunity for fruitful, decent, honorable existence as a separate community. We do not say that we are better than the blacks; only that we are different. Honestly, we *have* to find a solution; otherwise we will disappear. No solution is worth much if it does not hold out hope for the African as well. The Natives must retain their identity and pride; we must try to help them get over their inferiority. The only way out is to establish lines of *parallel* development."

Most Afrikaner "idealists" think that the best way to achieve true parallel development would be the creation of two separate states in South Africa, one white and the other black—a "Bantustan." They know full well that this might tranform part of the white section into a purely pastoral state like the old Boer republics; it would mean severe limitation on industrial development, partition of the Union, and poverty—"back to the ox wagon." Nevertheless a few say that they are willing to make this sacrifice, pay this enormous price, in order to maintain racial purity. The catch is that partition of the Union and the creation of a Bantustan is economically impossible—at least in the eyes of the present government. We talked to Strijdom, Dönges, and others about this in considerable detail. Complete geographical *apartheid* which, if set up and administered fairly, might be a good solution for the country under certain circumstances, is utterly impracticable for at least three reasons: (1) The government will not give up industrialization, which necessitates black labor in or near the cities. (2) Not enough land exists to make a Bantustan. The native reserves, as constituted today, cannot even support their present population. If, however, the Union took over Swaziland and Basutoland, there might be more elbowroom. We may note in passing that nobody in the government would dream of giving up any white areas, about 90 per cent of the country, to the blacks. (3) Africans as of the moment would probably not be capable of running a Bantustan by themselves, even granting that they would not be interfered with, because they have so few educated leaders, and have been systematically denied any opportunity for learning the elements of government and administration. There is no cadre of politically trained Africans ready to take over.

"Pure" *apartheid*, "idealistic" *apartheid*, is out of the picture. What the government wants is to make the present system work, and pretend cynically that it is "good" for Africans. Native labor will live in "buffer areas" near the towns, and will be pumped into industry as needed. But this system has already produced intolerable friction, and will produce more. For instance,

THE UNION: THE BLACKS AND THE BROWNS

Africans are, at the moment, forbidden to hold skilled jobs, but it is rapidly becoming impossible to draw the line in secondary industry between jobs skilled and unskilled. More and more Africans will, in time, be getting better and better jobs, unless industry chooses to commit suicide. This means that more Africans will inevitably get more earning power, which in turn will mean that they will demand more education and political advantages. Full industrial development can, in other words, only come at the steadily increasing risk of racial clash, which means that the government will necessarily have to become more (instead of less) repressive and totalitarian as time goes on.

Honest Afrikaners, when confronted with such dilemmas even in casual conversation, become almost desperate. Several times I heard remarks like, "You have no right to assume that we are not a decent people. You have *apartheid* in the United States, based on money. You have it in England, based on class. We have adopted our own special form of *apartheid* not because we want to suppress anybody, but because we believe that it is the *best* policy in the circumstances. If you can think of something better, let us know."

*

Even modified (as distinct from "total") *apartheid* cannot possibly work in the long run, if only because of the sheer, elementary, unavoidable fact that no state has much chance of functioning satisfactorily with four-fifths of its citizens denied even the most primitive rights of citizenship. No state of 12,600,000 people has much possibility of working well when ten million of these are not allowed to participate in its working. The worst thing about *apartheid* is not its villainy, but the fact that it is silly.

Some Afrikaners, even if they do not dare to say so, are coming around to this view. I have already mentioned that elements in the church are now feeling their way toward recommending some modification in the country's *apartheid* policy. In August, 1954, came an event that almost deserves the adjective sensational. An Afrikaner writer, Dr. G. D. Scholtz, who is also assistant editor of the *Transvaler* and thus, it would seem, a man who must be close to the Strijdom hierarchy, published a book called *Has the Afrikaner Nation a Future?* In this he says that the racial segregation laws will prove to be useless in the end, that Negroes are in no way inferior to the white man, that the Negro will sooner or later achieve a status in civilization equal to that of the white man, that the white community should learn to work with its hands instead of relying on Native labor, and that the lesson of history is that no minority so small as that of the whites in South Africa can hold down the majority without producing a "catastrophe."[13]

Extreme last-ditch *apartheidistas* are represented in the Union by the South African Bureau of Racial Affairs, known usually as SABRA. This has its headquarters at Stellenbosch, and was set up as a kind of counterpart to the liberal South African Institute of Race Relations in Johannesburg. It is close to the church, and its head is a professor of theology at Stellenbosch, Dr. G.B.A. Gerdemer. What the SABRA people think of the Scholtz book is unknown, but may be guessed.

*

One final odd point about *apartheid* is that a few old reactionary *Africans* believe in it, on the ground that it will serve to keep *African* culture pure.

COMMUNISM AT THE GATES?

The Union was the only country in Africa where we met and had long talks with avowed, official Communists. Of course we had to meet them surreptitiously, since the Communist party has been driven underground, and membership in it is a crime. The arrangements had to be made with some care. Several of the young men we met—Africans—had been to Moscow. I distinguished myself for naïveté by asking them how they had managed to get passports for leaving the Union, and one boy grinned in reply saying that passports had no part in the way *he* traveled. None of these people were well known. Their names had never been in any newspaper. They had never been "named" by the government, and were members of the rank and file. They were tough in a peculiar slap-happy way, well trained in the Communist dialectic, fixed in their ideas, and confident.

No one need ask why young Africans are so misguided as to become Communists. They have nothing else to turn to, nowhere else to go. The wonder is that there are not more of them. If South Africa goes Communist, it will be *apartheid's* fault.

Alan Paton has written in his pamphlet, *South Africa Today*, "No one can say what is the real present strength of Communism in Africa. I suspect it is not great but only a fool would take comfort from that, or conclude that 'Communism does not suit the African.' The truth is that Communism may well suit any person who has grievances against society, and who feels hindered and frustrated. And it would be true to say that there is not one

[13] New York *Times*, August 31, 1954.

THE UNION: THE BLACKS AND THE BROWNS

educated African in South Africa who does not cherish grievances against society, and who does not feel hindered and frustrated."

Communist influence is stronger in the Transvaal than anywhere else in the Union, but there are plenty of Communist sympathizers in the Cape. In Natal the party has scarcely any strength, and in the Orange Free State none. In the Cape, when we were there, several prominent citizens had been "named" as Communists, and it was possible to buy on the newsstands at least one periodical which, if not officially Communist, certainly showed Communist indoctrination. Many voters, particularly in the Western Cape, even today, steadily vote Communist, although the candidates call themselves "independent," and do not use any party appellation. Communists, *as such*, cannot run for office in the Union.

The government, to break the rise of Communism, and also because it wanted to tighten up security regulations in general (the Communists provided a highly convenient pretext to this end), passed in 1950 the celebrated Suppression of Communism Act. This law has provisions unique in the history of jurisprudence. Items in it would, if they were well known in the United States, make the most extreme red-baiters turn green, or some other appropriate color, with envy. Senator McCarthy at his wildest never went so far as the South African parliamentarians who drew up this fantastic law. (But we must always remember—South Africa is the *only* country south of the Sahara where the potential Communist threat is substantial. For this, most fair-minded people think, the government has only itself to blame.) The text of the Suppression of Communism Act runs to seventeen closely printed foolscap pages, and must contain 10,000 words or more. It is a document strangely hard to come by in the Union; I asked both the Ministry of Justice and the Public Information Department in Pretoria for a copy, but none was ever "available." However, we managed to find one. Strenuous debate attended passage of the Act and—something that is not often mentioned—it was passed in the Senate by only one vote. Many members of parliament thought that it opened the way to grave abuses in the whole field of civil liberties.

As I have already mentioned, the Act gives the minister of justice absolute power to decide whether a man is a Communist or not, and to outlaw anybody he calls a "Communist" from public life. Other penalties may be inflicted, such as a fine of £200 and imprisonment up to five years, and it seems that the law may be applied retroactively. The passage in the law defining Communism is lengthy, and very broad indeed. To be convicted of being a Communist, a person does not have to be a member of the Communist party. Not at all. Anybody who believes in "social change" or who is against the *status quo* in any respect, may find himself guilty of what is called "statutory" Communism, i.e., Communism as defined in the 1950 Act. Communism, by this definition, does not mean merely any doctrine or scheme founded on Marxian socialism "as expounded by Lenin or Trotsky" and based on the dictatorship of the proletariat, but any doctrine or scheme "which aims at bringing about *any* [italics mine] political, industrial, social, or economic change within the Union by the promotion of disturbance or by the threat of such acts," or ". . . which aims at the encouragement of feelings of hostility between the European and non-European races in the Union." In other words anybody who, let us say, expresses the opinion that housing conditions are bad in the Johannesburg locations, and influences Africans to protest against them, is a "Communist." The definition could not be more extreme.

Mr. Swart told us, however, that the Ministry of Justice was not worrying about "academic" Communists, although it knew who all of these were; the Act was designed to annihilate "active" Communist propaganda.

Quite aside from criminal penalties, anybody suspected of being a Communist may be "named." An official sits in the Ministry of Justice nicely known (it is his official title) as the "Liquidator." In 1953 the Liquidator was a senior magistrate, De Villiers Louw, who luckily enough is of unimpeachable character. Nevertheless the system of "naming" can, as is only too obvious, lead to the most flagrant and shocking of abuses. The process goes somewhat as follows. The Liquidator, acting on information received from the police or the Ministry of Justice, decides that Citizen A, who has some kind of public job or job in the trade unions, is a Communist or Communist sympathizer. The Liquidator thereupon writes him a letter, formally characterizing him as a Communist, and ousting him from his job. That is all there is to it. Once a man is "named," the authorities can put on him practically any kind of restriction. He may be forbidden to travel or appear in public or semi-public meetings, and his premises may be searched. The man "named" has a right to reply in writing to the Liquidator, but is not allowed to call on him in person. Also he may bring a court action. There have been several cases of mistaken identity and guilt by association; a man may be "named" as a Communist because he is supposed to have spoken at a rally on such and such a date, whereas actually he may have been in London at the time. About five hundred people have been "named" by the Liquidator so far. The names are not as a rule published. So far as I know nobody "named" has ever been "un-named," i.e., cleared by the courts and reinstated to his former position.

An official newssheet published by the South African Government Information Service in New York says that the Liquidator "can take over all the

THE UNION: THE BLACKS AND THE BROWNS 541

property and assets of [an] outlawed organization and after paying all debts distribute the balance of the assets to a charitable organization." The law says (Section Three, Paragraph Three) that the Liquidator himself—a most peculiar provision—"may be paid out of the assets of the unlawful organization such remuneration for his services as the Minister [of Justice] may determine." The judge, so to speak, collects the fine!

Shortly before passage of the Act, the Communist party of South Africa voluntarily dissolved itself, which of course means that it went underground.

MR. KAHN AND MR. SACHS

Two lively and pertinacious characters are Sam Kahn of Cape Town, a lawyer and former member of parliament, and E.S. ("Solly") Sachs, the best known trade union leader and organizer in the Union, who now lives in exile in London.

Mr. Kahn was elected to parliament for a Cape constituency in 1948, and served until 1952. He was "named," but "naming" was not sufficient under the law at that time to unseat an actual member of parliament. So a Select Committee of parliament went into the case—the testimony was exciting—and eventually decided that Mr. Kahn was a Communist. He was thereupon ousted from his seat. There is no doubt that Mr. Kahn himself, a most striking personality, considered himself to be a Communist at one time. I have on my desk a pamphlet entitled *Sam Kahn Speaks, the Parliamentary Record of South Africa's First Communist M.P.*, published by the Central Committee of the Communist Party of South Africa, PO Box 2098, Cape Town, and on sale for 1s. 6d. But it would be incorrect to call him a Communist now. The Communist party no longer exists legally, and Communism is a crime. Mr. Kahn is irrepressible. The day after he was thrown out of parliament, he appeared in the lobbies (any former MP has the right to enter the building), and there sold copies of the *Guardian*, an extreme left-wing publication, to ministers as they passed in and out. Mr. Swart even bought one.

Mr. Kahn is a brilliant lawyer and conversationalist, and has a sharp tongue. Once he said that "the only difference between Malan and Hitler is that Hitler is dead." During the parliamentary debate in 1949 on the Prohibition of Mixed Marriages Act the following exchange took place:

An HON. MEMBER: Would you marry a Coloured woman?
Mr. KAHN: Are you a marriage broker? Have you a client you are seeking to marry?
Mr. SPEAKER: Order, order!

Also Mr. Kahn said:

> This Bill, to my mind, is the immoral offspring of an illicit union between racial superstition and biological ignorance. Unfortunately for the Minister of the Interior, who is South Africa's leading political misanthropologist, humanity has been in the melting pot for unknown millennia, and it is far too late for any section of mankind now to seek to give the sanction of law to the pseudo-biological phantasies about race purity which are incorporated in the Bill before the House.

Considerable parliamentary confusion followed the expulsion of Mr. Kahn from his seat. A by-election had to be held, and Brian Bunting, editor of the *Guardian*, running as an independent, was nominated by Kahn's constituents. Minister Swart then served an order on Bunting forbidding him to run. Bunting ignored the order. Swart applied to the courts to keep him from running, but was overruled. Bunting was then duly elected by a big majority, and took Kahn's seat. But it was freely predicted when we were in Cape Town that he would not hold it long. The government will somehow manage to get rid of anybody it really dislikes.

"Solly" Sachs is an extraordinarily vivid and useful person. He was born in Lithuania and emigrated to South Africa at an early age. In some respects his career resembles that of the late Sidney Hillman in the United States. For many years he was general secretary of the Garment Workers Union of South Africa, which he built up from insignificance into one of the largest and most powerful unions on the continent. It was (and is) a mixed union, with white, African, and Colored members, and was admirably run. White Afrikaner girls from the *veld* worked side by side with Negroes without the slightest trouble or friction. Racial partnership in the Union of South Africa is not an "impossibility," the government to the contrary notwithstanding, as the example of the Garment Workers Union proves.

Mr. Sachs was a Communist years ago, but was expelled from the party for "deviationism" in 1931. He has not been a member since. Periodically, however, he has been called a "Communist" or a "concealed Communist" by nationalist newspapers. He has sued for libel on several occasions, and won one case triumphantly. He is thus one of the few personages in contemporary history who has been juridically declared *not* to be a Communist. In spite of this, the government "named" him after passage of the Suppression of Communism Act, and he was obliged to give up his union job, to which he had unselfishly devoted most of his adult life. One count against him, egregious even for South Africa, was that he used phrases like "comrade" and "fraternally" in union correspondence. Sachs, a fighter, defied the order "naming" him, and spoke at several public meetings, including one at the Johannesburg City Hall where 10,000 of his own garment workers greeted him. The police broke up the meeting, sixty-one people were injured, and Mr. Sachs was subsequently sentenced to six months in jail.[14]

*

Official relations between the Union of South Africa and the Soviet Union are "normal," although not cordial. The Russians maintain a small diplomatic installation at Pretoria.

SOUTH AFRICA: INTERNATIONAL

The Union government and the United Nations have been at loggerheads for a long time. One issue is the status of South-West Africa, Another, brought up by the government of India in 1946, has to do with discrimination against Indians, and is argued year after year by the General Assembly, with little tangible result. Third, the Arab-Asian bloc brought the *apartheid* problem into the UN arena in 1952, on the ground that the South African segregation laws violated human rights and were a threat to peace. The General Assembly set up as a result a special Commission on Racial Problems in South Africa, which has for several years held elaborate hearings in Geneva and elsewhere. The South Africa government will not, however, permit its members to visit the Union and inspect conditions on the spot. The United States supported establishment of the Commission in 1952, but in 1953 abstained from voting on the question of continuing it. The United Kingdom opposed setting up the Commission in the first place, and the South Africans not only boycott it but consider its activities to be an intolerable affront to their sovereignty.

In November, 1953, the Special Political Committee of the Assembly voted thirty-nine to two (with nineteen abstentions) for a resolution calling on South Africa to abandon its racial policy, condemning severely the *apartheid* legislation, and criticizing the Union government for ignoring the UN's Good Offices Committee. In April, 1955, South Africa withdrew from UNESCO, the United Nations Educational, Scientific, and Cultural Organization.

The United States has a major interest in South Africa for several reasons. One is strategy. The Cape will, if the Suez Canal should ever be blocked, control the seaways from Europe to the East. Another is that South Africa is the greatest gold producer in the world, and is a prime source of uranium. Twice recently the World Bank in Washington has made important loans

[14] *Atlantic Monthly*, "South Africa," August, 1952.

to South Africa, in part for improvement of the railways. Of course the United States could weaken the Union drastically overnight, and perhaps even destroy it, by stopping gold purchases or substantially lowering the price of gold. Professor Arthur Keppel-Jones of Witwatersrand University wrote some years ago a grim Wellsian fantasy called *When Smuts Goes*, describing what might be the results of such a step by the United States. South Africa goes Fascist, a black revolt occurs, and eventually the nation reverts to savagery, because the white elite has never permitted the education of enough blacks to administer the country properly.

South Africans are much puzzled by American attitudes. I asked one cabinet minister what he thought of United States policy toward Africa in general and South Africa in particular, and he answered testily, "That question is impossible to answer, because nobody here has ever been able to figure out what American policy is."

*

In Dakar, some months after we visited the Union, I met a seasoned, hard-minded French official who was not distinguished by any particular love of Africans. I asked him what he thought of the Union's white leaders. Answer: "They are the greatest danger to the white man ever known on this continent, because they will make Africans everywhere in Africa anti-white."

CHAPTER 27

The Union: Gold, Diamonds, and South-West Africa

A diamond is forever.
      —DE BEERS ADVERTISING SLOGAN

SURELY it is one of the nicest of contemporary paradoxes that South Africa, such a puritanical small state, so uncompromisingly dour, dry, and frugal, should have its economy based on commodities so extravagant and glittering as gold and diamonds. This, one of the most severely plain of countries, wears jewels in its hair.

South Africa accounts for 41.3 per cent of the gold production of the world, produces a major share of its diamonds, and is probably the world's biggest uranium producer.[1] Without minerals the Union would be a country of sheepherders and petty agriculturalists. Gold alone pays approximately 9 per cent of the total budgetary revenue of the country, and other mineral products account for another 3.4 per cent. This latter figure was correct for 1951, before the uranium boom reached its present prodigious development, and is probably substantially higher today.

Not only does the Union provide gold, diamonds, and uranium in fabulous quantities to the markets of the free world, but also minerals less aristocratic and spectacular—for instance manganese, chrome, lead, zinc, copper, coal, and asbestos. Chrome and manganese are of vivid importance strategically. South Africa produces a particularly valuable high-grade variety of chrome. The United States buys roughly 60 per cent of the Union's total output of chrome and 50 per cent of its manganese, and would like to have more, but the South African railways, burdened beyond capacity, cannot carry it

[1] Oddly enough the USA and the USSR each produces 7.2 per cent of the world's gold.

all expeditiously. Five hundred thousand tons of manganese have been stockpiled at Postmasburg, near Kimberley, and 400,000 tons of chrome sat immobile in 1953 in the northern Transvaal, awaiting transport. The World Bank recently loaned South Africa $30,000,000 to improve railway facilities.[2]

Gold is the king. In the last year for which figures are available, gold production was worth £147,000,000, whereas diamonds were worth only about £20 to £25 million (including South-West Africa); uranium climbed from nothing to £40,000,000—a staggering figure. Gold may not be the sleek king forever. Production of other minerals together was valued at £49,500,000. The discovery of diamonds (1867) preceded that of gold (1886), and it was diamonds that made gold "possible." Immense sums made out of diamonds overnight were used to finance and build up the great gold mines. Both diamonds and gold were, incidentally, discovered quite by accident. The details are of the utmost romantic interest, but are not part of our story here. One curious point is that Lord Bryce, author of *The American Commonwealth* and other works which have stood up for years as monuments of shrewd observation and insight and an almost uncanny prescience, could not have been more wrong than in his judgment about the importance of gold to South Africa. He wrote in 1899 that the mines would be soon "exhausted," and could not be a "permanent factor" in the development of the country. "The present gold fever is a fleeting episode."[3] I think that this is the only serious mistake Bryce ever made.

*

There are half a dozen leading gold-mining companies on the Rand today. They are sharp competitors but they have many problems in common, like labor procurement and relations with the government, and they are closely linked by a formidably powerful organization known as the Transvaal Chamber of Mines, which was founded in 1889. The president of this organization is also the chairman of the Gold Producers Committee, representing all the major companies, and has a semi-official status *vis-à-vis* the government. The biggest gold-mining groups are:

[2] Americans in the Union do not have much respect for the carrying power of the South African railways. The administration is overlaid with politics, and the white labor employed is of the lowest category. Any white man in the Union can (if he wants) get a job on the railway labor gangs. They are a kind of WPA. We heard one sour joke: "The government keeps the railways going here to keep the white man from going out into the bush and becoming African."

[3] *Impressions of South Africa*, by James Bryce, p. 466.

GOLD, DIAMONDS, AND SOUTH-WEST AFRICA 547

	Production (millions of ounces)	
Company	Current Financial Year	Last Financial Year
Consolidated Gold Fields of South Africa, Ltd.	1.25	1.16
Central Mining & Investment Corp., Ltd.	1.24	1.09
Anglo American Corp. of South Africa, Ltd.	.45	.34
Anglo-Transvaal Consolidated Investment Co., Ltd.	.34	.22
Union Corporation Ltd.	.30	.27
General Mining & Finance Corp., Ltd.	.18	.16

Of these the most interesting is Anglo American, because it is the Oppenheimer company. Consolidated Gold Fields, still the biggest, is the old Rhodes company. Central Mining and Investment, sometimes called the "Corner House" group, has the biggest single mine in the country, and has always been near the top. Anglo-Transvaal, known usually as "Anglo-Vaal," is the newest of the giants, and has American connections through Kennecott. The Union Corporation was for a long time headed by Sir Henry Strakosch, one of the world's foremost authorities on gold; its chairman nowadays is Lord Bracken, who, as Mr. Brendan Bracken, has had a long and effervescent career in British public life, and was one of Mr. Churchill's main coadjutors during the war. General Mining and Finance is the smallest of the leaders. Another important group is Johannesburg Consolidated Investment, usually called the "J.C.I." All of these companies, the shares of which are known as "Kaffirs," are controlled from London except Oppenheimer's Anglo American, which has very strong British connections but which is run strictly from Johannesburg. It has always been one of Oppenheimer's advantages that he could take instant decisions on the spot without having to consult London six thousand miles away.

The year 1954 was a very good year indeed for the mining companies, and 1955 may be better still. The working profits of the mines in 1954 reached £38,000,000, as against about £35,000,000 in 1953. Most South African gold goes to England in the first instance and eventually finds its way to the United States, where, a point we need not go into, it is promptly put underground again. Nor have we the space to describe the peculiar physiognomy of the earth in this region, whereby both gold and diamonds have been manufactured in such abundance by ancient geological processes. The chief value of gold is, as everybody knows, symbolic. If all the gold in the world should disappear overnight, *and nobody knew it,* the difference to humanity would be slight. The contemporary prosperity of South Africa is, in a manner of speaking, based on a fiction. The stuff is, however, undeniably handsome. In the Johannesburg offices of one company a gold brick is sometimes shown to visitors. Anybody who can lift it with one hand can keep it. Nobody ever has.

There are forty-five actively functioning gold mines in the Transvaal, and about a dozen in the Free State. The Rand mines are very deep, among the deepest in the world. Several are deeper than 8,000 feet, and one (Crown Mines) reaches 9,020 feet. Mining at such depths is difficult and expensive. Serious problems occur in ventilation, health of workers, the cost of haulage, and so on. What is more, white men will not work at such dangerous depths, and mechanization is impossible. Neither the mines (for this and other reasons) or South Africa would have much future without black labor. A glutton for statistics may be interested in the fact that the Rand mines paid in 1952 taxes of about £15 million, dividends of £19 million; taxes since the formation of the Union amount to £424 million. The deepest single hoist shaft is at No. 3, Vogelstruisbult (6,662 feet), and the deepest borehole (10,738 feet) is near Potchefstroom. The rope used in a single hoist can weigh 21 tons. Twenty million pounds of cyanide, enough to poison a lot of people, are used annually, and 143,000,000 passengers are carried in the mine cages every year. The fastest cage goes at thirty miles an hour, in case you want to know before taking it.

*

The Orange Free State mines are a new and sensational phenomenon. One qualified writer[4] says that their discovery and early development (1947-51) are events that may rank with the original discoveries of diamonds near Kimberley and gold on the Witwatersrand. What is going on in the Free State now has been called "the greatest gold rush in history." The life of the new fields is estimated at half a century, and the total yield may reach a value of £4,000 million, which is more than has come out of the Transvaal so far. By 1957 all the new Free State mines are expected to be in production. Also several uranium plants are being built. The companies most active in the Free State have been Anglo American and the Union Corporation. The Oppenheimers, who were the pioneers, invested £70,000,000 in the Free State development, and raised every cent of this without any government aid. The area covered by the new mines was, until the 1940's, largely uninhabited high *veld*. The chief Anglo American town, by name Welkom, did not exist in 1947; today the area has a population of 35,000

---

[4] "New Style Gold Rush," by a Special Correspondent of the London *Times*, December 13, 1954. Also see the *Times*, December 26, 1951.

Europeans and 70,000 Africans; the total population of the district as a whole will, it is estimated, be not less than 400,000 in time. Welkom will, in other words, starting from scratch, become the third or fourth most populous metropolitan area in the Union. The Oppenheimers have done their best to modify the compound system here, in order to avoid the creation of slums like those near Johannesburg. Their hope was that 10 per cent or more of the total African labor force would be permanent, not migratory, with provision for married men and their families. According to the *Times* article just mentioned, Dr. Verwoerd has insisted that this proportion be cut to 3 per cent, because the government does not approve of such amenities for Africans. The mining companies, for humanitarian and other reasons, want to get away from compounds in the new developments. A stable labor force, with Africans permitted to bring their families into the townships, makes production cheaper.

THE OPPENHEIMERS AND ANGLO AMERICAN

Sir Ernest Oppenheimer is, like Rhodes, a monarch of both gold and diamonds. He is not only chairman of the Anglo American Corporation, which is responsible for about 17 per cent of all South African gold production, but also of De Beers Consolidated Mines, Ltd., which controls 95 per cent of the world's diamonds. Gold is more important financially than diamonds, but Sir Ernest likes diamonds better. He has been a connoisseur of diamonds all his life, loves them, and is perpetually fascinated by their beckoning glitter. Gold is business. Diamonds are fun. (Not that diamonds are not big business too.)

Oppenheimer is a courtly man, not at all grasping or predatory; he is adroit, indefatigable, a most civilized host, with a nice sparkle of humor, and quick of tongue. He likes the good things of life—exquisite food, art, urbanity, and conversation. He showed us his pictures, and told us how, for fun, he once bought a celebrated *fake* Vermeer. He loves to tell stories, some of them mildly scandalous, about famous jewels. His house in the outskirts of Johannesburg is not in the least a "grand" house, although he must be one of the richest men in the world. It is not like the Frick mansion on Fifth Avenue, or even the kind of palace the California gold kings built on Nob Hill. It has beautiful gardens, and is large and comfortable. It reminded me somewhat of a really nice house on Long Island, owned by a modest rather than a resplendent millionaire. Lady Oppenheimer adds much grace and beauty to the scene. Oppenheimer family relationships are complicated. Sir Ernest married in 1906 Miss May Pollak, who died in 1934. At about the same time his nephew, Sir Michael Oppenheimer, was killed in an aviation accident. Sir Ernest subsequently married Sir Michael's widow. She has a son by her first marriage, also named Michael, who is thus both Sir Ernest's stepson and grandnephew. By his first marriage Sir Ernest had one son, Frank, who was drowned in a bathing accident, and a surviving son, Harry F. Oppenheimer, who is a director in most of his father's corporations, deputy chairman of Anglo American, and Sir Ernest's closest associate. People sometimes wonder why Oppenheimer has never received a peerage and is, in fact, merely a knight, not even a baronet. The reason is that South African citizens have for some years been forbidden by law to accept British titles.

Oppenheimer, who is a man who likes to be liked, told us cheerfully that he is six years older than the discovery of the gold on the Witwatersrand that made his fortune. He was born in 1880 in Friedberg, a small town in Hesse, Germany, of a Jewish merchant family. His father had a cigar business. Ernest was one of five brothers. At the age of sixteen he went to London, where several of his elder brothers were working, and got a job as an office boy with a firm of diamond merchants, Anton Dunkelsbuhler and Company. He worked here for six years and then, at twenty-two, was sent out to South Africa to be the company's representative in Kimberley. He has lived in South Africa ever since. He rose quickly in several fields. He became mayor of Kimberley in 1912, and served three terms. His friend Jan Christiaan Smuts persuaded him to go into politics on a broader scale, and he was elected member of parliament for Kimberley in 1924. Meantime, he had been knighted in 1921, when this was still possible. He held the Kimberley seat till 1938. His son Harry holds it now. The Oppenheimers have for years been a major force behind the United party.

Like Rhodes, Oppenheimer went from diamonds into gold. He formed the Anglo American Corporation in 1917, to develop mines on the Far East Rand. Four mines—later six—became big producers. He needed capital at the beginning, and borrowed £1,000,000 from the House of Morgan. An intermediary in this transaction was none other than that well-known mining engineer Herbert Hoover. Oppenheimer named his company "Anglo American" in appreciation of the help he got from the United States, but the title is a misnomer now. Very little, if any, American capital remains in the organization today.

Gold did well, but Oppenheimer could not keep away from diamonds. In fact Anglo American was originally formed with an eye to diamonds as well as gold. After World War I there came a scramble for the diamond properties in South-West Africa, when this German colony became a League

GOLD, DIAMONDS, AND SOUTH-WEST AFRICA

of Nations mandated area. Oppenheimer, through Anglo American, organized the Consolidated Diamond Mines of South-West Africa, Ltd., bought up various small producers, and consolidated them, much as Rhodes had done. Then slowly, using his South-West holdings as a lever, he bought his way into De Beers. The story is complicated. He became chairman of De Beers in 1929, and has been the undisputed world master of diamonds ever since.

Anglo American (which is a totally separate corporation from De Beers, although they are related) is the "father" organization of the Oppenheimer empire. This colossal holding company has more than two hundred subsidiaries, and its total wealth has been estimated at two and a half billion dollars. The Oppenheimer interests pay about 2 per cent of South Africa's total tax revenue. The home building, on Main Street in Johannesburg, is the handsomest skyscraper in the city, and, appropriately enough, is built directly on top of some of the earliest mine shafts. I asked an Anglo American director to work out for me a chart showing the company's family tree, and he replied amiably, "Impossible." But I inspected maps and charts showing the extraordinary range and variety of Anglo American ramifications and affiliations. It controls about 40 per cent of all coal produced in the Union, and has a half interest in African Explosives and Chemical Industries, Ltd. A sister company, the Anglo American Investment Trust, takes care of the diamond end of the business, and Rhodesian Anglo American has enormous interests on the Northern Rhodesia Copperbelt, as we shall see. Another subsidiary, the West Rand Investment Trust, deals with gold interests on the Western Rand. Then there are such companies as African Malleable Foundries, Ltd., the First Electric Corporation of S.A., Ltd., African Cables, Ltd., and the Springfield Colliery. Recently I skimmed through a technical magazine devoted to mining in South Africa and came across a series of company reports. The first seven statements dealing with seven different companies were all by Harry Oppenheimer.

URANIUM IN SOUTH AFRICA

Details of uranium production in most countries are the deepest of deep secrets, but the South Africans are proud of their new uranium industry, and talk about it freely, within certain circumscriptions. The atmosphere is different from that of the Congo, where officials recoil in stunned horror at the least mention of uranium. One day in Johannesburg I got an invitation that made uranium seem very cozy:

> The Chairman and Directors of
> Daggafontein Mines, Limited,
> request the pleasure of the company of
> John Gunther, Esq.,
> at the official opening of the Uranium and
> Sulphuric Acid Plants at the mine by
> Sir Ernest Oppenheimer
> at 11 a.m. on May 22nd, 1953,
> and to luncheon in the Daggafontein Mines
> Recreation Club afterwards.

On this occasion Sir Ernest pressed a button which registered a signal at Harwell, the great atomic energy installation in the United Kingdom; the signal was instantly transmitted back to South Africa, and the plant was officially declared open. Previously (on October 8, 1952) Dr. Malan had formally opened the first of the South African uranium plants, at the West Rand Consolidated Gold Mine near Krugersdorp. This is the date given for the inauguration of South Africa's "atomic age." But the Daggafontein operation is much bigger. There are at the moment twenty-three mines in the Union authorized to produce uranium. Not all are in actual production yet. Of this total seven are operated by Anglo American.[5]

Uranium is not "mined" in the Union in the sense that uranium-bearing ores are (as in the Congo) dug out of the earth. The process is much cheaper and simpler. (But, even though the method may be comparatively cheap, the initial investment in South African uranium development is calculated at £50,000,000.) The uranium industry in the Union depends altogether on the gold industry. Uranium is a by-product of gold. After the ore is crushed and the gold is removed, the residue or mash or "slime" is treated by a special process and uranium is extracted in the form of an oxide ($U_3 O_8$). This oxide, from all the mines involved, is then sent to a central plant, Calcined Products, Ltd., where it is further treated, refined,

---

[5] Daggafontein is on the East Rand, Western Reefs Exploration and Development is at Klerksdorp, and the other five (President Brand, President Steyn, Welkom Gold Mining Company, Western Holdings, Ltd., and the Free State Geduld Mines, Ltd.) are new mines in the Orange Free State.

and packed for export. The great mine dumps in and near Johannesburg, composed of "tailings" from the gold mines, also contain sizable amounts of uranium, which may be easily extracted.

Ownership of South African uranium is not vested in the mine companies, but in the Atomic Energy Board of the Union government. Proceeds which accrue to the state from the sale of uranium abroad are then paid back to the producers, and the state shares in the profits by complicated arrangements over leases and taxation.[6]

Most (if not all) uranium production goes to the United Kingdom and the United States, and South Africa has become almost overnight the chief source for uranium used in America. This, one political observer has suggested, is why "the United States, no matter how much it may dislike the Strijdom government, is going to go easy on it."

WE PROCEED TO DIAMONDS

We flew over the "Big Hole" at Kimberley, which has been called the "womb" of South Africa; it is three-quarters of a mile wide and 1,400 feet deep, and is supposed to be the largest hole on the earth's surface ever made by man. Out of it in less than half a century came something like fifteen million carats of diamonds, of a value probably reaching £50,000,000. Diamonds in New York City today are worth anywhere from $600 to $1,675 per carat (or more for exceptional stones) retail, and the point does not need to be labored that Kimberley produced a great deal of wealth in its time. Operations in the Big Hole stopped in 1915. One of the first mine sites near here was a farm owned by a Boer farmer named De Beer; hence the name of the company. Cecil Rhodes bought it for $18,000.

Then in Johannesburg we saw diamonds. A specialist in the field showed us a few rarities. The first was comparatively modest. It weighed 17 carats. It was absolutely pure and of the best blue-white color, but it had been chipped by careless handling, and in being recut lost a fraction of its value. Even so, it was worth around $75,000. "Diamonds are hard, but brittle, and can easily be damaged," our host told us gravely. Next we saw a stone of equal purity and brilliance (21.69 carats) that had been found in the Premier mine near Pretoria last year. Eighty per cent of the output of Premier consists of industrials, but it produces a fair quantity of gem stones too. Then came a dulcet glittering giant cut out of a stone originally weighing 283 carats. Number Four was a square diamond colored a rich deep

[6] "Uranium in South Africa," an article prepared in the Office of the Atomic Energy Board. *South African Journal of Economics*, March, 1953.

yellow. Value? "Don't know," said our host. "But it is interesting as a curiosity." Nobody knows what gives color to a diamond. Those found near gold mines are usually tinted green. "Wish we had a really big pink stone to show you. They are quite rare." The last stone we saw was blue, almost slate-colored, the size and shape of a small matchbox, and probably worth $300,000. "It makes the Hope look like nothing." There are only three blue diamonds bigger than 30 carats known in the world—the Hope, one now believed to be in Germany, and this one, which weighs 46 carats. "Look at it. You'll never see another." But I thought that its steel-like blueness seemed faintly sinister, even menacing.

There has never been a stone like the Cullinan. People still talk of this radiant gem as if it were something alive; it carries a legend, a mystery, an aura of incomparable romantic beauty, as does Miss Greta Garbo among actresses. The Cullinan was discovered at the Premier mine in 1905 by an executive named Wells. He saw half exposed in the ground something that sparkled, and dug it out with a penknife. It weighed 3024¾ carats, three times bigger than any diamond ever known. This means that, uncut, it was the size of a large man's fist. Mr. Wells was given a bonus of £2,000 for his discovery. The diamond could not be sold; it was too big; nobody in the world could have afforded it. Eventually it was cut into nine different stones and ninety-six brilliants, and, as I have mentioned above, was presented to the British royal family. To do the cutting took three skilled men, who worked fourteen hours a day, eight months.[7] The biggest fragment, the Star of Africa, is marquise-cut and measures 2⅜ by 1¾ inches; it is the majestic central stone in the British Royal Scepter. Cullinan II, the next biggest fragment, the size of a small apricot, adorns the Imperial State Crown.

I take the following from an article on the Cullinan in *Optima*, a quarterly review published by the Anglo American Corporation (December, 1954), in description of the first cutting:

> A crystal so big could not be faceted as a single gem. It would have to be cleaved or split, and herein lay danger. Every diamond has planes of cleavage just as wood has its grain, and, unless these planes are precisely and accurately determined, a single blow can reduce a priceless diamond to a heap of small fragments . . . J. Asscher [of I. J. Asscher & Company of Amsterdam], the celebrated cutter of "Excelsior" and other gems, studied the Cullinan for weeks and practised with oversized tools on glass and wax models. Finally, on February 10, 1908, after several days of rest, the master-cutter clamped the big diamond in a specially-made holder and inserted his cleavage blade in the ¼ inch

---

[7] Somebody who ought to know told me that the fee for the job was £25,000, but I do not vouch for this.

ORGANIZATION OF DE BEERS INTERESTS

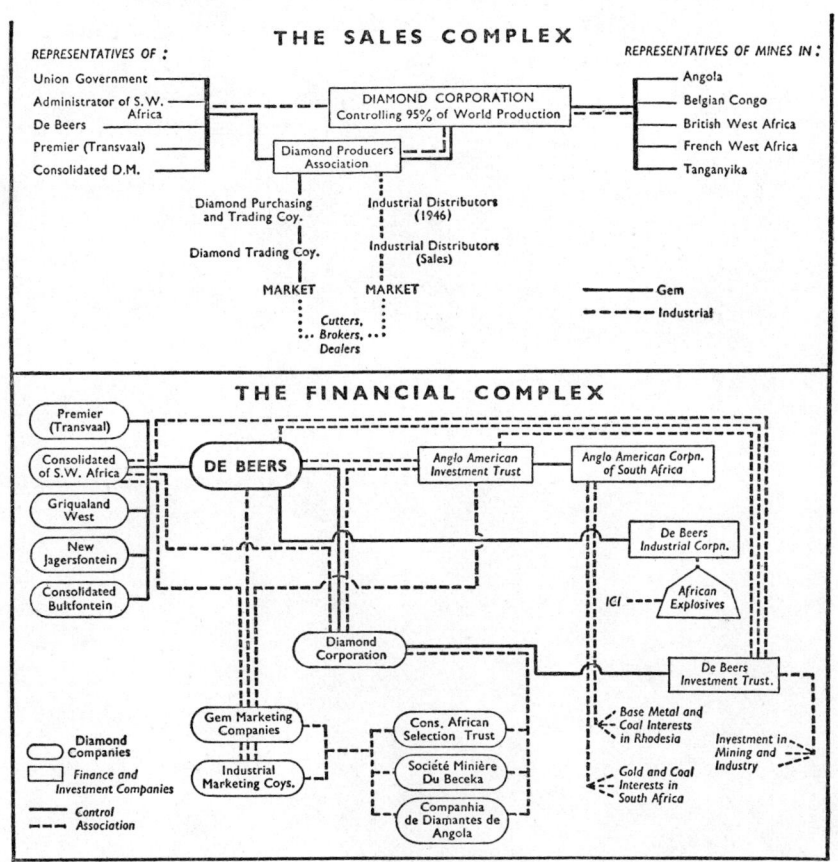

From the London *Economist*, June 19, 1954

notch he had ground in the diamond's surface. Then, as his assistants breathlessly watched, he struck the blade with a heavy rod. The blade snapped! With beads of cold sweat bedewing his face and in a tense silence stretched to breaking point, Asscher fitted a second cleavage blade and tapped it sharply. This time the diamond was split in two exactly as planned. As the portions fell apart, Asscher crumpled on to the floor in a dead faint.

We cannot in this space go into any details of the way diamonds are sold and marketed. Three-quarters of total production goes to the United States. De Beers, a syndicate of seven companies, has been called "the neatest, tightest industrial monopoly" the world has ever seen; it not only controls the sources of supply but also regulates the market and controls world sales through the Diamond Corporation and the Diamond Trading Company in London. In case the reader does not find the accompanying chart complex enough for his taste, we may add a detail or two. The Anglo American Investment Trust (Oppenheimer) owns 20 per cent of the De Beers equity. De Beers (Oppenheimer) holds 92 per cent of the preferred shares of the Premier (Transvaal) Diamond Mining Company, and 96.4 per cent of the equity of Consolidated Diamond Mines of South-West Africa, Ltd. The Diamond Corporation is owned by De Beers, Consolidated Diamonds, and Anglo American Investment Trust. And the De Beers Investment Trust is owned in turn by the Diamond Corporation, De Beers Consolidated, Consolidated Diamonds, and Anglo American. No matter which way you add it up, the answer always comes out the same—Ernest Oppenheimer.

Labor is better off in diamonds than in gold. The work is not so arduous nor so deep underground; wages are higher, and contracts shorter. As a rule African workers going into the diamond compounds serve from three to six months, not longer. But during this time they are never allowed outside the wire that fences in the mines, and, when they do leave, they are X-rayed and purged. A new radar device is also useful for detecting theft. It is illegal anywhere in the Union to buy or sell rough diamonds, except through the constituted authorities, and possession of an uncut stone is a crime. Men working with diamonds often have their suits cut without pockets, so that nobody can "plant" a stolen diamond on them. The diamond business is as slippery as a wet vitamin pill or cherry stone.

*

The diamond fields in South-West Africa, which are something quite apart from the mines in the Free State and Transvaal, lie at the mouth of the Orange River on the Atlantic. Dig with your toe in the sand here, and you may be arrested. Build a house, and the police will watch every detail of the excavation. Visitors to the area, even those most respectable, are searched with care when they emerge. This is because diamonds lie close to the top of the soil, and may even be picked up on the surface of the beaches. North of the river, which is the frontier between the Union proper and South-West Africa, the fields are owned by Consolidated Diamond Mines of South-West Africa, i.e., by De Beers, i.e., by Oppenheimer. South of the river, in the Union, they are nationalized—state-owned. This area is known as Namaqualand. The northern fields are much richer. They are, in fact, probably the richest diamond properties in the world, producing about 60,000 carats a month, mostly gem stones. Sizable areas in this region are not yet worked. Thus arose the widely accepted legend that "acres of diamonds" are deliberately kept off the market in order to raise prices. Actually very little stockpiling takes place these days. The market is too vigorous. But the De Beers organization can, if it wishes, feed stones into the world market at any rate it chooses, and this is an important factor in its prestige, success and wealth. It likes to keep supply just a little distance behind demand.

THE COMPOUNDS NEAR JOHANNESBURG

We are not done with Africans in the Union yet. I have in Chapter 25 described briefly the Johannesburg locations, and now to round out the picture we should have a word about the compounds. On a Sunday morning I drove out along the Main Reef Road to the Consolidated Main Reef Mine. A compound looks like an army barracks—or a prison. The dormitories are well built, the streets are paved with asphalt, and the accoutrements are clean. There are big somewhat dank kitchens, laundries, and lavatories. The physical circumstances of life are perhaps more attractive than in the locations, but the atmosphere is (no matter how well the workers are cared for) inhuman and forbidding.

At any given time in the Rand compounds there will be between 285,000 and 315,000 African workers. As I have already explained, they differ from Africans in the locations. Families are not allowed, workers have to be single or live apart from their wives for the duration of their contract, and 95 per cent are migratory. Contracts are for anything between nine and eighteen months. In the ordinary course of events a worker, no matter how strong, cannot work underground for longer than nine months, without danger of collapse. The Union does not have nearly enough black labor to meet the demand, and about 70 per cent of workers come from Basutoland, Nyasaland, Portuguese Africa, and elsewhere. At least one-third of the total force, around 100,000 men, comes from Mozambique every year. About 250,000 of the total number of workers work underground, where the temperature may reach 100 degrees or more, despite artificial cooling. Wages average somewhere between the equivalent of 33 cents to 45 cents per day. A day's work is eight hours, but the worker may spend an extra hour queuing up to the cages and still another walking to his post. Of course food, lodging, medical services, and so on are provided free. Workers are well fed—every calorie, every ounce of protein, is carefully measured—and often they leave the compounds in better physical shape than when they entered. For many, living conditions in the compounds are, in fact, much better than anything they have ever known before, from the physical standpoint. On the other hand, a miner working deep underground may easily contract tuberculosis, and he may transmit this to his family when he returns. Silicosis too has taken a heavy toll.

A worker in a compound is not, in the real sense of the word, a prisoner, although it is a crime to break his contract. But equally he is not free. If his behavior is good he will get a pass to go out into the city once a week. The authorities guard against his getting into trouble by giving him practically no money to spend. As a rule the greater part of the wages earned during the contract period is withheld, and paid in a lump sum when the man is discharged. Then, in theory, he can return home, rejoin his tribe, and buy a cow or a wife. Actually many boys, after a year or more in the compounds, go mildly crazy when they are released, and, before being shipped back to where they came from, go on spending sprees and buy almost any kind of weird object. Of course their total earnings (at 33 to 45 cents per day) do not provide a very large capital for extravagance. The Portuguese government, to keep their citizens from throwing away what they have earned, have an arrangement whereby they are not paid fully till they return safely home.

Labor is desperately short. Every year it becomes harder to entice 300,000 men into the mines. Many young men prefer to go into new industries where wages are higher and where there are no compounds. As a result, in order to attract labor, conditions in the mines have gradually tended to become better. No one has, however, suggested as yet a large raise in wages. Procurement for the mines is handled by the Chamber of Mines through two official recruiting organizations. An official of one of these, defending the system, told us that the essence of the process was that the workers "bought future leisure." But many (except those from Mozambique by and large) learn to like the circumstances of city life, and hate to go back to their reserves or other place of residence. Many return for a second contract period. One odd point is that to work in the mines is considered by many Africans to be a sign of manhood, equivalent to fighting in the wars in earlier days. They do not think that they are fit to acquire wives and raise families until their courage and virility have been proved by the ordeal of the mines. No doubt this piquant notion has been deliberately fostered by the recruiting companies to make it easier to get men.

The mine dances held in the compounds on most Sundays are one of the great sights of Africa. There are fifty-five tribes on the Rand, speaking forty-four languages. It is a tribute to the delight of Africans in music and dancing, and to their artistic capabilities, that almost every tribe, even the most primitive, has its own special and effective type of dance. The dances are set up by the mine authorities for several reasons. One is to let each tribe demonstrate its accomplishment in competition with the others, and provide entertainment for all. Another is that the dances give workers opportunity "to let off sexual steam." The boys are youthful and have no regular sexual outlet, with the result that homosexuality in some mines is a vexing problem.[8] But one seasoned social worker told us, "When a boy works a mile underground at a temperature of 105 degrees and breaks rocks with a jack hammer between his toes for eight hours every day, he does not have much energy left over for sex." In any case the dances we saw were enthralling. The performance took place in a sizable amphitheater; a large audience of blacks sat on the sunny side; a few whites had seats in the shade. First came Pondos doing an inflamed war dance. Then followed Amakwenkwes, who wore blue plumes, orange straps over their naked torsos, yellow shorts, and white wool anklets. Husky boys rolled in the dirt, pranced with an exaggerated erotic rhythm, did turns like those of tumblers in a circus, and danced sitting down. Then there were Mandaus, naked except for a loincloth, and Amakwayas who wore white feathers and carried long tufted spears. And if they were not letting off sexual steam, I do not know what it was.

SOUTH AFRICA: WHO RUNS IT?

There can be only one answer to this question. It is a double answer and peculiar. South Africa is run by two forces which, although they are not overtly hostile, have elements of bitter antagonism. South Africa, uniquely among nations, is run by an unwritten alliance between two groups which hate each other. One is the National party, i.e., Afrikaner nationalism, which

---

[8] One reason why some young married men go into the mines, leaving their wives behind, is that the wife may have just given birth to a child and a widespread taboo forbids the husband to have relations with her during the weaning period. Boys in some tribes are eager to get back to their homes on time because, if they are unduly late, an elder brother is entitled to marry the wife.

GOLD, DIAMONDS, AND SOUTH-WEST AFRICA 561

includes such factors as the Broederbond, the Dutch Reformed church, the universities of Stellenbosch and Potchefstroom, and personalities such as Mr. Strijdom. The other is the Chamber of Mines, i.e., financial interests concentrated largely in the City of London.

If open conflict should ever develop between these groups, Afrikaner nationalism would probably win. "In the long run, British capital has no alternative but to accept Afrikaner political domination," is the way one celebrated political economist phrased it to us.

There are plenty of Afrikaner nationalists who, in theory at least, would like to nationalize the mines, and take over gold production for the state. But at the present time this is a political impossibility. Even so, the Nationalists are in the driver's seat.

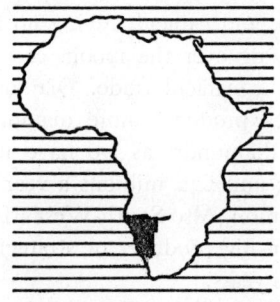

"GERMAN" SOUTH-WEST AFRICA

This is a curiosity among countries. South-West Africa, which was once called Damaraland, covers 317,725 square miles (about the size of France and Italy put together) and is three-quarters as big as the Union itself. The population is only about 450,000, of which perhaps 50,000 are white Europeans.[9] The area is divided roughly in two halves, the "Police Zone" in the south and the Native districts above. "Police Zone" means the territory where European administration functions fully. The name came into use because there are no police at all in the northern regions—only a handful of white administrators—and if any European gets into trouble there it would be necessary to send in a detachment of police to rescue him. As a matter of fact travel outside the Police Zone is rigorously restricted. The northern areas are the most "closed" part of Africa. The official in charge of the South-West African administration told us that even he could not give permission for

[9] There are also sixteen Malays and eleven Indians.

anybody to enter the north. Authority has to come all the way from Pretoria.

One geographical oddity is the Caprivi Strip. This is an arrow, flanked on one side by the Zambesi River, that shoots inland from the Atlantic and separates Angola and part of Northern Rhodesia from Bechuanaland and the Union. The Germans flung this arrow halfway across Africa, when they had ambitions to join their former colonies on the west and east coasts of the continent.

South-West Africa is mostly plateau and desert. Some towns have to import their water, and there "is not a river in the whole country that holds water all the year."[10] The Germans, when they occupied South-West Africa, pumped millions into this arid space, and it held more German colonists than any other German colony in the world, but they were never able to do much with it economically. Some years ago prosperity began, based on diamonds, other minerals, and caracul. Flying up to Windhoek from Cape Town was almost like flying over the moon, except for the ranches and a few towns built up on the caracul trade. Diamonds are a terrific moneymaker. South-West Africa produces more diamonds than Cape Province. They are Oppenheimer diamonds, as we have noted above. South-West Africa earns between £25 and £40 millions a year in foreign exchange, but most of this goes to the Union. Also South-West Africa has lucrative fisheries, and is rapidly becoming a big producer of strategic minerals. Exports have quintupled in the last five years.

The best known tribe in the Police Zone, and one of the most famous in all Africa, is the Herero. There are not many Hereros left. In the north the Ovambos, who number about 200,000, are outstanding. These are a markedly primitive people, who had no contact at all with the white man until about 1916. They pay no taxes to the government, live their own isolated lives, and have their own administration. Many of their young men are, however, now being recruited into the mines and diamond fields. Labor shortage is by far South-West Africa's chief economic problem.

People still called "Bastaards" (half-castes) form another striking community, centering on the town of Rehoboth. Another is that of the Bergdamaras, or "Klip Kaffirs," who still speak the Hottentot language. Still another, in a different category, is that of the "Angola Boers." These are white men, Afrikaners, of the poorest type, who derive from Boer trekkers who refused to stay in the Transvaal under British rule, and pushed up north and west into the Kalahari Desert. They have been called the "last dregs of

---

[10] Farson, *Behind God's Back*, p. 28. This book has some wonderful descriptions of South-West Africa and the "Southwesters."

the Great Trek." They penetrated into Portuguese Angola in about 1902, and unkind people say that they are "still surprisingly white, all things considered." They were repatriated into South-West Africa in the 1920's.

Penetration of South-West Africa by the Germans began in the 1880's, and continued until World War I. The Hereros several times revolted against German rule, and were mercilessly crushed.

*

Is South-West Africa a "country"? I asked this question of a leading official and got the answer, "Frankly, no one really knows." In practice, it is administered as a fifth province of the Union, but it is not a fifth province in fact—at least not yet. South-West Africa has its own legislative assembly, with considerably more power than the provincial assemblies in the Union, and has control of its own finances, education, roads, and post office. It has its own postage stamps. In theory the Union government has overriding power over legislation, but does not exercise it. Once a year or so the Administrator of South-West Africa (appointed by the Union government) goes to Pretoria for consultation. The Union retains control over defense, external affairs, transport, and security. Taxes are lower than in the Union, and sometimes people who forget how much foreign exchange South-West contributes to the Union say that "it is getting a free ride."

The man who really runs South-West Africa is not the Administrator, whose importance is largely titular, but a civil servant of exceptional attainments, John Neser. I doubt if anywhere in the world any official holds so many posts, and manages them more agreeably. Mr. Neser is secretary of the government. He is also Chief Native Commissioner, chairman of the Land Tax Board, chairman of the Diamond Board, chairman of the Tender Board, chairman of the Farming Interest Fund Board, Director of Internal Revenue, and Director of Prisons.

Behind all this (we will leave Mr. Neser to his various jobs) is an international legal situation very much tangled. The gist of it is that both the United Nations and South Africa claim authority over South-West Africa. It is difficult to treat of this story in a paragraph. The bare details are the following. During World War I, Union forces under Smuts and Botha beat the Germans there, just as Allied forces finally forced Von Lettow to quit fighting in German East Africa. In 1918 the country became a League of Nations mandate, administered by the Union. No one in the Union paid much attention to it for many years. In 1945 the old League mandates became Trust Territories of the UN, except South-West Africa. In 1946 the Union government gave notice of its desire to annex the territory. The UN said that it could not do so. After interminable wrangling the matter was put up to the World Court at The Hague in 1950. This issued an ambiguous advisory opinion to the effect that the Union was not under any obligation to transfer the territory to UN trusteeship, but on the other hand that it had no right to make any other change in the *status quo*, i.e., annex it. So the situation today is that South-West Africa is still a mandated territory with the UN as a kind of repository for the old League, which the Union administers and wants to take over. In 1953 came a significant development. The General Assembly of the UN took the position that it would not be doing its duty to the territory if it did not exercise as much scrutiny over it as was possible under the circumstances. So a committee (against fierce South African protest) was set up to get its own reports on South-West African affairs. This committee cannot visit the Union or the territory itself, but is empowered to receive documents, petitions, and the like, from the Hereros and others, much to Union chagrin.

The advent of Dr. Malan to power in 1948 made the issue sharper. In 1950, as we know, the Malanites "granted" to South-West Africa six seats in the Union House of Assembly, in which it had never previously been represented. By-elections were held, and the Nationalists won all six South-West seats. This helped substantially to give them a safe, stable parliamentary majority. In 1954 the National party adopted a resolution "terminating" the mandate and declaring the territory to be part of the Union. But formal annexation has not occurred to date.

The case might be made that annexation would probably have taken place by this time had it not been for the Reverend Michael Scott. Mr. Scott is an English missionary who went to South Africa for his health in 1926, when he was nineteen. He worked at a leper colony for a time, and became passionately interested in the welfare, political and otherwise, of Africans. This brought him into lively and painful contact with the authorities; he was sentenced to three months in jail in 1946 for assisting the Indian civil disobedience campaign, and was subsequently expelled from the Union. The Reverend Mr. Scott is a tall, extraordinarily handsome man, shy to the point of inarticulateness, gentle, and as innocent in some respects as a child flying a kite, but also a zealot, a fighting idealist, stubborn and tenacious to the last inch in defending what he believes to be right. He is a man of the highest religious and moral principles. Some people call him a crank, and no doubt he has taken on occasion an extreme view. The South African government has tried—vainly—to pin the "Communist" tag on him, as it does with most of its adversaries. When Mr. Scott visited the United States recently he received the kind of limited visa that severely re-

GOLD, DIAMONDS, AND SOUTH-WEST AFRICA

stricts a person's movements, even within New York City. The restrictions were waived on one occasion when he was invited to deliver a sermon in the Cathedral of St. John the Divine.

Mr. Scott took up the case of South-West Africa in 1947, and has been hammering at it ever since. It was his voice that, for years, helped to keep the issue alive, with the result that the 1953 resolution was passed giving the UN a kind of watching brief over South-West African affairs.

*

WINDHOEK, the capital, has great individuality and charm. Its altitude is 5,428 feet, and the atmosphere is brilliantly brisk and sunny. Windhoek has some 20,000 people, of whom half are Europeans. It takes three days to get from Windhoek to Johannesburg by train, cutting down below the Kalahari Desert, and three and a half hours by air. What makes Windhoek unique is its German texture. It might be a miniature Stuttgart or Dresden. The main street is still the Kaiserstrasse, and up in the hills nearby are three fantastic Rhenish castles, with fantastic histories. You call a waiter *Herr Ober*, drink a superlative light dry beer, and look at shopwindows filled with Hohner harmonicas, cuckoo clocks, Adler typewriters, Zeiss optical goods, and *Langspiel* records. The cuisine in the hotels is formidably Teutonic, and a good German newspaper, the *Allgemeine Zeitung*, has a bigger circulation than the English paper. Street signs are trilingual—in Afrikaans, German, and English; shops displaying *Skoene, Schuhe*, or Shoes may be *Oop, Offen*, or Open. The chief government building is called jestingly the *Tintenpalast*, or Ink Palace. One street is named for Goering's father, who was an early governor. There is a good German club, theater, and orchestra. This last is composed of forty members ranging in regular occupation from neurologist to manicure girl. The first violinist is the city electrician.

Windhoek has several other curious distinctions, for instance that truffles are abundant, and cost 6d. per pound. Jewelry shops, like those in Rio de Janeiro, are stocked with an extraordinary variety of semi-precious stones, including such rarities as the heliodore.

The German community, which probably numbers about 15,000 in South-West Africa as a whole, goes back to the 1890's. Unlike their compatriots in Tanganyika, the Reichsdeutsch did not go back to Germany after World War I, but stayed in Africa. During World War II many became Nazis, and a Gray Shirt movement flourished. One man, now a deputy in the Union parliament, took part in an attempt to burn down a synagogue. Since 1945 a slight, but steady, German immigration has taken place into South-

West Africa. Most German-descended citizens vote Nationalist, although they consider themselves vastly superior to the Afrikaners in culture. Lately, however, have come strong impulses for the formation of an "autonomy" party. Most Southwesters do not relish the prospect of being formally incorporated into the Union.

*

The Herero quarter in Windhoek is called simply "the" location. Shanties, in one of the most gruesome and nauseating slums I have ever seen, are made of old automobile fenders, cardboard, mashed-out petrol tins, and bits of old cloth and basketware. But the Hereros are a proud, dignified, and handsome people, who wear costumes of almost voluptuous regality. The dresses of the women are Victorian in mode, and sweep the ground. Some Hereros have aquiline noses, and are intensely superior in bearing. Color bar here is as severely applied as in the Union, perhaps more so. Curfew in Windhoek is at 9:00 P.M., and there is no single secondary school for Africans in the entire territory, or any facilities for technical training of any kind. There are no civil rights, no representation on any political body, and no local organization of the African National Congress. One lad we met was Berthold S. Himumuine, a Herero schoolteacher. He had just been granted a scholarship at Oxford. The South African authorities would not give him a passport and consequently he was unable to leave the country and accept the Oxford invitation. The case of young Mr. Himumuine and its manifest cruelty and injustice went all the way to the United Nations in New York, but to no avail.

The following is a prayer made recently by Hosea Kutako, a prominent Herero chief: "O God, Thou art the God of all the earth and the heavens. We are so insignificant. In us there are many defects. But You know all about us. For coming down from Heaven You were despised and brutally treated by the men of those days. For those men You prayed because they did not understand what they were doing, and that You came only for what is right. Help us to struggle in that way for what is right. O Lord help us who roam about. Help us who have been placed in Africa and have no dwelling place of our own. Give us back a dwelling place. O God, all power is yours in Heaven and Earth. Amen."

*

There is one American city in South-West Africa. It is a model city. It is a far cry from the Windhoek location. It is called Tsumeb, and is the seat of a large American mining development, owned by the Newmont Mining

GOLD, DIAMONDS, AND SOUTH-WEST AFRICA

Company. Tsumeb produces lead and copper, and is an important element in the territory's advancing economy. Another American enterprise at work in South-West Africa, but not yet doing any actual mining, is the Bethlehem Exploration and Mining Corporation, a subsidiary of Bethlehem Steel. This has a three-year exploration contract covering two million acres. The minerals sought—aerial surveys are promising—are iron and manganese. The Bethlehem development, if it is carried through, may entail an investment of $100,000,000. Not only will the mines have to be set up, but a town, railroad, and harbor will need to be built.

DEPARTURE

We should state again, in slightly different terms, the agonizing and dangerous dilemma that afflicts the Union. A huge majority of blacks and a small minority of whites divided amongst themselves are condemned to live in the same country. *Apartheid* forbids the development of racial partnership, and the cult of white supremacy adopted by Afrikaner Nationalists makes racial harmony impossible. Hence South Africa is bound to be tormented by continuing tension, fear, and strife.

Flying out of the Union we crossed the frontier, and our pilot, who travels in and out of the Union fifty times a year, said quietly, "The air is cleaner now. Every time I leave the Union I feel that I can look my fellow man in the face again."

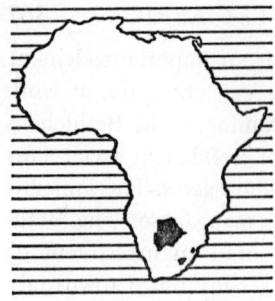

CHAPTER 28

Medicine Murder in Basutoland

> Let me and my people rest and live under the large folds of the flag of England before I am no more.
> —CHIEF MOSHESH

BASUTOLAND is one of the three "High Commission Territories" embedded in the Union. These are still British colonies or protectorates, under the authority of the British High Commissioner in Pretoria (whence their name) and ruled from London, although they are wholly or partially surrounded by Union territory. Basutoland, although small, is in some respects the most important of the three. It is a country extraordinarily distinctive and picturesque on any level. It is sometimes called the "Switzerland of Africa," sometimes "the country of the Lost Horizon." Indeed its horizons seem endless, leading from one gaunt sloping range of mountains to the next. Some peaks reach 11,000 feet. If Basutoland has a profile, it is that of a blue saw. Basutoland has practically no roads, except near the main towns, and three quarters of it can only be reached by horseback; there are 1,600 miles of bridle paths. The whole country, which seems to lie on a slant toward the sun, has at first glance an implausible, toylike character, with a fairy-tale sparkle. Not since Tamanrasset in the Sahara did we feel such an eerie impression of loneliness. But grim and formidable horrors—the most repellent we encountered in all Africa—lie hidden under Basutoland's isolated beauty and remoteness.

Basutoland covers no more than 11,000 square miles, and has only 600,000 people, of whom perhaps 1,600 are white Europeans. The capital, MASERU, lies about eighty miles by road from Bloemfontein in the Orange Free State. The country cannot easily be penetrated from any other direction. An arch outside Maseru (population 3,712) proclaims it to be a haven of peace. Maseru looks like an American Wild West town. It has no cinema or newspaper, and it is the only British capital we saw in Africa so small that it did not even have a Barclay's Bank. Two or three trading companies have shops heavily stocked with blankets, saddles, and other horsewear. Most Basuto are expert horsemen, their ponies are famous, and the national costume is the blanket. These are worn by men and women alike, draped from the shoulder. A human being looks like a tent. The best blankets come from Bradford, England, are known by the trade name "Victorian" (Queen Victoria still has commanding prestige in the country), and cost £7. Cheaper blankets come from Harrismith in the Union. They are made of the softest, furriest wool, and are mauve, pink, gray, or the color of orange juice mixed with milk; in the shops they are folded in a curious scalloped manner and hung on the walls for display like huge, pastel-colored butterflies.

The Basuto are a true nation, not a constellation of tribes, and they have a powerful, primitive national sense, deriving from their great King Moshesh. They have been wards of the British since 1884.[1] They are light-skinned Bantus, probably with Bushman admixtures. "Basuto" is the plural form of Mosuto; the name of the country is properly Lesuto, and the language is Sesuto. The Basuto are the best workers in southern Africa. They are a clean people physically, aloof, rugged, proud, and poor. The roadside greeting, when one Masuto meets another, is *Khotsa*, which means "peace." Mostly the Basuto live by grazing their flocks and growing mohair. Many have been converted to Christianity, and, as in Uganda, there have been fierce sectarian rivalries between Protestants and Roman Catholics. About 70,000 Basuto, more than 10 per cent of the population, go to the Rand every year to work in the mines, and probably 250,000 Basuto in all live in the Union. But items like these are not what makes Basutoland interesting. What does is medicine murder.

THE "DIRETLO" MURDERS

The peculiar thing about the recent wave of murders in Basutoland, of which the outside world knows little and which are the most appalling I have ever heard about, is that they are, in the literal sense, *medicine* murders. People are killed in the most hideous manner for the most prosaic ends. Bits of their flesh are severed from the body, and these are pounded into a smear, which is supposed to give magical powers to the person using it. If you

---

[1] Basuto historical development is as fascinating—and complex—as any in Africa, but it is too long a story to go into here.

want to find your son a job, get more land, or rise to a new political appointment, you may arrange for the murder of some completely innocent person and then use his remains as a baleful kind of sorcerer's charm.

Most Basuto murders are gruesome in the extreme, but this makes the medicine they produce more efficacious. They are not merely isolated acts of morbid violence, but a social and political phenomenon of great consequence, arising out of the most ancient and entrenched superstitions of the Basuto nation, and involving people of the highest rank.

How is the murder medicine used, and what makes it work? First, fragments of human flesh are mixed with blood, fat, and herbs, into a kind of paste, which is called *diretlo*. After this is boiled or brewed into the proper consistency, the person hoping to derive benefit from it smears it on various parts of his body, or rubs it into his skin, or even eats it. The medicine is always kept in a *lanaka*, or horn—the hollowed-out horn of an antelope, goat, or other beast. Basuto leaders have passed these horns down from father to son since the founding of the nation, and they are, naturally, objects of the most revered value. Every chief has one, whether it is filled with human flesh or not. The horn is always kept in some secret place. British (and native) police have been working on various Basuto murders for a generation, and some cases that date back to the 1930's are still being investigated today, *but no murder horn has ever been found*.

What makes the medicine in the horn so potent? No one can explain exactly. But, in brief, it seems that the ugly stuff symbolizes *power* to the primitive Basuto. Few have any conception that murder by this means is wrong. Magic is the black man's friend.

The British government, trying to cope with the *diretlo* murders and perplexed by the occult forces behind them, recently appointed a University of Cambridge anthropologist, G.I. Jones, to survey the subject. Mr. Jones's report, which has been published by Her Majesty's Stationery Office, tells the whole story,[2] and it makes grim reading. Here is one of his case histories:

> On a Saturday evening in January, 1948, Mochesela Khoto sat in a hut drinking beer with Dane Rachakana and a number of other people who had come to a wedding feast. . . . While the party was proceeding the Chieftainess of his ward [district] arrived. . . . Others were summoned . . . and they were told: "I want you to kill Mochesela for me, because I want to make a medicine horn which I will use in the 'placing' of my son [getting him an appointment]. Any one of you who disobeys this order will be killed. . . ." Dane got

[2] *Basutoland Medicine Murder.* A Report on the Recent Outbreak of "Diretlo" Murders in Basutoland. London. 1951. Cmd. 8209. I am drawing on this document for many of the details that follow.

up and said to Mochesela: "Cousin, let us go outside for a while." Mochesela followed him to where sixteen men were waiting for them with the Chieftainess and two of her women attendants. She greeted Dane . . . and told the men to seize Mochesela. As one of them caught hold of him, Mochesela cried out: "My father Pholo, are you going to kill me?" and when he did not reply, continued: "Let me free and I will give you my black ox." "I am not your father and I want you, not your ox," replied Pholo. He started to shout, but they gagged him and marched him off away from the village, while Dane threw stones to drive off some boys who had been attracted by his shouting. When they reached a satisfactory spot they removed their blankets, stripped the deceased of his clothes, and held him naked on the ground. An oil lamp was produced and by its light they proceeded to cut small circular pieces of skin from his body with a knife. Pholo cut a piece from the calf of his left leg, another man a piece from his groin, a third from beneath his right breast, a fourth from the biceps of his right arm. The pieces as they were cut were laid on a white cloth in front of Mosala, the native doctor who was going to make the medicine, and one of the men held a billy-can to collect the blood from these and later wounds. Then Dane took the knife and with it removed the entire face of Mochesela. He cut right down to the bone, beginning at the forehead and ending at the throat and he finished by taking out the throat, the tongue and the eyes. Mochesela died while his throat was cut. The Chieftainess who had stood by watching is then reported to have said: "I thank you, my children, for having killed this man for me. I know the Police will come here to investigate this matter and no one must tell them about it. If they do, I will kill them in the same way as I have killed Mochesela." . . . After this she left for her home. . . . The rest carried Mochesela's body to a hut where it remained wrapped in his blanket. . . . until Tuesday night. Then it was carried to some low cliffs near the village and after some of the clothing had been placed on the grass and on a tree nearby, it was thrown over and then dragged a little further downhill, to be found there the following morning.

The murderers were caught in this case and fifteen were brought to trial. The ward chieftainess and her leading accomplice were hanged. Three members of the gang got sentences of fifteen years, and three others seven years.

*

There have been about a hundred authenticated cases of medicine murder in Basutoland since 1895; sixteen took place in 1951, the second biggest number ever recorded in a single year. Forty cases have come to trial so far, and there have been nineteen convictions. Sixty-seven people have been hanged, including—as we shall see—two of the chief political personalities of the Basuto nation.

The Jones Report contains an analysis of ninety-three murders, dating from 1895 to 1949. Almost all conform to a basic pattern, and the motive is always the same, to get flesh for the sacred horns.

First, the victim is usually somebody inconspicuous. A chief never, it seems, murders another chief. If he needs medicine with which to oppose a rival chief, this is taken from a third person who is altogether innocent. Even worse, the victim is often a relative or close associate of the murderer. Apparently the power of the medicine is augmented if the murdered person is a kinsman.

Second, the murder is carefully planned and executed by a number of persons working together, never individually.

Third, flesh must be cut off the victim *while he or she is still alive.*

Fourth, the victim must then die, or be killed.

Fifth, the body of the victim, far from being hidden, is usually placed after an interval in some conspicuous spot where it is certain to be found.

Nevertheless, sixth, some attempt is made to give the impression that the death was accidental. But the authorities are never deceived by this, inasmuch as the victim will almost certainly have been subjected to the most frightful mutilations, which could not possibly have occurred by a fall or other accident.

Here is Case No. 47, as summarized in the Jones Report:

> First accused plotted with 10 other accused and 2 Crown witnesses to kill deceased for medicine to "strengthen" his village. The body was first "ironed" with hot stones then a portion of left eye, part of an ear, of the breast, of the flesh near kidneys and of the testicles were excised. Parts cut were "ironed" to stop bleeding. Deceased was left still alive in a donga where he was seen by a herdboy. He was killed a day or so later and he was eventually found under the "Vulture Cliff."

In one case the executioner was a doctor of medicine attached to a government hospital. In another a young woman was murdered by her father-in-law, who needed flesh particularly from her eyebrows. In another the victim was killed by having boiling water poured down her throat "and a hole made in the top of her head," and in still another the victim had to be blind, so that justice would similarly be "blind" if the case came to trial. Several case histories hinge on nothing more than a dispute over land. In one the victim had to be a woman who had just given birth to a child; the price paid to murder her was £5. In Case No. 37 a young man was ordered by a chief to find a victim for medicine; he failed to do so, and so was killed himself. In another the motive was to get medicine to assist a lawyer in "court cases and make grain plentiful."

MEDICINE MURDER IN BASUTOLAND

Perhaps the most revolting of all is No. 64 (October 19, 1947):

Deceased went off on a Sunday to fish. He was seized by the accused, carried under a cliff and mutilated. Persons who came on the scene were forced to join in; one Khoali refused but was asked to by the deceased who said: "Brother-in-law, agree to cut me so that they will let you live to look after my children." *Diretlo* included flesh from the tongue, eyelids, palate, armpits, testicles, buttocks, part of the intestines withdrawn through the anus, and blood drawn from a puncture made in the throat with an umbrella rib. Blood was kept in a bottle, the intestines in a dish. The body was hidden and later thrown into a river where it was found a fortnight later two miles lower down. First accused was said to need a person for medicine to strengthen his village.

*

The Basuto murders reach very high places indeed in the country, because of an extraordinarily complex and difficult dynastic situation.

The ruling class in Basutoland derives from Moshesh, who created the nation after the Zulu wars and ruled it singlehanded for almost fifty years, from around 1820 till his death in 1870. Moshesh was a very considerable personage indeed. His father was eaten by cannibals. He wore as a rule an American-style stovepipe hat. He had distinct statesmanlike qualities, and it was he who turned to the British for protection, although they would probably have taken the country over in any case sooner or later. Moshesh had, like most African chiefs, a large number of descendants, and these still completely dominate the political and social life of Basutoland. They are the chiefs and subchiefs in almost every district, they are all interrelated through their descent from the fountain-like Moshesh, and they call themselves the Sons of Moshesh. There are 1,330 Sons of Moshesh in all today, and every one is a cousin or some other relative to all the rest.

After Moshesh died the succession eventually reached one of his grandsons, by name Griffith, who ruled from 1913 to 1939 under the title paramount chief, and who was almost as strong a man as Moshesh. Griffith had three wives, all sisters, and two sons by two different wives, named Seeiso and Bereng. Seeiso succeeded to the paramountcy after Griffith, despite fierce opposition. Then, a year later, Seeiso died; probably he was poisoned, and his death threw the whole genealogical chart wide open.

By Basuto custom Seeiso's half-brother, Bereng, should have succeeded him. But for a variety of reasons Bereng was not permitted to succeed, and the paramountcy passed instead to Seeiso's senior widow, a remarkable lady named Amelia 'Mantsebo Seeiso, who—the kernel of the story—is paramount chieftainess today. (The apostrophe before the "M" in " 'Mantsebo" means, by Basuto terminology, that she is a mother.) 'Mantsebo has a daughter, but no sons. One of her stepsons was chosen to be heir apparent, but he was—and is—a minor. So 'Mantsebo today is not only paramount chieftainess, but regent, holding the paramountcy until this boy, who is now seventeen, becomes of age. Until then—under the British, of course—she is titular ruler of the country.[3]

But Bereng and his faction of chiefs bitterly opposed 'Mantsebo, just as they had contested the choice of Seeiso. Bereng wanted the paramountcy himself. And the British probably would have preferred Bereng to a complicated, unstable regency under a woman. But the decision to exclude Bereng had been taken by a solemn conclave of all the great chiefs, the Sons of Moshesh, and it is almost always British policy to let Africans settle their own dynastic affairs up to a point. Bereng brought suit in the High Court to oust 'Mantsebo, and lost. But he still sought rule, and even without it he remained the second most important personage in the country, as the son of Griffith and brother-in-law to 'Mantsebo.

Now another character must be mentioned—Principal Chief Gabashane Masupha, a grandson of Moshesh and as such a close relative to all the others. Gabashane, who ranked as the fourth most important person in Basutoland, had been one of the chiefs mainly responsible for choosing Seeiso instead of Bereng. Naturally, he expected to be rewarded when 'Mantsebo, Seeiso's widow, became regent. But it seems that he was not rewarded enough. So he left 'Mantsebo's camp, and joined Bereng in a relentless fight against her.

It is this sinister feud and its ramifications that have produced most of the recent murders. Both sides resorted to the murder of innocent people, to provide medicine, when other means to advance their ends failed. A sentence in the Jones Report conveys what many Basuto must have been thinking. "How was it that Seeiso's widow ('Mantsebo) was able to secure the rejection of Bereng's legitimate claim? There could be only one answer—by magic, by the use of *diretlo* medicine." The report goes on: "The primary cause of these murders or of their sudden increase is that they were employed *by the Regent* [italics mine] to support her claim against Chief Bereng." Then Bereng and Gabashane retaliated with more murders, and politics in Basutoland became a "kind of battle of medicine horns," with murder countered by more murder, and no end in sight.

[3] The boy, Constantinus Bereng Seeiso, went to London for the coronation of Queen Elizabeth in 1953. The paramount chieftainess bitterly opposed his going, because the trip might give him modern ideas. The two do not get on well together.

There was, however, an end for Principal Chiefs Bereng and Gabashane. The police were watching them. They were arrested for a ritual murder, tried, then arrested for a second murder, tried again, convicted, and eventually executed in 1949. Their execution came only after long delay and an appeal to the Privy Council in London. Most people in Basutoland never dreamed that they would actually be hanged. But they were hanged. And this caused, naturally, a great sensation in Basutoland. It was almost as if two prominent members of the cabinet should be hanged in Washington.

Murders tapered off after this for a time. Nobody, it seemed, could oppose the paramount chieftainess with any hope of success—her medicine was much too strong.

*

Cannot these murders be stopped? Why do the British tolerate 'Mantsebo as paramount chieftainess and regent? First, as we know, they are always loath to interfere with purely African quarrels, or to modify tribal customs, if their own interests are not at stake. Second, the young heir, 'Mantsebo's stepson, will accede to the paramountcy before long, and the British hope that under him things will be better. Third, dismissal of the regent now would make a first-rate political crisis, and might split the country. Fourth, even with the best will in the world, it would probably be impossible to abolish the tradition and practice of medicine murder altogether.

'Mantsebo is not spoken of with much affection in Basutoland, but I had the feeling that she is respected, as well as feared. The dominant trait in her character, people say, is suspiciousness. And no wonder. She has a small farm near Maseru, works hard on it, and is not eager to give up her salary as paramount chieftainess, which is £3,600 per year. By her own lights, she is a patriot. She knows well what Basutoland needs most—more schools, better communications, and above all agricultural improvement. She derives naturally from her environment. And it should be pointed out carefully that she has never been accused of any crime, although her name was mentioned in at least one trial and although the Jones Report explicitly puts responsibility for some murders on the quarrel between the Regency and Bereng.[4]

We met 'Mantsebo at a *pitso* (conclave or mass meeting) in Maseru, and then at a garden party given by the British Resident Commissioner. She came late, looked surly, and departed soon. She wore a dowdy hat and

[4] Her daughter, by name Ntsebo Nkhahle Lebona, has, however, been tried for murder (not a medicine murder—she was accused of poisoning a man with arsenic) but acquitted, and her closest friend, a chief named Matlere Lerotholi in her home district of Mokhotling, was also recently accused of murder and arrested, but released after investigation.

western dress—a dark red suit over an unbuttoned pink cardigan sweater—and stood rigidly among her courtiers, her head bobbing jerkily as she recognized people. She acknowledged the greetings of the company without smiling, and kept giving quick, nervous, grunting commands to underlings. She is somewhat fat, and her face has the color and almost the size and shape of a large baked potato.

A FEW WORDS MORE ABOUT BASUTOLAND

We took the Mountain Road out of Maseru; of this only twenty-four miles have been built so far, but eventually it will cut through the sandstone cliffs and wind-swept escarpments all the way to Natal. The season was summer, but at one pass (8,400 feet) we stepped out into the first snow we had seen since Kilimanjaro and, before that, the Atlas. We had two guides, the British head of the Agricultural Department, and a youthful African chief, Nksoke Molapu, who is a great-great-great-great-grandson of the immortal Moshesh. We passed Matsieng, where the paramount chieftainess has her farm and where she still likes to dig with her own hands, and Roma College, a Catholic institution run by French Canadian missionaries, where the heir apparent is being schooled. We saw the table mountain called Thababosiu, on which grows exactly one tree (sacred to Moshesh), and visited Morija, where the Paris Evangelical Mission (Protestant) has had headquarters since 1861, and where one of the best small printing presses in Africa (it issues books in thirty-three languages) is located. At one village we had political talk with a group of young, progressive chiefs, and in another learned something about what is even a more serious problem to Basutoland than medicine murder—soil erosion.

Catholic missionaries are very active here. If a new church has a corrugated iron roof, instead of straw, it is bound to be Catholic, because only the Catholics can afford such a luxury. Ironically enough, the money comes from Quebec, a country almost (perhaps I am exaggerating slightly) as poor as Basutoland. The Christian tradition goes far back. Moshesh had a French Protestant missionary as his "foreign minister" in the 1840's.

An American agricultural engineer visited Basutoland recently, and exclaimed, "This is the most *beautiful* erosion I have ever seen!" What he meant was that the country is being eaten to death by erosion on a truly spectacular scale. Much good work is being done to counteract this. One device is "rotational grazing," whereby flocks use alternately the warm and cold slopes of the steep, bleak mountains. Basuto officials called "grazing control caretakers" are posted throughout the country, and the scheme is paid for by the tax on mohair. One dangerous pest is a bush called the bitter karroo, which destroys grass. Basutoland has more livestock than it can handle, and "destocking" projects are under way. The authorities want to cut the goat population from 690,000 to 200,000, and are exporting goat meat to India. This is one part of Africa not touched by the tsetse fly, and so the herds proliferate. There are more than a million and a half sheep in the country, 400,000 cattle, and 100,000 horses.

Relations between Basutoland, the Union of South Africa, and Great Britain are extraordinarily intricate. We saw few external signs of color bar—a refreshing change from the Union. Africans are allowed to drink, and, wonder of wonders, even women may go into bars. Another cardinal difference between Basutoland and the Union is that the British permit no white settlement of any kind in Basuto territory. Whites are not allowed to own land, and all mineral and subsoil wealth belongs to the state.[5]

South Africa has an acute, compelling interest in Basutoland. This is the watershed for the Orange River, on which much of the Union's life depends. Moreover it is an essential reservoir of man power for the Rand mines. About two-thirds of all Basuto boys go to the mines at one time or other, and they are the best native labor force the mine operators have. They are recruited through an organization known as the Native Recruiting Corporation. But if the Union needs Basutoland, so does Basutoland need the Union. There are no jobs for the boys at home. As the Jones Report says, a young man to earn a living has to get out of the country. Also Basutoland is supported in part by a share of the Union's customs receipts, is completely surrounded by the Union geographically, and could not live without mealie meal imported from the Union. If trouble should occur between Great Britain and South Africa, the Union could starve out Basutoland in a matter of weeks. Few countries in the world are more vulnerable.

The Strijdom government wants, as a matter of prime policy, to absorb Basutoland and the other High Commission territories into the Union when possible. The Basuto nation wants at all costs to keep this from happening. The British certainly do not relish the idea of turning the Basuto over to the tender mercies of *apartheid*, which would obviously mean the end of the Basuto nation, but they have to adopt a cautious line. After all, Basutoland *is* incontrovertibly part of the Union, except politically, and they could not possibly prevent the Strijdom government from taking it

---

[5] Officially Basutoland is a full-fledged colony, not a protectorate, and Basutolanders are British subjects. But although it is a colony it is run by the Commonwealth Relations Office in London, not the Colonial Office—another example of the elasticity of British administrative methods.

over by force. One reason why the British tolerate 'Mantsebo is that she vigorously opposes incorporation of Basutoland into the Union. We heard her make a speech to this effect. Her line is, "Dear British, please keep us yours!"

Lively political development has occurred in Basutoland recently. A Basutoland National Congress has been organized, on the pattern of similar organizations we have seen elsewhere, under the leadership of N.M. Nts'ekhe, the secretary, and Ntsu Mokhehle, the president. One of its recent manifestos, an ably presented document, makes three main points—first, resistance to the uttermost against absorption of Basutoland by the Union; second, a demand for full self-government from the British; third, a plea to the British for racial equality in the Basutoland administration, appointment of more Basuto civil servants, and so on. The Basuto make much of such facts as that they are not a conquered nation, asked to be taken in by the British in the last century of their own free will, had close treaty relations with Queen Victoria, and have always been loyal to the British crown. "Britain," the manifesto says, "has no moral, political, or legal right to discuss Basuto affairs without our consent or behind our backs." One astringent issue is enlargement of the democratic process within Basutoland itself. At present administration is headed by an appointed body called the Basutoland Council. The Resident Commissioner (British) is chairman, and the Paramount Chieftainess nominates fifty-two of the hundred members. Recent reforms proposed by the British do not satisfy the Congress. In fact papers embodying them have been publicly burned in the Maseru streets. What the Basuto want—both the old-line sons of Moshesh and the younger chiefs—is a genuine Legislative Council, elected by the people, with progress toward responsible government assured.

In other words, the same type of political fermentation we have seen almost everywhere else in Africa exists even in such an isolated, inexpressibly remote little enclave as Basutoland. To ticket it with the formal word "nationalist" would probably be going too far, since Basutoland is hardly capable of existing alone as a nation. "Nationalism," here as elsewhere in southern Africa, is too blunt a term to convey satisfactorily the confused, wildly fluid mixture of protest, hope, unsettlement, despair, and desire for change that distinguishes native peoples just reaching the threshold of modern times. But nationalism is *part* of this effervescence. We met one white official of the mine recruitment organization, who said, "I am sending my children to Canada. This continent is washed up. What I mean is that *we* are washed up on this continent. All this part of Africa will be black within thirty years."

SWAZILAND: UP FROM GIN AND GREYHOUNDS

The Swazi are milder people than the Basuto, and their country is less angular and chill. Swaziland has mellow rivers, forests, and a low-lying "bushveld" adjoining Portuguese East Africa. It is hemmed in by the Transvaal and the Drakensberg mountains on the other three sides. Swaziland is one of the smallest countries in Africa—about the size of Wales—and has only about 200,000 people, of whom perhaps 3,500 are white South Africans or Europeans. Swazis are a derivative of the Zulus, but are less warlike in background, and have their own highly individual characteristics.

The ruler of Swaziland is Paramount Chief Sobhuza II, sometimes called the "King." His native title is the Ngwenyama (lion) of Swaziland. He belongs to a clan that has ruled for several generations, and was originally named Mona, which means "jealousy." Sobhuza II is a stout character. He was born in 1899, and has been paramount chief since 1921, after a long regency under his grandmother, a lady named Labotsibeni. He was educated at Lovedale in the Cape Province. His manner of rule (under the British) is both dictatorial and enlightened, within a democratic framework. Nobody knows as much about Swaziland as he does. He has family connections in every grove and crevice. He is supposed to have no fewer than ninety-three wives, selected from all parts of the country, and children beyond count or estimate. The legend that he has six toes on each foot is inaccurate.

King Sobhuza's mother is dead, but by inflexible Swazi custom the nation must have a Queen Mother, and one of his aunts therefore occupies this exalted position. She is known as the Ndhlovukati, or Cow Elephant. Her constitutional position is very important, and she must be consulted as a matter of right on all political and national affairs. Swaziland only covers 6,704 square miles, but it has three capitals. The headquarters of the British administration is at Mbabane, in the central high veld. Eleven miles away is Lozithlezi, the seat of Sobhuza's government. The Queen Mother lives at Lobamba, twenty-seven miles further away, where the royal kraal is situated. Most of the national festivals and ceremonial displays characteristic of the Swazi people occur at Lobamba, where the Queen Mother rules with a hand of iron. There are two kinds of rain in Swaziland, fierce rain accompanied by thunder and lightning, which is made only by the paramount chief, and gentle rain, which is made only by the Queen Mother. Even witch doctors cannot make rain, if the paramount chief and Queen Mother do not co-operate.

Inheritance is not by primogeniture in Swaziland, and nobody knows who Sobhuza's successor will be. The elders of the tribe will, when the time comes, select the new King (with British advice) on the basis of the reputation in the community of the boy's mother, not the boy himself. The fact that there is no heir apparent makes it impossible to educate and train a successor, a phenomenon widespread in Africa.[6] The British do their best consequently to give *all* the royal children as good an education as possible, which imposes a certain strain on the school system.

The Swazis are among the most colorful people in Africa. The women soak their hair with soap, and then (in the Zulu fashion) build it up in a kind of tower or mane. This they wear permanently, but the whole coif is cut off if the husband dies. Most Swazis carry assegais, and are fierce-looking; men are often dressed in nothing more than a loincloth, and women wear a soft skirt made of hide and smothered in grease. The Swazi do not circumcise. Witch-doctoring is illegal, and it is an offense to wear the secret beads associated with black magic. Legitimate herbalists are registered and licensed. Ritual murder is uncommon. One celebrated Swazi pageant is linked with the coming of the rain; a jet-black bull is led into the royal kraal, and slaughtered by being *pommeled* to death by Swazi youths. The process takes a long time. Then a holy fire is lit, which the new rain must put out. If rain does not come, something very serious indeed is the matter.

Swaziland has an excellent administration, one of the best in Africa, but certain primitivenesses still survive. The British took the country over in 1903. It had no postage of its own until last year; the courts still mete out three grades of punishment: imprisonment, fines up to £100, and "whipping not exceeding fifteen strokes."[7]

The old legend is that the Boers bought the Transvaal with beads and brandy—that is, got native chiefs to surrender their land for practically nothing—and that the British did the same thing in Swaziland with "gin and greyhounds." Before the turn of the century the Swazi King was Mbandzeni, a feckless ruler; he gave most of the country away to Britons from South Africa, concession hunters and other riffraff. He was crazy about greyhounds. Thousands of these were brought into the country as gifts, and some of their canine descendants survive today. Likewise a strong white settler group survives. Some farmers from the Transvaal have large tracts of grazing land, but do not live in the country. This makes the chief difference between Swaziland and Basutoland, where, as we have just seen, white settle-

---

[6] The same thing occurs in Moslem Africa; for instance, northern Nigeria. See Chapter 39 below.
[7] *Swaziland*, Colonial Reports, 1952, p. 39.

ment and the ownership of land by whites are forbidden. About half of Swaziland is, in sharp contrast, white-owned.[8]

Swaziland is much less advanced politically than Basutoland, but more advanced economically. The country is, in fact, the scene of some of the liveliest economic developments in southern Africa. The Colonial Development Corporation has here several of its most successful projects on the entire continent, in particular an afforestation program and the development of rice fields. Private investors are also busy. Swaziland is (or should be) a paradise for the hydroelectric engineer. Also there are important mineral deposits, and two-fifths of the country's income comes from a celebrated asbestos mine.

Swaziland has a European Advisory Council, elected by the European members of the community, which has advisory powers on purely European affairs, and on the African side, a National Council called the Ibandhla. Representative government does not exist as yet, nor has Swaziland any nationalist movement or political party or National Congress. Legislation proposed by the British must be approved by the Ibandhla, so that in effect a parallel system of government exists. *Every* adult male Swazi is, in theory, a member of the Ibandhla, and may attend its meetings once a year. This is democracy carried to the point of *reductio ad absurdum*, and the procedure is so unwieldy that another body functions, called the Iqoqo. But this, the "eyes and ears of the paramount chief," is also too large for comfort. What really counts is a small executive committee (all African) chosen out of the Iqoqo, which meets with the British Resident Commissioner once a week.

Race relations are good in Swaziland, and there is little racial tension, even though most of the Europeans are South African or of South African descent. Britons and Boers get along well together too. The agitations that afflict the Union and Basutoland are not much in evidence. Swaziland is still a backwater. It has no growing pains, because it has hardly begun to grow. The only political issue is that of future incorporation into the Union, a prospect which Britons and Swazis both view with extreme distaste.

TSHEKEDI KHAMA AND BECHUANALAND

Bechuanaland, in strong contrast to Basutoland and Swaziland, is a huge territory, covering about 275,000 square miles. It is bigger than Texas. The population is 290,000, and includes about 2,900 Europeans—exactly

[8] But an elaborate scheme has been put into effect recently whereby the Swazi are being helped to buy back their old holdings. About a third of the country is now solely for the use of Africans.

1 per cent of the total. Bechuanaland is bounded by the Union, South-West Africa, the Caprivi strip, and Southern Rhodesia, and at least half the area is taken up by the desolate wastes of the Kalahari desert. If anybody wants to have proof of what an empty continent Africa is, all he needs do is visit Bechuanaland. The economy is based almost exclusively on cattle. The country would be even less well known than it is, except for the fact that the single track north-south railway connecting Rhodesia with Johannesburg slices through its eastern edge, giving it a spine. Bechuanaland has one uniqueness: it must be the only country in the world whose capital is outside its own frontiers. This is Mafeking, a town on the railway in Union territory, a few miles from the Bechuana border.

But Bechuanaland, for all its sparse emptiness and infertility, has a vividly colorful history. Here Dr. Livingstone worked for some years, and married Miss Moffat, the daughter of one of the earliest and greatest of all British missionaries in Africa, Robert Moffat of Kuruman. The territory lay athwart the parched route of the first British adventurers working their way from the Cape to the Rhodesias, and some tiny isolated European communities still exist, like Ghanzi, which are white Tobacco Roads. Cecil Rhodes called Bechuanaland "the Suez Canal to the north." In 1895 the territory was annexed to the Cape of Good Hope, to keep it from the Boers, and has been British territory ever since. It is a protectorate these days, not a colony. Not only does the Union government covet it; so does Southern Rhodesia. The Rhodesians make a strong historical case for incorporation of the northern half of Bechuanaland at least into the new Central African Federation.

British administration is very loose, because Bechuanaland is not a country in any real sense, but an amalgamation of tribal groups, each of which have autonomous rule to a degree, under their own hereditary chiefs. The most important tribe, and one of the most distinctive in all Africa, is the Bamangwato, which numbers about 100,000 people, covers roughly half the country, and has its own capital, Serowe, thirty-two miles inland from the railway. Other tribes of consequence, each of which has a redolent history, and which are sturdily independent to this day, are the Bangwaketse (under Chief Bathoen), the Batawana (under a regent, Mrs. E.P. Moremi), and the Bakwena (Chief Kgari).

A great man named Khama III lived from 1838 to 1923, and ruled the Bamangwato for fifty-one uninterrupted years. He was a friend of Livingstone's and a devout Christian, full of reforming zeal. The legend is that he and Livingstone between them made Bechuanaland prohibitionist, which it has been ever since. It is a pity to have to pass over the life of a man as remarkable as Khama with a bare sentence. He lived to be ninety-three. Practically singlehanded, he created the Bechuanaland we know today. He was succeeded on his death by his eldest son, Sekgoma II, who died after a brief reign. The succession then passed to Sekgoma's son, who was only four years old, a boy named Seretse Khama. The Bamangwato system of rule is democratic in the extreme, and decisions on matters like these are taken by the tribe as a whole, through the *Kgotla* or tribal assembly. Obviously there had to be a regent during Seretse's minority, and the *Kgotla* decided that this should be a young man, Tshekedi Khama, who was Khama III's youngest son, and thus an uncle of Seretse's. Tshekedi was only twenty-three at the time his regency began in 1926. He ruled the Bamangwato for almost twenty-five years, and set up a record for progressive, stable, beneficent administration that has not been matched in contemporary Africa. He was a cattleman, like most of his people, and did much to improve the quality of the local stock by selective breeding. He was passionately interested in agricultural reform. He worked hard on educational projects and built the first (and only) secondary school in Bechuanaland. Tshekedi was tough, energetic, a realist, and a reformer. By any count, he is one of the ablest men in Africa, and I have heard seasoned Britons describe him as "the best African on the continent."

Not that he did not have lively brushes with the British. Once he refused to accept the legality of an administrative measure announced by the High Commissioner in Pretoria, and brought suit against him, an unheard-of act. In 1939 came something unprecedented and even more sensational. A white man in Serowe made persistent trouble, and was arrested on the charge of molesting native women. Tshekedi had him tried exactly as any other offender would be tried, black or white, and he was sentenced to be flogged. The storm created by this can be well imagined. A black man made a white man submit to corporal punishment! The Union rocked. A hotheaded, trueblue British naval officer was Acting High Commissioner in South Africa at the time, and sent a force (by land) all the way from the Cape of Good Hope to Serowe to avenge this infamy, and throw Tshekedi bodily out of office. Tshekedi was duly deposed. But he found strong support in liberal circles in London, and within a month he was back in office again, vindicated and triumphant.[9]

Meantime, he saw to it that his nephew, Seretse, for whom he was regent, got a good education. Seretse went to Balliol College, Oxford, studied law, and gave promise of a good career. In 1949-50 came the noisiest *cause célèbre* in recent British colonial history, which made gross headlines in the tabloid press all over the world. This cost Tshekedi his regency, Seretse his throne, and Bechuanaland its continuity of administration. What happened was that Seretse fell in love with and married a white English girl,

[9] Tshekedi Khama, a profile in the London *Observer*, June 3, 1951.

Miss Ruth Williams. Tshekedi vigorously opposed the marriage. He is proud of his color and inheritance even as white men are of theirs, and he did not think it right or wise for the ruling house of Bechuanaland to be mixed, with the possibility of a mulatto heir. He was willing, however, to put up the matter to the national *Kgotla*. This decided first for Tshekedi, and then reversed itself and took Seretse's side. Indignation began to rise vehemently and vindictively in the Union and the Rhodesias. The hard-shell whites were unspeakably shocked at the idea that a white woman should become the wife of a paramount chief—in effect a queen—in their area. In the end London had to intervene. Tshekedi voluntarily left Bamangwato territory, and went into exile in the Bakwena country nearby, in order not to prejudice the case; he did not want to be put in the position of seeming to be an opponent or rival to Seretse. The British took advantage of this situation with neat alertness, and suspended *both* Tshekedi and Seretse from their functions. Seretse was not allowed to remain in Bechuanaland, even though his wife stayed there for a time, and Tshekedi was forbidden to rejoin the Bamangwato. Few people have ever been able to understand why the British took action against Tshekedi. It seemed, and still seems, utterly unreasonable as well as self-damaging and self-defeating. Even the wisest of imperial powers make blunders, though not many as inexplicable as this. The whole affair became a dreary mess. No doubt the authorities in London felt that, if Tshekedi returned to power, agitation for the return of Seretse would be incessant, since Tshekedi wanted to abide by the decision of the *Kgotla*. The future of the *tribe* (so the British say) "demanded a solution."

But there has been no solution. Tshekedi has been allowed to return to the Bamangwato reserve as a private citizen, but he is barred from any political activity. Seretse and his wife live in England, but cannot come back to Bechuanaland, and he has been permanently excluded from the chieftainship. Rule is carried on by a "temporary" British administration. Time and time again the British have tried to persuade the Bamangwato to elect a new paramount chief, but they refuse to do so. The tribe is demoralized, and much of the sound hope that Tshekedi gave the country has been lost. The situation is almost what it might be in Denmark if the people were deprived of their King, or if the United States had no President for year after year.

*

We conclude now with the Union and its peripheral states. But for a considerable time to come the influence of the Union will still be with us.

CHAPTER 29

Portuguese Africa

In the region of the Unknown, Africa is the Absolute
—VICTOR HUGO

WE HAVE many times in these pages mentioned the Portuguese, their intrepid wayfaring and exploratory zeal. They contributed much to Africa quite apart from the indentations they made on its blunt shores all the way from the Gold Coast to Ethiopia, and the early forts and settlements they built. They brought into Africa for the first time commodities (which became basic crops) like corn, manioc, and tobacco, and some authorities think that they—not traders from Arabia—were the first to introduce the oil palm and even bananas, which they brought over from the West Indies. Many words used widely in Africa today by Europeans and Africans alike, particularly on the West Coast, have a Portuguese origin, like *palavar, dash,* and *fetish*. Also the Portuguese introduced to black Africans the hammock and the guitar.

The old Portuguese trading posts and settlements scattered along the coasts have long since disappeared, or were taken over by other European powers. Today Portuguese Africa consists mainly of two immense blocks of territory, Mozambique on the East Coast, and Angola on the West, separated from each other by the Rhodesias, the Belgian Congo, and the Union. They are all that remains importantly of the old Portuguese empire in Africa, but they are large enough to make Portugal the third biggest colonial power in the world, second only to Britain and France. Portuguese Africa is generally thought of as being nothing but a backwoods wilderness, inexpressibly remote, forlorn, and primitive. And this is indeed partly true. Very few people ever see Mozambique or Angola, and the Portuguese authorities do not encourage promiscuous visitation except by tourists in the coastal cities. The interior is largely terra incognita, and the natives living there are among the most backward and untutored on the continent. But, as always, Africa is full of surprises. Portuguese Africa is a hundred years behind the times—yes. But ports in Angola and Mozambique are connected by the only transcontinental railroad on the continent. Portuguese Africa is for the most part mangy and derelict—yes. But Lourenço Marques, the capital of Mozambique, has the best equipped high school we saw in all Africa, the most attractive little department store, and one of the best hotels.

These least known of all African countries have several other points of interest, as to wit:

Mozambique and Angola are not colonies, or protectorates, or dependencies, or even territories. They are, on the contrary, integral and organic parts of Portugal itself, with the rank of "provinces"; technically they do not differ from the suburbs of Lisbon, and from the point of view of administration, politics, law, and so on they are as much a part of Portugal as the Orkneys are part of the British Isles. This is a new development, dating from constitutional changes in 1951, whereby Portugal officially became an "*Afro*-European" power.

What this means, of course, is that Mozambique and Angola are run by the Ministério do Ultramar in Lisbon, which in turn, like everything else in Portugal, is run by the country's dictator, Dr. Antonio de Oliveira Salazar. The aim of the device is to perpetuate colonial rule forever. Lisbon is the boss, with no nonsense about it. A strong Governor General on the spot (like the present Governor General of Mozambique, Captain Gabriel Teixeira) may, of course, be a powerful influence on Lisbon; nobody at home would be likely to reject the doughty advice of Captain Teixeira. The fact remains that the Portuguese overseas provinces are ruled exactly as Portugal itself is ruled, by authoritarian methods. The press is censored, the secret police are proficient, and elections do not mean anything even if they do take place. It is quite true that Mozambique has a local "Governor General's Council," with five official and five non-official members (on the pattern of British Africa), and that it sends two deputies to Lisbon (on the pattern of French Africa south of the Sahara). But no faintest idea exists of development toward political freedom or self-government. Any such evolution is excluded. Nationalism is firmly suppressed, if it is even heard of, and political organization by Africans is unknown.

On the other hand, as we shall see below, Portuguese Africa has virtually no color bar. The character of Portuguese rule is difficult to describe fairly, because it reflects such conflicting elements. It resembles Belgian rule in the Congo to an extent, in that it has a strong paternalistic streak, but administration is not nearly so efficient as in the Congo. Both Angola and Mozambique are reminiscent of Brazil—racially mixed, easygoing, and full of "do-it-tomorrow-ism." But the Portuguese, for all their temperateness, employ some measures harsher than anything else we shall see in Africa. The Portuguese domains have, in a word, an atmosphere composed at one and the same time of backwardness, sterility, racial ease, ruthlessness, a vague feeling for future spiritual uplift, and, believe it or not, charm. The chief problems are poverty to an extreme degree (the average wage in Mozambique is about 10 cents a day) and lack of education. Most schools are run by Catholic missions, not by the state, and only limited funds have been available. Probably the percentage of illiteracy is higher than in any comparable region on the continent. In the whole of Angola there are exactly sixty-eight African high school students.

*

The worst thing about Portuguese Africa is forced labor. Not only does this still exist; the Portuguese authorities admit that it exists, say that it is necessary and even a "good thing" for its victims, and condone it. They call it "directed labor." In Mozambique every able-bodied man must work for six months a year unless he is a landowner and can prove that he has put in an equivalent amount of work on his own property. That every man should work is, the government holds, an "essential element in the civilizing process." But the system has manifest abuses. It is not quite—but almost—a form of slavery. The man becomes a chattel. The system works more or less like this. An upcountry planter informs the government that he needs so-and-so many men, and these are provided for him by the local *Chefe do Posto*, or district officer. Native recruiters go out into the villages, and collect the necessary number of men, who are then turned over to the planter. But the planter, to be sure of getting all the recruits he needs, usually has to pay off the *Chefe do Posto*, if this latter gentleman happens to be corrupt. The normal "pay-off" is ten times the contract laborer's wages for six months. Nothing more vicious can be imagined. The *Chefe do Posto* naturally contrives to gather up as many laborers as possible, in order to make more money. In any case he gets ten times what the laborer gets! On top of the initial iniquity of forced labor itself is a worse iniquity—government officials make a profit out of it. The pay-off system is illegal, but widespread. If a *Chefe do Posto* has a record particularly flagrant and malodorous, he may be transferred out of the bush and assigned to a post in some metropolitan area, like Beira, where no opportunity exists for cashing in on the forced labor traffic. I heard one high official say ironically, "Unfortunately there aren't enough jobs in Beira for everybody!"

The contractor or planter who employs forced labor must, by law, provide food and shelter of a sort for his workers, make medical facilities available, and pay them a minimum wage. But this is miserably small.

The government itself also "hires" forced labor for work on the roads, which as a rule is not paid any wage at all. The Africans conscripted are usually those who have failed to pay their hut tax. But sometimes a local *Chefe do Posto* simply corrals gangs of men and puts them to work if, for instance, the roads in his district are particularly bad and he wants to impress his superiors by improving them.

Some unlucky Africans, particularly those who have had trouble with the police or have been convicted of minor crimes, are deported to São Tomé and Principe, two small Portuguese islands in the Gulf of Guinea, which have pronounced labor shortages. Here they do forced or "directed" labor on the cocoa fields in circumstances barely distinguishable from slavery. São Tomé is a name Portuguese Africans dread, and with reason. The legend is that if a man is shipped there he never returns. Serious rioting occurred in São Tomé in February, 1953, largely because of intolerable working conditions. The authorities in Lisbon, be it said to their credit, took prompt steps to make things better, and the Governor was recalled and replaced. But the *system* still goes on.

A standard punishment in Portuguese Africa is beating of the hands with a weapon known as the *baramatola*, a kind of ping-pong bat pierced with holes. If a man is picked up for a minor offense, he is as a rule given a sharp bastinado with this, and then released. The palms of the victim usually blister painfully, because of the holes in the bat. But no lasting injury ensues, unless a bone or two happens to be crushed, and the Portuguese say that this method of punishment is simpler, cheaper, and more effective than sending men to prison. The death penalty has been abolished in some areas. A convicted murderer has shackles welded to his ankles, and then is let free to stumble where he wills out in the bush.

Every African servant in a European family must carry a book certifying his position, and this must be signed by the employer *every* day. If an employer forgets to do so and the police, checking on passbooks, happen to pick the boy up, punishment is swift—his head is cropped and he is sent out to work on the roads or imprisoned. The white employer is *not* informed, but if his servant fails to appear some morning he has a pretty good idea of what must have happened and he can go to the police and bail the unfortunate boy out, if anybody can find him.

THE ASSIMILADO SYSTEM AND COLOR BAR

All this being said, there is much to say on the other side. The most salient and striking characteristic of Portuguese Africa is that it has no official color bar. There are no signs "For Europeans Only," no segregated waiting rooms in the airports, no prohibition of alcohol (indeed Africans are actively encouraged to drink Portuguese wine), and no segregation in transportation, banks, shops, the post office, or even in the schools. I walked into a travel bureau. At adjacent desks were two full Negroes, one white man, two Indians, and two mulattoes. I went to the museum. The official in charge was an African. We met mulatto teachers, government servants, and nurses working side by side with whites. There are no pass laws except for domestic servants, and a white man mistreating a native is subject to severe punishment.[1] At once, arriving in Lourenço Marques from Johannesburg, the visitor feels an acute sense of social amelioration and relief. The stubborn bigotry and intolerance of the Union become yesterday's bad dream. One high official told us, "The color of the skin—pouf!—what does it matter?" What a contrast to the attitude in Durban or Pretoria!

Segregation does, however, still exist on social levels. No Portuguese governor would be likely to have a full Negro to dinner, nor would any of the foreign consuls resident in Lourenço Marques. But there is no ban for the most part on mulattoes, who are officially considered to be white. The excuse for discrimination against people fully black is that practically none have enough education or cultural background to be socially acceptable. One interesting point is that any African, even if he is as black as the Styx, may legally enter any hotel, restaurant, or café. Few, however, ever do so. It never occurs to them. They do not have money enough or proper clothes. But the fact that they *could* makes their resentment less acute. Also the circumstance that segregation is *not* enforced makes it (paradoxically enough) easier to enforce.[2]

Portuguese Africa has one unique phenomenon, the *assimilado* or *civilizado* system. Any native may rise from his status as an *indigena* and become "civilized" by a process of law. He passes certain tests (if he wants to) and

[1] So at least we were told in Lourenço Marques. In other towns circumstances may be different.
[2] Color bar trouble may come to Mozambique in the future, however, because of a general anti-black feeling among newly arrived white immigrants from Portugal. These are much less tolerant than the long-established white colonials, who are called "Mozambiquanos" or "Laurentinos," and who are proud of their sophistication and lack of bigotry.

then—presto!—becomes a white man instead of black, no matter what his color. This is a remarkable innovation, and serves a useful purpose in that it gives ambitious Africans opportunity, hope, and a kind of outlet, such as scarcely exists in the Union or the Rhodesias. The Portuguese think of it as a safety valve. It buys off potential discontent. When the time comes to cope with nationalism (so the Portuguese calculate), the Africans who count will already be assimilated, and will therefore make no trouble. It is interesting to note that the Belgians have recently begun to copy this system in the Congo; their *assimilados* are called *immatriculés*.

An African wishing to become assimilated and thus "civilized" applies to a local tribunal, which consists as a rule of one Portuguese official and two natives. He must prove to the satisfaction of the tribunal that he is literate in Portuguese, belongs to the Christian faith (which means in effect that he must be Catholic), has a certain financial standing, and is willing to give up native customs—for instance polygamy—and live in the European manner. The main thing is that he should be capable of adopting the white man's way of life. Once he becomes an *assimilado*, he assumes not only the privileges but the duties of full citizenship. He has the right to a passport, and may travel; his children are entitled to free education in the state schools; he takes precedence over other natives, has the right to vote, and does not have to pay hut tax, which is about $4.00 per year. On the other hand, he becomes subject to military service, loses the right of the unassimilated African to free medical service, and has to pay a European income tax higher than hut tax.

In the very long run the Portuguese (in theory) hope to assimilate *all* their Africans. Of course the catch to the whole system is that it is difficult almost beyond conception for an African to qualify. The Portuguese, at the same time that they open the door to *assimilados*, make it practically impossible for the average African to achieve a high school education or make enough money to live in the European manner, and thus have a chance to become assimilated. As of the moment, there are only a handful of *assimilados*—about 30,000 in Angola, and only 4,378 in Mozambique, out of a total population of more than nine million.

*

A proverb about Brazil in the slave trade days was that it was purgatory for a white man, hell for a Negro, and paradise for a mulatto. To a certain extent, this holds true for Portuguese Africa today. Many Portuguese cohabit with or even marry Negro women, and there is no stigma attached to being a mulatto. We heard one little story about a Portuguese official who arrived to take up a post in East Africa with seven children, who ranged in color from ebony to ivory. A far cry from Strijdom and Malan!

Mulattoes in Portuguese Africa, who are known as *Mistos* or *Misturados*, do not have to be assimilated since they are "white." If a European has a child by an African woman, even if the union is irregular, the child is treated automatically as a European, and may even be sent to Lisbon to school. There are, however, two classes among the *Mistos*—those descended from early colonists, who came of sound white stock and like as not from good African stock as well, and newer arrivals who represent a mixture of many nationalities and races, and are considerably less superior.[3]

Portuguese tolerance about color gives other Europeans in Africa headaches on occasion. I heard a British ambassador explode, "The Portuguese have no administration at all! They mistreat people horribly and are proud of their backwardness. Think of what would happen to us if we behaved in the Gold Coast the way the Portuguese do in Angola. But they are excused everything, because they have no color bar."

BENGUELA RAILROAD

This extraordinary railway was built largely by British interests to tap the Katanga ore fields in the Congo, and is still preponderantly British, owned through a company known as Tanganyika Concessions, Ltd., although Tanganyika is far away. The road cuts through some of the most desolate and primitive country any builder of railways ever faced. Its western terminus is Lobito, an Angolese port on the South Atlantic, and it traverses the great Angola plateau to a point above Elisabethville in the Congo. Then it links up with the Rhodesian railway system, serves Salisbury and other Rhodesian towns, and proceeds to Beira on the Indian Ocean, in Portuguese territory once more. The journey from Lobito to Elisabethville, the halfway mark, takes from 6:00 P.M. Friday to 8:00 A.M. Wednesday—one hundred and ten hours. A through service, with neat little *wagon-lits*, operates once a week. To get to Beira takes three and a half days more. The ocean to ocean journey, a distance of only 1,700 miles as the crow flies, requires almost nine full days, more than it takes the Trans-Siberian to cross Asia. If one should draw on a map of the United States a route analogous to that taken by this line, it would roughly go San Francisco-Minneapolis-Chicago-St.

[3] A powerful Indian community lives in Mozambique, mostly Goan. The Indians are white-collar workers, artisans, and in particular servants. No restriction on immigration from India exists, in strict contrast to the Union. But Indians, even if they are Portuguese citizens from Goa, are discriminated against in various petty ways.

Louis-Mobile-Atlanta-Jacksonville. Such convolutions! And there are only two main intersections on the whole crazy elongated route! But I should also mention that we traveled on Rhodesian Railways over part of this distance, and I have seldom ridden on a more comfortable, efficiently run train.

Perhaps it is incorrect to call this the "only" transcontinental line in Africa, since the Union can also be crossed by rail. But to do so involves a procedure even more involved and tedious, although the distance is shorter. The eastern terminus of this railway is also in Portuguese territory, at Lourenço Marques.

A WORD ON MOZAMBIQUE

Under the flamboyant trees and the jacarandas out of season
The avenue lies quiet, like a dog in the dust.
"Quite like home," they say,
And the paint on the concrete villas
Curls up like sunburnt skin on shoulders
Caressed by the indolent absent-minded sun.
Narrow shadows lie black, fixed to the roots of the trees:
"Just as at home, at Lisbon, at the hour of the siesta."
—C. H. WADDINGTON

Mozambique (correctly Moçambique) is a huge, oddly shaped wedge of territory bisected by the Zambesi River and almost cut apart by the downward thrust of Nyasaland. Sometimes it is called Portuguese East Africa. It covers 297,654 square miles (twice the size of Montana) and has approximately 5,700,000 people, of whom all but 100,000 are black Africans. The white European total is around 48,000, and there are about 50,000 Asians and mulattoes. Surprisingly enough the number of Moslems is large—almost 800,000. In the north, near the Tanganyika border, thousands of pagan Africans are converted to Islam every year, much to the chagrin of Roman Catholic and other Christian missionaries.

The Portuguese have been in Mozambique for 450 years—since 1505— but they almost lost it in the 1890's, when Britain and Germany were competing for East Africa. And on another occasion (in the early 1900's) the Portuguese offered to sell the whole area to London for £3,000,000, but the British had lost interest, and refused to buy. The British retain, however, a substantial strategic interest in Mozambique, because of its long frontage on the Indian Ocean, with good ports. Beira in particular is important, and is sometimes even called a British "sphere of influence," because it is an essential outlet for exports from the Rhodesias and Nyasaland. Mozambique has several anciently celebrated towns. Quelimane, above Beira, is the point where Dr. Livingstone reached the sea after traversing the continent. The old capital, Mozambique, is in the north and is almost completely derelict now.

Large tracts of land, fertile and fit for European habitation, are still unoccupied in Mozambique, but white settlement is not welcomed. Probably immigration from Portugal does not amount to more than two hundred people a year, and these are not assisted. The authorities would like to see experienced and soundly skilled farmers enter the country, if only for the example they might provide the Africans, but they do not want any urban riffraff, even from Portugal itself, that might create unpleasant problems in housing, color bar, unemployment, and the like. At all costs the Portuguese administration wants to avoid creation of a poor *white* class. (We shall see presently that the Belgians in the Congo pursue this same policy.) Ninety-seven per cent of the land of Mozambique is owned by the tribes, and their rights are carefully protected; no European may buy land without permission of the government. On the other hand, something known as the "Limpopo Project" has come into existence recently, a development scheme for the settlement of nine thousand European farmers, but without prejudice to the rights of Africans, on irrigated land in the Limpopo Valley.

Mozambique lives on tourists, sugar, cotton, tea, and the export of black labor.[4] The world's largest coconut grove is in Quelimane. American oil interests are active in the area, and there have been recent reports of uranium strikes. A Six-Year Development Plan has been worked out for the country as a whole. The safari business is lively, and every effort is being made to encourage it. Mozambique swarms with game. License fees are lower than in Kenya, and the Portuguese (who have four white hunters at their disposal) hope to draw off some Kenya traffic. You can get a terrific bag in Mozambique for license fees amounting only to £35. Moreover the animals have not been thinned out. Mozambique has a game park modeled on those elsewhere in Africa, by name Gorongosa. Colonel Mervyn Cowie, the director of the Kenya National Parks, came down to visit it recently, and saw something that startled him. In a deserted village lions were living in the houses.

LOURENÇO MARQUES, the chief port and capital, has about 100,000 people, of whom perhaps 40,000 are mixed or white. This is one of the most attractive little cities in Africa, and resembles strongly towns in Brazil. The churches are hung with bright pink lights—such a contrast to the dour, harshly architectured Calvinist churches in the Union—and the chief hotel looks like a bright old circus lady hung with tinsel. White

[4] One odd product is bat guana, found in caves along the coast and used as fertilizer. *African Affairs*, July, 1953.

lights outline its gay rococo façade. Lourenço Marques is the cleanest city I saw in Africa, bar none. It has sidewalks (which do not exist for the most part in such a metropolis as Bulawayo, Southern Rhodesia), and the empty lots look scrubbed. The market is spic-and-span, and even in the native quarter hardly a cigarette stub or fallen leaf lies on the streets. Lourenço Marques is a boom town, and is full of brightly colored new houses, like a community in Florida. Crime is virtually unknown, and there are only sixty-eight police in the entire city—again, what a contrast this makes to Johannesburg!

We spent a day visiting the schools. The new high school is a model structure. But it is the *only* high school in the whole of Mozambique. No wonder there are so few *assimilados*. Moreover the tuition is so high—about $30 per year—that few, if any, native children can afford it. In the primary schools classes are mixed, but white children predominate; even so it was startling, after the Union, to see Negro, Indian, mulatto, Chinese (from Portuguese Macao), and white children sitting side by side. The small children greet visitors to a classroom with the Fascist salute. I asked an official of the Education Ministry about schooling out in the bush. He replied blandly, "Ah, primary education is compulsory—*if* there happens to be a school available." He went on, "Frankly we do not want *many* educated natives, until they have an appropriate social background. They have no place to go. They become dissatisfied. What we want here is a stable society, a stable state. So we move very, very slowly."

The museum in Lourenço Marques has one of the most unusual taxidermical displays I have ever seen—a complete set of elephant foetuses, ranging from the age of two months to twenty. Hundreds of female elephants had to be shot before this could be mounted completely. At two months an elephant foetus is about the size of a grasshopper, and is ivory in color with a tiny clearly discernible pure white trunk; at seven months it resembles a teddy bear; at eleven, a sizable gray pig; at twenty, a fat black pony.

Lourenço Marques differs strikingly from the South African communities on the Rand, but this whole area—if the Portuguese will forgive my saying so—is virtually a colony of the Union of South Africa. Mainly this is because Lourenço Marques is Johannesburg's chief outlet to the sea, the biggest port for the whole Transvaal. Without railway traffic from the Union, it would shrivel to a quarter of its size and wealth. If you want to frighten a Laurentino, mention the possibility that the Union may someday build a competing railroad into Natal. Also South African tourist traffic is important. Lourenço Marques is only an hour and a half by air and overnight by train from Johannesburg, and thousands of South Africans come here for tropical winter holidays. Conversely, Mozambique (like Basutoland) sends a heavy human traffic into South Africa. Gold comes from Johannesburg to Lourenço Marques; the labor force that digs the gold goes from Lourenço Marques to Johannesburg. About one hundred thousand Portuguese African boys live in the Union legally (also 40,000 in Rhodesia), and about 200,000 illegally. They filter across the frontier because wages are so much higher in the Union. Legal recruitment of mine labor is in the hands of the Witwatersrand Native Labor Association, an official body. Its recruiters are known coloquially as "blackbirders." This labor is not forced, but voluntary; nevertheless the system is, as we know, vicious. Boys serve as a rule eighteen months in the South African mines, and then return for six months; after this they may do another eighteen-month tour, but two tours is the limit. Their average wage is three shillings a day (42 cents), of which they are paid half while they are at work; the other half is accumulated for them by the Portuguese government, and is given to them on their return. It is thus insured (in theory) that when boys come back to their homes they will have a modest capital; the whole proceeds of their labor will not be frittered away in Johannesburg. Meantime, the Portuguese government has the use of about £1 million gold a year. Few boys want to stay in the Union. They are not like youngsters from Vermont who migrate to Bridgeport, Connecticut, to find a job in a factory and then stay there. The idea is to amass enough money so that, on return to their Portuguese villages, they can buy a cow or a wife and settle down into their original society.

The Governor General of Mozambique, Captain Gabriel Mauricio Teixeira, is a robust, jovial, and energetic man who has made the country hum and whistle more than any governor in a generation. He is a former naval officer, and has a sun-and-salt-water freshness. Governors of Portuguese overseas provinces are usually political appointees chosen from outside the colonial service, but they must have a record of activity overseas. Captain Teixeira was for some years commissioner of lighthouses in Mozambique, and knows every inch of the country. His forthrightness and simplicity are reminiscent of Sir Edward Twining in Tanganyika. Everybody calls him "the G.G." He answers the telephone himself, and drives around the streets without an escort. He took us on a brief expedition, and we walked into half a dozen native houses without warning; in one I was astonished to see portraits of Cordell Hull and General Grant. Teixeira likes Africans, knows how to get the best out of them, and, within the circumscriptions of the Portuguese system, tries to protect their interests. He told us with a bluff laugh, "All of this country is one tribe, and I am the chief!"

Nationalism on an organized basis does not exist as yet in Portuguese Africa. The people are taught that they are *Portuguese,* so that a revolt would be a revolt against themselves. Several officials we met thought that, with luck, white rule might last longer here than anywhere else on the continent, because education is deliberately starved. But we met one young Portuguese who said frankly, "Of course nationalism will come in time. People will hear about what is happening on their borders, in Tanganyika and Nyasaland. You cannot seal a country off forever. People grow, even here. And they will sooner or later demand change." Last year a document of protest was smuggled out of Portuguese Africa and sent to a well-known American educator in New York. It adduced various grievances—such as that men impressed into labor gangs were wantonly flogged—and was soberly composed and well written. No fewer than 594 Africans dared to sign it.

To sum up and repeat: Mozambique is a curious mixture—Shangri La with a bullwhip behind the door.

ANGOLA, "THE BLACK MOTHER"

Angola, on the other side of Africa facing the Atlantic, is a huge squarish block of territory, fourteen times bigger than Portugal itself and roughly the size of Spain, France, and Italy put together. In all this vastness live only about four million people, of whom 80-90,000 are white Europeans. But this is a greater European population than that of the Congo. Once more we should underline the extreme emptiness of this part of Africa.

Most of Angola is, unlike Mozambique, a high semi-arid plateau, with desert areas going right down to the water as in the Union. Important quantities of manganese are exported to the United States. Angola has the smallest horse population of any country in the world—831—and is the only known habitat of a rare and carefully protected animal, the giant sable antelope. The currency is not the escudo but something called the "angolar," and the postage stamps, like those of the Congo, have signal beauty—they portray birds indigenous to the territory. Angola is probably the least known big country in Africa, and is only beginning to be developed. I don't think that more than half a dozen British or American journalists have visited it in twenty years. It is the only country in Africa we went to,[5] and one of the few in the free world, where a traveler needs an exit as well as an entrance visa. The chief problems are labor shortage and lack of food. One large district is known proverbially as "the Hungry Country."

[5] Except Egypt.

Perhaps I should mention again, even at the risk of repetition, the extraordinary and almost unbelievable possibilities for development that Africa offers. Here is a country one-sixth the size of the entire United States, largely temperate in climate and packed with no man knows what wealth—with only four million inhabitants![6]

Several differences exist between Mozambique and Angola, aside from the fact that Angola is potentially much richer and is much less known:

1. Angola carries less prestige in Portuguese eyes, and is less sophisticated. It was a penal colony in the old days, which gave it a certain stigma.

2. Angola does not export labor to the mines in South Africa or the Rhodesias. It needs all the men it has at home. (I met a European in Angola whose cook had just been bastinadoed on the hands for some minor dereliction, and I asked if this would do permanent injury. Reply: "No. The police do not inflict permanent injuries, because man power is so scant."

3. White settlement is encouraged, instead of the reverse. About 11,000 Portuguese immigrants entered Angola in 1951. Mostly they were—and are —a miserable lot. Creaking old boats dump them on the beaches; often as not they cannot find suitable work, but they are too proud to return to Portugal; inevitably they drift into native villages, take up with African women, live at a bare subsistence level, and "go native." Africa absorbs the European, instead of vice versa.

To remedy this state of affairs the authorities have set up several experiments. One is a colonization project near Cela. The government offers to any Portuguese farmer who is over thirty and married a twenty-hectare plot in this area—three hectares irrigated, seventeen dry—with a cow, sheep, a brood sow, six chickens, six ducks, and some rabbits. But out of a thousand colonists anticipated in 1953, only 124 actually arrived.

4. No one pays much attention to color bar. There is no curfew for natives. Many more Africans have become *assimilados* than in Mozambique.

Also Angola's historical development is quite different. The name of the country, which has a Latin sound, is not Portuguese, but comes fron an old native king called N'gola. The Portuguese have been in Angola since 1482, ten years before Christopher Columbus discovered America. One brief period of Dutch rule (1641-48) occurred, under Boers from the Cape. What particularly distinguished Angola for centuries was the slave trade, and this may be one reason why it is so underpopulated today. Angola is the "mother" of Brazil, and in time superseded the Guinea Coast as the

---

[6] American technical assistance, both through the MSA and privately, has begun in Angola. One American company is making an aerial survey of the whole territory, and another is mapping mineral resources.

chief source of slaves—"black ivory"—for markets everywhere in the New World. When the slave traffic stopped, Portuguese interest in Angola stopped too. Not till recent times has it begun to stir again.

One geographical curiosity is Cabinda, an enclave of Portuguese territory separated from the rest of Angola by the mouth of the Congo. Not much is known—or is worth knowing—about Cabinda.

The capital of Angola is in theory a town in the southern highlands, Nova Lisboa. This was laid out some years ago, but has never been used as the capital. The chief city, seat of government, and capital in fact is LUANDA, once called Saint Paul de Luanda, and known nowadays in tourist propaganda as "Luanda, *Cidade das Buganvílias.*" This is the oldest European settlement in all Africa south of the Sahara. On the surface it seems to be a completely European city; the Archbishop's palace, which is pink, sits next door to the lemon-yellow palace of the Governor. Old forts command the shore, and the shops are chic. The British journalist Henry W. Nevinson, writing in 1905, said that Luanda was "the only place that looks like a city" all the way between "Moorish Tangier and Dutch Cape Town." Even today this is true to an extent, and Luanda is probably the pleasantest city for Europeans on the whole West Coast of Africa. The population is about 160,000, of whom perhaps 45,000 are white. Businessmen complain that taxes are high, and that the Bank of Angola, the only bank in the country and a very rich institution since it has a monopoly, keeps credit tight. The bookshops are meager, but Luanda has three daily newspapers, more than Atlanta, Kansas City, or Milwaukee.

Angola has no politics to speak of. Everything is run from Lisbon. Organized nationalism is, as in Mozambique, unknown.

Forced labor is an essential part of the economic system, even more than in Mozambique. Probably 380,000 Africans work as forced laborers in Angola in circumstances of the utmost wretchedness and poverty. This is another factor that probably tends to keep the population down, since families are all the time being broken up. It is a crime not to work in Angola. Even a servant cannot quit employment without permission. The railway, the mines, the big plantation owners, all get labor from the government. The usual contract period is eighteen months. A European merchant in Luanda can even ask the government for a gardener, who is then obliged to work for him at a wage unbelievably low, whether he wants the job or not.

*

Far to the north, on the westward bulge of the continent, is Portuguese Guinea. A good many American travelers had at least a glimpse of this shabby, almost moribund fragment of territory during the war, because Pan-American clippers crossing the Atlantic stopped there if the weather was bad in the Azores. The chief ports are Bolama and Bissau, and the population is around 510,000.

Another Portuguese colony, the Fort of St. John the Baptist of Ajuda (S. Jôao Batista de Ajuda), must be the smallest political entity in the world. It lies in Dahomey, on the Guinea Coast, a few miles from the French post of Ouidah. The Portuguese have held it since 1680. The territory consists of nothing but the Fort, and the garrison comprises exactly *one* officer (who is also the Resident) and a handful of men.

My wife and I applied for visas to the Fort of St. John the Baptist, and were courteously given them by the Portuguese embassy in Washington. We were told that we were the first non-Portuguese in history ever to ask to go there.

THE "GREAT ISLE" OF MADAGASCAR

Because of transportation difficulties we did not visit Madagascar, and I don't like to write about places we did not see. As a matter of fact, Madagascar, although it lies in the Indian Ocean close to Mozambique, is not in the true sense African at all. Fauna, flora, people, customs, languages, even geology, are altogether different. Madagascar has close links, not with the African mainland, but with Ceylon, India, and places even further removed, such as the Polynesian and Melanesian archipelagos in the Pacific. Geologists say that, like the Seychelles and other nearby islands in the Indian Ocean, it may be part of a lost continent, now mostly submerged, that they call by the nice name Gondwana. At any rate the connection with southern India is close. Similarly the people of Madagascar are not of African or Negro stock, but derive from Asia and Oceania. They have a strong Malay streak, and are called Malagasys. The most important Malagasy tribe is the Hova.

There are no dangerous carnivorous animals on Madagascar, no anthropoid apes, and no poisonous snakes. But the island has a phenomenal number of different kinds of lemur, and many other zoological curiosities; in particular it is a paradise for the entomologist. In 1952 a coelacanth was caught in the deep waters off Madagascar. This made a sensation all over the scientific world. The coelacanth is a curious species of fish which scientists knew about from its fossilized remains, but which they assumed had been extinct for 70,000,000 years. This "living fossil" has "rotating pectoral fins," and is otherwise startling to experts in the field. Six or eight coelacanths have been found off Madagascar since 1952, but they die if they are not kept in very deep water.

Madagascar is the fourth largest island in the world, after Greenland, Borneo, and New Guinea, and is more than twice the size of Italy. Laid along the coast of the United States it would stretch from Nantucket to the middle of Florida. It was once called the Ile Dauphine. The population is 4,346,000, of whom about 50,000 are French nationals. The capital (population 180,000) is TANANARIVE, and the chief products are graphite and cassava. Madagascar is the first exporter of tapioca flour in the world. The British took it in World War II in order to deny it to Vichy, because of its great importance commanding the sea lanes around the Cape of Good Hope into the Indian Ocean.

The country has three sharply marked divisions. The north, with its port Diégo-Suarez, is one of the hottest and laziest places on earth. It was once a penal colony, and is now a naval base. "How the French treat their *own* people!" I heard a British officer exclaim. "Diégo-Suarez did not even have a tennis court or swimming bath when we got there." At one time four different pretenders to the old Madagascar throne lived here. In the center of the island are healthy, fertile highlands, centering on Tananarive, and the south has a lush Mediterranean appearance, like Mozambique. The narrow coastal strips are pierced by numerous luxuriant lagoons known as *pangalenes*. The island as a whole is fabulously colorful.

Madagascar is, of course, not Portuguese but French. The first French settlers landed in 1529. Today the country is part of the French republic, and a full-fledged member of the French Union. On a political level (as well as administratively and in matters of education, public health, and so on) Madagascar is a century ahead of Angola or Mozambique. More than 800,000 natives are entitled to vote, and it sends five deputies and five senators to Paris, as well as seven councilors to the Assembly of the French Union at Versailles. These are mostly strong and articulate nationalists, but loyal to France.

The Madagascar people, particularly the Hovas, have a marked sense of history and a lively political sophistication and nationalist spirit. The country had its own ruling house for centuries, and achieved a state of civilization far in advance of the African mainland. The last native sovereign, a woman of formidable quality, was Queen Rànavàlona III; she was forced to abdicate in 1895, when Madagascar became a French protectorate. She died in exile in Algiers in 1916. It is striking that Sultan Mohammed V of Morocco, who was deposed by France in 1953, should now be an exile in Madagascar. The French have a way of shipping sovereigns around.

In 1947 a serious revolt against French rule took place in Madagascar, few details of which ever became known to the outside world. The leaders were Hova intellectuals, who were inspired by the same instinct for self-determination that distinguished nationalists in Syria, the Lebanon, and North Africa. The Malagasy movement was perfectly legitimate for the most part, and had deep roots in native culture. The French paid little attention to warning signals, and refused to make concessions. In the fighting that followed thousands were killed. This was an uprising on a major scale, and it was mercilessly suppressed, Madagascar nationalists with whom I have been in touch say that *eighty thousand* of their people died; the French admit to 11,505 "known dead." Of these (according to official French information), 4,928 were killed outright in riots; the others fled into the jungle in order to hide, and either "disappeared," died of physical exhaustion, or starved to death.

Hardly a word about this shockingly bloody affair ever appeared in the American or British press. But even 11,505 dead—taking the French figure at face value—are a lot.

CHAPTER 30

The Rhodesias and Central African Federation

So much to do; so little done!
—CECIL RHODES ON HIS DEATHBED.

Your Majesty, what I want to know from you is if people can be bought at any price. . . . Your Majesty, what I want to know from you is: Why do your people kill me? Do you kill me for following my stolen cattle which are seen in the possession of the Mashonas . . . I have called all white men living at or near Bulawayo to hear my words, showing clearly that I am not hiding anything from them when writing to Your Majesty.
—CHIEF LOBENGULA, last King of the Matabele, in a letter to Queen Victoria.

HUGGINS is a character. In some ways he was, I thought, as interesting as any personality we met in Africa. He is a doctor of medicine, a surgeon, who came out to Africa in his youth, entered politics almost by accident, and has been a prime minister—first of Southern Rhodesia, then of the Federation of Rhodesia and Nyasaland—uninterruptedly for twenty-two years. He was elevated to the peerage in 1955—the first colonial prime minister ever to be made a peer—and is now known as Lord Malvern. But it is easier to write about him under the name his career has made celebrated all over central and southern Africa, Sir Godfrey Huggins.

Huggins, who is seventy-one, became prime minister of Southern Rhodesia, a British colony with a special self-governing status, in 1933. When this was incorporated into the new Central African Federation in October, 1953, he simply stepped out of one prime ministership into another. On February 17, 1955, he served his 7,829th consecutive day as prime minister, a record unparalleled in the Commonwealth. Mackenzie

THE RHODESIAS AND CENTRAL AFRICAN FEDERATION 603

King was prime minister of Canada for 7,828 days, but these were spread over three separate periods of office between 1921 and 1948. Sir Robert Walpole was prime minister of England from 1721 to 1742 without interruption—7,620 days—but nobody else in British history comes anywhere near the Huggins record.

The peculiar and controversial amalgam run by Huggins is the newest political entity in the world. As these lines are written, the Federation is less than a year and a half old, and Huggins is thus not only the oldest prime minister in the world from the point of view of length of service, but also one of the youngest.

Three states compose the new Federation—Southern Rhodesia, Northern Rhodesia, and Nyasaland. The latter two, even though federated, are still protectorates under the Colonial Office. Southern Rhodesia, although it is smaller in population than Nyasaland and is much less rich than Northern Rhodesia (which has the Copperbelt) has superior political experience and prestige and is the senior partner. The Federation is landlocked—this must be one of the few countries of equivalent size and importance in the world with no direct access to the sea. Its area as a whole is 488,000 square miles, about two and a half times that of Spain.

As to population, the Federation has about six and a half million Africans and 209,000 whites. Southern Rhodesia has a bigger European population than any country in Africa between French North Africa and the Union, and has a long history of being a white settler state; even so, the white population is only 160,000—as against more than two million blacks. Northern Rhodesia has roughly 45,000 whites to 1,860,000 blacks; Nyasaland only a tiny handful of whites—4,073—as against 2,400,000 blacks. The ratio of black to white is thirteen to one in Southern Rhodesia, forty-two to one in Northern Rhodesia, and 588 to one in Nyasaland.

South African influence is profound in both Rhodesias, but we have come a considerable way now from the racial policy of the Union. Plenty of white supremacy fanatics live and flourish in the Federation, and color bar is in some respects even more outrageously pronounced than in the Union, but officially this new country stands not for *apartheid* but on the contrary for racial partnership. Southern Rhodesia is white, more or less; Northern Rhodesia is "gray"; Nyasaland is black. The idea is to melt them down into a multiracial harmony, completely run by the whites (of course), but not under overt white *domination,* and with Africans being gradually permitted more share in government and administration. Six Africans are members of the new Federation parliament. They have practically no power, but they are there.

The Federation is self-governing (under certain limitations) and will presumably become in time a full dominion; if so, it will be the first truly multiracial dominion in the Commonwealth. (The Gold Coast will also probably reach Dominion Status fairly soon, but this will be something altogether different, a *black* dominion.)

Huggins is a smallish, alert, adroit man with iron-colored hair, a neat mustache, and the brightest of bright brown eyes. He smokes a pipe continually, and in conversation taps the table or makes other gestures with his eyeglass case. He looks twenty years younger than his years, and has a lively sense of humor. He is inquisitive, gay, and clever. He works very hard indeed. For sixteen years (1933-49) he was minister of native affairs as well as prime minister in Southern Rhodesia, and when federation began he became not only prime minister but federal minister for defense, external affairs, and finance.

Huggins relaxes, when he gets the chance, on his country property, Craig Farm, seventeen miles from Salisbury, the capital of both Southern Rhodesia and the Federation.[1] He has been happily married for many years, and has two sons; one helps run the farm, and the other is in the RAF in England. The farm is a full-sized operation. Huggins lays bricks himself, pours concrete, and so on. He likes to say, not altogether seriously, that the farm has made him a poor man, because he cannot resist buying the newest gadgets and machinery. Some years ago, setting up a new machine, something went wrong and he lost the tip of the index finger of his right hand. He growled cheerfully, "Serves me right. I should have let my African boys do that kind of job. They would have done it better, and not got themselves messed up."

Huggins suffers from deafness and plays on this defect occasionally, as many deaf people do. "He has a wonderful instinct," one of his best friends told us, "for hearing only what he wants to hear."

He was born in Kent, eleven miles from London, in an area that has long since been swallowed up by London. His father was on the stock exchange, and the family owned a brewery. After getting his medical degree, he served for some years as medical superintendent of a children's hospital in Great Ormond Street. His practice taught him a lot about human nature. Threatened by tuberculosis, he went out to Rhodesia for his health, and arrived in Salisbury on February 11, 1911. He remembers the date well. There were only four physicians in the whole of Salisbury then, and Huggins was offered a partnership in a local medical firm at £50 per month. In London he had been getting £100 a year. His health picked up, and he decided to stay on

---

[1] A new federal capital, not Salisbury, may be chosen in the future.

THE RHODESIAS AND CENTRAL AFRICAN FEDERATION 605

in Rhodesia. When he arrived, Salisbury had no electricity, proper streets, or public water supply. "I've seen it change a bit in forty years," he told us cheerfully. "There was no native problem then. The Africans were nice old souls. You lost one, you got another." He smiled ruefully, "We create our own troubles."

Young Huggins did practically every kind of surgery, but came to specialize in abdominal operations. Before long he was one of the best known surgeons in southern Africa. He kept up his practice till about ten years ago. He operated as a rule every morning at 7:30, and then spent the rest of the day with politics, if his patients were not too demanding. He entered public life out of a deep sense of service, but to an extent accidentally, not dreaming that politics would become his career. This was in 1924. Southern Rhodesia had just become self-governing, and was electing its first parliament. Friends asked him to stand for this, and he agreed to do so "to shake things up a bit." "I'll join your beastly party," he told them, "but I won't promise anything else." He only spoke twice during his first campaign. At one meeting he was asked whether, if he won, he would give up his medical practice. This question put him in "rather a spot." If he said no, it might cost his group the election. If he said yes, he might win! Anyway he won. He was treating a patient when the news of victory came. He exclaimed, in mock horror, "Good God! What will my partners think!"

Of the 1924 parliament Huggins is the only survivor still sitting as a member. He has never lost his seat. He has been the head of six different Rhodesian ministries, and is the only survivor of his own first cabinet. He has outlived and outlasted everybody.

Most anecdotes about Huggins have to do with medical matters. One of his cabinet ministers reported for duty after a boisterous late night. "My dear fellow," Huggins greeted him, "you have three minor hemorrhages in your left eye." Once an old acquaintance snapped at him rudely, and the prime minister replied, "I know what is the matter with you, and I will be taking it out within six weeks." Within six weeks, the acquaintance's gall bladder, the cause of his bad temper, was duly taken out.

A local newspaper correspondent called on him one morning. Huggins said, "I am going to interview you, not vice versa. You look ill. Tell me about your complaint." An hour later the prime minister had him in the hospital, and set about removing his appendix.

Huggins drinks little, but has a zest for the good things of life. He lived at the Salisbury Club when he was still a bachelor, and was a member of the wine committee. A kitchen fire scorched the cellar. Huggins constituted himself a subcommittee of one to drink a bottle from each bin, to see if any damage had been done. When he finished this chore he said mildly, "Nobody in the club even thanked me for all the hard work I did."

Few countries have ever been more of a one-man show than Southern Rhodesia since 1933, when he became prime minister. It is almost impossible to dislike him. As much as by anything, he rules by his good nature.[2] He has moved strongly with the times. Thirty-three years ago (in 1922) he advocated incorporation of Southern Rhodesia into the Union of South Africa. Then he decided to become an "amalgamationist," that is, he wanted Southern and Northern Rhodesia to combine into a single unitary state. This idea had to be given up, and Huggins became in time a chief advocate of federation.

Huggins has had to fight two elections recently, and he won both with ease. First (April, 1953) came the referendum in Southern Rhodesia whereby the electorate decided, by a two to one majority, that it wanted federation. More on this below. Second (December, 1953) occurred the first *federal* elections, whereby the new country chose its government. Huggins' victory was overwhelming. His newly formed Federal party won twenty-four out of twenty-six regularly contested seats. (The total membership of the parliament is thirty-five, but nine seats are especially assigned to Africans or to Europeans charged exclusively with representing African interests.) The opposition to Huggins, which is called the Confederate party and which stands for outright *apartheid*, got only one seat, and one went to an independent. Nothing could have been more complete than the Huggins landslide.

On color bar, the most harassing and important problem in the country, Huggins' attitude is mixed. No doubt he deplores personally the uglier excesses of segregation in Rhodesia, which are indeed revolting, but he is a white politician representing an almost solidly white electorate, and he must choose his path carefully. He is no Swart or Strijdom by a long way, but on the other hand he does not want to give Africans too much too soon, even though the Federation is supposed to be based on partnership. In 1954 he vehemently opposed a motion presented in the new parliament by an African member to the effect "that equal treatment for all races in public places should be enforced by legislation." He thought that any such legislation was premature, might split the country, and "would set back the clock of partner-

---

[2] But his tongue can be sharp on occasion. Serious rioting occurred in Nyasaland in protest at the federal scheme, and eleven Africans were killed in clashes with the police. Huggins blamed the Reverend Michael Scott for fomenting these disturbances, and said bitterly that "Scott's bag of eleven dead was not bad for a peaceful missionary." This was a flagrantly unfair statement. Scott, an idealistic and noble person, is a firm believer in *non*-violence, and was not even in Africa at the time, although he had been in Nyasaland some months before.

ship ten years," by alienating the white community.³ On the other side of the fence it was his decision that the new university now being constructed in Salisbury, the first in the history of the Rhodesias, shall be multiracial.

A TALK WITH HUGGINS

We called on the prime minister for what was to have been a brief meeting, and stayed for more than two hours. He is a most artful conversationalist. His office is modest, and the desk—even the floor—had a litter of papers. "Beastly campaign kept me busy—haven't had time to clean up yet." On the wall was a portrait of Rhodes, strong and faintly sinister, and photographs of some of the dignitaries Huggins has often met at Commonwealth conferences. He lit a pipe and began to trace out his political career. "I hate politics. I like administration." He explained how he had happened to vote for the incorporation of Southern Rhodesia into South Africa back in 1922. "I didn't know the Union well. I didn't think two men and a boy could run Rhodesia. The Union was a different thing then." I do not think that I should repeat the prime minister's remarks about the Union now, an awkward neighbor. He mentioned his old hope for amalgamation of Northern and Southern Rhodesia into a single state. "Both countries were largely empty—why shouldn't we make them one? Besides I was an imperialist—that's a terrible thing to be in the United States, isn't it? I wanted Africa to be a nice bright British pink, just as Rhodes did, all the way to Egypt." He chuckled. "I was willing to take Northern Rhodesia in when it was poor, and I still am even when it's rich!"

Time and again he came back to the subject of race relations, an obsession with almost all Rhodesians. "Education—that's the biggest problem." Sixty-five years ago the Africans were just "a lot of savages, sticking assegais into one another," and Nyasaland was "a zoo." Of course the new university would be multiracial. It had to be, because Africans must have opportunity for higher education, no matter how bitterly white extremists may object. Huggins' bright brown eyes flashed. "If education is segregated, it certainly can't be higher!"

On the other hand he fears close contact between black and white. He talked, almost as South Africans talk, of the danger of "mixing up people" and producing a *"café au lait"* society. Yet he conceded that Africans had to be given some kind of outlet, not only as a matter of justice but as a political necessity. Apparently he thinks that the only solution is gradual economic betterment. "It takes a long time to change human beings. You cannot alter

³ *East Africa and Rhodesia*, August 5, 1954.

the social patterns of a people by legislation. We cannot abolish segregation overnight, but at least we can give economic opportunity." But true, full economic opportunity is exactly what most Africans in Rhodesia do *not* have.

The prime minister said frankly that the fact that Africans are in such a large majority in the Federation as a whole made it necessary to give them steadily more and more concessions. "But if they try to take things over, we'll stop 'em dead!"

Rhodesia, Huggins thinks, is "the nut in the nutcracker," with the white nationalism of the Union on one side, the black nationalism of the West Coast on the other. The new Federation must be something in between; hence, it is committed to the principle of racial partnership. "The new parliament should be a *nursery* for the Africans. We must *nurse* them over their social grievances."

ENGINEER WELENSKY AND MISSIONARY TODD

Sir Roy Welensky, the deputy prime minister and federal minister of transport and development, will, it is generally thought, be Huggins' successor in time. He is a quite different type of personality, not so sophisticated or urbane, but with great force. Northern Rhodesia is his bailiwick, not Southern. He is a very large man (weight about 270 pounds) with a moon of a face, lively forked eyebrows, and a blunt, untutored manner. The legend is that he is so large that he cannot find pajamas or shirts in the shops, and his wife makes them for him. Welensky is a teetotaler and does not smoke. He has simple tastes, and likes to do work around the house. When we called on him in Lusaka, Northern Rhodesia, the first thing I noticed was a lawnmower propped casually against a wall in the living room.

Welensky was born in 1907, and was knighted in 1953. His father was a Polish immigrant, half-Jewish, who came out to Rhodesia in the nineties, one of the early pioneers. Roy had no schooling after the age of fifteen. He worked as a barman in a frontier hotel, in the mines, and on the railroads. He became a locomotive engineer, and pursued this trade for many years. "I'm just an engine driver," he kept telling us. He rose rapidly as a labor leader, became undisputed boss of the powerful white railwayman's union in Northern Rhodesia, and inevitably entered politics.[4]

For years he boxed as a hobby, and for a time was heavyweight boxing champion of Northern Rhodesia. He is proud of this attainment, and loves boxing to this day. He told me that when he visited the United States some years ago he had only one ambition—to meet Jim Jeffries, former heavyweight

[4] Some of these details are from a profile in the London *Observer*, June 17, 1951.

champion of the world. But he never made contact with Jeffries, who died subsequently. Jeffries was the only man for whom Welensky ever had hero worship. Welensky is interested not only in boxing, but most other forms of sport. He asked me (somewhat wistfully, I thought) if Jackie Robinson could be "partly white." Apparently he found it hard to believe that any really great athlete could be a full Negro. I did not ask him what his opinion was of Joe Louis.

Welensky, embarking on his political career, became such a power in his home constituency, Broken Hill, an important railway town, that nobody bothers to oppose him in elections there. As leader of the "unofficial," i.e., elected European members of the Northern Rhodesian legislature, he had a position unique in recent British colonial history, and was in fact—if not name—prime minister. More than in any British colony in Africa, the "unofficials" ran the LEGCO. In November, 1953, nine white members of the government resigned their posts suddenly, under Welensky's lead. This was because Oliver Lyttelton, then the Colonial Secretary, had proposed some very mild reforms giving Africans more power in the legislature and extending their franchise. The white representation was to be lifted from ten elected members to twelve, and the African from two to four. Welensky has never had much fondness for the Colonial Office. He protested vehemently that the change would increase African representation by "100 per cent, European representation by only 20 per cent." (It might also be pointed out that, even so, the 45,000 Europeans in Northern Rhodesia will have twelve seats, whereas two million Africans have to be content with four.)

Welensky has small love for the Africans, and has been in the past a vigorous supporter of color bar. But, as a leading member of the new Federal party, he is pledged to partnership and co-operation with the African community. Federation is supposed to create in the long run a multiracial state, and therefore he cannot officially take a white supremacy position any longer. But he certainly stands for "partnership" on what seems to be ambiguous terms, and he is probably still a believer in strict social segregation. I asked him (before Federation) why he favored the scheme so strongly. Answer: "Colonial rule is finished. We have to hold on here somehow, or we will lose everything the way we lost India."

*

The prime minister of Southern Rhodesia, who stepped into this post when Huggins became federal prime minister, is R. S. Garfield Todd, the first missionary ever to become a prime minister in the British Commonwealth. He is also minister for internal affairs and justice.[5] Mr. Todd was born in New Zealand. He left school at sixteen, and worked in a pottery. He decided to be a missionary, studied theology, and joined the New Zealand mission station at Fort Jameson, Northern Rhodesia, some twenty years ago. To equip himself further, he took a year's medical studies at Witwatersrand University, in the Union. He moved to Southern Rhodesia, and became head of the Church of Christ Mission at Dadaya. There were twenty African students when he arrived in Dadaya, and there are more than six hundred now. Mr. Todd not only taught good habits of work, but worked hard himself—as a bricklayer, stonemason, and gardener. He entered politics in 1946, and rose to be an MP and an important member of the Huggins party.

Also Mr. Todd became a settler, and owns a large ranch near the Lundi reserve. The white electorate likes him because, as a settler, he will presumably stand firmly for white interests. On the other hand some extremist settlers hold it severely against him that he is a missionary, and may therefore "pamper" the Africans. They call him "naïve." Most Africans with whom he is in contact admire his competence, high principles, and fairness of mind. Once, however, he got into trouble following a charge that he had used physical violence on African boys. Youngsters at his school were insubordinate, and he caned them—not a very serious offense. It is a revealing commentary on the habits of mind of the last-ditch Europeans that this episode became a big asset in Todd's favor when he entered politics.

BEFORE FEDERATION

Rhodesian history flows upward from the Cape, and the determining, vitalizing factor was Rhodes himself. He is still often referred to respectfully as "Mr." Rhodes, and several frontiersmen and early settlers who worked with him still survive.

The Rhodesias were a barren wilderness, utterly unknown except to a handful of traders and missionaries, until occupation from South Africa began in the 1880's. The area had, however, been intermittently penetrated by gold-seekers from the earliest times. This was the land of Ophir, and here is supposed to have been the site of Solomon's mines. Nobody knows for certain who built the stone monuments at Zimbabwe, one of the principal sights of Rhodesia, or when exactly they were built—possibly by invaders from Arabia or the Red Sea (or even India) in the eighth century AD. The

---

[5] Most Rhodesian ministers have double functions, because of the shortage of men available.

THE RHODESIAS AND CENTRAL AFRICAN FEDERATION 611

Zimbabwe ruins are among the most formidable and mysterious in the world.

In the early 1800's a ferocious Bantu king, by name Moselekatse, occupied most of what is now Southern Rhodesia. His tribe, the Matabele (properly, Amandabele), a branch of the Zulus, had been pushed out of South Africa by the Boers. He had a son, Lobengula, who became king in 1870, and ruled a vast area from his kraal in what is now Bulawayo. Lobengula was a very fat man, who had sixty-eight wives, wore as a rule nothing but a skirt of blue monkey skins, and was not quite so much a savage as he looked. His name means "He that drives like the wind." This was the monarch with whom Rhodes came into contact, and what followed is one of the nastiest, shabbiest episodes in imperial history.

Gold and diamonds still concerned Rhodes in 1883-84, and so naturally did his position as a member of the Cape parliament, but it was the undeveloped north that really challenged and gripped his imagination. He spent part of 1884 as Deputy Commissioner in Bechuanaland, and the next year the Bechuanaland Protectorate was proclaimed. In 1888 he sent emissaries to negotiate with Lobengula in the territory then known as "Zambesia." Rhodes had at least three motives: (1) Business—this was a country rich in minerals; (2) Extension of the empire; (3) Self-aggrandizement, Napoleonism. Lobengula was bullied, tricked, and swindled as neatly as a child in a gambling den. By an agreement reached in October, 1888, he gave up all metal and mineral rights in Matabeleland, over an area covering more than 75,000 square miles, exclusively to the Rhodes group for a payment of £100 per month, a thousand rifles, ammunition, and the promise of a gunboat on the Zambesi. He never got the gunboat.

Not since Manhattan island was bought from the Indians has any piece of real estate so valuable been had so cheaply. Many people in England were shocked. Lobengula, as an authentic monarch, had steady contact with Queen Victoria. She wrote him: "It is not wise to put too much power into the hands of men who come first, and to exclude other deserving men. A King gives a stranger an ox, not his whole herd of cattle, otherwise what would other strangers have to eat?"[6]

Rhodes took several of Lobengula's sons as his servants. He made it quite clear that the duty of these young princes would be to shine his boots and the like. There is no need to sentimentalize about the fate of these boys, who were savages and who were probably delighted to be introduced to the wonders and virtues of western civilization. The episode is worth mention only because it shows how the Rhodes magnificence had become almost casual—

[6] *Rhodes*, by Sarah Gertrude Millin, p. 111.

lighthearted. It seemed to him perfectly natural that the King's sons should be his servants. Alexander the Great might have had much the same attitude.

The British South Africa Company, organized by Rhodes to develop the northern territories, received its charter in 1889. It was hungry for more land and opportunity. A group of pioneers, equipped and managed by the Company (not by the British government), set out to occupy Mashonaland, the area to the north of Matabeleland, and hoisted the Union Jack at what is now Salisbury on September 13, 1890. Rhodes did not take part in the march, which was guided by a celebrated professional hunter, Frederick Courteney Selous.[7] Africans in the wild country traversed by the column were perfectly peaceable. They are almost always referred to as bloodthirsty barbarians and savages, but not a single shot against them had to be fired. The expedition cost only £89,000.

Mineral rights were not enough for Rhodes and the rapidly expanding chartered company. They had political ambitions too. Matabeleland would not be "safe," they thought, until it was more fully integrated into the British framework. Perhaps they were right. At any rate the so-called Matabele war occurred in 1893, which some historians think was deliberately instigated by Rhodes and his fellows. There were frontier "incidents" having to do with cattle between the Matabele and the Mashona, and these were seized upon by the pioneers as a pretext for hostilities. The Matabele were crushed promptly. Rhodes had his "little war," and won it. Lobengula retreated into the wild mountainous bush beyond Bulawayo, and died of smallpox the next year.[8]

In 1896 the Matabele—also the Mashona—rose again and were crushed again. Rhodes happened to be in England. He hurried back to Salisbury, and vigorously took affairs into his own hands. This is one occasion on which we see him acting with full vision as a great man should. He knew that permanent peace was impossible if the Africans did not—now that the period of conquest was over—have complete trust in British fairness and good intentions. Nobody but himself could possibly convey to them the necessary confidence. Unarmed and at the risk of his life, he met the native chiefs at a lonely rendezvous out in the wilderness, in the Matopo hills near Bula-

---

[7] Twenty years later, when Theodore Roosevelt visited Africa in search of game, Selous was one of his advisors.

[8] One of Lobengula's last recorded statements is the following: "Matabele! The white men will never cease following us while we have gold in our possession, for gold is what the white men prize above all things. Collect now all my gold . . . and carry it to the white men. Tell them they have beaten my regiments, killed my people, burnt my kraals, captured my cattle, and that I want peace." (Millin, *op. cit.*, p. 197.)

wayo, and persuaded them to lay down their arms. They agreed to do so, and it is a proud boast of the Rhodesians that from that date (August 21, 1896) to this, "no African in Rhodesia has ever been shot in anger."

The new region was formally named "Rhodesia" in 1895. Some people wanted to call it "Cecilia" in honor of Lord Salisbury, who was prime minister in London at the time and whose family name is, as everybody knows, Cecil.[9] But the Rhodes myth, the Rhodes prestige, carried everything before it. Rhodes always had immense pride in the fact that the Rhodesias were named for him, and with reason. Certainly he is the only man in history ever to have had two countries named for him. One of his biographers records that, when his decline began, he wanted to know plaintively if "Rhodesia" might ever be renamed something else. "People don't change the names of *countries*, do they?" he is supposed to have asked with anxiety.

Rhodes pushed the empire north, and that is his greatest achievement. The Jameson Raid, which broke him and ended his political career, set in motion events that in the long run turned the Union back to the Boers, but the Rhodesias are still British in fact as well as name. Not only did he open up the north, but, a point not often realized nowadays, he created a kind of east-west roadblock. The invention of Rhodesia made it impossible for the Portuguese to link Angola up with Mozambique, and impossible (something much more serious) for the Germans to establish a belt across the continent connecting German South-West with German East Africa. No one can doubt that Rhodes was one of the greatest empire builders who ever lived. Perhaps it is lucky that he died when he did. If he had survived long into the present century, he would almost certainly have made the ties between Rhodesia and the Union stronger, and the Rhodesias might conceivably be going the way of the Union now, instead of being part of a "safe" British federation.

*

From 1889 to 1914 the Rhodesias were administered, not by the British government, but by the British South Africa Company founded by Rhodes. The resident director of the company, although bound to consult with the British High Commissioner at the Cape, ran both Rhodesias. They were "owned," so to speak, by a private organization. The company's charter ran out in 1914, after twenty-five years. There were three alternatives. First, the company could have its charter extended. Second, the Rhodesias might join the Union, which was the original intention. Third, Southern Rhodesia

---

[9] Of course "Cecilia" would also have commemorated Rhodes, in that his own first name was Cecil. See *Cecil Rhodes*, by William Plomer, p. 65, an admirable short biography.

might become a colony of the British government. In the end the British government renewed the company's charter for ten years, with the proviso that the people might have self-government before the decade was up. In 1922, following bitter quarrels between the company and individual settlers, matters came to a head, and, in the best British tradition, the fate of the country was put up to the electorate. The rule of the company ended, and the voters, by a slim majority, chose not to join the Union but to become a self-governing British colony. So in 1923 Southern Rhodesia was annexed to the British crown.

The British South Africa Company still plays a consequential role in Rhodesian affairs, although it has had no governmental responsibility for many years. It must be the last of the great nineteenth-century chartered companies still to be functioning. The resident director in Salisbury today is American-born, and, fittingly enough, is a Rhodes scholar—Sir Ellis Robins. The company is proud of its record. For decades it plowed so much into administration and development that it paid no dividends. Now, however, it is a flourishing enterprise; net profits in 1954 were £3,295,898. The company has no direct mineral rights in Southern Rhodesia any longer, but it still owns *all* mineral rights and controls all prospecting rights in Northern Rhodesia, and the great mines on the Copperbelt pay it a handsome royalty. Also it has extensive interests in Nyasaland. Twenty per cent of its Northern Rhodesian royalties are, by terms of a recent agreement, paid back to the Northern Rhodesian government every year. Strong pressure by Welensky and others, who held that the company rendered no service commensurate with its profits, brought about this agreement. The company's charter will finally expire in 1986.

*

Southern Rhodesia for years could not afford proper facilities for its blind, aged, insane, and so on, and these were commonly sent to institutions in the Union. Similarly a few—very few—Rhodesian Negroes went to universities in the Union, since no university existed for them at home. This is one reason why the new university at Salisbury had to be built, and is to be multiracial. Dr. Malan refused some years ago to take in any more African students, and there was no other place for them to go.

Many other interrelations between the Union and the Rhodesias exist, so much so that at first glance much of Southern Rhodesia seems indistinguishable from its southern neighbor, but these will probably become less conspicuous as time goes on.[10] Federation will serve to pull the Rhodesias

---

[10] For instance, the two countries shared the same Supreme Court (at Bloemfontein) until federation.

THE RHODESIAS AND CENTRAL AFRICAN FEDERATION

away from South Africa, despite their close historical association and the large number of South Africans resident in Rhodesia. One Rhodesian told me, "The difference between us and the Union is that we have *hope!*"

*

Northern Rhodesian history follows roughly the same course as Southern, and need not concern us. But Northern Rhodesia was never conquered by force of arms. Its chiefs asked for British protection of their own volition, and made their own treaties with Queen Victoria. The principal chief was named Lewanika. Rhodes himself never set foot in Northern Rhodesia, which in those days could hardly be distinguished from the Congo. The Katanga area of the Congo would today be part of Northern Rhodesia (the mines there were discovered by the British) except for a series of outlandish accidents. Northern Rhodesia, after long rule by the chartered company, was taken over by the British crown in 1924. It did not have as big a white population as Southern Rhodesia or as much experience of democratic institutions and so its status became that of a protectorate, not a self-governing colony.

THE GIST OF FEDERATION

At one year old the Federation is still a rather ugly child, but there is every hope that before long it will become a beautiful boy.
—GODFREY HUGGINS IN 1954.

Seen in its best light, from the long-range British point of view, the gist of federation is that the new state forms a kind of barrier preventing the successors of Malan from coming north, and the disciples of Nkrumah from coming south and east. It is, in brief, a device to keep out of central Africa the influence of both the Union and the Gold Coast. Suppose South Africa should leave the Commonwealth, as many people think it will within the next ten years. At least the new Federation will give British interests a strong bulwark against the Union, if it should be hostile. Suppose (to look in another direction) the Mau Mau troubles should wreck Kenya and seep into Uganda and Tanganyika. Federation, if it works, should be an ideal mechanism for stopping it from spreading further. The aim of federation is, in a word, to make central Africa secure.

Seen in another light, as a good many critics see it, federation is no more nor less than a clever, hypocritical artifice for maintaining and extending white supremacy in central Africa. This is why almost all Africans in the region dislike and oppose it. They ignore the pledge that the new state shall be based on racial partnership, and do not take seriously the safeguards it promises Africans. Moreover—much worse—the white supremacy perpetuated will not be that of the comparatively benign Colonial Office, but will be a white *settler* supremacy, which is an altogether different thing. Southern Rhodesia will, people say, without question dominate the new Federation, and Southern Rhodesia itself may be dominated in time by white supremacy extremists. The hugely preponderant African mass has been "sold down the river to a handful of whites," who have no intention whatever of creating a genuine multiracial state. Perhaps these criticisms sound severe. But plenty of die-hard whites ardently support federation for exactly the same reasons for which Africans deplore it. I met one prominent Lusaka politician who said frankly, "Why do we want federation? Because it will insure white supremacy forever!"

In any case the British pushed federation through for a variety of motives, and several other factors came into play:

1. Federation will make for a better economy. Northern Rhodesia, because of copper, is rich as Midas; Southern Rhodesia, with a large adverse trade balance, has a pronounced deficit economy. Combined, the two will complement each other nicely, and there will be opportunity for fruitful over-all economic planning and development. Moreover black labor from Nyasaland will assist industrialization in the Rhodesias.

2. Imperial considerations, as mentioned above and otherwise. Federation assures British survival in this vital part of Africa. One strong country is better than three weak countries.

3. Federation is bound to help, not hurt, African interests in the future. It opens the door not merely to African advance in economic fields, but politically.

4. It will, if successful, set the pattern for the evolution of racial partnership in other states, like Kenya.

Crosscurrents of feeling among whites on the spot have been abstruse. Some Northern Rhodesians did not like the idea of "bailing Southern Rhodesia out." Some Southern Rhodesians did not want to see more of their precious coal, from the great Wankie Colliery, go to assist the Northern Rhodesian Copperbelt. Also some Southern Rhodesians think that Northern Rhodesia and Nyasaland are "too black to be saved," that nationalism cannot be stopped in these areas, and that they will in the end be swamped not only by their own Africans but by the heavily expanding African communities of the partner states.

Those Northern Rhodesians who vehemently welcomed federation did so largely because they feared that, under sole authority of the Colonial Office, which stands in the long run for training Africans for self-government, Northern Rhodesia would become in time a "Gold Coast." Those Southern Rhodesians who vehemently welcomed it did so more out of economic

THE RHODESIAS AND CENTRAL AFRICAN FEDERATION 617

motives, in that federation will make Southern Rhodesia more prosperous, and keep taxes down. Nobody liked the safeguards for Africans that the British government insisted on.

Sir Andrew Cohen, whom we met in Uganda, is generally credited with being the father of the federation concept. Cohen was, as we know, an important intellectual influence in the Colonial Office before he came out to Uganda. He "sold" the federation idea to James Griffiths, who was Colonial Secretary in the Labor government. A conference to explore the project took place in Victoria Falls (with Africans participating) in 1951; this was followed by a conference in London. A draft constitution was prepared and made public in June, 1952. This had to be approved, before federation could become a fact, by the British parliament on behalf of Northern Rhodesia and Nyasaland, as well as by a referendum in Southern Rhodesia, which, being self-governing, had its own say in the matter. Northern Rhodesia and Nyasaland had no opportunity to vote. One of the most vivid debates ever to attend a development in British colonial policy followed in England, publicly and privately. People took very strong stands indeed for or against federation. It is instructive today to read letters from citizens that poured into such organs of opinion as the *Times*. Liberals wanted to be particularly sure that African rights were being safeguarded amply enough. In the end the decision to set up federation passed in the House of Commons by a vote of 304 to 260.

The Southern Rhodesian referendum, as I have already mentioned, took place in April, 1953, and roughly 25,000 out of 40,000 white voters approved it. It seems remarkable that some 15,000 whites in Southern Rhodesia should have been *against* federation. I asked Huggins why, and he outlined several reasons.

First, there are about 70,000 white South Africans in Southern Rhodesia. Some Afrikaners among these felt that federation was a blow to the Union and cut off forever the possibility of junction between the Union, their spiritual homeland, and Southern Rhodesia.[11]

Second, the white artisan class—bricklayers, railwaymen, and the like—feared that federation would lead to "Africanization" of the European services.

Third, hard-shell whites thought that the scheme gave the African too

---

[11] In South Africa itself, however, one section of opinion *favors* federation instead of the reverse, and this attitude is shared by some Afrikaners in the Rhodesias, too. The reason is that federation will presumably serve to keep the Gold Coast and the Mau Maus further away.

much, and resented bitterly the idea of having Negro members in the federal parliament.

Fourth, many citizens felt that Southern Rhodesia, even if hard up financially, was getting along quite nicely on its own. It had a self-governing status, won in 1922-23 after a long fight, and it did not welcome being "pulled down" by Northern Rhodesia and black Nyasaland. It was free of the Colonial Office, and did not want to get more closely involved with London.

Details of the federal structure itself are complex. One innovation is the creation of an African Affairs Board, independent both of the legislature and executive, which, in the event of legislation that might be discriminatory against Africans, has the right to appeal to the British government in London. Six members of the thirty-five-man federal parliament are, as mentioned above, Africans, and three others are Europeans representing African interests. The divisions of power are not altogether easy to follow. The Federation has no fewer than four governments—the federal instrument at the center and the three territorial governments. One joke is that never have so few people been ruled by so many.[12]

African grievances against federation, echoed by much liberal sentiment in London, are vociferous. The Africans insist that the scheme was imposed on them without their consent, and that the safeguards are meaningless except on paper, especially if large-scale white immigration is encouraged. Africans in Northern Rhodesia and in particular Nyasaland suffer politically from federation much more than do those in Southern Rhodesia, because the latter are less developed and have little to lose. But Northern Rhodesia and Nyasaland have fairly strong nationalist organizations and were evolving (so they thought) steadily toward self-government. The Nyasalanders have always had great faith in British institutions and respect for British administration. Now they feel that, even if they are still under the protection of the Colonial Office, their political development in an entity of their own is gravely hampered. Some even think that they have been "betrayed," turned over to the mercies of Rhodesian white settlers totally against their will.

---

[12] Die-hard whites have already sought to modify the new system, in particular F. M. Van Eeden, who came up with a proposal recently whereby the federal state, so newly born, should be partitioned. Mr. Van Eeden, who represents strong Afrikaner sentiment, would like to have Southern Rhodesia and the Northern Rhodesia Copperbelt amalgamated into one state (white, with future Dominion Status), and the rest of Northern Rhodesia and Nyasaland (black) returned to the Colonial Office. Van Eeden's proposals caused such a storm that he was expelled from the Huggins-Welensky federal party, although he was a leading MP and government whip. Defending his point of view, Van Eeden said that federation would soon collapse and that Huggins himself had called the new constitution "one of the craziest of documents." *East Africa and Rhodesia*, January 20, 1955.

We happened to be in Blantyre, Nyasaland, a day or two before federation became a fact in London. We met at night with a group of twelve or fourteen African chiefs, schoolteachers, and intellectuals, who were trying to draft desperate last-minute appeals to the UN, the Queen, and personages in London. Not since Prague in 1948, when President Beneš died, have I seen anything so poignant in a political realm. We talked in a simply furnished room in a mission, after efforts to find a rendezvous. Inarticulate with grief (like the Czechs), the Nyasalanders told us their story, how—as they saw it—they were losing their country and all that was most precious to them, their freedom and national identity. They spoke without rancor, respectfully, and with great dignity. They could not believe that London would not, in the end, make some turnabout and rescue them from their impending fate. They hoped for a miracle. It did not come, and they watched their country die.

On their side the British and pro-British Africans make two or three main points. (1) *Six Africans sit in the new federal parliament.* Whether they are Quislings or not does not matter. They are present. The door has been opened. One liberal South African jurist told us with admiration, "Think what a difference it would have made to *our* whole political and emotional evolution if *we* had black MP's!"[13] (2) Segregation patterns are bound to be ameliorated, as more and more Africans get what they need above all—political education and experience. Social contact will inevitably follow official contact. (3) The tyranny of the white trade unions in the north will in time be diminished because Northern Rhodesia is now part of the federal state.

Be this as it may be, I never met a single African in the Rhodesias or elsewhere who favored federation. When I mentioned this to a prominent cabinet minister, he replied scoffingly, "Ah, they don't know their own minds! As well ask a child of two how to operate a battleship." Perhaps.

One word more. The real test will, of course, be whether or not the Federation does genuinely set up a racial partnership, on decent terms. This in turn will depend on two matters which we shall allude to presently, extension of the suffrage and color bar. Many earnest Britons in the Federation do not think that the pace toward reform is fast enough.

---

[13] On the other hand the Europeans will do their best to keep the African legislators completely powerless. Unless the Africans can produce concrete results and do something for their own people, bitterness and frustration may be intensified rather than the reverse.

CHAPTER 31

More about Rhodesia and Nyasaland

Africa is not polite.
—E. S. GROGAN

MUCH of Southern Rhodesia still gives a strong note of being open frontier, like Oklahoma or the Texas Panhandle until yesterday. Even the big towns, no matter how British they may be in character, have qualities of the American West; Salisbury might be York dropped into the middle of Wyoming, or even California, with clear hot sunshine by day, cool nights, flamboyant sunsets, long straight streets, and low white buildings with flowering shrubs built around patios. The people, too, have a marked frontier spirit, especially if they are descendants of the earliest pioneers. A man will say proudly, "My father was an 1890 pioneer," or, "My mother came up by oxcart in 1893."

Southern Rhodesia is a small country for Africa, about the size of Japan. It lies for the most part between the Limpopo and Zambesi, and has, curiously enough, no lakes. Its backbone is called the Great Dyke; this is a seam, or welt, cutting straight across the country for 330 miles, and containing much of its mineral wealth, including chrome, the second most valuable article of export. The first is tobacco. The United States is the major purchaser of Rhodesian chrome, which has high strategic value.

One-half the land (roughly 47 million acres out of 95 million) is owned by whites, although the whites are less than eight per cent of the population. The *best* land is mostly white-owned. As in Kenya, the Europeans took for themselves the healthiest and most productive areas; much African land is "under the fly" or has other disadvantages. Africans may, in certain circumstances, be peremptorily moved off their land in the reserves and transplanted somewhere else, whether they want to go or not, if mineral wealth is discovered on their property. Hundreds of families have been moved, sometimes to unhealthy areas where they do not even know the language. No injustice in contemporary Africa is more flagrant.

Of the white population, which has doubled in seven years, almost half is South African. Not all the South Africans are, however, Afrikaners. It is sometimes difficult to draw the line between "British" South Africans and "Dutch" South Africans; the best criterion is membership in the Dutch Reformed church, which claims about 19,000 members. There has been a tendency recently for emigrant Afrikaners to leapfrog Southern Rhodesia and settle in Northern. It is the British stock which prefers Southern Rhodesia. In any case Southern Rhodesia—although it desperately wants white immigration—has no intention of being swamped by whites from the Union, any more than it wants to be swamped by the blacks, and immigration from South Africa is now strictly controlled.

As to the Africans the two chief tribes are, as we know, the Matabele in the south, around Bulawayo, and the Mashona to the north. Rhodesians say that the Matabele are a phlegmatic people, who resemble Scandinavians in temperament; the volatile Mashona are more like Italians or Greeks. Tribal distinctions have tended to break down, partly because so many Africans have moved into the towns, partly because the original tribes have been much diluted by black labor from outside. Hardly any organized nationalism exists as yet, and there is no African community that comes anywhere near being as sophisticated or developed as the Baganda, say, or the Ibos in Nigeria.

SALISBURY (population about 150,000, of which roughly a third is white) lies at 4,825 feet, and the altitude makes the climate brilliant. Like Nairobi, it became the capital by accident. The flag was planted here, instead of higher up at Mount Hampden, which was Selous' favorite camp site and which had been selected as the capital, when the pioneers in the first column decided that they had come far enough. Salisbury—also Bulawayo—has extraordinarily broad streets; this is because Rhodes wanted them wide enough to hold comfortably an eight-pair team of oxen making a U-turn. Salisbury has blood-red London buses—bought second hand, shipped to Durban, and driven up from the coast. The train whistles sound American. Salisbury is the headquarters of the Capricorn Society, and has a successful and articulate African press under white management. Nearby is one of the best schools in southern Africa, by name Dumbushawa. Some old-style conventions still hold sway in Salisbury; women are, for instance, not allowed in bars. Until recently a block of flats had a sign, CYCLISTS, DOGS, AND AFRICANS NOT ALLOWED. Pressure of opinion brought it down.

The population of BULAWAYO (altitude 4,469 feet) has more than doubled in five years, and is now 123,000. There are about 35,000 whites. The housing shortage, both for Europeans and natives, is acute, as it is in Salisbury. Bulawayo, to my mind, has a good deal more character than Salisbury, and also has strong American overtones. The chief thoroughfare is called Main Street, and the avenues are numbered. Sidewalks are not paved, but consist of red dirt, which becomes mud when it rains. The seal of the city is copied from Lobengula's totem, and consists of three rock rabbits; the name "Bulawayo" means "Place of Slaughter," which it often was in Lobengula's day. Bulawayo is the center of pro-Union sentiment in Southern Rhodesia, the heart of the white labor movement, and an important communications center. The need for social services has far outstripped the financial ability of the government to provide them. I asked a leading citizen of Bulawayo if the local economy might not be improved by giving the Africans higher wages, so that they would have more purchasing power. Answer: "They're not worth the wages we pay now." But this is an outmoded view.

The Rhodes grave in the Matopo Hills twenty miles from Bulawayo, is, of course, one of the supreme sights in Africa. Rhodes fell in love with the Matopos when he penetrated here in 1896 to make peace with the Matabele chiefs, named the scene "World's View," and decided to be buried on a hill top, facing north. The site is wild, forlorn, and almost forbidding in its naked loneliness and grandeur. Lichens peculiarly colored—chartreuse, lemon, reddish green—make tufts of carpet over an enormous mound of black igneous rock slippery as ice. Leopards yawn in thickets below. The abrupt mound of rock, with its litter of boulders, has a curious scarification, supposed to have been made by the tracks of the gun carriage bearing Rhodes's body, when it was hauled by brute force up the steep slope. Rhodes left his imprint even on rock. The slab marking the actual grave carries only the inscription: HERE LIE THE REMAINS OF CECIL JOHN RHODES—with no other text or dates. Nobody can be buried in this area, which Rhodes bought outright and presented to the Rhodesian government, except by act of parliament. Jameson too is buried here, close to the friend he betrayed unwittingly. Sliding down the rock, which has something of the texture and even the appearance of a flat-iron, I thought that only a true megalomaniac, who nevertheless must on occasion have experienced neurotic insecurities, would choose for his grave a setting so majestically isolated and immovable.

Another of the supreme sights of Africa, VICTORIA FALLS, is shared by Southern and Northern Rhodesia. For some reason I have always been bored by great waterfalls, but it cannot be denied that this one is spectacularly wet, noisy, and possessed of profound beauty and momentum. The Victoria

MORE ABOUT RHODESIA AND NYASALAND

Falls (discovered by Livingstone in 1855, and named by him) lie on the Zambesi 290 miles from Bulawayo; the Africans call them "the smoke that thunders." So little known and inaccessible was this area until recent times that only forty-eight Europeans visited the Falls in all from Livingstone's discovery until 1900—forty-five years.[1] The Victoria Falls are broader than Niagara, and more than twice as high, 347 feet as against 167; the highest known flow of water was 169,000,000 gallons per minute, and the mean annual flow is 47,000,000 gallons per minute, which is a lot of water. This immense amount of river, crashing down into a narrow chasm, explodes upwards into huge flowers of spray, producing rainbows of unsurpassed purity and brilliance. Rhodes picked the site of the railway bridge that spans the Zambesi here, connecting Northern with Southern Rhodesia. Sometimes spray hits the trains, as Rhodes hoped it would. Interestingly enough, only two other bridges have ever been built across the Zambesi, which is the fourth most important river in Africa and is 1,600 miles long. Africa is a continent short on bridges.

Not far away from Victoria Falls is the Wankie Game Reserve; this covers five thousand square miles and is particularly distinguished for elephants. Southern Rhodesia, like the Sudan, has set about the wholesale extermination of big game in other parts of the country in an attempt to prevent the spread of the tsetse fly. Another animal menace is the red-billed weaver, a kind of finch. These fly in solid clouds three miles long and a mile wide, and eat their way through the sorghum fields. The best way to get rid of them is to dynamite the trees in which they rest at night, a noisy process.

*

Southern Rhodesia lives on tobacco, chrome, gold, and asbestos, among other things. Chrome is the biggest dollar earner. Tobacco goes mostly to the United Kingdom and Australia; we watched a million pounds of it being auctioned in Salisbury one sunny morning. Rhodesia grows no wheat and must import much of its food. One pressing economic difficulty is transportation. The country has grown too fast; the railway and roads are simply not able to cope with the burden put on them. The roads have to be heavily metaled and bound, or they will blow away. Many are "strip" roads, with parallel tracks just wide enough to hold the wheels of a car. The railway has been so drowned with traffic that, for a time, huge backlogs of chrome piled up on the sidings, and could not be moved for months. Recently the United States lent $10,000,000 to Southern Rhodesia for railway development

[1] *The Victoria Falls*, edited by J. Desmond Clark, a fascinating brochure published in Northern Rhodesia in 1952.

(through the FOA), following a £5,000,000 loan to Rhodesian Railways.

"The greatest wealth of Southern Rhodesia," an Indian friend in Salisbury told us, "is its emptiness." The country is, virtually speaking, still a vacuum.

One large and ambitious development is the Kariba Gorge scheme, which is to cost £54 million and which involves damming the Zambesi about three hundred miles from Victoria Falls. Fierce political dispute accompanied the inauguration of this project. Northern Rhodesians wanted a different site on their own territory, on the Kafue River. Had it not been for federation, which made it easier to establish a broad over-all view, the fight might still be going on. The Kariba Dam will be the largest in the world, and will store three times as much water as Hoover Dam in the United States, with a consequent prodigious production of electric power. The power generated will be a government monopoly. A large share of the cost of the Kariba scheme will, it is hoped, be provided by the World Bank or the United States. One point, mentioned by few, is that an estimated 29,000 Africans will have to be moved out of the flooded area, and given new homes elsewhere.[2]

NOW NORTHERN RHODESIA

Northern Rhodesia is almost twice the size of Southern, and is lower-lying, flatter, and more tropical. We are getting fairly close to the Equator now. The countryside looks, for the most part, dreary—unending miles of dry savanna and plateau. The towns have little of the metropolitan quality of Salisbury or Bulawayo, which are real cities. Northern Rhodesia, which lives mostly on copper, is like a Texas millionaire—somewhat dull and perhaps uncouth, but rich. The chief difference between Northern Rhodesia and Southern is that Southern is much whiter, or likes to think it is. Also Southern Rhodesia is self-governing (within federation) while Northern is still a protectorate. Southern Rhodesians are British "subjects," whereas Northern Rhodesians are merely British "protected persons."

The capital, LUSAKA, looks like a Wild West set in early, shabby movies. The European population is about 6,000; the African, about 50,000. The altitude is 4,198 feet. Weeds and rough scrub fill the two-channeled avenue leading out to Government House, and the long, broad main street, lined by arcaded wooden shops in bad need of a paint job, is nicknamed "High Street, Africa." Properly it is called Cairo Road, and indeed one wing of the Cape to Cairo highway, if such it can be called, passes through here. Lusaka has one cinema, but no daily newspaper. There is no direct rail connection with Salisbury, the sister capital. We visited one secondary school, Munali,

[2] New York *Times*, March 3, 1955.

MORE ABOUT RHODESIA AND NYASALAND 625

with a teaching staff half European, half African—the *only* secondary school for Africans in the entire country, which is almost twice the size of California. Lusaka has, however, one of the most fruitful and enterprising radio stations on the continent, ZQP, which has the biggest collection of African music (20,000 records) in Africa, reaches at least 100,000 people regularly, and has been picked up in places as far away as Scandinavia and the West Indies. Programs are broadcast in simple English, Nyanja (which covers most of Nyasaland), the Matabele and Mashona languages for Southern Rhodesia, and three principal Northern Rhodesian languages, Tonga, Bemba, and Lozi. The educational impact of a radio station like this is profound. One reason why adult education for Africans is so limited in much of the continent is that most homes have no light at night. But a radio set working on a simple battery reaches people through their ears.[3]

LIVINGSTONE (altitude 2,997 feet, European population 2,317) was the capital till 1935, and is the oldest municipality in Northern Rhodesia. It has one of the principal airports in southern Africa, the Zambesi Sawmills, and, seven miles away, Victoria Falls. Also here is the Rhodes-Livingstone Museum, a most stimulating, pleasant, and instructive institution. (Distinguished, too, is the Rhodes-Livingstone Institute at Lusaka, which does much valuable work in anthropology and similar fields.) The chief boast of the museum in Livingstone is, of course, its collection of letters, documents and the like having to do with the great explorer-missionary. What interested me more was something alive. A Bushman happened to be there, the only Bushman we saw in Africa. He had been brought up from Bechuanaland, and was en route to Bulawayo, where the Rhodes Centenary Exhibition was about to open. He was having a good time in Livingstone, where the museum authorities showed him every courtesy. Luckily a giraffe had just died in the nearby game reserve, and he was able to occupy himself by carving arrowheads out of its bones. Also he recorded some of his native music, and we heard him sing some strange, sad Bushman songs. I have often wondered what happened to this curious and appealing little creature after he finished being an exhibit at Bulawayo.

Northern Rhodesia has a new game reserve, the Kafue National Park, which is said to be the largest in the world, as well as several other reserves and good opportunity for shooting game in the Luangwa Valley. The

[3] I wish I had space to list samples of ZQP's programing—vernacular talks, English lessons, relays of BBC news, and instruction on such local issues as locust extermination. "Country" music (that is, recordings of authentic native music from out in the bush) is popular, and so is the more sophisticated "town" music, or *Saba-saba*, which sounds like calypso. "Adapted tribal music," with European instrumentation, is also widely liked.

Northern Rhodesian government would like very much to get more safari and tourist business. Two animals are to be found here unknown elsewhere in the world—Cookson's wildebeest and the Senga kob. Northern Rhodesia, unlike Southern, does not kill off game as a measure against the tsetse fly.

The European population has doubled since 1946, and is now almost 45,000. About half of this is South African. The South Africans are not kept out by a quota system, as in Southern Rhodesia. No settlers are allowed to buy crown land on freehold, but most leases on big farms run for 999 years, which is presumably long enough to make the purchaser feel at home. The price varies by locality, ranging from 6s. 6d. per acre to 30s. When land is alienated to a purchaser he pays one-third down and an annual rental of 4 per cent on the rest. To make a success of a mixed farm near a line of rail, the settler needs a capital of at least £4,000.[4] The native reserves are, of course, inalienable to European settlement, and these cover an enormous area. But, as in Kenya and Southern Rhodesia, much African land is uncultivable, inferior, or unhealthy.

The greatest of Rhodesian tribes is the Barotse, and Barotseland has a special protected status deriving from the early treaties with Queen Victoria. The Barotse are a conservative, closely knit people, who still seem to be living in the days of Livingstone. Their form of government is, in effect, a constitutional monarchy, under a king, Mwanawina III, a son of the great Lewanika, who first made overtures to the British when he thought that the Matabele might come up and destroy him. The Barotse have two capitals, Lealui on the plains and Limulunga on the sand belt, to which the court moves ceremoniously when the rains come. The movement is by royal barges and canoes, and is a bizarre spectacle.

Some of the most startlingly primitive and picturesque tribes in all Africa are Northern Rhodesian. The Tonga like to wear sticks of ivory through their nostrils. The Ila, south of Barotseland, dress their hair into large tapering cones as solid as a tusk and two feet high, made by packing the hair with eland dung and never removed. The most advanced tribe is probably the Lozi, and the Bemba are influential on the Copperbelt, where much intermingling has taken place. The Makishi are adept at "pole dancing," in which boys perform astonishing gyrations on the top of long poles.[5] In one tribe hunters are buried standing up, with their hands projecting from the grave and holding a stick. When an animal is killed, a spoonful of blood is poured

[4] These figures are from a government pamphlet, *Northern Rhodesia*, a *Pocket Book Guide*, 1953. The density of population of Northern Rhodesia is only 1.4 per square mile. In the Kasempa district (25,000 square miles) there are only twenty-seven Europeans—one to every 926 square miles.

[5] See *African Dances of Northern Rhodesia*, a brochure by W. V. Brelsford.

on this stick, and drips into the skull's mouth, as a libation to the gods of the chase. There is no cannibalism in Northern Rhodesia, but until recently necrophagy—eating of corpses—was quite common. It was not even against the law, provided that the person eaten had died a natural death, any more than it is among survivors in a lifeboat.

*

Northern Rhodesia has an incipiently powerful and articulate nationalist movement, focused in the Northern Rhodesian National Congress, the president of which is Harry Nkumbula. We had several talks with this lively personality. He went to the London School of Economics, and this, the British say, is what turned him into a rabid nationalist, not anything in Rhodesia itself. Nkumbula was recently expelled from Southern Rhodesia, when he made a visit there; this occurred soon after the President of the Nyasaland National Congress was prohibited from entering *Northern* Rhodesia.[6] Nationalists in the new Federation have a hard time getting around. Once Mr. Nkumbula called a "pan-African" conference in Ndola, Northern Rhodesia, of nationalists from Kenya, Tanganyika, Uganda, and Zanzibar, as well as from the Rhodesias and Nyasaland, but the meeting was a fiasco partly, it seems, because few delegates arrived. There was a good reason for this. The British authorities intercepted them on arrival in Rhodesian territory, and sent them back to where they came from. In January, 1955, Nkumbula was arrested and sentenced to two months' imprisonment at hard labor, after the police raided his house near Lusaka and found forbidden literature there.

A peculiar assortment of books and periodicals is prohibited circulation in Northern Rhodesia. The list includes Communist publications as a matter of course, as well as much religious and other literature, like the Jehovah's Witnesses yearbooks, various tracts put out in New York by the Watchtower Bible and Tract Society, *Fight Comics,* and, of all things, several books by the eminent Indian philosopher Sri Aurobindo, no doubt because he teaches civil disobedience.[7]

Not all nationalists in the country are as extreme as Mr. Nkumbula, but the chances are that, if suppressed unfairly, they will become steadily more extreme. We met one delightful old African gentleman who said that relations between the races had been good in Northern Rhodesia ever since "the death of the late Dr. Livingstone" (his exact words), and that he could not

---

[6] *African Digest,* September-October, 1954.
[7] Indignant questions were asked recently in the House of Commons about the propriety of this type of censorship, as well as about a new order empowering the Northern Rhodesian government to send prisoners to jails in *South Africa,* instead of at home, presumably because Rhodesian prison facilities are not ample enough.

believe that the British government would ever do deliberate harm to the Rhodesian people.

THE COPPERBELT

The Northern Rhodesian Copperbelt, which produces about 15 per cent of the free world's copper and is the second richest copper deposit in the world, lies adjacent to the Katanga fields in the Congo. What is known as the "Congo Pedicle" dips down sharply into Rhodesia, and the two areas are part of the same geological formation. Copper was discovered here long ago, but lay fallow in Rhodesia, where production did not begin until as recently as 1931. The Copperbelt is the newest of the great mining properties of the world. There are four principal mines, which between them produce about 450,000 tons of copper per year. These are, in order of size, Nchanga, Mufulira, Roan Antelope, and Nkana. All have been spectacularly successful. Their interrelations are abstruse, as may be seen on the chart on page 629. Nchanga and Rhokana (the name of the mine at Nkana) are controlled by the Oppenheimer interests in South Africa, through the Anglo-American Corporation; Mufulira and Roan Antelope by the Rhodesian Selection Trust and the American Metal Company of New York, although Anglo-American also has a one-third interest in Mufulira.[8]

Practically everything in Northern Rhodesia depends on the price of copper. This is high now, and has been high for some years, with the result that the country has had a fantastic boom. Its budget was only about one million pounds twenty years ago, and is around £30 million today. The mines have an annual output valued at £130,000,000, produce about 93 per cent of the export revenue of Northern Rhodesia, provide 85 per cent of its taxes, and earn a profit (before taxes) of about £40,000,000. As to the new Federation, it will depend on copper for not less than 50 per cent of its tax revenues and 60 per cent of its total exports. If a visitor asks what will happen in Rhodesia if the price of copper should fall catastrophically, people blanch and change the subject. Among other things practically all social services (those that exist) would have to be drastically reduced. Seldom has any country hitched itself to such a single star.[9]

---

[8] The "American" mines on the Copperbelt, that is, those controlled in part from New York, are Mufulira and Roan Antelope. There is very little American capital in the Anglo-American Corporation, despite its name.

[9] One difficulty is fuel. The mines need about 90,000 tons of coal per month, and the railway from Wankie, 500 miles away, cannot deliver more than 70,000 tons. The difference is made up by burning wood. The forests near Kitwe and the other mining towns are as a result rapidly disappearing.

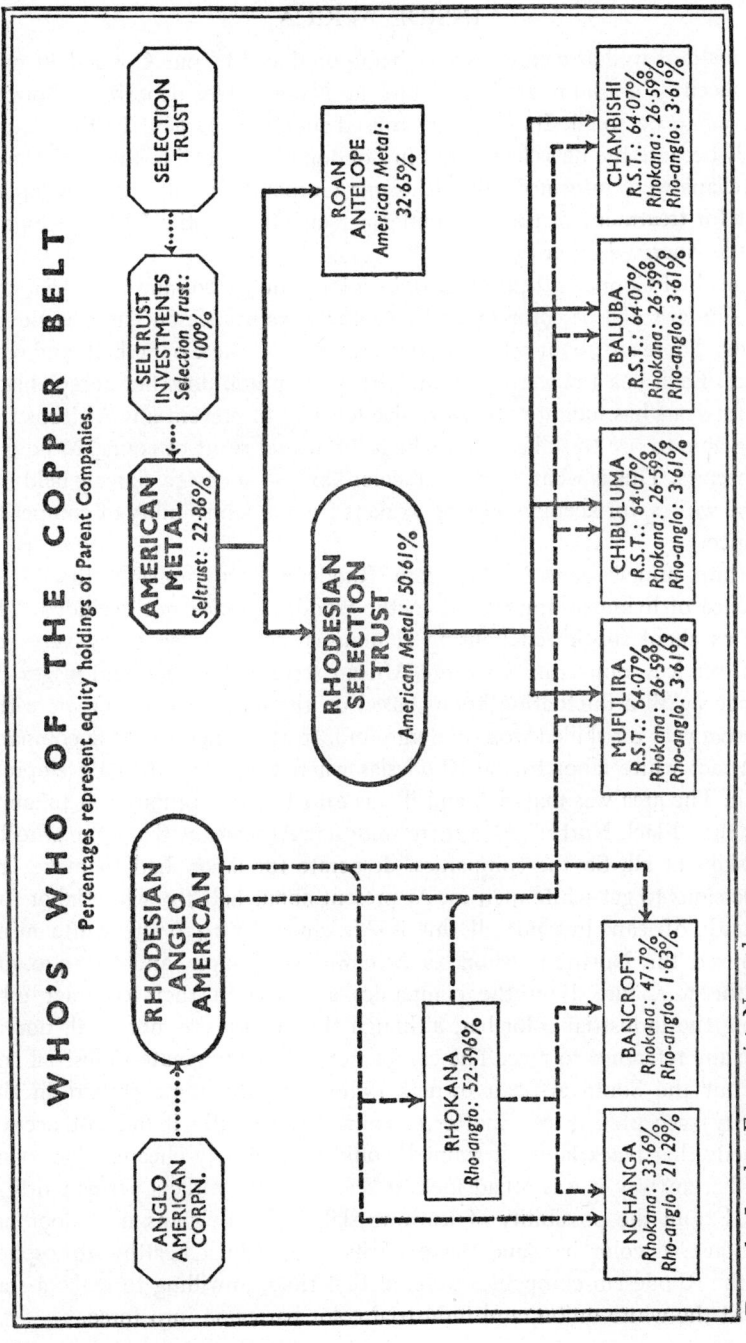

From the London Economist, November 27, 1954

Cobalt, as well as copper, is now being produced by one Copperbelt mine, and recently uranium ore was found at Nkana. The deposit is, however, believed to be small. Its discovery caused much excitement in the vicinity, if only because the news leaked out in London before the Northern Rhodesian politicians were informed. The Rhokana Corporation will presently build a plant for treatment of this ore, under agreement with the United Kingdom Atomic Energy Authority.

The chief Copperbelt problem is, by a long shot, labor and industrial color bar. The gist of this complex and in many ways unpleasant story is the following. There are about 37,000 African workers on the Copperbelt, and 6,000 whites. Each has a powerful union. The white union does not accept blacks, and for years has fought with aggressive tenacity to prevent any Africans from being able to rise to skilled jobs, which the whites want of course to hold for themselves. This is what "industrial color bar" is—a device, fiercely held onto by the whites, for keeping African workers from any possibility of competitive advance.

White mineworkers in Northern Rhodesia have probably the highest standard of living of any miners in the world, America not excluded. They have excellent subsidized housing at nominal cost, garden cities, very good social services, opportunity to hire African servants cheaply, and wages that average (with a fluctuating bonus based on the price of copper) more than £2,000 a year for skilled work underground. It was difficult for the companies to attract white labor to the Rhodesias when the Copperbelt development began. The area was malarial, and it was called contemptuously in Johannesburg the "Black North." Also there were few Africans at that time who had any skills at all. So the companies, desperate for labor, had to make large concessions to get white men in. At present about half the white labor force is South African, but not all this is Afrikaner. In 1936 the white miners organized the Northern Rhodesia Mineworkers Union, and in 1940, during the war, forced on the companies a clause in their contract establishing the industrial color bar, although this phrase was not used, nor was there any reference to race. The companies did not originate industrial color bar, but the South African owners (who have the same system in their country) accepted it as a matter of course. Apparently it did not occur to anybody that black labor, if trained, could be infinitely cheaper than white, and that anyway it was a bad idea to keep African workers permanently excluded from the possibility of learning skills. The Belgians next door have no industrial color bar, and make terrific profits in a healthy atmosphere. But the Rhodesian companies were, at that time, unwilling to make a stand against the white union, and industrial color bar came into force.

MORE ABOUT RHODESIA AND NYASALAND 631

The black union, called the Northern Rhodesia African Mineworkers Trade Union, was organized in 1949. It has a large membership, and is well run. In 1953 it fought and won an important strike. It struck again early in 1955, but was beaten. During this strike, which lasted for two months, the Federation lost about $150,000 per day in taxes, and the gross cost to the companies was calculated at $2,155,000 per week. The companies in the end took back 32,000 African strikers without penalty, and this made the white union (which hoped that the strike would destroy the black union) unhappy. There is a tendency among the operators to play one union off against the other.

African miners on the Copperbelt live in compounds, but they are not on contract. Unlike those on the Rand, they are free to come and go. The average tenure at Roan Antelope is about fifty months, and a beginning at least has been made to create a permanent, stable, non-migratory labor force. Moreover, married men are permitted to live with their families, in sharp contrast to South Africa. About 65 per cent of African miners on the Copperbelt have their families with them, and this helps greatly to improve morale and keep costs down.

The chief African grievance, aside from industrial color bar, is the acute disparity in wages. African wages have gone up (partly as a result of the successful strike in 1953), but not by much. The average wage of the European underground worker is £105 per month; that of the African can be as low as £6. It is true that Africans receive free some services that the European has to pay for, and their housing and food are also free. Even so the fact that the white man gets approximately *seventeen times* the cash wages of the black man is, to most observers, scandalous.

Several characteristics distinguish the African labor force, the mine operators say, but these are changing or disappearing. (1) Africans are not accustomed to a money economy, and are apt to squander cash. (2) It is difficult to keep them on a job year after year. (3) They are better at work with a repetition pattern than at tasks that call for originality. (4) They lack incentive, since, if they do manage to save any money, they feel compelled by custom to share this with their families or send it back to the reserves. (5) They do not like positions of responsibility, which may make it necessary for them to give orders to other Africans. This can disturb clan or family relationships and lead to retaliation by black magic.

Since 1948 repeated efforts have been made to eliminate or at least ameliorate industrial color bar. Various commissions have come out from England to explore the subject. The general conclusion is that the system is not only morally obnoxious but economically idiotic. The white union itself, realizing the invidiousness of its position, recently said that it would agree to lift color bar if the companies would agree to the principle of equal pay for equal work. The obvious catch was that the union knew perfectly well that the operators could not possibly agree to this, without upsetting the whole wage structure and adding greatly to their costs. The Rhodesian Selection Trust-American Metal Company group has lately taken a strong—in fact unprecedented—stand for reduction of industrial color bar, but the South African owners are much more cautious. The American group even went so far as to give notice of termination of its contract with the white union, which meant risking a *white* strike, in an effort to get rid of industrial color bar, but this notice was withdrawn later and negotiations began anew. The Oppenheimer interests have now reached the point of being willing to turn over 5 per cent of European jobs, but no more, to Africans over a period of five years. The Rhodesian Selection Trust-American Metal group does not think that this goes far enough, and advocates a system whereby African advancement is determined on the basis of capability alone.

Industrial color bar will probably hang on in Northern Rhodesia for a long time to come, but in the end it will disappear—if only because no industry can operate forever on the basis of discrimination against the huge majority of its own working staff. One American owner told us, "We will have to get around to the Belgian system sooner or later, not only as a means to avoid conflict but as a matter of simple decency and right."

COLOR BAR IN THE RHODESIAS

And now to other aspects of color bar. In some respects segregation is more pronounced in the Rhodesias than anywhere else in Africa, even Kenya and the Union. There are, no doubt, honest English people who have a sentimental attachment to Rhodesia, and for that matter honest Rhodesians who have no basis of comparison with other countries and who are blind to what is happening under their noses, ignorant of the fact that racial discriminations in Rhodesia are among the most barbarous, shameful, and disgusting in the world.

In Lusaka when we were there Africans were not allowed *in* most European shops, but had to use hatchways. They stood in line out in the dust or rain in dark passageways on the side of or behind the shop, where a kind of peephole with a small ledge was built into the wall. Through this hatch they called out their wants, and merchandise was (if the white salesman inside chose to pay attention) pushed out to them through the slot. Africans were not allowed to touch or handle articles; they could not feel the texture of a bit of cloth or try on things, and they had no opportunity for looking around or making any choice.[10] We visited a bank, Here too Africans had to do their business through a trap door in the wall, like a speakeasy window, while waiting outside in the mud. The white tellers inside might, or might not, pay attention to them. A British lady in Lusaka told us, "I do not like Africans. But I do not think that those hatches should be *allowed* in a British protectorate. They make me crawl with shame."

At the Lusaka airport (while we were there) a commercial airliner arrived with one African among its passengers. The plane, en route south, stopped here for lunch. The Negro was not allowed in the airport restaurant, and hence could get nothing to eat. This is a minor episode, of course. But such minor episodes multiplied endlessly leave a bitter sting.

There is no movie for Africans in Lusaka, no theater, and no facility for public recreation. In theory segregation has been abolished at the post office, but the one we saw had two entrances, with Africans squeezed into a dark passageway a quarter of the size of the white section. One social point is that Government House has to give official dinners and receptions in duplicate. To the first are invited a few Africans (members of the LEGCO for instance) together with whites who will bring themselves to break bread with them; the second is for whites only. I asked if Roy Welensky, who is scheduled to be Huggins' successor as prime minister of the Federation, had ever had a meal with an African. Answer: "Doubtful." Perhaps if a visitor arrives from the Union none of this will seem surprising; but if he comes from the Congo, where Africans just across the frontier are given decent facilities and fair treatment, he will find the atmosphere shocking beyond belief.

Africans in Northern Rhodesia are probably worse off than those in the Union from the point of view of educational opportunity, but better off in some economic respects. They have more chance of becoming bricklayers or minor artisans, and (unlike their countrymen in Southern Rhodesia) they can join effective unions and have the right to strike. Also they can become members of political organizations and their rights on the land are carefully safeguarded.

In Southern Rhodesia (much of what follows applies to Northern Rhodesia also), Africans cannot possess firearms, cannot enter a white hotel, cannot in metropolitan areas go out after curfew without a pass, and cannot drink liquor or European beer. Their housing is abominable—almost as bad as in the Union. Salisbury, with an African population of 109,490, has no movie or

---

[10] The hatch system has recently been abolished in the Copperbelt towns, like Ndola. Africans who could not endure the indignity any longer picketed the European shops to keep other Africans from buying. This hurt business so much that the shops gave way. London *Times*, February 10, 1954.

meeting hall for Africans, and they are not allowed in the European theaters. Segregation is complete in local transportation. Africans are permitted to travel second class on the trains, but in segregated compartments; they are not allowed to eat in the dining car. There is no provision whatever for African waiting rooms or restaurants in the stations. Africans may, however, buy coffee at a stall and drink standing up. There are practically no African civil servants in the upper brackets, and (except as demonstration pieces during royal visits) Africans are never invited to official functions. They are not allowed to use elevators in office buildings, and the post office and schools are rigidly segregated. The primary school system, such as it is, exists in triplicate, with separate facilities for Africans, Asians, and whites—an expensive way to run education. The most painful single experience I had in Africa was, I think, a trip to a Native Purchase Area near Salisbury. Here we visited, among other things, a country school. The poverty, the squalor, the pitiable lack of equipment, the sheer inhuman primitiveness, were bad enough. But what really hurt was that our white escort, a senior government official, refused ostentatiously to shake hands with the perfectly decent, perfectly respectable, and perfectly humble black schoolmaster.

African artisans in Southern Rhodesia have an embryo union, but it is not officially recognized; the mines are not yet organized. On the railways the train crews are all white, except the African coalman on the tender, who shovels coal to the white fireman, who in turn shovels it into the locomotive. The African coalman, who does most of the hard work, gets one-fifth of the white fireman's wages. But a senior railway official told me, "We will have African firemen in time. Do not tell anybody I said this." Ten thousand Africans walked out recently at the Wankie Colliery. European workers there get $250 a month or more; Africans get from 21 cents to 50 cents a day.[11]

All this is poisonous enough—in a state supposed to be committed to racial "partnership." Farsighted people are worried further by what is going to happen when, as industrialization proceeds inexorably, the white and black populations find themselves adjacent on a much broader front than at present. Thousands upon thousands of Africans will in the next few years erupt out of the reserves, and come into the factories and towns. The possibilities of conflict are, as is only too obvious, boundless. One Rhodesian executive told us blandly, "Things are not too bad for our Africans here, because they have not yet learned about passive resistance and all that rot, like Africans in the Union, so that we have not had to *retaliate*."

[11] *Time*, February 22, 1954.

*

Other white attitudes are more moderate. By and large (as in the American South), it is the poorer class of whites that is most Negrophobe. Among those educated, many Europeans have an acute sense of bad conscience about segregation, feel a deep responsibility for the plight of Africans, and want genuinely to make race relations better. One should not think that Rhodesia is populated by monsters. A distinguished parliamentarian said to me, "Yes, we will try to keep this a predominantly white country south of the Zambesi for as long as we can, but we will fail. White domination will not last more than fifty years. And perhaps it is a good thing that we shall fail. After all, we are all members of the human race."

Decent whites in Rhodesia are positively schizophrenic about the African, as many American southerners are about the Negro. The prevailing mood is not so much hatred or even "genetic fear" as a helpless sense of having lost contact and authority, plus irritation at African fecklessness and backwardness. I heard phrases like "What did these people do with self-government during the centuries they had it?" and "They will be done in in the end *by their own leaders*, if we do not protect them!"

I was much struck by a brochure put out by the Southern Rhodesian government called *Your Servant and You*—advice to the European housewife on how to treat African domestic servants. The servant should be given a pound and a half of mealie meal a day, half a pound of meat if available, vegetables (which he will not like), sugar, salt, and a "slice of bread and jam and tea or coffee remaining from the table." Also:

> The African has dignity. Do not allow your small children to give cheeky orders to a grown-up, or to speak or act rudely to him. Do not lose your temper with a native servant. His women are his inferiors, and it is asking for trouble for a woman to scold a native loudly (especially in the presence of other natives) or, above all, to strike him. . . . The African is a good mimic, and if you lose your dignity you will be laughed at.
> In giving orders, always be clear and concise. Say, "Do this," rather than "Don't do that." Be sure the African understands what you want, for he thinks it polite to say "Yes" even when he doesn't understand. Your servants will come from many different tribes, probably speaking many different languages. In common, they have only "Kitchen Kaffir," so you would be well advised to learn this easy lingua franca of the kitchen. Give directions one at a time, and don't nag.
> The African is modest. Be as modest before him as before any man of your own race. Respect his ideas about women. You may think him a savage—and in many cases his moral outlook has little in common

with ours—but he never allows even a small native girl to appear naked before a man or boy, so your little girl should not do this. . . . Although the African is naturally fond of children, you must never leave your daughter with an African male, nor allow her to wander alone in sparsely populated areas.

Make your own beds, wash your own underclothing and do not expect your houseboy to wash stained linen. It outrages his sense of what is proper.

The law forbids you to give the African alcoholic liquors. He has his own national drink (kaffir beer), which he likes and which is good for him, but sometimes he is misled into drinking *skokiaan* (a strange and often deadly brew of evil ingredients) or into accepting European drinks to which he is not accustomed.

The most important thing of all is that you should adopt the right attitude towards the African. He naturally looks for courtesy and justice.

Time and time again we heard from Europeans the analogy to the American Negro. One politician said boastfully, "This country is like the American South at its best." Of course, as scarcely needs to be pointed out, Rhodesia differs from the American South in at least four important particulars. First, Negroes in the United States are a minority of the population, not a large majority. Second, Negroes in Africa are not descendants of imported slaves, but were the original possessors of the country. Third, segregation in America is steadily on the decline, not the opposite, particularly in education. Fourth, the law by and large is on the Negro's side, not against him.

*

African attitudes in Rhodesia are, to a degree, what they are in Kenya. "We care nothing about being allowed into white hotels, but we want more education and economic opportunity." And, "The white man still thinks that we are children. He gives us no chance to express ourselves, to tell him what we are really like." And, "We respect some tories. The whites we dislike most are the liberals, who talk all the time about 'human rights' and then do nothing about it. We would even prefer honest *apartheid* to hypocritical racial partnership, because then at least we would know where we stand."

*

There are five different racial groups in Southern Rhodesia, each of which looks down on the next: (1) Europeans; (2) Asians, mostly Indians; (3) Coloreds; (4) Africans; (5) a few Chinese. The Coloreds are further subdivided into two communities, those deriving from the original Cape

Coloreds, who have been in the country for generations, and the "Eurafricans," who are mulattoes of more recent origin, born of irregular unions between the first European settlers, who did not bring white women with them, and African women.

Almost every gradation of color may be seen. Cases have been recorded (as in the Union) in which one of a pair of brothers has been classified as a Negro, the other as a white. The Coloreds (and Eurafricans) occupy an uncomfortable middle position. They cannot rise to a European level, and do not want to sink to the African level. A young colored girl, no matter how pale, will not be given employment as a salesgirl in a shop, or something similarly respectable; she must find work in the lowest class of factory, or become a servant or prostitute.

We met one Colored businessman, whose young daughter is almost white. "My wife and I will do our utmost to give her the best education possible, and then plead with her to get out of this country forever and forget us."

The Colored community takes in general a pro-Federation line, on the ground that Africans should, in time, be able to expand their power within the federal framework, and that anything making for African advancement will help the Coloreds too.

Indians number about five thousand in Southern Rhodesia. They have been forbidden entry into the country (except for a handful of schoolteachers) since responsible government began in 1923. If, however, an Indian already legally resident in Southern Rhodesia returns to India and marries, he may bring his bride back with him. Otherwise Indian immigration is prohibited, on the curious ground that Indians (the best trading people in Africa) "lower economic standards." Whites in Rhodesia greatly fear India's political influence, so much so that recent speeches by Mr. Nehru have been forbidden circulation in the country. Segregation against Indians is severe. They are, however, permitted to attend movies (but only if they sit in a segregated section in the balcony), and, at the hotels and bars, they are sometimes allowed to enter to buy a sandwich if they eat it outside. Most Indians, like the Coloreds, are pro-Federation, although they are not represented in the federal parliament. They think that the new system will augment economic opportunity, and in the end tend to diminish racial barriers. Certainly they could not be much worse off than they are.

Segregation patterns reach their most ferocious peak in regard to the Chinese. Recently a former cabinet minister of the Nationalist government of China visited Salisbury, and had to sleep in a laundry. No hotel or resthouse would take him in.

THE QUESTION OF FRANCHISE

Southern Rhodesia has been self-governing since 1923; it has an African population of 2,095,000, and the new Federation promises racial partnership. But in the last elections *only 429 Africans voted*. No African may vote in Southern Rhodesia unless (1) he earns £240 per year or has movable property worth £500, and (2) has had three years of schooling beyond primary school. In all Southern Rhodesia, only about two thousand natives fulfill these qualifications. A salary of £240 per year is enormous for an African, and, since there are only two government secondary schools in the entire country, it is not what you would call easy for an African to get three years of high school education. I asked Sir Godfrey Huggins how, in view of his hopes for the future, any such limitation on African suffrage could possibly be justified. Forty thousand white people voted in the last election, and—let me repeat—only 429 Africans. The prime minister's reply was that there should be an aristocracy in a democracy, and that people must "earn their vote." But there are other reasons too. One is the ingrained temperament of the white ruling class; another is the fact that the government does not dare to affront the *white* electorate; the most important is that the Europeans know full well that severe restriction of the native electorate is the best of all weapons for keeping African political development down.

In Northern Rhodesia, incredible as the figure is, exactly *three* Africans (out of almost two million) voted in the first federal election. In order to qualify, an African has to become a British subject, not merely a British protected person.[12]

A FOOTNOTE ON NYASALAND

This is a beautiful little country—mountainous, vividly green, fertile, heavily populated—in sharp contrast to the Rhodesias. "Nyasa" means "broad water," and the country is called "the Land of the Lake." It clings to Lake Nyasa like a long green caterpillar attached to a blue leaf. Of course the blue leaf is as big as Wales. Readers of Laurens van der Post's sensitive *Venture to the Interior* do not need to be told of the romantic, if somber, beauty and mysteriousness of the Nyasa landscape. If scenery were for sale, Nyasaland would be rich. (Actually, although fertile, the country is so densely populated that it is poor—people often call it the "Cinderella colony.")

---

[12] This only costs £5, but few Africans care to make the change. Of course it cannot be denied that most Africans are simply not ready for full voting privileges as yet.

MORE ABOUT RHODESIA AND NYASALAND

Outside Blantyre, in the Cholo region, the earth looks positively chocolate-colored. We climbed hills solidly studded, almost like a pincushion, with blue gums—tall trees that grow perfectly straight, and shed their own branches by a self-pruning process, so that they look like marvelously tufted poles. Little blue monkeys chatter in these trees, and never come down; they will not cross flat territory to the next hilltop, and so each grove has its own monkey colony. Even the birds, we were told, do not move around much from their chosen constellation of blue gums. Further up the road is Mlanji Mountain. This is a formidable monument, which in its own way contributes to Nyasaland almost as much atmosphere and folklore as Kilimanjaro contributes to Tanganyika. All this part of Nyasaland is carefully tilled and tended, inch by inch. The chief crops are the three "t's"—tobacco, tung, and tea.[13]

All this is Livingstone country. The footsteps of the magnificent doctor are everywhere, and one town—Livingstonia—commemorates his name. The Free Church of Scotland sent in its first mission in 1875, and in the next year the Church of Scotland founded Blantyre, named for Livingstone's own birthplace. A remarkable missionary, Dr. Robert Laws, was probably the most important personage in the country for more than fifty years—from 1875 until his retirement in 1927. Nyasaland has as strong a Christian heritage as any country in British Africa, and the devout, robust Scots in the field today are still a profound influence.

Nyasaland was never conquered by Britain or taken by force of arms. It did not need to be. Sir Harry Johnston entered the country in 1889 on behalf of the British South Africa Company, with £10,000 given him by Rhodes, to negotiate with the chiefs and keep Portugal and Germany out. For a time the country was known as the British Central African Protectorate. The chiefs made their own treaties with Queen Victoria and of their own free will entered into the British grasp.

ZOMBA (altitude 2,900 feet, European population about 600) is the capital, but is seldom visited. Nobody lives here but government servants. Until very recently it did not even have a hotel. There is, however, a restaurant in Zomba called the Pig and Whistle. The chief commercial town is BLANTYRE (altitude 3,400 feet, white population about 800) in the lovely Shire Highlands. Six mountains higher than 5,000 feet are within seven miles.

Blantyre is one of the few cities we went to in Africa to which Coca-Cola

[13] Along the lake many old houses have their backs to the water, and do not have gardens. This curiosity came about because the area is heavily malarial, and the first settlers, who did not know that malaria was carried by the mosquito, thought that it came from "vapors" in the lake, which they did not want to face, or from garden dampness.

has not penetrated, but we saw signs advertising another almost universal African phenomenon, Bata shoes. At the bank in Limbe, a town five miles away where I cashed a check, silver is not only counted but weighed before being given to a customer. The principal sight in Blantyre is, of course, the Scottish Mission church, a massive structure, and the settlement around it.

Color bar is not particularly noticeable in Blantyre, probably because of missionary influence. There are strong and articulate Indian and Colored communities. Segregation is not enforced in banks, government buildings, the airport, the post office, or shops, but pass laws are in effect, and Africans cannot be in the streets after 9 P.M. I did not see many Africans in the shops. "Their natural courtesy," our white guide said, "makes them keep back."[14]

*

Nyasaland is, as we know, an almost solidly black country—99.6 per cent. Although it is the smallest of the Federation sisters in area, its African population (about 2,400,000) is bigger than that of either of the Rhodesias. Among the principal tribes are the Yao, who were great purveyors of slaves to the Arabs in older days, and the Angoni, a Zulu offshoot. The chiefs are organized into a union.

The Nyasa people are modern-minded in many respects, but still are lively believers in black magic. I asked why they had, unlike other Bantus in central Africa, produced few works of art; the answer was that if anybody arose with exceptional talent the supposition was that he must be bewitched, and hence he was not allowed to express himself. Two favorite ways to propitiate spirits in Nyasaland are with (a) beer; (b) a black cloth. Practice of witchcraft is against the law. Necrophagy is, as in Northern Rhodesia, fairly common, but it is unlawful to eat a corpse if it is dug out of a grave or used for medicine. One little story I heard has to do with a tick, *Ornithodorus moubata*, which causes a kind of relapsing fever. Africans who move about carry with them a few of these ticks—in a segment of bamboo or a matchbox —and let the ticks bite them at regular intervals, on the assumption that this will maintain their immunity. If they are *not bitten*, they think that they will get the disease when they return home.

The story of Chief N. A. Maganga shows the vicissitudes which may come in the lifetime of an African in Nyasaland, as well as the closeness of yesterday to today. This worthy chief was born in about 1885, and when he was a boy of ten was captured by a notorious Yao slave trader. Yoked to a stick, he was walked all the way to Dar es Salaam, and there sold into slavery to a

---

[14] Another Briton told us, "Color bar is evil, but will last until enough Africans come forward whom we can respect."

rich Swahili family. He remained a slave until 1914, when, on the outbreak of World War I, the Germans released him. He enlisted in Lettow-Vorbeck's army, and became a skilled *askari*. The British took him prisoner after a battle, and at once, because he was such a good soldier, he was drafted into the King's African Rifles. He fought with the Germans against the British for the first half of the war, and then with the British against the Germans for the second half. In 1922 he returned to Nyasaland, and became an important Yao chief. In 1953 he visited London—one of the Nyasa leaders who sought to petition Queen Elizabeth against federation.

Thousands of Nyasaland boys go into the Rhodesias and the Union every year to find work, and about 130,000 adult males live outside the territory. At home, their wages may be no more than $2.80 per month;[15] on the Copperbelt they get a good deal more than that. Some, who leave their wives and children and stay away for years, are called *Achona*, or "lost ones." Some do not return to their homeland until extreme old age, when they may have forgotten their local language and even the names of their villages. The British try to help them locate themselves, and, even if they have been forgotten, they are invariably taken in by the community from which they came, if it can be found.

Like the Basuto, the Nyasalanders are exceptionally good workers—industrious, cheerful, and quick to learn skills. They have absorbed a lot from the Scots—loyalty, reliability, and a spirit of adventure. Above all they make good soldiers. (But I heard a European in Rhodesia say grimly, "The Nyasa are the source of all our woes, because they are so intelligent and able.")

Almost to a man, the Nyasalanders bitterly opposed federation. They do not want to be permanently under the thumb of Rhodesian white settlers or mine operators. The fact is as striking as any in contemporary Africa—*four hundred thousand* citizens of Nyasaland gave a penny or two each and raised a fund of £1,967, so that they could send to London a delegation of chiefs to protest against the federal scheme in 1953. They drew up a petition —a remarkably well-written and soberly worked out document—and sought, in all humility, to present it to Queen Elizabeth. Their fathers had, after all, once made treaties with another British queen. But Queen Elizabeth could not receive them, and their petition was curtly rejected by the Colonial Office, which at all costs wanted to push federation through. Empty-handed, the chiefs returned to Nyasaland.

Evil things happened that summer. The most respected African in Nyasaland was Chief Phillip Gomani, now dead. He had been paramount chief of the Angoni for thirty-two years, had always served the British with intense

---

[15] Campbell, *op. cit.*, p. 471.

loyalty and devotion, and had encouraged thousands of his young men to join the King's African Rifles and fight for the British crown on various fronts in both world wars and in postwar Malaya. Chief Gomani disliked federation, took a strong stand against it, and encouraged his people to do likewise. On the other hand he strictly forbade violence. He had learned about passive resistance from India (and from Christianity) and insisted that any demonstrations should be non-violent. He wanted to register a protest, but to do so peaceably. In association with him were eighty-two other Nyasa chiefs.

The British decided that, to prevent possible disorder, they must arrest Chief Gomani, in spite of his age and the fact that he was seriously ill. He was charged "with abusing his powers as a Native Authority and disobeying the law." The Reverend Michael Scott was with him at the time. Mr. Scott has written an instructive account of what followed, from which I would like to quote:[16]

> A big meeting with songs and dances of the Angoni people was to be held on May 22nd and 23rd, at which the Chief, who insisted on leaving hospital, was due to speak. . . . Non-violent resistance was to be the theme of the meeting. The police however objected to the meeting being held, and when application was made to the Court for permission, the magistrate upheld the police objection and forbade the meeting. By the time the decision was made, many thousands of people had congregated and had been waiting for five hours. The Chief's eldest son . . . asked and obtained the magistrate's permission for one of his father's headmen to ask the people to disperse quietly. This they did, despite their resentment and the provocative action of two white officials in going by car to the meeting place before the headman could reach it, and ordering the audience to go home. They remained, singing hymns until the arrival of the Chief's headman whose authority they recognized.
> During these days strenuous efforts were being made by officials to persuade the Chief to cancel his advice to his people to oppose the imposition of Federation. When he persisted in his refusal to do so, he was finally suspended and ordered to leave his District in twenty-four hours, and was told that the District Commissioner had now been appointed as Native Authority in his place.
> I was staying with Chief Gomani as his guest at Lizulu, his home and traditional headquarters, at the time he received his banishment order from the Governor. On arrival at his house, he had found that many of his people, hearing of the Chief's trouble, had come in from the surrounding districts. . . .
> Nights like this occur often in the lives of the African people. When

[16] *African Episode*, published by the Africa Bureau, London. Quoted by Mr. Scott's kind permission.

trouble comes, it is felt almost as a binding force, and the people foregather to protect their Chief and to comfort one another. The fires are kept burning all night under the stars. There is Bible reading by the light of a storm lantern; and there are prayers and hymns, and songs and dances, including on this occasion "God Save the Queen" in the Chinyanja language.

The Chief sat with his wife and counsellors round one of the fires. Although he is fully alert mentally, he suffers from Huntington's Chorea which keeps his limbs and body in a perpetual state of convulsion. He stood up to pray, his patient soft-spoken wife clasping him in her arms to prevent him staggering into the fire, his arms and legs thrusting back and forth as he called upon his people to put all their faith in God and Christ. The people were all exhorted not to resort to any acts of violence, no matter what happened, or how provocative the police might be if they came. There was no hatred or anger in his voice as he appealed to God, to Jesus Christ and to the Queen to behold the plight of his people and to take pity on them in all their fear and trouble. . . . They sat huddled in their ragged clothes, with blankets round their shoulders, and as they sang sparks and flames kept leaping upwards from the fires.

This whole episode can hardly be understood except in the light of an old tradition of the Angoni (and of many other African tribes) that their Chief must at all costs not be taken captive. Even if the people are killed, if the Chief can be kept free, the tribe remains unconquered. All were praying that there would be no banishment for their Chief.

There were fires on the distant hills, where people were collecting in neighbouring villages to hear the news. . . . The first light of dawn was coming as a rosy tinge in the East, and a chapter from Isaiah was being read in Chinyanja. The deep confident African voices went on reading in the growing light. The familiar friendly world of daylight seemed to dispel fear, and people went about their morning tasks.

Suddenly everybody was alert as a young boy came running with the news that police cars and trucks were arriving. The people cleared a passage for them, and the leading car drew up in front of the Chief's house, the others remaining at some distance. Two police stepped on to the verandah where a number of us were waiting. The Police Commissioner said:

"I think you know why we are here. I want to serve notice on the Chief. Where is he?"

I told him he should go and speak to the Chief; he went inside with his second-in-command and, not finding the Chief in the front room, began to call out his name. Receiving no immediate reply, he called out: "Oh! So the Chief has run away!"

This was naturally not well received. The Chief appeared, not fully dressed, and stood holding on to the door to support himself.

Conversation followed. The police realized that "they had an unpleasant task to perform" and appeared "rather white and their voices shook." Then:

The Chief ... wanted to explain to the people that he did not of his own accord want to leave his home and people. Also that it was not the wish of his people that he should leave. He was still the Chief of his people, though the Government might decide to suspend him as its Native Authority.

The Police Officer said that he was not a politician. He had to carry out his orders and not argue about them, and he wanted these orders carried out as quickly as possible.

Many people had come into the room and on to the verandah. Whenever the police made as though to seize the Chief by the arm, they protested and asked them not to lay hands on the Chief, who was being supported by his family. The people were saying they would prefer the police to imprison all of them rather than take the Chief. The police became flustered as more and more people gathered round and the Police Commissioner said to me: "If you have any influence with these people, now is the time to use it."

I said I should prefer to be arrested myself with any others he might consider responsible for obstructing the police, but that they should leave the Chief, who was a sick man, and report to the Governor on the situation, and on the state of the public mind. "That," he said, "would be silly. I have been given a warrant to take the Chief, and that is what I am going to do."

By coaxing and persuasion the argument was carried on, with the Chief moving in the direction of the front door. Eventually the police emerged on to the verandah and tried to force a passage through the crowd to the car.

When the Chief had been brought to within a few feet of the car, the Police Commissioner, apparently thinking it might be impossible to get him into the car, blew his whistle and the police began to launch a tear-gas attack. (It afterwards transpired that the African *Askaris* refused to make a baton charge.) The tear gas was thrown amongst the crowd, who did not know what it was, and believed it to be poisonous.

Then an astonishing thing happened. The chief was "hustled into his car and driven away." But lines of Africans stood against the path of the car, so that it could not move—and the chief was rescued by his own people, seized out of the car, and carried by his followers out into the bush. "The police made no attempt to follow." Perhaps they were too embarrassed.

Scott, the Chief, and some others, after arduous experiences, got across the frontier on foot and reached Portuguese territory. The Portuguese welcomed them at first, but then deported the chief back to Nyasaland, where he was put into a hospital to await trial. Scott—although no charges were made against him, and he was never given any opportunity to explain his position —was refused permission to re-enter Nyasaland and went back to England. Chief Gomani died soon after.

*

In August, 1953, active disorders broke out in the Cholo area and elsewhere in Nyasaland. For a time the British feared that they might have another Mau Mau rebellion on their hands, but the troubles were suppressed quickly. Not only did hatred of Federation enter into this, but also longstanding grievances over land. There are very few white settlers in Nyasaland, but they own about a million acres of the best land. Africans, as in Kenya, complain that their own areas are so overcrowded that economic well-being is impossible, whereas huge white-owned tracts are kept empty and undeveloped. About 200,000 Africans work on the European tea and tung plantations.

The president of the Nyasaland African Congress is J. S. Sangala; another important personality is W. M. Chirwa, a deputy to the federal parliament. Mr. Sangala is not allowed entry into the Rhodesias. The Congress is well organized, militant, and active. Some Britons say that, through a "shadow cabinet," it is the real ruler of the country. Nyasa leaders, even though they are now yoked to federation, steadily push for constitutional reform within their own area, and have gone so far as to announce that July, 1957, is their "target date for self-government."

*

A youthful Englishman told us in Blantyre, with characteristic frankness, "Of course we will have to go in the long run, but let us at least stay until we have taught Africans proper *standards*." But he did not explain what kind of standards he had in mind.

*

So much for the Rhodesias and Nyasaland. We pass on now to still another and altogether different and distinctive African world, that of the Belgian Congo.

CHAPTER 32

Congo I: Belgian Policy in Africa

*Then I saw the Congo, creeping through the black,
Cutting through the jungle with a golden track.*
—VACHEL LINDSAY[1]

IF you superimpose the Congo on a map of the United States, its western tip will touch Kansas, the north will spill upward into Canada, the east will strike the Atlantic coastline, and the south will reach all the way to Florida. Few people have adequate conception of the enormousness of the Congo, which covers more than 900,000 square miles. Perhaps an analogy to Europe will be more striking. The Congo, placed on a map of Europe, stretches from Paris to Riga, from Riga to Athens, and from Athens all the way back to Paris. It is seventy-seven times the size of Belgium, its parent. All of this—an area as big as the eastern third of the United States or western Europe—was until 1908 the exclusive property of one man, King Leopold II of Belgium. It was by far the largest and most opulent private domain ever known to history.

The Congo today, is, by African standards, fairly well populated; it has about 12,000,000 people, of whom perhaps 60,000 are Europeans.[2] But by European or Asiatic standards it is virtually empty. The density of population is only 1.8 per square mile. When Chester Bowles, the former American ambassador to India, visited the Congo in 1955, the first thing that struck him was its comparative emptiness, and consequent prodigious capability of development. The Congo is almost as big as India, and perhaps

---

[1] From "The Congo" from *Collected Poems of Vachel Lindsay*, reprinted by permission of The Macmillan Company. Copyright, 1914, 1942, by The Macmillan Company.

[2] These figures exclude Ruanda-Urundi, a UN trust territory administered by Belgium (area 20,120 square miles; population, 4,065,000), which we shall deal with in the chapter following.

richer. But India has 356,000,000 people, as against 12,000,000 for the Congo! The Belgians are very proud—justly so—of their physical accomplishment in the Congo, but on American or European terms development has scarcely begun. Take railways. In the whole of the Congo there are only 3,065 miles of rail, less than in Arkansas, and these are on three different gauges. Take roads. The Congo is supposed to be an "advanced" country and it is indeed highly advanced in some respects, but even today no road exists between Léopoldville, the capital, and Stanleyville, the third most important town in the country. This (the difference in terrain and distance being understood) is almost as if no road existed between New York and Boston. The Belgians hate to have things like this mentioned. They are almost morbidly sensitive about the Congo. They wince in embarrassment (and carefully conceal such facts in their tourist propaganda) when somebody points out that it is still impossible to cross the country by road or rail, either from north to south or east to west.[3]

Few countries in the world can match the Congo for sheer spectacular variety and density of color. We reach now the core of equatorial Africa. The Congo has majesty, mystery, and a commanding romantic spell. Also, quite aside from elements in the picturesque, it is an extremely important country not only to Belgium and to Africa but the world. Most of the Congo is a low plateau, and about half the total area is forest. One curiosity is that, although it is one of the biggest countries in the world, it has only twenty-five miles of coastline—the button of territory holding it to the Atlantic. It has mineral resources, including uranium and copper, that are formidably large, and it produces 70 per cent of the industrial diamonds of the world. The principal export is, however, palm oil. The Congo has the greatest undeveloped water-power potential of any country in the world. This is a rich country in almost all senses of the word. Its exports come close to being worth three billion dollars a year (as compared to less than $60,000,000 for Kenya, as an example) and the trade balance is fat and favorable.[4] One should also mention, I daresay, such facts as that the Congo has fewer than five hundred doctors of medicine for more than 12,000,000 Africans, and that its university (just opened, and the first one in the history of the country) has at the moment exactly twenty-eight students.

[3] It is true that Léopoldville and Elisabethville, the capital of the Katanga mining area, are connected by a road network of a kind. The distance is about 1,100 miles as the crow flies. The trip can, if the weather is good, be made by automobile in about ten days, but anybody who does it except for adventure is crazy. Even Sabena, the admirable Belgian airline, does not penetrate the deep interior of the Congo. Routes connect all the principal cities nicely, but they are in the form of a web *around* a central area still blank, as Sabena maps clearly show.

[4] E.C. Eggins, "The Belgian Congo, a Contented Colony," *Listener*, October 2, 1952.

Of the total European population (60,000), about fifty thousand are Belgians. There are (in strict contrast to East and South Africa) practically no Indians. The small retail traders, if not Belgian or African, are for the most part Greeks in the western half of the country, Portuguese in the east. One suggestive point, in sharp contrast to the Rhodesias, is that the number of white South Africans is minute—197. The Belgians, although they are the white masters of a black country, dislike *apartheid* and the theory of unmitigated white supremacy almost as much as they dislike black nationalism. Belgian racial policy (as we shall see) steers a careful, practical line all its own. On the African side, the Congo presents a brilliant, bewildering variety of peoples. It has the pygmies, the Watutsi giants (who are Hamites, not Negroes), and several important Nilotic tribes, like the Mangbeto, where it adjoins the Anglo-Egyptian Sudan. There are two hundred different tribes in all. Most are Bantu or Bantu intermixed with Negro, and they speak thirty-eight different *main* languages. One of these, Lingala, is a lingua franca like Swahili, and is known over wide areas. The tribes cover the broadest arc conceivable. We saw primitive peoples near the Equator who are almost, if not quite, naked savages; we also saw Africans operate complicated machine tools and drive locomotives. Near the lower Lualaba are the Basalampasu, some of whom are still active (if surreptitious) cannibals. The chief of one famous tribe, first seen by Livingstone, is never from enthronement to death allowed to put his feet on the ground. Even from bed to bath, he must be carried. Probably the best known Congo tribe is the Baluba, which has a dynasty going back at least three hundred years, and has produced works of art—masks, fetishes, and other sculpture—of the most astonishing beauty. The Baluba also create magnificent—if sometimes sinister—objects of art. The King of the Baluba is one of the most massively picturesque of African monarchs. He weighs 250 pounds and has 250 wives, one for each pound.

Africans in the Congo seem by and large much happier than those in the surrounding territories. The Belgian system denies them much; but it also gives them much. They are certainly far and away better off than their fellows in the Union and the Rhodesias. Men smile; children are fat; women look contented. And they have not succumbed to the pervasive, creeping drabness that afflicts so much of southern Africa. They wear costumes gleaming with intricate color; they prettify themselves with unashamedly barbaric devices; they preen and prance and giggle, showing off.

One striking contrast to Rhodesia is that white settlement is discouraged, not encouraged. White men run the Congo—true—and white entrepreneurs exploit without possibility of contradiction the country's inexhaustible mineral and vegetable wealth. But few individual whites *own land,* except

CONGO I: BELGIAN POLICY IN AFRICA 649

in the Kivu region. The Belgian authorities want at all costs to avoid the racial tension which, as in Kenya, is the inevitable result of large-scale white settlement. Likewise they want at all costs to make impossible the development of a "marginal" poor white urban class, as in South Africa. The Belgians know full well that without harmonious race relations the Congo could—in time—become a box of firecrackers. White officials come and go, and technicians for the mines serve their tours of duty, but nobody is encouraged to become a *permanent* Congo resident. In fact—a most unusual point—no Belgian is admitted to the country (tourists excepted) without the posting of a sizable bond, 50,000 Belgian francs or $1,000. This is forfeited if he fails to establish himself. It has been calculated that a Belgian settler, to make a success of life in the Congo, must have a capital of at least $30,000. Hence, all riffraff are kept out. What is even more startling is that white Belgians in the Congo have no political rights whatever. They are not permitted to form political parties, as in Kenya, or white trade unions, as in Rhodesia. Politically speaking, they are colonial subjects, no more and no less, just like the Africans. This is still a colony pure and simple. Nobody—black *or* white—has the vote,[5] and the European community in the Congo, numbering 60,000, must be the largest group of white people totally devoid of voting power anywhere in the free world.

*

The River Congo, the third of the great African rivers (the others being the Nile and Niger) and the sixth longest river in the world, flows for 2,900 miles. Several great tributaries feed it, like the Lualaba (Upper Congo) which was discovered by Livingstone, the Ubangi, and the Kasai. It is the only river in Africa that crosses the Equator twice. In some places it swells out to a width of eight or nine miles, and it contains no fewer than four thousand islands. No single bridge crosses it from Stanleyville all the way to the Atlantic, a river distance of some 1,900 miles. Bridges are, as we know, very rare objects indeed in Africa. Stanley, the first white man to explore the main Congo, wanted to name it the Livingstone, and the Portuguese call it the Zaire. Its basin covers more than 1,400,000 square miles, half the area of the United States, and when it reaches the sea its rate of discharge is still 2,000,000 cubic feet a second, the third largest of any river in the world. This is a river even more powerful than the Nile, and, although it does not flood, it plays a role in the life of the Congo fully equivalent to that of the Nile in Egypt.

This is largely because the Congo and its tributaries are still (except for

[5] With an exception to be noted below.

aviation) the basis of the country's communications. The Congo has 8,750 miles of navigable waters, constantly traversed by wood-burning steamers. Without these it could not function as a modern state. The Congo is the circulatory system of the Congo. But this mighty, voluptuous river is not harnessable or navigable for all its length. Twice impassable cataracts and rapids cut it off—at Stanley Falls near Stanleyville, and between Léopoldville and the sea. At this latter point the river drops 850 feet in 200 miles, and has thirty-two different cataracts. Short railways exist at both these intersections, so that the rapids can be bypassed, but this does not make for easy or efficient communications.

At the mouth of the Congo on the Atlantic is a town with the peculiar name Banana, the seat of the oldest trading station in the country. But ships do not stop here any more, but proceed up the estuary to Matadi, the port for Léopoldville. The railway from Matadi to Léopoldville is one of the most useful in Africa. Until it was built in 1898 there was no way at all to get into the Congo from the west, a factor contributing greatly to the country's early isolation and inaccessibility. The area it crosses is, incidentally, the scene of Joseph Conrad's somber and magnificent *Heart of Darkness*. The Matadi railway performs an indispensable function, but is an agonizing bottleneck. Sometimes to get freight from Matadi to Léopoldville (230 miles) takes longer than to get it from New York to Matadi.

Let us look into this matter of communications from another direction. Suppose you want to ship titanium or columbite from northern Ruanda to Antwerp or New York. There will be at least nine different stages to the journey. (1) Truck to Usumbura. (2) Boat down Lake Tanganyika to Albertville. (3) Train to Kabalo. (4) Train or boat up the Lualaba to Kindu. (5) Boat to Ponthierville. (6) Train to Stanleyville. (7) Boat along the main Congo to Léopoldville. (8) Train to Matadi. (9) Boat to New York or Europe.[6]

My wife and I had a day's flight along the Upper Congo, making six or seven stops. The pilot did not always know what his next stop would be, because this was determined at the last moment by what cargo he picked up. This was the roughest (and also most exhilarating) flight we had in Africa until we reached French Gabon some months later. The first airstrip we touched on, Kindu, looked like a deserted tennis court; the airport "office" consisted of nothing but a grass hut with a portable telephone.

[6] The extraordinary thing is that communications, despite all this, are as good as they are. For instance, large trucks carrying cotton, vegetables, and the like start out from points in the northeast and drive non-stop to Stanleyville. There perishable goods proceed by refrigerated boat to Léopoldville and are on the consumer's table within ten or eleven days, not bad time at all considering the circumstances and difficulties involved.

CONGO I: BELGIAN POLICY IN AFRICA 651

Yet Kindu is an important city, both a railhead and a steamer port. At another stop, Kongola, we saw a black boy with filed teeth lounging next to a new chartreuse-colored Chevrolet convertible. For a while the river looked like a lion's tail, a clear tawny yellow, and so sharply transparent that we could see the shadows of palms in the water cut out as if by a stiletto. Then it broadened out, fed by greasy streams which soak out over the land and take the shape of clover-leaf intersections on a big American highway. It looked, in fact, almost like a parkway itself, with long narrow islands in the middle resembling the grass strips that separate lanes of automobile traffic. We flew at palmtop level most of the time. The Congo is a wonderful place for bush flying. Even in the sizable towns, like Costermansville, the airstrip lies directly athwart the place where passengers wait; you can see the great ships lift themselves up and tuck their wheels in from a distance of thirty feet, like metal herons.

*

LÉOPOLDVILLE has been capital of the Belgian Congo since 1923. Before that the capital was Boma, down the estuary. Belgians on the spot usually call it simply "Leo," as they call Stanleyville "Stan"; the native name is Kintamo. It was founded by Stanley in 1881, and lies on the Congo next to a bulge in the river known as Stanley Pool.[7] Immediately below this the cataracts begin. But navigation is possible upstream all the way to Stanleyville, which is why Léopoldville was built where it is. Directly across the Congo from Léopoldville is Brazzaville, the capital of French Equatorial Africa, which we will describe in Chapter 34 below. The two cities are twins like Minneapolis and St. Paul, but the Congo is more of a barrier than the Mississippi.

Léopoldville has about 250,000 people, of whom perhaps 15,000 are white Europeans.[8] This represents an increase from corresponding figures of 40,000 and 2,500 fifteen years ago. No city in Africa is faster growing. It has big warehouses stacked like packing cases along the river, broad businesslike streets, one skyscraper (ten stories) known as "Le Building," and no charm. The atmosphere is European, but Léopoldville gives an altogether different impression from a city in the Rhodesias or in Portuguese Africa. It reflects strongly the Belgian national character. People are hardheaded, hard-working, frugal, bourgeois, and successful. There is no nonsense about aesthetics. Léopoldville puts forth a note of practicality, commerce, and

---

[7] Not to be confused with Stanley Falls at Stanleyville.
[8] If you ask a Belgian the population he will say, "Fifteen thousand." Conversationally at least the blacks are not counted.

good will. It reminded me of Belgium immediately after the war, when Brussels was a thriving metropolis while Paris still lay in the abyss.

Segregation patterns we shall go into later, but it is impossible to describe Léopoldville without mentioning that it consists of two cities, one European, the other African, with comparatively little contact between them. Africans are not allowed to enter the European city after 9:00 P.M. (except with a special pass), nor are Europeans allowed to enter the African city. The African quarter is well built, and has commendable amenities. It does not remotely resemble the slums around Cape Town. Sound, handsome housing projects are in process of construction, and Africans have their own cinemas, restaurants, and so on—not many, but more than in any city in southern Africa. Recently completed was a stadium seating 70,000. The week we were there a Belgian football team played a *mixed* Congo team. There were 65,000 blacks in the crowd, 5,000 whites. Imagine such a thing in Salisbury or Pretoria.

Léopoldville is sprayed by helicopters carrying DDT periodically, and mosquito nets are unnecessary. The average temperature is around seventy-eight degrees, and people become exasperated with the humidity during the long rainy season, but it is a healthy city. The worst months are between January and May. Several curiosities may be reported. Europeans pay ten dollars a bunch for faded carnations or other hothouse flowers flown from Brussels, although the Congo produces flowers of the most astounding tropical beauty and luxuriance.[9] But European flowers make the Belgians feel more at home and "civilized." The cost of living is very high; it is cheaper to have a chicken flown up from Johannesburg than to buy one in the local market. Parrots in considerable number fly across the river every morning from Brazzaville, and return to French territory at night—nobody knows why. At a European cocktail party, the African servants have a habit of mixing indiscriminately together in a washbasin all the drinks not consumed by guests; they drink copiously of this bizarre and explosive mixture, and are apt to pass out like flies hit with an insecticide.

ELISABETHVILLE, on the other side of the country, is the chief city of the Katanga mining district. It has about 110,000 blacks, 10,000 whites. A thousand of these latter are, curiously enough, Spanish-speaking Jews, who drifted to the Congo after long years in Smyrna, Rhodes, and other points in the Mediterranean. Elisabethville (founded in 1910) is laid out in the rectilinear pattern of an American city; it has, a rare thing for tropical Africa, street lighting at night, and, something rarer, illuminated shop windows. The elevation is 4,008 feet, and not a drop of rain falls for six

[9] Meeker, *op. cit.*, mentions this odd characteristic.

months every year. Elisabethville is much richer than Léopoldville, because of the mines; the hinterland is not, like that of Léopoldville, nothing but a swamp. Even more than Léopoldville, partly no doubt because it is cooler, Elisabethville conveys a note of bustle, vigor, and solidity. Africans living here have probably the highest standard of living of any on the whole continent. No fewer than eight thousand own their own homes, and thousands more are skilled wage earners.

On the upper loop of the Congo lies COQUILHATVILLE, the capital of Equator Province, with a European population of 527. Its main street lies directly on the Equator, and it has what are considered to be the most beautiful botanical gardens in the world. Stanley founded Coquilhatville in 1883, and called it "Equator Station." Further east is STANLEYVILLE itself, which Stanley called "Falls Station," and which has 30,000 Africans, 2,000 Europeans. It was destroyed by Arab slave raiders in 1886, and is now the capital of Oriental Province. Nothing could be more quintessentially the heart of tropical Africa than Stanleyville, but it has the liveliness and efficiency of a miniature Antwerp. The most attractive of all Congo cities, to my mind, is COSTERMANSVILLE, on Lake Kivu. This is now called by its native name, Bukavu, as a gesture to African sentiment and because "Costermansville" is too large a mouthful for most Africans to pronounce. Its location is ravishing—as lovely as Stresa. In the leading hotel, one of the best in all Africa, a Negro boy aged about eight wears a scarlet uniform and a flat gold hat, shaped like a tambourine, and assists in opening the elevator doors. One day he commanded abruptly, "Give me money." I asked him why. "Because my pay is very small." This seemed to be a good reason, and I gave him some.

CONGO HISTORY: A FIVE-MINUTE GLIMPSE

Listen to the yell of Leopold's ghost
Burning in Hell for his hand-maimed host,
Hear how the demons chuckle and yell
Cutting his hands off, down in Hell.
—VACHEL LINDSAY[10]

Africa is in me.
—HENRY M. STANLEY

The Belgian Congo was created by two men, both of them characters of the most relentless ambition, energy, and fixity of purpose—King Leopold II and Henry Morton Stanley. Neither was Belgian. Leopold was, of course,

[10] From "The Congo" from *Collected Poems of Vachel Lindsay*, reprinted by permission of The Macmillan Company. Copyright, 1914, 1942, by The Macmillan Company.

King of Belgium, but he was a German by origin. Stanley was a Welshman who became an American and toward the end of his life reverted to British nationality.

Before Leopold and Stanley the Congo had plenty of history, but this is largely misted over and ignored nowadays. The Portuguese explorer Diego Cão reached the Congo estuary in 1482, and even at that time a native kingdom of a sort existed, with ample traditions. The Portuguese could not get up the river, because of the rapids, but they made settlements to the south of it, in what is now Angola, and converted numerous kings of "Kongo" to the Christian faith. One monarch was Garcia Affonso II, who ruled from 1641 to 1665 over a limited area. The early Congolese (at least those near the coast) absorbed European influences rapidly. One of Affonso's sons, by name Enrique, studied theology in Lisbon, and in 1520 was consecrated as a bishop by Pope Leo X, the first Negro bishop in history. The Congo regularly sent emissaries to the Vatican for several centuries.[11]

Arab penetration from the east began around 1820, from Zanzibar and through Tanganyika, and Arab slave raiders decimated the population. The first European explorers also entered the Congo from the east, crossing Lake Tanganyika and seeking the source of the Nile. Livingstone thought that the Congo tributaries he discovered were part of the Nile system.

Henry Stanley's real name was John Rowlands. Few men have ever had a more spectacular life. Stanley was completely self-made. He was a soldier, politician, empire builder, an extremely accomplished journalist, and one of the greatest explorers who ever lived. He was harsh, impulsive, fiercely egocentric, and extravagantly inspired. He was a much more dashing character than the plodding, selfless Livingstone, and much less elevated.

Stanley was born in Wales in 1841, and grew up in the most crushing poverty. His family boarded him out for half a crown a week, and he became a "workhouse" boy. He fled to the United States, working his way across the Atlantic. In New Orleans a wealthy benefactor adopted him, and Stanley took his name. An exceptional circumstance is that he fought on *both* sides during the American Civil War. He joined the Confederate army first, and was captured in battle. He was imprisoned for a time in Chicago, of all places, and got out by volunteering to fight for the north. Briefly he served in the United States navy, and then traveled all over the American West, as a member of expeditions pacifying the Indians. He

[11] *Negro Art in the Belgian Congo*, by Leon Kochnitsky, p. 6.

CONGO I: BELGIAN POLICY IN AFRICA

became a journalist. He became, in fact, one of the best and most successful journalists ever known.

James Gordon Bennett of the New York *Herald* sent him to find Livingstone, after Stanley had proved his prowess on assignments in Tibet, the Caucasus, Ethiopia, and elsewhere. Duly he found Livingstone (1871), and thereafter Africa became his life. He traversed the continent from east to west and discovered the course of the Congo in an epochal journey (1874-77) that cost the lives of two-thirds of his men and took 999 days. It was this journey that led directly to the creation of the Congo Free State and the carving up of Africa by the European powers. Few events in history have ever been more seminal.

Leopold II ascended the throne of Belgium in 1865; Belgium itself had only become a country thirty-four years before. Leopold was a vain man, greedy, and overpoweringly ambitious. His Queen was a daughter of Archduke Joseph of Austria-Hungary and was called the "Rose of Brabant." His private life was floriferous. Leopold wanted prestige; he wanted acclaim; and Belgium was not big enough for his energies. He became fascinated by tales of Africa brought back by the first explorers. He sent an emissary to meet Stanley at Marseilles, when Stanley was returning to Europe in 1878, thus getting ahead of the other powers, and offered him employment in his service. Stanley accepted. It is an extraordinary fact that Leopold, who became the personal owner of the Congo, never once saw Africa or visited the Congo. He never bothered to glimpse his illimitable domain. Stanley did the job for him. He returned to the Congo, and spent four years there working for Leopold, a private empire builder for a ruthless King.

Officially, however, he was not Leopold's personal agent but the representative of something called the Congo International Association. We must retrace our steps slightly. In 1876 Leopold had summoned a group of experts on Africa to Brussels. He was genuinely interested in African exploration and development. He wanted to give European penetration a legal, international framework. Out of this Brussels meeting came the Congo International Association, on which several European countries were represented. Soon it became necessary to regularize their conflicting interests, and in 1884-85 a celebrated conference met at Berlin, which marked out spheres of influence in Africa and determined boundaries that exist to this day. Stanley returned from the Congo and became, interestingly enough, technical adviser to the *American* delegation at this conference. Leopold laid claim to the Congo, partly because of the treaties Stanley had signed with various chiefs, and the Berlin Conference made one of the most astonishing decisions in history—it gave it to him outright. The Congo Free

State was set up as a sovereign state under the personal suzerainty of Leopold. It was not a part of Belgium, but part of himself.[12]

Stanley's life remained full and productive until his death in 1904, but need not concern us here. He made a third fruitful expedition to Africa in 1887-89, when he discovered the Mountains of the Moon amongst much else. Also he relieved Emin Pasha, the Governor of Equatoria Province in the Sudan, who had been cut off by the Mahdi's dervishes. But much controversy still attends his behavior in performance of this feat. Many in his rear guard died, as he ruthlessly pushed forward regardless of cost.

Leopold ruled Stanley's creation, the Congo Free State, singlehanded from 1885 to 1908, when it was transferred to the Belgian government as a colony. Leopold died in 1909, and was succeeded by his gallant son, who became renowned the world over as Albert, King of the Belgians, when World War I broke out in 1914.

Leopold's rule was mercilessly exploitative. How much money he made out of the Congo, after his investment began to pay off, no man can know. He had to borrow large sums at first. Certainly he became one of the richest men in the world. As early as 1885 a decree made all "vacant land" in the Congo the property of the state, i.e., Leopold. This meant, in effect any land the white man wanted. Natives were simply pushed out into the bush. Rubber and ivory, the two chief objects of value in the Congo at that time, became state monopolies, and the government gained "an absolute proprietary right over nearly the whole country."[13] In 1896 came the creation (by secret decree) of the *Domaine de la couronne*, which gave Leopold special additional rights over not less than 112,000 square miles of territory, an area almost as big as Poland. But this was not all. The most heinous and ghastly atrocities ever to accompany the "development" of a primitive area by a presumably civilized power occurred. The appetite of Leopold's agents for rubber and ivory grew steadily more voracious and insatiable. African workers were made to fill quotas, and if they failed to bring in the required amount of rubber and ivory they were mutilated or shot. "Development?" Competent authorities say that the population of the Congo was about 20,000,000 in 1900; today it is 12,000,000. Leopold's regime is believed to have cost, in all, between five and eight *million* lives.

[12] The Belgian parliament agreed that ownership of the Congo should be "exclusively" personal by Leopold. The United States was the first power to ratify the arrangement, largely through the efforts of General Henry S. Sanford, who was American minister to Brussels at the time. See *Belgians in the Congo*, a pamphlet by G. D. Périer.

[13] Encyclopaedia Britannica, article on the Congo Free State.

That is certainly "development" of a peculiar sort. Most horrible was the practice of mutilation. If an African boy did not satisfy his bosses, a hand or foot—sometimes both—were cut off. Photographs of such amputations are part of the record, and may be scrutinized today if anybody wants to rake through the old documents. Africans themselves in the Congo had never used mutilation as a form of punishment. It was purely a European invention. To prove their efficiency in this business, the bosses of labor gangs brought in to their superiors baskets full of human hands. The right hand was always favored. To preserve them in the humid climate, they were sometimes *smoked*.

Word of this began to leak out, and all over the world decent people rose in protest. The British sent Roger Casement, their consul at Boma, to investigate what came to be known as the "red rubber" horrors. (Casement, an Irishman, was convicted of treason against the British and executed many years later, in World War I.) In the end Leopold was forced by the pressure of outraged international opinion to appoint a Commission of Inquiry to investigate the atrocities. Sir Edward Grey, the British foreign secretary, said in 1908 that the Congo Free State had "morally forfeited every right to international recognition."

Reforms were put into force, the atrocities ceased (although forced labor remained part of the system), and Leopold surrendered the Free State to the Belgian nation. He fought hard, however, to preserve for his own descendants his rights in the *Domaine de la couronne* and other properties. Meantime, Belgium itself was fiercely divided over the Congo question. Many Belgians did not want the Congo. They certainly did not want it subject to the extravagant stipulations made by Leopold. In the end the Belgian parliament agreed to accept Leopold's gift, but only after a sharp political crisis and on its own terms, namely, that the Congo should be administered as a colony subject altogether to the will of the Belgian nation. Lord Hailey suggests in his *African Survey* (p. 143), that Belgian policy today is based partly on the "general determination that . . . rule of the colony should be such as to present the strongest possible contrast to the history of the Free State under Leopold II."[14]

THE CONGO: WHAT RUNS IT

I asked Léon A. M. Pétillon, the Governor General, what ran the Congo, and he replied with a quick, alert, confident "I do!" M. Pétillon was not being egotistical. He was telling the truth, but not the whole truth. Three things

[14] For a contrary view of Leopold, see *African Journey*, by André Siegfried.

run the Congo: Belgium, which is represented by M. Pétillon; the Roman Catholic church; and big business.

About each of these three factors we should have a word:

(1) The Congo is as much controlled by Brussels as, say (on a very different scale), Guam is controlled by Washington. The Belgian Governor General, who almost invariably rises out of the colonial service and who as a rule has spent many years out in the bush, is responsible to the minister of colonies, who is in turn responsible to the Belgian parliament. He is, however, more of a free agent than British or French governors. In the first place, he is not troubled much by political events at home. Second, he has no local Legislative Council or assembly as a check on his powers, because representative government does not exist in the Congo. It goes without saying that no Congolese sit in the Brussels parliament. Within this framework Belgian rule reflects, just as does the atmosphere of Léopoldville, the national character. It is stern, just, practical, and with a delight in figures and results.

Belgian District Commissioners in the hinterland are conscientious men, who keep every element of rule under their fingertips. One interesting regulation is that a DC is not allowed to spend more than ten days a month in whatever town or village is his headquarters. During the other twenty he must keep moving, circulating from village to village and tribe to tribe. Nobody has a chance to be lazy. Also they are obliged to learn the local languages. Another point is that most Belgian officials, even those of highest rank, are middle-class folk. In the whole roster of the Congo administration only one man comes from the aristocracy. This is a government based on the rights and privileges of the average citizen. I asked what would happen to the Congo if a socialist government should take power in Brussels some day. Answer: "There would be no change. The socialists have no more desire than we to kill the goose that lays the golden egg."

The present Governor General, Léon Pétillon, has a brilliant administrative record. He is fifty-one, and has been in the colonial service all his adult life. He several times served as *chef du cabinet* to a renowned former governor, Pierre Rijckmans, who is now Belgian representative to the Trusteeship Council of the UN. Belgian officials rise (if they are good enough) with methodical precision, step by step. Pétillon has been Vice-Governor of the Congo and Governor of Ruanda-Urundi, which post is usually the stepping-stone to the Congo governorship. He helped write the Congo's Ten-Year Plan (which envisages a total investment of about $1.6 billion dollars) and has served on several of the great parastatal boards so important in Congolese economic life, like the Comité National de Kivu and *Otraco*, which runs transportation in the western Congo. Also Pétillon has been bold enough on occasion to crack down on eminent ecclesiastical dignitaries when they

CONGO I: BELGIAN POLICY IN AFRICA

sought to interfere in secular affairs. A career and vision like Pétillon's goes a long way to efface memories of Leopold.

Finally, it is the Congo that makes Belgium a first-class power; therefore it behooves Brussels to administer it as competently as possible. Belgium is like an iceberg; the exposed fragment of motherland gets most of its weight, wealth, and substance from the huge submerged Congo mass underneath. The contribution of the colony to Belgium is enormous, if indirect, in several fields. To change the metaphor sharply, the Congo is the Belgian ace of spades.

(2) The Roman Catholic church owes its terrific power to several factors. Belgium itself is more than 90 per cent Catholic, and naturally the local administration reflects this strong preponderance. One recent minister of colonies, M. Godding, was, it is true, a pronounced anti-clerical, but on the whole Catholics have always dominated the colonial ministry without question. The chief immediate influence of Catholics is on education. There are intricate elements to this story. Education in the Congo is not administered by the government, but by the missions. There are (incredible as it may seem) *no* state schools for Africans, only mission schools or those run by private interests. The state does, however, give extremely important financial assistance to the missions. Of the total number of schools (26,540), 80 per cent are Catholic. About 30 per cent of all Congolese children of primary school age go to school—a figure high for Africa—and recently for the first time African children in limited number have been admitted to the European secondary schools.

The first missionaries to penetrate into the Congo (in 1878) were British Protestants. The Catholics began to enter in the early 1880's, but for a generation most educational work was done by the Protestants, not the Catholics. In 1925 came a measure by the Belgian government giving the Catholic church an absolute monopoly on governmental subsidies to education for twenty years. Money (state money) poured in to aid the Catholic missions, whereas the Protestants had to keep afloat and maintain *their* schools by their own efforts. So they were rapidly outdistanced. No full accounting has ever been made of the billions of francs the Catholic missions received. They spent them well. Their educational plant is magnificent by African standards. In 1945 the twenty-year monopoly expired, and since that date the Protestant missions have received a share of government funds for education. The fact remains that for twenty critical years, when the Congo's educational system as it exists today was being established, the Catholics had everything their own way.

The Catholics are justifiably proud of their record in the Congo. Even in the remote bush a traveler will see on lonely roads Catholic schools, hospitals, social establishments and shrines. Almost three million Congolese have become Christian, and most of these are Catholics. The Catholic church has no fewer than twenty-six bishops in the Congo, of whom one is a Negro; there are about three hundred Negro priests.

I mentioned above that the Congo now for the first time (like Southern Rhodesia) has a university. This is at Lovanium, near Léopoldville, and is an adjunct of the University of Louvain at home. It is of course a Catholic institution. That the Belgian administration should have at last agreed to the creation of a university in the Congo is a significant forward step. There are fewer students than teachers at the moment, but many more students will come in time, when the secondary schools can turn them out. Courses in medicine, agriculture, and general education are planned, but none in law or engineering.

(3) *Big business.* This is the key to much. Nowhere else in the world (except in Communist areas) are the government and economy of a country so wedded and welded as in the Congo. The Congo probably represents the highest development of state capitalism ever attained by a country. There are, as we shall see, important British commercial companies in British West Africa, and important French companies in French West Africa, as well as ambitious development projects in which government plays a large role, but nowhere else on the continent does the state have the authority over private business that it has in the Congo. The Belgian government can dominate a corporation in a manner impossible to the British or French governments. Partly this derives, as is only too obvious, from the system set up by Leopold. The state inherited from him a vast and intricately enmeshed private property, and still runs it by a subtle and effective combination of public and private means.

Five enormous holding companies (or call them trusts or economic groups) control probably 70 per cent of *all* Congo business. This represents a concentration of economic power unparalleled in the modern world. In all five, the Belgian *government* holds a powerful interest, ranging up to 50 per cent. Moreover in organizations other than the big five the government has not merely a quarter or half interest but a controlling interest. The resultant situation is unique. The Belgian state not only extracts taxes from these corporations—naturally—but dividends as well. The Congolese cow is milked at both ends at once.

The five overriding giants are (1) Brufina (Société de Bruxelles pour la Finance et l'Industrie), which controls the Banque de Bruxelles and various industrial organizations; (2) Cominière (Société Commerciale et Minière du Congo), which ties in with the Nagelmackers financial interests and has huge agricultural properties; (3) Unilever (through its Belgian subsidiary,

CONGO I: BELGIAN POLICY IN AFRICA

Huilever); (4) the Banque Empain, with strong interests in transportation and much else; and (5) the fabulous organization know as the Société Générale de Belgique.[15]

This last immense and proliferating holding company was founded in 1822, has capital reserves of more than two billion Belgian francs ($40,000,000), and is the kind of colossus that might be envisaged if, let us say, the House of Morgan, Anaconda Copper, the Mutual Life Insurance Company of New York, the Pennsylvania Railroad, and various companies producing agricultural products were lumped together, with the United States *government* as a heavy partner. This is monopoly with a vengeance. The Société Générale is bigger than the other four combines put together. Its interests are extraordinarily multiform. It is much more than a mere bank or holding company. For instance it controls the CCCI (Compagnie Congolese du Commerce et Industrie) which in turn controls subsidiaries in cotton, sugar, pharmaceutical products, automobiles, and beer. It has interest in railroads, insurance, Sabena (the Belgian aviation company), diamonds, cattle, shipping, and cold storage. But none of this is what makes the Société Générale *really* count. What counts is the mines.

These we shall allude to in the chapter following. The financial structure is complicated. Under the Société Générale and the CCCI is an organization known as the Comité Special du Katanga. This, in theory, administers the government's interest in the mining industry, and holds 111,111,111 acres (the Belgians love neat figures) of property, comprising some of the world's most valuable mineral rights. Also an organization known as the Compagnie du Katanga is important. Underneath these is the celebrated Union Minière du Haut Katanga, one of the foremost and most successful mining companies in the world. The Belgian government owns a two-third interest in the CSK, which in turn owns 25 per cent of the Union Minière. Also British capital is involved. About 20 per cent of Union Minière stock is owned by the Société Générale. The Union Minière is, in any case, the tail that wags the Société Générale dog. It pays, for instance, between 45 and 50 per cent of *all* Congo taxes. Can one imagine any single American corporation rich and powerful enough to pay almost *half* of total United States taxes? Then consider what wealth the Union Minière must extract from the soil in order to support such a tax burden. A golden elephant indeed!

Visitors to the Congo cannot but be impressed by Belgian habits in financial nomenclature. Most companies have peculiarly abbreviated names, which carry a vaguely Russian sound, although that is not the intention.

---

[15] See "The Congo is in Business," by Herbert Solow, *Fortune*, November, 1952, an admirably informed article, and a dispatch by C. L. Sulzberger in the New York *Times*, January 30, 1953.

There are organizations called for short UTEXLEO, FORESCOM, SOKIMO, OTRACO (Office d'Exploitation des Transports Coloniaux), SYMÉTAIN (tin), GÉOMINES, CAFECONGO, COTONCO (cotton), and CONGOPALM. The Ford company in Léopoldville bears the strange name CEGEAC. One giant is FORMINIÈRE (Société Internationale Forestière et Minière du Congo) which owns Léopoldville's skyscraper and is the largest producer of industrial diamonds in the world.

THE CONGO: ITS GREATEST PROBLEMS

I asked a weighty Belgian authority what he considered these to be, and he replied: (a) transportation; (b) harnessing the cataracts below Léopoldville for the production of electric power; (c) soil conservation; (d) "assimilation," namely, the incorporation of more Africans into "civilized" society.[16]

I alluded to these points in a conversation with Governor General Pétillon, without mentioning their source, and he laughed, "Whoever told you that must be an economist." (He was.) M. Pétillon went on, "The chief problem of the Congo is *political education*—how to get the Africans fit for future responsibility."

THE BELGIAN SYSTEM AND COLOR BAR

> The weakness of the [Belgian] program appears to be their reluctance to allow the African to secure an advanced education—even a technical education—for fear that he will then demand a growing share of responsibility in the shaping of his own future. Any visitor who has seen the strength of the independence movement thoughout the world will wonder if the Belgians like King Canute are not trying to curb a force that eventually will become irresistible.
>
> But it would be a serious mistake to underestimate the intelligence of the Belgians and to assume that they will attempt to stand like a rock in the face of strong future demands from the people. The danger lies not so much in the possibility that the Belgians will not compromise eventually with the force of nationalism, but that when they do they will find the Africans almost totally inexperienced in handling the responsibilities which they are certain to demand and eventually to get.
>
> —CHESTER BOWLES

The essence of the Belgian system is to buy off African discontent by giving economic opportunity, widespread social services, and a comparatively high standard of living. A Belgian would define it differently by saying that a

[16] As mentioned in Chapter 29 above, the Belgians have adopted the Portuguese *assimilado* system to an extent. But so far only a few thousand Congolese have been, as the Belgians put it, "matriculated." Thousands of others are, however, known as *évolués*, Africans advanced enough not to need matriculation.

thoroughly sound economic structure, with Africans participating in its benefits to some extent, is an indispensable prerequisite for political advance. If you have a healthy economy, the Belgians say, other problems will in time solve themselves. The whole stress is material. The Belgians think that it is madness for the British to let Africans vote when they are still economically submerged, and worse madness for the French to work out an elaborate abstract political system and then try to fit Africans into it.

The average Congolese (as of today) has few civil or other rights. He is not even a citizen in our sense of the term. But his children have a fair chance of getting some education at least, medical services, skilled or semi-skilled jobs when they grow up, good pay, and, above all, freedom from the worst irritants of color bar. The Congo is not the Gold Coast by a long shot. But neither is it Mr. Strijdom's Union. It is—to put it as briefly as possible —a kind of welfare state without political advantages.

The Belgians like to say that color bar does not exist in the Congo, but this is of course not true. Africans are given opportunity, but not equality. We have already seen that Léopoldville and Elisabethville are double cities, with one compartment for blacks, one for whites. All manner of minor discriminations still exist. Africans cannot travel without a permit, cannot (in theory) drink anything stronger than beer, and cannot possess firearms. They are permitted vocational education, but only up to a point. The ceiling is a curious one. A Congolese Negro can become a first-class carpenter or mechanic, but not an engineer. He can be a bishop, a journalist, an accountant, a medical assistant, a teacher, a civil servant, or a pharmacist, but not an architect or attorney. There are thousands of Negro lawyers in British and French Africa, but not one in the Congo. The new university will, however, open a variety of professions to Africans before too long. One vivid point of difference between the Belgian and British (or French) systems is that the Belgians do their utmost to keep Congolese out of Europe and particularly Belgium. They do not want them to see how Europeans live in Europe. Hundreds of African students attend French and British universities in Europe, but practically none—perhaps two or three boys in all—have ever gone to a Belgian university. The barrier between the Congo and the home country is almost impenetrable. The Belgians do not want their Africans to become dissatisfied. For years if a Congolese seaman managed to skip ship at a Belgian port, he was made to remain in Belgium for the rest of his life—so that he could not return to the Congo and tell his fellows of the wonders he had seen. Few Africans, even officials of rank, are ever allowed to visit Belgium. When we were in Léopoldville a headline made big news—*Les notables Congolais en Belgique.* Most exceptionally, a small group of Negro leaders had been invited to Brussels for a brief "orientation" visit. Africans like to laugh. A cynical chuckle instantly spread around town to the effect that the chief of the mission, who was mayor of the black portion of Léopoldville, would soon be made a baron like the mayor of Brussels.

A Belgian official told us, "We have a duty to these people. We want to treat them like human beings. But surely it would be a disfavor to the Africans, not a favor, to communicate to them the achievements of European civilization *before they are ready*. Will it not ruin them to submit them to foreign intellectual influences *too soon*?" No doubt this remark was made in all sincerity, but a lot of false-face accompanies it. The real reason why the Belgians (until very recently) have withheld higher education from Africans and sterilized them from any contact with Europe at all was the fear that, once they knew more, they would be less malleable, less docile, less subject to the lulling glut of Belgian paternalism, and harder to handle politically. The Belgians do not want their Africans to go abroad and hear about things like habeas corpus, a free press, elections, and trial by jury.

If Africans are babied in the Congo, it is to keep them from getting a sense of responsibility. Babied? We first entered the Congo from Uganda, and our chauffeur was a Uganda boy. He was terrified of every Belgian we met. He had a bad cold, and we were up in the mountains in freezing rain. But he said that if we asked the hotel manager to give him a room (normally chauffeurs sleep in their cars), he would be "arrested." I said that this could not possibly happen, since he was a British subject, not Congolese. "Makes no matter, *bwana*." I asked him what advantages Africans had in the Congo that they did not have in British Africa. "*Bwana,* people here have no anything."

This was a gross exaggeration, but certain abuses do still exist in the Belgian Congo. One is forced labor on the roads or fields. Year by year, however, the incidence of this decreases, men in the labor gangs are paid and well treated, there is no corruption as in Portuguese Africa, and the system will be ended soon.[17] One punishment was (in older days) the dusting

[17] In British Africa the local District Officer tries to *teach* better agricultural methods. In Belgian Africa, like as not, the District Officer will say to a peasant, "Plant thirty trees here next month—or else!" The Belgians see nothing whatever wrong in this. On the contrary they say that it is a good thing to *force* peasants to adopt better agricultural methods. In British Africa, as time goes on, the African may forget what the Englishman has taught. But in Belgian Africa there will be lasting beneficial results, such as improvement in the quality of stock, control of erosion, and so on, because of work already done. The British *hope* that the Africans will remember what they have been taught. The Belgians concentrate on producing an efficient, well-balanced economy now, so that the country will be in good shape in any case.

of a culprit with a kind of nettle called a buffalo bean, which caused the most violent irritation but did not do lasting injury. Unpleasant, but better than Mr. Swart's cat-o'-nine-tails or the Portuguese ping-pong bat. One complaint I heard was that if any European housewife reported a servant for a dereliction fancied or real, he was subject—without trial—to a sentence of six months in jail. Another curious point (Africans told us) was that boys out in the countryside were made to marry very young, whether they wanted to or not. The Belgians demand a big, quickly expanding population.

Intermarriage between black and white is not against the law in the Congo, but almost never occurs. Belgians in remote areas, both officials and non-officials, sometimes have black mistresses, but a certain discretion is supposed to accompany such an affair, and by unwritten law the white father is required to make provision for any child.

Whites in the Congo live under certain strictures too, and the great majority are well behaved—much better than white settlers in Kenya, for instance. One word Africans hate is *macac*, which means "monkey." In theory any white man calling a Negro a *macac* is subject to a fine of one thousand francs, or $20. If any white man flagrantly and persistently abuses or affronts Africans, he is subject to peremptory dismissal from the colony, and is shipped back to Belgium. A Draconian punishment, but the threat of it works.

There is no segregation or color bar in shops, elevators, banks, post office, or local transportation. Africans must be in their own localities by 9:00 P.M. but no curfew is in force after that *within* the African city. Africans are—in theory—allowed into hotels and restaurants anywhere in the Congo, if they are correctly dressed and behave themselves. Recently in Léopoldville they were permitted to sit for the first time in the European sidewalk cafés. People thought that an explosion might occur, but nothing whatever happened. Still, it should be carefully pointed out that only an infinitesimal proportion of Africans care—or dare—to avail themselves of these privileges. And the rules are not hard and fast. An American Negro, representing the State Department, arrived in Léopoldville not long ago. Somewhat hesitantly, the local consul asked if he would be received in the leading hotel. The manager replied, "How black is he? If he isn't very dark, all right!"

I went to one big European shop which—such a contrast to Rhodesia!—was thronged with Africans. The shopkeeper told me, "Don't think that I would be such an idiot as to have color bar *here!* Africans outnumber Europeans by twenty-five to one in this community, and I want the business. Besides in ten years or maybe twenty there won't be any Europeans left."

The healthiest thing in the Congo is the development, which the good sense of the Belgian administration has made possible, of an African middle class. Belgians do not want Negroes at their dinner tables (although at big official parties a few chosen Africans may be present), but they want them to have economic opportunity. The more Africans who learn skilled trades and make money, the better the Belgians like it. This serves the national purpose. It increases purchasing power. And Africans do make money. Several in Léopoldville earn $20,000 per year or more; our host's cook had just put $1,000 into a new house. There are, believe it or not, no fewer than 130,000 Congolese with savings accounts in the local banks.[18] And how refreshing it was, after the Rhodesias and the Union, to see Africans at work as hotel clerks, airline dispatchers, post office employees, barmen, government servants, newspapermen, and traffic cops (imagine a Negro cop in Bulawayo!). Every stationmaster on the Matadi railway except one is an African. Africans are beginning to fulfill in the Congo, in other words, the role held by the Indians in East Africa. And this is as it should be.

The railway from Elisabethville to Ndola in Northern Rhodesia runs partly on Belgian soil, partly on British. At the frontier a white Rhodesian crew takes over from the African crew which was perfectly competent to run the train in Belgian territory, and could carry it on to Ndola without fault. It is, after all, the same train. But the Rhodesians cannot believe yet that an African can run a locomotive, nor will the white trade union tolerate black competition. The Belgians, getting richer every minute because African wages are lower than white, sit back and laugh. So do the Africans. Once on a Sabena airliner an irate South African passenger noticed that the steward was a Negro. He contemplated this indignity in shocked silence for a time and then asked him for something, rudely calling him "Boy!" The steward replied politely, "Am not boy, sir. Am air hostess!"

POLITICAL PICTURE AND THE FUTURE

The great bulk of Congolese do not think at all in nationalist terms, i.e., of freedom from Belgian rule, because they are not educated enough to know what nationalism is. The Belgian system works well, and organized discontent does not exist. There are, however, by official statistics some 3,800 political prisoners in the Congo—not an inconsiderable number. Most apparently belong to something known as the Kitawala Society, a body of fanatic religious revivalists. The authorities have done their best to suppress this, but on occasion it still makes trouble.

[18] New York *Times*, August 25, 1953.

CONGO I: BELGIAN POLICY IN AFRICA

A man named Kibangu arose in the area southeast of Léopoldville about thirty years ago, and organized a secret organization (strikingly like the precursors of Mau Mau in Kenya) based on protest, mysticism, and distorted Christianity. It was anti-white, and its members believed in the coming of a black Messiah. Kibangu was arrested, and died in jail. Another dissident leader arose, Simon Mpadi, one of Kibangu's disciples, who was also jailed. He had definite political objectives, but these were cast mostly in religious terms.

The Belgians dismiss "Kibanguism," which grew into the Kitawala or was absorbed by it, as inconsequential crackpot-ism, and say that, strangely enough, it is an offshoot of Jehovah's Witnesses. Two extremist Kitawala leaders, who had given themselves the names "Jesus Christ" and "Hallelujah" were hanged for sedition not long ago.[19] Shortly after the war a mutiny of Congolese troops took place at Luluabourg, an important provincial town, and was ruthlessly suppressed, but this seemingly had no political roots, and was not associated with Kitawala.

If you ask a Belgian why, by and large, the Congo is almost completely tranquil politically, and why practically no danger exists of any African uprising like that of the Mau Maus, he will give two main reasons. First, the Congo permits few white settlers. Second, economic factors. The Congo has no industrial color bar (always we get back to the question of race) and encourages its Africans to earn good livings. No trace at all exists of the fear and hysteria that deface the Union. "But we would be frightened," one Belgian friend told us, "if we had a million *white* men here."

The Belgian government, which is a very sound government indeed, knows, however, that the present situation cannot be held without alteration forever. There *must* be some political evolution, if only as an escape valve. This is the reason for an important reform now getting under way. The Congo is to have its first "elections," an unprecedented step. In certain towns, new municipal councils (half European, half African) are to be chosen by a limited, carefully controlled electorate.

Why cannot the Belgian system, which for all its arbitrary character gives substantial benefits to Africans, go on without modification forever? Why not let unmitigated colonial rule proceed indefinitely? It gives a good standard of living, and presumably keeps Communism out. One Belgian told us, sighing, "If we do ever have to go, at least we will have the satisfaction of leaving to the Africans a rich country." The reason why administration cannot, however, proceed without profound change in the future is that the people will sooner or later be in a position to demand change. Once a

[19] Basil Davidson in the *Reporter*, January 27, 1955.

certain standard of living is reached, education cannot possibly be withheld. The Congo cannot hide forever from the modern world, because it cannot exist without the rest of the world. No less a personage than the Apostolic Delegate to the Congo, Monsignor Sigismondi, told us, "Discontent is inevitable, and that is perhaps a good thing, since discontent is the price of progress. The people are beginning to realize, even here, that the mines are theirs, the land is theirs."

I asked a man who is quite possibly the single most powerful living Belgian how long Belgium could hold the Congo, how long the rule of the white man was going to last. He replied, "Sooner or later we will have to have elections. After that, five years."

CHAPTER 33

Congo II: Uranium, Pygmies, Giants

Africa cannot be developed without African cooperation.
—ERIC LARRABEE

PROBABLY not one American in a hundred thousand has ever heard the name Edgar Edouard Sengier, nor is he well known in Europe outside of a limited circle. So far as I know, no photograph of him has ever appeared in an American newspaper or magazine of wide circulation, and, although he has visited the United States forty or fifty times, I do not think he has ever been noticed or interviewed by a ship news reporter. Edgar Sengier is, in his field, one of the great unknowns of our time.

This is all the more remarkable because it was Mr. Sengier who made it possible for the United States to make the atomic bomb. Without Sengier, there would have been no bomb—none, at least, by the summer of 1945, when the Hiroshima and Nagasaki bombs ended the war against Japan. A great many other people contributed to the atomic project, of course. But if it had not been for Sengier, those first bombs would never have exploded when they did, because it was he who produced the deadly uranium without which they could not have been made.

Moreover, until fairly recently, *every* atomic bomb manufactured in the United States, *every* atomic bomb tested in Nevada or the South Pacific, has been made out of Sengier's uranium, or from plutonium which derives from uranium. Nor would it have been possible to make the first hydrogen bombs without Sengier's uranium, since these work by means of an atomic trigger, made of uranium. Nowadays uranium is being mined in a wide variety of places—Canada, Colorado, and South Africa. Sengier's uranium is not as indispensable as it was, and production in the Union probably exceeds that of the Congo today. Nevertheless Sengier's contribution has a considerable historic and dramatic interest.

The Sengier story has never been written before, and it is difficult to write for several reasons. First, Mr. Sengier's own self-effacement. When we met and dined with him in Paris he mentioned casually that, until 1951, he had never in his life talked to a foreign journalist. He said to us dryly, "If you are going to write about me, please try to keep me out of it." Second, security. If it were not for security, Sengier would be a household name. During the war and immediately afterward any details about uranium in the Congo were top secret to an extreme degree. Even now the Belgians have a violently hush-hush attitude to uranium. The South Africans welcome publicity about their uranium, as we know, but not the close-mouthed Belgians.

Quite without regard to uranium Sengier has a firm claim to fame, if he chose to assert it, because as much as any man he is responsible for the rise of the Haut Katanga mining interests, chiefly copper. He does not visit the Congo often nowadays, but he did a great deal to develop it. Sengier is seventy-four, and is Président du Comité Permanent (roughly, chairman of the board of directors) of the Union Minière du Haut Katanga. This, we have just seen, is the most powerful element in the Société Générale, the huge agglutination of financial and industrial power which holds a position in Belgium and the Congo comparable to that once held by the Rothschilds in Central Europe. Sengier runs the Union Minière, more or less, the Union Minière runs the Société Générale, more or less, and the Société Générale helps run the Congo.

Sengier was born in Belgium, and was educated to be an engineer. He spent five years in China, working with Belgian tramway companies in the coastal cities. He was adventurous, willing to take responsibility, tough, shrewd, and durable. When he was about thirty, he decided to move on to Africa, and became associated with the Union Minière, which had been created in 1906, as a result of a merger between Belgian and British financial interests, notably Tanganyika Concessions, Ltd. The Congo itself only became a Belgian colony in 1908. Elisabethville, the chief city of the Haut Katanga, was founded in 1910. Sengier arrived there in 1911. He, the Union Minière, Elisabethville, and the Congo all grew up together.

The Union Minière procured in the Katanga area a concession (7,700 square miles) more than half the size of Belgium itself, which does not expire till March 11, 1990. When Sengier arrived the principal mine was at Kambove, about a hundred miles from Elisabethville. He had to walk there. There was no other way to reach it. The railway had reached Elisabethville but had not bitten its way into the high, wild bush beyond. Elisabethville itself was no more than a disorderly nest of tents and tin shanties. I met there an old prospector who, in 1909, shot a rhinoceros at the spot where the post office stands today. Elisabethville has grown with extraordinary speed. Sengier helped to plan and lay it out. I saw here more new American automobiles than in any city in Africa, in proportion to population. (Also I saw more convicts—boys in striped uniforms cleaning up lawns, repairing sidewalks, and the like. The Belgian authorities, instead of putting prisoners in jail, sometimes assign them to miscellaneous labor in the town. Also, as in South Africa, convicts may be hired out by private contractors.)

Slowly, year by year, Sengier rose in the Union Minière hierarchy. The Union Minière likes to be sure of its men, and it does not promote fast. It began to rise too. There was a time when it had to import its coke all the way from Europe. It overcame unimaginable difficulties in beating down the harsh pressures of isolated Africa, and it has been called the most "brilliant" mining company in the world.

It produced in 1953 more than 200,000 tons of copper alone, and normally accounts for not less than 7 per cent of the total world production of copper, 80 per cent of cobalt, and 5 per cent of zinc, as well as substantial quantities of cadmium, silver, platinum, columbium, tungsten, and many other minerals. It has spawned all manner of subsidiaries—in electricity (SOGELEC), in chemicals (SOGECHIM), coal, zinc (METALKAT), transportation, dairying, flour mills, and water power (SOGEFOR). It produces 45 per cent of all Congo exports, and I have already mentioned that it provides nearly half of the country's total taxes. Net profits in 1953 were more than $60,000,000.

Mr. Sengier is a very rich man, and a favorite indoor sport in the Congo is to guess at the incomes of various Société Générale directors. But, wealthy as they may be, they live deliberately unostentatious lives. That is part of the Belgian pattern and tradition. The Union Minière guest house in Elisabethville, where officials and visitors are put up, is a very modest house indeed—a four-room cottage. When my wife and I arrived there we found one bottle of milk in the icebox, and nothing else. (More, I hasten to add, was provided soon.)

Sengier is, of course, pleased by the immense financial beam and bulk of the Union Minière, and the fact that business seems to get better and better every year. But this is not all that interests him. What he looks back to with particular satisfaction is the social contribution he and his company have made to the Congo, not least in the realm of race relations. The Union Minière takes wealth out of the country; therefore, as Sengier sees it, he has a duty to put wealth back, in order to improve the standard of living of the people as a whole. This is, of course, shrewd policy as well as altruism, since (a) a healthy economy will tend to keep Congolese nationalism down, and (b) a population with substantial purchasing power makes for good business all around.

The "population" of the Union Minière is about five thousand whites, including wives and children, and about 19,000 native workers. The Africans do not live in compounds, as in South Africa, but in well-planned villages with admirable housing. The cruelties and uglinesses of the Rand system do not exist. No fewer than seven thousand African children go to Union Minière schools, and a strong effort is made to keep them healthy. The hospitals are the best I saw anywhere in Africa. Babies' cribs even have sheets! We visited the clinics, schools, and welfare establishments surrounding the great mine at Kipushi, near Elisabethville, and marveled. Once Sengier happened to be inspecting this same mine. He exclaimed to his subordinates gruffly, "What are we doing here? Producing copper, or just babies?"

Union Minière labor policy is complex. (1) There is no recruiting system like that in the Union. Boys are not grabbed out of the bush from surrounding territories. Until 1928, contract labor was brought in from Rhodesia, but since that date the labor force has been largely permanent, not migratory. About three thousand workers do, however, come from Ruanda on three-year contracts. (2) Ninety per cent of workers are married and live with their families. (3) Wages are not as high on a cash basis as in Rhodesia, but social services are more advanced. The Belgians do not believe in too much cash. "The Africans *drink* cash," our guide in the Katanga put it. But workers get free clothing, food, housing, schools, and medical attention, and their emotional as well as physical circumstances of life are enormously better than in South Africa. Moreover a *skilled* worker in the Union Minière can get up to $100 per month, a very large sum indeed for Africa. The wages of a white man for equivalent work is about five times that of the African, but this is a better ratio than in Rhodesia. (4) An African can rise fairly high, but must always be under the orders of a white foreman. (5) Unionization is still vestigial, and a successful strike almost out of the question. Here we have a striking contrast and paradox. The worker in the Rhodesias may live in economic misery, but he has the right to organize. The worker in the Congo is a political slave, but may be much better off economically. (6) There is no industrial color bar.

Indeed the principal point to make about labor in the Congo has to do with race. We have noted in the preceding chapter that an African middle class is beginning to emerge. Also African *skilled labor* is beginning to emerge. The Union Minière no longer uses whites on shovels, cranes, or bulldozers. It is teaching the blacks new and much more complicated skills day by day. This is practical good sense as well as altruism, if only because African labor is so much cheaper than white. To a visitor from other parts of Africa, the results are astonishing. Our first night in Elisabethville we went to the fiery Lubumbashi smelter, with its smokestack 492 feet high—the third highest in the world. We could scarcely believe it when we saw Africans handling the huge overhead cranes, with their oscillating burdens of molten metal, and otherwise doing work of the most technically exacting sort, and doing it as well as a white man could.

Basil Davidson wrote recently (April 10, 1954) in the *New Statesman*:

> Industrial revolution is fast pushing the Congo into new economic patterns . . . This sharing of skills can easily seem the most hopeful event in Africa. For industrialism in the Congo not only lifts thousands of Africans out of their rural poverty, out of their subservience to a ruined tribalism; it also lifts them into the modern world. Industrialised Africans in the Congo begin to lose their helot status, begin to take new bearings, begin to be "people like everyone else," not only in their own eyes but also in those of the Europeans for whom they work.

At any rate the theory so tenaciously held in South Africa that Africans are incapable of skilled work or advancement in technical fields is plentifully disproved by these developments.

One word more. The creation of a genuine industrial proletariat in the Congo might, in the very long run, make the country vulnerable to Communist penetration. This would be a wry joke on the Union Minière and the Belgian government. But the stout Belgians realize this as well as anybody, which is one reason why they do their best to keep political development at the minimum.

$$E = mc^2$$

I saw uranium twice in the Haut Katanga. I even touched a piece of ore loaded with it—then wanted to wash my hands quickly, out of the silly fear that it might be radioactive enough to hurt. We went to the museum in Elisabethville, and there, at the entrance, saw on display a block of pitchblende, uranium ore, as big as a pig. It was colored black and gold, and looked as if it were covered with a green scum, or moss made of stone.

It came from Shinkolobwe, the uranium mine operated by the Union Minière; a small sign says "*Attention. Bloc radioactif!*"

Then we saw lumps of other uranium ores, a characteristic of which is their savage, morbid color—tobernite, which is bright yellow-green and silver, billietite (yellow-red), fourmarierite (a brilliant marbled orange), kasolite (fawn and gold), saleite (lettuce green), sklodowskite (dull black mixed with pea green), metatobernite (spinach colored), and, most extraordinary of all, vanderbrandeite, which is greenish-gray, yellow, black, and orange, in tiger stripes.[1]

We called on Maurice Van Weyenbergh, the chief of the Union Minière in the Katanga, and saw in his office more samples of this brilliant, hideous ore. One chunk looked like a metal watermelon, pink and green, but it also had flaming veins of gamboge, lemon, and orange. The reflection was trite, but difficult not to summon—rocks like these have fire in them not only figuratively but literally. The fate of civilization rests on a more slender thread than at any time in history, because of energies imprisoned in these flamboyant stones. Rock mined from this remote area in the Belgian Congo is capable of burning up the world.

The Shinkolobwe mine has a curious history. In 1915 or thereabouts an independent Belgian prospector, scratching for what he could find, came across some pitchblende. He brought a sample to the local manager of the Union Minière, who happened to be an American, and who said in effect, "Throw it away. I don't want pitchblende. All I want is copper." And, indeed, copper stood at a tremendous premium then, in the early days of World War I.

The prospector, penniless, ended up in London, and sold his chunk of pitchblende to a secondhand minerals dealer. Some months later, a Belgian professor of geology happened to visit this obscure shop, in quest of odd stones; he bought the pitchblende, and had it analyzed. It was the richest radium ore he had ever seen. He took it at once to the headquarters of Union Minière in London, and as a result the Shinkolobwe radium mine came into being.

Shinkolobwe is near Jadotville, which is eighty-seven miles northwest of Elisabethville. It began to produce radium after World War I. The ore body was first worked from the surface, in an opencut; later, as the surface ore became exhausted, digging progressed underground, and today Shinkolobwe is the only underground mine operated by the Union Minière, except

---

[1] Sengier is not a man much impressed by honors or distinctions, but of one thing he is proud. A new ore (composed of uranium, vanadium, and copper) has recently been named for him—sengierite.

the great Prince Leopold copper mine at Kipushi.[2] The radium mine was worked, not by the Union Minière itself, but by a sister company, the Société Générale Metallurgique de Hoboken. (Not Hoboken, New Jersey, but Hoboken, Belgium, a small town near Antwerp.) Radium ore went up to a place called Oolen, near the Meuse, and was processed there. Thus pure radium in minute but important quantities began to reach hospitals and laboratories all over the world.

In those early days, nobody thought that the uranium contained in the radium ore had any particular value. After a time, strangely enough, the Shinkolobwe mine went out of action. Radium ore was cheap to mine, but the extraction of pure radium at Oolen was fantastically expensive. A little radium went a long way, and the Union Minière produced enough ore so that, before World War II, there was no point in mining any more. The market was glutted. And radium constituted only an infinitesimal fraction of the Union Minière's total business. The Shinkolobwe mine went derelict, and eventually, as underground mines will, it became flooded, and hence incapable of use.

In 1938, Sengier, then president of the Union Minière, was approached in circumstances of the utmost secrecy and urgency by a British physicist, Professor Tizard. He told him that German scientists were working on atomic fission, and might be able to make an atomic bomb out of uranium. It was of the most critical importance, Tizard told Sengier, that no uranium should get into German hands. (A year or so later, almost the same thing happened in the United States, when Professor Einstein and other scientists first got in touch with President Roosevelt to tell him about uranium and atomic fission for military purposes.)

Sengier, on his own responsibility, did something extraordinarily far-seeing and dramatic. He knew that a sizable stockpile of very rich pitch-blende existed in the Congo, and he arranged to have more than a thousand tons of this shipped from Shinkolobwe to the United States—secretly, of course. "I did this," he told me, "without telling anything to anybody." The ore reached America safely in 1940, and was put in storage in a New York warehouse. So, when the American atomic project got under way, the essential uranium was already there. *Every bit of uranium that went into the first American bombs came from a "mine" aboveground, and in New York City!* Thanks to Edgar Sengier.

Between the arrival of this indispensable ore and its actual use, some

---

[2] We went down the shaft of this, an experience I do not care to repeat. An incidental point is that Rhodesia is only seven hundred yards away. One can almost walk underneath the frontier.

quaint episodes occurred. Sengier, in total secrecy, informed the proper American authorities that his uranium was available. The State Department was so impressed that it wanted to move the deadly stuff to Fort Knox at once. But, because of various confusions, a year passed before the American government acted to take advantage of Sengier's foresight and perspicacity. By this time (such was the veil of secrecy) people apparently forgot—or had never known—where the pitchblende actually was. In 1941 Colonel Nichols, an American officer representing the atomic project, walked into Sengier's New York office on Broad Street and asked him urgently for help to get ore—from the Congo! Uranium was, Nichols said, absolutely vital to American defense and the war effort. Not to be able to get it from the Katanga would be a disaster of unparalleled seriousness and magnitude. Sengier listened. Sengier smiled. Then he told Colonel Nichols that a sizable quantity of ore had been ready and waiting in *New York* for a year.

Nichols walked out with a memorandum quickly drawn up on a piece of yellow paper and signed by Sengier, making this uranium the property of the United States.

This was the first signal service that Edgar Sengier rendered the American and Allied cause. There came another.

The Shinkolobwe mine was, we have seen, flooded and out of use. The ore in New York would not last forever. American emissaries made contact with Sengier again, and he met them with General Groves, in charge of the Manhattan Project, at a secret rendezvous. He did not wait for the Americans to put their questions. In the first moment of conversation, he asked abruptly, "Do you want the uranium mine opened, or not?"

They wanted it opened.

Union Minière engineers proceeded to deflood the Shinkolobwe mine, and started it producing uranium again. One stroke of luck lay in the "tailings" of earth and rock piled around the pit. No one thought in the old radium days that these had any value, and they had simply been left there. They did not contain radium in sufficient quantity to be profitable. But they did contain uranium. To get the mine into full working operation was an appallingly difficult job, engineers have told me. Moreover all work had to be done in conditions of the most mortal secrecy. But by 1943 Shinkolobwe was producing uranium ore once more, and it has been producing it ever since.

Why did Sengier do the United States these signal favors? He was a Belgian and hated Nazi Germany. He was a decent human being, who wanted the democratic world to win. He believed in freedom, and he liked Britain and the United States.

Very few people have ever visited Shinkolobwe. Only one man, Sengier himself, can give permission to see the mine, even today. During the war, the fact that uranium was mined in the Congo *was* really a top secret. Shinkolobwe did not even appear on the maps. Now the existence of the mine is public knowledge everywhere. But, obviously, precautions must be taken. Luckily it is easy to guard Shinkolobwe against sabotage, because of its peculiar isolation; only one road gives access to it, and this is firmly controlled. Although the American (and British) interest in the mine is still marked, security since the war has been exclusively a Belgian matter. There is no representative of the Atomic Energy Commission at Shinkolobwe. Sengier insisted on this. He told the Americans that they must never let the Belgians think that they, the Belgians, were not considered to be fully discreet and competent.

Three things about uranium in the Congo are still ultrasecret. First, the amount of production. Second, price. Third, how the ore is transported to the United States, although anybody ought to be able to guess this by looking at a map.[3]

Only two Americans have, so far as I know, ever seen the Shinkolobwe mine. One was a technician, a mining engineer; the other is a lawyer, Joseph Volpe, Jr., of Washington, D.C. Although he was, incredibly enough, only a private at the time, Volpe was one of General Groves's right-hand men in the early negotiations with Sengier. Then he went out to the Congo to check up on various matters. When he arrived in Elisabethville and called on the Union Minière people, he saw a large lump of high-grade pitchblende in a geologist's office. He laughed, "Don't you boys know that this stuff makes you sterile?" The Belgians replied that they all had several children. Volpe told them calmly about research that had just taken place in the United States, proving how dangerous uranium could be. The next time he visited the geologist's office the pitchblende had disappeared.

Volpe asked, "Do you drink the water around here?"

"Of course! The radium content is infinitesimal."

No one drank water from that particular area from that day on.

The Belgians have been roundly criticized on occasion for what they charged for uranium during the war. Actually, at that time, Sengier set an arbitrary price that was not exorbitant. But he wanted to take care of his costs, and he insisted that the terms be "reasonable." Nowadays the price is reached competitively, because of South African, Canadian and American production.

When Sengier visited the United States in 1946, Mr. Truman presented

---

[3] One of the few specific items I have ever seen printed on these subjects was a brief dispatch from a Belgian news agency to the New York *Times* (January 4, 1948), saying that in 1946 the United States bought 3,650 tons of uranium ore from the Belgian Congo, paying $5,332,000 for it.

him with the Medal of Merit. He was, I am told, the first non-American civilian ever to receive this decoration. Even though the war was over, the ceremony was secret, and the record of the proceedings was impounded in the White House, for security reasons. But I have seen the text of the citation, which is harmless enough and reads:

> Edgar Edouard Sengier, for exceptionally meritorious services to the United States of America in accomplishments involving great responsibility and unfailing cooperation in connection with the supply of essential war materials. As Chairman of the Board of Directors of the African Metals Corporation, Mr. Sengier personally supervised and carried out certain contracts and other arrangements connected with the production of raw materials essential to the war effort. His sound judgment, initiative, resourcefulness and cooperation have contributed significantly to the successful conclusion of the allied war effort.
>
> Harry S. Truman

*

Sengier is a tallish man, somewhat portly, with pale skin, white hands, a fringe of shinily white hair, and a short silver mustache clipped with sharp neatness. He conveys that pleasant sense of benevolence which may come to an extremely successful man of affairs, after his major work is done. During the war he lived mostly at the Hotel Ambassador in New York City. His telephone rang early one August morning in 1945. Sengier told me, "The voice did not identify itself. But whoever was talking told me to stay close to the radio all that day." He chuckled dryly, "I daresay they thought that I had a right to hear what was going to be announced."

The announcement, from which the world has not yet recovered, was that the United States had exploded the Hiroshima bomb.

WE VISIT BOENDE

We had more experience of genuine back country, real tropical bush, in the Congo than anywhere else in Africa except Nigeria. We told Governor Pétillon that we wanted to see some totally primitive people, if possible, and he promptly sent us to a town called Boende, about ninety miles from Coquilhatville as the crow flies (there is no road) and on the Tshuapa River near the Equator. This was, to put it mildly, a far cry from the Haut Katanga. Nobody near Boende ever heard of industrial color bar or an industrial "revolution."

From Boende we drove out into the heart of the great equatorial forest.

CONGO II: URANIUM, PYGMIES, GIANTS

The rust-colored roads wound through lanes of trees so heavily hung with creepers that they had the shape of parasols, and seemed to be growing downward, not up. Giant leaves, pink and green, looked like a milky way of butterflies; a kind of tulip, bursting into a cup of scarlet and orange, rose as tall as a man on every side. The people here had no agriculture at all till the white man came; they lived on roots and maggots, which are still a delicacy. But it was interesting to note that the narrow little roads, cutting across the swamps that led down from the scummy green river, separated from the rest of the world as if by an enormous wet sponge and leading nowhere, were better marked than streets in the city of Johannesburg.

The tribesmen we saw were mostly Bakutu (not to be confused with Bakuba); they number 40,000, and speak a dialect of Lingala. Most have their teeth sharply filed, and the men wear wonderful scars on their bellies, branching out like leaves; some carry spears with a rattle at the tip. Men and women both wear a peculiar headdress—a cloth-covered wooden block attached to the hair—and red paint on their faces. The men adorn their throats with leopard teeth, and women with string after string—as many as thirty—of brightly colored beads, so close together that the effect is that of a scarf. They also wear scarlet beads around their loins. We saw one newly born baby that looked like a brown spider, and one albino. The albino, dead-white, about two years old, will have a hard life, because albinos are thought to be unlucky.

On the hot red road two women approached, and their calves shone with gold. The gold blinked at us in this steaming sunshine. I thought that they must be wearing gaiters, or boots, of some strange sparkling golden cloth. But no. These were metal greaves they wore, of solid polished brass, welded to the leg from ankle to knee, and weighing ten and a half pounds each. (I know this weight to be accurate, because we were given one of these greaves as a souvenir, and I have just weighed it on the kitchen scale.)

These shackles, which are at once sharply beautiful and repulsive, are worn by married women whose husbands are rich enough to afford them. A blacksmith fixes them on, and they are never taken off. They are called *kongas*, and are objects of great pride. Sometimes only the favorite wife in a family has them. We even watched women *dance* wearing this remarkable equivalent of the ball and chain. But if the husband dies, whereupon the *konga* may be chiseled off by the blacksmith, the woman will have to learn to walk all over again, because her legs have become so accustomed to the great weight of these brass manacles. Free of them at last, her muscles no longer have power.

Another peculiarity in this area is that many Bakutu, strolling along the roads, carry with them a light wooden curved stool, with one leg and no arms. When fatigued, they sit down on this. They carry their own chairs, like an English sportsman with a hunting stick. The dances we saw were somewhat placid—a ring of shuffling women around several drummers—as far as movement and music were concerned, but the barbaric nakedness of the bodies and glittering ornamentation made them superlatively picturesque.

These tribesmen have one meal a day, after sundown; men and women eat separately. They live on palm oil (the basis of the diet), manioc, sugar cane, and corn. They are expert hunters with spears, bows and arrows, and in particular nets. They can mimic closely the sounds of wild beasts, and trap them by calling to them out of the trees. They love to eat monkeys. Their tomtoms are hollowed out of redwood trees—the same tree that makes the crimson dye for their faces. When they wear out a patch of soil, they pick up their houses, made of portable reed slabs, and move somewhere else—exactly as did the first settlers in Virginia who progressively moved westward, although Virginia settlers did not carry their houses with them. Most have two wives, some three; one chief in the neighborhood has thirty. They marry as many wives as they can afford, since a woman is a useful animal. Since 1952, however, by terms of a new Belgian law aiming to reduce polygamy, only the first wife is considered to be legitimate.

Girls marry from the age of twelve, and most have had sexual relations long before that. A man will not, as a rule, marry a girl until she has proved her fertility by having an illegitimate child or two. The Bakutu and their neighboring tribes make love sideways, and the mother of the girl superintends her first experience of the sexual act. Wives are not only useful, but a good investment; bride-price (usually paid in the form of small *kongas*) can be as little as $3.00, and the woman then works for life. Taxes are about $2.00 per year, and the annual cash income in a good district is around $60 per year. The cash crops are rice and a form of solidified resin called copal, an important Congo article of export. The infant mortality rate is very high. On death, a Bakutu is put into a termite hill, a simple procedure and quite sanitary.

At Wema we spent the night at the Disciples of Christ Congo Mission, where Dr. Howard Horner and his wife, also a doctor, run a small hospital. Air travel and the opening up of communications, Dr. Horner told us, have brought to this part of Africa diseases never known before, like dengue fever and various obscure forms of dysentery. (When the Horners arrived in Boende twelve years ago, there was not a single automobile in the whole area. Now they are common.) We watched with admiration the work of this devoted American staff, under the Horners, so cheerful, courageous, and secure in the knowledge of their good works, all done in difficult circumstances thousands of miles from home, with only the scantiest funds. We saw lines of sick and maimed Africans waiting gratefully for treatment. This is one of the best bush hospitals in central Africa. One odd point is that it is impossible to teach African boys in the school softball, because they are unable to learn to catch. Nobody knows why. Suddenly we walked into a funeral. A woman had been brought to the hospital too late, and died of peritonitis following childbirth. She was carried away in a rough brown sack slung on a pole borne by two bearers, as a group of mourners wailed and moaned plangently. Her child was alive, and was being cared for at the hospital by a female relative wearing nothing but a raffia G-string. I lit a cigarette and tossed the match on the ground. A boy picked it up with extreme shy interest and curiosity, as if it were the first match he had ever seen. Maybe it was.

The visitor to places as utterly primitive and unconversant as the villages around Boende is bound to ask himself, no matter how fervently he may believe in the potentiality of African progress, "Can people as impenetrably backward as these ever be made fit to take part in a modern society, let alone develop toward democratic institutions?" The Belgian answer is, surprisingly enough, an emphatic yes, but with the qualification that the process may take a hundred years. Even today one should not disparage the basic intelligence and acumen of most Africans. They watch things carefully, and learn fast. The phrase for "white man" in the local language is *Lolema djola feka feka*, which means "the bat that flies hard without knowing where it is going."

THE KIVU COUNTRY AND THE PYGMIES

Far on the other side of the Congo, in its northeast corner near the Uganda frontier, lies the lake country. If anybody should ever be so insane as to want to visit Africa for just a week, this is where he should come. If any area on the whole continent is the "real" Africa, this is it. To your hand is anything from a pygmy to a gorilla, the native life is profusely colorful, and the scenery grandiose and varied almost beyond conception. One night at Butembo, where we slept in a hotel exactly a mile high in the shadow of the Mountains of the Moon, the sunset was so rich and reverberating that I thought that the sky was on fire. The next day we saw the earth on fire— near Kisenyi, where live volcanoes thrust out tongues of rosy glow over a landscape green and gray.

We crossed the Semliki River, which boils with crocodiles, on an ancient rickety float, poled by two boys. Our chauffeur took a half-smoked cigarette out of his mouth, and gave it to one of them; this was our total payment for the passage. We touched on the Ituri forest. I have used many synonyms for the word "black" in this book, and if I ever need to do so again, I shall say, "black as the Ituri forest." This is the kind of matted jungle the sun cannot get into at all. We climbed the Kabasha escarpment, before entering the Albert National Park with its magnificent quarries of game, and saw the flat misty platter of the Rift Valley four thousand feet below—straight down—a sea of land without end, tawny, dust-colored, ocher, green, with the colors merging, and emblazoned by rainbows of haze on each side. Other things we noticed too. Belgian officials wear sun helmets, and in the hotels *pâté de foie gras* is served for breakfast.

Approaching Ruanda-Urundi, we encountered for the first time in Africa severe tropical rain. We did not find it again until Liberia. This rain calls its punches. You can watch a thunderstorm build up, slowly, majestically, inexorably, with the clouds wallowing up over the sharp spiny mountains and then making curds in the sky still blue. The impact is as shattering as that of a cataract. The very roof of our car shipped water. But equatorial clouds discharge their splashing cargo in the quickest of bursts; fierce, biting sunshine lights up the shimmering landscape in between. Another car followed us half an hour behind, and it never even got wet. This road, from Kisenyi to Astrida, is the most spectacular and dangerous I have ever traveled on. Until the mid-1930's it did not exist. If a Belgian official wanted to go from Astrida on to Usumbura, he had to take a bicycle or walk, and the journey took anywhere from three days to a week. The road is well surfaced now and passable in all weathers, but so full of blind turns that traffic is permitted only in one direction until twelve noon every day, and then the other. A tomtom (or a hammer on a petrol drum) gives warning of the change. This road is part of the transcontinental route from Algiers to the Cape; I must say that both seemed far away.[4]

Up and down, round and around, the road circles, climbs, bobs, and twists. Round hills follow round hills, all of them cultivated. Never before have I seen agriculture carried on almost vertically. Every inch of available soil is used, and the intensely green fields climb the hills at angles steeper—literally—than thirty-five degrees. The basic crops are chick peas, corn, and beans. Farmers have to produce a certain quota, or face trouble. The rondavels, with overhanging thatched roofs, are neat as laundry pins. They are scattered over the corrugated hills in regular formation

---

[4] In fifty miles we saw three vehicles overturned; one was a bright new green Studebaker. It was all the way over on its back, with the wheels sticking up in the air, like a teddy bear lying supine.

so that they resemble bobbins that might be on a fisherman's net spread by a giant.

Men wear European hats, smoke pipes, and carry spears—all at once! Children, hordes of them, surrounded us whenever we stopped, but never begged—a sharp contrast to children in most of the rest of Africa. Costumes of the women differ from those in Uganda and Tanganyika. The colors are not so violent, but have the effect of batik or a Paisley shawl; the designs can be anything from a cock to a fish or something abstract. The predominant colors seemed to be yellow, dark blue, dark green, and a subdued grayish-violet. Almost never did we see a woman without a child. Women without children are as rare as a *Vogue* model with. Near Astrida we saw women carried slowly on litters. I thought that there must be a good deal of invalidism in the vicinity, until our guide explained that these were Watutsi noblewomen, who never walk, but are always borne by slaves.

Kivu has particular enchantment. It lies at 4,500 feet, and is I think the most beautiful lake I ever saw except Maggiore. Kivu was never seen by a white man till 1893—so "new" is this part of Africa. Its waters are, the local citizenry likes to boast, "three degrees too cold for crocodiles," and so saturated with mineral ash from the volcanoes, which kills snails, that bilharzia is not a problem.

*

The pygmies live in the deep forest between Beni and Irumu, farther north. We did not, I am sorry to say, visit the camp-hotel-hospital run here for many years by the late Patrick Putnam, the foremost American authority on pygmies. But it is not difficult to see pygmies if you want to see them. We had no guide, and no white man accompanied us. We made no preparation. Near Beni our African chauffeur told us that pygmies lived nearby. We bought some sugar and cigarettes and drove up the road for a few miles, and then walked for perhaps five hundred yards through the forest. We came to a hot, fetid saucer of rough ground, closed in by dense branches, and here some pygmies were. It was as simple as that.

Nobody knows surely the origin of the pygmies, who must be among the ugliest people in the world. If I ever had doubts of Darwin, a glimpse of these peculiar little creatures dispelled them. Some authorities think that the pygmies were the original residents of Africa, and they are almost certainly related to the Bushmen. A large controversial literature exists about their connection—if any—with other pygmy or pygmoid peoples in the world, like those in the Philippines and Indonesia.

The adult male pygmies we saw were, I should say, all under five feet in height, and some may have been no taller than four feet eight. All have filed teeth sticking out of their bright red gums like white thumbtacks. They were cheerful, friendly, and eager for our gifts, as children might be. They showed us their weapons proudly, including nastily fanged arrows, with teeth like a barracuda. They wore nothing but a scrap of bark or liana tied around the middle, with streaks of black—resembling coal dust smears—on their faces. Pygmies are monogamous. It was difficult to tell women from men. The empty, sagging breasts of the women hung down, in Negley Farson's phrase, "like razor straps." One woman—she might have been fourteen or forty—had a hole drilled through her upper lip, and in this was affixed a projecting bouquet of reeds. The children had swollen bellies, with their navels bulging out almost in the shape of small pears.

Pygmies in the Congo and Ruanda-Urundi are forest people, who seldom see the sun, grow no crops, do no work, and live on the game they spear or trap. They are predominantly meat eaters, but not cannibals. Sometimes they come into the villages, and trade meat for sugar, salt, and vegetables. They have no villages of their own. One story told by a renowned white hunter, the late Major Pretorius, is that if a gang of pygmies kills an elephant, they cut a hole in him and eat their way out. Pygmies are generally despised by other Africans. A black servant will say to his master, "There are four men outside, and two pygmies."

RUANDA-URUNDI AND ITS WONDERS

> We must get out of the habit of the Visiting Mission paying tribute to the Administration, and vice versa, and of all being polite about each other, and then ignoring the 4,000,000 people about whom we are talking.
>
> —V. A. KRISHNA MENON

This crowded, rich, fertile area once belonged to Germany, and is now a United Nations Trust Territory administered by Belgium, almost indistinguishable from the Congo. It was part of German East Africa—what is now Tanganyika—before World War I. The Germans would like to have it back. Ruanda-Urundi has the highest density of population (184 per square mile) of any country in Africa, and overpopulation—since the birthrate is tremendous—is a leading problem.[5] The Ruanda language is the sixth most widely spoken on the continent. About 40 per cent of the population is Catholic. The White Fathers have been here since the turn of the century. A White Sister in Ruanda-Urundi presents, incidentally, a curious picture;

---

[5] Compare this density of population to that of the Congo proper, which is only 1.8 per square mile.

CONGO II: URANIUM, PYGMIES, GIANTS

she wears a sun helmet (white of course) on top of her regular white headgear. Ruanda and Urundi are separate units historically, but are administered together; each has about two million people on roughly 10,000 square miles. Eight per cent of the people are still polygamous. There are only 5,406 Europeans in all. Urundi is a shade bigger, but Ruanda has more cattle, and cattle are the chief hallmark of wealth and consequence in the community. Cattle are the diamonds of the Ruanda people. The country has many more cattle than it can profitably support. The Ruandans will not kill their cattle for meat (except in exceptional circumstances) and have not, like their cousins the Masai, learned to live off the live animal by drinking its blood, a smart process of having your cow and eating it too.

One odd point is that practically all people in Ruanda, even women, smoke pipes; those in Urundi do not. No anthropologist has ever been able to explain this phenomenon. But the minute you cross the invisible frontier between Ruanda and Urundi, pipe-smoking stops. Another difference is that most Urundi women shave their heads; this derives from an old-time fear of typhus. Of course shaved or very close-cropped hair is common in all this part of Africa.

Most distinctly, the people of Ruanda and Urundi do not think of themselves as Congolese. Their roots are closer to Uganda and Tanganyika. They are, however, solidly loyal to Belgium, and I had the feeling that many did not even know that, technically speaking, they were wards of the UN. The Belgians, it is hardly necessary to add, do not exactly go out of their way to tell them what their true status is. Early in 1955, a visiting UN mission issued a report which somewhat tartly points out that United Nations emblems and symbols are not shown as conspicuously as they might be in Ruanda-Urundi, and that Belgian information policy is "far from satisfactory," in that it plays down instead of up the position of the UN in the country.

Ruanda is a fascinating little entity on several counts, but what makes it most distinctive is that it is the home of the Watutsi giants. Outside the hotel in Astrida, next to a woman cupping a child's head to her naked breast, we ran into the tallest man I have seen except in a circus. He made the American playwright Robert E. Sherwood, who is six foot seven, look like a dwarf. He must have been at least seven and a half feet tall.

The Watutsi[6] have lived in Ruanda for at least four hundred years, and have a dynasty going back eighteen generations. They are not Negroes, even

---

[6] Once more we encounter the confusions of African nomenclature. "Watutsi" is the Swahili form of the correct word for the tribe, "Batutsi." The singular is "Mututsi."

though they may be jet black. A Hamitic or Nilotic people, they were pastoral nomads and cattlemen who came down from the north, and they startlingly resemble Ethiopians—except that I never saw an Ethiopian seven feet tall. The Watutsi are the aristocrats of Ruanda-Urundi, and number about 15 per cent of the population. They are proud, sophisticated, and not particularly energetic. Several times we saw Watutsi lords sitting on bicycles and being pushed by their vassals. They do not look strong, and give the impression of being much inbred. They have small heads for their height, slim wrists, and delicate long thin arms.

They value women highly, almost as highly as cattle, and live on milk and peas. Divorce is condemned, because it breaks up complicated clan and family patterns. By tradition, when a landowner dies, the cattle are divided; bulls go to the vassals, cows stay with the lords. No anthropologist has ever explained satisfactorily why the Watutsi are so tall. Possibly diet has something to do with it. In any case tallness is the symbol of racial exclusiveness and pure blood.

Eighty per cent of the people of Ruanda are of normal stature, and belong to the Bahutu tribe. They are Bantus, the peasants who till the hilly soil. Some people think fancifully that these medium-sized folk are the result of interbreeding generations ago between the giant Watutsi and the pygmies. But this seems unlikely, because the pygmies are such a small element in the population. Little contact exists between the Watutsi and the pygmies nowadays.

The King of Ruanda is known as the Mwami. His name is Charles Mutara III Rudahigwa, and the Belgians consider him to be an authentic monarch, which indeed he is. They refer to him as the *"roi,"* but face to face call him simply "Mwami," in the democratic native fashion. He is about forty, very sober in character, even somber, lean, handsome, and six feet nine. I do not need to go into the dynastic confusions attending his accession. His predecessor was quietly removed from office by the Belgians because he had surreptitious contact with German agents before World War II. No one knows who will be the present Mwami's successor, because he has no children. An important influence is that of the Queen Mother, whom he goes to see twice a week. He has visited Belgium, speaks excellent French, and was baptized into the Roman Catholic faith in 1943, after long delay.

In the Mwami's palace I felt once more the acute contrasts of Africa, as well as the huge extremes that may be represented in the life, character, and habits of individual Africans. It is a wonder that the resultant tensions do not pull them apart. The palace is a European building, with leopard skins on the floor (one is from the first leopard the Mwami ever shot) and ornaments made of exquisite Ruanda basketware on the walls. The outer rooms are decorated with the traditional beautiful spears of the Watutsi, some shaped like harpoons, some as broad as airplane propellers, and some fringed like brooms. Then in a hall we saw an exercise machine that might have come from the most modern sporting goods store in London or New York, which the Mwami uses on occasion. Everywhere in this part of Africa, yesterday kisses tomorrow.

The Mwami gave us lunch, and this was the most stupendous meal I ever ate in my life. Belgians are solid eaters, and the Mwami has adopted their cuisine. He had lobster, shrimp, *jambon d'Ardennes,* eggs, and asparagus— all in copious quantities—as appetizers. Then came a thick steaming soup, then chicken in a cream and mushroom sauce, then a roast pork weighed down with six or seven vegetables, then a custard, and finally two inordinately rich cakes, one of which was decorated with rose-shaped ornaments made out of orange mousse. I sat next to the Mwami's Queen. The meal lasted several hours, but, paralyzed by shyness, she never said a single word, although she knows French quite well. She has not been out into the world much. She has never even been to Usumbura, the capital of Ruanda-Urundi, which is only eighty miles away. Her hair fascinated me. Most Ruanda women of the nobility shave and clip their stiff cones of hair into designs like those on a French poodle. But the Queen had her hair built up into a solid frizzy pyramid, at least a foot high and shaped so firmly that it looked like a hat.

After lunch male dancers of the tribe put on an exhibition for us in the palace yard. The court is lined by a circle of cypresses, with the round green hills behind. Watutsi dancing is so well known that I will not attempt to describe this spectacle, which was certainly one of the two or three most magnificent and exciting we saw in all Africa. The leading dancer, by name Butera, seven feet five inches tall, weighs something like three hundred pounds; he is so celebrated as a dancer and high jumper, and so typical of the old Watutsi, that his portrait appears on the local banknotes. The dancers carried spears and wore red and white cotton skirts, long-tailed white headdresses of monkey hair and beading, and bells around the ankles. Watutsi dances are altogether different from any other we saw in Africa— wild, violent, crashingly dynamic, and marked by tremendous jumps and bounds.

Part of *King Solomon's Mines* was filmed here, and we drove to Rusitira to see the royal enclosure and palace built (for purposes of the movie) by Metro-Goldwyn-Mayer. It is a painstakingly accurate and elaborate reproduction of the old Watutsi palaces, made largely of grass, with reed pouches over the doorways and circular rooms with movable reed walls. It was left intact, after the picture was made, and given to the people so that they could see how their regal ancestors lived. Of course their own houses are of the same type, but much smaller. I noticed that some wooden posts were breaking into leaf. Already the palace is returning to the jungle. The Mwami told us that he bitterly disliked *King Solomon's Mines*, first because the story was so silly, second because the film makes a point of scarification. But in actual fact the Watutsi are one of the few people in this part of Africa who do not scarify themselves.

I asked the Mwami if, as in Tanganyika, the people at large felt a double sense of security because of trusteeship by the UN. His reply was that the UN "made no difference." Belgium is the father. I asked him if there would ever be political parties in Ruanda, and he replied, "What good do parties do?" I asked him about nationalism, and he scarcely seemed to understand the meaning of the word.[7]

Urundi also has a Mwami, by name Mwambutsa. He is not called a king by the Belgians, but a sultan. He is not so tall as the Mwami of Ruanda, and is of less pure stock. He seemed, when we met him, to be cleverer and surer of himself than his Ruanda counterpart, but to have much less style.

Both Ruanda and Urundi have native capitals, but the administrative center for the area as a whole, where Belgian rule is centered, is USUMBURA. This is a hot, dreary little town (population about 30,000 with 3,000 whites) on the northern tip of Lake Tanganyika. Here we saw schools, clinics, factories, and the like which are a distinct credit to Belgian paternalism. Usumbura must certainly be the only city in southern or central Africa with a swimming pool for Africans. The hospital has actual beds, not pallets on the floor. But a hearty black lady who had just given birth to a child was nursing it sitting on the floor. She preferred this to the bed, which was empty. The Governor, M. Claeys-Bouüaert, took us on an expedition. There was no flag on his car, and we had no chauffeur or escort. Once we got stuck in the mud, and Africans who helped cheerfully to pull us out had no idea that this was no less a personage than the Governor himself. Claeys-Bouüaert is one of the best men in Africa—decisive, alert, industrious, and with strong sympathy for and understanding of the Africans.

The Ruanda-Urundi administration came in for some marked criticism during the last meeting of the UN Trusteeship Council in New York. An Indian delegate, Ali Khan, asked for more assistance by the state to educa-

---

[7] But the Mwami is not to be discounted as a political force. A Belgian official told me that if, for instance, he should ever be infected by Mau Mau, the Ruanda people would follow him to a man.

tion, reform of the curfew laws, and extension of the powers of the Governor's Council. He said, "In contrast to what is going on all around it, Ruanda-Urundi is somewhat like a fly embalmed in amber. The system of administration . . . is utterly anachronistic. . . . In the middle of a sea of rising nationalism, we observe this little island of cautious indirect rule where the local people merely carry out orders. . . . It would be tragic if these antiquated and semi-feudal methods lead to unrest."[8]

On the other hand Ruanda-Urundi has an advisory council on which Africans are represented (something that the Congo does not have), and the way is being opened to a rudimentary form of election. Claeys-Boüüaert would be delighted to give more Africans political opportunity, but he says that it is difficult to find any competent enough. We met several of his African councilors, and indeed they seemed to be fifty years behind Africans of comparable rank in Uganda or the Sudan—at least so far as political sophistication is concerned. But the basic reason for this and other backwardnesses should not be forgotten, namely that the Belgian system deliberately keeps education down.

CONGO MISCELLANY

The Congo has no fewer than 45,000 different species of birds and insects, and its postage stamps are the prettiest in Africa. It has one of the most useful anthropological institutions on the continent, IRSAC (Institut de Recherches Scientifiques au Congo), and, at a place called Gangala Va Bondio, a school where African elephants—hitherto thought to be untamable—are being trained. The Congo is the only known habitat of the okapi, a cross between an antelope and a giraffe, and it is where a celebrated German musicologist, Dr. E. M. Von Hornbostel, first traced out scientifically the rhythm of African drums.

The Congo is a rich country, yes, and does much for its Africans, yes, but in 1950 more than 75 per cent of its total income (32.5 billion Belgian francs) went to 3 per cent of the population. United States imports from the Congo increased from a value of $1,471,000 in 1937 to more than $52,000,000 in 1951.

Belgium is building at Kamina, which is halfway between the Atlantic and the Indian Ocean, an air base which will be one of the largest in the world—bigger than Randolph Field. One of its runways is eight miles

---

[8] Mr. Khan pointed out that instruction in some Catholic schools is in *Latin*. It is hard enough to teach an African boy French without inflicting on him the burden of learning another European language.

long, and it will be able to handle aircraft weighing up to 135 tons. Seventeen thousand Belgian pilots are to be trained here, where the flying weather is much better than in Belgium. American officers are in attendance.

The Congo is the first country in Africa to make experiments with artificial rain, in order to relieve drought in the Katanga, and has produced some of the most remarkable of all African works of art. It has the best beer I found in Africa, called Simba. No Congolese city has a *quartier réservé* and white women are not allowed to be prostitutes. If you open a Coca-Cola bottle, put three grains of rice in it, and then seal it up again, the ensuing fermentation will produce a spirited drink. So at least Congolese told me. I never tried it.

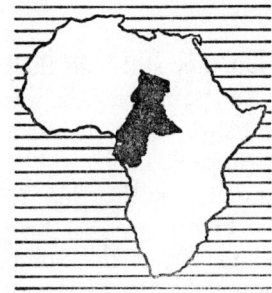

CHAPTER 34

French Rule in Black Africa

> *France shall form with the peoples of her Overseas Territories a Union based upon the equality of rights and privileges, without distinction as to race and religion.*
> —PREAMBLE TO THE CONSTITUTION
> OF THE FOURTH REPUBLIC, 1946
>
> *If God ever made a worse colonist than the French, He hasn't let me know about it.*
> —ALFRED ALOYSIUS HORN

BRAZZAVILLE, capital of the vast hot expanse of jungle and desert known as French Equatorial Africa, is situated directly across the Congo from Léopoldville. I have described these as twin cities, but they differ radically; much more separates them than the turbid, densely flowing Congo. Léopoldville might be Jersey City, except that it happens to lie in tropical Africa—businesslike, packed with bourgeois wealth, proud of its bustle, and almost totally devoid of grace. BRAZZAVILLE is still an African city, loosely constructed, colorful, relaxed, to which has been magically added a dash of Paris. In Léopoldville, everybody works. In Brazzaville, everybody—perhaps one should say almost everybody—smiles.

Léopoldville has, as we know, 250,000 people; Brazzaville is considerably smaller, with 100,000 Africans and between 5,000 and 6,000 Europeans. Léopoldville was founded by Stanley in 1881; Brazzaville a year later by one of the most romantically successful of all African explorers, Count Pierre Paul François Savorgnan De Brazza, known as the "father of slaves." This man, with the face of a tortured, ascetic poet, brought 500,000 square miles of Africa to France in two years. Stanley thought that De Brazza was a tramp, and the two were bitter rivals, as each raced to acquire territory on opposite sides of the river. De Brazza's first treaties with a native king,

Makoko, were called by Stanley "scraps of paper," but they still hold their writ. In those days—the 1880's—the technique of European conquest was to get to a place first, plant a flag, and buy off the native chiefs. It was a lovely process, and it went on until almost all West Africa was gone.

The Belgians say that Brazzaville is lazy and corrupt, but they like to cross the gummy Congo and make sport there. The French say that Léopoldville may indeed possess the first skyscraper in this part of the world, but that *they* have culture, which cannot be measured by the height of buildings. The fact is that Brazzaville is much poorer than Léopoldville, and the French are jealous of this unhappy fact. But the Belgians are jealous too —of Brazzaville's sophisticated charm. We heard this little story. Crossing on the Congo ferry were two Africans, one well dressed, the other so shabby that he looked like a scarecrow. The first African was a mechanic in the Ford plant in Léopoldville; the second a senator, no less, who represented Brazzaville in Paris, no less. The senator said, "I am sorry for you, my friend, since you live in political shadow." The mechanic replied, "Yes, but I have clothes on my back while I'm living there."

A Frenchman told us, "Of course we're poorer. On the Belgian side the authorities tell a farmer what crop to grow, and if he doesn't grow it, *zip*, off he goes to a forced labor gang! Here we cannot do such a thing. Our Africans are citizens, like you and me."

A Belgian told us, "On our side every African gets a square deal, even if he has no political rights. Our district commissioners speak the local dialects and get out into the most remote stretches of country, and really work there. On the French side if a native gets into trouble the French District Commissioner will say, 'Learn to speak French, *mon vieux*, and after you have mastered my language perhaps I can do something for you.' "

No bridge spans the Congo here, not even a ferry for heavy material or automobiles; if you want to take your car from Belgian to French territory, or vice versa, you must hire a barge. The Congo at this point is about 2½ miles wide; the journey from what is called "Le Beach" in Léopoldville on the small, stubby river steamer takes forty minutes in the wet season, twenty in the dry when the current is not so obstreperous. If your boat loses a motor, sirens shriek desperately up and down the river and a rescue craft sets out at once; otherwise you may be dragged into the rapids a few miles downstream. Service stops at 11 p.m., and if you are caught on the wrong bank at night you have to hire not one boat, but two, because a ship must have escort after dark for fear of the cataracts. (I am not sure I quite believe this but anyway it is what we were told.)

Stepping off on the Brazzaville side, you discover what a delight it is to

be in France. Paris is 3,750 miles away, but this is Paris, more or less. We had seventeen pieces of baggage. The customs officer—an African—spluttered with incredulity, his hands high held in mock horror, even desperation—and never opened one. To get visas for French Equatorial Africa takes time and trouble, but we made two separate entrances into Brazzaville and never had our passports stamped or even looked at. When I asked if anybody wanted to inspect our health certificates an official merely shrugged. Who cares? Then, emerging from the furiously disorganized but neat and efficient customs shed, the first things we saw were a bookshop erudite and classically aloof, if dog-eared, like all French bookshops; a pleasant café with a striped awning; an *épicerie* stocked with bright bottles of wine; and black children who didn't look frightened. What is it that makes French culture automatically and instantly recognizable, quite apart from such obvious items as good food, good beds, and good intellectual and artistic taste? The French, even in Africa, combine two things hard to reconcile, freedom and responsibility, anarchy and realism, a ravishing instinct toward laissez-faire together with punctilious respect for lucidity and order.

Brazzaville has an excellent hotel—in contrast to the deplorable hotel in Léopoldville—decorated like a supermodern French liner; the bathrooms are made largely of aluminum. We had the best meal we had had in a hotel for months. But I was more interested in something else. Across from us at lunch—in what was obviously a de luxe establishment—sat a well-dressed young Negro; that evening we watched a pretty African girl dine with two white escorts. Once again, color bar (or rather the lack of it in Brazzaville) was the first thing to intrude itself on our attention. This was the first hotel in Africa in which we saw white and black people dine together with elegance and ease.

Brazzaville has the most powerful radio station in the French Union, which was built in 1942 and broadcasts in a dozen languages. Its news is picked up and printed in cities as far away as Tokyo. It has one of the most unusually beautiful churches in the world, the Église Sainte-Anne, a masterpiece of the architect Roger Erell; it is distinctly a modern structure, built of ocher brick—without any steel—and with a bright green roof; its profile is almost that of a tall, narrow, icily triangular palm leaf. Brazzaville has a "daily" newspaper which appears triweekly. It has an art school in the Poto-Poto district, where African boys learn to paint and where they produce works of art both primitive and extraordinarily sophisticated. It has one delightful night club, to which patrons come mostly by bicycle, and where the girls wear bustles, dance with their shoulders utterly motionless and their hips swaying like canoes in a storm, and have bare feet. Even the waitresses, while taking your order, do the gentlest, most insinuating of pectoral bumps.

Also Brazzaville was, in a sense, the birthplace of Free France during the war; here General de Gaulle set up his first African headquarters. More on this below.

It is also the place where everything—including the French franc itself—costs roughly twice as much as in Paris. In France you get 350 francs for a dollar, more or less; in French Equatorial Africa, 200.

FRENCH EQUATORIAL AFRICA IN GENERAL

French Equatorial Africa (*Afrique Équatoriale Française*) is shaped something like a bluntly spiked boot, and covers almost a million square miles; it is three and a half times bigger than Texas, four and a half times bigger than France. It was once called "French Congo." It stretches in a northeasterly direction from the Congo estuary on the Atlantic all the way to the desert frontiers of Libya and the Anglo-Egyptian Sudan, almost two thousand miles distant. And what does this enormous mass of variegated territory contain, except emptiness? 4,436,500 people (of whom a scant 24,000 are Europeans); exactly 320 miles of railroad (the Congo-Ocean railway that connects Brazzaville with Pointe Noire on the sea); three million head of cattle, concentrated near Lake Chad; twenty airports (I will deal with some of these hereunder); a considerable mineral wealth not yet exploited; forty-six secondary schools, or roughly one for every 96,000 inhabitants. According to the well-known British authority Vernon Bartlett, only *one* per cent of the FEA budget went to education until recent years.[1]

French Equatorial Africa is the poorest country in the entire French Union, largely because of the villainous climate and appallingly backward communications. "French penetration," the New York *Times* said not long ago, "was accompanied by highly uneconomic methods of colonization . . . France simply assumed title to all the land and then proceeded to portion vast tracts of it out on a concession basis to large monopolistic companies . . . These companies depleted all the human and natural resources that they could easily get their hands on and returned virtually nothing to the economy of the country."[2] The French government took 15 per cent of the profits, and the sky was the limit as to exploitation. Lately, however, progress and reform have begun to come. In June, 1947, a Ten-Year Development Plan, supervised by the metropolitan government in

[1] *Struggle for Africa*, p. 148.
[2] Michael Clark in the New York *Times*, June 8, 1952.

France, got under way. Attempts are being made to repair the damage to looted and devastated forests, and to develop scientific agriculture, especially in the realm of oleaginous plant production. The chief resources are cotton (in the north), timber, oil palms and similar tropical produce, gold to a minor extent, coffee, and diamonds. Diamond production was 155,000 carats in 1952, a substantial figure. Recently the United States Steel Corporation became interested in manganese deposits near Franceville; the ore is rich, but hard to get at or to get out. A contract has been signed, and mining operations are to begin soon. The cost of the project, if it is fully worked out, will be $231,000,000.

French Equatorial Africa is subdivided into four great territories (Once they were called colonies, but the word "colony" is now taboo.)

Gabon. (Area 103,000 square miles; population 407,400). This is the most advanced region; it comprises the bulk of the coastal area, where the natives have been in touch with European influences for centuries. The capital is Libreville, and at Lambaréné is the celebrated forest hospital of Dr. Schweitzer, which I shall deal with in the chapter following. Libreville has the only statue to an African we saw anywhere in Black Africa, erected in honor of a gallant army officer, Captain N'Tchorere, who was killed in France in World War II. The town of Port-Gentil, at the mouth of the formidable River Ogowe, has the largest plywood factory in the world, and no hotel. Its bay is, like those further down the Atlantic on the shores of South-West Africa, famous as a haunt for whales. The name Gabon comes from the Portuguese. Among early explorers were Prince Joinville (who brought the body of Napoleon from St. Helena to Paris); Paul du Chaillu who discovered the gorilla in 1856; and the fabulous English lady Mary H. Kingsley, who—in Victorian petticoats—made in this region one of the most dangerous expeditions ever known. It cost her her life eventually, but the Ogowe gave to her secrets it had never divulged before. "Many a wild waltz" she danced with the wild river, as she put it. Miss Kingsley's written work should be better known. She had a gay, salty humor. Among missionaries she liked the Wesleyans best because they were "the only people who had a hearse with feathers."

Middle Congo. The capital is Pointe Noire, the area 132,000 square miles, and the population just under 600,000. It is separated from Belgian territory by the giant thrust of the Congo; much of it is impenetrably wild bush. But Brazzaville is in the Middle Congo, and so is the pitiable little railroad.

Ubangi-Shari. The population is 1,081,600 on an area of almost 250,000 square miles. The capital is Bengui. This territory is an anthropologist's paradise among other things, and contains almost every variety of tropical

African oddity. Here natives have their entire torsos, back and front, carved with scars as intricate and regulated as in a bas-relief, or, to change the metaphor, a really ornate broadloom rug; here one may see women with heads squashed and shaped to a point, and, more notably than anywhere else in Africa, those with lip plates—huge oval protuberances, made of clay or metal, on which the lips are stretched and permanently affixed, so that they look like unevenly-sized flat castanets.[3] But also in Ubangi-Shari are representatives of the modern African world, for instance a handsome mulatto lady, Jane Vialle, who has been a delegate to the United Nations in New York, and is now a distinguished senator in Paris. She is a writer by profession, and was a heroine of the resistance.

Chad. (Area 496,000 square miles, population 2,252,700, with its capital at Fort Lamy.) Chad is twice as big as France. This is a world totally removed from the simmering, green-black Congo swamps and forests; this is Saharan Africa again, dry Africa, Moslem Africa, the Africa of lunar emptiness and desert without end. Fort Lamy, a historic post, lies however on an important body of water, Lake Chad. The first white man ever to reach Chad was a British explorer, the intrepid Hugh Clapperton, who got there in 1823 and was also the first white man ever to see Kano, Nigeria. It is a familiar maxim of French military policy that "whoever holds Chad holds Africa." Indeed it was from Chad that General Leclerc leaped out on his celebrated and circuitous desert campaigns in World War II, and, presupposing an attack on Africa from the north in some future war, the French say that "Chad is the first fort for the defense of Cape Town."[4] There are 5,000,000 goats and sheep in the Chad area, and 200,000 camels. Women wear their hair tightly plaited in separate strands, so that it lies on the partly naked skull like rows of black beads. Anybody who wants to glimpse the Chad area while staying safely at home should read André Gide's *Voyage au Congo,* or look at the superlative photographs by Hoyningen-Huene in *African Mirage.* Economically Chad suffers from its geographical remoteness and lack of communications; there are no adequate routes to the sea.

*

The contemporary history of French Equatorial Africa (half of which is not truly "equatorial" since it is in the Sahara) begins with one of the most illustrious—and little known—of contemporary Negroes, Félix Éboué,

---

[3] Originally plated lips were a deliberate attempt to disfigure women, so that Arab slave raiders would not carry them off. Then gradually they became fashionable—a mark of being chic.

[4] See *Watch Over Africa,* by Denis Saurat, pp. 37 and 124.

who died during the war and whose widow, a well-known musician, lives now in Paris. Éboué was born in Cayenne, French Guiana (in South America) and made a great career in the French colonial service; he served variously as Acting Governor of the French Sudan and Governor of Guadaloupe in the West Indies, and was Governor of Chad when France fell in 1940.[5] Éboué risked not merely his career but his life by coming out instantly on the side of de Gaulle against Vichy. Chad, under Éboué, raised the flag of Free France on August 26, 1940; Brazzaville followed two days later, and Ubangi-Shari on August 30. Thus all of French Equatorial Africa except Gabon (which had a separate mixed history) stood at once with the democratic world against Hitler. We may take this as a matter of course now; it was a matter of extreme importance then. When Éboué, on his own initiative, took his courageous stand, almost the whole Mediterranean was in German or Italian hands. There were strong pro-Nazi elements in the Congo, the Union of South Africa, and elsewhere on the continent. Hitler and Mussolini might well have turned south, if they had taken Cairo. Moreover—if I may quote Walter White—"when France fell French West Africa, Morocco, Algeria, Syria, and Indochina all followed Pétain and Laval into the arms of Hitler. French Equatorial Africa, under the stimulus of Éboué, was the only French territory of importance not to take this course."[6] Strategically this had pivotal consequences. Éboué's action made it impossible for the Nazi armies to penetrate further into Africa, and also opened up a route for quick allied communication to Cairo and the Middle East. Lake Chad became an essential stop on the air trajectory that became our African life line. And not just Africa. For a substantial period the *only* way we could get high personnel or precious cargo quickly from New York and London all the way to India, China and beyond was through Lake Chad and its environs. For this, thank Félix Éboué.

In January, 1944, came what is known to history as the "Brazzaville Conference," to which Éboué was host. Here General de Gaulle and others transformed the structure of the French colonial system as it applied to Black Africa, and tried to transform its spirit. Most of the evolution toward reform that has taken place subsequently dates from this germinal conference, because it paved the way for such items as the abolition of forced labor and the declaration of the 1946 constitution giving complete rights of citizenship to Africans.

---

[5] He was also the author of a standard musical work on the language of the tomtom, in collaboration with Mme Éboué.

[6] In *A Rising Wind*, p. 105.

FRENCH RULE IN BLACK AFRICA

Nationalism, as an active political force, hardly exists as yet in FEA. The country is too heterogeneous, the Africans for the most part too undereducated. The ethnic medley is so inordinately complex over such a wide area with such hopelessly bad communications that a cohesive nationalist expression is impossible. Basically the population is Negro, speaking Bantu languages in the south and Sudanese in the north. There are Tuaregs, Tedas, pale Peuhls (Fulanis), and Nilotics black as Cerberus or Hitler's soul. Arabs from the north pushed the Bantus southward and the Bantus displaced the Negrillos. Just to list a few tribes—Gabon has Omines, Galoas, Pahouins, and Bandjas; the Middle Congo has Bayombi, Bateki, Bakota, and Ubangi; Ubangi-Shari has eight principal groups, according to a classification made by Éboué—Mangia, Banda, Zandi, Banziri, Sari, Pambla, Boonga, and, a nice name, M'Boom.

We found less color bar in French Equatorial Africa than in any European territory on our whole route thus far. In Libreville, the wife of the French Resident told us that her daughter was the only *white* child in the local school.

THE FRENCH SYSTEM

French policy in Black Africa, as I have already mentioned in Chapter 1 so many pages past, is based on the idea of assimilation, of the gradual—very gradual—absorption of educated Africans, when they are fit, into the realm of French culture and even French society. This process will, of course, be a long one, since nobody can create a class of African elite—the French call its members *évolués*—overnight, and since it depends above all on education, a field in which French policy has (until recently at least) been notoriously lax. The idea of assimilation must, if it is honestly applied, result in the long run in the creation of a mixed society, not merely a plural society. "If you eat with them, you sleep with them," says the adage. The French may or may not look forward to this. Let the next generation worry about it. But they are a lucid people, and realize full well—if grudgingly—that something has to be done now; they are aware that (in French Equatorial Africa as an example) 20,000 Frenchmen cannot rule more than 4,000,000 blacks indefinitely—no matter how primitive and underdeveloped the blacks may be today—without eventual expensive trouble. To this extent they have a much profounder vision than, say, leaders in the Union or the white settlers of Rhodesia. The French know that they have to bring Negroes into the functioning of the state *somehow*.

French policy, even if it gives Africans more rights than the British do in some areas, is diametrically different from British policy. The British—we have said this before but let us repeat it—train Africans for eventual *self-government*; the French train them to be *Frenchmen*. (It is extraordinarily striking that no word for "self-government" exists in the French language.[7]) The British, in theory at least, even where their administration is most reactionary, have the long-range aim of creating *African* domains within the Commonwealth; the French ambition is to make their Africa part of France. And why not? Is not France the most civilized community on earth? Should not any African be delighted by the opportunity of becoming French? And is not membership in the French Union by a French territory the same as membership by a British dominion in the British Commonwealth? As to this last point the answer is—by no means! Full-fledged members of the British Commonwealth are self-governing and in fact are to all intents and purposes independent, since they have the right of secession. Members of the French Union are ruled from Paris, and—make no mistake about it—Paris does not intend to stop being boss.

By and large, few Africans in French territories south of the Sahara are anti-French as yet. This is what makes French Equatorial Africa and French West Africa differ so markedly from Morocco and Tunisia. The Africans whom the French do succeed in turning into Frenchmen are, on the whole, more loyal to France than British-educated Africans of the same class are to Britain. In fact most of the African elite in French territories (south of the Sahara) do not want independence from France at all; on the contrary they want more complete inclusion into the French orbit. They do not want liberty; they want fraternity. The French system in Black Africa has, in a word, been extremely successful from this point of view. There is no problem even remotely like that in Morocco or Vietnam.

Officially, the French do not employ the word "native" any longer, just as they do not use "colony," because these terms are an affront to educated Africans. The Ministry of "Colonies" has been replaced by the Ministry of "France Overseas." Instead of *indigène* (native) they use the fancy word *autochtone*, which comes from the Greek and means "sprung from the land itself."

French policy in Black Africa differs from Belgian or Portuguese policy in that, in theory at least, all French Africans are citizens of France itself, with all the rights of citizens. There can be no *assimilados* as in Mozambique, because—again in theory—everybody is already legally assimilated. The constitution of the Fourth Republic, of date October 27, 1946, establishes com-

[7] See Sylvanus E. Olympio in the *Nation*, "Quest for Liberty; an African Speaks," December 26, 1953.

plete equality of rights without reference to race or color. Not all Africans are, however, allowed to vote, as things have worked out in practice. The franchise is limited more or less to French-speaking Africans who have a *carte d'identité*. And, in order apparently to restrict voting to those adult and responsible, a curious proviso forbids women to vote unless they have two or more children. This puts an odd political premium on maternity. Even so, statistics in French Equatorial Africa are illuminating. At least 700,000 Africans are privileged to vote, and of these some 400,000 actually voted at the last election, or 10 per cent of the total population. Few African countries can match these figures.[8]

At the top of the structure in FEA is a High Commissioner, also known as the Governor General, who is appointed by Paris (usually out of the old colonial service) and is responsible to the Ministry of France d'Outre Mer in Paris. He has a council, which includes the four provincial governors. There are local assemblies for each territory, elected indirectly by dual colleges, one French, one African, and a Grand Council on the federal level. This is elected out of the territorial assemblies and is overwhelmingly African, but it does not have much power. In the villages administration is carried out partly by native chiefs working under French administrators, but the chiefs do not have anything like the position they have in British Africa. All males are subject to military service in the French army. Administration of justice is purely French, and there are no native courts.

But French Equatorial Africa elects and sends *to Paris* seven deputies in the National Assembly (the former Chamber of Deputies), eight senators to the Council of the Republic (Senate), and seven councilors to the Assembly of the French Union at Versailles. Of this group of twenty-two, thirteen are *autochthonous*, i.e., black. No other colonial power permits a phenomenon of this kind. There are, as we know, no MP's in the House of Commons representing Kenya or Uganda, white *or* black. Many critics of French policy think that, in time, as more and more Africans are educated and become voters, this system may lead to an embarrassing and even dangerous situation in France itself. At the moment of writing the National Assembly in Paris has 626 deputies; of these no fewer than 59, or almost 10 per cent, are from Africa, debating the laws of *France*.[9] If representation were strictly in accordance with population, there would be several *hundred*

---

[8] In the third century AD all subjects of the Roman Empire received full citizenship, no matter where they lived or to what race they belonged. The historical parallel is interesting. Did the Roman grant of citizenship come too late? Cf. Hailey, *op. cit.*, p. 262.

[9] Cf. "Africa Is Next," by Theodore H. White, *Harper's Magazine*, February, 1952.

Negro deputies, and in time there might well be more blacks than whites.[10]

As of today the Africans in Paris call themselves a Bloc des Indépendants, and do not as a rule vote together. If they did, it is only too obvious that they might on any number of critical occasions provide the balance of power in *French* politics. They could upset any government. A splinter group of Africans might cast the deciding vote on such a matter as whether France should, or should not, withdraw from NATO, declare war on Russia, or—let us be fanciful—abolish the French franc.[11]

Cynics say that the French insure against eventual full assimilation by all manner of artful devices at present, and by making progress deliberately slow. The gist of the whole business is, of course, education, since without education—no matter what the law says—Africans cannot emerge into effective citizenship. And if they do become educated, the risk is that they will become nationalist too. In any case educational advance is coming. It is true that only 850 elementary schools, most of them primitively staffed and equipped, exist in the whole of FEA; of children of school age, only about 18 per cent go to school at all. On the other hand the French, who deny firmly that they deliberately starve education, point out that the enrollment of elementary students has risen from 15,921 in 1945 to 108,788 in 1952, a jump of not less than 580 per cent. As to advanced students no fewer than 185 attend universities in France, which is an impressive figure compared to those for Belgian, Spanish, Portuguese, or even British Africa.

Why is French administration in tropical Africa so much more enlightened, humane, and successful than in Morocco? First the people are less advanced, and therefore easier to govern. Second, the French can afford to take risks at Brazzaville, which is far away, that would be impossible at Rabat so close to home. Third, French policy in tropical Africa is a new development, which could not easily be made retroactive to include Morocco or Tunisia. Fourth, Morocco is a protectorate, with an altogether different technical status, and has in theory its own "government." But why, if a man from the jungles near Bangui, who was born in a hut dripping with filth, is considered fit to be a deputy in Paris, is a professor at Fez, who has six hundred years of culture behind him, not considered fit? If Éboué can be a governor in Chad, why cannot some African be a governor in Tunis? The conventional French answer to this is that Morocco and Tunis are not "developed" enough. But they are certainly more developed than the Middle

[10] Two French undersecretaries of state for Colonial Affairs have been African in recent years. At the moment the president of the Senate, Gaston Monnerville, is a Negro, but he was born in Latin America, not Africa. Dr. Aujoulat, a deputy from the Cameroons, was minister of labor in the Mendès-France cabinet.

[11] See Chapter Eight above.

Congo. The real answer is that they are too well "developed," so much so that they would kick over the traces and make a nationalist revolution if they had the opportunity. Perhaps the French have learned something from the Moroccan tragedy. They are trying to educate French Equatorial Africa to be French *in time*.

BUSH FLYING WITH THE FRENCH

We took off at Brazzaville early in the morning, in thick adhesive fog; I could not believe that any plane would dare to fly in such weather. We walked toward the runway and I did not even see our ship until we were ten yards away. Then, it turned out, this was not ours at all; ours was a few yards further on, but still totally invisible. It is an odd experience to get into an airplane you cannot see.

We bucked and burrowed through greasy clouds, with stops at Dolisie, at Pointe Noire, at Tchibanga, at Mouila, and finally at Lambaréné. The flight takes most of the day, though the distance is only a few hundred miles. The plane, an old DC 3 stripped down to its metal bones, held cargo as well as passengers, and at each stop, depending on what got off and what came aboard, the inner composition of the craft was dramatically changed. The cargo was strapped down by canvas belts on metal braces, first on one side, then the other, displacing the folding seats. I had the sense of being in a structure designed out of movable blocks by a mad child; we were moved around, seats and all, like people in a dream.

An old African, wearing orange-colored tennis shoes, sat across from us, wedged between a cage of parrots and sacks of grain. He was a member of the White Fathers, but did not have a beard. He had never flown before, and prayed steadily and crossed himself, moaning gently; when we put down at Dolisie, he knotted and unknotted his fists with the movement of a heart contracting.

I asked him how, inasmuch as he was a White Father, he could be beardless.

"I shaved it off last year."

"Why?"

"It scratched."

I asked if this was not contrary to discipline.

He swung his arms gaily. "Discipline? Do you know how old I am? Seventy-five! I was ordained forty-seven years ago, and you talk of discipline!"

The airstrip here, as we looked down, resembled a short green noodle. It has, the pilot told us, the shortest runway in the world. Yet I do not believe there has ever been a serious accident on this crazily difficult run. After Pointe Noire we became almost totally a cargo plane. I saw something that I have never seen in an aircraft before or since; one of our wingtips became invisible in a mass of steaming cloud, while the other was sharp and clear in flashing sunshine. At Tchibanga we were fueled up by boys using wooden hand pumps, like cradles. There were no blocks to put behind the wheels; the plane started to blow away, until other boys grabbed the tail and held it. Elegantly, with a gesture of mock despair, the pilot wrung his hands. Everybody in Air France in this part of the world is a d'Artagnan.

Then came Mouila. If ever there was a village lost in the middle of nowhere, back of the beyond, Mouila is it; one cannot describe places like this without using the most idiotic of clichés. We sat in a dirt-floored reed hut, moist with rot, in an isolated hollow scraped out of impenetrable jungle, and had lunch. And what did we have for lunch? It was one of the best lunches we had in all Africa, better by far than any I ever had at any airport in the United States—imported salami as hors d'oeuvres, a salad of peas and carrots, ravioli that might have been cooked by Alfredo in Rome, buffalo steak, and a *Pont l'évêque* of precisely correct maturity, together with copious quantities of an admirable Moulin du Vent, '47. And where did all this come from? I do not know. Ah, the exquisite satisfactions of *la belle France!*

After Mouila we became a passenger plane again. We scudded low over lagoons and gray-green muddy rivers sticking into the bush like fat, limp legs and arms drawn by Thurber. The pilot said that a plane crashing here would instantly be swallowed up by the forest, and might quite possibly never be seen again, like one falling into the ocean. Then the countryside became less dense; rivers spread and oozed out into brush-laden fields. At Lambaréné we talked to the lady who ran the bar. Her husband had carefully marked out a neat little garden with empty beer bottles. I have never seen anything so forlorn. The lady—she had been a nurse—told us that she had recently been poisoned but had recovered. Tribesmen near a mission station wanted to kill her because she had saved someone else from poison.

After Lambaréné we stopped at Port Gentil, Libreville, Mitzic, Bitam, Yaoundé, the capital of the Cameroons, and finally Douala, our destination. We skirted on three sides the little parallelogram of Rio Muni, belonging to Spain; French planes do not fly over this "lost" territory, which is also known as Spanish Guinea. When we put down at Douala at last our pilot, who had a face gnarled like the head of a blackthorn, said with

Gallic satisfaction and imperturbability that Douala was the most difficult airport of his whole experience. "It rains three hundred days a year, is completely surrounded by rivers, and has execrable hills."

THE CAMEROONS

About the Cameroons I can write little. This is a pity, because few places in Africa are more fascinating. But this book is getting to be uncomfortably long, and we still have a great deal of territory to cover. Portuguese slave traders dominated the Cameroons first, and gave the country its name from the piquantly edible prawns (*camarões* in Portuguese) found in its clouded waters. Every time the Cameroons have become a political issue among the European powers, erudite wits have been unable to resist making a mild joke, to the effect that the Cameroons are prawns in the game. After the Portuguese came the Dutch, and then the British. But British interests were, for most of the nineteenth century, commercial; the Foreign Office (which handled colonial affairs during this period) was reluctant to annex the Cameroons even though various native chiefs asked for British "protection," i.e., inclusion in the Empire; Whitehall and the merchant interests could not agree about apportioning the costs of the colonial administration that would have to be set up. Finally in 1883 a British emissary was sent into the Cameroons to negotiate treaties of annexation with the native kings, in particular one from the Efik country with the remarkable name Eyo Honesty VII.[12] He got to Douala just too late. German agents, working in secret, had signed an annexation treaty five days before. Indeed those were the days of the "scramble" for Africa!

So the Cameroons were German until the outbreak of war in 1914, when a joint Anglo-French invasion team conquered the country. The Cameroons were then split between Britain and France under a League of Nations mandate; France got by far the larger share, 166,800 square miles as against 34,000 for the British. The thin British slice is to the west, and adjoins Nigeria; the French area stretches upward along the borders of French Equatorial Africa toward Lake Chad. After World War II the Cameroons, still divided, became a trust territory under the United Nations, which it still is. The British end is administered from Nigeria; the French run theirs from Paris.

The Germans, as in Tanganyika, left an emphatic impression. Some of

[12] Another was King Duke Ephraim IX of Duke Town. Once he called on a British official wearing nothing whatever but a top hat. *The Story of My Life*, by Sir Harry H. Johnston, pp. 191-92.

their government buildings, put up before 1914, are still the best in the country. German rule was so severe that thousands of Africans fled to FEA or Nigeria; nevertheless—again as in Tanganyika—the Germans are still respected. Nowadays, an odd point, it is sometimes almost impossible for the British or French authorities to determine who is the legitimate chief in a community, because during German times the real chiefs were often hidden (by their own people) to spare them from punishments the Germans might inflict; various tribes put up false chiefs to bear the brunt of German ire. These false chiefs, if they survived, sometimes usurped power, with resultant hierarchical confusions that go on to this day. The German settlers were a strong and tenacious lot. Their banana and other plantations were confiscated during World War I; immediately after the armistice many returned to the Cameroons, and managed to buy their properties back. At the outbreak of World War II there were twice as many Germans in the British area of the Cameroons as British, even including British officials. Now the Germans are gone for good.[13]

There are wonders without end in the Cameroons both in the physical and human spheres. A live volcano called Mount Cameroon, across the bay from Douala, the chief seaport, is (13,370 feet) the highest peak in West Africa. The rainfall in one area reaches 400 inches a year, and a point called Debundscha is reputedly "the wettest place in the world" outside Assam. One local dignitary, the Fon of Bikom, who lives in the southern Cameroons near Bamenda, has, it is proudly asserted, more wives than any human being in the world. Grass huts in the savanna regions of the French Cameroons are, so far as I know, the only buildings in the world that wear hats; atop each is a small conical roof that fits the regular roof, in the shape of a Chinese coolie's headgear. One tribe has the picturesque name Fang, and red-purple orchids (*lissochilus*) grow to a height of fifteen feet. There are 20,000 pygmies in the Cameroons—probably they were the original inhabitants of the area—and tonal communication by drums is more advanced here than anywhere in Africa except the Congo. In the French Zone 75 per cent of the native population has syphilis, and there is one doctor for every 70,000 people.

*

The French Cameroons cover an area somewhat larger than California, and have 3,065,000 people, of whom—in the words of an official French document—13,173 are *non-autochthonous*, that is, white. This territory, at the crook of the African bulge, is a veritable "racial crossroads"; there are

[13] A. T. Steele in the New York *Herald Tribune*, January 15, 1948.

no fewer than two hundred different tribes. Mostly the people are Bantu-speaking Negroes in the south, Sudanese-speaking Negroes in the north.[14] Officially the Cameroons are known as an "Affiliated Territory" of the French Union, and send to Paris four deputies, three senators, and five councilors to the Assembly of the French Union. Of this total of twelve, eight are African.

Political fermentation is much more advanced than in French Equatorial Africa, and so is legislation. The Cameroons have, for instance, laws providing for the forty-hour week, collective bargaining, and the right to strike. There are no fewer than 138 local unions, and the influence of the Confédération Générale de Travail is considerable. Moreover several political parties, which hardly exist as yet in FEA, are active in the Cameroons. The noisiest is the UPC, or Union des Populations des Caméroun, which, as its name indicates, stands for amalgamation of the British and French sections of the country. This, though not Communist, is supported by the French Communist party in France. Its leader is a vehement nationalist with the odd name Um Noyobe Ruben. He was educated at the Edea Protestant Mission, near Douala, went to France for further study, became an official, and then went into political activity.[15] Another notable Cameroons leader, who takes the French side strongly, is a descendant of the old Efik kings, and is known as "Prince" Manga Bell. He is a deputy in Paris. He was educated in Germany before World War I, but during World War II fought with the French resistance.

The capital of the French Cameroons, YAOUNDÉ, has a population of about 30,000, of whom perhaps 2,500 are non-African. The cconomy of its hinterland is rich and varied. Yaoundé, like Léopoldville, is sprayed every night by helicopters bearing DDT, to keep disease down. When I asked a French official what the total white population was, I was rebuked with the words, "Please say 'European' instead of 'white.' We do not have color bar here." Of course this is an exaggeration. The Negroes have a long, long way to go before they achieve social, economic, and political "equality," though officially at least "popular representation exists without racial discrimination."

V.K. Krishna Menon, the Indian delegate to the UN, spoke before the Trusteeship Council in New York in February, 1954, and severely attacked French policy and administration in the Cameroons. He said that the economic position of the territory was "regrettable," not showing an ad-

[14] All are animists or pagan, except about 600,000 Christian converts and 600,000 Moslems.
[15] A Moslem party also exists, by name Grukr.

vance "consistent either with the purposes of the Trusteeship Agreement or the constitution of the French Union." A Trust Territory is supposed to "march toward self-government." But, said Mr. Krishna Menon, the French administer the Cameroons as if they were an integral part of France, almost as Pretoria administers South-West Africa; France has virtually "annexed" the Cameroons, making a forced *Anschluss* with it. There is an urbane "air of unreality" about the reports the French make to the UN. Discriminations against Africans *do* exist in all realms, according to Mr. Krishna Menon; for instance, some 12,000 Frenchmen are represented by eighteen persons in the territorial assembly; three million Cameroonians are represented by thirty-two. In other words one Frenchman is worth 140 Cameroonians.

The seaport, DOUALA, is more dynamic than Yaoundé, as well as bigger. It has roughly 100,000 people. Here French officials play tennis under yellow fog lights—an odd spectacle—because it is too hot to play till twilight, and twilight in the tropics is very brief. The leading night club, the Canne à Sucre, is owned by an African senator who spent ten years in the United States as a headwaiter. As to aspects of color bar, I was told that an African policeman could arrest a white man, but that a white could be tried only before a European judge. Douala is a flourishing port. One astounding item is that it receives 20,000 *tons* of wine from France every year, for local consumption and distribution inland. Most local traders are Greek; these are the "Indians" of the Cameroons. The chief banana port is Bonaberi, across the Wouri River; this, like Douala, was substantially helped by Marshall Plan funds after the war.

There are two short narrow-gauge railways in the Cameroons, both built by the Germans and not much improved since; one goes to the banana country from Bonaberi, and the other connects Douala and Yaoundé; together they span only 315 miles. This in a country bigger than California! I mention this not to enlarge invidiously on the backwardness of the Cameroons, but contrariwise to indicate once more what copiously fertile field this part of Africa could be for future economic development.

*

Four hours from Douala by launch, twenty minutes by air, is Brigadier E.J. Gibbons, who runs the British Cameroons and is one of the most successful British administrators in all Africa. His headquarters are in the pleasant town of Buea, which was the old German capital, on the slopes of Mount Cameroon. It is a minor instance of African hugeness that the base of this volcano covers seven hundred square miles.

What occupies Gibbons most these days is an important constitutional development—the creation of a new federal administration for the southern part of the British Cameroons, separate from the north. This follows changes in the political structure of Nigeria, which we shall inspect in a later chapter. The northern (British) Cameroons are almost indistinguishable from northern Nigeria, ethnically and otherwise; they do not even have towns of their own, and want to link up with the Nigerian North. The southern (British) Cameroons—partly because they fear penetration by Ibos from southern Nigeria—want on the other hand to be on their own. So they are to be given federal status with their own Executive and Legislative Council, a procedure far in advance of anything going on on the French side of the border.

One important economic factor in the British sector is the Cameroons Development Corporation, which has taken over former German holdings in bananas, cocoa, rubber, and so on, and works them for "the common benefit" of the population. Profits are plowed back into the country as a whole; schools and hospitals have been built, and social services improved. This has been one of the most successful experiments of its kind in British Africa; it has really worked—in contrast to such ill-fated schemes as the monkeynut project in Tanganyika. Moreover it points a way toward solution of a difficult and pressing problem—how to use the white man's efficiency for improvement of the living standard of Africans, give the white man a reasonable profit, and at the same time avoid exploitation. Africa needs development. But private European capital will not, in the main, enter Africa if it is not assured rates of profit that Africans think are exorbitant. The days of 20 per cent dividends are over. Hence a public company like the Cameroons Development Corporation fills a particularly useful role. Three Africans sit on its board, and it has 18,000 employees; wages have doubled in the past three years.

The Cameroons provided several lively passages in the 1954 meeting of the Trusteeship Council of the UN, in addition to Krishna Menon's assault on the French. Mr. Krishna Menon also attacked the British, though in gentler terms, saying that their failure to extend suffrage to women was a reflection of "Victorian" colonialism, and that they still made use of barbarous and archaic punishments such as the imposition of collective fines. To the latter charge Brigadier Gibbons replied with point. He agreed that collective punishment of a tribe is indeed archaic, and should be "scrubbed"; but he explained that he had to continue using it on occasion, to restore order and prevent bloodshed, because people will not respect any other measure. For instance, a people known as the Bali—a small, well-organized and martial tribe—came down from the north many years ago, and invaded and took over the territory of the Widekums; they were confirmed in this by the German rule of the time; and the two tribes have been bitter enemies ever since. The Widekums surround the Bali area, which makes the tension worse; and in March, 1952, they set out to attack the Bali, burning 1,900 Bali houses. The Balis prepared to take armed revenge. Then Brigadier Gibbons fined the Widekums £10,000 and told them to behave themselves under threat of further punishment. They paid up without a murmur, the Balis were satisfied, and there has been no bloodshed since.

The American delegate, Mason Sears, did something unusual at this same UN meeting—he openly (if cautiously) criticized the French in the Cameroons for being less advanced than the British, and cautioned them that this might, in the long run, lead to Communism. "We cannot," he said, "blind ourselves to the complications which could arise if self-government was being achieved by some peoples of West Africa while not yet being fully achieved by others. We believe that if such a situation is allowed to drift and becomes unduly prolonged it will . . . ultimately provide fertile territory for alien controlled agitators, disguised as local patriots, to introduce Communist activity."[16]

Mr. Sears concluded by saying that it would not be long before the various states of West Africa achieved independence and (barring a Russian veto) seats in the UN.

THE SPANISH ISLAND OF FERNANDO PO, OR PÓO

This island in the Gulf of Guinea may be seen on a clear day (if there ever is a clear day) from Douala, but few people ever visit it. Spanish administration is dreary and unkempt; this is the kind of place where officials will still be lounging in pajamas at 8 P.M. Fernando Po (an alternate spelling is Póo) was named for its discoverer, the Portuguese navigator Fernao do Po, who reached it exactly twenty years before another better known explorer, Christopher Columbus, reached the West Indies. For a time it was called, peculiarly enough, Formosa. The natives are known as Bubis; the mulattoes, of whom there are a considerable number, are called Portos. Fernando Po does not have enough men to work its cocoa fields, and imports labor from Nigeria. There are about 20,000 Nigerians working on contract—indeed Nigerians and Gold Coasters are an important constituent in the labor force all along the Cameroons and FEA coast. They have a British vice-consul nearby to protect their interests. They get perhaps twenty pounds for two

[16] New York *Times*, February 11, 1954.

years' work, and then return to their villages on the mainland, buy a sewing machine or other implement of trade, and set themselves up in business. Fernando Po was, for years, particularly deadly—from the point of view of health—in this generally deadly region. Sir Richard Burton was once British consul in Fernando Po, from 1861 to 1865. One legend is that his superiors could not brook any longer his imperious and idiosyncratic habits, and deliberately sent him there to die.

CHAPTER 35

A Visit to Dr. Albert Schweitzer

Whatever is reasonable is good. To be truly rational is to become ethical.
—ALBERT SCHWEITZER

You can burn a candle at both ends if it is long enough.
—ALBERT SCHWEITZER

INCONTESTABLY Schweitzer is a great man—one of the greatest of this or any time. The majesty of his thought and the breadth and force of his ethical sense are almost, if not quite, Olympian. Schweitzer is too lofty, too manifold to grasp easily—a "universal man" in the sense that Leonardo da Vinci and Goethe were universal men. Everybody knows that he is a teacher, seer, humanitarian, healer, and practical idealist. He has had four different professional careers, and is an authentic quadruple doctor—in philosophy, medicine, theology, and music. He has written learned books on Bach, Jesus, and the history of civilization, and is the world's foremost authority on the architecture of organs as well as a celebrated interpreter of organ music. Also Dr. Schweitzer knows a great deal—more than many men who have devoted their lives to these fields—about aesthetics, tropical zoology, anthropology, and agriculture, and is an expert carpenter, nurse, mason, veterinarian, boatbuilder, dentist, architect, repairer of pumps, draughtsman, mechanic, pharmacist, and gardener. Universal man indeed!

He has multitudinous disciples—Schweitzer "addicts"—and these talk about him with an almost frightened reverence, as people at Yasnaya Polyana talked of Tolstoy. Schweitzer's own view of himself is simpler, and partakes of his anthropomorphism. He said once, "I am a tall tree in the Vosges!"

Schweitzer would be intolerable if, together with his overwhelming intellectual and moral virtues, he did not have defects. He himself is quite conscious of these, and mentions in one of his books that he has often been "arrogant" and "lacking in love," and that he has even "hated, slandered, and defrauded." In plain fact the old man—he was turning seventy-nine when we saw him—has several frailties. His venerators are horrified if these are mentioned; they want their Great Man whole, untattered and undiminished. Few people ever visit Lambaréné, the Schweitzer lair in French Equatorial Africa, and dare to write anything except unrestrained eulogies. And indeed Schweitzer is a perfectly enormous personality, who has done sublime work; he is the "greatest living Christian," and his heart is august and good. But also he can be cranky on occasion, dictatorial, prejudiced, pedantic in a peculiarly Teutonic manner, irascible, and somewhat vain. And why not? It might even be whispered that Dr. Schweitzer's views on several subjects are obstinately old-fashioned. Again, why not?

Our chief interest was, naturally, to find out something of his relation to Africa. Actually Dr. Schweitzer does not know much about Africa except his own small and isolated corner, as he himself freely concedes. He has made eleven voyages to the continent, but, with the exception of a two-week sojourn in the Cameroons in 1924, he has never visited any African country except French Equatorial Africa. (Of course ships on which he is a passenger make brief stops at various West Coast ports, and these he saw briefly. He has never traveled by air.) He has lived in Lambaréné for an aggregate of twenty-eight years, but has never once even been to Brazzaville, the capital of the territory, which is 420 miles away. This is as if a man should, say, live in Oneida, New York, all his life, and never once go to New York City. It is also an interesting point that, so far as I know, Dr. Schweitzer has never learned any African language or dialect—except a few words of greeting—though of course he knows Latin, Greek, Hebrew, English, French and German.[1] As to his attitude toward Africans en masse that is a mixture of benevolence, perplexity, irritation, hope, and despair. He never talks about politics for public expression, but is vociferous privately. I would imagine that he has little if any belief in the capability of Africans—at least in his own area—for self-government. He hates oppression, of course, and believes devoutly in the brotherhood of man, but he has, it seems, almost no conception of the volcanic surges and stresses of modern Africa and its hungry zest for political advance. He knew and liked Félix Éboué, but I do not think he has ever encountered or exchanged a word with any contemporary African nationalist. He is, in short, one of those good old souls who would like to see the white man stay on in "colonial" areas forever.

Also I was much struck by something else. Dr. Schweitzer is a profound moralist, but he has comparatively little interest in human beings as such,

[1] He does not like to speak English but I had the feeling that he understands it well.

African or otherwise. His mind goes in, not out. Basically his interests are art and ideas. The hospital is run in a way somewhat difficult to explain. Some visitors find in it all that they are looking for spiritually; to meet Schweitzer and see his work is a magnificent emotional experience. Others—though they may not say so—do not quite regard it as the model of a Christian community. Discipline, though not overtly exercised, is somewhat strict; everything, as I heard it put, is "noted." Discussion at mealtimes or in the evening hardly exists, and acolytes do not sit at the feet of the master to absorb wisdom—because he seldom talks. His aloofness is remarkable, and he has small contact with most of his workers. Of course his mind is far too elevated for casual chitchat. If any trouble occurs, the disputants are called into Schweitzer's office one by one. With his eyes closed, the Doctor tells them what his ruling is—"Do this," or "I want no more of that"—without permitting apology or explanation. Schweitzer is totally just, and always fair, but he simply does not have much interest in minor personal problems. On the other hand he can be magically charming on occasion and is literally worshiped by his old associates. His laughter—when he laughs—is a striking indication of his inner sweetness. It is a shining laugh, a silvery laugh, and it tinkles.

No bush hospital can be tidy, any more than can a farmyard in South Carolina. There will always be things out of place, and innocent litter on the ground. But Schweitzer's hospital was, I thought, the most unkempt place of its kind I saw in all Africa. The sanitary arrangements are—how shall I put it?—picturesque. Of course Schweitzer is totally above such details. Another thing that struck me was that many African workers seemed unhappy and somewhat unfriendly—even surly. They wheedled for tips. Once, a hundred yards away from the hospital, I was openly solicited by two robust grinning Negro ladies. I laughed and pulled two francs out of my pocket, saying that this was all the money I had. With cheerful contempt they said it was not enough, and waved me on. It seemed an odd thing to happen so close to Dr. Schweitzer.

Later we watched him feed one of his pet antelopes; the hospital area swarms with animals, and on these the Doctor bestows the most tender care. He seems to be fonder of the animals in Lambaréné than the human beings, and perhaps—who knows?—they reward him more. As a whole the hospital gives a curious atmosphere of being a kind of abstraction, almost an exercise in penance. Schweitzer does his work for himself before God, as well as out of a sense of duty for the Africans. He is not only saving the bodies of men, but—as all men should—his own immortal soul.

A VISIT TO DR. ALBERT SCHWEITZER

LIFE AND WORK OF THE "THIRTEENTH APOSTLE"

The great secret of success is to go through life as a man who never gets used up.

—ALBERT SCHWEITZER

Some sort of demon has always possessed Schweitzer; he pursued both faith and reason, not easy bedfellows. Once he wrote that he belonged proudly to the fellowship of those who bear the Mark of Pain. To make his career at Lambaréné comprehensible we must go back to the roots.

He was born in Upper Alsace in 1875; his father was an evangelical pastor, and his mother the daughter of a pastor. The family moved to an Alsatian village named Gunsbach when Albert was an infant, and this is still his European home. One of his grandfathers was a schoolmaster and organist; three granduncles were also organists. Schweitzer told me, when I asked him about his parents, that he was strongly influenced by his father, but that he remembers his mother more. The Gunsbach community was small; both Catholics and Protestants held services in the local church. The father often talked to him, when he was a child, about the sacrificial life of missionaries in Africa. Schweitzer's mother met death in an extraordinary way; during World War I she was knocked down and trampled to death by German cavalry horses trooping up an Alsatian road.[2]

Puny children, if they survive adolescence, often grow up strong; nature, it seems, hoards her reserves and delays giving full vitality until it is really needed. Schweitzer was a sickly child, with a subsequent robustness that was, and is, phenomenal. Also—more strangely—he was a poor student, slow to read and write. Because of this, as he grew up he *made* himself master subjects that were particularly difficult for him, like Hebrew. He had a stern, glowing sense of duty. Schweitzer says that he lacked self-confidence when he was a youth, but he has certainly never lacked it since. He had a book published by the time he was twenty-three.

As a child he hated cruelty and injustice; he would not shoot birds, fish, or track animals as his playmates did; he wore clogs instead of shoes because other Gunsbach boys could not afford shoes. Also his passion for music began early, and in this as well as other fields he was an authentic prodigy. He composed a hymn at seven, began to play the organ at eight "when his legs were scarcely long enough to reach the pedals," and at nine substituted for the regular organist in a church service. He records that he almost fainted with emotion the first time he ever heard brass instruments playing

[2] *Out of My Life and Thought,* one of Schweitzer's best autobiographical works, gives exactly one sentence to this episode.

together—he had to prop himself against a wall to avoid falling. He heard a Wagner opera for the first time when he was sixteen, and was so inexpressibly moved that it was days before he could give "proper attention to his work in school."

In early manhood three of his four professional lives proceeded concurrently. He studied philosophy at the University of Strassburg, and a thesis on Kant brought him his first doctorate. He studied theology and in 1900, when he was twenty-five, was ordained curate of the St. Nicholas Church in Strassburg. He studied the theory of music, and began his career as an organist. He had degrees in philosophy, theology, and music at twenty-six, and became a *Privatdozent* on the Strassburg faculty.[3] A stream of books began to pour out from him, and has never stopped. In his early thirties appeared the biography of Bach, which is also an acute study in aesthetics, and which has never been excelled as a work of research on Bach; he wrote it first in French, and then completely rewrote it, much enlarged, in German. Then came his *Quest of the Historical Jesus*, which upset many theological assumptions of the time; a work on organ building, which has similarly remained a classic; a dissertation on the problem of the Last Supper; and a searching study of St. Paul.

His vigor was enormous. He records that sometimes he went to his organ studies early in the morning without having been to bed at all.

I asked Schweitzer in Lambaréné what his family had thought of all this. He answered, "When I was still a young man my father asked me what preoccupied me and I replied, 'A work on eschatology.' My father shook his head, saying, 'My son, I pity you. No one will ever understand a word you write.'"

Schweitzer worked a good deal in both Paris and Berlin in those days—he liked Berlin better—and it is interesting that, so far as I know, there is no mention at all in his work of politics or nationalism, not even Alsatian nationalism. Alsace was German when he was born, but had been French five years before; it became French again in 1918. Schweitzer grew up in both French and German, but is more instinctively at home in German. Mostly he has to speak French at Lambaréné; when he returns to Alsace, he turns completely to German to get a change. Even if he had no interest in nationalism, he has been a victim of it. He was a German citizen working in French Equatorial Africa when World War I came; he was promptly interned by the French as an enemy alien, and his hospital was kept under

---

[3] See *The Africa of Albert Schweitzer*, by Charles R. Joy and Melvin Arnold. This and Joy's *Albert Schweitzer, An Anthology*, are invaluable works on Schweitzer.

guard by black troops.[4] In 1917 he was brought back to France and spent ten grisly months in camps for enemy internees—concentration camps, we would call them nowadays. This was probably the bitterest experience of his life, and marked the only time when he has ever been severely ill. He never got dysentery in Africa; in France he did.

In Lambaréné, sitting in the garden by the river, I asked him which he thought himself to be most—French or German. His reply was quick, "*Homo sum!*"

*

When Schweitzer was twenty-one he vowed to give himself nine years of fulfillment in art and theological service; after that he would do something else. So, at thirty, seeking complete spiritual self-realization, he abruptly quit his three careers, having reached a very tidy summit in each, in order to become a doctor and go out to Africa for the rest of his life as a medical missionary. No act of renunciation could be more profound.

Why medicine? Would it not have been enough to be a non-medical missionary? Because, he records, he was tired of talk, and wanted action.

Why Africa? First, because of his father's early conversations. Second, because he had been strongly impressed in his youth by a heroic statue in Colmar, portraying a Negro in chains at the foot of a monument. (This statue, incidentally, was by Bartholdi, the sculptor of the Statue of Liberty.) Third, a communication from the Paris Missionary Society, which reached him at the critical time, emphasized the need of medical service in French Equatorial Africa.

Why Lambaréné? Because it was one of the most inaccessible and primitive spots in all Africa, one of the most dangerous, and one without any doctor at all in the area.

He worked at his medical studies at Strassburg from 1906 to 1912 and finally, aged thirty-eight, became an MD. His thesis was a psychiatric study of the mind of Jesus, with particular attention to "mental derangements of which other scholars thought He might have been a victim." A period of internship and special courses on tropical medicine in Paris followed. These years were the most difficult and fatiguing he ever spent, he records. A German medical education was a thoroughly grueling process in those days; yet while going through this Schweitzer managed to continue teach-

---

[4] He records that, on the day after he was forbidden to work at the hospital, he at once proceeded to start writing his *Philosophy of Civilization*. Previously, so that his music would not get rusty, he set out to learn *by heart* the organ compositions "of Bach, Mendelssohn, Widor, César Franck, and Max Reger." *Out of My Life and Thought*, p. 144.

ing philosophy, kept on with his activity as curate of St. Nicholas, and started work on a definitive edition of Bach's organ music, while giving organ concerts all the time!

He married in 1912. Before this a friendship with an elderly and distinguished noblewoman "rounded off many a hard angle" in his personality, as he puts it. His wife, by name Helene Bresslau, the daughter of a noted Strassburg historian, is Jewish. She learned nursing in order to be able to help him in Africa, and has been his devoted companion and assistant (though for reasons of health she has not been in Lambaréné recently) ever since. The Schweitzers have one daughter, Rhena, and four grandchildren.

Schweitzer records frankly how his relatives and friends "expostulated with me on the folly of my enterprise" when he prepared to set out for Africa. They said that "unfortunate love experiences" must be the reason. His own point of view was that he had to "give something in return" for all the happiness he enjoyed. He was obeying literally the command of Jesus, "Whosoever would save his life shall lose it, and whosoever shall lose his life for My sake . . . shall save it." Renunciation was his keynote. He was perfectly conscious of the difficulties that would confront him, because he always demanded that "idealists should be sober in their views." He sums up his qualifications for his task quite candidly: "In my own case I felt the venture to be justified . . . and credited myself with the possession of health, sound nerves, energy, practical common sense, toughness, prudence, very few wants, and everything else that might be found necessary by anyone wandering along the path of the idea. I believed myself, further, to wear the protective armor of a temperament quite capable of enduring an eventual failure of my plan."[5]

Schweitzer assembled his equipment, and paid for the entire expedition himself out of gifts from his parish and his earnings as a lecturer and organist. He records how the preparation of intricate shopping lists gave him high "artistic satisfaction." His theology was so unorthodox that the Paris Missionary Society, which had to give its approval of the venture, asked him to submit to an examination on his beliefs.[6] This he refused to

[5] *Out of My Life and Thought*, p. 89.

[6] Few today would think that Schweitzer's thought is dangerously heterodox. We cannot discuss in this space his theology. He is completely devout about both the historicity of Jesus and His position as the Son of God. But he considers that Jesus made human errors, such as thinking that the end of the world was imminent. He tried to see Jesus as Jesus saw Himself. And he continually asked pressing, rational questions, like "If the wise men brought such rich and precious gifts to the manger of the child Jesus, why were his parents always so poor?" See Joy's *Anthology*, op. cit., p. xv.

do, but he called on various members of the organization individually, explained his ideas, and was passed. He had to promise, however, to confine his activities solely to the medical field, and be "as silent as a carp" on matters of theology, for fear of "subverting" other missionaries in the field. Finally Schweitzer and his wife were ready. With seventy packing cases of supplies, they sailed for Africa from Bordeaux on March 26, 1913.

*

Lambaréné lies on the River Ogowe fifty miles south of the Equator, in the territory of Gabon. The Ogowe flows roughly parallel to the Congo five hundred miles north of it, and is the largest river between the Congo and the Niger. Near Lambaréné the celebrated character Trader Horn had some of his most colorful adventures; Schweitzer's hospital is, in fact, at a place called Adolinanongo, where Horn set up his first trading post. The easiest way to describe the area is to paraphrase Schweitzer himself, and say that it resembles the beginning of the world—clouds, river, and forest combine and melt into a landscape that seems literally antediluvian. Most of the year the air is like steam coming out of a green mist, and I, for one, would not have been surprised to see prehistoric lizards rise out of the swamps and swallow islets at a gulp.

Lambaréné lies about 175 miles above the mouth of the Ogowe at Port Gentil, and is an island. Further up the river there is little but *brousse*—bush. The island measures approximately ten miles by four, and has a population today of two thousand natives, forty-four French, and one Swiss.[7] Schweitzer's establishment is not on the island, but is a mile or two away on the mainland across a gray-green, soupy branch of the Ogowe. When Schweitzer arrived in 1913 there were already two French missions in the area, one Protestant, one Catholic, but neither had a doctor. One of these had formerly been an American mission.

Every inch of habitable land near Lambaréné has to be seized from the giant forest. The waterways are the roads. The tribesmen in the area had been cannibals not long before, and the forest was—and is—populated thickly with beasts of unamiable disposition, like pythons and gorillas. The rivers are heavy with crocodiles and hippopotamuses, and Schweitzer told us that the hospital was virtually isolated from Lambaréné itself from six every evening until the next morning, because at night hippopotamuses were likely to attack and tip over the *pirogues* (dugout canoes) that are his only means of transport. On the other hand there is no atmosphere at

[7] I asked the French commandant if the *indigènes* voted and he replied, "Some do but not very passionately."

all of danger, active or passive, except from mosquitoes.[8] The forest (it is particularly rich in enormous *okoumé* trees) seems to have been thoroughly intimidated by the Great Doctor, even if it isn't.

Here, then, forty-two years ago, Albert Schweitzer began his work. The story of his career in Africa is too well known to need repetition. To build a bush hospital from scratch—and Schweitzer did it practically with his bare hands—is something like swimming the Atlantic in a suit of armor. Once he had to move and rebuild the entire establishment, because the old huts were made untenable by a dysentery epidemic. For one period of eighteen *months*, he says that he scarcely had time to do any medical work at all! His labors were like those of Hercules, except that there were Augean stables to cleanse every day, not just once. One of his books describes with understated vividness how he and Madame Schweitzer had, on one occasion, to fill cavities in each other's teeth. African patients, suffering anything from leprosy to phagedenic ulcers, from strangulated hernia to elephantiasis, were not always easy to handle. For one brief period, after the death of a patient who arrived at the hospital too late for successful treatment, Schweitzer was considered to be a leopard in disguise, who deliberately took lives.

Once he records that he threw himself in a chair and groaned out, "What a blockhead I was to come out here to doctor savages like this!" Then his faithful African interpreter replied, "Yes, Doctor, here on earth you are a great blockhead, but not in heaven."[9]

But nobody can be more obstinate, more dogmatically purposeful, than an Alsatian theologian. Even in periods of complete despair Schweitzer was "intoxicated with delight at having to deal with realities which could be determined with exactitude." The plain fact is that, despite everything, he loved Lambaréné, and still loves it. Among other things it taught him his basic ethical concept, which is the root of his philosophy today and which he calls "reverence for life." Once in 1939 he returned to Europe intending to take a long recuperative holiday; after the barest glimpse of Gunsbach he changed his mind and returned to Africa forthwith, traveling back in fact on the return trip of the same boat that brought him to Europe. The demon was still pursuing.

Schweitzer, when he set out for Africa, thought that he was giving up forever what was dearest to him—art and preaching. He prepared to sacrifice three things—"to abandon the organ, to renounce academic teaching, and to lose his financial independence." (He says that, even today, he

[8] But once on the river my wife had to scratch a tsetse fly off her neck.
[9] *More from the Primeval Forest*, by Albert Schweitzer, p. 182.

cannot bear to look at the lecture building at the University of Strassburg, because it calls up poignantly all that he has missed.) But the old Doctor was spared the sacrifice. Or, to put it somewhat differently, all the sacrifices have, as it were, paid off. He has always had a piano with him in Africa, and so he has been able to keep up with his music, although it was certainly a deprivation not to have a proper organ. His Bach recordings, made when he was on holiday in Europe, have been a profound artistic success. As to academic work he lectures widely whenever he returns to civilization, and has been honored by universities without number. He became one of the two or three most famous men in the world, and won the Nobel peace prize for 1952.

FIRST ENCOUNTER WITH LE GRAND DOCTEUR

Nowadays it is easy enough to get to Schweitzer, if you do not mind old airplanes and eccentric flying. I have already described the Air France "milk run" that touches on Lambaréné several times a week. We put down at the airport across the Ogowe from Schweitzer's hospital. I have never seen an airport like this, because there was nothing whatever on it to indicate any connection with flying, except the stepladder on which we descended from the plane—not even a windsleeve or a drum of gasoline. When the plane took off, leaving us there, the stepladder remained where it stood, blankly alone in the middle of the field, stepping up to nothing—a perch to infinity. The effect was bizarre. I asked our pilot what Lambaréné was like. He replied in succinct English, "It stinks." I asked the Negro official representing Air France what it was like. He replied with the utmost solemnity, "It is purgatory on earth, monsieur." (Of course they meant the town, not Schweitzer's installation.)

The hospital startles some visitors because almost everybody thinks beforehand that it will be like an Indian *ashram*, an aseptic harbor of tranquillity, spirituality, and out-of-worldness.

Schweitzer sent his assistant, Miss Emma Haussknecht, in a *pirogue* to meet us at the riverbank, but the French authorities insisted on giving us a lift on their official launch. This cut swiftly across the swollen, solid-seeming river. We disembarked at a point where other *pirogues* were clustered, and climbed up a rough, hot, bushy path. Schweitzer's hospital, on first glance, looks like what, in fact, it is—a native village. Patients come from miles around, often with their families. Miss Haussknecht, an Alsatian nurse who has been Schweitzer's dedicated companion since 1925, is general manager to the whole establishment, and serves as interpreter from French or German into English. She wore a white sun helmet and carried a large white umbrella. (It is one of the Doctor's theories that the tsetse fly is less likely to attack white objects than those darker.) This admirable lady is a most determined character—once, many years ago, she *walked* from Lambaréné to the coast. She led us to our room, gave us the key, and told us to be careful always to lock the door. "Please never leave your room unlocked, even for a moment." This remark was something of a shock.

The fear of theft is, of course, natural. There are Africans who steal, just as there are Europeans who steal. But Schweitzer's camp, we found out later, was positively obsessed by fussiness about stealing. It was sharply disillusioning, in this community dedicated to good works, to find that there should be so much overt distrust. *Every*thing at Schweitzer's is kept rigidly under lock and key. We even had to give our key to the roomboy each morning when he made up the room. The servants are not permitted to carry keys.

Our building was a long, low, narrow structure, set so closely under trees that it almost seemed to be bearing foliage itself. Schweitzer designed it, and has every reason to be proud of his work. The rooms have cross ventilation, and are cool. The windows are screened, but without glass. Each room has one or two narrow iron beds, a simple washstand, wicker chairs, shelves, and a table. There are no closets, bathrooms, running water, or electric light. Nevertheless it was not only comfortable, but extremely pleasant.

A dozen or more of these narrow cubicles face the long shady veranda. Two doors down from us was a European woman convalescing from sleeping sickness. She was holding a parrot, and she warned us not to play with it, since it was *méchant*, and would bite. We met then a young man, one of Schweitzer's associates, carrying a sick baby mandrill. Most of the African servants, I noticed, had bandages stained with gentian violet on their hands or feet. It did not occur to me then that they were lepers.

Slop basins from the rooms are poured into an open drain flowing directly in front of the veranda, and bits of bandage, broken crockery, scraps of grapefruit peel, and the like, are scattered in it. But somehow this was not offensive, and the building itself gave the impression of being spotlessly clean. Five feet away were three rude wooden crosses; children had put them up to mark the graves of dead animals. Miss Haussknecht led us past a nearby rockpile where a dozen Africans were at work, swinging hammers. These too were lepers. One youth sat alone, without hammer or pick, crooning, while goats, dogs, pigs and chickens scrambled near him. "He is a mental patient, but not violent," Miss Haussknecht said. "We call him *Petit Poisson*, because those are the only words he understands."

We strode up a dirt path, through brush and fruit trees, for a quarter of an hour. There was a sense of aliveness in the trees; they seemed to vibrate with heavy, hidden, sodden life. This path is nicknamed "Philosopher's Walk," and leads to the new leper village that Schweitzer is building half a mile away. We passed a small cemetery, and saw a homemade monument to an African, one of Schweitzer's first nurses, who had been cook to none other than De Brazza. As always, the generations are close in Africa. Near a ragged clearing Schweitzer himself came forth. He has a powerful aquiline nose, dripping gray mustache, and eyes that really *fix* you. He is strongly built, and wore an open white shirt, tattered pants, and heavy black shoes. Force, repose, command, sensitiveness—all these characteristics are reflected in his proud, grizzled, piercing face. It is a wonderful face, and he is a magnificent-looking man.

Courteously he asked us if his *pirogue* had been comfortable, and Miss Haussknecht explained that we had come by the government launch. Schweitzer seemed to be disconcerted by this, and responded with a curious gesture, a kind of sweeping, mocking bow, as if to indicate ironically that he was delighted that we had received such unusual official hospitality. Then he asked us, horrified, why we were not wearing sun helmets. We discovered later that sun helmets are practically a fetish at Lambaréné. Nobody at the hospital ever stirs out of doors by day without a *casque*, and the Great Doctor even wears a hat—a crumpled old fedora—when he goes out at night. He attributes his good health to the fact that he always covers his head except indoors. At least a dozen times in the next few days people rushed after us every time we stepped out, offering us headgear. Vainly I tried to explain that I had been in Africa for eight months, had visited places much hotter than Lambaréné, and had not worn a hat yet, much less a sun helmet. Then I pointed to the sky. Not a trace of sun was visible. This was June, the dry season in this part of the world; the sky was heavily overcast with low-lying, dirty wool clouds; it was a meteorological certainty that there would be *neither* rain nor a single ray of clear sun until August. But Schweitzer's folk kept pursuing us—for our own good, of course. Sun helmets are completely archaic in most parts of Africa now, but not here. There is a good reason for this. The sun helmet is the badge of the old colonial. Also Schweitzer himself has had several minor sunstrokes (he got them indoors, when he was not wearing a hat, from sunshine piercing holes in thatched roofs) and is excessively sensitive about the subject. When, the next day, he saw that we were still bareheaded, he stared at us as if we obviously must be demented, and then shrugged cheerfully as if to say the responsibility was no longer his.

Schweitzer led us forward briskly to the leper village, where he wants to erect substantial structures, with iron roofs like those at the hospital proper, to replace the present miserable huts which could be blown away by the next tornado. Immediately he got to work, and it was striking to see him devoting himself to this activity, that of being foreman of a labor gang. But Schweitzer begins and ends each day with this occupation. *Somebody has to do it*. A group of lepers stood by. They were, I admit freely, the worst workmen I have ever seen. They used their spades (they were supposed to be digging foundations) with about as much animation as corpses. If they had spines, they were made of blotting paper. They were not too ill to work, but just plain lazy, as well as numb with boredom and indifference, dazed like zombies. Schweitzer strode amongst them with explosive and hortatory grunts. He argued, threatened, and cajoled. He took a spade himself. Then he chanted a kind of tune, to mark time for the digging: *"Allez-vous OPP! Allez-vous OPP-upp-O P P! Hupp, upp, Hup, upp, OPP!"*

We asked Schweitzer a question or two about the workmen, such as what they got to eat.

"Seven bananas a day."

I asked, "Would they work better if they got eight bananas?"

Dr. Schweitzer's eyes flashed. (And they really do flash.) "No. That would disturb discipline and morale. If somebody does particularly good work, I may give him extra fare, but I do so secretly, so that the others will not know."

We toured the village, smoky with little outdoor fires, and with ebony children underfoot in the greenish dusk. We passed some bad leper cases, and Schweitzer asked them to show us their hands. "Do not touch the hands," Dr. Schweitzer said.

FOREST HOSPITAL AND ITS ROUTINE

All thinking men must renounce the attempt to explain the universe.
—ALBERT SCHWEITZER

Schweitzer's encampment lies on a low, sloping bluff and has forty-five or more buildings; these are all home-built, simply made, and serviceable. Everybody knows what a frightful toll the tropical heat and dampness impose on any structure; that Schweitzer's should be so substantial and in such good condition is amazing. And he built most of these with his own

A VISIT TO DR. ALBERT SCHWEITZER

hands! The hospital has between 350 and 400 African patients, depending on circumstances, and 75 paid African helpers, mostly lepers. There are some 500 mouths to feed every day. The area is hilly and heavily wooded, under a festoon of oil palms and mango trees. There are of course no paved walks or roads. The French authorities offered to put in a telephone line to connect Schweitzer with Lambaréné, but the old Doctor would not hear of it. There is no running water, no hot water (except what is boiled in pots), no electricity except just enough for the operating room, no radio since the departure some years ago of a physician who had one, no motorboat, and no chapel.

Animals drop their refuse everywhere. One afternoon we saw a sick dog lying in one corner of the dispensary, while an orange-colored cat lay next to the crude board that was the treatment table. The hospital has about 150 goats, which fertilize the fruit trees. Near the dining hall are a wild pig in a cage, and a monkey on a six-foot leash, tied to a tree. Chickens, other birds, goats, and piglets scratch near the rations laid on the bare ground, before these are distributed to the African help. Four graceful antelope stand in a rough wire enclosure; the Doctor feeds them through the wire after dinner every night. In one cage are both guinea pigs and parrots. One European nurse has a pet civet cat, another a big red pig named Tecla, and another a chimpanzee, by name Fifi. The sick mandrill we saw is called Monsieur Obama by the natives, and Charles by his white master. It will have to be disposed of when it is about three, since it cannot be permanently tamed, and will bite. Schweitzer told us that of all animals the bite of the human being is the most dangerous; after that, serpents; after that, monkeys. For a time (one visitor to the hospital records) Schweitzer even kept a litter of baby rats, although he did not try to make pets of them. The pets are treated with the utmost affection and at the same time are made useful, if possible. As we walked in to lunch one day Schweitzer encountered Tecla, the red pig, and calmly wiped his shoes on her. Obviously the pig enjoyed this process, and her stiff bristles gave the Doctor's shoes a formidable shine.

What appears to be the main hospital ward is a long one-story structure, cut apart into narrow dark rooms, each of which opens to a courtway. The patients do not lie actually on the floor, as they do in most bush hospitals, but on wooden bunks covered with matting. I did not see any sheets or pillows. Outside each door a small, smoky fire is burning; here the family of the patient does the cooking. It is good to have these fires; they keep the mosquitoes down, and thus tend to lessen the incidence of malaria and sleeping sickness. (Yellow fever and acute sleeping sickness cases are, incidentally, the province of a new government hospital on the island, and are no longer dealt with by Schweitzer.) If a man has no family, and is too sick to cook for himself, he becomes a serious problem. Most patients will not accept food from anybody not a member of their own tribe out of fear of being poisoned. A far cry from Medical Center!

Schweitzer has saved thousands of lives, which is the more extraordinary considering the primitiveness of his equipment. There is, so far as I could see, no mechanism at all for sterilizing bandages under pressure; water has to be boiled in kettles propped up on stones, underneath feeble wood fires out in the open. For years drugs and bandages were in short supply. Every safety pin is precious. Things that we would take utterly for granted in a European hospital are objects of wonder, if they exist at all. I was told that Schweitzer did not like elaborate modern gadgets. For one thing they are difficult to maintain or repair in a tropically humid climate. What point is there to having hot-water bags, if they rot in a week? For another, he wants the Africans to feel comfortable, in circumstances that make them think they are at home, so that they will not be timid about coming to him when they are ill.

We came across a nurse at work on a sheet of board that served as a table. Projecting from a blanket was something that looked like the greenish, decayed trunk of a small tree. She was scraping blotches of what appeared to be fungi off this. It was a man's leg.

We peered into the operating room one morning; it was startling to be able to look right in from the courtyard. On the table lay a naked Negro, his abdomen streaming with blood. I looked more closely. It was not blood, but mercurochrome. The doctor who performed the operation—it was a routine hernia—came in to lunch an hour later. He had not had time to wash up completely and, in his shirt sleeves, sat down with his arms still scarlet with mercurochrome up to the elbow. I do not mean to indicate by this that surgery at Schweitzer's is rough or incompetent. It is not. Standards are very high.

One bizarre sight is the insane asylum. It is a small square box without windows, with two padlocked cells on each side. A certain amount of light gets in through a criss-cross aperture. There are no sanitary facilities, but at intervals the occupants are led down to the river to bathe. The violently insane must be locked up not only to protect the community, but to keep them from being murdered by their families. Schweitzer records in one of his books his delight that he was able to build this structure, because it replaced one smaller. The smaller one must have been even more ghastly. Yet it is a remarkable tribute to Schweitzer's thoroughness and humanity that there should be room for the insane at all. Most bush hospitals do not have such facilities.

In a crowded open space near the dining hall Africans busily carry produce in rude barrows made by putting short poles on packing crates. Women squat on the ground, binding palm fronds together for roofing; others are busy on sewing machines, and still others iron the wash with primitive irons heated by a lump of wood coal. The Doctor strides back and forth, amid this orderly animation, seeing that everybody works. The bustle and clatter is that of a frontier camp. The great moment here comes when the rations are distributed. Each African entitled to a ration gets seven large bananas a day, plus two sticks of manioc wrapped in leaves, the native equivalent of bread. Also, on occasion, the ration includes palm oil, rice, and soap. The bananas (which are really plantains) are measured out with scrupulous care, so that everybody gets fruit of identical size. Some workers get a cash wage as well as their ration, but this is small, averaging only about 7½¢ a week.

One should interpolate a word about Schweitzer's fruit. In our residential hall, when we arrived, I saw one room which seemed to be carpeted by a luxurious pebbly golden rug. It was a layer of grapefruit, put there for storage. Now strangely enough fresh fruit is rare in Africa, except bananas. This is partly because of a native superstition which holds that a man planting a fruit tree will die before it bears its first crop—and most fruit trees take a long time to bear. But Schweitzer grows almost every kind of fruit, from trees which he himself planted with laborious devotion. One can more than forgive his irritation at Africans who are too stupid or lazy to help him tend his trees. Also his vegetable garden is a delight. It is one of his proudest achievements that he has made Lambaréné practically self-sufficient as to food.

One nurse in the establishment is senior even to Miss Haussknecht; she is another Alsatian, Miss Matilda Kottmann, who came to Lambaréné in 1924. She is a most saintly and delightful person. Other veteran nurses, equally devoted, are Dutch—Miss Lagendyk and Miss Silver. The chief doctor at present (Schweitzer himself does not do much active medical work nowadays) is Hungarian; another is one of the old man's nephews. The nurses are dedicated utterly to their work. One told me that their health is generally good, but that they are likely to get malaria if they are very tired after taking care of a *European* patient, since these need more attention than Africans. (The Europeans come mostly from the logging camps nearby, and have separate hospital quarters.) It is a most remarkable thing that Schweitzer himself has never once had malaria. For a time, years ago, sores on his feet were apt to become ulcerated, but this aside he has *never* been seriously ill in Africa, which is another proof of how much he likes it.[10]

There are almost always visitors at the Schweitzer board, and some of these—even those who come uninvited—may stay for months or even years. Schweitzer's hospitality is boundless, and nobody is turned away. One of the chief buildings at the hospital bears the inscription, fingered rudely into the cement, *Schweitzer et Schatzman Entrepreneurs*. Mr. Schatzman was a Swiss who arrived without warning one day, and became an expert builder. Usually guests, if they stay any length of time, do some sort of work, like helping call the hospital roll or distributing the bananas.[11]

Miss Haussknecht said one morning that she had arranged an expedition up the river in a *pirogue*. "Four of our best lepers will row you. Do not touch their hands or paddles."

By this time—after only a day or two—we had lost or managed to conceal most of the instinctive apprehension we felt about lepers. As a matter of fact Miss Haussknecht's warning meant little; we had already been in contact a dozen times a day with things that had been touched by lepers, even if we did not touch *them*. To enforce strict segregation of leprous patients would be altogether impossible in a community like Lambaréné. The worst cases are restricted to a certain area, but others wander about freely. The truth is that leprosy is not nearly so unpleasant a disease as some that are widely prevalent in our western world, and it is not particularly contagious (though, after contact, a person cannot be absolutely sure he has not caught it for five years). Probably it is less contagious than tuberculosis. It is an odd medical point that the bacillus of leprosy is almost indistinguishable from that of tuberculosis, even to a skilled eye under the microscope. Incidentally Schweitzer has never seen a case of appendicitis in an African, and cancer is virtually unknown.

The hospital day is regulated by a series of bells—reveille at 6:30 A.M., breakfast at 7:30, and lunch at 12:30. A brief siesta is then supposed to be obligatory, but *le Grand Docteur*, which is what the natives call him, seldom sleeps. At 6:30 P.M. a bell announces the end of the day; at 7:30 comes the dinner bell and at 8:30 a final bell after which the *indigenès* are not allowed out of doors. Europeans, too, seldom stir outside after this hour, because of the danger from mosquitoes. But once we joined the whole staff at the riverbank, when Schweitzer celebrated a saint's day by building a large

---

[10] The sunstrokes I mentioned above were minor.

[11] Nothing about Schweitzer impressed me more than his letter asking us to stay with him. It ended with a medical homily advising us not to eat underdone meat while in Africa and always to wash our hands after shaking hands with a native.

fire of palm fronds and watching it burn fiercely. That was all that happened, but it was a beautiful and impressive ceremony. The Doctor's face was rapt, and the flames sounded like surf.

The dining table is long enough to hold twenty or more people, and is lit by a row of kerosene lamps. Schweitzer's cook is a Swiss lady, and the meals are simple, ample, and altogether delicious. At breakfast pots of tea and coffee are waiting, with toast and several kinds of jam made out of local fruit. At lunch there will be a vegetable or fruit stew—for instance of papaya and carrots mixed together—plain boiled sweet potatoes in their jackets, noodles, bread-fruit fritters, palm nuts, fresh salad, and steamed bananas. Once we had meat—some lamb sent over by a neighboring mission. Eggs or fish are served every day, sometimes twice a day. At dinner tureens of healthy thick soup are placed on the table as the company assembles, and this is followed by rice or macaroni, other vegetables, and great bowls of fresh fruit cut up into a macédoine.

Schweitzer sits at the middle of the long table flanked by Miss Haussknecht and Miss Kottmann, with guests of honor opposite. Gently the two nurses offer him special delicacies, like radishes from his preciously tended garden, tidbits of salad, or brown beans. At each meal, including breakfast, Schweitzer eats steamed bananas. Sometimes he puts food into a soup plate, and eats with a spoon. When fresh fruit is served he pulls a large penknife out of his pocket, and peels an orange or grapefruit with it.[12]

Immediately before each meal Schweitzer says a brief grace in French; immediately after dinner (no meal takes more than half an hour) he announces a hymn in a decisive voice, and hymnbooks are passed around. He walks to an upright piano at one end of the room, and plays briefly but with great vigor and precision as the company sings. He returns to his place at the table, inspects carefully a list of Bible passages, slowly opens the Bible and reads a few lines from scripture.

Schweitzer is a most incisive, alert, and authoritative conversationalist. His mind is sharp as a saw, and he gives forth opinions with a wonderful quick dogmatism. The epigrammatic quickness of his mind is as astonishing as its spiritual breadth and profundity. He is a true German "thinker." But he seldom talks much at meals these days—he is too tired.

After dinner doctors and nurses gather at one end of the long room, and have cinnamon tea or some similar mild stimulant. Schweitzer may, or may not, join them. One evening he left the table at once, because an argument—he called it a "palaver"—with some workmen had exhausted him. Another evening he sat with us until after nine, at which time Miss

---

[12] Incidentally he adores *pâté de fois gras* from his native Alsace, but of course this is unobtainable in Africa.

Kottmann reminded him that it was time to deal with his mail. Always on leaving the dining hall he takes with him odd bits of food, which he gives to the antelopes. Then—after curfew has descended on the rest of the camp—he will work till midnight or beyond.

GRACE NOTES

Once, when most of his helpers were ill, Schweitzer had to drag some heavy beams under cover before an outburst of tropical rain. This was tedious physical labor. The Doctor noticed a Negro—in a white suit—sitting near a patient whom he had come to visit. Schweitzer called out, "Hello, friend! Won't you lend us a hand?" The Negro replied, "I don't drag wood about. I am an intellectual." Schweitzer replied, "How lucky you are. I tried to be an intellectual too, but didn't succeed."

He has a shrewd sense of values, and a nice sardonic sense of humor. When he visited the United States for the first (and only) time in 1949, to attend the Goethe Festival in Aspen, Colorado, he was much impressed by the attention he got from the news photographers. "Dear me!" he exclaimed. "You obviously think that I must be as important as a prize-fighter!"

He never wears a necktie (while in Africa) unless he is officiating at a funeral or similar occasion. In fact he owns only one necktie, which he bought in 1928. When questioned about this by one of his biographers he replied, "Why have more than one tie? After all I can only wear one at a time."[13]

When he finishes writing a chapter of whatever book he is working on he loops a string through the pages, and hangs them behind his desk, "like a bag of pheasants." (Of course metal clips cannot be used in Lambaréné, since they rust at once.)

He will not step on a flower needlessly, and would never dream of harming an animal. One reporter in Paris has, however, recorded that he saw Schweitzer, in a moment of irritation, squash a moth that was bothering him.

He is good-humoredly proud of his *pirogues*, which he calls "my fleet" and of the fact that his hospital runs on its own time, fifteen minutes ahead of Lambaréné time.

He saw me writing notes one afternoon, and asked me if I kept a carbon.

---

[13] From *The Africa of Albert Schweitzer*, by Charles R. Joy and Melvin Arnold, *op. cit.* The anecdote about intellectuals is from Schweitzer's *Out of the Primeval Forest*.

I said no, and he said that he didn't either, but that when he is working on a manuscript he writes a message on the first page—"Dear Thief: If you happen by chance to *find* this, please return it to the above address, and you will have my eternal gratitude."

He writes everything in a neat round longhand, and can only find time to write at night when the day's work is done. He told me, "Writing costs a man a lot."

He shocked the customs officers at Bordeaux on one occasion when he boarded his ship carrying with him some unanswered mail. It filled four potato sacks.

SOME MISCELLANEOUS ATTITUDES

The tragedy of music is that it can only express with limited intelligence the concrete image from which it has sprung.
—ALBERT SCHWEITZER

It is hard to keep oneself really humane.
—ALBERT SCHWEITZER

He admires greatly Romain Rolland, the Stoic philosophers, Frederick the Great, Lao-tse, and, among musicians aside from Bach, César Franck (also an organist), Wagner, Schubert, Beethoven, and Mozart. He likes Russian music if it is "real." Somewhat grudgingly he concedes that Shostakovich is real, and he has a certain regard for Rimsky-Korsakoff. He has, or so it seemed from his conversation with us, more appreciation of Goethe than of Shakespeare. He thinks that Socrates was a "demagogue," and that most real progress in Europe has come in periods of enlightened, benevolent despotism. I asked him if he had hated Hitler. Miss Haussknecht answered for him saying that he hated nobody, but that if Hitler had been drowning he, Schweitzer, would have hesitated a moment before taking off his shoes to dive in and rescue him.

Everything, he thinks, must have a moral basis—particularly art. He has profound regard for Tolstoy for this among other reasons. André Gide he cannot understand, because Gide carries self-analysis to such intricate and exasperating lengths. "One day he writes in his journal that he takes tea for breakfast, and the next day coffee. What difference does it make?" When I asked him if he thought that Napoleon was a great man he snorted a rough "*Non!*" He had correspondence with Gandhi on occasion; apparently he thinks that Gandhi was politically naïve. Freud, whom he knew and liked, puzzled him. "He was better as a man than in his work." He had great respect and liking for Dr. Einstein. He mentioned Hegel once and when I said that Hegel was the father of Marx, he replied with a snort of contempt, "Only Marx made Marx!" I asked him whether he thought that any war could ever be justifiable, and he answered that he could not answer—he did not know. I asked him what had given him most pleasure in life, and he replied, "Whatever I am working at."

ATTITUDE TO THE AFRICANS

> The idea of the rights of man was formed and developed . . . when society was an organized and stable thing . . . In a disordered society the very well-being of man himself often demands that his fundamental rights be abridged.
> —ALBERT SCHWEITZER

Africans try Schweitzer's patience sorely, no matter how much he loves them in the abstract. So many are shiftless; so many lack any sense of responsibility or joy in achievement. He says that his Negroes have nothing whatever to do after work is finished each afternoon, but that it never occurs to them to fish in the river—yet they complain of protein deficiency! If they get any education at all, they promptly move into the towns, and try to become stenographers. Yet he, Schweitzer, out in the hinterland, cannot for the life of him find a good carpenter, or even somebody to tend a field. He smote himself on the breast telling us this. "I am the only peasant!"

It shocked him frightfully that there had been recent riots in Port Gentil, with bloodshed. Apparently he attributed these to the free-and-easy ways Africans have been encouraged to assume. Much in contemporary French policy does not please the Doctor. There was even a "revolt" in the Schweitzer hospital itself a year or so ago, which the staff had to put down; Schweitzer himself was away in Europe at the time. Patients armed with knives marched on the inhabitants of the leper village, saying that the lepers had threatened them.

He did not seem to have much faith in the educability of Africans in his vicinity, or even their good will. He said, "I put a mango here, a banana here, a breadfruit here. The Africans do not know enough to tell which tree is which. I explain. They walk away and by the time they reach the river in ten minutes they have forgotten."

He reported a colloquy with one of his native boys, who asked him why he was not as good as Schweitzer was. "I'll tell you," the Doctor replied. "Each of us goes out into the forest with an ax, a hammer, and a saw. A tornado comes. You drop your tools and run. I retreat more slowly, and pick up the tools you have dropped. So, when we return, I have six tools, you have none. Is that not so?" The boy replied, "Yes." Schweitzer went on, "And does this not prove that I am better than you are?" The boy shook his head, not seeing the point at all.

To be civilized, the Doctor thinks, a person must pass four tests. He must not lie, he must not steal, he must prove that he values property, and he must be kind to animals.

The following is a striking passage:

> A word about the relations between the whites and the blacks. What must be the general character of the intercourse between them? Am I to treat the black man as my equal or as my inferior? I must show him that I can respect the dignity of human personality in everyone, and . . . the essential thing is that there shall be a real feeling of brotherliness. How far this is to find complete expression in the sayings and doings of daily life must be settled by circumstances. The Negro is a child, and with children nothing can be done without the use of authority. We must, therefore, so arrange the circumstances of daily life that my natural authority can find expression. With regard to the Negroes, then, I have coined the formula: "I am your brother, it is true, but your elder brother."

And:

> Have we white people the right to impose our rule on primitive and semi-primitive peoples? . . . No, if we only want to rule over them and draw material advantages from their country. Yes, if we seriously desire to educate them and help them attain to a condition of well-being.[14]

We sat on upturned boxes in the garden, and Schweitzer gave us a little lecture. Boys passed bearing pails of water, which, like much else in the hospital, are marked sternly with the initials A.S.B. (the "B" stands for the maiden name of his wife); Schweitzer saw that the paint was rubbed off one, and he groaned aloud, "Now they will steal it!" A boy moved slowly. The Doctor turned to him with a resigned, exasperated plea: *"Voulez-vous marcher? VOULEZ-vous!"* A moment later he was telling us that the only way to reach the African was "through the heart." We climbed toward the camp and saw a baby chicken with its eyes scratched out. Schweitzer comforted it tenderly.

FAREWELL

On our last night at the hospital we were invited after dinner to accompany Schweitzer to his small bedroom and adjoining office. Here is a tatterdemalion assortment of books, papers, stores, tools—a saw was lying

[14] Joy's *Anthology*, pp. 179-80.

across a sheaf of manuscript—empty tins, piles of music, and bits of carpentry. On a wall I saw the portrait of a bearded dignitary—Charles Darwin. I could not have been more surprised if it had been Beelzebub. "Darwin sought the truth," said Schweitzer calmly. We peeked further, and saw his favorite antelope, Theodora, behind a rude net of wire, and two chimpanzees in a cage, Romeo and Juliet. All sleep in close proximity. Schweitzer led us to his celebrated piano, which has organ-like pedal attachments; this is lined with zinc to keep termites out, weighs three tons, and was presented to him by the Paris Bach Society when he first set out for Africa forty-two years ago. Schweitzer, my wife, and I all sat squeezed together on the small bench—indeed there was no other place to sit down—and he played some Bach superbly. This brief nocturnal recital was the last touch, the authentic Schweitzer ceremony of farewell. He was not playing for us particularly. He plays every night, especially when his eyes are tired. He said to one recent visitor, "I play for my antelope." But it was a fascinating privilege to hear him play, and it is this picture of him, sitting at that battered old wreck of a piano in the middle of the silent jungle, that I shall always remember as most typical of him—this crusty old Bismarck of the spirit, this magnificent tyrant with a heart of gold.

CHAPTER 36

Introduction to British West Africa

In Africa it is always five minutes to twelve.
—ANONYMOUS

We reach new vistas now, and deal with an entity markedly different from any we have met in this whole book so far—British West Africa. Four countries comprise this challenging region: Nigeria, the Gold Coast, Sierra Leone, and the Gambia. Nigeria and the Gold Coast, the most important, lie on the underside of the African westward bulge, facing the Gulf of Guinea. Sierra Leone and the Gambia are further west, on the Atlantic. From Bathurst, the capital of the Gambia, to the eastern edge of Nigeria is as far as from San Francisco to the tip of Texas. Much of this area—including French and other territories interspersed between the British units—was known in older days as the Slave Coast, for the good reason that most African slaves who came to the West Indies and the United States derived from here. Perhaps "derivation" is not the proper word to describe a process which entailed the most frightful suffering, as Africans were plucked out of the bush, caged as if they were animals, abominably whipped, and transported across the seas. Almost the entire Negro population of the United States, to say nothing of the Negro and semi-Negro peoples in Central and South America, is descended from forebears on these Guinea shores. Put in another way, one-tenth of the population of the United States—roughly fifteen million Negroes—has a West African origin. One out of every ten living Americans has an ancestor from Nigeria or nearby.

This Slave Coast not only imprisoned and killed blacks; it killed whites too, and is the part of Africa known to legend as the "White Man's Grave." The undisputed king of the Guinea Coast was, for centuries, the mosquito. Yellow fever, blackwater fever, malaria, were this king's chosen and malign weapons. The sinister deadliness of the West Coast climate is not merely a matter of remote record, but a living memory. A favorite anecdote describes the consular officer who, not too long ago, found himself assigned to Nigeria and asked about his pension. "Pension?" his chief in the Colonial Office replied. "My dear fellow, nobody who goes to Nigeria ever lives long enough to be retired."

Graham Greene (incidentally, the scene of his *The Heart of the Matter* is Freetown, the capital of Sierra Leone) wrote recently, "The phrase 'the White Man's Grave' has become a music hall cliché to those who have never seen the little crumbling cemeteries of the West Coast . . . Mungo Park in the course of his second expedition reported: 'I am sorry to say that of forty-five Europeans who left the Gambia in perfect health, five only are at present alive, viz. three soldiers (one deranged in his mind), Lieutenant Martyn and myself.'" Park, one of the boldest of West African explorers, was drowned (1805) shortly after sending back this report. Not a single member of his expedition survived.

I have heard it argued that the most important single human being in the whole history of Africa is Sir Ronald Ross, who never even saw it except for a brief trip (in 1899) to Sierra Leone. Ross did not discover the malaria parasite, but it was he who proved that malaria was carried by the Anopheles mosquito, and who worked out consequent techniques in mosquito control that have been adopted all over the world, and have saved countless millions of lives. Without Ross, large parts of the earth's surface now flourishing would be uninhabitable.[1]

Several other factors have, of course, contributed to eliminating or diminishing disease along the Guinea Coast—refrigeration, drugs, wire screening, DDT and other insecticides, and above all the airplane. If you get sick these days, you can be flown out. The air distance between Lagos and London is 3,442 miles but you can fly this in eighteen hours. Between Nigeria and the rest of the world there are about forty flights by major airlines every day.

The White Man's Grave is a grave no longer, and, with reasonable luck and if you pick the season right, Lagos is not more uncomfortable than St. Louis or Atlanta in summer. Still, nobody should be too cavalier about the forces of African nature. The Guinea Coast is not the healthiest place in the world by any means; British civil servants there still get ten weeks

[1] Ross was an odd fish. He failed to pass his examinations in medical school because he was more interested in music and epic drama. Midway in his career, working in India, he "collected malarious Hindus the way a terrier collects rats." He wrote some weird verse. He won the Nobel Prize in 1902, and died in 1932. See Paul de Kruif, *Microbe Hunters*, pp. 278-298.

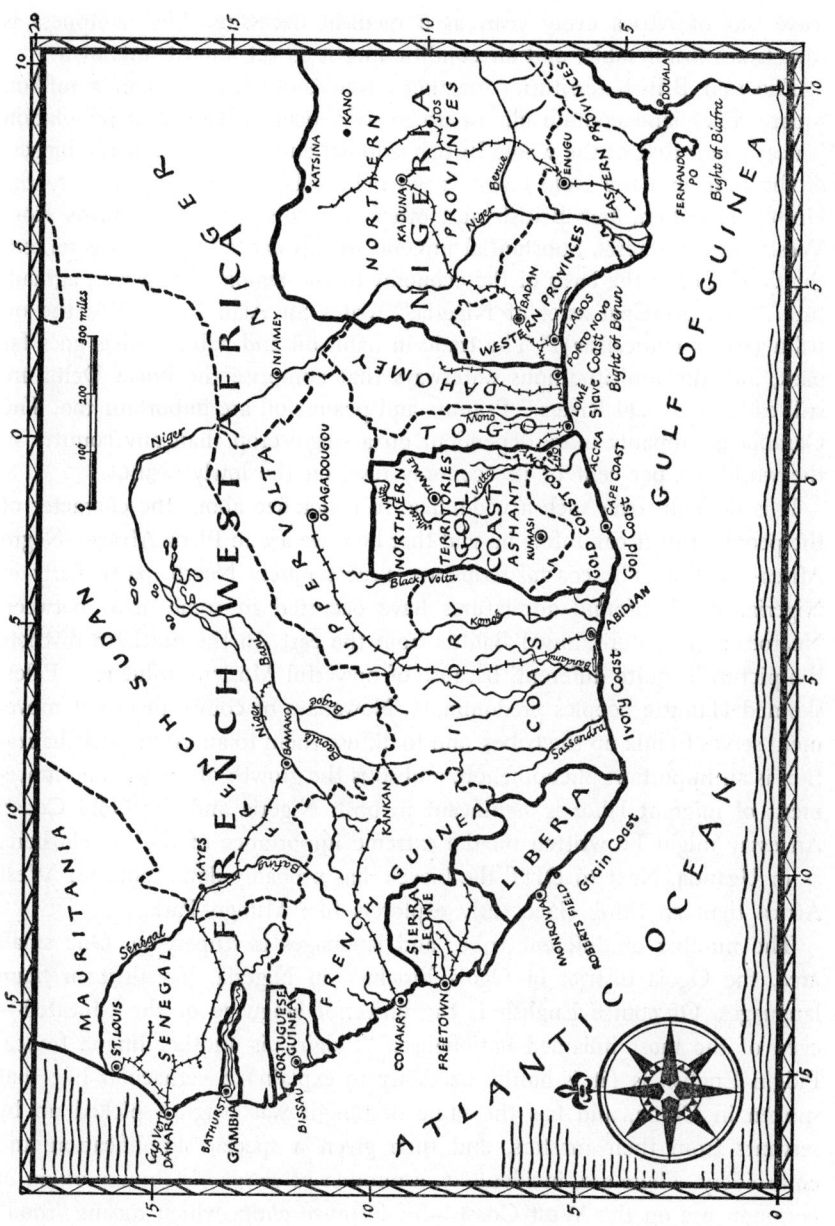

leave out of Africa every year, as a medical necessity. The dampness is sometimes insufferable, and air conditioning is as yet almost unknown.

The four British territories together cover something like half a million square miles, and contain almost 40,000,000 people. The total population is nearly half that of the whole British colonial empire. Nigeria is the biggest of the four, and the Gold Coast is the richest. None pays any taxes to the United Kingdom, but British and other investors get large returns from West Coast interests. Substantial mineral wealth exists in both Nigeria and the Gold Coast; the basis of the economy of the region is, however, agriculture. "The principal asset of Nigeria," writes Sir Alan Burns,[2] "is the oil palm (*elaeis guineensis*)." The trade in palm oil and palm kernels goes far back, and the multitudinous waterways that comprise the Niger Delta are still called the "Oil Rivers." Peanuts and peanut oil are important too. The Gambia is probably more dependent on a single crop than any country in the world; 97 per cent of its economy rests on the lowly peanut.

It is difficult, over such a wide area, to generalize about the character of the people. But it can safely be said that here we are in Black Africa—Negro Africa—at last. The coastal strips are almost purely Negro, particularly in Nigeria. But profound admixtures have occurred in some areas between Negroes and lighter-skinned Bantus from the east. In the northern districts the picture is quite different, because of powerful Moslem influences. Paler-skinned Hamitic peoples predominate. Nowadays of course incessant movement serves to mix up the tribes, and to diffuse them to an extent; detribalization is an important phenomenon, and so is the growth of towns. The movement of migrant labor is significant in both Nigeria and the Gold Coast. An essay might be written on the extreme importance of the bicycle here, as in Uganda. Next to DDT the bicycle has probably done more for West Africa than anything since early explorers like Mungo Park.

The number of different tribes and languages is stupefying. One small area, the Ogoja district of Ogoja Province in Nigeria, has thirteen *main* languages. Of course English is the universal language of the educated—even of the most inflamed nationalists. "Pidgin" is another lingua franca. Pidgin English is (it is hardly necessary to explain) a vernacular like that spoken in China, and has the same origin—it was English picked up by servants from their masters, and then given a special simplification and embroidery. There are, incidentally, a number of words of Chinese origin in common use on the West Coast—for instance *chop*, which means "food" or "to eat." This has even penetrated into French. In Brazzaville people say,

---

[2] In his admirable *History of Nigeria*. Sir Alan Burns is a former Governor of the Gold Coast and a distinguished specialist on Nigeria.

"*Voulez-vous chopper chez nous ce soir?*" or "*Avez-vous eu votre chop?*"
The following is a passage from Genesis transposed into pidgin:

> An de Lawd, He done go work hard for make dis ting dey call um Earth. For six day de Lawd He work an He done make all ting—everyt'ing He go put for Earth. Plenty beef, plenty cassava, plenty banana, plenty yam, plenty guinea corn, plenty mango, plenty groundnut—everyt'ing. An for de wata He put plenty fish, an for de air He put plenty kinda bird.
>
> After six day de Lawd He done go sleep. An when He sleep, plenty palaver start for dis place dey call um Heaven. Dis Heaven be place where we go live after we done die, if we no been so-so bad for dis Earth. . . .
>
> De headman of dem angels, dey call um Gabriel. When dis palaver start for Heaven there be plenty humbug by bad angel, dey call um Lucifer. An Gabriel done catch Lucifer an go beat um. An palaver stop, one time.
>
> An de Lawd tell Gabriel he be good man too much an He go dash Gabriel one trumpet . . . An Lucifer go for hellfire where he be headman now.
>
> After, de Lawd done go look um dis ting dey call um Earth an He savvy dat no man be for seat. So de Lawd take small piece earth an He go breathe—an man day. An de Lawd He go call dis man Hadam.
>
> De Lawd He say: "Hadam, you see dis garden? Dey call um Paradise. Everyt'ing for dis garden be for you—but dem mango tree that be for middle garden dat no be for you. Dat tree be white man chop, dat no be black man chop. You no go chop um or you get plenty pain for belly. You savvy?"
>
> An Hadam He say: "Yessah, Lawd, I savvy."

Later comes the fall:

> Den de Lawd dun come back for Earth an He go call Hadam. But Hadam he no be for seat. He go fear de Lawd an done go for bush, one time. Again de Lawd call: "Hadam!" An Hadam he say with small voice: "Yessah, Lawd." An de Lawd He say "Close me, Hadam, close me." An Hadam he close de Lawd.
>
> De Lawd say: "Wassa matta, Hadam, why you go for bush?" An Hadam say: "I no get cloth Lawd, so I no want dat you dun see me naked." An de Lawd He be vex too much. He say: "What ting dis who tell you you be naked?" Den He say: "Ah-ha, you dun go chop dem mango from tree for middle garden." An Hadam say: "I no chop um Lawd. Dem woman you dun make for me, she go put um for groundnut stew."
>
> Den de Lawd He make plenty palaver an He dun drove Hadam an Heva from Paradise.[3]

[3] In the pidgin version of the story of Noah, the Ark is a ship of the Elder Dempster Line, the foremost shipping company in West Africa. Incidentally, there is a legend, probably untrue, that courses in pidgin were given in German universities when Germany ruled Togoland and the Cameroons.

Nationalist Africans are not amused by the above. They dislike pidgin, just as they hate talk of *juju*, the name for black magic in Nigeria. Pidgin and *juju* are behind them, they like to think. From this it is an easy transition to an important, vitalizing point. The chief generalization to make about West Africa as a whole is that it is educated enough, despite its huge illiteracy, to want more and more education. What this part of the continent stands for most of all is *advance* and confidence that it can make its own good future, under its own government. Today's fetishes are an English grammar and the polling booth.

WEST AND EAST AFRICA—HOW THEY DIFFER

1. West Africa has known European penetration of one sort or another for well over three hundred years, whereas in Kenya and elsewhere in East Africa, as we know, substantial European influence only began in the 1890's. Hence, West Africa (at least on the coastal strip) has had a much longer and more productive contact with western civilization than East. Nigerian students, mostly mulatto, were sent to London for education as far back as the 1700's. In the Gold Coast we met Africans, members of the upper class, partly of Danish, British, and other European blood, who have a tradition of education centuries old. (There is no African "upper class" in Kenya).

2. Paradoxically, West Africa was penetrated by a class of Europeans inferior on the whole to those who came to East Africa. Europeans who opened up the West Coast were mostly of the "gin and slavery" school, ruffians and adventurers; in the East they were merchants, government servants, and missionaries. Hence, Africans on the West Coast today, if they look into history, are likely to be more resentful of white influences. They suffer from a longer background of outrage and hate.

3. European influences quite aside, West Coast Africans derive from a higher stage of culture than those in the East. There are no surviving works of art in Tanganyika, say, or Nyasaland, to compare with the Benin bronzes and other objects of art in Nigeria. Even the northern, interior regions of West Africa have a very definite *African* history. This may have been defaced by various barbarisms, but it was a real history, and quite rich. Kano, the chief town of Northern Nigeria, has written records going back to AD 900.

4. Climate and the mosquito. The highlands of East and Central Africa are healthy by and large; the swampy, deliquescent West Coast is not. This has tended to keep white settlement in West Africa at the minimum, and it is this which makes the chief political and social difference between the

INTRODUCTION TO BRITISH WEST AFRICA 741

two regions today. Europeans came to West Africa to administer or exploit, but not to stay. There is no white settler class at all as in Kenya or the Rhodesias. And, as we know, white settlement can be the most irritating and dangerous of all impediments to the development of an orderly society. No possibility of a Mau Mau uprising in Nigeria exists, because no white settlers exist, and there is no incentive for Africans to revolt against whites whom they consider to be encroaching on their land. Here in the West, these are *African* countries. The population ratios are startling. I have already mentioned that in Nigeria (population probably 31,500,000) there are only 11,750 whites. In the Gold Coast there are only 6,770 whites to 4,500,000 Africans; in Sierra Leone only 598 to 2,000,000; in the Gambia exactly 222 to 275,000. Moreover the West African governments now being consolidated are not white or plural, as in East or Central Africa; they are *black*— indigenous African native governments.

5. No Indian "problem" exists in West Africa, for the simple reason that there are practically no Indians. This means that West Africa is free, for good or ill, of the fermentation and enlivenment that Indians bring to a community. Only about 1,900 Asians live in Nigeria; most of these are Syrians or Lebanese who play no political or intellectual role. Compare this figure to that for Kenya, where, in a country much smaller, more than 150,000 Asians live. For Accra or Lagos to have Asian mayors (as do Kampala and Dar es Salaam) would be inconceivable. Nor can there be any persecution of an Indian community, as in South Africa. As to commerce, the great trading companies in West Africa are European— for instance two French companies, the Société Commerciale de L'Ouest Africain (SCOA) and the Compagnie Française de l'Afrique Occidentale; a famous Swiss company; and above all the United Africa Company, the largest trading company in the world, which is a branch of the huge Unilever empire and has widespread economic power.[4] Small retail trade is largely in the hands of Africans themselves—mostly women.

6. Land tenure. There are exceptions to the rule but basically *white Europeans are not allowed to own land in Nigeria and the Gold Coast.* They may procure timber or mineral concessions,[5] and they are an obvious factor in the business life of the community, but they do not own land. No European, not even an Englishman, is so much as allowed by the British to *enter* Nigeria without being required to prove that his presence is "necessary," and without posting a sizable bond. This is a matter of strict law and

---

[4] One big Indian trading company does, however, exist—the house of Chellaram.
[5] But all mineral wealth belongs to the state; concessionaires are merely given rights to work it.

policy. Even if settlers came, they could not settle. Lord Lugard, the proconsul who was the founder of modern Nigeria, set it down some fifty years ago—and set it down once for all—that "the land was the property of the people, held in trust for them by their chiefs," and not purchasable by foreigners. No European may buy, sell, or speculate with land. "This was held to be essential for the moral and material welfare of the inhabitants ... The duty of the white man is mainly that of administration and his material advantage lies in trade."

7. All these and other interrelated factors have combined to produce the dominant and unique political characteristic of Nigeria and the Gold Coast today, namely, that they have made (under the British) such marked political progress that they are on the brink of self-government. Here, although it is colonial territory still, Africans are running Africa. The ministers, mostly African, not only administer policy but make it. A largely *black* bureaucracy has grown up. The Gold Coast has virtually complete independence within the Commonwealth now, and parts of Nigeria are not far behind; Nigeria is fiercely jealous of the Gold Coast's progress. The target date for Nigerian independence, accepted by the British, is 1956.

8. Industrialization scarcely exists; a factory is as rare as a mangrove swamp in Yorkshire, or a cocoa palm in Massachusetts. Economy rests mostly on raw materials.

9. The country (at least along the coast) for the most part *looks* altogether different from East Africa; we have left behind us now, except in a few localities, high grasslands and brittle, eroded plateaus. The weather is different; here rain is really rain. And above all the towns are different. Lagos and Accra are *black* cities, not mixed or white. Lagos no more resembles Salisbury than Addis Ababa resembles New York.[6]

10. West Africa is not as much of a unit as East Africa. Various unifying agencies exist, but the four countries of the West Coast do not have the tendencies to cohesion of Kenya, Uganda, and Tanganyika.

SIERRA LEONE AND THE GAMBIA

It disturbs geographical and political sequence to describe these two dependencies at this juncture, but serves convenience. Sierra Leone is a sizable block of territory (27,925 square miles) lying between Liberia and French Guinea. FREETOWN, the capital, has an annual rainfall of about 150 inches (which means that it is very wet indeed), a temperature that hovers

---

[6] A small (perhaps not so small) incidental point is that few West Coast ports have docks or proper harbor facilities; ship have to be unloaded by lighters plunging through the surf.

in the low eighties during most of the hot season, enchanting hills, and one of the finest natural (if undeveloped) harbors in the world. During World War II it was a staging point for Atlantic convoys, and on one remarkable occasion no fewer than 250 ships were anchored here at the same time, including both the *Queen Elizabeth* and *Queen Mary*. Freetown is also the site of Fourah Bay College, which has been affiliated to Durham University since 1876, and is one of the most notable institutions of learning for Africans in Africa. The Carnegie Corporation of New York donated $8,000 to Fourah Bay last year. Estimates of the population of Sierra Leone range from 1,700,000 to 2,000,000. There are about thirteen different tribes, the most important being the Mende and the Temne. The country is 99.8 per cent black.

Sierra Leone has an intriguing and romantic history, which resembles closely that of Liberia. It was founded, like Liberia, as a haven for freed Negro slaves, but the company promoting this worthy enterprise was, of course, not American but British—the Sierra Leone Society. The first settlers (1787) were four hundred Africans rescued from slave ships by the British navy; with them came thirty white prostitutes from the slums of London. These together are the foundation of contemporary Freetown society. The Sierra Leoners made a much better thing of their country than the Americo-Liberians made of Liberia. To this day the major line of cleavage is that between the Creoles, as descendants of the first settlers are called, and the backwoods natives. The pure Creoles are few in number (perhaps only 30,000 in all) but until comparatively recent times they altogether dominated the country, as the Americo-Liberians ran—and still run—Liberia.[7] The aristocratic Creoles still look down on the primitive aborigines with supercilious contempt. Here we have social, political, and economic stratifications within a black society.

Sierra Leone has traditionally been one of the most loyal of British colonies. I asked a British official about the nationalists, and he replied, "Our nationalists have so much better *manners* than those in the Gold Coast and Nigeria!" Be this as it may be nationalist pressures are emphatic these days, and are getting more emphatic all the time. The British, bending before the wave, have given substantial political reform to the country. There are two parties, the National Council for the Colony of Sierra Leone (NCCS), and the SLPP, or Sierra Leone People's Party. One important nationalist leader is Wallace Johnson, a father of the independence movement not only in Sierra Leone itself but elsewhere on the West Coast; he has paid particular attention to the development of trade unions, and in

[7] See Chapter 43 below.

1946 set up a West African National Secretariat in London, to correlate nationalist propaganda and activity in all the West African dependencies. In February, 1955, Sierra Leone suffered some fierce rioting, following a strike declared by the Artisans and General Workers Union. Again let us emphasize the point that, here in British West Africa, we have come a long distance emotionally and politically from East and Central Africa. Imagine an independent labor union being permitted to exist—much less make a strike—in Mozambique or the Congo!

The biggest economic issue in Sierra Leone has to do with diamonds. Taxes on diamond production contribute about 15 per cent of the country's revenue. But smuggling has been so phenomenally widespread and successful that more diamonds leave the country illegally than legally. So the authorities are doing their best to keep illicit diamond buying and smuggling at a minimum. Diamonds are a monopoly of the Sierra Leone Selection Trust.

*

The Gambia is one of the most oddly shaped countries in the world; it looks like an earthworm, and fits around the Gambia River like a long, tight, wrinkled sleeve. This is the oldest, smallest, and poorest British colony in West Africa. It has been British since 1661, and was governed for a time by a company called romantically the Royal Adventurers of England. The Gambia as it exists today covers about 4,100 square miles and has roughly 275,000 people. Strange as it may seem, most are Moslem. The chief tribe is the Mandingo, and in the whole country only about 4,000 people are literate. BATHURST, the capital (population about 20,000) has no hotel other than a government resthouse with six beds, and no restaurant. President Roosevelt stayed in Bathurst briefly after his wartime visit to Casablanca in 1942, and did not like it much. The Gambia was the scene recently of an ambitious "poultry project" operated by the Colonial Development Corporation, to grow eggs for export to Great Britain. It did not do well.

The Gambia, despite its poverty and extreme lack of development, is advanced politically and has an articulate nationalist movement. The British, marching with the times, gave it a new constitution in 1954, which strongly increases African power both in the Executive and Legislative Councils. There are three African ministers (more than Kenya has). Two active political parties exist, and the first general election in the country's history took place in 1954.

Nationalists in the Gambia have every reason to be proud of these

INTRODUCTION TO BRITISH WEST AFRICA 745

developments. Gambia has a right to be free like any other country. But it could hardly survive alone as a free state without substantial outside help. African nationalists themselves concede that the Gambia—by itself—has little future, and in curious fact one important nationalist grievance against the British is that the West Coast is "Balkanized"—split into too many fragments. The British, they think, should not only give national liberation, but at the same time lay the groundwork now for a future federation of all the West African communities.

*

Now we proceed to Nigeria, which is as different from Sierra Leone and the Gambia as Einstein is from Copernicus.

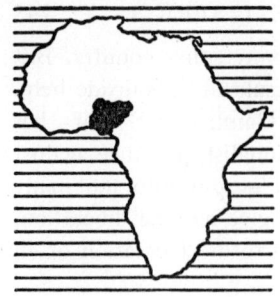

CHAPTER 37

Complexities and Achievements in Nigeria

*Beware and take heed of the Bight of Benin
Where few come out though many go in.*
—ANONYMOUS

The only way to train people for self-government is to let them govern.
—WILLIAM CLARK

WHEN Sir John Stuart Macpherson became Governor of Nigeria in 1948 he went out into the hinterland on a forty-day tour and made many speeches. He was well aware of Nigerian complexities and was not surprised to find out that, in one town, he had to have three different interpreters. But it did surprise him, and surprised him greatly, to discover that the first interpreter took twelve minutes to translate his four-minute speech, the second interpreter eight, and the third interpreter four. The explanation came later—the first interpreter was translating into three different Nigerian languages, the second into two, and the third merely into one!

Indeed Nigeria, the largest country in Africa from the point of view of population, has many different tribes—probably 250 in all—and different languages. When the Nigerian government prepared recently a series of pamphlets to explain the new constitution, these had to be published in twelve languages besides English—Yoruba, Urhobo, Sobo, and Bini in the West; Ibibio, Efik, and three varieties of Ibo in the East; and Hausa, Fulani, and Kanuri in the North.

I would not go into details like this—we have encountered often enough a bewildering variety of peoples and languages within a limited area—except for the fact that the lack of homogeneity of Nigeria is by all odds **its** overriding political and national problem. The curse of this great country

COMPLEXITIES AND ACHIEVEMENTS IN NIGERIA

is, in fact, sectionalism. Nigeria is a geographical monstrosity—three countries in one. There are three immense regions each with its own independent character, Northern, Western, Eastern. West and East together are commonly known as the "south." In unusual circumstances, which I will describe later, we met Obafemi Awolowo, one of Nigeria's leading politicians. He said, "West and East Nigeria are as different as Ireland from Germany. The North is as different from either as China."

Nigeria is the biggest British colony in the world. By the census of 1952-53 it has a population of almost 31,500,000; in other words, it has two and a half times more people than the Union of South Africa, which is often thought of as the "biggest" country on the continent, and is a third more populous than Egypt. Of the total population, as I have mentioned in the preceding chapter, only 11,750 are Europeans. We are on the West Coast now; this is *Black* Africa and make no mistake about it.

What else is this extravagantly colossal and turbulent Nigeria? It covers some 373,000 square miles and is thus larger in area than any European country except Russia. Its politics are more confused and tumultuous than those of any country I have ever been in except possibly Chile, and its national income has sextupled since 1939. A case might be made that the handsomest skyscraper in the world—the Lever Building in New York, floating on Park Avenue like a luminous glass box—could not have been built without Nigeria, since the Lever interests have vast holdings in the country, and this is where the palm oil comes from that goes into soap.

Nigeria has 509 doctors, 41 cinemas, and 12 daily newspapers—for more than 30,000,000 people. Nevertheless, by African standards, it is an advanced community. There are only about 20,000 Nigerians who have the equivalent of an American high-school education, but Nigeria competed for the first time in the Olympic Games in 1952. The rail trip from Lagos, the capital, to Port Harcourt covers roughly a thousand miles; the journey will take three long days, if you are lucky. But Nigeria has an excellent broadcasting service. The country has a celebrated wind, the *harmattan*, the "wind of the white horsemen"; and in Lagos I saw a witch doctor with a mask made solidly of small scarlet beads. The UN does admirable work in Nigeria through such of its agencies as the World Health Organization, UNICEF, and a "Language Clearing Center." But isolated spots still exist where natives have never seen a white man. There are, however, no "closed areas" as in Kenya, and no place in the entire country (except possibly near the Cameroons border) where a white man or woman is not perfectly safe to wander about alone. But *Africans* do not like to go out alone at night in some areas for fear of cannibals.[1] I met a British official in the interior. He had a thin brittle voice, profound erudition, and hands like little puddings. He said, "You must remember that this is a mad country—*quite mad!*"

Define Nigeria further. It is a British dependency still ruled in the last analysis by the Colonial Office in London. But—the details are abstruse, and we will go into them later—it has a functioning *African* government (under a British governor) and substantial autonomy. It is nearer complete independence, within the Commonwealth, than any British region in Africa except the Gold Coast. Here for the first time in Negro Africa we confront *black nationalism on the governmental level.* Yet Nigeria is probably 95 per cent illiterate!

One more preliminary point: Nigeria as we know it today was not born till 1914, and hence is only a little more than forty years old.

TO BEGIN WITH

We will get nowhere in Nigeria without introductory mention of two giant factors, color bar and nationalism. Practically speaking color bar does not exist. We have come a long, long way now from Kenya and the Rhodesias. A visitor from Johannesburg will be stunned by Lagos. The day I arrived I asked the kind of question I had been asking all over Africa. "Can an African drink here?" Answer: "Good God, yes!" "Is there any curfew keeping Africans off the streets at night?" "Good God, no!" I asked if African children had trouble getting into the schools, and the answer was that there is no provision for the education of *white* children in Nigeria. I asked—a supreme test of color bar—if an African policeman could arrest a white man, and heard the answer that this happened all the time, and caused no comment. On that very day, the trial had begun of a white man charged with manslaughter, before an African judge.

This is, in other words, the first country we have encountered since the Sudan and Ethiopia where the African is not discriminated against on account of race. Africans shop in perfect freedom anywhere, go to any bank or post office, and hold any kind of job. Nigeria pullulates with Nigerian officials, although most high civil servants are still British. I sat next to an African lady at a formal dinner party and asked her about color bar and

---

[1] Perhaps they have not forgotten what their grandfathers told them. Not more than a hundred years ago in the Calabar region cannibalism was still rife. Missionaries saw such things as "two men grinding human skulls into powder which they put in the palms of their hands and licked off like sugar" (*Calabar, the Church of England Mission*, by Donald F. McFarlan, p. 5).

she replied that she had never heard the term. An Englishman told me, "No one even *thinks* of color here." He was exaggerating. Discrimination does still exist in social and other minor spheres. There are few friendships—outside the office—between Briton and African, and Nigerian ladies whom I met in British houses were shy, uncomfortable, and aloof, not out of fear that they might be snubbed—which would not be likely to happen—but out of a subterranean, ineffaceable feeling that they did not belong.

On the other hand, the best club in Lagos, *the* club—and this is another supreme test, since the Englishman's club is often more important than his home—has now accepted its first African member, and a few (not many) mixed marriages have taken place in fairly high levels of society. A well-known gynecologist in Lagos, Dr. Adekoye Majekudunmi, has an English wife, and so has one minister from the Eastern Region. District Officers in the North have on occasion formed relationships with African women—the beautiful Fulanis—and sometimes even marry them.[2]

I made the mistake (I had made the same mistake in the Cameroons) of using the word "native" when I arrived in Lagos. The Governor himself chided me gently, "We do not use the word 'native' here; we say 'Nigerian.'" And this, of course, is as it should be. Nigerians *are* Nigerian. Sensitiveness about the word "native" has even reached the political zone. A member of the Legislative Council introduced recently a motion to forbid its use in debate, and even to expunge it from the record of previous sessions. The British agreed in principle, but in the end the proposal could not be carried out because it was too impracticable.

Again, what a massive and exciting contrast all this is to most of the rest of Africa! One day before lunch at Government House we had cocktails with two or three smart young *Negro* officers of the West African Frontier Force, a famous regiment. And they were *officers!*[3] They were having drinks in Government House! More than this, all had been former aides-de-camp to the Governor himself! To become an ADC is, of course, the dream of any young officer, white or black. But this was the only place on the continent where I ever met a black ADC. The next night we dined with Sir John Macpherson. I blinked. I could not believe my eyes. Sir John had an African lady on his right as a matter of course; of the total assembly of perhaps thirty persons of high rank, half were African. This dinner was

---

[2] Nigeria does not have District Commissioners. Officers in the field are known as Senior District Officers or District Officers.

[3] The King's African Rifles on the East Coast, a corresponding regiment, has no black officers.

one of the most interesting I went to in all Africa.[4] Three Northern ministers were present, in their glowing, gleaming ceremonial dress. The Honorable Mallam Muhammadu Ribadu, MBE, minister of national resources, wore a pink turban, and looked something like a Falstaff in Oriental costume; the Honorable Mallam Abubakar Tafawa Balewa, OBE, minister of works and transport, had an ultramarine blue cloak and embroidered scarlet cap; the Honorable Shettima Kashim, MBE, minister of social services, wore stiff gold and crimson robes. Another minister (from the East), Dr. E.M.L. Endeley, was present in western dress; he represents the British Cameroons. He is the grandson of a warrior chief; he is also a trade union leader and doctor of medicine. Nigeria spans centuries in a generation.

We proceed now to nationalism, which is at a fierce pitch in Nigeria. I have seldom known such violent sensitiveness about nationalism. The easiest way to introduce the subject is by mentioning Government House again, this time in connection with myself. My wife and I were guests there. We were delighted to accept Sir John Macpherson's hospitality, and had no idea that this would provoke exacerbated polemics in the press.

But I should explain that, at this particular time, a severe constitutional crisis was at its peak. The African ministers representing one important political party, the Action Group, had adopted a non-fraternization policy, and would not accept hospitality from the Governor, although their Northern colleagues did. They were perfectly willing to talk business with Sir John Macpherson in Government House, but they would not accept "hospitality" from him, not even a glass of water. There was nothing particularly personal in this. Macpherson was widely liked as an individual. But Government House symbolizes the Crown, and both West and East were at that time boycotting the Crown as a matter of principle.

Anyway, a day or two after we arrived in Lagos, the following editorial appeared in the *West African Pilot*, the organ of the nationalist leader Dr. Azikiwe, known everywhere as "Zik":

> Mr. John Gunther, an American with a country as young as our great great great grandparents, is in Africa whose written and unwritten histories date back much further than the first Caucasian ape men.

Caucasian ape men? I began to read with more interest:

> And what does this American want in this ancient land, shrouded in mystery, enveloped in enigma, and replete with as yet insoluble conundrums? He wants to write a book not on America, but on Africa.

---

[4] It was also the only occasion when I have ever dined under a punkah with no fewer than six blades.

COMPLEXITIES AND ACHIEVEMENTS IN NIGERIA 751

Has Mr. Gunther ever visited this part of Africa before? No. Has he ever lived in Africa? No. *Are his ancestors African?* [Italics mine.] No. Yet . . . Mr. Gunther of America is here . . . to tell us all about the inside of Africa.

Next day the *Pilot* returned to the attack:

> A man came to Nigeria a few days ago to collect material for a book . . . But he does not stay inside the homes of Africans in order that he may better appreciate their public and private activities. Instead, he lives with a British-born and bred Governor. *How can the people of Africa be sure that Mr. Gunther will not come under the influence of Sir John Macpherson?* It would have been most fitting if this American author were compiling a book on "Inside Britain" or "Inside Government House." However we cannot stop Mr. Gunther from writing his book. . . . But we definitely wish to remind him that authorship is a sacred responsibility. American taste for books is wedded to a nauseatingly refractory sensationalism. . . . Out of our own kindness, we wish to inform Mr. Gunther that Africa is aflame and blazingly indignant against alien rule. For Nigeria freedom comes in 1956 with or without outside consent or assent. Let Mr. Gunther mark that down.

I might have replied that (a) a writer is not necessarily prejudiced by the roof under which he sleeps and that (b) I wrote some chapters of *Inside U.S.A.* that were certainly not anti-Negro while staying in some of the most glaringly white hotels in the American South. But to go on—

The *Daily Service*, another nationalist organ, soon warned me that I must be careful not to portray Africans as "a race of savages living in the forest with animals and beasts," and then the *Daily Success*, which carries under its masthead the slogan TRUTH HAS COME, FALSEHOOD VANISHES, used me as a pretext for the following extraordinary nationalist paean:

> They [the Africans] know that they are Hannibal crossing the Alps when snows were young. They remember that they are the little black Bambino, the pet of the Italian church. They are Chrisna, the Black Christ of India. They observe portraits of Black Virgins strewn all over Europe. They reminisce over paintings in the caves of Austria, of Germany, of Spain, of Portugal, of France.
>
> They know their warm Negro blood flowed in the veins of Cleopatra and that Caesar fell in love with her just the same . . .
>
> They know that these and more are no dreams . . . They know that if they once built pyramids on the Nile, fought with Caesar's battalions, ruled over Spain and dominated the Pyrenees, they the same very black people can be great again and be slaves no more.

At another dinner—also in Government House—I met a high Nigerian official who talked vividly about the "shameful" violence in Kenya. It took me some time to realize that he meant by this British violence against the Mau Maus. He was convinced that the British had willfully incited the Mau Mau rebellion in order to have a pretext for remaining in East Africa.[5]

NIGERIA: ITS HISTORY IN BRIEF

The country was named for the Niger, which means "black." This is the ninth longest river in the world, and is the third great river of Africa, along with the Congo and Nile. For a time it was known as "the Nile of the Negroes," and early geographers thought that it might have a common source with the Nile, rising in the Mountains of the Moon. The Niger begins its slow, heavy flow in the Sahara in French territory, bends around in an enormous loop, bisects Nigeria, and reaches the sea after 2,600 miles. It is longer than the Missouri, and drains a basin (500,000 square miles) about one-sixth the size of the entire United States. Its delta, an amazing sponge dripping with little rivers, covers 14,000 square miles and is bigger than the Delta of the Nile.

Nigerian history along the coast, like that of Sierra Leone and the Gambia, begins with the Portuguese. A Portuguese ship reached the Bight of Benin in 1472. Traders of other countries, including the British in particular, then began to reach this wild, forlorn, fragrant coast—they sought "pepper, Elephant's teeth, oyle of palm, cloth made of Cotton wool very curiously woven, and cloth made of the barke of palme trees."[6]

Soon came traffic much more lucrative, that in human beings. Indeed slavery dominates Nigerian history for almost three hundred years, with all its bizarre and burning horrors. We have already touched on slavery in East Africa; on the West Coast its history was different. *First,* the origin of the Atlantic trade was the discovery of America and the consequent development of rich sugar plantations in the West Indies. When the American aborigines were killed off, as they were promptly, a labor force had to be found somewhere, and slaves from Africa were a marvelously cheap and convenient device to this end. The trade brought fantastic profits. In the Cameroons in the early days the purchase price of a slave was "two measures of Spanish wine" and he could be sold for a thousand ducats, the profit being 5,000 per cent. As late as 1786, a slave could be bought in Nigeria for £2 and sold in America for £65. In that period 100,000 slaves or more were shipped across the Atlantic each year. For every three slaves that got to Amer-

---

[5] This is also the Russian party line. See Chapter 20 above.
[6] Burns, *op. cit.,* p. 65. Also see Burns for fascinating details about the Niger and the slave trade.

ica alive—so frightful were conditions in the boats or on shore before departure—seven died. *Second*, aside from the British and Portuguese there were slave traders of several other nationalities, but Britain got a monopoly of the business by the Treaty of Utrecht in 1712. *Third*, Africans were as much involved in the overseas slave traffic as Europeans, since the latter did not dare as a rule to penetrate inland from the sea. The interior was too dangerous. Instead they bought slaves from warlike African tribes—the Ashanti on the Gold Coast, for instance—who seized and collected other Africans and marched them to the coast. As much barbarity accompanied these raids on Africans by Africans as accompanied the actual voyage across the ocean. *Fourth*, Africans also sought and captured slaves for themselves. In Northern Nigeria, for example, slavery was almost universal until the most recent times; slavery did not become illegal in Nigeria till 1901, and a few domestic slaves are still alive, who have never been emancipated.

A case can be made for slavery and even for the slave trade. It is that tribal wars took place in the African interior without cessation, and that it was better for a man to be taken prisoner and made a domestic slave, or even sold into slavery, than to be killed and perhaps eaten. On a slave raid the object was to get the prisoner alive, and, with luck, he might survive the trip to America or Arabia. On balance, the slave trade (despite its inferno-like horrors) may have saved more lives than it cost. In any case it is the origin of a great many healthy, useful and progressive Negro communities in the United States and elsewhere in the western world.

The British outlawed the slave trade in 1807, after Denmark had done so, and after the United States (1804) forbade the further importation of slaves. But the traffic continued to flourish illicitly, so much so that in the year 1847, for example, more than 80,000 slaves were shipped out of Africa "to all destinations." What finally killed the illicit traffic was a combination of factors—moral feeling in Great Britain, the fact that legitimate trade with Africa was becoming increasingly profitable, and the abolition of slavery by the United States in 1865.

Turn now to British political penetration of Nigeria, a story which we must foreshorten greatly. It began in the North in the 1790's with the extraordinary explorations of Mungo Park and others along the Niger, promoted by private societies in London. It was Park, dressed in a blue coat and tall beaver hat, who first saw the Niger near Timbuktu (in what is now French West Africa)—"the long sought for, majestic Niger, glittering to the morning sun, as broad as the Thames at Westminster, and flowing slowly to the Eastward." Before this it had been thought that the Niger flowed west. Not for many years did the British succeed in establishing themselves securely in Nigeria, so appalling were the difficulties of climate and terrain. Three different entities grew up. In the North administration was carried on largely by the Royal Niger Company, which operated in the traditional manner of chartered companies in those happy imperialist days. Commercial penetration, as in East Africa, preceded political penetration. In the south were two separate governments, first the Oil Rivers Protectorate and later (1893) the Niger Coast Protectorate. Not till 1900 were these and other anomalies resolved by the formation of two over-all units under the British crown—the Protectorate of Northern Nigeria and the Protectorate of Southern Nigeria. (Lagos, however, was not finally absorbed by Southern Nigeria till 1906.) At last in 1914 the two protectorates were amalgamated under the governorship of Lord Lugard, and a united Nigeria as we know it today came into being for the first time.

Slavery was not the only trade that disfigured early Nigerian history. Grotesque stories may be told about the liquor traffic. European traders flooded the country with oceans of the cheapest possible liquor, which they sold to Africans at an enormous profit.[7] Soon "trade spirits," as this kind of infamous cheap liquor was called, became an important political and economic factor in government, because it was heavily taxed. Africans who could afford to do so stocked up large reserves of gin. "By hoarding this they accumulated wealth, since the price always went up as taxes rose," as one historian puts it. Gin almost became a form of currency. One chief, when the government advanced upon him, had a cache of 8,300 cases. In time not less than *half* the total revenue of Nigeria came from the customs duty on trade spirits. Lord Lugard thought that this was a disgrace, and after many years of effort the traffic was abolished, although smuggling still continued. The situation today is that anybody, European or African, can buy reputable brands of liquor in Nigeria exactly as in London or New York. There are several deductions to be drawn from this little story, aside from the fact that Africans, in common with many others of the human race, like to amass capital and to drink. First, they were undeniably debauched and exploited by individual Europeans. Second, this was in time stopped by the moral sense of the European community as a whole.

Constitutional development in Nigeria since World War II has been very fast. In 1946 came a new constitution establishing a central legislature for the first time. The previous council had not legislated for the North. In 1952 came another new constitution (the "Macpherson constitution"), making substantial concessions to nationalist pressure and greatly extending Nigerian power both in the regional assemblies and central legislature. Now

---

[7] *Calabar*, cited above. Some trade spirits cost Europeans only 9½ *d*, a case, shipping included. One can imagine what it tasted like.

COMPLEXITIES AND ACHIEVEMENTS IN NIGERIA

this constitution has been supplanted in turn by another establishing a federal system and giving still more authority to the people. Nigerian nationalism is on its final march. "Slaves no more."

LAGOS, THE CAPITAL

Lagos (pronounced with a long "a"), the capital of Nigeria, deserves more words than I can give it. Its population is around 270,000—with perhaps four thousand Europeans—and people say that it will become "the Bombay of Africa."[8] Its location on a lagoon made it ideal for the slave trade in older days, and its name derives from "lagoon" in Portuguese. (The vernacular name is Ikko.) There has been a connection for five hundred years between the Lagos in Nigeria and a town named Lagos in Portugal. Americans in Lagos, the few who live there, think of it as being somewhat remote—"beyond the double track"—because it is not on the route of Pan-American World Airways to West Africa. Pan-American stops at Accra in the Gold Coast, but not at Lagos.

Most African cities which are not yet altogether absorbed by the twentieth century have prevailing colors, caused in part by architecture, in part by local costumes. Marrakesh is a pink city, Ibadan is tin-colored, Khartoum ocher, and Accra white. The color of Lagos is, I should say, indigo.

Lagos is a kind of Washington, D.C. It is the capital of the country but not of any province, and is administered separately. Although it is located in the Western Region, the West has its own capital, Ibadan. Nothing is ever simple in this part of Africa.

The first thing I saw in Lagos, looking out from Government House to the Marina (the waterfront street—again the name is Portuguese) was an immaculately slender palm, leaning against the sea, and with the breeze tossing the fronds back as if they were a young girl's hair.

The second thing was the worst slum we ran into in all Africa, except in Johannesburg. In the very middle of the town, 28,000 people live on 60 acres. Here land is worth £1 per yard, and a room costs 25 shillings a month. A room? Perhaps it could be called such. But the houses are so ramshackle that a visitor can walk *through* them from street to street; each, open at the ends, is so grotesquely dilapidated that it can serve as a passageway. The entrances to collapsed buildings are hung with dirty matting, and sewage flows in open drains under the actual floorboards. One small thing surprised me; in these festering catacombs of filth there was one miserable factor lacking—I saw no flies. I mentioned this to our guide, and he replied,

[8] E. D. Morel mentions this in his *Nigeria*, published as far back as 1911.

perhaps not seriously, "Flies? They do not live here. They could not stand it."

Nearby is the Idumagbo market, as colorful and vivacious as the slum is morbid. We saw bolts of sumptuous cloth, mostly white and dark blue; there were blindingly gay trays of bright beads—as alive as small fruit—coral-colored, magenta, scarlet, turquoise. In the cosmetic stalls you can buy lumps of alum (to clean the tongue), raw powdered antimony (to make eye shadow), mint for sweetening the breath, and chalk—the two favorite colors seemed to be lemon yellow and deep violet—which is the Nigerian equivalent of face powder. And indeed several customers who had come into the town from nearby villages had wide, thick chalk marks on their faces. What were they buying? Alarm clocks, flashlights, razor blades, safety pins.

Of course we stayed longest at the *juju* (magic) stall, where we saw objects with important sorcerous qualities, like monkey skulls. There were carcasses of small golden birds, dried mice impaled on sticks, parrot beaks, gizzards delicately blown up into little balloons, a bouquet of sheep's intestines, snake fangs, "luck powder" made of herbs and heaven only knows what else, snake heads in varying stages of decomposition, and, inside a sheaf of cornhusk, a fine dead parrakeet.

Then I noticed something else, a cluster of oddly shaped greenish objects suspended in a bunch from the ceiling; their color and texture was that of mistletoe. They were dried monkey penises.

Europeans like to talk about *juju* in Lagos, and at lunch one day we heard a curious story. The local broadcasting studio invites people to come in and record anything of interest. A sixteen-year-old boy arrived on one occasion, and told this tale. At school, his teacher informed him that *juju* was nonsense—pure superstition, to which he should pay no attention. The boy reported this to his father, who laughed, saying jovially that *juju* might after all—who could tell?—exist and that the boy should be careful or he might be eaten. The boy was much disturbed by something in his father's tone. He went to his mother, who reassured him, saying that *juju* was, indeed, a silly carryover from ancient times, which should be ignored. One night came drumbeats in the suburb where the boy lived. He slipped out of bed to see a procession of dancers winding down the dark road. And at the head of this was his own father, dressed as a magician or *jujuman*, preparing for some kind of feast. The most remarkable thing about this story is, of course, that the boy was courageous and modern-minded enough to want to tell it on the radio.

Lagos had a handsome, small semi-European quarter, called Ikoyi, but it does not remotely resemble Nairobi or even Dar es Salaam. Things taken

COMPLEXITIES AND ACHIEVEMENTS IN NIGERIA 757

for granted in most communities—a comfortable hotel, a good bar, easy transportation, an up-to-date pharmacy—simply do not exist.[9] I do not recall having ridden in a single elevator. Most shops are stalls, open like caves and facing directly onto the street; they bear rudely printed legends, like "Considerate Medicine Place." At night merchants crouch along the curbs (if there are any curbs) selling bits of soap or single cigarettes by the light of kerosene lamps or even candles. A vitalizing sense of stir, of commotion, gives life. But how primitive it still is! Women are great traders, and throng the densely packed streets, which for the most part have no illumination except that provided by the feeble flares of the curb-side merchants. Incidentally a substantial American influence has begun; in a meadow in the center of town I saw boys playing softball, not cricket. The two most popular brands of cigarettes, Bicycle and Pirate, come in American-style soft packs, not British tins.

One day we called on His Highness the Oba Adeniji Adela II of the Royal House of Addo, the principal chief of Lagos, whose family has been ruling here for 260 years. "Oba" means "king." This was the first West African chief we met. He is president of the Lagos Town Council, and is a member of the House of Chiefs, Western Region. He worked as a government civil servant for thirty-six years before becoming Oba. His palace, not an imposing structure, has the familiar African dirt-paved courtyards; as we entered two unkempt retainers were lounging against the wall, one naked to the waist, and the other in a white undershirt. In the opposite corner, out in the sunlight, a woman was having her hair cut. Even after months in Africa we were still capable of being shocked by the extraordinary way formality and informality are often juxtaposed. The Oba's secretary, who had on blue pajamas, nothing else, took us into the Ga'opoide, or throne room, and there we met His Highness, a dignified figure, who wore a gold-braided blue turban, cream-colored robes, and slippers in silver and cloth-of-gold. He carried a gold-tipped wand, and a page stood nearby with his orange umbrella. The Oba speaks perfect English, but has never been outside Nigeria. When an aide came in to deliver a telegram, he prostrated himself full length on the floor before handing it to the Oba. The Oba said one thing of interest during our interview: "God did not make Nigeria. The British did."

I have already mentioned that Nigeria has no color bar, and a striking demonstration of this is the Island Club. (Perhaps there is a color bar *against* whites—people told me that Africans on the streets and in the shops were becoming steadily ruder to Europeans, but I never encountered

[9] But the all-powerful United Africa Company maintains a modern, well-equipped shop—swarming with African customers.

any pushing or bad manners.) The Island Club is one of the few mixed social clubs in Africa. It has more black members than white, and some stiff-backed whites hold it in contempt, but that it exists at all, even if it is somewhat crude and dreary, is refreshing. Our party there one night comprised two Government House officials (white), an African dignitary (black), his wife (white), the doyen of Nigerian journalism (black), one of his assistants (white), and an important cabinet minister (black), who wore an old brown sweater, with no coat or jacket. Later we crossed the broad lagoon and visited some night clubs, which are at once sordid, amateurish, explosive, and delightful in the extreme. Outside are long ranks of parked bicycles. The clubs resemble waterfront dives in Havana more than the Stork Club, but never mind. They have music that positively burns the skin, their dancing is the most sinuous and rhythmic I saw in Africa, they are full of shy, pretty, delicately graceful little girls, and they do not really get going till 4:00 A.M. I mention all this because it affords such an acute contrast to most of the rest of Africa. After the Rhodesias and the Congo, such freedom and relaxation, such an easy-flowing mixture of black and white, is startling to say the least.

Lagos is served, as I have already indicated, by an inflammatory press. Several of the dailies look like wet blotters. They are apt to be smeary in another sense too—valuable men of state have quit their posts because they could not endure any longer the reckless abuse put on them by a press so undisciplined.

Two topics of conversation when we were in Lagos were the local crematorium and nudity. The town has no more space for graves, and the authorities decided to build a crematorium. But this had to be given up, because of opposition from the Moslems, who must bury their dead, and local converts to Catholicism. As to nudity southern members of the House of Representatives, being modern-minded, sought to pass a law making it obligatory for all Nigerians to wear clothes. There are, of course, multitudes of pagans in the North and East who, if not actually naked, do not wear much in the way of clothing, and the Northern deputies opposed the idea so vigorously that it had to be dropped. They said, in effect, "To pass this law will put all law into contempt, since it will be unenforceable." Their motive was not merely to preserve indigenous customs but to make Nigeria more easily viable as a modern state.

It was in Lagos that we first began to hear about the worst thing in Nigeria, corruption. A tip or a gift is known as *dash,* and "dashing" exists almost everywhere. This phenomenon is probably unavoidable in any community like Nigeria, convulsed as it is by the most violent fermentations, and where people thrown up from the bottom suddenly find themselves able to exert power through money. Nevertheless it is regrettable. Multitudes of people—in the Gold Coast too—have become, let us say, physicians or lawyers or civil servants almost overnight, without having had the opportunity to absorb the ethical equipment that should accompany these professions. We of the West should not, however, be too much horrified by corruption and bribery in Nigeria. Think of the Kefauver investigation in the United States. Probably nothing in Africa has ever been as corrupt as Kansas City under Boss Pendergast.

Most Nigerian corruption—to date anyway—is minor. A boy in a hospital will have to "dash" the nurse a penny to get a bedpan. Horrible, of course. But, on a different level, have you ever given a headwaiter in a New York restaurant a dollar or two to get a good table?

Recently, however, the Lagos Town Council had to be dissolved, following a report that exposed fantastically ornate—if petty—corruption in municipal affairs. The Nigerian government is doing what it can to cope with this general problem, and I carried out of the country one remarkable souvenir—an enrollment blank for joining an organization called the Nigeria League of Bribe Scorners. Members of this swear not to offer or take bribes, form units in various communities like Alcoholics Anonymous in America, and wear proud badges, "Fight Bribery and Corruption."

In the general sphere of shady practice, Nigeria can produce some choice items. Some boys were active recently in a novel industry. They picked up gobs of chewing gum from the streets, straightened them out, and then sold them as new in counterfeit wrapping. On the other hand, consider a story like the following. Nigeria had the first general election in its history in 1951. In some hinterland constituencies, voters who could not read or write expressed their choice by advancing to the polling officer, and *whispering* to him the name of their candidate; the polling officers, who were African, not British, then recorded the vote. And there was no cheating of any kind in most constituencies, though it did occur in some.

*

When people say that Nigeria is a "mad" country what they really mean is that it is so full of explosive, tumultuous contrasts between old and new.

NIGERIA: ITS GEOGRAPHICAL SUBDIVISIONS

These, as mentioned above, are three:

1. *The East*. Area about 30,000 square miles, population probably 8,000,000. The predominant tribe is the Ibo, and the capital is a brisk little town, Enugu, which has coal mines almost on its main street. Dr. Azikiwe, the

creator of modern Nigerian nationalism, is its most important politician.

2. *The West.* This is separated from the East by the long muddy thrust of the Niger. Area 45,000 square miles; population probably 6,300,000; capital Ibadan; chief tribe, Yoruba; principal leader, Mr. Awolowo. East and West are bitterly jealous of each other, but often combine politically against the feudal North. They are much more Europeanized than the North. Their watchwords are emancipation and advance. The West is far richer than the East, and more developed politically. Of children of school age in the West, no fewer than one-third go to school, an extremely high ratio for Africa. I heard people say, "The West could be like the Gold Coast if it were on its own." That is, it could almost at once become a functioning national state.

3. *The North.* Area, 281,000 square miles (it is twice as big as East and West put together); population 16,800,000, of whom roughly 10,000,000 are Moslem. Capital, Kaduna. The languages of the North, like Hausa, are totally different from those of the South. From other points of view as well, the North is such a special and important entity that we will deal with it separately in Chapter 39 below.

IBOS IN THE EAST

There are some four million Ibos, who are divided into at least two thousand separate units;[10] they are nothing if not individualists. This is one of the most distinctive and important of all African tribes. Ibos live in multitudinous villages, fragmented into small family groups; they do not (unlike tribes in the West and North) have chiefs. Every Ibo is, more or less, his own master. They are a mobile, vividly industrious people—sometimes they are called "the Jews of Africa"—and they have spread all over Nigeria as traders and small merchants. (Again, let us mention the bicycle as a decentralizing force.) The population of Lagos, far to the west, is 35 per cent Ibo. Most Ibos have a lively sense of humor; they are clannish despite their individualism and hold together closely in non-Ibo communities; they are often unpopular because they push hard to make money; they can do anything on this good earth, I heard it said, except govern themselves. But in fact the Ibos today are so effervescent politically that the British sometimes differentiate between the "good East" and the "disruptive East," meaning by the latter the radical Ibo strongholds.

Many Ibo tribesmen still practice female circumcision, and have a complicated system of bride-price; this may be paid in cattle, brass rods, labor,

[10] Hailey, *op. cit.*, p. 21.

dane guns (the antediluvian muskets still used by hunters), or even cash. Most Ibos do not kiss when making love (unless they have become westernized by seeing movies). The word for "make love" in one Ibo tongue is, literally translated, "to look into the eyes." It is an abomination to make love by daylight, or on land newly ploughed. There have been isolated cases of cannibalism in Iboland as recently as 1946; in some remote towns people will not buy meat if it is not attached to a bit of hide, to prove that it is not human. Leopard-men—ritualistic killers who wear leopard pelts and maim their victims with steel hooks, as if they were claws—still exist. In fact a veritable epidemic of leopard murders took place in 1947, and seventy of these macabre killers were caught, tried, and executed.[11]

THE WEST AND THE YORUBA

We drove from Lagos to Ibadan, the capital of the Western Province, on a hot, misty morning in July. The red laterite road cuts through mangrove swamp and palm-oil bush; hundreds of minor waterways curl and gurgle beneath small bridges. We sloshed past "mammy wagons" by the score—small overloaded trucks so-called because they are owned as a rule by women traders, and are sometimes driven by women. To find women active in trade and otherwise in such numbers is startling; they play a role in public life and commerce that would be unimaginable in the Rhodesias or the Union. Most "mammy wagons" have slogans painted on them, like "God Is Good," or "We Believe in the United Africa Company."

In a marsh I stared at a piece of canvas draped and sagging on a wooden frame. It moved. It was a cow. Cattle driven down here from the North do not get much to eat.

We passed through a fascinating town, Abeokuta (population 54,000). This community had a newspaper in English in 1862[12]—more than ninety years ago—and is full of rude bookshops; some of these are no more than stalls or shelves in front of mud shacks, and contain mostly textbooks and self-help manuals. New arrivals among books are advertised by chalk signs on blackboards. Nigeria likes to read anything. The avidity for education is obsessive. The Alake—ruler—of Abeokuta is an eminent noble, one of the four principal chiefs of the whole West, who is known as "First of the Equals." He is reputed to be the richest man in Nigeria with the exception of some Northern emirs. Modern times struck him recently. He was accused of some dereliction in connection with water rates, and his subjects thought

[11] "Nationalism in British West Africa," by Vernon MacKay, *Foreign Policy Reports*, March 15, 1948.
[12] Burns, *op. cit.*, p. 21.

that his taxes were too high. The indignant citizenry deposed him. The movement to do so was led by a resolute little woman, Mrs. F. Ransome-Kuti, a well-known feminist and head of the local Union against Unjust Taxation. The British had nothing to do with this. They tried to save the Alake, but even so he was forced into exile by his fellow Africans. Later, on promise of improved behavior, he was reinstated and forgiven. Even in feudal domains these days, the people count.

IBADAN (pronounced Ee-bahd-un) is one of the most extraordinary places I have ever seen. It is by far the largest city in Nigeria, with something like 500,000 people, and is not only the biggest black city in the world (there are only a handful of whites) but the fourth or fifth biggest city of any kind in all Africa. Yet, I imagine, not one reader out of a hundred thousand has ever heard the name Ibadan. It lies high on comparatively healthy terrain. It was originally a military camp, pegged into the bush by Yoruba warriors, and has a history dating back 150 years. It is astonishing to look at, because the whole vast city seems to have a metal top; the tin roofs of thousands of houses, packed closely together in an endless sloping expanse, are like an iron lid. Ibadan, like so much in Nigeria, is inextricably mixed up between old and new. Five sacred crocodiles are carefully protected by the municipality. It also has University College, which looks almost like the Museum of Modern Art in New York. This college, a handsome glassy structure opened in 1952, is affiliated with the University of London, and gives degrees of wide variety. It offers to Nigerian youth substantial new vistas of education, and many Nigerians are prouder of it than of anything in the country. It resembles Gordon College in Khartoum and Makarere in Uganda to an extent, but is much more modern in equipment; presumably it will do for Nigeria what these institutions have done in their respective countries, namely, produce an intellectual elite that in time will dominate the new society. Some critics, however, think that its plant is too elaborate—it has a library with 100,000 books—and too expensive. Visiting it I might have forgotten that we were in tropical Africa had not our guide told us that, within a square mile of the site, an entomologist had collected two hundred different varieties of butterfly.

People often think of Africa as a continent without towns, and indeed this is true in a manner of speaking, but it is not true of West Nigeria. Urbanization is proceeding at a phenomenal pace. Near Ibadan are no fewer than four cities, not merely towns, with populations of 100,000 or more—Iwo (100,006), Ife (110,690), Oshogbo (122,746), and Ogbomosho (139,247). Ife and Iwo have important and excessively romantic histories.

All this is Yoruba country. The Yoruba are one of the master tribes of the continent—a proud folk, claiming Nilotic descent, and with an active culture.

They are a sophisticated people, and look down on Ibos as barbarians. There are about three million Yorubas. Many are intellectuals and dreamers, "but strenuous beyond any comparison with the Bantu."[13] Some of their customs are unique; for instance, a father's property is inherited by his sons, a mother's by her daughters. In their chamber of deities there are four hundred gods; the chief of these is named Olorun, which means "Owner of the Sky."[14] One minor deity is the smallpox god.

The most important Yoruba chief is probably Sir Adesoji Aderemi, KBE, CMG, MHR, the Oni of Ife, who until recently was a minister in the central government. Though he has a British knighthood he is a prominent member of the Action Group, one of the leading Nigerian nationalist parties. The Yoruba people had their mythical birthplace in his capital, Ife, and he is spiritual head of the tribe as a whole. Until about 1900, when a lesser Yoruba chief died, his head had to be sent to the Oni of Ife as a gesture of respect. But his subjects at least waited until the chief died before chopping off his head, which shows that they were considerably more advanced than some of their neighbors. The present Oni is sixty-five, and in ceremonial costume looks as if he had been plunged into a pool of green, orange, and fuchsia-red dye. He represented his people at the Coronation of Queen Elizabeth in 1953.

Other great Yoruba chiefs, who, however, do not play much of a political role, are the Alafin of Oyo (a Moslem) and the Awujale of Ijebu Ode. Chiefs like these do not resemble even remotely the kind we have met in Central or Southern Africa; they are not peasant leaders growing crops on sparse hillsides, or civil servants paid to collect taxes dutifully. They are elevated and ornate. They resemble to a degree maharajas in India in prewar days. And probably they will disappear from public life much as the maharajas did, when the Nigerian revolution progresses, and becomes, as it is inevitably bound to become, more and more a people's affair. The day of flamboyant chiefs is over. Not all Nigerian chiefs are, incidentally, simon-pure marionettes of the British as most Indian maharajas were. If they have political

[13] Margery Perham, London *Times*, December 29, 1932. Miss Perham, whose authority carries magisterial weight, talks with admiration of the way the Yoruba have jumped the gap to modern times, although generally in Africa "sophistication means disruption."

[14] A number of Yoruba communities exist in the New World, particularly in Cuba. See an article by an American anthropologist, William T. Bascom, in *Nigeria*, No. 37, 1951. Mr. Bascom describes how Cuban descendants of Yoruba slaves retain some of their old tribal characteristics while at the same time they are progressive Cubans. They eat Yoruba food and sacrifice animals in the Yoruba manner. Several of their deities have become merged with characters in Christian theology; for instance, St. John the Baptist is the Yoruba god Ogun. Songs in mixed Yoruba-Spanish "are played on the Havana wireless station and can be bought on commercial Cuban gramophone records."

direction at all, it is nationalist. The fermentations of modern Nigeria reach almost everywhere.

Then there is the Oba of Benin. Recently he founded a new religion. He is a most imposing figure. It is a pity that we cannot mention Benin except in passing—a city celebrated in legend as well as fact for two reasons, blood and bronzes. Until a few generations ago its kings held annual ceremonies known as "the customs"; these were carnivals of human sacrifice. Enough human blood might be spilled for small boats to sail on. On the other hand the lords of Benin were, it seems, more merciful than Roman emperors, because they generally stunned their victims before crucifying them.[15] But anyway Benin ran with blood; courtyards were paved with human skulls, and a favorite article of food on really big ceremonial occasions was the human heart. The British took Benin in 1897, and cleaned it up. It is an extraordinary fact that, in addition to atrocities more horrible than anything known in modern Africa, Benin should also have produced bronzes which, almost beyond dispute, are among the most magnificent works of art in the world. Nobody knows the origin of the delicately modeled Benin bronzes. Probably they date back to the fifteenth century. There are still folk who deny that any true African civilization has ever existed. Perhaps they measure civilization purely in terms of written records. But if civilization includes art, then the Africans who made the Benin bronzes and Ife terra cottas were certainly civilized, at least in so far as they were capable of producing works of art. Most of the bronzes were carried off as loot after the British expedition in 1897, and have been scattered all over the world. Now the Nigerian government, which is setting up a national museum in Lagos, is doing what it can to get them back. Two bronze leopards were located in New York recently but at a fancy price—$25,000. Nevertheless the Lagos museum bought them.

TO SUM UP

Nigeria may seem overwhelmingly and exasperatingly complex, but the main channels of development are clear. There are three sharp, overriding phenomena or issues. First, the precipitous climb of the people from tribalism to modern times overnight. Second, sectionalism versus unity—that is, the fierce struggle to establish and maintain cohesion between North, East, and West. Third, nationalism versus the British. Let us go on.

[15] Sir Richard Burton, who had "the brow of a god and the jaw of a devil," visited Benin in 1863 and escaped alive. He saw much. See *West African Explorers* (Oxford, 1951) for an enthralling account of this.

CHAPTER 38

Nigeria—Its Inflammatory Politics

It is almost as difficult to get rid of an Empire as to build one.
—ANONYMOUS

NIGERIA is, in some respects, the most exciting country I have ever been in in my life. Its politics are incandescent, and flicker violently. To say that it is more fully evolved toward self-government than any British colony except the Gold Coast is to make it sound far too tame and simple.[1]

As of the time we visited Nigeria there were three regional Houses of Assembly, for East, West, and North. Also the West and North had Houses of Chiefs, more or less like the House of Lords in London. Members of the regional assemblies are elected by the people, through a combined system of direct primaries and electoral colleges, and membership in all three is overwhelmingly Nigerian. These are not merely advisory bodies, but have substantial legislative power. We have come a long way now from the embryonic Legislative Councils of East Africa.

A federal legislature also exists, called the House of Representatives, which sits in Lagos and is, in effect, the Nigerian parliament. It too is overwhelmingly African and has wide legislative powers on a national basis. It has ninety-two members from the North, as against fifty-six each from East and West. This ratio was established to give the North, which comprises more than half the country, a fair share in representation; it might be added that it also serves to protect British interests to an extent, since the North is much more pro-British than the southern areas. In the old house there were also twelve "injected" or appointed members, who were British. These, in a pinch, could combine with the North to hold the balance of power.

Nigeria has as yet no federal prime minister, as the Gold Coast has. But

[1] Readers not interested in the intricacies of African local politics may, however, skip this section.

the Council of Ministers, the executive body of the government, has when fully constituted a clear and unalterable African majority. Again we have come a long way from the Executive Councils in Kenya and elsewhere in East Africa, which are little more than instruments of the British Governor.

Nigeria has, at the top of the structure, a Governor General who represents the Crown and who is sent out by the Colonial Office, and he has "reserved powers," as have the governors (also British) of the three regions. That is, he can "certify legislation," which means that he can make a law if after a reasonable period the House of Representatives refuses to do so, in order that government may go on, and he can veto any legislation imperiling British imperial (as apart from domestic) interests. The present Governor General, Sir John Macpherson, has never used these reserved powers, nor would any governor be likely to use them except in an extreme emergency.[2]

What nationalist Nigerians (at least those in East and West) want is to progress further from this framework and reach complete independence. But this desire is seriously compromised by the sectional rivalries within the country. Few mature nationalists want independence at the price of splitting the nation, as India was split by the formation of Pakistan. What the British want is harder to explain. Most are reconciled to the concept that Nigeria must be free. But they think, both altruistically and for the sake of their own interests, that freedom should not come too soon, and should await a further period of tutelage. Roughly their position corresponds to that which they formerly held in the Sudan.

I heard it said in Lagos, "The British must rule in Nigeria, or get out." But this remark, if fully analyzed, is meaningless. The British cannot rule by arbitrary means any longer; they cannot risk any such crisis as that which attended the dismissal of the Kabaka in Uganda. It is basic and unalterable British policy to *assist* the Nigerians toward freedom, within certain limitations. Nor can the British simply "get out." They have responsibilities. They have commitments. They do not want chaos. Nigeria, if they withdrew today, might split not merely into three countries, but five or six—North, Ibo East, non-Ibo East, Yoruba West, non-Yoruba West, with the Cameroons out on a lonely limb. The lack of cohesion in the country gives them a pretext for staying on.[3] But it is important to reiterate that developments in

---

[2] MacPherson retired as Governor General early in 1955, and was succeeded by Sir James Robertson.
[3] But one of the lieutenant governors told me, "We are accused on the one hand of inventing the concept of a united Nigeria, and on the other of splitting it into fragments. Both accusations cannot be true."

Nigeria are not a series of concessions made by the British out of weakness, but steps in the logical working out of a policy. A final point in this connection: *Why* is British policy so ameliorative on the whole? Mainly it is because the British do not want to risk losing Nigeria altogether. They make certain concessions in the hope that, by "soft" rule, they will at least be able to keep Nigeria, when or if it becomes free, safely within the Commonwealth.[4]

There are two dominant political parties in Nigeria (not including the North for the moment), both aggressively nationalist. One is the Action Group, which has its main strength in the West among the Yorubas; the other is the NCNC—National Council of Nigeria and the Cameroons—which exists in all three regions but is strongest in the Ibo East. In 1953—the details are too complex to go into—some NCNC leaders split off to make a splinter party allied to the Action Group. Its members were called "Nippers," from the initials for National Independence Party. These parties have been flamingly antagonistic. Each seeks to woo the intractable North, and outstrip the others in working for complete independence for the country as a whole. Nationalism has become a kind of football. Each party tries to kick or carry this further along, to advance its own party ends. The two main parties compete in extremism to get support.

In March, 1953, came a positively savage crisis. Its effect was to paralyze government. An Action Group deputy, Anthony Eronsele Oseghale Enahoro,[5] rose in the central House of Representatives and introduced a resolution demanding complete self-government by a specific date—1956. This seemed to many to be going too fast, although 1956 was a convenient "magic" date in that the last legislature, elected in 1951, was due to expire after five years. In particular the North, which knows that it, at least, cannot possibly be ready for full independence by 1956, pleaded for caution, and a Northern deputy offered an amendment to the original motion, omitting the specific date 1956 and saying instead "as soon as practicable." This led to such a confused storm that, when the President of the House accepted the amendment, members from both East and West noisily walked out. The East and West leaders, "Zik" and Awolowo, who had been fighting like scorpions the night before, publicly embraced, and pledged themselves to make common cause.

One word more about Nigerian attitudes toward the British. We never

[4] Somewhat ruefully the British say that in Nigeria they are "the only government in the world without a voice." No newspaper represents Government House, and the radio is non-partisan.

[5] This young man, born in 1923, is a firebrand. He was for some years a member of Zik's party, and then switched over to the Action Group. He has been imprisoned three times for sedition.

met an educated Nigerian who was not a nationalist (although there are some "armchair" nationalists and a few appeasers or "Uncle Toms"), but to be a nationalist does not necessarily mean being belligerently anti-British. Most moderates want to keep some kind of British tie, even after self-government. But a lesson from the Sudan and elsewhere is that it is very difficult to maintain such ties. Moderates are likely to be swallowed up.

A conference to amend the constitution took place in London in the summer of 1953, which to the surprise of almost anyone was successful, because the three outstanding regional leaders—"Zik," Awolowo, and the Sardauna of Sokoto representing the North—all wanted, in essence, the same thing, more power for their respective regions. The main result of the conference—a signal development—was to assure self-government by 1956 on a regional basis, if the people so desire. Each region may, if it wishes, become completely self-governing with its own prime minister, within a central federation. Presumably East and West Nigeria will at once proceed to do this. The North may not. So, in the same "country," we may have the spectacle of two quasi-independent states living side by side with another state, the North, that is still colonial.

In November, 1953, the West threatened to "secede" from the new federation (before it was formed) following a bitter quarrel over the status of Lagos. Oliver Lyttelton, at that time still the colonial secretary, replied in sharp language that any such step would be "resisted," presumably by force. Nigerian ministers flew up to London to protest, challenging Lyttelton on various points and warning him bluntly that he could no longer rule colonial people by threats. This angry crisis was resolved by a conference held in Lagos early in 1954. Since then events have moved fast. A new constitution, the third in eight years, was written and promulgated embodying the results of the London and Lagos conferences. Nigeria got a new name—the Federation of Nigeria. The Governor became a Governor General. The Cameroons were divided, as had been anticipated, into two administrations, with the northern area attached to Northern Nigeria and the southern sector formed into a new "quasi-federal territory." In November came the first *federal* elections in the country's history; Dr. Azikiwe's NCNC won handily not only in his own East, as was expected, but in the West as well.

SOME MINISTERS

The Nigerian ministers, in or out of office, are an interesting lot. Their names are totally unknown to most of us, but they are administering a country bigger than Germany. They may wear dress strange to our eyes, but it is hardly necessary to point out that they are about as far removed from *jujumen* in the bush as is, say, John Foster Dulles from an Ozark mountaineer. They are paid exceptionally good salaries for Africa—up to £2,500 per year, which is more than a British MP gets. Some in the regional Houses have names picturesquely representative of the eruptive flux that has created modern Nigeria. One Northern deputy is named Sambo, the Ciroma of Hadejia. And consider Sunday W. Obani-Ukoma, Davied D. Tom-George, Theophilus Owolabi Shobowale Benson, and Jackson Mpi. Many deputies are Christian, and got their given names from missionaries. Thousands of Nigerians are named Patrick, Jeremiah, and so on.

One consequential personality is the Honorable Eni Njoku, former minister of mines and power. We had a good talk with him in Ibadan, where he is professor of botany. His wife is British. He was educated at a celebrated missionary school, the Hope Waddell Institute at Calabar, in the East, and at the Universities of London and Manchester. This is a common pattern— education at a local mission, which the boy manages to enter against no matter what obstacles, further education in England if he is bright and lucky enough, and then, on return to Nigeria, an almost automatic absorption into public service and politics. The Honorable Okoi Arikpo, former minister of land, survey, and local development, went to a Church of Scotland school in Nigeria, studied anthropology and law in England, returned to Nigeria to become a teacher, was a leader of the Nigerian Youth Movement, and is a fellow of the Royal Anthropological Society and the Royal Economic Society in London. We met another well-known minister (as of that time) at the Island Club, the Honorable Chukudifu Nwapa. He ran commerce and industry. He went to Cambridge, and had a good career there; his wife is a physician. Most Nigerians of this type are as modern-minded as tomorrow. They are also inclined to be somewhat doctrinaire, to be painfully sensitive and unsure of themselves, and to be carried away by splinter partisanship.[6]

Another personage is the Honorable S.L. Akintola, the former minister of labor and a powerful, stormy figure in the Action Group. He is certainly not unsure of himself. He was one of the ministers who resigned from the

[6] See *Our Council of Ministers*, by Ernest Ikoli, in the Crownbird Series. There are all manner of titles in this series of pamphlets published by the Nigerian government—*Our Next Generation, Our Festival of the Arts, Our Progress in the Air, Our Marketing Boards, Our Folklore*, and so on. A crane known as the crownbird is the national emblem of Nigeria. The pamphlets are an interesting experiment in public education on the part of the Nigerian government, as an effort to stimulate the interest of people in their own new country.

cabinet in the fierce crisis of March, 1953.[7] Akintola, a Westerner, went to the Baptist School at Ogbomosho and then made a career as a teacher, a journalist, and in law. He told me that to get freedom for Nigeria, he would even sacrifice unity; that is, although the south would do everything possible to bring the North in, it was prepared to go ahead toward independence without the North if necessary. The British, he went on, "are goading the North to secede." Akintola, as minister of labor, had a great deal to do with the trade union movement in Nigeria, which is a rapidly growing force. The biggest employer in Nigeria (as in the Sudan) is the government, partly because the government runs the railways, and the government and railway workers are solidly organized in a powerful, politically conscious union. The tin mines, spinning, and timber industries have also been organized. The most successful union so far is probably the NUT, or Nigerian Union of Teachers.

COMMUNIST DANGER IN NIGERIA

I asked these and other ministers about Communism. Mr. Awolowo declared, "No Communist danger exists in southern Nigeria, though we have a few Communists. There could be a Communist danger in the North, when the feudal system there breaks down." In general it seems that young Nigerians who become Communists do so without much realization of what Communism is, and mostly to annoy the British. Some Britons, on their side, are apt to call anybody a Communist if he is an extreme nationalist. Then too some Nigerian youngsters flirt with Communism because in theory it is the enemy of imperialism, and apparently these innocent souls think that Communists are anti-imperialist; also there is a natural tendency to side with anybody who is anti-British. On the whole most Nigerians seem to think that Communism has little to offer them at present, although a small Communist party exists and some penetration has occurred in the trade unions.

One minister told me (a) "We take care of our own poor and our own children—we do not need society to do this for us," and (b) "Our conception of God is totally different. No political creed can succeed in Africa that does not take account of religion."[8]

[7] So did the minister of communications at the time, Chief Arthur E. Prest, Akintola's close associate. Chief Prest has a background differing somewhat from these others. At the age of twelve he shipped as a messboy on a merchantman sailing between Lagos and New Orleans. Later he became an intelligence officer in the police.

[8] See Chapter 46 below for a general recapitulation of the subject of Communism.

But one morning I saw this in the *Daily Service,* the organ of Awolowo's Action Group:

> As far as we are concerned this is not the time for us to bother our heads about Communism or Capitalism. Our immediate objective is complete independence from British rule within or outside the Commonwealth. It is after independence that we may, if we so desire, consider whether Communism or Capitalism will suit us best.
>
> If the Communists can help us to attain our objective we shall welcome them just as Britain recently gave King Tito of Yugoslavia a royal reception in the capital of the British Empire.

Once again we encounter the nationalist obsession.

In July, 1954, the Nigerian government issued an important order prohibiting importation of Communist literature from abroad, including various trade union publications. A few months later the federal and regional governments went further and (following the example of the Gold Coast) barred "active Communists" from all key departments in public service—administration, education, labor, police, communications, and the like. This was done frankly as a counterstep to the infiltration of Communism into countries "on the threshold of self government."[9]

ZIK AND AWOLOWO

Finally we reach the top. The best known and most powerful Nigerian man of politics is "Zik"—Dr. Nnamdi Azikiwe (pronounced Ah-*zik*-way)—who was born in the East in 1904, and who is Premier and Minister of Local Government in the Eastern Region. The term "prime minister" is not used. Zik is a strong Ibo. Unlike most of his colleagues he was educated not in Great Britain, but in the United States; he went to Howard University in Washington, D. C., and did graduate work at both Columbia and the University of Pennsylvania. One of his teachers was Dr. Ralph Bunche. Perhaps he should have absorbed more of Dr. Bunche's calm discernment and wisdom. Zik is a master of science, a master of laws, and both a Litt.D. and an LL.D.

From the earliest days he has been an aggressive, inflammatory nationalist. He wrote a book on African freedom while he was still at Howard; his thesis dealt with the social organization of the Ibos. He was also (at Howard) a formidable soccer player. He returned to Africa, took up journalism on the Gold Coast, got into trouble with the authorities, and was expelled from the country for sedition. One of his concepts is that "by the year 2944 Black

[9] London *Times,* October 14, 1954.

Africa will have destroyed Europe and brought the United States to the verge of extinction." Negro missionaries will then redeem the world.[10]

Dr. Zik is an explosive man, handsome, magnetic, and versatile in several fields. He runs a bank, and one of his big enterprises is Zik's Press, Ltd., which gives him a wide audience all over southern Nigeria. He organized the NCNC—National Council of Nigeria and the Cameroons—in 1947, and he was so powerful for a time that Nigerian nationalism as a whole got the nickname "Zikism." He believes violently in a unitary Nigeria, and that, under self-government, the Ibo, Yoruba, and Hausa can live in peace together, although naturally he wants to safeguard the interests of his own Ibos. Zik lives in Lagos and for a time was a member of the Western, not Eastern, regional Assembly, even though he is a fanatic Easterner. Later he won election to the Eastern House, and in 1954 he became Leader of Government Business in the Eastern cabinet. His party won the first federal elections by a sizable margin. He visited the United States briefly in 1954, and his wife took courses in home economics at Storer College in West Virginia.

There is no orator in Nigeria like the dynamic, magnificent-looking Zik. He is a wonderfully effective demagogue, and mobs spring up anywhere in southern Nigeria to hear him speak. They sing "Zee-ee-ek . . . Zee-ee-ek . . ." like a chant.

Some British like Zik for the odd reason that he is a great sportsman. "He watches football," one Englishman told me, "like an Englishman"—the ultimate in compliments. He is president of the Lagos Football Association and vice-president of the Nigeria Boxing Board, and he loves to referee boxing matches. Other Britons cannot endure him; once—some years ago—he fled from Lagos for a time, out of fear that white hotheads might assassinate him. Plenty of people call Zik cynical. I heard one Briton say, "All that Zik is really interested in is money." This is probably an unfair statement. But the London *Economist*, a temperate organ, wrote recently,[11] "There is a story that when Zik was asked what he would do if the British were to leave Africa on October first in any year he answered, 'Take the boat for England on September thirtieth.'"

The NCNC is, of course, rabidly nationalist. It was created in Zik's image. It stands for universal adult suffrage, direct elections, control of the civil service by African ministers, and complete "Nigerianization" of the country's military forces. It sought to boycott the local coronation festivities in 1953. Zik's own sources of power are several, aside from his personal

[10] *Time*, February 9, 1953.
[11] August 23, 1952.

qualities and his strenuous revolutionary history. For one thing he controls several influential newspapers. For another he is undisputed leader of the Ibos. These are so important not merely for their geographic position in the East but because, spreading out, they make up the personnel of most government departments all over Nigeria; also they dominate the police. Recently a semi-Christian sect in an Ibo village canonized Zik as a "saint." Much more is going to be heard of this man in coming years.

*

The leader of the Action Group, and Zik's chief political rival, Obafemi Awolowo (pronounced A-*wa*-luwa), has an altogether different quality. He is not a demagogue, but an intellectual. There has never been a breath of scandal about him. He is a man with a good deal of reserve, conscientious, precise, and somewhat stiff-backed. I heard an Englishman say, with genuine regret, "If only Awolowo would *relax*, and have a glass of sherry with us sometimes!" His intellectual arrogance is marked, although he seemed reasonable enough when we talked to him.

The Action Group, which has its principal strength in the Yoruba West, is a newer party than Zik's, and grew out of a semi-religious group, the Egbe Omo Odudua, founded by Awolowo to give voice to Yoruba nationalist and tribal aspirations. In theory at least it would like to remain on friendly relations with the British, when and if they go. But many of its members are extremists, and Awolowo himself was a prime mover for fixing 1956 as the target date for independence. Recently an Action Group member, commenting on the troubles in Kenya, went so far as to say that Mau Mau, in spite of its horrors, might "still be the way out of Nigeria's bondage."[12]

Awolowo has a tidier mind and more planning capacity than Zik. Awolowo, people say, seized the Nigerian nationalist movement away from Zik, by organizing his own party in the West. Before this, Zik had a claim to be leader everywhere. Overnight, there were two parties, which is a healthy enough sign of democratic evolution if they are not too rigidly regional. The Action Group uses scabrous language in attacking Zik's East. One of its newspapers recently characterized the Eastern Assembly as a home "of terrorism, gangsterism, blackmail, shameless lying, and mob politics." At one juncture, when they were quarreling ferociously, Awolowo and Zik sued each other for libel for considerable sums; the two awards more or less canceled each other out. Then, after the crisis in 1953, the two began to work together again, each keeping his own sphere of influence, with Awolowo stronger in the West, Zik in the East. But in 1954 and later came other bitter quarrels, and they split venomously once more.

[12] Quoted by the *Economist*, May 2, 1953.

Awolowo was born in a small Yoruba village in 1909; he was poorest of the poor, and is entirely self-made. This is unusual in Nigeria; an intelligent youngster, if destitute, will in the normal course of events be taken in by some family. Awolowo, on his own, managed to get a British education at a mission school in Ibadan, and then made his way to London, where he studied law. He is a barrister of the Inner Temple. Returning to Nigeria he became an advisor to the trade unions. He did not take a strong political line against the British until about 1948. Awolowo is an extremely cultivated and intelligent man. He speaks, of course, perfect English. His book *Path to Nigerian Freedom* was well received by intellectuals in London. He has a world sense somewhat unusual among Africans (if only because few Africans ever have opportunity to acquire it) and recently visited India and Egypt; Jawaharlal Nehru made a great impression on him—and vice versa. In 1954 he became Premier of the Western Region, which means that he is in effect prime minister.

We met Awolowo in odd circumstances, on a lonely road out in the bush, driving back to Lagos from Ibadan. We had missed him in Ibadan, and were pursuing him to his home village, by name Ikenne. To catch Awolowo at Ikenne, we had to be there by 5 P.M., since he was proceeding elsewhere. The British said, "He will not wait for you—get there on time." But we were delayed, and when we finally reached the outskirts of Ikenne at about seven we had given up hope of seeing Awolowo. It was becoming dark, and a soft, steamy rain came down. Then a shiningly bright new American car appeared suddenly over the crest of the red road, like a metallic apparition charging out of tropical dusk. In it was Awolowo. Our chauffeur recognized him as we slithered past. We stopped. He had been waiting for us but could wait no longer. So we stood out there in the rainy twilight, talking. We became conscious of a strange buzz and stir—the sound of myriads of insects. It became darker, and the shafts of light from the two cars made furrows into the green mask of jungle. Rain fell harder, and Awolowo stepped into our car, saying, "I can give you a quarter of an hour." We could still hear the solid, strident call of insects. It was a strange place to have a conference.

Awolowo is of medium height, with a studious look; he wore Nigerian robes, and a dark red and gold turban. His manner is suave, considered, and aware. I asked him if Nigeria would, after independence, become a republic. He thought not. The Nigerian chiefs would not like the word "republic." He went on, "We have to consider our princes. They do not resemble princes elsewhere. They fight for independence *with* us." He discussed briefly constitutional anomalies within the Commonwealth. I asked him what his principal grievances against Britain were, considering the British record of accomplishment in Nigeria. He replied, first, that it was morally wrong for one nation to govern another, second, that British administration was carried out by incompetent, inferior officials, third, that the British did not have the true interests of the country at heart. "In fourteen months, under the present government, we have done more for Nigeria than the British did in 120 years."

NATIONALISM: ONE WORD MORE

Is Nigeria fit for complete self-government today? Of course not—judged by western levels. The pace of advance has been quick and powerful in recent years, but a long way to go remains. But, if I may repeat a familiar theme, the fact that the country is not yet ideally equipped for self-government has little to do with the impending course of events. Nigeria is striking out for full independence whether it is ready or not. The British know that they cannot possibly dam up the nationalist flood; what they wisely try to do is give it channels. The real question at issue is whether the flood will break over these before the foundations are fully laid, and so make chaos.

But Nigeria is in no danger, as some other African countries might be, "of going back to the tribes." The people are committed enough to education and modernization to keep anything like that from happening. Nor is Nigeria likely to become a tyrant state under a ruthless or unscrupulous dictator. Citizens are too diversified and individualistic, too conscious of their own growing stake in the community. But democracy is not an easy form of government to make work and this is a consideration that Nigerians themselves recognize clearly and worry about vociferously. A writer in the *Nigerian Handbook*, 1953, sums it up this way: "The issue of whether self-government will come is a dead one. It will come, but the pertinent questions are, What kind of self-government? And self-government for whom?" This reflects the cardinal apprehension of the North, to which we must now turn.

CHAPTER 39

The Nigerian North

Nigeria is a place where the best is impossible but where the worst never happens.
—OLD SAYING

FROM Lagos we flew up to Kano, the ancient and historic city of the North, over mangrove swamps along the coast and a thick humid belt of rain forest. The North, let us repeat, has all the appurtenances of a totally different country. I suppose that the first thing I noticed on this upland plateau was that English was no longer a lingua franca. And here we are in Moslem Africa once more. Kano might be Marrakesh across the Sahara. Here we return to oceans of corrugated sand, the stately walk of camels, women behind veils, minarets like tall chessmen, and the soft, gliding handshake of the Arabs.

I had seen Kano during the war, when it was a base for military aircraft crossing Africa. Stepping out of the plane, then and now, is like stepping into a blast furnace. Lagos was hot as Baltimore may be hot on a sultry afternoon; Kano has the dry burning heat of the desert. It has not changed much, except that there are more bicycles, and it has a big new bright mosque with a blue-green dome. The bicycles flash by in confused intersecting streams, almost as fish do in a bowl.

KANO (population 130,000, pronounced "Kahno") is famous for being a walled city, like Peiping, but the walls, even if they have a circumference of eleven miles and are intersected by imposing gates, are disappointing. They are little more than embankments, crumbling at the top. The population is 99,000 within the walls, 31,000 outside. Kano, as I have already noted, has a history dating back more than a thousand years. No white man saw it till Captain Hugh Clapperton got there in 1824. His description[1] proves once more that, for a reason nobody can fully explain, British explorers in Africa had a magic hand with prose. Lord Lugard did not capture Kano and bring the area into the framework of British rule till 1903.

[1] See again that fascinating little book, *West African Explorers*.

THE NIGERIAN NORTH

The Kano market throbs and sings with color. It is open to the sun and therefore sparkling. It makes the market in Lagos, say, look like a cave. It is the kind of place Aladdin and Scheherazade might have liked to shop in, and its celebrated dye pits demonstrate that, in some respects, Africa has its own peculiar unities. The Tuareg of the Hoggar, whom we talked about so many pages past, come all the way here to buy cloth dipped in Kano's pools of indigo.[2]

But what I noticed most in Kano was something else. The surface of the city, both within and outside the walls, is pierced by a multitude of tall, sharp, geometrically perfect green pyramids. I thought, "This is the most curious architecture I have ever seen." The pyramids consist solidly of the *Arachis hypogaea*, or peanuts. These are not edible peanuts, not decorticated peanuts, but peanuts for oil, and billions of them are packed into the pyramids, covered with green tarpaulin, and left standing in the open till the overburdened railway can get them to the coast. In each pyramid are 760 tons of peanuts. In each ton, there are 13 bags; in each bag, approximately 172 pounds. (The British ton is 2,240 pounds, not 2,000.) Figure out for yourself the total number of peanuts in a pyramid, if you know what a single peanut weighs.[3]

The airport at Kano is one of the busiest and most important in Africa. British, Dutch, French, Belgian, and other lines use it as an essential stop on their north-south routes across the continent. It handles six hundred aircraft movements a month, and 74,000 passengers a year. Near the control tower is a splendid sign, with arrows pointing next door:

Mombasa	—	2,409 miles
Cairo	—	1,933
Jerusalem	—	2,176
Cape Town	—	3,244
Buenos Aires	—	5,479
Wellington	—	10,251
Mecca	—	2,189

Mecca? Yes, indeed! West African Airways has a regular service from Kano to Jiddah, via Khartoum—one of the most unusual air routes in the world. Its purpose is to fly Moslem pilgrims to the holy city and back. (The last

---

[2] In older days caravans came to Kano all the way from Tripoli. They had as many as 1,200 camels, and carried £40,000 worth of goods. The journey took eleven months. See *Our Roads*, by Sir Hubert Walker, a pamphlet published by the Nigerian government in its Crownbird series.

[3] The Nigerian peanut harvest last year amounted to 430,000 tons, of which 200,000 are still interred in the pyramids. The nut can make oil after three years. But this is an expensive method of storage.

brief segment of the trip, Jiddah-Mecca, is done by automobile, since Mecca itself has no airport.) The round-trip fare from Kano to Mecca is £149, and last year 1,159 passengers went; this year the number will be well over two thousand. Many pilgrims are very old when they are at last able to achieve this final fulfillment of their lives, a pilgrimage to Mecca, and some die—twenty did in 1952—en route. The airline seldom, however, has demands from a relative for a refund on the round-trip fare, since the seats are apparently grabbed up at once by Arabians at the other end, who want to leave Saudi Arabia. The pilgrimage to Mecca from Kano overland and across the Red Sea was once an undertaking of the most arduous and prolonged difficulty, taking several months. Now it can be done in less than twenty-four hours. I asked the late Emir of Kano if this did not make it too easy for the faithful to get to Mecca, and so become entitled to be called by the precious name Hadji. "Won't there be so many Hadjis soon that the title will no longer carry distinction?" I inquired. The old Emir chuckled. "The price is too high for most. Anyway it is a good thing to have many Hadjis."

Let no one doubt the puritanical authority of the Moslem religion in these parts. The penalty for public drunkenness, as established by Koranic law and the native courts in Kano, is still—even today—forty lashes. It is true that the lashing is administered lightly. But it is done in public, and is thus a gross humiliation to the recipient.

Kano is two cities. The quarter outside the walls is known as the Saba N'Gari, or Town of Strangers. Here lives a colony of some 20,000 southern Nigerians, most of them Ibos but with some Yorubas. These are not allowed into Kano proper at night, when the gates close. The northerners hate them, particularly the Yorubas, who have little discipline. In the North intermarriage sometimes occurs between a northerner and an Ibo, but with a Yoruba almost never. The Ibos are expanding very fast. They are industrious, they are pugnacious, and they know how to organize. "If an Ibo has to be arrested, you will need four police to hold him," a magistrate told me.

Why do many southern Nigerians live in Kano? The answer could not be simpler—few northerners have even an elementary education, and southerners must be imported to fill essential jobs. The Ibos and Yorubas are stationmasters on the railroad, telegraph clerks, post office employees, airline dispatchers, and so on, everywhere in the North, because practically no northerners are capable as yet of doing this kind of work. This has led to much bitter feeling, and there were severe riots in Kano early in 1953. People fought with machetes, dane guns, and even—yes—bows and arrows. No one knows how many people were killed; the official figure is forty-six.

The riot followed the visit to Kano of a southern politician we have named, S.L. Akintola, who was trying to influence the North to agree to the southern demand for independence in 1956. Most northerners despise their southern brethren. Of course they only see southerners *in the North*, some of whom are bad types, and judge the whole south accordingly.

In Kano we were guests of our good friend Dr. Arthur Bryson, and he showed us the city hospital, the largest hospital in West Africa. In the yard I saw fat, slimy blue and yellow parrots crawling—oddly enough—on the ground. I looked again. They were lizards.

In one ward, we encountered a case of elephantiasis of the scrotum—the patient had a black sack the size of a large basket, bigger than a pumpkin, dangling between his legs. In another lay the most pitiable medical case I have ever seen. A boy fell asleep on a road, and a hyena bit off the lower part of his face. The boy lost tongue, lips, and the whole lower jaw, but would not die. I asked what would happen to him, if, on leaving the hospital, he was not poisoned by his family. Answer: "He may make a good living as a beggar."

Dr. Bryson's division of this hospital has the highest possible standards, and does work of notable and devoted quality. In equipment it compares to Dr. Schweitzer's hospital in Lambaréné as, say, Claridge's compares to a pub in Lambeth. But this does not mean that Dr. Bryson does not often encounter typically African difficulties. Recently he operated on a boy for tropical ulcer; the operation was successful, but, to lengthen a tendon in the leg, a second operation was projected. Dr. Bryson did not know why the youngster, terrified, did his best to avoid and delay the second operation. He learned the reason later. A nurse had told the boy that, unless he gave her fifteen shillings "dash," she would see to it that the anesthetic in the next operation would kill him.

*

Officially the Emir of Kano is known as the Emir Alhaji Abdullah Bayero, the Galadima Dawakin Kudo of Kano. He rules 2,300,000 people.[4] "Galadima" means "leader of the foot army"; chiefs in the North bear titles which indicate their ancient ceremonial position. We have met enough Moslem potentates in this book, and so I will be brief. The Emir is seventy-eight, and has some forty children. He is of the sixth generation of his line to hold the throne. We were taken to pay our respects to this eminent and highly feudal old gentleman. His palace, inside a sizable courtyard, is dec-

---

[4] The Emir died in December, 1953. He was succeeded by his eldest son, the Chiroma of Kano, mentioned below.

orated with prongs made of baked ocher-red mud in the familiar desert style, and one court leads to the next, but not in mazes so complicated as those we saw on the other side of the Sahara, in the Berber country. The Emir's bodyguard was lined up as we approached; its uniforms are a loud, handsome mixture of red and green. Then we became conscious of courtiers greeting us. I was startled because, as they smiled, I thought that all must have bleeding gums. But no. They were chewing kola nut, a well-known Nigerian delicacy. This is supposed to contain minute quantities of strychnine, and thus acts as a stimulant. Addicts (like the Emir) chew the nut for a period, then spit the remains on the floor. The juice is bright red.[5]

The Emir himself, who has considerable stateliness, met us at the outer gate, and showed us into his throne room. This large conical stucco chamber has decorations depicting, of all things, airplanes. The Emir sat down, placing us next to him; his attendants and eldest son squatted at a respectful distance. He wore a white turban that contained a kind of bib fore and aft, with two spurs stuck out over his ears; this symbolizes the spelling of the word "Allah." The Emir gets £7,000 per year salary from the Native Authority (local administration) plus £3,000 for his establishment. At once, when our interview began (he talked in Arabic, not Fulani), we discovered that he was intelligent and well informed. He knew about Idris in Libya and what was going on in the Sudan, and said one thing about events in the local sphere that was enlightening. We asked him about the political situation in the North and he replied enigmatically but not too enigmatically that it was "like Pakistan."

The word I heard most, both from the Emir and his courtiers, was "*to*," pronounced "tow." It is uttered with the most artful, melodiously soft, grave intonation, "To . . . To . . ." again and again, and means "indeed."

Outside the palace, when we left, some convicts were busy cutting away grass. They all carried long knives. The lone guard was totally unarmed.

The Emir's most important son is known as Alhaji Mohammadu Sansusi, the Chiroma of Kano. He is about forty-eight. He is clever and modern-minded. Succession is, as we know, a complex subject in most of Africa. It must go to somebody in the royal house, but not necessarily to the Emir's own branch of this. Genealogy is wildly confused in Moslem lands, and there are usually any number of people to choose from. This has both good and bad effects. It encourages bright young men of royal blood to work

---

[5] This marks an advance to modern living, not the reverse, since the Northern nobles, like the Tuareg, never used to show their mouths at all. The lower part of the face was customarily hidden by a snatch of veil held in the teeth, so that the beholder could not view the chief's expression.

THE NIGERIAN NORTH 781

hard and be on their best behavior, if they want to be chosen, but on the other hand it makes it impossible to give special education to an heir presumptive, because nobody knows who the heir will be.

We spent one afternoon inspecting a village with one of the Emir's brothers, who is seventy-eighth in line to the succession. This amiable gentleman wore a marvelous pink turban the color and almost the consistency of pink spun sugar—what one buys for children at a circus. He is advanced, so much so that he likes to sit in the front seat of his automobile, or even drive himself. (Normally, an emir sits alone in the back of a car, and in the exact middle of the seat.) He took us to a meeting of his village council, and this was an enlightening experience. We listened to these villagers, so miserably poor, half naked, so unutterably primitive, as they sat first in a council chamber and then outdoors under the trees, with their faces scarred by tribal identifications and their children squirming nearby smeared with ceremonial ash-marks, talk with businesslike solemnity about the new fig trees they had planted, about the sick and the maimed and how they must be fed, about the night watchman they contemplated hiring for a shilling a month, and, miracle of miracles, about the bulldozer they wanted to rent to clear a neighboring field. They were spanning the immense arc between camel caravans and mechanized agriculture overnight, and doing so by a simple, collective democratic process.

There are fifty-two emirs in the Nigerian North in all, of whom twenty are important enough to be known officially as "first-class" emirs. They are feudal chieftains still, but they have felt the beginning, at least, of the impingement of the modern world. The emirs no longer have personal financial control of their areas, and do not levy taxes any more.

THE NORTH IN GENERAL

I have mentioned that Northern Nigeria has 16,800,000 people, which means that it is more populous than Norway, Sweden, and Denmark combined. Administration is carried on largely (under the British system of Indirect Rule) by a Native Authority in each area. One index of the extreme isolation and remoteness of this territory is that only *one* Northern Nigerian (a schoolmaster at Zaria) has ever visited the United States. An incidental point is that not a single Jew lives in the entire vast region.

Feudalism, particularly in a rigid Moslem area, brings familiar evils. The people, no matter how charming and picturesque they may be, are not only poverty-stricken to an extreme, but unbelievably ignorant. Broadcasting has to be in the simplest vernacular. If you ask even the most rudimentary questions about government, people will not understand. There are a few cinemas in Kano; Europeans often find it difficult to hear the sound track, because the bulk of the audience shouts continually in surprise and delight, uttering aloud such remarks as, "Look—a horse!" As an example of backwardness, let me mention that, until twenty years ago, a doctor could not amputate a man's leg even to save his life without the laboriously gained permission of the local Moslem elders. I hardly need to go into such obvious items as the position of women. Here we find the usual Moslem conventions enforced with limitless orthodoxy, so much so that it is almost impossible to obtain female nurses or schoolteachers. As a rule women in the new adult education classes are, and have to be, prostitutes. No other women exist to recruit from. A doctor we met needed assistants for his leprosarium, and prostitutes were the only women he could get. And these, it may be added, did their jobs very well.

The principal Northern tribe is the Hausa, but this term is so all-embracing as to be almost meaningless. To use it is like saying "European." There is no such person as "a" Hausa, just as there is properly speaking no Bantu.[6] There are Hausa-*speaking* people, like Bantu-speaking people. The Hausa folk are generally Negro or negroid in appearance, but their language is Hamitic. It is an old language, having certainly been in use for a thousand years or more; a contemporary Hausa-English dictionary is a thick book indeed, and it is the second most widely spoken language in Africa. Like Berber, Somali, and Galla, it is an "advanced" language, with grammatical rules. But the Hausas produced no culture. They are a people without any creative spark or illumination at all, it seems—without art, literature, or even crafts. The average Hausa woman cannot sew. Her hands are so slippery with henna, used to make them soft, that it is impossible for her most of the time to hold a needle.

In the early 1800's another African people, the Fulani, descended on the Hausa and conquered them in the name of the Prophet. Under a great warrior Othman Dan Fodio they made a *jehad* (holy war) and established the Fulani empire. Descendants of these Fulani, a Hamitic folk who belong technically to the white race, are today tall, slim, much lighter-skinned than the Hausa, more graceful and with finer features.[7] Some even have blue eyes, and some Fulani women are extravagantly beautiful. The Fulani promptly intermarried with their Hausa vassals, and many Nigerians today bear traces of both heritages. Generally it is the ruling class that has

---

[6] We will, however, violate this dictum, as we have violated it with Bantu.
[7] Fat women are, however, generally admired. When, in the old days, an emir wanted concubines, he stood a line of women with their noses against a wall; those who projected most behind were chosen.

the most Fulani blood, and some emirs claim to be pure Fulani. The proudest are those palest in color. Most Fulani today are what their forefathers were—nomads, cattle raisers, with no fixed habitation; when they move, their women carry their reed houses with them. There are also "town Fulani," whom the nomads consider to be degenerate. Incidentally Fulani is one of the most complicated and abstruse of languages. There are *seventeen* genders, and the plural of a noun may have no resemblance whatever to the singular.

Partly because Indirect Rule has worked well the Nigerian North has always been a region highly favored by the British.[8] This is the land par excellence of the loyal, devoted, and sometimes idiosyncratic Resident or District Officer who in a perfectly genuine sense gives his whole life to the service of the country. We have seen the same phenomenon in East Africa. Of course British officers in Nigeria have an excellent career and gain substantial rewards. But most have an almost completely unselfish attitude toward their mission. If I met one District Officer I met a dozen whose philosophy had the ring of utter sincerity, "We are here to do a job. We are training these people to do *their* jobs. Of course we are going to get out in time. This is *their* country. There is no exploitation here."

One Northern province, Sokoto, is twice the area of Holland.[9] It has 1,500,000 people and is run by exactly thirty white officials, who have at their disposal three hundred unarmed African police. Disparities like this produce beautiful legends. One District Officer was told by his African sergeant, on a Wednesday, that a riot was taking place outside his door, with tribesmen massing to sack the establishment. The Briton did not look up from his desk. "Tell them to go home. In this area we do not have riots on Wednesdays. Let them come on a Saturday if they wish, when I have more time." Recently a DO near the Cameroons border went mad, after he had survived an attack by natives with poisoned arrows. He tore down a hut, and walked about in a suit made of its tin roof.

The British in Nigeria have been strongly influenced by the country's sectionalism, and some even seem to be more "nationalist" than the Nigerians. Up here in the North, they say, the Africans are *men*! Similarly in southern Nigeria, British officials can be strongly pro-Ibo or pro-Yoruba. I heard an Englishman say, "If it was up to me I'd live in Yorubaland all my life, even after Nigeria gets self-rule. I hope they'll hire me when *we*

---

[8] The British, as always, do their best never to interfere with the native satraps. Sometimes, however, these behave so disgracefully or are so unmanageable that they have to be removed. The Emir of Dikwa was deposed in 1954.
[9] Vernon Bartlett, *Struggle for Africa*, p. 117.

go." Even Africans make jokes about this. They say that they will have to have a sizable army in the new Nigeria, for fear that the British who are pro-Hausa, pro-Ibo, or pro-Yoruba will start a civil war.

The upper tier of Northern Nigeria (which has twelve large provinces in all) is Moslem; the southern is still largely pagan. With the British came Christianity, and the missions have been responsible for practically all the education the country has. Many pagans have become Christianized.

*

Northern Nigeria is feudal, yes, but it is also part of Nigeria, the modern state. The chief political figure in the North is Ahmadu, the Sardauna of Sokoto, the head of the Northern People's Congress. He is a very considerable personage indeed, and for a variety of reasons. First, Sokoto is big and heavily populated. Second, the Northern People's Congress is by far the most important political organization in the North. Third, the Sardauna has commanding vigor, intellect, and prestige. Fourth, from a religious point of view, his capital is a holy city, and he is the spiritual head not merely of all Moslems in Nigeria, but on the whole West Coast of Africa.

The Sardauna, who is a descendant of the old Fulani kings, had a partly European education. He is a moderate nationalist. For a long time—perhaps not now—he thought that 1956 was too early a date for independence, in that the North was not anywhere so mature politically as the precocious south and would be sucked under by it. When the central legislature broke up in March, 1953, he walked out of the chamber muttering, "Ah! Now we pay for Lugard's mistake in 1914!" By this he meant presumably that Lord Lugard should not even have attempted to unify the country.

Another political party exists in the North, called NEPU, or Northern Elements Progressive Union, an offshoot of Zik's forces. This is much more radical and inflammatory than the Sardauna's NPC. It has stood for self-government in 1956 all along.

Several other Northern emirs have large territories and substantial power. One is the Shehu (sheikh) of Bornu. He is one of the richest men in the world. His "kingdom," which is bigger than Scotland or Maine and lies to the northeast of Kano, as Sokoto lies to the northwest, was never conquered by the Fulani; his people are a famous independent race, the Kanuri. His remote capital, Maiduguri, was seen—oddly enough—by many Americans during World War II, because it was a stop on the Air Transport Command's route to the Middle East. His chief source of power, like that of most of his colleagues, is that the uneducated serfs are solidly behind him.[10]

Now we recapitulate the basic political situation insofar as it concerns the North. Constitutional reform in Nigeria as a whole means simply to bring the North in. The North is extremely loath to lose British administration, if this is to be followed by a Nigerian administration that may turn out to be much inferior. The North knows that it has not the personnel with which to run its own government. On occasion inflamed northerners have even threatened to secede and establish a separate country of their own, "Hausaland," rather than accept submission to the south. There are firebrands who say that the North will invade and conquer the south, as the Fulani warriors once tried to do. But the North, if it should sever all ties with the south, would have no seacoast, a crippling disadvantage; on the other hand it has most of Nigeria's great mineral wealth, particularly tin. I heard northerners say, "If we secede, we can ship our goods out to French Africa, along the Niger." But this would be a difficult process.

In Kano we had one lively morning talking about all this with a group of young Nigerians. One said, "The southerners despise us, but we despise them more. We had culture when the Ibos were eating their own grandmothers. Of course we want self-government, but we must be educated up to it first. We must preserve our identity. The choice of the date 1956 was an unscrupulous political device on the part of the south. They chose this date knowing that we will not be ready when the British go; hence the south will be able to absorb us more easily. To say that the British are 'goading us to secede' is nonsense."

This was one of several occasions when we were asked questions about American history in the period 1776-87; Nigerians want to know how the United States managed to establish unity. This morning one official said soberly, "What a pity it is that Northern and Southern Nigeria differ so much more than Virginia and Massachusetts."

We asked how education could possibly come to Northern Nigeria while women were still not emancipated. What happened then was what always happens when this question is asked in an Islamic community. Our meeting broke up in an excited storm.

*

One further point might be mentioned—the future position and influence of the Sudan. It is commonly assumed that Nigeria will always, in

[10] Political scientists are sometimes vexed by a curious paradox—that by and large Moslems in the Mediterranean sector of Africa are flamingly radical, whereas those in the desert below are equally anti-nationalist and conservative. The reason of course is that the desert dwellers have not yet emerged from feudalism.

the end, do what the Gold Coast does, but the Sudan is emotionally much closer, at least to Nigerians of the North. If the Sudanese experiment in self-government works well, this will have a strong effect on Nigeria as a whole.

WE VISIT JOS

We flew to Jos, two hours by air from Kano, high up on the central plateau. Here too is a new Nigerian world. Jos sits at 3,900 feet, in healthy upland country; it has more of the texture of a European city than any I saw in Nigeria. The population is 30,000, of which 1,500 are white. Jos has a splendid little museum of African anthropology and antiquities. Seventeen miles away is the oddly named town of Vom,[11] the seat of the West African Institute of Trypanosomiasis Research, where Colonel H. W. Mulligan and his associates do admirable work. One of the roads out of Jos—we traveled on it a few inches—leads all the way to Lake Chad.

Jos is the center of tin and columbite mining—which, strange as it may seem, makes it of considerable strategic interest to the United States. Nigeria produces a large proportion of the world's columbite, a mineral indispensable for the manufacture of special heat-resisting steel. No jet plane can fly without columbite or some similar alloy; the American air force could not exist without columbite from Jos and elsewhere. The tin mines here are an old story. They have been operated for many years.[12] Until recently nobody paid any attention to columbite, a rare mineral associated with tin, because no market for it existed. Residue from the tin operations was tossed aside as worthless, and soon became covered with grass and bush. Now it is being dug up again inch by inch for columbite, just as the slag heaps near Johannesburg are being worked over for uranium. Apparently mining in Africa always has to be done twice. The United States pays a bonus of 100 per cent beyond the regular price for all the columbite that Nigeria produces.

Everybody in Jos talks about the mining boom, almost as if it were Butte, Montana, and almost everybody, it seems, has a claim. This remote little town will be one of the first in Africa to have residential apartment buildings, because, hemmed in as it is by mine leases, no room is left to expand horizontally. Some villagers resent the mines. They say that mining takes their land away, but this is not true—native holdings are carefully pro-

---

[11] But there are towns in Texas with such odd names as Ace, Box, Nix, and Pep.
[12] The major company is Amalgamated Tin Mines of Nigeria, usually known as ATMN. Tin is mined by an open cast process, since the ore lies close to the surface; there are no deep shafts.

tected, and it is against the law to lease any mine sites within areas actually lived on by Africans.

Jos is a European toy metropolis, but a few miles away live people more uncompromisingly primitive than any we saw in Africa, except possibly in Tanganyika and the Congo. We went to a village inhabited by a tribe known as the Birom. Its people cannot have changed much in a thousand years. The Fulani horsemen and slave traders could not get up here; the plateau was too high, and they were ambushed on the rocky trails. So we saw villagers almost completely untouched by any modern influence. The Birom are stark naked except for a small napkin made of grass and hung over the loins fore and aft. The breasts of the women, flat, empty, and drooping, look like spaniel's ears. These folk live mostly on a variety of wild rice called *atcha*, which is also made into beer and is used in fertility rites; the favorite local poison comes from the bark of the sasswood tree. Forbidding cactus fences surround each group of huts. Our guide told us something of the customs of the Birom. Even in a small village people are divided into two exogamous clans, with marriage between them forbidden. Children who are born feet first are considered to be unlucky and in older days were strangled promptly; so were children born of a marriage between members of the same clan. The man in the moon is the patron of drummers in this tribe, and one method of murder is to insert a peculiar kind of thorn in the victim's throat; this kills him, but is then completely absorbed by the bodily tissues, so that no trace exists and murder cannot be proved. Ordeal by poison is also common. The smallpox god was powerful among the Birom until recently, and perhaps still is. Corrupt priests of this cult, who are supposed to be able to cure smallpox, sometimes went out and deliberately spread this malady, in order to be able to "treat" more patients and thus collect more fees.

Nigerians have, in contrast to unpleasantness like this, some exceptionally charming folklore, and they love tall tales. Their fables in this and other areas have an amazing resemblance to Aesop, and usually concern animals —why the oyster has no fat, how the mosquito got its buzz, and so on. One well-known Nigerian story is called "The Suitors of the Princess Gorilla," and one renowned creature of local folklore resembles startlingly the American Brer Rabbit.

WE VISIT KATSINA

From Kano we drove northwest to an important emirate, Katsina, a few miles from the frontier of French West Africa. Here the ruler is the Hadj Osuman Nagogo, Emir of Katsina, CBE. He has been a minister without portfolio in the central Nigerian government, and is one of the best polo players in the country. He is in his middle forties, and has been on the throne since 1944. His father, of whom he was the fourth son, was Emir for forty years. The Emir of Katsina rules 9,000 square miles of territory, with a population of 1,400,000. He is religious as well as political head of his people, and is both an enlightened ruler and, from the pan-Nigerian point of view, a moderate nationalist. He sat in the same cabinet with such extremists as Akintola and the late Chief Bode Thomas. Africa, let us say once more, is a very mixed-up continent.

I will not describe the circumstances of our audience with this personage, because they resemble generally the one we had in Kano. This Emir was, however, much more westernized. As we talked, his counselors (including his eldest son) were permitted to sit twelve feet away, which is considered close. But the occasion was quite informal; during the audience one of his grandsons entered the throne room without warning, dressed in a little *riga* (robe). The boy bowed, then crawled for about ten yards, then laid himself down flat on the floor before the Emir, not in the gesture of prostration, but almost like a friendly dog. One adviser present was the development secretary, whose talk, in this archaic palace built of mud, was roughly what one would hear if Governor Harriman, say, summoned a consultant to explain what was going on in New York in the realm of road development, public health, and municipal finance. And the Emir himself gave us a strong impression of being cosmopolitan, sophisticated, and progressive.

Moslem officials are known by titles here, rather than by name. I asked the identity of another man, who had been introduced merely as the Magajin Gari (Keeper of the Town). The British Resident said that he had known him well for four years, but had never even heard his name. We learned on this visit something about other phenomena of chiefdom. In this part of Nigeria, authority goes by chain of command almost as it does in the American army; every field of activity has its chief, with stratifications underneath. There was until recently a *Kaigama* or Chief Slave. There is a Chief Beggar, who rides on horseback. There is a Chief Butcher, and a Chieftainess of Prostitutes.

*

En route back we stopped briefly at Kankiya, to visit Dr. Gordon Butler, the public health officer of the area. We watched a snake charmer put on an exemplary performance with two cobras ("If a snake hasn't fed for a couple of days, and hits you with both fangs, you've had it.") and heard about local medical problems, which are grievous. We even saw one. In the outpatients room, an African fully clothed was lying inert on the floor, like a limb off a tree. He was a madman, and Dr. Butler had just given him a soporific, to keep him quiet till the ambulance could get him to Katsina. In this district there are 40,000 cases of leprosy, and the bilharzia rate is near saturation—80 per cent. Dr. Butler sends town women out into the villages to look for the earliest signs of leprosy in people, so that they may be brought to him and treated. The first symptom of sleeping sickness is, paradoxically enough, insomnia. This comes when the trypanosome first begins to irritate the brain. When a villager is far gone with sleeping sickness—emaciated, languorous, and half stupefied—his fellows take him out in the bush and leave him there to die.

*

So now we conclude with Nigeria, its immense complexities and vitality, its color without end and high-charged, hot, multifarious development. Next—the Gold Coast.

CHAPTER 40

Prime Minister Nkrumah of the Gold Coast

I came out of jail and into the Assembly without the slightest feeling of bitterness to Britain.

—KWAME NKRUMAH

DR. KWAME NKRUMAH, Prime Minister of the Gold Coast, is one of the most remarkable personalities in Africa. He is the first Negro ever to become prime minister of a British colony, and as leader of the Gold Coast revolution he personifies the hopes of black nationalism everywhere on the continent where people are educated enough to have heard of him. He has been called "the African Nehru," the "Giant of Ghana"—Ghana being the vernacular name for the Gold Coast—and, depending on the zoological predilections of his admirers, both the "Eagle" and the "Lion" of Africa. His nickname is "Show-Boy," but not in the sense of "showing off"; it indicates merely that his fanatically devoted followers think of him as a prize demonstration piece.

Dr. Nkrumah was educated largely in the United States, and is forty-six. He is a socialist who flirted with Communist ideas in his youth, but he is not a Communist. His personality and career demand serious study, not only because of his intrinsic interest and importance but because he obviously portends so much. The Gold Coast is the pacemaker for African nationalism, and as it goes, so may much of the rest of the continent go in time. Nkrumah's Gold Coast, as I have mentioned several times, will probably become before long the first Black Dominion in the Commonwealth, if the other dominions approve. Conversely if it blows up and the experiment fails—on account of inexperience, corruption, or what not—independence movements will be set back elsewhere.

Dr. Nkrumah (pronounced En-krooma) reached his present elevated position through a combination of factors: (a) his own personal qualities, which are striking; (b) the evolution of British policy, which gave these qualities substantial play. We will discuss these in turn.

Also Gold Coast characteristics played a role. This country is altogether different from Nigeria, for example, although the two have many problems in common and their historical origin is similar. But the Gold Coast is much more homogeneous than Nigeria, smaller, more compact, and far richer. Like Nigeria it is divided into three distinct areas, but these have closer links. There is no risk of fragmentation as in Nigeria. Prime Minister Nkrumah is the creator and head of a *national* party, and has a national following. Politics here are more advanced, stable, and sophisticated, despite perennial sharp crises. Nkrumah can afford to be moderate and make his own pace, because he has no serious competitor for leadership of the nationalist movement, and does not have to inflame the country artificially to get votes.

The Gold Coast evolution toward Dominion Status, or independence within the Commonwealth, is being watched with electric interest by Europeans nearby. For instance, the Gold Coast (including British Togoland) is completely surrounded by French territory except where it faces the sea. What will be the effect of an independent Gold Coast, if it is successful, on these French areas? The French try to scoff at Nkrumah, but they are perturbed. How will it be possible for France, even in a country as far away as Morocco, to assert that Africans are incapable of self-rule, if the Gold Coast under Nkrumah rules itself well? And what about the Congo? As to British Africa the repercussions may be felt far afield. Already Nkrumah is talking about a future federation of West African free states. If the Gold Coast turns out to be capable of efficient and enlightened self-government, then it will be logically difficult to deny that, given a further period of tutelage long or short, the same thing may be true for Uganda, or Kenya, or even Tanganyika. Open one door; the draft will blow open other doors.[1]

Also the point might well be made that the more the Gold Coast succeeds the worse may circumstances become for Africans in those countries where they are already suppressed. Dr. Malan talked of the Gold Coast with contempt and loathing, and his successors are certainly not going to take any chances and allow anybody like Nkrumah to rise in *their* domain.

However let us proceed, and sketch a brief portrait of Nkrumah the man.

[1] Of course it is official British policy that all their territories shall have *eventual* self-government.

SHOW-BOY

I stand for no racialism, no discrimination against any race or individual, but I am unalterably opposed to imperialism in any form.
—KWAME NKRUMAH

Government House in Accra is a marvelous old castle built right up out of the sea so that a lather of surf slaps without pause against the walls. Christiansborg Castle it is called, and it was built by Danish slave traders in 1661. The stone came from Denmark—ballast in the outgoing slave ships. The structure is the purest, most dazzling white, with tall palms leaning against the crenelated battlements, and kingfishers nesting in the moldy cannon. In the garden are maroon, salmon-pink, scarlet and pale yellow cannas, as regal as any flowers I ever saw.

Christiansborg has a history almost as romantic as its appearance. The Danes bought the promontory where it sits in stately radiance for seven gold bars, from African chiefs in the neighborhood. Then the Portuguese took it from the Danes and then the Danes took it back from the Portuguese. It is the only fort in all Africa which was once recaptured by an intrepid band of Africans themselves. The British, when they took over the Gold Coast, used Christiansborg as a lunatic asylum for a time. Its wild and isolated beauty, the crashing of the waves against its towers, the salt moisture seeping endlessly through the thick walls, must have made it almost indecently appropriate for this purpose. It has been Government House since 1900.

The Governor, Sir Charles Noble Arden-Clarke, asked Dr. Nkrumah to dinner. No ban on fraternization between British and Africans at Government House, as in some British territories, exists on the Gold Coast.[2] But no one knew, until he arrived, whether the Prime Minister would actually

[2] Arden-Clarke tactfully but firmly settled the business of hospitality at Government House in Accra once and for all on the very day that Nkrumah got out of jail in 1951. By tradition members of a new ministry are entertained at a garden or sherry party at Government House. Arden-Clarke reminded Nkrumah and his colleagues of this, and went on to say that he assumed that the nationalist ban on social contacts with the British did not apply to representatives of the Crown. The new ministers accepted the invitation at first, but then changed their minds and refused it. Arden-Clarke, a stout character and one of the ablest British governors in Africa, then calmly reminded a nationalist spokesman that "the invitations had only been issued after consultation with the ministers," and that he "would not tolerate" a refusal to accept the invitation, because this would be an insult to the Crown. The Governor let it be known that he expected Nkrumah and his men to come, and they did. There has never been any trouble about official hospitality since.

appear for dinner or not. He would not have been so rude as to have neglected to come without warning, but his secretary might well have sent word at the last moment that, owing to some emergency, he would be unable to be present. Anyway he came. It was interesting to meet the Prime Minister in such a setting. The Union Jack flew stiffly in the dark breeze on a terrace overhead. Here was an African nationalist, pledged to terminate British rule, breaking bread at the Governor's own table. But I do not want to stress unduly the dramatic impact of this. Relations between British and Gold Coasters are gracious on the whole, and the atmosphere of the dinner was cordial, even casual. Everybody seemed to be a friend, without the shyness and stiffness that usually accompanies African-British social intercourse.

Nkrumah has a high, narrow, fully domed forehead, a receding crown of hair, a nose only moderately broadish at the tip, the perfect white teeth typical of Africans, and big lips nicely shaped, like slices of a tangerine. He is of medium height, supple, graceful, and assured. All his movements and gestures have power, ease, and magnetism. He neither struts nor shows exaggerated reserve. People often describe him as having "melancholy" or "brooding" eyes, and perhaps this is true, but we discovered soon enough that he likes to laugh.

Nkrumah wore African dress, which struck me deeply if only because I had never seen anything like it before. The national costume of the Gold Coast differs from any other in Africa; it is a robe worn like a Roman toga, with the left arm and shoulder exposed. Some people, depending on the weather, wear a kind of thin shift under their togas, and the Prime Minister did so this evening—it was white with an embroidery of tiny gold stars. The toga itself was magnificent. It differed from those worn by people on the streets as a Valentina gown, let us say, differs from one from Seventh Avenue. It was of a dusty golden color, with a rectilinear design in deeper gold, yellow, red, and pale green. The silk that goes into togas like these, which are customarily worn only by chiefs, is called *kente* cloth. It is designed and made locally, and is thus distinguished from the plebeian "mammy cloth" which comes from England or North Carolina. *Kente* cloth is woven in long narrow strips, and these, when sewn together to make the robe, give it a characteristic pattern. It is very costly. Enough for a good robe may cost three hundred dollars, but many people buy them. The rectangular designs always have an esoteric meaning, like Scottish plaids.

We met Nkrumah the next time in his own quarters, and here he wore much simpler, less flamboyant dress. He lives in an Accra suburb in a house strangely named—Lutterodt's Memorial Inn. This belonged, or belongs, to a prosperous African photographer, one of his close friends, and he and his staff have the use of it. It is of European design but has striking African touches. The brick walls are painted the brightest possible pink with thick white stripes on the intervening lines of mortar. The shutters are green on one side of each window, red on the other. In the garage I saw a black Cadillac, which gave rise to a minor scandal lately. Nkrumah, his enemies alleged, may have received this as a gift from somebody of dubious reputation who wanted favors. The Prime Minister, denying these allegations, says that he bought the car himself with legitimately borrowed money. Far from being rich through corruption, he did not even have enough capital to buy an automobile. The controversial vehicle is notable for another and quite different reason. Nkrumah's adherents told me that, whenever he traveled out from Accra into the villages, people would recognize the car as his and polish it with their robes. They did this as a gesture of affection and respect. Nkrumah's simplicity has always been one of his chief qualities. Out in the country, he gives no thought at all to where he sleeps. He will share a beggar's *kenke* (mealie meal) anywhere. He sits on the muddy ground and talks on terms of complete familiarity and equality with any citizen, in a way that Zik and Awolowo in Nigeria almost never do.

Courtyard and corridors at Luttorodt's are full of tatterdemalion retainers, as in the headquarters of any African dignitary. We were led upstairs to a small bare study where the Prime Minister received us. With him was his secretary, an intelligent and very pretty girl from the British West Indies named Joyce Githens. Sometimes she led the talk when a question did not interest him. I asked him what he did for relaxation, and he replied dryly, "Work." Miss Githens suggested that he should add, "See people." He drives into the hinterland every Sunday, to maintain his close contact with the masses. I asked him what intellectual influences he remembered most, and he replied, "Hegel." Other influences make a mixed bag. Christianity is certainly one; his speeches are peppered with the names of saints. So was Gandhi, who taught him the meaning and power of civil disobedience. So was Roosevelt and the American New Deal. Nkrumah lived in the United States in the middle thirties, and Roosevelt's giant brush touched him as it touched the whole world at that time.

I asked him if he were a socialist, and he replied, "Of course"; then he added that he was a "Christian Marxist," without, however, defining this peculiar term. He denied firmly that he was, or ever had been, a Communist. Marxism has interested him, he went on, merely as a philosophical point of view, not in the realm of practical political affairs. His voice was emphatic when he said, "We have no Communist party here!"

The Gold Coast revolution is, Nkrumah thinks, a forerunner of the inevitable emancipation of all Africa, particularly West Africa. His fondest political hope is that the Gold Coast, Nigeria and the rest of West Africa will, in the future, be able to combine into a free federation; creation of a truly African Africa is his greatest dream. Recently he paid a state visit to Liberia. He wants the closest possible relations with all the nearby territories.

There is, he thinks, no danger of disunity in the Gold Coast like that in Nigeria. For one thing the Gold Coast chiefs are no problem from the nationalist point of view. "We are building on the old heritage of the chiefs, not superimposing something from above. Our chiefs are much more democratic than most outsiders think. Our biggest asset is that our movement rises from people who *understand* our goals."

Nkrumah's fourteen months in prison did not, it seems, embitter him against the British. He told us that after independence he would be quite prepared to hire private British advisers under contract. He has the greatest respect for men like Arden-Clarke. In jail he was subject to the regular prison discipline, and got no favors. "But it wasn't too bad. I made fish nets and wove baskets." His behavior in prison was exemplary, as it was in court. The British like him for this—he "plays the game"—and for such minor reasons as that he has amicable relations today with the judge who sentenced him. A British official who gave testimony against him was the one assigned to greet him when he was released from jail. Nkrumah stuck out his hand warmly, laughed, and said, "Well, sir, I'm glad to see you again in God's fresh air!"

When we prepared to leave him after an hour Nkrumah said that he wanted us to meet his mother. She came out of the kitchen downstairs. She is about sixty-five, a tiny, dignified, and immensely proud old lady. The Prime Minister talked to her affectionately in her native tongue; she knows no English. I asked her (with Nkrumah interpreting) if she had known when her son was a little boy that he was going to be a great man. Tartly she replied, "No one can know things like that. But—" She finished the sentence by putting a hand on Nkrumah's shoulder, in a gesture denoting at once satisfaction, pride, skepticism about the reality of all this, and a cozy confidence that she, at least, was not going to have any nonsense from her son even if he was prime minister.

PERSONAL QUALITIES OF THE PRIME MINISTER

Nkrumah is a bachelor. He likes the company of women, including white women, but says that he has no time to get married. One of his best known remarks is, "Every woman in the Gold Coast is my bride."[3]

[3] See a well-informed cover story on Nkrumah in *Time*, February 9, 1953, and "Letter from the Gold Coast," by Oden and Olivia Meeker, *New Yorker*, December 20, 1952.

He neither smokes nor drinks, though very occasionally he may have a sip of champagne. Mostly he is a vegetarian, and when we saw him he did not touch coffee. Many nationalist leaders or dictators in prewar Europe cultivated similar puritanisms, but they are somewhat rare in Africa, except among Moslems. Nkrumah's salary as prime minister is high—£3,500 per year.[4] He has no interest in sport, worldliness, or the frivolities that waste the time of most men, but he is fond of music, both classical and the local dance music, which resembles calypso and is called Highlife.

He works long hours, but without much sign of strain. His manner is almost always suave. He talks well when he wants to, but is sometimes guarded—especially with Europeans—and even inarticulate. He gets up at six, does paper work, and then receives for an hour anybody who wants to see him. This is in the orthodox tradition of African leaders. *Anybody* may walk in. And hundreds do. At about nine he goes for several hours to the headquarters of the Convention People's Party, of which he is president, and then proceeds to the Prime Minister's office or the Legislative Assembly if it is in session. Here he does his administrative and parliamentary work. He returns home, has a brief dinner, and then has conferences or does more paper work till midnight.

His best friends in the political sphere are two cabinet colleagues, Kojo Botsio, the Oxford-educated minister of state, and K. A. Gbedemah, minister of finance. More on Gbedemah later. Mr. Botsio is a red-hot socialist (and, incidentally, one of the handsomest Negroes I ever met). He and Gbedemah, who is practical-minded and more moderate, compete to an extent for Nkrumah's favor. People watch at a function to see which of them will be on the Prime Minister's right, which on his left. (Similarly at a political banquet at the Waldorf-Astoria people may crane their necks to see the order of precedence among speakers on the dais.) Another close political associate is the youthful Krobo Edusei, who is chief whip and ministerial secretary in the Justice Department. Socially Nkrumah's best friend is probably a British doctor, resident in Accra, whose wife is African. Nkrumah sometimes slips away to the movies with them. He reciprocates hospitality as a rule through Sir Emanuel Quist and Lady Quist. Sir Emanuel, an African who is supposed to have Danish blood from far back, is Speaker of the House.

Nkrumah has guts. Consider the cocoa story. Some years ago Gold Coast

---

[4] Other ministers get £3,000. These figures were suggested by Arden-Clarke. The Colonial Office was reluctant at first to establish salaries on such a high level. But as a matter of fact £3,000 does not go far in Accra if a person lives in the European manner. Also, I heard it put, this figure gives three thousand good reasons for a minister to stick at his job.

cocoa, which is by far the country's chief source of wealth, became afflicted by a disease called Swollen Shoot; this is caused by an insect known as the mealy bug, and is extremely difficult to extirpate. The only sure way to keep Swollen Shoot from spreading and ruining the crop is to destroy the diseased trees root and branch. But the trees continue to bear cocoa beans for several years after Swollen Shoot first attacks them, even though they are bound to die eventually. Orders went out to chop down and burn the infected trees, but the peasant farmers refused to do this. It was like asking them to cut off their own heads. At first Nkrumah opposed obligatory destruction of the trees. He wanted a voluntary system. Then, when he came to realize that the blight of Swollen Shoot, if unchecked, might ruin the entire cocoa industry, he reversed himself and made the farmers destroy all their diseased growth. Up to 1953 sixteen million trees have been destroyed. For Nkrumah to impose this Draconian measure on his own people, many of whom were too ignorant to understand why it was necessary, took signal political courage.[5]

Nkrumah's first quality is, people say, his animal spark, his magnetism and vitality. You can feel this across a room. Second, his ability and resilience. He is not in the least fixed or doctrinaire, and can bounce back from almost any blow. He works by intuition more than intellect, and is a highly skilled negotiator. Third, he has more serenity and confidence than most Africans. Fourth, his charm and sense of humor. He never goes in for the kind of vituperative tub-thumping that distinguishes politicians in Nigeria. Nkrumah, like Nehru in India, is a gentleman.

But do not forget that the hub of his character is nationalism. What he believes in above all is freedom for his country. He has not, however, committed his party to a specific date for independence. If you ask him, as we did, when the Gold Coast is to be fully free, he will reply warily, "Soon," or "Next year." He knows full well that, before he can rule alone successfully, he needs a better administrative structure and more trained men, and he is far too shrewd to tie himself to any unalterable date. In this too he differs from leaders in Nigeria.

The Gold Coast revolution has three aspects—youth against age, the people against the chiefs, the nationalists against the British. It is Nkrumah's greatest source of power that he combines in himself leadership in all these spheres.

Most of the men around him are young, in their forties or even younger.

---

[5] Strangely enough, another mortal enemy of the cocoa tree is mistletoe, which strangles the growth of the young shoots. For more about Swollen Shoot see Chapter 42 below.

They will presumably dominate the Gold Coast for a generation, and they can grow up with it. The situation is unlike that which obtained in India, for example, where the majority of nationalist leaders were old men when independence finally came. One of Nkrumah's biggest assets is that he has captured the imagination of the youth, and works from the bottom up. The Gold Coast is not likely to go to pieces, because the young people are aroused. This country could never be a Liberia.

His second most important source of power is probably his gift for concrete political organization. He learned a good deal about this in London, by watching the tactics of Herbert Morrison. The CPP (Convention People's Party) is organized throughout the Gold Coast down to the smallest village. Nkrumah handles it like a man winding a watch. The party has loudspeakers, automobile caravans, and other paraphernalia hitherto unknown to Black Africa. It has its own party colors (red, green, and white), its own uniformed brigades of women and youth, its own salute, which is the open palm displayed at arm's length, and its own insignia. Its motto is "Freedom," pronounced with the accent on the second syllable, and its slogan "Forward Ever, Backward Never." Some performances put on by the CPP may seem naïve to Europeans, but they have undeniable effect.

Nkrumah was brought up as a Roman Catholic, but now calls himself a "non-denominational Christian." Some people say that he still occasionally consults a *juju* or medicine man, and this is quite possible. Once again we encounter the extraordinarily pungent contrasts of Africa. Few Africans, even those most emancipated, can shake off their tribal heritage overnight. This is, as we know, the basic reason for their self-division, their so-called "schizophrenia." They go to Cambridge, they read the *Times*, they belong to clubs, they even marry white women; but they are rooted nevertheless to a past of which they are often ashamed, but which they can seldom totally exorcise if only because their skin stays black. Color is the core of everything. But Nkrumah shows few signs of self-division or inferiority. What his movement means, in essence, is the substitution of a modern fetish—nationalism—for the tribal fetishes of his fathers. Therefore he must use such symbols as motorcars brightly painted green, red, and white. He has to make the new "mystique" attractive and understandable in *African* terms. As to *juju*, why should he not, if he wants, visit a witch doctor? Similar phenomena are not unknown in the West. Mackenzie King, who was Prime Minister of Canada for twenty years, had crystal balls all over his office, indulged steadily in the fanciest kind of "spiritual" hocus-pocus, and never moved an inch without consulting an astrologer.

PRIME MINISTER NKRUMAH OF THE GOLD COAST

SATURDAY'S CHILD

Dr. Nkrumah was born in 1909 in a small village, Nkroful, in the Nzima area near the frontier of the French Ivory Coast. His native tongue is a dialect of Twi, one of the Akan languages. At the time of his birth there were no roads at all in this region, only tracks through bush. He was named Kwame, which is a word associated with "Saturday," because he was born on that day. Later he was given a Christian name—Francis—but he seldom uses it. His father was a goldsmith, an artisan who made trinkets; his mother was a mammy trader, a small shopkeeper.

Catholic mission schools—first near Nkroful, then at a town called Sekondi—gave him his early education. He was intelligent and ambitious and, when he was about eighteen, became a teacher. He saved enough money to go to Achimota College near Accra. He would have gone to England for further study, but could not get a scholarship. One of his uncles staked him to a trip to the United States, and he entered Lincoln University in Pennsylvania. This is one of the oldest and best known Negro institutions of learning in America, which has made a speciality of hospitality to African Negroes. Nkrumah worked his way through Lincoln at all manner of jobs, and saw a good deal of America and the West Indies during vacations. He got no fewer than four degrees—in theology and science as well as a B.A. and M.A.—and became for a time an instructor at Lincoln.[6] I met recently one of his classmates, who said: "Nkrumah was sober, reserved, and conscientious, as well as brilliant. The main thing about him was that he acted as if his whole life were planned."

An American writer[7] who saw Nkrumah not long ago asked him if he had ever been subjected to any particular racial humiliation in the United States. The Prime Minister replied that, at a bus station in Baltimore, he once asked where he could get a drink of water, and the clerk pointed to a spittoon. We could be fanciful about the mysterious processes of history and point out what extraordinary personal accidents have influenced events —for instance, the Dollfuss dictatorship in Austria came about partly because a member of parliament went to the washroom during a critical vote— but anybody who asserted that Great Britain is on the point of losing its richest African colony, the Gold Coast, and that Nkrumah is prime minister today, because of the barbarian rudeness of somebody in Maryland twenty

---

[6] His doctorate—an LL.D.—is an honorary degree from Lincoln, which he received on a visit to the United States in 1951, after he became prime minister.

[7] Wolfgang Langewiesche in the *Saturday Evening Post*, March 7, 1953, "He Wants to Rule West Africa."

years ago, would almost certainly be wrong. The incident may have annoyed Nkrumah at the time, but he took it with good humor. His basic philosophy was formed long before this episode. When he was still a youthful undergraduate he was writing to friends in Accra, "If I fail to bring self-government to the Gold Coast, bury me alive!"

He became president of the African Students Association of America and Canada, and his classmates at Lincoln wrote this about him when he got his first degree:[8]

> Africa is the beloved of his dreams;
> Philosopher, thinker, with forceful schemes,
> In aesthetics, politics, he's "in the field,"
> Nkrumah, "très interessant," radiates appeal.

One legend is that Nkrumah was powerfully influenced in the United States by Paul Robeson, but the truth is that he never saw Robeson but once, and this was at a public meeting. Later, however, another American Negro did make a strong impact on him—the venerable Dr. W. E. B. Du Bois, whom he met in England. He attended a Pan-African Congress in Manchester organized by Dr. Du Bois, an ardent spokesman for Negro rights who is now far to the Left.

Nkrumah spent several years in England; he studied at the London School of Economics, and met a good many British intellectuals, some of them Communists. The Communists, then as now, kept their eyes out for bright young Africans, cultivated them, and took them into their homes. Indeed it was almost impossible for an impoverished African student in London at that time to have tolerable social relations with anybody who was not a Communist or extreme left-winger. Nkrumah's so-called "Communist period" derives from this. He was considerably influenced by Communists for a brief time. When he was arrested in Accra years later, a membership card in the British Communist party was found among his papers. However, it had never been signed. Nkrumah laughs about this today, saying that he had used the card on occasion to get into Communist meetings and the like, but that it had no other significance at all and that he was never an actual party member.

In London, Nkrumah kept in close touch with Gold Coast political developments. Now came the turning point of his life. A political leader named J. B. Danquah was head of the chief nationalist party of that day, the United Gold Coast Convention, or UGCC. This, following an evolution too complex for mention here (Gold Coast nationalism has a long and

---

[8] *Time, op. cit.*

PRIME MINISTER NKRUMAH OF THE GOLD COAST 801

emphatic history), was expanding strongly. Dr. Danquah needed men, particularly an organizer. So he communicated with Nkrumah—whom he had never met—in London and invited him to become secretary of the organization. Nkrumah accepted, and arrived back in the Gold Coast on December 16, 1947. He had been twelve years away.

We must try to compress what followed, though it is, or should be, a suggestive study of how revolutions are made.

NKRUMAH IN ACTION

1. He set to work with ruthless drive, enthusiasm, and acumen to consolidate his position in the party. He was nominally under Danquah, but soon supplanted him. Then, he took advantage of an angry local situation to challenge the British. There had been a crisis in the cocoa industry and desperate Africans were boycotting European shops. On February 28, 1948, only two months after Nkrumah's arrival, some Negro war veterans marched toward Government House to demonstrate there. They were dispersed by the police and two were killed, which caused bitter public indignation. Rioting broke out all over the town, mobs burned and pillaged in the streets, and twenty-nine deaths occurred. A British official told me, "On February 27 the Gold Coast was a model colony. On March 1 it was a shambles."

2. On February 29, while rioting still went on, Nkrumah in his capacity as secretary of the UGCC telegraphed an appeal to the Colonial Office in London, saying that the local authorities could no longer maintain order and demanding the immediate recall of the Governor, one of Arden-Clarke's predecessors. "People demand self-government immediately," Nkrumah wired. "Send commission supervise formation constituent assembly. Urgent." It is interesting that, in this moment of extreme stress, he found time to send copies of this telegram to a dozen newspapers all over the world, including the London *Daily Worker*, the Associated Negro Press (Chicago), the Moscow *New Times*, and the New York *Times*. On the same crowded day he dispatched a much longer telegram, also to the Colonial Office, describing the background of the crisis in full. This telegram ends with the words, "God Save the King and *Floreat* United Gold Coast."

3. The Governor assumed emergency powers and on March 13 issued an order sending into exile Danquah, Nkrumah, and other UGCC leaders. There was no trial, and no direct accusation that Nkrumah had any relation with the February bloodshed. His banishment was decreed solely on the ground that this was "expedient for securing the public safety and the

maintenance of order." Nkrumah was at once packed off to a remote village in the Northern Territories.

4. A commission of inquiry was set up to look into the disturbances. This made a long report, which contained various charges against Nkrumah, mainly that between his arrival on the Gold Coast and the outbreak of the riots he had greatly stimulated the organization of nationalist activity. (Of course that had been his job, but it amazed the British that he could have done so much so quickly.) This report did not overtly accuse him of being a Communist, but said that he had studied Communist "techniques." Also it alleged that Nkrumah had organized a society known as the "Circle," a secret body the members of which swore personal fealty to him. The aim of this was national unity and independence for West Africa, and the eventual creation of a Union of West African Socialist (not "Soviet") Republics, but with a pledge not to resort to violence "except as a last resort." Nkrumah, when he gave testimony about the riots, dismissed his plans for this organization as an old "dream"; it was something he had played with in London. Apparently no society such as that projected by the "Circle" ever actually came into being, but it is still the main "evidence" held against Nkrumah by those who are convinced that he is an overt revolutionary conspirator.

5. In London the Colonial Office did not like the look of things. It did not want anything further to happen that might provoke disorders in the Gold Coast, and after careful investigation issued a policy report which took what was on the whole a strong pro-African line. It said that the Gold Coasters did not have enough share in government (which was Nkrumah's main point) and urged prompt constitutional reform. Its foreword contains a summary of the basic British position that is perhaps worth quoting:

> It is an axiom of British colonial policy that progress, whether political, social, or economic, and whether in local affairs or at the centre of government, can be soundly achieved only on two conditions: first that it rests on the foundations of tradition and social usage which already exist, and second that changes and developments carry with them the substantial acceptance of the people. It is not impossible, within these limitations, to banish abuses, to adjust anachronisms and to introduce the framework of modern civilization, but the process must be evolutionary. *A European system cannot be imposed arbitrarily on an African society* [italics mine].[9]

6. Then early in 1949 the British made an extraordinary gesture. They appointed an all-African committee of forty, under the chairmanship of an

---

[9] *Report of the Commission of Enquiry into Disturbances in the Gold Coast, 1948.* His Majesty's Stationery Office, 1948.

PRIME MINISTER NKRUMAH OF THE GOLD COAST

African judge, Sir J. Henley Coussey, to write a new constitution. "Both the composition of this all-African commission," a British observer has said, "and the far-reaching political changes which it proposed, marked an event without precedent in British colonial history." What the British were doing, it seemed, was to give the Gold Coast away. The people of the Gold Coast were to be given the opportunity to determine for themselves the kind of government they wanted.[10] The Coussey report was accepted by the Colonial Office with certain qualifications, and the way was thus opened to a general election, the first in Gold Coast history.

7. Nkrumah was released from internment in the north. At first he rejected the Coussey proposals because he thought that they did not go far enough. He called the new constitution "bogus and fraudulent," and, not a man to go halfway, demanded immediate Dominion Status. Later he modified this view, and decided to give the new constitution a try. But at the same time he set up the machinery for a civil disobedience campaign, which he called "Positive Action."[11]

8. Now came an internal fight. Nkrumah thought that the UGCC, under Danquah, was moving much too cautiously. He outmaneuvered Danquah, the man who had brought him back to the Gold Coast, and in June, 1949, captured his movement by forming a new party of his own, the Convention People's Party, or CPP. This is the party which he still heads, and which runs the government today. At its first mass meetings CPP organizers sang songs like "Lead Kindly Light" and "Onward Christian Soldiers." But their tactics were anything but pious. It was a party with a punch.

9. Meantime Sir Charles Arden-Clarke had come out as governor. He was, and is, as impregnably British as a bulldog or Piccadilly Circus, but he understood the temper of the times. He decided to get into direct touch with Nkrumah, and sent a senior British official, R.H. Saloway (later minister for defense and external affairs and now Sir Reginald Saloway) to see him. Some old-line Britons were scandalized by this—it shocked them that Arden-Clarke should delegate anybody to *talk* to Nkrumah, "that scalawag." But if the government did not treat with Nkrumah at once, he was in a position to make a revolution. "The lorry was running wild." The meeting took place on January 5, 1950, and marked the first time that Nkrumah ever had a political meeting with a British official.

The two got along well, but reached no agreement. Nkrumah insisted on going ahead with civil disobedience. Saloway urged prudence. Nkrumah replied, "We are a desperate people, and will adopt desperate measures if

[10] See *The Gold Coast Revolution*, by George Padmore, p. 56.
[11] At about the same time Colonel Nasser in Egypt also put forward the idea of "Positive Action," but he meant a different thing by it. See Chapter 13 above.

necessary." He proceeded to put on a general strike, but it was non-violent. Arden-Clarke forbade the police to use firearms, and there was no bloodshed. Nkrumah was, however, arrested, on the charge of having fomented an illegal strike, tried (by a correct judicial process this time), and sentenced to two years in jail.

10. His imprisonment made him even more of a hero to his fanatic followers than before. The word spread that the jail could not hold him, and that he slipped out every night in the guise of a white cat. People chanted to the tune of "John Brown's Body":[12]

> Kwame Nkrumah's body lies amold'ring in the jail,
> But his soul goes marching out.

11. The new constitution was duly promulgated on January 1, 1951, and the election campaign began. The CPP barnstormed the country with great success, even though Nkrumah and most of its other leaders were in jail, and won in February by a tremendous majority. Nkrumah had been chosen to stand for a constituency in Accra, although he was unable to campaign, and got 22,780 out of 23,122 votes.[13] In the country as a whole the CPP won thirty-four out of thirty-eight constituencies, with its slogan of "S.G. Now." ("S.G." meant, of course, self-government.) The voting was completely orderly and conducted with great efficiency, although the Gold Coast had never had an election before, and in some areas as many as 50 per cent of the people went to the polls.[14]

12. Now the British were in a quandary. It was clear that the CPP would have an overwhelming majority in the Legislative Assembly just elected. But Nkrumah was in prison. How could a new government function with its leader in jail? Arden-Clarke decided to exercise his power of clemency, and let him out. This was a bold and statesmanlike step. On February 12, 1951, Nkrumah was released from the James Town prison in Accra—100,000 people were waiting for him on the streets—and went to Government House to confront Arden-Clarke personally for the first time. It is important to remember that at this time the CPP had had no experience whatever with administration. The legend is that Arden-Clarke, after the first conference, arranged for classes, staffed by teachers at Achimota, to instruct the new ministers in parliamentary procedure. In actual fact well-attended lectures did take place, but the initiative came from Achimota. Arden-Clarke and Nkrumah, after their first encounter, became

---

[12] *New Yorker, op. cit.*
[13] Padmore, *op. cit.*, p. 116.
[14] Of course the over-all number of citizens eligible to vote was relatively small.

good friends and established a fruitful relationship. The new Gold Coast owes much to the wisdom, friendly tact, and farseeing firmness of Sir Charles Noble Arden-Clarke.

13. Nkrumah set up three principles for his men to follow. First, African ministers must not live in the choice European bungalows that the British had always provided for members of the government. Second, only a minimum of social admixture with individual Britons would be permitted. Third, members of his cabinet must pay back one-third of their salaries into the party funds.

14. At first Nkrumah was called "Leader of Government Business." A new constitutional advance came in March, 1952, and he assumed the title and position of prime minister.

*

The Gold Coast government consisted when we were in Accra of eight African ministers (six of whom were CPP men) and three British members who held their posts ex-officio. These were in charge of the three most important portfolios, finance, justice, and defense and external affairs, but the Africans had the majority and could outvote them. In the Assembly of eighty-four there were only nine Europeans. In theory Nkrumah's men could legislate about anything, subject only to the brake of the Governor's reserved powers, which have never been used. This was a genuinely *African* government, although the ultimate power was still British.

The partnership between Nkrumah and the British has worked well, but the Gold Coasters have pushed steadily for a bigger share of authority pending attainment of their final aim—complete self-government. It was difficult for the British to resist this, for reasons we shall go into later. The first three objectives of the CPP were (a) an all-African cabinet, in other words elimination of the British members responsible for justice, finance, and external affairs and defense; (b) an all-African legislature, chosen entirely by direct elections; (c) gradual but complete Africanization of the civil service.[15]

---

[15] Points (a) and (b) were duly achieved in 1954. The Gold Coast now has the first responsible legislature and the first all-African cabinet in British colonial history. As to point (c) Nkrumah's policy has been temperate. He offered "secure employment in the Gold Coast civil service to all British officials who would opt to remain there." Thus he hoped to avoid the kind of administrative breakdown that occurred in the Sudan. He wants to keep on hand "the best and most experienced British officials during the critical years of early independence." See "Gold Coast Comes of Age," by Gwendolen M. Carter, *Foreign Policy Bulletin*, August 15, 1954, and "Growing Pains in West Africa," *Economist*, March 20, 1954.

As to full independence that is a matter of timetable. Nkrumah, as I have already pointed out, has not fixed a firm date. For one thing a date would upset the north, as it did in Nigeria. The government must first bring the north up to the level of the rest of the country. On the other hand he must keep abreast not only of his own restless followers, but of his African opposition. This explains what happened on July 10, 1953, when he presented to the Assembly an important motion, which was worked out in full accord with the British and which was overwhelmingly passed. It authorized the Gold Coast government—*as soon as the necessary constitutional and administrative arrangements are made*—to request Her Majesty's Government in Britain to pass an act in the Houses of Parliament declaring the Gold Coast "to be a Sovereign and Independent State within the Commonwealth." Of course the phrase "as soon as" was the operative clause in this motion. But even so the black peasant boy from the Akan country, the student at Lincoln University and the lonely expatriate in London, has come a long, long way.

CHAPTER 41

House of Commons in Black Miniature

> While Britain is committed, both by her political ideals and by the inherent political forces of her empire, to the progressive abdication of power and the transformation of authority into influence, her moral responsibility does not decrease. . . . For the devolution of power . . . is the most delicate, difficult, and exacting of all the roles that can be played by an imperial state.
>
> —ATTITUDE TO AFRICA

MY WIFE and I happened to be in Accra on the date Dr. Nkrumah presented his independence resolution to the Legislative Assembly, and we watched these carnival proceedings. The hall is an airy modern structure, pleasantly functional, and the procedure, the standards of which are high, closely follows that of the House of Commons. The Negro Speaker wears a white wig, and before him is a golden mace. Ministers, most of them black, sit along a front bench, facing the equally black opposition, and there is a question period as at Westminster. Everything is taken down by youthful and expert African stenographers, and appears the next day in a local Hansard (price 3d.), corresponding to the *Congressional Record*. Debate is, of course, in English. There are constant interjections of "Hear, hear!" as in London (but the pronunciation is more like "Heeyah, heeyah") and cries of "Shame." The cut and parry of debate mimics closely what one would hear in the mother of parliaments, with occasional gaucheries. Recently an African member interrupted an English member who represents the mining industry, with cries of "Big imperialist! Sit down!" Or a member will shout, "I am confused." If a remark evokes both laughter and cheers, members call out, "Ho! Ho! Ho!" The Speaker, Sir Emanuel Quist, often quotes from British handbooks of parliamentary law, and occasionally rises in wrath to chide members who become obstreperous.

The debate on self-government produced some lively passages. Mr. W.E.A. Orfori Atta, second rural member from Akim Abuakwa, started to tell an anecdote. "A certain chief had three wives," he began, "and all three were pregnant—"

Mr. Bediako Poku: How many have you? (*Laughter*)
Mr. Orfori Atta: I will tell you in private later. (*Laughter*)

During argument on the date of independence this interchange took place:

Mr. Asafu-Adjaye: Now, self-government is not a thing in our pocket. (*Laughter*) Now, if it is in our pocket, we would have taken it out long ago.
Mr. Kwesi Lamptey (Municipal Member, Sekondi-Takoradi): Don't we get it from the top of a coconut tree?
Mr. Asafu-Adjaye: We have reached the top of the coconut tree and what we are doing now is that we are requesting the United Kingdom Government to give the Act of Independence so that it will come down from that tree to us.
Mr. Danquah: On a point of order. I would like to climb the coconut tree myself.

A recalcitrant member taunted Nkrumah for being dilatory. The Prime Minister replied with mild but Olympian scorn, "Go drink some orange juice." (*Laughter*)

Debate is generally on a high level, and this is remarkable in that it is not always easy to cope with the thorny intricacies of British parliamentary procedure. Ringing through every session is, above all, a note of pride. Again and again members mention that the Gold Coast has reached in three years a goal that it took Ceylon twenty years to achieve, and India a generation. Another point of interest is the tendency to quote often from fathers of the American Revolution, like Tom Paine and Jefferson.

Of course one factor making this Assembly so picturesque is that most faces are black or brown, and many legislators wear native costume, which means that their naked shoulders gleam. Chiefs from the north dress in moderately resplendent robes and turbans. Some chiefs, even in this modern parliament, do not speak except through the mechanism of another person who crouches close by and who is known as a "linguist"; convention forbids that a really big chief ever talk publicly except in the voice of someone else.

I asked why Nkrumah and his fellows on the front government bench wore such strange headgear—white rimless caps, somewhat like the Gandhi cap, embroidered in gold with the initials "P.G." This means "Prison Graduate." Ministers who went to jail in 1950 wear these as a reminder and a badge of honor. Then I saw one minister with a cap marked in red,

"D.V.B.," which means "Defender of the Veranda Boys." He was a distinguished lawyer, who was not sentenced to jail himself but defended those who were. The Nkrumah colleagues were called "Veranda Boys" because they seldom had a regular place to sleep.

First, on the day we watched the Assembly, came singing of the Gold Coast anthem, and then the question period. Ministers handled themselves with marked aplomb. The questions this morning ranged from the ravages of Swollen Shoot to the disappearance of an ambulance in a remote provincial town, from the quality of the tin used in roofing for a housing project to telephone facilities in a village called Mim. One legislator who asked several pertinent questions in flawless English was a locomotive driver till two years ago. Give-and-take was sometimes lively, but always in the most lordly parliamentary manner. As to wit:

> *Mr. Bediako Poku:* What percentage of the population of the country are victims of venereal diseases?
> *Mr. Donkoh:* This requiring a detailed answer, I need notice.
> *Mr. Jantuah:* Is it not correct to suggest that venereal diseases can cause insanity?
> *Mr. Donkoh:* Yes, sir.
> *Mr. Kusi:* In view of the answer that the Honourable Member's request will receive consideration, do you suggest that it will receive priority consideration?
> *Mr. Donkoh:* Any demand that necessitates priority will receive priority; those that do not necessitate priority will not receive priority.

And:

> *Mr. Kusi* asked the Minister of Agriculture and Natural Resources—
>   (a) What is the estimated population of the tsetse fly?
>   (b) Is there any evidence that the number is increasing?
> *Mr. Casely-Hayford:* (a) There is no available record of tsetse fly population.
>   (b) In view of the answer to Part (a) of the question the answer is "No."

At 9:45 A.M. the Prime Minister arose, and was greeted by cheers from all parts of the house. He wore a cotton smock, white with vertical black stripes; this is a well-known costume, which several ministers affect; it symbolizes simplicity in contrast to the ornate regalia of the chiefs. Nkrumah's voice is nicely modulated, resonant, and full of color. He spoke for sixty-five minutes without any letdown in pace, and with no manuscript except a few notes. He was calm from first to last, logical, and eloquent. First came a quotation from Burke about political maturity. Nkrumah went on, "I pray God to grant me the wisdom and . . . endurance to do my duty as it should be done . . . The range of this debate must be national not regional, patriotic not partisan." (*Hear, hear!*) Then he quoted Aristotle: "In practical matters the end is not merely speculative knowledge of what is to be done, but rather the doing of it. It is not enough to know about virtue . . . We must endeavor to possess it." Then: "As with virtue, so with self-government; we must endeavor to possess it, and to use it." (*Hear hear!*) He proceeded to discuss why, in his view, the Gold Coast demand for self-government was just, and stated, "The slightest concession on matters of principle infers the abandonment of principle." (An Honorable member: "That's a philosophy!") He gave then a vivid brief history of British colonial policy, and, rising to a language more emotional, an account of Gold Coast nationalism:

> In the very early days of the Christian era, long before England had assumed any importance, long even before her people had united into a nation, our ancestors had attained a great empire, which lasted until the eleventh century, when it fell before the attacks of the Moors of the North. At its height, that empire stretched from Timbuktu to Bamako, and even . . . to the Atlantic . . . Lawyers and scholars were much respected in that empire, and the inhabitants wore garments of wool, cotton, silk, and velvet. . . . Thus may we take pride in the name of Ghana, not out of romanticism, but as an inspiration for the future. It is right and proper that we should know about our past. (*Hear, hear!*)

But:

> The heroes of our future will be those who can lead our people out of . . . serfdom, into the valley of light where purpose, endeavour and determination will create that brotherhood which Christ proclaimed two thousand years ago, and about which so much is said, but so little done.

Laughter came when he said that, of course, there were certain advantages to being ruled by somebody else: "As long as somebody else has charge of us, we can lay our mistakes at their door." He proceeded:

> There is no conflict that I can see between our claim and the professed policy . . . of the United Kingdom. We have here in our country a stable society. Our economy is healthy . . . In many respects, we are very much better off than many Sovereign States. And our potentialities are large. Our people are fundamentally homogeneous . . . and, above all, we have hardly any colour bar. In fact, the whole democratic tradition of our society precludes the *herrenvolk* doctrine. The remnants of this doctrine are now an anachronism in our midst, and their days are numbered. (*Hear, hear.*)

He alluded to the cordial relations between Britain and the Gold Coast, paid respect to Queen Elizabeth, and demanded of Her Majesty's Government that it should comply without delay to the Gold Coast's request for self-government. Then:

> In our daily lives, we may lack those material comforts regarded as essential by the standards of the modern world, because so much of our wealth is still locked up in our land; but we have the gifts of laughter and joy, a love of music, a lack of malice, an absence of the desire for vengeance for our wrongs, all things of intrinsic worth in a world sick of injustice, revenge, fear, and want.

Finally:

> We prefer self-government with danger to servitude in tranquillity. Doubtless we shall make mistakes as have all other nations. We are human beings, and hence fallible . . . And while we are making our claim for self-government I want to emphasize, Mr. Speaker, that self-government is not an end in itself. It is means to an end, to the building of the good life for the benefit of all. (*Loud cheers.*)

Nkrumah's speech ended with a nicely apt quotation from Tennyson, whereupon the Speaker, not to be outdone in knowledge of British verse, rose and with great emotion murmured a line from Rupert Brooke, "Now God be thank'd Who has matched us with His hour."

Nkrumah left the assembly hall, and we joined him in an anteroom. He went outside, and then all resemblance to the House of Commons ceased. A group of dispatch riders, who are also his bodyguard, stood by in smart uniforms—black shirts, red caps, and short white coats—as did members of a woman's party organization wearing the CPP colors, with red hats, white blouses, and brilliant green short skirts. At once Nkrumah, when he reached the courtyard, was lifted off his feet. Deputies, party friends, colleagues, seized him and while he was laughing and struggling carried him on their hands around and around the open square. There was a mad clatter of excitement and the parliamentarism we had just seen exploded into a wild, cheerful frenzy, and people began to sing and dance. Breathless, Nkrumah got off the shoulders of his partisans. If Sir Winston Churchill were ever to be captured outside Downing Street and hoisted into the air by Yeomen of the Guard dancing a jig, the scene would be equivalent. Or suppose Mr. Eisenhower should dance on the White House lawn to calypso music played by girl scouts.

An African onlooker, as excited as if he were drunk, pinioned us and said, almost weeping, "The Prime Minister's speech is the turning point of my life. All my life I have thought that the white man was my enemy. Now I know that he is my friend!"

OPPOSITION TO THE GOVERNMENT

Soon it was the turn of the opposition to reply to the Prime Minister. Several opposition parties exist on the Gold Coast, which had perhaps a dozen representatives in the Assembly at that time; the most important is the Ghana Congress Party.[1] The chief opposition figure is none other than Dr. Danquah, who brought Nkrumah to Accra from London and shared his imprisonment in the north. Nkrumah, as has already been mentioned, then leapfrogged Danquah by demanding a quicker tempo in the fight for independence; now Danquah is leapfrogging *him*, hoping thus to win back leadership.

Danquah rose to speak, and demanded independence by a near and specific date, March 6, 1954. Given its premises, his speech was an extraordinarily able performance. He is a witty and effective parliamentarian, and he rocked the house. He asked why Nkrumah should go to London "to beg" for independence on some future date not even specified, and then mentioned George Washington. "Let us do what the British colonists in America did and make a *declaration* of our Gold Coast independence." (Some Honorable members: "Declaration of war?") Then he talked sagely about constitutional anomalies in the British colonial system and demanded to know exactly what *kind* of Dominion Status the Gold Coast was going to get. (*Cheers*) He said then that if Britain refused assent to the Gold Coast demands there were "many other countries waiting around the corner" which might co-operate. (An Honorable member: "And even Russia!") Dr. Danquah: "I do not want to mention Russia."

Toward the end of Danquah's speech parliamentary decorum almost broke down. Somebody yelled, "Shut up!" and other members cried out hysterically, "Withdraw, withdraw!" But the general tone remained good-humored, and the debate that followed was sober, accomplished, and full of point. It lasted several days, without much waste motion, and it compared favorably, I thought, to almost any debate one would hear on the European continent and was far above the usual level of the House of Representatives in the United States.

[1] Some opposition to Nkrumah exists on personal and *social* grounds. Members of the old Negro coastal families resent it that a "bushboy" should be prime minister. Even in a country where few people are educated it does not follow that the educated stick together, as they should.

MEN AROUND THE PRIME MINISTER

After Nkrumah the most interesting and powerful Gold Coaster is K.A. Gbedemah (pronounced "Beddama"), who was at first minister of commerce and industry and then became minister of finance. What makes him outstanding is not merely his ability and close friendship with Nkrumah, but the fact that he is the *party* boss. Gbedemah went to jail with the other nationalists in 1950, but got a shorter sentence. Hence, when he was released, it fell to him to do everybody else's work, particularly in organizing the CPP for the elections. He was the only man, and he did a stunning job. Without him Nkrumah would never have been voted into power so triumphantly. He is still doing a stunning job. The party membership, including women and boys over sixteen, now numbers one million, and increases day by day; it is by far the largest African political party in Africa.[2] Gbedemah likes to call himself the party "ace," because—under Nkrumah of course—he controls its funds. He takes every detail of CPP organization with extreme seriousness. On the day that Nkrumah laid his independence motion before the Assembly, he was much upset because through some error only six sound trucks had arrived, instead of the seven he had ordered.

Gbedemah was born in 1912 in Togoland, which was at that time German. He derives from the great Ewe tribe, and his family may have German blood far back. He certainly has a European mind, and is Teutonic in his thoroughness. He went to mission schools first—the pattern is familiar—and then Achimota. He told us that he became an ardent nationalist when he was still a "toddler"; he wanted to be a doctor, but was "cheated," as he puts it now, out of a medical degree. So he set himself up as a candy manufacturer in Accra, and taught school (at a salary of £9 a month) on the side. After six years of this he launched out as a timber contractor. Then Nkrumah came back to the Gold Coast, and Gbedemah gave up a prosperous business to join him in the nationalist movement. He had known Nkrumah at Achimota, but they had not been particularly close. After 1947 the two became inseparable. Nkrumah lived in Gbedemah's house in Accra, and when they went around the country together, organizing it, they sometime found themselves in lodgings so primitive that they had to sleep in the same bed.

The British have respect for Kimla Agbeli Gbedemah. As minister he does his homework, takes decisions wisely, and sticks to them. I have heard

[2] With the possible exception of the Liberation Rally in Egypt, which is not really a party.

him called "the best administrator in Africa," and "the brains behind Nkrumah." His influence is all toward practicality, and he does his best to keep the Prime Minister's nose firmly to the ground. He visited the United States for the first time in 1954, as a member of the British delegation to the UN Trusteeship Council.

Mr. Gbedemah is, incidentally, the only CPP minister who did not have a British (or American) education. Kojo Botsio, formerly minister of education and now minister of state, went to Brasenose College, Oxford, and taught school in London. He is a Catholic. T. Hutton-Mills, ex-minister of health, is a member of a distinguished old African family and a Cambridge bachelor of arts. The son of one of the historic figures of Gold Coast nationalism, Archie Casely-Hayford, minister of interior, went to British public schools and Cambridge. E.O. Asafu-Adjaye, minister of local government, is a graduate of University College, London, and a member of the British bar.

THE BRAIMAH AFFAIR

Late in 1953 came a small but unpleasant scandal, the echoes of which still roll. The minister of communications and public works, J. A. Braimah, suddenly reported to Governor Arden-Clarke (it is significant that he went to an Englishman, not to Nkrumah) that he had taken bribes from people doing business with his department, felt bad conscience about this, and wanted to make a clean breast and amends. Arden-Clarke, shocked, told him to go to the police. Braimah did so, and brought with him a bundle of currency that had been given him, but which he had never put in a bank or spent. The total sum involved was $5,600. Braimah resigned his high office, and was brought to testify before a commission of inquiry— all-African—that was at once set up. According to Braimah's charges, corruption was widespread in the Nkrumah government, and the Prime Minister himself had accepted "dash." Crooked European interests seeking contracts for road building and the like were involved. Nkrumah went on the stand in turn, and in a three-hour session denied Braimah's allegations categorically. Shortly thereafter two junior ministers—one in the Finance Department, and one who had been Braimah's ministerial secretary—resigned and were committed to trial on charges of corruption.

We met Mr. Braimah on several occasions while we were in Accra, and were much struck by him. He is a man from the north, a minor chief, and was one of the two members of the government who did not belong to the CPP. He wore a blue turban shaped like a child's stocking cap, and has tribal scars on his cheeks. He is only thirty-seven, and never had any education beyond primary school. When we talked to him he discussed with the utmost pride and seriousness the work of his ministry, and the responsibilities he had to shoulder, although he had only recently entered politics. His department had, in fact, the reputation of being one of the best run in the government. Braimah had a most attractive personality. He was shy. He was innocent. He would try to make his face impassive, and then be unable to keep a winning smile from bursting out. That he should have become enmeshed in this scandal is a great pity, and a warning to all budding African politicians who do not understand the difference between simple "dash" and outright bribery, or are unaware of the pitfalls likely to be spread in their path by unscrupulous Europeans. Actually in this affair the real villains were local Greeks and others who thought that, with the British on the way out, they could turn the Gold Coast into a kind of Levant. It is striking too that this unpleasant little game was stopped by the aroused consciousness of the Africans themselves.

FURTHER EVOLUTION OF THE SHOW-BOY

> *As colonial territories approach self-government in the twentieth century, they face difficulties and hazards which were unknown in earlier periods. Most of them spring from the new levels of expectation which the western welfare state has created in the minds of the local electorate. The people not only expect independence, a vague term in any case. They also demand health services, better education, improved diets and an increasing standard of living. And they demand all these things without any understanding of the fact that they are unobtainable without an increase in real wealth and the services of efficient and well-trained administrators . . . The problem is . . . no longer independence, but independence with prosperity and progress.*
>
> —BARBARA WARD

Important—in fact, resounding—events came in 1954. A new constitution was written, which provided for an enlarged legislature elected directly by the people (instead of elections only partially direct as before), the first fully "responsible" parliament in colonial Africa, and an all-African cabinet, the first ever to be installed in a British colony. The three ex-officio European ministers disappeared, although the British still maintain certain reserved powers. The governor no longer presides at cabinet meetings.

Elections took place in June, and the CPP won handsomely. The campaign was one of the most vivid and colorful ever waged anywhere. One slogan was "Cipipify the country!"—from the initials CPP.[3] Nkrumah's men got 54 per cent of the total vote, and 67 seats out of 104.

---
[3] "Gold Coast Comes of Age," *op. cit.*

FINAL WORD ON BRITISH ATTITUDES

Now for the last time we discuss British policy. So far as the Gold Coast is concerned this can be summed up in the phrase "creative abdication."[4] This means that the British are pulling out, because they must, but that they intend to hold on to something even after they have gone.

Sir Charles Arden-Clarke told us, "Thirty-three years ago I was instructed that it was my job to teach Africans to stand on their own feet." Another high British official said, with a certain lonely magnificence, "Why am I here?—to preside over my own liquidation." There are still some 1,500 British civil servants in the Gold Coast—working themselves to death to give the country away.

The policy to "give—and keep!" only works if you give before you have to give. The secret of successful British policy, as we have mentioned before, is *pace*—to judge the timing right. The British do not consider the advance of the nationalist movement to be a defeat, but—if things turn out well —almost as a victory. In 1949 Nkrumah stood for immediate and complete independence *outside* the Commonwealth. Today he is fully prepared to accept Dominion Status within the Commonwealth, and does not even say when he wants it. The British have given up a lot. But so has Nkrumah.

The British, particularly in West Africa, are a continual source of bewilderment and exasperation to practitioners of other colonial methods, like the French. They blandly contrive to pave the way for their own withdrawal in such a manner that they, the hated imperialists, become popular even with the most ardent nationalists. These have even been known to say to Britons, "You are going too fast for us. Slower, please!"

One reason why the British support Nkrumah is, of course, that if he should fail or be pushed out, the "wild" CPP would take over and his successor might well be an extremist much more radical and violent. Nobody wants a Communist government on the Gold Coast. Also I have heard cynical reasons advanced to account for English policy. One American businessman told us, "The British will make any concession here in order to keep the Gold Coast in the sterling area." And I heard an American Negro say, "The British are getting out of the Gold Coast for two reasons. First, they have to—they will be pushed out if they don't go. Second, they want to make the Gold Coast a demonstration piece, to take the pressure off else-

---

[4] This phrase has come into widespread use recently. I have never seen its source accurately traced, and I do not know who coined it.

where. So long as they can adduce their good will in the Gold Coast they have a pretext for remaining longer in Kenya and elsewhere."

Some well-meaning people in London, who think that the Colonial Office goes too far too fast, ask such questions as these: "Is the Gold Coast more important to us than South Africa? If we give Dominion Status to the Gold Coast, will not South Africa secede from the Commonwealth?" Answer: The Gold Coast is more important, because (a) South Africa is in effect lost anyway, and (b) if the Gold Coast is refused Dominion Status, then all the rest of Africa may be lost.[5]

Is Nkrumah a British tool or puppet? Certainly not. Are the British *his* unwitting tool? Certainly not. It is a strange development, but Nkrumah and Government House are working together more or less for the same end—a tranquil, politically adult Gold Coast that will take its place among the fully independent states of Africa when ready, presumably by the end of 1956. One development which, however, is worrying to Britons on the spot is a steep recent rise in xenophobia, like that in the Sudan.

THE COMMUNIST ELEMENT

The Gold Coast has, like Nigeria, a handful of noisy Communist intellectuals; Communist influence is particularly strong in the trade unions. Some time ago Nkrumah began to take measures against further Communist penetration. He did this reluctantly, because ideally he does not want to interfere with free political expression by anybody. But he is sophisticated enough to realize full well that Communist imperialism could be a menace much more unpleasant, to put it mildly, than British imperialism ever was, and he certainly did not want any alien Communist infiltration into his own precious nationalist movement.

In October, 1953, Nkrumah took the serious step of suspending from the CPP two powerful figures, Anthony Woode, a member of the legislature, and Turkson Ocran, general secretary of the Gold Coast Trade Union Congress. Ocran was the man who, some years before, had helped organize the strikes that brought Nkrumah into power. But also Ocran was the chief instrument working to bring Gold Coast trade unions under Communist

---

[5] Dr. Malan's successors may, of course, try to blackball admission of the Gold Coast to the Commonwealth, as if it were a kind of club. But the constitutional position is obscure, and it is uncertain if they could do this legally. One theory is that, if the Gold Coast is admitted to full membership in the Commonwealth without South African consent, the Union will retaliate by taking over one or all of the three British High Commission territories—Bechuanaland, Swaziland, Basutoland.

control. The Prime Minister said, "There can never be any question of exchanging British masters for Russian masters. It is not in the best interests of our country for any nationalist . . . to allow himself to be used by a Communist organization."[6]

Responsible Gold Coasters are glad, of course, that Nkrumah was prudent enough to take this and other anti-Communist measures, but they do not think that, as of the moment at least, Communism is a particularly vital issue. First, it does not have much appeal to peasants on the land, because on the Gold Coast most land is individually owned by small holders. Exploitation by rapacious big landowners does not exist. Second, in the towns and among the educated, the nationalist movement takes precedence over anything, and the industrial proletariat is small. Third, Communism is regarded in the Gold Coast as a *white* movement, which indeed it is, and most people are suspicious of it for this reason.

Meantime Nkrumah has to face vexing problems in civil liberties. He does not want to interfere with the right of people to read anything, even if it is outright Communist propaganda. On the other hand he feels that, in a society largely uneducated, the government has a duty to protect those who might become Communist dupes because they cannot think for themselves. He has to draw a line between those who are capable of reading Communist literature without being inflamed or seduced by it and those who cannot. A considerable number of Communist books have been banned recently, but only after scrupulously careful investigation. Those most likely to be outlawed are the ones that cleverly mix half truth with truth.

NKRUMAH: TO CONCLUDE

I have already mentioned the varied influences in Nkrumah—Christianity, Marxist socialism, the concept of civil disobedience borrowed from Gandhi, the example of Roosevelt and the New Deal, and, above all, African nationalism. These make a mixed pudding, but one quite typical of modern Africa. The main thing to say about Nkrumah is that his struggle is twofold—first, to continue to work out his subtly meshed program vis-à-vis the British, and get independence when he wants it without disorder or hostility; second, to maintain his delicate equilibrium with his own people, who may be tempted to kick up their heels on other issues now that the self-government issue is more or less settled. He has to talk with two voices. He cannot go too fast, but if he goes too slowly he will be pushed ahead willy-nilly by the machine he himself created.

[6] In March, 1954, the Gold Coast government forbad employment of Communists in important government departments.

CHAPTER 42

The Gold Coast and the Golden Stool

One country, one people, one destiny.
—KWAME NKRUMAH

Now we must swallow a few mild statistics. The population of the Gold Coast is about 4,500,000, of which 6,770 are non-African. Four thousand of these latter are British. The country is 99.8 per cent black. The Africans are 66 per cent animist or pagan, about 30 per cent Christian, and about 4 per cent Moslem. Illiteracy is variously calculated at something between 75 and 85 per cent. Among the principal languages are several with names that seem uncommonly short, like Ewe, Ga, and Twi (pronounced *chwee*). But let us not condescend to them, strange as they may sound. As many people speak Twi as live in Cincinnati and Cleveland combined, and the Ga speakers are equivalent in population to every man, woman, and child in Utah, Montana, Idaho, and Wyoming put together.[1]

The Gold Coast is shaped like a sloping wedge and covers 79,000 square miles, almost the size of the United Kingdom. Its frontiers, like all those on the West Coast, do not rise out of any natural geographical phenomena, but are purely arbitrary. Like Nigeria it is divided into three separate sections, the Gold Coast Colony, which is the steamingly hot strip along the coast, the "kingdom" of Ashanti in the middle, and the desiccated, primitive Northern Territories above. There are only about twenty people in the north (population 1,097,000) with a high-school education. The north is largely administered, as Northern Nigeria is, by southerners who have moved up to fill the vacuum.

[1] When I was in Accra during the war I remember asking a boy at the Air Transport Command mess what tribe he belonged to. He answered, "Me, oh, I city boy, not bushboy." I asked him then what his native language was. He replied "Ga," pronouncing it with a hard "g." I did not understand and he repeated, "Ga— just same word, sir, as one of your states." I was bewildered until I realized that he must have seen "Ga," as an abbreviation of "Georgia," on some envelope.

In the Northern Territories women wear their little grass fig leaves over the behind, not in front. The minarets in Moslem areas, with their crude ledges, look like lumps of *shashlik* on a spit. Some men have as ornate facial scars—virtual monograms—as any we saw in Africa. I asked one northern chief in Accra—his name was Tolon Naa, and his title the Wulana of Yana —if having his cheeks carved had hurt much. He said that it had happened when he was seven days old, and he had no memory of the event at all. The Gold Coast north differs radically from the Nigerian North. For one thing the veneer of Islam is much thinner, and the social organization is not so feudal. For another most of the chiefs are not so regal as the Nigerian emirs. For another it is poor whereas the Nigerian North is rich, and has less than a quarter of the total population of the country. Most important, the Gold Coast north is not anywhere nearly so acute a political problem.

GOLD COAST CHIEFS

These are a mixed bag, ranging from the illustrious Asantehene of Ashanti, on whom we will have a word below, to the pettiest of princelings. There are about sixty paramount chiefs in the Gold Coast Colony. Until recently most were amenable British puppets and they largely dominated the old Legislative Council; they served to give a convenient native cloak to the old imperialist rule. Most were (and are) old, and they inevitably blocked the progress of younger, brighter men. Nkrumah's idea is to restore the chiefs to the position they had in the community before the British made political use of them, in other words pull their teeth. He would like them to maintain their ceremonial role and to be mouthpieces of the people, but without power. The more radical CPP ministers think of the chiefs as obsolete relics of a dreary past, and probably would like to get rid of them altogether. This they cannot do. The Coussey report stated, "The whole institution of chieftaincy is so closely bound up with the life of the nation that its disappearance would spell disaster." Even Nkrumah, addressing the legislature in the session we saw, was always careful to pay special attention to the chiefs; he used locutions like "the chiefs and people of the Gold Coast," rather than "people" alone.

Not all Gold Coast chiefs were—or are—autocrats by any means, and few were ogres. If they were autocrats or ogres, they did not last long. They were "destooled." This is the most interesting of all phenomena in regard to Gold Coast chiefdom. Every important chief has a stool, corresponding to a throne, as a symbol of his high office, along with other paraphernalia such as his umbrellas.[2] The stool is a kind of low wooden bench with projecting short wings. People use the term stool, or its derivatives, in several ways. The chief's property is known as "stool land," and if a quarrel occurs between heirs to a chieftaincy, the claimants are said to be "contesting the stool." When a chief reaches his throne he is "enstooled"; if he is deposed he is "destooled." Destooling occurs more frequently than most people think. In one royal state, the Dua Yaw-Nkwanta kingdom, where the dynasty goes back to 1630, the last three chiefs have all been destooled, in 1915, 1936, and 1941.[3] Now it is important to point out that the British almost never destool a chief directly. This is done by the people themselves in state council; they *vote* to remove a ruler. Gold Coast chiefs, for this and other reasons, are unique in Africa. Also since succession to a chiefdom is not necessarily hereditary in the direct sense, extraordinary dynastic and administrative anomalies occur. A man who was your clerk yesterday may be chief tomorrow.

More important than the chief in some tribes is the principal chieftainess or Queen Mother, since the succession almost always passes through the *female* line. Even in plebeian society, the oldest grandmother is usually the most important person in a village. Most Gold Coast chiefs are polygamous and have plenty of sons, but *nephews* (not sons) usually inherit rule.

The most interesting chief I saw on the Gold Coast was, strange as it may seem, an American. A former missionary, he retains his American citizenship although he is chief of an African tribe and also a British civil servant. His name is Lloyd Shirer, and he has his headquarters near Tamale, the remote capital of the Northern Territories. He was born near Pittsburgh and came out to Africa for the Assemblies of God Mission, first in the Haute Volta in French territory, then in the northern Gold Coast, many years ago. He and his wife have given their whole lives to Africa, and have made a remarkable contribution. First they had unprecedented success teaching illiterates to read and write by use of the Laubach method. The British liked Mr. Shirer's work so much that, eventually, they asked him to accept appointment as a Community Development officer, which he still is. The Africans liked him so much that he became the Malgu Naa, or negotiating chief, of an important branch of the great Dagomba tribe. He does not sit on a stool, but on a sacred skin. When he became chief, he had to promise three

---

[2] Also every important chief has in his retinue an official known as the "linguist," as mentioned in the preceding chapter. A chief is not supposed to talk to strangers or even to his own people aloud. He whispers what he wants to say to his linguist, who then transmits the message in a normal tone of voice. The linguist usually carries a wand, topped by a gold ball or other emblem.
[3] See *Akan Traditions of Origin*, by Eva L.R. Meyerowitz, p. 142.

things—to own no locust trees (which might give him undue wealth), to possess no streams (to indicate that the fish belonged to the tribe as a whole) and never to pull anybody's ear, that is, punish someone without just cause.

Mr. Shirer has done a great deal for his territory. His methods were concrete, sympathetic, and step-by-step. He would ask a community, "What do you need most?" The answer would invariably be water first, firewood next. So he would suggest tentatively the idea of building a small dam and planting experimental fruit trees. And presently the dam would be built, and the trees planted, as if by the initiative of the people themselves. Next the villagers would ask for more food, and for ways to make money. So, little by little, Shirer tempted them to launch out into small but ambitious new projects like irrigation schemes and rice cultivation. Before long the village became transformed, with fish flourishing in a nearby stream, which replaced an old muddy waterhole, teal swarming in the rice fields, and new crops growing. Result: food. Further result: cash. The by-products paid for the original investment, and the work was done eagerly by the Africans themselves, even old men of the tribe, who as a rule never work at all. All they had needed was a lead.

GHANA, COCOA, AND THE U.S.A.

Gold Coast history has deep and ancient overtones. About a thousand years ago a kingdom known as "Ghana" (=Guinea) existed in the western Sudan. Its people drifted across the Sahara, where they were decimated by battle and driven south. Remnants arrived eventually in what is now the northern Gold Coast, and were called the Guans, or Akans. This is one reason why most nationalists today want to rename the country "Ghana." "Gold Coast" connotes the slave trade, and has too much of a British smack. Besides nationalists everywhere these days have a penchant for going back to historic names. Persia became Iran. Incidentally the British first called the country "The Golden Coast of Guinney."

French navigators reached the Gold Coast in the fourteenth century (and there may have been Phoenician and Greek navigators long before that), but the first permanent settlement was by our old friends the Portuguese in 1471. Christopher Columbus is supposed to have touched on the Gold Coast at about this time. In 1482 the Portuguese built a fort, Sao Jorge del Mina, on the site of Elmina today, named for the gold mines nearby. After the Portuguese came Dutch, Danes, Swedes, Prussians, and Brandenburgers. (Similarly did Dutch, Swedes, French and Spanish establish posts on the east coast of North America at about this time, and the Danes went into

THE GOLD COAST AND THE GOLDEN STOOL 823

the Caribbean.) The British did not establish a substantial foothold till the sixteenth century. Promptly they became dominant. It might be interpolated that the Danes did not abandon their interests in the Gold Coast till 1850, and the Dutch till 1872.

Meantime the African tribes of the interior—the early Akans and their descendants—fought aborigines along the coast, and sold slaves to the Europeans. In time there came to be two main divisions, the Fanti on the coastal strip, and the Ashanti in the middle of the country. The powerful and militant Ashanti have had an established kingdom since 1660. They were a proud people dwelling deep in the rain forest, who did not know the wheel or plow until modern times. They had no livestock (because of the tsetse fly), no cultivation, and no roads. When they could no longer sell slaves to Europeans in the south, they sold them to Moslems in the north. They had, and have, a very peculiar mythology, and believe themselves to be descended from a Queen Mother named Nyamkomaduewuo, which means "She who makes death sacred." Some Ashanti, even today, bury pythons with human funeral honors.

There were eight different Ashanti wars, packed with fierce and vivid incident. The British interceded to help the more civilized Fanti tribes along the coast resist aggression by the warlike Ashanti. These wars caused so much trouble that a powerful segment of opinion in London wanted to pull out of the Gold Coast altogether. As Joyce Cary once wrote, "We didn't want the damned place." But in 1874 the British consolidated the various coastal settlements into the Gold Coast Colony, and it became part of the Empire. A similar evolution, we have already seen, occurred in Nigeria. The British marched against Kumasi, the Ashanti capital, in 1874, and burned it to the ground. There followed a famous treaty between Queen Victoria and an Ashanti monarch named Kofi, who was known as "King Coffee." In 1895-96 the British demanded of another ruler, King Prempeh, head of the Ashanti Confederacy, that he accept a protectorate, i.e., submit to imperial domination. When he refused, he was conquered, deposed, and removed to exile in the Seychelles. (The British, like the French today, always had islands remarkably convenient for the forced detention of recalcitrant or independent-minded native monarchs.)[4] Ashanti was annexed to the British Crown in 1901, after a signally dramatic military event— the investment and relief of Kumasi, its stubborn capital.

Now we must tell the story of the Golden Stool. This throne, sacred to the Ashanti kings, is much more than a mere symbol; it is supposed to have

[4] A good brief account of Gold Coast background is in *World Today*, March, 1950.

been handed down from heaven in a black cloud, and is considered literally —not figuratively—to *be* the soul of the Ashanti people. The British Governor of the Gold Coast at the turn of the century was not a very intelligent or informed man. He demanded that the Ashanti surrender their revered and holy stool. They declined to do so, and this caused the eighth and last Ashanti war. The British won the war, but did not get the stool. Patriotic Ashantis hid it, and hid it so well that it was not found till 1921, when it was discovered accidentally by workmen digging up a road. The Ashanti people then served notice that if the British took the stool, they would go to war once more. London had learned a lesson by this time, and the stool was permitted to remain in Ashanti possession. Then King Prempeh was brought back from exile, and, in 1935, Britain formally recognized the Golden Stool as an inalienable sacred symbol of the Ashanti nation. Since that time, relations between British and the Ashanti have been smooth.

The Northern Territories of the Gold Coast also have a curious and appealing history, which we cannot go into here. The frontiers were surveyed and the way opened to annexation of the area not by any Englishman—it was impossible for an Englishman to get into the region and survive—but by a remarkable African, George Ekam Ferguson, who negotiated the first treaties with the local chiefs for the British. The French refused to accept the frontiers at first, because they said that a black man could not have been capable of drawing them.

As to the south—the coastal strip and Gold Coast Colony proper—the main thing to say is that it has had a longer experience of democratic procedures than any region in British Africa.[5] The people had the advantage of a double fermentation. They had close relations with Europeans, and at the same time were ardent nationalists. As far back as 1844 Fanti chiefs united themselves into a "Bond," under British law, and six years later a "Legislative Assembly of Native Chiefs Upon the Gold Coast" was created. This, it may be observed, happened when Kenya was still a completely unknown wilderness, when Morocco was still a Turkish no-man's land, and when Stanley had never heard of Livingstone. In 1868 came the first attempt by the Fanti to establish independent government, and in 1885 the first African member was nominated to the Legislative Council—something that has not happened yet in, let us say, Basutoland. Later came the formation of the first real political party ever known to Black Africa—the Gold Coast Aborigines' Rights Protection Society. A West African National Congress was established as early as 1920. The Gold Coast got its first modern constitution, the Guggisberg Constitution, in 1925, and in 1946 came another

[5] Except the Union if you consider the Union to be "British" Africa.

THE GOLD COAST AND THE GOLDEN STOOL

under the governorship of Sir Alan Burns. The Legislative Council chosen under this had a Negro majority, the first in the history of British Africa, and Burns appointed two Africans to the Executive Council. Then came Nkrumah, and the rest we know.

*

The Gold Coast is, after Malaya, the richest of all British dependencies. It is the largest producer of cocoa in the world, supplying more than one-third of the total world crop, and the largest exporter of manganese. (Russia has a bigger manganese production, but does not export so much.) Also the Gold Coast has substantial wealth in timber, gold, and diamonds, and when the fabulous Volta River project gets under way, the country will become one of the world's foremost producers of bauxite, aluminum, and hydroelectric power.

There are no European settlers on the Gold Coast—settlement by whites is strictly forbidden—and no European ownership of land, although mineral rights may be leased. No European may enter the Gold Coast to seek employment without government permission. The British want this to be an *African* country, and it is. One fact so striking that it can scarcely be believed is that every cocoa farm in the country, of which there are many thousand, is African-owned. Moreover the Gold Coast Cocoa Marketing Board, a semi-state organization like the great marketing boards in Nigeria, is African-managed; of its ten members eight are African. This supervises the industry on a broad basis, buys the crop, sells it, accumulates funds for lean years, and contributes widely to other elements in Gold Coast economy. It has piled up so far a reserve of almost £100,000,000.

One could write about Gold Coast cocoa endlessly. The first pod was imported into the country from Fernando Po, by an African blacksmith, in 1879. For a time only *one* tree existed in the country, and its owner got £1 per pod for the cocoa it produced. Then the industry began to grow. Swiss missionaries and traders played a large role in this. Production from 1892 to 1896 was a total of twelve tons; in 1951 it was around 275,000 tons. But cocoa has been threatened by one of the most lethal menaces ever to confront an agricultural industry anywhere—the epidemic of Swollen Shoot to which I alluded in Chapter 40. Of the 500,000,000 cocoa trees in the country, about 10 per cent may have this fatal malady already, and it has been spreading. Apparently the first infection came from Togoland in about 1930, and the east is the region worst afflicted. Swollen Shoot is so difficult to wipe out partly because of an exceptional zoological phenomenon—the mealy bug that carries the virus is usually associated with an ant, the *crematogaster* ant, which protects it. Then the ant feeds on the mealy bug's honey, while the bug destroys the cocoa tree. Recently, however, a new chemical has been introduced which may operate successfully against these formidably intertwined destroyers.

My authority for part of the foregoing is a recent article in the *New Statesman*,[6] "Can We Save Cocoa?" by Roy Lewis. Let me quote Mr. Lewis:

> The Gold Coast is cocoa. The measure of its political consciousness and social advance lies in an overseas trade worth £30 per Gold Coastian, compared with, say, £6 per Nigerian. That income, which . . . has brought an African professional class into existence, nearly all comes from cocoa. But cocoa is more than the foundation of the Gold Coast's progress towards nationhood. It is the symbol of African achievement. . . . It is the cash-crop of hundreds of thousands of sturdy peasant-farmers. It is also almost the perfect crop for the soil and climate of the "cocoa belt." Its destruction would shake the country to its foundations. And it *is* being destroyed.

No one on the Gold Coast minimizes the danger of Swollen Shoot—a recent official pamphlet says flatly that "the spread of the disease threatens the future *existence* of the cocoa industry"—but people hope strenuously that Mr. Lewis may be too pessimistic. If cocoa *should* be destroyed, the political effects could of course be catastrophic. Cocoa provides almost 70 per cent of Gold Coast exports, and the export duty on it pays for harbors, schools, hospitals and government finance. A sharp fall in cocoa revenue could smash the government—any government. In other words the future of nationalism in the Gold Coast depends to an extent on a bug having a liaison with an ant. Nkrumah could be destroyed by the mealy bug. He is not only fighting the British, but a disease.[7]

Finally a word about the importance of the Gold Coast to the United States, and vice versa. We do not need to mention that, by and large, every American who nibbles on a chocolate bar is probably contributing to the economy of this Negro state. The United States takes normally about 38 per cent of total cocoa exports. American imports from the Gold Coast increased from $17,937,000 in 1937 to more than $80,000,000 in 1951. Another point is in the realm of strategic raw materials—we critically need Gold Coast manganese. Another is in more abstract considerations of defense. If the Mediterranean should be cut off in a new world war, Accra would reassume the position it had in World War II as an indispensable base for American and Allied communications across Africa.

[6] December 20, 1952.
[7] But cocoa has had several terrific boom years lately, and Swollen Shoot seems to have been largely checked in the last year.

A good many bright young Gold Coast boys go to America these days instead of England for education. There are about 140 in the United States at present. Most are flaming nationalists—as was their spiritual father, Dr. Nkrumah, when he went to an American university appropriately named Lincoln.

THE VOLTA PROJECT

This is one of the most ambitious development projects in all Africa. The Volta, a triple river—there are White, Black, and Red Voltas—flows steeply down to the sea through an area in the Gold Coast that contains the richest bauxite deposits in the world. The reserves probably amount to 200,000,000 tons. For many years schemes to harness the Volta, like the Nile at Owen Falls, with the consequent production of an aluminum industry and enormous amounts of hydroelectrc power, have been advanced. In the spring of 1953 agreement was reached to this end by the Gold Coast government, the United Kingdom government, and private British and Canadian aluminum companies. The total cost will be roughly £144,000,000, of which the Gold Coast contributes £40,000,000, and the work will have three phases—a dam on the Volta at Ajena capable of generating 564,000 kilowatts of power, a smelter to produce 210,000 tons of aluminum per year, and a new port (cost £10,000,000) at Tema, east of Accra. The project as a whole has ten times the magnitude of Owen Falls, and will be—if all goes well—a kind of African TVA. Every physical circumstance seems to favor it. Nowhere in the world are bauxite, the raw material from which aluminum is made, and potential water power so conveniently adjacent. The British favor the scheme strongly because, at present, they have to buy four-fifths of their aluminum with dollars, and the Volta enterprise will give them this vital material, which in turn is "packaged power," from a sterling area.

Nkrumah was wary about the project at first, even if the fact that both the British government and private investors were willing to risk capital in such a gigantic venture showed, it would seem, that they had great political confidence in his regime. But nationalist Gold Coasters thought that the whole business might be a Machiavellian trick, a device, whereby the wicked British replaced political by economic exploitation. After acrid debate the Africans at last accepted the proposals, but Nkrumah demanded —and got—plentiful safeguards. The Gold Coast government, not the British, will control the project, and the private aluminum companies have bound themselves to be subject to Gold Coast tax laws. There will be no forced labor or conscription of labor. The Gold Coasters do not want to destroy the economy of peasant farmers by tempting them to go into the smelters at higher wages. Of course the country gets tremendous advantages. For one thing the project will, when completed, give its economy as a whole a broader base, by lessening its critical dependence on cocoa.

The sociological as well as economic ramifications of all this are obviously profound. Even geography will be changed. For instance, the reservoir above Ajena will create a new lake (to be called Lake Nkrumah) which will cover not less than two thousand square miles, and be one of the largest lakes on the continent. Severe precautions will have to be taken against the spread of diseases like onchocerciasis. Ajena will, it is predicted, become almost overnight a town of 100,000 people; this vast community will have to be fed ("we must get more protein into 'em"), housed, and educated. There will be problems in fields so various as fish-hatching, race relations, afforestation, soil control, irrigation, communications with the north, metallurgical innovations, and public recreation. And it must all be done through voluntary, sympathetic partnership between black and white with a single supreme end in view, raising the standard of living of the nation as a whole.

The man in charge of this whole Volta operation is a youthful Australian engineer, Commander Robert G. A. Jackson, a former assistant Secretary General of the UN. His wife is Barbara Ward, the well-known British economist and political writer, a former editor of the *Economist*, governor of the BBC, and author of *The West at Bay*.[8]

---

[8] I cannot resist, even so late in this book as this, the temptation to quote another nugget of African journalism. Here are passages from an account of Commander Jackson's first press conference in the Accra *Daily Spectator*, by a staff reporter:

"'Ah, here is the Press Gang!' I said to myself as I entered the bright hall of the Hon. Mr. Gbedemah. . . . But I was looking out for the Commander Jackson of whom there has been much talk. And there he stood quite tall and slim. A man of many parts including faultless dressing. His tie matched with his breastpocket handkerchief . . . Often, as he spoke, he waved his tie like a woman sampling a Nylon stocking, and said with a smile, 'I wear the Gold Coast tie!' He wore it indeed.

"With a medium-sized head and a comparatively small face which may look harsh when he stops talking, Commander Jackson is a man of the World. He has the fashion of illuminating his talk with smiles which make him charming and a human . . .

"The gentleman's repertorie of facts and figures on economics generally, to say nothing of aluminum and allied material in particular, is fabulously enormous.

"You will readily understand why they selected him for such a job. At one time I felt his head might crack with all the relevant knowledge he had stored up.

"Of course, all the while we were drinking—drinking and eating titbits and talking, as Commander Jackson told us of his world experiences with rare wit . . .

"Then the Hon. Mr. Gbedemah spoke in an amazingly faultless manner."

ACCRA, CAPITAL OF THE GOLD COAST

Accra is not what you would call a tidy town. But few cities in Africa are more interesting. The sewers are mostly open drains, like those in prewar Teheran, and it has no traffic lights. ACCRA resembles Lagos, but is smaller (population roughly 136,000). It looks like a collection of tin hovels, interspersed with dilapidated frame buildings and tawrdy hole-in-the-wall shops under moldy arcades. The first impression a visitor is apt to get is of an almost desperate physical squalor together with a contrary note of extreme animation. The streets are thronged with people in their Roman-like togas. The airport and its hotel and restaurant look like a prodigious crazy dance hall in Harlem. I saw no sight in Africa more exhilarating. Accra is drippingly moist most of the year; Europeans have electric lights in their closets (as do Americans in Panama) to keep clothes from rotting; books and shoes fall to pieces in a month, and important officials store their private papers in "hot" rooms, which are fanned with hot baked air to keep them dry. The contrasts of Accra are, of course, startling. It even has smartly uniformed policewomen. In the tourist agencies (which sell tickets to Mecca or Springfield, Illinois) youthful Africans behind the counter wear badges proclaiming them to be "trainees." A favorite local stew is made of ground nuts and palm oil, and the phrase for closing a deal is "to cut guaha," guaha being a kind of twine. I saw outside a tailor shop the legend "Trained in His Majesty's Prison." There are two hundred registered goldsmiths, and in the big trading company stores, which look like rough warehouses, you can get anything from rude ivory ornaments to DDT. Advertisements in the local press tell you whether "frock ladies" or "cloth ladies" will be present at various entertainments—the latter being those dressed in the African manner. Several night clubs are named for American states; we went to one called "Weekend in Colorado." Curiously enough, this phenomenon is something that I often observed in the Balkans before the war. The best night club in Budapest was called the Arizona; Bucharest had a Wyoming and Sofia a Florida. Apparently American state names give a provocative hint of vice, and carry a fine high tone.

This city is the capital of a black—not a mixed—society, and color bar has virtually disappeared.[9] This is not to say that Africans are not still

[9] There are several mixed marriages in Accra. One well known was that of Joseph Manuel Appiah, formerly the personal representative of the Prime Minister in London, to a daughter of Sir Stafford Cripps. Recently Captain Hamish Millar-Craig, assistant financial secretary of the Gold Coast, married Miss Rosebud Ohne, the niece of a local chief.

effervescently self-conscious about color. If you should happen to mention the British Commonwealth in conversation, you should not compare it to a "club," but say "family" instead, because the word "club" still carries an association with segregation.

The distinguished American writer Richard Wright happened to be in Accra when we were there, and he was having trouble. This came because a local journalist, interviewing him, had asked what specific part of Africa his family originally sprang from. Wright did not have the faintest idea, any more than would most American Negroes born in Natchez, Mississippi. To cover up his ignorance with a joke, he blithely suggested to the journalist that the Accra authorities should set up an institute for genealogical research so that the lineage of any Afro-American could be traced. To Mr. Wright's consternation this proposal was taken with complete seriousness, and caused no end of polemics in the press and on the radio.

Nationalism is lively on almost every level. When Oliver Lyttelton arrived in Accra on an official visit, he was astonished to see a picket line of ebony children, mere tots, carrying placards which said DOWN WITH THE GOVERNOR'S RESERVED POWERS.

Strange and wonderful are the uses put to the English language in Accra. A northern chief, in the course of a description of the British Isles, crystallized his thought with the expression "Scotland be Englishman's bush country." When Sir Alan Burns retired as governor in 1947, a newspaper story, intending to be complimentary, carried the headline, "Governor's Departure Hilariously Cheered on All Sides."[10] The newspapers are, in general, even more inflammatory than those in Lagos, and similarly look as if they were printed on a tablecloth.

One newspaper in Kumasi has a kind of personal column, signed by Wamba. Here are some items:

> Wamba wants to know if that lady teacher at Wesley College will reform AND if she knows that insolence does not pay.

> Train Guards, Kumasi—I hear some of you try to find out if a girl is old—above the lower rate for passengers—by feeling her breasts. If it's true, stop it. Try and treat the passengers with respect.

> The tall sanitary inspector at the meat factory has a stoogeic [sic] attitude.

This same paper recently printed an attack on the Ashanti Goldfields Corporation, accusing it of being "capitalist." The headline was A.G.C. MINES—SHUT YOUR MONSTROUS MOUTH.

[10] McKay, op. cit.

Not long ago an Accra paper failed. One of its contemporaries, delighted to see it pass from the scene, gave it this vigorous obituary:

> Men and women of Ghana, brethren, to-day we are gathered to pay tribute to our dear comrade, Talking Nonsense alias Talking Drums, Talking Rubbish, Talking Dross, Talking Rot, Talking Drunkard and Talking Balderdash.
> It was a sad day when the bells tolled and the drums beat to tell the tale that Talking Rubbish was no more.
> I was present at the funeral and there I saw the chief mourners in grey tails and toppers—the same tails and toppers which missed the ministerial coach and bungalows.
> The scene was weird and eerie; bluish phosphorescent light twinkled on the ghostly mourners. Doctors Damquack, Bourgeoise and Armytoad were gloomy and solemn at the graveside. Lawyers Busman Conductor, Beastie Lampshade, Bus Boy Unholysnook, Ocoocoo Haddock, Akoko Hedgehog and Messrs. Dangling Daftie, Quasi-Smoky Lamp, Ashes Nitwit, Wily Oaf Hatter, Wuta Saggitarius Cocoabags, Joker Clownman, and the rest of the unholy crew.
> Dr. Armytoad, A.S.S., I.D.I.O.T., S.N.E.A.K., etc. etc., well known international boaster and scientific failure (now a sixth rate politician) gave the funeral oration.
> "High Ministers of the future Ghana Dynasty, we are here to-day to say farewell to our beloved Talking Nonsense. Our great friend and denationalist died of heroditusviz-kipsillasstism, the scientific name for jealousy, the green-eyed monster. This brought about high blood pressure and eventually apoplexy. The Editor Boy Donkey did his worst, circulation was twenty (20) all over Ghana. . . ."
> As the Oxford and Continental intonation of Dr. Armytoad filled the air, Bourgeoise shouted Quality! Quality! and great crocodile tears rolled down the cheeks of Dr. Damquack. Then loud wailings and lamentations and the ghostly figures with flying coat tails waved their grisly arms in the air, "Earth to earth, ashes to ashes" intoned Armytoad, and with one accord they all jumped into the open grave.[11]

Accra is a highly litigious community, and is vociferously full of lawyers. The courts have a great many land cases in particular. Young men lucky enough to get any higher education at all usually favor the law over other professions—as, indeed, do students in Montevideo and Istanbul. When an intelligentsia is created, law is always likely to be its first love because this paves the way for politics, public service, and, if worst comes to worst, revolutionary activity. I met one Accra judge who said that he could not understand why anybody bothered to be a judge any more, since practically all cases are appealed. "Anything over £500 goes all the way to the Privy Council."

[11] From *African Affairs*, July, 1953.

Corruption is another characteristic, although I had the feeling that Accra was not so sensationally corrupt as communities in Nigeria. If you have business at the post office, it may cost you an extra penny or two to get attention. Recently came a movement to clean up petty corruption in the schools. We heard tales of backward parents who resented this development, and were dismayed by it particularly if their youngsters were stupid. Previously they had been able to arrange for their children to pass a course by "dashing" the teacher 30 shillings. Now it is impossible to tell who will pass or not!

Superstition and *juju* (which is usually known by the more formal term "fetishism" on the Gold Coast) still plays a vivid role in Accra. We met one distinguished, western-educated judge who, every time he has his hair cut, has the shorn bits burned, and who never allows his robe or particularly his wig to be touched by anybody else, out of fear that *juju* will be "put," as the phrase is, on these objects.

The Gold Coast is a rich country, yes, and Accra is a thriving city as African cities go, but by our standards most people are miserably poor. But nobody starves. The tribe, the village, the family, take in the indigent. Prices are very high to the African (or European) consumer. Gold Coast beef is more expensive than beef imported from Australia. Incidentally Accra is one of the few cities in Africa to which Coca-Cola has not yet penetrated. A lawyer in Accra who earns, let us say, £80 per month is considered to be a rich man. A schoolteacher gets about £10 per month, a policeman £8; a cook gets from £5 to £7, and a "small-boy," the junior domestic servant, about 30 shillings.

The two things that make Accra most picturesque are the togalike dress of the people and the signs on trucks and buses. Never, not even in the Congo, did we see so many exotic and brightly colored designs on mammycloth. A lady may wear pictures of a rhinoceros, pop bottles, top hats, or Dr. Nkrumah. The legends on the trucks and lorries are even more fancifully bizarre than those in Nigeria.[12] I saw God's Time Is the Best, Safety First with God, Proud Old Man, All the World's a Stage (on a cinema van), See Before You Say, My Happiness, Abomination Has No Remedy, and God The Killer.

Finally one must have a word on Achimota, which is probably the best known educational institution in British Africa. It is situated a few miles inland from Accra, and is now officially known as University College of the Gold Coast. Its influence has been profound. Nkrumah, Gbedemah, Botsio

[12] Truck drivers are a powerful political force, because they are organized into an effective union, and it is they who carry first-hand news from town to town.

THE GOLD COAST AND THE GOLDEN STOOL 833

and almost the entire contemporary generation of Gold Coast public men went there. The student body numbers 510 at present; this will be expanded to 800 by 1956. Degrees given are recognized by the University of London. Achimota means "Speak No Name," and the origin of this goes far back—slaves trying to escape would steal away from the coast, and, if lucky, get as far as Achimota for their first stop. Then friendly Africans would hide them, as American slaves were hidden by the underground railway in the United States. The motto of Achimota comes from a famous Gold Coast philosopher and educator, the late Dr. James Aggrey—"In the harmony of the world as in the harmony of an organ or a piano, the black and white keys are both essential."

THE ASANTEHENE OF ASHANTI

We flew up to Kumasi, the capital of Ashanti, and there met the ruler of this ancient land, the land of the Golden Stool. So for the last time in this book we confront the phenomenon of a native African potentate of exalted rank.

The most curious tradition associated with the Asantehene—any Asantehene—is that he must be whole, without blemish or alteration. If he should lose a finger in an accident or operation, he would have to be destooled at once. He cannot be circumcised or have his tonsils or appendix out. I did not ask what would happen if he had a tooth pulled.

The present Asantehene, who derives from a dynasty almost three hundred years old, and who succeeded to the Golden Stool in 1931, is correctly entitled Otumfuo, the Asantehene, Nana Sir Osei Agyeman Prempeh II, KBE, King of Ashanti. Otumfuo, the appellation with which he is addressed, means "All Powerful"; "Nana" means grandfather. "Hene" is the native word for chief, and "Asantehene" is Chief of the Ashantis.

This eminent personage was, before he became Asantehene, a wealthy trader. He was the nephew of the previous ruler—the Prempeh who was exiled to the Seychelles—and the succession will presumably pass to one of his nephews in time.

I found the Asantehene to be a somewhat stagnant character, although amiable. He is a tall man, heavily Negroid in feature. We were disappointed that he wore a simple blue and white costume instead of his blazing ceremonial robes, but he made up for this by showing us a recent portrait of himself painted by a Hungarian artist, which presents him in full and magnificent regalia. The Asantehene has four wives, and these made the work of the artist somewhat difficult, since each wife had to approve of the work day by day, and one wanted the Otumfuo's skin to be somewhat paler than it actually is. The portrait shows the monarch dressed in sumptuous golden *kente* cloth, and wearing a green velvet necklace studded with gold, huge golden rings projecting on each finger, large bracelets of gold and velvet around the biceps, and a ponderous golden triangle hanging down from the naked throat. The Asantehene carries a golden flywhisk, and his sandaled feet rest on a stool smothered in leopard skins, near a pot of gold dust accompanied by the traditional Ashanti golden weights. It is a most resplendent work of art. When the portrait was completed, the Asantehene hung it facing the wall for two years, until any *juju* that might have got into it should be dispelled.

Another picture of the Asantehene shows him in a costume even more ceremonial, which he has worn only three times—when his uncle died, when King George V died, and on the occasion of his own accession. It consists entirely of feathers. Near this was a faded tintype photograph, which looks like one of a gorilla. But it portrays a distinguished old-time ancestor of the Asantehene. Also in this room was an object of furniture somewhat unusual in the palaces of African chiefs—a bookcase. The titles included G.D.H. Cole's *Intelligent Man's Guide to the Post-War World,* a compendium called *One Hundred Great Lives,* and some self-help manuals.

Prempeh II is a very rich man, since in theory he owns the entire Ashanti nation. He thinks of himself as a good, solid member of the Church of England, even though he is polygamous. Nobody knows how many children he has. He likes to play golf, and talks all the time while playing. He entertains by giving ornate and diffuse garden parties, at which he wears a white dinner jacket, dispensing for the moment with his ceremonial umbrellas (which are on the modest side, considering his exalted rank). A number of eunuchs are still supposed to be members of his court.

The Asantehene is a middle-of-the-road nationalist, and has considerable political force. He rules, under the British, through a council consisting of himself and the twenty-seven Ashanti paramount chiefs. The Asantehene's principal power resides in the fact that it is he who appoints all the subchiefs, with the concurrence of this council. Nkrumah sees him at once on any visit to Kumasi. They talk Twi together, and get along quite well. The Asantehene knows that he must reflect the prevalent mood of the people, or lose his stool. The CPP carried Ashanti overwhelmingly in the 1951 elections.

We did not, I regret to say, see the Golden Stool, but we heard a good deal about it. Rumors are that it is not of solid gold, which would make it too heavy to carry, but is gold-plated, and looks somewhat shabby now,

THE GOLD COAST AND THE GOLDEN STOOL 835

with bits of gold leaf peeling off. In the old days any unauthorized person who caught a glimpse of the stool, even inadvertently, was blinded, and the penalty for touching it was to wash out the touch with blood. The Golden Stool does not, of course, rest on the ground, but sits on its own stool, a larger article of furniture, or on an elephant skin, and it has its own umbrella as if it were human. It precedes the Asantehene at a public ceremony, and is usually tipped slightly so that no devil may perch on it. It is commonly thought that *nobody* is ever allowed to sit on the Golden Stool, under any circumstances, but the Asantehene himself told us that he goes to the secret place where it is hidden once every forty days, and there, utterly in private, sits on it for a few minutes.

One of the major sights in Kumasi is the new 510-bed hospital being built; this will probably be the best hospital in West Africa, and will cost £ 2,500,000. It will have a training school for nurses, something desperately needed. It was difficult to proceed with work on this hospital recently, because one wing came perilously close to a certain tree, which marks the place where the Golden Stool descended from heaven, and is a formidably sacred monument. We inspected this tree with appropriate curiosity. It rises sixty feet, gnarled and broken at the top, and is hung with ugly creepers. You could no more get an African to climb up to cut off a rotting branch than you could get him to slit his own throat. The hospital premises had to be built around it, so powerful is its dark magic. Also in this area is an extraordinary walled pit where public executions took place until recent times. Here, still stuck into the earth, we inspected the Akofokye, or sacred executioner's sword, which is named for the priest who brought the Golden Stool from the skies. Part of this projects about three feet from the ground, and looks like a broken bulldozer blade. The legend is that no one has ever been able to yank it out. The truth is that nobody, not even the British, would dare to try. An end of pipe, near the huge notched blade, is also visible. At mass executions, this drew off the blood.

When a member of the royal family dies nowadays, the procedure is curious. First he, or she, is buried in a sacred cemetery four or five miles out of town, where the body rests until the dead person's *successor* dies. Then it goes to a permanent mausoleum, and the successor's body duly takes its place in the cemetery, where it may wait for years, until the *next* successor comes along, whereupon it proceeds to its appointed place in the mausoleum. The process is like that of a celestial conveyor belt. When a chief died in older days, several members of his retinue, particularly children, were at once killed, so that he would not be lonely in afterlife. Older days? Only a few years ago several people of high rank were convicted of murder and hanged, for having murdered a subchief so that he might "go along" with a deceased chief. Even today, if a chief of rank or even a chieftainess happens to die, the streets of Kumasi will be empty. Servants, houseboys, and the like fear that they will be picked up and killed to lend weight and color to the funeral festivities.

The Asantehene has a body of irregular troops, a kind of combination Gestapo and bodyguard, known as the Zongo Volunteers. These are a ferocious lot, at least in appearance. They wear steel helmets painted with the initials "Z.V." and cover their faces with masks like Halloween masks, false whiskers, or other frightening ornamentalia. Their function is to keep public order, and they are privileged to stop any car at night, to inspect its occupants. If they catch a thief, they may deal with him at once and in their own fashion. A favorite method of execution in the Ashanti country is to drive a nail through the victim's forehead.

*

Kumasi has about 60,000 people, of whom perhaps seven hundred are European. It is a pungently colorful small town and rich, being the center of both the cocoa and gold-mining industries. Even children—boys of six— are busy traders, making money. I could not believe my eyes when I saw some headlines in the Kumasi press. One said HITLER STILL TERRORIZING PUBLIC and another NKRUMAH JAILED FOR THREE YEARS! These are jokes, put in the paper to get circulation. African journalism *is* really something. One local problem has to do with migratory labor. Just as youths come in from Basutoland to the mines in South Africa, so do they pour into Kumasi from the French territories to the north. Kumasi is Mecca. The government has built rest camps for these migrants, and takes care of them as best it can, as they trek down the crowded, muddy roads. There is a vast stir over the whole Ashanti region. Once again let us point out that Africa is a continent in ferment.

Nearby is what is called the "richest square mile in Africa," at Obuasi where the Ashanti Goldfields Corporation has its center of operation. This company "is the largest tonnage producer of high grade ore in the world, recovering more than an ounce of gold per ton milled."[13] Its chairman is General Sir Edward Louis Spears, who was one of Churchill's close associates during the war and whose wife, born in Chicago, is the well-known novelist Mary Borden. The Ashanti company is the largest employer of labor in the Gold Coast, the government excepted. Unlike the mining companies on the

---

[13] *Africa South of the Sahara*, p. 211.

THE GOLD COAST AND THE GOLDEN STOOL 837

Rand, it is strongly unionized.[14] At Nsuta the manganese mines operated by the African Manganese Company, Ltd., are another important source of wealth. One result of industrialization is that the old crafts are dying out. The Ashanti have been famous for their woodcarving and particularly their weaving of cloth of gold and other fabrics. But nobody wants to spend a month making a strip of *kente* cloth if he can get good wages and tolerable living conditions in the cocoa fields or mines.

Kumasi has been pro-Nkrumah in the past, but we heard here more pointed criticism of the government—from African intellectuals—than anywhere else in the country. An editor told us, "Of course Nkrumah is a success, because he preaches Utopia, and everybody likes Utopia. But there is a risk that he is taking our roots away. We must become detribalized, yes, but not too fast. Also Nkrumah ought to cultivate an opposition. There can be no successful democracy without the two-party system."

Serious riots occurred in Ashanti in January, 1955. One reason was dissatisfaction over cocoa prices; another was political discontent. The Ashanti people, taking advantage of the impending departure of the British, decided that they wanted more control over their own affairs. A "National Liberation Council" asked for establishment of a federal system, which the central government refused.

A TRIP TO TOGOLAND

Togoland, a former German colony, is now a trust territory under the United Nations, like the Cameroons, with the British administering the western strip, the French the rest. The capital of the British section is a few hours' drive from Accra, across the Volta, and has the nice name Ho.

The road slithers and burrows through surly bush. We passed through cocoa—the trees have mottled, whitish, skinny trunks, and are huddled together in the shadow of tall forest trees. At one spot we saw a fire-bearer—the man who carries a torch of palm fronds from one village to the next, not so much because matches are expensive but for occult ceremonial reasons. We hopped across the Volta ferry, drove through two small native states, and heard about the nearby battlefield at Dodowa. Here, in one of the Fanti-Ashanti wars, British troops used a novel weapon—rockets—and the Ashanti fled. Their chiefs were so overcome by shame that two or three sat themselves on kegs of gunpowder and blew themselves up.

HO itself has had a burst of growth lately; its European population rose from twelve to twenty-four. (The total non-African population in all British

[14] Total trade union membership on the Gold Coast is about 32,000.

Togoland is fifty-one.) The Africans in Ho number about five thousand. American missionaries have, incidentally, been here since 1847, and the Ewe Presbyterian Mission is the third oldest in West Africa.

This is all Ewe country. The Ewes (pronounced "Evvies") are an advanced tribe, who have spread out widely, get jobs almost everywhere on the West Coast, and have a lust for education. There are few Ewe villages without a school. But the rural Ewes are still somewhat primitive in some respects. Traditionally they have a four-day week, consisting of (1) Market Day, (2) The day after Market Day, (3) Farming Day, (4) The day before Market Day. If a girl becomes a prostitute, she is not allowed to live in her native village, but moves to Accra. I was assured that no woman in the entire tribe above the age of twelve was a virgin. It is an extremely serious offense to commit adultery with the wife of a chief. The Ewes have a powerful *juju* and in some ceremonies swear what is called the Great Oath; if anybody violates this, he may be punished by having a skewer stuck through the cheeks and tongue. Or this grievous measure may be taken to keep somebody *from* taking the oath.

When the 1919 treaties broke up German Africa, the British and French took their slices of Togoland without much regard to natural frontiers or the feelings of the inhabitants. Villages were sundered, farm land fragmented, and families split apart. (The same thing happened at the same time in eastern Europe, particularly when Czechoslovakia and the other succession states were carved out of the old Hapsburg empire.) Ever since 1919 —and particularly since World War II—the vocal and adhesive Ewes have wanted unification. This is the chief preoccupation of the Togoland peoples. There are about 400,000 Ewes on the French side, and about 170,000 on the British side in *Togoland.* But also a substantial Ewe community, numbering perhaps 250,000, lives in the eastern Gold Coast, along the frontier. This makes for complications. Ideally Ewe leaders would like to see all their folk united. Dr. Nkrumah, on his side, wants British Togoland to be part of the Gold Coast, since this would considerably enlarge the area of the country. The French of course take a totally different line. They want to hold on to their part of Togoland at all costs, and oppose ferociously any attempts by the Ewes to establish unification.

The Ewes of British Togoland have a right of petition to the United Nations, and use this frequently and with vigor. The Ewes in the Gold Coast do not, but presumably most of these are fairly content with their lot, and do not need it.

The British favor some sort of unity between the Gold Coast and British Togoland, so that the Volta River, which is the frontier, will have the same

THE GOLD COAST AND THE GOLDEN STOOL 839

administration on both sides—particularly since the aluminum project is getting under way. On the other hand they do not want to give Nkrumah too much for nothing. Now enters another bristly complication. Two political groups exist among the Ewes in British Togoland. Members of the first group, fanatic nationalists, hate the *French* so much that they prefer to take the long chance of getting rid of them some day, thus uniting all of Togoland proper into a free national unit, instead of merging with the Gold Coast now, which would end the hope of complete unification. The second and stronger group is allied to Nkrumah's CPP, wants amalgamation with the Gold Coast, and is working for it hard.[15]

The dominant political personality in Togoland lives not in the British sector but in LOMÉ, the capital of the French area. He is one of the most interesting of contemporary African leaders. We met him not in Togoland, but in New York; he is vice-president of the Comité de l'Unité Togolaise and as such visits the United States frequently to present briefs on behalf of his people to the UN. His name is Sylvanus E. Olympio. He speaks perfect English, French, Portuguese, and German, as well as Ewe. He was managing director for many years of the large United Africa Company interests in Togoland, and he is proud—with a chuckle—of the fact that his family derives not from African slaves but from an African slave *trader* who, some generations ago, emigrated to the West Indies and then lived in Brazil. It was Olympio's father who brought the family back to Africa. Olympio learned German as a child, and then went to the University of Dijon and the London School of Economics. One of his childhood memories is of gangs of Togolanders being led through the streets of Lomé in chains; the Germans, who ran Togoland then, were strong masters. Olympio's political views are, of course vehemently nationalist. But he is an intelligent man and he knows what realities are. He would like to reconstitute the two trust areas, the British and French segments of Togoland proper, into a single autonomous state (excluding the Ewes on the Gold Coast), but with the hope that the Gold Coast and Togoland will some day be federated. In particular he dislikes the possibility that Nkrumah may in time absorb British Togoland, because this would give the French an excuse for absorbing *their* section and incorporating it into Dahomey, the adjacent territory, which is part of French West Africa.[16] Mr. Olympio fears that if British

---

[15] In December, 1954, the Trusteeship Committee of the General Assembly of the UN voted 42 to 1 to authorize an election in British Togoland whereby its inhabitants might decide their own future. The lone dissenting vote was cast by Belgium.
[16] Brief mention of Dahomey will be found in Chapter 45 below.

Togoland ceases to be a trust territory, this will sound the doom of other UN territories elsewhere. The Belgians will take over Ruanda-Urundi and so on. He would deplore this (as would most African nationalists) because the UN, even if ineffective, gives nationalist Africans such a useful forum.

Most Ewes, it seems, prefer British administration to French. There are virtually no civil liberties on the French side, and French Togoland did not have a single secondary school (for 400,000 people) until 1947. French Togoland is run from Paris, like the French Cameroons, almost as if it were an outright colony.[17] The French do not allow members of Nkrumah's CPP to enter their territory. They even seek to deny that an Ewe nationalist movement exists, while at the same time they do their best to keep it submerged. They are, in other words, pursuing much the same tactics that they pursue in Morocco and run the same risk, namely, that by trying to eradicate nationalist sentiment they may in the end defeat themselves by making nationalism stronger. Here in Togoland, as Mr. Olympio puts it, the French "don't think that the world will ever change." On the other hand one should be careful to point out that about 50,000 French Togolanders have the vote, and one African deputy from French Togoland sits in Paris. To this the nationalists reply that they care little about having a deputy in Paris, who is powerless; what they want is more self-government at home.

On account of the UN, conditions are probably better for Africans in French Togoland than in Dahomey next door. Thousands of Dahomey citizens seek to cross the border each year and take up residence in the trust territory. In the latter region nationalists at least have the advantage of being able to put some pressure on the French by adducing what the British do for their Africans in *their* segment of the country.

*

To return to British Togoland. The Ewe region is a good example of the peculiar but innate democracy—rudimentary of course—of Africans in this part of Africa, with their own special checks and balances. Not only does each community, as a rule, have a family from which the chiefs come; also they have what is called a "stool family," which is in some respects superior. There is a royal line and also a separate "stool line," the head of which is the "stool father." If a chief is destooled for incompetence, mal-

---

[17] Incidentally Dr. Ralph Bunche wrote his doctor's thesis in 1932 on the difference between French rule in Dahomey, a colony, and Togoland, which was then under the old League of Nations mandate system. He did not find much dissimilarity, nor would he find much today.

feasance, or some other offense, the stool reverts to the stool family which holds it in trust until a new chief is elected. The British cannot destool a chief in this area. If he commits a crime they can throw him into jail, but they cannot take him off his stool. The Africans (not the British) pay the salaries of chiefs, and these are modest. Sometimes it is a considerable sacrifice for a man to become a chief, if he has a prosperous business or even if he is a government servant at a tolerable salary.

We happened to be in Ho on a historic day, when the Trans-Volta-Togoland Council was set up and held its first meeting. Creation of this body, something unprecedented, was the first step toward knitting the eastern Gold Coast (Trans-Volta) and British Togoland together. The ceremonies were a brave display. Umbrellas of every color waved in the hot wind like flags. (There is a special umbrella "language" in this region—you can all but thumb your nose with an umbrella.) The more important chiefs not only had their linguists with them, but their ceremonial umbrella carriers—boys in outlandish, almost teratoid costumes. These boys, who seemed to be a naughty lot, knelt by the side of their chiefs, giggling, watching us while we watched the ceremonies. Togbe Yepre Hodo III was elected president of the new Council, after a spirited public session. He wore green robes, a long gold chain around his neck, a black velvet cap with crownlike golden ornaments, and on one finger a ring of gold the shape and almost the size of a shrimp. His attendants carried before him two objects—a wand tipped with a golden orb, and his executioner's sword, a weighty silver object with the hilt made in the shape of a large chicken. His umbrella was a royal red. I watched these medieval splendors. I also watched Mr. Gbedemah, at the time the minister of commerce and industry, in his neat western business suit, and his CPP sound caravans assembled for the occasion. And most of all I watched something quite prosaic—the ballot box. This was held aloft and publicly taken apart and then screwed together again, to show all voters beyond peradventure of a doubt that it was empty.

The big news this day, next to the actual creation of the Council, was that the Gold Coast government had appropriated £2,000,000 to build a bridge across the Volta—none exists now. The money will come from the Cocoa Marketing Board. Chiefs and councilmen cheered almost with the emotion of children getting a long-wanted but unexpected toy at Christmas.

WHAT THE GOLD COAST NEEDS

We asked several prominent Gold Coasters what they thought the country needed most. Answers: (1) More honesty in the public service. Abolition of corruption. (2) The Volta project. (3) Education, education,

education. (4) More technicians with special skills, like engineers, architects, veterinarians, irrigation experts, pharmacists, accountants. But as far as primary education is concerned, the Gold Coast has a right to be proud of its record, even if an enormous lot remains to be done. There are 85,000 girls, 220,000 boys, in the primary schools today, a record in proportion to total population that no other country in Africa can match.

*

During all the early part of our trip, friends and councilors kept urging us to save time for the end. "Don't skimp the British West Coast, no matter what!" I hope I haven't.

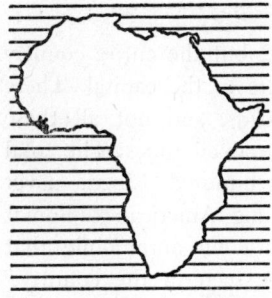

CHAPTER 43

Mr. Tubman of Liberia

This is a sick country—maybe it will get well.
—AN AMERICAN OFFICIAL IN MONROVIA

THE President of Liberia is a plausible and enterprising man in his middle fifties named William Vacanarat Shadrach Tubman, sometimes called by the nickname "Shad." The Honorable Mr. Tubman has been Chief Executive of Liberia since 1944, and will probably remain president for a considerable time to come. He is a character of the utmost originality and interest, who gives forth a certain waggish note.

Liberia itself is *sui generis*—unique. I could use any of several adjectives about it—"odd," "wacky," "phenomenal," or even "weird." It is, as is well known, one of the five independent countries in Africa, and for a great many years (until Egypt became a republic in 1953) it was the only republic on the continent. Haiti in the West Indies aside, it is the only Negro republic in the world.

Monrovia, the capital, was named for President Monroe, and is practically the only city I have ever seen without either taxis or buses. What is more, it does not even have many bicycles. The people are too poor, too mercilessly exploited. A village in Uganda or in the wastes of Northern Nigeria will have bicycles in profusion, but not the capital of Liberia. There was no successful public telephone service in Monrovia until last year, and the system does not extend beyond the city; it was impossible (at the time of our visit) to telephone to the airport, Roberts Field, fifty miles away, or even to the Firestone plantation which plays a paramount role in the economic life of the country. One European official in Monrovia answered his new telephone proudly soon after it was installed. Wrong number. His Liberian assistant asked him, "If it was the wrong number, why did you answer it?"[1]

[1] A postal service exists, but it does not function regularly outside Monrovia. A

Liberia is roughly the size of Ohio or Tennessee, but the entire country has only *ten miles* of paved road, five of which are in the capital. There are no more than 260 miles of "all-weather" roads, and not all these (except in the Firestone area) are actually passable at all times. The total road mileage—including dirt tracks—is only eight hundred. Liberia never had a road at all until 1916, when an enterprising American diplomat built one in Monrovia itself, so that he could use an automobile that had arrived there by mistake, the first ever to be seen in the country.[2] Today Liberia produces enough rubber for thousands of American cars to ride on, but two-thirds of the country cannot be reached except on foot. In the Hinterland,[3] porters carry folk on hammocks; communication is by what people ironically call the "ankle express." My wife and I drove from Monrovia to a village called Totota, perhaps sixty miles away, to have lunch with President Tubman at one of his country estates. An army truck had to escort us—to pull us out of the mud if we got stuck. This was the worst road I have ever been on in my life. It is also Liberia's best road. We traversed on that day about *half* of the total "improved" Liberian road system. Bridges are often slippery planks laid across chasms. Of course this was in the rainy season, and Liberian rains are really something. Last year 260 inches of rain fell in the Monrovia area, all of it in six months. Early in 1953 so much rain came in one twenty-four-hour period that the deluge broke the instruments of a Point Four meteorologist.

Consider public health and education. Only two native Liberians have ever become doctors. There are also two naturalized Haitian MD's, but in the whole country there are probably not more than half a dozen reputable physicians, outside of Firestone and the missions.[4] Infant mortality among Africans runs as high as 75 per cent in some areas.[5] No public health service at all existed till 1931—and Liberia has been an independent republic since 1847! More than 90 per cent of the population is illiterate. In 1946 the total sum allotted to education in the national budget was only around $50,000 (80 per cent of education was taken care of by

---

foreign consul, no longer serving in Monrovia, told me that it was the custom for the postmaster to visit new arrivals in town, and ask for a loan of $100, more or less, to insure that mail would be delivered "promptly."

[2] This odd bit of history is mentioned in *Liberia, 1847-1947*, by Charles M. Wilson, p. 91. Also see "Letter from Liberia," by Oden and Olivia Meeker, *New Yorker*, November 29, 1952.

[3] The back country is officially called the Hinterland, spelled with a capital "H."

[4] Dr. George Way Harley, for many years the head of a justly celebrated hospital at Ganta in the interior, is one of the best known American missionary doctors in all Africa.

[5] The rate in the United States is 2.92 per cent.

missionaries); it is substantially higher now, roughly $1,500,000 out of a budget of $10,088,810. Liberia College, the chief institution of "higher" learning in the country, where several of its leading contemporary citizens were educated, had for years no library, laboratories, or scientific equipment; a former head of this school calmly appropriated all its funds on one occasion, and with this loot sent his daughters to be educated in Italy.[6] Recently Liberia College was reconstituted as the University of Liberia, and its functions are now taken more seriously. Another institution, the Cuttington College and Divinity School, is run by the Protestant Episcopal church (which has been established in Liberia since 1836). It operated at a place called Cape Palmas for many years, but the buildings there gradually disintegrated—melted away in the rain. Then after nineteen years in which it did not function at all it was rebuilt in a healthier location, at Suakoko in the interior. One American missionary group worked in Liberia for seventy-five years without ordaining a single minister.

The poverty of most Liberians is formidable. An American businessman got this note from his chief boy one morning:

> Dear Sir:
> Will you please buy me one Umbrella or Hat? I have already get my Rain's Coat but I did not have Umbrella either hat. So that is the reason why get me so late this morning.
> Obediently yours.

The 1953 national budget was $10,088,810.96. This may seem a pitiably small figure, but it represents an almost sensational advance. In 1934 the budget was only around $467,000 and in 1945 $1,500,000. It is difficult to get a copy of the actual budget document; only a few copies are printed, and these are not distributed freely. The 1953 budget provided $618,149.39 for the Executive Department—not all for Mr. Tubman personally, of course. His salary is a modest $25,000 per year. But it is startling that more than 6 per cent of the entire national income should go to administration of the presidency. The average income of a Liberian out in the bush is 25 cents a day.

Recently a distinguished visitor from abroad, representing an agency of the United Nations, was taken out into the Hinterland to inspect a new agricultural station. The delegation accompanying him included a cabinet minister, no less, whom we may call Mister X. Some cabbages, grown at the station, were on proud display. These were so good that anybody might well have coveted them; nevertheless the UN man was somewhat surprised when he saw Mr. X pick one up surreptitiously and toss it into his car.

[6] Raymond Leslie Buell, *Liberia: A Century of Survival*, pp. 16-18.

Mr. X.'s chauffeur then darted forward and seized one too, and others in the official party followed suit.

Thievery—the cities swarm with thieves—is most conspicuous during the rains. First, rice is short then, and people are hungry. Second, the noise of the rain makes it easy for thieves to get around.[7] Stealing is, however, by no means confined to professional criminals or to the poor, who are so miserable that petty theft may easily be forgiven. It is almost a national sport. Newspapers talk openly of "wholesale stealing" in government departments. Recently the Italian legation lost, of all things, its safe. Even at a fashionable cocktail party in Monrovia, an unwary guest may have his pocket nimbly picked or his wallet rifled. Liberians love to wear top hats, and the joke is that these are useful as well as decorative in that they are so convenient for the temporary disposal of minor loot. A hostess may even find rolls of her toilet paper missing, and a top hat is an admirable place for concealing objects of this nature.

As to corruption in Liberia that, too, like the rains, is really something. It exists on all levels. Money is, let us say, assigned to some government department for a worthy project. But it is rare for the entire sum to reach its proper destination. Underlings help themselves to a share of the appropriation as it moves along, like mice nibbling at a piece of cake. This would not matter much in a rich country, but it is a disaster in one with such a small budget as Liberia. Precious funds are wasted. "Kansas City," I heard it said, "can afford graft; Monrovia cannot." But obviously in a nation so pathetically poor corruption is bound to occur. It cannot be stopped until the standard of living of the people as a whole is raised. Bizarre tales may be heard in this general realm, and some, I am sure, must be apocryphal. An American expert came out to train the police; he went home on leave and, when he returned, he found that his entire collection of fingerprints had disappeared. If a man is important enough, he can run up hundreds of dollars' worth of bills in the local shops; maybe he will settle them at some future date, but maybe not. In the field of *political* corruption Liberia has had some wonderful distinctions. One President of the Republic (not Mr. Tubman) got 243,000 votes in a certain election, though only 15,000 persons were privileged to vote. That is really laying it on. It might have happened in Missouri. But not even in Missouri would any politician have quite dared to do what one Liberian candidate for office did in the early 1940's, just

---

[7] The day I arrived in Monrovia I heard something that shocked me—prisoners in the public jails are not fed. Their families feed them, or they starve. Later I was told that provision *did* exist in the budget for feeding prisoners—the annual sum allotted is $12,000—but this does not mean that they get much to eat.

for fun—he dressed a monkey in a frock coat, took him to the polls, and let him "vote."

Most educated Africans in neighboring countries pay lip service to Liberia because it is an independent republic, created by freed Negro slaves, but they despise it inwardly, because it constitutes a betrayal of what modern Africans stand for. Even Ethiopia has higher standards. Liberia might almost be called a kind of perverse advertisement for imperialism, since, although the country is free, the people are so badly off compared to those in most French and British colonies. Liberia has not had the advantages in education and similar fields that enlightened colonialism provides. This does not, however, mean that Africans are not capable of advance, in Liberia or anywhere else. What it does mean is that Liberian governments in the past have not been good enough. Members of the ruling class, which happens to be Negro, have not done a tithe of what they should have done for their own Negro people.

There are times in Monrovia when even a sympathetic observer has the feeling that many Liberians are backward and eccentric children, playing at statecraft. Vernon Bartlett mentions in his *Struggle for Africa* that at one time the appropriation for brass bands exceeded that for public health. On the other hand much improvement has come recently, and will presumably continue. Mr. Tubman has done more for Liberia in ten years than any president in its history.

AN AMERICAN STEPCHILD

Liberian backwardness and squalor strike an American visitor doubly hard, because the country is so closely associated with the United States. The flag is red, white, and blue (but with only one star and eleven stripes) and American dollars are the legal tender. The constitution is closely patterned on that of the United States, and was drawn up by a dean of the Harvard Law School. One Liberian county is named Maryland, and there is a town called Philadelphia. Most Liberians, at least in Monrovia, wear western dress, not African tribal costume. American officers train the Liberian Frontier Force, the country's "army." But if you suggest to a patriotic Liberian that his country is a "colony" or "protectorate" of the United States, he will wax extremely wroth. Liberians have a natural sensitiveness about their status as a nation. In blunt fact Liberia is not an American "colony" or even sphere of influence in the sense that Washington directs its policy in any overt manner. Sometimes Liberia votes against the United States in the United Nations.

On the other hand American influence is profound. American advisers, through the Foreign Operations Administration of the Mutual Security Program and otherwise, are doing staunch and beneficial work in several fields. The country could not exist economically without Firestone, and an American mining company at work on Liberian iron ore deposits will greatly increase the national wealth. The only bank of consequence in the country, the Bank of Monrovia, is a Firestone subsidiary.[8] Total exports of the country were valued at $30 million in 1953; of these $25 million worth went to the United States.[9] On the governmental level, Washington has alternately neglected, bullied, and supported Liberia. As recently as 1938 the United States sent a warship to Liberian waters to warn another country (it happened to be Germany) to keep out. But not till the Roosevelt era did America pay much attention to Liberia on a sustained or substantial basis. World War II—and communications across the Atlantic —made it strategically important, and for several years, beginning in 1942, the United States maintained a garrison (of Negro troops) in the country, partly in order to protect the American-built air bases at Fisherman's Creek and Roberts Field.

*

One brief word on Liberian history. Almost everybody knows something of this romantic tale. The area was once called the "Pepper" or "Grain" coast. Liberia was created by the American Colonization Society, a private organization (its first president was a nephew of George Washington) formed in 1816 to transport freed American slaves to Africa, where they might settle and start a new life on their own. The motive was only humanitarian in part. A good many American slaveowners *wanted* to get freed slaves out of the country; it was dangerous to have them around. Also in 1819 the American navy was empowered to seize slave ships on the high seas, free any slaves found, and return them to Africa, as part of an attempt to suppress what remained of the organized slave trade. The American government (under President Monroe) and the American Colonization Society worked together. An expedition was sent out to explore the possibility of settlement on the Liberian coast. The British had already done the same thing in Sierra Leone. The expedition arrived safely in 1822 at a site which the pioneers named Providence, and land was bought. Payment, "after long and tedious palavers with the native kings," consisted among other things of "six muskets, one box beads, two hogsheads of tobacco, one cask gunpowder, six iron bars, six pieces blue baft, three pairs

[8] Odd as it may seem this bank was chartered in New Mexico.
[9] Total Liberian exports in 1938 were less than $2 million.

MR. TUBMAN OF LIBERIA 849

shoes, one box soap, one barrel rum, one dozen knives and forks, ten iron pots, and a dozen spoons."[10]

The new community suffered every known privation. Of the first eighty-eight Negroes to arrive, twenty-nine died of disease. The survivors are the foundation of contemporary Liberian society. Authorities differ on the total number of Negroes who, from beginning to end, created Liberia out of America, but it was not large. Probably the Americo-Liberians, as descendants of the pioneers are called, and who comprise Liberia's tightly interlocked ruling class, do not number more than 15,000 today. If the country as a whole has 1,500,000 people (nobody knows, since there has never been a census, but this is a reasonable guess) this dominant and exclusive Americo-Liberian *bloc* makes up only 1 per cent of the total population.

The American Colonization Society administered Liberia for some years, and the early governors (one was a cousin of President Buchanan's) were white. Joseph Jenkins Roberts, for whom Roberts Field is named, was the first non-white governor; he was an octoroon from Virginia. In 1847 the Society withdrew, and Liberia became an independent Negro republic, but the most southerly province, Maryland, did not join the new nation till 1857. For some reason that has never been totally clear the United States, whose foster child Liberia was, did not recognize its independence till the 1860's. "It is almost miraculous," wrote Raymond Leslie Buell, "that [a handful of] captured Africans and freed slaves from America should have succeeded as well as they did in making a new life for themselves in West Africa." Poverty was the worst curse. Since there were no roads, no real contact with the Hinterland was possible. No Liberian president ever ventured into the back country until President Edwin Barclay took a trip by hammock in the early 1930's. The British and French steadily nibbled off bits of Liberian territory; Liberians assert that they lost 44 per cent of their nation through various "rectifications" of the frontier. Of course nobody could say with much precision what the original frontiers were. The worst crisis in the history of modern Liberia came between 1926 and 1936, because of financial troubles and a scandal over slavery. For a time it seemed that the country would be taken over by some foreign agency.

THE PRESIDENT: PERSONAL

Mr. Tubman, the eighteenth president of his country, derives from an old Americo-Liberian family; his mother's forebears came from Sparta, Georgia, and his father's from Atlanta. It is often said, however, that his heritage also includes admixtures of "native" blood. A Tubman helped

[10] *Top Hats and Tom-Toms*, by Elizabeth Dearmin Furbay, p. 6.

finance the first trip of the American Colonization Society to Liberia, and a lady named Harriet Tubman, who lived in Maryland (USA) in the 1850's, is a character well known to American Negro history. Whether or not she was an actual ancestor of President Tubman is uncertain.

Tubman's father was a minister of the gospel, who rose to be Speaker of the Liberian House of Representatives. He gave his son as good an education as the country provided in those days, which was not much, and the young Tubman became a lawyer. He worked hard, advanced quickly, and served both as a senator and an associate justice of the Liberian Supreme Court, before his rise to the presidency. He has always been an astute, shrewd, and farseeing politician.

The President is of medium height; he looks tough, shrewd, and supple. He likes the company of women, and has been married several times. His present wife, a cousin of former President Barclay's, is a pretty, shy, smiling woman. One of his sons went to a Massachusetts preparatory school and entered Harvard in 1954.

Before we met Mr. Tubman we inspected carefully his photographs, which may be seen everywhere. In one he wears a top hat (of course), a morning coat of the most severe and formal cut, and several medals; the President is a Grand Master of the Order of the Star of Africa, among other things. In his right hand is an ebony stick; in his left an exceptionally long cigar. Other manifestations of Mr. Tubman's omnipresence are at once apparent to a visitor to Monrovia. We saw the William V.S. Tubman Bridge and other public monuments. The William V.S. Tubman School of Music exists, as does the President Tubman Dramatic Institute.

Mr. Tubman is a *bon vivant*, and likes to sit around with the boys. His favorite haunt is the well-known S.A.C. Club, the impregnable inner citadel of the Americo-Liberian aristocracy. It has about thirty members, and is expensive and exclusive; a member told me that (with assessments for parties) it can cost up to $500 per year. I asked, immediately on arriving in Monrovia, what ran Liberia. The universal answer was, "Tubman, the S.A.C. Club, and the 125 leading families." When the President visits the S.A.C. after nightfall the roof (which has four squat towers) is illuminated, to show that he is there, discussing matters of state with his chosen friends.

Mr. Tubman is a staunch Methodist—in fact he is a lay preacher and likes to be called "Doctor"—but he sometimes carries a gun. With this he is, on occasion, playful. By Liberian etiquette, no automobile may pass the presidential vehicle (a Cadillac presented to him by an American businessman) and other cars must draw up to the side of the road and stop if the

President is passing. Last summer somebody did not pull over, no doubt because he did not know that it was the Chief Executive behind him. The tale is told—it may well be apocryphal—that Mr. Tubman then drew out his pistol calmly and shot out the rear tires of the offending car. When he saw that the occupants of the automobile he had halted so dramatically were an American and his wife, he gallantly picked them up, and, amid much laughter, drove them to their destination.

Much talk in Liberia centers on Mr. Tubman's yacht, the *President Edward J. Roye*.[11] This 463-ton vessel, which has a passenger capacity of thirty-six, was bought in Holland, where it had been a coastwise steamer. No one knows exactly what it cost, but its upkeep is estimated to be around $125,000 a year, or more than 1 per cent of the *total* national budget. Mr. Tubman dispatched no less a personage than the country's secretary of state to shop for it in European marine circles. One story is that the yacht could, in the event of a Liberian revolution (a prospect unlikely in the extreme), be a convenient mechanism for the quick escape from the country of the entire cabinet. Reports that the *President Edward J. Roye* is not seaworthy are manifestly untrue; it carried Prime Minister Nkrumah of the Gold Coast to and from Monrovia on his recent state visit, and in 1952 Mr. Tubman used it—part way—for a trip to Spain. Tubman partisans say that the yacht, far from being a personal luxury on the part of the President, is a national necessity. It is, in fact, the Liberian navy. When Tubman was a senator he, like everybody, found it appallingly difficult to get around the country; sometimes the Senate had no quorum, simply because the roads were impassable. A yacht, which can fetch people up and down the coast, removes some of these impediments to official travel. Liberia is no longer at the mercy of cargo boats which may, or may not, stop at the local ports. Be this as it may the Tubman yacht has provoked controversy. Liberia has one independent (or more or less independent) newspaper; this printed a dispatch from Washington early in 1953 announcing that President Eisenhower did not intend to keep *his* presidential yacht in commission. There was, of course, no mention of Mr. Tubman's yacht, but that such an article should be printed at all, criticizing the Chief Executive by even the faintest implication, was considered to be extremely daring. Not all has been smooth aboard the yacht itself. According

---

[11] Roye was the first all-black President of Liberia (1870-72); his predecessors were mulattoes or octoroons. Mr. Roye was born in Ohio, and had a stormy career in Liberia. He was deposed as President and put into jail. Seeking to escape the country, he was drowned when his canoe capsized in the surf.

to the authoritative British journal *West Africa*,[12] four of its Dutch officers were suddenly replaced by Germans not long ago. They were alleged "to have been concerned in a mutiny on board."

In 1952 Mr. Tubman paid a state visit to Spain. This was an exceptional event. He had never been in Europe before, and he and Mrs. Tubman were received in the most sumptuous fashion by Generalissimo Francisco Franco. Relations between Liberia and Spain have always been close, partly because of shipments of Liberian labor to the Spanish island of Fernando Po. Mr. Tubman was, by all accounts, inordinately impressed by Spain under Franco; in 1953 a treaty of friendship was signed between Liberia and Spain, and this was followed in the next year by a trade agreement. Voices were not lacking to suggest that, by this and other maneuvers, President Tubman was seeking to show that he is no mere tool or puppet of the United States. In Monrovia the Spanish envoy has conspicuously high prestige. Mr. Tubman has been in the United States three times, once to attend a Methodist congress many years ago and once in 1943, when he was president-elect; he was a member of a mission returning the brief visit President Roosevelt made to Liberia after the Casablanca Conference. Mr. Tubman then waited until 1954 before going to the United States again. For a considerable period no invitation from Washington was forthcoming. But when the visit at last occurred it was a lively and colorful affair, although several untoward events took place.

The President is a jovial and relaxed person socially, but his official life is marked by the most extreme punctilio. Everything official in Liberia is, for that matter, sternly formal. At Tubman's second inaugural, which is supposed to have cost a sum truly grandiose, *gray* cutaways and top hats had to be worn. One luckless photographer got into trouble by taking a picture of a Liberian dignitary arriving for a function—the inaugural festivities lasted a whole week—dressed in gray formal clothes of the most impeccable cut, but riding in an open pickup truck; that the truck should have been included in the photograph was deemed tactless. People like to be addressed by their titles as well as names. Almost everybody is an "Honorable," and the proper mode of address is "Mr. Undersecretary" and so on. Life at the Executive Mansion, which is on the corner of Ashmun and Randall streets, is strictly regulated. In the garden of this building, however, I saw something startlingly informal—statues of an elephant, a leopard, and a bush cow. The elephant's trunk is adorned

---

[12] April 11, 1953.

with a colored electric light, as is the forehead of the bush cow and the leopard's fiercely open mouth.[13]

Liberians are, of course, sensitive about demeanor, exactly like Paraguayans, the ancient Toltecs, or citizens of Fort Worth, Texas. If a member of the *corps diplomatique* should happen inadvertently to affront the President, even on the most trivial matter, his usefulness would be abruptly ended. The Liberian solicitor general, S.R. Horace, lost his job not long ago in circumstances not fully explained. He was discharged for "political and *social* reasons," misconduct in social relations, and "disregard of special considerations due to the Head of the State."[14]

Mr. Tubman can, however, be merciful on occasion. The manager of the local radio station, by name John West, called on him wearing a dusty sport shirt; the scene was the presidential farm. Another official, Mr. Dunbar, had an audience with the Chief Executive at about the same time, encountered Mr. West, and wrote a letter to the *Listener*, a local newspaper, saying that Mr. West's improper costume was an insult to the President. Thereupon Mr. Tubman himself wrote a letter, which was also published, clearing Mr. West of this charge, and saying indeed that Mr. Dunbar, who had informed on Mr. West, must have washed up at the nearest creek before entering the presidential area. Mr. Tubman proceeded: "You will remember that I was in my disaabilles [sic] when you arrived and that I remained in that condition for the duration of your stay at the farm; that was for the benefit of relaxation . . . I consider Mr. Dunbar's letter to be the quintessence of officiousness and totally unwarranted."

The Chief Executive is a wealthy man, and has property in Monrovia (several houses said to be his were pointed out to us), a sizable rubber estate near Cape Palmas, and Konoyale, a cocoa plantation near Totota.

Of course the President has defects, but he is sharply intelligent, alert, and accessible; that he keeps his fingers on everything is his chief source of power. He is certainly the hardest working man in Liberia, and, I heard it said, the *only* man with the real interests of the country at heart. He has done more to stamp out petty corruption among officials than any president in Liberian history. No government payment over $250 may be made without his personal approval, and, together with the secretary of the treasury, he signs *all* government requisitions. When he was in Spain the

---

[13] The following notice appeared on the front page of a leading Monrovia daily on April 25, 1953: "The Social Secretary to the President of Liberia discovered a pair of gloves left by one of the President's guests . . . and would be pleased if the owner applies for them at my Office."

[14] *West Africa*, March 7, 1953.

transfer of an automobile from one government department to another had to await his express authorization.

No president has ever traveled in the Hinterland as much as he; intermittently he goes upcountry to have palaver with the native chiefs. Practically all the Liberian tribes support him now, except perhaps some dissident Krus. Most important of all, a full 20 per cent of the national budget goes nowadays to a new Economic Development Program, which is being administered with Point Four co-operation, as we shall see below. If rubber and iron ore continue to bring good prices, Mr. Tubman will have more revenue at his disposal for public improvements and education. He certainly needs everything he can get if Liberia is to become a mature, self-respecting state.

We drove from Monrovia to Totota to have lunch with the Chief Executive, and both the trip and lunch were interesting. It took us three and a half hard hours to go sixty miles. This was the wettest stretch of jungle I saw in all Africa. Mr. Tubman's house looks something like an Alpine château, and has a wonderful view of green hills bathed in mist. In the large salon the furniture was of bamboo, and various ornate trophies stood against the walls. The President's desk is of the French style, heavily decorated with gold, and, oddly enough, is informally placed in a corridor near his bedroom. In the main reception room the elaborate large rug was covered with a transparent plastic sheath to keep mud off.

Mr. Tubman greeted us affably, and introduced us to several of his retainers, who sat by in attitudes of extreme stolidity. He was gay and talkative, as if to make up for the total silence of his staff, members of which apparently do not often dare to express themselves if visitors are present. Mr. Tubman drank Bass ale, and offered us hearty slugs of whisky as an *apéritif*. Lunch, when it came, was ample and delicious. We had sherry, red wine, champagne, and a half a dozen stoutly substantial courses including corn on the cob. I sat next to Mrs. Tubman who did not say more than two or three words during the entire meal, which lasted several hours. But the President was effervescent, although at the same time guarded. He told jokes about his doctor, asked us about the difference between French and Spanish methods of colonization, and made some shrewd observations about German character. He never mentioned the United States.

THE PRESIDENT: POLITICS

Mr. Tubman was first elected to the presidency in 1943, and took office early the next year, his term being for eight years. In those days a Liberian president could not succeed himself, but the constitution was amended so that, in 1951, Mr. Tubman was able to stand for a second term, which he won without difficulty. This term was, however, limited to four years. In 1953 the Senate and House passed a petition urging him to accept a national "draft" in 1955, and succeed himself once more, and this he agreed to do. Originally—in the early forties—Mr. Tubman was a "Barclay man," handpicked by the then President, Edwin Barclay, to be his malleable successor. Under Barclay government was a completely closed circle, with the backwoods natives tightly frozen out. But Mr. Tubman, once in office, refused to be a Barclay stand-in. Instead of being a puppet, he broke open the old Barclay clique, pursued his own policy, and became president in fact as well as name.

I have already mentioned that the people of Liberia are sharply divided into two groups (1) the Americo-Liberians and (2) the natives, who are the huge majority. The basic cleavage is that between the ruling Americo-Liberian minority and the overwhelmingly more numerous mass of natives. If there is any struggle for power, it is between these two sections of the population. But the natives have practically no power. One can appreciate readily how the first Americo-Liberians, expanding from their original tiny nucleus and seeking to hold themselves together, feared and despised the aborigines in the Hinterland. But as Liberia developed and became stable the natives were treated worse, not better. They were denied the most elementary rights and decencies. The Liberian government behaved toward them even in modern times as backward white colonial powers did fifty years ago. There was no political fraternization within the bond of color. Here *black* settlers exploited a black countryside.

On the other hand a certain amount of mixing up inevitably took place. People held hands, so to speak, and many Americo-Liberians had what are called "outside" children. Tribal youngsters often took the names of their masters in the towns, so that, after a generation or two, nobody could tell with much precision what name meant what. I heard one estimable lady, a leader of Monrovia society, groan aloud, "You cannot tell the wheat from the chaff any more. *Every*body is a native." Hence the ruling caste is extraordinarily sensitive about its aristocratic purity. Almost everybody has a different guess as to the number of authentic Americo-Liberians; I have given it as 15,000, but it may be less or more. The ruling families among these are almost as interlocked and pervasively powerful as those that ruled prewar France. On the way to visit the President, we passed the rubber estates of several. Most are cousins, and a few names predominate. One Tolbert is vice-president of the republic, another is assistant secretary of agriculture, and another is a senator. One Cooper is ambassador to London.

one is secretary of agriculture, and one is (or was) a wealthy businessman. One son of ex-President King is an executive assistant to Mr. Tubman. One Barclay is an associate justice of the Supreme Court, and another is one of the two living Liberian MD's. One Dennis is secretary of state, another is secretary of the treasury, and another is an undersecretary.[15] And so on.

Take the natives now. Of the estimated total of 1,500,000 some 60,000, who live along the coast, are considered to be "civilized." There are twenty-three tribal groups, among them the Krus, who are great fishermen, the Bassas (who provide most of the servants in the towns), the Grebos, and the Vais. These latter were the ruling class before the Americo-Liberians came, and were advanced enough to have achieved a written language, one of three written African languages on the entire continent.[16] Liberia also has a considerable number of Moslems, and many of the Hinterland people have become Christianized.

The great bulk of natives is still excluded from the fruits of government or business in Liberia, but Tubman has done more for them than any other president ever has. He had the good sense to see that, considerations of justice quite aside, Liberia could not be made into a viable state if something like 1 per cent of the nation permanently oppressed 99 per cent. He knew, if only as a gesture of political prudence, that he must make some effort to tap the strength of the submerged tribal masses. The natives have not got much from Tubman, but they have got something. For the first time, there are several in the House of Representatives (but none in the Senate), and a few have lately reached administrative posts. E.C.B. Jones, of partly Grebo descent, is secretary of war, and the chief justice of the Supreme Court, Nimley Russell, is a full Grebo. Dr. J.N. Togba, director general of the Public Health Service, is a Kru, and Oscar Norman, a Gola, is director of the Bureau of Tribal Affairs. It is fascinating to watch developments like this—Negroes permitting other Negroes to emerge. Liberia feels the same winds, though they are faint as yet, that have blown with such vigor on Nigeria and the Gold Coast. The yeasty tribal masses cannot be permanently kept down.

*

The Liberian political system is closely modeled on that of the United States. The cabinet, appointed by the President, functions much like ours. There are ten senators, two from each county, and thirty-one representatives;

---

[15] Gabriel L. Dennis, secretary of state, died in 1954.
[16] The others are Amharic and Tamachek (Berber). See Duncan MacDougald, Jr., *The Languages and Press of Africa*.

the Vice-President presides over the Senate, just as does the Vice-President in Washington. In theory all citizens over twenty-one, including women, are entitled to vote if they are property owners or pay a modest hut tax. But elections, even today, are apt to be a burlesque, because there is seldom any choice of candidate. Liberia is a one-party state. What is known as the True Whig party, the Tubman party, has held power without serious interruption since the 1870's. Mr. Tubman is not only president, head of state, chief executive, and commander-in-chief of the army, but party boss.[17]

Not long ago a resident of Monrovia complained to a high Liberian official that a certain person was giving him trouble. "Why not arrest him?" the official suggested. "On what charge?" "Oh, any charge."

Mostly Mr. Tubman rules by means of patronage, exactly as a President of the United States may rule. His enormous, unchallengeable weapon is jobs. The government (Firestone excepted) is by far the largest employer in the country, and all government jobs go—naturally—to members of the True Whig party. The party is financed in turn by a levy on every officer who earns $25 a month or more, amounting to two weeks' salary during normal times, a month's salary in an "election" year. Nobody can possibly get a job if he is known to be in opposition, and no opposition can exist effectively because nobody outside the government has any funds. No neater system of political domination has ever been devised.

Mr. Tubman knows as well as anybody that there are crooks and grafters in Liberia. But he cannot get rid of them all until an educated class arises out of which he can find better men. Close to him are the ablest people in the country. He is careful, however, to see that nobody is an obvious Number Two man. He plays politics by balancing one associate against another, as politicians have done from Pericles to Roosevelt.

Overt criticism of the President is considered to be sedition, and a person guilty of giving information of a deleterious nature to foreigners is, in theory, subject to a jail sentence. As a result people in Monrovia are somewhat guarded in their expressions of opinion. There is no Gestapo (as is sometimes alleged) because there is little need to have one; everybody tells Mr. Tubman everything, if only to curry favor. All this being true, it is astonishing that public criticism, of a veiled sort (and never aimed at the President directly), is sometimes heard. One newspaper, a remarkable journalistic phenomenon called the *Friend*, is not against Tubman, but tries to take its own line. In March, 1953, it wrote that "high job seekers" were among those urging Mr. Tubman to come out for a third term. The Presi-

[17] Reports are heard, however, that in forthcoming elections Tubman will be opposed by a group calling itself the "Independent" True Whig Party.

dent issued a statement denying this and saying that the editor was a disappointed job-seeker himself. The editor replied in a front page editorial, "We feel that we owe it to the public to correct the statement made by the President in which he alleges that the editor of the *Friend* is 'disgruntled, mortified, and chagrined' because of his disappointment in not being appointed consul general to Germany. We call on High Heaven to refute this statement, and we hasten to make it cristal [sic] clear that we are not disgruntled, mortified, or chagrined."

On another occasion, when this editor was being attacked by the True Whig old guard, he replied, "There is one object all these super loyal citizens seem to have in view, and that is to increase the President's sensibility and thereby move him to either imprison the editor of the *Friend* for life or close down the *Friend* or have the Frontier Force *shoot the editor down*." (Italics mine.)

One opposition leader of consequence has, despite all obstacles, managed to rise, a man named Dihdwo Twe. He is a Kru, and for years sought to represent the crushed masses in the Hinterland. Back in the 1920's he helped bring to light before the League of Nations the role of leading Liberians of that time in the slave traffic, and the ruling classes have hated him ever since. In 1951 Mr. Twe achieved something almost impossible— he organized a genuine opposition party and set out to oppose Tubman for president. A further miracle might have occurred and he might have won the election, but at the last moment the outraged True Whig forces managed to prevent him from running owing to "a technicality." Mr. Twe was then charged with sedition, but managed to escape from the country. His movement was called "treasonable," and several of his adherents were arrested. Recently the Institute of Ethnic Affairs in Washington petitioned the Human Rights Commission of the UN on behalf of Mr. Twe, who is now living in Sierra Leone. Witch doctors were employed to try to poison Twe, this document alleges. Mr. Twe, who was educated in the United States, wrote Mr. Tubman a perfectly dignified letter (before he fled the country) urging electoral reform. Mr. Tubman's reply was as follows: "For the present time, my reply to your note is that you are inherently a traitor to your country, a consummate liar, a senile visionary, a sophisticated bigot, and an uncompromising egotist, the truth of which you will be made to realize."

CHAPTER 44

Monrovian Doctrine

FROM ROBERTS FIELD, where the Pan-American clippers land, to MONROVIA, capital of Liberia, is about fifty miles. During the rains it will take a car several hours to traverse this distance, if it is possible to get through at all. Recently a new concrete bridge collapsed. The easiest way to make the trip is by air, if you are lucky enough to catch a shuttle service operated by Liberian National Airways. This company has one DC 3, and its general manager is also the chief pilot. The journey was the shortest I ever took on a commercial airliner—twelve minutes—and the fare is $5.00.

The population of Monrovia is, according to some, 17,000; according to others, 35,000. Liberians are proud of this city and there are, indeed, a few stately but down-at-the-heel old-style mansions, built in the manner of the American south. The town has one modern office building. A modern port, built during the war by American Lend-Lease funds (cost, $19,000,000), permits liners to be loaded directly from a wharf, instead of by means of lighters plunging through the surf. The port aside, Monrovia looks like something afflicted by scurvy. It is not merely crumbling with rot, but deliquescent. The streets are for the most part slippery ditches oozing with red mud. Houses are mostly wooden, and cannot be kept up on account of the whiplike rain. The hospital, originally the premises of a German cable station, has been called "the worst single sight in Africa." There is no insane asylum or poorhouse. Lebanese and Arab traders run the dank, scrofulous waterfront, and I saw a headline in a local paper, HOGS INFEST THE TOWN—SANITARY INSPECTORS NOT CONCERNED. In the police station men awaiting trial sleep in "pools of urine." One area not far from the Executive Mansion looked to me like a swamp, but it is apparently the most fashionable part of town. Here, if the mud will permit their passage, one may encounter automobiles of the most flamboyant contemporary cut —cream-colored, chocolate-colored, or painted green-and-silver—carrying important officials or their mistresses on various errands, and which resemble fireflies trying to skip through muck.

Socially Monrovia is reminiscent of what Natchez or Savannah might have been in the old days, except that the leading families are, of course, black instead of white. Everybody knows everybody else, and people have an easy courtesy, with a sense of dignified tradition. They dance the Virginia reel. I heard one lady say, "We took our dances with us to America, and now we have brought them back here." The late secretary of state, Gabriel L. Dennis, was an accomplished performer on the piano and musical saw. Social notes in the daily press are picturesque. A lady may be called her husband's "solar star." A new rum factory opened while we were in Monrovia, and was described as being "aristocratic." An official memorandum, signed by the secretary of state on behalf of the President, announced rules for the behavior of guests at the last Independence Reception and Ball at the Executive Pavilion. "At the ball there should not be any shaking of hands." The report of an official picnic at about the same time said that "Tommy guns announced the arrival of guests of honor."

The aristocracy, like all good aristocracies, has close ties to the land. Almost everybody has a patch of rubber. Land is a very serious matter in Liberia, and so is citizenship. Nobody not of Negro blood may become a citizen, and only citizens may purchase land. Liberia does, however, encourage foreign enterprise in certain particular fields. The country has, for instance, considering its poverty and lack of maritime development, an astoundingly large merchant fleet, amounting to not less than 2,349,978 tons. A similar situation exists in Panama. Foreign shipowners register vessels under the Liberian flag, which gives them freedom of movement and other advantages, and fees from this process provide the Liberian government with an unusual and handsome revenue.

It is a striking phenomenon that three of the independent states of Africa—Ethiopia, Libya, and Liberia—should be the poorest and most backward on the continent, much poorer than most of those dominated by white powers. I asked a Monrovian of consequence a simple question, "Why is Liberia so poor?" His answer was a jovial, "You tell me!"

OUT OF SLAVERY, SLAVERY

Liberia—a Devil's Paradise
—SIR JOHN HARRIS

One of the most horrifying official documents I have ever read has to do with Liberia, the report made in 1931 by an international commission inquiring into the slave traffic.[1] For years rumors had been heard, which the Monrovia government persistently denied, that Liberia tolerated organized slavery. At last in 1929 pressure, largely from the United States, forced an investigation. Henry Stimson, secretary of state at the time, wrote to the Liberian authorities, "It would be tragically ironic if Liberia whose existence was dedicated to the principle of liberty should succumb to practices so closely akin to those which its founders sought forever to escape."[2]

Facts discovered by the commission were—and are—appalling. It found that "slavery as defined by the 1926 anti-slavery convention" existed in the country, that contract laborers "were recruited under conditions of criminal compulsion scarcely distinguishable from slave raiding and slave trading," and that high officials of the Liberian government not only connived at this traffic but made money out of it. Outrages took place, according to the report, in three separate but related fields.

First, Liberian natives were forcibly exported to the Spanish island of Fernando Po and the French Gabon, where they had to work for whatever period their "contract" stipulated. The worst offenders outside Liberia were Spaniards. The Spanish cocoa planters wanted as much cheap labor as they could get. Their recruiting agents in 1928 "entered into an agreement with a number of Liberians, some of whom were officials and relatives of President King, agreeing to pay $45 per boy for each group of 3,000 boys exported, plus a bonus of $5,000 for every additional group of 1,500 boys."[3] Boys were hunted almost like animals, herded to the ports, and shipped aboard Spanish or German steamers. The report gives texts of numerous telegrams proving beyond doubt the nature and extent of this traffic. Sometimes boys were seized out of the jungle by the Liberian Frontier Force itself, an agency of the government.

The President of Liberia at this time was Charles Dunbar Burgess King. The Vice-President and second most important person in the country, Allen N. Yancy, was boss of Maryland county. Yancy's record, as demonstrated by the commission's report, is one of the most malodorous ever known in Africa. One has to go back to the history of agents of King Leopold in the Congo to match it. Mr. Yancy murdered people, it seems, almost as casually as he doffed his hat. He boasted that he would soon be President of the Republic, and that no man could possibly halt or hinder him. If

[1] *Report of the International Commission of Inquiry into the Existence of Slavery and Forced Labor in the Republic of Liberia*, U. S. Government Printing Office, 1931.
[2] Buell, *op. cit.*, p. 35.
[3] "The Reconstruction of Liberia," *Foreign Policy Reports*, August 3, 1932, p. 124.

even a paramount chief should refuse to provide him with enough boys, he would have him publicly flogged in front of his people. One chief testified before the commission that Yancy said to him, "If I want to ship you to Fernando Po now I can do so, who can stop me? I can turn you over to the soldiers to take you to the barracks in the interior, and then give them orders to kill you on the way, and when the report gets to Monrovia I will simply write and tell the President that you died from sickness, and whatever reason I give for the cause of your death will be accepted by him."

Families of boys of the Wadebo tribe sang this song:

> We were here when trouble came to our people;
> For this reason Yancy came to our country—
> He caught our husbands and our brothers,
> Sail them to 'Nana Poo
> And there they die!
> And there they die!
>
> Tell us
> Yancy, why?
> Yancy, why?
> Wadebo women have no husbands,
> Yancy, why?
> Wadebo women have no brothers,
> Yancy, why?
> Mothers, fathers, sons have died,
> Waiting for the return
> Yancy, why?

One boy, returning from Fernando Po after serving out his contract, reported that his wages in fourteen months amounted to £1.12.3.

Mr. Tubman, the present President of Liberia, was a senator during this period, and served as one of Yancy's lawyers. He is mentioned in the report twice, each time in connection with the receipt of fees from native chiefs.

Second, the report revealed the existence of a hideous practice known as "pawning." This means just what the word says, but the pawn was a human being. People, to get desperately needed money, would be forced to pawn their close relatives for indefinite periods; these became in effect slaves of the pawn-holders. Records exist of innocent persons being held in pawn for forty years. Some never got out of pawn. Sometimes—in fact often—chiefs or subchiefs had to pawn *their own children* in order to raise money for fines which the government levied on them, as punishment for not having delivered enough contract labor. It is difficult to conceive anything more pernicious. A man who was decent enough to refuse to sell his fellows into slavery could be forced to make his own child a slave!

Sometimes women were taken as pawns "to attract male labor" on the land; young girls were pawned for as little as £5. Here is a specimen of a pawn contract:

>   Gbowah Compound
>   Bharzon Dist. #4
>   May 25th, 1928.
> this is to certify that I Sidi Weah at Gbhowah Section have pawned one little girl and one boy to Seargeant Johnny Williams until the amount £13.10 thirteen pounds ten shillings sterling which I due him be pay to him at any time.
>
>   Principal
>   Side Weah
> Witness
> Moses: S. Weah
>   Approved
>   J. C. Phillips
>   D. C. Coast
>   District L.F.F.
>   23, May, 1928

Third, forced labor within Liberia itself. I quote the Foreign Policy Association pamphlet cited above. "Men were invariably forced to work . . . without pay, and both men and women laborers had frequently been subjected to cruel treatment. Many natives exhibited to the commission the bruises and scars they had received from government overseers; in addition to being flogged, some natives had been tortured by being strung up to the rafters of a hut and literally smoked over a fire. Others had been subjected to 'basket punishment,' by which an immense basket, filled with earth and heavy stones, was lifted by four soldiers and placed upon the head of the prisoner, who was then required to walk. Usually the basket was so heavy that it either immediately broke the native's neck, or caused such injury that he later died."

Here is a sample of testimony before the commission:

> We must give 20 labourers. If you do not agree, they fine you. My two children, I pawned them. I was sub-chief once, but they broke me. . . . When you send your labourers on the road they make them pay fifty cents if they are late, and then work. If they do not work, they catch them, throw them down, and the whip they get is their money. The only pay they get for their work is whip. They call for rice, chicken, eggs, and then if they call for chicken and you don't give them, they flog you. No time for us to do our work. If you do not send the boys on the road they fine you; they tie you with a long stick on your back. If you do not get money you have to take your

son and pawn him to get money to pay and then you fight hard to get the money to redeem the child.

Knowledge of the commission's findings caused, naturally, wide and startled stirrings in Liberia. There were attempts to equivocate and delay but in the end Vice-President Yancy was impeached and criminal prosecution of other officials took place. President King was forced to resign,[4] and was succeeded by his secretary of state, Edwin Barclay. This is the Barclay whom Tubman in turn succeeded. The United States, partly because Liberia seemed to be somewhat slow in instituting the reforms it promised, did not recognize the Barclay regime for four years—until 1935.

Pawning and its attendant horrors have, so far as is known, now disappeared.

FIRESTONE AND ITS ACCOMPLISHMENT

Firestone went into Liberia in the 1920's. At this time American appetite for rubber had become voracious, but various restrictions impeded rubber purchases abroad. Harvey S. Firestone, Sr., the founder of the Firestone Tire and Rubber Company, wanted to make the United States independent of British and Dutch production. To this end he procured immense quantities of land in Liberia, and set up plantations there. The original agreement (1926) gave the Firestone interests the right to lease up to a million acres, which is roughly 4 per cent of the area of the entire country, at a price of 6 cents per acre developed, for a period of ninety-nine years. Rubber is not indigenous to Liberia (although a local vine, the lobelia, does produce a kind of latex) and the trees were brought in from Brazil. Liberia seemed ideal for the growth of *Hevea braziliensis*. Firestone has, however, never used anything like the million acres it has the right to use; only about 80,000 acres are in active production today, with 7,000 more planted to rubber still immature. But 8,885,160 trees are being tapped and the Harbel Area of the Firestone Plantations Company is the largest contiguous rubber plantation in the world. Firestone produced in 1952 72,706,554 pounds of rubber. This was roughly 7 per cent of total American needs for that year.

Rubber plantations existed in Liberia long before Firestone came in, but they were not particularly successful. Today Firestone controls 95 per cent of Liberian production. The company co-operates closely with the small

---

[4] After retirement for seventeen years Mr. King re-emerged to become Liberian minister to Washington in 1947. He is now one of Firestone's attorneys in Monrovia.

private producers, and encourages them if only because it is advantageous to have the country "rubber-conscious."

The Firestone agreements were, in the early days, severely criticized on occasion. Following the plantations contract came a loan agreement, also in 1926, whereby a Firestone subsidiary, the Finance Corporation of America, agreed to lend Liberia up to $5,000,000 for forty years—at 7 per cent interest—in order to help Liberia pay off previous indebtedness. Only half the loan was issued, and its terms remained secret for almost five years. It was a loan not very productive for Liberia, since most of the $2,500,000 went to pay off existing obligations. "Service charges and adviser's salaries amounted to a fixed charge of nearly $270,000 a year, constituting 20 per cent of government revenues in 1928, and about 50 per cent in 1931." The loan was "one of the few refunding operations in history which actually increased the burden on the debtor government."[5] All this took place, of course, in the era when "dollar diplomacy" was considered respectable, and when the ethics of international bankers were seldom questioned. In 1932 the League of Nations sent a commission to Liberia to study these matters and try to put the country on its feet. Various spokesmen for the League criticized Firestone sharply. One recommendation was that its rental payments should be increased from 6 to 50 cents an acre.

The international commission investigating slavery cleared Firestone of charges that it employed slave labor. The report found that the company did, indeed, get about 10 per cent of its workers from "government sources," which could mean almost anything, but that "there was no evidence that the Firestone Plantations Company consciously employs any but voluntary labor." Workers got fair pay considering the standards of the country, and were free to leave the plantation at will.

The 1926 loan was a severe burden to the country, but on the other hand Firestone, as the years went by, contributed greatly to Liberian economy. At least a quarter of the total national income came from Firestone directly or indirectly. In 1951 Mr. Tubman announced that the old loan was no more—Liberia had at last succeeded in paying it off, every penny. Also in 1951 Liberia passed an income tax law, with which Firestone agreed to abide. The company paid 12 per cent tax on net profits at first, then 14. In 1953, after stiff negotiations, the rate was raised to 25

[5] These quotations are from Buell, *op. cit.*, pp. 32-33. Liberia was virtually helpless in the first negotiations because it needed money so badly and wanted American support in a frontier dispute with France. Firestone "threatened to transfer his interests to Borneo or the Philippines if his terms were not accepted."

per cent, which will give Liberia an annual revenue of about $3,000,000 from Firestone. Wonderful local language celebrated this event. The *Friend* headlined its story, PRESIDENT TUBMAN TEARS DOWN FIRESTONE'S IRRESISTIBLE DEFENSE . . . BAGS MILLIONS OF DOLLARS FOR LIBERIA.

We drove from President Tubman's estate to the Firestone properties, and through them to Roberts Field. The differences, when you cross the Firestone "frontier," are almost those between night and day. Here are red laterite roads well kept up, passable even in the rains; here the whole countryside has been made neat, orderly, and productive. The atmosphere of wild, irascible jungle disappears. We saw housing developments, schools, clinics, laboratories, workshops. The golf course is so good that people come all the way from Sierra Leone to use it. All this is, of course, indication that the rest of Liberia could immensely improve its own miserable physical plant, if the will and even a modicum of means were available, if graft and plunder were stopped, and if the Monrovia government thought more in terms of the needs of the country as a whole.

Firestone employs 25,362 Liberian workers, and its labor policy is good. It has looked with close attention on the example of the Union Minière du Haut Katanga in the Congo. Workers are not altogether encouraged to bring their families with them, but they may do so if they prefer; there are no compounds as in South Africa. About 1,100 African children go to the admirable Firestone schools. Adult workers are trained to be bricklayers, carpenters, truck drivers, and the like. What Liberia needs above all is a middle class—people independent of employment by a slatternly government —and the company is helping to produce this by being a kind of school for trades. And it is a striking fact that Firestone spends as much on medical services for 25,000 people as the government spends for the entire population.[6] All its workers have access to clinics—free.

Liberians criticize Firestone mainly on two counts. First, very few Africans get managerial posts. The company's answer is that these are open to any Liberians capable of filling them, but that not many are capable so far. Second, wages are shockingly low—only 28 cents a day for the lowest paid unskilled labor. But to raise wages might upset the economy of the entire country, the company says. Skilled employees get salaries that are huge for Liberia; a clerk can earn $75 per month.

One Firestone subsidiary, the U. S. Trading Company, is agent for various American imports, and has the local Coca-Cola bottling franchise. The government recently put a one-cent tax on soft drinks, raising the price of

[6] The American Foundation for Tropical Medicine has an important installation on the Firestone properties. Recently Harvey S. Firestone, Jr., gave it $250,000.

Coca-Cola from 7 cents to 8 cents a bottle, but this did not diminish its sales, about 10,000 cases a month—an extraordinary amount for a population so small and poor. There is scarcely a village in Liberia without Coca-Cola.

Liberian nationalists will, in time, want to get rid of Firestone—some want to get rid of it already—because it is "exploitative" and has an economic power so overshadowing. But countries like Liberia need capital investment, technical know-how, and imported brains, on the understanding that foreign investors deal fairly and do not abuse their privileges. Firestone may have been greedy in the past, and it certainly makes a handsome profit out of Liberia, but it has fulfilled a necessary historical role. When its usefulness is over, it may disappear, as the old chartered companies in Nigeria disappeared. The era is past when any private—or public—company can be in a position to control a nation's destiny. Meantime Firestone justifies itself amply by doing more for its workers than the government itself does for the majority of citizens. That it has done a great deal for Liberia cannot be doubted or denied.

*

A vital new factor in the economic life of Liberia is development of the iron ore reserves in the Bomi Hills. Lansdell K. Christie, the president of the Liberian Mining Company (the stock of which is 61.57 per cent owned by Republic Steel) is the major actor in this substantial and worthy enterprise. At present he is shipping out of Liberia more than a million tons a year of the richest iron ore in the world (1,300,000 tons in 1953); it is so rich that it can be used almost like scrap. Liberia has a railway now, thanks to Mr. Christie; this, the first railway in the country, runs from the Bomi Hills to Monrovia, and is forty-three miles long. Shipments of ore began in June, 1951. There are estimated reserves of more than 130,000,000 tons. By terms of the original contract, the mining company was not subject to Liberian income tax, but paid on a royalty basis. The rate was low at first. Then the Liberian government demanded—and got—a better arrangement. It will (after a preliminary period) take 25 per cent of the net profits of the company for five years, then 35 per cent for ten years, and then 50 per cent. Already Mr. Christie and his coworkers are contributing to the national exchequer a sum greater than the whole annual budget a few years ago.[7] Even in a country as backward as Liberia one-sided exploitation by outside interests is a thing

[7] "A Visit to Liberia," by Cecil Sprigge, *Manchester Guardian*, January 21, 1954. Also see the New York *Times*, July 5, 1952.

of the past. If a foreign entrepreneur wants to make money, he has to share some of the proceeds with the government, which should in turn use revenue for the benefit of the people as a whole.

*

In 1947 Edward R. Stettinius, Jr., former American Secretary of State, organized a corporation, the Liberia Company, owned half by himself and his associates, half by the Liberian government, for widespread economic development in the country. The project encountered various difficulties, and is little heard of in Monrovia today. About 4,000 acres of a 25,000 acre concession have been planted to cocoa.

POINT FOUR AND THE FUTURE

More than eighty American experts, representing the Technical Co-operation Administration, were at work in Liberia when we visited Monrovia. The head of the mission was a Negro, Dr. John W. Davis, formerly president of West Virginia State College and an able, devoted citizen. "Liberia was the first country," an official announcement reads, "to sign a general Point Four program embracing its entire economy." No nation, as is only too obvious, needed such a program more. The agreement was signed in Washington in December, 1950, and work urgently needed in several fields got under way—public health, public works, agriculture, government services (which will include the taking of a census), and above all education.

The United States government contributed $1,300,000 to this program in 1953, and the Liberian government $1,497,000. The former sum means little to American economy; it is like a speck of dust on the floor. But $1,497,000 means a great deal to Liberia, since it is not less than one-seventh of the total national budget. Mr. Tubman deserves substantial praise for this. Moreover the Liberian contribution will increase as the Five-Year Development Plan gets under way. Further American credits, to the amount of $6,250,000, came to the country since 1952 from the Export-Import Bank, largely earmarked for basic public services like roads, water, and sewerage projects. Other examples of American activity may be cited; for instance, a team from Cornell University is codifying the country's laws. Also Liberia has lately begun to import specialists from several nations besides the United States; an Indian, a Dane, a Norwegian, and a Canadian are among recent arrivals, and the administration may, in time, take on a multinational texture like that in Ethiopia. Finally Liberia has made specialized agreements with various UN organs, like the World Health Organization and UNESCO. We saw several WHO cars on our trip upcountry. All this is an excellent augury for the future.

As to Point Four, the organization is somewhat like that we inspected in Libya many pages past:

(a) *Public Health.* The first problem is malaria, the incidence of which is probably 100 per cent; another is onchocerciasis, which causes blindness. No one has much accurate knowledge of what particular kinds of disease-carrying mosquitoes Liberia has. A FOA physician is now attached to a rural demonstration project at Gbarnga; here people are taught (if they will listen) rudiments of public health, like spraying, protection of the water supply, and better methods of midwifery. There are only four public hospitals in all Liberia. Anything that the Americans can do will be welcome, even if this is no more than the collection of statistics. The country needs reliable statistics almost as much as it needs honesty and cash.

(b) *Public Works and Natural Resources.* Work in this field means, in the main, roads. Six hundred miles of new roads are planned, and the road to French Guinea and the Ivory Coast will be "rehabilitated." An allied project is a complete photogrammetrical survey of the country, from the air, which is now 87 per cent accomplished. (It is an interesting sidelight that only 42 per cent of the United States has ever been similarly mapped.) Also weather observation stations will be built. This will not make it rain less, but it will give people some knowledge of how the rains behave.

(c) *Agriculture.* Point Four specialists are now stationed in several key areas; their function is roughly that of county agents in the United States. Demonstration farms have been set up, seedlings distributed, and instruction given in soil chemistry, animal husbandry, insect control, and the like. An agricultural research station with eight Americans has been established at Suakoko. Efforts are being made to increase the export of a fiber called piassava, used in making rough brooms. Forestry reserves are being investigated, and a marine biologist is at work on fisheries. But the chief emphasis is on food production, if only because the local agriculture has been so backward that the country cannot feed itself. Liberia never even had a department of agriculture until five years ago.

(d) *Education.* On this, of course, everything else will ultimately rest. In the entire country at present there are only 325 public schools (most of the buildings being dilapidated beyond belief) and about 1,480 teachers. During the six months' rainy season most schools shut down. Of the 1,480 teachers (and Liberia should have 24,000 to meet the needs of its population) many have never even had elementary schooling. About 30,000 Liberian youngsters—10 per cent of those of school age—are now going to some sort of school or other. Only nine secondary schools exist, and four of these are run by the missions. "Functional" illiteracy—that is, inability to read, write, or comprehend in English at the fifth-grade level—is between 90 and 95 per cent. Obviously anything that the United States, or other nations, can do to give Liberia a lift in education will be worth while.

Point Four and other American agencies are often criticized in Liberia and elsewhere for being inefficient and having mediocre personnel. But they represent a phenomenon new to the world, constructive, and of the utmost promise. This is "imperialism" in a new, commendable, and exciting dress. We are giving backward nations blood and sinew out of our own resources, instead of exploiting them. Some day Liberia may be able to look tomorrow in the eye.

LIBERIAN MISCELLANY

This is the only country I have ever visited where people have a special, "national" handshake, which takes place with a mysterious noisy snap of the thumb. To be able to make three snaps in a row, during one handshake, is a highly regarded accomplishment. Most Liberian villages have a "palaver house" or community center, which is usually no more than a hut of mud, dung, and reeds, and Liberian girls have the prettiest breasts I saw anywhere in Africa. Liberians have one unique animal, the pygmy hippopotamus, and out in the country some people are so lazy that, even if they are on the point of starvation, they will work only ten or twelve days a year.

CHAPTER 45

Dakar and French West Africa

The less intelligent the white man is, the more stupid he thinks the African.
—ANDRÉ GIDE

Now FINALLY we reach French Africa once more. The end is the beginning, as it is in life itself and should be in works of art. This book began forty or more countries ago with the tricolor in Rabat; it concludes with the tricolor in Dakar. We have come full circle.

French West Africa is one of the largest geographical entities in the world, if it may properly be called an entity—it stretches from the Atlantic bulge to the far end of the Sahara, from the frontiers of Morocco to Nigeria. It is six times bigger than Texas, eight times bigger than France, one-half the size of all Europe, three-fifths the size of the United States; and it covers one-sixth of all Africa. The population is around 17,000,000, of whom 63,000 are, as the French say non-autochthonous or not African.

Let us bolt down other facts and figures. French West Africa has two formidable rivers, the Senegal and Niger, although much of it is desert as blank as any known to man; 2,404 miles of railway, only slightly more than the state of Maine; thirty-four airports; a budget totaling $300,000,000 (about three-fifths that of the city of Chicago); some 23,000,000 acres under cultivation of which only 291,000 are owned by Europeans; fifty-four cinemas; and 360,000 camels. For 17,000,000 people there are only *thirty-six* secondary schools; in one territory exactly seven Africans have had a college education. On the other hand school enrollment—I am quoting an official source—"increased by fifty-six per cent from 1946 to 1951 and by another ten per cent the following year," and let it be said proudly that Dakar has an actual university (founded in 1950), which is something that Kenya and Northern Rhodesia do not have.

Countries which we have discussed recently, like Nigeria, the Gold Coast,

Sierra Leone, Liberia, and the Gambia, all stick into the huge mass of French West Africa like blunt fingers in a mass of dough, but without touching each other. All are enclaves (of course they face the sea) in the embrace of French territory. British historians make much of this. Smart and tricky Frenchmen, they like to say, outwitted the honorable but stupid British in the heyday of African land-grabbing, so that French West Africa is a cohesive unit, whereas British possessions are unfortunately scattered.

For the last time in this book we mention the labyrinthian diversity of African tribes in a given area. The people of French West Africa (which was once called Senegambia) speak no fewer than 120 different languages, and are divided into twenty-seven large ethnic groups.[1] Almost as an exercise in desperation we may mention the Wolofs, Sarakolés, Sérères, Bambaras, Malinkés, Sonraïs, Bozos, Sorkos, Dogons, Mossis, Bobos, Lobis, Gouronsis, Djermas, Soussous, Kissis, Tomas, Guerzés, Coniaguis, Baoulés, Agnis, Sénoufos, Minas, Sombas, and Baribas. These are largely black. The French classify as "white" the Berbers and Tuareg, of whom there are about a million, and call two million others—Moslems of Hamitic origin who have strayed to Senegal all the way from the Nile—"mixed." Then there are the "gray" people, like the Fulani. Of the total about nine million are pagan, six and a half million Moslem, and perhaps a million Christian.[2]

Non-human phenomena are also varied. The French gravely report that, in the field of climatology, there are three important winds, the *alizé* which blows from the north in winter, the *mousson*, a wet wind uncomfortable in the rainy season, and our old friend the *harmattan*, which contains sand.

POLITICS IN FWA: NOT WITHOUT RISKS

The Ivory Coast, an important division of French West Africa, some years ago elected a distinguished Negro lawyer, Victor Biaka-Boda, as a senator to Paris. Mr. Biaka-Boda returned to his constituency in 1950 to do some electioneering, and disappeared out in the bush. All efforts to trace him failed. On March 30, 1953, he was officially declared dead by a court sitting at Bouaflé which, on inspecting the evidence, decided that he had been eaten by cannibals. "*Debris humain*" was the proof. There are cases innumerable in the world of senators feasting with their constituents, but this must surely be the only instance on record of constituents feasting on a senator.

---

[1] Some of these items are from a bulletin published by the French *Service de Presse et d'Information* in New York.
[2] French West Africa has about sixty American missionaries.

ADMINISTRATIVE DIVISIONS OF FRENCH WEST AFRICA

*The Forest Belt is passed
And Timbuctoo is reached at last.*
—THE MODERN TRAVELLER.

It has always been French policy to decentralize overseas; a curse of Syria and the Lebanon in the old days, and of Indochina recently, was sectionalism, splitting up of a country into segments to make ultimate rule by Paris easier. (Of course there were other reasons too for a sectionalist policy.) In French West Africa decentralization was a necessity, if only because the country is so huge, heterogeneous, and diversified. Timbuktu is as different from Abidjan as Birmingham, Alabama, is from Birmingham, England—perhaps more so.

French Equatorial Africa, as we saw in Chapter 34, has four great territories; French West Africa (*Afrique Occidentale Française*) has eight:

Senegal. This Atlantic region, which contains the federal capital (Dakar), is the best known part of French West Africa, as well as the most westernized. Senegalese—among the blackest blacks in Africa—have served in the French army for generations, and make good soldiers; the territory is an important reservoir of French military man power. The educated class, deriving from four old towns called the "Quatres Communes," is immaculately cultivated, and has been sending political representatives to the French parliament since World War I. Senegal completely surrounds the British colony of Gambia, which looks like a crude mouth cut into Senegal's head. Senegal was first settled by the Normans. The capital is St. Louis, 150 miles north of Dakar on the Senegal River, and an early governor—very distinguished—bore the odd name Schmaltz. Many women have a lively political consciousness, and even Moslem women (who are unveiled for the most part) vote. Senegal has rich phosphate deposits, and is the biggest peanut producer in the world. One important project for the mechanized cultivation of peanuts is at Ziguinchor, on the Casamance River. This is run by the state (with some private capital) somewhat on the line of various British colonial development organizations, and is called the Compagnie Générale des Oléagineux Tropicaux.

Mauritania. Whereas Senegal has 2,092,700 people on 80,600 square miles, Mauritania has only half a million people on more than 400,000 square miles. The capital of both territories is the same town, St. Louis. This is because Mauritania is too poor, too sparsely inhabited, to be able to afford its own capital; the largest town, Port Etienne, a seaport on the edge of the Spanish colony Rio de Oro, has only four thousand inhabitants and has to import all its water from Dakar. To describe Mauritania one needs only to employ the word "desert." The inhabitants are mostly Moors, who in older days were avid and successful slave traders; every year they descended into Senegal, and reaped a crop of human loot. Mauritania has important deposits of iron ore. Also it has exactly two secondary schools.

French Sudan. Capital Bamako; area more than 450,000 square miles (three times as big as Germany); population 3,346,900 (about that of Chicago). This, with the possible exception of Morocco, is the most "romantic" of all French possessions overseas, because it contains the celebrated city Timbuktu, a synonym for extreme remoteness and inaccessibility.

Actually Timbuktu, or Tombouctou as it is spelled in French, is not particularly isolated or inaccessible. It lies close to the Niger, it is not far from the important town of Gao (once the center of an "empire"), and it can be reached by *piste* for part of the year at least from Bamako, though only a fanatic chauvinist would claim that the road is good. Air France touches on Bamako four times a week. Nor is Timbuktu particularly romantic these days; it is little more than a languidly provincial Saharan outpost. A more picturesque and exciting town, remarkable for its spiked-beehive architecture, is Goundam nearby. Timbuktu has, on the other hand, an exceptionally pungent history. It was founded in the eleventh century, and developed an important Moslem culture; Portuguese river navigators were the first Europeans to reach it (in 1487), and it was not occupied by the French till as late as 1893.

A good many places in Africa vie for the honor of being the hottest, and Bamako has a just claim. It is, in fact, almost as hot as Senator McCarthy's collar, or Needles, California, in July.

The French Sudan is headquarters for the *Office du Niger*, an important hydroelectric and irrigation project. Some 27,000 Africans have been settled on a 95,000-acre tract reclaimed from the desert, following completion of the Sansanding Dam. The Niger Office is a non-profit agency, and has been called an African TVA. All over French West Africa planned economy is a watchword.

French Guinea. Area 106,200 square miles; population 2,260,600. Here we are on the Guinea Coast again. The capital is Conakry, on the sea, where a literally phenomenal industrial expansion is proceeding, caused by the development of iron and bauxite mines, hydroelectric power, and enlargement of the port. The reserves of iron ore in French Guinea are estimated at two billion tons. A few years ago, Conakry was one of the few Gulf cities where young women stark naked still walked without shame down the chief streets; now this amiable sight is becoming rare. Wherever the white man comes in force, African picturesqueness goes.

Ivory Coast. This is an exceptionally important territory. Its area is 123,200 square miles and it has roughly 2,000,000 people. Abidjan, the capital, is like Conakry, but bigger. Ten years ago it was nothing; perhaps it exported a few bananas, but little else. Today, largely as a result of the creation of an artificial harbor, made by cutting a canal through sandbanks and lagoons, it has 110,000 people, and is growing at a fantastic rate. More Europeans live in Abidjan than in the whole Gold Coast. Its port traffic exceeded 750,000 tons last year, and it is supposed to have "the greatest industrial future of any port in the French Union." Abidjan bounces with vitality, and potentially the Ivory Coast is the richest colony in French Africa.[3] Its principal products, aside from bananas, cocoa, coffee, palm oil, and the like, are manganese and diamonds; it produced in 1952 not less than 136,000 carats of these latter. Diamond smuggling is a lively preoccupation. Motorboats in Abidjan harbor carry names almost as picturesque as those on lorries in Nigeria, for instance *Tout Passe, Le Destin n'a pas de Choix, La Souffrance, Des Deux Frères,* and *Ma Gloire.*

Nowhere in French Africa are contrasts historical and otherwise more acute than on the Ivory Coast. Only seventy years ago savage kings crucified their slaves *upside down,* and then cut off their heads the better to draw off blood.

Haute Volta. This is for the most part wild and primitive bush country (area 105,900 square miles; population 3,108,600). It sits atop the Gold Coast and below the French Sudan, and has 1,400,000 sheep and goats. The capital is Ouagadougou; the chief commercial town is Bobo Dioulasso, with 52,000 people. A French lady who lived in the Upper Volta for some time told us, "Our natives are not so *évolués* as the Africans of the Gold Coast; hence they are simpler and friendlier." The French say that Gold Coast Africans seep steadily (but in small numbers) across the frontier, because they "fear" Nkrumah's reforms. The chief Haute Volta exports are livestock, an edible fat called karité, and sisal.

Dahomey. This, with its capital at Porto Novo, is the smallest province in FWA; it lies like a narrow wedge between Togoland and Nigeria, and has an extraordinarily bizarre history. No African kings have ever quite rivaled those of Dahomey for vices and virtues both. The people, of pure Negro stock for the most part—at least along the coast—call themselves Fons and have a unique tradition. A great king, Gozo, ascended the Dahomey throne in 1818, and reigned for forty years. His subjects were intensely

---

[3] Beg pardon. The French, as we know, never use the nasty word "colony" officially.

warlike; they fought each other, and several times made deep invasions into Nigeria. (The British annexed Lagos in 1861 largely to keep it safe from Dahomeyan raiders.) What was chiefly remarkable about the Dahomey army was that it contained a large number of professionally trained women troops—Amazons. There were 18,000 of these at one time, and their fierceness and valor knew no bounds. Also Dahomey has been famous—or infamous—because like Benin in Nigeria it practiced the "customs," wholesale human sacrifices. These were designed to give a dead king or nobleman satisfactory company in the hereafter. Gozo was a conspicuous reformer (as well as warrior), although the walls of his palace were made of human skulls, and "his sleeping chamber was paved with the heads of his enemies." On his deathbed, however, he asked that his family and retainers be spared. Usually when a man died his nearest of kin were the first to be crucified.

The name "Dahomey" comes from that of an older king, and means literally "belly of Dan." King Dan was accustomed to eat his victims. The French had a troublesome war with Dahomey as recently as 1892, but today the country is as peaceful as an empty barnyard. In older days the territory produced exceptional works of art, in particular small bronzes. Dahomey has eight secondary schools, and the chief exports are palm kernels and palm oil.[4]

Niger. This is a large back-country province, stretching (area 494,500 square miles) all the way from Nigeria to Libya, a formidable distance indeed. The capital is Niamey, and the population something over two million. Much of this enormous territory—partly jungle, partly savanna, partly desert—is still terra incognita. Hunters chase oryx and addax in "the strip of herbage strown that just divides the desert from the sown." A project for the large-scale production of rice recently got under way.

MEN AND ISSUES IN FWA

French West Africa is much more alive and energetic politically than French Equatorial Africa or even the Cameroons. Parts, at least, of this giant country are almost as advanced as Nigeria and the Anglo-Egyptian Sudan. The number of registered voters has significantly increased in recent years—for instance, in the French Sudan the jump has been from 159,000 to 916,000. There are 80,000 people on the electoral lists in Dakar alone, and half of these voted in the last election.

[4] Professor Melville J. Herskovits of Northwestern University, to whom every student of African anthropology owes a great debt, is the author of a superlatively interesting two-volume history of Dahomey.

At the top of the structure is a French High Commissioner and Governor General, Bernard Cornut-Gentille, an able and ambitious administrator. As in French Equatorial Africa, a Grand Council exists on a federal level, and each territory has an Assembly elected (indirectly) without regard to race or color. But these bodies have little actual legislative power. Moreover they are heavily weighted to French advantage. For instance, in the Ivory Coast 15,000 Frenchmen elect 18 members to the local assembly, whereas 2,000,000 Africans only elect 32. Roughly the same proportions apply to the other territories.[5] To Paris, French West Africa sends a big delegation—twenty senators, twenty deputies, and twenty-seven counselors of the French Union. Of this total of sixty-seven, no fewer than forty-five are black or *métis*, mixed. (Officially the French consider all *métis* to be white.) They belong to seven different French political parties, ranging from extreme right to left. None are Communists.

Most FWA political leaders have attained a considerable sophistication. French policy *has* worked; they are almost indistinguishable from Frenchmen. They may want more rights and privileges for their territories, but few are outright nationalists like Nkrumah or the men who run the Anglo-Egyptian Sudan. Practically no anti-French sentiment exists to an important degree. It might even be said that some Africans in FWA want to run *France*, not merely themselves. Oddly enough, however, several conspicuous senators and deputies who sit in Paris think on the other hand that it is preposterous for Paris to have so many black legislators. Though loyal to France, they consider this to be a wily artifice by the French to drown them in domestic French affairs and thus make them neglect Africa. "Representation in Paris does the African cause more harm than good," I heard it said. What these deputies want instead is more chance for political expression and development at home—above all the creation of a genuine legislative structure, with eventual autonomy within the French Union.

Léopold Sédar Senghor, a deputy for Senegal in the National Assembly, is probably the leading politician in FWA as a whole. An exceptionally cultivated man, he is a renowned poet and professor as well as politician; he was a prominent member of the drafting committee that wrote the new French constitution in 1946, and had the exacting job of putting this into as perfect French as possible. He is Senegalese, in his early forties, Catholic-educated, an agnostic now, a former socialist, and a son-in-law of the late Félix Éboué, the wartime Governor of Chad. People say that he

[5] Professor Rayford W. Logan in *African News*, February, 1954.

knows French much better than he knows Wolof, the Senegalese lingua franca. Here is one of Senghor's poems, dedicated to Pablo Picasso:

Masque Nègre

Elle dort et repose sur la candeur du sable.
Koumba Tam dort. Une palme verte voile la fièvre des cheveux, cuivre le front courbe.
Les paupières closes, coupe double et sources scellées!
Ce fin croissant cette lèvre plus noire lourde à peine—ou le sourire de la femme complice?
Les patènes des joues, le dessin du menton chantent l'accord muet.
Visage de masque fermé à l'éphémère, sans yeux, sans matière.
Tête de bronze parfaite et sa patine de temps
Que ne souillent fards ni rougeurs ni rides ni traces de larmes ni de baisers.
O visage tel que Dieu l'a créé avant la mémoire même des âges
Visage de l'aube du monde, ne t'ouvre pas comme un col tendre pour émouvoir ma chair
Je t'adore, ô Beauté, de mon oeil monocorde.

Senghor's party, deriving from the Bloc Democratique Sénégalais, is known as the I.O.M. and stands for what it calls "federalism" or *indépendance d'outre-mer*. It wants to revise the French constitution so that overseas territories will be *equal* partners with France itself. Senghor, like many farseeing and intelligent Africans in French Africa, thinks, as outlined above, that the *autochtones* have too much representation in Paris, not too little; he wants more black power in black areas where blacks should be in charge of their own affairs.

Another powerful politician, Lamine Gueye, is mayor of Dakar. He has given the city an excellent administration. He is Senegalese, a Moslem, a former judge in the West Indies (his wife is a West Indian), a former deputy in Paris, a successful lawyer in France, a representative of France on the UN, a former chairman of the Grand Council of FWA, and the chief of the local Socialist party. Two years ago Senghor beat him for a seat in the National Assembly. Gueye stands for the present constitutional system, and wants French West Africa to be an "integral" part of the French Republic, in opposition to Senghor's idea of federation.

Gueye was succeeded as chairman of the Grand Council in Dakar by another notable figure, Maître Léon Boissier-Palun, a lawyer and close friend of Senghor's. He is a *métis*.

The leading political figure on the Ivory Coast is Félix Houphouet-Boigny, the son of a local chief and a wealthy plantation owner. He is a deputy in Paris, the strong man of the Ivory Coast, and founder and leader of an important party, the RDA or Rassemblement Democratique Africain. This is, in fact, more than a party; it is a kind of "rally" or assembly, standing for quick, full "development" of FWA "within" the French Union. Once the RDA sought to be a bridge between urban intellectuals and the impoverished countryside, and was markedly radical. In fact Houphouet-Boigny made an alliance with the Communists when they were part of the government of France in the postwar period; people tend to forget nowadays that Maurice Thorez, the Communist leader, was once vice-premier in a French cabinet. Later came bloody riots on the Ivory Coast, Communist-inspired, and in 1950 the RDA cut itself off from the Communists.[6] Houphouet-Boigny's chief assistant at this time was a *métis* named Gabriel D'Arboussier, the son of a former French governor and an African mother. Promptly he founded his own independent splinter group, which still exists but has little power; it is nicknamed the "RDA-Cominform." D'Arboussier, who is vice-chairman of the Assembly of the French Union in Versailles, denies that he is a Communist but acts like one most of the time.

The Communist party is, in theory, perfectly legal in FWA, as it is in France, and Communist influence is more pervasive here than anywhere else in French Africa. There are, however, no local party units functioning openly as such. Mostly Communist penetration and agitation take place through the powerful Confédération Générale de Travail. Probably future developments will closely follow those in France itself. Meantime repeated serious strikes—strikes that are genuinely effective—have taken place in French West Africa. In 1947 a railway strike (the railway workers are the strongest local union) completely tied up the economy of the country for some weeks, so that no produce could be moved; the strikers wanted equal pay for equal work and the abolition of all manner of anti-black discriminations. Later came strikes on the Ivory Coast, largely because the legal forty-hour week was not, the African workers said, being equitably applied. In 1954 more strikes came in Senegal—affecting hospital orderlies, telegraphic employees, and pharmaceutical workers among others—and there are bound to be still more if working conditions are not improved. Above all Africans want more *opportunity*.

Finally—to resume this brief catalogue of politicians—there are two important African leaders in French Sudan, both deputies and both socialists, Jean Silvandre and Fily Dabo Sissoko. Monsieur Sissoko heads what is called the French Union "Intergroup," and has several times visited the

---

[6] But in Paris the RDA often votes the Communist party line.

United States as a representative of UNESCO. In Dahomey a consequential leader is Sourous-Migan Apithy, who is a deputy in Paris and a member of the Grand Council in Dakar.

*

Each of the eight FWA regions has a Ten-Year Development Plan. The chief obstacles to economic progress are wretched communications, and, as in so much of Africa, lack of fuel. All coal and oil have to be imported. Incidentally more than a third of all imports come from the United States.

No discussion of French West Africa, no matter how brief, can be representative without at least bare mention of the organization (which operates in other parts of French Africa also) known as FIDES, the Investment Fund for Economic and Social Development. This promotes large-scale capital investment—for roads, harbors, and the like—and helps to finance education, through funds provided partly by the metropolitan government in France, partly by each territory. Its activities resemble somewhat the work of British organisms like the Colonial Development Corporation.

White settlement on the land is not yet a problem in FWA; there are comparatively few agricultural *colons*. But the same kind of evolution that led inevitably to violent friction in Morocco is beginning. "The visitor to French West Africa," writes a British authority, "is greatly impressed by the numbers of private traders, shopkeepers, and craftsmen who have come from France and established themselves with their families as butchers, bakers, chemists, hairdressers, dressmakers, *garagistes*, transporters, mechanics, middlemen, and so on. These people feel that they have a real stake in the country. They can make a decent living, and some of them have become rich. They become interested in local politics and in the finances and economics of the country, and one feels that they are really settlers . . . changing the aspect of life in French West Africa. There is the impression of a growing overseas community with its own individual life."[7]

Let me fire a final salvo of statistics. The French, their critics are apt to say, give only the most meager support to education and health services. But, according to French figures, seventeen per cent of the FWA budget went to education in 1952. As to public health there are 612 physicians and twenty-five hospitals, seventeen leprosaria, 213 maternity centers, sixty-one centers for treating sleeping sickness, and 579 other specialized medical centers (including mobile units) of one sort or other. Last year more than five million people were vaccinated against various complaints.

[7] *World Today*, July, 1951.

DAKAR AND FRENCH WEST AFRICA

DAKAR AND DEFENSE

Dakar sits on a peninsula which marks the extreme westerly projection of Africa, and it has been fittingly called "the boomingest boom town on the continent." It is a real city, in the European manner, and resembles a smaller Casablanca; we have come a long way now from West Coast towns like Lagos and Accra, which are camps made of mud and tin, or the shabby, disgraceful squalor of Monrovia. DAKAR is somewhat tawdry at the edges like any provincial town built practically overnight, and looks like a Florida real estate development; its harbor is one of the most important in Africa but it has no substantial hinterland; it lives on government, the sea, and peanuts. Building activity is lively, and rents are high; a six-room flat in a new building can cost 75,000 African francs per month, or $420. The joke is that Dakar is being fitted out to be the capital of France if the French are beaten in World War III. There is also a native city, the *medina*, which vibrates with brilliant color. The Mauretanian women wear purple-blue gowns, and have sumptuous headdresses, with bows sticking out like artificial ears. A native housing project is built of identical spherical structures, in the shape of bubbles; the French naughtily call this Nichonville, or teat-town.

The velocity of Dakar's growth is startling. Its population has more than quintupled in twenty years and doubled in ten. It has today 267,000 people, of whom 32,050 are European; this classification is divided into 22,700 metropolitan French, 1,950 *métis*, who are considered to be European no matter how dark they are; 6,200 Lebanese and Syrians, who are the old trader class; and 2,100 *étrangers*. Most of the Africans are Senegalese, who have been thoroughly detribalized. Once more—for the last time—we take note of the impact of the western world on primitive Africa. The bush feeds people into the towns almost like a funnel feeding grain into a hopper. But Africans in Dakar do not have too bad a time. They can vote; they can even belong to trade unions and political parties. They can buy and actually own their own homes, by payments over a ten-year period, which is something almost unique in Africa, and 15 per cent of their children of school age go to school.

What color bar there is has little to do with color, per se; it rests much more on social stratification. Officially, of course, there is no discrimination of any kind. The mayor of Dakar, as we have noted above, is an African. So are multitudinous lesser officials. Minor irritants like curfew or proscription of the sale of alcohol do not and cannot exist, since every African is a French citizen, with rights in theory equal to those of any white man.

In the schools European and African children sit side by side. Even in the sexual realm there are no official taboos. People of any color sleep together; intermarriage is, however, comparatively rare.[8]

I liked the museum of the Institute Français d'Afrique Noire; this, known as IFAN, is one of the foremost anthropological organizations on the continent. We saw "jewels" of the most intricate loveliness from the Sonrai people in the Sudan, made of straw and silk; wildly feathered masks from the Cameroons six feet high; from Bouaké exquisitely fashioned tiny iron weights, in the form of swords and scorpions; and serpent fetishes from French Guinea that might have been designed by Braque. African art is, as always, a combination of the savage and the fastidious.

The chief importance of Dakar, and its chief interest to the United States, is in the realm of strategy. Practically all maritime traffic between Europe and South America goes by way of Dakar; similarly it is the jumping-off place for most aircraft crossing the South Atlantic. At least twelve international air services use the Dakar airport, because it is not only an essential link in routes from Europe to Brazil and the Argentine, but from New York to South Africa. Dakar controls the "throat" of the Atlantic between Africa and Brazil; the distance is only about 1,600 miles, less than that between Newfoundland and Ireland. From New York to Dakar is only 3,300 miles, roughly the same distance as from New York to Southampton. Geography is full of optical illusions. Jet liners, incidentally, now fly the Paris-Dakar route (3,071 miles) in six hours and forty minutes. In the event of war Dakar would, of course, resume the place it held in World War II (the origin of its boom) as an essential American-European base. Dakar was, and is, vital, because if the Mediterranean should be closed this African port perched on the Atlantic would control routes to South Africa, the Middle East, India, Australia, and beyond.[9]

FINALE TO THE FRENCH

I wrote in Chapter 34 above that, from a strictly logical point of view and in the long, long run, a complete policy of assimilation must eventually

---

[8] Before the new constitution an African with a French wife could become a citizen if the marriage produced children, or lasted twenty years (Hailey, p. 199). Today, according to *Time* (February 9, 1953), "French colonial officers may claim family allowances for their illegitimate half-caste offspring, some get allowances for thirty or more little half and halfs."

[9] A seven-power conference to co-ordinate defense arrangements in Africa south of the Sahara took place in Dakar early in 1954. The participating countries were Britain, France, Belgium, Portugal, the Central African Federation, Liberia, and the Union of South Africa. The United States sent observers. New York *Times*, February 21, 1954.

tend to create not merely a plural but a mixed society. That is, blacks and whites will combine to produce a sort of Brazil, which, one might add, is an extremely attractive country. It might be assumed that responsible Africans would welcome this prospect, which offers them so much more than they can ever possibly hope to get in, say, the Congo or the Union. Some extreme nationalists, however, abhor French assimilationist ideas. Recently in the New York *Times* an African writer put forth his feelings on this subject with great vigor, saying that the French concept of turning Africans into Frenchmen on a permanent basis was not only preposterous and unworkable but came close to being a crime. "Any process by which an alien government attempts to deculturize and denationalize members of another race finds no sanction in divine or natural law."[10] But would the author contend that the French system in Black Africa was "worse" than the French system in Morocco, or the Portuguese system, or the white settler system in the Rhodesias? I think not.

One last point should be made, that of the potential role of Islam in French Africa in the future. The Moslem vote is overwhelmingly preponderant in Senegal, Niger, French Sudan, and Mauretania, and Moslems are becoming more politically articulate day by day. Here, as in the Moslem areas of Nigeria, a great deal will depend on future developments in the Anglo-Egyptian Sudan, when this becomes free in 1956. Already something that might loosely be called a "Khartoum-Kano" axis is shaping up, emphasizing a close, vital community of Moslem interest halfway across the Sahara. If this stretches further to become a Khartoum-Dakar axis in time, the French will have to do a lot of hard thinking. The assimilation policy may become more difficult. What has been going on in Morocco has not had a good repercussion in French West Africa. One administrator in Dakar told me, "We worry about Morocco every minute." What he meant was not merely that Morocco, a Moslem state, may become the symbol of Islamic resentment against France elsewhere, but that France cannot possibly afford to have the turbulence of Morocco duplicated in French West Africa.

A second powerful external factor in determining the future of FWA will, of course, be the United States, so long as Paris and Washington are in alliance. Dakar is as much a part of the Atlantic community as Baltimore or Le Havre.

[10] Ndukwe N. Egbuono, executive secretary of the American Council on African Education, December 20, 1953.

CHAPTER 46

... And to Conclude

> *There seems to be no remote possibility that white domination [in South Africa] will last a hundred years.*
> —ALAN PATON
>
> *If a man can read the instructions for servicing a tractor he can also read the Communist Manifesto.*
> —STUART CLOETE

IT REMAINS to pull a few loose threads together. As to separate regions and territories, one might make the following rough summary:

A serious potential revolutionary situation exists in both Morocco and Tunisia, and armed insurrection has spread even to an area long considered to be safely part of France—Algeria. Morocco and Tunisia are the last Moslem countries left in the world that have not achieved national independence. The French position is bound to become steadily more difficult if Moroccans and Tunisians are not given more share in their own government.

French rule in Black Africa is more temperate, wiser, and more likely to produce a stable future, than on the troubled shelf of the Mediterranean. The French policy of assimilation is working fairly well—if slowly—and citizens of French West Africa and French Equatorial Africa, though a long way from being able to stand on their own feet, are approaching the threshold of political responsibility.

Of the independent states Libya is still a largely inert waste land, with a feeble economy and paralyzed by factional difficulties. In Ethiopia the Emperor is working manfully to replace feudalism by a modern administration, and knit the country together. Liberia has made more progress in the last ten years than in the previous hundred, but it still has a long distance to go. Egypt, which is the most important country in Africa from several points of view, is in the full stream of revolutionary turmoil and reform.

... AND TO CONCLUDE

Likewise the Sudan—probably a country with more vitality than any other in the Moslem world—is staking out an intrepid new life of its own, with its future (complete independence or unity with Egypt) not yet decided.

Kenya is the worst trouble spot in Africa from the criterion of public order, in consequence of the prolonged, bloody Mau Mau rebellion. Racial relations are, as always, most subject to strain in countries with substantial white settlement. Tanganyika is still politically asleep for the most part, but not Uganda. Here an articulate nationalist movement will sooner or later have to be dealt with in mature long-range terms.

On the surface the experiment of Central African Federation seems to be working well. The easiest way to summarize this is to repeat what I have already said, that it is an attempt to keep Nkrumah from coming east and the inheritors of Malan from coming north. A grave demerit to the scheme is that the predominant African majority accepts it only with desperate reluctance.

In the Union we have inspected one of the most unpleasant and exacerbated political situations in the world. *Apartheid* cannot work as its inventors hoped it would work, but the governing authorities will make no concession that might conceivably lead to a harmonious relationship between white and black. This country, with its unique and admirable old heritage, has become a prisoner of its own bigotry and intolerance.

Portuguese Africa has not yet entered the modern world; the Belgian Congo has. Belgian rule is bourgeois, practical, and stern; it has done a good deal for the Africans, and before time runs out much longer will be obliged (from the point of view of Belgian self-interest) to do more. Sixty thousand Belgian whites cannot permanently deny political expression and civil rights to more than 12,000,000 blacks.

On the British West Coast we have encountered the highest advance of colonial peoples toward effective self-government. Nigeria has profound problems still to solve particularly in the realm of national unity, and the Gold Coast is not finding the last miles of the highroad to freedom paved with roses, but these countries are stimulating auguries for tomorrow.

*

Taken all in all, British rule is the best. If I were an African I would rather live in a British territory than any other. The British do not give as much economic opportunity in some realms as the Belgians and perhaps not as much political and racial equality as the French in Black Africa, but the average African in British territory has more copious access to the two things Africans need most—education and justice. No doubt the British make blunders on occasion. But Great Britain is the only colonial power that has as its official policy the systematic training of Africans for self-government.

Interesting—but not surprising in view of what we have seen on this long trip—is that comparatively little pan-African sentiment exists. Not only tribal and linguistic barriers but European rule have made it difficult if not impossible for most Africans to think in continental terms. There are, however, a number of nascent unifying factors. The Arab League strives to speak for all Moslems, particularly in North Africa. Prime Minister Nkrumah and other personages of the West Coast talk in terms of a future federation of West Africa. Tendencies in this direction, toward the development of an all-African consciousness, are bound in time to increase. One suggestive development is steadily closer contact between the free or semi-free African countries and the newly independent states of Asia, as at the Bandung conference early in 1955.

Nationalist success in one African country may—in the present historical period—frustrate similar success in others. For instance, South Africa increases repression step by step as Nigeria and the Gold Coast march step by step nearer freedom. The Congo, as a result of what is happening in Kenya, tends to tighten up its administration. *Und so weiter.*

*

Now as to over-all trends and issues. It is risky to generalize, but—

1. Almost the whole of the African continent is, we have seen, trembling and astir with acute nationalist uplift. If Africa has any single common denominator, it is the desire (latent or positive) by most Africans to get rid of colonial rule, or at least modify its oppressive terms. Why cannot the white man stay forever, without conflict? Because of the temper of the times. Because his record, whether good or bad, calls forth intense resentment. And above all because he is overwhelmingly outnumbered in a continent not his own. In any case in most of Africa the days of arbitrary, universal, unmitigated white domination are gone forever.

2. The two things Africa needs most are development and education. If the colonial powers do not give education, this will cause in time fatally serious discontent; if they do give it, the black man will in the long run be strong enough to kick the white man out. We have several times elaborated on this root paradox. The answer to it is that education, no matter at what risk, must be given.

3. Race relations are at the bottom of most contemporary friction in Africa. What Africans hate and deplore even more than their submerged political status is color bar. If whites and blacks can learn to live together,

not necessarily melted down into a solidly gray continent, but peaceably side by side in communities gradually becoming harmonious (as in much of the United States), Africa is saved. If not, it may be lost—to chaos, to civil war, to feudalism, or the Communists.

4. In addition the white man, if he hopes to survive peaceably in Africa, must make large economic concessions. Exploitation of blacks by whites purely for the benefit of whites will not be possible much longer, except perhaps in the Union.

5. Most of these topics have been dealt with at length in these pages, but perhaps we should have a final word on nationalism. This, whether in Africa or anywhere else, is not necessarily a cure-all by itself; it is not a universal magic key. There are a great many problems that cannot be solved merely by going to a ballot box. Just to be nationalist is not enough. *Colonial abuses are wrong, but this does not mean that nationalism is always right.*

The plain fact of the matter is that the nationalist awakening cannot be stopped, but that large areas of Africa are not yet ready for the effective practice of nationalism, namely, full self-government. This is the central African dilemma above all other dilemmas. Some danger exists that, if nationalism succeeds too soon, the new governments may be exploited by corrupt *African* charlatans, underseasoned intellectuals, and illiterate politicians on the make. Beyond doubt Africa *does* need further tutelage. The nationalist inflammation should not blind Africans to their immense debt to colonialism as well as their formidable lack of experience. But European tutelage, European experthood and enterprise and know-how, will not be accepted except on a basis of trust and should promise the African more opportunity, better race relations, and fair economic rewards.

Ideally, backward peoples should be able to develop most readily and fruitfully through what has been called "the free interplay of cultures." But white nationalism in South Africa, to say nothing of black nationalism in Uganda, Nigeria and the Gold Coast, makes this comfortable type of evolution difficult if not impossible.

Xenophobic Africans might well reflect on their economic vulnerability, since they depend to such an extreme degree on world markets. "A change in the United States tariff, quotas, or stockpiling policy can upset completely the economy of . . . undeveloped countries."[1]

6. Until recently it was generally assumed, particularly in liberal British circles, that when the white man's job was finished and he was ready to go, he could go leaving a reservoir of good will behind him. Now tensions are so acute, and there has been so much bungling and disharmony, that this hope

[1] Walter Lippmann, "On Colonialism," New York *Herald Tribune*, June 15, 1954.

seems vain. On the other hand (as an example) the British and Indians get along well together these days, with old-time frictions largely forgotten.

7. Tomorrow's Africa will be largely leftist. Nationalism in almost all underdeveloped countries takes on an inevitable leftward character, if only because white rule has been largely based on economic as well as political exploitation.

8. A third world war, if it comes, will almost certainly serve to break European strings to Africa. It was Hitler and the Japanese war lords who, in a manner of speaking, made it possible for India and Indonesia to become free. A convulsion let loose by some demented would-be conqueror in the future, or a war made by blunder, will do the same thing for much of Africa.

9. Africa is almost completely defenseless from the military point of view, and is the richest prize on earth.

THE COMMUNIST PROBLEM: SUMMING UP

Soviet Russia has, as we have already pointed out, no official installation—embassy or consulate—anywhere in North Africa, nor on the whole of the West Coast with the exception of a satellite consulate[2] in Léopoldville. The only points in all Africa where it maintains diplomatic posts are Cairo, Addis Ababa, and Pretoria. Nor is there any outright Communist party anywhere in Africa on an important scale, except in Algeria, Tunisia and French West Africa.

Several reasons exist for this somewhat puzzling state of affairs. One is that Africa is not high on the Soviet list of priorities at present. The Russians prefer to deal with countries *after*—not before—they achieve national independence, on the assumption that the nationalists are convenient cat's-paws. Nationalists sometimes unwittingly serve an eventual Communist purpose by stirring up trouble, weakening imperialist prestige, and reducing the grip of the western powers on colonial territories. Why should the Soviets bother to instigate a struggle against the British today in, let us say, Nigeria, if Nigerian nationalists are already doing the job for them?

But it is important to state at once—emphatically—that it is by no means certain that nationalism in undeveloped territories necessarily *will* (as the Russians hope) pave the way for Communism. Indeed the contrary is probably true. (Russians have made mistakes before.) Look at the example of Asia. No fewer than ten Asian countries have won national independence since World War II, and not one has become Communist—India, Indonesia,

[2] Czechoslovak.

Pakistan, Syria, the Lebanon, Burma, Ceylon, the Philippines, Jordan, Israel.[3]

Even though the Russians are not officially active in most of Africa, there are plenty of expressions of Communist influence. We have noted several, and let us recapitulate. In French territories penetration takes place through the Confédération Générale de Travail, which is affiliated with the Communist-run International Federation of Trade Unions. Jomo Kenyatta went to Moscow. Soviet broadcasts are heard to some extent in parts of Africa, and in North Africa the Budapest radio has been pernicious. Perhaps the chief focus of Russian interest is in African students in London, Paris, and elsewhere in Europe; Soviet sympathizers do their best to get their hands on these, and convert them. But the total number of African university students abroad is probably not more than seven thousand.[4] Finally, the Russians assiduously propagandize among Africans by indirect use of the UN. They make long speeches about the evils of colonialism at every meeting of the Trusteeship Council, and give close support to grievances expressed by Africans.[5]

Take country X. Suppose the European governing power withdraws, and the African nationalist successor proves incapable of maintaining stable rule. Will Moscow fill the vacuum? Will Communism necessarily inherit? On balance the chances are that it will not.

In general—summing up tendencies we have seen in various parts of Africa—the following forces make *for* Communist advance:

1. Ignorance. Most Africans have no idea what Communism is, and therefore may succumb to its blandishments. Moreover Africa is a continent in violent transition, and thus doubly vulnerable. People are not educated enough or are too mixed up intellectually to understand the true significance and menace of Communism. An allied point is that several things which we of the west dislike most about Communism—for instance its suppression of civil liberties—are of small interest to most Africans, who have never had much liberty to lose.

2. Poverty. Obviously any continent as poor as Africa, with consequent miserable housing, undernourishment, wretched medical services and the like, is a prime field for Communist infiltration. Poverty alone will never

---

[3] Of course North Korea and part of Vietnam are Communist, but these are special cases.

[4] Of whom 1,702 are in the United States.

[5] A brilliant exposition of the Communist problem in general is "Communist Exploitation of Anti-Colonialism and Nationalism in Africa," by Vernon McKay, a chapter in *The Threat of Soviet Imperialism*, edited by C. Grove Haines, Johns Hopkins University Press, 1954.

make a nation go Communist, or such countries as Eire, Afghanistan, and Ecuador, among others, would have become Communist long ago. But poverty without opportunity, without hope, can breed almost any kind of misery, which Communists will be quick to exploit.

3. Educated Africans want three things above all, freedom from colonial rule, freedom from economic exploitation, and freedom from color bar. All this, it happens, is exactly what the Communists say (mendaciously) that *they* stand for.

4. Abuses by present governments, both white and black. The fact that Liberia, as an example, has no more than ten miles of paved road could, in the long run, do more to promote Communism than all the propaganda in Moscow ever printed. Portuguese Angola is 97 per cent illiterate; nothing could benefit the aims of Communism more. In the Union it is political repression, more than any other factor, that turns desperate men into Communists.

5. A positive feeling among many Africans, particularly the youth, that Russia and Communist China are working well, produce a "beneficent" economy, and become stronger daily. In other words (some Africans think), the Communists will win the world struggle for power, and they want to be on the winning side.

6. Russia is the enemy of Britain and France, the "enemies" of nationalist Africa, and therefore is to be regarded as a friend.

Also we may list forces tending to operate *against* Communist advance.

1. Russia is not geographically contiguous, and Communism is still a remote concept to most Africans.

2. Land in much of Africa is held by the tribes in trust for the people or by individual small holders. There are comparatively few large landowners (except in the white settler areas) crushing a landless peasantry; there are few big estates to be broken up and held out as bait by Communist agitators. Also the industrial proletariat is scant and hard to reach. Moreover millions of Africans have a "communal" society; Communism promises them nothing new.

3. The great mass of Africans are poor, yes, but the fruit of the trees feeds them even if they are undernourished. *Africa is the continent where people do not have to work to eat.* The community (for the most part) takes care of the indigent, and everybody belongs to somebody.

4. Religious factors. The Mohammedan religion in its wide areas is a strong deterrent to Communism, although some individual Moslems may be Communists.

5. Educated Africans, on the way to getting rid of one set of imperialisms,

do not want to become subject to another. Many dislike Communism intensely, as I have already noted in reference to intellectuals on the West Coast, if only because it is a *white* movement. (The fact that China, a nonwhite country, has been captured by Communism may, however, tend in the future to modify this factor).

6. In countries like the Congo, the Union of South Africa, and elsewhere, Communism has little chance of becoming an active force because the authorities have complete power to put it down.

7. Above all, education, political democracy, and reform. The best guaranty against Communism is the establishment of stable, progressive nationalist governments, if possible with strong links to a friendly Europe. By far the most sensible way to discourage Communism in Africa is to give political opportunity to the native populations. Deprive them of their legitimate aspirations to be free, and the Communists will certainly make trouble. For instance, if the Gold Coast experiment fails, the blow to the rest of Africa—and Europe—could be terrible.

Africa may not be ready for full self-government as yet, but at least it deserves *good* government, which it does not always get. So long as colonial powers misrule, Russian exploitation of any local situation is a possibility.

AMERICAN POLICY AND THE FUTURE

The United States came to direct diplomatic interest in Africa somewhat late. The State Department did not have an African division till 1943, and even today Africa is not dealt with on a continental basis. Part of it belongs to the British Commonwealth "desk," part to Western Europe, and part to a large conglomerate division known as the Bureau of Near Eastern, South Asian, and African Affairs. Correlation and over-all leadership are lacking. Out in the field in Africa itself the United States has several good men, but by and large African posts do not get the superior personnel that their contemporary importance deserves.

American policy toward Africa is double-edged, as I have mentioned in Chapter 5 and elsewhere. It is to sympathize in the abstract with colonial peoples in their desire to be free, but to do nothing that will embarrass their European masters. Nothing, obviously, could be more self-nullifying. We refuse to assist countries; and then we resent it if, like Egypt, they retaliate by taking a neutralist position. But State Department people say that it is impossible, in the present world situation, for our policy to be otherwise. Traditionally the United States has never been an imperialist power. We won our freedom by a nationalist-white-settler revolt against a colonial administration; we set up the Monroe Doctrine for Latin America and stood for the Open Door in China; we did not linger long in Cuba and we freed the Philippines. Woodrow Wilson was the father of the principle of self-determination for small nations. On the other hand, in its contemporary phase, American foreign policy is absolutist and has to protect our interests. We are engaged in a Cold War and cannot afford to see our principal allies, Great Britain and France, weakened. We do not want newly freed people to be absorbed by force or trickery into the Soviet orbit before they are capable of defending themselves, and at all costs we hope to prevent the spread of turmoil and disorder throughout the world.

Recent statements of American policy try to solve the foregoing basic contradiction—sympathy both for colonial peoples and their masters—by setting up various qualifications, for instance, that progress by colonies toward self-government should be made "without delay," but that a country must prove, if proof is possible, that its desire for self-determination is "real" and that it can "endure." This means little. Africans laugh at us for being so cautious and ambiguous. What the United States ought to do is take a much bolder position, announce its unshakable faith in freedom for all peoples, and enormously multiply our assistance to Africa in fields of technical aid, education, and the like. *That* is the only effective way to beat Communism. We shall be stupid beyond belief if we allow Africa to go by default, and let the Soviet Union usurp our historical role as the protector of young nations.

The tendency of most emergent Africans is to be neutralist. In other words the United States has lost ground so far, not gained it; among educated Africans anti-American sentiment is often pronounced. Jawaharlal Nehru is more likely to be the spiritual father of the new Africa than Dwight D. Eisenhower.

In any case Africa is part of our frontier nowadays, whether we like it or not. The world is our frontier these days. Cold wars, even more than hot, are global. Nationalist Africa is not remotely strong enough to be able to get rid of Europe in the near future, but it can make Africa unpleasantly expensive and troublesome for Europeans. Europe is stuck, so to speak, with Africa, and Africa is stuck with Europe, and America is stuck with both. So at least we should give Africa our most seasoned, scrupulous, and long-minded attention. The challenge to American as well as European statesmanship is undeniable. Africa is awake, Africa is alert, it has seen the example of Asia, even if its circumstances are different from those of Asia, and for good or ill it is marching with the times.

Acknowledgments, Bibliography, and Sources

I have so many people to thank for their help on this book that I do not know how to begin. At first I planned to print a full list of the names of all those whom we met and who shared their wisdom with us—a list like that in *Inside U.S.A.*—but this book is long enough already, and such a list is of small interest to the general reader. We took notes, as I have mentioned in the Preface to this volume, of conversations with no fewer than 1,503 people. They cover a very wide range indeed of African specialists and others, from one end of the continent to the other. Some I have already mentioned in various passages in the text. To one and all, my profound and earnest thanks.

Some who helped us in New York, Washington, London, and Paris before we reached Africa, and who gave us valuable advice on things to watch for and other tutelage, or who assisted us otherwise in several fields after our return, are the following: David K. E. Bruce, former American Ambassador to France and Undersecretary of State; Vernon McKay of the State Department; Mr. and Mrs. Faubion Bowers; Dr. Ralph Bunche; the late Walter White of the National Association for the Advancement of Colored People; Goddard Lieberson of Columbia Records; David E. Lilienthal; Major C. B. Ormerod and Richard E. Webb of British Information Services in New York, to whom my debt is indeed inestimable; Paul Auriol; Henri Bonnet, former French Ambassador to the United States; Roger Vaurs, director of the French Press Service in New York; Robert Lemaignen of Paris and Casablanca; Sir Alan Burns, former governor of the Gold Coast; former governor Pierre Rijckmans of the Congo; Edgar Sengier of the Union Minière du Haut Katanga; Serge Fliegers (to whom our debt is particularly marked) of Intercontinental Press; Bishop Fulton Sheen; Thomas K. Finletter; Anna Rosenberg; Mr. and Mrs. H. V. Kaltenborn; Mr. and Mrs. Harry Scherman; Mr. and Mrs. Sacheverell Sitwell; A. J. Friedgut who helped us particularly in relation to the Union; El Abed Bouhafa, who gave us introductions to various personages in North Africa; James W. Ivy and Henry Lee Moon of the NAACP; Dr. W. O. Brown, formerly of the State Department and now head of African studies at Boston University; Harold K. Hochschild of the American Metal Company; Jennifer Chatfield of the Brooklyn Museum, New York; Dr. H. A. Wieschoff of the UN; Kenneth Thompson, former British colonial attaché in Washington; Dr. Emory Ross, one of the best known of American missionaries; and

Dr. Ruth Sloan, formerly of the State Department and now the publisher of *African News*.

In London dozens of people gave us stout assistance and enlightenment—Vernon Bartlett, former MP, journalist, broadcaster, and author of *Struggle for Africa*; Charles Y. Carstairs of the Colonial Office; Lord Hemingford; the Reverend Michael Scott (whom we saw on several occasions in Africa and New York) and Miss Mary Benson of the Africa Bureau; David Astor and several of his well-informed colleagues on the *Observer*, like Colin Legum; the Marquis and Marchioness of Salisbury; John Foster, MP; Irene Worth; George Padmore, veteran Negro journalist; H. Muoria Mwaniki and Mbiyo Koinange, exiles from Nairobi; and Sir Christopher Chancellor, head of Reuters.

All over Africa, a continent where good hotels are scarce, pleasant people put us up. I want to thank with the utmost cordiality the governors of every British colony and protectorate we visited. It is invidious to name some of our hosts and hostesses and not others, but it is impossible for us not to render specific acknowledgment to the efficient and delightful hospitality of Sir John and Lady Kennedy in Salisbury, Southern Rhodesia, and Sir Charles N. Arden-Clarke on the Gold Coast. Similarly French officials showed us the utmost kindness almost everywhere. And there was no city on the continent with American representation where we did not receive generously bestowed help from State Department and other United States officials. To American ambassadors, ministers, chargé d'affaires, consul generals, consuls, Point Four administrators, United States Information Service officials, and other Americans in the field—our profound thanks are due. Particularly we want to thank those who gave us beds when we badly needed them.

Four people during the course of our trip were kind enough to put private or government airplanes at our disposal: Henry S. Villard, at that time American Minister to Libya; D. M. H. Evans of Khartoum; Léon Pétillon, the Governor General of the Belgian Congo; and that stimulating and enlightened personage Sir Edward Twining, governor of Tanganyika.

Among Africans who helped us in various localities were Dr. Xuma, Dr. Moroka, and Chief Luthuli, all of them former presidents of the African National Congress in the Union of South Africa; among Indian leaders and officials, Manilal Gandhi of Phoenix, South Africa; Shri Apa B. Pant, who was High Commissioner to East Africa when we visited Nairobi; and the Hon. Ibrahim E. Nathoo, now a member of the Kenya government.

Taking other names almost at random let me mention with our warm thanks Colonel Mervyn Cowie, director of the Royal Kenya National Parks; Michael Dunford of Nairobi; Michael Blundell; Richard Wright, author of *Black Power*, whom we met in Paris and Accra; Dr. Arthur Bryson of Kano, Nigeria; Sylvanus E. Olympio, who has several times represented Togoland at the UN; Mr. and Mrs. Albert H. Garretson of Addis Ababa, whose help to us was inestimable; Robert Scheyven of Ruanda-Urundi, Belgian Delegate to the Trusteeship Council of the United Nations; A. Claeys-Bouüaert, governor of Ruanda-Urundi and one of the ablest administrators in Africa; Mr. and Mrs. Robert Jackson of Accra; Frances Gunther, who met us in Accra; Mr. and Mrs. Quintin Whyte of Johannesburg, through whom we met other amiable folk; T. C. Robertson, also of Johannesburg; Graham Young, who "made" Port Elizabeth for us in a crowded hour; Alan Paton, author of *Cry the Beloved Country*; Sir Ernest Oppenheimer; Prime Minister

SELECTED BIBLIOGRAPHY 895

Nkrumah of the Gold Coast; and Dr. Albert Schweitzer. Names of other hosts, guides, and friends are mentioned in the source lists below. Some people, amongst them several to whom our debt is particularly great, I deliberately do not mention, for fear of getting them into trouble.

Finally, this book could not have been written without the patient and discerning guidance of Cass Canfield, Chairman of the Editorial Board of Harper & Brothers. Also I want to thank Beulah Hagen of Harper & Brothers, without whose staunch help this manuscript would never have reached the press, and Eric Larrabee of *Harper's Magazine*, who read and checked it all. So did my friend Alexander Lindey, attorney-at-law. Hamish Hamilton and Roger Machell, my British publishers, rendered stout service from beginning to end of the project; I want to express my special appreciation for their friendly encouragement in down-draft moments. Equally important was the assistance in every phase of the work of De Witt Wallace, Alfred S. Dashiell, Robert Littell, and Hobart Lewis of the *Reader's Digest*. Without Mr. Wallace and the *Digest* our trip would not have been possible—nor the writing of the book. Twelve chapters have appeared in the *Digest* in abbreviated form.

Susan Walthew Elliott typed the manuscript in several versions, and struggled ably to cope with my idiosyncrasies in spelling, grammar, and punctuation, much more than this, she helped greatly with development of the work as a whole, from first to last.

Superfinally, hardly a line of this book could have been written without the penetrating and luminous day-to-day co-operation of my wife, Jane Perry Gunther. Many of the ideas are hers, as much of the over-all concept and spirit. In the best sense of the word, she has been a collaborator—a co-author as well as expert editor. Moreover she accompanied me on every inch of the trip, and never missed an hour of it. I worked much harder on this book than on any I have ever written before, largely because of her sensitiveness to things seen and stimulus.

SELECTED BIBLIOGRAPHY

I have been collecting material on Africa for many years, and have in my files innumerable articles on the continent, mostly from British journals, that go back almost a quarter of a century. In active preparation for this book recently I did a great deal of reading, although as in the other Inside books my principal and determining sources are personal—what I saw with my own eyes and heard by word of mouth. But I believe that I have looked at every article of consequence that has appeared on an African subject in the past three years in the London *Times*, London *Observer*, Manchester *Guardian*, *Economist*, *New Statesman*, *New York Times*, New York *Herald Tribune*, *Foreign Affairs*, *Reporter*, *Time*, and *Life*. In addition I watched attentively a good many specialized publications, like *African News*, published by the Ruth Sloan Associates in Washington; *Africa Digest*, published by the Africa Bureau in London, and of marked value; *African World*; *West Africa*; *East Africa and Rhodesia*; and, in different categories, *Africa*, the journal of the International African Institute; *Corona*, an unofficial publication of the Colonial Office; and *Optima*, a quarterly issued in Johannesburg. The two periodicals

I used most were *World Today*, published by the Royal Institute of International Affairs, and *African Affairs*, the journal of the Royal African Society. Both are invaluable.

The reference books I used most were the *Encyclopaedia Britannica*, the *Statesman's Year Book* (1952), the *World Almanac*, the *Information Please Almanac*, and the *World Geo-Graphic Atlas*, published in Chicago by the Container Corporation of America (1953). This is the best atlas I have ever seen. As to pamphlets I have fed on them by the score. Those put out by the Colonial Office and British Information Services were particularly useful.

*

ABRAHAMS, PETER. *Return to Goli*. Faber and Faber, Ltd., London, 1953.
African Challenge, The Story of the British in Tropical Africa. British Information Services, New York, 1945.
AKELEY, CARL E. *In Brightest Africa*. William Heinemann, Ltd., London, 1924.
Algérie-Tunisie. Les Guides Bleus. Libraire Hachette, Paris, 1950.
ALPORT, C. J. M. *Hope in Africa*. Herbert Jenkins, London, 1952.
ARMSTRONG, H. C. *Grey Steel*, J. C. Smuts. Methuen & Co., Ltd., London, 1951.
ASHMEAD-BARTLETT, E. *The Passing of the Shereefian Empire*. William Blackwood and Sons, London, 1910.
ASHTON, HUGH. *The Basuto*. Oxford University Press, London, 1952.
Atlas of the Tanganyika Territory. Dar es Salaam, 1948.
AWOLOWO, OBAFEMI. *Path to Nigerian Freedom*. Faber and Faber, Ltd., London, 1947.

BARTLETT, VERNON. *Struggle for Africa*. Frederick Muller, Ltd., London, 1953.
BELLOTTI, FELICE. *Fabulous Congo*. Andrew Dakers, Ltd., London, 1954.
BEY, M. RIFAAT. *The Awakening of Modern Egypt*. Longmans, Green and Co., London, 1947.
BLACKWELL, LESLIE, and MAY, HENRY JOHN. *This Is South Africa*. Shuter and Shooter, Pietermaritzburg, 1947.
BLUNT, WILFRID SCAWEN. *Gordon at Khartoum*. Stephen Swift and Co., Ltd., London, 1912.
———. *Secret History of the English Occupation of Egypt*. Alfred A. Knopf, New York, 1922.
BODLEY, R. V. C. *The Warrior Saint*. Little, Brown and Co., Boston, 1953.
———. *Wind in the Sahara*. Robert Hale, Ltd., London, 1942.
BOXER, C. R. *Salvador de Sá and the Struggle for Brazil and Angola, 1602-1686*. The Athlone Press, London, 1952.
BRADLEY, KENNETH. *Copper Venture*. Mufulira Copper Mines, Ltd., and Roan Antelope Copper Mines, Ltd., 1952.
BROCKELMANN, CARL. *History of the Islamic Peoples*. Routledge and Kegan Paul, Ltd., London, 1952.

SELECTED BIBLIOGRAPHY

BRODRICK, ALAN HOUGHTON. *North Africa.* Oxford University Press, New York, 1943.

BRYANT, A. T. *The Zulu People.* Shuter and Shooter, Pietermaritzburg, 1949.

BRYCE, JAMES. *Impressions of South Africa.* Macmillan and Co., Ltd., London, 1899.

BUELL, RAYMOND LESLIE. *Liberia: A Century of Survival, 1847-1947.* University of Pennsylvania Press, Philadelphia, 1947.

BURNS, SIR ALAN. *History of Nigeria.* George Allen & Unwin, Ltd., London, 1951.

BURTON, ISABEL. *The Life of Captain Sir Richard F. Burton.* 2 volumes. Chapman & Hall, Ltd., London, 1893.

BUSCH, NOEL F. *My Unconsidered Judgment.* Houghton Mifflin Co., Boston, 1944.

BUXTON, DAVID. *Travels in Ethiopia.* Ernest Benn, Ltd., London, 1951.

CALDER, RITCHIE. *Men Against the Desert.* George Allen & Unwin, Ltd., London, 1952.

CALVERTON, V. F., editor. *The Making of Man,* An Outline of Anthropology. Modern Library, Inc., New York, 1931.

CAMPBELL, ALEXANDER. *The Heart of Africa.* Alfred A. Knopf, 1954.

CANSDALE, G. S. *Animals of West Africa.* Longmans, Green and Co., London, 1946.

CARRINGTON, J. F. *Talking Drums of Africa.* The Carey Kingsgate Press, London, 1949.

CARY, JOYCE. *Britain and West Africa.* Longmans, Green and Co., London, 1946.

———. *The Case for African Freedom.* Secker and Warburg, London, 1944.

CERAM, C. W. *Gods, Graves, and Scholars.* Victor Gollancz, Ltd., London, 1952.

Chasse en Mozambique. Litografia Nacional, Oporto, Portugal, 1952.

CHILVERS, HEDLEY A. *The Story of De Beers.* Cassell and Co., Ltd., London, 1939.

CHURCHILL, WINSTON. *The River War,* an account of the Reconquest of the Soudan. Eyre & Spottiswoode, London, 1933.

———. *A Roving Commission.* Charles Scribner's Sons, New York, 1944.

———. *My African Journey,* London, 1908.

CLARK, F. LE GROS; COLLINS, HENRY; HODGKIN, THOMAS; and OKAFOR, AMANKE. *The New West Africa.* George Allen & Unwin, Ltd., London, 1953.

CLARK, J. DESMOND, editor. *The Victoria Falls.* Commission for the Preservation of National and Historical Monuments and Relics, Livingstone, Northern Rhodesia, 1952.

CLOETE, STUART. *African Portraits.* Collins, London, 1946.

The Colonial Territories, 1951-1952. Her Majesty's Stationery Office, Cmd. 8553, London.

COON, CARLETON S. *Caravan:* The Story of the Middle East. Jonathan Cape, London, 1952.

———. *Measuring Ethiopia and Flight into Arabia.* Little, Brown and Co., Boston, 1935.
COUPLAND, SIR REGINALD. *Livingstone's Last Journey.* Collins, London, 1945.
CURTIS, LIONEL. *With Milner in South Africa.* Basil Blackwell, Oxford, 1951.

DAVIDSON, BASIL. *Report on Southern Africa.* Jonathan Cape, London, 1952.
DAVIS, RICHARD HARDING. *The Congo and Coasts of Africa.* Charles Scribner's Sons, New York, 1907.
DE LUBICZ, R. A. SCHWALLER. *Le Temple dans L'Homme.* Le Caire, Imprimerie Schindler, 1949.
DINESEN, ISAK. *Out of Africa.* Random House, New York, 1938.
DUNDAS, CHARLES. *Kilimanjaro and Its People.* H. F. & G. Witherby, London, 1924.
DU PLESSIS, I. D. *The Cape Malays.* Maskew Miller, Ltd., Cape Town, 1947.

EDWARDS, I. E. S. *The Pyramids of Egypt.* Penguin Books, London, 1947.
EL-BARAWAY, DR. RASHED. *The Military Coup in Egypt.* Renaissance Bookshop, Cairo, 1952.
EVANS, HAROLD, editor. *Men in the Tropics,* A Colonial Anthology. William Hodge, London, 1949.
EVANS-PRITCHARD, E. E. *The Sanusi of Cyrenaica.* Oxford University Press, London, 1949.
———. *Witchcraft, Oracles and Magic Among the Azande.* Oxford University Press, London, 1947.

Facts and Figures About French North Africa. Office of Technical Publications of the French Prime Minister, 1952.
FARSON, NEGLEY. *Last Chance in Africa.* Harcourt, Brace & Co., New York, 1950.
———. *Behind God's Back.* Victor Gollancz, Ltd., London, 1940.
FITZGERALD, WALTER. *Africa. A Social, Economic, and Political Geography of Its Major Regions.* Methuen & Co. Ltd., London, 1950.
FLAVIN, MARTIN. *Black and White,* From the Cape to Cairo. Harper & Brothers, New York, 1950.
From Darkness to Light, New Developments in British Africa. British Information Services, 1949.
FURBAY, ELIZABETH DEARMIN. *Top Hats and Tom-Toms.* Ziff-Davis Publishing Co., Chicago, 1943.

GAFFÉ, RENÉ. *La Sculpture au Congo Belge.* Editions du cercle d'art, Paris.
GALE, W. D. *Heritage of Rhodes.* Oxford University Press, London, 1950.
GIBBS, HENRY. *Twilight in South Africa.* Philosophical Library, New York, 1950.
GIDE, ANDRÉ. *Travels in the Congo.* Alfred A. Knopf, New York, 1929.

SELECTED BIBLIOGRAPHY

GITHENS, THOMAS S. *Drug Plants of Africa.* University of Pennsylvania Press, Philadelphia, 1949.

GITHENS, THOMAS S., and WOOD, CARROLL E., JR. *The Food Resources of Africa,* University of Pennsylvania Press, Philadelphia, 1943.

GORER, GEOFFREY. *Africa Dances.* John Lehmann, London, 1949.

GRAHAM, R. B. CUNNINGHAME. *Mogreb-el-Acksa,* A Journey in Morocco. Duckworth & Co., London, 1921.

——. *Success and Other Sketches.* Duckworth & Co., London, 1912.

GRAY, JAS. *Payable Gold.* Central News Agency, Ltd., South Africa, 1937.

Great Britain and Egypt, 1914-1951. Royal Institute of International Affairs, London, 1952.

GREENE, GRAHAM. *Journey Without Maps.* William Heinemann, Ltd., London, 1950.

GROGAN, EWART S., and SHARP, ARTHUR H. *From the Cape to Cairo.* Hurst and Blackett, Ltd., London, 1902.

GRUBB, NORMAN. *Christ in Congo Forests.* Lutterworth Press, London, 1945.

GWYNN, DENIS. *Traitor or Patriot,* The Life and Death of Roger Casement. Jonathan Cape and Harrison Smith, New York, 1931.

HAGEDORN, HERMANN. *Prophet in the Wilderness,* the Story of Albert Schweitzer. The Macmillan Co., New York, 1947.

HAHN, C. H. L., and others. *The Native Tribes of South West Africa.* Cape Times, Ltd., Cape Town, 1928.

HAHN, EMILY. *Congo Solo.* The Bobbs-Merrill Co., Indianapolis, 1933.

HAILEY, LORD. *An African Survey,* second edition. Oxford University Press, London, 1945.

HAMILTON, ANGUS. *Somaliland.* Hutchinson and Co., London, 1911.

HANSON, LAWRENCE and ELISABETH. *Chinese Gordon.* Funk and Wagnalls Co., New York, 1954.

HARRIS, WALTER B. *France, Spain and The Rif.* Edward Arnold & Co., London, 1927.

——. *Morocco That Was.* William Blackwood and Sons, London, 1921.

HARRIS, CAPT. WILLIAM CORNWALLIS. *Selections from the Wild Sports of Southern Africa.* Macmillan & Co., Ltd., London, 1947.

HATTERSLEY, ALAN F. *Portrait of a City.* Shuter and Shooter, Pietermaritzburg, 1951.

——. *South Africa 1652-1933.* Thornton Butterworth, Ltd., London, 1933.

HELLMANN, ELLEN, editor. *Handbook on Race Relations in South Africa.* Oxford University Press, London, 1949.

HEMINGWAY, ERNEST. *Green Hills of Africa.* Charles Scribner's Sons, New York, 1935.

HERSKOVITS, MELVILLE J. *Dahomey, An Ancient West African Kingdom.* J. J. Augustin, New York, 1938.

HINDEN, RITA, editor. *Local Government and the Colonies.* George Allen and Unwin, Ltd., London, 1950.
HOLLINGSWORTH, L. W. *A Short History of the East Coast of Africa.* Macmillan & Co., Ltd., London, 1951.
HOWARD, C., editor. *West African Explorers.* Oxford University Press, London, 1951.
HOYNINGEN-HUENE. *African Mirage.* B. T. Batsford, Ltd., London, 1938.
HUNTINGFORD, G. W. B., and BELL, C. R. V. *East African Background.* Longmans, Green and Co., Ltd., London, 1950.
HURST, H. E. *The Nile.* Constable, London, 1952.
HUXLEY, ELSPETH. *Four Guineas,* A Journey Through West Africa. Chatto and Windus, London, 1954.
——. *The Sorcerer's Apprentice,* Chatto and Windus, London, 1949.
HUXLEY, JULIAN. *Africa View.* Chatto & Windus, London, 1933.

INGRAM, JIM. *The Land of Mud Castles.* John Long, Ltd., London, 1952.
Introducing East Africa. His Majesty's Stationery Office, London, 1950.
Introducing West Africa. Her Majesty's Stationery Office, London, 1952.
Introduction à la Connaissance du Maroc. Bureau des Questions Musulmanes, Casablanca, 1942.
ISKANDER, ZAKY, and BADAWY, ALEXANDER. *Brief History of Ancient Egypt.* Jos Minerbo, Cairo, 1949.

JACOBSSON, D. *Fifty Golden Years of the Rand, 1886-1936.* Faber and Faber, Ltd., London, 1936.
JOHNSTON, HARRY H. *The Story of My Life.* The Bobbs-Merrill Co., Indianapolis, 1923.
JOY, CHARLES R., editor. *Albert Schweitzer,* an anthology. Harper & Brothers, New York, 1947.
——. *The Animal World of Albert Schweitzer.* The Beacon Press, Boston, 1951.
——., and ARNOLD, MELVIN. *The Africa of Albert Schweitzer.* Harper & Brothers, New York, 1948.

KAMM, JOSEPHINE. *African Challenge,* The Story of the British in Tropical Africa. Thomas Nelson & Sons, Ltd., London, 1946.
KEARTON, CHERRY, and BARNES, JAMES. *Through Central Africa.* Cassell and Company, Ltd., London, 1915.
KENYATTA, JOMO. *Facing Mount Kenya.* Secker and Warburg, Ltd., London, 1953.
KEPPEL-JONES, ARTHUR. *South Africa.* Hutchinson's University Library, London, 1953.
——. *When Smuts Goes.* Shuter and Shooter, Pietermaritzburg, 1953.
KJERSMEIER, CARL. *African Negro Sculptures.* A. Zwemmer, London, 1947.
KOCHNITZKY, LEON. *Shrines of Wonders.* Clark and Fritts, New York, 1952.

SELECTED BIBLIOGRAPHY

KRIGE, EILEEN JENSEN. *The Social System of the Zulus.* Shuter and Shooter, Pietermaritzburg, 1950
―――― and KRIGE, J. D. *The Realm of a Rain-Queen.* Oxford University Press, London, 1947.

L'Algérie Contemporaine, Coulouma S. A., Paris, 1954.
LANDAU, ROM. *Moroccan Journal.* Robert Hale, Ltd., London, 1952.
――――. *The Sultan of Morocco.* Robert Hale, Ltd., London, 1951.
LANGER, WILLIAM L. *An Encyclopaedia of World History.* Houghton Mifflin Co., Boston, 1948.
LANHAM, PETER. *Blanket Boy's Moon.* Collins, London, 1953.
LEAKEY, L. S. B. *Mau Mau and the Kikuyu.* Methuen & Co. Ltd., London, 1952.
LEGEY, FRANÇOISE. *The Folklore of Morocco.* George Allen & Unwin, Ltd., London, 1935.
LEGUM, COLIN. *Must We Lose Africa?* W. H. Allen & Co., London, 1954.
Le Missioni Cattoliche. Rome, 1950.
LEWIS, ETHELREDA, editor. *Trader Horn.* Garden City Publishing Co., Inc., New York, 1927.
LEWIS, W. ARTHUR; SCOTT, MICHAEL; WIGHT, MARTIN; and LEGUM, COLIN. *Attitude to Africa.* Penguin Books, London, 1951.
LEWIS, WYNDHAM. *Filibusters in Barbary.* National Travel Club, New York, 1932.
LEYS, NORMAN. *Kenya.* The Hogarth Press, London, 1926.
L'Habitat au Cameroun. Éditions de l'Union Française, Paris, 1950.
LIGHT, RICHARD UPJOHN. *Focus on Africa.* American Geographical Society, New York, 1941.
LIVINGSTONE, DAVID. *A Popular Account of Dr. Livingstone's Expedition to the Zambesi and its Tributaries.* John Murray, London, 1875.
――――. *A Popular Account of Missionary Travels and Researches in South Africa.* 2 volumes. John Murray, London, 1875.
LONGRIGG, STEPHEN H. *A Short History of Eritrea.* Oxford University Press, London, 1945.
LOTI, PIERRE. *Morocco.* David McKay, Philadelphia.
LUDWIG, EMIL. *Genius and Character.* Jonathan Cape, London, 1927.
――――. *The Nile.* The Viking Press, New York, 1937.
LUMB, SYBIL V. *Leaders of Africa.* University of London Press, Ltd., London, 1952.

MCCORD, J. J. *South African Struggle.* J. H. De Bussy, Pretoria, 1952.
MCCULLOCH, MERRAN. *The Southern Lunda and Related Peoples*, International African Institute, London, 1951.

MCFARLAN, DONALD M. *Calabar*, The Church of Scotland Mission, 1846-1946. Thomas Nelson & Sons, Ltd., London, 1946.
MABBATT, J. A., editor. *The Cape Peninsula*. Maskew Miller, Ltd., Cape Town, 1952.
MACDOUGALD, DUNCAN, JR. *The Languages and Press of Africa*. University of Pennsylvania Press, Philadelphia, 1944.
MACMILLAN, W. M. *Africa Emergent:* A Survey of Social-Political and Economic Trends in British Africa. Pelican Books, London, 1949.
MAISEL, ALBERT Q. *Africa, Facts and Forecasts*. Duell, Sloan and Pearce, New York, 1943.
MALLERY, RICHARD D. *Masterworks of Travel and Exploration*. Doubleday and Co., Inc., 1948.
MARQUARD, LEO. *The Peoples and Policies of South Africa*. Oxford University Press, London, 1952.
MARVEL, TOM. *The New Congo*. Duell, Sloan and Pearce, New York, 1948.
MATHEW, DAVID. *Ethiopia*. Eyre and Spottiswoode, London, 1947.
MAUGHAM, ROBIN. *North African Notebook*. Chapman & Hall, London, 1948.
MAYALL, R. C. *Recent Constitutional Developments in the Sudan*. Royal Institute of International Affairs, London, 1952.
MAYNE, PETER. *The Alleys of Marrakesh*. Little, Brown & Co., Boston, 1953.
MEAKIN, BUDGETT. *The Moors*. Swan Sonnenschein & Co., London, 1902.
MEEKER, ODEN. *Report on Africa*. Charles Scribner's Sons, New York, 1954.
MELLOR, F. H., Major. *The True Morocco*. Argus, Casablanca, 1952.
Merchant Adventure. John Holt and Co. Ltd., Liverpool.
MEYEROWITZ, EVA L. R. *Akan Traditions of Origin*. Faber and Faber, Ltd., London, 1952.
MILLIN, SARAH GERTRUDE. *General Smuts*, 2 volumes. Faber and Faber Ltd., London, 1936.
———. *The People of South Africa*. Alfred A. Knopf, New York, 1954.
———. *Rhodes*. Central News Agency, Ltd., South Africa, 1952.
MOREL, EDMUND D. *Affairs of West Africa*. William Heinemann, London, 1902.
———. *Nigeria*. Smith, Elder & Co., London, 1911.
———. *Red Rubber*. The Nassau Print, New York.
Morocco Under the Protectorate. Morocco Office of Information and Documentation, New York, 1953.
MORTON, H. V. *In Search of South Africa*. Dodd, Mead & Co., New York, 1948.
MURABET, MOHAMMED. *Tripolitania*. United States Information Service, Tripoli.

NADEL, S. F. *A Black Byzantium*. Oxford University Press, London, 1951.
NASSAU, ROBERT HAMILL. *Where Animals Talk*. Duckworth & Co., London, 1914.
NESBITT, L. M. *Abyssinia Unveiled*. Albatross, Hamburg, 1935.
NEVINSON, HENRY W. *A Modern Slavery*. Harper & Brothers, New York, 1906.

SELECTED BIBLIOGRAPHY

NEWMAN, BERNARD. *Morocco Today.* Robert Hale, Ltd., London, 1953.
NIETZSCHE, FRIEDRICH. *The Genealogy of Morals.* Modern Library, Inc., New York.
NIVEN, C. R. *A Short History of Nigeria.* Longmans, Green and Co., London, 1952.
NOON, JOHN A. *Labor Problems of Africa.* University of Pennsylvania Press, Philadelphia, 1944.

Official Year Book of Southern Rhodesia. Salisbury, Southern Rhodesia, 1952.
O'HANLON, DOUGLAS. *Features of the Abyssinian Church.* Society for Promoting Christian Knowledge, London, 1946.
O'LEARY, DE LACY. *The Ethiopian Church.* Society for Promoting Christian Knowledge, London, 1936.
OLIVER, ROLAND. *The Missionary Factor in East Africa.* Longmans, Green and Co., Ltd., London, 1952.

PADMORE, GEORGE. *Africa: Britain's Third Empire.* Dennis Dobson, Ltd., London, 1949.
―――. *The Gold Coast Revolution,* Dennis Dobson, Ltd., London, 1953.
PANKHURST, E. SYLVIA. *Ex-Italian Somaliland.* Watts & Co., London, 1951.
PARENT, PIERRE. *The Truth About Morocco.* Moroccan Office of Information and Documentation, New York.
PARKINSON, JOHN. *The Dinosaur in East Africa.* H. F. & G. Witherby, London, 1930.
PARNWELL, E. C., editor. *Stories of Africa.* Oxford University Press, London, 1949.
PARRINDER, GEOFFREY. *West African Religion.* The Epworth Press, London, 1949.
PASHA, RUDOLPH C. SLATIN. *Fire and Sword in the Sudan.* Edward Arnold, New York, 1896.
PATON, ALAN. *Cry the Beloved Country.* Charles Scribner's Sons, New York, 1948.
―――. *The Land and the People of South Africa,* J. B. Lippincott Co., Philadelphia, 1955.
PATTERSON, J. H. *The Man-Eaters of Tsavo.* Macmillan and Co., Ltd., London, 1952.
PEATTIE, RODERICK. *Struggle on the Veld.* The Vanguard Press, Inc., New York, 1947.
PEDLER, F. J. *West Africa.* Frederick A. Praeger, New York, 1951.
PENN, PETER, and STREET, LUCIE. *To-Morrow's Continent.* Sidgwick & Jackson, Ltd., London, 1948.
PERHAM, MARGERY. *The Government of Ethiopia.* Faber and Faber Ltd., London, 1948.
―――― and SIMMONS, JACK. *African Discovery.* Penguin Books, Ltd., London, 1948.
PLOMER, WILLIAM. *Cecil Rhodes.* D. Appleton & Co., New York, 1933.

POSTEL, A. WILLIAMS. *The Mineral Resources of Africa.* University of Pennsylvania Press, Philadelphia, 1943.
PRELLER, GUSTAV S. *Argonauts of the Rand.* Central News Agency, Ltd., South Africa, 1935.

RADIN, PAUL and others. *African Folktales and Sculpture.* Pantheon Books, New York, 1952.
RASMUSSEN, RENÉ. *Art Nègre.* Presses du Livre Français, Paris, 1951.
REED, DOUGLAS. *Somewhere South of Suez.* Jonathan Cape, London, 1950.
REEVE, ALAN. *Africa, I Presume?* Macmillan Company, New York, 1948.
Report of the International Commission of Inquiry into the Existence of Slavery and Forced Labor in the Republic of Liberia. United States Government Printing Office, Washington, 1931.
ROBESON, ESLANDA GOODE. *African Journey.* The John Day Company, New York, 1945.
RODD, FRANCIS RENNELL. *People of the Veil.* Macmillan and Co., Ltd., London, 1926.
ROOSEVELT, THEODORE. *African Game Trails.* Charles Scribner's Sons, New York, 1910.
RUKAVINA, KATHALEEN STEVENS. *Jungle Pathfinder.* Hutchinson & Co., Ltd., London, 1951.

SACHS, E. S. *The Choice Before South Africa.* Turnstile Press, London, 1952.
ST. JOHN, ROBERT. *Through Malan's Africa.* Doubleday & Co., New York, 1954.
SANDFORD, CHRISTINE. *Ethiopia Under Haile Selassie.* J. M. Dent & Sons, Ltd., London, 1946.
SAURAT, DENIS. *Watch Over Africa.* J. M. Dent & Sons, Ltd., 1941.
SCHAPERA, I. *The Bantu-Speaking Tribes of South Africa.* Maskew Miller, Ltd., Cape Town, 1950.
SCHMALENBACH, WERNER. *L'Art Nègre.* Les Éditions Holbein Sa-Bâle, Paris, 1953.
SCHWEITZER, ALBERT. *On the Edge of the Primeval Forest and More from the Primeval Forest.* Macmillan Company, New York, 1948.
———. *Out of My Life and Thought.* Henry Holt and Co., New York, 1950.
SEGY, LADISLAS. *African Sculpture Speaks.* A. A. Wyn, New York, 1952.
SELOUS, FREDERICK COURTENEY. *Sunshine and Storm in Rhodesia.* Rowland Ward & Co., Ltd., London, 1896.
SIEGFRIED, ANDRÉ. *African Journey.* Jonathan Cape, London, 1951.
SILLERY, A. *The Bechuanaland Protectorate.* Oxford University Press, London, 1952.
SITWELL, SACHEVERELL. *Mauretania.* Gerald Duckworth & Co., Ltd., London, 1951.
SMITH, EDWIN W. *Knowing the African.* United Society for Christian Literature, London, 1946.

SMUTS, JAN CHRISTIAN. *A Biography of J. C. Smuts.* William Morrow & Co., Inc., New York, 1952.
SOMMER, FRANÇOIS. *Man and Beast in Africa.* Herbert Jenkins, London, 1953.
SOWDEN, LEWIS. *The Union of South Africa.* Doubleday, Doran and Co., Inc., New York, 1943.
SPENCE, C. F. *The Portuguese Colony of Moçambique.* A. A. Balkema, Cape Town, 1951.
STALEY, EUGENE. *The Future of Underdeveloped Countries.* Harper & Brothers, New York, 1954.
STANLEY, DOROTHY, editor. *The Autobiography of Sir Henry Morton Stanley.* Sampson, Low, Marston and Co., London.
STEPHENSON, J. E. *Chirupula's Tale.* Geoffrey Bles, London, 1937.
STERN, JACQUES. *The French Colonies.* Didier Publishing Co., New York, 1944.
STEVENSON, BURTON. *The Home Book of Quotations.* Dodd, Mead & Co., New York, 1937.
STRACHEY, LYTTON. *Eminent Victorians.* Modern Library, Random House, New York, 1933.
Sudan Almanac 1953. Sudan Government Public Relations Branch, Khartoum, 1953.

THOMAS, H. B., and SCOTT, ROBERT. *Uganda.* Oxford University Press, London, 1935.
TOLLIVER, CATHERINE. *Moroccan Horizons.* Edita, Casablanca, 1952.
Towards Self-Government in the British Colonies, I. D. 598 (revised). British Information Services, New York, January, 1950.
TRACEY, HUGH. *African Dances of the Witwatersrand Gold Mines.* African Music Society, Johannesburg, 1952.
Traditional Sculpture from the Colonies. His Majesty's Stationery Office, London, 1951.
Traveler's Guide to the Belgian Congo and Ruanda-Urundi. Tourist Bureau for the Belgian Congo and Ruanda-Urundi, Brussels, 1951.
TRIMINGHAM, J. SPENCER. *Islam in the Sudan.* Oxford University Press, London, 1949.
TROLLOPE, ANTHONY. *South Africa.* Chapman & Hall, London, 1879.

UNDERWOOD, LEON. *Bronzes of West Africa.* Alec Tiranti, Ltd., London, 1949.
———. *Figures in Wood in West Africa.* John Tiranti Ltd., London, 1947.

VAN DEN BOSSCHE, LOUIS. *Peintures du Katanga.* Abbaye de Sainte-André-lez-Bruges, Belgium.
VAN DER POST, LAURENS *In a Province.* Hogarth Press, London, 1953.
———. *Venture to the Interior,* William Morrow & Co., New York, 1951.
VANDIER, JACQUES. *Egyptian Sculpture.* A Zwemmer, London, 1951.

VON LETTOW-VORBECK, General. *My Reminiscences of East Africa.* Hurst and Blackett, Ltd., London.

WALDECK, THEODORE J. *Treks Across the Veldt.* The Viking Press, New York, 1944.
WARD, W. E. F. *A History of the Gold Coast.* George Allen & Unwin Ltd., London, 1948.
WAUGH, EVELYN. *Waugh in Abyssinia.* Longmans Green and Co., London, 1936.
The Way to the West, Economic and Railway Survey of Certain Areas of West Uganda. Entebbe, Uganda, 1951.
WELCH, GALBRAITH. *North African Prelude.* William Morrow and Co. New York, 1949.
WELCH, SIDNEY R. *South Africa under John III, 1521-1557.* Juta & Co., Ltd. Cape Town, 1948.
WELLS, CARVETH. *Introducing Africa.* G. P. Putnam's Sons, New York, 1944.
WELLS, H. G. *The Outline of History.* Garden City Publishing Co., New York, 1949.
WELSH, ANNE, editor. *Africa South of the Sahara.* Oxford University Press, London, 1951.
WHARTON, EDITH. *In Morocco.* Macmillan & Co., Ltd., London, 1920.
WHITE, WALTER. *A Rising Wind.* Doubleday, New York, 1945.
WIESCHHOFF, H. A. *Colonial Policies in Africa.* University of Pennsylvania Press, Philadelphia, 1944.
WILLIAMS, BASIL. *Botha, Smuts and South Africa.* The Macmillan Company, New York, 1948.
———. *Cecil Rhodes.* Constable and Co., Ltd., London, 1938.
WILLKIE, WENDELL L. *One World.* Simon and Schuster, New York, 1943.
WILSON, CHARLES MORROW. *Liberia, 1847-1947.* William Sloane Associates, Inc., New York, 1947.
WILSON, CHRISTOPHER. *Before the Dawn in Kenya.* The English Press, Ltd., Nairobi, 1952.
WINGERT, PAUL S. *The Sculpture of Negro Africa.* Columbia University Press, New York, 1951.
WRIGHT, RICHARD. *Black Power.* Harper & Brothers, New York, 1954.
WYNDHAM, RICHARD. *The Gentle Savage.* Cassell and Co., Ltd., London, 1936.

Year Book and Guide to Southern Africa. Edited by A. Gordon-Brown. Robert Hale, London, 1953.

NOTES, NAMES, AND SOURCES
Preface

The quotation from George H. T. Kimble is from "Africa Today: The Lifting Darkness," *Reporter,* May 15, 1951. *The Modern Traveller,* verses by H. B., pictures by B. T. B., is a well-known little book published in London in 1898.

NOTES, NAMES, AND SOURCES

Chapter 1

Africa as Europe's "last frontier" is mentioned by Theodore H. White, "Africa Is Next" *Harper's Magazine*, February, 1952. *African Challenge*, a pamphlet by Josephine Kamm, published by the British Information Services, is useful. The best short overall book on Africa I have read is Vernon Bartlett's *Struggle for Africa*. Almost all writers on African geography mention the impenetrability of the coastline. An eloquent and poetic article is "Africa," by Laurens Van der Post, *Holiday*, March, 1954. Hailey mentions Africa as "the most tropical" of continents, *An African Survey*, p. 11. For statistics on raw materials, see the *Life* special number on Africa (May 4, 1953); "Africa in World Affairs," by George H. T. Kimble, New York *Herald Tribune*, November 14, 1953; and "Struggle for Africa South of the Sahara," *Nation*, December 26, 1953. "Africa in Perspective," by Harry H. Rudin, in the *Journal of International Affairs*—a special issue called "Crisis in Africa"— is a stimulating treatment of economic and historical factors in general. Consult also *Attitude to Africa* in the Penguin series, a most valuable survey, and Padmore, cited in the bibliography. For communications see *Tomorrow's Continent*, by Peter Penn and Lucie Street. The item about tribal wars in Nigeria is from Sir Richard Burton, quoted in Burns, *History of Nigeria*, p. 128. Kingsley Martin in recent articles on West Africa in the *New Statesman* mentions that Africans have no old culture to feed on. Bushmen paintings are described in H. G. Wells, *The Outline of History*. Basil Davidson, *Report on Southern Africa*, has valuable details on exploitation. Alexander Campbell (*The Heart of Africa*, p. 166) mentions that white settlement depends on black labor. Also see Farson, *Last Chance in Africa*, p. 12. Margery Perham, "African Facts and American Criticisms," *Foreign Affairs*, April, 1944, discusses the speed of modern African development. Population figures are mostly from the *National Geographic Magazine*, March, 1950.

Chapter 2

The quotation from the ex-Sultan at the head of the chapter is paraphrased from the *Economist*, March 27, 1954. Some authorities give 1649 instead of 1668 as the date of the formation of the Alaouite dynasty. For historical details see *North Africa*, by Alan H. Brodrick. This small handbook is an expert guide to things North African. The *Economist* is authority for my statement that the present Sultan is related to the Pasha of Marrakesh, May 17, 1953 and August 22, 1953. Details about female inheritance are from F. H. Mellor, *The True Morocco*. *Caravan*, by Carleton S. Coon, is an authoritative guide to Arabic spelling. For the Sultan and President Roosevelt, see Robert E. Sherwood, *Roosevelt and Hopkins*, and Rom Landau, *The Sultan of Morocco*. For the Juin incident and other background a *Time* article (April 30, 1951) is valuable. Details of the struggle between the Sultan and Glaoui are in "Morocco, Yesterday and Today," by Nevill Barbour, *Political Quarterly*, October, 1951. For dismissal of the Sultan see the New York *Times*, August 15, 20, 21, and 23, 1953; *World Today*, October, 1953; and *Time and Tide*, October 16, 1953. *Time*, August 31, 1953, mentions that the new Sultan asked people to wear slippers in his presence, instead of going barefoot. Professor Harry R. Rudin in the article cited above mentions that "Africans can be placed in the front line of a third world war without a say in the matter." I owe much in this and the following chapters to the hospitality of the Pasha of Marrakesh and General Augustin Guillaume.

Chapter 3

An admirable article in the *Reporter* (April 13, 1954) by Claire Sterling, "Morocco: The Struggle Neither Side Can Win," mentions that of 400,000,000 Moslems in the world all but 40,000,000 have now achieved national independence. That the word "Moor" is not used by "Moors" is from an old book on Morocco, *The Moors*, by Budgett Meakin. Almost all writers on Morocco,, for instance Bernard Newman, have picturesque passages on Moulay Ismail. Nevill Barbour, *op. cit.*, is authority for the statement that there was no printing press in Morocco till the French came. That Cervantes was imprisoned in Salé is from Mellor. For the Casablanca riots see the New York *Times*, January 30, 1953; the London *Observer*, February 1, 1953, and a pamphlet, *The Truth about Morocco*, by Pierre Parent, published by the Moroccan Office of Information and Documentation in New York. Sitwell, cited in the text, describes Marrakesh as a sister town to Seville and says that parts of it were torn down to build Meknes. Details of the 1937 typhus epidemic are from Sitwell. For population figures and other economic details see the *Harper's* article by Theodore H. White already mentioned, and a series of articles in the London *Observer* by Philip Deane, November 1, 8, and 15, 1953. Michael Clark discusses hydroelectric development in the New York *Times*, November 2, 1953.

Chapter 4

The figure for Arab tribes is from a French publicity brochure, *Facts and Figures About French North Africa*, published by the office of technical publications of the French prime minister. This also has background on the Berbers. I have paraphrased some passages in the section about Mohammed from my *Inside Asia*. The quotation about paradise is from Bertram Thomas, *The Arabs*, p. 44. A good account of Arab expansion and culture is in H. G. Wells, *The Outline of History*. For Islamic expansion in Africa see Michael Clark in the New York *Times*, November 16, 1953. That the Berber only "thinks" that he is a good Mohammedan is from the Encyclopaedia Britannica. For Vichy's treatment of Jews in North Africa, see *Crusade in Europe*, by Dwight D. Eisenhower, p. 108. A thorough treatment of Jewish problems is in "Cross-Tides of North African Revolt," by Herbert Luethy, *Commentary*, November, 1952. The remark about Jews living in "a protectorate within a protectorate" is from this. Paul Bowles mentions in "Fez" (*Holiday*, July, 1950) that no distinction exists in Koranic law between legitimate and illigitimate children.

Chapter 5

The quotation from Abdel Krim is from a conversation he had with Miss Dorothy Thompson. For General Guillaume see "French Morocco, Torch plus Ten," by Charles R. Codman, *Atlantic Monthly*, July, 1952. That only one hospital existed in Morocco in 1912 is from *Facts and Figures about French North Africa*, cited above. A letter to the *Atlantic Monthly* (October, 1953), by Abderrahman ben Abdelali, states the anti-French case ably. For a good brief

NOTES, NAMES, AND SOURCES 909

history of the nationalist movement see *World Today*, March, 1948. Some of my statistics about French achievements come from information sheets of the French press service in New York. The best statement of the French viewpoint I have read is "The French Accomplishment in Morocco," by General Augustin Guillaume, *Foreign Affairs*, July, 1952. The quotation from Marshal Lyautey is from Emil Ludwig's *The Nile*, p. 239. William O. Douglas, associate justice of the United States Supreme Court, writes brilliantly about Moroccan nationalism in "The French Are Facing Disaster Again in Morocco," *Look*, October 19, 1954.

Chapter 6

The quotation at the beginning of the chapter is paraphrased from *Time*, August 31, 1953. A charming and competent description of a visit to the Pasha is "Morocco's Man of Destiny," by Christa Armstrong, *Réalités*, March, 1954. For Berber dances, see Tolliver, cited in the text. Sitwell (p. 138) mentions the Saharan or Sudanese influence on the architecture of Tinherir.

Chapter 7

The quotation describing Tangier as the most successfully governed international city in the world is from a pamphlet, *International Tangier*, by Dr. Graham H. Stuart, published by the International Bank of Tangier. Recent informative articles on Tangier are "Anything Goes," by Joseph Wechsberg, *New Yorker*, April 12, 1952, and "Tangier," by William S. Schlamm, *Fortune*, August, 1950. My chief source for Spanish Morocco is *World Today*, May, 1954. For Spanish Africa in general, see "Spain as an African Power," by Robert Gale Woolbert, *Foreign Affairs*, July, 1946, a well-informed study of a subject little known. The word "subtenant" is used by Rom Landau, "Morocco," *International Conciliation*, September, 1952. Our guide to Tetuán was Paul Bowles, composer and author of *The Sheltering Sky*.

Chapter 8

Basic sources for this chapter are "Politics and Economics in Algeria," *World Today*, February, 1948, and "North African Dilemma," by Philip Deane, *Observer*, November 8, 1953. Also see Claire Sterling in the *Reporter*, May 25, 1954, and two articles in the London *Economist*, April 26 and May 23, 1952. The remark about Algerian pirates trading in white slaves as well as black is paraphrased from Edith Wharton, *In Morocco*, p. 250. The Constantine riots of 1945 are mentioned in *Africa*, by Harold R. Isaacs and Emory Ross, a valuable pamphlet published by the Foreign Policy Association. For the 1954 disturbances see two articles in the London *Times*, "Rule and Riot in Algeria," November 10 and 11, 1954.

Chapter 9

For Père de Foucauld see R.V.C. Bodley, *The Warrior Saint*. "The Secret Sahara," by Paul Bowles, *Holiday*, January, 1953, describes oases brilliantly. For camel lore I am indebted to the table talk of Mr. L. Cabot Briggs, an American physical anthropologist resident in Algiers. My debt to M. Claude Blanquernon of Tamanrasset, our guide to the Tuareg country, is manifest. The item about Richard St. Barbe Baker's work in the Sahara is from the New York *Times*, June 25, 1954.

Chapter 10

The quotation at the head of the chapter comes from Vernon McKay, "France's Future in North Africa," *Middle East Journal*, July, 1948. Some of my Tunisian statistics are from "Basic Facts on Tunisia," issued by the Service de Presse et d'Information of the French Embassy in New York. For Tunisian background see "Crisis and Reform in French North Africa," by Charles-André Julien, *Foreign Affairs*, April, 1951, and the Deane articles in the *Observer* already cited. See also Brodrick. My list of things the French might do to ameliorate conditions in Tunisia comes from an American source who prefers to remain anonymous. For labor problems consult "Nationalism and the Trade-Unions in French North Africa," *World Today*, June, 1952, and articles by Alexander Werth in the *New Statesman*, July 12 and 19, 1952. Bourguiba's remark about Communism is from "Tunisian Tinder Box," by Andrew Roth, *Nation*, February 9, 1952. I have also read various pamphlets put out by the Tunisian Office for National Liberation in New York, as well as *The Tunisian Question in the United Nations*, by Professor Ahmed S. Bokhari, former Pakistan delegate to the UN. Our amiable hosts in Hammamet were Mr. and Mrs. Jean Henson.

Chapter 11

Tripolitania, the Country and Its People, published by the United States Information Service in Tripoli, is a useful handbook. See also articles by Robert Doty in the New York *Times*, February 12 and 15, 1954. For Gadamès, see an article in the London *Times*, December 5, 1938. My historical survey of Libya is based on a private memorandum. That freedom was "forced" on Libya is mentioned in Bartlett, *Struggle for Africa*, p. 157. The *Economist* (May 31, 1952) mentions Idris as a "shepherd chieftain." That the royal palace is a former Italian casino is from Michael Clark in the New York *Times*, December 27, 1950. Recent events are described in the article from the London *Times* cited in the text, another *Times* article (November 2, 1954), and "Libya: Trinity in Disunity," *Economist*, November 20, 1954.

Chapter 12

The Emergence of Modern Egypt by John S. Badeau and Richard H. Nolte, published in the Headline Series by the Foreign Policy Association, is a useful pamphlet. See also Leigh White, "Egypt's 'Blessed' Revolution," *Harper's Magazine*, January, 1953, and Kermit Roosevelt, "Egypt's Inferiority Complex," *Harper's Magazine*, October, 1947. Aneurin Bevan, MP, has given it as his opinion that the Egyptian revolution is merely "a coup d'état with a revolutionary façade." (*Time*, January 11, 1954.) A. J. Toynbee, *A Study of History* (abridged edition, p. 72), quotes a passage from V. G. Childe mentioning the similarity between ancient and modern Egyptians. The article by Dorothy Thompson cited in the text appeared in the *Saturday Review of Literature*, January 2, 1954. Some of my figures on land come from *The Philosophy of the Egyptian Revolution*, published by the Institute of Current World Affairs in New York. This is a translation of the Nasser articles quoted in the text, with a commentary by Richard H. Nolte. Figures on the amount of property confiscated from members of Mohammed Ali's family are from the

New York *Times*, December 20, 1953. For the Rockefeller Foundation report on Egyptian villages see the New York *Times*, May 3, 1952. See Vincent Sheean, "England and Egypt," *Saturday Evening Post*, April 25, 1936, for the early background of British rule. Berberines on the Nile are described in "Servants in Clover," London *Times*, October 11, 1934. I mentioned the triple struggle for power in Egypt in articles in the Chicago *Daily News* as far back as 1926.

Chapter 13

I owe much in this chapter to the conversation of General Naguib and, in the opposite camp, of Abdul Rahman Azzam, former secretary general of the Arab League. Also I want to thank Mr. Charles R. Payne, head of the United States Information Service in Cairo, for his courtesy. The lines from Sagittarius are from "Eau de Nil," *New Statesman*, April 26, 1952. Two recent sketches of Nasser are by James Bell in *Life*, March 8, 1954, and Robert C. Doty, New York *Times Magazine*, September 19, 1954. Also see "After the Cairo Storms," London *Times*, June 23, 1954. The amount of Farouk's income is from a profile in the *Observer*, February 3, 1952. Figures on the Moslem Brotherhood are from *Time*, December 6, 1954. Naguib's own story of the July, 1952, coup, as told to David Douglas Duncan, appeared in *Life*, August 25, 1952. Nasser's statement about mutual defense pacts is from the New York *Times*, August 20, 1954. For German maneuvers in Egypt see *Time*, February 16, 1953 and Albion Ross in the New York *Times*, December 5, 1954. The invaluable chronology in *African Affairs* (October, 1953) compiled each quarter by Henry Swanzy, is my authority for the statement that students from Soviet Moslem countries attend Al Azhar university. Sources for the Suez are "Richest Ditch on Earth," by Ernest O. Hauser, *Reader's Digest*, May, 1949; *Time*, May 4, 1953; *World Today*, May, 1954; *Life*, August 9, 1954; various articles in the *New Statesman*; "Suez Marks End of Era," by Hanson W. Baldwin, New York *Times*, July 18, 1954; and an article by B. B. Rowe, New York *Herald Tribune*, November 25, 1951. The Institute of Current World Affairs has allowed me to quote from Nasser's *The Philosophy of the Egyptian Revolution*.

Chapter 14

Plato and Winston Churchill are among writers who have compared the Nile to a palm tree. Churchill in *The River War*, p. 5, has a vivid passage about the Nile's rate of discharge; my paragraph parallels this but was independently arrived at. Incidentally both Keats and Shelley wrote sonnets entitled "To the Nile." An indispensable source for things Sudanese is the *Sudan Almanac*, published annually. *Life* (November 20, 1950) has some superb photographs of Nilotic tribesmen by Eliot Elisofon. The line about black Sudanese "patronizing" whites is from the London *Times*, February 11, 1953. The phrase "petrified ocean" is from Hoyningen-Huene, p. 7, cited in the bibliography. For a photograph of a *haboob* see the *National Geographic* (February, 1953), "South in the Sudan," by Harry Hoogstraal. *Time* (June 23, 1952) says that Kitchener ordered the Mahdi's bones thrown into the Nile. The item about hiring Indian technicians is from the London *Times*, December 9, 1954. For the British record in general see the London *Times*, March 6, 1953 ("A Self Governing Sudan"); "Delicate Transfer of Rule in the Sudan," by Margery Perham, London *Times*, June 16, 1954; and "Britain in the

Sudan," by A. T. Steele, New York *Herald Tribune*, January 22, 1952. All the Steele articles on Africa are of high value. G. H. Bacon, director of agriculture of the Sudanese government, was our expert guide to the Gezira. Also I want to thank Governor W.H.T. Luce of the Blue Nile province for his hospitality at Wad Medani.

Chapter 15

Evelyn Waugh, *Waugh in Abyssinia*, p. 20, mentions £9,000,000 as the cost of the Napier expedition. For Ethiopian prowess in the Korean War, see Homer Bigart in the New York *Herald Tribune*, December 16, 1952. See David Buxton, *Travels in Ethiopia*, for the early Christian churches, p. 191. That one man in every five is a priest is stated by A. T. Steele in the New York *Herald Tribune*, July 28, 1948. For Ethiopian Jews, see Sandford, *Ethiopia Under Haile Selassie*, p. 10. One source of rumors about Russian activity in Ethiopia was the *Intelligence Digest*, June, 1952. Also see C. L. Sulzberger in the New York *Times*, December 22, 1952, a Reuters dispatch in the same newspaper (October 26, 1952), and an article in the London *Times*, January 15, 1954. The item about dead children hung in trees is from Coon, cited in the text, p. 74. That very few Ethiopians know their own ages is from "My Four Years in Ethiopia," by William H. Seed, *New Leader*, April 6, 1953. *Time* (October 13, 1952) says that the Emperor opens incoming diplomatic pouches himself. The quotations about Haile Selassie's sole authority and the lack of modern administration are from the *Economist*, "Ethiopian Outlook," October 9, 1954.

Chapter 16

For the Münzinger story see *A Handbook on Eritrea*, published by the British Information Services in Asmara. Various spellings of Mogadiscio are given in *Ex-Italian Somaliland*, by E. Sylvia Pankhurst. Items about Somali nationalism are in Padmore, *Africa, Britain's Third Empire*, p. 241. For locust control, see the New York *Times*, August 28, 1953.

Chapter 17

Elspeth Huxley (*The Sorcerer's Apprentice*, p. 191) mentions the fame of Bahaya women as prostitutes. Alexander Campbell points out in *The Heart of Africa*, p. 244, the relationship between "laziness" and low wages. Charles R. Joy (*The Animal World of Albert Schweitzer*, p. 94) talks about the African's "morbid craving" for meat. All the Joy-Schweitzer books have illuminating passages about native lore. Negley Farson (*Last Chance in Africa*) has much that is valuable on cattle, tribal customs, etc. William Graham Sumner has a famous chapter on cannibalism in *Folkways*. For codes of behavior see *Knowing the African*, by Edwin W. Smith, pp. 36–37, an excellent small book. Carveth Wells mentions (*Introducing Africa*, p. x) that really black Africans are a rarity. See Vernon Bartlett's *Struggle for Africa* for theories about laziness, disease, sweat glands, etc. Polygamy among the Kikuyus is discussed by Leakey, cited in the text, pp. 16–17, as is bride-price as a form of "marriage insurance." I am uncertain of my authority for the fact that "Syphilis" is the name of a Tanganyika age group. The veteran journalist H. N. Brailsford mentions infibulation in a letter on African mutilation in the *New Statesman*, April 2, 1949. Freud in *Totem and Taboo* discusses the taboo on mothers-in-law. Huntingford, *East African Background*, is invaluable on all tribal matters. For female circumcision see Leakey and Farson, *Behind God's Back*, pp. 208–209. Huntingford (*op. cit.*) ably explains the differences between magic and witchcraft. The quotation from Frazer is from *The Golden Bough*. A good article on sleeping sickness is "War in Africa—on the Tsetse Fly," by George Kinnear, New York *Times*, May 29, 1949. For drums see Carrington, cited in the text. Anyone interested in African music should obtain an album called *African Coast Rhythms: Tribal and Folk Music of West Africa* (Riverside RLP 4001), collected and edited by Arthur S. Alberts. It is a most remarkable collection.

Chapter 18

The best description of the Rift Valley I have ever come across is by Julian Huxley in "More Aspects of Africa," London *Times*, March 10, 1930. "Report on Mau Mau," by R. H. S. Crossman in the *New Statesman*, January 23, 1954, mentions that the Kikuyu word for "village" is "ridge." *Introducing East Africa* has valuable material on early Kenya history and the Arab slave trade. Most of my details on the Uganda railway come from this. The quotation from Professor Robb is from a report by Sir Philip Mitchell, *Land and Population in East Africa*, 1952. Hailey, *op. cit.*, pp. 317–318, has material on early Indian influence in Africa. W. M. Macmillan discusses the appeal of colonial life in *Africa Emergent*, p. 13. As to the emergency, interesting periodical literature is the following—articles by Dr. L. S. B. Leakey, the foremost living authority on the Kikuyu, in the *Observer*, July 25 and August 1, 1954, and the Manchester *Guardian*, July 1 and 8, 1954; a profile of Dr. Leakey in the *Observer*; "The Enigma of East Africa," by Elspeth Huxley, *Yale Review*, June, 1952; "Life Goes on Under the Mau Mau's Shadow," by Santha Rama Rau, New York *Times Magazine*, July 19, 1953; articles in the *New Statesman* by Kingsley Martin; "Struggle Against Mau Mau," by Margery Perham, London *Times*, April 22, 1953; other articles in the *Times*, November 13 and December 3, 1952, April 22 and October 19, 1953 and March 1, 1954; and "The Mau Mau: Death in the Dark," by Richard Llewellyn, *Saturday Evening Post*, May 23, 1953. Some of Mr. Blundell's opinions are from an article in the *New Statesman*. One person who shared his wisdom with us, and whom I want particularly to thank, is Archbishop David Mathew, the Apostolic Delegate to Kenya, who is a fascinating human being quite without regard to his ecclesiastical rank or his work in Africa. He was a midshipman at Jutland, has written several works of history, and is a novelist of distinction.

Chapter 19

Julian Huxley, *Africa View*, p. 395, mentions the difficulty of defining "paramount" interests. Enoch E. K. Mulira in "Crisis in Africa," *Journal of International Affairs*, says that British rule in East Africa is indirect in principle, but direct in practice. For the difference between colonies and protectorates see a British government pamphlet, *Toward Self Government in the British Colonies*, p. 7. An invaluable summary of British colonial techniques, which I have drawn on for some observations in this chapter, is a leaflet put out by the British Information Services in New York, *Constitutional Rule in British Territories*, by Kenneth Robinson. For Tanganyika and Uganda resentment against Kenya see the New York *Times*, May 30, 1954. Colonel Henry Howard, the governor's principal private secretary, shared with us a valuable memorandum. Our debt to the hospitality of Mr. and Mrs. Michael Blundell is manifest. We also want to thank Sir Evelyn and Lady Mary Baring. The quotation at the head of the Zanzibar section is from *Introducing East Africa*, which I have also used for historical details. Faubion Bowers writes revealingly of Zanzibar in the *New Yorker*, October 31, 1953. The item about *Theraptus* is from the chronology in *African Affairs*, July, 1954. Sir John Rankine, the British Resident, helped us courteously in Zanzibar, and so did Mr. M. E. Jessa of the Indian community.

Chapter 20

The Crossman quotation is from the *New Statesman*, January 23, 1954. Leakey, cited in the text, is an indispensable source for Mau Mau and the Kikuyu. Santha Rama Rau, "The Trial of Jomo Kenyatta," *Reporter*, March 16, 1954, describes brilliantly the background and circumstances of the Kenyatta trial. Miss Rau's article appeared in the *Reporter* in abbreviated form, but I have had access to the full manuscript. Elspeth Huxley (*The Sorcerer's Apprentice*, p. 124) mentions that "a law passed in one generation to prevent Europeans from exploiting Africans by selling them cheap intoxicants is resented by the next as an instance of racial discrimination." I want to thank particularly our Kikuyu chauffeur in Nairobi, Benjamin Gichan.

Chapter 21

For much in this chapter we have Colonel Mervyn Cowie to thank. I have drawn some details on game from the official guidebook of the Nairobi Royal National Park. Carl Akeley describes his encounter with the leopard he killed in *In Brightest Africa*, p. 97. Farson (*Last Chance in Africa*, p. 278) mentions the way elephants help other elephants. Experiments on blood pressure in the giraffe are mentioned in one of the chronologies in *African Affairs* (October, 1953). Elephants and their water holes are described in the New York *Times*, March 29, 1954, quoting a report by Colonel Cowie to the Fauna Preservation Society in London. Rhinos sometimes fill these holes up, out of stupidity or meanness. Our host at Treetops was Eric Sherbrooke Walker. The friend who signaled us in Amboseli was the photographer A. S. Milotte, who has won one Academy Award after another for the nature films he has taken for Walt Disney.

Chapter 22

The classic source on Kilimanjaro tribes is Dundas, *Kilimanjaro and Its People*. Light (*Focus on Africa*) has the best pictures of the mountain I have ever seen. Theodore Roosevelt in *African Game Trails* (published in 1910) noted the resemblance of the Masai to ancient Egyptians. Hollingsworth, mentioned in the bibliography, says that bananas (not indigenous to Africa) were introduced to the continent by early Negro peoples coming from Southern Asia. Most African fruits are not native to Africa. The quotation from Krishna Menon is paraphrased from his speech to the Trusteeship Council of the UN on March 10, 1954. The fact that only 450,000 Africans in Tanganyika are gainfully employed comes from *A Note on Tanganyika and the Constitutional Issue*, by E. F. Hitchcock. I have drawn some details about Von Lettow from his own book, listed in the bibliography. Among

NOTES, NAMES, AND SOURCES 915

friends who helped us greatly in Tanganyika were Governor Twining, Provincial Commissioner Hugh McCleery, who had us in his efficient charge for some days, Sir Eldred Hitchcock of Tanga, and Mr. A. L. G. Bennett of the Kilimanjaro Native Cooperative Union, one of the wisest white men in Africa. I will never forget the luncheon we had on Mr. G. R. A. M. Johnston's farm.

Chapter 23

Uganda (1949) and other documents published by the Protectorate Government in Entebbe are valuable. Mrs. Paul Robeson (*Africa Journey*, p. 118), mentions edible ants. The chronology in *African Affairs* is my source for the number of bicycles recently stolen in Uganda. That the Kabaka must always marry a commoner is from *East Africa Background, op. cit.*, p. 24, and is mentioned in Meeker's observant and penetrating *Report on Africa*. Background to the 1945 and 1949 disturbances, as well as much else of value, may be found in a pamphlet published by the Fabian Colonial Bureau, *Troubled Uganda*, by E. M. Mulira. Joyce Cary in "Africa Yesterday: One Ruler's Burden" (*Reporter*, May 15, 1951) mentions the extreme importance of continuity in African affairs. For the Kabaka crisis see the Crossman article cited in the text, several letters from Africans in the London *Times*, and a brilliantly prophetic article in the *Times*, "Uganda's Uncertain Future," November 21, 1953, as well as a profile of Mutesa II in the *Observer*, (December 6, 1953) and several articles by Colin Legum. That Christian congregations in Kampala "dissolved overnight" is from an article in the *Times* (June 18, 1954) by Roland Oliver. This chapter owes much to the hospitality of Sir Andrew and Lady Cohen.

Chapter 24

Useful recent pamphlets on South Africa are *South Africa*, by Gwendolen M. Carter, published by the Foreign Policy Association in its Headline Series, Number 109; *Civilization Indivisible*, by Michael Scott, published by the African Bureau, London; *Shadow over Africa*, also by Mr. Scott, with an introduction by Tom Driburg, MP, published by the Union of Democratic Control, London; *Race versus Reason in South Africa*, by Julius Lewin, published by the Council for Social Action, New York; *White Domination or Racial Peace?* by Adrian Hastings; *Sam Kahn Speaks*, the Parliamentary Record of South Africa's First Communist M.P.; *This is South Africa*, edited by Henry M. Moolman, director of the South African Information Office in New York; *The Racial Tensions in South Africa*, by Quintin Whyte, published by the South African Institute of Race Relations; *Some Aspects of the South African Industrial Revolution*, by Dr. H. T. Van Eck; *The Road Through the Wilderness*, by Patrick Duncan; and *South Africa's Heritage*, published in Pretoria. Duncan mentions that the Britons in South Africa are the "only English group of any size in the world . . . that is a ruled, subordinated minority." The *Veldtrust*, edited by T. C. Robertson, is an interesting periodical devoted largely to problems of the land, soil, and erosion. Marquard, whose *The Peoples and Policies of South Africa* is the best short book available on the subject, defines "Afrikaner" fully. This is also my authority for the statement that the parliament of the Union has three elements, Queen, Senate, and assembly, and for other background details. The phrase "pigmentocrat" was, I believe, invented by Mr. Sam Kahn. That Smuts invented the term "Commonwealth" in its present meaning is from *Time*, May 5, 1952. Source for my material on the Broederbond is a private memorandum. See also Gibbs, cited in the bibliography. I have drawn some details about Malan, Strijdom, and Swart from profiles in the London *Observer*, August 31, 1952, December 5, 1954, and March 1, 1953. The quotation from Schoeman is from the admirable cover story in *Time*, May 5, 1952, as is the quotation from Malan.

Chapter 25

The quotation from Rhodes is from Plomer, cited in the bibliography; that from Kruger is from Cloete, similarly cited. *The Peoples of South Africa*, a brochure issued by the State Office of Information, Pretoria, has material on Hottentots and Bushmen. For Kruger in general, see Cloete. Millin, Basil Williams, Plomer, and Cloete are basic sources for Rhodes. Also see a Historical Catalogue issued by the British South Africa Company on the occasion of the Empire Exhibition, Johannesburg, 1936-37. Cloete (p. 188) is authority for the statement that Rhodes died worth "between twenty-five and forty-five million pounds," and for the item about the thirteen states. For the influence of the Rhodes scholarships today, see the *Economist*, June 27, 1953. It is a nice index of Rhodes's ego that, when the scholarships were set up, it was stipulated that German students should be chosen by Kaiser Wilhelm himself (Plomer, p. 167). Rhodes did not want any scholarships to go to women. The line about "Prester John and the King of Calicut" is from a tourist pamphlet. Cape Town is mentioned as a "tavern of the seas" by du Plessis, *The Cape Malays*. Alan Paton, *op. cit.*, mentions that Paarl has the largest wine cellars in the world. Farson, *op. cit.*, p. 34, mentions that whales make love in Walvis Bay. That the Durban rickshas come from Burlington, New Jersey, is noted by Busch, p. 16. The possible position of Natal as a kind of Ulster is described in the London *Times*, December 23, 1954. Recent good periodical literature on South Africa includes "I Speak for the African," by Stuart Cloete, and "Impending Tragedy in South Africa," by Alan Paton, both of which appeared in the special African number of *Life*, May 4, 1953; two articles entitled "Politics and Opinion in South Africa," *World Today*, April and May, 1947; "South Africa and Its Problem," photographed by Margaret Bourke White, *Life*, September 18, 1950; "Men Against Malan," the *Economist*, February 28 and March 7, 1953; and "Advent of a Supernationalist," by John Hatch, *New Statesman*, January 29, 1955. Also see a number of articles in *Foreign Affairs*—"The Realities of Africa," by W. E. Burghardt Du Bois, July, 1943; "The African Response to Racial Law," by Z. K. Matthews, October, 1951; "Hard Choices in South Africa," by C. W. M. Gell, January, 1953, which I have several times cited in the text; "South Africa Swing-Over," by Edgar H. Brookes, October, 1948; "Alternatives to Apartheid in South Africa," by J. W. Patten, January, 1952; and "South Africa in Afrikaner Hands," by G. H. Calpin, April, 1951. Patrick Duncan in *African News*, March, 1955, outlines the importance of South Africa to Great Britain. Among many people who showed us courtesy in South Africa and helped us in various ways, aside from those already mentioned, are René de Villiers, editor of the *Friend* in Bloemfontein; Father Trevor Huddleston, C. R.; Miss Eleanor Ponsonby; A. E. Harmel of the Schlesinger Organization; Patrick Bell of Pan-American World Airways; the Hon. Colin Stamp; Marcus Sacks; Lt. Col. B. W. Martin, who showed us Pietermaritzburg; and Mr. and Mrs. Erwin Schuller. For obvious reasons

NOTES, NAMES, AND SOURCES 917

Chapter 26

I am not mentioning many other personal sources in the Union. To one and all, my thanks.

The quotation from Trollope appears in Millin, *The Peoples of South Africa*, p. 5. Details about the visit of the cruiser *Midway* to Cape Town are from the *New York Times*. That the introduction of work for wages broke up the Native reserves is mentioned in the Du Bois article cited above. Figures about overcrowding in the reserves are from Bartlett, *op. cit.*, p. 34. The quotation from the Transvaal constitution is from Hailey, *op. cit.*, p. 130; that from Sir Stephen King-Hall is from *East Africa and Rhodesia*, December 30, 1954. For the Communist problem in general, see "Africa: Next Goal of Communists," by Dr. Max Yergan, *U.S. News and World Report*, May 1, 1953. Davidson, *op. cit.*, p. 188, mentions that "Solly" Sachs was banned by the Liquidator for having used terms like "Fraternally yours" in his correspondence. That Sachs is one of the few people ever officially declared *not* to be a Communist is mentioned by *Time*, quoting the Johannesburg *Star*. A distinguished authority, Professor Cornelis W. de Kiewiet, mentions in "African Dilemmas," *Foreign Affairs*, April 1955, that the United States has "no" African policy. As handsome as any small brochure I have ever seen put out by a government is *Native Life in South Africa*, published by the South African Tourist Corporation. South Africans are very proud of their Natives so long as they can be presented as picturesque, sequestered children.

Chapter 27

Figures for gold production by the leading companies are from a private memorandum. Some miscellaneous statistics come from *As a Matter of Fact*, a pamphlet published by the Transvaal Chamber of Mines. *Time* (February 12, 1951) says that the Anglo American Corporation is "worth" $2.5 billion. Authority for the statement that Rhodes bought the original De Beer property for $18,000 is "South Africa in Diamond Boom," by John Worrall, *New York Herald Tribune*, October 14, 1953. Also see "Diamonds Are Big Business," by Ernest O. Houser, *Saturday Evening Post*, April 26, 1947. Details about the interlocking Oppenheimer structure are from the *Economist*, June 19, 1954. Campbell, *op. cit.*, outlines the complexities of Oppenheimer family relationships. The Herero prayer by Chief Kutako appears in "Experiment in Time," by Michael Scott.

Chapter 28

Our host in Basutoland was E. P. Arrowsmith, the Resident Commissioner. Also I want to thank Brian Marwick, the government secretary, for his help. Study of the Jones Report, cited in the text, is indispensable for anybody interested in Basutoland. *Life*, May 11, 1954, contains some spectacular photographs of Basutoland by Ernest Haas. Three authoritative articles on Basutoland, Swaziland, and Bechuanaland, by the Colonial Correspondent of the London *Times*, appeared on April 15, May 27, and July 12, 1954. Also see two articles by Basil Davidson in the *New Statesman*, "The Country of King Sobhuza," and "Paternal Colony," September 19 and October 3, 1953.

Chapter 29

The quotation from Victor Hugo comes from an old book by H. W. Nevinson, *A Modern Slavery*. Meeker, *op. cit.*, mentions that the Portuguese introduced the hammock to Africa. Macmillan (*Africa Emergent*) and Joy (*The Africa of Albert Schweitzer*) list other Portuguese contributions. Campbell, *op. cit.*, p. 389, makes the point that a vote in Mozambique is a vote for Dr. Salazar. The quotation about mulattoes in Brazil comes from a scholarly and illuminating book, *Salvador de Sá and the Struggle for Brazil and Angola, 1602-1686*, by Professor C. R. Boxer. The poem "Home Thoughts from Lourenço Marques," by C. H. Waddington, of which I quote the first stanza, appeared in the *New Statesman*, December 11, 1954. The spread of Islam in Mozambique is mentioned in "Portugal's Strategic Territory," by José Shercliff, *Foreign Affairs*, January, 1953. For forced labor see A. T. Steele in the New York *Herald Tribune*, February 2, 1948, a news dispatch by Albion Ross in the New York *Times* (June 9, 1954), and "Africa's Modern Slavery," by Basil Davidson, *Harper's Magazine*, July, 1954. The coelacanth is described in the London *Observer*, February 27, 1954.

Chapter 30

Our hosts in Salisbury were Sir John and Lady Kennedy; in Lusaka, Sir Gilbert Rennie; in Ndola, Provincial Commissioner Geoffrey Fane-Smith; in Blantyre, Provincial Commissioner W. H. J. Rangeley. Also I want to thank Mayor C. M. Newman of Bulawayo, the Taylor family of Que Que, Mrs. J. Desmond Clark of the Rhodes-Livingstone Museum at Livingstone, and W. E. Arnold, who helped us greatly in Salisbury. The quotation from Lobengula is from *Rhodes*, by Sarah Gertrude Millin, p. 191. Millin Plomen and Cloete are all indispensable for Rhodes and Lobengula. Also I have consulted *Rhodes and Rhodesia*, *The Man and His Movement*, published by the British South Africa Company, and *The Story of Cecil Rhodes*, published by the Central African Rhodes Centenary Exhibition, Bulawayo, 1953. Details about the tenure of Huggins, Mackenzie King, and Walpole are from the *Newsletter* of the Federation of Rhodesia and Nyasaland, March 9, 1955. For Prime Minister Todd, see Albion Ross in the New York *Times*, July 11, 1954, and *East Africa and Rhodesia*, July 8, 1954. Marquard, cited in the bibliography, mentions that Rhodes prevented a junction of German territories across Africa. Bartlett, *op. cit.*, notes that Lobengula never got his gunboat. Patrick O'Donovan (*Africa: Which Way Now?* a pamphlet published by the Africa Bureau) records that "it is nearly sixty years since any African was killed in a public disorder" in Rhodesia. The alternatives before Southern Rhodesia in 1922 are sketched in the Encyclopaedia Britannica. The remark that "never have so few people been ruled by so many" as under federation appeared in the New York *Times*, October 26, 1954.

Chapter 31

For Copperbelt figures see "The Northern Rhodesian Copperbelt," by R. D. Prain, president of the Rhodesian Selection Trust Group, *African World*, February, 1955, and an article in the London *Times*, May 20, 1954, "African Miner's Fight for Advancement," by C. W. Guillebaud. Statistics on the cost of the 1955 Copperbelt strike appear in a bulletin (by Peter Bird Martin) issued by the Institute of Current World Affairs, New York. The phrase "genetic fear" is from a provocative article in the *Listener*, July 1, 1954, "Rival Colonial Policies in Africa," by Louis Kraft. For physical items about Nyasaland see *Nyasaland Calling*, a visitor's guide published to celebrate the diamond jubilee in May, 1951. Details about Chief Gomani are from the pamphlet by Michael Scott quoted in the text. Another Africa Bureau pamphlet publishes the petition to Queen Elizabeth II, with a postscript by A. Creech Jones. This is my authority for the statement that 400,000 Nyasalanders contributed to the cost of the mission to London. Recent political developments in Nyasaland are covered by various issues of the *Africa Digest*, as well as in a memorandum by Colin Legum.

Chapter 32

I want to thank particularly M. Willaert, Secretary General to the Governor of the Congo, for his kindness. An old book by Richard Harding Davis, *The Congo and Coasts of Africa*, picturesquely describes the geographical immensity of the Congo. The remarks about the Congo and India by Chester Bowles are from a private memorandum, as is the quotation from him, used by permission. For details of hydroelectric power in the Congo (the potential is greater than that of the United States) see the New York *Times*, August 28, 1953. The *Nation* (December 22, 1951) mentions that the Congo has only 464 white doctors. An admirable brief survey of recent Congo problems appeared on July 3, 1954, in the London *Times*. *Life* and the *National Geographic* have both printed photographs of King Bope Mabinshe of the Bakuba. Details about Congo cities and early history may be found in Marvel, *The New Congo*. For Leopold and Stanley I have followed largely the Encyclopaedia Britannica. *Red Rubber*, by E. D. Morel, has photographs of the Congo amputations and other atrocities, including one of an African surveying the remains of his child, who had just been eaten by Belgian-employed cannibals. The New York *Times* (October 27, 1954), mentions that Belgians may be summarily sent home to Belgium for mistreating Negroes. The *Times* is also authority for the statement that it can cost $30,000 to be a colonist.

Chapter 33

In Elisabethville we were in the good hands of Colonel Jean de Ryckman de Betz of the Union Minière, among others. Our host in Léopoldville was the late Philippe de Braconnier, and our escort to Boende was Victor Brabant, a director of the *Affaires Indigènes et Main d'Oeuvres*. I have already mentioned the staunch service rendered us in Ruanda-Urundi by Robert Scheyven, alternate delegate of Belgium to the Trusteeship Council of the United Nations. A useful monograph is *Union Minière du Haut Katanga*, published by the company. Also see a very full article "The Congo Is in Business," by Herbert Solow, *Fortune*, November, 1952. Solow and Campbell, *op. cit.*, mention the Russian flavor that accompanies Congo nomenclature. Basil Davidson, "Some Congo Contrasts," *West Africa*, June 26, 1954, describes the differences in status between labor in the Congo and the Rhodesian Copperbelt. Since writing the text of this chapter I have found that at least one other American, Bob Deindorfer, has visited the uranium mine at Shinkolobwe. See his "Top Secret," *American Weekly*, November 30, 1952. I wish we had seen it. Davidson (*Report on Southern Africa*, p. 110) points out that the example of the Congo disproves the South African thesis that Africans are incapable of skilled work in highly technical fields. For Major Pretorius, pygmies, and elephants, see *Jungle Man*, p. 117. Figures on Congolese national income are from the Foreign Policy Association pamphlet already cited, p. 15. For other economic figures see the special African number of the *Nation*, December 26, 1953. The new airport at Kamina is described in the New York *Times*, August 30, 1953. *Fabulous Congo*, by Felice Bellotti, has the best Congo photographs I have ever seen.

Chapter 34

The quotation from *Trader Horn* refers, of course, to French colonization half a century ago. For De Brazza see Stern, *The French Colonies*. Several details about Fernando Po are from Burns, *History of Nigeria*. For statistics in general in this chapter I have used the lucid information sheets (on FEA and the Cameroons) put out by the French Embassy Press Service in New York. Also I want to thank Robert Mason, British Consul General in Brazzaville, and Brian Philpotts, British Consul in Douala, as well as M. Paul Chauvet, the High Commissioner and Governor General.

Chapter 35

Source of the line about the Vosges is Hagedorn, *Prophet in the Wilderness*, p. 8. The passage quoting Schweitzer on his own defects is from Joy, *Albert Schweitzer: An Anthology*, p. 157. "Greatest living Christian" is from an article by Eugene Exman in *Presbyterian Life*, November 24, 1951. It was to Mr. Exman that Schweitzer said he "played to his antelopes." The "bag of pheasants" anecdote is from *Out of My Life and Thought*, p. 273. The moth anecdote is from Lionel Durand, in the *New Era*. Almost all the quotations under sub-chapter headings are from the *Anthology*. The quotation about not being glad to be alive is from *Out of My Life and Thought*, p. 240. See also an admirable article in the *Progressive* (August, 1952), by Dr. Homer Jack.

Chapter 36

A pamphlet by Lord Hemingford, *Nationalism in Africa*, contains the quotation at the head of the chapter. Graham Greene's quotation from Mungo Park comes from his review of *West African Explorers* in the *New Statesman*, June 21, 1952. Also see Joyce Cary, *Britain and West Africa*, p. 19. A friend in Lagos gave me the full text of Genesis in pidgin; it is a rare document and hard to come by. McKay, "Nationalism in British West Africa," *Foreign Policy Reports*, March 15, 1948, mentions the concentration of shipping in Freetown harbor during the war. The item about diamonds is from *West Africa*, November 20, 1954.

Chapter 37

The first quotation at the head of the chapter appears in Burns, *History of Nigeria*, as well as several other works. Burns is my authority for much in this chapter, including some details on the slave trade and the item about the chief who cached 8,300 cases of gin. The detail about Mungo Park's clothing is from Kamm, p. 13, as is the description of Burton "with the brow of a God and the jaw of a devil." Basic statistics are from *Introducing West Africa*. Also see *Time*, February 9,

1952. The quotation about land tenure is from the Encyclopaedia Britannica, vol. 16, p. 444. For Lagos, see "Nigeria from the Bight of Benin to Africa's Desert Sands," by Helen T. Gilles, *National Geographic*, May, 1944, and an article by L. C. Lelard in *Nigeria*, No. 39, 1952, "Lagos in Portugal and Lagos in Nigeria." Eric Larrabee, "The Afterglow of Empire," *Harper's Magazine*, June, 1953, brilliantly discusses corruption and much else on the Nigerian scene. The detail about Yoruba inheritance is from the Encyclopaedia Britannica. Meeker, cited in the text, saw some of the same things we saw in West Africa, and quotes from some of the same sources. In particular I want to thank that able and enlightened canny Scot, Sir John Stuart Macpherson, who was governor when we were in Nigeria, for his help and hospitality.

Chapter 38

The quotation heading the chapter is paraphrased from the *Economist*, April 26, 1952. For the new constitution, see *World Today*, October, 1953, "The Nigerian Constitution Conference," and November, 1954, "Nigeria's New Constitution." Valuable background to Nigerian politics may be found in "Nationalism in British West Africa," by Vernon McKay, cited above. Also see "Politics and Pigment" in the *Economist*, August 23, 1952, and "The New West Africa," by Basil Davidson, *New Statesman*, June 21, 1952. The *Nigerian Yearbook*, 1953, p. 121, discusses some differences between Zik and Awolowo.

Chapter 39

The quotation at the head of the chapter is from the *Economist*, April 18, 1953. One of the Crownbird pamphlets deals with Nigerian folklore. Also see an odd old book, *Where Animals Talk*. There is mention of Brer Rabbit in *Introducing West Africa*, p. 27.

Chapter 40

Much in this chapter came from Prime Minister Nkrumah himself. I have already indicated our debt to Governer Arden-Clarke. The quotations from Nkrumah are from Padmore, *The Gold Coast Revolution*. The *Economist* cogently mentions possible repercussions on the Gold Coast experiment in French Africa. For Christiansborg Castle, see *A Brief Account of the Gold Coast*, a pamphlet containing information on all the old castles. For Mackenzie King see *Life*, March 23, 1953. Sources on Nkrumah are "The Magic of Nationalism," by Patrick O'Donovan, *Reporter*, September 18, 1951; a profile in the London *Observer*, February 11, 1951; and the valuable *Time* and *New Yorker* articles mentioned in the text. Alport, cited in the bibliography, mentions Nkrumah's "undenominational Christianity." The quotation about the Coussey Committee is from *World Today*, March, 1951. Padmore, *op. cit.*, is valuable on the historical period, but written from a strongly African point of view. Among a multitude of people who helped us in Accra I must mention J. V. A. Lillie-Costello, who was Chief Information Officer at the time, Finance Minister Gbedamah, and Sir Reginald Saloway.

Chapter 41

Time, February 9, 1953, quotes a BBC broadcast to the effect that if Nkrumah fails, "a great hope will die in Africa." Kingsley Martin in the *New Statesman* has discussed the differences between "dash" and bribery in connection with the Braimah scandal. William S. White wrote for the New York *Times* in 1952 (May 15 and 17) two highly discerning and prophetic articles about the Gold Coast. Also see Barbara Ward Jackson, "The Gold Coast: An Experiment in Partnership," *Foreign Affairs*, July, 1954, an article which describes ably among other things the Gold Coast's immensely lucrative export trade and its need for technical manpower.

Chapter 42

Much in this chapter comes from the conversation of Michael Ensor, who took us to Ho, and R. J. Moxon, our escort to Kumasi. The figure 99.8 per cent is from the London *Economist*, May 16, 1953, "Who Rules in Africa: A Summary." I used the anecdote about the house boy and "Ga" in an old book of mine, *D-Day*. Mr. Shirer's work is mentioned briefly in "An Area of Light in the Dark Continent," by Elspeth Huxley, New York *Times Magazine*, June 11, 1953. So is the inveterate Gold Coast interest in litigation. A Colonial Office spokesman in London is my authority for the story of George Ekam Ferguson. I have never seen it in written records. For early Gold Coast history, see Joyce Cary, *Britain and West Africa*. For cocoa see two admirable pamphlets published in Accra by the Information Services Department, *Golden Harvest, the Story of the Gold Coast Industry*, and *The Gold Coast, 1951*. For Ashanti history, see Meyerowitz and *West African Religions*, by Geoffrey Parrinder.

Chapter 43

Details about corrupt elections are from Buell, *Liberia, a Century of Survival*, as is the anecdote about the monkey. *Top Hats and Tom Toms*, a book not altogether complimentary to Liberia, is source for the item that one American denomination has worked in Liberia for seventy-five years without producing a single minister. Several other historical details are from this volume, including the item that a Tubman helped finance the American Colonization Society. For a grim account of conditions in the Liberian interior, see Graham Greene's *Journey Without Maps*. The article in the *New Yorker* by Oden and Olivia Meeker, cited in the text, is an exceptionally good survey. The late Gabriel L. Dennis, Secretary of State when we were in Liberia, arranged our visit to Mr. Tubman.

Chapter 44

The figure on Liberian merchant shipping is from the Manchester *Guardian*, February 4, 1954. For our visit to the Firestone plantation we have Mr. Ross Wilson, the general manager, to thank.

Chapter 45

The New York *Times* (July 12, 1953) is authority for the story of the French senator eaten by cannibals. The quotations in reference to Dahomey and Niger are from the Encyclopaedia Britannica. For racialism and nationalism see "France's Colonial Stake in Africa," by Virginia Thompson, *Foreign Policy Reports*, June 15, 1944. The Senghor poem is from a brochure called *Le Senegal*, published by Plaisir de France. For the "Kano-Khartoum Axis" see Michael Clark in the New York *Times*, November 14, 1953. Names of boats in the Abidjan harbor are from

NOTES, NAMES, AND SOURCES

West Africa, March 13, 1954. In Dakar M. Roger Chamburd, diplomatic councilor to the High Commissioner, helped us.

Chapter 46

The quotation from Alan Paton is from a special African issue published by the *Saturday Review*, May 2, 1953; that from Stuart Cloete is from *Life*, May 4, 1953. Rudin (*op. cit.*) calls the present changes in Africa "the biggest" revolution in history. Margery Perham (London *Times*, October 28, 1952), mentions the "almost impossible task of trying to ensure that African peoples, while demanding European civilization, do not make it impossible for Europeans to help them to attain it." Julian Huxley in *Africa View* (p. 434) is eloquent about the opportunities Africa provides for intelligent planning. That Africa deserves good government was a point made by Winston Churchill (A *Roving Commission*, p. 201) thirty years ago. *Attitude to Africa* (p. 14) discusses African nationalism as part of a world movement, and is valuable on Communism. The "free interplay of cultures" as a solution for the nationalist problem was advanced by the late Raymond Leslie Buell in his *Liberia: A Century of Survival*. Harold Isaacs, "Western Man and the African Crisis," *Saturday Review*, May 2, 1953, has some cogent words to say on Communism. See also Rudin, *op. cit*. McKay, cited in the text, gives five main reasons why African and Asian political development is apt to be dissimilar. (1) The presence of five million Europeans in Africa, strategically concentrated in north and south. (2) Africans cannot obtain weapons as Asians do. (3) The geographical proximity of the Soviet Union to Asia. (4) Western Europe is close to Africa. (5) The European powers are pouring hundreds of millions of dollars into African development. The New York *Times* (July 29, 1954) mentions that the colonial powers have given freedom and independence "to 600,000,000 people at the same time that Communists enslaved a like number."

So now *Inside Africa* is done.

Index

Aba Dina, 251
Abalessa, 134
Abbas, Ferhat, 126, 127
Abdel Aziz, 95, 118
Abdel Krim, 72, 114, 115, 147 n., 908
Abdelali, Abderrahman ben, 908
Abdelhai el Kittani, 52
Abdullah, Si, Caid of Fetouaka, 97
Abdullah Bayero, Emir of Kano, 779-780
Abdullahi, Khalifa of the Sudan, 232-233, 235
Abdullahi Issa, 283
Abeokuta, 761
Aberdares Range, 312
Abidjan, 873, 875
Abrahams, Peter, 523
Abu Bakr, Caliph, 62
Abu Simbel, 231
Abuna of Ethiopia, 254
Accra, 741, 742, 755, 801, 807, 826, 829-832
Achimota (University College of the Gold Coast), 428, 804, 813, 832-833
Act of Union, South Africa, 450, 462, 512, 520
Action Group, Nigeria, 750, 763, 767, 769, 771, 773
Adams College, South Africa, 528
Addax, 383
Addis Ababa, 248, 256, 257, 258, 259, 260, 262, 263, 264, 265-266, 270, 274, 278, 888
Aden, 256
Adeniji Adela II, Oba of Lagos, 757
Aderemi, Sir Adesoji, 763
Adola, 264 n.
Adolinanongo, 719
Adolph, E. F., 139 n.
Adowa, Battle of, 252
Afforestation, 142 n., 150, 581
Afghanistan, 35 n.
Afoot in the Desert, A Contribution to Basic Survival, 139 n.
Africa as a whole, 3-19; colonialism in, 13-14, 16-18; color bar in, 14-15; history of, 10-12; modern, the pattern of, 15-18; physiognomy of, 4-7; problems of, 8-10
Africa, Britain's Third Empire (Padmore), 912

Africa: New Crises in the Making (Isaacs and Ross), 8 n., 909
Africa: Which Way Now? (O'Donovan), 918
Africa of Albert Schweitzer, The (Joy and Arnold), 716 n., 730 n., 918
Africa Bureau, 337, 894
Africa Emergent (Macmillan), 317 n., 913, 918
Africa Journey (Robeson), 915
Africa Minor, 39 n.
Africa South of the Sahara, 836 n.
Africa View (Huxley), 289 n., 913, 923
African Affairs, 374 n., 593 n., 831 n., 911, 914, 915
African Affairs Board, 618
African Angelus, 64
African Cables, Ltd., 551
African Challenge (Kamm), 907, 920
African Children's Feeding Scheme, 508
African Coast Rhythms: Tribal and Folk Music of West Africa, 913
African Dances of Northern Rhodesia (Brelsford), 626 n.
African Digest, 627 n., 919
African Discovery (Perham and Simmons), 410 n.
African Episode (Scott), 642 n.
African Explosives and Chemical Industries, Ltd., 551
African Game Trails (Roosevelt), 914
African Journey (Siegfried), 657 n.
African Malleable Foundries, Ltd., 551
African Manganese Company, Ltd., 837
African Mirage, 697
African National Congress, 454, 498, 500, 526, 527, 528, 533, 894
African News, 352 n., 894, 916
African Students Association of America and Canada, 800
African Survey, An (Hailey), xi, 291 n., 296 n., 498 n., 657, 701 n., 760 n., 907, 913, 917
African World, 918

Afrika Korps, 166, 199
Afrikaans, 454, 461-463, 468
Afrikaner party, 458
Afrikaners, 452, 453, 454, 455, 457, 458, 511, 522, 526-527, 530, 532, 535, 537, 617, 621; attitudes and characteristics of, 459-467. *See also* Union of South Africa
Afrique noire. See Black Africa
Afrique Occidentale Française. See French West Africa
Aga Khan, 61, 325-326, 353, 355, 407
Agadès, 134
Aggrey, Dr. James, 833
Agni tribe, 872
Agoni tribe, 287
Agriculture, Bantu, 286; in British Somaliland, 282; in British West Africa, 738; in the Congo, 682; in Ethiopia, 276; in French Equatorial Africa, 696; and irrigation, 191; in Kenya, 317, 318, 321, 330, 365; in Liberia, 869; in Libya, 178; in Morocco, 55; in South Africa, 492, 496, 498, 523, 524; in Tanganyika, 405, 408. *See also* Livestock raising
Agulhas Current, 494
Ahmadu, Sardauna of Sokota, 768, 784
Ahmed, Si, 97
Ahmed Ou Tzoujjouart, 103
Ahmed Tazi, Si, Mendoub of Tangier, 113
Aida, Princess, 269
Aïda, 219
Aide-de-camp, 340-341, 749
Air France, 703-705, 874
Ajena, 827
Akan Traditions of Origin, 821 n.
Akans, 822, 823
Akeley, Carl, 382, 385, 914
Akhamouk, King, 135
Akher Saa, 202
Akintola, S. L., 769-770, 779, 788
Akofokye, 835
Al-Alem, Mohammed Abu Al-Asad, Grand Mufti of Libya, 176
Al Azhar University, 162, 189, 216

925

926 INSIDE AFRICA

Al Senussi, Sherif Moheiddin, 173, 174
Al Shalhi, Ibrahim Ahmed, 173, 174, 176
Alaouite dynasty, 22, 907
Alafin of Oyo, 763
Alake of Abeokuta, 761
Albert, King of the Belgians, 656
Albert, Lake, 312
Albert National Park, 385, 682
Albert Nile, 224
Albert Schweitzer, An Anthology (Joy), 716 n., 718, 733 n., 920
Alberts, Arthur S., 913
Albertville, 650
Alcohol, ban on, 57, 62, 376, 412, 517, 633, 636, 663
Alcoholism, 531
Alexander the Great, 188, 612
Alexandria (Egypt), 188
Alexandria (South Africa) 509 n.
Algeciras Conference, 37, 110, 111
Alger Republicain, 127
Algeria, 7, 38, 66, 120-122, 884; compared with Morocco, 122-123; government of, 124-125; nationalism in, 125, 126-128; political status of, 120, 123-125; revolt of, in 1954, 128-129; Southern Territories of, 132 (*see also* Sahara); women in, 123
"Algerian Front," 127
Algiers, 120, 121
Ali, Caliph, 22, 62, 63
Ali Khan, 688-689
Alizé, 872
All-African Congress (Egypt), 218
All-African Convention (South Africa), 527, 528
Alport, C. J. M., 921
Aluminum, 825, 827
Aly Maher, 199, 202, 205
Amakwaya tribe, 560
Amakwenkwe tribe, 560
Amalgamated Tin Mines of Nigeria (ATMN), 786 n.
Amazons, 876
Amboseli country, 388-390, 395
Amer, Tahar Ben, 155
American Colonization Society, 848, 849, 850
American Commonwealth, The (Bryce), 546
American Council on African Education, 883 n.
American Foundation for Tropical Medicine, 866 n.
American Metal Company, 628, 629, 632, 893
American Presbyterian Mission, 258
American Weekly, 919
Americo-Liberians, 743, 849, 855
Amhara, the Amharas, 253, 255, 256, 261, 286
Amharic, 6, 250, 259, 261, 856 n.
Amin El Husseini, Grand Mufti of Jerusalem, 202

Amoebic dysentery, 192
Anglican church, 460
Anglo American Corporation of South Africa, Ltd., 547, 548, 549, 550, 551, 552, 554, 628, 629
Anglo American Investment Trust, 551, 557
Anglo-Transvaal Consolidated Investment Company, Ltd., 547
Angola, 18, 407 n., 585, 586, 587, 590, 591, 596-598, 654, 890
Angola Boers, 562-563
Angoni tribe, 298, 410, 640, 641-644
Animal sanctuaries. *See* Game reserves
Animal World of Albert Schweitzer, The (Joy), 912
Animals, antelope, 382, 384, 389, 474, 596, 714, 723, 734; baboons, 383-384, 494; birds, 237, 387, 389, 391, 399, 429, 623, 779; buffaloes, 382, 383, 385, 388, 389, 390, 392, 393, 394; cheetahs, 382, 385; crocodiles, 382, 399, 426, 719, 762; domestic, *see* Camels, Cattle, Goats, Livestock raising, *and* Sheep; East African, 379-395; elephants, 228, 380-382, 383, 386, 389, 391, 392, 393, 394, 594, 623, 689; giraffes, 382, 389, 391, 914; hippopotamuses, 228, 380, 383, 393, 394, 407, 426, 719, 870; hyenas, 384, 389, 390; at Lambaréné, 714, 719, 725; leopards, 382, 384, 389, 391, 622; in Libya, 178 n.; ligers, 499; lions, 317, 379-380, 383, 394, 395, 430, 593; locusts, 284, 399; monkeys, 382, 388, 391; in Northern Rhodesia, 626; okapi, 689; ostriches, 389, 391; rhinoceroses, 380, 383, 384, 388, 389, 394, 391, 496, 914; snakes, 383, 394, 420, 497, 719, 788; in Tanganyika, 399; zebras, 389, 401
Ankole, 422 n., 430
Antelope, 382, 384, 389, 474, 596, 714, 723, 734
Anti-American sentiment, 892. *See also* Xenophobia
Anti-Catholicism, 460
Anti-Semitism, 461, 468, 473, 479, 503
Anti-Slavery Society, 337
Antimony, 54
Anton Dunkelsbuhler and Company, 550
Antricycle, 307
Aouache, 101
Apartheid, 450, 453, 454-455, 456, 459, 464, 465, 469, 473, 474, 475, 480, 481, 485, 511, 514, 516-522, 526-527, 535-538, 543, 567, 577, 606, 648, 885; geo-

graphical, 460, 475, 495, 509-510, 536
"Apartheid Bridge," 496
Aphrodisium, 149
Apithy, Sourous-Migan, 880
Appiah, Joseph Manuel, 829 n.
Arab bloc, 35, 63, 543
Arab League, 164, 173, 176, 212-213, 886
Arabi, Ahmed, 196
Arabian Nights, The, 43
Arabic, 39, 59-60, 63 n.
Arabs, 38-39, 43, 56-71; and Berbers, 66; birth rate of, 128; in the Congo, 654; cruelty of, 57, 119; in Egypt, 186; in Fez, 51; influence of, on East Coast, 287; in Kenya, 314, 315; in Libya, 167, 181; in Nigeria, 776; slave trade carried on by, 11; in the Sudan, 227; in Tanganyika, 404, 408; in Tunisia, 146-147; in Uganda, 434; in Zanzibar, 352, 353, 354, 356
Arabs, The (Thomas), 908
Arak, 140, 141
Archer, José, 108, 111, 112
Arden-Clarke, Sir Charles Noble, 406, 792, 803, 804-805, 814, 816, 894, 921
Arikpo, Okoi, 769
Aristotle, 810
Armstrong, Christa, 909
Arnold, W. E., 918
Arrowsmith, E. P., 917
Art, art objects, 10-11, 164, 189, 289, 308-309, 404, 485, 524, 648, 690, 740, 764, 876, 882
Arthur of Connaught, 471
Arusha, 398-399
As a Matter of Fact, 917
Asafu-Adjaye, E. O., 808, 814
Asantehene of Ashanti, 833-836
Asbestos, 545, 581, 623
Ashanti, 753, 819, 823-824, 833, 837
Ashanti Goldfields Corporation, 830, 836
Ashigga party, Sudan, 245
Asia, influence of, in North Africa, 40. *See also* India, *and* Indians
Asmara, 278, 280-281
Assab, 280
Asscher, J., 554-555
Assemblies of God Mission, 821
Assimilado system, 18, 589-590, 597, 662 n.
Assimilation, French policy of, 75, 79, 86, 120, 160, 882-883, 884
Associated Negro Press, 801
Astor, David, 894
Astrida, 682, 683, 685
Aswan, 224; Aswan Dam, 225
Asyut, 186
Atbara River, 224
Athlone, Earl of, 471
Atlantic Charter, 13, 126
Atlantic Monthly, 74 n., 76 n., 320 n., 543 n., 908

INDEX

Atlantide, L' (Benoit) 134
Atlas ranges, 42
Atomic bomb, 669, 678. *See also* Uranium
Atomic Energy Authority (United Kingdom), 630
Atomic Energy Board (South Africa), 553
Attitude to Africa, 338 n., 376 n., 907, 923
Auda, Abdel Kader, 208
Augustine, St., 66
Aujoulat, Dr., 702 n.
Auriol, Paul, 893
Auriol, Vincent, 32, 34, 72
Aurobindo, Sri, 627
Autochtones, 700, 878
Authoritarianism, 586
Awolowo, Obafemi, 747, 760, 767, 768, 770, 773-775, 921
Awori, Wycliff Wyasya Work, 346, 367
Awujale of Ijebu Ode, 763
Axum, 252, 253, 275
Azikiwe, Dr. Nnamdi ("Zik"), 750, 759, 767, 768, 771-773, 921
Azzam, Abdul Rahman, 188, 213, 911
Azzedine Bey, 152

Baasskap, 474, 480, 519
Baboons, 383-384, 494
Bacchouche, Salah Eddine Ben Mohammed, 156
Bach, 731
Bacon, G. H., 912
Badeau, John S., 910
Baganda, 286, 425, 430, 431, 432, 433, 434, 435, 441, 443, 445, 621
Bahaya tribe, 287
Bahutu tribe, 686
Bairu, Tedla, 280
Baker, Richard St. Barbe, 142 n., 909
Bakota tribe, 699
Bakutu tribe, 679-680
Bakwena tribe, 582, 584
Balbo, Marshal, 173
Baldwin, Hanson W., 911
Balewa, Mallam Abubakar Tafawa, 750
Bali tribe, 709
"Balkanization" of West Africa, 745
Ballinger, Senator Margaret, 515
Baluba tribe, 648
Bamako, 874
Bamangwato tribe, 582, 583, 584
Bambara tribe, 872
Bambridge, George, 185 n.
Bamenda, 706
Banana (town), 650
Bananas, 400, 429, 585, 706, 724, 727, 875, 914
Banda tribe, 699
Bandja tribe, 699
Bandung Conference, 886
Bangui, 702
Bangwaketse tribe, 582
Banque Empain, 661

Bantu Africa, Bantus, 5, 8, 64, 285-309, 425, 486, 487, 496, 569, 611, 648, 686
Bantu Authorities Act, South Africa, 482, 534
Bantu Education Act, South Africa, 482, 522
Bantu Forum, 498
Bantu languages, 6, 287-288, 699
Banziri tribe, 699
Baoulé tribe, 872
Baraka, 61, 211-212
Baramatola, 588
Barbary, Barbary Coast, 39
Barbour, Nevill, 40 n., 84 n., 907, 908
Barclay, Edwin, 849, 855, 864
Bariba tribe, 872
Baring, Sir Evelyn, 196, 243 n., 341, 343, 344, 371, 373, 914
Baring, Lady Mary, 324, 341, 343, 914
Barotse, Barotseland, 287, 302, 626
Barracan, 174
Bartlett, Vernon, 406 n., 532 n., 695, 783 n., 847, 894, 907, 910, 912, 917, 918
Basalmpasu tribe, 648
Bascom, William T., 763 n.
Bassa tribe, 856
Bastaards, 529, 562
Basutoland, 336, 512, 536, 558, 568-578, 817 n.; government of, 573-574; medicine murders in, 569-573, 574-575; political development in, 578; South Africa and, 577, 578
Basutoland Council, 578
Basutoland Medicine Murder, 570 n.
Bat-eared fox, 387
Bata shoes, 640
Batawana, 582
Bateki tribe, 699
Bates, J. Darrell, 281 n.
Bathoen, Chief, 582
Bathurst, 735, 744
Bauxite, 825, 827, 874
Bayombi tribe, 699
Beachrangers, 485 n.
Beaton, K. de P., 392
Beaufort West, 479
Bechuanaland, 336, 512, 581-584, 611, 817 n.
Bediako Poku, 808, 809
Bedouin, 147, 163, 187
Bedri, Sheikh Babikar, 244
Beecher, Rt. Rev. Leonard J., 328
Beeswax, 409
Beethoven, 731
Behind God's Back (Farson), 562 n., 913
Beira, 587-588, 591, 592
Beirut, 64
Beja tribe, 228
Belafrej, Hadj Ahmed, 84
Belgian Congo. *See* Congo
Belgians in the Congo (Périer) 656 n.

Belgium, administration of the Congo by, 18, 586-587, 590, 593, 647, 648-649, 652, 656, 657-668; administration of Ruanda-Urundi by, 18, 405 n., 646 n., 684-685, 688-689; on Committee of Control, Tangier, 111
Bell, C. R. V., 287 n.
Bell, James, 911
Bell, Manga, 707
Bell, Patrick, 916
Bellotti, Felice, 920
Bemba tribe, 287, 298, 626
Ben Guerir, 89
Beneš, 619
Benghazi, 164, 166, 180-181
Benguela Current, 494
Benguela Railroad, 591-592
Bengui, 696
Beni, 683
Beni Hillal, 167
Beni Suleim, 167
Benin, Bight of, 752; bronzes of, 11, 740, 764; Oba of, 764
Bennett, A. L. G., 400, 915
Bennett, James Gordon, 655
Benoit, Pierre, 134
Benson, Miss Mary, 894
Benson, Theophilus Owolabi Shobowale, 769
Bent el-Nil, 188
Berber language, 6, 66, 782
Berbers, 10, 39, 46, 51, 52-53, 65-67, 93, 104, 121, 146, 164, 167, 255, 403, 872
Berdugo, Albert E., 94
Bereng, 573, 574, 575
Bergdamaras, 562
Beshir Bey Sadawi, 176
Besse, A., and Company, 256
Beteng Seeiso, Constantinus, 574
Bethlehem Exploration and Mining Corporation, 567
Betz, Colonel Jean de Ryckman de, 919
Bevan, Aneurin, 910
Bevin, Ernest, 17, 221 n., 339
Bevin-Sforza plan, 170, 279
Biaka-Boda, Victor, 872
Bicycles, 291, 430-431, 738, 760, 776, 843
Big business, 546-547, 549, 550-551, 557, 660-662, 670, 671-673
Bigart, Homer, 35 n., 912
Bilharzia, 7, 193, 234, 308, 426, 683, 789
Biljon, Dr. F. J. Van, 513
Billietie, 674
Bini language, 746
Birds, 237, 387, 389, 391, 399, 429, 623, 779
Birom tribe, 787
Birth control, 194, 297
Birth rate, Algerian, 128; Moroccan, 55
Bishaftu, 268, 277
Biskra, 123, 128
Bismarck, 12, 150, 354
Bissau, 599
Bitam, 704

INSIDE AFRICA

Bizerte, 146, 155
Black Africa, 7, 17, 285, 738, 741, 742, 743, 747, 884; Egyptian attitude to, 217-218; French rule in, 691-708. *See also* British West Africa *and* French West Africa
Black Djebel, 104
Black magic, 299-303, 362, 363, 368, 570, 640, 740. *See also* Juju, Superstition, *and* Witch doctors and witchcraft
Black mamba, 383
Black Mischief (Waugh), 263
Black Power (Wright), 894
Blackwater fever, 308, 735
Blanquernon, Claude, 136, 137, 138, 909
Blantyre, 619, 639-640
Blindness, 192, 308, 426, 869
Bloc Democratique Sénégalais, 878
Bloc des Indépendents, 702
Bloemfontein, 450, 460, 500, 518, 614 n.
Blood River, Battle of, 487
Blue Nile, 224, 225, 254
Blue Nile Province, 236
Blundell, Michael, 315, 331-333, 339, 342, 343-344, 346, 347, 894, 913, 914
Blundell, Mrs. Michael, 914
Bobo Dioulasso, 875
Bobo tribe, 872
Bodley, R. V. C., 909
Boende, 678, 680
Boer War, 455, 456, 477, 488, 489, 501, 527
Boers, 12, 314, 455, 457, 459, 462, 486, 487-488, 516, 532, 580, 581, 597; Angola, 562-563
Boghdady, Abdel Latif, 207
Boissier-Palun, Maître Léon, 878
Bokhari, Professor Ahmed S., 910
Bolama, 599
Boloki, 299
Boma, 651, 657
Bomi Hills, 867
Bonaberi, 708
Bongo, 382, 383
Bonnet, Henri, 893
Boonga tribe, 699
Bope Mabinshe, King, 919
Borden, Mary, 836
Bornu, Shehu of, 784
Botha, General Louis, 456, 457, 485, 527, 563
Botha, Smuts, and South Africa (Williams), 456 n.
Botsio, Kojo, 796, 814, 832
Bou Regreg River, 48
Bouaflé, 872
Bouaké, 882
Bouhafa, El Abed, 893
Boulhaut, 89
Bourdet, Claude, 95
Bourguiba, Habib, 157-158, 160, 910
Bourke White, Margaret, 916
Bousbir, Casablanca, 49
Bowers, Faubion, 893, 914

Bowers, Mrs. Faubion, 893
Bowles, Chester, 447, 646, 662, 919
Bowles, Paul, 908, 909
Boxer, Professor, C. R., 918
Bozo tribe, 872
Brabant, Victor, 919
Bracken, Brendan, 547
Braconnier, Philippe de, 919
Brahim, Si, Caid of Telouet, 96-97, 102-103
Brahimi, Sheikh Bachir, 127
Brailsford, H. N., 912
Braimah, J. A., 814-815, 921
Brand, Sir John Henry, 500
Brazil, 11, 338, 464, 587, 590, 883
Brazza, Count Pierre Paul François Savorgnan De, 691, 723, 920
Brazzaville, 651, 691, 692-695, 696, 698, 703, 713, 738
Brazzaville Conference, 698
Brelsford, W. V., 626 n.
Bremer, Dr. Karl, 480-481
Bride-price, 297, 496, 680, 760-761
Brief Account of the Gold Coast, A, 921
Briggs, L. Cabot, 909
Britain and West Africa (Cary), 920, 922
British Central African Protectorate, 639
British East Africa, 285, 286, 315. *See also* Kenya, Tanganyika, Uganda, *and* Zanzibar
British Guiana, 345
British Information Services, 893
British Somaliland, 282
British South Africa Company, 490, 612, 613-614, 639
British Togoland, 837-839, 840-841
British West Africa, 735-742, 885. *See also* Gambia, Gold Coast, Nigeria, *and* Sierra Leone
Brodrick, Alan H., 60, 64, 66 n., 116, 907, 910
Broederbond, 469-471, 561
Broken Hill, 609
Brooke, Rupert, 811
Brookes, Edgar H., 916
Brooklyn Museum, 893
Brown, Dr. W. O., 893
Browne, Sir Thomas, 547
Bruce, David K. E., 32, 893
Brufina (Société de Bruxelles pour la Finance et l'Industrie), 660
Bryce, Lord, 500, 522, 546
Bryson, Dr. Arthur, 779, 894
Bubis, 710
Buchanan, James, 549
Budo, 428
Buea, 708
Buell, Raymond Leslie, 845 n., 849, 861 n., 865 n., 922, 923
Buffaloes, 382, 383, 385, 388, 389, 390, 392, 394

Buganda, 422, 425, 427, 433, 434, 435, 436; Kabaka crisis in, *see* Kabaka crisis
Bukavu (Costermansville), 651, 653
Bukirabasai Ja Agutamba, 422 n.
Bulawayo, 594, 611, 621, 622
Bulletin of International News, 110 n.
Bunche, Dr. Ralph, 424, 771, 840 n., 893
Bunson, Bernard de, 427
Bunting, Brian, 542
Bunyoro, 422 n.
Bureau for African Industrialization (BEIN), 142 n.
Bureau of Near Eastern, South Asian, and African Affairs, 891
Burger, Die, 468, 474, 475
Burgess, H. E., 419, 420
Burke, Edmund, 809
Burma, 35 n., 80, 335, 889
Burnouse, 58
Burns, Sir Alan, 738, 752 n., 761 n., 825, 830, 893, 907, 920
Burton, Isabel, 197 n.
Burton, Sir Richard, 197, 354, 711, 764 n., 907, 920
Busch, Noel F., 916
Bushmen, 5, 485-486, 683
Busoga tribe, 317
Butembo, 681
Butera, 687
Butler, Dr. Gordon, 788, 789
Buxton, David, 912
Byzantines, 39

Cabinda, 598
Cachalia, Yosuf, 533
Cadmium, 671
Caesar, Julius, 167
CAFECONGO, 662
Caffery, Ambassador, 244
Caids, 27, 33, 36
Cairo, 186, 188-189, 200, 220, 223, 224, 888
Calabar, 748, 769
Calabar, the Church of England Mission (McFarlan), 748 n., 754 n.
Calanscio, Sand Sea of, 182
Calcined Products, Ltd., 552
Calder, Ritchie, 149, 150
Calla tribe, 254
Calpin, G. H., 916
Caltex Company, 266 n.
Camels, 144-145, 178 n., 697, 776
Cameroon, Mount, 706, 708
Cameroons, 16, 44, 705-710, 752, 766, 768, 882
Cameroons Development Corporation, 709
Campbell, A., 350 n.
Campbell, Alexander, 412 n., 506 n., 534 n., 641 n., 907, 912, 917, 918, 919
Camus, Albert, 123
Canal Zone (Suez), 219-222
Cancer, 308
Candler, J. H., 359-360, 361, 362-364, 371
Cane rats, 382

INDEX

Canfield, Cass, 895
Cannibalism, 292, 648, 748, 761
Cão, Diego, 654
Cape Argus, 504
Cape Coloreds, 529-531, 636-637. *See also* Coloreds
Cape Malays, 452, 485, 494, 499, 529, 531
Cape Malays, The (du Plessis), 916
Cape Palmas, 845
Cape Province, 450, 452, 461, 462, 488 n., 493-496, 518, 539
Cape Times, 504
Cape Town, 450, 474, 494, 517, 518, 521; University of, 462, 519
Capitalism, state, in the Congo, 660
Capitulatory treaties, 49
Capricorn Society, 352, 621
Caprivi Strip, 562
Caracal, 387
Caracul, 562
Caramanli, Ahmed, 167
Caravan (Coon), 907
Carnegie Corporation of New York, 743
Carothers, Dr. J. C., 372
Carrington, John F., 288, 913
Carstairs, Charles Y., 894
Carter, Gwendolen M., 483 n., 520 n., 805 n., 815 n., 915
Carthage, 10, 39, 148, 167
Cary, Joyce, 823, 915, 920, 922
Casablanca, 41, 42, 45, 48-50, 71, 109, 118, 744; Pasha of, 37; riots in, 33, 50
Casablanca Conference, 31
Casamance River, 873
Casely-Hayford, Archie, 809, 814
Casement, Roger, 657
Cassava, 600
Castello at Tripoli, 174
Catholic church. *See* Roman Catholic church
Cattle, 286, 291, 292, 307, 401, 430, 485, 486, 523, 577, 582, 685, 695. *See also* Livestock raising
Cavendish-Bentinck, F. W., 346
Cayenne, 698
Cecil Rhodes (Plomer), 490 n., 493 n., 613 n.
CEGEAC (Ford Company), 662
Cela, 597
Cement industry, Uganda, 423
Censorship, 476, 627, 818
Central African Federation, 16, 336, 378, 436, 582, 602, 603-604, 615-619, 885; opposition to, 606 n., 615-616, 617-619, 641-645, 885; racial partnership as basis of, 606, 608, 609, 615, 619, 638. *See also* Northern Rhodesia, Nyasaland, and Southern Rhodesia
Central America, African strains in, 11
Central Legislative Assembly, Kenya, 351

Central Mining and Investment Corporation, Ltd., 547
Ceram, C. W., 190 n.
Cervantes, 908
Ceylon, 80, 335, 889
Chaamba, 144
Chad, 697, 698; Lake, 134, 695, 786
Chagga tribe, 286, 287 n., 296, 402-403
Chaka, 487, 496, 524 n.
Chamber of Mines (Transvaal), 546, 559, 561
Chamberlain, Neville, 408
Chambard, Roger, 922
Chancellor, Sir Christopher, 894
Chandos, Lord. *See* Lyttelton, Oliver
Chatfield, Jennifer, 893
Chauvet, Paul, 920
Cheetahs, 382, 385
Chellaram, house of, 741 n.
Chenek, Mohammed, 161
Cheops, funeral ship of, 190; Great Pyramid of, 189, 190
Chewa, 298
Chiefs, chiefdom, 228, 289-290, 337, 365, 403, 433, 528, 573-574, 701, 706, 757, 763, 779, 781, 788, 795, 820-822, 840-841, 854
Chigango, 301
Childe, V. G., 910
Children's Emergency Fund, 215, 747
China, 890, 891, 892
Chinese, segregation against, 637
Chinzali district, 302
Chiroma of Kano, 779 n., 780
Chirwa, W. M., 645
Cholmondeley, Hugh (Lord Delamere), 317-318
Cholo region, 639, 645
Chopra, L. C., 418
Christianity, 6, 13, 64; among the Kikuyus, 365-366; in Basutoland, 569, 576; in the Congo, 654, 659-660; the Copts, 186-187, 253, 254, 260, 278, 279, 280; in Ethiopia, 252, 253-254; in French West Africa, 872; in the Gold Coast, 819; in Liberia, 856; in Nigeria, 769, 784; in Nkrumah's life, 794, 798; in Nyasaland, 639; in Ruanda-Urundi, 684; sectarian rivalries within, 305, 435, 569; in South Africa, 524 (*see also* Dutch Reformed Church); in the Sudan, 229; in Uganda, 425, 427, 434, 435. *See also* Islam, Missionaries, *and* Religion
Christiansborg Castle, Accra, 792
Christie, Lansdell K., 867
Chrome, 5, 545, 546, 620, 623
Churchill, Sir Winston, 58, 61, 94, 98, 221, 222, 224 n., 232, 234, 244 n., 245, 310, 320, 421, 423, 428-429, 445, 456, 547, 811, 911, 923

Cicatrization, 303-304. *See also* Scarification
"Circle," 802
Circumcision, 297-298; female, 298, 760
Citizenship, of *assimilados*, 590; denial of rights of, 537; in Liberia, 860; rights of, to Africans, 698, 700-701. *See also* Franchise
Citrus farms, 498
Civet, 387
Civil disobedience, 37, 327, 478, 498, 528, 530, 533, 534, 564, 627, 794, 803
Civil liberties, denial of, 81-82, 157, 663, 840, 889; in the Gold Coast, 818; in South Africa, 476-477, 539
Civil service, Morocco, 78
Civilizado system. *See Assimilado* system
Civilization Indivisible (Scott), 508 n., 915
Claeys-Bouüaert, A., 688, 689, 894
Clapperton, Hugh, 697, 776
Clark, J. Desmond, 623 n.
Clark, Mrs. J. Desmond, 918
Clark, Michael, 695 n., 908, 910, 922
Clark, William, 746
Clawless otter, 387
Cloete, Stuart, 884, 916, 918, 923
Cloves, 352, 354, 356
Coal, 545, 616
Cobalt, 54, 630, 671
Cobras, 383, 497, 788
Coca-Cola, 57, 104, 350, 639, 690, 832, 866-867
Cocoa, 5, 797, 825-826, 837, 868, 875
Cocoa Marketing Board, 841
Coconuts, 593
Codman, Charles R., 908
Coelacanth, 600
Coexistence. *See* Plural society
Coffee, 261, 286, 400, 402, 421, 423, 696, 875
Cohen, Sir Andrew, 339, 341, 436, 438, 439, 440, 442, 443, 444, 445, 617, 915
Cohen, Lady, 915
Cold War, 88, 892
Cole, G. D. H., 834
Coleridge, Samuel Taylor, 247
Collected Poems of Vachel Lindsay, 646 n., 653 n.
Colobus monkey, 382, 391
Colomb-Béchar, 123
Colonial Development Corporation, 581, 744
Colonial Development and Welfare Fund, 350
Colonial Office, 311, 344, 345, 603, 609, 615, 616, 617, 618, 736, 748, 766, 801, 802, 803, 817, 894
Colonialism, 13-14, 44-45, 125; American support of, 115 n.; Belgian, *see* Belgium, admin-

istration of the Congo by; British, 335-357, 403, 709; debt to, 887; French, 74-77, 153-155, 161-162; hatred of, 217-218, 327, 440; Italian, in Libya, 168-169; Russia as enemy of, 88, 115, 889. *See also* Policy in Africa

Colons, in Algeria, 121, 122, 124, 125, 126; in French West Africa, 880; in Morocco, 77-79; in Tunisia, 153, 155, 156-157, 158, 169. *See also* White settlement

Color bar, 14-15, 17, 18, 886; Catholic church and, 305; in the Congo, 662-666; in French West Africa, 881; industrial, 440, 454, 466, 483, 630, 631-632; in Kenya, 310-311, 326, 327, 328-329, 333, 373, 376, 378; in Morocco, 79; in the Rhodesias, 603, 606, 609, 619, 631-637; in South Africa, 454, 457, 482, 516-522 (*see also Apartheid*); in South-West Africa, 566; in Tanganyika, 405, 406; Relative lack of: in Algeria, 125-126; in Angola, 597; in Basutoland, 577; in the Cameroons, 707, 708; in French East Africa, 694, 699; in the Gold Coast, 829; in Islam, 64; in Nigeria, 748-750, 757-758; in Portuguese Africa, 586, 589, 591; in Spanish Morocco, 116; in Uganda, 423, 424. *See also* Discrimination *and* Segregation

Color Bar Act, South Africa, 518
Color prejudice, 464, 466, 469, 530, 798. *See also* Color bar
Colored People's National Union, 530
Coloreds, 452, 465, 479, 483, 485, 494, 495, 499, 500, 517, 518, 529-531; in Nyasaland, 640; in Southern Rhodesia, 636-637
Columbite, 786
Columbium, 671
Columbus, Christopher, 822
Cominière (Société Commerciale et Minière du Congo), 660
Comité Special du Katanga, 661
Comité de l'Unité Togolaise, 839
Commentary, 122 n., 908
Commission for Technical Cooperation in Africa South of the Sahara, 336
Commonwealth Relations Office, 577 n.
Communication *and* transportation, in the Cameroons, 708; in the Congo, 647 n., 650; difficulty of, 7-8, 498, 506, 535, 623, 695, 844, 880; and disease, 680; by drums, 706 (*see also* Drums and tomtoms); in East Africa, 351; in Ethiopia, 260, 262, 271, 274-276; in French West Africa, 871; in Kenya, 316-317; in Liberia, 867; in

Libya, 180; in Eritrea, 281; in the Sahara, 131-132, 138-142, 144-145; segregation and, 517; in South Africa, 545, 546 n.; in Tanganyika, 404; via the Congo River, 650
Communism, 19, 31, 888-891; in Algeria, 123, 123 n., 127; among Moslems, 65; in the Congo, 673; in Egypt, 184, 216; in Ethiopia, 250, 260; in French West Afria, 879; in the Gold Coast, 817-818; in Morocco, 83-84, 86-88, 92; in Nigeria, 770-771; not a factor in Mau Mau, 374-375; in South Africa, 476, 477, 525, 527, 528, 533, 538-542; in the Sudan, 245; in Tunisia, 160
Comorians, 353
Compagnie Congolese du Commerce et Industrie, (CCCI), 661
Compagnie Française de l'Afrique Occidentale, 741
Compagnie Générale des Oléagineux Tropicaux, 873
Compagnie du Katanga, 661
Compounds, 506, 557, 558-560, 631
Conakry, 874
Concentration camps, 157
Confederate party, Southern Rhodesia, 606
Confédération Générale de Travail, 83, 84, 86, 127, 707, 879, 889
Congo, 12, 14, 78, 224, 292, 305, 382, 392 n., 428, 586-587, 591, 593, 615, 628, 646-684, 689-690, 885, 886, 891; administration of, 648-649, 656-661; Albert National Park in, 385; *assimilado* system in, 590; color bar in, 662-666; economics of, 647, 653, 660-662, 666, 667, 670, 671-673; history of, 653-657; political situation in, 662, 666-668; pygmies of, 683-684; superstitions of, 300; uranium in, 647, 669, 670, 673-678; witch doctors in, 299
Congo and Coasts of Africa, The (Davis), 919
Congo International Association, 655
Congo-Ocean railway, 695
Congo Pedicle, 628
Congo River, 649-650, 654, 655, 692
Congo treaties, 376 n.
CONGOPALM, 662
Congress of Peoples Against Imperialism, 337
Coniagui tribe, 872
Conrad, Joseph, 650
Consolidated Diamond Mines of South-West Africa, Ltd., 551, 557, 558
Consolidated Gold Fields of South Africa, Ltd., 490, 547

Consolidated Main Reef Mine, 558
Constantine (Algeria), 120, 123
Constitutional Rule in British Territories (Robinson), 913
Contract labor, 557, 558, 672, 861-864
Convention People's Party (CPP), Gold Coast, 796, 798, 803, 804, 805, 813, 815, 816, 820, 834, 839
Convict labor, 671
Cookson's wildebeest, 626
Coon, Carleton S., 252 n., 907, 912
Co-operatives, 400, 403, 423, 425
Copal, 680
Copper, 5, 545, 567, 647, 670, 671, 674, 675
Copperbelt, 551, 603, 614, 616, 618 n., 626, 628-632, 641
Copts, 186-187, 253, 254, 260, 278, 279, 280
Coquilhatville, 653
Coriolanus, 384
"Corner House" (Central Mining and Investment Corporation), 547
Cornut-Gentille, Bernard, 877
Corona, 281 n., 895
Corporal punishment, 478-479, 583. *See also* Punishment
Corruption, among Birom priests, 787; in "directed labor" system, 587-588; in Egypt, 204, 207; in Ethiopia, 264; in the Gold Coast, 814, 832, 841; in Liberia, 846, 857, 866; in Nigeria, 758-759
Costermansville, 651, 653
Costumes. *See* Dress and ornamentation
COTONCO, 662
Cotton, 190-191, 228, 421, 423, 425, 593, 696
Council of Revolutionary Command, Egypt, 206
Coupland, Professor Reginald, 304
Couscous, 101
Coussey, Sir J. Henley, 803, 820, 921
Cowie, Colonel Mervyn H., 380, 385, 593, 894, 914
Cox, T. R. F., 430
Creech Jones, A., 919
Creoles, 743
Crime, South Africa, 478, 503-504, 520
Criminal Law Amendment Act, South Africa, 534
Cripps, Sir Stafford, 339, 829 n.
Crocodiles, 382, 399, 426, 719, 762
Cromer, Lord, 46, 196, 243 n.
Crossman, R. H. S., 364, 443 n., 913, 914, 915
Crown Lands Ordinance, 319
Crown Mines, 548
Crusade in Europe (Eisenhower), 908

INDEX

Cry, the Beloved Country (Paton), 455, 894
Cuba, 763 n., 892
Cullinan, Sir Thomas, 499
Cullinan diamond, 456, 554-557
Current History, 63 n.
"Customs," 764, 876
Cutch (India), 356
Cuttington College and Divinity School, 845
Cyprus, 150, 167
Cyrenaica, 164-166, 167, 168, 169, 181, 182; Defense Force of, 181
Cyrene, 164

Dadaya, 610
Dadoo. Dr. Y. M., 533
Daggafontein Mines, Ltd., 552
Dagher, Ibrahim, 63 n.
Dagomba tribe, 821
Dahomey, 303, 599, 839, 840 n., 875-876, 880
Dahomey, an Ancient West African Kingdom (Herskovits), 303 n.
Daily News (Chicago), 911
Daily Service (Lagos), 751, 771
Daily Spectator (Accra), 828 n.
Daily Success (Lagos), 751
Daily Worker (London), 801
Dakar, 871, 873, 876, 878, 881-882, 883
Damaraland. See South-West Africa
Dan, King, 876
Danakil Desert, 252 n., 254
Dancing, art objects used in, 309; Berber, Arab, 101-102, 103, 104; in the Congo, 680; in Nigeria, 758; pole, 626; in South Africa, 560; in Tanganyika, 420; in Uganda, 431-432; Watutsi, 687; western, banned, 431-432
Dane Rachakana, 570-571
Danquah, Dr. J. B., 800, 801, 803, 808, 812
Dar es Salaam, 351, 352, 404, 407, 741
D'Arboussier, Gabriel, 879
Darfur Province, 228
Darwin, Charles, 734
Dashiell, Alfred S., 895
"Dashing," 758, 779, 814, 832
Davidson, Basil, 667 n., 673, 907, 917, 918, 919, 921
Davis, Dr. John W., 868
Davis, Richard Harding, 919
D-Day (Gunther), 922
DDT, 177, 736, 738
Deane, Philip, 65 n., 122, 125 n., 908, 909, 910
De Beers Consolidated Mines, Ltd., 489, 545, 549, 551, 555, 557, 558, 917
Debundscha, 706
"Defiance" movement, South Africa, 528, 533-535
De Gaulle, General Charles, 72, 129, 695, 698

Deindorfer, Bob, 919
Dejazmatch Balcha Hospital, Addis Ababa, 260
de Kruif, Paul, 736 n.
Delamere, Lord (Hugh Cholmondeley), 317-318
Delom, Guy, 52
Delta Barrage, 225
Democracy, among the Arabs, 58; among the Baganda, 432; among the Kikuyus, 365; in Basutoland, 578; in Bechuanaland, 583; in British colonies, 344-347; in the Gold Coast, 824, 837; in Islam, 64; in Swaziland, 579, 581; in Togoland, 840; tribal, in Nigeria, 781; in tribal organization, 290
Democratic Union of the Algerian Manifesto, 126-127
"Demographic colonization," 168-169
Demnat, 98
Dengue fever, 680
Denmark, in the Gold Coast, 792, 822, 823; outlawing of slave trade by, 753
Dennis, Gabriel L., 856 n., 860, 922
De-oathing ceremony, 362-364
Departmental Ditties and Ballads and Barrack Room Ballads (Kipling), 185 n.
Deressa, Yilma, 272
Desert, climatic and man-made, 150
Dessie, 269
Desta, Ras, 257, 268, 269
Desta, Princess Ruth, 269
Destooling, 820-821, 841
Destour, 156
Detribalization, 516, 738, 837, 881
De Valera, Eamon, 469
Development plans, in the Congo, 658; in French Equatorial Africa, 695; in French West Africa, 880; in Kenya, 350; in Liberia, 854, 868; in Mozambique, 593; in the Sudan, 237; in Tanganyika, 409
Devonshire, Duke of, 334
Devonshire White Paper, 334-335
Diamond Corporation, 557
Diamond Trading Company, 557
Diamonds, 5, 416-420; in the Congo, 647, 662; in French Equatorial Africa, 696; in French West Africa, 875; in the Gold Coast, 825; in Sierra Leone, 744; in South Africa, 488, 489, 499, 545, 546, 549, 550-551, 553-558; in South-West Africa, 546, 557-558, 562
Diaz, Bartholomeu, 11
Dickson, Reverend William Scott, 370
"Dieback," 356
Diégo-Suarez, 600
Dienbienphu, 72
Diet, 228, 266, 291-292, 400, 401,

429, 432, 508, 577, 635, 680, 686, 724, 727; an Arab banquet, 98-101
Diffa, 98-101, 102-103
Dik-dik, 389
Dikwa, Emir of, 783 n.
Dingaan, King, 487, 497
Dinkas, 228
Dioch, 399
"Directed labor" system, 587-588. See also Labor, forced
Diretlo murders, 569-573, 574-575
Disciples of Christ Congo Mission, 680
Discrimination, 328-329, 589, 663, 708; against Indians, 532, 533, 543, 591 n. See also Color bar and Segregation
Diseases, 5, 13, 76, 177-178, 306-308; bilharzia, 7, 193, 234, 308, 426, 789; blackwater fever, 308, 735; conquering of, 218, 736; dengue fever, 680; dysentery, 192, 680, 720; East Coast fever, 317; in Egypt, 192-193; livestock, 317-318, 382 n.; elephantiasis, 308, 779; filariasis, 308; hernia, 308; insanity, 726-727; leprosy, 308, 722, 723, 724, 728, 789; malaria, 76, 308, 727, 735, 736, 869; malnutrition, 308, 432, 508; onchocerciasis, 308, 426, 828, 869; plant, 356, 797, 825-826; pneumonic plague, 192; relapsing fever, 640; Schistosomiasis, 193; silicosis, 559; sleeping sickness (Trypanosomiasis), 306, 307-308, 392, 725, 789; smallpox, 192, 787; trachoma, 177, 192-193; tropical ulcer, 308, 779; tuberculosis, 308, 559; typhus, 54, 192; venereal, 57, 136, 177-178, 193, 278, 308, 401, 402, 706; worms, 192, 308, 508; yellow fever, 725, 735
Disney, Walt, 914
Disraeli, Benjamin, 219
Djellaba, 58
Djemma el Fna, Marrakesh, 53
Djerba, 149
Djerma tribe, 872
Djezira-el-Maghreb, 39
Djibouti, 256, 282
Dodowa, 837
Dogon tribe, 872
Dolisie, 703
Dollar diplomacy, 865
Dönges, Dr. Theophilus Ebenhaezer, 178 n., 470, 474-476, 518, 536
Doppers, 459, 470, 471
Dorobo tribe, 298
Doty, Robert C., 179 n., 910, 911
Douala, 704-705, 706, 708
Douglas, William O., 909
Drake, Sir Francis, 493
Drakensberg Mountains, 496
Drakenstein Valley, 491, 494
Dress and ornamentation, 58, 80

n., 174, 290, 300-301, 365, 401, 407 n., 430, 566, 580, 626, 648, 679, 683, 697, 755, 793, 820, 829, 832, 833-834, 841, 881
Driburg, Tom, 915
Drum (Johannesburg), 505, 523, 528 n.
Drums and tomtoms, 288, 309, 438, 443, 680, 682, 689, 706
Du Bois, W. E. B., 349 n., 800, 916, 917
Du Chaillu, Paul, 696
Du Plessis, I. D., 916
Dua Yaw-Nkwanta, 821
Dual Mandate, 338
Dube, Dr. John, 527
Duiker, red forest, 388; yellow-backed, 383
Duke Ephraim IX, King, 705 n.
Duke Town, 705 n.
Dulles, John Foster, 91, 769
Duluti, Lake, 398
Dumbushawa (school), 621
Duncan, David Douglas, 911
Duncan, Patrick, 534-535, 915, 916
Dundas, Charles, 304 n., 410, 914
Dunford, Michael, 388 n., 894
Durand, Lionel, 920
Durban, 497-498, 518
d'Urban, Sir Benjamin, 498
Durham University, 743
Dutch East India Company, 485, 529
Dutch Reformed church, 459-461, 462, 470, 471, 561, 621
Dutch settlement, in Angola, 597; in the Cameroons, 705; in the Gold Coast, 822, 823; in South Africa, 484-486, 487-488, 493 (see also Boers)
Dysentery, 192, 680, 720

East Africa, 351-352; animals of, 379-395; United States position on, 350
East Africa Command, 351
East Africa High Commission, 351
East Africa and Rhodesia, 359 n., 375 n., 607 n., 618 n., 917, 918
East African Background (Huntingford and Bell), 287 n., 298 n., 912, 913, 915
East African Railways and Harbors, 317
East Coast of Africa, Arab influence on, 287; color bar in, 17; compared with West Coast, 289, 291, 316, 344 n., 349, 740-742, 749, 752; language of, 287; primitive and not-so-primitive aspects of, 288-289. See also various countries
Éboué, Felix, 697-698, 699, 702, 713, 877
Éboué, Mme Felix, 698
Eck, Dr. H. T. Van, 915
Economic development program, Liberia, 854

Economic opportunity for Africans, 18, 662, 663, 666, 667
Economic situation, Bantu, 291; in Bechuanaland, 582; in British West Africa, 738, 741, 742, 744; in the Congo, 671; in Egypt, 190-192, 216; in Ethiopia, 261-262; in French West Africa, 880, 881; in the Gold Coast, 797, 825-826; in Kenya, 311; in Liberia, 854, 865-868; in Madagascar, 600; in Morocco, 54-55, 83; in Mozambique, 593; in Nigeria, 747; in the Rhodesias, 616, 623-624, 628, 633; in South-West Africa, 562, 567; in Swaziland, 581; in the Sudan, 237; in Tanganyika, 407-409; in Uganda, 421-422, 423; in the Union of South Africa, 465-466, 503, 510, 511, 518, 545-546; in Zanzibar, 356
Economist, 75, 481 n., 514 n., 773 n., 805 n., 828, 907, 909, 910, 912, 916, 917, 921, 922
Edea Protestant Mission, 707
Eden, Sir Anthony, 169
Education, in Algeria, 126; British policy on, 349; in British West Africa, 740; in the Cameroons, 709; colleges and universities, 51, 235, 366, 377, 427-428, 519, 576, 607, 614, 743, 845; in the Congo, 647, 659, 660, 662, 663, 668; effects of, 19, 71; in Egypt, 186; in Ethiopia, 259, 264-265, 266; in French Equatorial Africa, 695, 699, 702; in French Togoland, 840; in French West Africa, 871, 874, 876, 880; in the Gold Coast, 819, 842; Kikuyu system of, 366; in Liberia, 844-845, 866, 869-870; in Libya, 178-179; missionaries and, 12, 305, 306, 519, 784, 799, 870; in Morocco, 59, 76, 82; in Mozambique, 594; need for, 886, 891; in Nigeria, 747, 760, 761, 762, 769; "nomad schools," 136; political, 662 (see also Political development); in Portuguese Africa, 586, 587; in the Rhodesias, 607, 614, 621, 624-625, 634, 638; Roman Catholic church and, 305, 659, 660; in South Africa, 462, 482, 518-519, 522; in South-West Africa, 566; starving of, by colonial powers, 15, 59, 82, 278, 294, 376, 377, 412, 413, 596, 689, 699; in Tanganyika, 412, 413; thirst for, 51, 82, 117, 178-179, 251, 294, 740, 761, 838, 841; in Tunisia, 154; vocational, 294; for women, 71, 244, 428
Edusei, Krobo, 796
Edward, Lake, 312
Eeden, F. M. Van, 618 n.
Efik tribe and language, 705, 746

Egbe Omo Odudua, 773
Egbuono, Ndukwe N., 883 n.
Eggins, E. C., 647 n.
Église Sainte-Anne, Brazzaville, 694
Egypt, 15, 35 n., 63, 164, 183-222, 335, 336, 884; British in, 184, 196-200, 201; civilization of, derived from Europe, 7; corruption in, 204, 207; economy of, 190-192, 216; history of, 195-200; influence of, in Libya, 173; international considerations on, 212-218; irrigation in, 225; length of civilization of, 10; military coup in, 183, 200, 204, 205; nationalism in, 183, 185, 196, 198, 233; and the Nile, 224; physical picture of, 185-195; position of women in, 188; present government of, 184, 203, 204, 205-207; social and political revolution in, 205-206; and the Sudan, 226, 227, 231, 232, 241-242, 245
Einstein, 675, 731
Eiselen, Dr. W. W. M., 461, 495
Eisenhower, Dwight D., 811, 892, 908
El Azhari, Sayed Esmail Ahmed, 245
El Baida, 173
el-Din, Fuad Serag, 207
El Djema Sahim, 89
El Fasher, 228
El Goléa, 131, 140, 142-144
El Hodeiby, Hassan, 208
Eland, 389
Elder Dempster Line, 739 n.
Electricity production, 54, 55, 423, 446, 624. See also Hydro-electric power
Elephantiasis, 308, 779
Elephants, 228, 380-382, 383, 386, 389, 391, 392, 393, 394, 594, 623, 689, 914
Elgon, Mount, 312
Elisabethville, 591, 647 n., 652-653, 663, 666, 670, 671
Elisofon, Eliot, 911
Elizabeth, Queen Mother of England, 479
Elizabeth II of England, 245, 250 n., 387, 418, 421, 444, 445, 449-450, 467, 469, 574 n., 641, 763, 811, 919
Elliott, Susan Walthew, 895
Elmina, 822
Emergence of Modern Egypt, The (Badeau and Nolte), 195 n., 910
Emerson, Ralph Waldo, 20
Emin Pasha, 656
Eminent Victorians (Strachey), 229 n.
Enahoro, Anthony Eronsele Oseghale, 767
Encyclopaedia Britannica, 656 n., 908, 918, 919, 920, 921, 922
Endeley, Dr. E. M. L., 750

INDEX 933

Endelkachau, Bitwoded Makonnen, 272
Endymion (Keats), 278
Enfidaville, 149
Enrique (son of Affonso II), 654
Ensor, Michael, 922
Entebbe, 286, 423, 426-427, 430
Enugu, 759
Equator Province, 653
Equator Ranch, 317
Equatoria, 229, 230
Equatorial forest, 678-679
Erasmus, F. C., 480
Erell, Roger, 694
Eritrea, 261 n., 278-281
Ermelo district, 486
Erosion, 5, 452, 576
Erskine, General Sir George W. E. J., 373, 377
Eshowe, 496
Ethiopia, 12, 15, 63, 168, 199, 224, 247-266, 273, 884; federation of Eritrea and, 279-280; finance in, 269-270; foreign influence in, 255-258, 267, 275, 277; history of, 252-253; Imperial family of, 267-271; language of, 6; in League of Nations, 262, 268; religion in, 253-254, 258; United States and, 258-259
Ethiopia Under Haile Selassie (Sandford), 912
Ethiopian Air Lines, 258, 274-276
Eugénie, Empress, 219
Eurafricans, 637
European Defense Community, 31 n.
Evans, D. M. H., 894
Evans, Harold, 434 n.
Evans-Pritchard, E. E., 168 n.
Évoluées, évolués, 71, 147, 662 n., 699, 875
Ewe Presbyterian Mission, 838
Ewe tribe and language, 229, 813, 819, 838, 839, 840
Executive Council (EXCO), 344, 345, 346, 347, 709, 744, 766, 825
Ex-Italian Somaliland (Pankhurst), 912
Exman, Eugene, 920
Experiment in Time (Scott), 917
Exploitation, economic, 15, 83, 125, 239, 316, 656, 695, 754, 843, 876, 887, 888
Exploration and discovery, 11, 12, 39, 167, 185, 252, 315, 354, 397, 433, 654, 695, 696, 736, 752, 753, 822, 874
Export-Import Bank, 868
Exports and imports, of Angola, 596; of Basutoland, 577; of the Cameroons, 708; of the Congo, 647, 671, 680, 689; of French West Africa, 875, 876; of the Gold Coast, 826; of labor, *see* Labor, migrant; of Liberia, 848; of Mozambique,

593; of the Rhodesias, 620, 623; of South-West Africa, 562; of the Sudan, 228; of Tanganyika, 407-408; of Uganda, 421-422. *See also* Economic situation *and* Trade
Extraterritoriality, 49, 50 n.
Eyo Honesty VII, 705

Fabian Colonial Bureau, 337
Fabulous Congo (Bellotti), 920
Facing Mount Kenya (Kenyatta), 297 n., 298, 367
Facts and Figures About French North Africa, 908
Falaq, Al, 356
Falashas, 255
Fane-Smith, Geoffrey, 918
Fang tribe, 706
Fanti tribe, 823, 824, 837
Farhat Hached, 159 n.
Farouk, former King, 173, 195, 199, 200, 201, 204, 205, 213, 233, 911
Farson, Negley, 334, 335 n., 366 n., 377 n., 562 n., 684, 907, 912, 913, 914, 916
Fascism, 467, 483. *See also* Nazism *and* Totalitarianism
Fashoda crisis, 233 n.
Fassi, Allal el, 84
Fatalism, 58
Fath, Mahmoud abul and Hussein abul, 207
Fathia (sister of Farouk), 187
Fatima, Queen (of Libya), 172, 173
Fawzy, Dr. Mahmoud, 188
Federal Independence party, Kenya, 347
Federal party, Southern Rhodesia, 606
Fellagha, 161
Fellahin, 195
Feminism, 188, 762. *See also* Women, emancipation of
Ferguson, George Ekam, 922
Fernando Po (Poó), 710-711, 825, 852, 861
Fetishism, 832. *See also* Black magic *and* Juju
Feudalism, 781, 785 n.
Fez, 43, 44, 46, 47, 50-52, 106, 109, 702; Ulema of, 20, 22
Fezzan, 166, 178
FIDES (Investment Fund for Economic and Social Development), 880
Figueras, Garcia, 113
Filariasis, 308
Fillmore, Millard, 37
Finance Corporation of America, 865
Finletter, Thomas K., 893
Firbank, Ronald, 149
Firestone, Harvey S., Jr., 866 n.
Firestone, Harvey S., Sr., 864, 865 n.
Firestone Plantations Company, 843, 844, 848, 864-867

Firestone Tire and Rubber Company, 864
First Electric Corporation of South Africa, Ltd., 551
Fisheries, South-West Africa, 562; Uganda, 292
Fisherman's Creek (Liberia), 848
Fliegers, Serge, 893
Flogging, 478-479, 534
Flooding of the Nile, 224
Focus on Africa (Light), 914
Folkways (Sumner), 912
Fon of Bikom, 706
Fondouk, in Fez, 51-52; in Tamanrasset, 134
Fons, 875
Forced labor, 18, 520, 587-588, 598, 657, 664
Foreign Affairs, 65 n., 76 n., 151 n., 191 n., 197, 216, 321 n., 349 n., 456 n., 470 n., 478 n., 496 n., 907, 909, 910, 916, 917, 918, 922
Foreign Operations Administration, 350, 624, 848, 869
Foreign Policy Bulletin, 805 n., 815 n.
Foreign Policy Reports, 761 n., 861 n., 863, 920, 922
FORESCOM, 662
FORMINIÈRE (Société Internationale Forestière et Minière du Congo), 662
Fort Hall, 320
Fort Hare, 519
Fort Jameson, 610
Fort Jesus, Mombasa, 315
Fort Lamy, 134, 697
Fort Miribel, 142
Fort of St. John the Baptist of Ajuda, 599
Fortune, 661 n., 909, 919
Foster, John, 894
Foucauld, Père de, 134, 137, 143, 909
Foum Tatahouime, 157
Fourah Bay College, 428, 743
Fourmarierite, 674
France, in Algeria, 38, 120, 123; in the Cameroons, 705, 707-708; colonial policy of, 16-17, 67, 75, 79, 86, 120, 153, 155, 160, 344, 873, 882-883, 884; on Committee of Control of Tangier, 110, 111; in Ethiopia, 256, 267; in French Equatorial Africa, 692, 694, 695-696, 698, 699-703, 705, 707-708; in French Somaliland, 282; in the Gold Coast, 822; in Indochina, 72, 335; in Madagascar, 600; and Morocco, 20-21, 24, 26-27, 29-30, 31, 32-37, 38, 41, 42, 43, 44-46, 50, 52, 66-67, 72-85, 86, 89, 90, 104, 105, 335; relations of, with Spain, 115; in Togoland, 837, 838, 839-840; in Tunisia, 38, 146, 150, 153-156, 161-162, 169
Franceville, 696

INSIDE AFRICA

Franchise, in the Congo, 667; denied Africans and Coloreds in South Africa, 483, 518, 530-531; in French Equatorial Africa, 701; in French West Africa, 873, 876, 881; in Liberia, 857; in Nigeria, 759; in Southern Rhodesia, 638; for women, 701, 857, 873
Franck, César, 731
Franco, 34, 90, 115, 116-117, 118
Franks, 39
Franz Joseph, Emperor of Austro-Hungary, 219
Frazer, Sir James, 299, 913
Frederick the Great, 731
Free France, 695, 698
Free Officers Committee, 203, 204
Freedom, and desire for education, 422; individual, absence of tradition of, 10
Freetown, 736, 742-743
French Colonies, The (Stern), 920
French Equatorial Africa, 44, 63, 691, 694, 695-708; bush flying over, 703-705; the Cameroons, 705-708; French policy in, 699-703; government of, 701-702; history of, 697-698; territories of, 696-697
French Foreign Legion, 52, 95, 123, 166
French Guinea, 874
French North Africa, 38-40. See also Algeria, Morocco, and Tunisia
French Press Service, 872 n., 893
French Somaliland, 282
French Sudan, 227, 874, 876, 879
French Togoland, 6, 837, 838, 839-840
French Union, 38, 45, 282, 600, 694, 695, 700, 707, 877
French West Africa, 63, 700, 753, 871-883; administrative divisions of, 873-876; government and politics in, 876-880
Freud, 731, 912
Friedberg (Germany), 550
Friedgut, A. J., 893
Friend (Liberia), 857, 858, 866
Friend (Orange Free State), 500, 916
Fruit, at Lambaréné, 727
Fruit farms, South Africa, 492, 493, 498
Frumentius, St., 254
Fuad, King, 199
Fulani tribe and language, 699, 746, 749, 782-783, 872
Fuller, Thomas, 65
Furbay, Elizabeth Dearmin, 849 n.
Furnivall, J. S., 338 n.
Fuzzy Wuzzys, 228

Ga, 819
Gabashane Masupha, 574, 575
Gabon, 696, 698, 699, 719, 861
Gadamès, 166

Galla tribe and language, 262, 276, 782
Galoa tribe, 699
Gama, Vasco da, 11, 315, 325, 495
Gambia, 735, 741, 744-745, 873
Game hunting. *See* Hunting
Game reserves, Albert National Park, 385, 682; Gemsbok Game Reserve, 486; Gorongosa, 593; Hluhluwe Game Reserve, 496; Kafue National Park, 625; in Kenya, 384-387; Kruger National Park, 385, 386, 499; Queen Elizabeth Park, 392-393; Serengeti Plains, 386; Tsavo National Park, 386, 395; Wankie, 623
Gandhi, Mahatma, 61, 327, 498, 533, 534, 731, 794
Gandhi, Manilal, 498, 533, 534, 535, 894
Gangala Va Bondio, 689
Ganta, 844 n.
Gao, 134, 140, 874
Garcia Affonso II, 654
Garcia Valiño, 114, 117
Garment Workers Union of South Africa, 542
Garretson, Albert H., 259, 894
Garretson, Mrs. Albert H., 894
Gbarnga, 869
Gbedemah, Kimla Agbeli, 796, 813-814, 828 n., 832, 841, 921
Geez, 261 n.
Gell, C. W. M., 470 n., 478 n., 916
Gemsbok Game Reserve, 486
General Mining and Finance Corporation, Ltd., 547
Genet, 387
"Genetic fear," 635
GÉOMINES, 662
George VI of England, 387, 479
Gerdemer, Dr. G. B. A., 538
Gerenuk, 389
German East Africa, 410-411, 414, 613, 684
Germany, in the Cameroons, 705-706; and Egypt, 217; in Ethiopia, 257, 267; interest of, in Africa, 44, 45, 217, 316, 354, 397, 434 n.; missionaries from, 304; Nazi, analogy of South Africa with 458; in South-West Africa, 562, 563, 565-566, 613; sympathy for, in World War II, 457, 467, 473, 698
Germiston, 513, 534
Gezira project, 236-237
Ghana Congress party, Gold Coast, 812
Ghanzi, 582
Ghardaia, 121
Ghibli, 163, 172
Giant sable antelope, 596
Gibbon, Edward, 247
Gibbons, Brigadier E. J., 708-709, 710
Gibbs, Henry, 916

Gibraltar, 40, 116
Gichan, Benjamin, 914
Gide, André, 56, 149, 697, 731, 871
Gilles, Helen T., 920
Giraffes, 382, 389, 391, 914
Giralda, in Seville, 52
Giraud, 72
Githathi, 363
Githens, Joyce, 794
Githunguri, 366
"Give—and keep," 17, 239 n., 816
Gladstone, 196, 316, 474 n.
Glaoui, Pasha of Marrakesh, 24, 31-32, 33, 36, 37, 52, 93-98, 100, 101, 115
Gluckman, Max, 372 n.
Goans, 314, 591 n.
Goats, 577, 697, 875
Godding, M., 659
Gods, Graves, and Scholars (Ceram), 190 n.
Goethe, 712, 731
Gogoland, 409
Gojjam, 253, 271
Gola tribe, 856
Gold, 5; in French Equatorial Africa, 696; fugitive, in Tangier, 108-109; in the Gold Coast, 825, 836; in South Africa, 488, 490, 492, 501, 502, 511, 543, 544, 545, 546-549, 550-551, 552, 553, 595; in Southern Rhodesia, 623
Gold Coast, 10, 15, 63, 78, 336, 338, 344 n., 367, 428, 436, 525, 604, 735, 738, 740, 741, 742, 753, 790, 791, 819-837, 841-842, 885, 886, 891; British policy in, 791 n., 816-817; Communism in, 817-818; debate in, on self-government, 808-811, 812; German interest in, 217; government in, 805, 806, 807-811, 824; history of, 822-825; leaders of, 790-806, 808, 809-811, 812, 813-814, 818; opposition to government in, 812; revolution in, 794-795, 797, 801-805
Gold Coast, The, 922
Gold Coast Aborigines' Rights Protection Society, 824
Gold Coast Cocoa Marketing Board, 825
Gold Coast Colony, 819, 820, 823, 824
Gold Coast Revolution, The (Padmore), 803 n., 804 n., 921
Gold Coast Trade Union Congress, 817
Gold Producers Committee, 546
Golden Bough, The (Frazer), 913
Golden Harvest, the Story of the Gold Coast Industry, 922
Golden Stool, 823-824, 833, 834, 835
Golding, George J., 530
Golien, Waldo G., 275, 276
Gomani, Chief Phillip, 641-644, 918-919
Gondar, 269, 274

INDEX 935

Gondwana, 599
Gonorrhea, 178, 193
Gordimer, Nadine, 505
Gordon, General Charles George, 229, 232
Gordon Memorial College, 235, 428
Gorillas, 719
Gorongosa game park, 593
Goundam, 874
Gouronsi tribe, 872
Government of Ethiopia, The (Perham), 253 n., 262 n., 264
Government House, Accra, 792-793; Lagos, 749-750; Lusaka, 633; Nairobi, 311, 340, 341, 342-344
Governor, British, institution of, 339-341, 344, 345
Governor General's Commission, Sudan, 245
Gozo, King, 875, 876
Graaff, Sir de Villiers, 513
Graaff Reinet, 493 n.
Grahamstown, 519
Grand Mufti of Jerusalem, 61
Grand Vizier El Mokri, 96
Grant, General U. S., 595
Granville, Lord, 197
Graphite, 600
Graziani, Marshal, 168, 257
Grazing, 523, 569, 576, 577, 697, 875. *See also* Cattle, Goats, *and* Sheep
Great Britain, attitudes of, 347-349; in Basutoland, 574, 575; in Bechuanaland, 582; in British Somaliland, 282; in British West Africa, 738, 743, 744, 745; in the Cameroons, 705, 708-710; in the Canal Zone, 219-222; colonial policy of, 17-18, 75, 196-198, 229, 239 n., 242 n., 334-357, 403, 411, 435, 574, 575, 617, 766-767, 791 n., 816-817, 885-886; and Egypt, 184, 196-200, 201; in Eritrea, 278, 279, 280; and Ethiopia, 252, 256, 267; financial contribution of, to Africa, 350; freedom of Asian colonies of, 80, 335; in the Gold Coast, 792-793, 802, 816-817; hostility to, 217-218, 231, 336, 468, 477, 487, 488 (*see also* Xenophobia); interest of, in Mozambique, 592; in Kenya, 310-311, 315-316, 317-318, 319, 320, 321, 331, 334-347, 365, 370, 372; and Libya, 164, 166, 175, 176, 177; in Madagascar (in World War II), 600; measures of, against the Mau Mau, 359-360, 361-364, 373-374; missionaries from, 304; in Nigeria, 748, 753-754, 764; Nigerian attitudes toward, 767-768, 770; in Ogaden, 284; outlawing of slave trade by, 753; in the Rhodesias and Nyasaland, 611-614, 615, 618, 639, 641-645; in South Africa,

449-450, 452, 454, 465, 471, 472, 486-487, 496, 497, 498, 500, 501, 510-513; in the Sudan, 230, 232, 233, 234, 239, 240-241; in Swaziland, 580; in Tanganyika, 411-413; in Tangier, 110; techniques used by, 349-350; in Uganda, 435-436, 438-439, 441-445; in Zanzibar, 353, 354-355, 357
Great Dyke, 620
Great Fish River, 486
Great Lakes, 312
Great Oath of the Ewes, 838
Great Pyramid of Cheops, 189, 190
Great Trek, 487-488
Great Western Emptiness, Great Eastern Emptiness, 140
Grebo tribe, 856
Greeks, explorations of, in Africa, 11, 39, 822; in the Cameroons, 708; in the Congo, 648; in Libya, 167; in Tanganyika, 398, 405
Greene, Graham, 736, 920, 922
Grey, Sir Edward, 657
Grievances, African, 357, 412, 631, 634, 645, 745, 775
Griffith (grandson of Moshesh), 573
Griffiths, James, 617
Griqualand West, 488 n.
Griquas, 485
Grogan, E. S., 620
Groix, 158
Group Areas Act, South Africa, 481, 509, 530, 534
Groutville, 498, 528
Groves, General, 676, 677
Guans, 822
Guardian (Manchester), 11 n., 263 n., 372 n., 541, 542, 867 n., 913, 922
Guerzé tribe, 872
Gueye, Lamine, 878
Guggisberg Constitution, 824
Guide Michelin, 44 n.
Guillaume, General Augustin, 25, 28, 30, 32, 33, 34, 35, 40, 46 n., 72-73, 74, 75, 76, 98, 120, 908, 909
Guillebaud, C. W., 918
Guinea Coast, 599, 874
Guinea worm, 308
Gum arabic, 228
Gunther, Frances, 894
Gunther, Jane Perry, 895

Haas, Ernest, 917
Haboob, 228
Hached, Farhat, 50, 158-159, 160
Hadi, Ibrahim Abdel, 207
Hadj, Messali, 127
Hadrumetum, 149
Hagedorn, Hermann, 920
Hagen, Beulah, 895
Haggard, Rider, 524
Haile Selassie, 247-251, 253, 254, 255, 258, 259, 261, 262, 264, 265, 267-268, 269, 270-271, 272,

275, 277, 279, 280, 281, 884, 912
Haile Selassie Imperial University, 265
Hailey, Lord, xi, 291 n., 296 n., 320, 498 n., 657, 701 n., 760 n., 882 n., 907, 913, 917
Haines, C. Grove, 889 n.
Haiti, 843
Halifax, Lord, 61
Hamilton, Hamish, 895
Hamilton, Thomas J., 87 n.
Hamitic peoples and language, 5, 6, 38, 39, 227, 229, 255, 278, 281, 286, 401, 425, 648, 686, 738, 782, 872
Hammamet, 149
Hampden, Mount, 621
Hancock, Sir Keith, 444
Handbook on Eritrea, A, 912
Hannington, James, 434
Hanno, 11
Harar, 254, 262, 267; Duke of, 269, 270
Harbel Area, Firestone Plantations, 864
Hargeisa, 282
Harley, Dr. George Way, 844 n.
Harmattan, 747, 872
Harmel, A. E., 916
Harper's Magazine, 701, 895, 907, 908, 910, 918, 921
Harris, Sir John, 860
Harun el Rashid, 43
Has the Afrikaner Nation a Future? (Scholtz), 537
Hassan, Si, 97, 98
Hassi, Sidi, Pasha of the Kasbah, 94
Hastings, Adrian, 915
Hatch, John, 916
Hatch system, 632-633
Haud, 284 n.
Hausa language and tribe, 746, 760, 772, 782
Hauser, Ernest O., 911
Haussknecht, Miss Emma, 721-722, 723, 728, 729, 731
Haut Katanga. *See* Katanga district
Haute Volta, 821, 875
Havelock, W. B., 346, 347, 371
Havenga, Dr. N. C., 458, 468, 470
Health, public, in French Somaliland, 282; in French West Africa, 880; in Liberia, 844, 869; in Morocco, 76, 83
Heart of Africa, The (Campbell), 412 n., 534 n., 641 n., 907, 912, 917, 918, 919
Heart of Darkness (Conrad), 650
Heart of the Matter, The (Greene), 736
Hegel, 731
Hehe tribe, 298
Helgoland, 13, 354
Helwan, 192
Hemingford, Lord, 894, 920
Hemingway, Ernest, 397
Henry the Navigator, 11
Henson, Mr. and Mrs. Jean, 910

Herald, George W., 151 n.
Herald (New York), 655
Herald Tribune (New York), 35 n., 90 n., 188 n., 423 n., 473 n., 706 n., 887 n., 907, 911, 912, 917, 918
Herero tribe, 287, 562, 563, 566
Hermanus, 493
Hernia, 308
Herskovits, Melville J., 303, 876 n.
Hertzog, General James Barry Munnik, 455, 456-457, 458, 470, 477, 500, 518, 527, 530
Heydias, 27
High Commission Territories, 512, 817 n. *See also* Basutoland, Bechuanaland, *and* Swaziland
High Court of Parliament Act, South Africa, 483
Hillman, Sidney, 542
Himumuine, Berthold S., 566
Hindorf, 408
Hindus, 325
Hinterland, Liberia, 844, 854, 858
Hippopotamuses, 228, 380, 383, 393, 394, 407, 426, 719; pygmy, 870
Hiroshima, 669, 678
Hisbia Dighil Mirifle, 283
History of German East Africa, A (Dundas), 410 n.
History of Nigeria (Burns), 738 n., 752 n., 761 n., 907, 920
Hitchcock, Sir Eldred F., 407, 408, 914, 915
Hitler, Adolf, 267, 411, 457, 458, 467, 468, 698, 731, 888
Hluhluwe Game Reserve, 496
Ho, 837-838, 841
Hochschild, Harold K., 893
Hofmeyr, 499
Hoggar, 130, 131, 777
Holiday, 907, 908, 909
Holism, 456
Hollingsworth, L. W., 287 n., 914
Holstein, Marda Von, 472-473
Homosexuality, 57, 66, 523, 560
Honor's List, 349
Hoogstraal, Harry, 911
Hoover, Herbert, 550
Hope diamond, 554
Hope Waddell Institute, 769
Horace, S. R., 853
Horn, Alfred Aloysius (Trader), 691, 719, 920
Hornbostel, Dr. E. M. Von, 689
Horner, Dr. and Mrs. Howard, 680
Horses, 577
Hospitals, 527, 680-681, 688, 696, 709, 714, 719, 721-722, 724-730, 779, 835, 844 n., 859, 869, 880
Hottentots, 485, 529; language of, 562
Houphouet-Boigny, Félix, 878-879
Howard, Colonel Henry, 342, 913
Howard-Williams, Mark, 388 n.
Hoyningen-Huene, 697, 911
Huddleston, Father Trevor, 916
Huggins, Sir Godfrey, 602-603,
604-608, 615, 617, 618 n., 638, 918
Hugo, Victor, 585
Huguenots, 485
Huizinga, J. H., 335 n.
Hull, Cordell, 595
Human sacrifice, 764, 876
Hunting, 390-392, 593, 625-626
Huntingford, G. W. B., 287 n., 298 n., 912, 913
Hutton-Mills, T., 814
Huxley, Elspeth, 317, 912, 913, 914, 922
Huxley, Julian, 289 n., 913, 923
Hydroelectric power, 39, 54, 581, 624, 825, 827, 874
Hyenas, 384, 389, 390

Ibadan, 49 n., 428, 755, 760, 761, 762
Ibandhla, 581
Ibibio tribe, 746
Ibn Saud, 96 n., 213
Ibo tribe and language, 365, 621, 709, 746, 759, 760-761, 763, 766, 767, 771, 772, 773, 778, 785
Idris I of Libya, 164, 170-174, 179 n., 355, 780, 910
Idumagbo market, 756
Ife, 762, 764; Oni of, 763
Ifni, 118
Ikenne, 774
Ikko. *See* Lagos
Ikoli, Ernest, 769 n.
Ikoyi, 756
Ila tribe, 626
Illiteracy, 8, 9; in Algeria, 126; in Egypt, 192; in Ethiopia, 253, 264; "functional," 870; in the Gambia, 744; in the Gold Coast, 819; in Kenya, 294; in Liberia, 844; in Libya, 180; in Morocco, 24; in Nigeria, 748; in Portuguese Africa, 587, 890; in the Sudan, 227; in Tanganyika, 411; in Tunisia, 151; in West Africa, 740. *See also* Education
Imézouaren family, 95
Immorality Amendment Act, South Africa, 482
Impala, 389
Imperial British East Africa Company, 316, 435
Imperial Police Staff College, Ethiopia, 251
Imperialism, 12-13, 44-45, 150, 196-198, 316, 407, 692, 705, 753-754, 770, 817, 820, 823, 847, 870, 872, 888. *See also* Colonialism *and* Exploitation, economic
Impressions of South Africa (Bryce), 546 n.
Imru, Ras, 268
In Brightest Africa (Akeley), 914
In Morocco (Wharton), 44 n., 909
Independent Schools Association (Kikuyu), 366, 368, 377
"Independent" True Whig party, Liberia, 857 n.
India, 14, 35 n., 80, 230 n., 294, 335, 349, 356, 532, 534, 543, 564, 599, 637, 798, 888
Indians, American, 80; in Kenya, 314, 317, 322, 324-328; in Mozambique, 591 n.; in Nyasaland, 640; segregation against, 532, 533, 637; in South Africa, 452, 455, 469, 476, 479, 481, 495, 496, 498, 499, 500, 501, 517, 531-533, 543; in Southwest Africa, 561 n.; in Southern Rhodesia, 637; in Tanganyika, 404, 407; in Uganda, 425; in West Africa, 741; in Zanzibar, 353
Indirect Rule, 17, 337-338, 365, 783
Indochina, 45, 72
Indonesia, 35 n., 356, 888
Industrial color bar, 440, 454, 466, 483, 630, 631-632
Industrial Conciliation Act, South Africa, 482-483
Industrialization, in the Congo, 673; in Egypt, 191-192, 194; in French West Africa, 874, 875; in the Gold Coast, 837; in Rhodesia, 616, 634; in South Africa, 466, 495, 498, 500, 516, 536, 537
Infant mortality, 194, 844
Infibulation, 296
Ingalls, Leonard, 477 n.
Inheritance, matrilineal, 299. *See also* Succession
Insanity, 726-727
Inside Asia (Gunther), 908
Inside U.S.A. (Gunther), 751
Institut Français d'Afrique Noire (IFAN), 882
Institut de Recherches Scientifiques au Congo (IRSAC), 689
Intelligence Digest, 912
Intelligent Man's Guide to the Post-War World (Cole), 834
Intermarriage, 465, 482, 665, 749, 829 n., 882
International Conciliation, 909
International Confederation of Free Trade Unions (ICFTU), 160
International Federation of Trade Unions, 889
International Locust Control Organization, 336
International Tangier (Stuart), 909
Intestinal worms, 192, 308, 508
Intrepid, USS, 175
Introducing Africa (Wells), 912
Introducing East Africa, 317 n., 354 n., 913, 914
Introducing West Africa, 920, 921
Investment Fund for Economic and Social Development (FIDES), 880
Iola, 395
I.O.M. (*indépendance d'outre-mer*), 878
Ionides, C. J. P., 383

INDEX 937

Iqoqo, 581
Iran, 35 n., 221
Iraq, 35 n., 215, 335
Irene, Princess, of Uganda, 438
Iron, 567, 848, 854, 867, 874
Irrigation, in Egypt, 191, 225; in Morocco, 55; in the Sahara, 141-142; in the Sudan, 236, 874
Irumu, 683
Isaacs, Harold L., 8 n., 909, 923
Iscor (Iron and Steel Corporation of South Africa), 498
Islah (Reform party), Spanish Morocco, 117
Islam, 7, 39, 40, 56, 60-64, 65, 86, 127, 217, 229, 252, 253, 254-255, 267, 592, 820, 883
Island Club, Lagos, 757-758
Ismail, Khedive, 195, 196, 219
Ismailia, 220
Ismailis, 325
Israel, British withdrawal from, 335; and Egypt, 187 n., 213-214; Jewish emigration to, 68, 147 n., 174; South Africans and, 503
Istiqlal movement, 24, 29, 30, 31, 33, 46 n., 66, 81-84, 86, 112, 117
Italy, administration of Somalia by, 168, 279, 282, 283; on Committee of Control for Tangier, 111; conquest of Ethiopia by, 168, 199, 252, 267; in Eritrea, 278, 279, 280; in Libya, 164, 166, 167, 168-169, 172; present influence of, in Ethiopia, 257-258; in Tunisia, 147
Ituri forest, 682
Ivory, 656
Ivory Coast, 872, 875, 877, 878, 879
Ivy, J. R., Ltd., 499
Ivy, James W., 893
Iwo, 762

Jabavu, 506
Jack, Dr. Homer, 920
Jackson, Andrew, 49
Jackson, Barbara Ward, 922. *See also* Ward, Barbara
Jackson, Commander Robert G. A., 828
Jackson, Mr. and Mrs. Robert, 894
Jacobsdal, 479
Jadotville, 674
Jameson, Dr. Leander Starr, 491, 492, 493, 622
Jameson Raid, 492, 613
Janissaries, 166
Jansen, Dr. Ernest George, 471-472
Jebb, Sir Gladwyn, 87
Jebel el Akhdar, 173
Jebel Auliya Dam, 225, 236
Jeffries, Jim, 608-609
Jessa, M. E., 914
Jessup, Philip, 279
Jews, 39; in Algeria, 121; in the Congo, 652; in Egypt, 187;

in Ethiopia, 255; in Fez, 51; in Johannesburg, 503; Kenya Highlands offered to, as National Home, 318; in Libya, 174, 181-182; in Morocco, 67-68, 94; in South Africa, 461, 503; in Tangier, 108, 112; in Tunisia, 147, 149
Jinja, 426, 429, 430
Johannesburg, 286, 293, 462, 466, 498, 501-505, 517, 518, 538, 551, 553; the compounds, 558-560; the locations, 505-509
Johannesburg, South Africa's Metropolis, 502 n.
Johannesburg Consolidated Investment, 547
Johnson, Wallace, 743-744
Johnston, G. R. A. M., 399, 915
Johnston, Sir Harry, 423, 435, 639, 705 n.
Joinville, Prince, 696
Jones, E. C. B., 856
Jones, G. I., 570, 572, 574, 575, 577, 917
Jordan, 335, 889
Jos, 786-787
Joubert, 499
Journal of International Affairs, 8 n., 907, 913
Journey Without Maps (Greene), 922
Joy, Charles R., 716 n., 718, 733 n., 912, 918, 920
Juba, 230
Juin, Marshal Alphonse-Pierre, 31, 32, 73, 84, 85, 151 n.
Juju, 740, 756, 798, 832, 838. *See also* Black magic *and* Witch doctors and witchcraft
Julien, Charles-André, 151 n., 910
Julius Caesar, 447
Jungle Man, 919

Kaapse Kleuring, 529
Kabaka of Bugando, 433
Kabaka crisis, 424, 435, 436-438, 439, 441-445
Kabalo, 650
Kabasha escarpment, 682
Kabyles, 121
Kaduna, 760
Kaffir wars, 486
"Kaffirs," 455, 530
"Kaffirs" (shares in gold-mining companies), 547
Kafue National Park, 625
Kafue River, 624
Kahn, Sam, 467, 541-542, 915
Kairouan, 148
Kairouyine mosque, 22, 51
Kaiser Wilhelm Point, 397
Kalahari Desert, 486, 494, 562, 565, 582
Kaltenborn, Mr. and Mrs. H. V., 893
Kamba tribe, 298, 349 n., 375
Kambove, 670
Kamina, Belgian air base at, 689

Kamm, Josephine, 907, 920
Kampala, 317, 351, 424, **425**, 426, 427-428, 438, 741
Kane-Berman, Louis, 515
Kankiya, 788
Kano, 134, 697, 740, 776-780, 782, 785, 883; Emir of, 779-780
Kansas City (Missouri), 759, 846
Kanuri, 746, 784
Kanyenyena, 361
Kapenguria, 369
Karamoja, 436 n.
Kariba Gorge scheme, 624
Karimjee, Abdulkarim, 407
Karité, 875
Karroo, 485, 494
Kasai River, 649
Kasbah of Algiers, 120
Kasbah country, 102-106
Kasempa district, 626 n.
Kashim, Shettima, 750
Kashmensky, Dr., 260
Kasolite, 674
Katanga district, 591, 615, 628, 647 n., 652, 670, 673
Katsina, 787-788
Keats, 278, 911
Kefauver investigation, 759
Kele, 288
Kemal Ataturk, 65
Kennedy, Sir John and Lady, 894, 918
Kente cloth, 793, 834
Kenya, 12, 229, 255, 284, 286, 291, 292, 297, 298, 310-333, 504 n., 525, 615, 740, 741, 885; British rule in, 310-311, 315-316, 317-318, 319, 320, 321, 331, 334-352, 365, 370, 372; color bar in, 310-311, 326, 327, 328-329, 333; education in, 15, 294; government in, 344-347, 378; history of, 315-318; Indian community in, 314, 317, 322, 324-328; the land, 311-314, 318-322; Mau Mau crisis in, 324, 327, 336, 358-378; national parks in, 384-387, 395; nationalism in, 326, 327, 348, 366, 372; the people, 314-315; poll tax on Africans in, 350; roads in, 7; self-government for, 334-335, 349, 377, 378; White Highlands of, 293, 312, 318, 319-321, 376; white settlement in, 6, 17, 78, 79, 311, 317-321, 329-333, 338, 342-344, 345, 347, 352, 370, 377, 399
Kenya, Mount, 304, 312, 397
Kenya: Your Queries Answered, 330 n.
Kenya African Union, 366-367, 368
Kenya Elector's Union, 347
Kenya Teachers College, 366, 377
Kenya Weekly News, 335 n.

INSIDE AFRICA

Kenyatta, Jomo, 297 n., 298, 341, 348, 366, 367-369, 371, 372, 375, 889
Keppel-Jones, Professor Arthur, 485 n., 544
Ker and Downey, 390
Kgari, Chief, 582
Kgotla, 583, 584
Khalifa, of Spanish Morocco, 114; of the Sudan, 232-233, 235; of Zanzibar, 355
Khama III, 582-583
Khamsin, 282
Khartoum, xii, 224, 226, 228, 230, 234-235, 245, 246, 755, 883
Khatmia sect, 243
Khedives, 196
Khoja Moslems, 325
Khologhli, 166
Kiambu Reserve, 320
Kibangu, 667
Kibo, Mount, 396, 397, 398
Kidaha, Chief Makwaia, 403
Kiewiet, Professor Cornelis de, 496 n., 917
Kikuyu tribe, 286, 289, 291, 297, 298, 312, 324, 333, 346, 347, 348, 349, 364-367, 370, 399, 402, 428; the Mau Maus, 358-378; women of, 295-296
Kikuyu Central Association, 366
Kikuyu Independent Schools Association, 366, 368, 377
Kikuyu Land Unit, 320-321
Kilimanjaro, Mount, 286, 304, 396-398
Kilimanjaro and Its People (Dundas), 304 n., 914
Kilimanjaro Native Co-operative Union, Ltd., 400, 403
Kimberley, 488 n., 494, 550, 553
Kimble, George H. T., ix, 906, 907
Kindu, 650-651
King, Charles Dunbar Burgess, 861, 864
King, Mackenzie, 602-603, 798, 918, 921
King-Hall, Sir Stephen, 535, 917
King Solomon's Mines, 687-688
King's African Rifles, 349, 370, 375, 422, 641, 642, 749 n.
King's College, Uganda, 428
Kingsley, Mary H., 696
Kinnear, George, 913
Kintamo. *See* Léopoldville
Kipling, Rudyard, 185, 500 n.
Kipsigi tribe, 296, 349 n.
Kipushi, 672, 675
Kisenyi, 681, 682
Kishwamba, 392, 430
Kissi tribe, 872
Kitale, 369
Kitawala Society, 666-667
Kitchen Kaffir, 635
Kitchener, General Sir Horatio, 232, 233, 234, 911
Kitchener School of Medicine, 235

Kitwe, 628 n.
Kivu Lake and region, 312, 649, 653, 681-683
Klerk, Dr. Jan de, 473, 480
Klerk, Susanna de, 473
Klerksdorp, 475, 552 n.
"Klip Kaffirs," 562
Kliptown, 506
Knowing the African (Smith), 297 n., 912
Kochnitsky, Leon, 654 n.
Kofi, King, 823
Koinange, Mbiyo, 894
Koinange, Peter, 366
Kola nut, 780
Kongas, 679, 680
Kongo tribe, 287
Kongola, 651
Konoyale, 853
Koran, 61, 62
Kordofan, 233
Korean war, 277, 281
Kottmann, Miss Matilda, 727, 729, 730
Koutoubia, in Marrakesh, 52
Kraft, Louis, 918
Krapf, Ludwig, 304
Krishna Menon, V. K., 294, 404, 412, 684, 707, 708, 709, 914
Kru tribe, 854, 856, 858
Kruger, Paul, 484, 488-489, 492, 496, 499, 916
Kruger National Park, 385, 386, 499
Krugersdorp, 552
Ksar-es-Souk, 106
Kufra, 182
Kumasi, 823, 830, 833-837
Kutako, Chief Hosea, 566, 917
Kwesi Lamptey, 808

Labonne, Eirik, 84
Labor, convict, 671; contract, 557, 558, 672, 861-864; in diamond fields, 557, 558, 559-560; Firestone policy toward, 866; forced, 520, 587-588, 598, 657, 664, 710, 861-864; migrant, 558-559, 593, 595, 641, 710, 738, 836, 852; organized, *see* Unions, unionization; Union Minière policy toward, 672-673
Labor movement, in Morocco, 83-84, 86; in Rhodesia, 608, 622, 630-631; in the Sudan, 231, 244-245; in Tunisia, 159-160
Labotsibeni, 579
Lacoste, Charles, 73
Lacoste, Francis, 72, 73
Ladgham, Bahi, 159 n.
Ladysmith, 496
La Galite, 158
Lagendyk, Miss, 727
Lagos, 741, 742, 747, 748, 754, 755-759, 760, 764, 768, 876
Lalla Aisha, 29
Lalla Henia, 25
Lalla Malikn, 29

Lambaréné, 696, 703, 704, 713, 715, 717, 719-720, 721
Land and Population in East Africa (Mitchell), 913
Land problems and policies, in Egypt, 195; in Kenya, 318-322, 330 n.; in Liberia, 860; in Nigeria and the Gold Coast, 741-742; in Uganda, 423-424
Landau, Rom, 907, 909
Langewiesche, Wolfgang, 799 n.
Lanaka, 570
"Language Clearing Center," 747
Languages, 6; Afrikaans, 454, 461-463, 468; Akan, 799; Amharic, 6, 250, 259, 261, 856 n.; Arabic, 39, 59-60, 63 n.; Bantu, 6, 287-288, 707; Bemba, 625; Berber, 6, 66, 782, 856 n.; Bini, 746; of the drums, *see* Drums and tomtoms; Efik, 746; Ewe, 229, 819; Fulani, 746; Ga, 819; Galla, 782; Geez, 261 n.; Hausa, 746, 760, 782; Ibibio, 746; Ibo, 746; Kanuri, 746; Kele, 288; Lingala, 648, 675; Lozi, 625; Luganda, 287; Mashona, 625; Matabele, 625; Negro, 6, 287; Nyanja, 625; Osmania, 284; Pidgin English, 738-740; Ruanda, 684; Sobo, 746; Somali, 782; Sudanese, 229, 707; Swahili, 287-288, 648; Tamachek, 6, 135, 856 n.; Tigrinya and Tigré, 278; Tonga, 625; Twi, 229, 799, 819, 834; Urhobo, 746; Vai, 6, 856; Wolof, 878; Yoruba, 229, 746; Zulu, 287
Languages and Press of Africa (MacDougald), 856 n.
Lao-tse, 731
Lapaillonne, Colonel René de Benoit de, 152 n.
Laperrine, Mount, 134
Lari, 374
Larrabee, Eric, 669, 895, 921
Lashing, 778. *See also* Flogging
Last Chance in Africa (Farson), 335 n., 366 n., 377 n., 907, 912, 914, 916
Lathbury, Major General G. W., 373 n.
Latimer, Hugh, 314 n.
Laubach method, 821
Lavigerie, Cardinal Charles, 143
Laws, Dr. Robert, 639
Lead, 54, 545, 567
League for Colored Peoples, 218
League of Colored People, 337
League of Nations, 199, 262, 268, 405 n., 456, 550-551, 563, 705, 858, 865
Leakey, Dr. L. S. B., 297 n., 366 n., 370, 912, 913, 914
Lealui, 626
Lebanon, 35 n., 889
Leclerc, General, 166, 697

INDEX

Lecointre, Captain, 133
Legislative Council (LEGCO), 345, 346, 357, 367, 412, 435, 578, 609, 633, 709, 744, 749, 765, 820, 824, 825
Legum, Colin, 373 n., 377 n., 894, 915, 919
Leland, L. C., 920
Lemaignen, Robert, 893
Lemma, Menassi, 272
Lemurs, 600
Lend-Lease, 859
Lennox-Boyd, Alan, 346 n.
Leo X, Pope, 654
Leonardo da Vinci, 712
Leopard-men, 761
Leopards, 382, 384, 389, 390, 622
Leopold II of Belgium, 12, 646, 653-654, 655-657, 660
Léopoldville, 647, 650, 651-652, 662, 663, 666, 691, 692, 888
Leprosy, 308, 722, 723, 724, 728, 789
Leptis Magna, 167, 174
Les Sables-d'Olonne, 127
Lesseps, Ferdinand de, 218
Lettow-Vorbeck, Paul von, 413-416, 563, 914
Levant, 64
Lever interests, 747
Lewanika, Chief, 615, 626
Lewin, Julius, 519, 915
Lewis, Hobart, 895
Lewis, Roy, 826
Leyte, 173
Liberals, in South Africa, 465, 467, 515
Liberation Rally, Egypt, 183, 207, 813 n.
Liberia, 12, 15, 35 n., 743, 795, 843-870, 884, 890; divisions of population of, 855-856; economy of, 864-868; Firestone enterprises in, 864-867; history of, 848-849; opposition to Tubman regime in, 857-858; Point Four in, 350, 868, 869-870; political system of, 856-857; slave traffic in, 11, 861-864
Liberia: A Century of Survival (Buell), 845 n., 861 n., 865 n., 922, 923
Liberia, 1847-1947 (Wilson), 844 n.
Liberia College (University of Liberia), 845
Liberian Frontier Force, 847, 861
Liberian Mining Company, 867
Liberian National Airways, 859
Libreville, 696, 699, 704
Libya, 15, 39, 63, 163-166, 335, 884; American interest in, 164, 179-180; British influence in, 166, 167-168, 175, 176, 177; Egyptian influence in, 164, 173; government of, 175-176; history of, 166-169; independence for, 168, 169-170; Italy in, 164, 166, 167, 168-169; Jews

in, 174, 181-182; King Idris I of, 170-174; nationalism in, 169, 179 n.; Point Four in, 177-179, 181, 350
Lieberson, Goddard, 893
Liesching, Sir Percivale, 472
Life, 907, 911, 916, 917, 919, 921, 923
Life of Sir Richard Burton (Burton), 197 n.
Ligers, 499
Light, Richard U., 914
Lilienthal, David E., 893
Lillie-Costello, J. V. A., 921
Limbe, 640
Limpopo Project, 593
Limpopo River, 620
Limulunga, 626
Limuru, 322
Lincoln University (Pennsylvania), 799, 806
Lindey, Alexander, 895
Lindsay, Vachel, 299, 392, 646, 653
Lingala, 648, 679
"Linguist," 809, 821 n.
Lions, 317, 379-380, 383, 394, 395, 430, 593
Lippmann, Walter, 887 n.
Liquor traffic, 754
Listener, 647 n., 853, 918
Littell, Robert, 895
Livestock raising, 523, 569, 697, 875. *See also* Cattle, Goats, and Sheep
Livingstone, David, 12, 291, 293, 304-305, 336, 348, 354, 409-410, 582, 592, 623, 639, 648, 649, 654, 655
Livingstone (town, Northern Rhodesia), 302, 625
Livingstone's Last Journey (Coupland), 304
Livingstonia, 639
Lizards, 779
Llewellyn, Richard, 913
Lobamba, 579
Lobengula, Chief, 602, 611, 612, 622
Lobi tribe, 872
Lobito, 591
Locations, Johannesburg, 505-509
Locusts, 284, 399
Lomé, 839
London, University of, 762
London Calling (Legum), 377 n.
Longrigg, Stephen H., 255 n.
Look, 909
Loti, Pierre, 107
Louis IX (Saint Louis), 148
Louis XIV, 43
Louis Napoleon, 37
Lourenço Marques, 586, 589, 592, 593-595
Louw, De Villiers, 540
Louw, Eric Hendrik, 479, 518
Lovanium, 660
Love, Kennett, 193 n., 213 n.
Lovedu tribe, 523
Lozi tribe, 626

Lozithlezi, 579
Lualaba River, 648, 649, 650
Luanda, 598
Luangwa Valley, 625
Lubumbashi, 673
Luce, Governor W. H. T., 912
Ludwig, Emil, 190 n., 196 n., 909
Luethy, Herbert, 122 n., 908
Luganda, 287
Lugard, Lord, 337, 338, 435, 742, 754, 776, 784
Lukiko (parliament) of Uganda, 432, 433, 438-439, 443-444, 445
Luluabourg, 667
Luo tribe, 286, 298, 346
Lusaka, 608, 624-625, 632, 633
Lusson, Father, 144
Luthuli, Chief Albert J., 498, 528-529, 894
Lutterodt's Memorial Inn, 794, 795
Luxor, 230
Lyautey, Marshal Louis Hubert Gonzalve, 38, 42, 45-46, 47, 65, 74, 95, 909
Lyttelton, Oliver, 346, 347, 441, 443, 609, 768, 830

MacArthur, Douglas, 46
McCleery, Hugh, 915
MacDougald, Duncan, Jr., 856 n.
McFarlan, Donald F., 748 n.
Machell, Roger, 895
McKay, Vernon, 761 n., 830 n., 889 n., 893, 910, 920, 921, 923
Mackinder, Sir Halford, 312
Macmillan, W. M., 4, 223, 311, 317 n., 913, 918
Macpherson, Sir John Stuart, 746, 749, 750, 751, 766, 921
Madagascar, 45, 354 n., 599-601
Madani, Si, 95, 96
Mafeking, 582
Mafia Island, 408
Magajin Gari, 788
Maganga, Chief N. A., 640-641
Maghreb-el-Aksa. *See* Morocco
Magic. *See* Black magic
Mahdi of the Sudan, 232, 235, 242-244, 244 n., 355, 911
Maiduguri, 784
Maini, A. N., 425
Majekudunmi, Dr. Adekoye, 749
Maji-Maji rebellion, 410
Makerere College (University College of East Africa), 235, 427-428, 441
Makhzen, 26
Makishi tribe, 626
Makoko, King, 692
Makonnen, Ras, 267
Malagasys, 599, 601
Malakal, 228
Malan, Adolph Gysbert, 514
Malan, Dr. Daniel F., 331, 373, 399, 449, 452, 455, 457, 458, 459, 461, 464, 467-469, 470, 473, 479, 480, 493 n., 501, 503, 512, 514, 515, 517, 519, 552, 564, 614, 791, 916

940 INSIDE AFRICA

Malaria, 76, 308, 727, 735, 736, 869
Malgu Naa, 821
Malherbe, Professor E. G., 497
Malindi, 315
Malinké tribe, 872
Malinowski, Bronislaw, 367
Malnutrition, 308, 432, 508. See also Diet
Malraux, André, 129
Malvern, Lord. See Huggins, Sir Godfrey
Mammy-cloth, 832
Mammy wagons, 761
Mamounia Hotel, Marrakesh, 52
Man Eaters of Tsavo, The (Patterson), 380 n.
Manan, Empress, 268-269, 270
Manchester *Guardian. See Guardian,* Manchester
Mandau tribe, 560
Mandingo tribe, 10, 744
Manduza, 301
Manganese, 5, 54, 545, 546, 567, 596, 696, 825, 826, 837, 875
Mangat, N. S., 326
Mangbeto tribe, 287, 648
Mangia tribe, 699
'Mantsebo Seeiso, Amelia, 573-574, 575-576
Marabouts, 61
Marchand, Colonel, 233 n.
Marco Polo, 325
Mardazmach Asfa Wasan, Crown Prince of Ethiopia, 269
Marealle, Chief Tom, 398, 402, 403, 406
Maritz, Gert, 497
Marquard, Leo, 462 n., 463 n., 464 n., 479 n., 482 n., 515, 518 n., 530 n., 915, 918
Marrakesh, 46, 52-54, 102, 755; Pasha of, 24, 31-32, 33. 36, 37, 52, 92-98, 100, 101, 115
Marriage, mixed, 465, 482, 665, 749, 829 n., 882
Marriage customs, 57, 64, 68-70, 296-297, 680. See also Sex customs
Marshall Plan, 54, 708
Martin, Lieutenant Colonel B. W., 916
Martin, Kingsley, 907, 913, 921
Martin, Peter Bird, 918
Marvel, Tom, 919
Marwick, Brian, 917
Marx, 731-732, 794
Masai, Bitwoded Andargachaw, 269, 280
Masai tribe, 8, 229, 286, 298, 318, 319, 320, 370, 375, 400-402, 685
Maseru, 578
Masfin Makonnen, Prince, 269
Mashona, Mashonaland, 301, 612, 621
Mason, Robert, 920
Masonry, 470
Massawa, 248, 278 n., 280
Massouna, Abdel Khalek, 213

Masters and Servants Act, South Africa, 506 n.
Matabele, Matabeleland, 287, 611, 612, 621, 626
Matadi, 650
Mateinzo, Eduardo Anze, 279
Mathew, Archbishop David, 913
Mathu, E. W., 346, 367
Matopo Hills, 612, 622
Matriarchal system of inheritance, 136
Matsieng, 576
Matthews, Dr. Z. K., 523, 916
Mau Mau uprising, 17, 286 n., 293, 296, 310, 311, 327, 332-333, 336, 341, 342, 348, 358-378, 399, 458-459, 615, 752, 773, 885
Mau Mau and the Kikuyu (Leakey), 297 n., 366 n.
Mauretania, 39, 873-874, 881
Mauretania (Sitwell), 53, 149 n., 167 n.
Mauriac, François, 50
Mauritius, 356
Mawanda, Prince George, 439
Mawenzi, Mount, 396
Mbabane, 579
Mbandzeni, King, 580
Mbarara, 430
M'Boom tribe, 699
Mbunda tribe, 287
Meadowlands, 509
Meakin, Budgett, 908
Meals, Arab, 98-101. See also Diet
Mealy bug, 797, 825-826
Mecca, pilgrimages to, 777-778
Measuring Ethiopia (Coon), 252
Mechoui, 100
Medicine man, 299. See also Witch doctors and witchcraft
Meeker, Oden, 373 n., 795 n., 844 n., 915, 917, 921, 922
Meeker, Olivia, 795 n., 844 n., 922
Méharistes, 144
Mehdi, Si, 97
Meknes, 43, 51, 52
Mellor, F. H., 47 n., 907, 908
Melotti beer, 279
Men in the Tropics (Evans), 434 n.
Mende tribe, 743
Mendès-France, Pierre, 73-74, 128, 129, 155, 156, 161, 702 n.
Menelik I of Ethiopia, 253
Menelik II of Ethiopia, 252, 265, 267
Meru, Mount, 396 n., 398
Meru tribe, 298, 349 n.
Messalis, 127
Methodists, 460
Metatorbernite, 674
Meyer, Hans, 397
Meyerowitz, Eva L. R., 821 n., 922
Microbe Hunters (de Kruif), 736 n.

Middle class, African, 653, 666, 672-673
Middle Congo, 696, 699
Middle East, 14
Middle East Defense Organization (MEDO), 214, 215, 250
Middle East Journal, 156 n., 910
Middle Eastern Affairs, 40 n., 215 n.
Midelt, 106
Midway, USS, 521
Millar-Craig, Captain Hamish, 829 n.
Miller, Hymie, 503
Millin, Sarah Gertrude, 456 n., 491 n., 611 n., 612 n., 916, 917, 918
Milotte, A. S., 914
Milton, 315, 379
Mina tribe, 872
Minerals, 5; in Angola, 597 n.; in the Congo, 647, 670, 671, 674; in the Gold Coast, 738, 741, 825, 826, 827; in Liberia, 867; in Morocco, 54; in Nigeria, 738, 741, 785, 786; in the Rhodesias, 620; South Africa, 545, 546; in South-West Africa, 562, 567; in Swaziland, 581. See also Coal and various metals: Copper, Gold, etc.
Mining, in the Congo, 661, 670, 671-673, 674-675, 676-677; in French Equatorial Africa, 696; in French Guinea, 874; in the Gold Coast, 836-837; in Liberia, 848, 867; in Nigeria, 786; in Morocco, 39, 54; in South Africa, 546-549, 551, 552, 557, 558, 559. See also Copperbelt, Gold, and Diamonds
Miscegenation, 465; fear of, 464. See also Marriage, mixed
Misr. See Egypt
Mission schools, 519, 784, 799, 870
Missionaries, 12, 13, 64, 256, 258, 298, 304-306, 354, 366, 397, 410, 425, 433, 434, 528, 564, 576, 582, 592, 610, 639, 659, 696, 748 n., 769, 838, 844 n., 845, 872 n.
Mistletoe, 797 n.
Mistos (Misturados), 591
Mitchell, Sir Philip, 288-289, 329, 340, 371, 372 n., 913
Mitzic, 704
Mixed marriage. See Marriage, mixed
Mixed Marriages Act, South Africa, 482
Mixed society, 338, 464, 475, 699, 758, 829, 883
Mlanji Mountain, 639
Mochesela Khoto, 570-571
Modern Slavery, A (Nevinson), 917

INDEX 941

Modern Traveller, The, ix, 163, 285, 379, 906
Moffat, Robert, 582
Mogadiscio, 282
Mohair, 569
Mohammadu Sansusi, Chiroma of Kano, 779 n., 780
Mohammed (the Prophet), 22, 61-62
Mohammed, Si, Caid of Ait Ourir, 97
Mohammed V (Mohammed Ben Youssef) of Morocco, 26-35, 94, 95, 115, 601
Mohammed VI (Mohammed Ben Moulay Arafa el Alaoui) of Morocco, 20, 22-26, 34, 35, 36-37, 94
Mohammed Ahmed. See Mahdi of the Sudan
Mohammed Ali of Egypt, 195-196, 232, 910
Mohammed ben Maziàm, 117
Mohammed bin Abdullah, 282
Mohammed El Mokri, Grand Vizier of Morocco, 37
Mohammed Lamine Pasha. See Tunis, Bey of
Mohammedanism, 6, 60-65, 217, 531, 890. See also Islam and Moslems
Mokhehle, Ntsu, 578
Moluccas, 356
Mombasa, 311, 315, 325, 350, 373 n.
Moncef, Mohammed El, 151
Mongu, 302
Monk, General, Duke of Albemarle, 110
Monkeys, 382, 388, 391
Monnerville, Gaston, 702 n.
Monroe, James, 843, 848
Monroe Doctrine, 892
Monrovia, 180, 843, 859-860
Monsoons, 356
Montagne, Robert, 65 n.
Moolman, Henry M., 915
Moon, Henry Lee, 893
Moors, 21-22, 39, 40, 58, 59, 112, 874
Moors, The (Meakin), 908
More from the Primeval Forest (Schweitzer), 720 n.
Morel, E. D., 755 n., 919
Moremi, Mrs. E. P., 582
Morija, 576
Moroccan Horizons (Tolliver), 70 n.
Morocco, 12, 403, 884; Berber population in, 66; civilization of, derived from Europe, 7; cities in, 46-54; color bar in, 79; Communism in, 83-84, 86-88, 92; compared with Algeria, 122-123; divisions and characteristics of, 40-42; economy of, 54-55; French in, 20-21, 24, 26-27, 29-30, 31, 32-37, 38, 45, 72-85, 86, 104, 105, 702-703; government in, 26, 27; history of, 39, 43-46; illiteracy in, 24; Jewish community in, 67; nationalism in, 24, 29, 30, 33, 36, 38, 43, 45, 50, 52, 73, 74, 75-76, 81-86, 87, 90-91, 92, 106, 112, 117, 118, 213; Spanish influence in, 41-42, 51; Spanish Zone of, 35, 68, 71, 113-118; Sultan of, 20, 22-37; United States interest in, 29-30, 35, 48, 49, 88-90, 91, 214; women in, 25, 27-28, 85-86
Morocco under the Protectorate, 46 n.
Moroka, Dr. James, 506, 527-528, 894
Moroka Methodist Missionary Hospital, 527
Moros, 40
Morrison, Herbert, 798
Moru tribe, 228
Moselekatse, King, 611
Moshesh, King, 568, 569, 573, 576
Moshi, 309, 398, 400, 404, 430
Moslem Brotherhood, 184, 207-208, 220, 222, 255
Moslem Confraternities of Morocco, 52
Moslems, 6, 39, 40, 57, 60-65, 144, 171, 785 n.; in British West Africa, 738; in Egypt, 186; in Eritrea, 278, 280; in Ethiopia, 253, 254-255; in French West Africa, 872, 883; in the Gambia, 744; in the Gold Coast, 819; in Kenya, 325; in Liberia, 856; in Mozambique, 592; in Nigeria, 760, 776, 777-778, 782, 784; in Somaliland, 281, 282; in Tanganyika, 412; in Uganda, 434; women among, 296; in Zanzibar, 242, 353. See also Islam and Mohammedanism
Mosquitoes, 652, 720, 725, 728, 735, 736, 740, 869
Mossi tribe, 872
Mouila, 703, 704
Moulay Hafid, Sultan, 37
Moulay Hassan, 25, 29, 30
Moulay Hassan Ben Ali Quazzani, Pasha of Port Lyautey, 48
Moulay Hassan Ben el Mahedi, Khalifa of Spanish Morocco, 114
Moulay Ismail, Sultan, 43-44, 52
Moulin, General Boyer de Latour du, 161
Mountains of the Moon, 425-426, 656, 681, 752
Mousson, 872
Movement for Triumph of Democratic Liberties (MTLD), 127, 129
Moxon, R. J., 922
Mozambique, 18, 559, 585, 586, 587, 589 n., 590, 591 n., 592-596

Mozart, 731
Mpadi, Simon, 667
Mpi, Jackson, 769
Mtwara, 408
Mubwa, 302
Mufulira mine, 628, 629
Mujaji, 523
Mulattoes, 590-591, 637, 710, 740
Mulira, Enoch E. K., 421, 913, 915
Mulligan, Colonel H. W., 786
Multiracial government, 346-347, 378
Multiracial society, 338-339, 352, 403, 406, 515, 542, 603, 604, 606-607, 608, 609, 614, 615, 619, 638
Munali (school), 624-625
Muntasir, Mahmoud Bey, 176
Münzinger, Baron, 278 n., 912
Murabet, Mohammed, 60 n.
Murad, 151
Musaka, Ham, 434
Musazi, Ignatius K., 440, 443
Muscat, 354 n., 355; Sultan of, 354, 355
Music, 308, 309, 625 n.
Mussolini, Benito, 146, 168, 169, 267, 268, 278, 698
Mustafa ben Halim, 176
Mutara III Rudahigwa, Charles, 686-687
Mutesa I of Buganda, 433-434
Mutesa II of Buganda, 438
Mutilation, as punishment, 657
Mutual Security Program, 177, 848
Muumbi, 371
Mwadui, 417
Mwalule, 302
Mwambutsa, 688
Mwami, of Ruanda, 686-687; of Urundi, 688
Mwanawina III of the Barotse, 626
Mwanga, 434, 435
Mwaniki, H. Muoria, 894
Mwanza, 417
Mwians, 407 n.
My African Journey (Churchill), 320 n., 421, 429 n.
Mysticism, 59
M'zabites, 121, 133

Nadiope, William Wilberforce Kajumbala, 433 n.
Nabagereka of Buganda, 438, 443
Nagasaki, 669
Nagelmackers interests, 660
Nagogo, Osuman, Emir of Katsina, 787-788
Naguib, General Mohammed, 61, 183, 184, 185, 187, 188, 191, 195, 200, 204, 205, 206, 208, 209-212, 213, 214, 242, 911
Nahas Pasha (Mustafa el Nahas), 199, 200, 207
Nairobi, 286, 310, 314, 317, 321, 322-324, 328-329, 341, 347, 350,

942 INSIDE AFRICA

351, 352, 369, 374, 386-387, 414
Nakuru, 331
Nalinya of Buganda, 439
Namaqualand, 558
Nandi tribe, 286, 298
Napier expedition, 252
Nasser, General Gamal Abdul, 30, 173, 183, 184, 185, 186, 188, 191, 192, 194, 195, 196 n., 197-198, 200, 201-209, 212, 213, 214, 215, 217, 221, 222, 242, 803 n., 911
Natal, 290, 300, 450, 469, 496-498, 531, 532, 539; University of, 497, 519
Nathoo, Ibrahim E., 326, 347, 894
Nation, 700 n., 907, 910, 919, 920
National Association for the Advancement of Colored People, 893
National Council for the Colony of Sierra Leone (NCCS), 743
National Council of Nigeria and the Cameroons (NCNC), 767, 768, 772
National Geographic Magazine, 907, 911, 919, 920
National Independence party ("Nippers"), Nigeria, 767
National Parks, Albert, 385, 682; Gorongosa, 593; Kafue, 625; Kruger, 385, 386, 499; Queen Elizabeth, 392-393; Tsavo, 386, 395. *See also* Game reserves
National Unity party, the Sudan, 244, 245
Nationalism, 3, 7, 13, 14, 19, 883, 885, 887, 888; Afrikaner, 560-561, 567; Arab, 63, 65; in Basutoland, 569, 578; in British Somaliland, 282; in British West Africa, 740; in Egypt, 183, 185, 196, 198, 233; Egyptian fostering of, in other countries, 217; in French Equatorial Africa, 699; in the Gambia, 744-745; in the Gold Coast, 790, 791, 793, 795, 797, 798, 800-806, 810-811, 813, 815, 816, 817, 818, 824, 826, 827, 830, 839; in Kenya, 326, 327, 348, 366, 372; in Liberia, 867; in Libya, 169, 179 n.; in Madagascar, 601; Mohammedanism and, 65; Moroccan, 24, 29, 30, 33, 36, 38, 43, 45, 50, 52, 73, 74, 75-76, 81-86, 87, 90-91, 92, 106, 112, 117, 118, 213, 703; in Nigeria, 748, 750-752, 755, 764, 766, 767-768, 771, 772, 773, 784; in Portuguese Africa, 586, 596; in Rhodesia, 616, 618, 627; in Sierra Leone, 743-744; in Somalia, 283, 284; in South Africa, 454, 455, 456-458, 466, 467, 468, 480, 511, 518, 525, 527; Sudanese, 227, 229, 233, 240; Tunisian, 38,

147, 152, 153, 154, 155, 156-160, 161, 213, 703; in Uganda, 435, 444; West Coast, 608; white, 608, 887 (*see also* Nationalism, Afrikaner, *and* Nationalism, in South Africa) Afrikaner, and Nationalism, in South Africa)
Nationalism in Africa (Hemingford), 920
National party, South Africa, 460, 467, 469, 470, 471, 473, 474, 480, 483, 495, 500, 503, 511, 512, 519, 526, 527, 530, 531, 560, 564, 566
Nationalization, of industry, 423, 558; of railways, 770
Native Lands Trust Board, 320
Native Life in South Africa, 917
Native Purchase Area, 634
Native Recruiting Corporation, 577
Native reserves, 320-321, 322, 323, 486 n., 494, 496, 516, 522-525, 536, 626
Natural resources, 5; in Angola, 597 n.; in Basutoland, 577; in the Congo, 647, 670, 671, 674; in Ethiopia, 261-262; in French Equatorial Africa, 696; in the Gold Coast, 738, 825, 826, 827; in Liberia, 867; in Morocco, 54; in Nigeria, 738, 785, 786; in the Rhodesias, 620 (*see also* Copperbelt); in South Africa, 488; in Swaziland, 581
Nazism, 31 n., 457, 467, 470, 482, 565
Nchanga mine, 628, 629
Ndhlovukati, 579
Ndola, 627, 666
Ndonga tribe, 287
Nechiskwa, 301
Necrophagy, 627, 640
Negrillos, 699
Negro Art in the Belgian Congo (Kochnitsky), 654 n.
Negro languages, 6
Negroes, 5, 10, 285, 286, 287; aesthetic sensibility of, 309; American, 11, 80, 521, 636, 735, 753; as bishops and priests, 654, 660; in British West Africa, 738; in the Congo, 648; in Dahomey, 875; economic opportunity for, 662, 663, 666, 667; in French Equatorial Africa, 694; in high positions, 702 n.; intelligence and educability of, 293-294, 480, 537; Islam and, 64; as an issue in South Africa, 458, 459; in Morocco, 39; origin of, 10; in Portuguese Africa, 590; in the Sudan, 227. *See also* Bantu Africa
Nehru, Jawaharlal, 61, 326, 327, 464, 512, 532, 637, 774, 892
Nelson, Lord, 110
Néo-Destour, 147, 155, 156-158, 160, 161

Neser, John, 563
Netherlands, on Committee of Control for Tangier, 111. *See also* Dutch
Netherlands India (Furnivall), 338 n.
Neutralism, 92, 214, 250, 891, 892
Nevinson, Henry W., 449, 598, 917
News Chronicle, 150 n.
New Congo, The (Marvel), 919
New Deal, 794
New Era, 920
New Leader, 83 n., 912
New Statesman, 83 n., 142 n., 149, 283, 443 n., 673, 826, 907, 910, 911, 912, 913, 914, 916, 917, 918, 920, 921
New Times (Moscow), 801
New Yorker, 795 n., 844 n., 909, 914, 921, 922
Newman, Bernard, 908
Newman, C. M., 918
Newmont Mining Company, 566-567
Newsletter of the Federation of Rhodesia and Nyasaland, 918
Newspapers, in Africa, *Alger Republicain,* 127; in Angola, 598; Associated Negro Press, 801; *Bantu Forum,* 498; *Burger,* 468, 474, 475; *Cape Argus,* 504; *Cape Times,* 504; *Daily Service,* 751, 771; *Daily Spectator,* 828 n.; *Daily Success,* 751; *Drum,* 505, 523, 528 n.; *Falaq,* 356; in French Equatorial Africa, 694; *Friend* (Liberia), 857, 858, 866; *Friend* (Orange Free State), 500, 916; in the Gold Coast, 828 n., 830-831, 836; *Kenya Weekly News,* 335 n.; in Liberia, 851, 853, 857, 858, 866; in Nigeria, 750-751, 758, 761, 771, 772; *Rand Daily Mail,* 504; in Rhodesia, 621; in South Africa, 504-505, 522; *Star* (Johannesburg), 504, 917; *Sun* (Cape Town), 530; *Transvaler,* 473, 479, 499, 537; *West African Pilot,* 750-751
N'gola, King, 597
Ngorongoro, 386
Ngubane, Jordan K., 498, 528 n.
Ngwenyama of Swaziland, 579
Niamey, 876
Nicholls, Senator Heaton, 497
Nichols, Colonel, 676
Nietzsche, 38
Niger Coast Protectorate, 754
Niger Office, 874
Niger Province, 876
Niger River, 738, 752, 753, 760, 871
Nigeria, 6, 11, 12, 15-16, 17, 49 n., 63, 316, 336, 337, 338, 340, 365, 404, 428, 435, 436, 621, 735, 738, 740, 741-742, 746-764, 885, 886; absence of

INDEX

color bar in, 748-750, 757-758; the East, 760-761, 766, 767; German interest in, 217; government and politics of, 748, 765-775, 785; history of, 752-755; Lagos, capital of, 755-759; nationalism in, 748, 750-752, 755, 764, 766, 767-768, 771, 772, 773, 775, 784; the North, 776-789; subdivisions of, 759-760; the West, 761-764, 766, 767, 773
Nigeria, 763 n., 921
Nigeria (Morel), 755 n.
Nigeria League of Bribe Scorners, 759
Nigerian Handbook, 775
Nigerian Union of Teachers (NUT), 770
Nigerian Yearbook, 921
Nile, The (Ludwig), 190 n., 196 n., 909
Nile River, 12, 193, 223-226, 421, 433, 445, 654
Nile Waters Agreement, 226
Nilotic peoples, 228, 229, 286, 401, 425, 684, 686, 699, 762
Njoku, Eni, 769
Njoro, 317
Nkana mine, 628, 630
Nkanga, 299
Nkroful, 799
Nkrumah, Dr. Kwame, 30, 367, 368, 790-806, 808, 809-811, 812, 813, 814, 816, 817-818, 820, 826, 827, 832, 834, 838, 839, 877, 886, 895, 921
Nksoke Molapu, 576
Nkumbula, Harry, 627
Nolte, Richard H., 910
Non-violence, 534, 606 n., 642, 643. *See also* Civil disobedience *and* Passive resistance.
Norman, Oscar, 856
North Africa, 7, 38; conquests in, 39; European character of, 39-40. *See also various countries.*
North Africa (Brodrick), 64 n., 66 n., 907
North African Prelude (Welch), 44 n.
North Korea, 889 n.
Northern Elements Progressive Union (NEPU), 784
Northern Frontier Province, Kenya, 312
Northern People's Congress, Nigeria, 784
Northern Rhodesia, 16, 302, 603, 606, 607, 608, 609, 610, 614, 615, 616, 617, 618, 624-632, 633, 638, 640, 666; Copperbelt in, 551, 603, 614, 616, 618 n., 626, 628-632, 641; South Africans in, 626, 630. *See also* Central African Federation, Rhodesias *and* Southern Rhodesia
Northern Rhodesia, 626

Northern Rhodesia African Mineworkers Trade Union, 631
Northern Rhodesia Mineworkers Union, 630
Northern Rhodesian National Congress, 627
Northern Territories, Gold Coast, 819, 820, 821, 824
Norwegians, in Ethiopia, 256
Note on Tanganyika and the Constitutional Issue, A (Hitchcock), 914
Nouasseur, 89
Nova Lisboa, 598
Nsibirwa, Martin Luther, 440
Nsuta, 837
N'Tchorere, Captain, 696
Nts'ekhe, N. M., 578
Nubians, 187
Nuer tribe, 228
Numidians, 167
Nwapa, Chukudifu, 769
Nxumalo, Henry, 523
Nyamkomaduewuo, Queen Mother, 823
Nyanja tribe, 287, 625
Nyanza tribe, 346
Nyasa, Lake, 312, 638
Nyasa tribe, 291
Nyasaland, 6, 16, 336, 558, 592, 596, 603, 606 n., 607, 617, 618, 619, 638-645
Nyasaland African Congress, 645
Nyasaland Calling, 918
Nyasaland National Congress, 627
Nyerere, Julius K., 412
Nyeri Reserve, 320
Nylstroom, 473
Nyzam of Hyderabad, 325
Nzima area, 799

Oases, 140, 141, 142-144, 180, 182
Oath taking, 361-364
Obani-Ukoma, Sunday W., 769
Observer, 65 n., 125 n., 202 n., 314 n., 337, 367 n., 373 n., 456 n., 478 n., 482 n., 583 n., 894, 908, 909, 910, 911, 913, 915, 916, 918, 921
Obuasi, 836
Ocran, Turkson, 817
Odede, F. W., 346, 367
O'Donovan, Patrick, 918, 921
Office du Niger, 874
Ogaden Province, 284
Ogbomosho, 762, 770
Ogoja Province, 738
Ogowe River, 696, 719
Ogun, 763 n.
Ohanga, A. B., 347
Ohne, Miss Rosebud, 829 n.
Oil (petroleum), in Algeria, 121-122; in Mozambique, 593; in Saudi Arabia, 213; search for: in Egypt, 191; in Ethiopia, 258; in Kenya, 350; in Tanganyika, 408
Oil, palm, 5, 647, 680, 696, 738, 747, 875, 876; peanut, 777
Oil Rivers Protectorate, 754
Okapi, 689

Ol Tukai, 389
"Old Turbans," 156
Oliver, Roland, 915
Olorun, 763
Olympio, Sylvanus E., 700 n., 839-840, 894
Oman, 354
Omar, Caliph, 62
Omar Al Mukhtar, 168
Ombo, Governor of, 269
Omdurman, 232, 234, 235, 243
Omine tribe, 699
Onchocerciasis, 308, 426, 828, 869
One Hundred Great Lives, 834
1001 Facts about the Sudan, 228 n., 236 n.
Oni of Ife, 763
Oolen, 675
Open Door in China, 892
"Operation Anvil," 374
Oppenheimer, Sir Ernest, 549-551, 552, 557, 558, 894
Oppenheimer, Lady, 549, 550
Oppenheimer, Frank, 550
Oppenheimer, Harry F., 550, 551
Oppenheimer, Sir Michael, 550
Oppenheimer interests, 417, 499, 514, 547, 548, 562, 628, 632, 917
Optima, 554
Oran, 120
Orange Free State, 450, 459, 485, 486, 488, 500-501, 516, 527, 539, 548-549, 552 n.
Orange River, 487, 488, 557, 577
Order of the British Empire (OBE), 349
Orfori Atta, W. E. A., 808
Oriental Province, 653
Orlando, 506, 535
Ormerod, Major C. B., 893
Oryx, 389
Oshogbo, 762
Osmania, 284
Ossewa Brandwag, 467
Ostriches, 389, 391
Othman, Caliph, 62
Othman Dan Fodio, 782
OTRACO (Office d'Exploitation des Transports Coloniaux), 662
Otumfuo, the Asantehene, Nana Sir Osei Agyeman Prempeh II, 833-836
Ouagadougou, 875
Ouarzazate, 103, 104, 105
Oudtshoorn, 495
Ouidah, 599
Oujda, 53, 54
Ouled Nails, 121 n.
Our Council of Ministers (Ikoli), 769 n.
Out of My Life and Thought (Schweitzer), 715 n., 717 n., 718 n., 920
Out of the Primeval Forest (Schweitzer), 730 n.
Outline of History, The (Wells), 907, 908
Ovambo tribe, 287, 562
Overgrazing, 523. *See also* Cattle

944 INSIDE AFRICA

Owen Falls, 224; Hydroelectric Scheme, 421, 445-446
Oyo, Alafin of, 763

Paarl, 493
Padmore, George, 803 n., 804 n., 894, 907, 912, 921
Pahouin tribe, 699
Paintings, rock, 10-11, 404. *See also* Art
Pakistan, 35 n., 80, 215, 314, 335, 889
Palestine, partition of, 115 n.
Palm oil, 5, 647, 680, 696, 738, 747, 875, 876
Pambla tribe, 699
Pan-African sentiment, 886
Pan-American World Airways, 755
Pangani River, 399
Pankhurst, E. Sylvia, 283, 912
Pant, Shri Apa B., 327, 894
Paradise Lost (Milton), 315, 379
Parent, Pierre, 908
Paris Evangelical Mission, in Basutoland, 576
Park, Mungo, 736, 753, 920
Parrinder, Geoffrey, 922
Parsees, 325
Partito Democratico Somalo, 283
Pashas, 27, 33, 36, 183 n., 194-195
Pass laws, 519-520, 534, 640
Passfield, Lord (Sidney Webb), 334-335
"Passing," 530
Passive resistance, 37, 327, 528, 533, 634, 642
Pastilla, 100-101
Patel, A. B., 326, 347
Paternalism, Belgian, 664, 688
Path to Nigerian Freedom (Awolowo), 774
Paton, Alan, 455, 466 n., 479, 510 n., 515, 538, 884, 894, 916, 923
Patronage, political, 857
Patten, J. W., 916
"Pawning," 862-864
Payne, Charles R., 911
Payne, John Howard, 148
Peanuts, peanut oil, 738, 777, 873, 881
Pemba, 353, 356
Pendergast, Boss, 759
Penn, Peter, 292 n., 907
Peoples and Policies of South Africa, The (Marquard), 462 n., 463 n., 464 n., 479 n., 482 n., 518 n., 530 n., 915
Peoples of South Africa, The (Millin), 916, 917
Perham, Margery, 12, 253 n., 262 n., 264, 410 n., 763 n., 907, 911, 913, 923
Périer, G. D., 656 n.
Pétain, 72
Peters, Dr. Karl, 410
Pétillon, Léon A. M., 657, 658, 662, 678, 894
Petits Frères du Sacré Coeur, 134
Peuhl tribe, 699

Phadogenic ulcer, 308
Philip II of Spain, 474 n.
Philippines, 35 n., 889, 892
Philosophy of the Egyptian Revolution, The, 910, 911
Philpotts, Brian, 920
Phoenicians, 11, 39, 167, 254, 822
Phoenix (South Africa), 498
Pholo, 571
Phosphates, 54, 873
Photography, 391-392
Physiology of Man in the Desert (Adolph et al.), 139 n.
Pickering, Neville E., 491
Pidgin English, 738-740
Pietermaritzburg, 497
"Pigmentalists" ("Pigmentocrats"), 464, 522, 532
Pimville, 506
Piracy, 39
Pirow, Oswald, 467
Place to Live, A, 507
Plague, 76, 192
Planned economy, 874
Platinum, 671
Plato, 911
Pliny the Elder, ix
Plomer, William, 490 n., 493 n., 613 n., 916, 918
Plural government, 346-347, 378
Plural society, 9, 338-339, 352, 403, 406, 515
Plutonium, 669
Plywood, 696
Po, Fernao do, 710
Poaching, 385 n., 386 n.
Point Four, 305, 350; in Egypt, 191, 215-216; in Ethiopia, 250, 256, 259, 261, 284; in Liberia, 350, 868, 869-870; in Libya, 177-179, 181, 350
Pointe Noire, 695, 696, 703
Police brutality, South Africa, 519, 520
Policy in Africa, Belgian, 18, 593, 648-649, 657, 662-666, 667; British, 17, 75, 196-198, 229, 239 n., 242 n., 334-357, 403, 435, 574, 575, 617, 700, 766-767, 791 n., 802, 816-817, 885-886, (*see also* Self-government); French, 16-17, 45-46, 67, 74-77, 79, 120, 153, 155, 344, 699-703, 873, 882-883, 884, (*see also* Assimilation, French policy of); Italian, 168-169; Portuguese, 17 (*see also Assimilado* system); Spanish, 116-118
Political development, 4, 9; African and Asian, 923; Arab, 63; in Basutoland, 578; in the Cameroons, 707; in the Congo, 662, 667, 673; in French West Africa, 876-880; in the Gambia, 744; in the Gold Coast, 742, 791, 798; Kikuyu, 366-367; in Madagascar, 600, 601; in Nigeria, 742, 754-755, 760, 775, 785; in the Rhodesias and Nyasaland, 618, 619; in Ruanda-Urundi, 689; in Somalia,

283-284; in South Africa, 525; in Uganda, 440; in Zanzibar, 353. *See also* Nationalism *and* Political parties
Political parties, in the Cameroons, 707; in Egypt, 183, 198, 199, 200, 204, 207, 233, 813 n.; in French West Africa, 877, 878, 879, 881; in the Gambia, 744; in the Gold Coast, 796, 798, 812, 813, 815, 824 (*see also* Convention People's Party (CPP), Gold Coast); in Kenya, 347; in Liberia, 857, 858; in Nigeria, 750, 763, 767, 784 (*see also* Action Group, Nigeria); in Sierra Leone, 743; in Somalia, 283-284; in South Africa, 456, 457-458, 467 (*see also* Nationalist party, South Africa); in Southern Rhodesia, 606; in the Sudan, 244, 245
Political Quarterly, 907
Pollak, Miss May, 549
Polygamy, 57, 64, 70, 296, 365, 680, 685, 821, 833
Pondo tribe, 523, 560
Pondoland, 492, 522
Ponsonby, Miss Eleanor, 916
Ponthierville, 650
Poor white class, South Africa, 466
Population Registration Act, South Africa, 482
Port Elizabeth, 495-496, 517
Port Etienne, 873
Port Gentil, 696, 704, 719, 732
Port Harcourt, 747
Port Lyautey, 48
Port Said, 220
Port Sudan, 230
Porto Novo, 875
Portos, 710
Portugal, on Committee of Control, Tangier, 111
Portuguese, in the Belgian Congo, 648; early explorations and conquests by, 11, 39, 110, 252, 315, 354, 585, 654, 705, 752, 822, 874; in the Gold Coast, 792
Portuguese Africa, 14, 18, 217, 407 n., 558, 585-599, 885. *See also* Angola, Mozambique, *and* Portuguese Guinea
Portuguese Guinea, 598-599
"Positive Action," 803
Post, Laurens van der, 638, 907
Postmasburg, 546
Potchefstroom, 460, 498-499, 548; University of, 561
Poto-Poto district, Brazzaville, 694
Poultry project, 744
Poverty, 8, 108, 125, 163, 291, 292, 311, 405, 437, 587, 598, 744, 781, 820, 832, 845, 846, 849, 889-890
Prain, R. D., 918
Premier Diamond Mining Company, 499, 553, 554, 557
Prempeh I, 823, 824, 833

INDEX 945

Prempeh II, 833-836
Presbyterian Life, 920
President Edward J. Roye, 851
Press. See Newspapers
Prest, Arthur E., 770 n.
Pretoria, 450, 498, 499-500, 521, 528, 888
Pretoria University, 462, 470
Pretorius, Major, 499, 684, 919
Prince Leopold mine, 675
Principe, 588
Pritt, D. N., 347-348, 369
Professional Hunters Association, 390
Progressive, 920
Prohibition, 582. See also Alcohol, ban on
Prohibition of Mixed Marriages Act, South Africa, 482
Prophet in the Wilderness (Hagedorn), 920
Prostitution, 49, 57, 482, 838
Protectorates, British: British Somaliland, 282; High Commission Territories, 336, 568, 582, 611; Kenya, 318, 339; Nigeria, 754; Northern Rhodesia, 615, 624; Nyasaland, 639; Uganda, 318, 422, 435, 436; Zanzibar, 339, 354-355; French: Madagascar, 601; Morocco, 20-21, 38, 45, 81, 702-703; Tunisia, 38, 146; German East Africa, 410-411, 414
Protestant Episcopal church, 845
Protestant missionaries, 305, 434, 435, 659, 707. See also Missionaries
Providence (Liberia), 848
Public Safety and Criminal Law Amendment Acts, South Africa, 482
Punch, 435
Punishment, African attitudes to, 294; in Bechuanaland, 583; collective, 709-710; in the Congo, 657, 664-665; in Nigeria, 778; in Portuguese Africa, 588; in South Africa, 478-479, 520, 534; in Swaziland, 580
Purdah, 109, 123, 243; abolition of, 269 n., 355
Purified Nationalist party, South Africa, 457, 458
Pushkin, 260 n.
Putnam, Patrick, 683
Putput, 149
Pygmies, 286, 683-684, 706
Pygmy hippopotamus, 870
Pyramids, 189-190
Pyrethrum, 400
Pythons, 394, 420, 719

"Quatre Communes," 873
Quawa, 410
Que Que, 918
Quebec, 498, 576
Queen Elizabeth, Queen Mary, 743
Queen Elizabeth Park, 392-393
Quelimane, 592, 593

Quest of the Historical Jesus (Schweitzer), 716
Quist, Sir Emanuel, 796, 807
Quist, Lady, 796

Rabambasai, 422
Rabat, 30, 34, 46-48; Pasha of, 48
Race relations, 14-15, 886-887; British attitudes toward, 347-349; in the Congo, 648-649, 671-672; in the Gold Coast, 793, 811, 824, 828; in Islam, 64; in Kenya, 364, 373; in the Rhodesias, 607-608, 627, 634, 635-636; in South Africa, 457, 458, 463-465, 516-522, 528; in Swaziland 581; in Tanganyika 405-406; and white settlement, 885. See also Color bar
Race versus Reason in South Africa (Lewin), 915
Racial groups, 5
Racial partnership. See Multiracial society
Racial problems in South Africa, UN Commission on, 543
Racial Tensions in South Africa, The (Whyte), 915
Racism, 453, 454, 460, 461, 469, 470, 475, 483, 498, 511, 536. See also Apartheid
Radio, Brazzaville, 694; Dar es Salaam, 407; Lusaka, 625; Tangier, 109
Radio Marina, 280-281
Radium, 674-675
Radziwill, Princess Catherine, 491-492
Railways. See Communication and transportation
Rain, 226, 452, 524, 579, 580, 652, 682, 705, 706, 742, 844, 859, 869; artificial, 690
Rànavàlona III, Queen, 601
Rand Daily Mail, 504
Rand compounds, 558-560
Rand mines, 286, 498, 502, 503, 548, 550, 551, 560, 577
Rangeley, W. H. J., 918
Rankine, Sir John, 914
Ransome-Kuti, Mrs. F., 762
Ras Desta Hospital, Ras Hotel, Addis Ababa, 257
Rassemblement Democratique Africain (RDA), 879
Rats, 399
Rau, Santha Rama, 371 n., 914
Raw materials, 5. See also Natural resources
Reader's Digest, 895, 911
Réalités, 909
Rebmann, Johannes, 304, 397
Red-billed weaver, 623
Red Hand, 158, 159
Red Rubber (Morel), 919
"Red rubber" horrors, 657
Reeves, Right Reverend Ambrose, 507
Rehoboth, 562
Religion, 6; and apartheid, 537; in Arab nationalism, 65; and

art and music, 308, 309; in the Gold Coast, 819; in Morocco, 25; politics and, 242; and racism, 469; in South Africa, 459-461, 462, 524; in tribal affairs, 291; in Uganda, 427, 440 n.; wars in name of, 435. See also Christianity and Islam
Rennie, Sir Gilbert, 918
Report on Africa (Meeker), 373 n., 915, 917
Report of the International Commission of Inquiry into the Existence of Slavery and Forced Labor in the Republic of Liberia, 861 n.
Report on Southern Africa (Davidson), 907, 917, 919
Reporter, 78 n., 170, 371 n., 667 n., 906, 908, 909, 914, 915, 921
Republic Steel, 867
Republican party, South Africa, 467
Republicanism, South Africa, 450, 474, 512-513
Reserves, game. See Game reserves
Reserves, native, 320-321, 322, 323, 486 n., 494, 496, 516, 522-525, 536, 626
Resistance, French, 697, 707
Retief, Pier, 497
Reusch, Dr. R. R., 397
Rhinoceroses, 380, 383, 384, 388, 389, 391, 496, 914
Rhodes, Cecil John, 3, 484, 489-493, 547, 553, 582, 602, 607, 610, 611-613, 621, 622, 623, 639, 916, 917
Rhodes (Millin), 491 n., 611 n., 612 n., 918
Rhodes Centenary Exhibition, 625
"Rhodes Fruit Farms," 492
Rhodes-Livingstone Institute, 625
Rhodes-Livingstone Museum, 625
Rhodes scholarships, 493
Rhodesian Selection Trust, 628, 629, 632
Rhodes University, 519
Rhodes and Rhodesia, The Man and His Movement, 918
Rhodesian Railways, 592, 624
Rhodesias, 306, 339, 378, 602-638; British in 611-614, 615; color bar in, 17, 603, 606, 609, 619, 631-637; the Copperbelt, 628-632; economic situation in, 616, 623-624, 633; history of, 610-615; nationalism in, 616, 618, 627; race relations in, 607-608, 635-636; racial groups in, 636-637; white settlement in, 603, 610, 626. See also Central African Federation, Northern Rhodesia, and Southern Rhodesia
Rhokana Corporation, 628, 629, 630
Ribadu, Mallam Muhammadu, 750
Rice, 581, 680, 876
Rida, Deputy King of Libya, 172

Riebeeck, Jan van, 459, 465, 484, 516
Riebeeck West, 468
Rif, 114
Rift Valley, 312-314, 682
Rijckmans, Pierre, 658, 893
Rimsky-Korsakoff, 731
Rinderpest, 382 n.
Rio de Oro, 118, 873
Rio Muni, 704
Riotous Assemblies Acts, South Africa, 482
Ripon Falls, 421, 445
Rising Wind, A (White), 698 n.
River War, The (Churchill), 224 n., 244 n., 911
Rivlin, Benjamin, 156 n., 157 n.
Road Through the Wilderness, The (Duncan), 915
Roan Antelope mine, 628, 629, 631
Robb, Professor R. L., 318, 913
Roberts, Joseph Jenkins, 849
Roberts Field, 848, 849, 859
Robertson, Sir James, 237, 766 n.
Robertson, T. C., 894, 915
Robeson, Paul, 800
Robeson, Mrs. Paul, 915
Robins, Sir Ellis, 614
Robinson, Jackie, 609
Robinson, Kenneth, 913
Rock paintings, 10-11, 404, 485
Rockefeller Foundation, 193 n.
Rolland, Romain, 731
Roma College, 576
Roman Catholic church, 258, 305, 434, 435, 460, 576, 659-660, 684; schools run by, 587, 659, 660, 799. *See also* Missionaries
Romans, ancient conquests by, 39, 167
Rommel, Marshal, 166, 199
Roosevelt, F. D., 30, 31, 142, 675, 744, 794, 848
Roosevelt, Theodore, 289, 317, 612 n., 914
Roosevelt and Hopkins (Sherwood), 907
Rooyen, Dr. J. C. van, 470
Rosen, Count C. G. von, 277
Rosenberg, Anna, 893
Ross, Albion, 162 n., 412 n., 911, 918
Ross, Dr. Emory, 8 n., 893, 909
Ross, Sir Ronald, 736
Roth, Andrew, 910
Roving Commission, A (Churchill), 232 n., 923
Rowe, B. B., 911
Rowlands, John. *See* Stanley, Henry Morton
Royal Adventurers of England, 744
Royal African Society, 337
Royal East African Navy, 351
Royal Kenya National Parks, 894. *See also* National parks
Royal Niger Company, 754
Roye, Edward J., 851 n.
Ruanda-Urundi, 16, 229, 305, 309, 405 n., 646 n., 684-689
Rubber, 656, 657, 844, 854, 864

Ruben, Um Noyobe, 707
Rudin, Harry R., 8 n., 907, 923
Rudolf, Lake, 312
Rukirabasai Ja, Mukama of Toro, 422 n.
Rusitira, 687
Russell, Nimley, 856
Russia, as enemy of colonialism, 88, 115 n.; manganese production in, 825; Moslem population in, 87; nonparticipation of, in administration of Tangier, 111; not represented in French Africa, 127-128; policy of, in Africa, 86-87, 88; relations of, with African countries, 216, 259-261, 375, 543, 888-889, 890
Ruwenzori Range, 425-426, 429

Saad el Ali scheme, 191
Saba-saba, 625 n.
Sabaean peoples, 255
Sabena, 647 n., 661, 666
Sabratha, 167, 174
S.A.C. Club, Monrovia, 850
Sachs, E. S., 541, 542-543, 917
Sacks, Marcus, 916
Sadek, Si, 97, 98
Safari, 388-392, 593, 626; "gameviewing," 391
Safariland, Ltd., 388 n., 390
Safi, 55 n.
Sagittarius, 201, 911
Sahara, 7, 121, 130-145, 150, 752; communication in, 131; search for oil in, 122; Spanish, 118; travel across, 138-142, 144-145
St. Germain en Laye, Treaty of, 376 n.
St. Louis (French West Africa), 873
Salah, 140, 141
Salazar, Dr. Antonio de Oliveira, 586, 918
Salé, 39, 48
Saleite, 674
Salem, Dr. Ben, 152
Salem, Major Salah, 213, 216, 242
Salisbury, 286, 352, 491, 591, 604, 605, 612, 620, 621, 623, 633-634
Salisbury, Lord, 150, 354, 613
Salisbury, Marquis and Marchioness of, 894
Saloway, Sir Reginald, 803, 921
Salvador de Sá and the Struggle for Brazil and Angola, 1602-1686 (Boxer), 918
Sam (El Sayed Sir Ali Mirghani Pasha), 242, 243
Sam Kahn Speaks, 541, 915
Samaii, Davis, 521
Sambo, the Ciroma of Hadejia, 769
Samson, Prince, 269
Sand Sea of Calanscio, 182
Sandford, Christine, 912
Sanford, General Henry S., 656 n.
Sangala, J. S., 645
Sansanding Dam, 874
Sanusi of Cyrenaica, The (Evans-Pritchard), 168 n.

Sao Jorge del Mina, 822
Sao Tomé, 588
Sar (El Sayed Sir Abdel Rahman el Madhi Pasha), 242-244
Sarakolé tribe, 872
Sardauna of Sokoto, 768, 784
Sari tribe, 699
Sarro range, 104
Saturday Evening Post, 799 n., 911, 913
Saturday Review of Literature, 910, 923
Saudi Arabia, 35 n., 41, 163, 213
Sauer, Paul Olivier, 480
Saurat, Denis, 289, 304, 697 n.
Sbanya, 273
Scandinavian Lutherans, 258
Scarification, 303-304, 688, 697, 820
Schacht, Dr. Hjalmar Horace Greeley, 217
Schatzman, 728
Scherman, Mr. and Mrs. Harry, 893
Scheyven, Robert, 894, 919
Schistosomiasis, 193
Schlamm, William S., 909
Schlesinger, I. W. and John, 503
Schmaltz, Governor, 873
Schmidt, Dana Adams, 191 n.
Schoeman, Barend Jacobus, 480, 916
Scholtz, Dr. G. D., 537
Schubert, 731
Schuller, Mr. and Mrs. Erwin, 916
Schuman, 155
Schweitzer, Dr. Albert, 11, 56, 696, 712-734, 895, 920; attitudes of, 731-733; hospital of, 714, 719, 720, 721-722, 724-730; life and work of, 715-721; philosophy of, 720, 731; quoted, 712, 715, 724, 731, 732, 733
Scientific Council for Africa South of the Sahara, 336-337
Scoones, General R. D., 240
Scotland, Church of, 639; settlers from, in Nyasaland, 639
Scott, Reverend Michael, 337, 507-508, 564-565, 606 n., 642-644, 894, 915, 917, 919
Scott, Ohlin and Robert K., 259
Scottish Mission church, 640
Sears, Mason, 284, 710
Sébha, 166, 173
Sectionalism, 747, 766, 783, 873
Seed, William H., 263 n., 912
Seeiso, 573
Segregation, 79, 338, 619; absence of, in Uganda, 424; in the Congo, 652; defense of, 521-522; of Indians, 532, 533; in Nairobi, 328-329; in Rhodesia, 606, 609, 632-637; on social level, 589; in South Africa, 454, 457, 459, 464, 469, 475, 509, 536, 537, 543. *See also Apartheid and* Color bar
Segura, Francisco (Pancho), 521

INDEX

Sekgoma II, 583
Sekia el Hamra, 118
Sekondi, 799
Self-determination, 74, 892
Self-government, 14, 15-16, 185, 348, 886, 887; for Basutoland, 578; British policy of training for, 17, 334-335 (*see also* Policy in Africa, British); for British West Africa, 885; for the Gold Coast, 742, 804, 805, 806, 808-811, 812; gradual movement toward, 153, 155, 218, 892; for Kenya, 331, 349; for Morocco, 81, 85, 106, 117; for Nigeria, 742, 765, 767, 768, 772, 773, 775, 784, 785; for Northern Rhodesia and Nyasaland, 618, 645; for Southern Rhodesia, 605, 614, 617, 618, 624; for the Sudan, 239, 240, 245; for Tanganyika, 411, 413; for Uganda, 444
Selous, Frederick Courteney, 612, 621
Seme, Dr. P. I., 527
Semitic languages, 6, 59-60
Semitic peoples, 38, 39, 255
Semliki River, 681
Senegal, 293, 873, 877, 879
Senegal, Le, 922
Senegal River, 871, 873
Senegalese, 53, 873, 878, 881
Senegambia, 872
Senga kob, 626
Senghor, Léopold Sédar, 877-878, 922
Sengier, Edgar Edouard, 669-672, 674 n., 675, 676, 677-678, 893
Sengierite, 674 n.
Sennar Dam, 225, 236
Sénoufo tribe, 872
Senussi tribe, 164, 166, 168, 169, 171
Separate Amenities Act, South Africa, 482
Separate Registration of Voters Act, South Africa, 483
Sephardic Jews, 67
Severus, Septimius, 167 n.
Serengeti Plains, 386
Sérère tribe, 872
Seretse Khama, 341, 583-584
Serowe, 582
Seventh-Day Adventists, 258
Seville, 52
Sex customs, 57, 296-298, 760-761
Sexual fear, South Africa, 463-465
Sexual symbolism, 57-58
Seychelles, 599, 823
Seyyid Sir Khalifa Bin Harub. *See* Zanzibar, Sultan of
Seyyid Soud bin Ali, 355
Sfax, 149
Shadow over Africa (Scott), 915
Shafik, Madame Doria, 188
Shakespeare, 1, 193, 384, 447, 463, 731
Shallal, 230
Shanghai, 107

She (Haggard), 524
Sheba, Queen of, 252-253, 271
Sheean, Vincent, 115 n., 911
Sheen, Bishop Fulton J., 64, 893
Sheep, 493 n., 494, 577, 697, 875. *See also* Livestock raising
Shehu of Bornu, 784
Shell Company, 266 n., 408
Shelley, 911
Sheltering Sky, The (Bowles), 909
Shepheard's Hotel, Cairo, 189, 220
Shercliff, José, 918
Sherifian Empire, 20, 22, 41, 113, 114, 118
Sherwood, Robert E., 685, 907
Shilluk tribe, 228
Shinkolobwe mine, 674-675, 676, 677
Shinyanga, 417, 420
Shirazi, 353
Shire Highlands, 639
Shirer, Lloyd, 821-822, 922
Shoa, 253, 268
Shooter and Schuter, 497
Short History of Eritrea, A (Longrigg), 255 n.
Short History of the East Coast of Africa, A (Hollingsworth), 287 n.
Shostakovich, 731
Siam, 35 n., 256
Sidi bel Abbes, 123
Sidi Bou Said, 148
Sidi Chedley Ben Mohammed Lamine, 152
Sidi Mohammed Lamine, *See* Tunis, Bey of
Sidi Slimane, 89
Sidky Pasha, 221 n.
Siegfried, André, 657 n.
Sierra Leone, 6, 11, 428, 735, 741, 742-744, 848
Sierra Leone People's Party (SLPP), 743
Sierra Leone Selection Trust, 744
Sierra Leone Society, 743
Sigismondi, Monsignor, 668
Sikhs, 325
Silicosis, 559
Silvandre, Jean, 879
Silver, 671
Silver, Miss, 727
Silver City Airways, 180 n.
Simba beer, 690
Simmons, Jack, 410 n.
Simonstown, 495, 511
Sinclair Petroleum Company, 258
Sisal industry, 405, 407-408, 875
Sissoko, Fily Dabo, 879-880
Sisulu, Walter Max, 527
Sitwell, Sacheverell, 53, 149 n., 151 n., 167 n., 893, 908, 909
Sitwell, Mrs. Sacheverell, 893
Sklodowskite, 674
Slave trade, 11-12; abolition of, 229, 304, 316 n.; in Angola, 597-598; in British West Africa, 735; in the Cameroons, 705; in the Congo, 654; in East Africa, 325; in the Gold Coast, 822, 833; in Kenya, 315, 325;

in Liberia, 848; Moorish, 874; in Nyasaland, 640; recent, in Liberia, 858, 861-864; on the West Coast, 752-753; in Zanzibar, 315, 354
Slavery, 11-12, 13, 43; abolition of, in South Africa, 487; abolition of, in the Sudan, 229; in Ethiopia, 262; Europeans as slaves, 39, 44; forced labor as, 587; in South Africa, 485
Sleeping sickness, 306, 307-308, 392, 725, 789
Sloan, Dr. Ruth, 894
Smallpox, 76, 192, 787
Smara, 118
Smith, Edwin W., 297 n., 912
Smuts, Jan Christian, 1, 415, 416, 455-456, 457, 458, 468, 471, 485, 487, 550, 563, 915
Smuts, "Ouma," 416
Snakes, 383, 394, 420, 497, 719, 788
"Snows of Kilimanjaro, The" (Hemingway), 397
Sobhuza II, 579
Sobo, 746
Socialism, 423
Socialist party, French West Africa, 878
Socialist Republican party, the Sudan, 244
Société Commerciale de l'Ouest Africain (SCOA), 741
Société Générale de Belgique, 661, 670
Société Générale Metallurgique de Hoboken, 675
Société Universelle du Canal Maritime de Suez, 219
Socrates, 731
Soeurs Blanches, 143
SOKIMO, 662
Sokoto, 783, 784; Sardauna of, 768, 784
Solomon, 252-253, 255, 271
Solow, Herbert, 661 n., 919
Somali area of Ethiopia, 254
Somali language, 782
Somali tribe, 63, 281, 282, 283, 284, 315, 349 n., 387, 404
Somali Youth League, 283, 284
Somalia, 16, 168, 282-284; as trusteeship under Italy, 279, 282, 283
Somalilands, 281-284
Somba tribe, 872
Some Aspects of the South African Industrial Revolution (Van Eck), 915
Sonraï tribe, 872, 882
Sons of Moshesh, 573, 574
Sophiatown, 504, 509-510
Sorcerer's Apprentice, The (Hurley), 912, 914
Sorko tribe, 872
Souk, 51; in Tetuan, 114
Sousse, 149
Soussou tribe, 872
Soustelle, Jacques, 129

South Africa. *See* Union of South Africa
South Africa (Carter), 483 n., 520 n., 915
South Africa (Keppel-Jones), 485 n.
South Africa Today (Paton), 466 n., 538
South Africa's Heritage, 915
South African Bureau of Racial Affairs (SABRA), 538
South African Christian Council, 528
South African Indian Congress, 533
South African Institute of Race Relations, 538
South African Journal of Economics, 553 n.
South African party, 457
South America, African strains in, 11
South-West Africa, 458, 543, 546, 550, 557-558, 561-567
Southern Protectorate of Morocco, 118
Southern Rhodesia, 16, 17 n., 301, 491, 504 n., 602, 603, 605, 606, 610, 611, 613-614, 616-618, 620-624, 633-638. *See also* Central African Federation, Northern Rhodesia, *and* Rhodesias
Southern Territories of Algeria, 121
Soviet Union. *See* Russia
Soysambu, 318
Spain, American Air bases in, 90; on Committee of Control, Tangier, 111; and Egypt, 215; emigration of Jews from, to Morocco, 67; in Fernando Po, 710-711; influence of, in Africa, 41-42, 51; and Liberia, 852; and Libya, 167, 173; nonrecognition of Mohammed VI by, 34-35, 41; in North Africa, 39, 44, 113-118; relations of, with France, 115; in Tangier, 108
Spanish Africa, 18, 118, 704, 873. *See also* Spanish Morocco
Spanish Civil War, 435
Spanish Morocco, 40-41, 68, 71, 113-118
Spears, General Sir Edward Louis, 836
Speke, J. H., 12, 354, 433
Spencer, John H., 259
Spices, 281, 282, 352, 354, 356
Sports, color bar in, 521
Sprigge, Cecil, 867 n.
Springbok, 474
Springfield Colliery, 551
Squatters, 321, 361
Stack, Sir Lee, 199, 233
Stamp, Colin, 916
Stanley, Henry Morton, 12, 409-410, 426, 433, 649, 653, 654-656, 691, 692
Stanley Falls, 650
Stanley Pool, 651
Stanleyville, 647, 650, 651, 653

Star (Johannesburg), 504, 917
Star of Africa, 554
Statut de l'Algérie, 124
Stealing, 845-846
Steele, A. T., 706 n., 912, 918
Stel, Simon van der, 493
Stellenbosch, 538; University of, 462, 471, 493, 561
Sterling, Claire, 78 n., 81 n., 908, 909
Stern, Jacques, 920
Stettinius, Edward R., Jr., 868
Stevenson, Sir Ralph, 221
Stimson, Henry, 861
Stirling, Colonel David, 352
Stoics, 731
Stool, symbol of chiefdom, 820-821, 840-841; *see also* Golden Stool
Story of Cecil Rhodes, The, 918
Story of My Life, The (Johnston), 705 n.
Strachey, Lytton, 229 n.
Strakosch, Sir Henry, 547
Strauss, Jacobus Gideon Nel, 513, 514
Street, Lucie, 292 n., 907
Strijdom, Johannes Gerhardus, 449, 455, 461, 468, 472-474, 481, 505, 512, 530, 536, 561, 577, 916; opposition to, 513-515
Strikes, 244, 535, 631, 633, 634, 744, 804, 879
Struggle for Africa (Bartlett), 406 n., 532 n., 695 n., 783 n., 847, 894, 907, 910, 912, 917, 918
Stuart, Dr. Graham H., 909
Study of History, A (Toynbee), 910
Suakoko, 845, 869
Succession, 135-136, 780-781, 821, 833
Sudan, 38 n., 63, 224, 226-246, 293, 335, 336, 428, 883, 885; civil service in, 237-240; condominium over, 226, 231, 233; economy of, 237; Egypt and, 226, 227, 231, 232, 241-242, 245; French, 874; Great Britain in, 230, 232, 233, 234, 239, 240-241; history of, 232-233; nationalism in, 227, 229, 233, 240; politics in, 242-245; self-government for, 15, 185, 221, 226, 239, 245, 441, 785-786; slaves in, 262
Sudan Agency, 233
Sudan Almanac, 225 n., 911
Sudan Interior Mission, 258
Sudan Political Service, 237-240
Sudanese Defense Force, 240, 241
Sudanese languages, 6, 699
Sudd swamps, 224, 225
Sudden Death, 356
Suez, Anglo-Egyptian agreement over, 215, 218-222; British base in, 219-222; British evacuation of, 185
Suez Canal, 12, 196, 218-219, 316, 543

Suffrage. *See* Franchise
Sugar, 496, 532, 593
Sukuma tribe, 403-404
Sukumaland reclamation project, 409
Sultan of Morocco, The (Landau), 907
Sulzberger, C. L., 114 n., 661 n., 912
Sumner, William Graham, 912
Sun (South Africa), 530
Superstition, 291, 296, 300, 308, 361, 398, 570, 727, 756, 832. *See also* Black magic, *Juju,* and Witch doctors and witchcraft
Suppression of Communism Act, South Africa, 477, 481-482, 527, 539-541, 542
Survival, 139
Sus, 93
Swahili, 287-288, 648
Swahili Coast, 63
Swanzy, Henry, 911
Swart, Charles Robert, 467, 477-478, 479, 481-482, 500, 528, 529, 540, 541, 542, 916
Swaziland, 301, 336, 512, 536, 579-581, 817 n.
Swaziland, 580 n.
Sweden, influence of, in Ethiopia, 248, 251, 255-256, 257, 277
Swift, Jonathan, 449
Swollen Shoot, 797, 825-826
SYMÉTAIN, 662
Syphilis, 308, 401, 706
Syria, 35 n. 889

Taberer, W. H. M., 395
Table Bay, 484
Table Mountain, 494
Tademait Plateau, 142
Tafilalet oasis, 106
Talking Drums of Africa (Carrington), 288
Tamachek, 6, 135, 856 n.
Tamale, 821
Tamanrasset, 130, 132-134, 136
Tana, Lake, 224, 273
Tana River, 311
Tananarive, 600
Tanga, 408, 414, 416
Tanganyika, 5, 16, 78, 224, 286, 290, 298, 309, 352, 375, 383, 396-420, 596, 615, 654, 684, 885; basic structure of, 404-409; history and politics of, 410-413; Serengeti Plains, 386
Tanganyika, Lake, 312, 404, 650, 654, 688
Tanganyika African National Union (TANU), 412
Tanganyika Concessions, Ltd., 591, 670
Tangier, 41, 67, 71, 107-109; administration of, 107, 111-113; history of, 110; Mendoub of, 108, 112, 113
Tangier Statute, 110, 112-113
Taourirt, *kasbah* of, 103-104
Tapioca, 600
Tas, Sal, 83 n.

INDEX 949

Taylor family of Que Que, 918
Tchibanga, 703, 704
Tea, 639, 645
Tebessa, 123
Technical Co-operation Administration, 868
Teda tribe, 699
Teixeira, Captain Gabriel Mauricio, 586, 595
Telecommunications Authority, Ethiopia, 256
Tell Freedom (Abrahams), 523
Teller, Judd L., 170 n.
Telouet, 96-97, 102
Tema, 827
Temne tribe, 743
Temps Moderne, 95 n.
Tenaghne Worq, Princess, 269
Tennyson, 811
Tetuan, 68, 114, 116, 117
Thababosiu, 576
Thabanchu, 527
Thailand, 35 n., 256
Thami Glaoui el Mezouari. *See* Glaoui, Pasha of Marrakesh
Theraptus, 356
This Is South Africa (Moolman), 915
Thomas, Bertram, 908
Thomas, Bode, 788
Thompson, Dorothy, 191, 908, 910
Thompson, Kenneth, 893
Thompson, Virginia, 922
Thomson's gazelle, 389
Thoreau, H. D., 8
Thorez, Maurice, 879
Thousand Hills, Valley of a, 497
Threat of Soviet Imperialism, The (Haines), 889 n.
Thuku, Harry, 366
Tifoultout, 104
Tigrai, 253, 271
Tigré, 278
Tigrinya, 278
Timber, 696, 825
Timbuktu, 10, 753, 873, 874
Time, 216 n., 226 n., 279 n., 305 n., 470, 506 n., 510 n., 634 n., 772 n., 795 n., 882 n., 907, 909, 910, 911, 912, 916, 917, 920, 921
Time and Tide, 907
Times (London), 173 n., 180, 216 n., 365 n., 370 n., 462 n., 472 n., 510, 548 n., 549, 617, 633 n., 763 n., 771 n., 909, 910, 911, 912, 913, 915, 916, 917, 918, 919, 923
Times (New York), 50 n., 68 n., 87 n., 114 n., 152 n., 162 n., 179, 191 n., 193 n., 213 n., 350 n., 412 n., 463 n., 477 n., 510 n., 521 n., 538, 624 n., 661 n., 666 n., 677 n., 695, 801, 867, 882 n., 883, 907, 908, 909, 910, 911, 912, 913, 914, 917, 918, 919, 920, 921, 922, 923
Timgad, 123
Tin, 785, 786
Tinerhir, 105-106

Tito, Marshal, 250 n.
Tizard, Professor, 675
Tlemçen, 123
Tobacco, 620, 623, 639
Tobernite, 674
Tobruk, 164, 173
Todd, R. S. Garfield, 609-610, 918
Togba, Dr. J. N., 856
Togbe Yepre Hodo III, 841
Togoland, 16, 813, 837-841
Tolliver, Catherine, 70 n., 909
Tolon Naa, 820
Tolstoy, Leo, 712, 731
Toma tribe, 872
Tom-George, Davied D., 769
Tomorrow's Continent (Penn and Street), 292 n., 907
Tomtoms. *See* Drums and tomtoms
Tonga tribe, 626
Top Hats and Tom-Toms (Furbay) 849 n., 922
Torch-Commandos, 514-515
Toro, 422 n.
Toro tribe, 286
Torres, Abdel Khalek, 117
"Tot" system, 505
Totalitarianism, 458, 511, 525, 537
Totem and Taboo (Freud), 912
Totota, 844, 854
Tourist business, 350, 593, 594, 626
Toward Self Government in the British Colonies, 913
Toynbee, Arnold J., 150 n., 910
Trachoma, 177, 192-193
Trade, clove, 356; in the Congo, 647; Egyptian, with Russia and Britain, 216; in Kenya, 311; in Rhodesia, 620, 623; in South Africa, 495, 511; in Tanganyika, 407-408; in Uganda, 421-422; in West Africa, 741. *See also* Economic situation *and* Exports and imports
Trade spirits, 754
Trade unions. *See* Unions, unionization
Trans-Volta-Togoland Council, 841
Transkei, 494, 522
Transvaal, 450, 459, 460, 469, 486, 488, 492, 498-500, 516, 520, 523, 535, 539, 546, 548, 580
Transvaal Chamber of Mines, 546, 559, 561
Transvaler, Die, 473, 479, 499, 537
Travels in Ethiopia (Buxton), 912
Treetops, 387-388
Tribal customs, 9, 10, 289-293, 296-299, 760-761, 763, 787, 823, 835-836
Tribal organization, 289-290, 337-338, 365, 401
Tribal wars, 104, 753, 837
Tribes, Agni, 872; Agoni, 287; Akan, 822, 823; Amakwaya, 560; Amakwenkwe, 560; Angoni, 298, 410, 640, 641-644; Amhara, 286; Arab. 56;

Ashanti, 753, 823-824, 837; Baganda, 286, 621; Bahaya, 287; Bahutu, 686; Bakota, 699; Bakutu, 679-680; Bakwena, 582, 584; Bali, 709-710; Baluba, 648; Bamangwato, 582, 583, 584; Bambara, 872; Banda, 699; Bandja, 699; Bangwaketse, 582; Bantu, 286-287, 289-290, 486, 496, 648; Banziri, 699; Baoulé, 872; Bariba, 872; Barotse, 287, 626; Basalampasu, 648; Bassa, 856; Basuto, 569; Batawana, 582; Bateki, 699; Bayombi, 699; Bedouin, 187; Beja, 228; Bemba, 287, 298, 626; Beni Hillal, 167; Beni Suleim, 167; Berber, *see* Berbers; Birom, 787; Bobo, 872; Boonga, 699; Bozo, 872; Chaamba, 144; Chagga, 286, 287 n., 296, 402-403; Chewa, 298; Coniagui, 872; Dagomba, 821; Dinka, 228; Djerma, 872; Dogon, 872; Dorobo, 298; Ewe, 813, 838, 839, 840; Fang, 706; Fanti, 823, 824, 837; Fulani, 782-783, 872; Fuzzy Wuzzy, 228; Galla, 254, 262; Galoa, 699; Gola, 856; Gouronsi, 872; Grebo, 856; Guerzé, 872; Hausa-speaking, 772, 782; Hehe, 298; Herero, 287, 562, 563, 566; Hova, 599, 601; Ibo, 365, 621, 709, 759, 760-761, 763, 766, 767, 771, 772, 773, 778, 785; Ila, 626; institution of, 286-287, 291; Kabyle, 121; Kamba, 287 n., 298, 320, 349 n., 375; Kel-Rela, 136; Kikuyu, *see* Kikuyu tribe; Kipsigi, 296, 349 n.; Kissi, 872; Kongo, 287; Kru, 854, 856, 858; Lobi, 872; Lovedu, 523; Lozi, 626; Luo, 286, 298; Makishi, 626; Malagasy, 599; Malinké, 872; Mandau, 560; Mandingo, 744; Mangbeto, 287, 648; Mangia, 699; Masai, 8, 229, 286, 298, 318, 319, 320, 370, 375, 400-402, 402; Mashona, 612, 621; Matabele, 287, 611, 612, 621, 626; M'Boom, 699; Mbunda, 287; Mende, 743; Meru, 298, 349 n.; Mina, 872; Moru, 228; Mossi, 872; M'zabite, 121; Nandi, 286, 298, 349 n.; Ndonga, 287; Nigerian, 746; non-primitive aspects of, 289; Nubian, 187; Nuer, 228; Nyanja, 287; Nyasa, 291; Omine, 699; Ovambo, 287, 562; Pahouin, 699; Pambla, 699; Pondo, 523, 560; Sarakolé, 872; Sari, 699; Sénoufo, 872; Sérère, 872; Shilluk, 228; Somali, 281, 282, 283, 284, 315, 349 n.; Somba, 872; Sonraï, 872; Sorko, 872; Soussou, 872; Sukuma, 403-404; Sudanese,

227-228; Swazi, 579, 580; Taï-tok, 136; Tanganyika, 405; Tedjehe-Mellet, 136; Temne, 743; Toma, 872; Tonga, 626; Toro, 286; Tuareg, 130, 136, 286, 872; Ubangi, 699; Vai, 6, 856; Waarusha, 399, 402; Wagogo, 286; Wameru, 404; Wanyamwezi, 286; Wasukuma, 286; Wataware, 301; Watutsi, 229, 648, 683, 685-688; Widekum, 710; Wolof, 872; Xhosa, 287, 486, 523; Yao, 287, 640; Yoruba, 760, 762-763, 766, 767, 772, 773, 778; Zandi, 699; Zenete, 143; Zouave, 132; Zulu, 287, 290, 298, 410, 487, 496, 497, 523, 524 n., 579, 611, 640
Tripoli, 164, 169, 172, 173, 174, 175, 180
Tripolitania, 164
Tripolitania, The Country and Its People (Murabet), 60 n., 910
Troglodytes, 166
Trollope, Anthony, 495, 516, 917
Tropical ulcer, 308
Troubled Uganda (Mulira), 915
Trud (Moscow), 375
True Morocco, The (Mellor), 47 n., 907
True Whig party, Liberia, 857, 858
Truman, Harry S., 677-678
Trust Territories, United Nations, the Cameroons, 16, 705-710; Ruanda-Urundi, 16, 405 n., 646 n., 684-689; Somalia, 16, 279, 282, 283-284, 563; Tanganyika, 16, 352, 404, 406, 412, 413; Togoland, 16, 837-841
Trusteeship Council, 709, 710
Truth about Morocco, The (Parent), 908
Trypanosomiasis, 306, 307-308
Tsahai, Princess, 269 n.
Tsavo National Park, 386, 395
Tsetse fly, 5, 306-307, 319-320, 392, 404, 409, 426, 620, 623, 720 n., 722
Tshekedi Khama, 583, 584
Tshuapa River, 678
Tsumeb, 566-567
Tuareg, 53, 130, 133, 134, 135-138, 255, 286, 699, 777, 780 n., 872
Tuberculosis, 308, 559
Tubman, Harriet, 850
Tubman, William Vacanarat Shadrach, 173, 843, 849-855, 856, 857, 858, 862, 864, 865, 868, 922
Tung, 639, 645
Tungsten, 671
Tunis, 147-148, 150, 155, 702-703; Bey of, 146, 150-153, 158
Tunisia, 146-162, 884; civilization of, derived from Europe, 7; disappearance of Berbers from, 66; French in, 38, 146, 150,

153-156; 161-162, 169; government of, 161; nationalism in, 147, 152, 153, 154, 155, 156-160, 161, 213; women in, 71
Tunisian Question in the United Nations, The (Bokhari), 910
Turbans, 58
Turkey, early conquests by, 39, 41; in Ethiopia, 252, 267; interest of, in Libya, 167, 176; Iraq pact with, 215; U.S. pact with, 215
Tutankhamen, King, 189
Twe, Dihdwo, 858
Twi, 229, 799, 819, 834
Twining, Sir Edward, 339, 406, 407, 412, 417, 595, 894, 915
Twining, Lady, 406 n.
"Two streams" policy, 456
Typhus, 54, 76, 192

Ubangi River, 649
Ubangi tribe, 699
Ubangi-Shari, 696-697, 698, 699
UDMA (Democratic Union of the Algerian Manifesto), 126-127
Uganda, 224, 235, 262, 286, 290, 292, 295, 305, 307, 336, 337, 338, 352, 375, 421-446, 491, 615, 885; government of, 432, 433, 435-439; history of, 433-435; Kabaka crisis in, 424, 435, 436-438, 439, 441-445; nationalism in, 435, 440-441, 444; physical aspects of, 424-428
Uganda, 915
Uganda Agreement, 435
Uganda National Congress, 440, 443, 444
Uganda Railroad, 316-317
Ujiji, 409, 410
Ulema of Fez, 20, 22
UMMA (Independence) party, Sudan, 243, 244
Umvoti Mission Reserve, 528
Unilever interests, 408, 660, 741
Union against Unjust Taxation, 762
Union Corporation Ltd., 547, 548
Union Federalist party, South Africa, 497
Union Générale des Travailleurs Tunisiens (UGTT), 160
Union Minière du Haut Katanga, 661, 670, 671-673, 674-675, 676-677, 866, 893, 919
Union des Populations des Caméroun, 707
Union of South Africa, 12 n., 14, 15, 331, 335, 336, 338, 617 n., 817 n., 824 n., 885, 891; African leaders in, 526-531; *apartheid* in, 516-522, 526-527, 535-538 (*see also Apartheid*); and Basutoland, 577, 578; British in, 486-487, 490, 496, 497, 498, 500, 501; Cape Coloreds in, 529-531; Communism in, 527, 528, 533, 538-542; controlling interests in, 560-561; "Defi-

ance" movement in, 528, 533-535; diamonds in, 545, 546, 549, 550-551, 553-558; economics of, 465-466; geography of, 450-452; German interest in, 217; gold production in, 545, 546-549, 550-551, 552, 553; government of, 450, 453, 471-472; history of, 484-489; Indian community in, 531-533; international relations of, 532, 543-544; Johannesburg, 501-509; Kruger National Park, 385, 386; language in, 454, 461-463, 468; native community in, 522-526; opposition to present regime in, 465, 467, 513-515; political figures in, 455-459, 467-476, 477-478, 479-481; population of, 452; provinces of, 493-501; race problems in, 463-465, 466, 481; recent measures passed in, 481-483; religion in, 459-461, 462; segregation patterns in 516-522; South-West Africa, 561-567; status of, 449-450; uranium in, 545, 546, 548, 551-553; Western Areas Removal Scheme, 509-510. *See also* Afrikaners, *Apartheid*, Boers, *and* Nationalism, in South Africa
Unions, unionization, in Algeria, 127; black, 631, 633, 634; in the Cameroons, 707; of chiefs, 640; in the Congo, 672; in French West Africa, 879, 881; in the Gold Coast, 817, 837; mixed, 542; in Morocco, 83-84; in Nigeria, 770; in Sierra Leone, 743-744; in the Sudan, 244-245; in Tunisia, 159-160; white, 608, 619, 630. *See also* Labor movement
United Africa Company, 408, 741, 757 n., 839
United Country party, Kenya, 331, 347
United Gold Coast Convention (UGCC), 800-801, 803
United Kenya Club, 329
United Nations, Arab bloc in, 35, 63; and Egypt, 215; and Eritrea, 279, 280; Ethiopia and, 257, 259, 284; and Liberia, 868-869; and Libya, 164, 168, 177-178; and Nigeria, 747; and South Africa, 543; and South-West Africa, 563-564, 565; Technical Assistance Administration of, 257; Trust Territories, *see* Trust Territories, United Nations
UNESCO, 543, 869
UNICEF, 215, 747
UNRWA, 215
United Nations Charter, 13, 16, 91
United Nations World, 151 n.

INDEX 951

United party, South Africa, 456, 457, 458, 495, 503, 513, 514, 550
United States, abolition of slavery by, 753; as an administrator of Tangier, 110, 111; air bases of, in Spain, 90; areas of backwardness in, 9; assistance of, to Angola, 597 n.; atomic bomb dropped by, 678; colonialism supported by, 115 n.; columbite imported to, from Nigeria, 786; and Egypt, 214-216; and Ethiopia, 256 n., 258-259, 275; exports of, to French West Africa, 880; importance of Dakar to, 882; importance of the Gold Coast to, 826-827; imports to, from the Congo, 689; imports to, from South Africa, 545, 547, 553, 557; influence of, in Nigeria, 757; interest of, in Libya, 164, 177-180, 181; interest of, in Mozambique, 593; and Liberia, 847-849, 864, 868, 869-870; military base of, in Eritrea, 280-281; mining developments of, in South-West Africa, 566-567; missionaries from, 305; loan to Southern Rhodesia by, 623; and Morocco, 29-30, 35, 49, 54, 88-90, 91, 109, 214; naval base of, at Port Lyautey, 48; Negroes in, *see* Negroes, American; nonrecognition of Italian occupation of Ethiopia by, 250, 259; nonrecognition of Spanish Morocco by, 114 n.; and Pakistan and Turkey, 215; Point Four, *see* Point Four; policy of, in Africa, 73, 91-92, 115 n.; 891-892; position of, in East Africa, 350; and South Africa, 543-544; treatment of Negroes and Indians in, 80; and the Tunisian "case," 161-162; uranium shipped to, from the Congo, 675-677; and Zanzibar, 354, 356
United States Information Service, 179, 350, 517
U.S. News and World Report, 917
U.S. Steel Corporation, 696
U.S. Trading Company, 866
University College of the Gold Coast (Achimota), 428, 804, 813, 832-833
University College of Nigeria, 762
Upper Nile Province, 228
Upper Volta, 875
Uranium, 5, 543, 545, 546, 548, 551-553, 593, 630, 647, 669, 670, 673-678
Urbanization, 460, 762, 881
Urengzeb, Emperor, 325
Urhobo, 746
Usumbura, 650, 682, 687, 688
UTEXLEO, 662

Utrecht, Treaty of, 753

Vaal River, 487
Vai tribe, 6, 856
Valley of a Thousand Hills, 497
Vandals, 39, 167
Vanderbrandeite, 674
Vanne, Marda, 472-473
Vasey, E. A., 344, 346
Vaurs, Roger, 893
Veld, 498
Veldtrust, 915
Vendaland, 522
Venereal disease, 57, 136, 177-178, 278, 401, 402
Venture to the Interior (van der Post), 638
Verdi, 219
Versailles Treaty, 456
Verulam, 498
Verwoerd, Hendrik Frensch, 467, 479-480, 508, 549
Vialle, Jane, 697
Victoria, Lake, 224, 312, 426, 433
Victoria, Queen, 397, 435, 491, 578, 602, 611, 615, 626, 639, 823
Victoria Falls, 617, 622-623, 625
Victoria Falls, The (Clark), 623 n.
Vietnam, 889 n.
Vieux Ksar, 143
Villard, Henry S., 180, 894
Villiers, René de, 916
Viniculture, 485
Virginia Quarterly Review, 115 n.
Voice of America, 246
Voizard, Pierre, 161
Volcanoes, 681, 706
Volkswil, 467, 468
Volpe, Joseph, Jr., 677
Volta River, 837, 838
Volta River project, 825, 827-828
Volubilis, 43
Vom, 786
Voortrekkers, 487, 499 n.
Voss, Dr. Wilhelm, 217
Vote. *See* Franchise
Voyage au Congo (Gide), 697
Vryheid, 496

Waarusha tribe, 399, 402
Wad Medani, 236
Waddington, C. H., 592, 918
Wadi Halfa, 228, 230, 231
Wafd, 183, 198, 199, 200, 204, 233
Wagner, 731
Wagogo tribe, 286
Walker, Eric Sherbrooke, 914
Wallace, De Witt, 895
Wallega country, 269
Walpole, Sir Robert, 603, 918
Walvis Bay, 494
Wameru tribe, 404
Wankie, 628 n.
Wankie Colliery, 616, 634
Wankie Game Reserve, 623
Wanyamwezi tribe, 286
Ward, Barbara, 815, 828, 922

Warrior Saint, The (Bodley), 909
Waruhiu, 373
Washington, George, 109, 812, 848
Wasukuma tribe, 286
Wataware tribe, 301
Watch Over Africa (Saurat), 697 n.
Water control, 409. *See also* Irrigation
Water power, 5, 54-55. *See also* Hydroelectric power
Waterberg, 473
Waterboer, 488 n.
Watutsi tribe, 229, 648, 683, 685-688
Wau, 228
Waugh, Evelyn, 12 n., 263, 912
Waugh in Abyssinia, 12 n., 912
Webb, Richard E., 893
Webb, Sidney (Lord Passfield), 334-335
Wechsberg, Joseph, 909
Wedding ceremony, Comorian, 353; Moorish, 68-70. *See also* Marriage customs
Weizmann, Dr., 318
Welch, Galbraith, 44 n.
Welensky, Sir Roy, 608-609, 614, 633
Welkom, 548-549
Wells, Carveth, 912
Wells, H. G., 907, 908
Wema, 680
Werth, Alexander, 83 n., 910
West, John, 853
West Africa, 852, 853 n., 919, 920, 922
West African Explorers, 764 n., 776 n., 920
West African Frontier Force, 749
West African Institute of Trypanosomiasis Research, 786
West African National Congress, 824
West African National Secretariat, 744
West African Pilot, 750-751
West African Religions (Parrinder), 922
West African Students Union, 337
West at Bay, The (Ward), 828
West Coast of Africa, 285, 735-736; compared with East Coast, 289, 291, 316, 344 n., 349, 740-742, 749, 749 n., 752; nationalism in, 608. *See also various countries*
West Rand Consolidated Gold Mine, 552
West Rand Investment Trust, 551
"Western Areas Removal Scheme," 509-510
Weyenbergh, Maurice van, 674
Wharton, Edith, 44 n., 909
Wheelus Field, Libya, 164, 179-180
When Smuts Goes (Keppel-Jones), 544
Where Animals Talk, 921
Whipping Bill, South Africa, 478

952 INSIDE AFRICA

White, Leigh, 910
White, Theodore H., 701 n., 907, 908
White, Walter, 698, 893
White, William S., 921
White Domination or Racial Peace? (Hastings), 915
White Fathers, 143-144, 148, 684, 703
White Highlands, Kenya, 293, 312, 318, 319-321, 376
White Man's Country (Huxley), 317
White Man's Grave, 735-736
White Nile, 224, 225
White settlement, 6; in Algeria, 121, 124, 125; in Angola, 597; barred in Uganda, 423-424, 433; in British Togoland, 838; in British West Africa, 747, discouraged in Belgian Congo, 648; forbidden in Gold Coast, 825; forbidden in Nigeria, 17; in French West Africa, 871, 880; in Kenya, 17, 78, 79, 311, 317-321, 329-333, 338, 342-344, 345, 346, 347, 352, 370, 377; in Morocco, 39, 77-79; not permitted in Basutoland, 577; not welcomed in Mozambique, 593; resentment against, 364, 366, 372-373, 376-377, 410, 412, 428, 740; in the Rhodesias and Nyasaland, 603, 610, 620, 622, 626, 638, 645; in South Africa, *see* Union of South Africa; in South-West Africa, 561; in Swaziland, 579, 580-581; in Tanganyika, 399, 404-405; in Tunisia, 153, 155, 156; in West Africa, 740-741
White Sisters, 684-685
White supremacy, 17, 311, 331, 338, 347, 377, 449, 474, 512, 519, 531, 567, 603, 615-616, 635, 648, 886. *See also* Color bar *and* Apartheid
Whitman, Walt, 456
Whittlesey, Derwent, 321 n.
Whyte, Quintin, 894, 915
Whyte, Mrs. Quintin, 894
Widekums, 710
Widows, 297
Wieschoff, Dr. H. A., 893
Wildebeest, 626
Wilhelm, Kaiser, 44, 397, 496, 916
Willaert, 919
Williams, A. F. Basil, 456 n., 916
Williams, Ruth, 584
Williamson, Dr. John Thoburn, 416-420
Williamson, P. B., 418
Willkie, Wendell, 15
Willowmere, 473
Wilson, Charles M., 844 n.
Wilson, Ross, 922
Wilson, Woodrow, 13, 156, 456, 892
Windermere, 494

Wingate, Sir Reginald, 233
Windhoek, 562, 565-566
Winds, *alizé,* 872; *ghibli,* 163, 172; *haboob,* 228; *harmattan,* 747, 872; Khamsin, 282; monsoon, 356; *mousson,* 872
Witch doctors and witchcraft, 291, 299-303, 361, 362, 363, 411 n., 524 n., 640, 747, 858. *See also* Black magic *and* Juju
Witwatersrand, 488, 502. *See also* Rand mines
Witwatersrand Native Labor Association, 595
Witwatersrand University, 462, 519
Wold, Ato Makonnen Abte Ato Akilou Abte, Ato Akaele Abte, 272
Wolde Guiorguis Wolde Yohannes, Tsahafi Taezaz, 272
Woldemarian, Woldeab, 280 n.
Wolof tribe and language, 872, 878
Women, in Algeria, 123; allowed in bars in Basutoland, 577; Amazons, 876; in Bantu Africa, 295-299; as beasts of burden, 295; in Black Africa, 295-299; in Casablanca, 71; education for, 71, 244, 428; in Egypt, 188; emancipation of, 70-71, 85-86, 147 (*see also* Feminism); in Ethiopia, 269 n., 273; *évoluées,* 147; Kikuyu, 295-296; in Morocco, 25, 27-28, 68-70, 85-86; Moslem, 25, 178, 181, 236, 776, 782, 785, 873; nonextension of franchise to, 709; on police force, 829; political consciousness of, French West Africa, 873; in Rhodesia, 621; in the Sudan, 236, 243; In Tanganyika, 403; in Tangier, 109; in trade, 741, 757, 761, 799; in Uganda, 422; voting rights for, 701, 857, 873; Watutsi, 686
Woode, Anthony, 817
Wool trade, 495. *See also* Sheep
Woolbert, Robert Gale, 909
World Bank, loans of, to South Africa, 543-544, 546
World Health Organization, 747, 868-869
World Today, 27 n., 124 n., 168 n., 208 n., 461 n., 480 n., 823 n., 880 n., 907, 909, 910, 911, 916, 921
World War I, 13, 95, 267, 457, 563, 656, 706, 716-717
World War II, 13, 30, 95, 110, 166, 167, 182, 199, 267, 268, 282, 283, 457, 565, 600, 695, 696, 697, 698, 706, 707, 743, 848, 882
Worms, intestinal, 192, 308, 508
Worq Kidane Wold, Ato Tafarra, 250
Worrall, John, 917

Worth, Irene, 894
Worthington, Dr. E. B., 337
Wouri River, 708
Wright, Richard, 830, 894
Wulana of Yana, 820

Xauen, 68, 118-119
Xenophobia, 817, 839, 886, 887. *See also* Anti-American sentiment *and* Great Britain, hostility to
Xhosas tribe and language, 287, 486, 523, 526
Xuma, Dr. A. B., 526-527, 894
Xuma, Mrs. A. B., 526

Yacob, Prince, 269
Yale Review, 913
Yana, Wulana of, 820
Yancy, Allen N., 861-862, 864
Yao tribe, 287, 640
Yaoundé, 704, 707, 708
Yasu, Lij, 267, 268
Yaws, 308
Yellow fever, 725, 735
Yemen, 35 n.
Yergan, Dr. Max, 917
Yeshash Worq, Princess, 272
Yoruba tribe and language, 229, 746, 760, 762-763, 766, 767, 778
Young, Graham, 894
"Young Tunisians," 156
Your Servant and You, 635

Zaghlul Pasha, 198, 199, 204
Zakia, Princess, 152
Zambesi River, 562, 592, 611, 620, 623, 624
Zambesi Sawmills, 625
Zande, 237
Zandi tribe, 699
Zanzibar, 12, 13, 63, 242, 315, 352-357, 654; British in, 353, 354-355, 357; history of, 354; lack of education in, 294; Sultan of, 311-312, 352-353, 355, 357, 410; Sultana of, 343, 355
Zaria, 781
Zauditu, Empress, 267, 268
Zawia, 171-172
Zebras, 389, 401
Zeinab el Wakil, 207
Zellidja, 54
Zenetes, 143
Zenj Empire, 354
Zetland, Lord, 196 n.
Ziguinchor, 873
Zik's Press, Ltd., 772
Zimbabwe ruins, 610-611
Zinc, 54, 545, 671
Zinder, 134
Zomba, 639
Zongo Volunteers, 836
Zorilla, 387
Zouaves, 132
Zulu, Cyprian Bhekuzulu, 496
Zulu language, 287
Zululand, 306, 496, 522
Zulus, 287, 290, 298, 410, **487,** 496, 497, 523, 524 n., 611, 640